Twentieth-Century Literary Criticism

Guide to Gale Literary Criticism Series

For criticism on	Consult these Gale series
Authors now living or who died after December 31, 1999	***CONTEMPORARY LITERARY CRITICISM (CLC)***
Authors who died between 1900 and 1999	***TWENTIETH-CENTURY LITERARY CRITICISM (TCLC)***
Authors who died between 1800 and 1899	***NINETEENTH-CENTURY LITERATURE CRITICISM (NCLC)***
Authors who died between 1400 and 1799	***LITERATURE CRITICISM FROM 1400 TO 1800 (LC)*** ***SHAKESPEAREAN CRITICISM (SC)***
Authors who died before 1400	***CLASSICAL AND MEDIEVAL LITERATURE CRITICISM (CMLC)***
Authors of books for children and young adults	***CHILDREN'S LITERATURE REVIEW (CLR)***
Dramatists	***DRAMA CRITICISM (DC)***
Poets	***POETRY CRITICISM (PC)***
Short story writers	***SHORT STORY CRITICISM (SSC)***
Asian American writers of the last two hundred years	***ASIAN AMERICAN LITERATURE (AAL)***
Black writers of the past two hundred years	***BLACK LITERATURE CRITICISM (BLC)*** ***BLACK LITERATURE CRITICISM SUPPLEMENT (BLCS)***
Hispanic writers of the late nineteenth and twentieth centuries	***HISPANIC LITERATURE CRITICISM (HLC)*** ***HISPANIC LITERATURE CRITICISM SUPPLEMENT (HLCS)***
Native North American writers and orators of the eighteenth, nineteenth, and twentieth centuries	***NATIVE NORTH AMERICAN LITERATURE (NNAL)***
Major authors from the Renaissance to the present	***WORLD LITERATURE CRITICISM, 1500 TO THE PRESENT (WLC)*** ***WORLD LITERATURE CRITICISM SUPPLEMENT (WLCS)***

ISSN 0276-8178

Volume 133

Twentieth-Century Literary Criticism

**Criticism of the
Works of Novelists, Poets, Playwrights,
Short Story Writers, and Other Creative Writers
Who Lived between 1900 and 1999,
from the First Published Critical
Appraisals to Current Evaluations**

Janet Witalec
Project Editor

GALE®

THOMSON
GALE

Detroit • New York • San Diego • San Francisco • Cleveland • New Haven, Conn. • Waterville, Maine • London • Munich

THOMSON

GALE

Twentieth-Century Literary Criticism, Vol. 133

Project Editor
Janet Witalec

Editorial
Jenny Cromie, Scott Darga, Kathy D. Darrow,
Julie Keppen, Allison Marion, Linda Pavlovski

Research
Michelle Campbell, Tracie A. Richardson

Permissions
Shalice Shah-Caldwell

Imaging and Multimedia
Lezlie Light, Daniel W. Newell, Dave G.
Oblender, Robyn Young

Composition and Electronic Capture
Gary Leach

Manufacturing
Stacy L. Melson

LIBRARY OF CONGRESS CATALOG CARD NUMBER 76-46132

ISBN 0-7876-6337-9
ISSN 0276-8178

Printed in the United States of America
10 9 8 7 6 5 4 3 2 1

Contents

Preface vii

Acknowledgments xi

Literary Criticism Series Advisory Board xiii

Preface

Since its inception more than fifteen years ago, *Twentieth-Century Literary Criticism* (*TCLC*) has been purchased and used by nearly 10,000 school, public, and college or university libraries. *TCLC* has covered more than 500 authors, representing 58 nationalities and over 25,000 titles. No other reference source has surveyed the critical response to twentieth-century authors and literature as thoroughly as *TCLC*. In the words of one reviewer, "there is nothing comparable available." *TCLC* "is a gold mine of information—dates, pseudonyms, biographical information, and criticism from books and periodicals—which many librarians would have difficulty assembling on their own."

Scope of the Series

TCLC is designed to serve as an introduction to authors who died between 1900 and 1999 and to the most significant interpretations of these author's works. Volumes published from 1978 through 1999 included authors who died between 1900 and 1960. The great poets, novelists, short story writers, playwrights, and philosophers of the period are frequently studied in high school and college literature courses. In organizing and reprinting the vast amount of critical material written on these authors, *TCLC* helps students develop valuable insight into literary history, promotes a better understanding of the texts, and sparks ideas for papers and assignments. Each entry in *TCLC* presents a comprehensive survey on an author's career or an individual work of literature and provides the user with a multiplicity of interpretations and assessments. Such variety allows students to pursue their own interests; furthermore, it fosters an awareness that literature is dynamic and responsive to many different opinions.

Every fourth volume of *TCLC* is devoted to literary topics. These topics widen the focus of the series from the individual authors to such broader subjects as literary movements, prominent themes in twentieth-century literature, literary reaction to political and historical events, significant eras in literary history, prominent literary anniversaries, and the literatures of cultures that are often overlooked by English-speaking readers.

TCLC is designed as a companion series to Gale's *Contemporary Literary Criticism,* (*CLC*) which reprints commentary on authors who died after 1999. Because of the different time periods under consideration, there is no duplication of material between *CLC* and *TCLC*.

Organization of the Book

A *TCLC* entry consists of the following elements:

- The **Author Heading** cites the name under which the author most commonly wrote, followed by birth and death dates. Also located here are any name variations under which an author wrote, including transliterated forms for authors whose native languages use nonroman alphabets. If the author wrote consistently under a pseudonym, the pseudonym will be listed in the author heading and the author's actual name given in parenthesis on the first line of the biographical and critical information. Uncertain birth or death dates are indicated by question marks. Single-work entries are preceded by a heading that consists of the most common form of the title in English translation (if applicable) and the original date of composition.

- A **Portrait of the Author** is included when available.

- The **Introduction** contains background information that introduces the reader to the author, work, or topic that is the subject of the entry.

- The list of **Principal Works** is ordered chronologically by date of first publication and lists the most important works by the author. The genre and publication date of each work is given. In the case of foreign authors whose works have been translated into English, the English-language version of the title follows in brackets. Unless otherwise indicated, dramas are dated by first performance, not first publication.

- Reprinted **Criticism** is arranged chronologically in each entry to provide a useful perspective on changes in critical evaluation over time. The critic's name and the date of composition or publication of the critical work are given at the beginning of each piece of criticism. Unsigned criticism is preceded by the title of the source in which it appeared. All titles by the author featured in the text are printed in boldface type. Footnotes are reprinted at the end of each essay or excerpt. In the case of excerpted criticism, only those footnotes that pertain to the excerpted texts are included.

- A complete **Bibliographical Citation** of the original essay or book precedes each piece of criticism. Source citations in the Literary Criticism Series follow University of Chicago Press style, as outlined in *The Chicago Manual of Style,* 14th ed. (Chicago: The University of Chicago Press, 1993).

- Critical essays are prefaced by brief **Annotations** explicating each piece.

- An annotated bibliography of **Further Reading** appears at the end of each entry and suggests resources for additional study. In some cases, significant essays for which the editors could not obtain reprint rights are included here. Boxed material following the further reading list provides references to other biographical and critical sources on the author in series published by Gale.

Indexes

A **Cumulative Author Index** lists all of the authors that appear in a wide variety of reference sources published by the Gale Group, including *TCLC*. A complete list of these sources is found facing the first page of the Author Index. The index also includes birth and death dates and cross references between pseudonyms and actual names.

A **Cumulative Nationality Index** lists all authors featured in *TCLC* by nationality, followed by the number of the *TCLC* volume in which their entry appears.

A **Cumulative Topic Index** lists the literary themes and topics treated in the series as well as in *Classical and Medieval Literature Criticism, Literature Criticism from 1400 to 1800, Nineteenth-Century Literature Criticism,* and the *Contemporary Literary Criticism* Yearbook, which was discontinued in 1998.

An alphabetical **Title Index** accompanies each volume of *TCLC*. Listings of titles by authors covered in the given volume are followed by the author's name and the corresponding page numbers where the titles are discussed. English translations of foreign titles and variations of titles are cross-referenced to the title under which a work was originally published. Titles of novels, dramas, nonfiction books, and poetry, short story, or essay collections are printed in italics, while individual poems, short stories, and essays are printed in roman type within quotation marks.

In response to numerous suggestions from librarians, Gale also produces an annual paperbound edition of the *TCLC* cumulative title index. This annual cumulation, which alphabetically lists all titles reviewed in the series, is available to all customers. Additional copies of this index are available upon request. Librarians and patrons will welcome this separate index; it saves shelf space, is easy to use, and is recyclable upon receipt of the next edition.

Citing *Twentieth-Century Literary Criticism*

When citing criticism reprinted in the Literary Criticism Series, students should provide complete bibliographic information so that the cited essay can be located in the original print or electronic source. Students who quote directly from reprinted criticism may use any accepted bibliographic format, such as University of Chicago Press style or Modern Language Association (MLA) style. Both the MLA and the University of Chicago formats are acceptable and recognized as being the current standards for citations. It is important, however, to choose one format for all citations; do not mix the two formats within a list of citations.

The examples below follow recommendations for preparing a bibliography set forth in *The Chicago Manual of Style,* 14th ed. (Chicago: The University of Chicago Press, 1993); the first example pertains to material drawn from periodicals, the second to material reprinted from books:

Morrison, Jago. "Narration and Unease in Ian McEwan's Later Fiction." *Critique* 42, no. 3 (spring 2001): 253-68. Reprinted in *Twentieth-Century Literary Criticism.* Vol. 127, edited by Janet Witalec, 212-20. Detroit: Gale, 2003.

Brossard, Nicole. "Poetic Politics." In *The Politics of Poetic Form: Poetry and Public Policy,* edited by Charles Bernstein, 73-82. New York: Roof Books, 1990. Reprinted in *Twentieth-Century Literary Criticism.* Vol. 127, edited by Janet Witalec, 3-8. Detroit: Gale, 2003.

The examples below follow recommendations for preparing a works cited list set forth in the *MLA Handbook for Writers of Research Papers,* 5th ed. (New York: The Modern Language Association of America, 1999); the first example pertains to material drawn from periodicals, the second to material reprinted from books:

Morrison, Jago. "Narration and Unease in Ian McEwan's Later Fiction." *Critique* 42.3 (spring 2001): 253-68. Reprinted in *Twentieth-Century Literary Criticism.* Ed. Janet Witalec. Vol. 127. Detroit: Gale, 2003. 212-20.

Brossard, Nicole. "Poetic Politics." *The Politics of Poetic Form: Poetry and Public Policy.* Ed. Charles Bernstein. New York: Roof Books, 1990. 73-82. Reprinted in *Twentieth-Century Literary Criticism.* Ed. Janet Witalec. Vol. 127. Detroit: Gale, 2003. 3-8.

Suggestions are Welcome

Readers who wish to suggest new features, topics, or authors to appear in future volumes, or who have other suggestions or comments are cordially invited to call, write, or fax the Project Editor:

Project Editor, Literary Criticism Series
The Gale Group
27500 Drake Road
Farmington Hills, MI 48331-3535
1-800-347-4253 (GALE)
Fax: 248-699-8054

Acknowledgments

The editors wish to thank the copyright holders of the criticism included in this volume and the permissions managers of many book and magazine publishing companies for assisting us in securing reproduction rights. We are also grateful to the staffs of the Detroit Public Library, the Library of Congress, the University of Detroit Mercy Library, Wayne State University Purdy/Kresge Library Complex, and the University of Michigan Libraries for making their resources available to us. Following is a list of the copyright holders who have granted us permission to reproduce material in this volume of *TCLC*. Every effort has been made to trace copyright, but if omissions have been made, please let us know.

COPYRIGHTED MATERIAL IN *TCLC*, VOLUME 133, WAS REPRODUCED FROM THE FOLLOWING PERIODICALS:

American Imago, v. 35, Spring-Summer, 1978. © The Johns Hopkins University Press. Reproduced by permission.— *American Literature,* v. 57, October, 1985. Copyright © 1985 by Duke University Press. Reproduced by permission.— *The Blade,* May 19, 1988. Reproduced by permission.— *Bulletin of Hispanic Studies,* v. 63, July, 1986. Reproduced by permission.— *Cahiers Victorians et Edouardiens,* v. 46, October, 1997. Reproduced by permission.— *The Christian Science Monitor,* January 27, 1984. © 1984 The Christian Science Publishing Society. All rights reserved. Reproduced by permission from *The Christian Science Monitor.—CLA Journal,* v. 29, June, 1986; v. 35, December, 1991. Copyright, 1986, 1991 by The College Language Association. Both used by permission of The College Language Association.— *Critical Quarterly,* v. II, Winter, 1960. Reproduced by permission of Blackwell Publishers.— *Essays in Literature,* v. 11, Fall, 1984. Copyright 1984 by Western Illinois University.— *Extrapolation,* v. 13, 1972; v. 20, Summer, 1979. Copyright © 1972 by The Kent State University Press. Reproduced by permission.— *Hispanofila,* v. 119, January, 1997. Reproduced by permission.— *Inter-American Review of Bibliography,* v. xxxiii, 1983. Reproduced by permission.— *Journal of Modern Literature,* v. 18, Fall, 1993. © Temple University, 1994. Reproduced by permission.— *Latin American Literary Review,* v. 15, July-December, 1987; v. 17, January-June, 1989; v. 23, January-June, 1995. All reproduced by permission.— *The Los Angeles Times Book Review,* June 10, 1984. Copyright, 1984, Los Angeles Times. Reproduced by permission.— *Modern Language Notes,* v. 115, March, 2000. © 2000 by The Johns Hopkins University Press. Reproduced by permission.— *The Modern Language Review,* v. 81, January, 1986. Reproduced by permission.— *Mosaic,* v. 34, March, 2001. Reproduced by permission. — *The Nation* (New York), v. 129, July 21-28,1984. © 1984 The Nation Magazine/The Nation Company, Inc. Reproduced by permission.— *New Novel Review,* v. 1, April, 1994 for "A Conversation with Jose Donoso," by Nivia Montenegro and Enrico Mario Santi. Reproduced by permission of the publisher and the authors.— *Notes on Modern American Literature,* v. viii, Winter, 1984 for "Wrapped in a Winter Rug: Richard Brautigan Looks at Common Responses to Death," by Brooke K. Horvath. Reproduced by permission of the author.— *The Northwest Ohio Quarterly,* v. 70, Summer-Autumn, 1998. Reproduced by permission.— *Ohioana Quarterly,* v. 27, Autumn, 1984. Reproduced by permission.— *Philological Quarterly,* v. 69, Spring, 1990 for "Eat or be Eaten: H. G. Well's 'Time Machine,'" by Kathryn Hume. Copyright © 19990 by The University of Iowa. Reproduced by permission of the author.— *PMLA,* v. 84, May, 1969. Reproduced by permission.— *Publishers Weekly,* v. 232, October 9, 1987. Copyright 1987 by Reed Publishing USA. Reproduced from *Publishers Weekly,* published by the Bowker Magazine Group of Cahners Publishing Co., a division of Reed Publishing USA., by permission.— *The Review of Contemporary Fiction,* Fall, 1988; v. 12, Summer, 1992; Reproduced by permission.— *Revista de Estudios Hispanicos,* v. ix, January, 1975; v. 19, January, 1985. Reproduced by permission.— *Romance Languages Annual,* v. 10, 1998. © 1998 by Purdue Research Foundation. Reproduced by permission.— *Salmagundi,* v. 82-83, Spring-Summer, 1989. Copyright © 1989 by Skidmore College. Reproduced by permission.— *Science Fiction Studies,* v. 3, July, 1976; v. 3, November, 1976; v. 6, March, 1979; v. 8, November, 1981; v. 14, July, 1987; v. 26, July, 1999. Copyright © 1976, 1979, 1981, 1987, 1999 by SFS Publications. All reproduced by permission.— *Studies in Short Fiction,* v. 17, Spring, 1980. Copyright 1980 by Newberry College. Reproduced by permission.— *Studies in Twentieth Century Literature,* v. 23, Summer, 1999. Copyright © 1999 by *Studies in Twentieth Century Literature.* Reproduced by permission.— *Symposium,* v. 41, Fall, 1987; v. 42, Summer, 1988. Copyright © 1987, 1988 Helen Dwight Reid Educational Foundation. Both reproduced with permission of the Helen Dwight Reid Educational Foundation, published by Heldref Publications, 1319 18th Street, NW, Washington, DC 20036- 1802.— *The Wellsian,* v. 17, Winter, 1994; v. 22, 1999. Reproduced by permission.

COPYRIGHTED MATERIAL IN *TCLC*, VOLUME 133, WAS REPRODUCED FROM THE FOLLOWING BOOKS:

Borinksy, Alicia. From *Theoretical Fables: The Pedagogical Dream in Contemporary Latin American Fiction.* University of Pennsylvania Press, 1993. Reproduced by permission.—Boyer, Jay. From *Richard Brautigan.* Boise State University,

Literary Criticism Series Advisory Board

The members of the Gale Group Literary Criticism Series Advisory Board—reference librarians and subject specialists from public, academic, and school library systems—represent a cross-section of our customer base and offer a variety of informed perspectives on both the presentation and content of our literature criticism products. Advisory board members assess and define such quality issues as the relevance, currency, and usefulness of the author coverage, critical content, and literary topics included in our series; evaluate the layout, presentation, and general quality of our printed volumes; provide feedback on the criteria used for selecting authors and topics covered in our series; provide suggestions for potential enhancements to our series; identify any gaps in our coverage of authors or literary topics, recommending authors or topics for inclusion; analyze the appropriateness of our content and presentation for various user audiences, such as high school students, undergraduates, graduate students, librarians, and educators; and offer feedback on any proposed changes/enhancements to our series. We wish to thank the following advisors for their advice throughout the year.

Richard Brautigan
1935-1984

American novelist and poet.

The following entry provides criticism on Brautigan's works from 1984 through 2001. For criticism prior to 1984, see *CLC,* Volumes 1, 3, 5, 9, 12, 34, and 42.

INTRODUCTION

Brautigan's avant-garde poetry and fiction made him a transitional figure between the Beat movement of the 1950s and the counterculture movement of the 1960s, as well as a precursor of the postmodernists. In his novels, Brautigan employs lyrical prose, simple syntax, and a whimsical narrative style while exploring such themes as death, sex, violence, betrayal, loss of innocence, and the power of imagination to transform reality. Several critics have argued that Brautigan is an unclassifiable author, most closely allied with Kurt Vonnegut.

BIOGRAPHICAL INFORMATION

Brautigan was born on January 30, 1935, in Tacoma, Washington. He never met his biological father and had few happy memories of his childhood. Though a troubled teenager, he began to write stories in high school. Brautigan was once placed in a mental hospital after being diagnosed as a paranoid schizophrenic. Upon his release in the mid-1950s, Brautigan went to San Francisco where he encountered poets of the Beat Generation, including Lawrence Ferlinghetti and Philip Whalen. Brautigan then began to frequent poetry readings in North Beach coffeehouses. In 1957 he married Virginia Dionne Adler, with whom he had a daughter. Brautigan first published poetry but began to write fiction in the 1960s, which were his most productive years. Brautigan divorced in 1970 and in 1977 married a Japanese woman after he had achieved a measure of literary success in Japan. In 1976 Brautigan bought a ranch in Montana, where he continued to write despite his waning popularity. Another divorce, numerous other personal disappointments, and a heavy dependence on alcohol contributed to his death in September of 1984 from a self-inflicted gunshot wound.

MAJOR WORKS

Brautigan's first important volume of poetry, *The Galilee Hitch-Hiker* (1958), an outgrowth of his experiences with the Beat poets in San Francisco, is the surrealistic

odyssey of a man who drives a Model A Ford across Galilee and the United States. Brautigan plays with language, especially similes and metaphors with humorous twists, in *Lay the Marble Tea* (1959) and in *The Octopus Frontier* (1960) uses objects in the natural world to construct a world of imagination. Another poetry collection, *All Watched Over by Machines of Loving Grace* (1967), was followed by *The Pill Versus the Springhill Mine Disaster* (1968), which became his most popular volume of poetry. His novel *A Confederate General from Big Sur* (1964) is a play on the concept of historical accuracy. Brautigan's lasting fictional legacy was probably fixed by his 1967 novel *Trout Fishing in America,* which found its first audience among the counterculture then beginning to flourish in San Francisco. This novel, set mostly in the American West, is a lament for the loss of the natural landscape told in a picaresque and absurdist way. *In Watermelon Sugar* (1968) takes place in a postapocalyptic utopian commune called iDeath, where people manufacture everything they need from watermelon sugar and have no hope for uplift or progress. Brautigan's *The Abortion: An Historical Romance 1966* (1971) is a parody of a genre novel which tells the story of a trip to Tijuana to secure an abortion for the author's girlfriend. Another parody, *The Hawkline Monster: A Gothic Western* (1974), takes on the western novel genre in a bizarre tale of a monster who lives in ice caves under an estate in Oregon. Three more novels in this parody series included *Willard and His Bowling Trophies: A Perverse Mystery* (1975), *Sombrero Fallout: A Japanese Novel* (1976), and *Dreaming of Babylon: A Private Eye Novel 1942* (1977). Brautigan produced just one volume of short stories, *Revenge of the Lawn: Stories 1962-1970* (1971), composed of very short vignettes on specific themes. He published several minor volumes of poetry in the 1970s, ending with *June 30th, June 30th* (1978), a collection of his impressions as an outsider in Japan in 1977. A novel, *The Tokyo-Montana Express* (1980), also grew out of his experiences in Japan and his new life on his Montana ranch. *So the Wind Won't Blow It All Away* (1982), Brautigan's final novel, was marked by the pessimism which pervaded the last part of his life.

CRITICAL RECEPTION

Brautigan's critics have found him hard to classify. Some called him a last vestige of the Beat Generation, a hippie writer, or a modern-day Thoreau; others thought he was an early postmodernist or a Zen Buddhist. In the 1960s his experimental fiction was well received, although some reviewers felt his work was simplistic and lightweight. *Trout Fishing in America* received considerable critical attention for its unusual style and humorous tone. This book became something of a cult classic, especially on the west coast. Brautigan's *In Watermelon Sugar* and *A Confederate General from Big Sur* were also reviewed and widely read. Brautigan's later genre novels, however, were given much less attention. His poetry gained mixed reviews, called uneven by some and linguistically and imaginatively interesting by others. In the 1970s and early 1980s Brautigan's work was out of fashion and received few reviews, except in Japan, where he had gained a new audience. Those western critics who did comment on Brautigan's work often labelled him an aging hippie whose literary time had past. By the time of his death, most critics had dubbed Brautigan a minor writer of the counterculture period. In the mid-1980s and in the years after his death, however, critics began to take a renewed look at Brautigan's work, finding in it considerable complexity and an originality. The publication of a biography, three biographical-critical studies, and a detailed bibliography helped to rekindle interest in Brautigan's life and body of work.

PRINCIPAL WORKS

The Galilee Hitch-Hiker (poetry) 1958
Lay the Marble Tea (poetry) 1959
The Octopus Frontier (poetry) 1960
A Confederate General from Big Sur (novel) 1964
All Watched Over by Machines of Loving Grace (poetry) 1967
Trout Fishing in America (novel) 1967
The Pill Versus the Springhill Mine Disaster (poetry) 1968
In Watermelon Sugar (novel) 1968
The Abortion: An Historical Romance 1966 (novel) 1971
Revenge of the Lawn: Stories 1962-1970 (short stories) 1971
The Hawkline Monster: A Gothic Western (novel) 1974
Willard and His Bowling Trophies: A Perverse Mystery (novel) 1975
Sombrero Fallout: A Japanese Novel (novel) 1976
Dreaming of Babylon: A Private Eye Novel 1942 (novel) 1977
June 30th, June 30th (poetry) 1978
The Tokyo-Montana Express (novel) 1980
So the Wind Won't Blow It All Away (novel) 1982
An Unfortunate Woman: A Journey (novel) 2000

CRITICISM

Brooke K. Horvath (essay date winter 1984)

SOURCE: Horvath, Brooke K. "Wrapped in a Winter Rug: Richard Brautigan Looks at Common Responses to Death." *Notes on Modern American Literature* 8, no. 3 (winter 1984): Item 14.

[*In the following brief analysis of "Winter Rug," Horvath discusses the manner in which the characters come to terms with death.*]

"Winter Rug," a story included in ***Revenge of the Lawn: Stories 1962-1970,*** reveals in brief compass the preoccupation with death central to Richard Brautigan's fiction.[1] Whereas Brautigan's major imaginative efforts present characters who typically bring radical tactics into play in their efforts to gain psychological control over death (the retreat into fantasy in ***A Confederate***

General from Big Sur, death's imaginative revision in *Trout Fishing in America,* the attempt of the iDEATH inhabitants to live in and with death in *In Watermelon Sugar,* and the mock-heroic triumph over death achieved in *The Abortion*), "Winter Rug" examines the paltry efforts of two characters to defuse death's sting through recourse to society's less drastic, habitual ploys.

The story concerns an old dog "dying very slowly from senility."[2] Owned by a wealthy old woman, the dog is eventually wrapped in an expensive Chinese rug and buried in the garden following the woman's reluctant decision to have her pet put "to sleep," a euphemistic expression that, like the rug, serves to hide death's reality. "Winter Rug," however, proves interesting not because of its plot but because of the responses the dog's death elicits from the narrator and his friend (the woman's gardener and the source of the story). Indeed, the first page of this stubby tale concerns not the dog and its owner but the narrator, who commences by presenting credentials to establish his competence to speak of death. His funereal vita begins:

> My credentials? Of course. They are in my pocket. Here: I've had friends who have died in California and I mourn them in my own way. I've been to Forest Lawn and romped over the place like an eager child. I've read *The Loved One, The American Way of Death, Wallets in Shrouds* and my favorite *After Many a Summer Dies the Swan.*

The narrator goes on to cite funerals he has witnessed (from a distance) and recalls once seeing a corpse, "done tastefully in a white sheet," carried out of a skid row flophouse to an ambulance solemnly waiting to drive it away, his friend remarking at the time that "Being dead [was] one step up from living in that hotel." The narrator concludes simply, "As you can see, I am an expert on death in California."

The narrator's opening lines thus disclose several common means of masking death's horror. His mourning, like the tasteful winding sheet and stately processional bestowed upon a flophouse resident, witnesses to society's usual practice of blanketing death in distracting legalities and honors (the ambulance "was prohibited by law from having a siren"); of wrapping it in ritualized, symbolic acts that serve to sooth us survivors; of handing it over to professionals to be disguised and distanced: all ways of removing death from the sphere of daily life, ways ably dissected in Jessica Mitford's *The American Way of Death.* Reading this book and the others mentioned suggests a second common attempt at conquering death's strangeness: the acquisition of knowledge, the knowledge-is-power routine.

The narrator also tells of visiting Forest Lawn and romping "like an eager child," as though life's final mystery could be familiarized, made the object of happy

expectation, rendered innocuous (ploys Brautigan characters attempt elsewhere, as in *The Abortion* and *In Watermelon Sugar*), made part of a game (an attempt made in many of the stories of childhood in *Revenge*: for instance, "The Ghost Children of Tacoma," "A Need for Gardens," and "Sand Castles"). His child-like behavior suggests further a denial of time's passage, a willed return to innocence, to that time when, necrobiotically speaking, one is as far from death as one will ever be. Finally, the friend's joke, with its allusion to the notion of death as the doorway to one's reward, seeks to deflect a discomfiting confrontation through humor, which serves to distance the fact of death and to deflate its seriousness.

Beginning his account of the dog's death, the narrator observes that "the dog had been dying for so long that it had lost the way to death." Dwelling upon the dog's suffering, the narrator resorts implicitly to the perennial wisdom, seeing death as a release from suffering, a kindness: it is the animal's "time"; death is for the best. In short, this "metaphysical war" (as the narrator describes the enterprise of funeral directors) is won by giving death a purpose, by transforming it from end to means (another tactic in the *Revenge* stories: compare "A Complete History of Germany and Japan").

Finally, the story closes with the friend cursing the dog and having second thoughts about burying a rug worth $1000. Although someone earning a gardener's wages might well regret the lost opportunity of possessing such a treasure, more importantly the friend's comment reveals another prevalent means of controlling death anxieties: by reducing death's place in the scheme of things, by pretending that other things are worthier of one's concern, things whose loss constitutes sounder reason to mourn.

"Winter Rug" presents its thanatopsis with unusual guilelessness, but its catalog of life-enhancing illusions is far from unusual. Although the narrator claims to be "an expert on death," clearly he is no more experienced than most of us, and his attempts at controlling his responses to life's irremediable end are among society's routine strategies, as he must know from his reading. The defensive tone with which he begins—as well as his limiting his area of expertise to "death in California"—exposes self-doubts vis-a-vis that mastery of death's mystery his introduction is supposedly establishing, just as his story reveals one old woman's pathetic attempts first to deny death's reality ("When the old woman [first saw the death doctor's] little black bag, she paled visibly. The unnecessary reality of it scared her . . .") and then to control death by choosing the time and means of her pet's departure.

But the inadequacy of the narrator's ploys and those of his friend are perhaps best suggested by the fact that an unknown dog's death has so captured the narrator's imagination, has thrust the problem of death so unavoidably before him, that he must transform it into a story, into art. Particularly in the absence of religious belief (an absence present in this story), such an act, according to psychologists and literary theorists alike,[3] is inherently concerned with giving our endings meanings, with creating illusions that make endings part of a comprehensible, hence meaningful and possibly acceptable whole. If the narrator of **"Winter Rug"** has gained any control over death, he has done so—as, perhaps, has his creator—by capturing it in a fiction.

Notes

1. On the death-obsessiveness percolating through Brautigan's work, see, for example, Tony Tanner, *City of Words: American Fiction 1950-1970* (New York: Harper & Row, 1971), and Jack Hicks, *In the Singer's Temple: Prose Fictions of Barthelme, Gaines, Brautigan, Piercy, Kesey, and Kosinski* (Chapel Hill: University of North Carolina Press, 1981).

2. Richard Brautigan, *Revenge of the Lawn: Stories 1962-1970* (New York: Pocket Books, 1972). The story runs from page 59 to page 62; because it is so short, I will not include page references for individual passages cited.

3. See, for example, Ernest Becker, *The Denial of Death* (New York: The Free Press, 1973); Frank Kermode, *The Sense of an Ending: Studies in the Theory of Fiction* (New York: Oxford University Press, 1967); and Peter Brooks, *Reading for the Plot: Design and Intention in Narrative* (New York: Knopf, 1984).

Brooke Horvath (essay date October 1985)

SOURCE: Horvath, Brooke. "Richard Brautigan's Search for Control over Death." *American Literature* 57, no. 3 (October 1985): 434-55.

[*In the following essay, Horvath examines the ways in which Brautigan's fiction deals with the illusion of cheating death.*]

Ludwig Wittgenstein once noted that "Death is not an event in life. Death is not lived through."[1] However, as Keirkegaurd and others have forcefully argued, the prospect of death is life's central fact and the repression of this fact life's primary task. For Ernest Becker, moreover, man's heroism lies in his impossible efforts to transcend creatureliness, to deny death by means of "life-enhancing illusion."[2] Among such illusions might be placed statements such as Wittgenstein's and the fiction of Richard Brautigan.

As Becker writes early in *The Denial of Death,* "The irony of man's condition is that the deepest need is to be free of the anxiety of death and annihilation; but it is life itself which awakens it, and so we must shrink from being fully alive" (p. 66). For Becker, this dilemma is inherent to consciousness, a consequence of human nature more than nurture. His views thus oppose those of Marcuse or Norman O. Brown, whose works speak to the desire for unrepressed living while pointing an accusing finger at society as the cause of repression. Yet throughout the Sixties, Brautigan created characters seeking not greater freedom but greater control over their lives: over their creatureliness, their thoughts and emotions. But further, although shrinking from life should not be seen exclusively as a result of social antagonism toward freedom and self-expansiveness, society can exacerbate this existential timidity. And in *Trout Fishing in America* (completed 1961, published 1967), *A Confederate General from Big Sur* (completed 1963, published 1964), *In Watermelon Sugar* (completed 1964, published 1968), and *The Abortion: An Historical Romance 1966* (1971) the global village falls to ataractic communes and isolated dreamers seeking escapes from history, time, and change.

I

The American 1960s was often violent and deadly. The decade brought the country Vietnam and nightly body counts, the Cuban missile crisis and renewed atmospheric nuclear testing, Birmingham Sunday and the Days of Rage, Watts and Newark, Charles Whitman and Richard Speck, assassinations and alarms of overpopulation and eco-death. Strange, unnatural death and explicitly detailed acts of irrational, unexpected violence clearly obsessed the decade's fiction. Brautigan suggested the inseparability of death from his vision of the Sixties in the title of his fourth novel, *The Abortion: An Historical Romance 1966,* thereby underscoring the death-obsession which his critics have frequently noticed percolating through his work.[3] This obsession underlies the now-famous vignettes of blighted landscapes and polluted streams, perverted myths, frustrated hopes, corrupted values, corporeal and spiritual death in *Trout Fishing in America.* Brautigan's disappointment with our times underlies as well the sense of degeneration informing *A Confederate General,* evoked through the novel's contrast of present-day America with the Civil War years and of the heroic images that war typically conjures up with both the imagined behavior of Lee Mellon's ancestor Augustus and the observed behavior of that border psychopath Lee. *In Watermelon Sugar* reveals its author's critique of society in its images of an alternative community and of the Forgotten Works: those remains of a self-destructive civilization so far fallen into ruin that its survivors, 171 years later, can no longer identify many of its simplest artifacts.

Additionally, Brautigan's *idée fixe* habitually works itself out in stories of dropouts or of those living along the mainstream's more ragged tributaries, for his characters customarily sound retreats: to Big Sur, to what remains of the wilderness, to the emotionless science-fiction commune of iDEATH, to the cloistered utopia Vida and the narrator share in *The Abortion.*[4] Such a conjunction of death, destruction, and disaffiliation suggests that Lee, Vida, and the rest share a countercultural view of the dominant culture as dealing and desiring death; in which case, disengagement from society might understandably follow. But further, to the extent that fear of death may be considered the primary motivational factor in men's lives, disengagement may result not only because death is ubiquitous within the confines of the establishment but because, even when most admirable, most heroic, the dominant culture offers promises of transcending death that no longer convince. When such promises fail to inspire belief, the individual is forced back upon himself to create his own illusions of control, his own means of defusing death fears. In short, our world makes closet neurotics of us all when we must forego, in some measure giving allegiance to the dominant culture as savior and attempt instead to erect private stays against dissolution.[5]

To free themselves from the anxiety of death, Brautigan's heroes seek to control the life that awakens it, seek the know-how of dominating life through self-imposed restraints upon life and self. Lee Mellon, for instance, may possess a certain amount of barely serviceable survival know-how, but, as importantly, he also has the know-how to shape his life into a denial of death. In that connection, Hugh Kenner has recently observed how-to literature's venerable tradition in America. Infiltrating the work of our best writers (Kenner points to *Walden, Moby-Dick, Life on the Mississippi,* and *Death in the Afternoon*), how-to literature has over the years metamorphosed into "a genre sui generis, the indigenous American literature of escape."[6] Similarly, Brautigan's Sixties seekers put a premium on self-reliance, on know-how, as a way of creating the illusion that one is master of one's life, hence of one's destiny. In this respect, *The Abortion* is in a sense only a terribly *au courant* how to manual (how to resolve a problematic pregnancy easily, safely, and relatively emotionlessly); *In Watermelon Sugar,* a mock blueprint for structuring utopia; and Lee Mellon, that "Confederate general in ruins,'"[7] a half-assed, latter-day Thoreau.

Brautigan's is, however, a curious brand of how-to self-reliance. Two comments reprinted on the back cover of the Dell edition of *Trout Fishing* clarify the nature of these novels as how-to literature. A reader at the Viking Press noted that "Mr. Brautigan submitted a book to us in 1962 called *Trout Fishing in America.* I gather from reports that it was not about trout fishing." *Fly Fisherman* magazine, on the other hand, told its readers that "reading *Trout Fishing in America* won't help you catch more fish, but it does have something to do with trout fishing."[8] The point is that Brautigan, foregoing even a facade of practical instruction, foregrounds instead the escapism underlying America's indigenous genre no less than it underlies the musings of armchair and weekend anglers. He focuses on the how-to of escape: not only from a particularly deadly society but from too much life generally, and from the fear of being overwhelmed by this life, the life awakening fears of death.

Such concerns may be described as religious insofar as they manifest a preoccupation with death and its transcendence and insofar as the desire to transcend death lies at the heart of religious belief. Brautigan's fiction as how-to, then, involves creating a private religion that promises a triumph over death. This combination of self-reliance and spiritual necessity—requiring the reshaping of a received but no longer viable tradition or, more drastically, the constructing of a private alternative to fit personal needs—characterizes as well a large part of religious thought in America. America's history of do-it-yourself religion might be seen to begin with the Puritans' covenant theology and their vision of the New World as the New Israel. This tradition informs the Enlightenment appropriation of Puritanism, the Transcendentalist and Romantic revisions of Puritanism and Unitarianism, the merger of civil and millennial expectations that became so centrally a part of nineteenth-century thought, the Campbellites and Millerites (indeed, America's history of utopian communities in general), the work of Joseph Smith and Mary Baker Eddy, Emerson's plea for religious self-reliance and James's *Varieties of Religious Experience,* Henry Adams and the Beats. In short, whenever spiritual dissatisfaction has flowered, Americans have been quick to "make it new," to clear some imaginative ground upon which to raise their personal solutions.

II

As man's capacity for killing increased in scale, as incomprehensible death seemed increasingly omnipresent, as conventional religious belief as a means of resolving death fears continued to collapse, literary theorists began speaking more and more of literature's function in terms of its ability to give endings meaning.[9] It is art's ability to control its ends, its power to resee and to reorder reality, that Brautigan foregrounds in his first completed novel, *Trout Fishing in America.* "Rembrandt Creek," one of the novel's two "lost chapters" (published in *Esquire* three years after the book's appearance), seems to offer a heuristic for interpreting *Trout Fishing*'s intention: "Often I think about Rembrandt Creek and how much it looked like a painting hanging in the world's largest museum with a roof that went to the stars and galleries that knew the whisk of comets."[10] Like the name arbitrarily assigned to the creek, this passage reminds the reader of the possibility of transforming life into art. More explicitly still, Brautigan emphasizes fiction's ability to legislate endings by the conclusion he here offers. The penultimate chapter of the novel ends with the narrator expressing his desire to "write a book that ended with the word Mayonnaise" (p. 181). Then, on the next and final page, postfixed to the letter concluding **Trout Fishing** but having nothing to do with this letter, the following appears: "Sorry I forgot to give you the mayonaise" (p. 182). (Not to strain, but the fact that "mayonnaise" is here misspelled—in all editions of the novel, as far as I can tell—may suggest that the narrator's wish to control his story's ending has been at best imperfectly realized.) Finally, the book's overall style and structure highlight art as symbolic transcendence: through its collage construction and lack of narrative line, the novel seems intent on converting time into space and thereby halting America's progressive decay, while this tactic of atemporality likewise creates a sense of timeless presence that erases mortality as a function of time-boundedness.[11]

On the other hand, like the Biblical prophet, who assumes a countercultural stance to speak against his culture's numbness to death, Brautigan as controlling author has constructed a witty, dispassionate jeremiad to criticize his country's passionless capitulation to death, America's degeneration and forgetfulness concerning its hopes and dreams: which he does by ironically mirroring in his book's construction the sense of that eternal now that Walter Brueggemann labels "the lewd promise of immortality" and argues is always an illusion the establishment finds necessary to maintain to deny the possibility of newness, of alternative beginnings. By voicing through its series of koan-like sketches the despair over death and dissolution America has provoked, is blind to, and cannot countermand, **Trout Fishing** expresses the grief that must precede dismantling and energizing toward a new beginning. That is, through its language of grief, through its dark humor, through its awareness of death fears suppressed so long they have been forgotten in numbness, Brautigan's first novel opens the possibility of controlling death insofar as the novel now allows the future to be imagined alternatively.[12]

However, Brautigan's fiction attempts to solve the problem of death not only by finding an energizing language of grief and hope, not only by imposing "coherent patterns" providing ends consonant with beginnings and middles,[13] but also by intercalating within these patterns accounts of characters who themselves seek controls over death, controls they would like to think proffer freedom, dignity, and hope—characteristics of the "best" illusions, according to Becker (p. 202). Toward this end, the characters of **A Confederate General, In Watermelon Sugar,** and **The Abortion** resort, variously,

to fantasy, simplification of perception and response, ritualized and routinized behavior, and an effort at shutting down the self by maintaining a cool aloofness from emotion, from too much introspection, and from anything else that might cause a loss of self-control. Self-reliance for these characters is achieved not by expanding the sphere of their competence but by reducing life's scope and possibility (the less-is-more approach) or by wrapping themselves in private myths that imaginatively render life harmless. The problem with such ploys lies in the fact that rather than penetrating a numbness to death and so engaging in that "embrace of deathliness [that] permits newness to come,"[14] these characters typically spin illusions enhancing numbness by camouflaging its underlying anxiety: those fears of death with which they refuse to wrestle.

III

A Confederate General, with its hard-drinking, dope-smoking, gun-toting, womanizing dropouts Lee and Jesse, might seem to illustrate not the characterization of Brautigan's heroes just drawn but that craziness that may easily result from the need to contrive private rituals. Yet neurosis and psychosis are ways of seeking to control life and to neutralize the terror of eventual annihilation—though such strategies cost too much, which is part of the reason why Lee and Jesse seem finally to be leading unenviable lives.

In an early discussion of **A Confederate General** Terence Malley objected that Jesse's replacement of Lee as the novel's center of attention works to the book's detriment. Malley found Jesse's slide into psychological instability too radical a change from his earlier role as humorous sidekick, and the melancholic temperament he comes to exhibit, too perplexing.[15] Yet from first to last the book is Jesse's, not only because he is its narrator and central consciousness but because what **A Confederate General** in fact chronicles is Lee's effect on Jesse: the gradual undermining of this shy loner's precarious psychological balance through his acquaintance with Lee, that "end product of American spirit, pride and the old know-how" (p. 93).

The reader learns little about Jesse's life prior to his meeting Lee, but one suspects it was quietly desperate. Well read, given to paying visits on the elderly woman living below him, conscientious he leaves a newfound lover's bed, for example, to recover a drunken Lee before the police find him), Jesse finds his days nonetheless clouded by depression. The most unlikely experiences emerge from his mind in metaphoric shrouds: "a rush of wind came by the cabin. The wind made me think about the Battle of Agincourt for it moved like arrows about us . . ." (p. 111). Against this habitual disposition, Jesse favors small life-enhancing illusions, such as humor—which attempts to distance despair and to deflate its seriousness—or the book about the soul he reads shortly after joining Lee at Big Sur: "The book said everything was all right if you didn't die while you were reading the book, if your fingers maintained life while turning the pages" (p. 66). Similarly, after obsessively reading and rereading Ecclesiastes, Jesse finds a way of bringing its gloomy world view under control by reducing the text to its punctuation marks, which he then carefully tabulates night by night, Qoheleth's vision mastered by being reduced to a "kind of study in engineering" (p. 74).

Yet at the time Jesse is practicing such pathetic rituals, he has already fallen into the manic world of Lee Mellon. Lee's exuberance doubtless attracts the withdrawn Jesse, who finds fascinating material for his death-suffused outlook in Lee's martial fantasy and violent behavior. Throughout the novel, Jesse has occasion to relate instances of Lee's sadism, as when Lee threatens to shoot two teenagers caught trying to siphon gas from his truck (pp. 76-80). If heroism is, at root, the courage to face death, and sadism, like mental illness generally, "a way of talking about people who have lost courage" (Becker, p. 209),[16] Lee's sadistic behavior is a logical consequence of his lifestyle, as is the fantasy role he assigns himself: the outlaw descendent of the fictitious Confederate general Augustus Mellon.

Lee leads a life of petty violence, squalor, and penury; as a self-reliant outlaw, he is inept: his hold-ups net him petty cash; he cannot shoot straight because he is "excitable" (p. 65); and although while holed up in an abandoned house in Oakland he successfully taps a gas main, he cannot control the resulting flame and is consequently seen for a time minus eyebrows. To give such a life meaning and the heroic dimension that would justify it, Lee must resort to sadism and fantasy: as the Confederate General of Big Sur, he gains self-worth by proxy and a precedent for abandoning the conventions by which lesser men must live.

The martial imagery draping Lee and the book is, however, primarily Jesse's doing, for he has masochistically bought into Lee's fantasy life to add vicarious grandeur to his own failed heroics. As Jesse observes while the two teenagers grovel at gunpoint and he stands by, ax in hand, "Do you see how perfect our names were, how the names lent themselves to this kind of business? Our names were made for us in another century" (p. 78). But eventually, these fantasies become themselves too overwhelming, no longer a means of controlling life but now a threat to self-control. Johnston Wade may be the final straw here, for, unlike the fantasies of the others (even Lee, threatening the teenagers, knows his gun is not loaded), Wade's are so out of control and dangerous that Lee finally resorts to chaining Wade to a log to keep everyone safe. Further, Wade, as a deranged insurance magnate on the lam because convinced his family

is out to get him, offers an unsettling reminder not only of society's power to destroy but also of both the trapped individual's recourse to fantasy-control and the destructive potential of fantasy itself.

After a few hours of Wade, Jesse confesses, "I wanted reality to be there. What we had wasn't worth it. Reality would be better" (p. 126). But life at Big Sur will continue to tip Jesse's delicate balance: "I was really gone. My mind was beginning to take a vacation from my senses. I felt it continuing to go while Lee Mellon got the dope" (p. 152). By the final chapter, Jesse has fallen into sexual impotence and, looking back, concludes, "The last week's activities had been a little too much for me, I think. A little too much of life had been thrown at me . . ." (p. 154).

Jesse fails to find the illusions he needs, leaning instead on the crutch of others' fantasies, which offer him small hope, smaller dignity, and at best a loser's kind of freedom. Unable to discover a way of ordering his life into a meaningful, heroic whole, Jesse, not surprisingly, finds no satisfying end for his story but rather five alternative conclusions followed by "more and more endings: the sixth, the 53rd, the 131st, the 9,435th ending, endings going faster and faster, more and more endings, faster and faster until this book is having 186,000 endings per second" (p. 159).

IV

According to Nietzsche, most men employ either "guilty" or "innocent" means in their struggles against life's "deadening dull, paralyzing, protracted pain," which only the courageous have the capacity to experience without a soporific. Guilty means always involve "some kind of an *orgy of feeling,*" whereas innocent means include a "general muting of the feeling of life, mechanical activity, the petty pleasure, above all 'love of one's neighbor' . . . the communal feeling of power through which the individual's discontent with himself is drowned in his pleasure in the prosperity of the community."[17] In *A Confederate General* Lee and Wade represent the employment of guilty expedients, which submerge Jesse and his more innocent stratagems. Well aware of the dangers of excess, and more fortunate than Jesse in avoiding these dangers, the characters of *In Watermelon Sugar* and *The Abortion* likewise favor innocent maneuvers. In both books, characters find asylums wherein carefully regulated and ritualized fantasies—do-it-yourself religions—achieve a drastic shutting down of self that masks a failure of heroism and voids death anxiety more successfully than anachronistic secession and more predictably than dope.

In the world of Watermelon Sugar, simple, quietly routine days pass without disturbing emotions, thoughts, or desires. Whatever happens is seen to have happened for the best and as it must, and whatever displeases tends to disappear from view, like Margaret's note: "I read the note and it did not please me and I threw it away, so not even time could find it."[18] Personality has been so repressed that most of the community's art, to choose one telling example, stands as the work of anonymous artists who typically favor harmless subjects, electing to produce statues of vegetables and books on innocuous topics like pine needles and owls. In iDEATH, the community's spiritual center, as in Watermelon Sugar generally, "a delicate balance" obtains, as the narrator acknowledges (p. 1). To safeguard this life's emotional and intellectual deep sleep, virtues conducive to placidity must be cultivated; consideration and politeness are fetishized, and small, unsophisticated pleasures prevail. To experience such innocent joys, emotion must be carefully monitored, and even sexual desire must be satisfied with passion well under control (p. 34).

Further, all actual or potential threats to the community's well-being must be neutralized. Books, for example, are unvalued. Written by those who can find no satisfaction in more communally useful employment, books are seen as odd, solitary pursuits. If they do not, as in *Farhenheit 451,* represent such subversive dangers as curiosity and originality of thought, this is because no one pays them any mind. Although only twenty-three books have appeared in 171 years, even these go largely unread (pp. 11, 135), the possibility of life's growing too large averted by simple disregard, which also serves to defuse the nearby evil of the Forgotten Works:

> Nobody has been very far into the Forgotten Works, except that guy Charley said who wrote a book about them, and I wonder what his trouble was, to spend weeks in there.
>
> The Forgotten Works just go on and on and on and on and on and on and on and on and on. You get the picture. It's a big place, much bigger than we are.
>
> (p. 82)

Other sources of unrest fade from view as readily. The tigers, the once-great threat to Watermelon Sugar, required the most active opposition. Exterminated and subsequently mythologized, the tigers, symbols of human aggressiveness and instinctual need, have taken the theological problem of Blake's tyger with them, leaving only their remembered virtues—their math prowess and beautiful singing voices—for souvenirs. On the other hand, inBOIL and his gang, like Margaret, obligingly remove themselves through suicide, the end of their restless dissatisfaction with iDEATH. However, their deaths, although violent, trouble utopia only momentarily because Watermelon Sugar is a world with the knowhow to repress death anxiety by masking death's reality behind numbing familiarity, spurious immortality, and soporific funereal wisdom. InBOIL may kill himself to reveal iDEATH's true meaning, what the

death of the self really entails: that it means more than the death of the ego (Ideath), of the id (IDeath), of thought (IDEAth); that Charley and the rest have made a mockery of iDEATH, have, in fact, failed to confront it. Yet nestled firmly in their numbed, death-in-life existence, iDEATH's inhabitants cannot be flushed by literal death so easily. In the midst of the mass suicide of inBOIL and his gang, the narrator's girlfriend responds only by fetching a pail and mop to clean up the "mess" their bleeding to death has made. And although other deaths may elicit more sympathetic responses, they do not provoke much more emotion. Watching in the Statue of Mirrors (in which "everything is reflected") as his former girlfriend Margaret hangs herself, the narrator remarks, "I stopped looking into the Statue of Mirrors. I'd seen enough for that day. I sat down on a couch by the river and stared into the water of the deep pool that's there. Margaret was dead" (p. 136; see the similar reaction of Margaret's brother, p. 142).

Naming its center iDEATH, a place as changeable as death is various (pp. 18, 144-45), the community can pretend to be living with and in "death," which is further familiarized through elaborate burial rituals that leave the dead "in glass coffins at the bottoms of rivers" with "foxfire in the tombs, so they glow at night and we can appreciate what comes next" (p. 60). However, the community must pay a great price for this anxiety-free life. The shutting down of self practiced in Watermelon Sugar has reduced tremendously the scope of human response-ability. Moreover, the elaborate defensive armor forged here is not without chinks: unpacified dissidents like inBOIL; unhappy, ostracized souls like Margaret; and the restless, nameless narrator as well. Not only does the narrator see behind the shared illusions of iDEATH ("We call everything a river here. We're that kind of people," p. 2); he has written a book ("I wonder what his trouble was"): a book very different from the others written in Watermelon Sugar; a book that builds toward the suicide of iDEATH's latest dropout and ends on the day of the black sun; a book that implicitly gives the lie to the utopian triumph over death this world seems to represent by showing Watermelon Sugar as the restricted, dehumanizing, hopeless, and deadly place it finally is.

V

The Abortion continues Brautigan's interest in characters attempting to retreat from life. The narrator, again nameless, appears in the novel's first two books as a recluse operating a library to which San Francisco's lonely, frustrated residents can bring manuscripts to be recorded in the Library Contents Ledger, shelved (but never borrowed or read), and eventually moved to caves for permanent storage (where "cave seepage" will insure their destruction). Life, the narrator confesses, "was all pretty complicated before I started working here,"[19] but now, safe within the library—tellingly described as a prison, a church, a funeral parlor, an asylum, a time machine, a monastery (pp. 71, 77, 84, 85, 105, 178)—the ritualized, isolated life he leads in this building he has not left once in three years insulates him from history, time, and change. As he remarks upon finally emerging, "Gee, it had been a long time. I hadn't realized that being in that library for so many years was almost like being in some kind of timeless thing. Maybe an eternity" (p. 70).

The cause behind the narrator's re-entry into life is Vida, a relentlessly beautiful girl who arrives one evening with a book for the stacks. She also is in retreat from life; as she tells the narrator, "I can see at a glance . . . that you are something like me. You're not at home in the world" (p. 51). Vida's unease centers upon her body, not despite but because of its beauty: "My book is about my body, about how horrible it is to have people creeping, crawling, sucking at something I am not," she explains (p. 45).

If the library represents a refuge from life, Vida (Spanish for life) enters as a threat to the narrator's innocent defenses: mechanical activity, petty pleasures, muted feeling. "'Yes,' I said, feeling the door close behind me, knowing that somehow this at first-appearing shy unhappy girl was turning, turning into something strong that I did not know how to deal with" (p. 49). The narrator rightly feels such qualms, for Vida's beauty—the terrible beauty of life—is a perilous thing capable of wrecking havoc wherever it reveals itself. A middle-aged man, for instance, spotting Vida in the airport, "stood there staring on like a fool, not taking his eyes off Vida, even though her beauty had caused him to lose control of the world" (p. 117). And Vida's beauty can conjure death anxieties even more directly: "The driver continued staring at Vida. He paid very little attention to his driving. . . . I made a mental note of it for the future, not to have Vida's beauty risk our lives" (p. 177).

Yet Vida's beauty does risk their lives. The narrator finds himself far from the library riding in a taxi because Vida's appearance has caused life to enter his world in one particularly troublesome fashion: she has become pregnant, and the two must seek a Tijuana abortion, endangering Vida in obvious ways (and through the very source of her existential dis-ease), endangering the narrator insofar as this fall into physicality constitutes the immediate cause for his forced return to the world. "It looks like our bodies got us," Vida concludes, to which the narrator replies, "It happens sometimes" (p. 67), seeking comfort, like Jesse, in the assumption of a lighthearted attitude.

Indeed, although the narrator's good-natured stoicism falters momentarily as he waits in the doctor's office for the abortion to begin, for the most part he and Vida respond splendidly to life's sudden eruption in their midst. Just as Vida drags the narrator from his womblike existence to "live like a normal human being" (p. 189), so he more than reconciles her to her body. By novel's end, Vida is in fact supporting him by working in a North Beach topless bar (p. 191).[20] Similarly, the narrator's outlook changes during the course of his adventure. Flying to San Diego en route to Tijuana had left him green with nausea and desirous of a return to timelessness (p. 120). However, by the time of his return flight, mere hours later, he can remark cavalierly, "From time to time the airplane was bucked by an invisible horse in the sky but it didn't bother me because I was falling in love with the 727 jet, my sky home, my air love" (p. 183). And even earlier, only minutes after leaving the abortionist's, he finds it hard to keep a straight face when the hotel desk clerk reveals his belief that "People should never change. . . . They are happier that way" (p. 173). Returning to find he has lost his library position, the narrator adjusts quickly, moving into an apartment with Vida, Foster (his only other friend and a former library employee), and Foster's girlfriend and raising money for the library at a table across from Sproul Hall at Berkeley, where he becomes the hero Vida had assured him he would be (pp. 113, 192).

But in what sense is the narrator a hero? And how have he and Vida made their rapid transition from passive withdrawal to active participation in the world? The answer to the first question usually involves the narrator's personality. Beatle-like in appearance, gentle, caring, tranquilized, the narrator embodies, ostensibly, the virtues of heroism as redefined by the counterculture. Thus Malley describes him as a "strange, passive, low-keyed hero of our time" desiring an escape from the American experience, and Charles Hackenberry, plugging into the story's allegorical possibilities, sees in Brautigan's romance a "portrait of the peace movement's heroism and efficacy, its solution to the unwanted pregnancy of American intervention in Asia."[21] But I would suggest that the narrator considers himself heroic because he has triumphed over death. This feat accounts as well for his and Vida's altered attitudes toward the world, attitudes that in fact begin to change when they decide to seek an abortion, for this decision seems to place control over death (choosing its time and means) and so over life in their hands.

Although Hackenberry illustrates that *The Abortion* enacts the archetypal heroic quest, he carefully notes that the book is as much a parody of the romance as it is a romance-proper. It is parodic for the same reasons the narrator's control over death fails as a liberating, dignifying, and hopeful life-enhancing illusion. Like Lee and inBOIL, *The Abortion*'s narrator has attempted to control life and death by becoming the agent of death (in this case, the indirect agent). But his triumph is ephemeral. He has not seized control of his life; he has not even severed his connection with the library. But more to the point, his triumph lacks heroism, involving as it does a Foster-financed, antagonist-free trip to Tijuana for a relatively guiltless, untroubling termination of his girlfriend's pregnancy. The hotel clerk's wish may cause the narrator to smile, but the object of his quest is the fulfillment of this wish: to remain the same, to deny life and change: "Vida's stomach was flat and perfect and it was going to remain that way" (p. 133). The abortion was inexpensive and painless, and one gets what one pays for: in this case, a cheap, temporary illusion that will be obsolete in a few years.

VI

A Confederate General, In Watermelon Sugar, and *The Abortion* present searches for illusions capable of allaying death anxiety and of controlling the life that awakens this anxiety by overwhelming us self-conscious animals with the knowledge of our inherent finitude and biological enslavement. These searches end no more successfully than the search in *Trout Fishing* for pristine trout streams or for the continuance of traditional American myths and ideals, and one might conclude that Brautigan holds no hope of discovering a saving illusion that does not necessitate shutting down the self, smothering emotion, limiting human possibility. Yet stepping back, so to speak, beyond these stories and their narrators to the level on which both become components of Brautigan's imaginative acts, one returns to the sphere of art as life-enhancing illusion. In **"Tire Chain Bridge,"** a brief, three-page stop along the route of *The Tokyo-Montana Express* (1980), Brautigan presents in small compass a paradigmatic exploration of the possibilities and limits of art as death-defying illusion.

"Tire Chain Bridge" takes the form of a parable about the Sixties. It begins:

> The 1960s:
>
> A lot of people remember hating President Lyndon Baines Johnson and loving Janis Joplin and Jim Morrison, depending on the point of view. God rest their souls.
>
> I remember an old Indian woman looking for a tire chain in the snow.[22]

The story, set in 1969, is quickly told. Its narrator and his girlfriend are driving across New Mexico after a snowfall, looking for "some old Indian ruins." They find them, after a fashion, in the persons of an old Indian man and his sister. The man is encountered first, "standing patiently beside a blue Age-of-Aquarius pickup truck parked on the side of the road." He is not in any trouble; in fact, "Everything's just fine": he only waits for his sister, who is a mile or so down the road looking for a lost tire chain valued at three dollars. The

narrator is pleased to learn that road conditions improve ahead but has trouble believing someone is really "out there," searching in such wintry weather beneath the indifferent mesas for a used tire chain. But driving on, he soon finds her and asks foolishly if she has found the chain yet. Glancing "at the nearby 121,000 square miles, which is the area of New Mexico," she answers simply, "It's here someplace."

> "Good luck," I said, ten years ago in the Sixties that have become legend now like the days of King Arthur sitting at the Round Table with the Beatles, and John singing "Lucy in the Sky with Diamonds."
>
> We drove down the road toward the Seventies, leaving her slowly behind, looking for a tire chain in the snow with her brother waiting patiently beside a blue pickup truck with its Age-of-Aquarius paint job starting to flake.

So the story ends. Although brief, seemingly artless, and lightly told in a style matching the content's superficial slightness, **"Tire Chain Bridge"** means more than meets the casual eye, but what? Surely one must push beyond Edward Halsey Foster's opinion that the story illustrates an ability to laugh good-naturedly at the world's left over hippies.[23] True, the narrator's retrospective glance back does appear to offer a biting (though hardly acerb) assessment of the decade's foibles and delusions. Its heroes and villains, once as large and seemingly eternal as the New Mexican mesas, barely survived the decade, and—like the narrator's road, which disappeared into "a premature horizon"—they have already vanished into legend. Yet what sort of legends have they left us? Is the Age of Aquarius a fit substitute for Camelot? Are the Beatles the best the period could serve up in the way of heroes worthy to sit beside Arthur and his knights? Is "Lucy in the Sky with Diamonds" what we have in lieu of *Morte d'Arthur*?

If a parable, the lesson of **"Tire Chain Bridge"** would seem to be that the Sixties was a time of hopeless searching and of passive complacency: both inadequate responses to a cold world in which life exists, like this story, between death and dissolution. Further, these quests, however solemn and sincere, were worse than hopeless: they were so absurd as to be unbelievable ("'What?' I said, not quite hearing or maybe just not believing . . ."). The boon sought was trivial, the seekers caricatures of knights errant capable of mistaking a used tire chain for the Holy Grail. But if the searches were ludicrous, the alternative response was an exercise in misguided smugness: to wait beatifically in the assurance that "everything's just fine" while another conducts one's search, seeks one's solutions. Hoping to salvage a three-dollar investment but oblivious to his truck's slow corruption, the brother would seem to be the man who knows the price of everything and the value of nothing. Similarly, the Age of Aquarius itself—

self-satisfied, commercialized, soon bogged down in trivialities and (like the Beatles) in internal feuding—was already beginning to chip and fade even as it was being proclaimed a *fait accompli*.

Such a reading follows Brautigan's recent critics in their efforts to free his work from a too-narrow and perhaps spurious identification with the counterculture.[24] But I think the reading just offered does not tell the entire story. In the first place, metamorphosis into legend is not necessarily a shameful fate; to seat the Beatles beside Arthur may be a means not of undercutting their stature but of enhancing it. And with its acid-induced celebration of wonder, of emancipation from an overly repressive and joyless sense of reality, "Lucy in the Sky," the lay of Woodstock Nation, may be in its way a fitting successor to the songs of the troubadours, an appropriate anthem for the Children's Crusade of the Sixties.

But in terms of a close reading of Brautigan's story, it is perhaps more important to note that the Indian couple is heading not out of but into bad weather, and so the tire chain is well worth looking for: it could save their lives. To see the chain only in terms of its meager monetary worth discloses not only a faulty but a dangerous value system, just as it is wrong to fault the brother for worrying more about the chain than about his pickup: for want of the chain, the truck may be lost. Moreover, direction of motion is problematic here. Although the Indians seem to be dawdling "in the middle of nowhere" and the narrator ostensibly heading toward better weather, the road he travels is, like the year in which the story is set, a bridge into the Seventies, a decade equated in the opening and closing paragraphs with death—Joplin in 1970, Morrison in '71, Johnson in '73—and with disintegration: the flaking paint, the Beatles' death as a group in 1970, the evaporating sensibility of the Sixties. This dissolution hits closer to home for the narrator in that he and his "long since gone girlfriend" broke up after their travels together; and it is emphasized structurally by the girlfriend's disappearance into an infrequent "we" after paragraph six, the only paragraph in which she is spoken of.

Yet looking back to tell his tale, the narrator recalls as his talismanic figure not his girlfriend, not the mesas, not the Indian ruins he was looking for and presumably found, not the decade's dead or disbanded culture heroes, but a woman "looking for a tire chain in the snow." It is she who orients his perspective on the past. The narrator, apparently, cannot recall this woman without the accompanying thoughts of death and deterioration framing her story, yet in recollection her eyes "[echo] timelessness," placing her symbolically among those mesas that "had been witnesses to the beginning of time." Just as she stands alone in the snowy landscape—her patient searching akin to neither her brother's iner-

tia nor the narrator's heedless forward progress into the Seventies and the end of the road—so she stands apart from the decade's famous dead and their failed heroics.

Tire chains are, of course, a means of controlling one's movement along dangerous routes. The woman's search becomes, then, a defiance of death, a search for control in a deadly environment. There is no reason to suppose she enjoys her cold, lonely task, undertaken possibly only to please her brother, who lingers metaphorically closer to the Seventies, content to let whatever will be, be. Yet unlike him, she acts, purposefully if hopelessly, her actions sounding a small triumph of life over death, her conviction that the chain is "here someplace" becoming, however unconvincingly or absurdly, a denial of death: a denial echoed by the story's surface tone, which implies that nothing terribly fearful or serious is here at issue.

However, a sorrow underlies the story's placid surface. This sadness derives not so much from the narrator's necrology or wistful recounting of things past as from his recognition of the futility of the woman's paltry stay against destruction (and, by extension, of the limits of his own death-defying art). Her seeking may bridge the loss surrounding her, but the narrator has located these structurally peripheral memento mori at the story's thematic center. He has anchored his story-proper—of the salvific bridge the woman's action erects—in death at both ends: in the physical deaths with which **"Tire Chain Bridge"** begins and in the symbolic, spiritual death with which it ends. This latter anchorage involves the extinction of a way of seeing, of imagining the world: possibilities flatten out and dead-end, like the mess-topped horizon behind the narrator's forward-fleeing Jeep. Structurally, then, **"Tire Chain Bridge"** gives in to death. And so it is no wonder that the narrator's style has been affected by his acknowledgment of death's centrality, of the limits of control, of the losing battle recollection as an artistic method wages against entropy. And consequently, it is no wonder that the story should sound so flat and artless, that beneath its surface calm should be heard a "melancholy, long, withdrawing roar."

The story, in fact, would seem to deflate its own implicit pretensions as a stay against decay, just as and because it undermines the promise of the woman's seeking. Yet if seeming to succumb to the death it argues is inescapable, **"Tire Chain Bridge"** acts upon us as it does only by virtue of its remaining an accomplished fact even while proclaiming itself a fading, futile, gesture. The story's telling establishes a small, coherent world of order, and, through its direct engagement of death, **"Tire Chain Bridge"** permits the "fruitful yearning" that alone allows newness and hope to come.[25] Perhaps Becker is correct when he writes that, in the face of death's inevitability, "The most that any one of us can seem to do is to fashion something—an object or ourselves—and drop it into the confusion, make an offering of it, so to speak, to the life force" (p. 285). The woman has fashioned herself; the narrator, his story. It would seem that, like his creator, he cannot do otherwise.

VII

Several years ago John Clayton complained that Brautigan's "politics of imagination," with its implied hope of "salvation through perception," was not only insufficient but dangerous because its vision might seduce readers into abandoning the struggle to make this world a better place.[26] One can understand Clayton's objection, yet he is wrong to dismiss Brautigan's work as unrebelliously or merely escapist, as lacking a social consciousness. Clayton's error lay in missing the centrality in Brautigan's fiction of death and the anxiety an awareness of death engenders. This awareness is ineradicable; as the narrator of one short story observes, "you cannot camouflage death with words. Always at the end of the words somebody is dead."[27] Death-obsessed, Brautigan's characters find they must dissociate themselves from a culture that both throws death constantly in their paths and fails to give it meaning. These characters typically retreat into private life-enhancing religions, but habitually this ploy does not, as in **Trout Fishing** or **"Tire Chain Bridge,"** engage life-and-death fears head-on and fruitfully; rather, it intensifies that hopelessness and numbness that make death so fearsome within the establishment. A year ago, Richard Brautigan committed suicide; why, I would not presume to say. His work, however, continues to forward an especially severe critique of American society, one that moves beyond politics into prophecy, implicitly sounding a call for repentance, for a turning from death toward life.

Notes

1. *Notebooks 1914-1916,* 2nd ed., trans. G. E. M. Anscombe, ed. G. H. von Wright and G. E. M. Anscombe (Chicago: Univ. of Chicago Press, 1979), p. 75e.

2. *The Denial of Death* (New York: Free Press, 1973). Further references are to the paperback edition (New York: Free Press, 1975) and are included parenthetically within the text.

3. See, for example, Tony Tanner, *City of Words: American Fiction 1950-1970* (New York: Harper & Row, 1971); Ihab Hassan, *Contemporary American Literature: 1945-1972* (New York: Ungar, 1973); and Jack Hicks, *In the Singer's Temple: Prose Fictions of Barthelme, Gaines, Brautigan, Piercy, Kesey, and Kosinski* (Chapel Hill: Univ. of North Carolina Press, 1981).

4. Brautigan's characters as dropouts have been the subject of much commentary. See one example, John Clayton, "Richard Brautigan: The Politics of Woodstock," *New American Review,* 11 (1971), 56-68; Terence Malley, *Richard Brautigan,* Writers for the Seventies (New York: Warner, 1972); W. T. Lhamon, Jr., "Break and Enter to Breakaway: Scotching Modernism in the Social Novel of the American Sixties," *boundary* 2, 3 (1975), 289-306 and Manfred Pütz, *The Story of Identity: American Fiction of the Sixties* (Stuttgart J. B. Metzlersche Verlagsbuchhandlung, 1979).

5. My discussion here is much indebted to Becker; see pp. 198-99 particularly.

6. "The Wherefores of How-To: Pascal, BASIC, Call Up a Literary Tradition," *Harper's,* March 1984, p. 92

7. *A Confederate General from Big Sur* (1964; rpt. New York: Delta / Seymour Lawrence, 1979), p. 18. Further references are included parenthetically within the text.

8. *Trout Fishing in America* (New York: Dell, 1967). Further references are included parenthetically within the text.

9. See, for example, Frank Kermode, *The Sense of an Ending: Studies in the Theory of Fiction* (New York: Oxford Univ. Press, 1967) and Peter Brooks, *Reading for the Plot: Design and Intention in Narrative* (New York: Knopf, 1984).

10. "Rembrandt Creek," in *Revenge of the Lawn: Stories 1962-1970* (New York: Pocket Books, 1972), p. 42.

11. According to Frederick Hoffman, fictions positing no hopes for an afterlife often, in attempting to articulate their "mortal no," work to convert time into space. See *The Mortal No: Death and the Modern Imagination* (Princeton: Princeton Univ. Press, 1964).

12. Brueggemann develops the notion of prophecy sketched here in his book *The Prophetic Imagination* (Philadelphia: Fortress Press, 1978).

13. See Kermode, p. 17.

14. Brueggemann, p. 113.

15. Malley, pp. 104-09.

16. In this quotation, Becker is summarizing Alfred Adler. See Adler's *The Practice and Theory of Individual Psychology* (London: Kegan Paul, 1942), chap. 21.

17. Friedrich Nietzsche, *On the Genealogy of Morals,* trans. Walter Kaufmann and R. J. Hollingdale ed. Walter Kaufmann (New York: Vintage, 1969), p. 136.

18. *In Watermelon Sugar* (1968; rpt. New York: Dell, 1973), p. 65. Further references are included parenthetically within the text.

19. *The Abortion: An Historical Romance 1966* (1971; rpt. New York: Pocket Books, 1972). p. 53. Further references are included parenthetically within the text.

20. Even earlier, Vida had mellowed to the point where Foster (keeper of the caves and arranger of the abortion) could make her laugh by swearing, "My God, ma'am, you're so pretty I'd walk ten miles barefooted on a freezing morning to stand in your shit" (p. 78). That Vida can laugh at such a remark is particularly revealing, for as Becker explains, "excreting is the curse that threatens madness because it shows man his abject finitude, his physicalness, the likely unreality of his hopes and dreams" (p. 33).

21. Malley, p. 75, and Charles Hackenberry, "Romance and Parody in Brautigan's *The Abortion*," *Critique*, 23, ii (1981-1982), 34.

22. In *The Tokyo-Montana Express* (New York: Delacorte / Seymour Lawrence, 1980), p. 94. Because the story is so short (running from p. 94 to p. 97), I will not include page references in the text.

23. *Richard Brautigan* (Boston: Twayne, 1983), pp. 120-21.

24. The two most recent book-length studies of Brautigan, for example, assert among their principal intentions the desire to free the novelist from the critical error of reading him primarily in terms of Sixties concerns. Foster in his Preface claims that "Brautigan's best works were in fact never quite what they were alleged to be. Although they certainly do reflect a special time in American history, the time they reflect has little to do with America in the late 1960s and early 1970s." Marc Chénetier, *Richard Brautigan* (New York: Methuen, 1983), offers the thesis that Brautigan "has always been much more akin to the metafictionists of the seventies than to the naive flower-children of what I should like to call the pre-Nixapsarian sixties" (p. 16).

25. The phrase is Brueggemann's, p. 113.

26. Clayton, pp. 56, 59.

27. "The World War I Los Angeles Airplane," in *Revenge of the Lawn*, p. 169.

Jay Boyer (essay date 1987)

SOURCE: Boyer, Jay. *"Trout Fishing in America."* In *Richard Brautigan*, pp. 19-24. Boise, Idaho: Boise State University, 1987.

[*In the following excerpt from his short study of Brautigan, Boyer discusses the ways in which* Trout Fishing in America *is an attempt to transcend reality through the use of the imagination.*]

Rendering experience in self-contained little sections, and relying upon the cumulative power of these sections for dramatic effect, would be a technique Brautigan would become identified with, but one he used to greatest advantage in his first novel, **Trout Fishing in America.** Like his stories and poems, each of these sections relies upon voice and tone and the appeal of the speaker for its charm. And there's often a "serial" quality to be found here as well. The degree to which we can appreciate what's going on has to do with how willing we are to allow the speaker his unique path of logic. For instance, "Knock On Wood (Part One)," the second section of the fifty that make up the novel, begins in this way.

> As a child when did I first hear about trout fishing in America? From whom? I guess it was a stepfather of mine.
>
> Summer of 1942.
>
> The old drunk told me about trout fishing. When he could talk, he had a way of describing trout as if they were a precious and intelligent metal.
>
> Silver is not a good adjective to describe what I felt when he told me about trout fishing.
>
> I'd like to get it right.
>
> Maybe trout steel. Steel made from trout. The clear snow-filled river acting as foundry and heat.
>
> Imagine Pittsburgh.
>
> A steel that comes from trout, used to make buildings, trains and tunnels.
>
> The Andrew Carnegie of Trout!
>
> (*Trout* [*Trout Fishing in America*] 3)

There is a sense throughout the novel of a mind-in-progress, a mind that would like to, as the speaker says here, *get it right,* and too a reminder that no matter how casual and familiar the writing may seem, communicating with people is no simple matter. The world is always elusive—*When did I first hear about it? From whom?*—and accounting for it is always a tentative business, as in the speaker's caveat above, *I guess it was.* Then too, what's real often has little to do with what's actual. The time and place (recalled here only in the broadest terms, *Summer of 1942*), as well as the people involved (*a stepfather,* apparently one among several, one described here no more completely than *the old drunk*), are of less importance than what the mind of the speaker can do with the material.

The last line of this section, *The Andrew Carnegie of Trout!,* is meaningless in and of itself; but that's not true once we're aware of the process of the mind which works its way toward this conclusion. Trout, to the speaker's stepfather, are currency, of value only in terms of what they can buy. But that bit of profanity can be reworked until it takes on almost magical qualities. A precious metal leads the speaker to think in terms of silver, to reject silver as the word he would choose, to move from silver to steel, from steel to the city that boasts of itself as the steel center of the world, to move from the industrial wastelands of Pittsburgh, Pennsylvania, to the making of a civilized America, and from that to Pittsburgh's Andrew Carnegie—acquisition personified.

None of this imaginative word association dilutes the fact that the speaker's stepfather was "an old drunk," nor that his notion of trout is ill-conceived and distasteful; nor does it deny that Andrew Carnegie may have been one of the great robber barons of his time. What it does instead is to suggest a thaumatropic and idyllic vision which can emerge when the mind is given a chance, an ordering—or perhaps re-ordering—of the cold hard facts, when cold hard facts are understood to be of less importance than the person who would wrestle with them.

Trout Fishing in America, Brautigan said, was "a vision of America," and that seems to be as good a way of putting it as any, for he was holding out the possibility of transcending the world before us. Transcending the day-to-day realities of modern life through the use of imagination seems to be the structuring principle of the novel, in fact. As the novel gradually develops through its individual passages, simple comparisons seem to become metaphors, and these metaphors finally take on a life of their own. As many critics have noted, it's as if the speaker's imagination becomes more powerful and more transcendent as the novel progresses.

But it's a mistake to become too trusting of the speaker's gentle voice and manner and his pastoral vision in general. Let's look at two of the most often quoted—and most often compared—sections of the novel, the first, "Knock On Wood (Part Two)," an early one, and the other, "The Cleveland Wrecking Yard," from among the final sections.

> One spring afternoon as a child in the strange town of Portland, I walked down to a different street corner, and saw a row of old houses, huddled together like seals on a rock.
>
> Then there was a long field that came sloping down off a hill. The field was covered with green grass and bushes. On top of the hill there was a grove of tall, dark trees. At a distance I saw a waterfall come pouring down off the hill. It was long and white and I could almost feel its cold spray.
>
> There must be a creek there, I thought, and it probably has trout in it.

> Trout.
>
> At last an opportunity to go trout fishing, to catch my first trout, to behold Pittsburgh.
>
> It was growing dark. I didn't have time to go and look at the creek. I walked home past the glass whiskers of the houses, reflecting the downward rushing waterfalls of night.
>
> (4)

But when he returned to fish the trout stream, equipped with fish hook made from a bent nail and white bread from which to make dough balls for bait, the stream was not the same.

> But as I got closer to the creek I could see that something was wrong. The creek did not act right. There was a strangeness to it. There was a thing about its motion that was wrong. Finally I got close enough to see what the trouble was.
>
> The waterfall was just a flight of white wooden stairs leading up to a house in the trees.
>
> I stood there for a long time, looking up and looking down, following the stairs with my eyes, having trouble believing.
>
> Then I knocked on my creek and heard the sound of wood.
>
> I ended up by being my own trout and eating the slice of bread myself.
>
> (5)

In the later passage, "The Cleveland Wrecking Yard," the speaker goes to a junkyard and discovers that a trout stream—with insects and animals and foliage available at an extra charge—is being sold off as scrap. The similarities between the two passages are obvious. In both we're dealing with a trout stream situated in a city, in both we're dealing with streams which do not physically exist, and in both the climax of the scene takes place when the speaker puts his hand to the stream and tests it against his own existence. But the climaxes are also distinctly different—as the lines from the end of "The Cleveland Wrecking Yard" clearly witness.

> O I had never in my life seen anything like that trout stream. It was stacked in piles of various lengths: ten, fifteen, twenty feet, etc. There was one pile of hundred foot lengths . . . I went up close and looked at the lengths of stream. I could see some trout in them . . . It looked like a fine stream. I put my hand in the water. It was cold and felt good.
>
> (*Trout* 106-07)

The central difference here has to do with the way the speaker's vision functions. In the earlier section, the vision of the child transcends the world before him, if only for a few hours, as a stairway becomes what he would wish it to be, a trout stream, one in which he can catch the trout that his father has told him about earlier.

This is a child's magic, pure Piaget. But it's not any more than that. The powers of the child's imagination transport him temporarily beyond the limits of Portland and his blue-collar life—that's all. Finally that magical thought is testable against a world of very real dimensions: touch the stream and it turns back into stairs; hear your mother call, and it's time to go home.

That isn't true in the second passage. Here the speaker's vision doesn't just transcend reality. What begins as one more playful examination of the potential of America (trout fishing in America) being tested against its modern condition (a wrecking yard) assumes literal—and troubling—dimensions: conjure a trout stream in your mind, and there will be water that's cold to the touch.

Rather than reality determining the metaphor, then, here the metaphor determines the speaker's reality. And what we seem to be witnessing may well be less significant as a demonstration of the powers of the imagination, albeit they're impressive throughout the novel, than it is as a warning that the speaker is in danger of losing touch, both literally and figuratively, with the world all around him.

Keith Abbott (essay date fall 1988)

SOURCE: Abbott, Keith. "Shadows and Marble: Richard Brautigan." *Review of Contemporary Fiction* 8 (fall 1988): 117-25.

[*In the following essay, Abbott discusses the critical neglect of Brautigan's work and attempts a reevaluation of his skill at dialogue and narrative.*]

> "What I desired to do in marble, I can poke my shadow through."
>
> —Richard Brautigan, from an unpublished short story
> *"The F. Scott Fitzgerald Ahhhhhhhhhhh, Pt. 2"*

Since Richard Brautigan's death, his reputation has hardly been cast in marble. His writing has been relegated to the shadowland of popular flashes, that peculiar American graveyard of overnight sensations. When a writer dies, appreciation of his work seldom reverses field, but continues in the direction that it was headed at the moment of death, and this has been true for Brautigan. Even during Brautigan's best-seller years in the United States, critical studies of his work were few in number. What there were never exerted a strong influence on the big chiefs of the American critical establishment.

Since he was both a popular and a West-Coast writer, his work has been easy to ignore. There are no critical journals on the West Coast which can sustain a writer's career, as there are on the East Coast. His popularity among the young dumped his work with literary lightweights, such as Richard Bach or Eric Segal, and counterculture fads as Abbie Hoffman, Jerry Rubin, or Charles Reich.

Curiously, a critical climate of open hostility to Brautigan's work prevailed on the eastern seaboard and his work was perceived as a threat. From the first, it was an object of ridicule, receiving much the same treatment as Jack Kerouac's novels did in the 1950s. Brautigan's literary position for his generation also was similar to the one Kerouac provided for the Beats: Brautigan became the most famous novelist for a social movement whose literary constituency was almost solely poets. Speaking politically, most poets have little recourse to effective literary power, lacking steady income, steady publication and/or reviewing positions. Brautigan did not have the safety of a group of novelists or a regular circle of reviewers friendly to his aesthetics; consequently, he had few defenders. Brautigan did not write reviews himself, or even issue manifestos. He was perceived as the stray, and so to attack his work risked no reply. In the *Vanity Fair* article published after Brautigan's death, the playwright and poet Michael McClure acknowledged this hostility and offered this reevaluation: "His wasn't a dangerous voice so much as a voice of diversity, potentially liberating in that it showed the possibilities of dreaming, of beauty and the playfulness of the imagination."

With the burden of a ridiculed sociological movement attached to his work, positive literary criticism was sparse. Often what commentary there was tried to talk about both the hippie community and Brautigan's fiction, and failed at both. Ironically, his first four novels were written before the hippie phenomenon, and the relationship between the two was an accident of chronology at first, and then a media cliché.

While his prolific output generated plentiful newspaper reviews, these usually functioned as simple indicators of his perceived fame. Most echoed previous prejudice that he was a whimsical writer for cultural dropouts, and neither his writing nor his supposed subjects were to be considered important. What has to be remembered about criticism is that even serious critics seldom create much lasting literature themselves, and most newspaper reviewers are inevitably trafficking in fishwrap.

The true test of a creative writer is whether the literature is remembered by good writers and begets more excellent work. Other authors have acknowledged Brautigan's influence. Ishmael Reed applauded Brautigan's courage in experimenting with genres in his later novels and claimed this had an effect on his own experimental and highly acclaimed novels of the 1970s. In 1985, the popular and respected novelist W. P. Kinsella published

The Alligator Report, containing short stories which he dubbed "Brautigans." In his foreword he spoke of how this work arose directly from Brautigan's fictional strategies, stating, "I can't think of another writer who has influenced my life and career as much."

The spare early stories of Raymond Carver have always seemed to me to show a strong connection, stylistically and culturally, to Brautigan's first two novels and short stories. Both writers create a similar West-Coast landscape of unemployed men, dreaming women, or failed artists trapped in domestic and economic limbos while attempting to maintain their distinctly Western myths of self-sufficient individuality.

Implicit in most negative criticism of Brautigan is the charge that he wrote fantasies about cultural aberrations, such as the hippies, with little connection to important levels of American life. I think this is mistaken. A strong cultural reality can be found in his work, that of people on the bottom rungs of American society, living out their unnoticed and idiosyncratic existences. Traditionally this class has been one of the resources for American literature. While discussing *Huckleberry Finn,* V. S. Pritchett writes that one of America's cultural heroes is "a natural anarchist and bum" and called the book "the first of those typical American portraits of the underdog, which have culminated in the poor white literature. . . ." Many of Brautigan's works are rooted in this underclass and his people are, in Pritchett's words, the "underdog who gets along on horse sense."

It is often the fate for writers of American popular culture that their work is not taken seriously here, and they find an audience in foreign countries. During his lifetime, Brautigan's writing was translated into seventeen languages. Internationally, Brautigan's work commands respect and continues to generate comment. In Japan, where twelve of his books have been translated, he is considered an important American writer. (And it is of interest that Carver's fiction now enjoys an equally high level of popularity in Japan.) In Europe, West Germany continues to publish his work and a television documentary on him is under way. In France, Marc Chénetier's excellent book-length study was published with accompanying translations of three Brautigan novels. This critical work was later translated into English as part of Methuen's excellent Contemporary Writers series.

In the America of the 1980s, Brautigan's work is treated only as an object for nostalgia, and confined to rehashes of the love generation. When roll calls of fictional innovators are published in critical articles, his name has been dropped off the list of Ishmael Reed, John Barth, Donald Barthelme, Robert Coover, and others.

Brautigan's work remains the best way we have to regard him, other than as an historical figure. As a writer, I have to think the work is what really matters. What-

ever follies, sins or beauties a writer might be said to possess, they are secondary considerations to the complete body of writing.

In a useful observation on Brautigan's poetry, Robert Creeley commented, "I don't think Richard is interested in so-called melopoeia, he said he wants to say things using the simplest possible unit of statement as the module." Simple sentences and minimal rhythms occur in Brautigan's fiction, too, but they work with his metaphors to obtain a more complex effect than in his poetry. By controlling the colloquial sound of his prose, Brautigan developed a strategy for releasing emotion while utilizing the anarchic and comical responses of his imagination.

"The Kool-Aid Wino" chapter in *Trout Fishing in America* provides an example of this strategy:

> When I was a child I had a friend who became a Kool-Aid wino as the result of a rupture. He was a member of a very large and poor German family. All the older children in the family had to work in the fields during the summer, picking beans for two-and-one-half cents a pound to keep the family going. Everyone worked except my friend who couldn't because he was ruptured. There was no money for an operation. There wasn't even enough money to buy him a truss. So he stayed home and became a Kool-Aid wino.

What can be said about this? First, except for the fanciful notion of a Kool-Aid wino, this paragraph has the sound of the English plain style. Brautigan wrote in a colloquial voice, but sometimes it had a curiously unmelodic and muted quality. The voice sounded as if the speaker were talking, but not always consciously aware of being heard. This might account for what other people have dubbed the naive quality of Brautigan's fiction: the tone of a child talking to himself. And for all his colloquial rhythms, slang or common nursery-rhyme devices, such as alliteration and internal rhyme, are carefully rationed, because both require that the reader *hear* them. In the paragraph, two incongruous states, being ruptured and being a wino, are joined, but the last has a rider attached, modifying it with a fairy-tale quality of special powers derived from common objects:

> One morning in August I went over to his house. He was still in bed. He looked up at me from underneath a tattered revolution of old blankets. He had never slept under a sheet in his life.
>
> "Did you bring the nickel you promised?" he asked.
>
> "Yeah," I said. "It's here in my pocket."
>
> "Good."

While the scene is being set, Brautigan slips in the metaphor of the blankets, but in a sentence that has the same declarative rhythm as the sentences just before and after it. This blanket metaphor sounds rhythmically no more important or remarkable than the lack of an operation or the absence of a truss, but the metaphor is, in this context, spectacularly surreal.

He also used very little rhythmic speech in his dialogue. Often his dialogue is even more uninflected than his narrative passages. As Tom McGuane writes, "His dialogue is supernaturally exact." Muting rhythm in dialogue and in narrative passages dampens down the emotional content. This has an interesting effect because hearing a voice calls for a much more emotional reaction than silent narrative passages. This is why "dialect" novels are so exhausting to read. They require much more concentration and emotional response. First-person narrative calls for more effort from the reader than third-person because we are listening and responding to one person. Brautigan often got a third-person objectivity while writing in first person.

Brautigan's strategy was to control and minimize the reader's responses until he was ready to tap into them. For both his dialogue and narrative, Brautigan habitually tried for emotionally neutral sentences. While still maintaining a colloquial tone, the narrative sentences *sound* normal, the dialogue sounds minimally conversational, so they may slide by unchallenged by a reader's emotional response. What is crucial to Brautigan's style is that both dialogue and narrative strike a similar *sound* and that a neutral equality be created between them.

Once Brautigan establishes this pattern in a work, then simple statements of fact could be followed by a simple sentence bearing a fantastic and imaginative statement. The strategy is, accept A, accept B, therefore accept off-the-wall C. The poet Philip Whalen explains the effect of Brautigan's style this way, finding "in Brautigan for example complete clarity and complete exact use of words and at the same time this lunatic imagination and excitement all going 100 miles an hour."

To change to a biological metaphor, what happens in Brautigan's prose is that the parasitical imagination invades and occupies the host of precise, orderly prose, subverting, disrupting and eventually usurping the factual prose's function.

> He was careful to see that the jar did not overflow and the precious Kool-Aid spill out onto the ground. When the jar was full he turned the water off with a sudden but delicate motion like a famous brain surgeon removing a disordered portion of the imagination. Then he screwed the lid tightly onto the top of the jar and gave it a good shake.

To give a realistic base for his fiction, Brautigan often started with mundane social situations and built from there, carefully placing one rhythmically neutral sentence on top of another. This lulls the reader into a false sense of security, and a false sense of security is a good first step for comic writing. By doing this, Brautigan sensed the emotional vibrations that are inevitable in the simplest sentences, so he could then upset these and introduce that lovely sense of comic panic.

Of course, there is a problem with this strategy. No matter how short, factual, or laconic sentences may be, writing always carries some shade of voice. The human voice resonates feeling and Brautigan knew this. By creating a kind of equal neutrality between the factual sound and fanciful content through the use of similar sentence structures, Brautigan tried to solve the problem of how to return to a realistic narrative once he had disrupted it with his metaphors. At times he simply alternated between the two, giving the fantastic equal time with the mundane.

> "Hello," said the grocer. He was bald with a red birthmark on his head. The birthmark looked just like an old car parked on his head. He automatically reached for a package of grape Kool-Aid and put it on the counter.
>
> "Five cents."
>
> "He's got it," my friend said.
>
> I reached into my pocket and gave the nickel to the grocer. He nodded and the old red car wobbled back and forth on the road as if the driver were having an epileptic seizure.

Or, at times, he would let the metaphor grow from a single sentence about a commonplace until it took over the paragraph. In this example from *Confederate General,* the rhythm speeds up as the metaphor expands.

> Night was coming on in, borrowing the light. It had started out borrowing just a few cents worth of the light, but now it was borrowing thousands of dollars worth of the light every second. The light would soon be gone, the bank closed, the tellers unemployed, the bank president a suicide.

Fiction must have drama, however minimal, but given this strategy in Brautigan's prose, often the drama is on the surface of the writing itself. The tension between the two poles of Brautigan's style, the plain and the metaphorical, creates the conflict in his fiction. In the passage quoted above, the first-person character/narrator is so hyped up about visiting his eccentric Kool-Aid wino friend and witnessing his rituals that his imagination runs wild. But no one in the story notices this, so this potential conflict is confined to the prose itself. Just as the "I" character remains undercover in the mundane tale of buying Kool-Aid, the fantasy remains undercover in a plain prose.

Brautigan's writing has been called undramatic, because in a conventional sense it is. His style provides what drama there is more often than his characters. His metaphors function as dramatic resolutions, if subversion of common reality with imaginative thought can be called a resolution. (One of Brautigan's themes is that ultimately this strategy subverts and disrupts the very act of writing fiction.) The fanciful notion of a Kool-Aid wino provides the impetus to continue reading, not any drama between the characters. The Kool-Aid wino will nowhere insist on the strangeness of his behavior while the narrator will provide the tension with his perceptions of that behavior as *being very special in a magical world*. Often the rhythms do not insist that this is a special occasion any more than does the Kool-Aid wino. The sentences chart a rather unremarkable exchange between the two characters but this exchange is seen by a quite metaphorical intelligence, and so the prose itself enacts the eventual theme of the piece, that illumination comes from within: "He created his own Kool-Aid reality and was able to illuminate himself by it."

Besides a plain, slightly colloquial style, Brautigan also favored the structure of facts to give a neutral tone to his sentences. Facts are meant to be understood, not heard and savored on their own. Brautigan loved to infiltrate and sabotage them. Here's an example from the opening chapter of *A Confederate General From Big Sur.*

> I've heard that the population of Big Sur in those Civil War days was mostly just some Digger Indians. I've heard that the Digger Indians down there didn't wear any clothes. They didn't have any fire or shelter or culture. They didn't grow anything. They didn't hunt and they didn't fish. They didn't bury their dead or give birth to their children. They lived on roots and limpets and sat pleasantly out in the rain.

During this masquerade of historical prose, the manipulation of a catalog style develops a strange emotional equivalency between the sentences which their content quietly disrupts. One source of this technique comes from the Western tall-tale, where a narrator, disguised as an expert, mixes the fantastic with the normal in equal portions. This passage somewhat reminds me of Twain in his role as the seasoned traveler in *A Tramp Abroad*:

> The table d'hote was served by waitresses dressed in the quaint and comely costume of the Swiss peasant. This consists of a simple gros de laine trimmed with ashes of roses with overskirt of sacre blue ventre saint gris, cut bias on the off-side, with facings of petit polanaise and narrow insertions of pate de foie gras back-stitched to the mise en scene in the form of a jeu d'espirit. It gives the wearer a singularly piquant and alluring aspect.

In both Twain and Brautigan's paragraphs, an anarchy is hatched inside the standardized English. Twain's prose has the trotting rhythm of standard fill-in-the-blanks travel or fashion writing. Brautigan's prose creates his bland rhythms through the careful alternation of "and"s and "or"s in factual sentences designed to be read and forgotten. Twain's intent is burlesque, while Brautigan's opts for a quieter anarchy. But the strategies for both seem similar.

A more complicated example of Brautigan's technique with this factual sound can be found in his short story **"Pacific Radio Fire."** The opening paragraph begins: "The largest ocean in the world starts or ends at Monterey, California." There's no sense of who is saying this. Since the story title has a radio in it, the voice could be someone on the radio, but it doesn't have to be, it could be anybody. Then Brautigan adds the next fact: "It depends on what language you are speaking." These two statements are acceptable, reasonable, and dispassionate. Nothing in their rhythm seems emotional or unusual. Put them together and they enact only a slightly different way of viewing the universe: "The largest ocean in the world starts or ends at Monterey, California. It depends on what language you are speaking." However, one thing has changed. With the use of *you,* the reader is now addressed, and his presence is acknowledged, giving a slightly more colloquial edge to the second sentence than the first, an intimacy. Then the third sentence plunges us into an emotional, very intimate situation—but *without* any corresponding passionate rhythm: "The largest ocean in the world starts or ends at Monterey, California. It depends on what language you are speaking. My friend's wife had just left him." Now, these three sentences present a fact followed by another fact followed by a third fact, but the last one is wildly removed from the reality of the first two. More importantly, the third sentence is *colloquially* factual. The first two have the tone of the mundane media facts that wash over us daily, while the third sentence belongs to the everyday world of emotional distress. The third sentence is something that any private person could say, just as any public commentator could say the first two.

This sequence establishes what I call an equal neutrality between the three sentences. The shift cracks the emotionless facade that the paragraph starts with and abruptly releases humor. While the language remains low-key, its arrangement yields the drama.

This linguistic shift is also curiously realistic, and I mean realistic in the manner that these verbal traumas occur. To my ear, this shift mimes the kind of dislocations that result when someone is trying to tell you how something bad happened, but doesn't know how to start. Instead they talk about the weather, the scenery, and then suddenly blurt out their distress without any rhythmic or emotional buildup. A familiar "out-of-the-blue" quality to the rapid shift from impersonal to personal occurs. Here, it works as comic timing:

The largest ocean in the world starts or ends at Monterey, California. It depends on what language you are speaking. My friend's wife had just left him. She walked right out the door and didn't even say goodbye. We went and got two fifths of port and headed for the Pacific.

What makes this more than a mere joke is that there is a vibration set off by the word "language" in the second sentence and the fact that the wife left without using any language. Brautigan at his best discovers a taut, underground humor in his prose by suppressing connections that other writers might make obvious. Someone else might have written, "and didn't even use language to say goodbye." One of the strengths of Brautigan's style is that he leaves the right things unsaid and trusts the placement of his language to supply the emotions.

When Brautigan tries to reverse this progression, going from the colloquial emotional truth to the dry facts, from the fantastic to the mundane, the humor sometimes is less natural, a tad more bizarre. Here are the opening paragraphs from a chapter in *A Confederate General From Big Sur,* "The Tide Teeth of Lee Mellon":

> It is important before I go any further in this military narrative to talk about the teeth of Lee Mellon. They need talking about. During these five years that I have known Lee Mellon, he has probably had 175 teeth in his mouth.

> This is due to a truly gifted faculty for getting his teeth knocked out. It almost approaches genius. They say that John Stuart Mill could read Greek when he was three years old and had written a history of Rome at the age of six and a half.

The reverse doesn't work as humor quite as well as the previous example because the neutral sentences are not part of the set-up, but are used to finish the joke. There's a deadpan humor to this strategy, of the bizarre masquerading as the everyday, but the implied connection between the historical fact of John Stuart Mill's genius and the asserted "genius" of Lee Mellon's losing his teeth either seems funny or it doesn't. At his best, Brautigan doesn't allow that much leeway for the reader's responses.

Timing was an essential ingredient in Brautigan's finest writing, and he understood the virtues of the simple buildup. According to his first wife, and Brautigan's own account of his early apprenticeship as a writer, he worked for years on writing the simple sentences of his prose. In a notebook located in Brautigan's archive at UC Berkeley, an early draft of the chapter "Sea-Sea Rider" in *Trout Fishing* showed how he divided the prose into lines of verse, carefully trying to isolate each of the phrases by rhythm, by their cadence, revising for the simplest sound possible. Accompanying this draft is

an aborted journal, written in 1960 and titled "August." In a rare moment of self-analysis, Brautigan wrote: "The idea of this journal is I want to make something other than a poem. . . . One of the frustrations of my work is my own failure to establish adequate movement. . . . I want the reality in my work to move less obviously, and it [is] very difficult for me." What Brautigan means by movement is, I would guess, the switch from his metaphorical intelligence in and out of his mundane situations. In order to be less obvious, the transition between the fantastic and quotidian had to be eased by giving both the same rhythms.

His poetry sometimes forced the connection between the mundane and his imaginative fancies by combining them in one sentence. The effect was artificial and clever, and so it lacked the careful, timed setups of his prose. What made his prose remarkable was his ability to sense those moments when his imagination could occupy the larger factual rhythms of his paragraphs. This might be what he meant by "adequate movement." When he strayed too far from the mundane and/or factual setups, the cleverness had only itself to sustain, and his fiction suffered from the same defects as his poetry.

His fiction has its own peculiar vision and a sometimes satori-like sharpness. There's a humanity to Brautigan's discoveries that sets them apart from mere humorous writing. The opening paragraphs of the chapter "Room 208, Hotel Trout Fishing in America" serve as a final example of Brautigan's skills as a writer, how in a few words he could blend a prosaic vision of the world and at the same time infiltrate it with his own imagination and turn the mundane into something quicksilver, moving and alive:

> Half a block from Broadway and Columbus is Hotel Trout Fishing in America, a cheap hotel. It is very old and run by some Chinese. They are young and ambitious Chinese and the lobby is filled with the smell of Lysol.

> The Lysol sits like another guest on the stuffed furniture, reading a copy of the *Chronicle,* the Sports Section. It is the only furniture I have ever seen in my life that looks like baby food.

> And the Lysol sits asleep next to an old Italian pensioner who listens to the heavy ticking of the clock and dreams of eternity's golden pasta, sweet basil and Jesus Christ.

Carolyn F. Blakely (essay date December 1991)

SOURCE: Blakely, Carolyn F. "Narrative Technique in Brautigan's *In Watermelon Sugar*." *CLA Journal* 35, no. 2 (December 1991): 150-58.

[*In the following essay, Blakely analyzes the narrative technique in one Brautigan novel, asserting that Brautigan has more literary worth than many critics have admitted.*]

Richard Brautigan, one among many contemporary writers who have been either ignored or brushed aside by numerous critics as passing fads or as transitory appeals to the fancies of the young generation, should not be dismissed so lightly. One may not assume from a cursory reading of his work that he is shallow or that he has no message to convey. On the contrary, it seems that his message is just as profound and valid as that of more established writers, in spite of the fact that his prose style is revolutionary and that his ideas are couched in a language which is frequently implied rather than overt in its statements. It is sometimes necessary to go beyond what is said in *In Watermelon Sugar* and concentrate on what is not said, for that is where the statement seems to lie. Some critics ignore this possibility, however, casually dismissing Brautigan as possessing no literary worth but seeing him instead as the response to the Beat Generation's need for a vehicle through which to vocalize its cynical outlook on life.

Michael Feld explains Brautigan as being a writer who is "namedropped in most places where there's lots of sensitivity and modernity and drugs and no common sense going on, where cool languid personalities slump about passing joints like sweaty kisses, speaking of power to the people and freedom and the plight of gipsies [and who] displays above anything else . . . a distaste for work."[1] Jonathan Yardley's estimation of Brautigan is no higher than Feld's because he says that "sooner or later . . . Brautigan is going to go the way of many minor literary figures, and even some bigger ones . . . who appeal to the peculiar needs of later adolescence."[2] Apparently these critics see Brautigan as only a response to the younger generation's radical cry for a return to nature in order to get it all together. They think that his style is casual and offhand, but in vogue, creating a certain charm for these youthful readers. In the opposite camp is Neil Schmitz, who labels *In Watermelon Sugar* a pastoral myth with

> all its objectives in fiction: the denial of history, its passion for loveliness (all those exquisite suns), its desire to represent the normative life, the "natural" way. And yet it is wrong, this perfected world. The balance that suits them also stylizes them and the result is a disfiguring of their humanity."[3]

Indeed, the perfected world of this novel does not work. Brautigan's silence speaks loudly as he presents what seems to be a parody of the pastoral. This society may represent what modern man might *wish* it to be—an answer to or a substitute for the mechanistic, profit-seeking, inhumane world of social and moral decadence in which he finds himself, but the distortion in the new society is also obvious and just as unattractive. Viewing this book, then, as a parody of the pastoral, one might consider the ideas that are implied by the silence and attempt to determine what Brautigan's attitude is toward this "perfect" society.

Admittedly the novel does present some of the images of the pastoral tradition when one observes its characters engaged in happy labor, in solitary walks along the river, and in contented existence in little shacks in the hills. Pauline, for example, is the healthy, happy maiden who is delighted to whip up hearty stews for the communal workers; and the schoolmaster who leads his pupils into a meadow to study nature is reminiscent of Goldsmith's portrait of the schoolmaster in the pastoral setting of *The Deserted Village*. These images, however, seem to camouflage the weaknesses in a society which is a fantasy or a postholocaustal world set in some idyllic future tense. Initially, this appears to be a nostalgic yearning for a pastoral America which has disappeared or has been destroyed by such elements as crime and violence until we realize that the reality of the past America has been replaced by a dream that is inadequate. Tony Tanner says that it is "a pastoral dream in which the dominance of fantasy and imagination over the Forgotten Works and the wrecking yard is perhaps too effortlessly achieved."[4] A summary of the novel reveals the pastoral dream:

> The narrator lives in a happy commune in an unlocated realm called, mysteriously, iDeath. The prevailing material there is watermelon sugar . . . which may be food, furniture, or fuel. More generally it is the sweet secretion of the imagination. There is still death in iDeath, but it has been made into something mysterious and almost beautiful: the dead are buried in glass coffins which are laid on the riverbed. Foxfire is put inside. . . . There was once a more violent time—the time of the tigers—but they have been killed off. More recently there has been a defection from iDeath by a drunken foul-mouthed figure called inBoil. . . . He and his gang have gone back to live in an ugly place called the Forgotten Works . . . an endless panorama of all the machines and things which made up a vanished way of life. . . . But inBoil returns to the commune insisting that the tigers were the real meaning of iDeath. . . . He and his followers say that they will bring back the real iDeath. They do this by gradually cutting themselves to pieces in front of the disgusted members of the community. Afterwards their bodies are taken down to the Forgotten Works, burned up, and forgotten. Everyone is relieved. Except for . . . Margaret who had started to show an inquisitive interest in the things heaped up in the Forgotten Works. . . . She commits suicide. But after the funeral the community gathers together for a dance, and the musicians are poised with their instruments.[5]

And so the book ends, but the problem remains; this perfect society is void of emotions and as such Brautigan implies that there is much to be desired in this fantasy also. In the delineation of this less-than-perfect society, he uses the techniques of fragmentation, repetition, and juxtaposition in order to establish the prevailing sense of loss. Although it is utopian in atmosphere, it offers no notations of progress, neither materialistically nor emotionally.

In discussing the structure of **In Watermelon Sugar,** Patricia Hernlund argues that the book has a fragmented time scheme which focuses on three deaths and that this organization permits the revelation of the narrator's (and his society's) responses to negative elements. The first of these time sequences is the distant past where the Forgotten Works began. The second time sequence concerns the major portion of the narrator's life. The third occurs during the narrator's present years but before the present time and is presented in a flashback to the first sign of trouble indicated by the rumor that in-Boil is plotting some scheme, which is almost simultaneous with the beginning of trouble between the narrator and Margaret. Finally, the fourth sequence is the present time of the novel which covers about three days.[6]

Obviously the book does not adhere to a linear, chronological plot, but if it is put to the test, this fragmented time scheme seems to work. In the first sequence the narrator says, "Nobody knows how old the Forgotten Works are, reaching as they do into distances that we cannot travel nor want to."[7] But one can speculate, however, that they mark the beginning of this new society that replaces a rejected past society which was plagued by the tigers and which was also the time of the birth of Charley, inBoil, and Old Chuck—a time before the narrator.

The second sequence is a time of the narrator's, Margaret's, and Pauline's childhood and young adulthood, when inBoil told them stories and when the tigers killed his parents and were eventually killed themselves. It is also a time when inBoil drew away from iDeath and turned to the Forgotten Works, when Margaret and the narrator became lovers, and when he began making statues.

It is during the third period that inBoil dies and that the narrator implies some connection between inBoil and Margaret which is suggested to him by her inquisitive delving into the Forgotten Works. He says, "Sometimes Margaret went down into the Forgotten Works by herself. It worried me. She was so pretty and inBoil and that gang of his were so ugly. They might get ideas. Why did she want to go down there all the time?" (p. 90). Later, specifically questioning Margaret about in-Boil's scheme, Charley asks, "What do you know about this, Margaret? You've spent a lot of time down there lately" (p. 95). Although this implied connection is denied by some of the characters, the narrator allows his suspicions to overwhelm him, severs his ties with Margaret, and starts his relationship with Pauline.

In the fourth and final sequence we see Old Chuck recounting a dream about the tigers and the narrator remembering their killing his parents. It is here, too, that Margaret commits suicide, and the citizens prepare for her funeral and a dance immediately after sunset.

The instances of repetition in the novel promote the suggested lack of emotion, sense of boredom, and feeling of loss. The only real sign of emotion of any major kind occurs in the chapter that describes the suicide of inBoil and his followers. The narrator's description of Pauline's rage at their messing up the hatchery with their blood places her in a peculiar light: "Pauline did not act like a woman should under these circumstances. She was not afraid or made ill by this at all. She just kept getting madder and madder. Her face was red with anger" (p. 113). There is a total absence of human sympathy or of any type of positive feelings, and this impression is emphasized by Pauline's methodical mopping up blood and wringing it out into a bucket.

In the two-page chapter entitled "My Name," the narrator repeats the sentence "That is my name" twelve times, establishing a hollowness and a situation that allows him to become whatever the reader wishes him to be. Harvey Leavitt suggests that the narrator is a part of a society in which the individual self is unimportant (I Death), in which the psychological is suppressed by the physiological (Id Death), in which knowledge is no longer desirable (Idea Death), and in which "the first person pronoun is dead in a social order that makes itself conscious of the interdependency of its parts. . . ."[8]

The almost total absence of emotion is even more obvious in the chapter entitled "Arithmetic," where the narrator describes, with alarming and disquieting calmness, his lack of response to the killing of his parents by the tigers. This startling attitude is strongly emphasized as the youth repeats and stresses the importance of learning his arithmetic rather than the tragic death of his parents. In the middle of the disaster he says to the tigers, "You could help me with my arithmetic" (p. 39) and continues to reiterate in the rest of the chapter how helpful the tigers were with his arithmetic. To cite a further example of this emotional void and atmosphere of boredom created through the device of repetition, one might note the conversation in the "Meat Loaf" chapter:

> "Today's special is meat loaf, isn't it?" Doc Edwards said.
>
> "Yes, 'Meat Loaf for a gray day is the best way,' that's our motto," she said.
>
> "I'll have some meat loaf," Fred said.
>
> "What about you?" the waitress said. "Meat loaf?"
>
> "Yeah, meat loaf," I said.
>
> "Three meat loaves," the waitress said,
>
> (p. 129)

Here the boring routine is established: on every "gray day" the special is meat loaf.

The sense of loss is also apparent in other instances. In the chapter "Statue of Mirrors" the narrator describes the visions that he has in the mirrors and the emptiness that he feels as he stands for hours allowing his mind to drain. When the visions begin to occur, he describes them in a repetitive pattern. Half of the sentences in that chapter begin with the same sentence structure, establishing the loss and emptiness that lead up to the climactic ending of the chapter: "I saw Old Chuck on the front porch . . . , I saw some kids playing baseball . . . , I saw Fred directing his crew . . . , [and] I saw Margaret climbing an apple tree beside her shack. She was crying and had a scarf knotted around her neck. She took the loose end of the scarf and tied it to a branch covered with young apples. She stepped off the branch and then she was standing by herself on the air" (p. 135). Even then the narrator displays no emotion, in the very next chapter he says simply, "I stopped looking into the statue of Mirrors. I'd seen enough for that day" (p. 136).

In what she sees as another of Brautigan's negative statements about his society, Hernlund says that "pleasure is negated by sudden introduction of an opposing emotion."[9] One may point to many instances in which the pleasant is juxtaposed with the unpleasant. In one of those instances the narrator speaks of how beautiful the tigers were in the same sentence in which he mentions the fact that they ate his parents; in another, Fred praises Pauline's good stew and the pleasure he derives from eating it in the same breath that he quietly hints at the displeasure of eating carrots; and in the middle of the whole idyllic scene describing Pauline's prettiness and pleasant watermelon sugar aroma, one is suddenly and unexpectedly told how most of the citizens did not like Margaret anymore because they thought that she might be involved in a conspiracy with inBoil and his gang.

In a society where the narrator insists that its citizens take pride in their communal life style, it seems that this style is peculiarly static. It refuses whatever is different from itself, as evidenced by the failure to name the "beautiful" things that Margaret finds in the Forgotten Works. Schmitz thinks that "Margaret's curiosity is the first step toward wisdom . . . but wisdom that is destructive of the innocence the writer strives to sustain."[10]

Leavitt, in a very extensive analogy, labels iDeath as "an Eden without the built-in supremacy order that was established for Adam I [He sees the narrator as Adam II] and Eve. Classification begets power, and power begets pride, and pride is an emotion."[11] Since emotion is considerably absent from iDeath, inaction is created through the mundane tasks of existence. Life in iDeath is void of such emotions as pity and joy, the absence of which could be presumed to be worse than anything that could be imagined in the old society. On this same issue, Hernlund concludes that "the delicate balance in iDeath is the delusion that they can maintain a neutral position disjunct from violence and death without also cutting themselves off from life's fullness. The basic error results in boredom, ritual, and sterility devoid not only of pleasure but of all feeling and thus all real curiosity, vitality, or a reason for existence."[12]

Life in the new utopian society is a farce and does not represent a satisfactory escape for man from his tainted, modern world. At the extreme, however, one might view life here as being equal with death. Certainly the one birth recorded in the novel does not offset the twenty-two suicides. At any rate, Brautigan must be reckoned with, not dismissed lightly. He recognizes the problem inherent in society, and this may be his shock therapy to awaken society itself to that problem, much the same way that Jonathan Swift did in "A Modest Proposal."

Notes

1. Michael Feld, "A Double with Christina," *London Magazine* (August-September, 1971), 150-51.

2. Jonathan Yardley, "Still Loving," *New Republic,* 164 (20 March 1971), 24.

3. Neil Schmitz, "Richard Brautigan and the Modern Pastoral," *Modern Fiction Studies,* 19 (1973), 120.

4. Tony Tanner, *City of Words: American Fiction, 1950-1970* (New York, 1971), p. 413.

5. Ibid., pp. 412-13.

6. Patricia Hernlund, "Author's Intent: *In Watermelon Sugar,*" *Critique: Studies in Modern Fiction,* 16 (1974), 5-8.

7. Richard Brautigan, *In Watermelon Sugar* (New York: Delacorte, 1968), p. 82. Subsequent references to this novel will be to this edition and page numbers will be noted parenthetically.

8. Harvey Leavitt, "The Regained Paradise of Brautigan's *In Watermelon Sugar,*" *Critique: Studies in Modern Fiction,* 16 (1974), 23.

9. Hernlund, p. 15.

10. Schmitz, p. 120.

11. Leavitt, pp. 23-24.

12. Hernlund, p. 16.

Mark Pietralunga (essay date 1998)

SOURCE: Pietralunga, Mark. "Luciano Bianciardi Translates Richard Brautigan: *Rebellion at Big Sur.*" *Romance Languages Annual* 10, no. 1 (1998): 345-49.

[*In the following essay, Pietralunga compares Brautigan's* Confederate General from Big Sur *to some of the work of its Italian translator, finding biographical and literary similarities between the two writers.*]

In his "Diario americano 1959-60," Italo Calvino writes about his impressions of Northern California and, in particular, of those scenic locations near the Monterey peninsula where a number of well known writers had established their residences. In the section entitled "Questi paradisi terrestri," Calvino observes:

> dove viv ono gli scrittori americani, non ci starei morto. Non c'e' altro da fare che sbronzarsi. Un giovanotto che si chiama Dennis Murphy o qualcosa di simile che ha scritto un best-seller, *The Sergeant,* che ora gli ha tradotto Mondadori nella Medusa gli e' arrivata proprio ora la copia e me la mostra e crede che sia un piccolo editore—arriva al mattino con tutti i polsi feriti. La notte si e' sbronzato e ha spaccato a pugni le vetrate della sua villa. Di Henry Miller che vive qui a Big Sur sappiamo gia' che non riceve piu' nessuno perche' sta scrivendo. L'ultrasettantenne scrittore che ha sposato da poco una moglie diciannovenne dedica tutto il resto delle sue forze allo scrivere per finire prima di morire i libri che ancora vuol scrivere
>
> *(Eremita a Parigi* 103).

It is here in this so-called Pacific paradise where Richard Brautigan sets his 1964 novel *Confederate General from Big Sur.* A lengthy exchange of letters between the work's main characters, the narrator Jesse and his charismatic friend Lee Mellon, captures the tone of the novel and seems to corroborate Calvino's impressions of this haven of American writers. In these letters the lovelorn Jesse, who is unable to cope with big city life in San Francisco, hopes to join Lee Mellon at his makeshift retreat in Big Sur. Upon hearing of Jesse's wish to follow him to Big Sur, Lee Mellon replies: "Great! Why don't you come down here? I haven't got any clothes on, and I just saw a whale. There's plenty of room for everybody. Bring something to drink. Whiskey!" (54). Farther along in their correspondence when Jesse asks Lee Mellon how he keeps alive at Big Sur, the latter responds: "I've got a garden and it grows all year round! A 30:30 Winchester for deer, a .22 for rabbits and quail. I've got some fishing tackle and The Journal of Albion Moonlight. We can make it OK. What do you want, a fur-lined box of Kleenex to absorb the sour of your true love Cynthia, the Ketchikan and/or Battle Mountain cookie? Come to the party and hurry down to Big Sur and don't forget to bring some whiskey. I need whiskey!" (60). Jesse and Lee Mellon had met in San Francisco. Lee had just hitchhiked up from Big Sur where, along the way, he steals some money, a watch, and the keys to the car of a wealthy homosexual who had wanted him "to commit an act of oral outrage" (23) but was nevertheless quite content with a blow to the head with a rock from the "good looking, dashing, toothless raider" (24). After a series of unconventional experiences, including Lee's "siege" of Oakland and a "daring cavalry attack" to tap a gas line of the Pacific Gas & Electric Company for light and heat, Lee resumes his wanderings, this time to Big Sur, where he settles in a ramshackle cabin that he

had built with yet another disturbed friend. Jesse, after finally letting himself be convinced to join Lee Mellon, learns that life in Big Sur is far from being the Pacific paradise that he had been led to believe, particularly when money is lacking and you are constantly being hounded by the nightly croaking of thousands of frogs in a nearby pond. However, they soon come into some money ($6.72), which Lee Mellon takes from two teenagers whom he catches attempting to steal gasoline from his truck. With their "riches," Lee proposes to hitchhike to Monterey to get drunk. In a small bar in Monterey, with Lee "passed out underneath the saloon" (89), Jesse meets the lovely Elaine, and the two are soon off to the young woman's place. The next morning the couple retrieve Lee, still "under a saloon covered with cardboard" (93), and return to Big Sur, bringing with them two alligators purchased by Elaine in order to take care of the frog problem. Back in Big Sur Elaine decides to set up house with Jesse, while Lee Mellon finds himself being comforted by the enchanting Elizabeth—a beautiful free spirit who works three months a year as a high-priced call girl in Los Angeles.

Their seemingly idyllic world is soon disrupted by the arrival of Jonathan Wade (of the "Johnston Wade Insurance Company"), a psychotic middle-aged millionaire, who has run away from his greedy wife and children, convinced that they are determined to put him in a mental hospital. After directly experiencing the aggressions of Lee Mellon, Wade, appearing to regain his sanity, suddenly feels the urge to return to his routine and sets off for a business appointment. The two friends and their girlfriends "go down to the Pacific and turn on and go with the waves" (152) with Jesse unable to perform during a sexual encounter initiated by Elaine. The novel concludes by offering more and more endings unraveling faster and faster, leading to what Brautigan calls "186,000 endings per second" (160). These endings are the only real revolution that takes place in the novel.

In his book-length study of Brautigan, Terence Malley places *Confederate General from Big Sur* within a category of American literature that has been broadly defined as American Pastoral. The stories that belong to this pattern, writes Malley, deal with "a man going off alone (or two men going off together), away from the complex problems and frustrations of society into a simpler world close to nature" (93).[1] As Calvino's opening observations remind us, Brautigan is not the first American writer to locate his "Paradise Regained" in Big Sur. Malley makes reference to two works about Big Sur that bear an important relationship to *Confederate General*: Henry Miller's *Big Sur and the Oranges of Hieronymus Bosch* (1957) and Jack Kerouac's *Big Sur* (1962). In fact, in *Confederate General* we catch a glimpse of Henry Miller, sitting in his old Cadillac near his mailbox, waiting for his mail to be delivered. In this casual observation, one intuits a general indifference on the part of Brautigan's characters toward Henry Miller and his literary reputation. Nevertheless, as Malley accurately notes, Miller's presence in this environment is unavoidable: "The gigantic figure of Henry Miller casts its long shadow across *Confederate General* [. . .] In some respects, Brautigan's Big Sur corresponds closely to Miller's—a place of beauty and privacy and freedom and (that word and quality Miller likes so much) ambience. For the most part, Jesse and Lee act out the advice that Miller repeats to himself and to us in the first section of his *Big Sur*: 'Stay put and watch the world go around!' (96). However Malley is quick to note that, while Miller has served, if only partly, as Brautigan's literary guide to Big Sur, "Brautigan's depiction of Jesse and Lee Mellon's Eden is ultimately very different from Miller's (or anyone's)" (96). Instead, in *Confederate General* everything is built on, and perceived through Lee Mellon's "wonderful sense of distortion" (83) to which Jesse has religiously ascribed. After all, Lee Mellon, observes Jesse, is "the battle flags and the drums of this book" (20). This "sense of distortion" is most evident in Mellon's claim that his great grandfather was a courageous Confederate general at the Battle of Wilderness, a battle which proved to be a turning point in the Civil War. Even after Lee and Jesse fail to find any references to a Confederate General Augustus Mellon in Ezra J. Warner's *Generals in Grey,* this fact does not prevent Lee Mellon, as Marc Chenetier writes, "from living in the imagination of his descendent and acting as a control on the wild antics the text will perform in its claims to freedom"(23). That freedom, or what Chenetier calls a "wilful violation of reality"(23), dictates the entire course of the novel.

As Edward Halsey Foster notes, *Confederate General from Big Sur* is "about people who cultivate an attitude of emotional and intellectual detachment that was to be found at the very center of the existential, alienated culture characteristic of the hipsters and the beats of the 1950s"(5-6). At Big Sur the ultimate awareness, rebellion, and resignation take place on the farthest extreme, geographically and intellectually, of contemporary America. *Confederate General from Big Sur* offers a vision, concludes Foster, "in which there is no historical progress, but in which all possibilities can be realized"(47). From this perspective, Lee Mellon's ability to live the life of a Confederate general one hundred years after the South has been fought and lost is beside the point. As we have mentioned, his life seems to be a strange series of echoes from American literature and myth, particularly the literature and myth of rebellion. For the beats, rebellion was a personal matter. A man did not change the system he changed himself. Together

with a distrust or loss of faith in historical progress, what the beats shared was their individual horror at what a nation in the name of economic progress had done to itself.

In an essay written not long after his return from America in 1960, Calvino analyzes Italy's so-called "miracle years" and argues that there was a scarcity of rebels in Italian literature.[2] He points out that Italy had nothing comparable to the "beat generation," the "beatniks," or England's "angry young men;" instead, the Italian writers expressed quite differently their lack of faith in history: "I libri che escono e che hanno piu' fortuna portano anch'essi come segno dell'epoca un accentuarsi della sfiducia nella storia, ma ad affermarlo non sono voci di arrabbiati o di nichilisti, ma caso mai sono le quete ragazze casalinghe di Carlo Cassola" (78). The successful novels in the period of the late 1950s and early 1960s were written by authors who turned their backs from an Italy that bathed in the euphoria of its modernity. For Cassola, it was a withdrawal to the traditional myths of the provinces and to characters, like Mara of *La ragazza di Bube,* who possess such positive qualities as a strength of spirit and a genuineness of feelings. This return to the traditional values of the provinces is accompanied by a stylistic return to traditional narrative forms.

Luciano Bianciardi's *La vita agra* is one of the few "angry" voices of protest to come out of the "miracle years." Although those same traditional myths of the provinces are operative in Bianciardi's 1962 novel, the world of "buoni sentimenti" exists as part of a distant place of memory and salvation, which enables the protagonist, a self-proclaimed anarchist who has come to Milan to execute a hostile mission against the chemical giant Montecatini, to survive in the grim, inhuman metropolis. Unlike Cassola, Bianciardi felt the need to leave the security of the provincial life and to seek some connection with the world of the Insiders, for he believed this was the only way possible to expose the depressed state that lie hidden under the mask of progress. He hoped to prevent the miracle that was taking place in Milan from infecting the rest of the country. *La vita agra* is a novel of protest against this miracle and the angry statement of his failure to defeat it. Both the protest and failure are depicted by the protagonist's attempt to undermine the capitalistic system that ultimately consumes him. His reluctant but eventual integration into the consumer society is accompanied by the complete disintegration of the self. At the novel's conclusion, the narrator, who is lost in the chaos of words, is totally deprived of the self. The mechanical routine of his job as translator, at a time when translators found themselves inundated by the new consumer's demand, has affected his most intimate actions (his loss of a sexual drive) and forces him to seek refuge in sleep.

In drawing comparisons between Bianciardi's "angry" novel and the "beat" writers, critic Giuseppe Nava has written: "Come i 'beat,' il protagonista di Bianciardi vive tutto nel presente, ormai scisso dal passato e reso incapace di progetti per il futuro dalla condizione in cui e' murato. Non gli resta, per sentirsi vivo, che la rabbia come reazione istintuale ed estrema difesa: una rabbia che e' impotente pratica e sogno consolatorio di un futuro utopico di vita rurale e di libera azione sessuale, quale appunto nella letteratura 'beat" (17). In the midst of the confusion of voices between his world and that of the languages and lives of the characters of his translations, such names as Jack Keruoac and Henry Miller appear and, like all else in this Babel, are distorted.[3] Prompted by Bianciardi's reference to Miller and Keruoac, Rita Guerricchio writes:"La ricorrenza di questi ultimi due assicura la consapevolezza da parte dell'io narrante di indubbie suggestioni subite da parte di entrambi, afflitto anch'egli, come in particolare l'io esorbitante dei *Tropici,* da un'ansia predicatoria di grana moralista proprio laddove piu' smodata si fa la proposta oscena, piu' anarchica e ribelle l'avversione alla civilta' meccanica. Non c'e' dubbio che sull'inarrestabile fluire del monologo della *Vita agra* abbiano agito anche altri modelli del cote' 'bitinicco' e arrabbiato, autori tradotti nello stesso giro d'anni come Kerouac e Burroughs [. . .] e Patchen e Donleavy e Behan, tutti portatori di un anarchismo protestatorio variamente modulato fra provocazione e sberleffo, e sopratutto affidato a un io personaggio ribaldo e guastatore" (79).[4] Bianciardi's attraction to works that question, mock and rebel against the status quo and the acceptance of majority values, explains, in many ways, his decision to translate Brautigan's *Confederate General from Big Sur.* It is important, however, to keep in mind that Bianciardi translated *A Confederate General from Big Sir* after *La vita agra,* which is one man's failed attempt to change the system from within. After the experience of *La vita agra,* Bianciardi sees himself transformed from a rebel with a cause to a rebel without a cause. In a letter to his friend Mario Terrosi, Bianciardi wrote about his attempt to oppose the system by writing a novel of protest: "Quel che potevo l'ho fatto, e non e' servito a niente. Anziche' mandarmi via da Milano a calci nel culo, come meritavo, mi invitano a casa loro e magari vorrebbero . . . Ma io non mi concedo . . ." (99). Subsequently, Bianciardi, artistically and personally, retreats from the "real" world, opting for a self-imposed exile at Rapallo. Alberto Gessani describes this point in Bianciardi's life: "non ha il cinismo autentico del pennivendolo, e quello d'intrattenere la gente con la letteratura facile del *boom* non e' stato mai e non puo' essere il suo mestiere. E allora, chiuso ogni conto con il presente e con il futuro, non gli rimane che il passato: il passato storico piu' o meno lontano, vissuto o no, che sfuma insensibilmente nella fantasia e si fa mito: mito evocato come luogo nel quale far parlare l'anima e come fuga momentanea dal

'labirinto di griglie scure' in cui si deve pur vivere" (57-58). By evoking once again the ghosts of the Risorgimento and Garibaldian campaign, Bianciardi attempts to cope with the present and give vent to his anger. In the introduction of his personal interpretation of the Risorgimento, *Daghela avanti un passo!,* Bianciardi describes the events and human passions of this historical period as "eroicamente festosi, coloriti, un poco matti persino"(8). Inherent in the term "matti" is that element of rebellion against organized authority and a spirit of freedom that attracted Bianciardi to such writers as Henry Miller and Jack Keruoac, who infused their poetic world with an irrationality, linguistic or otherwise, as well as a sense of anarchy. These are the same characteristics that Bianciardi brought to his very personal treatment of history.[5] Through a sense of irony and a great deal of fantasy, Bianciardi's vision of history acquires an unreal quality enabling him to mix characters and events of the present and past. Bianciardi's strong interest in popularizing, as well as fictionalizing, Italian history and his desire to raise the Risorgimento to the same epic level as the American Civil War are, one can deduce, other reasons behind his eventual decision to translate *Confederate General from Big Sur.* An affinity between Bianciardi's own phantasmagoric view of history, best depicted in his final novel *Aprire il fuoco* and Brautigan's treatment of the historical past, is immediately evident in the novel's Italian title *Il generale immaginario.* In his brief preface to the novel, Bianciardi poses the following questions: "Tanto per cominciare, il problema e' questo: credere o non credere che fra gli stati confederati ci fosse anche il Big Sur? Chilometri di rocce, sabbie, gabbiani, patelle, nuvole, flutti, ranocchi, e in piu' certi indiani cosi selvaggi che non coltivavano la terra, non cacciavano, non raccoglievano bacche, non si riparavano dalle intemperie: possibile che tutto questo fosse un giorno uno Stato, capace di mandare al fronte i suoi volontari, agli ordini del favoloso generale Mellon?"[6] Bianciardi concludes this short introduction with an observation that further explains his attraction to the work: "C'e' persino Henry Miller, fermo ad aspettare il postino nella sua vecchia Cadillac. E c'e' infine l'autore, che e' un matto, anzi un poeta. La letteratura che chiamiamo *beat* ha trovato il suo umorista." Perhaps following the trails of their mythic mentor Henry Miller, both Brautigan in the *Confederate General from Big Sur* and Bianciardi in *Aprire il fuoco,* have their main characters escape from the city and seek refuge (or freedom) near the sea. By merging, or distorting, the present and the past in their respective works each author appears both to exalt the past from a nonconformist perspective (Brautigan: "while all around them waged the American Civil War, the last good time this country ever had," 148; Bianciardi: "il piu' grandioso avvenimento [the Risorgimento] della storia italiana moderna," Terrosi, 93) as well as to emphasize history's failings in changing the present.

Brautigan's present day general is a "Confederate General in ruins" (20), while Bianciardi's adaption of the historical Five Days of Milan in 1848 to a contemporary setting of 1959 is viewed as a "Rivoluzione che ando' fallita" (170). In both works, past ideals which motivated the events like the Civil War, the desire to explore new frontiers, and the Risorgimento are now lost, distorted, or misdirected in a confused present, where freedom is more a state of mind, often induced by drink or other forms of drugs, rather than a reality. Ultimately, watching the whales at Big Sur in *Confederate General* or waiting for the dolphins to appear at Nesci[7] (fictitious name for Rapallo) in *Aprire il fuoco* reflect the sense of resignation and futility that pervades each novel. Consequently, both novels conclude with the narrator's recognition that paradise or freedom have not and cannot be regained, that the good world or the glorious past are unattainable. In the *Confederate General,* this is reflected in the feeling of vacancy or tedium that overwhelms Jesse at the novel's conclusion (just a few short days after his arrival) as he is unable to find an authentic identity in an illusory world. The fact that he is ultimately more attracted to Elizabeth, the beautiful call girl from Los Angeles, who is on hiatus in Big Sur, than to the rebel Lee Mellon seems to imply that he still feels an urge to drop back into that society in which he felt so alienated. In other words, Big Sur is not, he learns, a long-term solution to his feeling of alienation. Similarly, from his exile in Nesci the revolutionary professor in *Aprire il fuoco,* having been deprived of a cause, sees no values in which to believe. The fact that he sees himself as a permanent "inquilino" confirms his sense of alienation and a feeling of not belonging. Having failed to re-ignite the mythical passions of the past, his only solution is death. In fact, the signal the revolutionary is waiting for to "aprire il fuoco" is really a presentiment of death. The bottle of grappa, always "a portata di mano" (22) of our "professor" in exile, is perhaps a momentary solution but not a conclusive one. On this note Maria Clotile Angelini writes: "l'alcol, che negli anni precedenti era stato la 'carica' necessaria per affrontare le conseguenze dell'isolata ribellione di 'formica' indocile, e' divenuto poi la droga e lo strumento di morte con cui annullare il fallimento di un'esistenza e lo scacco" (109). Henry Miller's advice "Stay put and watch the world go around!" does not seem to work any longer for either novelist. Miller, who inspired a literary spirit of rebellion in both Brautigan and Bianciardi, like the myths of the Civil War and the Risorgimento, seems to be a thing of the past and no longer a place to turn for solace. In fact in a letter dated February 23, 1968 Bianciardi writes about Miller: "sto traducendo un volume di saggi di Henry Miller, il quale invecchiando e' diventato mistico, e parla di continuo di Cristo, dicendo oltre tutto delle solenni fesserie" ("Brani di lettere inedite" 30). Similarly, the "beat's" life-style of drink and "dropping

out" leads to a moribund existence, dictated by a deadening routine, as Bianciardi eloquently demonstrates in *Aprire il fuoco.* Calvino's description of Big Sur during his visit to the United States in 1959 appears to be prophetic, at least for Bianciardi. The latter's escape to his Big Sur in Liguria ultimately leads to drink and death. Calvino's observation that Henry Miller, a type of father to the beat generation and to Bianciardi "non riceve piu' nessuno" and that he [Calvino] "non ci starebbe morto" in Big Sur confirm his own rejection of isolation as the intellectual's way of combatting the system. In fact, Calvino further substantiates this conviction at the conclusion of his essay "I Beatniks e il 'sistema'": "Vi diro' solo che non vorrei che la nuova generazione fosse una *beat generation,* ma vorrei che ereditasse insieme al nostro atteggiamento positivo verso la vita anche la nostra insopprimibile, amareggiante, sacrosanta insoddisfazione" (81). While Bianciardi clearly shares Calvino's dissatisfaction with the system, he, as an outsider, chooses to fight the battle alone. Bianciard's own experience, as depicted in *La vita agra* and *Aprire il fuoco,* tells us that his connection with the "Insiders" has been short-circuited. Consequently, Calvino's letter to Bianciardi of September 7, 1962, in which he expresses his dismay in the latter's choice of publishers for *La vita agra,* captures both Bianciardi's spirit of freedom as well as his inability to live within the system: "Caro Bianciardi, vedo il tuo libro annunciato nella pubblicita' di Rizzoli. Sei diventato matto?" (*I libri degli altri* 105).

Notes

1. Malley refers to Leslie Fiedler's study *Love and Death in the American Novel* in which the latter notes that this theme of man/men fleeing society is at the heart of many American literary classics. Malley writes: "In fact, Fiedler finds the legend of 'Rip Van Winkle'—the man who cops out of his domestic duties by boozing off to sleep in the mountains—to be the central myth of our literature" (93).

2. This discussion of Bianciard's novel as an "angry" novel within the context of Calvino's essay "I beatniks e il 'sistema'" was previously included in my essay "The Emotional Deterioration of an Ordinary Man: Luciano Bianciardi and the 'Miracle' Years in Milan." See 140-42.

3. In *La vita agra,* Bianciardi writes: "L'avrei pensata e l'avrei scritta come un bitnicco arrabbiato, dieci anni o sono, quando il signor Jacques Querouaques forse non aveva nemmeno imparato a tirarsi su i calzoni [. . .] Provero' l'impasto linguistico, contaminando da par mio la alata di Ollesalvetti diobo,' e 'u dialettu d'Ucurlais, il Molinari Enrico di New York [. . .] (33-34).

4. We are reminded that Bianciardi translated both *Tropic of Cancer* (1962) and *Tropic of Capricorn*

(1962), which resulted in legal battles and scandals due to content and language. In addition, Bianciardi translated in 1961 the anthology *The Beat Generation and The Angry Young Men,* choosing as his title *Narratori della Generazione Alienata,* just a year before the publication of *La vita agra.*

5. In his introduction to the novel *Aprire il fuoco,* Oreste Del Buono describes Bianciardi's non-conformist treatment of historical events and, in particular, to those related to the Risorgimento: "Il protagonista [of the novel], infatti, si dice in esilio per avere partecipato in Milano all'insurrezione armata del 1959. Del marzo 1959. Gia' perche' Bianciardi rifa' la storia delle cinque giornate care alla retorica risorgimentale spostandole, pero,' in tempi piu' prossimi, e confondendo e rimescolando personaggi di allora con personaggi di ora. Il risorgimento, lo studio non conformista, ma appassionato del risorgimento, costante della carriera di scrittore di Bianciardi" (iv-v).

6. Bianciardi's introductory comments to his translation of *Il generale immaginario* appear in the edition's back cover.

7. Zolita Louise Vella notes that Nesci is a "play on the Latin verb 'nescio:' to know not, to ignore, and a commonly used word in the Ligurean dialect that means idiot, stupid, ignorant" (154).

Works Cited

Angelini, Maria Clotilde. *Luciano Bianciardi.* Florence: La Nuova Italia, 1980.

Bianciardi, Luciano. *La vita agra.* 1962. Milan: Rizzoli, 1980.

———. *Aprire il fuoco.* 1969. Milan: Rizzoli, 1976.

———. *Daghela avanti u passo!* 1969. Milan: Longanesi & C., 1992.

———. "Brani da lettere inedite." *Confronti 3* (October 1972): 29-33.

Brautigan, Richard. *Confederate General from Big Sur.* New York: Grove Press, 1964.

———. *Il generale immaginario.* Trans. Luciano Bianciardi. Milan: Rizzoli, 1967.

Calvino, Italo. "I beatniks e il 'sistema." *Una pietra sopra.* Turin: Einaudi, 1980.

———. *I libri degli altri.* Ed. Giovanni Tesio. Turin: Einaudi, 1991.

———. *Eremita a Parigi.* Milan: Mondadori, 1994.

Chenetier, Marc. *Richard Brautigan.* London: Metheun, 1983.

Feldman, Gene and Max Grettenberg, eds. *The Beat Generation and The Angry Young Men.* New York: The Citadel Press, 1958.

———. *Narratori della Generazione Alienata.* Trans. Luciano Bianciardi. Parma: Guanda, 1961.

Foster, Edward Halsey. *Richard Brautigan.* Boston: Twayne Publishers, 1983.

Guerricchio, Rita. "La vita agra." *Luciano Bianciardi tra neocapitalismo e contestazione.* Rome: Editori Riuniti, 1992.

Malley, Terrence. *Richard Brautigan.* New York: Warner, 1972.

Nava, Giuseppe. "L'opera di Bianciardi e la letteratura dei primi anni Sessanta." *Luciano Bianciardi tra neocapitalismo e contestazione.*

Pietralunga, Mark. "The Emotional Deterioration of an Ordinary Man." *Italiana IV: Literature and Society.* West Lafayette: Bordighiera, 1992.

Vella, Zolita Louise. *Luciano Bianciardi: His Life and His Works. Image of a Dilemma.* Diss. Columbia University, 1976. Ann Arbor: UMI, 1976. 76203998.

Kathryn Hume (essay date March 2001)

SOURCE: Hume, Kathryn. "Brautigan's Psychomachia." *Mosaic* 34, no. 1 (March 2001): 75-92.

[*In the following essay, Hume analyzes the aesthetics of Brautigan's narratives, noting that he consciously used Zen principles to evoke a special kind of reader response.*]

Richard Brautigan's novels rouse readerly uneasiness. Now accustomed to the gigantism of Don DeLillo's *Underworld* and David Foster Wallace's *Infinite Jest,* we wonder whether slender books can offer anything but wispy charm. The violent emotional substrate is also disquieting, tainted *ex post facto* by the author's suicide. Add to that the strangeness: Brautigan offers no authorial guidance on how we should respond to a trout stream described as a series of horizontal telephone booths. Is this a bizarrely accurate simile, or does it physicalize the metaphor of wilderness being commodified and reshaped by technology?

The current critical picture reflects our difficulties. In addition to readings of individual novels, we have many attempts to relate Brautigan to the American tradition, as if this will make his weirdness safer because more familiar. William L. Stull and Edward Halsey Foster derive a genealogy from Thoreau. Ancestor status is granted to Melville (Stull; Vanderwerken), Hemingway

(Vanderwerken; Locklin and Stetler), and Fitzgerald (Locklin and Stetler; Willis). Terence Malley identifies beat precursors, Kerouac in particular. Marc Chénetier, more concerned with unique than derivative elements, makes the case for Brautigan's experimentalism. Psychological approaches explain the strange by other means. Josephine Hendin's observations on repressed anger in the early works could be extended to all the novels, and Brooke Horvath traces Brautigan's fear of death throughout the corpus. Revealing and persuasive though these psychological approaches are, they tend to read the books as by-products of neurosis and emphasize the implicit author at the expense of his or her literary effects.

In this essay, I construct Brautigan as an aesthetician and writer, as a conscious artist who used Zen principles rather than simply becoming the victim of psychic furies. Overall, I ask, What is the nature of his *narrative* enterprise? I disentangle the artist from characters and view what he does as a series of narrative experiments in portraying emotions and in working out the philosophical and political dimensions of certain strong feelings that interested him. The emotions that fascinate him naturally stem from his own experience, but my concern is what he constructs from them artistically. The eleven novels (the last one published posthumously) constitute a series of battlefields in which he sets up emotional conflicts and tries to find narrative forms appropriate to his vision. Hence my term *psychomachia,* for in formalized schema he tests certain feelings and kinds of narrative much as medieval writers formalized into allegory the temptations besetting a Christian soul. In the course of tracing the artistic projects that Brautigan sets himself, I show how he invites an unusual sort of reader response modelled upon Zen observation and why two radical shifts take place in his method of plotting stories.

Brautigan's name flared vividly into national popularity in 1967, the publication of *Trout Fishing in America: A Novel* coinciding with media curiosity about hippies and the Haight-Ashbury phenomenon (Abbott, ch. 1). The first four novels constitute a group defined by several shared features: dissatisfaction with America, passive male protagonists, Zen as a philosophy for handling emotions, and an unusual kind of reader response provoked by deliberate lack of affect.

America's shortcomings surface in *Trout Fishing in America* (published second, in 1967, but written first, in 1961). Like trout, however, those faults do not hang around to be analyzed to death. The narrator of the novel occasionally implies an opinion—as he does about the hungry being given spinach sandwiches (2)—but that deadpan description is demonstrably judgemental only because he invokes Kafka immediately thereafter. Most of his musing observations are delivered without overt evaluations. He ponders poisoned coyote bait and deformed trout, winos and wilderness hermits. He mentions drawbacks of being poor. Vignettes like these provide a largely unarticulated rationale for the narrative movement in the following three novels, for in these books Brautigan imagines three forms of withdrawal from America. *A Confederate General from Big Sur* is a late beat reprise of *Walden* (E. Foster 63-64) and of Leslie A. Fiedler's American pastoral involving two men together in the wilderness (Malley 93). *In Watermelon Sugar* tests a communal group retreat. In *The Abortion: An Historical Romance, 1966,* the librarian retreats within the social structure rather than outside it.

The lack of overt emotion in these four books has been explained as neo-Transcendentalist (Pütz 105-29), but Chénetier (86-98), Claudia Grossmann (90-104), Edward Halsey Foster (16-24), and Jeffrey M. Foster (89-90) all persuasively link it to Brautigan's interest in Zen. Zen masters claim that defining Zen in words is impossible, but, as part of Brautigan's aesthetic, Zen can be said to provide a habit of meditative observation applied to everyday experience. The person meditating centres on the here and now and observes emotions and thoughts that ripple through the mind but does not try to control them (Suzuki 31-34). Guilt or desire to change have no role in this dispassionate observation. Maintaining an analytic focus empty of judgement can protect one from being overwhelmed by the emotions being observed, and Brautigan seems to have embodied versions of this detachment in his main characters because it seemed to him a philosophically helpful approach to emotion. Brautigan as writer can be flashy—as he is when imagining trout streams stacked in a wrecking yard—but his narrator remains calm throughout this fantasia.

Readers become uneasy when the narrator observes but offers no guiding response. Robert Adams, for instance, complains that Brautigan's "art lies in making things out of a scene, and the things he chooses to make aren't moral judgments, they're not even compatible with moral judgments" (26). Implicit is the question, Why read the works at all? Ideally, by contrasting their own response to that of the disturbingly bland focal figure, readers could learn something about their own motives and beliefs. This is the reader response I think Brautigan was aiming for. What critics have done, though, is pour their own reactions into the carefully constructed voids rather than analyze their responses against the neutral ground.

An episode in *Trout Fishing in America* will illustrate what happens when Brautigan's neutral narrator offers readers no guidance. The narrator describes Worsewick Hot Springs without showing any response to the green slime attached to the edges and bottom of the pool, the orange scum growing in the hot-water stream, the dead fish, the relaxing warmth, and the aquatic act of coitus interruptus (43-44). The narrator accepts what he finds, but unsanitized nature goads critical rejection. Gretchen Legler (68) invokes a passage from *Walden* in which "crystals" and "pure" and "fairer" serve to denigrate these springs. However, the dead fish have died from swimming too close to a natural hot spring, not from morally troubling pollution. Pulling out rather than risking an unwanted pregnancy need not be discredited as "fertility gone sour" (Tanner 408). The description of the swirling spermatic fluid satisfies idle curiosity as well as the demands of painstaking observation. Distortions in critics' analyses of the seminal event betray the acute uneasiness caused by lack of narrator response. Tanner calls the springs a "lake coated with dead fish and green slime" and the sperm a "stringy mess" (408), although a wide spot in a stream is no lake, the slime does not coat the water, and the narrator also reports the sperm to be "misty" and "like a falling star" (44). Neil Schmitz places the lovemaking "beside" the creek, which has been "carelessly" dammed, and the sperm hangs in the "green scum" "beside" the dead fish, none of the terms being accurate (123). Because the narrator refuses to relieve readerly uneasiness by displaying his own emotions, the critics reflexively pour theirs into the vacuum and thereby relieve the pressure of their judgemental reactions rather than study those feelings.

Responses to *In Watermelon Sugar* are more diverse. The passive narrator and his commune are condemned for creepy inhumanity (Blakely; Hernlund; Horvath; Schmitz) or hailed for flower power serenity or Zen detachment (Clayton; Leavitt; Grossmann). Michael L. Schroeder grants both interpretations and explains the contradictions as reflecting Brautigan's divided personality. The so-called Confederate general, Lee Mellon, is sadistic, a borderline psychopath (Horvath 441, 435), cruel but true to his own nature (E. Foster 30, 41) and unneurotic (Tanner 406). When Brautigan gives us a trout stream being sold by the linear foot in a wrecking yard, Clayton enjoys the bravura vision (57); Kenneth Seib latches onto the adjacent plumbing fixtures and identifies the scene as a satiric critique of the American pastoral (70); and Tanner identifies this and other junkyards as signifying the end of the American dream (410).

All these readings are worth considering, but they reject the narrator's careful voids. Critics who find the emotional blankness most repulsive are those who show no awareness that detachment has been considered culturally and psychologically admirable. Classical Stoics, Christian monks, and Zen meditators need not be rejected as neurotic for distancing themselves from frantic emotions, desires, and obsessions. In Brautigan's case, the philosophical justification comes from Zen, and the aesthetic experiment involves creating such

voids to initiate a reader response. In their haste to assume the universal humanity of certain attitudes and emotions, critics lose the chance to compare their own reaction analytically to the neutrality of Brautigan's presentation and learn to understand their own assumptions better.

If we consider the novels as a loosely linked psychomachia, the first novel written shows the writer attempting to present a narrator who is detached from emotions, many of those emotions provoked by America. Brautigan achieves his effect by focussing his narrative on individual observations and by projecting as neutral and unjudgemental a stance as possible. The next three novels (in order of writing) continue to explore dissatisfactions with life in America, and in each a different social configuration for detaching oneself is tried out. In *A Confederate General from Big Sur* (actually the first published), Lee and Jesse hang out in a hut on the California coast. One might expect that the emotional payoff for abandoning society would be ecstasy (the beat/hippie reading). If *Walden* is the prototype, then the hermits ought to enjoy their labours and self-sufficiency. Should they not soar mentally when they throw hundred-dollar bills into the Pacific, a ritual shown in one of the alternative endings? In fact, that moment is carefully emptied of any such feeling, and so are many other moments where the reader might anticipate elevated emotions—sex on the wild beachscape of Big Sur, for instance. Transcendence seems called for by the narrative conventions, but the characters refuse to cooperate. We expect serenity, but Jesse only registers confusion and unhappiness. His multiple endings seem calmer and emptier than earlier adventures, though hardly serene. Withdrawal from America did not produce detached stability, and the withdrawal itself does not settle the discontent over America. The two men are no more truly independent of society than Thoreau was, as Manfred Pütz notes (127), so, philosophically and emotionally, the book resists closure.

Individual retreat to the primitive offers only short-term sanctuary, so the next novel investigates communal withdrawal. Can one avoid the pressures from American society to enslave oneself to work, family, and suburban life? Most of the tranquil characters in the commune of iDEATH achieve a very even-tempered life and feel no need for bourgeois marriage, split-level ranch, and nine-to-five job. Those whose possessive and aggressive emotions are stronger commit suicide. Such narrative brutality correlates with the emotional substructure of the novel. Hendin (48) argues that the narrator's uncanny calm in the face of tigers eating his parents represents Brautigan's angrily visiting upon parental figures the pain they inflicted upon him. Whatever his plot's source in hot anger, Brautigan tries to transmute such feelings to something else. The narrator shows us the attractions of the tigers as well as their dangers; like romanticized outlaws or gangsters, they do not war on children and do what they must to survive, and they make endearing mistakes with their arithmetic. The setting of iDEATH suggests that the prior civilization, evidently urban America now lost through some catastrophe, has in a sense committed suicide, as do those whose temperaments make them prospect through its ruins. Many readers do not like the Zen ego-death of "I"-DEATH, but the alternative lifestyle of churning emotions and alcoholism leads to gruesome suicide through slicing off one's own extremities.

In the last of these four interrelated novels, the passive narrator tries withdrawing from the pressures and expectations of American life by working and living in an eccentric library. The exigencies of befriending someone who subsequently becomes pregnant by him force this narrator to emerge from his den. His managing to manoeuvre in the big world makes this novel a transition piece toward the next four novels, all of which devote themselves to action. This protagonist gets to keep his gorgeous girlfriend, and he gains a strange reputation as a hero, evidently analogous to Brautigan's own fame as writer, and described here in 1971, just when Brautigan's actual acclaim was waning and he was seeking new ways to attract readers. Critics dispute whether the narrator's heroic status is ironic (Cabibbo) or straight (Hackenberry), but that question is difficult to answer when the puzzle has been carefully emptied of all clues. As usual, all we can really assess is our own reactions.

As I turn to Brautigan's action plots, the next distinct phase in his writing, let me make a point about the politics of his passive protagonists. Their extreme passivity is not necessarily identical to masochism, but such submissiveness and lack of visible affect in a male protagonist runs completely counter to American notions of male individualism, which are based on a man's pursuing male passions and aggressions (Rotundo 5-6). The passivity disquiets readers accustomed to culturally sanctioned patterns. In her article on male masochism, Carol Siegel argues that, by laying aside claims to the power of the phallus, the male masochist undercuts patriarchy and unsettles "the dominant discourse on masculinity. [. . .] The man who could be king but 'would prefer not to' is potentially powerfully disruptive" (2). Brautigan's experiment with passive protagonists has political implications, and, insofar as America is one evident target for his disaffection, the protagonists are part of that critique. They reject American cultural patterns. While they fail to change America, America also fails to change them, thanks to their quiescence.

What happens when someone who has cultivated Zen detachment and passivity takes up action narration? We get a strange hybrid, in which the plot line matches those of various fast-moving popular genres—gothic, western, mystery, love story, war story, hard-boiled detective story—but Zen-like observation produces a series of observed tableaux that freeze motion. Brautigan focusses on non-significant frames, thus rendering the action aimless. In *The Hawkline Monster: A Gothic Western,* the narrative rush to kill the monster is interrupted by seemingly endless chatter about burying a butler or about gravy at supper.

Anyone who reads these novels as un-ironized examples of their genres will be repelled by the freeze-frame effect. As Keith Abbott puts it, "Violence, irrational hate, grief, and loss of innocence via the modern sexual diseases—[. . .] [these] themes demanded either psychological characterization or bold dramatic action, neither of which [Brautigan] could use effectively, given his style" (123). If we accept irony and absurdity, then we can enjoy the slippery play of our responses to the disparity between genre-fiction clichés and what actually happens. Some of the momentum of a monster-killing plot normally derives from the monster: we understand the pull exerted by dragons on knights, or murderers on detectives. We are balked of such known narrative tensions by a monster consisting of conscious light followed by a stumblebum shadow, both of which arise from a mixture of chemicals. Even if we accept Gordon E. Slethaug's theory that the chemicals represent recreational drugs (144), we cannot anticipate the form that a fight with conscious chemicals might take, yet the urgency of genre fiction derives from our having such expectations. The gothic and western elements are also rendered absurd by the kaleidoscopic description of the main characters' later lives.

By making his focal figures his men, whose profession demands lack of feeling, Brautigan has simplified the narrative challenge facing him in this first attempt to change his style and win back his audience. He could work on the action plot, so different from the pacing in his previous novels, without having to find narrative forms for representing feelings as well. Having found the ironized perspective on action that felt right to him, he was ready in future works to add roiling, violent emotions and play them off against action. In each of the next three novels, he sets up interlace structures consisting of the same three elements: an unhappy plot, a happy plot, and an action plot. Brautigan draws on his Zen focus for short, vibrant scenes, and in these novels he explores the links between unhappy plots and action plots, and he tries to see where the happy option might fit in. Must happiness be forever beyond one's reach? Or can it become narratively as well as psychologically and philosophically assimilated?

Brautigan applies his own powers of unjudgemental observation to capture the experiences of his characters, but they, themselves, are no longer presented as detached. They seethe with volatile emotions. In *Willard and His Bowling Trophies: A Perverse Mystery,* the action strand is a vendetta. Robbed of their bowling trophies, the Logan brothers vow vengeance and become criminals to support their search. The unhappy narrative concerns Bob and Constance as their marriage collapses under guilt and venereal warts. The happy story describes the cheerful, sexy marriage of John and Patricia, who have found the bowling trophies in an abandoned car and have installed them as ornaments in their little flat. Narrative tensions rise in both the unhappy and the action plot, and Brautigan releases these by having the Logan brothers mistakenly murder the unhappy couple.

Can actions blot out unhappiness? In a sense, yes. Narrative tensions are released, but characters' emotions are not. Stolen bowling trophies are a poor excuse for murder, let alone murder of anyone but the original thieves, and part of what Brautigan does is render the vendetta action absurd. If one compares this novel to the next two, one sees where it has failed to solve a narrative problem to Brautigan's satisfaction. He does not manage to create significant connection among the three plot lines. Nothing relates the unhappy couple to the Logan brothers. Nor does the brothers' anguish invoke any larger issue—the failure of the American Dream, for instance. Since Brautigan goes on to link his subplots more closely, one deduces that rendering everything absurd was not an aim that satisfied him.

Since E. Foster despises *Sombrero Fallout: A Japanese Novel* as the worst of Brautigan's novels (103), and since almost no one else has written on it, I may seem perverse in calling it arguably his best and most polished performance. True, it is less experimental than *Trout Fishing in America* and less poetic than *The Tokyo-Montana Express.* For humour, effective resonance between the plots, and devastating satire, however, this novel seems to me uniquely successful in solving Brautigan's problems of linking action and emotion. A writer of humor suffers agonies from the breakup with his Japanese lover. One hour in an evening of woe is his contribution to the novel, his every rippling change of emotion carefully observed without judgement by the implied author—this is the unhappy plot. The action narrative derives from his tearing up the start of a story and tossing it in the wastebasket. The characters described on that paper, like the characters of Flann O'Brien and Gilbert Sorrentino, take control of their own lives and go on without the author. Their wastebasket activities turn into an absurd and explosive riot that kills thousands in an American town. The contrasting happy strand of action consists of the former girlfriend, Yukiko, and her serene dreams during that same hour. The dreams are suffused with the spirit of her dead father, who had committed suicide in anger over his wife's infidelity but who offers a benign pres-

ence here. Not only is Yukiko relaxed and at peace, but also we see atonement with a parental figure, a highly significant motif coming from Brautigan's pen.

In contrast to *Willard and His Bowling Trophies, Sombrero Fallout* manages to make the three strands resonate meaningfully together. When the writer in one plot cries copiously, two men in the wastebasket world start crying uncontrollably, and their unmanly behaviour arouses such uneasiness in bystanders that it triggers a cascade of violent events that embody the writer's repressed anger. The psychological and political construction of the Orient by America, present in the writer's love for a Japanese woman who caters to his sexual and emotional needs, has its echoes in an invocation of Vietnam in the wastebasket action plot. The guns that fall into townspeople's hands are the "finest collection of hardware outside of Indo-China during the great Vietnam War days" (132). The writer's agonies abate when he turns his experience into a country-and-western lyric. The banality of the lyric's wording is paralleled in the wastebasket President's speech, whose thundering clichés provide rhetorical quietus to the insane massacre. In contrast to this intertwining of emotion and violence, Yukiko sleeps, enjoying oneiric rapprochement with her father. Like her cat, she is efficient and serene, and her cat's purr is the motor that runs her dreams. Her serenity makes us understand both why the writer wants her back so badly and also why his behaviour drives her to break off the relationship. All three strands thus achieve an emotionally logical lessening of tensions both in the action and in the characters' minds.

Another improvement over *Willard and His Bowling Trophies* is the re-emergence of America as a significant issue. The Logan brothers' loss is idiosyncratic, whereas the wastebasket town, inflamed by riot, resonates with American inner-city violence—as the fictional foreign newspaper headlines make clear. The Americanness of the wastebasket mop-up is brilliant satire. The insane mayor who chants his license plate number is transformed by suicide into a hero, that being easier for the public to assimilate than absurdity. The sombrero that falls from the skies and starts the riot (violence "at the drop of a hat") turns from black to white, a bad-guy to good-guy shift in television western codes. By the time the media are through, everyone and everything has been recast as tragically heroic and typically American, and watchers can congratulate themselves on America's greatness. Norman Mailer, ideologue for macho violence, makes an amusing cameo appearance as a war correspondent to tell the great American public what it should think. Brautigan never renders America with more satiric gusto than in this novel, and he puts similar enthusiasm and skill into portraying the emotions of the writer. Untouched by all the explosive tensions are Yukiko's harmonious slumbers and her cat's elegant sufficiency. As readers, we can enjoy and approve the fashion in which the writer laments her departure, but the novel's creator allows us to see that she was right to reclaim her independence. The book manages both hysterics and even-handed fairness.

Having succeeded in representing emotions and action, and having managed to connect the two, why launch another three-strand novel? What aesthetic problems remained unsolved in *Sombrero Fallout*? I suggest that the synthesis that Brautigan worked out at an artistic level did not entirely satisfy him emotionally because of Yukiko's being female, oriental, and asleep and therefore withdrawn from the other actions. Her serenity and her gender make her unsatisfactory as a narrative conduit for the tensions over America and parents that so clearly obsess Brautigan as writer. Her atonement with her father is promising, but only as a first approximation toward releasing oedipal tensions between son and father. Hence, the next book faces a male protagonist with parental problems and life in America.

In *Dreaming of Babylon: A Private Eye Novel, 1942,* we again find the three narrative strands. The unhappy strand is the miserable, guilt-filled parental relationship in which Card as a child has accidentally caused his father's death and is still nagged about it by his mother. The violence-filled action plot involves Card as a private eye stealing a corpse. The happy material consists of Walter Mitty-like daydreams in which Card imagines himself the best baseball player or general or private eye in Nebuchadnezzar's Babylon. The parental plot is obviously responsible for the life-destroying power of the daydreams; as Mark Hedborn puts it in Lacanian terms, "We can postulate that Card forecloses the Name-of-the-Father when his father dies. From that point on whenever he tries to enter fully into the Symbolic realm he cannot, because the Imaginary (Babylon) intrudes to ruin his opportunity" (108). Significantly, Card's action story ends with his hiding the stolen body of a dead whore in his refrigerator. Brautigan has physicalized metaphors since *Trout Fishing in America,* and this one reifying frozen passion reminds us of the importance of ice caves of the Hawkline house, the iciness of the sombrero that started the wastebasket riot, and the chilly calm of trout in their streams.

What distinguishes *Dreaming of Babylon* from *Sombrero Fallout* is the failure of the plot lines to integrate emotion with action. The gumshoe story is just parody (analyzed by Grimaud and Grimes). It takes on a literary form, but no grander issue, such as America. The unhappy childhood and happy daydreams are technically all part of the one man's life, but they dis-integrate rather than integrate his mentality. Both operate to render him accident prone in the real world, and he achieves no Zen-like ability to contemplate them with detachment. At this point in his narrative development,

Brautigan is coming to realize that trying to make his characters act rather than be passive has not helped them achieve freedom from their emotional baggage. Action does not cancel out unhappiness. The Zen observations that he as author brings to describing them and their emotions does not trickle down to the protagonists and help them gain perspective. Only in *Sombrero Fallout* does he manage to make action and emotion correlate effectively, and obviously what he is doing is sufficiently unusual that it does not communicate to many readers.

Having failed to integrate action with the emotions that matter most to him, Brautigan shifts his narrative strategies yet again. His final two lifetime novels do not resemble each other on the surface, but both hark back to the early experiments in passive Zen observation, both are structured about contrasts, and both conjoin his original affectlessness with the emotional extravagance that grace the action plots. Pure neutrality and undiluted emotionality—the modes of the first four and next four novels respectively—have not worked separately, so Brautigan the narrative experimenter tries combining them.

The reliance upon Zen is easier to document for *The Tokyo-Montana Express* than for any of his other books. In trying to describe Zen values to me, colleague John Whalen-Bridge remarked that the observer experiences the death of Princess Diana as a ripple in the mind, and that ripple is of no more importance than the ripple caused by the naked lunch on the end of one's fork. This value judgement does not apply to the personage and food but to the perceptions of each in the meditator's mind. Brautigan makes just such a comparison when the emotions caused by the death of President Kennedy are equated with those that the narrator feels about pancakes at a restaurant. Another echo of Eastern thought is Brautigan's reducing barriers between ego and the rest of the world when he says the "I" of the book is the voice of the stops on the Tokyo-Montana Express; he diffuses his narrator into the dual landscape. The novel is emotionally warmer than any of the earlier texts. While the narrator himself expresses little feeling directly, other characters with whom he interacts to display their emotions. The narrator also offers readers something other than emotional void at every scene. He presents opportunities to feel obviously acceptable emotions, such as sympathy for the woman whose life's savings have disappeared with her unsuccessful Chinese restaurant, for the discarded Christmas trees cluttering the cityscape, for the caged wolf. Occasionally his meditations are pleasant: his experience with the shrine-of-carp cab and the fantasy on orange trees in Osaka, for instance. The dominant trope, though, is the "alien being." The classical musician Francl, who came to the American west in 1851 and died in the snow in 1875, is one such alien. So are the live eels imprisoned in a kitchen bucket, the domestic pets abandoned by the road, the various suicides, the makers of pizza in Japan, the centuries-old intelligence serving time in Ancona, the woman searching the snow for a tire chain, and the mid-winter crows trying to eat bits of rubber tire in the road. All these creatures are isolated. They operate as if they had been plucked from their home world and dropped into one that is indifferent or hostile. The narrator feels just as alien in Montana as he does in Japan.

Episode by episode, the sense of not belonging to this world remains bearable, although the cumulative effect is fairly oppressive for emotional readers. Zen perspective does encourage dispassionate detachment, though, so the narrator neither invites us to get greatly roused, nor does he do so himself. As in the earlier novels, he mostly avoids telling us what to think, making us view our own emotions and understand them. In the chapter devoted to the death-row menu, for instance, he tells us that he and friends are upset by the menu but never explains why. We are left to mull over possibilities. Is he bothered because this high-calorie complex menu is served to murderers while poor children go hungry? Is it the contrast between the state's hypocritical solicitude and its intention to execute the men? Is it gourmet revulsion at what an institutional cafeteria considers fancy food? Is it the irony that the prisoners have been eating this last-meal food for years because they inhabit death row? Are we meant to liken the prisoners to the penned chickens who get fed exotic leftovers, Italian and Chinese? We must grope our own way to appropriate emotions. The feelings in *The Tokyo-Montana Express* are not resolved, but they do not get out of hand as they did in *Dreaming of Babylon*.

Having achieved a much greater degree of literary calm in *The Tokyo-Montana Express* than in *Dreaming of Babylon*, Brautigan once again takes up explosive feelings, in *So the Wind Won't Blow It All Away.* He sets up three tranquil, passive portraits and contrasts them with Whitey growing up and coping with frenzied guilt over shooting a friend. The narrator, Whitey as an adult, says he is describing the calm people as if understanding them could help him understand himself; if he could reach their state of mind, he could come to terms with his past.

The three have indeed achieved notable serenity in their lives. The alcoholic watchman seems placidly if cynically at peace with the world. The old man with the elaborately carved dock and boat has achieved monk-like serenity. He is a gas-injured veteran of World War I, living on a tiny pension. His minuscule shack is tidy, and he makes no unnecessary movements. He grows most of his own food. Despite the years of work that have gone into the ornamental carving on his dock and boat, he accepts that some day a sheriff will run him off the land because he is a squatter. His ability to face the

probability that an ungrateful society will deprive him of his modest squat and his extraordinary handiwork indicates an admirable measure of detachment. The eccentrics portrayed in most detail are the bovine couple who set up their entire living room (down to *National Geographics* and doilies) on the bank of a pond every evening where they fish. The Depression has uprooted this couple, but they have created a compensatory world for themselves.

The three portraits all echo earlier Brautigan creations from his first, passive, affectless phase. The watchman, with his trick postcard of a catfish, has some of the serenity of various trout fishermen. The dock carver resembles Old Charley from iDEATH. The couple's ritual act of world creation links them to the "Kool-Aid Wino" in *Trout Fishing in America* who similarly makes his reality by an act of will. Brautigan thus draws on the calm creations of the early books to balance or contain Whitey's frenzies, similar in their roiling intensity to the emotions of Brautigan's second, action, phase of writing.

Whitey does not achieve complete serenity, although some atonement between himself and his mother takes place. His early comments on her are very negative. She "just barely tolerated my existence. She could take me or leave me" (44). She is responsible for his being exposed to a number of unsatisfactory stepfathers. Her panic over being lodged in a flat with a gas stove reduces family life to shambles. Nevertheless, when Whitey has spent months obsessing over the hamburger he nearly bought instead of the fatal bullets that he did purchase, she enters his obsession and agrees that maybe he should have bought a hamburger. Almost magically, as sometimes happens when an outsider enters a fantasy, it loses its hold on Whitey, and he is able to burn his compulsive writings. He observes a caged coyote and bear in a neighbourhood zoo. They appear outwardly tranquil, if not precisely happy. Their endurance seems a more liveable state of mind to him than his orgies of guilt. With his emotional temperature thus lowered, Whitey ponders the couple by the pond and imagines their commenting on his having disappeared. He becomes invisible in the dusk, and they remain, placid amid their furnishings. Brautigan almost seems to be trying a cinematic fade-out from Whitey to them, from his unhappiness to their acceptance of what is. In terms of the technical portrayal of Whitey's emotions, this is a highly successful novel, in part because emotions and action are so tightly conjoined. The happy and miserable elements mingle enough to lessen the misery, though not yet enough to reach complete equilibrium.

Brautigan's daughter has issued a posthumous novel by her father, entitled *An Unfortunate Woman: A Journey.* In this, Brautigan largely eschews action and avoids giving his characters dramatic emotions. The narrator (who is either Brautigan himself or a very Brautigan-like writer) admits to being depressed (57-58, 86-90). To counter that anomie, he focusses on the minutiae of lives and emotions around him. He notes out-of-place creatures and objects such as a brand-new woman's shoe in a Hawaiian intersection and a spider in the hairs on his arm. His thoughts repeatedly return to the death from cancer of a thirty-eight-year-old female friend and the suicide of a woman whose house he rented. The narrator opines that in describing weather and thunderstorms he is describing himself (99). This narrator, the two dead women, and the alienated objects all seem projections of Brautigan's own melancholy. The narrator's plan to record daily experience (1-2, 107) resembles that of Scheherazade: he puts forth words to avoid being engulfed by death. In this novel, Brautigan's observations are as sharp as always, but he finds no actions that can block awareness or create a distance between himself and the temptation of nothingness.

Brautigan has lapsed into critical oblivion. Why attempt resurrection? Does he have a place in the canon of American literature? His early books once seemed to chime with 1960s flower power, but most critics realize that the 1960s ethos is not very central to his endeavour. As experimenter, he is interesting, but many more radical writers have succeeded him. His angers, directed at parental figures and America, put him right in the mainstream. A man's search for his father is the Maxwell Perkins ticket to writing the great American novel, and it hardly matters whether one wishes to find or kill the father.

Brautigan's whole novelistic output is an ongoing experiment in which intense emotion is channelled into plots whose surface concerns only glancingly reflect the causes of the emotion. The characters are not allegorical as they were in the medieval psychomachia, but the emotions well up at a distance from those characters and flow through them as their actions or their Zen observations attempt to contain the psychic energies. To this inner dynamic Brautigan adds his own aesthetic, a certain wry charm, acutely observed detail, an occasionally dazzling sense of vision, a spare efficiency of means, and a vein of high fantasy. He also invites an unusual reader response; the unjudgemental narrative stances or characters play foil to readers' reactions and invite self-analysis.

How should readers respond to Brautigan outside the 1960s' context? We find strong feelings swirling about recurrent issues, expressed in economically sketched vignettes. Like soap bubbles, their form is simple, their tension, immense. In novels, we perhaps expect powerful emotions to be the province of sprawling books. Norman Mailer novels reverberate with vivid feelings. However, Mailer is producing a fictional equivalent to

Géricault's famous painting "The Raft of the Medusa," while Brautigan gives us the Chinese master's perfect frog in one continuous brush stroke. The one works on heroic scale with heroic bodies in torment, while the other is postcard sized, with very subtle variation in the shades of gray and black on the background paper. It *looks* simple. Simplicity rarely is, though. Formally, Brautigan's novels strive for the compressed simplicity of haiku. They are sparely poetic and small scaled, if not actually miniature. In the land where bigger is better, he has tried looking at life from a different angle and has reflected that perspective in his art.[1]

Note

1. I owe thanks to John Whalen-Bridge, University of Singapore, for introducing me to Zen and for reading more than one draft of my argument.

Works Cited

Abbott, Keith. *Downstream from* Trout Fishing in America: *A Memoir of Richard Brautigan.* Santa Barbara: Capra, 1989.

Adams, Robert. "Brautigan Was Here" [an omnibus review of the first four novels and a volume of poetry]. *New York Review of Books* 22 April 1971: 24-26.

Blakely, Carolyn F. "Narrative Technique in Brautigan's *In Watermelon Sugar.*" *CLA Journal* 35.2 (1991): 150-58.

Brautigan, Richard. *A Confederate General from Big Sur.* 1964. Boston: Houghton Mifflin, 1991.

———. *Trout Fishing in America: A Novel.* 1967. New York: Dell [Delta ed.], 1980.

———. *In Watermelon Sugar.* 1968. New York: Dell [Laurel ed.], 1973.

———. *The Abortion: An Historical Romance, 1966.* New York: Simon and Schuster [Touchstone ed.], 1971.

———. *The Hawkline Monster: A Gothic Western.* 1974. Boston: Houghton Mifflin, 1991.

———. *Willard and His Bowling Trophies: A Perverse Mystery.* New York: Simon and Schuster [Touchstone ed.], 1975.

———. *Sombrero Fallout: A Japanese Novel.* New York: Simon and Schuster [Touchstone ed.], 1976.

———. *Dreaming of Babylon: A Private Eye Novel, 1942.* 1977. Boston: Houghton Mifflin, 1991.

———. *The Tokyo-Montana Express.* 1980. New York: Dell [Delta ed.], 1981.

———. *So the Wind Won't Blow It All Away.* 1982. New York: Dell [Delta ed.], 1984.

————. *An Unfortunate Woman: A Journey.* New York: St. Martin's, 2000.

Cabibbo, Paola. "*The Abortion: An Historical Romance, 1966,* di R. Brautigan, ovvero, l'aborto dell'eroe." *Sigfrido nel Nuovo Mondo: Studi sulla narrativa d'iniziazione.* Ed. Paola Cabibbo. Rome: La Goliardica, 1983. 209-16.

Chénetier, Marc. *Richard Brautigan.* London: Methuen, 1983.

Clayton, John. "Richard Brautigan: The Politics of Woodstock." *New American Review* 11 (1971): 56-68.

DeLillo, Don. *Underworld.* New York: Simon and Schuster, 1997.

Fiedler, Leslie A. *Love and Death in the American Novel.* Rev. ed. New York: Stein and Day, 1966.

Foster, Edward Halsey. *Richard Brautigan.* Boston: Twayne, 1983.

Foster, Jeffrey M. "Richard Brautigan's Utopia of Detachment." *Connecticut Review* 14.1 (1992): 85-90.

Grimaud, Isabelle. "'Stranger than Paradise': *Dreaming of Babylon: A Private Eye Novel, 1942,* by Richard Brautigan." *Caliban* 23 (1986): 127-35.

Grimes, Larry E. "Stepsons of Sam: Re-Visions of the Hard-Boiled Detective Formula in Recent American Fiction." *Modern Fiction Studies* 29.3 (1983): 535-44.

Grossmann, Claudia. *Richard Brautigan: Pounding at the Gates of American Literature: Untersuchungen zu seiner Lyrik und Prosa.* Heidelberg: Carl Winter, 1986.

Hackenberry, Charles. "Romance and Parody in Brautigan's *The Abortion.*" *Critique* 23.2 (1981-82): 24-36.

Hedborn, Mark. "Lacan and Postmodernism in Richard Brautigan's *Dreaming of Babylon.*" *Literature and Film in the Historical Dimension.* Ed. John D. Simons. Gainesville: UP of Florida, 1994. 101-10.

Hendin, Josephine. *Vulnerable People: A View of American Fiction Since 1945.* New York: Oxford UP, 1978.

Hernlund, Patricia. "Author's Intent: *In Watermelon Sugar.*" *Critique* 16.1 (1974): 5-17.

Horvath, Brooke. "Richard Brautigan's Search for Control over Death." *American Literature* 57.3 (1985): 434-55.

Hume, Kathryn. *American Dream, American Nightmare: Fiction since 1960.* Urbana: U of Illinois P, 2000.

Leavitt, Harvey. "The Regained Paradise of Brautigan's *In Watermelon Sugar.*" *Critique* 16.1 (1974): 18-24.

Legler, Gretchen. "Brautigan's Waters." *CEA Critic* 54.1 (1991): 67-69.

Locklin, Gerald, and Charles Stetler. "Some Observations on *A Confederate General from Big Sur.*" *Critique* 13.2 (1971): 72-82.

Malley, Terence. *Richard Brautigan.* New York: Warner, 1972.

Pütz, Manfred. *The Story of Identity: American Fiction of the Sixties.* Stuttgart: Metzler, 1979.

Rotundo, E. Anthony. *American Manhood: Transformations in Masculinity from the Revolution to the Modern Era.* New York: Basic, 1993.

Schmitz, Neil. "Richard Brautigan and the Modern Pastoral." *Modern Fiction Studies* 19.1 (1973): 109-25.

Schroeder, Michael L. "Rhetorical Depth or Psychological Aberration: The Strange Case of Richard Brautigan." *Mount Olive Review* 3 (1989): 45-49.

Seib, Kenneth. "*Trout Fishing In America*: Brautigan's Funky Fishing Yarn." *Critique* 13.2 (1971): 63-71.

Siegel, Carol. "Postmodern Women Novelists Review Victorian Male Masochism." *Genders* 11 (1991): 1-16.

Slethaug, Gordon E. "*The Hawkline Monster*: Brautigan's 'Buffoon Mutation'." *The Scope of the Fantastic: Culture, Biography, Themes, Children's Literature.* Ed. Robert A. Collins and Howard D. Pearce. Westport, CT: Greenwood, 1985. 137-45.

Stull, William L. "Richard Brautigan's *Trout Fishing in America*: Notes of a Native Son." *American Literature* 56.1 (1984): 68-80.

Suzuki, Shunryu. *Zen Mind, Beginner's Mind.* 1970. New York: Weatherhill, 1996.

Tanner, Tony. *City of Words: American Fiction, 1950-1970.* New York: Harper and Row, 1971.

Thoreau, Henry David. *Walden.* Edited and with an introduction and notes by Stephen Fender. Oxford: Oxford UP, 1997.

Vanderwerken, David L. "*Trout Fishing in America* and the American Tradition." *Critique* 16.1 (1974): 32-52.

Wallace, David Foster. *Infinite Jest: A Novel.* New York: Little Brown, 1996.

Willis, Lonnie L. "Brautigan's *The Hawkline Monster*: As Big as the Ritz." *Critique* 23.2 (1981-82): 37-47.

FURTHER READING

Bibliography

Barber, John F. *Richard Brautigan: An Annotated Bibliography.* Jefferson, N.C.: McFarland & Company, 1990, 236 p.

Detailed overview of primary and secondary works, annotated and organized by type. Also includes chronology and a brief biography.

Boyer, Jay. "Selected Bibliography." In *Richard Brautigan,* pp. 51-2. Boise, Idaho: Boise State University, 1987.

Selected list of primary and secondary works.

Biographies

Abbot, Keith. *Downstream from Trout Fishing in America: A Memoir of Richard Brautigan.* Santa Barbara, Calif.: Capra Press, 1989, 174 p.

A readable, chronological account of the author's eighteen-year friendship with Brautigan.

Chénetier, Marc. *Richard Brautigan.* London: Methuen, 1983, 96 p.

Short biographical-critical study which stresses the self-referential and "metafictional" aspects of Brautigan's work.

"Fishing for Truth." *People Weekly* 53, no. 23 (12 June 2000): 73.

Profile of Brautigan and his daughter Ianthe, also a writer.

Kerouac, Jan. *Trainsong,* pp. 154-57. New York: Henry Holt and Company, 1988.

Account of a 1983 meeting with Brautigan in Amsterdam, written by the daughter of Jack Kerouac.

Criticism

"Blame It on Brautigan." *Harper's* 281, no. 1684 (September 1990): 42-5.

Excerpts from the catalogue for the Brautigan Library of unpublished works in Burlington, Vermont—an institution suggested by a Brautigan novel.

Morton, Brian. "How Hippies Got Hooked on *Trout Fishing in America.*" *The Times* (London) *Literary Supplement* (16 November 1984): 12.

Discussion of *Trout Fishing, In Watermelon Sugar,* and *The Tokyo-Montana Express,* emphasizing that too many critics have incorrectly labelled Brautigan an ephemeral writer.

Schroeder, Michael L. "Rhetorical Depth or Psychological Aberration: The Strange Case of Richard Brautigan." *Mount Olive Review* (spring 1989): 45-9.

Schroeder attempts to resolve the coexistence of gentleness and violence in Brautigan's *In Watermelon Sugar,* suggesting that Brautigan's own divided personality accounts for the tone of the book.

Wright, Lawrence. "The Life and Death of Richard Brautigan." *Rolling Stone* (11 April 1985): 29ff.

Offers a memoir of Brautigan's life with some commentary on his works.

Additional coverage of Brautigan's life and career is contained in the following sources published by the Gale Group: *Beacham's Encyclopedia of Popular Fiction: Biography & Resources,* **Vol. 1;** *Contemporary Authors,* **Vols. 53-56, 113;** *Contemporary Authors New Revision Series,* **Vol. 34;** *Contemporary Literary Criticism,* **Vols. 1, 3, 5, 9, 12, 34, 42;** *Dictionary of Literary Biography,* **Vols. 2, 5, 206;** *Dictionary of Literary Biography Yearbook,* **1980, 1984;** *DISCovering Authors Modules: Novelists;* *DISCovering Authors 3.0;* *Literature Resource Center;* *Major 20th-Century Writers,* **Ed. 1;** *Reference Guide to American Literature;* *St. James Guide to Fantasy Writers;* **and** *Something about the Author,* **Vol. 56.**

José Donoso
1924-1996

Chilean novelist, short story writer, playwright, poet, journalist, and translator.

The following entry provides criticism on Donoso's works from 1975 through 2000. For criticism prior to 1975, see *CLC,* Volumes 4, 8, 11, and 32; and for an obituary entry on Donoso, see *CLC,* Volume 99.

INTRODUCTION

José Donoso was known as the best Chilean novelist of his generation. His complex, multi-layered fiction encompassed the best of the "the Boom" period in Spanish American literature during the 1960s and 1970s and beyond.

BIOGRAPHICAL INFORMATION

Donoso was born on October 5, 1924, in Santiago, Chile, to a physician's family of unstable fortunes. When Donoso's hopes for a substantial inheritance were dashed, he spent some time wandering about the country, even taking a job as a shepherd. Eventually he attended the University of Chile and Princeton University and became an English teacher, at the same time struggling to get his first works published in the provincial cultural environment of Chile. Journalistic assignments in Santiago and Mexico City, as well as teaching opportunities at Princeton and Dartmouth College, broadened his horizons. He began to be recognized as a writer of substance during the 1960s. In 1961 he married Maria del Pilar Serrano, a translator. Escaping from the stifling of creativity by the Marxist government in Chile, Donoso began a period of voluntary exile in 1964, spending time in Mexico and at the University of Iowa before settling in Spain. By the mid-1980s he had returned to his native land and in 1990 received Chile's highest literary award, the Chilean National Literature Prize. He died of cancer on December 7, 1996.

MAJOR WORKS

Critics note that it is difficult to characterize Donoso's work, which is a complex mixture of pessimism, social commentary, and observations on the relationship be-

tween an artist and his creations. His works reflect, without didactic intent, the tensions between rich and poor and the political upheaval which has characterized Chile from the Marxist Salvador Allende period in the 1960s to the brutal dictatorship of Augusto Pinochet beginning in the 1970s. Donoso's first novel, *Coronación* (1957; *Coronation*), partly a portrait of his insane grandmother, combines realism and fantasy. A second novel, *Este Domingo* (1966; *This Sunday*), explores the chasm between rich and poor with subtlety and sophistication and experiments with differing points of view. *El lugar sin límites* (1966; *Hell Has No Limits*), a novella, is an extremely pessimistic commentary on the futility of human effort. Donoso's greatest novel, *El obsceno pájaro de la noche* (1970; *The Obscene Bird of Night*), is a dreamlike exploration of the mind of a schizophrenic. After the success of *The Obscene Bird of Night* Donoso wrote his own account of the literary history of his times, *Historia personal del "boom"* (1977; *The "Boom" in Spanish American Literature: A Personal*

History). During his period of exile, Donoso's style began to veer away from dreams and hallucinations. In 1978 he produced *Casa de campo* (*A House in the Country*), a political allegory with echoes of the repressive Pinochet takeover of Chile. *La desesperanza* (1986; *The Curfew*), a novel written after his return to Chile, concerns the fate of the political left in the Pinochet period. Two later novellas, combined in *Taratuta; Naturaleza muerta con cachimba* (1990; *Taratuta; and, Still Life with Pipe*), explore the interaction between art and reality—in particular, the intricate relationship between the artist and his creations.

CRITICAL RECEPTION

Today recognized as the greatest Chilean novelist of his time, Donoso had difficulty getting his early work published and reviewed. Critics at first labelled him one of the so-called "Generation of 1950"—a group of well-educated, middle-class writers who moved fiction in Chile from a preoccupation with nativism to a new-found cosmopolitanism—and categorized him as a writer of "new novels" which combined both realistic and fantastical elements. Little English-language criticism appeared on Donoso until the translation of *Coronation* in 1965. The publication of *The Obscene Bird of Night* in 1973 and a full-length bio-critical study of Donoso in 1979 further encouraged scholarly work on Donoso in English. Critics have often disagreed over whether Donoso was directly criticizing the Allende or Pinochet regimes in Chile, or simply chronicling the decline of personal creativity or the existential angst of individuals in difficult circumstances. Critical approaches to Donoso's work have been as diverse and complex as Donoso's own fictional output. Earlier English-language critics outlined prominent themes in Donoso's work and pointed out the ways in which he expressed a particular "Latin American" consciousness. Other critics used structuralist theory or commented on Donoso's fluid use of narrative techniques. A number of critics have used a comparative literature or intertextual approach to connect Donoso with other literary traditions. Still others have engaged in psychoanalytic, mythological, existential, reader-response, or deconstructive criticism. After 1970 Donoso was often called "postmodern" since his work increasingly relied on ambiguity, inner-directedness, a non-integrated subject, a fragmented narrative, and the interweaving of fantasy and reality. Many critics have agreed that a central theme in Donoso's work is a condemnation of the world of social convention which prevents an individual from achieving self-fulfillment. The sheer volume, variety, and intellectual richness of Donoso criticism since 1965 seem to reinforce Donoso's own stated wish to avoid "simplification."

PRINCIPAL WORKS

Veranea y otros cuentos [*Summertime and Other Stories*] (short stories) 1955

Dos cuentos [*Two Stories*] (short stories) 1956

Coronación [*Coronation*] (novel) 1957

El charlestón [*Charleston and Other Stories*] (short stories) 1960

El lugar sin límites [*Hell Has No Limits*] (novella) 1966

Este domingo [*This Sunday*] (novel) 1966

El obsceno pájaro de la noche [*The Obscene Bird of Night*] (novel) 1970

Cuentos (short stories) 1971

Historia personal del "boom" [*The "Boom" in Spanish American Literature: A Personal History*] (literary history) 1977

*Tres novelitas burguesas [*Sacred Families: Three Novellas*] (novellas) 1977

Casa de campo [*A House in the Country*] (novel) 1978

El jardín de al lado [*The Garden Next Door*] (novel) 1981

La misteriosa desaparición de la Marquesita de Loria (novel) 1981

Poemas de un novelista (poetry) 1981

Cuatro para Delfina [*Four for Delfina*] (novellas) 1982

Sueños de mala muerte [*Dreams of a Bad Death*] (play) 1985

Seis cuentos para ganar (short stories) 1985

La desesperanza [*The Curfew*] (novel) 1986

Taratuta; Naturaleza muerta con cachimba [*Taratuta; and, Still Life with Pipe: Two Novellas*] (novellas) 1990

Donde van a morir los elefantes (novel) 1994

*This collection contains the novellas "Chatanooga Choo-choo," "Green Atom Number Five," and "Gaspard de la Nuit."

CRITICISM

Harley D. Oberhelman (essay date 1975)

SOURCE: Oberhelman, Harley D. "José Donoso and the 'Nueva Narrativa.'" *Revista de Estudios Hispanicos* 9 (1975): 107-17.

[*In the following essay, Oberhelman says that Donoso's* El obsceno pájaro de la noche *shows both a concern for national social problems and an adherence to the so-called "new narrative" of contemporary Spanish American letters which combines realistic and metaphysical elements.*]

The latest novel of José Donoso, *El obsceno pájaro de la noche,* is a complex statement of the metaphysical problems faced by humanity in the twentieth century. Published in 1970 at a time when Chile's political system was turning to state socialism in search of solutions to age-old nagging social and economic injustices, a careful reading of Donoso's text reveals a deep concern for national problems and at the same time marks the author as a major practitioner of the "nueva narrativa" in contemporary Spanish American letters.

Donoso, whose *Coronación* (1958), *Este domingo* (1966), and *El lugar sin límites* (1967) announced his principal theme, the inner world of the collapsing Chilean oligarchy, achieves a masterpiece of major proportions with *El obsceno pájaro,* a work which required some eight years to produce. It is clearly within the current of the innovative Spanish American novel of today in its cataloguing of the decline of bourgeois systems and values and in its creation of a new realism based on multiple mutations of the author's (and the reader's) creative imagination. There is a double axis on which Donoso's concept of reality is based; the novel moves simultaneously on an exterior and an interior plane, leading eventually to a negation of both levels of action. A new socio-economic system must replace the exterior reality of Chilean life just as the negation of the traditional protagonist points the way toward new novelistic forms.

The great complexity of *El obsceno pájaro* offers the critic a variety of approaches to its interpretation. The present study will limit itself to a consideration of the aforementioned dual aspects of exterior and interior reality which form the framework, as it were, of this innovative work. Action in the novel is fragmented so that the reader must constantly reconstruct the basic thread: a history in retrospect of the wealthy, landed Azcoitía family and especially of the family's charitable asylum for aging women, the Casa de Ejercicios Espirituales de la Encarnación de la Chimba. The origin of the Casa is lost in centuries of myth and folklore, but it was most certainly founded as a refuge by eighteenth century progenitors of the Azcoitía family for their only daughter who was described diversely by regional folklore as a witch, a deeply religious saint, or the mother of a bastard child. Through various generations the Casa remained in the hands of the family's male heir while the Church enjoyed usufructuary rights to the institution. Don Jerónimo de Azcoitía and his wife, Inés Santillana de Azcoitía, are the twentieth century heirs to the refuge and its forty old women, three nuns, and five orphans.

A second important setting in the novel is La Rinconada, Don Jerónimo's own artificial world created as a home for his son who was born a distorted monster. La Rinconada has a complete staff of servants, adminis-

trators, workers, and a doctor, who themselves are all carefully selected monsters. Boy, the Azcoitías' only issue, is therefore to grow up in a hermetically sealed environment where the grotesque is the norm, and where his own horribly deformed face and body will never cause him unhappiness or anxiety.

If the principal purpose of the contemporary Spanish American novel is to chronicle the profound transformations which are causing a restructuring of a whole society,"[1] then this latest novel of Donoso fully measures up to the assignment. While it fails to offer dramatic linguistic innovations such as those seen in Julio Cortázar's *Rayuela* and Guillermo Cabrera Infante's *Tres tristes tigres,* it does create an effective picture of the decay of an entire society similar in many respects to the vision of Macondo in Gabriel García Márquez and of Comala in Juan Rulfo.

Chile at the time of the action of most of the novel, roughly the decade prior to 1970, was still effectively in the hands of an oligarchy, which in the words of the author had been "incapaz de reunir más que mugres aquí."[2] If the Casa de Ejercicios Espirituales is to be considered the primary legacy of the Azcoitía family, this affirmation is entirely apropos. The decrepit existence of the forty old women, whose interminable monologues and dialogues fill nearly two hundred pages, can be reduced to the musty packages containing their nondescript earthly possessions which each jealously guards beneath her bed. Hanging over the Casa is the threat that Don Jerónimo may never produce a male heir and that at any time he may decide to demolish this monument to his family's eleemosynary concern and subdivide and sell the land it occupies.

There are rays of hope, however. Inés, Don Jerónimo's wife, is in Rome, ostensibly for the purpose of convincing the Holy See that the Azcoitía ancestor for whom the institution was originally founded should be beatified and ultimately canonized. Such action would most certainly save the Casa, and at the same time it would seem appropriate for a family whose right to a giant's share of Chile's land and wealth is considered divine: "El repartió las fortunas según él creyó justo, y dio a los pobres sus placeres sencillos y a nosotros nos cargó con las obligaciones que nos hacen Sus representantes sobre la tierra. Sus mandamientos prohíben atentar contra Su orden divino . . ." (*Pájaro,* p. 174) Rome, nevertheless, fails to grant this signal recognition to the Azcoitía family, which would incidentally have been a boon to Don Jerónimo's candidacy to the national congress.

It is through Don Jerónimo's secretary, one Humberto Peñaloza, that the complicated relationship between exterior and interior reality in the novel comes into focus. Peñaloza is one form of a multiple protagonist whose constant metamorphoses create a series of unusual characters: Mudito, the mute caretaker of the Casa de Ejercicios Espirituales; a yellow dog which follows one of the orphans from the Casa, Iris Mateluna, on a series of nocturnal wanderings through the streets of Santiago; Iris Mateluna's "miraculously" conceived baby; one of the old women in the Casa, the seventh in an unholy coterie organized to care for Iris' baby; a humid spot on the wall—the mutations are endless. Other cases of the multiple protagonist will be pointed out later, but the Humberto Peñaloza episode is of special significance in the question of social and economic injustice.

The son of an impoverished elementary school professor, Peñaloza was from the days of his childhood faced with the desire to be "someone," to escape from the limbo of the masses. But an insurmountable barrier stood between the masses and the Chilean middle class; few were able to reach this promised land where there existed the possibility of a dignified career. Peñaloza vividly recalls the first time he laid eyes on the debonaire figure of Don Jerónimo de Azcoitía shortly after his return from Europe and just prior to his marriage to Inés Santillana. Peñaloza makes the inevitable comparison: "Yo, en cambio, no era nada ni nadie" (*Pájaro*, p. 105).

It is years later during Don Jerónimo's congressional campaign that the cleavage between the oligarchy and the masses reaches its climax. Peñaloza, now his secretary, accompanies him to a mountain village where the rival Radical party has aroused the miners and where the boxes containing the ballots were stolen during the course of the election. The situation is tense. Don Jerónimo as a representantive of the Conservative party is *persona non grata* in the village. Violence appears probable as Don Jerónimo takes refuge with his cohorts and secretary behind the doors of the Club Social in the central plaza. The confrontation which follows results in one serious injury: a bullet penetrates Peñaloza's arm.

In the confusion that follows, Don Jerónimo is quick to take advantage of the situation; blood from Peñaloza's wound is liberally applied to his arm. The sight of the "wounded" candidate is enough to quell the forces of rebellion; it is also enough to elect a new senator. Peñaloza views the event as "el momento culminante del poder de una oligarquía que, a partir de entonces, comenzo a declinar." (*Pájaro*, p. 105) Donoso in this incident conveys the thesis that the strength of the oligarchy was possible only at the cost of the sacrificial blood of a commoner. But such an unwilling sacrifice would not always rescue Chile's aristocracy.

Humberto Peñaloza, one of the principal forms of the central multiple protagonist, provides an entrée into the vertiginous inner world of Donoso's novel. The almost endless succession of metamorphic changes results in a variety of narrative points of view, all of which ultimately coalesce into a single undefined "yo." Paralleling these changes is a similar line of development in the multiple character of Inés Santillana de Azcoitía, who throughout her lifetime was so influenced by her mysterious, witch-like nurse, Peta Ponce, that she eventually assumed the personality of the person who ultimately destroyed her mind. Donoso chronicles the change in the following manner: Inés, Inés-Peta, Peta-Inés, Peta, Peta Ponce. The confusion of characters reaches its zenith in the mysterious process of the procreation of Boy, the monstrous "version of chaos" who is to continue the noble Azcoitía lineage. Jerónimo and Inés are unable to bear a child without the intervention of a variety of "substitute" progenitors. At one point Humberto Peñaloza and Peta Ponce serve as the physical agents of Jerónimo and Inés in the act of conception. Others also intercede in the act; Iris Mateluna, the promiscuous orphan in the Casa de Ejercicios Espirituales, lends her body as a place for the unborn Boy to grow. Mudito, the caretaker who is really another form of Humberto Peñaloza, serves both as witness to Iris Mateluna's participation in the "miraculous" conception of Boy and as the suspected father of the child. Near the end of the novel it is even announced that "El Mudito es el hijo (de Iris Mateluna) que estuvimos esperando tanto tiempo y nació hace tanto tiempo que ya no hay nadie aquí en la Casa que recuerde cuándo nació. . . ." (*Pájaro*, p. 512).

Such a juxtaposition and multiplicity of characters results in a confused, schizophrenic world of inner reality. Inés suffers from advanced schizophrenia as the novel ends, and Boy is clearly the deformed product of a chaotic society in the last stages of decay. In a sense La Rinconada, the artificial world in which Boy is to lead a Segismundo-like existence, is a universe in miniature which should be viewed as a copy of Chilean society. Its staff of carefully chosen monsters duplicates the political and administrative bureaucracy which dominated Chile under the hand of the oligarchy. Donoso meticulously delineates the guidelines which governed the special world enclosed within the walls of La Rinconada: "El niño debía crecer encerrado en esos patios geométricos, grises, sin conocer nada fuera de sus servidores, enseñándole desde el primer instante que él era principio y fin y centro de esa cosmogonía creada especialmente paraél . . . era una sola su exigencia: que Boy jamás sospechara la existencia del dolor y del placer, de la dicha y de la desgracia, de lo que ocultaban las paredes de su mundo artificial, ni oyera desde lejos el rumor de la música" (*Pájaro*, p. 235).

Under the careful tutelage of Emperatriz, a distant relative of Don Jerónimo, the whole enterprise moved ahead despite the fact that the directress was a dwarf with an enormous head and distorted features, and her cohorts were the most gruesome collection of monsters ever assembled. In such a hermetically sealed world of the grotesque, Boy theoretically would never recognize his own deformities.

Donoso's creation of La Rinconada with its false system of values and goals is a direct attack on a system of government which exploits the unfortunate masses as a foundation for its power. Boy ultimately escapes from La Rinconada and discovers for himself the joys and sorrows of the world. The monsters realize that they have all been victimized by Don Jerónimo, but in the end it is Don Jerónimo himself who is a victim of his own creation, drowning in a lagoon on the grounds of La Rinconada, probably as a result of too much drinking at a masquerade ball organized by Emperatriz.

The national consternation caused by the death of Don Jerónimo is reminiscent of the turmoil which followed the death of Mamá Grande in the celebrated short story by Gabriel García Márquez. His death also represents the end of an era in Chilean politics, and at the same time it heralds the termination of the power of the oligarchy. The relationship of the event to a masquerade ball underlines a secondary motif in the novel: the need for masks to establish the idea of personal values in an impersonal world. Perhaps the most cogent example of this idea is in the form of a papier-mâché giant's head which makes the rounds of the district near the Casa de Ejercicios Espirituales. Originally a commercial advertising stunt, the head falls into the hands of neighborhood boys who acquire a feeling of strength and manhood by wearing it. Iris Mateluna on her nightly wanderings near the Casa readily succumbs to the amorous advances of anyone who wears it. Its ultimate destruction leads to the end of Iris's promiscuity, and at a later point in the novel the lack of masks leads Humberto Peñaloza to question the belief in a God "que fabricó tan pocas máscaras, somos tantos los que nos quedamos recogiendo de aquí y de allá cualquier desperdicio con que disfrazarnos para tener la sensación de que somos alguien. . . ." (*Pájaro,* p. 155).

Following the death of Don Jerónimo, the announcement of plans to demolish the Casa de Ejercicios Espirituales marks the final negation of the legacy of a decadent aristocracy. Significantly, the occupants of the Casa are to be moved to bright, new quarters made possible by the bequest of one of the late residents in her final will. This monument to the Azcoitía family and to the memory of their ancestor for whom it was first constructed is doomed to die amid the rubble and dust of the Casa itself. Coupled with the symbolic destruction of the physical representation of external reality is a most surprising final scene which negates the multiple "yo," i.e., the narrator of the novel. Abandoned in the vacated Casa, the narrator is placed in a series of sacks, all of which are carefully sewn shut. "Me meten dentro

del saco. Las cuatro se arrodillan alrededor mío y cosen el saco. No veo. Soy ciego. Y otras se acercan con otro saco y me vuelven a meter y me vuelven a coser . . . este paquete soy yo entero, reducido, sin depender de nada ni de nadie. . . ." (*Pájaro,* p. 525).

Donoso reduces the inner level of reality in the novel, the first person narrator, to the physical limitations of a bundle which a nameless old woman carries from the Casa into the brisk winter night. The final action develops under a bridge where a fire has been built to warm the bodies of a group of impoverished drifters. The old lady offers the contents of her sack to increase the fire: sticks, boxes, stockings, rags, newspapers, trash. Such is the ultimate form of Donoso's protagonist, and the destruction of inner reality is complete in the ashes of a sputtering fire.

In *El obsceno pájaro de la noche* Donoso reaches a new level of achievement within the framework of the "nueva narrativa." His use of fragmented and distorted protagonists parallels his destruction of temporal unity. He accuses Peta Ponce of taking the same liberties with time which he himself takes in the novel: "Las viejas como la Peta Ponce tienen el poder de plegar y confundir el tiempo, lo multiplican y lo dividen, los acontecimientos se refractan en sus manos verrugosas como en el prisma más brillante, cortan el suceder consecutivo en trozos que disponen en forma paralela, curvan esos trozos y los enroscan organizando estructuras que les sirven para que se cumplan sus designios." (*Pájaro,* pp. 222-223) The negation of time is an aspect of the more general negation of reality which abounds in the novel. For Donoso the complete rejection of the traditional social and economic order points the way toward a "new" reality; it is suggested that the new home to which the inhabitants of the Casa de Ejercicios Espirituales are to move is symbolic of the new social and economic systems which must replace the decadent past.

In an interview granted by Donoso shortly after the completion of *El obsceno pájaro,* the novel is described as a "happening" both for its author as well as for its readers. "Yo no escribí esta novela. Esta novela me escribió a mí. No podía elegir una estructura determinada porque las estructuras me estaban eligiendo a mí."[3] As is so often the case with the contemporary Latin American novel, the work itself takes on life and rushes forward spontaneously to ends not originally envisioned by its creator. Ernesto Sábato describes a similar experience in the genesis of his own works. "Y así sucede que los planes que inevitablemente empezamos haciendo para escribir, que en buena medida son cerebrales, terminan por ser arrollados por los personajes, que una vez en marcha cobran vida propia. Es muy difícil decir, en tales condiciones, lo que una novela significa en cada uno de sus aspectos, aún para el propio autor."[4]

What is certain is that Donoso in no instance seeks to present his protagonists as single psychological unities. His statement, ". . . soy una persona y soy treinta,"[5] clarifies the reasoning behind the multiplicity of characters in this work, which goes back directly to Carlos Fuentes' *Aura* for a model of the metamorphic protagonist. As readily admitted by Donoso, this novel would not have been possible if he had not previously read Fuentes, Gabriel García Márquez, Manuel Puig, Julio Cortázar, José Lezama Lima, and Mario Vargas Llosa. *El obsceno pájaro* is, in a sense, a synthesis of the new realism described by Fuentes in the following terms: "Lo que ha muerto no es la novela, sino precisamente la forma burguesa de la novela y su término de referencia, el realismo, que supone un estilo descriptivo y sociológico de observar a individuos en relaciones personales y sociales."[6] Fuentes' description of the death of traditional realism aptly describes the metaphysical contents of *El obsceno pájaro de la noche.*

Notes

1. For a more complete statement concerning this point see the prologue to Luis Harss, *Los Nuestros* (Buenos Aires: Editorial Sudamericana 1969), pp. 9-50.

2. José Donoso, *El obsceno pájaro de la noche* (Barcelona: Editorial Seix Barral, S. A., 1970), p. 26. Subsequent references to the same edition of this novel are cited in the text itself.

3. Donoso, "José Donoso: La novela como 'happening.' Una entrevista de Emir Rodríguez Monegal sobre *El obsceno pájaro de la noche,*" *Revista Iberoamericana,* 76-77 (julio-diciembre 1971), 518, 527.

4. Ernesto Sábato, *El escritor y sus fantasmas* (Buenos Aires: Aguilar, 1964), p. 20.

5. Donosa, "La novela como 'happening.' . . . ," p. 521.

6. Carlos Fuentes, *La nueva novela hispanoamericana* (Mexico City: Editorial Joaquín Mortiz, 1969), p. 17.

Guillermo I. Castillo-Feliú (essay date spring 1980)

SOURCE: Castillo-Feliú, Guillermo I. "Aesthetic Impetus Versus Reality in Three Stories of José Donoso." *Studies in Short Fiction* 17, no. 2 (spring 1980): 133-39.

[*In the following essay, Castillo-Feliú examines three short stories by Donoso, concluding that the creative deterioration of the characters is influenced less by the outer circumstances of Chile's deterioration than by an inner sense that creativity does not provide an escape from reality.*]

With the publication of his first story in Spanish titled **"China"** in 1954, José Donoso began a writing career which up to now includes a total of fourteen short stories, five novels and three *novelle.* Although all fourteen short stories appeared between 1954 and 1962, they provide a firm thematic foundation for the longer narratives which have been published between 1957 and 1978. The critic who is familiar with Donoso's prose fiction as a whole is aware that certain themes and character types are consistently treated by the author and that this apparently creative obsession has a logical starting point in the first literary experiments which are those fourteen tales.

Donoso is interested in those characters who most clearly evidence rebellion against the normal canons of society. As a social being, every individual who wishes to be admitted to the nucleus which society is realizes that acceptance of certain norms is required. The process is difficult for it is solely by means of accommodation and discipline that the individual succeeds in overcoming those characteristics which isolate him and accepts the regularity expected by a society which exacts his subordination to the group.

Certain characteristics prevail throughout Donoso's prose fiction. The majority of his characters are children, adolescents or persons who have reached what is commonly referred to as the *âge de retour* for it is these groups which most clearly evidence man's anarchy before society. In an interview of the author, he explained the basis for this interest this way:

> Esto es una organización estructural y has tocado uno de los puntos más neurálgicos de lo que es toda mi literatura. En ninguna de mis novelas aparece una generación intermedia. . . . Siempre son niños o viejos, o abuelos o nietos. Es la pauta más corriente: lo que me interesa a mí son los estados marginales, los estados anárquicos. La niñez es una anarquía; la neurosis es una anarquía.[1]

The author's interest for marginal states begins to be evidenced with his short narrative. When adults do appear, their lives seem empty and devoid of much interest. On the other hand, Donoso directs his attention to creating beings who exemplify strange, exotic or out-of-the-ordinary characteristics. Progressively, however, these protagonists exhibit a process of mental and creative deterioration which transforms them from positive and imaginative individuals into marginalized, abulic and constricted beings for whom there is no longer a creative outlet for self-expression. Up to the present, much of the criticism of Donoso's narrative has tended to attribute this progressive creative deterioration to the stifling social degeneration of Chile's bourgeois society. In this study, three of the Donoso stories are employed to present findings which at least point toward the plausibility that there exists a more primordial impetus in the author's creative motivation than the rationale commonly presented by present criticism.

Two of the stories treated seem to be especially appropriate for they stand at the beginning and at the end, up to the present, of Donoso's experiments with the short narrative. These are **"China"** and **"Santelices."** The third story, **"La puerta cerrada,"** is certainly his most outstanding example of creative obsession.

"China," written in the first person, tells of a child protagonist who ventures from his home to discover the vast world which exists outside in the hustle and bustle of the large metropolis. His first expedition he undertakes with his mother who has him accompany her through a certain street of the city. An exclamation by his mother provides him with a name for the exotic street which is full of small shops and people scurrying in and out of them and along the sidewalk. He names it "China." He tells of his feelings and sensations as he walks, his hand in his mother's: "Yo llevaba los ojos muy abiertos. Hubiera querido no solamente mirar todos los rostros que pasaban junto a mí, sino tocarlos, olerlos, tan maravillosamente distintos me parecían."[2] On subsequent occasions, the protagonist leads his younger brother, Fernando, on odysseys to "China" trying to imbue in him the same fascination for the exotic world that he has discovered, but he is unsuccessful. The protagonist's greater sensitivity is incapable of being transmitted to the other child. At the same time, the experience is solely the protagonist's and, thus, **"China"** continues to exist only in his realm of the imagination. As time passes, however, even he finds himself unable to sustain the fantasy of **"China"**: "'China' fue durante largo tiempo como el forro de color brillante en un abrigo oscuro. Solía volver con la imaginación. Pero poco a poco comencé a olvidar, a sentir temor, sin razones, temor de fracasar allí en alguna forma" [***Cuentos,*** p. 170].

As the story ends, years have passed and the child is an adult. With his new maturity comes a certain loss which he expresses in the following manner:

> Más tarde salí del país por varios años. Un día, a mi vuelta, pregunté a mi hermano, quien era a la sazón estudiante en la Universidad, dónde se podría adquirir un libro que me interesaba muy particularmente, y que no hallaba en parte alguna. Sonriendo Fernando me respondió: "En 'China'." Y yo no comprendí.
>
> [***Cuentos,*** p. 171]

In spite of the brevity of this early story, it clearly exhibits the author's predilection for child protagonists. It is they who possess that spirit of creativity which is released by the fertile and as yet untainted imaginative capacity inherent in the child. It is also the first mature literary demonstration of the solitude of the Donosian character; a solitude, maintained by the incomprehensibility of the personal world of each of the children who pass through that stage of life. Although the child exhibits characteristics relatively typical of his age, he already exemplifies those elements which place him within the Donosian frame. As a child, he takes refuge from his surrounding reality, creating for himself one which is more in harmony with his own imagination and circumstances. It is also as adults that these protagonists begin to lose their creative impetus and frame themselves within a stratified and regimented society.

"La puerta cerrada," written in 1959, is the story of an obsession. Sebastián, who lives in a boarding house with his widowed mother, discovers that he truly enjoys sleeping above any other activity. As the years pass, he devotes more and more time to his soporiferous vocation as his aging mother and uncomprehending employer resent and rebuke him for his lack of interest for any other activity. When questioned by don Aquiles Marambio, his superior at work, Sebastián explains his vocation: "Es que se me occurre que durmiendo, en lo que sueño voy a descubrir algo importante, algo más importante que . . . , bueno, que vivir." Don Aquiles questions him: "Y si te demoras toda la vida en averiguarlo y te mueres antes? Significa que perdiste toda tu vida durmiendo y que no sacaste nada." Sebastián's commitment to his vocation is clear in how he answers don Aquiles: "Se me ocurre que es tan maravilloso lo que voy a encontrar que estoy dispuesto a arriesgarme" [***Cuentos,*** p. 108].

Speaking with his mother, Sebastián attempts to transmit to her the depth of his commitment. Referring metaphorically to the impediment he always finds in his search during his dreams as a "closed door," he exhibits his frustration at his inability to cross that threshold in the following way: "Quizás descubra que haber dejado de vivir como los demás fue una equivocación, que tal vez no valía la pena saber lo que ocultaba la puerta. Pero no importa. El hecho de seguir un destino que yo siento auténtico me justifica y le da una razón a toda mi vida" [***Cuentos,*** p. 105].

Upon his mother's death, Sebastián leaves his job and wanders from place to place, working just enough to be able to sustain himself during the ever-increasing number of hours which he now devotes to sleeping. Falling asleep, which Sebastián at first had been able to control, now has become a form of narcolepsy. Ultimately, he dies. Don Aquiles, who had broken in disgust with Sebastián, finds him dead at his doorstep. Sebastián's face appears transfigured by such an expression of joy, that don Aquiles seems to accept that the dreamer has finally crossed that threshold that he had so earnestly sought.

It is important to note that it is only at the moment of his death that Sebastián is able to realize the object of his vocation. That creative impetus becomes a reality only outside the realm of the reality in which the protagonist lives. The intermittent departure from reality occasioned through his dreams is the only medium within which he can be creative.

"Santelices" is Donoso's last published short story up to the present time. Santelices is a bachelor in his early fifties who lives, like Sebastián, in a boarding house owned by don Eusebio and his old-maidish daughter, la Bertita. She clearly manifests the symptoms brought on by her lonely life style: her sterile life and her sexual frustration; disappointments that she hopes to overcome, at least emotionally, through Santelices. Her pensioner has problems of his own and has no intention of succumbing to her supplications, tenuous and indirect as they are. He has a unique means to effect his escape from the frustration that he feels. His greatest pleasure comes from looking at photographs and drawings of wild animals, a vocation which fuels his imagination and removes him from his sterile and depressing milieu:

> Aquí en las fotografías sensacionales que contemplaba con la nuca fría de emoción, la proximidad de la amenaza, la crueldad desnuda, parecían acrecentar la belleza, dotarla de eficacia agobiadora, hacerla hervir, llamear, cegar, hasta dejar sus manos transpiradas y sus párpados temblorosos.
>
> [*Cuentos,* p. 178]

La Bertita, upon discovering this eccentric hobby of her pensioner, accuses him of being abnormal, a devoté of the animals he so admires. She goes so far as to qualify his relationship with the animals as a display of bestiality.

The deception that Santelices subconsciously seeks carries him to the point in which his photographs and drawings slowly cease to satisfy him and he looks for a reality which might involve him more directly and personally. The city's zoological park provides an attraction that is more synesthetic but which, nevertheless, is short-lived in its interest for him.

From the window of his office, Santelices begins to weave a new reality which will allow him to create the world that he yearns for. Five floors below him and for several days, he has been observing a young girl who is playing with some domestic cats. In the beginning, his eyes transmit to him a true and objective vision of a common scene. Slowly, his imagination begins to transport him to a new reality which he has been creating from one day to the next. Expressing his own yearnings and anxieties, Santelices contemplates a scene which becomes savage and violent. The young girl that he has been observing now seems to be surrounded by animals which are advancing and threatening her:

> Las sombras se hundieron, cayendo bloque sobre bloque en el patio exiguo, iluminado por el fulgor de ojos verdes, dorados, rojos, parpadeantes . . . Los animales eran docenas, que circulaban alrededor de la muchacha: ella no era más que una mancha pálida en medio de todos esos ojos que se encendían al mirarla codiciosos.
>
> [*Cuentos,* p. 190]

The anxiety that he feels becomes an obsession to enter the new world that his imagination is creating. That world he now perceives is more fulfilling and offers him a special place where he will be able to feel that he truly belongs for it is his own. Santelices transports himself completely into the scene that he faces, five floors below, coming not only to see it but to hear it as well:

> Allá estaba la muchacha esperándolo; tal vez gemía; no podía oír su voz en medio del trueno de alaridos, rugidos, gritos, pero tenía que salvarla. Santelices se trepó al alféizar. Sí, allá abajo estaba. De un grito espantó a una fiera de la rama vecina, y, para bajar por ella, dio un salto feroz para alcanzarla.
>
> [*Cuentos,* p. 193]

George McMurray interprets this final act of the protagonist in the following manner:

> El acto temerario del protagonista enloquecido puede explicarse mediante su identificación con la joven, a quien considera como a una de las víctimas de la vida, y sobre la cual proyecta sus propios temores, frustraciones y resentimientos. Su salto final representa su último intento desesperado para echarse a un mundo de acción y así salvarse a sí mismo, escapándose de una existencia insoportable.[3]

It seems more plausible and less melodramatic to speculate that by his final actions, Santelices believes that he is escaping into a world which is the product solely of his imagination and, thus, more satisfying. This final act is obviously the end result of his progressive search for a world that is the product of his imagination. It is a world which satisfies him in a way that others' creations (the photographs, drawings) and the living animals (objective reality) cannot. The tragedy, then, lies in the fact that the creation of this new reality is carried out through the psychosis of the protagonist, a psychosis that puts an end to creativity.

The more obvious explanation that the process of marginalization is a direct consequence of the rigidity of a stratified bourgeois society is not one that satisfies. It seems to promote the premise that Donoso's motivation is social and detracts from the author's aesthetic impetus. In response to a query regarding critics' assertions that he is a thesis writer whose motivation is social, the author stated:

> No tengo ninguna visión social. Es un ejercicio interior. No hay ninguna actitud o propósito mío con respecto a la sociedad. Uso dos niveles sociales porque son los

que conozco mejor. Parte de la base que yo nunca, o muy raras veces en mis novelas, quiero hacer prototipos; rehuyo de hacerlo. Me parece la negación de la novela de calidad. La novela puede tener reflejos, facetas de ser social.[4]

Alexander Coleman states that Donoso's protagonists are:

Pathetic and at times comic figures . . . pilgrims of their own brand of truth, vague searchers for a freer self and society, constantly at odds with the reality of their own spiritual suffocation. A groping for a sense of transcendence, a whole process that inevitably entails the encounter with the monster that is within them, engendered out of the mathematical rigidities with which societies function in apparent order.[5]

Coleman's statement penetrates much more deeply into Donoso's creative motivation than McMurray's asseveration that "cuando el rechazo individual de la consagrada ética burguesa se haga general se derrumbará el dique" or these lines from the concluding paragraph of his article titled "La temática en los cuentos de José Donoso": "El rechazo de la realidad banal por parte de la mayoría de los personajes de Donoso y su incapacidad de actuar en una forma positiva sugieren una condenación de la sociedad chilena."[6]

The process of marginalization seems to transcend the patently obvious degenerative explanation based on a social struggle premise and emerges more basically as a kind of "sentimiento trágico de la vida." From this standpoint, the creative mind is progressively stifled by the growing realization that the ultimate result of creativity can be, and as Donoso's characters demonstrate tragically, proves to be, dejection brought on by a personal awareness that a particular instance of creativity does not provide a permanent escape from the real world. Since creativity must be constant and expanding, the creator must repeatedly transcend any plateau which has already been reached.

José Donoso's "sentimiento trágico" is one which is personally his as an individual creative force. Under differnt social circumstances, the frustration of his characters would perhaps be exposed in different ways but his own reality as a writer would still present him with a set of circumstances which would constantly constrict his realm of possibilities or take him into such unviable solutions as those found by Sebastián and Santelices. It seems not so much to be the bourgeoisie that limits his creativity as it is the constricting pervasiveness of reality itself.

Notes

1. Guillermo I. Castillo-Feliú, "An Interview of José Donoso," *Hispania,* 54 (December 1971), 958.

2. José Donoso, *Los mejores cuentos de José Donoso* (Santiago: Zig-Zag, 1965), p. 168. All further references to this work appear in the text.

3. George McMurray, "La temática en los cuentos de José Donoso," *Nueva Narrativa Hispánica,* 1 (Septiembre 1971), 136.

4. "An Interview with José Donoso," p. 958.

5. Alexander Coleman, "Some Thoughts on José Donoso's Traditionalism," *Studies in Short Fiction,* 8 (Winter 1971), 157.

6. McMurray, "La temática," p. 138.

John M. Lipski (essay date 1982)

SOURCE: Lipski, John M. "'Evolution Through Paradox: *El obsceno pájaro de la noche* and *Casa de campo.*'" In *The Creative Process in the Works of José Donoso* edited by Guillermo I. Castillo-Feliú, pp. 35-46. Rock Hill, S.C.: Winthrop Studies on Major Modern Writers, 1982.

[*In the following essay, Lipski examines two of Donoso's best-known novels, articulating their intertextuality and their intended interactions with the reader.*]

Like the majority of other major writers of his generation, José Donoso has been at work creating an extensive intertext, not through overlapping plots and characters but rather by means of a progressive narrative evolution, a gradual expanding and enriching of epistemological and linguistic possibilities as each work gives rise to the succeeding one. Donoso excels in reinforcing thematic elements of his works by the narrative structures in which he chooses to present them and his writing represents a continual confrontation with the reader, whose participation covers an entire spectrum of possibilities. It is particularly useful to explore the evolutionary process exhibited by the structures of *El obsceno pájaro de la noche* and the more recent *Casa de campo,* which promises to be equally rich, although exploring other directions. Since Donoso does not separate the thematic elements from the narrative devices these latter may be taken as epistemological statements of the manner of presenting information to the reader, the characterization of the reader and the act of reading, and a complete presentation of the writer vis-a-vis his intertextual production.

Attempting to summarize *El obsceno pájaro de la noche* is a virtually impossible task, and trying to reduce the plot to a one or two line summary is absurdly futile. Suffice it to say that among the variety of innovative structural devices the most salient one is the all pervasive, essential and cohesive use of ambiguity, of textual multiplicity which cannot be resolved from within the bounds of the text itself, but which points ever outward to the non-ending participation of the reader, the endless chain of readers which such a work presupposes. Nearly every plot element is presented in such a way that it is impossible to extract a unique interpretation; at times the text explicitly contradicts itself, and at times partially or potentially contradictory bits of information are scattered throughout the narrative so that only by reassembling all the pieces is the reader able to grasp the magnitude of the indeterminacy. Central to the text is a refined and highly stylized version of the paradox posed by many philosophers and made most famous by Descartes in his 'malevolent demon'. In essence the puzzle asks whether it would be possible to discern a superior intelligence or meta-force whose sole design is to confuce our minds into thinking that a certain set of elements, as presented and manipulated by this superior force, represent what we consider as 'reality' (as defined by an objective external observer) whereas reality is radically different from what we have been led to believe. Clearly this puzzle has no solution, at least if we insist on remaining within our own sphere of consciousness, for Descartes' demon would cover its tracks sufficiently well to preclude all possibility of discovering the artifice. If one postulates the possibility of stepping outside of the realm of our own senses then there is no way of avoiding an infinite regress, since each level of observation might just be confounded by a demon on a still higher level, and so forth.[1]

Donoso poses this puzzle in the form of the Azcoitía family, their monstruous son Boy and the mythical land of monsterdom that has been created by the novel's manipulative demon (in this case the father) in order to keep him from learning the truth about his own nature. At first it looks as though Donoso is going to place the reader in the position of the omniscient demon, Jerónimo de Azcoitía, to observe the construction, peopling, deterioration and eventual destruction of La Rinconada, as Boy, able in the literary artifice to leap out of the level of the text and into the meta-level inhabited by his father, by El Mudito and the other main characters, makes the devastating discovery about himself. Despite such apparent simplicity, this easy interpretation does not form part of the overall reading, for the essential ambiguity prevents the reader from categorically establishing the very identity of Boy, of the monster kingdom, of the relations between El Mudito and his spiritual double Jerónimo, and of the other double pair Inés de Azcoitía/Peta Ponce. The text contains explicit statements to the effect that Ines did give birth to the deformed child and equally telling testimony that she remained childless throughout her life. The same holds for the veracity of La Rinconada, which according to textual clues may or may not exist. The very narrator shifts identity among a variety of centers of consciousness, some of which are clearly identified while others are much more diffuse. Boy as the monster son is also confused with the young playboy Jerónimo, with the perhaps mythical offspring of El Mudito and/or

Jerónimo with Peta Ponce, and with the equally doubtful child of Iris Mateluna. The biography of the Azcoitías which El Mudito has written is similarly placed in a way that defies a single interpretation. As a matter of fact it is possible to characterize the entire novel as a pair, a set of narrative elements and its double, a novel and its corresponding anti-novel.[2] The reader is unable to extract a single interpretation and this is deliberate, for there is a continuous epistemological progression from the writer, through the text, to the reader. The reader must participate, not in the explicit formative way as the reader of Cortázar's *Rayuela* for example, but rather as the receiver of intelligence that is not in a format that can be passively digested. Rather than a narrative *fait accompli* the ambiguous structure of **El obsceno pájaro** signals the leap into the unknowable, the possibility of a text whose internal attempts at diabolical deception (Jerónimo isolating his son) are precisely mirrored in the way that Donoso isolates his readers from a single interpretation. Obviously the intent has not been to offer a finished package, nor is the reader free to rearrange the puzzle's pieces to arrive at his own customized version; rather the reader is made to confront the entrance to a higher level of epistemological awareness to which he can never ascend. By implication the author himself is not exempt from this ever-receding set of meta-levels. The narrative universe is presented as open, ever increasing via the impossibility of establishing an omniscient point of reference. Donoso has not offered an answer to Descartes' puzzle, he has merely restated it in literary form and has reinforced the fact of paradox, the impossibility of stepping outside our own frame of knowledge.

Casa de campo, while superficially less complex narratively than **El obsceno pájaro de la noche,** offers an epistemological structure equally elaborated around another puzzle. In this case the situation is that of two groups of people one of which, at a given moment, departs on a voyage. Upon returning the second group finds that time has passed much more slowly for them than for the group that was left behind, and the confrontation of the two groups provides a discontinuous epistemological leap. This configuration has become highly popularized in the world of modern physics, in the theory of relativity as now taught in freshman physics courses, and takes the form of the 'paradox of the twins'. Basic relativity theory teaches the essential interchangeability of all frames of reference and the impossibility of establishing any absolute Newtonian point of reference. It also states that for a rapidly moving body (moving with a speed approaching that of light), as measured by an external observer time will be slowed down, although within the internal system of the rapidly moving frame of reference no change will be noted. Suppose now that one man takes off from Earth on a rocket which travels at a very high velocity, while his twin brother remains behind. If at some point the traveller reverses his direction and returns to Earth he will presumably find that his brother has aged far more than he; in extreme cases, what seems like only a year to the traveller will be 100 years or more on Earth. The paradox, for the physicist, revolves around the need to establish a preferred frame of reference, but the (seeming) paradox for the layman lies in the much simpler fact of time bifurcating, so to speak, and then coming back together for comparison at some distant point. The intricacies of this problem have been widely discussed by physicists and philosophers,[3] and while no true concensus of opinion exists, most scientists agree that this seemingly impossible situation can indeed occur, and may be observed in the not too distant future.

In *Casa de campo* we are presented with the wealthy and decadent Ventura family, who spend each summer at the country estate Marulanda, a mythical domain lost in the midst of a vast grassland. While the children of the family engage in elaborate fantasies the elders, whose ability to come to grips with the real world is equally underdeveloped, plan an excursion to a fabulous picnic spot which subsequent remarks reveal to have been concocted in the overactive imagination of certain members of the family. The parents, seeking as much an escape from their children as a visit to an enchanting place, arrange to travel without their off-spring, and elect to take with them the army of servants, all the carriages and all the usable animals, killing those that are of no use. Their outing is planned for a single day, and they feel that nothing can happen to their children during this short time, particularly given their isolation and the lack of facilities for communicating with the outside world. Right from the beginning, certain of the children, most notably the precocious Wenceslao, doubt their parents' intentions, feeling that they have been abandonded forever. As soon as the adults leave, chaos breaks out, Wenceslao's father Adriano Gomara is released from the cell in which the Ventura family has kept him imprisoned, the indigenous population which had been subjected by the family generations ago regains its hegemony over the region, and the children become split into a group of young savages and a reactionary element favoring the old family system and awaiting the return of the parents. Reckoned from the point of view of the children, a year passes before the parents make their eventual return, first in the form of an advance assault by the servants. The adults, however, insist throughout that they have only been away a single day and thus adamantly refuse to accept the evidence which continually assaults them that a considerably greater period of time has elapsed. The stage is thus set for the paradoxical and all-annihilating encounter between the two groups whom a unitary time has abandonded and reunited only for this chaotic clash. A variety of elements paves the way for this configuration.

Remaining within the frame of reference of the children in the house, at first it appears that Wenceslao's fears have been borne out, and that the family has indeed abandoned them for more than the promised day. As night is falling on the first day the children refuse to light candles, since this would represent an admission of the failure of the parents to keep their word, an unthinkable occurrence. Eventually they do succumb to the necessities of continued survival and life in the house, while becoming more and more altered from the previous order, goes on. The natives take up the dislodged lances which had formed a fence around Marulanda, Adriano Gomara reassumes his position as spiritual leader of the indigenous population, and the entire house is turned into a commune, due to the necessities of producing food, sheltering the Ventura children and members of the native population, and the growing awareness of the need to defend themselves against the eventual return of the elders. Time continues to pass at the accustomed rate, and the reader of the novel learns, at various points, of the escape by Malvina, who has robbed the family hordes of gold and has travelled to the capital to set herself up in business, of the children's survival of the onslaught of the vast clouds of seeds that signal the beginning of the cold season on the grasslands, of the natives' taking possession of their ancient ceremonial costumes which had been hidden in the cellars of the house, and of other equally valid indications of the normal time scheme. Attention is completely diverted from the adults until the first half of the novel abruptly ends and the second half, entitled 'El regreso', focuses on the vacation party, leisurely beginning the return voyage after having spent a pleasant day at a spot which, while perhaps not the one originally conceived, was evidently beautiful enough to more than fulfill all expectations. No sign of anomaly is evidenced until the group, upon stopping at a chapel, discovers Fabio and Casilda, the two children who had escaped with Malvina in the cart laden with gold and had been abandonded by her. Casilda has given birth to a child, which the perplexed adults, in keeping with the family tradition of ignoring anything not in their plans, pretend is a rag doll and drown. The adults, unable to accept the double anomaly of Casilda having reached puberty so quickly and having had time to conceive and give birth to a child, assume that this is merely an extension of the children's fantastic passtimes, although this time things have gone too far. The two children, dressed in rags and at the end of their forces, tell of the changes that have occurred in the house, of the takeover by Adriano Gomara and the return of the natives to their rightful territory. At first, although dismayed by the outward appearance of the children, the elders still do not take them seriously. It is only after they mention that the entire yearly production of gold has been stolen and that Malvina is at that time already in the capital disposing of it, that the family tradition of shutting off all unpleasant circumstances within the famous 'tupido velo' must be hastily abandoned. Still the family members do not react as though to a true story, but rather as though checking out a rumor which is probably false but which must nonetheless be investigated. The servants, it is clear, are not so disbelieving, and exhort the Venturas, to hand over to them the entire cache of hunting arms in order to carry out an assault on the apparently entrenched house. The Venturas, ostensibly still refusing to believe the truth of the children's accusation, nonetheless comply, leaving themselves for the first time at the mercy of superior forces. After this abandonment of their undeniably superior position, many more of which will follow, the family decides to take a temporal side-step and await the return of the servants with the news that the way has been cleared. Meanwhile they conceive the idea of selling the entire property of Marulanda to the exotic Nordic merchants who have been their chief clients for the beaten gold.

Returning to the reference point of the house, its inhabitants are well aware that more than a day has passed, and yet in another sense time for them has also begun to stand still, for they have been lulled into thinking that the elders will never return to reestablish their absolute dominon over the children and the natives. Although Adriano Gomara, Wenceslao and a few others keep alive the theme of vigilance, no one seriously takes any step toward formulating an active defense. Since the Venturas had taken all the arms with them, the occupants of the house will rely on the ceremonial lances, now in the possession of the natives. When the servants at last attack, time begins to move again for the occupants of the house. The servants first attack the nearby village and discover several of the children who, through having defied Adriano's new regime, have been sent there for slave labor. The children greet the servants as liberators while the natives are eliminated almost without struggle. The conquest of the house is almost as easy. Adriano Gomara and most of his lieutenants are killed, the remainder of the children swear allegiance to the reestablished old order, or at least pretend to, while Wenceslao and his companion go into hiding to provide the last tangible bit of evidence that the insurrection is not entirely dead.

Throughout the entire 'reconquest', the servants are the only ones who appear to enjoy the perspective of both temporal points of reference. On the one hand they have accompanied their masters on the 'one day outing', have enjoyed themselves and have been allowed extraordinary liberties by their masters. On the other hand, they are aware that what has happened in the house took more than a day to accomplish, and in their greed they are faced with a paradox: if they admit that only a day went by then the Venturas will give them one day's wages, while if they insist that a year has elapsed their very jobs and even existence will be endangered through

having broken the ritual refusal to accept facts at face value, which characterizes the Ventura family. Only the Mayordomo and the ambitious and deceitful Juan Pérez cannot see things totally clearly, the former through adulation of the all-powerful family and the latter through extreme hatred. The Mayordomo, in order to consolidate his own power and also in unconscious emulation of the Venturas, tries not only to stop time after his arrival, but also to set it back to the day of the departure: he has the windows painted over so that no one can see daylight come and go, he has the children fed at all hours so that they lose track of the periodic demands of hunger, and he attempts the impossible task of restoring the physical aspect of the devastated house and gardens to their previous state. The children at this stage are still operating within their own framework and although they too sense that something is radically amiss, they are not ready to admit that their parents' absence has been any less than a year. Wenceslao and his companion, hiding in a distant cellar, measure time by the loaves of bread that are periodically slipped to them by a co-conspirator, while other children devise ingenious ways of reckoning the passing of time, but it is still the time of the house, an extension of the year that has passed since their parents set off for their picnic.

At last the elders themselves arrive, together with a group of foreigners who are potential buyers of Marulanda. The homecoming scenes are reminiscent of the fable of the Emperor's New Clothes, since the Venturas, spearheaded by the empty but yet prescient ramblings of the blind Celeste, pretend that nothing is amiss, while the foreigners, expressing their disdain in a form of Spanish even more stilted and artificial than that of the Ventura adults and children, see clearly through all the subterfuges and comprehend immediately the enormity of the situation. It is only out of a combination of deference and sadism that they prefer to let the Venturas discover things for themselves. Such discoveries are not long in coming. Balbina, the half-crazed mother of Wenceslao and the recent widow of Adriano Gomara, refuses to continue the farce that the destroyed house and its battered and starving inhabitants are merely the result of an exceptionally animated day of fantasies, and hysterically tears open the 'tupido velo' and calls for her husband and her son, whose fate she does not yet know, but surely suspects. She meets the same fate that the Venturas had earlier bestowed upon her husband; she is locked away to keep her madness from becoming contagious, but this act in itself signals that the family has finally acknowledged a discrepancy between their internal perception of elapsed time and the outward appearance of matters at the house.

Another irrefutable proof comes in the form of Malvina, now a dazzling concubine in a fancy carriage who turns on the decadent Venturas the disdain with which they had once treated her. Malvina has formed a partnership with the foreign gold merchants and it is she who masterminded the plot to strand the Venturas in the house to await the onslaught of the choking clouds of seeds which wipe out the final vestiges of the once proud family.

One could multiply and analyze further specific examples of the temporal anomalies, but of much greater interest is the epistemological perspective permitted by the author. The reader of *Casa de campo* is in the same relatively omniscient position with respect to the two groups of characters as the omniscient scientist with respect to the rocket travelling man and his earthbound twin in the relativistic thought-experiment. That is, we are able at nearly all points on the time scale, to make an instant comparison between the two sets of elapsed times (although we are given far less information regarding the moment-to-moment activities of the Venturas on the outing) and we are also present at the chaotic reencounter when the two time systems are revealed to have slipped with respect to one another. Time has moved slower for the Venturas not because they travelled at velocities approaching the speed of light but because they are characters in a literary work whose author is free to exercise his imagination in any way he sees fit in order to create a situation that captivates the reader's interest. There is no fundamental ambiguity about the outcome of *Casa de campo* (although one could perhaps argue that the Venturas were in fact away a year by anyone's frame of reference and that their reasons for insisting otherwise have nothing to do with incongruent time frames); the reader is placed in a superior position from which he can observe the characters flailing about in their self-created dilemmas. This is the basic narrative distinction between *El obsceno pájaro de la noche* and *Casa de campo,* the exalted epistemological perspective afforded by the latter and thereby the greatly reduced participation of the reader in giving structure and meaning to the work.

Almost from the beginning of *Casa de campo* the narrator, that is Donoso, intrudes ostentatiously into the reader's awareness, offering comments on the literary nature of the work and the necessity of never slipping into the complacent feeling that the narrated events are in any way real. At the beginning of the second chapter (53) Donoso clarifies his intentions even more, stating that he wishes to keep for himself, as author, the entire work, holding the reader at a distance which has been steadily decreasing in many recent novels. "Si logro que el público acepte las manipulaciones del autor, reconocerá no sólo esta distancia, sino también que las viejas maquinarias narrativas, hoy en descrédito, quizás puedan dar resultados tan sustanciosos como los que dan las convenciones disimuladas por el "buen gusto" con su escondido arsenal de artificios".[4] This audacious statement represents both reaction against empty liter-

ary posings and presumptuous readers and an attempt at innovation through refurbishing literary devices which disappeared from common acceptance more than a century ago. At several other points Donoso explicitly returns to this same theme, that of maintaining ever foremost the creative personality of the author and the artefactual nature of the work being read. He admits (372) that the speech and actions of the children and the adults is highly unreal, and that the characters are 'emblematic'; there is even a curious chapter in which Donoso the author, armed with the finished manuscript of *Casa de campo,* runs into member of the 'real' Ventura family, which turns out to be much different from that described in the novel. The 'real' Silvestre Ventura cannot understand why Donoso has had to elaborate the family's history to the point of creating a bizarre plot and insists that the family is in no way exceptional. In addition to providing yet another explicit glimpse of the work in the process of its own creation (very similar to that offered by Ernesto Sábato in *Abaddón el exterminador*) this chapter once more suggests the epistemological freedom enjoyed by the author, who can add as many meta-levels as he wishes and delete them equally easily in order to slip back into the main narrative. The reader is peeking over the author's shoulder, so to speak, and the author is occasionally turning around to tweak the reader's nose. At the end of the novel Donoso even refuses to wrap up all the loose ends, stating that to do so would take too long, and underlining even more definitely the fact that one is reading a novel, a work of fiction, a universe where time does not have to obey any consistent laws and does not even have to flow on forever. It can simply stop, leaving at the termination point a series of uncompleted episodes which while perhaps not a common maneuver, is completely legitimate within the scope of fiction.

In *El obsceno pájaro* the reader could not remain passive, awaiting explanations for the anomalies of the text; he had to constantly sort out the ambiguities and create a total meaning for himself which precluded the existence or at least attainability of any meta-level from which all ambiguity and insufficient information would vanish. The shifting narrative voices, the mutually contradictory elements and the overall Cartesian paradox posed by the plot all work together to open the work, and place the reader in the middle of it. *Casa de campo* presents a diametrically opposed achievement: the text, through the possibility of explicitly observing a bifurcation of time and the parallel existence of two universes, places the reader in a position of meta-knowledge that in and of itself defines a work of fiction. In the substance of the text Donoso makes clear this same fact: that the author has not solicited the complicity of the reader. *Casa de campo* is as much a 'meta-novel' as *El obsceno pájaro de la noche.* we see the novel being written and even discussed, much as we witness the creation of *El obsceno pájaro* in the tormented imagination of El Mudito and Jerónimo de Azcoitía. None-theless, *Casa de campo* presents a vastly different con-figuration of reader, writer and text. In each novel the epistemological structures themselves define the catego-ries involved; Donoso has exercised his options as au-thor to add explicit commentary in both cases: in *El ob-sceno pájaro* we have the textual ambiguities, while in *Casa de campo* the author's presence has evolved into the self-interpretative statements which provide a run-ning commentary. The intertext of Donoso's writings provides a scoresheet for the evolution of the narrator as author and of the incorporation of autocritical ele-ments which, with the appearance of creating a her-metic text, yet paradoxically continue to attract other readers.

Notes

1. See for example the treatment of this philosophi-cal program in J. M. Jauch, *Are Quanta Real?* (Bloomington: Indiana Univ. Press, 1973), esp. first and fourth dialogues.

2. Cf. J. Lipski, 'Donoso's *Obscene Bird of Night:* novel and anti-novel' *Latin American Literary Re-view* 4 (1976) 39-47.

3. Cf. for example R. Schlegel, *Time and the Physi-cal World* (East Lansing: Michigan State Univ. Press, 1961), esp. pp. 111-124 and references therein; cf. also M. Benton, comp., *The Clock Problem (Clock Paradox) in Relativity* (Bethesda, Md.: US Naval Research Laboratory, 1959).

4. 'If I can get the public to accept the author's ma-nipulations, they will recognize not only this dis-tance, but also that old narrative devices, currently in disfavor, may give results that are every bit as substantial as those which arise from the conven-tions made more subtle by 'good taste', the hid-den arsenal of artefacts'.

Philip Swanson (essay date 1983)

SOURCE: Swanson, Philip. "Concerning the Criticism of the Work of José Donoso." *Revista Interamericana de Bibliografía/Inter-American Review of Bibliography* 33 (1983): 355-65.

[*In the following essay, Swanson reviews criticism on Donoso through the early 1980s.*]

The last decade or so has seen a proliferation of critical articles on José Donoso. During this period, differing critical attitudes have emerged and there is as yet no general consensus of opinion on the meaning of his fic-tion, or on the best ways to approach his work. It is proposed here to examine briefly some trends in Donoso

criticism and to suggest some possible developments. My intention is to ignore merely introductory or exposi-tory criticism (e.g., that represented by such articles as those of Guillermo Carnero or Jaime Siles on *El ob-sceno pájaro de la noche,* or the general chapters on Donoso in books)[1] and to concentrate instead on what seem to be the more important and representative criti-cal works.

A sizeable group of critics avoids trying to interpret Donoso's work at all, taking refuge in the idea that his novels (especially *El obsceno pájaro*) are impenetrable. Pamela Bacarisse points out that in *El obsceno pájaro:*

> many pieces of information given to the reader are contradicted, many of the events recounted are then said not to have happened, there are conversations which may or may not have taken place and characters are themselves then someone else, or themselves *and* someone else. What the reader believes, on a narrative level, is up to him.
>
> (p. 19)

She goes on to say that "it is surely impossible to know how to choose between the various versions of the truth we are given" (p. 21). Certainly, *El obsceno pájaro* does contain many contradictory elements, and on a narrative level, it is difficult, therefore, to decipher fully. However, this does not mean that the novel is impos-sible to *interpret*. Indeed, Bacarisse herself goes on to give a highly plausible analysis of *El obsceno pájaro,* showing that the narrator's condition of ontological in-security turns the novel into a willed process of evasion.

John M. Lipski, meanwhile, claims that the various fac-ets of *El obsceno pájaro* "destroy the multiple signifi-ers and ultimately disappear in a dazzling verbal explo-sion" (p. 46), and Z. Nelly Martínez seems to believe equally that the multiple viewpoints of the novel and its many possible interpretations make it undecipherable. She considers that it shows "la derrota del Logos-Logos que apunta a un significado trascendente o presentido," which is replaced by "el juego de un sentido por siem-pre diferente y por siempre diferido" (*RevIb,* p. 55). Martínez thus reduces the novel either to "la noción del diferimiento del significado último de un texto al ser aquél (el significado) arrebatado por la praxis de una in-finita postergación," or to "la sucesión de diferencias de significado (de diferentes significados)" (p. 58).

In another article, the same critic comments that "así como las caretas simbólicas del narrador se invalidan mutuamente, también los diversos discursos se cancelan mutuamente revelando que la escritura misma es una máscara que enmascara el hecho de serlo" (Lo neobar-roco . . .", p. 641), and goes on to claim that "al final de la novela, cuando la conciencia narradora se hunde en la oquedad, sólo quedan 'astillas, cartones, medias, trapos, diarios, papel, mugre', vale decir sólo restan pa-labras, objetos inservibles, vaciados de significación" (p. 641).

However, she produces no hard evidence to show that this is the significance of the final scene of *El obsceno pájaro.*

Her words clearly echo those of Severo Sarduy who, in writing about *El lugar sin límites,* compares the transvestite Manuela to literature itself. He feels that the "planes of intersexuality are analogous to the planes of intertextuality which make up the literary object" (p. 33). He sees literature, like transvestism, as a kind of mask; just as the mask of transvestism merely hides "the very fact of transvestism itself" (p. 33), so writing is merely a mask which covers up an emptiness beneath.

Such views are shared by other critics. In an article on *El obsceno pájaro,* Alicia Borinsky says that "los elementos de la obra . . . se presentan como superficies," but that "no guardan nada en su interior" (p. 294). She concludes that, "Leemos un juego de superficies que nos engaña porque no son, como estamos inclinados a desear, signo de interioridad. No hay nada detrás, sólo subsiste la ilusión de la máscara en una línes horizontal" (p. 294).

Similarly, Sharon Magnarelli claims that "the word in the novel becomes a surface, a simple *envoltorio,* the wrapping that never yields the object or subject that it pretends to cover" (*MLN,* p. 271), and that "the novel becomes a game with the discovery of the impossibility of unmasking or unwrapping the essence, with the impossibility of finding a centre, a core" (*MLN,* p. 272).

Ignoring any possible social, existential and metaphysical implications of *El obsceno pájaro,* Magnarelli declares that Donoso is "presenting literature and the written word as the principal themes of the novel" (*MLN,* p. 284) and even suggests that "la mancha negra" of Mudito's ashes, at the end of the novel, merely reflects his reduction to words, his being nothing more than "a dark stain on a white page" (*MLN,* p. 276). In another article, she makes her position quite clear: "The presence of the signifier once posited the presence of the signified; now the text accentuates the inevitable, eternal abscence of the signified" (*HR,* p. 418).

A similar conclusion is drawn by Alfred J. MacAdam: "What the narrator . . . says is in effect irrelevant. What matters most is the telling itself, the imposition of order (grammar) on arbitrarily chosen things (signs)" (p. 115).

It seems clear that such critics are not actually analysing or interpreting the text itself; rather, they are bringing certain literary theories to bear on to the text. Sarduy's article relies heavily on quotations from Lacan, Barthes, Jacques Derrida, and Jean-Louis Baudry. Similarly, Z. Nelly Martínez spends about half of her first above-mentioned article discussing the post-structuralist theories of Jacques Derrida, with only an occasional reference to *El obsceno pájaro* itself. But can the implication that it is not worth trying to find any meaning in Donoso's work be justified? Not according to D. L. Shaw, who has written:

> toda tentativa de presentar *El obsceno pájaro de la noche* como una serie de significantes sin significado está condenada de antemano al fracaso. Donoso es ante todo un hombre de ideas, un hombre con una cosmovisión muy definida, de la cual debe partir todo cafeque válido de su obra.
>
> (p. 147)

Hugo Achugar, in his book on Donoso, makes a similar point, though less consciously and less directly than Shaw: "la producción literaria en tanto producción social propone un proyecto ideológico que da cuenta—a pesar incluso de la voluntad del propio escritor—de un modo peculiar y determinado de entender y reaccionar frente a la realidad social" (p. 12).

It is interesting to note that while Achugar actually chooses to emphasise ambiguity and indeterminacy as the essential features of the author's novels and stories, he is ready to assert of the short stories, for example, that "los textos . . . tienen una unidad que les viene de ser producidos por un hablante con una concepción del mundo determinada" and that "el conjunto de textos . . . tiene como todo acto humano un significado" (p. 39). It would seem, then, that for these critics the inherent ambiguity of the texts is not necessarily a barrier to understanding.

Donoso's own words might help. While on many occasions he has implied that there was no specific intention behind the writing of *El obsceno pájaro,* for example, and in a recent interview he goes so far as to claim that "el arte es irreductible a su significado" (*Literatura y sociedad,* p. 104), this is not at all the same as saying that there is no meaning in his work. Indeed, in many other interviews Donoso has frequently discussed the ideas behind his novels and has even commented on some specific themes or symbols. Thus, in one interview he recognises that it is "perfectamente aceptable" for different critics to see different meanings in his work: "es mejor que una obra pueda ser vista y entendida en muchos distintos niveles. A mí me agrada que los críticos digan que mis novelas son sociales, políticas, eróticas, etc.; que presenten otros niveles que vengan a ampliar o a negar los que yo veo" (Díaz Márquez, p. 8).

What this suggests is that art should not be brought down to a *single* meaning: He does not wish critics to "reducir la novela a una parte de sí misma" (*Literatura y sociedad,* p. 105). In other words, his work may have multiple and complex meanings but meanings, nonetheless. He explains this idea to San Martín:

Una novela tiene tantos niveles que elegir; uno no me satisfaría. Decir que es algo, y negar las otras posibilidades. Quisiera que fuera una cosa tremendamente polifacética, tremendamente vital, tremendamente movible, tremendamente barroca . . . como las ciudades medievales que de alguna manera tienen un sentido.

(*Car,* p. 202)

Having argued, then, that there *are* meanings to be found in Donoso's work, let us now turn to how some critics have applied themselves to finding them. An obvious first category is that of eccentric readings. A novel like *El obsceno pájaro,* for example, is an extremely complex work of art and one which presents many difficulties for reader and critic alike. This has resulted in a batch of rather odd interpretations. Silvia Martínez D'Acosta, for example, in an essay full of mysterious references to Indian rituals, suggests that Humberto Peñaloza feels a homosexual attraction to don Jerónimo de Azcoitía, the repression of which causes his paranoia. Humberto's desire for Inés is seen as in reality only a front for his sexual attraction to don Jerónimo. The same critic also claims that Humberto sees Peta Ponce as a mother figure, whom he rejects out of a fear of incest, and Dr. Azula is said to be the father figure who condemns the idea of incest. In an article on *Coronación,* Ramona Lagos treats us to a phychoanalytical explanation of the importance of the colour pink to Andrés, and later puts forward some curious interpretations based on an analysis of the significance (as she sees it) of the names of the characters in the novel. She also asserts that Andrés' collection of sticks represents a phallic symbol, and in analysing his relationship with Lourdes, she claims that the servant was in love with Andrés but that now "ha transferido sus sueños de amor hacia el gusto por el comer" (p. 302). Equally curious offerings come from Anita L. Muller, who sees Mudito's death by fire in *El obsceno pájaro* as representing "su unión con Dios, su purificación y la destrucción de las fuerzas malignas" and the pumpkins as "el milagro del maná para las viejas hambrientas" (p. 94), and from Francisco Rivera, who sees the frustrated hopes for a miraculous child as a parallel for Humberto's frustrated attempt to become a writer.

Other critics disguise pedestrian observations with rhetoric, sometimes to a point at which the critic's comments seem to be almost devoid of meaning. This is the case of Paul West, among sundry others. He writes of *El charlestón:* "this Donoso in a minor key is still an iridescent vertical invader of horizontal categories" (p. 66). As for *Tres novelitas burguesas,* West says: "the surprises . . . are irrevocable and, for all their sheen of ephemera gloatingly pinned onto cork, diagnostic of the human brain itself, done almost with a brain-side manner" (p. 66).

Fortunately, however, there have been more convincing attempts at interpretation. A frequent approach is via

social comment, and some critics heavily emphasise this element in Donoso's work. Guerra Cunningham, for instance, sees *Coronación* as a novel concerning "la caída total del mundo aristocrático en decadencia" (p. 421), while in reference to the characters of the same novel, John S. Brushwood claims that "their obvious function as a commentary on the Chilean oligarchy . . . transfers the reader's attention to a specific political situation" (p. 239). Similarly, Charles M. Tatum sees the "central theme" of *El obsceno pájaro* as "the demise of a feudal society" and "the decay of an oligarchical system" (*LALR,* p. 100). Even Antonio Cornejo Polar sees it as "la gran novela de la decadencia burguesa" (p. 110).

The problem with this approach is that it tends to oversimplify, for clearly there is much more even to Donoso's early work than social criticism. Several critics (including, for example, José Promis Ojeda, Isis Quinteros, and even Tatum himself in a different article) have pointed out that there are as many similarities as contrasts between the social classes in Donoso's novels. Others (such as Kristen F. Nigro and John J. Hassett) have actively attacked social interpretations. In fact, Donoso's himself has insisted that "no tengo ninguna visión social" (Castillo, "José Donoso . . . ," p. 958), and has elsewhere declared: "Nada me irrita tanto como los críticos que reducen mis novelas a sus elementos sociales, esos que quieren que yo haya escrito 'el canto del cisne' de las clases sociales chilenas" (*Libre,* p. 74).

A substantial amount of Donoso criticism, while avoiding such reductivism, nevertheless, has centred on a fundamental theme of Donoso's work which does have some social relevance. This is the idea that the rational world based on the principles of social convention prevents the individual from fulfilling himself on an instinctual level because it forces him to suppress his more natural inclinations. This concept is central to Tatum's approach. He believes that "Donoso's fiction leaves the impression that a rigid set of conventions, mores, and values dominates his characters of all social classes, frustating spontaneous self-expression" (*LangQ,* p. 49).

George R. McMurray points out, in his book on Donoso, that this theme is linked with the surrealists' dream of "the liberation and transformation of man which they hoped to accomplish through the establishment of a direct link between the objective and the subjective realms and through the elimination of the contradiction between the real and the imaginary" (p. 110). Perhaps the most thorough treatment of this theme is that offered by Hernán Vidal in his book *José Donoso: surrealismo y la rebelión de los instintos.* Vidal interprets all of Donoso's novels from this point of view and supports his argument with extensive references to the theories of Carl Jung. The book is cogently argued and well written, but it contains, in my view, a number of misinterpretations of specific aspects of Donoso's work and, once more, it often tends to overemphasise the more social implications of its main theme. Equally, it sometimes appears to offer interpretations that are rather too optimistic. Although he recognizes that the liberation of the unconscious can have disastrous consequences, Vidal often seems to think that Donoso really does believe that man can achieve fulfilment in this way. McMurray is more cautious: He emphasises Donoso's pessimism and suggests that "the surrealists' aspiration of ameliorating the human condition through their artistic endeavor would more than likely strike him as naïve" (p. 150), a thought echoed by Quinteros in her book (pp. 196-7). Nevertheless, the basic theme of Vidal's book reflects a central concern of Donoso's writing, and this is a subject to which critics (such as Promis Ojeda, Tatum, and many others) have returned again and again.

Plainly, interpretations like those of Vidal and McMurray must in some way relate to a consideration of the mental states of the protagonists of Donoso's stories and novels. This leads us on to a fifth trend in Donoso criticism, namely that which attempts to analyse his work on the basis of a psychological or psychoanalytical examination of the texts. Many critics have pointed out Donoso's lack of faith in the unity of the personality and his obsession with its disintegration. John Caviglia puts the emphasis on the mental collapse that follows any attempt at rebellion against the collective values of our society: "the abandonment of the norm . . . leads not to unique individuality but to disintegration and chaos" (p. 38). This reminds us of Vidal's stress on Jung's concept of the repressive effect that the collective unconscious has on the individual, a point taken up by Helen Calae de Agüera in her useful article on *Tres novelitas burguesas.* There is also a great interest in actually describing the process of mental disintegration. McMurray, for example, details the symptoms of schizophrenia and goes on to show how Humberto Peñaloza of *El obsceno pájaro* manifests the characteristics of a schizophrenic patient (Ch. 5). Pamela Bacarisse similarly sees Humberto's condition as one of schizophrenia with elements of ontological insecurity, and she puts forward an excellent analysis of the text based on this diagnosis.

However, there have also been many less satisfactory attempts at this kind of analysis. The unwisdom of taking the psychoanalytical process too far was mentioned à propos of Ramona Lagos' article on *Coronación.* Sometimes, too, this kind of approach results in the substitution of closely argued analysis by vague and unhelpful comments. Typical of many is Emir Rodríguez Monegal, who sums up the author's work as the expression of "una realidad torturada y pesadillesca, una realidad que complete el mundo de la superficie, que lo lastra de sombras, que lo duplica es claves terribles" (p. 85). Such nebulous statements are sadly familiar to students of Donoso.

The same problems occur when criticis try to establish relationships between myth and Donoso's work. Prominent here are Quinteros, Richard J. Callan, and G. Durán. Although Quinteros and Callan do make some stimulating points in their work, one can not help feeling that they sometimes go too far in their desire to seek out mythical elements in Donoso's novels. This tends to deflect them from the task of analysing what the works under consideration, in the end, are about. Such an approach is perfectly valid when it aids our understanding of the texts, but, as Donoso himself has suggested, this is often not the case. In an interview with McMurray he said: "I believe some critics tend to over emphasize mythical interpretations which often do not greatly increase the reader's understanding of a literary work" (*Hispania,* p. 392).

It may be time for critics to place less emphasis on psychological or mythical examination of Donoso's work, and to turn directly to the texts themselves in order to try and find out what it is that Donoso has to tell us about the human condition. There is now, I think, a need for an approach which will pay more attention to the levels of meaning in his novels, while, at the same time, bearing in mind the essentially ambiguous nature of much of his work and taking into account the multiplicity of elements that go to make it up. This would contribute to a greater understanding of Donoso's work without contravening the author's own wishes that his novels should not be interpreted reductively.

A major area of thematic significance which has been particularly neglected is that relating to the existential and metaphysical aspects of Donoso's work. Apart from the vague references to nothingness and hopelessness that recur in Donoso criticism, there have been very few attempts to analyse exhaustively and clearly this side of the Chilean author's writings. Only a few critics have explicitly and unambiguously referred to the importance of this theme. Shaw insists that it is "un tem fundamental en la obra de Donoso: su nostalgia de la fe, de un Dios garante de un 'orden' existencial sin el cual no hay más que caos" (p. 148). Robert Scott observes that "Donoso has always been concerned with death and its horror" (p. 134), and in a useful article (despite its jargon and its obsessive desire to relate the argument to the theories of Ernest Becker), he suggests that *El obsceno pájaro* dramatises the individual's need to fight against the annihilation represented by death. In an article on the short stories, McMurray points out the importance is Donoso's work of "la angustia existencial del hombre moderno en un caótico desprovisto de Dios" (*NNH,* p. 134). He develops this idea more fully in his book on Donoso, especially in relation to *El lugar sin limites* and *El obsceno pájaro.*

However, the theme has not been dealt with as fully as it deserves, since most critics have hitherto chosen to see man's anguish mainly as a result of sociological or psychological factors, or, as in the case of Achugar, as a result of his awareness of the inherent ambiguity of reality. This is especially true of **Coronación** and **Este domingo.** The metaphysical aspect of these novels has really only been discussed in relation to the individual characters' expressions of fear. There has been no real attempt to see the existence of this obsession on a symbolic level underlying the plot of these two novels. Even in considerations of **El lugar sin límites** and **El obsceno pájaro,** critics have tended to couch their language in vague abstractions whenever they have touched on this aspect of the novels.

Hitherto, we have mainly been concerned with thematic interpretations of Donoso's work. One reason for this is that the majority of Donoso criticism actually takes the form of content analysis, most of it being concentrated on **El obsceno pájaro.** Apart from the would-be socialists and structuralist approaches mentioned at the beginning of this study (which do not always clarify our understanding of Donoso's work), there have been very few convincing attempts at a sophisticated, formal analysis of his fiction.

Nevertheless, we can begin to distinguish several types of critical reaction to the formal aspect of Donoso's novels. Some critics simply include a few passing references to the novel's structure in the course of a largely thematic or generalized study. Rodríguez Monegal, for example, contrasts briefly what he sees as the traditionalism of **Coronación** with the more professionally executed **Este domingo** and comments on the importance of symbolism and juxtaposition, without investigating their technical impact on the novels in any depth. The formal level of Hassett's general article on **El obsceno pájaro** merely involves references to the novel's "unique narrative structure" (p. 29), which he sees as "an endless series of repetitions, substitutions and transformations," which has the effect of "forcing the reader to constantly adjust his visual apparatus to accommodate the next wave of images passing before him" (p. 30).

Other critics make more specific observations about the structure of the novels, but these often stand in isolation and do not constitute a genuine departure from content analysis. Isaac Goldemberg and Ramona Lagos, for instance, both offer essentially thematic interpretations of **Coronación.** But, at the same time, the former does suggest that the novel is structured around the interaction of a social and psychological axis and points to the existence of three layers of isolation. Lagos, meanwhile, emphasises the novel's division into three parts and the parallels between Misiá Elisa's two parties. It is a pity that these ideas were not developed more fully.

We see a similar pattern of approach in Caviglia's article on **El obsceno pájaro.** His analysis is not essentially formal, but he does make a brief attempt to demonstrate how the novel's jubling of different points in time shows "the distance between disillusion and an adolescent's illusory desires" (p. 43). Promis Ojeda's article on Donoso's work is also largely thematic, but he, too, includes useful formal observations, especially on **El obsceno pájaro,** whose structural basis he sees as one of contradiction and ambiguity. He also makes the interesting point that Donoso's work progresses from the presentation of the process of conflict (**Coronación, Este domingo**) to a situation where the reader is given a more general image of the actual state which results from such conflicts (**El lugar sin límites, El obsceno pájaro**).

The most common type of critical approach to the formal aspect of Donoso's novels (especially **El obsceno pájaro**) is to introduce a general comment on style and structure without making an adequate attempt to develop or explain it. Thus, Eyzaguirre refers to **El obsceno pájaro** as an "obra mucho más ambiciosa que las anteriores" which "no deja lugar a dudas del gran dominio de Donoso sobre el arte de novelar" (p. 277). However, this is all that he says about the novel. He does not attempt to explain the *functioning* of Donoso's artistry in **El obsceno pájaro.** Similarly, J. Marco comments on the same novel that "la forma es también el contenido" and states that, despite the novel's apparent chaos, Donoso's "maestria organizadora" points to the existence of a hidden structure which makes sense of the novel as a whole (p. 318). What Marco does not explain is the relationship between form and content, or what the hidden structure of **El obsceno pájaro** actually is.

It is of some interest that of the books devoted to Donoso none takes an exclusively or even predominantly formal approach. When their authors do consider the technical aspects of Donoso's work, they tend to discuss them in relation to features of the new novel as a whole. In other words, their most common feature is to point out how Donoso's use of ambiguity and audacious structures constitutes a challenge to the traditional novel's simplistic perception of reality. To be sure, Quinteros goes some way beyond this, particularly in her comments on **Este domingo** and **El obsceno pájaro,** and McMurray includes useful, if rather general, remarks on Donoso's technique in the creation of mood and his use of symbolism and stream of consciousness. When Vidal, on the other hand, comes to grips with the structure of **El obsceno pájaro,** the account he gives is, in my view, confused and even contradictory. Perhaps the best general work in this respect so far is Achugar's. Although his approach is more thematic than formal, an awareness of the importance of Donoso's fictional technique is implicit throughout his study. His book emphasises the process of development in Donoso's presentation of ambiguity within reality, seeing his work as having moved from the simple opposition of appearance and reality to a total denial of objective reality in *El obsceno pájaro.* While there is room for disagreement with some areas of Achugar's analysis, his book is a significant contribution to Donoso criticism and certain aspects of his general thesis are closely relevant to any formal analysis of Donoso's work.

It is clear, then, that although some kind of consensus exists on a few points, there has as yet been no over-all assessment of Donoso's fictional technique. With regard to *Coronación,* the critics seem to be polarised into two groups: those who emphasise the traditional elements of the novel and those who see important innovative elements in it. Critics like Cedomil Goic, for instance, have attempted to show that *Coronación*'s technique is not as transparent as it might seem at first. Goic argues that Donoso's skilful manipulation of point of view gives the reader a more convincing and more ambiguous vision of reality. Goic is the only critic to really develop this idea (although G. I. Castillo-Feliú and Quinteros paraphrase him in their studies of *Coronación*), and this important article must be seen as marking a major development in the critical interpretation of Donoso's first novel. Achugar, too, is one of the few critics to emphasise the fact that traditionalism and innovation are "elementos coexistentes en el texto" (p. 73). This is an important pointer towards the path that future criticism of *Coronación* should follow. It is not enough simply to show the existence of realist or avantgarde elements in the work: We must endeavour to demonstrate the transitional nature of the novel by examining analytically the tensions created by the coexistence of two potentially conflicting elements within a single literary artefact.

The structure of *Este domingo* has received more critical attention. This is probably because the novel's symmetrical structure is relatively easy to identify, and it is not surprising, therefore, that the vast majority of formal analyses of this novel have been descriptive in nature. Joan Rea Boorman's section on *Este domingo,* in her book on the new novel, and Quinteros' structural analysis of it both fall into this category. While both critics point out that the novel's technique creates a more ambiguous picture of reality, they do not clarify sufficiently *how* this is achieved. Even McMurray, in his chapter on *Este domingo,* only offers general observations about the novel's organization and about Donoso's evocation of mental processes. So, it must be said that most of the formal discussions of *Este domingo* have not progressed far beyond straightforward descriptions of Donoso's arrangement of his material. Analyses of *El lugar sin límites* have also tended either to ignore its formal aspects, or to offer only passing comments of a very general nature.

The majority of formal criticism, meanwhile, has been concentrated on *El obsceno pájaro.* Lipski makes some relevant points about Donoso's style and his use of "paradigmatic interpenetration" in order to generate ambiguity But at the end of his article, he unfortunately slips into vague, semiotic jargon, and instead of clarifying his stance, he seems to plump for the idea that the novel is ultimately undecipherable. Several other critics, including Achugar, Quinteros and Gertel, also advance the view that ambiguity and indeterminacy are fundamental to the novel's structure. But we seem to have been slow in developing critical techniques which are adequate for dealing with the extremely complex form of works like *El obsceno pájaro,* Fuentes' *Terra Nostra* or Sábato's *Abaddón el exterminador.* It is possible, however, that the recent article by Georgescu on the last-named novel may indicate a way forward based on modified Barthesean principles[2].

Meantime, some of the best analyses of Donoso's technique are to be found in *José Donoso. La destrucción de un mundo,* edited by Antonio Cornejo Polar. Indeed, Cornejo Polar himself, both in his introduction and in his article on *El obsceno pájaro,* emphasises the importance of the relationship between form and content. He says of *El obsceno pájaro,* for example: "no se trata de 'decir' destrucción; se trata, más bien, de encontrar algo así como un significante no arbitrario que plasme, encarn`ndolo, ese significado" (p. 109).

His identification of a law of substitution as the structural basis of Donoso's work is a significant critical achievement. Adriana Valdés shows the importance of substitution and reversability in her article on *El obsceno pájaro* in the same book. She examines the motif of the "imbunche" on a verbal, syntactic and semantic level, and suggests that the various motifs, with all their contradictions, help to bind the novel together in some kind of over-all unity. Raúl Bueno Chávez applies the law of substitution to *Este domingo,* and, although his study limits itself to a small area of analysis, it shows an important aspect of the organizational basis of the novel. Fernando Moreno Turner, meanwhile, offers a description of the narrative technique of *El lugar sin límites* and shows how the rule of inversion can be applied to almost all of the characters.

While Valdés and Moreno Turner sometimes fail to relate their points fully to the meaning of the novels and some of the other articles are only partial studies of the aspect of technique under consideration, they do point the way forward for future criticism to follow. A more sophisticated formal approach to Donoso's work is vital for a more complete appreciation of this author's fiction.

Future criticism, of course, also will have to incorporate Donoso's later work. The bulk of work on Donoso comes to a rather abrupt halt after *El obsceno pájaro.*

This is perhaps due to the disappointment of some critics, like Shaw, at what they see as the relative simplicity of the later work after the tortuous complexities of *El obsceno pájaro*. However, it is plain that the quality of a novel does not depend on its stylistic and structural complexities. Indeed, Donoso's later work is, to a certain extent, a reaction against the tendency to see a good novel as one which maximises complexity. The new novel emerged as a reaction against certain stereotyped forms of literature and Donoso may be worried that it is now close to replacing one set of stereotypes with another.

The criticism to appear so far on *Tres novelitas burguesas* has been very sparse and in general rather superficial[3]. There has been little, too, as yet on *Casa de campo*[4], and practically nothing on *La misteriosa desaparición de la marquesita de Loria, El jardín de al lado* [5] or *Cuatro para Delfina*. If past experience is any guide, future considerations of these novels will emphasise, as usual, their more specific themes (such as the political aspect of *Casa de campo* and the more personal aspects of *El jardín de al lado*). However, it will also be interesting to consider whether or not we can detect any change in Donoso's narrative technique and attitude toward literature, or see any development from the position of metaphysical anguish and pessimism that, for the most part, characterises Donoso's work up to and including *El obsceno pájaro de la noche*. The movement away from the darkness, chaos, and complexity of *El obsceno pájaro* to the lighter, more simple and more humorous tone of the later work may indicate, if not a change in attitude, then at least some kind of progression or evolution. The seriousness and the sense of despair are, without doubt, still there, but we can perhaps intuit a greater sense of calm and acceptance.

To conclude: Despite sporadic allusions to its partial incomprehensibility and a few eccentric aproaches, Donoso's work has given rise to a first phase of criticism which has been largely concerned with interpretation of content. Different approaches, social, psychological, and mythical, are already well represented, though greater emphasis remains to be placed on Donoso's basic existential malaise, its possible sources and development. While considerable areas have been explored and some quite closely mapped, there is more systematic work to be done here, especially with regard to novels other than *El obsceno pájaro* and with regard to the latest works, where a change of outlook may be under way. Far less has been done, however, on Donoso's literary technique, the structural arrangement of his narratives, the devices employed, the narratorial stance, or the ways in which effects are achieved. There is room for comparative study of his symbolism, his use of irony and the actual *means* by which he presents the ambiguity of reality. Finally, the development of his style remains to be examined. Only when we begin to give systematic attention to Donoso's works as what they are, that is, literary artefacts, and not merely vehicles for the expression of ideas, can we consider that Donoso criticism has really taken off.

Notes

1. Bibliographical items referred to in the text are as follows (where there is no ambiguity, page references alone are given; where there is ambiguity, appropriate abbreviations, of which there is a key at the end of this note, are also supplied): H. Achugar, *Ideologia estructuras narrativas en José Donoso (1950-1970)*. Caracas, 1979; P. Bacarisse, "*OPN:* A willes process of evasion," *Contemporary Latin American fiction,* ed. S. Bacarisse. Edinburgh, 1985, 18-34; E. Bendezú, "Donoso: fabulación y realidad," Cornejo Polar, 161-70; J. R. Boorman, *La estructura del narrador en la novela hispanoamericana contemporánea.* Madrid, 1976, 111-21; A. Borinsky, "Repeticiones y máscaras: *OPN,*" *MLN,* 88 (1973), 281-94; J. S. Brushwood, *The Spanish American novel.* Austin, Texas, 1975; R. Bueno Chávez, "*ED:* la autenticidad del relate novelesco," Cornejo Polar, 59-72; H. Calae de Agüera, "Desintegración de la personalidad on *TNB,*" *CHA,* 320, 1 (1977), 478-87; R. J. Callan, "Animals as mana figures in José Donoso's 'Paseo' and 'Santelices,'" *ELWIEU,* 2 (1975), 115-22; G. Carnero and J. Siles, "Dos comentarios sobre José Donoso," *CHA,* 259 (1972), 169-78; G. I. Castillo-Feliú, "José Donoso y su novela," *Hispania,* 54 (1971), 957-9, and "Reflexiones sobre el perspectivismo en *C* de José Donoso," *Hispania,* 63, 4 (1980), 699-705; J. Caviglia, "Tradition and monstrosity in *OPN,*" *PMLA* 93 (1978), 33-45; A. Cornejo Polar, "Introducción" and "*OPN:* la reversibilidad de la metáfors. José Donoso. *La destrucción de un mundo.* Buenos Aires, 1975, 7-11 and 101-12; R. L. Díaz Márquez "Conversando con José Donoso," *Horizontes,* 37 (1975), 5-12; J. Donoso, "Entrevista a José Donoso: a propósito de *OPN,*" *Libre,* 1 (1971), 73-6, and "La obra literaria del novelista José Donoso," *Literatura y sociedad en América Latina,* eds. V. Tascón and F. Soria. Salamanca, 1981, 103-11; G. Durán, "*OPN:* la dialéctica del chacal y del imbunche," *RevIb,* 42 (1976), 251-7; L. F. Eyzaguirre, *El héroe en la novela hispanoamericana del siglo XX.* Santiago, 1973, 267-77; I. Gertel "Metamorphosis as a metaphor of the world," *Review,* 9 (Fall 1973), 20-3; C. Goic "*C:* la espectacularidad de lo grotesco," Cornejo Polar, 43-57; I. Goldemberg, "*C* de José Donoso o los límites del aislamiento," *MNu,* 36 (June, 1969), 74-80; R. Gómez Palmeiro, R. "José Donoso, el retorno de la novela psicológica," *Nueva Estafeta,* 43-4 (1982), 75-7; L. Guerra Cunningham, "La prob-

lemática de la existencia en la novela chilena de la generación de 1950," *CHA,* 339 (1978), 408-28; J. J. Hassett "The obscure bird of night," *Review,* 9 (Fall 1973), 27-30; R. Lagos, "Inconsciente y ritual en *C*", *CHA,* 335 (1978), 290-305; J. M. Lipski, "Donoso's *Obscene bord:* Novel and anti-novel," *LALR,* 4 (1976), 39-47; A. L. MacAdam, *Modern Latin American narrative.* Chicago, 1977, 110-18, and "José Donoso: *CC*," *RevIb,* 47 (1981), 257-63; L. I. Madrigal, "Alegoría, historia, novela: a propósito de *CC* de José Donoso", *Hispam,* 25-6 (1980), 5-31; S. Magnarelli, "*OPN:* Fiction, monsters and packages," *HR,* 45 (1977), 413-9, and "Amidst the illusory depths: The first person pronoun and *OPN*," *MLN,* 93 (1978), 267-84; J. Marco, *Nueva literatura en España y América.* Barcelona, 1972, 313-9; Z. N. Martínez, "Lo neobarroco en *OPN* de José Donoso," *El barroco en América,* various authors, Madrid, 1978, 635-42, "*OPN:* la productividad del texto," *RevIb,* 46 (1980), 51-65, "*CC* de José Donoso", *Narradores latino american 1929-79,* Caracas, 1979, 261-8, and "*CC* de José Donoso: Afán de descentralization y nostalgia de centro," *HR,* 50, 4 (1982), 439-48; S. Martínez D'Acosta, *Dos ensayos literarios: Barrios y Donoso.* Miami, 1976, 69-84; G. R. McMurray, "La temática en los cuentos de José Donoso," *NNH,* 1, 2 (Sept. 1971), 133-8, "Interview with José Donoso," *Hispania,* 58 (1975), 391-3, and *José Donoso.* New York, 1979; F. Moreno Turner, "La inversión como norma: a proposito de *LSL*," Cornejo Polar, 79-100; A. Muller, "La dialéctica de la realidad en *OPN*," *MNH,* 2, (Sept. 1972), 93-100; K. F. Nigro, "From *criollismo* to the grotesque: Approaches to José Donoso," *Tradition and renewal,* ed. M. H. Forster, University of Illinois, 1975, 208-32; J. Promis Ojeda, "La desintegración del orden en la novela de José Donoso," Cornejo Polar, 15-42; L. Quinteros *José Donoso: una insurrección contra la realidad.* Madrid, 1978; F. Rivera, "A conflict of themes," *Review,* 9 (Fall 1973), 24-6; E. Rodríguez Monegal, "El mundo de José Donoso" *MNu,* 12 (June 1967), 77-85; M. San Martín, "Entretien avec José Donoso", *Car,* 29 (1977), 195-203; S. Sarduay "Writing transvestism," *Review,* 9 (Fall 1973), 31-3; R. Schwartz, *Nomads, exiles, and emigrés. The rebirth of the Latin American narrative, 1960-80.* Metuchen, N. J. and London, 1980, 100-11; R. Scott, "Heroic illusion and death denial in Donoso's *OPN*," *Symposium,* 32 (1978), 133-46; D. L. Shaw, *Nueva narrativa hispanoamericana.* Madrid, 1981, 141-53; C. M. Tatum, "*OPN:* The demise of a feudal society," *LALR,* 1, 2 (Spring 1973), 99-105, and "*Los medallones de piedra:* The hermetic beings of Donoso," *LangQ,* 13 (1974), 43-8; A. Valdés "El

'imbunche': estudio de un motivo en *OPN*," Cornejo Polar, 124-60; H. Vidal, *José Donoso. Surrealismo y la rebelión de los instintos.* Barcelona, 1972; P. West, "The Sanskrit everyone knows," *Review* (Spring 1977), 64-7. (Abbreviations used above for Donoso's novels are as follows: *C: Coronación; ED: Este domingo; LSL: El lugar sin límites; OPN: El obsceno pájaro; TNB Tres novelitas burguesas; CC: Casa de campo.*)

2. Paul Alexandru Georgescu, "Ernesto Sábato y el estructuralismo," *Nueva Estafeta,* 41 (April 1982), 47-58.

3. For example, see note 1 above: Bendezú, Calae de Agüera, McMurray, Schwartz, Shaw, and West.

4. For example, see note 1 above: MacAdam, Madrigal, Martínez, and Shaw.

5. For example, see note 1 above: Gómez Palmeiro.

Philip Swanson (essay date January 1985)

SOURCE: Swanson, Philip. "Binary Elements in *El obsceno pájaro de la noche.*" *Revista de Estudios Hispanicos* 19, no. 1 (January 1985): 101-16.

[*In the following essay, Swanson examines duality as a central organizing principle of* El obsceno pájaro de la noche.]

A notable feature of much recent criticism on José Donoso's **El obsceno pájaro de la noche** is the number of references to the text's inherent duality. Isis Quinteros sees the mythical level of the novel as being organized around a series of "relaciones en oposición binaria,"[1] while Adriana Valdés has commented that: "es constante la estructuración anverso/reverso en la narración."[2] Josefina A. Pujals also asserts that "toda la novela es un juego sobre dos tensiones o polaridades opuestas, de unión y desunión, de aglutinamiento y fragmentación representados por los factores imbunche y desmembramiento respectivamente."[3]

However, critics have so far tended to emphasize the ways in which binarism intensifies the complexity and ambiguity of the novel. Thus Promis Ojeda writes: "*El obsceno pájaro* es . . . una genial expresión de ambigüedad al mostrar la coexistencia permanente de los dos lados de la realidad."[4] Cornejo Polar agrees: "la reversibilidad enfatiza la caducidad de la oposición real/ficticio, cumple una clara función desjerarquizante y cancela toda opción de vertebrar causalmente el relato."[5] Achugar analyses the "dialéctica del afuera-adentro, de la verdad-mentira," "la dicotomía mínimo-máximo, instante-eternidad" and the motifs of "máscara y disfraz que son anverso y reverso de una misma noción: la de persona:"[6] but he sees these oppositions mainly as a manifestation of the futility of man's attempts to apply logical norms to fictional or non-fictional reality. The same outlook is implicit in the comments of Gertel and Hassett: the former feels that the element of reversibility indicates "la total negación de la realidad,"[7] while the latter claims that "the stability between signifier and signified begins to lose its customary integrity, so that a *mundo al revés* emerges in which objects tend to be signs to their opposites."[8] Such views are summed up by Lipski:

> Above all else, Donoso's novel is a novel of duality. Throughout the expanse of the text, a number of possible events or propositions are narrated, together with their opposites. The ensuing picture is one of total ambiguity.[9]

This systematic questioning of the nature of reality is indisputably an integral part of the text: the numerous oppositions and contradictions in the novel do plainly constitute a direct attack upon the notion of a reality that can be easily understood and transferred to the written page. The author himself has remarked, in an interview with San Martín, that *El obsceno pájaro* is characterized by "el binarismo como negación del maniqueísmo."[10] However, in the same interview, he also suggests that this ambiguity is not necessarily a barrier to identifying the novel's internal form:

> Quisiera que fuera una cosa tremendamente polifacética, tremendamente vital, tremendamente movible, tremendamente barroca, no en un sentido de Carpentier; barroca como las ciudades medievales que de alguna manera tienen un sentido . . . De alguna manera, las ciudades medievales tienen un urbanismo propio interior que es como una acumulación de cosas en que se llega a una forma extraordinaria, maravillosa, que es un pueblo en que no hay un propósito inicial, sino que hay una sobreposición de vidas y tiempos que van creando un conjunto; que van creando una forma. . . . Yo quisiera que la novela tuviera esa forma que va más allá de la forma, esa metaforma, digamos de la ciudad medieval, que tiene todo el contenido, todo el significado y toda la contradicción que puede tener una ciudad medieval.

> (Pp. 202-3)

Although the binary elements in *El obsceno pájaro* create uncertainty, they also provide a pointer towards part of the novel's hidden form. It is proposed here to examine the importance of binarism—not so much as a vehicle for ambiguity—but as an illustration of one of the novel's central organizing principles.[11]

A consideration of Donoso's use of binarism necessarily involves the modification of certain *purely* formal approaches which do not always clarify our understanding of complex Latin American works like *El obsceno*

pájaro. In a recent article on the novels of Sábato,[12] Paul Alexandru Georgescu highlights some of the limitations of the Barthesean approach in a way equally applicable to Donoso's novel. He posits the notion of a third structural layer beyond that of functions and signs, what he calls "signos numenales": this level involves the use of metaphor, temporal perspective and parallel narratives in order to expand the significance of the text. In other words, the key to our understanding of the novel lies not in our ability to break it down into causal sequences but in an awareness of the inter-relationship of episodes and motifs on a wider, symbolic plane. As Valdés writes in a study of the "imbunche" motif in *El obsceno pájaro*:

> la relación entre motivos no podrá depender sólo del argumento, del tiempo o del personaje: su sentido se irá constituyendo en parte muy importante por resonancias inesperadas, por una ligazón casi mágica entre los episodios.

> (P. 139)

This third level of symbolic interpenetration unifies the novel's disparate narrative threads. Its internal coherence is based on one central opposition: that of order-versus-chaos, what Solotorevsky calls "el mundo luminoso y el mundo oscuro."[13] This is reflected symbolically in the stories of all the main characters: their actions may be seen as representing the invention of a construct or what Scott calls "heroic illusions or immortality myths."[14] Their sense of existential alienation leads them to develop an artificial order as an alternative to the reality of chaos. Practically every symbol or motif reinforces this idea. A whole series of lexically diverse elements combine on a semantic level provoking a free flow of associations between motifs that enhances the reader's appreciation of the text. It is this system of binary oppositions deriving from the order-versus-chaos conflict that forms the true internal syntax of the novel. It is not, of course, intended to suggest that the system is mechanically imposed on the novel with total consistency, nor even to imply that order and chaos are presented as utterly separate entities: each is seen to contain the seeds of the other, or even—as is the case with order—to exist simply at the level of aspiration. None the less it is the binary element which receives the main emphasis.

Images associated with order (or the desire for order) are systematically opposed to images of chaos, each individual image linking up in turn with a new variation on the same motif. A fundamental opposition is that between youth (representing order) and age (representing chaos). "Youth" here refers to the post-adolescent phase of the upper middle classes. The orphan girls, for example, represent chaos: but this is due not only to their age, but also to their status as orphans—social outcasts from the lower classes. There is, however, an interesting contrast between the early and later years of Jerónimo and Inés. Their superficially happy, youthful relationship soon gives way to the reality of frustration and old age. Inés consciously attempts to transform herself into an old woman: the anarchy of senility is "una forma de libertad"[15] because it represents freedom from rational laws. Equally it is a state of neutrality, for this is nothing to look forward to: "soy libre, ya no *podría* sentir, pertenezco al sexo sintético que es el sexo de las viejas" (p. 400). It is significant that Inés explains her position to misiá Raquel Ruiz in sexual terms: if sexual activity is a symbol of the quest for fulfillment then Inés's withdrawal from the sexual world brings out her loss of hope and surrender to chaos.

The old women, along with Inés, constantly oppose games to reality. They prefer the fictional construct of the game to the real world. At the same time the game image, like the "viejas", emerges as a representation of chaos. Games after all are based on chance. The game in which the old women stick fragments of saints' statues together in order to "organizar identidades arbitrarias" (p. 372) reflects, like the telephone game, the fragility of the human personality and the pervasive ambiguity of reality. Their withdrawal into the world of the game brings out another aspect of their immersion into a world of chaos.

The final chapter shows the order represented by the new home being overrun by this chaos the old women personify. Padre Azócar and the young priests come to move them but the women argue crazily about Brígida's surnames, go looking for pumpkin seeds and end by boarding the buses in a state of total disorder. Padre Azócar realizes that it is useless to organize "estos seres anárquicos" for "las mentes de las viejas se enredaban en una maraña que impedía todo intento de iniciar un orden" (p. 529).

The youth-age dichotomy finds its correlation in the masters-servants opposition. Servants are said to confront the unpleasant side of reality that their masters choose to ignore. Masters feel "pavor de las cosas feas e indignas" (p. 66). But in forcing their servants to perform distasteful tasks they lose part of themselves to their employees, "la mitad inútil, descartada, lo sucio y lo feo" (p. 64). The servants "fueron robándose algo integral de las personas de sus patrones al colocarse en su lugar para hacer algo que ellos se negaban a hacer" (p. 65). Consequently, they build up "algo como una placa negativa" (p. 65), achieving "el reverso del poder" (p. 66). Thus the ruling groups cling to a false notion of order while the servile class are seen as embodying the dark, negative, chaotic side of life their masters choose to ignore.

This opposition is taken a stage further by the establishment of several more specific dichotomies stemming from the master-servant idea. Misiá Raquel Ruiz, al-though Brígida's mistress, is forced to look after the servant's finances to the extent that she becomes a "prisionera de la plata de la Brígida" (p. 313), her life having been made a misery. This inversion suggests the encroachment of chaos upon an ordered vision of the world. Moreover, a whole series of related oppositions, operating on various levels, suggests that the same crisis is present in the Azcoitía family. The Azcoitías barely acknowledge of the existence of the Casa, inhabited as it is by such representatives of chaos as ex-servants and old women:

> La falta de interés de los Azcoitía por esta Casa es secular. Como si le tuvieran un miedo que no se confiesan ni a sí mismos y prefieren desentenderse de ella en todo sentido menos en el de mantener el derecho de propietarios.
>
> (P. 55)

A more specific opposition encapsulating the order-chaos, youth-age, master-servant idea is that of Jerónimo and Peta Ponce. Jerónimo imposes his own artificial order on to a world which he chooses to see in terms of a series of logically interlocking medallions. Peta, however, lives in "un desorden de construcciones utilitarias sin pretensión de belleza: el revés de la fachada" (p. 181). She is part of "el mundo de abajo, de la siniestra, del revés, de las cosas destinadas a perecer escondidas sin jamás conocer la luz" (p. 183). This human embodiment of chaos does not fit into any of his rationally conceived medallions, but belongs to "la leyenda enemiga que contradecía a la suya" (p. 182).

The opposition is given added force by other groupings in the binary chain of linking pairs. The first comes when Jerónimo's medallions are set against Peta's handkerchiefs. The beauty and perfection of the handkerchiefs she gives him contradicts the system of reasoned laws upon which he has so far based his life: "un tizonazo de admiración hizo trastabillar su orden al reconocer en la Peta Ponce a una enemiga poderosa" (p. 183). The second important related opposition is that created between the classical beauty of Jerónimo's four noble, black dogs and the "perra amarilla" (which is associated with Peta Ponce and the nursery-maid witch of the old legend). Significantly, his dogs are unable to capture the yellow bitch which steals their meat: the idea of chaos holds sway over the artificial concept of order. The conflict between historical time and mythical time underlines this point. In Achugar's view, both represent man's attempts to define reality. The old hag (possibly Peta Ponce) prevents Mudito from escaping at the end of the novel: "el triunfo de la Peta Ponce es derrotar las vanas construcciones que el hombre ha erigido contra el tiempo" (p. 266). Peta's ability to distort time makes her an embodiment of chaos and ambiguity: her apparent victory over Mudito emphasizes the ascendancy of the qualities she represents.

It would be interesting at this point to consider the role played by the various chaotic elements mentioned so far in Donoso's presentation of sexuality in *El obsceno pájaro,* for this too indicates yet another binary opposition within the novel. Stabb has remarked that "The erotic is clearly a defining characteristic of that *obscene* nightbird chattering in the 'unsubdued forest.'"[16] There does seem to be a very definite relationship between sexuality and fatality here: this again relates to the order-versus-chaos conflict because it involves the juxtaposition of an image of hope of fulfillment with an image of decay, death and despair. When Iris Mateluna is pretending that Damiana is her baby, her washing of the old woman's vagina provokes an orgasm in the aged lesbian (p. 125). When people are making love in the Gigante's car the yellow bitch appears at the window. When Jerónimo and Inés make love in the open the yellow bitch appears again sniffing and licking at the secretions left by their bodies (p. 194). Humberto thought he had made love with Inés on the night of Boy's conception but later suspects that the act took place with Peta Ponce:

> en las tinieblas yo puedo no haberle dado mi amor a Inés sino a otra, a la Peta, a la Peta Ponce que sustituyó a Inés por ser ella la pareja que me corresponde, a la Peta raída, vieja, estropeada, sucia, mi miembro enorme la penetró a ella, gozó en su carne podrida, gemí de placer con la cercanía de sus manos verrugosas, de sus ojos nublados por las legañas, mendigando el beso de su boca acuchillada por las arrugas, sí, en las tinieblas de esa noche sólo los ojos del tordo vieron que fue el sexo de la vieja, agusanado por la cercanía de la muerte, que devoró mi maravilloso sexo nuevo, y esa carne deteriorada me recibió.
>
> (Pp. 223-4)

He now feels terrified that Peta will return to repeat the sexual act with him. He still desires Inés but, through ageing she has now adopted the characteristics of Peta:

> Así tiene que ser, así he sido siempre, Inés, Inés-Peta, Peta-Ines, Peta, Peta Ponce, jamás he podido tocar la belleza porque al desearla la convierto en desastradas dueñas de pensión.
>
> (P. 431)

Significantly, when he attempts to seduce Inés she is transformed into the wrinkled old hag, Peta. The effect of this juxtaposition of the horror of old age with the supposedly youthful, vigorous activity of sexual intercourse is that it reinforces the novel's central existential message. Sexual activity, a bodily function, may represent the quest for transcendence, but by introducing the motif of old age into a sexual context Donoso suggests the inevitability of bodily decay. As we are so eloquently reminded in many of Vallejo's poems, we are in fact prisoners of our own body. Thus at the point at which the characters feel they may be achieving a symbolic fulfillment, they are in reality confronted with a terrifying image of chaos and death.

The order-chaos conflict present in the above-mentioned contrasting binary motifs is reaffirmed in a series of other oppositions less central to the plot. There is an ironic contrast established in the double presentation of don Clemente: when we first read of him he is described as an old lunatic who used to run naked around the convent; we later see him as he used to be, a wily politician in apparent command of his senses. The order in which the reader is given these two images of the same man expresses Donoso's view that the seeds of destruction are present in all of us. Madre Benita is set against the "viejas". She develops her own construct in the form of charitable work in order to ward off the chaos represented by the emptiness of the old women's lives: "pobre (sic) viejecitas, hay que hacer algo por ellas, sí, usted se ha matado trabajando para no conocer el revés de la Brígida" (p. 29). The opposition of men and women also corresponds to the order-chaos polarity. Gutiérrez Mouat sees this in terms of a conflict between two approaches to narrative—the traditional (men) and the modern (women)[17]—but an existential reading can also be advanced. The motif runs throughout the novel but is most fully developed when Inés moves to the Casa. Inés, we are told, "ha ido impidiendo que su marido se desprenda de esta Casa, siempre por motivos irracionales, totalmente subjetivos, imposible comprender esos motivos que hicieron que generaciones de mujeres Azcoitía hayan ido intrigando y urdiendo una red de protección para esta Casa" (pp. 376-7). She compares the irrationality of women with the reason of men who take control of everything because "ellos entienden lo que significa y saben explicarlo, y explican tanto que las cosas dejan de tener significado" (p. 377). Just as men are false symbols of order and women symbols of chaos, Europe appears in the novel as representing order while Latin America is associated with chaos. Again the references are numerous; one striking example comes when Humberto describes Jerónimo's return from Europe: "el hecho es que la presencia de Jerónimo era una lección de armonía, incómoda porque era imposible emularla en estas latitudes bárbaras" (p. 163). The interesting feature of the presentation of these motifs is the way they all link together, providing structural unity and reinforcing the novel's central ideas.

So far we have been considering oppositions stemming basically from a youth-age, masters-servants dichotomy. Another obvious polarity is that set up between the Casa and La Rinconada. These are more than mere "metáforas de la ficción," as Gutiérrez Mouat claims (p. 147). La Rinconada is an attempt to impose order on to chaos. Jerónimo wishes to destroy "ese inmundo laberinto de adobe, de galerías y corredores" and replace the wild trees and plants with "matorrales podados en estrictas formas geométricas que disfrazaran su exuberancia natural" (p. 230). This leads to two further oppositions—Jerónimo-versus-the-freaks and Jerónimo-versus-Boy. Jerónimo tries to suppress the sense of disorder implied by Boy and the monsters, refusing to "ceder, incorporarse al caos, ser víctima de él" (p. 161). However, the freaks themselves adopt La Rinconada as a construct against chaos too. The estate and the world beyond its walls are systematically opposed. They fear the collapse of "el paraíso del que ninguno se atrevía a salir" (p. 406). Emperatriz sees the outside world as an "infierno" (p. 407). After breaching the boundaries of the estate, Boy asserts that: "ahora que conozco la realidad, sólo lo artificial me interesa" (p. 485). He asks Dr. Azula to perform an operation on his brain to remove his memory of the real world so that he can return to "el orden inicial" (p. 485).

Humberto's mental crisis is also expressed in terms of this system of binary oppositions corresponding to the notion of order-versus-chaos. His problems are engendered by his father who instills in him the urge to become a person of stature and significance: this provokes his obsession with assuming the identity of don Jerónimo. From now on Humberto fluctuates between the need to become "somebody" and the desire to be "nobody", between power and weakness, expansiveness and withdrawal, between what Goić calls "la voluntad de ser y la voluntad de autoaniquilamiento."[18] The problem is reflected in his ambiguous attitude to Iris Mateluna. During the telephone game he thinks he can control her thoughts but simultaneously fears her: if she wins he feels that "la sangre que el doctor Azula me robó volverá a correr por mis venas, dejaré de ser una mancha de humedad en una pared, me rescatarás, o no, quizás oyendo su voz me repliegue más, hasta quedar anulado" (p. 441). Sometimes he dominates Iris, sometimes he obeys her, "ciego y sin voluntad" (p. 82). It is interesting to note that the power-weakness opposition is reinforced by another symbol in the chain of interconnecting elements, namely that of the Chalet Suizo. It is something more than "the unattainable ideal home" referred to by McMurray:[19] it brings out the contradiction between the reality of Mudito's situation and his absurd aspirations. He addresses himself to Iris:

> Arranco mi mano de tu pecho. Enciendo una luz discreta y te muestro la cajita de música, abro la tapa, oyes el *Carnaval de Venecia,* tus ojos se van a iluminar, los haré asomarse a los espejitos de la puerta y de la ventana: te indico la puertecita, quiero que entres, ahora, ahora, ahora mismo, cazarte dentro de la caja de música.
>
> —¿Creís que soy huevona? ¿Que vai a poder hacerme lesa con ese juguete?
>
> No sé qué contestar.
>
> (P. 142)

The conflict within Mudito is presented largely in sexual terms. He dreams of seducing Emperatriz. He will:

> agarrala en sus brazos, penetrarla con su sexo, matarla de placer al ensartarla gritando con su sexo immenso . . .
>
> Sintió su pantalón mojado. Su miembro decayó.
>
> (P. 269)

At times he imagines he has a large, red, potent penis; but on other occasions it is a "trozo de carne inerte" (p. 431), "una cosa inútil" (p. 463). He feels his look controls don Jerónimo's virility: he has "la mirada cargada de poder" (p. 84) and thinks that his ex-master is desperate to "recuperar su potencia que yo conservo guardada en mis ojos" (p. 96). Yet he too is dependent upon the look of other people; referring to Iris he says:

> Estoy acostumbrado a ser una presencia sobre la que los ojos se resbalen sin que la atención encuentre nada en qué fijarse. ¿Por qué me seguías, entonces, si ni siquiera me ibas a conceder existencia con una mirada?
>
> (P. 76)

This conflict is, of course, as Bacarisse,[20] McMurray and others have pointed out, a symptom of Mudito's schizophrenia. At the same time though it fits into the general order-chaos binary system, the desire for sexual power and self-control corresponding to the need for a sense of order, and the reality of sexual feebleness equaling the process of succumbing to chaos and despair.

The taut web of inter-relations within the binary system is given added unity by a further layer of symbolic interpenetration. A whole series of images stems from one central symbol: that of enclosure. This image is itself binary in nature, for it suggests a conflict between inside and outside, appearance and reality, hope and despair, integration and withdrawal, order and chaos. There are two essential aspects of the enclosure image as presented in ***El obsceno pájaro.*** The first is its association with the concept of the construct, with the attempt to find meaning in things that have no meaning. A striking example is that of the packet. Although some critics (notably Borinsky, Gutiérrez Mouat, MacAdam and Magnarelli)[21] see this image in purely literary terms (that is, as a reflection of the text as a series of linguistic signs behind which there is no deeper meaning), a metaphysical reading is, in my view, more convincing. Like Colonel Aureliano Buendía's production of golden fish in *Cien años de soledad* and Amalia's hopeless hunt for the missing finger from the statue of St. Gabriel, the process of wrapping things up is a symbol of the absurd, pointless activity that is life. The search for something of significance inside the packages corresponds to man's futile quest for meaning in life. Mudito asks:

> ¿No ve, Madre Benita, que lo importante es envolver, que el objeto envuelto no tiene importancia? . . . ¿Para qué sigue abriendo y rompiendo envoltorios . . . si tiene que saber que no va a encontrar nada?
>
> (Pp. 30-1)

Other symbols link up with this one to reinforce the notion of the conflict between the desire for meaning (order) and the reality of despair (chaos). Mudito attempts to climb through a non-existent window, a recurring image in the novel; the window is illusory, only there "para que creyera que existía una afuera" (p. 303). The cells in the Casa are used as storage space for discarded oddments: Inés visits to search for "una sombrerera de cuero donde podía haber un envoltorio donde podía haber un sobre donde podía haber guardado hace años miles cierto certificado importante o cierta fotografía" (p. 55)—but as usual her quest is fruitless.

A second important feature of the chain of images of enclosure is their relation to the idea of withdrawal or escape. Solotorevsky has observed that "los ámbitos cerrados . . . representan la protección y la libertad, pero también el estatismo y la anulación. Asimismo el mundo de afeura . . . es mostrado como peligroso y terrible" (p. 161). As the characters attain an increasing symbolic awareness of the chaos surrounding them they attempt to recede even further into their own artificial constructs of order. As we have seen, the freaks prefer to stay within the boundaries of La Rinconada and Boy expresses his wish to languish in a mental limbo. The Casa, though itself a labyrinthine image of anarchy, is equally a symbolic refuge from chaos. Inés moves there after her hysterectomy (an operation which recalls Mudito's references to Iris's body as a "cáscara superflua" (p. 76), a mere "envoltorio" (p. 437), and indeed his description of himself as a worthless "corteza" (p. 217). Mudito thinks that "es terrible la ciudad" (p. 341), living in fear of the "abismo de la calle" (p. 347) as opposed to the Casa where he experiences the relief of being "adentro, libre" (p. 347) and enjoys "la paz de los corredores y las galerías" (p. 79). He begins to wall up parts of the Casa so that he can retreat even deeper into it (pp. 400-1).

Mudito's withdrawal also involves the destruction of his previous identities as he heads along the path to oblivion:

> he quemado mi nombre definitivamente, mi voz la perdí hace mucho tiempo, ya no tengo sexo porque puedo ser una vieja más entre tantas viejas de la Casa, y mis papeles incoherentes de garabatos que intentaron implorar que se me concediera una máscara definida y perpetua, los quemo . . . .
>
> (p. 156)

He imagines that Dr. Azula's operation has robbed him of 80% of his organs. He is now merely "un pedazo de hombre" (p. 336), even "esta manga exangüe a la puerta de un convento" (p. 148).

This process of withdrawal links up with another image in the chain, that of the "imbunche". Valdés has made a careful study of this motif identifying both positive and negative aspects in it: it thus forms part of the binary system identified earlier. It is much more than a representation of "la tradición histórica chilena" as Vidal suggests.[22] The notion of becoming an "imbunche" ironically constitutes an attempt to escape chaos by retreating into self-annihilation. Boy's operation transforms him into a kind of "imbunche". This is a state to which the mentally disturbed Mudito also aspires. For him this would be "la paz total" (p. 288). He cries out to Peta Ponce:

> déjame anularme, deja que las viejas bondadosas me fajen, quiero ser un imbunche metido adentro del saco de su propia piel, despojado de la capacidad de moverme y de desear y de oír y de leer y escribir, o de recordar . . .
>
> (P. 433)

Thus, via the linking up of motifs on a symbolic plane, the story of a mythical creature effects our interpretation of the present. The pattern of events is developed further as Donoso introduces more variations on the "imbunche" theme. One is Mudito's identification with Iris's baby, the so-called saviour child. He is wrapped up in a kind of strait-jacket so tight that "me está reduciendo más y más, ya estoy tan pequeño que una anciana me podría cargar en sus brazos" (p. 391)—recalling the way the size of the clothes Inés knits for her longed-for child decreases concurrently with the decline of her hope. The process is taken a stage further with the introduction of the image of the sack. The old women sew Mudito up in sacks, transforming him into a "paquetito sin sexo" (p. 525). However, there is still an element of binarism present here:

> sívenme, no quiero morir, terror, estoy débil, tullido, inutilizado, sin sexo, sin nada, rasado, pero no gritaré porque no hay otras formas de existencia, estoy a salvo aquí dentro de esto de donde jamás he salido . . .
>
> (P. 538)

Yet, despite the comfort and security that the sack represents for him, he feels terror when the old hag carries him off. Although the struggle between order and chaos is present right to the end, Mudito's complete destruction in the novel's closing lines seems indicative of the triumph of the latter.

The ascendancy of chaos, then seems evident. Indeed order and chaos turn out to be ultimately inter-related: youth gives way to age; sexual activity leads only to frustration; the desire for power is contradicted by the truth of weakness; masters assume the characteristics of their servants, just as normal people assume those of the freaks. However, the binary system of interconnecting images identified in *El obsceno pájaro* suggests that the novel's structure is not as chaotic as is often supposed: Donoso may not have approached his task with any preconceived plan, but he has clearly arrived at some kind of internal form. He debunks the myths of love, religion and reason but replaces them with a construct of his own: art. Thus the binary system extends to the novel's very structure: the act of writing itself is, if not exactly an attempt to impose order on chaos, then an attempt to achieve some sense of order by confronting the reality of chaos. It is therefore through the professionalism of his artistry that Donoso finds his own defense against the "unsubdued forest where the wolf howls and the obscene bird of night chatters."

Notes

1. Isis Quinteros, *José Donoso: una insurrección contra la realidad* (Madrid: Hispanova de ediciones, 1978), p. 220. After the first note, subsequent references to all items will be given in brackets in the main body of the text.

2. Adriana Valdés, "El 'imbunche'. Estudio de un motivo en *El obsceno pájaro de la noche*," in *José Donoso. La destrucción de un mundo,* ed. Antonio Cornejo Polar (Buenos Aires: Fernando García Cambeiro, 1975), p. 143.

3. Josefina A. Pujals, *El bosque indomado donde chilla el obsceno pájaro de la noche. Un estudio sobre la novela de José Donoso* (Miami: Ediciones Universal, 1981), p. 85.

4. José Promis Ojeda, *La novela chilena actual* (Buenos Aires: Fernando García Cambeiro, 1977), p. 170.

5. Antonio Cornejo Polar, "*El obsceno pájaro de la noche:* la reversibilidad de la metáfora," in Cornejo Polar, op. cit., p. 108.

6. Hugo Achugar, *Ideología y estructuras narrativas en José Donoso (1950-70)* (Caracas: Centro de estudios latinoamericanos "Rómulo Gallegos", 1979), pp. 251, 260, 270.

7. Zunilda Gertel, "*El obsceno pájaro de la noche:* des-encarnación, transformación, inexistencia," *Chasqui,* II, No. 1 (November 1976), p. 18.

8. John J. Hassett, "The obscure bird of night," *Review,* No. 9 (Fall 1973), pp. 28-9.

9. John M. Lipski, "Donoso's *Obscene Bird:* novel and anti-novel," *Latin American literary review,* 4, No. 1 (1976), p. 43.

10. Mercedes San Martín, "Entretien avec José Donoso," *Caravelle,* 29 (1975), p. 201.

11. The importance of binarism is not limited to *El obsceno pájaro de la noche:* much of what follows in this article is equally applicable to Donoso's other novels, for the same basic oppositions discussed here (youth-age, masters-servants,

men-women, power-weakness etc.) recur constantly in his work. For reasons of space, it has been decided to limit the present study to Donoso's best-known novel: it is hoped, nevertheless, that this examination of *El obsceno pájaro* will promote further insights into Donoso's work as a whole.

12. Paul Alexandru Georgescu, "Ernesto Sábato y el estructuralismo," *Nueva estafeta,* No. 41 (April 1982), 47-58.

13. Myrna Solotorevsky, "Configuraciones espaciales en *El obsceno pájaro de la noche* de José Donoso," *Bulletin hispanique,* 82 (1980), pp. 150-151.

14. Robert Scott, "Heroic illusion and death denial in José Donoso's *El obsceno pájaro de la noche,*" *Symposium,* 32 (1978), p. 135.

15. José Donoso, *El obsceno pájaro de la noche* (Barcelona: Seix Barral, 1979), p. 399.

16. Martin S. Stabb, "The erotic mask: notes on Donoso and the new novel," *Symposium,* 30 (1976), p. 177.

17. Ricardo Gutiérrez Mouat, *José Donoso: impostura e impostación. La modelización lúdica y carnavalesca de una producción literaria* (Gaithersburg: Hispamérica, 1983), p. 187.

18. Cedomil Goic, *Historia de la novela hispanoamericana* (Valparaíso: Ediciones Universitarias de Valparaíso, 1972), p. 262.

19. George R. McMurray, *José Donoso* (New York: Twayne, 1979), p. 134.

20. Pamela Bacarisse, "*El obsceno pájaro de la noche:* a willed process of evasion," in *Contemporary Latin American Fiction,* ed. Salvador Bacarisse (Edinburgh: Scottish Academic Press, 1980), 18-34.

21. Alicia Borinsky, "Repeticiones y máscaras: *El obsceno pájaro de la noche,*" *Modern Language Notes,* 88 (1973), 281-294; Alfred J. MacAdam, *Modern Latin American Narratives* (Chicago: University of Chicago Press, 1977), 110-118; Sharon Magnarelli, "*El obsceno pájaro de la noche:* fiction, monsters and packages," *Hispanic Review,* 45 (1977), 413-419;—"Amidst the illusory depths: the first person pronoun and *El obsceno pájaro de la noche,*" *Hispanic Journal,* 2, No. 2 (Spring 1981), 81-93.

22. Hernán Vidal, *José Donoso: surrealismo y rebelión de los instintos* (Barcelona: Ediciones Aubí, 1972), p. 217.

Pamela Bacarisse (essay date January 1986)

SOURCE: Bacarisse, Pamela. "*El obsceno pájaro de la noche*: The Novelist as Victim." *The Modern Language Review* 81, no. 1 (January 1986): 82-96.

[*In the following essay, Bacarisse examines Donoso's narrative devices to discover the relation of the narrator to the author, as well as the dominant emotional state in* El obsceno pájaro de la noche.]

> . . . es como si él mismo se hubiera perdido para si-
> empre en el laberinto que iba inventando lleno de oscu-
> ridad y terrores con más consistencia que él
> mismo. . . .[1]

One of the fundamental problems when reading José Donoso's *El obsceno pájaro de la noche* is that of sorting out what the author himself has referred to as the 'múltiples versiones' (p. 356) of what we are told and, even more important for the purpose of this essay, of discovering who is narrating them. Nothing can be sure. The 'voice' of the apparent narrator—el Mudito—is, so to speak, scrambled in order to defy recognition and his various chameleon-like personalities make the task of identification all the more difficult. Is he Humberto Peñaloza? Was he ever an author? Did he once control the closed colony of freaks called the Rinconada? Is he, in fact, deaf and dumb? Was he Jerónimo de Azcoitía's secretary? Was his father a primary school-teacher? Were he and his sister brought up by their parents in one of the poorer suburbs of the city? Or was he a foundling, brought into the *Casa de Ejercicios Espiritu-ales de la Encarnación de la Chimba* to be looked af-ter? Is he a hunchbacked, harelipped dwarf? Was he ac-tually born in the *Casa*? Was he hawked around as a child by beggars who found his pitiful gaze profitable? Did he ever study Law? Is he really Jerónimo? Is he Jerónimo's son, Boy? Is he, indeed, anyone at all, or is the dumb narrator actually the text itself, with what Sharon Magnarelli has referred to as 'the illusory depths of the first person pronoun' representing an absence rather than a presence?[2]

It will come as no surprise to anyone familiar with the complexities of this novel that not a few critics have classified it as self-referential, and some of their sup-porting arguments are undeniably convincing. 'At last', claims Magnarelli in her remarkable article, 'the narra-tive *I* has overtly come to be what the structural lin-guists and some of the Russian formalists had proposed all along: a vacuum, an absence.' She goes on to say that 'the *I* in *El obsceno pájaro* emerges as a fluctuat-ing entity, a compendium of voices, and appears to cor-roborate Benveniste's theory that the *I* has never had a referent apart from the moment of discourse'.[3] El Mu-dito 'becomes a dramatization of the very process of fictitious discourse', his dictum that 'lo importante es

envolver' because 'el objeto envuelto no tiene importancia' (pp. 30-31) takes on an extra dimension; it is significant that both the *Casa* and the Rinconada are closed areas 'so that there can be no interaction with the outside world', that the Mudito 'tells of the other characters as *he* and then assumes their voices as *I*' and that the Rinconada inhabitants are freaks, since they constitute 'the word, twice removed from a referent or the possibility of a referent [the Rinconada is seen as existing only within the covers of the book Humberto has written], a double artifice [which] must engender monsters'. The white laboratory where el Mudito's black blood is taken from him is seen as representing the white page, with creation achieved by the blood, which is ink.[4] Another critic who sympathizes with the self-referential interpretation of the novel, Alfred J. MacAdam, maintains that what the narrator actually says is 'in effect irrelevant'. For him, what matters most is 'the telling itself', for 'to tell "what happens" in *El obsceno pájaro de la noche* is virtually impossible'. The narrative is 'a monstrous creator, incapable of do-ing anything except narrating, creating stories in its own image'.[5] Yet another who supports this point of view is Alicia Borinsky: indeed, she was one of the first to express it. As we read the novel, she claims, the *yo* is 'calificado como una persona que nombra el Mudito', but 'este *yo* . . . es una ilusión creada por el lenguaje' and, when all is said and done, 'no hay nada detrás': there are 'superficies [que] no guardan nada en su interior' and 'máscaras que al descubrirse presentan una nueva máscara y así sucesivamente'.[6]

It seems to me that some of the best Donoso criticism has been written by those who see *El obsceno pájaro* in this way. It all—or nearly all—appears to fit together and is very persuasive indeed. Furthermore, it is emi-nently reasonable that a solution of this kind should ap-peal, since the text is full of disconcerting pronominal shifts (sometimes within the same sentence) and appar-ently arbitrary selection of the first, second, and third persons for the narration. Then, too, it revolves around a protagonist whose identity is constantly fluctuating. El Mudito, if he exists, is an unknowable character. On the other hand, this 'explanation' fails to satisfy completely. Donald L. Shaw is convinced that it will not do at all: in his view its authors 'rechazan todo intento de inter-pretación y se refugian en el cómodo concepto de una narrativa creadora de sí misma'. He rejects this, even as a possibility:

> Digamos sin ambages que toda tentativa de presentar
> *El obsceno pájaro de la noche* como una serie de sig-
> nificantes sin significado está condenada de antemano
> al fracaso. Donoso es . . . un hombre con una cosmo-
> visión muy definida, de la cual debe partir todo en-
> foque válido de su obra.[7]

My own position is, perhaps, a curious one. I should not be prepared to go as far as Shaw in rejecting the validity of seeing the novel as language for its own sake, but I feel that in fact this starting-point is not incompatible with the psychoanalytic approach I have elaborated elsewhere.[8] The amazing thing about this novel, in my opinion, is that so many different and apparently mutually exclusive interpretations of it can coexist and that almost all of them are acceptable. So it is that I am prepared to see it as a text gradually bringing itself to an end while simultaneously struggling to survive; however, at the same time there is a human psyche occupied in precisely the same activity. The book is *not* totally self-referential; its referent is a combination of contagious and haunting human emotions that come together in an elusive, protean narrative voice. The present study of one of its linguistic features may at first glance suggest that I do see the work as self-referential, but ultimately it helps to reveal the nature and source of these emotions.

I should be prepared to go even further. My premise—that a linguistic device used by the narrative voice represents a particular emotional state—suggests that it is convenient and possibly profitable to see the novelist and the narrator as virtually one and the same, to consider Donoso's 'message' as one that comes to us directly. It goes without saying that there is never any excuse for the *automatic* identification of the narrative voice of a novel with the real author's, and even in those cases where it is extremely tempting to make this equation, most modern critics would prefer not to do so.[9] They feel that it would represent an extremely ingenuous critical position and that it might well be seen as an indication of their ignorance of literary theory. Even avowed autobiographical material is often thought to be suspect at the very least, and evidence based on what the author himself says about his work is frequently dismissed as too subjective, too interested, or even irrelevant.[10] The intentional fallacy is an everpresent trap. Furthermore, any critic utilizing the psychoanalytic approach runs the risk of being accused of reductionism, of diverting attention away from many of the important features of the text and in that way diminishing its possibilities, In a brilliantly-argued rejection of the psychoanalytic method, Harold Skulsky is sceptical of what he judges to be its various claims and he highlights the pitfalls that beset its practitioners. In the end, he admits that his basic objection is that the method is seen by some as 'part of the transaction between writers and readers that is generally (if tacitly) understood to constitute literary communication'.[11] It is precisely because this is not the case with *El obsceno pájaro,* where—as I see it—the intention is to avoid communication, that this method is an efficacious interpretative tool. I do not assume that I have been totally successful in cracking some kind of code or opening a window onto all there is to know about the text or about the author himself. On the other hand, I am unrepentant in aligning myself with those critics who have fallen into what Harold Skulsky calls 'the reductionist fallacy',

which claims that '*semantic* analysis may sometimes be "a question of building bridges between the poem and the psychic condition from which it arose"'.[12] Furthermore, I do not accept that a psychological approach necessarily excludes sociological considerations, or that a *psychocritique* emphasizes the division between 'the psychic and the social, phantasmagoria and history, inside and outside', as William Rowe has claimed.[13] I am convinced, though, that some texts are more susceptible to psychoanalytic analysis than others, and that often the alternative methods are inefficacious when used in isolation: the self-referentiality explanation of *El obsceno pájaro* is acceptable, but this is one example of a novel where the use of several methods seems to be called for.[14]

If semantic analysis is suspect, how much more provocative is my claim that a stylistic study can achieve the same end? 'El psicoanálisis alcanza sólo el contenido de la obra y no la forma', claimed Yvon Belaval on one occasion with what appears to be some justification.[15] If that is in fact true, it would seem that what we are left with after psychoanalytic criticism will be no more than an impression of the banality of human complexes in sharp contrast with what we see as the excitement of great works of art. After all, as Charles Mauron once observed, basically everyone shares the same complexes, just as we all have a liver or a spleen.[16] Yet I am sure that at least some literature should be considered from the point of view of form as well as of content in the course of an attempt at a psychoanalytic interpretation. Art, it has often been said, should delight. With modern art in particular, 'excite' may be a more appropriate term, and Freud was surely right when he declared that although the artist's conscious intention is unlikely to excite us, if we discover what the text's real meaning is, this may well do so. Perhaps to understand a work of art, albeit only partially, is to go a little way along the path to both delight and excitement.[17] As Mauron says: 'La psychocritique . . . recherche les associations d'idées involontaires sous les structures *voulues* du texte.'[18] It is clear that 'idées involontaires' can be attributed only to the original author: his 'structures voulues', the language used by the narrative voice can, and often should, be used in psychological analysis.

One of Skulsky's objections to this approach is that frequently a critic will 'eke out his evidence . . . by admitting gossip and fortuitously available biographical information. The result will be a powerful temptation to annex these materials to the text in an arbitrary pattern of conjecture that can be called an explanation only if one defines "explanation" to match'.[19] He is undoubtedly right that the temptation to use biographical evidence is great indeed, and it is one I cannot resist. My defence is that the method appears to work.

There are many superficial connexions between the author and the (literally) self-effacing narrator of *El obsceno pájaro de la noche.* It goes without saying that most of these prove nothing in themselves and, of course, all writers draw on personal experience for the creation of both plot and character. Yet in this case, I suggest, the numerous coincidences are significant and revealing. If taken all together they constitute evidence that it is difficult to ignore. Although it would be tedious to list them all it is, for example, worth bearing in mind Donoso's admission that with this book he was interested in 'la experiencia de hacer un personaje que no pudiera ser personaje. Que fuera treinta personajes a la vez' and which nevertheless would have to be remembered 'como uno, como una identidad'. He followed this up with: 'Soy treinta personas y no soy nadie.'[20] It is important, too, that the motivation of a search for identity that so many critics have attributed to him does not seem unacceptable to him.[21] Less important, certainly, is the fact that Donoso spent his childhood in a rambling old house with eccentric elderly aunts, that his father was an obsessive card-player and gambler, that he was fond of assuming new identities by dressing up, or that he was irresistibly fascinated by his unbalanced cousin, Cucho, who used to lock the family cats inside minuscule drawers when he came to visit. Perhaps, too, it is not vital to our understanding to know that his maternal grandmother went gradually and distressingly insane, making life impossible for the family for many long years, or that, like Humberto Peñaloza, he managed to sell copies of his first book only by means of private subscription.[22] But if we add that the stomach pains he feigned as a child in order to avoid going to school were diagnosed—and by his own father at that—as appendicitis and that he was forced to have an operation, and that some years later the pains got out of control again and he developed an ulcer so that, like Humberto Peñaloza, every time he tried to write his great work he was laid low, the parallels begin to look more interesting. Can it really be irrelevant that he underwent psychoanalysis in the early 1960s? Or that in more recent years he has suffered from hypochondria and was kept 'despierto sólo a medias' for four months by order of his psychiatrist? Or that later, after emergency surgery, his hitherto-undetected allergy to morphia reduced him to a state of total insanity? He himself recalls that period: 'Pasé varios días enloquecido, con alucinaciones, doble personalidad, paranoia e intentos suicidas. Cuando me recuperé . . . los efectos retardados de esta locura demoraron un par de años en desaparecer.' Then, 'todavía sufriendo de pesadillas y paranoia', he started *El obsceno pájaro de la noche* all over again and rewrote it in only eight months.[23] Donoso's comments on the relationship between himself and his novel add weight to my argument. When asked by Jaime Alazraki if he could explain 'cómo se dio el puente entre la obra anterior de José Donoso y *El obsceno pájaro* . . .*', he replied: 'Responder esa pregunta equivale a contar mi vida', and he goes on to admit that during his convalescence, after what he refers to as 'un momento en que estuve loco', he read R. D. Laing's *Politics of Experience* and, even more revealing, the same author's *The Divided Self.*[24]

I emphasized the word 'voulues' in Mauron's distinction between the conscious and the unconscious intention of any author because the background to the writing of *El obsceno pájaro* suggests that here the 'structures voulues' are relatively few. The novel was incredibly difficult to write, the process suffered many setbacks, and in the end the author declared himself puzzled by his own creation. For the original version, 'hice cuarenta borradores', he admits;[25] then illness prevented him from concentrating on writing and the years passed. In the end, his comments reveal an extraordinary lack of planning and conscious control:

> 'En el fondo no sé de qué se trata mi novela'; 'Es algo que me ha sucedido más bien que he escrito'; 'Yo no escribí esta novela. Esta novela me escribió a mí. *No podía elegir una estructura determinada porque las estructuras me estaban eligiendo a mí*'; 'Escribí esta novela un poco para saber quién soy'; 'La forma no cambió porque yo quise cambiarla, sino que la forma se *me* cambió'; 'Escribo la novela para preguntarme si sería capaz de hacerme una pregunta'; 'Es una novela en que me he buscado'; 'Es una cosa que *tenía* que venir'; 'El plan de la novela está dictado por el hecho de escribirla'; 'Creo que el campo de la literatura es una cosa mucho más onírica, mucho más inconsciente [than that of merely expressing ideas]'; 'El "hack" elige su tema, mientras que el escritor es elegido por su tema.'[26]

One of the major elements in all Donso's writings is, indeed, lack of control. It is very clear that things can easily get out of hand and that, ironically, it is often a question of ideas, desires, inventions, even creations, that originally came from the person who, in the end, falls foul of them. Schizophrenic patients frequently complain of the sensation that someone or something outside themselves is controlling them. But in the Donoso novels and short stories, we go a step further with the sinister realization that we set our own persecutors in motion. Just one apparently positive and potentially fruitful move is all that is needed, one innocuous word, a seemingly safe idea, a misleadingly trivial-looking action—*anything at all* can set off hostile forces. The line between normality and abnormality is a narrow one, as the grotesque Rinconada freaks clearly demonstrate, and even Jerónimo's classically handsome features can turn into something abnormal in a split second (p. 504). Creating new life is fraught with danger, and the grossly deformed Boy, his son, is an example of this. To take up a new activity is to become vulnerable: the activity, or an element of it, will take over, as the gambling *viejas* in this novel and the female protagonist of the short story 'Paseo' show.[27] Literary creation is no exception. Humberto Peñaloza is constantly afraid that his fictional offspring may gain control over him: after all, 'él los había inventado a ellos, no ellos a él' (p. 255). Thus the great act of *hubris* when he tells Jerónimo that he *is* a writer is another moment at which he starts something that will turn out badly for him: it leads not only to the necessity of keeping his word (a significant phrase in the context of this study) and being obliged actually to get on with it and write something, but also to becoming a kind of servant to the characters he has created. Donoso has said of his own position that once he had written the phrase 'El Mudito tiraba su carro', that was that. '¡Qué sé yo! ahí empezó él [el Mudito] a dominar la novela, ¡y se comió la novela! ¡*fue* la novela! Pero, no sé cómo ocurrió.'[28] It is all a question of power versus impotence; this is a Donoso common denominator.

One aspect of this power struggle is made up by the way that language itself traps the narrator-author. Situations are actually *created* by language, and the vast majority of them are menacing. The much-quoted passage from *Alice Through the Looking-Glass* in which Alice is discussing language with Humpty Dumpty is particularly appropriate here again. Humpty Dumpty has no doubts on the subject of who is in control: 'When I use a word, it means just what I choose it to mean—neither more nor less.' The conversation then goes in a direction that is even more relevant:

> 'The question is', said Alice, 'whether you *can* make words mean so many different things.' '*The question is*', said Humpty Dumpty, '*Which is to be master—* that's all.'

In *El obsceno pájaro de la noche,* one of the 'masters' is language and there is a process of what I shall call 'literalization' throughout the work. Metaphors and idioms turn themselves into facts and events. The components of the weave of the plot trap the weaver himself like a spider's web that traps the spider, and the very language the narrator uses contributes to his downfall. It should, perhaps, be added that it is by no means the first time that an author has made use of this literalization device. Rafael Sánchez Ferlosio's *Industrias y andanzas de Alfanhuí,* for example, is a work full of what its creator calls 'materialización de la metáfora',[29] and a fascination for the process was what inspired him to write the book in the first place.[30]

In the Donoso novel the user of language (the author) wishes to signify something and makes use of many metaphorical locutions which are apparently innocuous and which in any case are almost unavoidable if he is to express himself at all. The problem is that he finds that language is not doing what he intends it to do, and he is far from being in control. In the same way that his

invented servants have power over their masters, language is stronger than he is, and dangerously so: we are reminded of the arrogance of his character Jerónimo 'que se creía dueño del mundo porque sólo lo inventó' (p. 493). And unlike Sánchez Ferlosio, Donoso is not writing in a lighthearted way. It is all deadly serious. There would be little cause for resentment, perhaps, if it could be claimed that he plays with language and that language then turns out to be one of the forces that play so horrifyingly with him. Indeed, there would be a kind of rough justice there. But that is not how it is: it is far more sinister and unreasonable. Donoso-el Mudito-Humberto merely *uses* language—something as normal as living itself—and in so doing loses his autonomy and security.

We can only speculate as to how conscious Donoso's use of the literalization device is. It is, of course, found with great frequency at levels far inferior to that of good literature, both in jokes and in advertising copy, and the author is undoubtedly aware of it in these contexts. Indeed, at one point in *El obsceno pájaro* we hear about 'precios tan bajos que hay que agacharse' (p. 83). Even jokes, though, can get out of hand.

There is a kind of intermediate group, examples of conscious literalization that although planned produce situations beyond themselves. For instance, the author is clearly aware of what he is doing when the concept of 'the naked truth' is literalized and the Rinconada freaks are not permitted to wear clothes. In fact, his character Emperatriz, in vengeful triumph (since she is jealous of her husband's interest in another), is delighted to note how flat-chested her rival is once she has undressed, and that her husband can now see 'la verdad literalmente desnuda' (p. 480). Then, when el Mudito burns a piece of newspaper that bears a photograph of a 'líder barbudo con su mano en alto', probably Fidel Castro, 'el olor a barbas chamuscadas' is carried away by the breeze (p. 79); the photograph, like the word, is a signifier but it is what is inadvertently signified that intervenes in the action.[31] Furthermore, it is almost certainly intentional that the physical abnormality that afflicts the Rinconada telephone operator who might hear too much is 'orejas enormes como alas de murciélago' (p. 247). But what I have called the intermediate group is not very large; there are relatively few examples where the author is still, as it were, in command, and it is not long before the game can no longer be seen as amusing and it begins to reflect an increasingly speedy decline into total impotence and, in the end, annihilation.

There is, of course, a certain irony in the fact that the protagonist of this novelistic search for survival should be a dumb man. If, as Freud and then Lacan have claimed, verbalization is essential for successful therapy, the presence of danger in both the spoken word and the written word does not suggest a happy outcome. There is yet another indication of a dreadful end to it all in Lacan's theory that 'the unconscious is the sum of the effects of speech on a subject, at the level at which the subject constitutes himself out of the effects of the signifier'.[32] It is appropriate that what is perhaps the most striking example of el Mudito's vulnerability is found when he involuntarily utters one single word, and that word is reported as being 'nada'. Verbalization brings no relief, and what is said could only too well act as a signifier for the subject. He is horrified that he might have betrayed himself, and the word burns his throat: 'Nada, nada, esa palabra delatora que se me había escapado iba quemándome la garganta', he recalls. It is no time at all before we find him with 'fiebre, temblores [y] la garganta hinchada', a condition that would prevent his talking even if he wanted to. 'Imposible tragar con este dolor', he goes on. 'Las papilas de la lengua enrojecidas, el paladar sangriento, la laringe áspera, nada, nada . . .' (p. 87). Another example of prophetic literalization comes when, later in the book, Humberto is alluded to metaphorically as a 'montón de escombros' after he has collapsed over his typewriter (p. 269). This locution truly tempts providence for at the very end, when Humberto-el Mudito's body has been burned, all that is left is ashes and cinders.

Some of the instances of the author's conscious use of the device are reduced similes, some even come from implied similes, though in the second group it is clearly impossible to say just how intentional the technique is. An obvious reduced simile is found when Dora, one of the old women in the *Casa,* is described as being 'inclinada sobre sus rábanos, examinando minuciosamente los tubérculos sangrientos como muñones que las viejas devorarán' (p. 304). This is referred to again later as: 'La Dora y la Rita arrancando muñones ensangrentados' (p. 307). Then Peta Ponce, an old hag who has always haunted the narrator, is said to be 'viva como una hoguera' (p. 471) and ultimately he is destroyed in an *hoguera.* 'Me echas a la calle como a un perro', el Mudito complains to one of the orphan girls, Iris Mateluna (p. 341), as he is 'maniatado y con una correa al cuello guiándome como a un perro' (p. 345); the next stage is that the old women leave plates of food around the *Casa* so that he can eat when he wants to, 'como un perro' (p. 447). There are more references to his being *like* a dog, and it is not long before this becomes the truth: one of the *medallones,* the versions of himself that the narrator gives us, is 'el perro de la Iris' (p. 89). Even if the author is aware as he uses the technique, he is not in command, as is illustrated by el Mudito's musings as he lies convalescing after his major operation: 'Miré la ventana, la calle interminable, fija como la fotografía de algo cotidiano, sin interés, sin belleza, fotografía sacada porque sí, sin propósito . . .' (p. 294). Soon he becomes aware of the 'truth': 'pero la ventana no es ventana, ahora me doy cuenta del engaño, es la ampliación fotográfica de una ventana que han pegado en la pared de adobe' (p. 302); and later he applies this 'knowledge' to his prognosis of Inés's immediate future in the asylum to which she has been taken: 'Despertarás', he says to her, 'en una habitación blanca con una sola ventana que no será ventana sino una gran fotografía que creerás que es ventana de verdad' (p. 470). The author-narrator knows what is happening but he can do nothing about it.

Where implied similes are concerned, it has to be admitted that some may exist only in the mind of the reader; some, though, are clearly intentional. For example, the bars of a hospital bed are, as everyone knows, similar to window bars. Here, 'los cuatro barrotes del pie de la cama no son los barrotes del pie de la cama sino los barrotes de fierro de la ventana', el Mudito discovers, and he adds: 'me tienen prisionero en este cuarto' (p. 279). Less consciously-worked, perhaps, is the text's development of Jerónimo's implied *sangre fría* when he apparently shows great courage during a dangerous skirmish in an election campaign. It turns out that the blood the crowds can see is really cold, since it is not his but Humberto's, and he has deliberately daubed it on his arm. What is not debatable is that all these locutions turn into something unpleasant—even Jerónimo's 'cold blood' is a source of distress to Humberto. When, as el Mudito, he is unable to see because he has been sewn into a sack, the implication is that he is *like* a blind man; it is only a short step to becoming one: 'Me meten adentro del saco. . . . No veo. Soy ciego' (p. 525). When Humberto's father cuts out the review of his son's published book from the newspaper, the implication is that the action resembles a surgical operation: 'Pidiéndole la tijera a mi madre [like a surgeon with a theatre sister] la hincó con crueldad en el papel para recortar ese artículo' (p. 283). This is then underlined when the narrator says: 'Le grité que me estoy muriendo de dolor al estómago desde que usted me pinchó con las tijeras para robarme mi triunfo' (p. 284). Ultimately, of course, the terrible operation materializes: 'Sentí el dolor aquí, en un sitio que ahora está cubierto por capas de algodón y gasa y tela emplástica' (p. 285).

Sometimes the chronology—if one can use the concept in relation to this novel—is reversed, and the 'literal truth' precedes the figure of speech. For example, we are well into the narrative and el Mudito is now weak and ill when Madre Benita comments: 'El Mudito anda como si fuera otra vieja más' (p. 362). Earlier he had actually become an old woman in one of his *medallones:* 'Me permitieron ser la séptima bruja', he tells us (p. 47), and then: 'Soy la séptima vieja' (p. 67). Another instance is when the experience, as it were, of Misiá Raquel and her old servant Brígida being identical and interchangeable comes before the locution that, I suggest, is its source. When recounting that she used to give Brígida all her discarded clothes, Misiá Raquel says: 'Toda mi ropa le quedaba regia porque teníamos el mismo cuerpo' (p. 309). That this is 'true' is underlined (and again this is before the phrase has been uttered) when we discover that her late servant has been buried in Misiá Raquel's family tomb: 'Le cedí mi nicho en el mausoleo', she explains, 'para que ella se vaya pudriendo en mi lugar' (p. 15). 'El mismo cuerpo' indeed.

Interestingly enough, there is another kind of reversal: this time is a question of those few cases where the truth is ironically turned into a metaphor. It is true, for example, even if it is not explicitly stated in the novel, that the shape or form of a child is something inherited from its parents. In **El obsceno pájaro de la noche,** this accepted fact becomes a figure of speech when Humberto says of his father: 'Ansiaba legarme una forma' (p. 99). Then it is 'true' that Jerónimo was not in fact wounded when fleeing from hostile voters, and the implied cliché that his injury was 'nothing' takes on an added dimension: 'Él no se cansaba de insistir en que no era nada' (p. 207). One of the most obvious examples of this particular kind of locution/truth connexion is found in the fact that the protagonist of *any* novel is unreal, an invention that does not really exist and cannot be heard. This is turned into a sort of linguistic game in **El obsceno pájaro;** when someone telephones the *Casa* and asks to speak to Humberto Peñaloza, this is what we find:

> No pudieron hablar con Humberto Peñaloza porque al oír ese nombre huyó por los pasadizos hasta el fondo de la Casa, no existe Humberto Peñaloza, es una invención, no es una persona sino un personaje, nadie puede querer hablar con él porque tienen que saber que es mudo.
>
> (p. 447)

The author, just because he is an author, sets inadvertent linguistic traps for himself; in the same way, living is seen by Donoso as a process of self-destruction. It is so easy for the world to be turned into chaos, for nothing is stable. The house of Azcoitía, in the metaphorical sense of the word, may well fall because of the lack of a male heir. The concept is literalized, or in this case truly materializes, and becomes a real house, the *Casa de Ejercicios Espirituales,* which is going to be demolished. The birth of a child would save the metaphorical house, so a new-born child can save the convent: 'Será dueño de esta Casa. La salvará de la destrucción' (p. 98). When el Mudito's life appears to have been saved, he sees himself as literally conserved: 'Me tendrán para siempre en este conservatorio' (p. 289). When he thinks that Peta Ponce is increasing the speed of the flow of his blood transfusion, he turns red: 'Abre la válvula un poco más, más, mucho, y me enciendo, me pongo rojo' (p. 278). The theory that old women can be dangerous ('el poder de las viejas es

inmenso' (p. 64) and 'no son tan tontas como parecen' (p. 66)) becomes something more than a theory when the old destitute women actually begin to terrorize the neighbourhood, a 'bandada sangrienta', a group of 'pordioseras ancianas quién sabe de dónde' (p. 523). The labyrinthine corridors of the *Casa* in which, metaphorically, one could lose oneself really do swallow people up: there was once a lady who 'un buen día salió a andar por los pasillos y se perdió . . . y nunca más la volvieron a encontrar' (p. 367). (We remember that, implausibly, even Madre Benita has no idea of where el Mudito's cell is.) When Boy wants an inconvenient and painful memory removed from his mind, this turns into a question of an actual surgical operation: 'Tendría que extirpar un trozo grande de su cerebro', the doctor warns him (p. 499). The usual meaning of the verb *servir* is extended when Humberto makes love to Inés: he has become the 'servidor que le estaba sirviendo' (p. 217). The concept of the spiritual Virgin turns into all-too-solid flesh when the old women assume that Iris Mateluna has given birth to a miraculous Christlike baby. When Iris sneezes, one of the *viejas* automatically says: 'Ave María Purísima.' And when the 'baby'—el Mudito sneezes immediately afterwards, she adds: 'Sin pecado concebida' (p. 325). If the rich need the poor as witnesses of their luxurious and fortunate lives, this is soon turned into the literal need on the part of Jerónimo for the power of Humberto's gaze, which Humberto refers to as the 'principio activo de mi mirada' (p. 93).[33] At first it was true that Jerónimo and Inés were not capable, metaphorically speaking, of living 'sin la presencia de [su] mirada envidiosa creando su felicidad' (p. 84); later this is literalized in a situation in which Jerónimo is unable to enjoy sexual intercourse at all without Humberto's presence. 'No salgas de la habitación, Humberto', he says to him when they visit a brothel, 'préstame tu envidia para ser potente.' Then he adds: 'Tú eres dueño de mi potencia . . . necesito tu mirada envidiosa a mi lado para seguir siendo hombre' (p. 227). When Jerónimo was young and leading a somewhat bohemian life, many thought it a good thing for him to enter politics—after all, 'ya tenía edad para hacerlo, asentara por fin cabeza' (p. 178). It is, perhaps, a tenuous connexion, but it is difficult not to recall Jerónimo's later sortie wearing the huge cardboard head belonging to the *Gigante,* another figure of speech brought to life. When Inés grows old, she is not, as they say, herself any more. 'No eres la de antes', el Mudito comments (p. 427), and to him she actually *is* someone else: he accuses her of undergoing surgery so as to change into Peta Ponce 'que siempre quiso encarnarse en ti y tú en ella' (p. 429). Her hysterectomy, if that is what it was, converted her into an old woman overnight: the idea that this operation signifies the end of a woman's youth is literalized. 'Tú . . . te internaste en la clínica del doctor Azula', el Mudito claims, 'para envejecer definitivamente' (p. 428). Earlier, of course, when she was young, Humberto had desired her, had wanted to be her husband; this is made literal when he actually becomes Jerónimo, who is her husband. It is consistent therefore that when he does make love to her, it is after the political skirmish in which he took Jerónimo's place. When Inés says goodbye to him afterwards, he is sure that she knows: 'Me lo dijo sin decírmelo, tú eres él' (p. 215). Yet another example of the device can be found in the early relationship between el Mudito and Iris Mateluna. Sexy and provocative, she disturbs him by her very presence, perhaps even to the point where he is obsessed by her. It is implied that she haunts him, and this is converted into real persecution, which invariably takes place at night: '¿Por qué me seguías? ¿O me perseguías? . . . invadiendo el equilibrio de mi vacío nocturno?', he asks her, as she trails him around the convent (pp. 75-76). Then when el Mudito runs away into the tangle of passages after the telephone call that terrifies him, his motivation is blind terror, so that he really is 'sin vista casi . . . casi sin vista' (p. 448).

Images and expressions connected with the question of identity are fruitful areas for literalization. Humberto, in one of the versions of his life story, was the child of insignificant parents. He is, in other words, one of the faceless masses: 'Mi padre me aseguró', he recalls, 'que no tenía rostro y no era nadie' (p. 433). And, of course, a set of features is essential, as the pressing need to paint them on the 'rostros borrosos' of the broken statuettes of saints found in the Chapel reveals (p. 327).[34] In Humberto's case, facelessness really is his condition when, as el Mudito, he tries to escape from his persecutors: 'Huí solo, al frío, sin facciones ya porque el doctor Azula sólo me dejó el veinte por ciento' (p. 297). The eighty per cent removed by surgery includes his face. Then to be without a name is also turned into a real condition: from not having an important name he moves to not having a name at all.[35] 'Since when have you had a name?' Humberto shouts at his father, slamming the door as he leaves the family home for ever (p. 284). Ultimately he becomes el Mudito, with no name and no means of knowing who he once was. He is a 'sombra sin nombre' (p. 447) and in the end admits that he is searching for (literally) vital information: 'Hay alguien afuera esperándome para decirme mi nombre' (p. 539). The point is underlined by the fact that in the case of another character of lowly birth, Brígida, no one can even remember her surname: the *viejas* argue about it, and her ex-employer, about to endow a home with money that actually belonged to her late servant, is at a loss as to what name to give it: 'La "Institución Brígida . . . Brígida . . .". ¿Va a creer que no me acuerdo ni siquiera de su apellido?' (p. 314).[36] Another haunting truth for the narrator has always been that life is just a game of masks, or assumed social identities. His father once told him this, and he continues to believe it as the years go by. Real disguises, and

especially masks, are the extension of this, and in a sinister way people can adopt another role and deceive their victims. For example the practical, medical masks of doctors and nurses hide their true identities. El Mudito, of course, is sure that he knows who his nurse really is: 'Es ella. Pese a la mascarilla blanca, alzada sobre coturnos, disimulada por la toca . . .' (p. 278); it is Peta Ponce. Later, he says: 'Emperatriz, te reconozco bajo el dominó galante de raso blanco con el que pretendes hacerte pasar por enfermera' (p. 299), for the *monstruos,* too, are 'disfrazados de enfermeros con delantales y con mascarillas que no ocultan sus monstruosidades' (p. 271); our social masks are turned into tangible, dangerous disguises. Humberto's present troubles were caused originally when he committed himself to a particular role: 'Soy escritor', he said to Jerónimo at their first meeting (p. 280), and he has, in a way, given his word and is bound by it. From then on images of binding imprisonment proliferate. In uttering this phrase, he now says: '*me até* a la Rinconada, a Inés, a la Peta, a usted [Jerónimo], a la Casa, a la Madre Benita, a estas figuras blancas del baile que Emperatriz dio hace años: "En el Hospital"' (p. 280). Jerónimo's glove brushed against his arm, this turned into a challenge (pp. 104, 288), and then became a wound, 'quemándome todavía después de tantos años' (p. 104) on the spot where he is injured when he 'becomes' his employer: 'Mil testigos me vieron encogerme con el dolor de la bala que me rozó el brazo justo aquí, Madre Benita, en el lugar donde años antes me había rozado el guante perfecto de don Jerónimo' (pp. 204-05). Now he cannot escape. '¿Me tienen amarrado?', he asks (p. 297), as he had previously asked: '¿Quién sabe cuánto tiempo me tienen amarrado en esta cama?' (p. 289). When he sleeps with Iris in her bed, he is bound up like a baby, so much so that not only is he unable to move, but he is in great pain (p. 338). Lack of identity causes real pain, both here and in the scene when Jerónimo's features dissolve in the reflection in the Rinconada *estanque:*

> Bajo los ojos para ver lo que sé que veré, mis proporciones clásicas, mi pelo blanco, mis facciones despejadas, mi mirada azul, mi mentón partido, pero alguien tira una piedra insidiosa al espejo de agua, triza mi imagen, descompone mi cara, el dolor es insoportable, grito, aúllo, encogido, herido, las facciones destrozadas.
>
> (p. 504)

Lack of control is terrifying. The image of blood in the sense of caste, the source of personality and social class, becomes real as the *monstruos* donate their blood to el Mudito, and he is 'cargado con sus monstruosidades' (p. 292), acquiring their 'caste': 'Me están monstruificando', he cries (p. 271) and there is nothing he can do about it.

Before his total loss of identity, he passes through a phase where it is *as if* he were no one. No notice is taken of him and nobody will come to his aid. His voice, in other words, cannot be heard, and it makes little difference whether he uses language or he is dumb. He is sure that the old women are also conscious of this kind of impotence. They dislike the darkness of the labyrinthine corridors of the *Casa* because once lost 'no se puede encontrar la voz para pedir auxilio' (p. 25). If, as it seems, his dumbness is feigned, then this must mean that he is accepting this terrible possibility for the sake of the anonymity the consequent lack of identity means. Throughout the novel, mutually incompatible attitudes coexist: the need to be someone and the need to live only a *vita minima* for the sake of personal, ontological safety is one of these cases, 'Quiero ser un imbunche', says el Mudito, 'metido adentro del saco de su propia piel' (p. 433), and this becomes the sack into which the *viejas* sew him at the end of his days. The final scene, with the wind carrying away the remains of his identity definitively, is prefigured when he claims that 'el viento se traga mi voz y me deja mudo' (p. 46), and there are repeated affirmations that his voice 'no se oye', for he is too insignificant. The literalization of this statement is found after his major operation: 'El doctor Azula me extirpó la garganta', he says, and 'no quiero gritar porque [this time literally] nadie me oirá' (p. 303). Imitating the fears he once attributed to the *viejas,* he says to Madre Benita: 'Mi voz no se oye en la oscuridad' (p. 316);[37] and of course, it is true that light is needed to read a text!

Many literalizations are found when the narrator is recovering from surgery. In his half-comprehending semiconsciousness he hears the medical staff say they have extirpated 'el ochenta por ciento', and left 'el veinte' (p. 277). He is now literally reduced in size: 'Tiene que ser difícil ver en una cama tan grande como ésta el veinte por ciento a que me dejaron reducido' (p. 297). He is '*reducido* y enclenque, centrado alrededor de [su] mirada' (p. 332), and at one point he declares: 'Soy el Mudito . . . o lo que queda de él, menos y menos cada día' (p. 348). He then begins to get even smaller, and we are reminded of Inés's diminishing hope earlier in the book of ever having a child. The author refers to this as the 'cronología de la desesperación', which was manifested in baby-clothes that were 'disminuyendo de tamaño' (p. 210). El Mudito, once referred to metaphorically as a 'pedazo de hombre', becomes just that on more than one occasion: he is either the *Gigante*'s cardboard head or a phallus. It is very easy to become less than you really are.

Like the dance that goes on until the dancer drops dead in the early Donoso short story 'Charleston', the pretty puppy that turns into a wild animal in 'Santelices',[38] the plastic dog that becomes real in Inés's board game here (p. 418), and all the other interests, pastimes, and desires that get out of hand, to embark upon telling a tale is dangerous. 'You listen to me because you think it is a novel', says el Mudito to Iris, and truth is that it *is* a

novel (p. 341). Characters are created and they take the creator over: 'Estoy en tu poder', he has previously said to Iris (p. 338). And when the demiurge is no longer in control, there can be nothing but disorder, the chaos of the abandoned Estación El Olivo in *El lugar sin límites,*[39] of the Rinconada when Humberto has left, of the *casa de campo* in the novel of that name when the parents leave the children alone, of the *Casa de Ejercicios Espirituales de la Encarnación de la Chimba* when Madre Benita temporarily abandons the inmates. As demiurge-author, Humberto created Jerónimo, who created monsters who, in their turn, control Humberto-el Mudito and the *Casa* (pp. 498-99). Language for the narrator is not neutral, but is one of the innumerable hostile forces that make up existence.

The only solution, apparently, is to be elusive, to attempt to escape from the countless dangers that threaten the individual and his fragile identity. It is here that paradoxes arise. A positive strategy is based on something negative—evasion, inaccessibility. The narrator searches for recognition and individuality while all the time realizing that his only hope of survival is a *vita minima* and anonymity. The text itself struggles on despite a pressing need to finish itself off. There is no escape when all is said and done, and this is one reason why the novel is claustrophobic and haunting, for this is powerfully communicated. On the simplest level, the aim to survive, both on the part of the text and the characters that comprise it, is doomed to failure. The reader's conventional expectation of termination in linear structures and his incapacity to appreciate circular infinity lead to what Frank Kermode has called 'the sense of an ending'.[40] The text, and life, must end; the struggle exists for its own sake. Any attempt at a *vita minima* is also pointless, as the case of Boy incontrovertibly demonstrates: there was never any real hope of keeping him 'en el limbo' (p. 409). Secure anonymity, too, is a state that simply cannot be achieved. A protean existence, a series of metamorphoses, of shifting *medallones,* dumbness, actual disguises, isolation, are all too positive, are all part of the activity of living, however strange that may seem. To live, in however negative a fashion, is to be vulnerable, to be in danger. The portmanteau narrative voice of *El obsceno pájaro de la noche* can be seen as nonexistent in a way, but the fact that it uses language at all gives it enough of a claim to existence to make it a victim. It is made up of language, and language threatens it. Speech is voluntarily rejected, but language still traps its user.

The narrative voice, then, indulges in all kinds of evasive techniques but is doomed to annihilation. Its raw material delivers it up to what it most fears, and ultimately we are no nearer to locating any individual human being who could be seen as the source of that voice. Yet this is surely not the only interpretation of the literalization device. If it is no more than an exercise, a linguistic game, a set of patterns, there remains a great deal that is unexplained and, indeed, inexplicable. A psychoanalytic reading adds something to an understanding of the novel, for without it even the terminology of criticism and the semantic insights that come out of the text are meaningless. How can we discuss fear and panic, the desire to escape, the sense of an ending, of being trapped and being doomed, without the realization that this terminology refers only to human beings? Why have so many critics referred to this book as 'haunting' if there are no contagious human emotions in it? And if there are, what is their source? I suggest that, in more ways than one, they emanate from the real author. The reader's delight and excitement, faced with this book, are based on recognition and sympathy and a *frisson* of fear: they are reactions to a human predicament. There is a narrative voice that is controlled by language, but it is impossible, in my view, not to treat this voice as a person, or at least, as Donoso said, as 'una identidad'. It is also a literary artefact, as those who support the self-referential view claim, but it is worth mentioning that most of these critics find it necessary to treat the narrative voice as a person for what they call tactical reasons. Can it be unworthy of consideration that the novel abounds with semantic examples of lack of control? The reader may suspect that few writers are as much in control as they themselves suppose, but in this case authorial helplessness is striking. The total incapacity of the novel's language to create a single, recognizable person can perhaps be seen as a reflection of the author's much-discussed and unsuccessful search for identity. Ultimately psychological insight comes about as a result of semantic *and* linguistic insight: linguistic insight is not enough on its own to provide answers for the many puzzles of the text or to account for the reader's emotional response to it. One of the accusations made by those who denigrate the psychoanalytic approach is that it makes the false claim that 'the perennial concerns to which literature ostensibly owes its appeal are infantile preoccupations in disguise, and yield their secrets to psychoanalysis alone'.[41] Largely about identity and fear, the Donoso novel certainly does appear to be concerned with these 'infantile preoccupations'. It is a kind of Freudian censored text. If we reject neither approach, we may come closer to understanding why Humberto, or el Mudito, or—in my opinion—Donoso writes: 'Lo que da más miedo de todo [es] que a uno lo persigan y uno se inventa motivos y urde dramas en que protagoniza hechos que jamás ocurrieron para justificar ese miedo . . .' (p. 341).

Notes

1. José Donoso, *El obsceno pájaro de la noche* (Barcelona, 1970). Quotations are taken from the third edition (1972). The epigraph can be found on page 488. Unless otherwise stated, all italics are mine. This article is a revised and extended version of a paper given at the Annual Conference of the Association of Hispanists of Great Britain and Ireland at the University of Manchester, March 1983.

2. Sharon Magnarelli, 'Amidst the Illusory Depths: The First Person Pronoun and *El obsceno pájaro de la noche*', *MLN,* 93 (1978), 267-84. Donoso himself has said: 'Yo no veo que mi novela tenga un narrador. Yo diría que es la novela de la búsqueda de un narrador.' See Mercedes San Martín, 'Entretien avec José Donoso', *Caravelle,* 29 (1977), 195-203 (p. 198).

3. Magnarelli, pp. 267, 268. For Benveniste, see *Problèmes de lingüistique général* (Paris, 1966).

4. Magnarelli, pp. 269, 278, 279, 282.

5. Alfred J. MacAdam, *Modern Latin American Narratives: The Dreams of Reason* (Chicago, 1977), p. 115.

6. Alicia Borinsky, 'Repeticiones y máscaras: *El obsceno pájaro de la noche*', *MLN,* 88 (1973), 281-94.

7. Donald L. Shaw, *Nueva narrativa hispanoamericana* (Madrid, 1981), p. 147.

8. See my '*El obsceno pájaro de la noche:* A Willed Process of Evasion', in *Contemporary Latin American Fiction,* edited by Salvador Bacarisse (Edinburgh, 1980), pp. 18-33.

9. That *El obsceno pájaro de la noche* is indeed one of these cases is confirmed by William Rowe, 'José Donoso: *El obsceno pájaro de la noche* as Test Case for Psychoanalytic Interpretation', *MLR,* 78 (1983), 588-96. He collates personal and literary factors in his opening paragraph, citing the author's real-life psychological problems and the narrator's neurotic and psychotic symptoms in order to justify the choice of this novel for his investigation.

10. See, for example, Frederick Crews, *Out of My System* (New York, 1975): 'Art is not . . . wholly explainable by reference to the troubled minds that made it' (p. 168).

11. Harold Skulsky, 'The Psychoanalytical "Reading" of Literature', *Neophilologus,* 67 (1983), 321-40 (p. 339).

12. Skulsky is quoting from Meredith Anne Skura, *The Literary Use of the Psychoanalytic Process* (New Haven, 1981), p. 152.

13. 'José Donoso', p. 593. Clearly the social cannot be excluded in any psychoanalytic interpretation. Humberto's father's wanting him to be someone is a good example of a concept that contains both social and psychological elements.

14. Steven Knapp and Walter Benn Michaels, 'Against Theory', *Critical Inquiry,* 8 (1981-82), 723-42, argue that 'the whole enterprise of critical theory is misguided and should be abandoned'. What I am suggesting, of course, is that there should not be exclusive adherence to one kind of theory.

15. See the Prologue to Anne Clancier, *Psicoanálisis, literatura, crítica,* translated by María José Arias (Madrid, 1976), p. 24.

16. Charles Mauron, *Introduction à la Psychoanalyse de Mallarmé* (Neuchâtel, 1950), pp. 25-26.

17. Freud expressed this view several times, but particularly in the 'Paper on Applied Psycho-Analysis', *Collected Papers,* IV (London, 1925), pp. 171-472. Another judgement of Freud that is relevant here is that 'writers [have] the courage to give voice to their own unconscious minds' (p. 192). P. D. Juhl, *Interpretation: An Essay in the Philosophy of Literary Criticism* (Princeton, 1980), is convinced that in interpreting any work critics are at the same time necessarily attempting to establish the author's intention (p. 12).

18. Charles Mauron, *Des Métaphores obsédantes au mythe personnel* (Paris, 1962), p. 23.

19. 'The Psychoanalytical "Reading"', p. 331.

20. Emir Rodríguez Monegal, 'José Donoso: La novela como "happening"', *Revista Iberoamericana,* 76-77 (July-December 1971), 517-36 (pp. 520, 521).

21. See, for example, Milagros Sánchez Arnosi's interview with Donoso at the time of the publication of *El jardín de al lado:* 'José Donoso o la búsqueda de la identidad', *Insula,* 416-17 (July-August 1981), 25.

22. José Donoso, *Historia personal del 'boom'* (Barcelona, 1972), p. 33.

23. See José Donoso, 'Cronología', *Cuadernos Hispanoamericanos,* 295 (January 1975), 5-18.

24. R. Luis Díaz Márquez, 'Conversando con José Donoso', *Horizontes,* 19, no. 37 (1975), 5-12. For Laingian connexions in *El obsceno pájaro,* see my 'A Willed Process'. This article was published before I was aware of the Díaz Márquez interview.

25. Rodríguez Monegal, 'José Donoso: La novela como "happening"', p. 527.

26. Rodríguez Monegal, pp. 518, 527, 528, 529 (author's italics), 531, 536.

27. José Donoso, *Cuentos* (Barcelona, 1971), pp. 203-30.

28. Rodríguez Monegal, p. 522 (author's italics).

29. Rafael Sánchez Ferlosio, *Industrias y andanzas de Alfanhuí* (Madrid, 1951). The author's view of 'la materialización de la metáfora' is found on page 23 of the London, 1969 edition. Myrna Solotorovsky, in 'Configuraciones espaciales en *El obsceno pájaro de la noche* de José Donoso', *Bulletin Hispanique,* 82 (1980), 150-88, draws attention to literalization here as a means of expressing 'el pensamiento mítico', as it involves 'la disolución de límites entre lo figurado y lo literal' (p. 180). See too Tzvetan Todorov, 'Poétique', in *Qu'est-ce que le structuralisme?* (Paris, 1968), pp. 98-166, for a discussion of 'littéralité'.

30. There are, in fact, many parallels between *Alfanhuí* and *El obsceno pájaro:* it is not just a question of literalization.

31. Photographs become real again in Donoso's latest book, *Cuatro para Delfina* (Barcelona, 1982). In 'Los habitantes de una ruina inconclusa' (pp. 93-147), the 'hirsutos mendigos y peregrinos con su saco en la espalda y su cayado en la mano' (p. 101) from a book of photographs of pre-Revolution Russia come to life as 'lujosos personajes harapientos del libro de fotos' (p. 138) and invade the comfortable world of a middle-aged Santiago couple.

32. Jacques Lacan, *The Four Fundamental Concepts of Psychoanalysis,* translated by Alan Sheridan (Harmondsworth, 1979), p. 126.

33. Though outside the confines of the present study, a consideration of the motif of the *mirada* in *El obsceno pájaro de la noche* based on the Lacanian view of the *regard* may well prove fruitful. Indeed, many images and other aspects of Donoso's writing could be interpreted in accord with Lacanian theory, even though Rowe does not concede that it provides 'a rationality into which Donoso's text can be fitted' ('José Donoso', p. 591, note).

34. This literalization is also found in *Cuatro para Delfina:* in the last story, 'Jolie Madame' (pp. 211-68), the subjects are the sinister fishermen who live rough on the beach at Cachagua. 'No quiero verte', says the female protagonist when one of them frightens her, and she tells her young daughter to close her eyes to them (pp. 264-65). They turn out to be literally faceless. '¡No tiene cara', she says of one of her potential assailants, 'por eso es que ni él ni los otros la muestran y miran siempre para otro lado!' (p. 262). The danger of the faceless poor on the doorstep is a key image in two of the stories in this book and is the latest manifestation of a preoccupation that can be found in much of Donoso's work, for example in *Casa de campo* (Barcelona, 1978), where the servants are interchangeable and individually unrecogniz-

able even to those who espouse egalitarian causes. See my 'Donoso and Social Commitment: *Casa de campo*', *Bulletin of Hispanic Studies,* 60 (1983), 319-32.

35. As Rowe has noted, Humberto's writing 'was first an attempt to acquire a Name'. This is literalized: 'The hundred copies of his book on Jerónimo's shelves signify to him the repetition of his name thousands of times' ('José Donoso', p. 592).

36. In 'Señas de mala muerte' (*Cuatro para Delfina*) a hitherto retiring nobody, Osvaldo, becomes someone when he discovers that he does indeed have a name and is from an old, monied family. His relationship with his fiancée changes. Now the dominant character, he makes love to her in an almost peremptory fashion and forces her to recognize him: 'Osvaldo la mandó:—Dime cómo me llamo.' After a pause: '—Osvaldo Bermúdez García-Robles—suspiró colmada.' 'Sólo entonces', says Donoso, 'él la besó en la boca . . .' (p. 44).

37. In 'Los habitantes de una ruina inconclusa' (*Cuatro para Delfina*) great emphasis is placed on communication: the hippy who visits the protagonists' house, a *muchacho de mochila,* speaks an incomprehensible language; when he returns some time later, it is only to show his hosts the bloody stump where his tongue once was. There may well be political implications here, as the Russian Revolution is seen as the event that destroyed free speech among the poor.

38. *Cuentos,* pp. 135-50, 255-84.

39. *El lugar sin límites* (Mexico City, 1966).

40. Frank Kermode, *The Sense of an Ending: Studies in the Theory of Fiction* (New York, 1967).

41. Skulsky, 'The Psychoanalytical "Reading"', p. 321.

Philip Swanson (essay date July 1986)

SOURCE: Swanson, Philip. "Structure and Meaning in *La misteriosa desaparición de la marquesita de Loria.*" *Bulletin of Hispanic Studies* 63, no. 3 (July 1986): 247-56.

[*In the following essay, Swanson describes* La misteriosa desaparición de la marquesita de Loria *as a metaphor that masks its complexity.*]

Donoso's seventh novel, *La misteriosa desaparición de la marquesita de Loria,* is at first sight a surprising departure from the author's profound, intellectual outlook. Humberto Rivas sees it merely as 'un divertimiento de

José Donoso', a light-hearted sexual fantasy whose tasteful treatment never threatens 'el tono festivo de toda la narración'.[1] However, as Pérez Blanco has correctly observed, *La marquesita de Loria* 'es mucho más que una novela erótica y galante'.[2] Unfortunately, the latter critic's position is equally limited, for he considers the novel simply to be a reworking of Blest Gana's brand of social realism. Although there is an implicit element of social criticism here, it is little more than a backdrop against which Donoso develops his wider concerns, most notably those concerned with the existential malaise of modern man. The novel can only be properly understood as a metaphor; the superficial exterior hides an inner complexity as great as that of any of Donoso's major works.

This *apparent* simplicity of content is matched by an equally apparent simplicity of style and form. The linear plot, chronological sequences, and standard third person omniscient narration conspire to give the effect of a traditional novel—with all its implications of comfort and order. The gentle nostalgia, the inoffensive eroticism and the element of intrigue also contribute to the impression of a straightforward 'good read'. Indeed, despite the occasional piece of comic exaggeration, the style of the novel is overwhelmingly realistic in tone, in that it presents us with an amusing tale which the reader accepts as true—within the fictional context—and which does not at first appear to question his attitudes too scathingly. This sensation of security is strengthened by the presentation of the story of the marquesita de Loria as a kind of case history, with the author clearly borrowing from the conventions of the detective story. This is evident from the precise nature of the title which also evokes the vocabulary of traditional mystery stories: 'The strange case of . . .'. The documentary style also adds to this sense of being involved in a relaxing, familiar format. This can be seen in the novel's opening line: 'La joven marquesa viuda de Loria, nacida Blanca Arias en Managua, Nicaragua, era . . .'[3] The tone is repeated in the account of Paquito's death:

> Ese invierno andaba mucha difteria por Madrid: falleció dos días después del miércoles de carnaval, Francisco Javier Anacleto Quiñones, marqués de Loria, antes de cumplir los veintiún años, dejando a toda su parentela desconsolada, muy especialmente a su joven viuda—nacida Blanca Arias, hija del recortado diplomático nicaragüense . . .
>
> (40-41)

The feeling of the veracity of the documentary style is reinforced also by a number of minor interventions by the imaginary compiler of this chronicle: 'si queremos ser rigurosos hay que precisar que . . .' (13); 'lo menos que se diga sobre la boda misma, mejor' (31); 'sería demasiado tedioso describir las ocasiones en que . . .' (35); and, with reference to the phantom dog, 'todavía corre por Madrid la leyenda . . . de que . . .' (173).

However, many of these interventions seem to have a tongue-in-cheek quality about them: the allusion to the 'marquesito de Loria, cuyo lamentable fallecimiento . . .' (13); to 'el banquete—si de banquete puede calificarse a tan rústico ágape' (31); to Almanza's vulgar 'retazos de fandangos absolutamente irrepetibles' (155); to the difficulties of today's police-force who 'con las cosas como ahora están, claro, deben preocuparse de problemas más serios' (174); and to phrases like 'Pero no se puede pasar por alto aquella memorable tarde de invierno . . .' (35), or 'Este propósito tuvo el lamentable fin que se conoce' (51). Furthermore, as in *Casa de campo,* Donoso often takes stock narrative styles to their extremes, indulging in a kind of deliberate exaggeration. The artificial language describing the ardour of Blanca's romance with Archibaldo Arenas simply highlights the folly of her fleeting faith in love:

> Lo besó tan prolongada y dulcemente, allí donde estaban, entregada tan sin urgencia a esa caricia elemental, que era como leer sólo el título de un libro del cual se podía inferir algo de su contenido. Tenían toda la vida, volúmenes enteros, por delante: este beso pulsaba el primer resorte del placer que los haría—como lo aseguraban todos los novelistas—vibrar al unísono.
>
> Cuando después de un siglo terminó el dulce beso que parecía haber encendido otra luz en el estudio, Archibaldo y Blanca se enlazaron por la cintura . . .
>
> (123)

A similar effect is achieved by the last five pages of the novel. They comprise a species of post-script or epilogue, a traditional summing-up of the fates of the other characters. Once again, the language is deliberately self-mocking, as, for example, when Donoso writes: 'Y para terminar con otra nota alegre . . .' (197).

Such interventions seem designed to satirize the very style the novel purports to employ: that of the realistic documentary. The point is impressed upon the reader by the blatant intrusion of the author Donoso when he is recounting the chauffeur's reaction to Blanca's disappearance: '. . . montó en el Isotta-Fraschini para ir a toda velocidad al puesto de policía más cercano, donde contó lo que el autor de esta historia acaba de contar en este capítulo y que está a punto de terminar' (193-94). This technique—a constant in *Casa de campo*—is even more shocking here because it appears in such striking isolation. As with Donoso's previous novel, it emphasizes the fact that realism cannot hope to depict reality, for man himself is incapable of comprehending that reality. Thus the novel's simplicity, far from postulating the idea of a structured universe, actually undermines the traditional concept of order by questioning the assumptions on which the novel itself is based.

La marquesita de Loria plainly lacks the '*colle* logique' which Barthes sees as fundamental to the 'readerly' text.[4] The effect of the title is to set forward an enigma: what is the reason for and the nature of the young marchioness' disappearance? The answer is never given in the text (we can only deduce answers via a symbolic analysis). We are faced with an incomplete hermeneutic code, an open-ended enigma. The detective or mystery story format is also broken down: the pleasure of reading such tales usually relies upon a gradual evolution towards the resolution of the puzzle. However, just as Borges' detective stories confront the protagonist with the futility of detection, so too does Donoso deny the reader the comfort and satisfaction of a logical conclusion to his tale. The technique is to dupe the reader into the false security of the realist novel, only to weaken that sense of security by systematically questioning the presuppositions upon which the text itself appears to be based.

This is reflected in the plot itself, which asks more questions than it answers. A cheery account of youthful sexuality gives way to the opaque symbolism of Luna's eyes and the imperspicuity of Blanca's apparent evanescence. This gradual introduction of an abstruse, uncertain motif and the disturbing distortion of the climax—both within a pseudo-realistic context—is even more discomforting than the hallucinatory complexities of *El obsceno pájaro de la noche.* In that novel the reader is plunged into a nightmarish world from the start; in *La marquesita de Loria* the shock is even greater, for the reader is projected from one extreme to the other—he is allowed to experience a sense of order, only to be then confronted by the falsity of that position and faced with the reality of chaos. This tension of opposites is dramatized in the novel's closing pages. The account of the other characters' settled lives may be reassuring, but Donoso stabs at the reader's smugness in the last line: Archibaldo and Charo are always 'seguidos por Luna, su gran y fiel perro gris' (198). This raises all sorts of questions, for Luna, after apparently abandoning his master, faded out of the action at the time of Blanca's disappearance. What is he now doing with Archibaldo? The answer is that we simply do not know. Donoso allows his readers to relax, but only to re-introduce the enigma of the dog on the very last line. We are thus made to close our copies of *La marquesita de Loria* in a mood of confusion and disquiet.

The essential structural principle of the text, then, is to overturn its own internal logic. This results in the creation of an up-down, rising-sinking, ascending-descending pattern. The two poles of this contraposition are, on the one hand, Blanca's symbolic search for fulfilment through materialism and sexuality, and, on the other, her relationship with Luna. The two sides of the antithesis correspond respectively to order and chaos. The fact that the latter movement displaces the former indicates the predominance of chaos.

The sexual quest dominates the novel's development, but its value is consistently neutralized. The first four chapters, after all, are each marked by the shadow of death despite their delineation of Blanca's growing awareness of her physical desire. In the first she is a widow; the second tells of Paquito's death; don Mamerto expires in the third; and his funeral takes place in the fourth. This juxtaposition of death and sexuality invalidates the hope inherent in eroticism. The point is pressed by two important pieces of ironic symbolism. When Paquito and Blanca go to the opera *Lohengrin* in the opening chapter, a relationship is established between the opera's main characters and those of the novel: Paquito is Lohengrin; Blanca is Elsa; Casilda is Ortruda; and Almanza is Telramondo. The association between opera and fictional reality is visible in the mixing of the two levels, as when Paquito ventures a furtive kiss:

> . . . Paquito no pudo resistir la tentación de arriesgarse a besarle el lóbulo. Ortruda se puso de pie con ademán furioso . . .
>
> (21)

The interesting aspect of the parallel though is the one not stated by the author. The chapter ends before we reach the opera's finale: the unhappy outcome of *Lohengrin* is still to come. This foreshadows Paquito's tragic fate, accentuating the hopelessness of the sexual quest. The feeling is reinforced by another symbol—that of Icarus. Paquito is to go to the fancy-dress party dressed as Icarus: but the informed reader knows that Icarus fell to his death when his wings melted—thus the tragedy is hinted at again. Wings are usually symbols of hope (as in **'Gaspard de la nuit'** where the image of the swallow suggests the possibility of transcendence). Here, however, they represent the opposite: 'las malhadadas alas sin estrenar colgaban del respaldo de la silla como la esperanza de algo que jamás se llegaría a cumplir' (49).

The pattern of growing sexual/spiritual desire is further undermined by Donoso's consistent contradiction of our expectations. The first chapter charts the courtship of Blanca and Paquito. Social convention prevents them from attaining total sexual satisfaction, but:

> Se consolaban de que las circunstancias no fueran propicias para pasar más allá diciéndose que era todo un estupendo simulacro para que cuando llegara el momento en que el amor total pudiera atravesarlos, tanto amago realzara lo que sin duda sería un asombroso premio.
>
> (16)

However, the conclusion of this proairetic sequence is never reached.[5] The text suggests that sexual fulfilment will arrive with marriage: but this is not the case. Thus the idea of the deceptive nature of the human construct is embedded in the very structure of the text itself.

The process is continued in the following chapters as the rising-falling / hope-frustration / order-chaos movement is initiated. Chapter 2 starts with the wedding, another stage in the proairetic sequence describing the young couple's relationship. However, there is a twist here: weddings are usually associated with joy, but this chapter begins with the sentence, 'Lo menos que se diga sobre la boda misma, mejor' (31), continuing with an account of the frugality of the reception. The next stage in the sequence is marriage: but again the normal pattern is inverted, for 'el matrimonio, en su sentido más estricto, fue una cruel desilusión para Blanca' (32). Paquito is unable to achieve orgasm and the reader's expectations, raised in the first chapter, are shattered. His death in the same chapter simply underlines the collapse of the upwards sexuality movement.

But despite the demise of both her husband and then don Mamerto, Blanca presses on with her search for sexual fulfilment. The most significant figure in this respect is Archibaldo Arenas. Her affair with him is the novel's most striking portrayal of the sexuality-frustration duality. The couple do not actually make love until Chapter 6: yet Archibaldo has appeared in Chapters 3, 4 and 5, cutting across her previous affairs. The significance of the delay between the two poles of the proairetic sequence (sexual attraction and sexual intercourse) is that it draws the reader's attention to Archibaldo, suggesting that after all her searching Blanca has eventually found, in this man, her passport to fulfilment. Each of the three chapters previous to their erotic encounter systematically puts off the moment of pleasure. Chapter 3 stresses the attraction she feels towards him, but the scene breaks off, heightening the impact of this new stage of increasing sexuality. On the one hand, by changing the thrust of the narrative at this point Donoso plays on the reader's growing sense of sexual excitement: he is forced to wait for further erotic delights and is thus drawn even more deeply into the story. Equally, the suspension of the action throws Archibaldo into higher relief, tricking the reader into believing he holds the answer to Blanca's needs. The process is continued in the next chapter where we are presented with two more significant links in the proairetic code: the first kiss and the arrangement of a time for the consummation of their mutual desire. But again the action is suspended: it is only two chapters later that the meeting takes place. Our expectations are fuelled once more though in Chapter 5, with an account of Blanca's masturbatory fantasies concerning the painter.

However, the technique is again to undermine the reader's assumptions. Despite the thrilling spontaneity of their coition, Archibaldo does not afford Blanca the liberation she seeks. Indeed, she feels let down as soon as she arrives at the flat. After his extensive documentation of Blanca's excitement, the author begins the passage on her visit with the words:

> Fue tan cordial la bienvenida de Archibaldo que Blanca no dejó de sentir cierta desilusión ante la ausencia de un ataque sexual instantáneo . . . La sencilla cortesía del pintor fue tal, en cambio, que hasta llevaba cierto dejo de timidez que Blanca no estaba muy segura si le gustaba o no.
>
> (119)

It transpires that the presentation of Archibaldo is totally ironic. He is not a great painter but a humble portrait artist, a favourite who obtains commissions by ingratiating himself with wealthy, middle-aged, female circles. Despite 'un aparente desorden', his life is determined by an 'estructura interna' (121); he is not a paragon of vitality but an extremely conventional being whose main aspirations in life are marriage and children. By the end of the chapter Blanca already mistrusts Archibaldo; by Chapter 7 she has rejected him completely.

It is her relationship with Archibaldo which forms the axis of the overall rising-falling sexuality/hope pattern. He represents the ultimate hope of the material world: but the novel builds up towards a climax which never materializes. The movement away from order to chaos is then initiated, with Blanca's obsession with Luna becoming the dominant feature of the latter part of the book. Archibaldo is a pivotal figure because he not only signifies the deception of the construct of love—he also provides Luna, the symbolic key to the novel's downward movement.

The arrival of Luna at Blanca's house introduces the thematization of a new hermeneutic code; the enigma is—who sent Luna? Blanca presumes that Archibaldo is responsible. This corresponds to what Barthes would call 'le *leurre*', the snare: Blanca (and perhaps the reader) are tricked by a false assumption. When she arrives at Archibaldo's flat another stage is introduced, 'la *réponse suspendue*': '¿O sería vergüenza por haber dejado escapar el perro? Se propuso no preguntarle nada sobre él: que él se lo explicara todo como parte de su gran amor por ella' (119). However, the final stage of the sequence—'le *dévoilement*, le *déchiffrement*'—does not emerge. When Blanca mentions the word 'Luna', Archibaldo does not respond:

> Pero Archibaldo no reaccionó como esperaba que lo hiciera, lamentándose que se había escapado, al oír la palabra luna. ¿Por qué lo callaba? ¿Qué secreto le escondía? Ella no se lo iba a preguntar. Si la amaba de verdad, entonces él, sin que ella se lo preguntara, tenía que explicarle la inexplicable . . . ausencia de Luna.
>
> (132)

The reader shares Blanca's confusion, for the answer to the enigma is suspended indefinitely: there is no conclusion to the hermeneutic sequence. The effect of this

is to associate Luna with the mysterious, inexplicable forces of chaos, to delineate his independence of his master, and to suggest that he is the answer to Blanca's pursuit of fulfilment.

This final point is reinforced by the general symbolism surrounding Luna; it shows him to be the only valid alternative to Archibaldo and to the sexual/spiritual quest as a whole. Such is the implication of the textual juxtapositions of Chapter 5. Blanca's memories of the previous night's session of sexuality with the Count are constantly interrupted by the barking of a dog, later revealed to be Luna. She turns her thoughts to Archibaldo, masturbating with satisfaction as she contemplates the future with him. However, the lengthy, luxurious crescendo of the prose, paralleling the growth of her sexual desire, is brought to an abrupt halt:

> . . . Archibaldo la esperaba, amante, bello, divertido. Iba a llevarla más allá del simple placer con el fin de que éste fuera completo. Evocando la figura del pintor junto al agua gris-limón del crepúsculo reflejada en sus ojos, Blanca, casi sin moverse, sin tocarse, llegó como nunca antes justo al borde y estaba a punto de zambullirse en el agua de esos ojos cuando los insoportables ladridos se alzaron como una llamarada justo al pie de su ventana, insistentes, dementes, exigentes. Rabiosa, Blanca saltó de su cama y abrió la ventana. Abajo, en la calle oscura, reconoció por entre las rejas una forma animal más oscura que la noche, que caracoleaba y gemía. Dos ojos color gris-limón brillaban mirándola por entre los barrotes.
>
> —Luna . . .—exclamó muy bajo y se escondió tras el postigo.
>
> (102)

The juxtaposition and the climactic build-up suggest that it is not Archibaldo but his dog who will provide fulfilment. This is also the effect of the contrasts within the novel's pattern of eye imagery. As Blanca observes Luna's eyes her urge to masturbate returns:

> . . . ella y Archibaldo eran como dos lunas que eran dos ojos, pero una sola luna, una sola mirada, un solo placer. Quiso incorporar la fantasía de Archibaldo a su juego solitario pero justo en el momento de proponérselo las dos lunas se extinguieron porque el perro las cubrió con sus párpados y ella se quedó dormida hasta la mañana siguiente.
>
> (106)

The play on the contrast in eye imagery is also developed in relation to colour. Early on in the novel, Blanca 'vio que los ojos del pintor no eran en absoluto negros como había creído, sino transparentes, grises o color limón . . . , exactamente del mismo color de los ojos del perro' (77). But when she visits Archibaldo, 'los ojos de ella, tan cerca de los suyos, vieron que los ojos del pintor no eran gris-limón porque se los había enviado de regalo a ella con su perro. Vio, en cambio, sonriéndole, los ojos negros del primer día' (120). Yet the painter does not admit to having sent the dog. Luna thus emerges, not as 'una extensión del espíritu de (Archibaldo)'—as Rivas would have it—, but as a separate entity to his master, the reverse of what his owner represents. The suggestion is again that the goal of Blanca's quest is not the artist but his canine companion. Hence the Marchioness asks of Archibaldo: '¿Quería arrebatarle la fiebre de los pálidos ojos inalterables, con los que fascinaba y luego traicionaba al presentar unos simples, aunque bellos y vivaces ojos negros? . . . ¿Qué podía comprender él de ese perro terrible y maravilloso en cuyas pupilas ella podía hundirse como no podía hundirse en las pupilas negras del pintor ni en ningunas otras?' (166). Archibaldo's eyes soon come to have no meaning for her: 'sintió tal aburrimiento al ver sus negros ojos implorantes a los que faltaba lo esencial' (168).

The text clearly sets forward, via a number of techniques, the idea that Luna offers an alternative to the sexuality of Archibaldo and others. The significance of this alternative is made evident through a series of symbolic interrelationships. The symbol of the dog relates back to that of the yellow bitch in *El obsceno pájaro de la noche.* The opening paragraph of Chapter 8 is an account of the legend of a dog who interrupts the sexual activities of young lovers stationed in their cars in the Retiro—a situation which echoes the yellow bitch motif. In *El obsceno pájaro,* the bitch (through its association with Peta Ponce) represented the intervention of death an chaos in a world of apparent order (sexuality corresponding to the search for meaning and harmony). It is natural to assume therefore that in this novel Luna is also to be associated with the forces of chaos. Blanca's attraction to the dog is symbolic of her growing acceptance of the absurdity of life—a more honest and consequently more satisfying outlook.[6]

Blanca's situation is dramatized by the system of order-versus-chaos symbolism connected with Luna. The dog is repeatedly paired with the recurring motif of the blacks, indians and half-castes of the Caribbean. These women (who read tarot cards and cling to strange superstitions) are typically Donosian characters: outcasts, old women, servants and witches—the very embodiment of chaos. When the dog refuses to leave Blanca alone after an early meeting with Archibaldo, the following exchange takes place:

> —¿Qué te pasa, Luna, corazón?
>
> —Quiere irse contigo.
>
> —¡Pobre . . . !
>
> —¿Por qué lo compadeces?
>
> —Los que se encariñan conmigo, sufren.
>
> Paquito. Don Mamerto. Pero riendo, el pintor la desafió:

> —No éste.
>
> —Podría ser la excepción.
>
> —Podría . . .
>
> —En todo caso, si no sufre uno, sufre el otro.
>
> Eran cosas que le habían dicho las negras . . .
>
> (81)

This passage is of great pivotal importance. By linking the dog and the negresses it suggests that Luna too is an image of chaos. It also implies that in this relationship it will not be Blanca who is the dominant figure but her partner, Luna: chaos will triumph. Yet the bond between the dog and the legends of the Caribbean indicates the preferability of this option. Blanca thinks back to her childhood: 'la carne demasiado hermosa, como la suya, era cuestión de la hechicería, susurraban las oscuras viejas de su infancia en la noche cuando ella era una niña que no podía dormir porque no salía la luna' (85). This ties Blanca to the forces of witchcraft and chaos, intimating that she will suffer a dark, mysterious destiny; equally the double-entendre of the suggestion that 'la luna' brings her calm, infers that the dog Luna will lead her to an inner peace through her acceptance of chaos. Contemplating Luna's eyes after returning to the wreck of her room, she thinks:

> . . . las mestizas de su niñez en las noches de miedo le señalaban las dos lunas idénticas en el horizonte para calmarla. ¿Pero por qué había producido esta hecatombe doméstica, Luna, su Luna, su perro querido a quien, ahora se daba cuenta, había echado de menos durante todo el día, sobre todo a sus ojos suspendidos en el horizonte mismo de su imaginación.
>
> (141-42)

Clearly, she feels drawn towards the salvation these eyes represent. The fact that they are her only hope is made apparent by her earlier thoughts on 'esas dos lunas castas y gemelas que la observaban—una luna muy baja, allá en el cielo junto al horizonte; otra luna reflejada en el caluroso mar del nocturno caribeño, dos lunas que eran una sola—como estos dos ojos que conformaban una sola mirada mirándola sin comprender pero yendo más allá de toda comprensión' (106). The moon and its reflection in the sea appear as two moons but are really one. Similarly, Luna's eyes form a single entity. Unlike the false unity of her relationship with Archibaldo, they offer Blanca a kind of wholeness, totality or fulfilment: the idea that man can only attain completion if he accepts the terrifying reality of a senseless life in an anarchic universe.

The presentation of the quest for order (via sexuality) and its counteraction by chaos (in the form of Luna) is given an extra dimension by the introduction of a general pattern of binary order-versus-chaos symbolism. A series of oppositions are set up between Europe (order) and Latin America (chaos), the most interesting coming at the end of the novel when Blanca abandons the material world to join Luna: despite being in the Retiro, she feels as if she is back 'en la noche vegetada y salvaje como la del trópico' (191). Linking up with this opposition are a number of other binary motifs: rich-versus-poor, masters-versus-servants, adults-versus-children, instinct-versus-convention. This interpenetrating pattern of binary symbolism is an evocative portrayal of the path Blanca takes to freedom, for it simultaneously brings out her desire for order and her progression towards chaos. The duality of the hope-hopelessness movement is summed up in the power-weakness binarism, present here as in Donoso's previous work. The equation between sexuality and strength is made evident in her first two erotic encounters: both Paquito, and don Mamerto in particular, die following their relationships with her. Despite the apparent virility of Almanza and Archibaldo, both men are soon shown to be fawning weakly after her favours (as indeed are Tere and Casilda). However, with Luna the positions change. Blanca feels that 'las heridas y rasguños causados por sus patas y sus dientes le dolían mucho ahora, como si su carne lozana, que en otro tiempo tuvo pretensiones asesinas, comenzara a descomponerse y a morir' (176). Her sexuality has no power over him: hence her reference to 'ese cuerpo al que no podía satisfacer con su sexo capaz de saciar, hasta de matar, a cualquiera' (143). Her attempt to train him is a complete failure, for she is now submissive to him. The dog pins her to the floor but does not rape her: 'los que son verdaderamente dueños de una situación no tienen para qué ser crueles ni despóticos: bastaba tener esos ojos pálidos, quietos' (143). Donoso does not, as Rivas suggests, simply avoid a scene of bestiality so as not to break up the story's jocular tone: this is a climactic illustration of the fact that the key to understanding lies not with sexuality (the hope of spiritual fulfilment) but with Luna (the acknowledgement of the absurdity of life).

The movement towards this final recognition is paralleled by an account of the destruction Luna effects in Blanca's room. This begins in Chapter 5 when the dog urinates and defecates over her splendid furnishings. This is the start of the materialization of Blanca's growing inner sense of chaos. The idea that this chaos offers a form of fulfilment is brought out by a clever double contrast in the next chapter. Blanca returns in a state of confusion after her visit to Archibaldo. Her bewilderment is expressed over several pages, but is set against the peace offered by Luna. Then there is another switch in the tone of the prose, which now goes on to highlight the havoc Luna has wrought in the room:

Y cerró la puerta en las narices de su doncella.

Las dos lunas la miraban desde la oscuridad, desde su nido de raso al pie de la cama. Eran dos nítidas redomas gris-oro, gris-crepúsculo, a esa hora que, en el Re-

tiro, no se sabe si las personas son árboles secos, o figuraciones de la fantasía. Tenían algo de sacramentales esas dos redondelas fijas que le devolvieron la serenidad que hacía media hora creía haber perdido para siempre. Hubiera querido permanecer por el resto de sus días en esa oscuridad, observada por esas dos lunas distintas que constituían una sola mirada. Pero para poder avanzar debía encender.

Cuando lo hizo lanzó un grito. Todo estaba destrozado, la ropa de la cama hecha jirones, las butacas destripadas, las mesas con espejos y cristales derrumbadas, su bata de brocato hecha tirillas, sus chinelas mordisqueadas, chupadas, desfiguradas, era una inmundicia, un mundo cochambroso que nada tenía que ver con ella . . .

(140)

The effect of this double juxtaposition is to suggest, on the one hand, that there *is* an alternative to Archibaldo; and, on the other hand, that that alternative involves an admission of chaos. Meanwhile, the movement towards chaos is accelerated in the next two chapters. The seventh starts with a description of the devastation caused to Blanca's room and to her person. She is now openly referring to 'ese caos' (148), and sees Luna as an 'habitante de la destrucción y el caos y lo desconocido' (164).

As the downward spiral continues Blanca withdraws even further. In Chapter 7 she rejects the possible excitement of an erotic adventure with Almanza and Tere Castillo, and is equally unmoved by their comments on Archibaldo. The accent on her boredom is carried on until she decides to leave, at which point there is another pivotal contrast within the prose:

. . . Cerró la puerta de calle compadeciéndoles, pero, sobre todo, mortalmente aburrida.

Al abrir, en cambio, la puerta de su dormitorio oscuro sintió que su corazón daba tal brinco de sobresalto en su pecho que casi le cortó la respiración: allá estaban los dos ojos como dos lunas nadando en ese infinito espacio oscuro y caliente y aromado.

(162-63)

The suppression of the numerous possible proairetisms between the two stages of the sequence (leaving/arriving) lends greater immediacy and power to the juxtaposition. She has clearly left one side of life behind in favour of another. She becomes more and more disillusioned, retiring from existence further still as she hacks at her once pretty hair and dresses her scarred, bruised body with the simplest and drabbest of garments. The last line of the chapter makes plain her position:

—¡Qué pitorreo!—se dijo al abrir la puerta de su dormitorio que fue tan hermoso en un tiempo y que ahora era esa fétida ruina que la satisfacía.

(170)

This closing line of Chapter 7 reflects the entire structural system of the novel. It contrasts the beauty and elegance of Blanca's life as depicted in the first part of the novel with the accelerating pattern of chaos in the second, emphasizing that this second movement contains her only chance of satisfaction. The quest for fulfilment through wealth and sexuality was based on the principle of hope. The displacement of this movement by an evolution towards union with primeval chaos suggests the idea of an inverted quest: the paradox that chaos brings fulfilment. This is confirmed by yet another contrast in the prose, this time in the final chapter. Casilda offers Blanca both riches and eros:

> Blanca cerró sus muslos porque nada de todo esto le importaba absolutamente nada. Quería ir a ver a Luna.
>
> (184)

Blanca has now completely rejected the artificial structures men impose upon life: she therefore follows Luna into 'la oscuridad total' (189) and disappears forever. The climactic moment of chaos and destruction has arrived; the descending phase of the dualistic pattern has been completed.

The order-chaos (sexuality-Luna) structure of the text, backed up by an interrelating system of corresponding binary symbolism, situates **La marquesita de Loria** firmly within the tradition of Donoso's writing as a whole. Its concentration on eroticism does not make it a surprising departure from his usual vein, as initial reactions to the novel suggested. It lacks the implied optimism of **'Gaspard de la nuit'** and *Casa de campo* (despite the epilogue's grudging acknowledgement of the partial value of the human construct); in many ways it marks a return to the spirit of Donoso's earlier work. But the main difference is in the way the subject matter is treated. The humour, eroticism, directness of style and linear structure hide the basic sense of existential Angst which underlies the novel on a symbolic plane. The anguish is brought out by the author's deliberate overturning of the literary conventions within which he appears to be writing, his main weapons being the neutralization of the story's natural progression towards sexual fulfilment, and the repeated indefinite suspension of the final sequences of the hermeneutic codes. Thus Donoso continues the process of evolution in his writing initiated after *El obsceno pájaro de la noche*. The main achievement of **La marquesita de Loria** is that it goes beyond the conventions of the 'nouveau roman'. The author is no longer attacking the realist tradition by means of an alternative narrative structure: the postboom Donoso is subverting realism from within.

Notes

1. Humberto Rivas, 'Un divertimiento de José Donoso. Una marquesita no encontrada', *La Semana de Bellas Artes*, CLII (29 October 1980), 9.

2. L. Pérez Blanco, 'Acercamiento a una novela de denuncia social. *La misteriosa desaparición dè la marquesita de Loria*', *Revista de Estudios Hispánicos*, (Alabama), XVI, 3 (1982), 399.

3. José Donoso, *La misteriosa desaparición de la marquesita de Loria* (Barcelona: Seix Barral, 1980), 11. All subsequent references will be to this edition and will be included in the main body of the text.

4. Roland Barthes, *S/Z* (Paris: Éditions du Seuil, 1970), 162.

5. The term 'proairetic' is simply used for a series of actions which together form a sequence (e.g. meeting-courtship-marriage-consummation etc.). 'Proairetic' sequences differ from 'hermeneutic' ones in that the latter code refers to the ways in which an enigma is introduced, held in suspense and finally disclosed. The technique of this novel is to break down each type of sequence or to withhold its final link.

6. For a more detailed explanation of the yellow bitch/Peta Ponce motif and of the comments to follow on binary order-versus-chaos symbolism in Donoso's work, see my 'Binary Elements in *El obsceno pájaro de la noche*', *Revista de Estudios Hispánicos* (Alabama), XIX (1985), 101-16.

José Donoso and Amalia Pereira (interview date July-December 1987)

SOURCE: Donoso, José, and Amalia Pereira. "Interview with José Donoso." *Latin American Literary Review* 15, no. 30 (July-December 1987): 57-67.

[*In the following interview, Donoso talks about such topics as his literary education, changes in his literary techniques, other Latin American writers, and his attitudes toward exile and toward the political situation in Chile.*]

The following interview was conducted at [the home of José Donoso] in Santiago on August 4, 1986.

[*Amalia Peroira*]: *Some of your earliest stories, such as* **"The Poisoned Pastries"** *and* **"The Blue Woman,"** *were written in English when you were a student at Princeton University. Being a very young man, how were you affected by this immersion in the North American intellectual and cultural world?*

[José Donoso]: Well, for me it was really the English world that I became immersed in when I came to study at Princeton. I studied English literature, and I also did read some American literature; for one thing I was introduced to Henry James, for example. But I was most impressed with the sensation that "this was the real thing," and that I was a part of it. I studied with great scholars, and I felt involved in the original thing; in contrast, in Chile my studies had always seemed like the shadow of all this. It was a very exciting time. . . .

Many important Chilean writers have spent long periods of their literary careers outside of Chile. (Neruda, Mistral, Huidobro, Donoso, for example). Do you think there are any common reasons or circumstances that impelled these writers to practice their profession abroad?

The most common reason, naturally, is the political reason. In the case of, for example, the English Romantics like Byron, Shelley, Keats, the reason, though not precisely political, had to do with the dissatisfaction with the social life and customs of the age, don't you think? In the case of Byron, especially, enamored as he was with the libertarian ideals of the epoch. Later on, in the Twenties, let's say, there was a sensation among writers of the need to go abroad; among the Latin Americans who went to Paris, for example, there were Huidobro and Rubén Darío. There was a need for a sense of perspective on their own countries. A need for a more cultured, more complicated world, a world more culturally complex.

Do you mean something similar to wanting to be immersed in "the real thing"?

I'm not sure if that's true in the case of Rubén Darío, for example, because he did not have that sensation that we had of living with copies. Modernism grabbed hold of him, the idea of modernism, after reading Verlaine and the other writers of that circle. He read them for the first time when he was here in Chile.

What constants do you see in Latin-American narrative, starting with the so-called literary "boom" up until today?

Well, quite a number of things. A grandiosity of concepts, in the first place, and a need to experiment. . . . These are novels about identification, about the exploration of identity: the problem is one of identity, a search for national identity and for personal identity is behind all of them.

In your book **A Personal History of the "Boom"***, you mention various Latin-American women writers as members of the literary boom of the 60's and 70's. Why haven't these writers reached the high level of recognition that some of the male writers have attained? (Beatriz Guido, Sara Gallardo, M. Aguirre)*

Simply for socio-economic reasons, I would say. Most of these women have not been solvent enough to really practice writing as a profession; being married and having children must make it difficult.

Do you mean that the women writers don't receive the same editorial support?

No, they all have that. There is no one that I know of that does not have editorial support. But they themselves, the events of daily life swallow them. The women, I mean. In addition, they don't have the training, the habit of working as a writer. They are somewhat bourgeois, these women that I am talking about, they belong to the upper middle classes; and since most of the women of the upper classes do not have the habit of working, they never get beyond a certain point.

So writing is sort of a "pastime" for these women?

Right, an adornment, something ornamental. They themselves do not take themselves seriously.

What did you feel with the death of Borges?

Well, the disappearance of a friend, in the first place. I knew him rather well. And, well, what can one feel in the face of the death of a man who has more than completed his life? He had completed his life both in terms of age and in terms of his profession. Borges did not lack anything. He was a friend, and I felt the pain and sadness that comes with the disappearance of a friend, and the sadness at the disappearance of the most prophetic writer in Latin-American literature, to be sure.

You discovered Borges when you were quite young, didn't you?

Not so young. But Borges was totally unknown then. In my youth I read an Argentinian writer who was at that time much more famous than Borges, a contemporary of his, a writer called Eduardo Mallea. I adored Eduardo Mallea, really; I liked his books very much. I discovered Borges ten years later.

Today there are many people who say they know his work, but I don't know if they have really read his books, or they just know the name.

It is true, yes, Borges' name has an enormous magic.

You lived your childhood and adolescence in Chile. What influence do your memories of these first stages of your life have in your work?

They are very important. Let us say that it is like the great stewpot from which all the broths of my creation issue. The memories, the sorrows, the frustrations of that age, the joys—they are all materials which transformed, become the idiom of literature.

Did you keep a diary, or are these just remembrances?

No, just memories. My diary begins only in 1958.

You once commented in an interview: "My experience has been very limited by my emotions and my tastes." What relation does this observation of yours have with one of the most characteristic traits of your work, the experimentation with masks and disguises, both real and symbolic?

Well, there you have a desire to broaden one's scope of action, one's scope of knowledge and vitality. One desires to live more lives, everyone desires to live more than one life. And so, these five-minute masks, which are, as you say, imaginary or real, are always symbols of the multiplication of lives, and consequently, of the multiplication of death.

The publication of **Casa de Campo** [**A House in the Country**] *signified a new stage in the recognition of your work in the U.S. Now there are two principal points of reference for those that study your works:* **The Obscene Bird of the Night** *and* **A House in the Country.** *What developments have there been in your work between and including these two novels?*

I see my work as something I am much more conscious of. At times **The Obscene Bird of the Night** was for me a way of becoming aware of the form of what I was doing. I do not mean that I was not conscious of the form that I was taking with my writing—this is already clear in **A Place Without Boundaries** mainly, and also in **Este Domingo** [**This Sunday**]. But most certainly, in **The Obscene Bird of the Night,** the form becomes part of the narrative itself. The form is the argument, let us say.

Something like in Ulysses?

Right. This coincides with the most intense moment in novelistic experimentation in Latin America. All of the writers of that time are experimenting with the form of the novel, and I include myself a bit in that.

Was that a conscious decision on your part?

Oh yes, by all means. Each one of us knew what we were doing. In the ten years that follow, between one novel and the next, there occurs a change of form, of aesthetic intentions in my writing, basically because what is so evident in **The Obscene Bird of the Night** no longer exists; that is, a sense of disquietude towards human existence with respect to the existence of the novel. In my earlier novels, these elements balance and unbalance themselves; they create and destroy, and then once again recreate themselves and each other. This process comes to its solution—I resolve it, let us say—in **The Obscene Bird.** Afterwards, my novels become much more even and level, "planar," if you will, until **A House in the Country,** in which once again I reflect upon the form "Novel."

The way in which you ponder this issue in **A House in the Country** *differs from that in* **The Obscene Bird.**

Yes, they do differ markedly; I would say that my approach to this problem in **The Obscene Bird of the Night** is a modernist approach, while the form this approach takes in **A House in the Country** is a postmodernist one.

You write a great deal about the Chilean upper middle class. And, as a Chilean professor once commented to me, you really drag them through the mud. (Laughter) Do you think that the people of the Chilean high society read your books, and if they do, what must they think of the ways in which you represent the bourgeois class?

I couldn't care less. (Laughter)

After living abroad for seventeen years, has your perception of Chile changed in the six years that you have been back?

Yes, it has changed a great deal. Before returning to Chile, I did not believe that we had the ability to degenerate as much as we have degenerated. We have fallen so low, and in a way so iniquitous, that I did not believe we were capable of it. No, I had never imagined such abject faculties as existing among the Chileans, such as I have seen now. Something like the betrayal of judicial power, for example, which is one thing the Chileans have done that I simply cannot grasp inside my head. I still have not been able to metabolize this.

Do you think that you or your writing have become "Chilenized" in some way after living here these past six years?

Yes, but I hope that my work has not become limited, that it has not been "Chilenized" in the sense of becoming limited. I hope that it has remained universal.

What was it like for you to collaborate with the theatre group ICTUS in the theatrical production that they did of your story, "Sueños de mala muerte" ["**Dreams of a Bad Death**"]?

It was one of the most marvelous experiences that I have had in this country. I think that writers in general lack the experience of working in a group, of having colleagues. Being a writer is a very solitary profession. Working with the theatre group was wonderful in the sense that I felt companionship, and in the sense that I always had a job to go to, with other people, and with continuous feedback. It was an excellent experience.

Have you given this experience as advice to other writers?

(Laughs) I do not think that solutions can be passed along; I think that solutions are totally personal, unique.

It is not usual for you to be referred to as a writer who utilizes folkloric concepts in your work. Nonetheless, a variety of popular and folkloric Chilean symbols can be found in your novels. What conception do you have, not necessarily as a writer, of the Chilean people and their folklore?

I know very little about Chilean folklore. I know it inasmuch as it was told to me by the servants in my house when I was a small boy. I do not know the Chilean commonfolk, almost. I am familiar with the upper middle class, with the intellectual class and with the servants' class. Therefore, my contact with the commonfolk has always been through the servants; the servants are the ones who related the folkloric stories to me. In general, the servants here are originally from the country, and they are brought to Santiago by their employers. These women were the ones who told me about these things. It has something to do with becoming emotionally close to them. The memories I have are very affectionate, very loving. These stories are surrounded by a world of affection for me.

Do you have memories of spending time in the country, of going to a summer house?

Yes, my family spent the summers in the country, near a place called Talca, where my family is from. We have had property there since the colonial period. Not that we still have it; it has been sold off through the years. But we did have land there, and that's where we would summer, in the houses of my uncles, of my grandparents.

Your novel **A Place Without Boundaries,** *for example, contains many popular, or folkloric symbols, and also themes that have come to be regarded as typically Latin-American, such as the wealthy landowner, the exploitation of the peasant, the "machista" society. This demonstrates a profound understanding of the life of the popular classes.*

Probably so, but it is an understanding absorbed through intuition, let us say . . . through intuition, through "flashes," and not through actual experience. Through poetic transmittance, let us say, more than through information. I could not give you any statistics on Chilean country folk, for example.

What role does the writer, the intellectual, the artist play in today's Chilean society?

I suppose that the answer has to do with preserving some of the human qualities in a world that is purely a struggle for power. It has to do with preserving human qualities such as the faculty for understanding, and for measuring and balancing. The writer's role has to do with conserving pleasure, and knowledge for knowledge's sake.

How does the turbulence that Chile is now experiencing affect the process of writing?

It is impossible to write about anything else. We are all condemned to this. I cannot stand writing about it, but nonetheless I cannot write about anything else. I find myself so completely obsessed by this problem, that I have no other option. May it be damned! But what other option is there?

Can you tell me something about the novel you have just finished writing, **La Desesperanza***?*

La Desesperanza is probably the most realistic of my novels, and the most Chilean. It is a novel that begins during the wake of Matilde Neruda, Pablo Neruda's wife, who died about a year ago. The second part of the novel is about a couple and an excursion they make throughout Santiago during the curfew hours, which ends up at Matilde's funeral. Everything occurs within eighteen hours, and, well, the novel has a sense of great urgency. The novel is significantly committed to the actual situation of the country. I both enjoyed and suffered very much writing it.

You taught at the Iowa Writer's Workshop for two years in the late Sixties. Here in Santiago you have conducted a literary workshop for a number of years. How do these experiences compare?

Here in Chile my classes are very elemental; the students are not widely read, and they have little literary training. In contrast, in the U.S., writing students have made the separation between literature and real life, and they understand very well what they are doing. A literary professionalism exists there. Here that does not exist.

The number of publishing houses in Santiago has recently increased, and it seems that there is increased support for the new generation of Chilean writers. Writers such as Diamela Eltit and Raúl Zurita, for example, receive a fair amount of attention in the press. What is your impression of the new generation of Chilean writers and of the literary world in Chile today?

Well, I find it to be somewhat shabby, if you want the truth of the matter. And this is for one reason: basically because of economic problems. For example, the number of books of short stories that are published in Chile is immense. Thin little books of stories, about eighty pages long, of short little stories. This is certainly an economic problem; the problem is the dismantling of the actual society in Chile, in the sense that people do not have the time nor the money to be able to write something longer, broader. I do not mean that the short story is inferior as a literary form to the novel. But there is something more of a commitment to writing a novel, and that commitment cannot be assumed by writers because of economic reasons, because of a sense of social insecurity. Because of this I think that Chile will remain for a time a country of writers of short story books—fifty pages long, of poetry books thirty pages long, those that can be read in one sitting. It is very sad if one compares this to the very large number of novelists my age who were beginning to write a generation ago. There were really a great number of novelists, and they had an enormous impact on the country. In contrast, there is no one like that now.

Except for Isabel Allende, who must have a great influence on other Chilean writers.

No, not really, she has not become a very significant influence. The problem is that she was a momentary flash; she did not continue, although they say that she is writing something else now.

Who are the young writers that most interest you?

For me, the term "young" is such an ample one (laughs); for me, at sixty, almost everyone is young. There is an Argentine writer that I like, called Juan Carlos Martín; there is a Cuban writer I like called Reinaldo Arenas.

Are you familiar with the works of contemporary North American writers like Alice Walker and Raymond Carver?

Well, of Alice Walker I have read the same work that everyone else has read, *The Color Purple*. I read it a year and a half ago, and it impressed me very much. But it is not a style of writing that I like very much.

Another American writer that I like a great deal is John Edgar Wideman.

John! John! He was a student of mine!

John Edgar Wideman?

Yes, of course! In the Writer's Workshop. Is he very well-known now?

Well, he won the PEN/Faulkner Award in 1985.

Oh, how wonderful! And for what novel?

A wonderful novel called Sent For You Yesterday.

Would you believe that my wife and I always wonder: what happened to John Wideman, has he stopped writing, has he fallen into obscurity? This news you've given me brings me great happiness. He was an intimate friend of ours, intimate, intimate. Adored personage! We have a series of photographs from the last time we were in the United States, of my daughter Pilar with his children. We were looking at them yesterday and wondering, What has happened to our friend John! We commented that, well, we had lost contact with him, like with so many others.

I almost did not mention him because I thought that you would not know his work.

Of course, but he was a personal friend. What wonderful news you have given me!

You have traveled a great deal as part of your profession. What are your sensations when you leave Chile?

To breathe, to breathe, to move, to rejuvenate myself. Chile is a country that ages one, that causes one to age. There exists a great deal of sadness in this moment; I hope that it is not always like this.

What do you miss when you are away from Chile?

Probably that which caused me to escape (laughs). It is a vicious circle, don't you think?

You mean that what you don't like about Chile is also a part of what you are?

Right, exactly. . . .

What do you miss when you are away from Latin America?

The language, of course, the language not only meaning Spanish, but also signifying a series of symbols that come into being through the participation within a culture. There are certain symbols that exist in Latin America that cannot be found outside of the Americas. There is a certain facility for expression, a certain joyousness, a certain ease that you find neither in the U.S. nor in Europe.

There is a significant number of writers, both from Latin America and from other parts of the world, that have been exiled or have self-exiled themselves from their countries for political reasons. What are your impressions of these writers and of the literature that proceeds from political exile?

Well, I think that it is quite necessary for this literature to exist. Political exile is one of the great themes of this generation. I think that it has performed quite brilliantly on various occasions. The elements of blame and nostalgia that are a part of the experience of exile have to make good material for a novel.

It is common for writers in exile to write about their countries even though they cannot return to them.

Sure, notice that all of the well-known novels of the "Boom" were written not in exile, but by writers working outside of their countries. One has only to realize that Mario Vargas Llosa wrote *The City and the Dogs* in Paris, that Cortázar wrote *Hopscotch* in Paris, that García Márquez wrote *One Hundred Years of Solitude* in Mexico; everyone wrote their novels abroad; it was a way of recovering one's birthplace, one's native land, from without.

Have you ever discussed why this was so with any of these writers you've mentioned?

No, no.

You will be going to the U.S. soon for a few months. What do you find attractive about living and writing in the U.S.?

I do not know if I am attracted to living and writing in the U.S.; I like the idea of being in the U.S. for a time. There is something invigorating about the U.S.; it is a country that is not totally obsessed by the political phenomenon; it is a country that enjoys freedom. A country that is obsessed by the political phenomenon is a country that does not enjoy freedom. And here in Chile we are obsessed by the political phenomenon.

So in the U.S. you feel that you can breathe more easily?

Right. I have a sense of freedom. Also, many more things are accessible in the U.S., things that are not accessible here in Chile.

What about the literary world in the U.S.; are you familiar with it?

I know something of the literary world in New York; I know Vonnegut, Sontag, Doctorow. I know John Irving, who was also a student of mine. Some of these people are good friends, but in general, I participate very little in the "literary" life. I don't know why, really; I have never been attracted to the "public" thing. The demands, the exigencies have always been distasteful to me. "To be a Personality!": the Americans call it Personality! I can't stand it; I hate it!

You mean you consider it to be a façade?

Yes, it is so false!

"The Imagination of the Writer and the Imagination of the State": this was the theme of the 1986 PEN Conference. What ideas does this theme provoke for you?

It is a very long and painful theme for one; imagine, writers do not have a place in the actual state of Chile. In Chile today we are peripheral to the system. And so,

of course, all of this is horrible for me. We do not have the right to participate in public life. In the past it was quite to the contrary; one of the characteristics of the Latin-American writer was his tendency to become involved. It was expected of him to take part in public life; the South American writer has always been a tribune. Now this is no longer so, at least in this country in which I live. It seems that it is different in other countries; but here, this is what we have.

What are the greatest satisfactions of being a writer?

Well, it is always the most usual ones, the satisfactions are the most common ones, really: recognition, respect, admiration, money, and being able to earn a living doing what one has a vocation for.

That must bring you a great deal of satisfaction.

It is something very ordinary, if you will, a very modest satisfaction, but it is very fine, after all. The recognition is very good also. I think that one has a right to it. Things become different with age. The satisfactions change; one looks for other satisfactions, don't you think so, different from those one looked for as a young person?

How does one feel when this happens, when things change like this?

It is a part of the evolution of each person. I mean, people adapt to time, to exterior time and to interior time. I think that this is a part of it: it is a pretty phrase, at least! One goes through changes; there is no reason for one to be the same person always. I find myself to be a completely different person from what "I set out to be."

What did you set out to be?

Oh, I set out to be violent, and a rebel, and scandalous. My evolution was, no, things did not turn out badly. . . . What's more, at my age, I can say that all of the objectives change.

Do you think that one gets to know oneself better with age?

Naturally, there is an important element, which is that one's opportunities get more and more limited; the world becomes more limited to a person of greater age. But it becomes limited in terms of breadth, not in terms of depth. That is to say, that which was ample, is transformed into something more profound. Therefore, one no longer has one thousand friends, you see, or calls thirty people, or is intimate with fifty people. One has two, three friends, but these friends are enough, and that is the change. I used to be quite gregarious, very,

very gregarious. I knew all kinds of people. I am still very curious about people, but if you get down to it I am less gregarious. For example, this upcoming trip to the U.S. has me up to here; I don't have any desire to go. I will have to meet people, whom I don't know if I wish to meet. So you see, I am no longer so outgoing.

But that does not mean one loses interest in the people one already knows . . . ?

Not in the people one knows.

. . . or the people one loves. . . .

Or those that one loves, or even new people that one meets. One becomes more choosy, that's all. One wants to have time. . . . And have time more for oneself.

Do you think that you are more aware of time?

Very much so, very much so. How to use it; to use it and not to use it up. To inscribe oneself in time, and not allow it only to pass. To do things without urgency, to look for a harmony.

That's all. . . .

Is that all? Ah, well, it's very short.

Thank you very much.

Thank you. You are very welcome.

Priscilla Meléndez (essay date fall 1987)

SOURCE: Meléndez, Priscilla. "Writing and Reading the Palimpsest: Donoso's *El jardín de al lado*." *Symposium: A Quarterly Journal in Modern Literatures* 41, no. 3 (fall 1987): 200-13.

[*In the following essay, Meléndez discusses the multiple texts and subtexts of* El jardín de al lado.]

To introduce the concept of palimpsest in a technological and computerized era might be perceived as an unnecessary irony or as the sign of reliance on an already exhausted metaphor. But the proliferation of intertexts, both perceptible and veiled, in José Donoso's **El jardín de al lado** (1981) reveals an archaic system, the palimpsest, linked to a process of writing or "publishing." This system functions as a literary metaphor in which the substitution of the object and its referent for one or more other objects and referents does not imply the disappearance of the first set. Although in the medieval practice of "scraping again" the text substituted is not necessarily linked to what it covers, the dialectical implications suggested by the palimpsestic metaphor in

Donoso's novel connect and unmask the multiple covert/overt texts that demand to be read. The recognition of texts over a text is, in essence, an incomplete enterprise, since the established fictive boundaries between them disappear with the identification of each fragment as a single entity. This contradictory phenomenon—boundaries vanish just as they are discovered—leads us to juxtapose the multiple texts and their readings and simultaneously reveals the subordinate nature of both the explicit and implicit discourses. Therefore, within this framework, literary intertextuality becomes a useful notion only if conceived not exclusively as an echo of other texts or as mere sharing of a stock of literary codes and conventions, but as a nonhierarchical interplay of discourses. The illusory discovery of footprints, of ruins, submerges the observer (reader) in a world that has apparently disappeared and upon which new worlds—or texts—have been built or written.[1]

The recognition of a consequent multiplication of texts and subtexts imposed by the palimpsestic metaphor obliges us to heed warnings in Paul de Man's *Allegories of Reading* against the debate that opposes intrinsic to extrinsic criticism, which in formalistic terms states that "form is now a solipsistic category of self-reflection, and the referential meaning is said to be extrinsic."[2] From the standpoint of the inherent plurality implied in the title of the present essay, my concern is the "obligation" of reading and decoding both the superimposed text and the one(s) being removed. That is, I shall be dealing, not with the inside/outside metaphor that de Man seriously questions—although he often has recourse to it—but with the notion of covert and overt writing, which has more to do with a rhetorical development than with a structural one. The relationship between the act of interpretation and the use of the metaphor of the palimpsest suggests a process of elucidation, of revealing something else.

But my goal is not to "translate" into intelligible or familiar language what has been explicitly presented or indirectly concealed, even less to put the overt discourse in the place of the one that remained obscured. It is to expose a proliferation of texts that thematically and formally clash with one another and, in this encounter, to examine their genesis/destruction as linguistic and fictive entities. Nevertheless, the possibility of reading these multiple "manuscripts" that are constantly emerging and simultaneously being substituted presents the reader with a rhetorical dilemma. The metaphorical and/or literal nature of the text's language creates another level of intra- and extra-textual structures that are part of the overt/covert writings. The garden, for example, not only characterizes the proliferation and elusiveness of its meanings but also questions the distinction between what is understood as literal and what is figural. In other words, which one is the "real" garden, who represents the authoritative voice of the text, which novel are we, in any case, reading?

In *El jardín de al lado* the protagonist and narrator, Julio Méndez, is a slightly recognized Chilean writer whose most recent novel has been rejected for publication by the well-known editor from Barcelona, Núria Monclús, although she encourages Julio to revise and rewrite his text. Five of the first six chapters of Donoso's novel consist of Julio's narration of the ordeal of revising his manuscript during a summer in Madrid. Parallel to his need for writing, the other strong force in Julio's life is his wife, Gloria. Fusion and confusion of past and present events transforms Julio's narration of his professional and personal life into an autobiography. But when, in the sixth chapter, we discover that it is Gloria who has written and implicitly narrated the entire preceding text, *El jardín de al lado*'s clear commentary on its self-begetting and fictional nature becomes problematic. What was first taken for Julio's autobiography—Julio's text and narrative voice—turns out to be Gloria's recreation of their survival as writers. This moment of recognition, which coincides with the end of Donoso's novel—and also with that of Gloria's work—invites the reader to look for an alternate and more reliable writing that has been concealed. The act of rereading, either literal or metaphoric, implies substitution of the former interpretative text (where the garden was observed by Julio) for a text where the narrative discourse has been drastically altered and where the point of view (that of the observer of the garden) has been replaced. "Erasing" the first reading to set forth a new interpretation is reminiscent of Julio's painful exercise of rereading and rewriting his rejected text.

Overt thematization of the acts of writing, reading, publishing, and interpreting in *El jardín de al lado* leads us to pose a question similar to the one de Man proposed while trying to "explain" the passage in Proust's *A la Recherche du temps perdu* where Marcel engages in the act of reading a novel: "The question is precisely whether a literary text is *about* that which it describes, represents or states" (p. 57). In his attempt to answer his query, de Man examines the possible coincidence between the meaning read and the meaning stated in the *Recherche*. If, as de Man says, "reading is the metaphor of writing" (p. 68), then *El jardín de al lado* is a clear example of an act of reading both explained and redefined by its counterpart, the act of writing. The process of interpretation becomes, therefore, a paradigm of both reading and writing. De Man's Proust is comparable to Donoso: *El jardín* is a work in which the story-telling and the story-told are intermingled, the meaning read and the meaning stated blend together. Gloria's fictionalization of Julio's political and existential dilemmas documented in his rejected novel reveals the difficulty

of writing about a writing saturated with historical and political overtones. It is Julio-narrator who reproduces part of Núria Monclús' verdict of his novel: "Falta una dimensión más amplia, y, sobre todo, la habilidad para proyectar, más que para describir o analizar, tanto situaciones como personajes de manera que se transformen en metáfora, metáfora válida en sí y no por lo que señala afuera de la literatura, no como crónica de sucesos que todo el mundo conoce y condena, y que por otra parte la gente está comenzando a olvidar. . . ."[3] De Man's concerns for autobiography as a genre—"what is at stake is not only the distance that shelters the author of autobiography from his experience but the possible convergence of aesthetics and of history"[4]—highlight not only the autobiographical connections between Donoso's own life and *El jardín* but, more substantially, Julio's inadequacy to recreate his political experience within his literary creation. On the other hand, to what extent does Gloria's own text succeed or fail to make of her literary discourse a metaphor—something that, as she immediately discovers, Julio is incapable of doing? Can we, as readers of Donoso's novel, recognize our own forgetfulness of historical events that are foreign to our experience, or that, even if experienced, are eventually buried in our memory? Can we describe the ethical/aesthetical dialectic that obsessed Julio and Gloria as an aporia which, in spite of its contradictions, they both try to reconcile in their writings—Julio through overt incorporation and description and Gloria through a false act of rejection?

Julio's "intention" in writing his novel-document (as he alludes to it) is precisely to transform the six days spent in a Chilean jail into what he calls a source of telling, in other words, a discourse. But this enterprise is threatened not only by the course of time (which turns the narration pale and causes it to fade away), but more evidently by the superimposition of other texts, by the invasion of other "experiencias menos transcendentes y más confusas, mezquinas experiencias personales que no me aportaban otra cosa que humilliación . . ." (p. 31). The weakening of Julio's "heroic experience," the weakening of his initial hate produced by the imprisonment, begins to transform itself into a marginal text where the remains and footprints are being replaced by other writings: "todo este cúmulo de vejaciones se había sobreimpreso a aquella experiencia cuya jerarquía yo tan desesperadamente trataba de mantener mediante las páginas de notas que escribía como quien riega una planta moribunda, pero que, ay, al fin se iba secando pese a tanto esfuerzo" (p. 32).[5] It is not until Julio completes the revision of his novel that he is able to criticize his manuscript, recognizing in it the lack of two central aspects of the creative process: "Al avanzar por mi copioso escrito se me fue haciendo indudable que la pasión que pretendía animarlo no era ni convincente como literatura ni válida como experiencia" (p. 114).

As de Man suggests, Marcel's act of reading reconciles imagination and action. Marcel realizes that the sedentary act of reading is powerful enough to recreate the outside world and even to draw a more holistic perception of it. Although in *El jardín de al lado* Julio's ethical conflict between imagination and action is restructured in a different manner, it also dramatizes the confrontation of the inner and the outer worlds (jail-garden) as experienced by the protagonist. Julio's anxiousness to transform his political experience—which is not transcendental—into a transcendental writing is precisely what establishes the parameters and the inevitable failure of his text. But one of the ironic forces of *El jardín* is that Julio not only fails to recreate asthetically his Chilean imprisonment, but also fails to participate, while in self-imposed exile, in an active political life. Gloria constantly accuses him of his ideological "impotency," of his weak liberalism, and describes his "moderate humanism" as pedantic cowardice. Therefore, the emptiness of both his literary work and his own life is filled neither by imagination nor by action. Contrary to Marcel's relationship with the act of reading, neither of these activities is capable of satisfactorily replacing the other. When Julio mentally blames Gloria for living her life in his shadow—that is, through him—he is ironically describing his own pseudoliterary discourse which lies under the shadow of historical facts and, indeed, is eclipsed by Gloria's successful story. In a similar way, the garden translates into metaphor and simultaneously deconstructs its own allegorical meaning, particularly in its dual incarnation of the literal and the metaphorical and of the action and the imagination.

After a long period of procrastination, provoked by his weaknesses, his abuses of drugs and alcohol, his mother's death, his contemplation of the garden, Julio completes the revision of his novel. But his second version is the result of an imprisonment different from the one that inspired the original text. The endless series of dramatic events in Gloria's life—from Julio's refusal to sell the family house after the death of his mother to Bijou's theft of one of Salvatierra's paintings—pushes her to a state of depression, having as one of the consequences her absolute silence, particularly towards Julio. In their own special ways, both Julio and Gloria become convalescents from different "diseases," prisoners of different jails where, as Julio says: "Incomunicada [Gloria], sólo tolera su situación de encarcelamiento dentro de su enfermedad. Pienso en mis seis días de calabozo en Santiago, en lo distinto y en lo igual a esta enfermedad que fueron, y lo igual que son, también, a esto en que se está transformando mi novela" (pp. 208-09). Not by mere coincidence, *El jardín* is divided into six chapters. This fact suggests the possible infinite exchange between the literal and figurative vision of the garden and the six days spent by Julio in jail—a substitution that can even take place in the title. Julio asks

himself: "¿Hubiera podido terminarla sin el silencio de su enfermedad, sin la paz que me ha proporcionado su dolor y su encarcelamiento?" (p. 212). Once his novel is revised and Julio recognizes his wife's symptoms of recovery, he gives his new text to Gloria, whose muteness is now directed only toward him. Gloria's reading is staged, as de Man would have it, in his *Allegories of Reading* in "an inner, sheltered place . . . that has to protect itself against the invasion of an outside world, but that nevertheless has to borrow from this world some of its properties" (p. 59). The jail, in Gloria's text, has become a garden. But the garden turned out to be as oppressive for Gloria as she had intended to make it for Julio. In other words, the metaphorical connotation of the garden has expanded to include both the creation and the creator.

Gloria's reading of the new manuscript—that took place after Julio's revision of his own text—questions the first act of rereading that he experiences, since it suggests that the end result will not only be an act of criticism on her part but also of re-writing. We are forced to ask then: to what extent is Gloria's novel—that is, her writing—the consequence of her reading of Julio's novel? Is her own creation a "revision" of her husband's defective text? Núria's negative response to Julio's novel comes precisely from Julio's inability to "see" his own creation. Since he is incapable of "looking over" his text, his rewriting is as faulty as the first version: "No sé lo que he escrito, ni lo que a mí me ha ocurrido al escribir. No logro verme, ni 'verla'" (p. 211).

But the reader does "see" and recognize the confused causality of the acts of (re)reading and (re)writing in the identities, also confused, of Julio and Gloria. Their marital struggles, where harmony and discord coexist as a single entity and where dissatisfaction with the physical and sexual decadence of the partner's body can only be destroyed by the other's presence, dramatize their battle to reconcile their antagonistic discourses in a single body—or text—as a means of becoming one. Julio repeatedly questions himself about his tendency and Gloria's to invade the other's very being, to deny it by their intrusions: "¿Por qué sólo nos satisface la devoración mutua, el escarbar incansable de uno dentro del otro hasta que no queda ni un rincón turbio ni oscuro ni privado, ni una sola fantasía conservada como algo personal, sin exponerla?" (p. 234). The duality—reading and writing and their repetition—exercised both by Julio and Gloria, represent part of that struggle of identity where there is a confusing relationship between creator and reader. Within this profusion of readings, writings, and interpretations, Gloria raises these acts to the level of themes in her novel and experiences them in her chaotic life:

> Escribí mis quejas en mi diario, tan desgarrador que ahora no me atrevo a releerlo; pero al releerlo entonces

para escarbar mi rencor, y al volver y volver a escribir esas páginas, y darles vueltas y más vueltas, fui como depurándolo todo, en ese tiempo tan largo que las estaciones me han obsequiado junto al Mediterráneo, depurando la imagen de mí misma, la de Julio, la de nuestro matrimonio, hasta darme cuenta de que para que este examen tuviera fuerza de realidad era necesario que yo construyera algo fuera de mí misma, pero que me contuviera, para "verme": un espejo en el cual también se pudieran "ver" otros, un objeto que yo y otros pudiéramos contemplar afuera de nosotros mismos, aunque todo lo mío sea, ahora, en tono menor.

(pp. 252-53)

This is precisely why the famous editor of Latin American fiction, Núria Monclús, is willing to publish Gloria's novel. In opposition to the accomplishments of her text, Gloria realizes that the only footprint left by Julio's manuscript was a vague chronicle of injustice. But is Gloria's success, in any case, the result of her refusal to give Núria access to her diary and in a way risk a rewriting of her text by an "outsider," as they both did to Julio? Or is this not what actually happens when, during a meeting between editor and writer, Núria expresses dissatisfaction with the end of Gloria's novel, and after listening to her narration of Julio's vicissitudes in Tangiers, suggests that this become the end of the novel:

—¡Please do not disturb! ¡Qué irónico final feliz para una novela tan amarga!—dijo [Núria].

—¿Cómo . . . ?

—Bueno, ¿no es éste el capítulo que falta, el que no has escrito . . . ? preguntó Núria Monclús.

(p. 264)

Needless to say, this also happens to be the end of *El jardín de al lado.* Ironically, Núria-(re)reader has provided her own writing; she has imposed her own ending to Gloria's novel. But, is this a metaphor for what the reader of fiction experiences while engaged in the act of (re)reading—that is, the imperative to interpret and rewrite what (s)he is reading? When Núria suggests that Gloria's real challenge is to write a second novel, is she implying that the public's reading of her first text will immediately produce an infinite number of rewriters demanding their active participation in the process of creation?

This "struggle for authority," or even the recognition of it—to use Lucille Kerr's terms[6]—is not limited to the two narrator-writers, Gloria and Julio, who represent the overt powers. But the causal line of development between the act of (re)reading and the need to (re)write unveils the fragility of those powerful overt structures of creation which, ironically, become subject to the strength of other readings and writings, such as Núria's or even our own. The "new" texts discovered do not represent the substitution of the original one, but an interplay of discourses that weakens the entire system of authority, including the authorial figure.

According to Kerr, when we finish reading *El jardín de al lado* and discover Gloria's voice as creator and manipulator of the narration, "we virtually see one image of authority usurp the position of the other: an apparently secondary subject of authority replaces another whose primary position seems to have been authorized and then denied by that very subject who literally follows, but also virtually precedes, him as the 'original' author(ity)" (p. 44). The truth of this statement is subject to an endless process of substitution that is not limited to Julio and to Gloria's manipulations or even to the direct or subtle allusions to Donoso's reality as a Chilean writer, but to the very nature and power of reading and writing. In this case, Donoso is equally subject to the process of substitution, and his text is also threatened by our reading and inevitable rewriting.[7] The ironic overtones of the readers' discovery of Gloria's new position provoke the dismantling of the first reading, where the autobiographical first-person narration becomes a biographical account presented by one of the characters of the "former" text. Gloria's takeover demands an act of rereading—which for de Man (*Allegories,* p. 57) is "a play between a prospective and a retrospective movement" (p. 57)—an act of revising not the truth or falseness of the overt and covert texts, but their rhetorical structures. As already implied, Gloria's literary account is also subject to a process of dismantling and reconstruction.

To decode the layers of rhetorical structures that a plurality of narrations—through the proliferation of readings and writings—imposes on the text, has been one of my tasks. Let us turn now to the recurrent trope of the garden. The first allusion to the duke's garden, which is next to Salvatierra's apartment, is immediately diverted to a different garden populated by other flora and by other figures:

Mientras Gloria termina de abrir la cortina me levanto de la cama y miro: sí, un jardín. . . . Florecillas inidentificables brotan a la sombra de las ramas. . . . Ramas de un jardín de otro hemisferio, jardín muy distinto a este pequeño parque aristocrático, porque aquélla era sombra de paltos y araucarias y naranjos y magnolios, y sin embargo esta sombra es igual a aquélla, que rodea de silencio esta casa en que en este mismo momento mi madre agoniza.

(p. 65)

Julio's memories of his Chilean house and its inhabitants (his dying mother, his dead father, his German-speaking niece, himself as a youth) come forth through the presence of an immediate and physical space already mentioned in the title. In addition, the fusion, confusion, and multiplication of gardens and feelings remind the reader of a parallel proliferation of texts and narrative voices in *El jardín.* But this frantic reproduction of spaces and referents ironically creates a sense of oppression, isolation, claustrophobia, which is reflected in Julio's perception of the outside world through various windows or, as he later says, "desde mi ventana chileno-madrileña de exilado" (p. 144). As a space of enclosure, the garden is where Julio's historical past, his political experience, and his imaginative world clash to recreate the linguistic and narrative paradox of the text.[8]

When Monika Pinell de Bray, that is, "la condesita," leaves with her family for the traditional summer vacation out of Madrid (their departure also coincides with the death of Julio's mother), Julio experiences a profound emptiness as he faces the deserted garden. His new enigma is how and with what he should fill the empty space. Surprisingly, what comes to Julio's mind is Marcelo Chiriboga's poetics of writing: "Al fin y al cabo uno no escribe con el propósito de decir algo, sino para saber qué quiere decir y para qué y para quiénes" (p. 159). The uninhabited garden, in Julio's words, is available now for a luminous inquisition; he is now "free" to write his own text—his own garden.

The garden represents the linguistic and narrative paradox of the text. Throughout the novel, this particular space is destroyed as a single unit while its various expressions become the paradigm of the emerging texts already conceived in the palimpsestic metaphor. In other words, the literal and metaphorical presence of the garden also works as a mirror image of the figural and literal meanings of the multiple overt and covert texts. Within this rhetorical distinction, what has to be taken into account is that *El jardín,* with all its linguistic and literary images—above all, the garden—is inherently metaphorical and its literal dimension impresses us also as a metaphor. The notions of reading and writing—an overt theme in Donoso's novel—compel Gloria and Julio (characters, writers, narrators) and us as readers, to engage in a process in which both of these activities are challenged by their own repetition. Rereading and rewriting endlessly multiply those subtexts that we have been in search of through the medieval practice of "scraping again." The text's deconstruction of its own writing is achieved in the infinite replacement and flow of previous writings that show no hierarchical bounds but which have been rhetorically concealed.

De Man's allusion to the traditional meaning of the metaphor sheds light on *El jardín*'s ultimate expression of the palimpsestic structure: "Conceptualization, conceived as an exchange or substitution of properties on the basis of resemblance, corresponds exactly to the classical definition of metaphor as it appears in the theories of rhetoric from Aristotle to Roman Jakobson" (*Allegories,* p. 146). The exchange or substitution that

takes place in the act of conceptualizing, of metaphorizing, leads the reader to ascertain Julio's strong desire to become someone else (Bijou, Pato, Gloria, Chiriboga, or the "guapo-feo"), to possess other people's bodies, discourses, identity, as he simultaneously erases his own decadent codes and footprints, which had traced his failure as a writer, a father, a husband, and as a political activist. Julio suddenly discovers the meaning of his attraction for Bijou: "De repente comprendí . . . que no era tan sexual mi atracción por Bijou sino otra cosa, un deseo de apropiarme de su cuerpo, de *ser* él, de adjudicarme sus códigos y apetitos, mi hambre por meterme dentro de la piel de Bijou era mi deseo de que mi dolor fuera otro, otros que yo no conocía o había olvidado; en todo caso, no mi código tiránico ni los dolores que me tenían deshecho . . ." (p. 84).

Julio's desire for transmutation is not only dramatized by his obsessive desire to become a Cortázar and write a *Rayuela* for Gloria, or to possess García Márquez or Vargas Llosa's literary discourse. It is in Julio's last chapter as narrator that the reader is confronted with his almost insane willingness to get lost in a jungle of unintelligible codes, which, in the eyes of a Westerner, are represented by the enigmas of the Arab world. Julio's desire for anonymity is not provoked by his fame as a writer but, ironically, by his endless failures. As he constantly suggests, his disappearance alone will guarantee freedom from his unsuccessful life. But is the need for transformation a way of searching for another mask, for another disguising source, or is it an act of unmasking that is indirectly linked to the activity and nature of literature?

His eagerness to unfold himself and experience a mental and physical metamorphosis reaches its highest point when, on a Tangiers street, he glimpses a scene in which a beggar is lying beside a rubbish dump and is accompanied by a naked one-year-old child who is feeding (his father?) with garbage: "Envidia: quiero ser ese hombre, meterme dentro de su piel enfermiza y de su hambre para así no tener esperanza de nada ni temer nada, eliminar sobre todo este temor al mandato de la historia de mi ser y mi cultura, que es el de confesar esta noche misma—o dentro de un plazo de quince días—la complejidad de mi derrota . . ." (p. 239). Julio goes a step further and even contemplates the possibility of killing the beggar. He recreates the scene: while he exchanges his breath and soul with the dead man, they also exchange their identities, allowing Julio to walk away from himself. The garden—in all its forms— and Tangiers are the two spaces in which signs are deprived of their traditional meaning and values: the former by the juxtaposition of past experiences with an unreadable present (the duke's garden with all its characters), and the latter by cultural differences. Who is Núria Monclús or Marcelo Chiriboga, Julio asks himself, in a space ruled by a completely different set of codes? Parallel to the unexpected narrative transition from the fifth to the sixth chapter in *El jardín de al lado,* which demands a rereading and reinterpretation of signs and "messages," the mysterious gardens and the indecipherable happenings at Tangiers challenge the reader to retune his/her reading codes or habits.

Similarly, the narrative, psychological, and existential unmasking that characterizes Julio's discourse can be compared with his claim for physical transformation. Julio's writing tries arduously to detach itself from bourgeois codes and Western standards as a way, among other things, of challenging the "boom" writers. But as readers watch Julio disappear from the scene, witness Gloria's takeover, and later discover her husband's return to the hotel at Tangiers, they realize that Julio's search for otherness has also been a failure. What he seems incapable of appreciating is that one of the effective ways to become someone else (a metaphor of himself) is achieved through writing. Even Gloria's success does not come without pain and a certain fear of experiencing that same transformation that she will later embrace with determination: "Tuve la certeza, en esos minutos que siguieron a su desaparición del hotel, que no volvería a ver a Julio nunca más. . . . ¿En qué se transformaría Julio? ¿En ese mendigo que ni siquiera sé si vio, tirado a la puerta de una mezquita, mientras yo me transformaba en una señora latinoamericana, sola y madura, dedicada a traducir o a los telares en Sitges?" (p. 260).

The profound irony of *El jardín de al lado* is that Gloria, the writer of Julio's desire for transformation, is ultimately the one who experiences metamorphosis. As the creator of Julio's narrative voice, she (to some extent out of envy) impersonates his discourse, codes and sufferings, but only to free herself from anonymity. She happens to be the observer, the *reader* of the next-door garden which, as she suggests at the end, inspired the *writing* of her novel. As I have been stressing, the proliferation of intra- and extra-textual readers, narrators, and writers in *El jardín* and their constant exchange of roles not only creates a flow of texts within texts demanding to be read but also gives language a sense of otherness, where a frequent transformation toward aesthetic discourse takes place: the garden is framed through the image of the window; Gloria becomes the perfect "Odalisca de Ingres"; Bijou the *angelo musicante;* and Monica Pinell "la Brancusi."

Because *El jardín de al lado*'s main concern is the dialectic between reading and writing and the endless repetition of these two acts, the characters' explicit discussion of the ethical/aesthetical question in relation to both art and their own lives cannot be ignored. For example, it is Julio, himself, who poses the ethical/aesthetic conflict at the beginning of the novel: "¿Por qué—me preguntaba cada vez que hablaba con él [Pancho Salvatierra], cada vez que veía su casa o su pintura—, por qué Pancho tenía la terrible virtud de replantearme el problema, que yo ya daba por resuelto, de la relación entre arte y ética?" (p. 18). In Pancho's world—by contrast with Julio's philosophical views of art and life—things lack history, purpose, and even future (p. 15). And it is in this absence that the antagonism between Pancho's art and Adriazola's becomes even more evident. The tension between Adriazola's weekly murals, permeated with propaganda against political and social injustice, and Pancho's lack of compromise represents one of Julio's moral conflicts. Julio's attachment to his political experience in Chile hinders his writing. But, ironically, when Gloria confronts him with his lack of political commitment, he indirectly associates himself with Pancho's perception of art and life: "No nací para héroe, ni siquiera para tener razón, lo que puede señalarme como un ser limitado y comodón, pero qué le voy a hacer: es lo que soy. Después de todo lo que ha pasado, es muy duro darse cuenta que me interesa más la música de piano del romanticismo y las novelas de Laurence Sterne que tener razón en cualquier campo que sea" (p. 116). Julio's allusion to Sterne should not go unnoticed, since that eighteenth-century author's art represents one of the most important efforts to break with traditional literary codes. *Tristram Shandy* is an overt exaltation of literariness and of self-conscious fiction that has often been interpreted as a departure from a contextual commitment.

Not by mere coincidence, one of Salvatierra's most discussed paintings in the novel is precisely the one that reproduces a deceptive reality: between the two symmetrical and barred windows of his apartment there is a painting—of the same dimensions as the windows—that reproduces the white curtains of the entire house. Pancho Salvatierra, through his paintings, and, surprisingly, Gloria, through the text that "we" are reading, are perceived by Julio and Núria, respectively, as successful reconcilers of the "dual" scheme of art and ethics. Gloria acknowledges: "Te quiero explicar que yo, como persona, no es que no siga exaltada, políticamente, y sobre todo en relación a Chile. Haría cualquier cosa para que la situación cambiara en mi país. Pero sé que eso es ajeno a la literatura, quiero decir, ajeno por lo menos a mi literatura" (p. 262). Far beyond this confession, what she actually does is closer to what Julio and Núria perceive than it is to her own statement. Gloria's achievement is the incorporation of a political discourse through apparent rejection. That is, her own text about Julio's failure as writer incorporates—through storytelling—those same elements that contributed to his novel's unsuccessful outcome. Although Gloria theoretically pretends to stay away from nonliterary discourse, the reader is constantly exposed to the ideological developments of the protagonist creating, not a contradictory level of expression, but a dynamic relationship between ethics and art.

Within a thematic context the ethical issue is frequently translated into a deep sense of guilt, particularly expressed by Julio. Although he forcefully condemns Bijou's immoral behavior, Julio commits similar crimes. Directed by Bijou, Julio uses a "fixed" phone to call his mother in Chile; he steals Salvatierra's painting the way Bijou stole one sometime before, but with the additional burden that Julio falsifies the object painted, selling it as Gloria's portrait. Directly or indirectly, the idea of fraud is always present: fraud in the political development of Latin America, in Julio and Gloria's marital relations, in the subtle allusions to plagiarism, and even fraud on the part of the narrator-creator, inevitably posing the question of the intrinsic falseness of literature.

But our interest goes beyond strict concern for a moralistic view of ethics, to the multiple texts and subtexts unveiled and substituted, and their demand to be read and deconstructed. The "reconciliation" of ethics and aesthetics that the reader experiences both in Donoso's novel and in Gloria's is not the result of a mere fusion but the claim of each text to be (re)written and (re)read. The act of writing and reading represents the literal and figurative space where the creative process is conceived. But it is simultaneously the space that also generates its own destruction. The reader's perception of Julio's guilty conscience is not so much the recognition of the protagonist's incapacity to write a text that accurately fuses the ethical/aesthetical dialectic, but the realization that Gloria's multiple levels of narration, of writing, and of reading incarnate the ethical demands of a fictional enterprise; that is, to reread and rewrite Donoso's and Gloria's *El jardín de al lado*.

Paul de Man's discussion of the image of the fountain in Proust's *A la Recherche du temps perdu* suggests that the fountain—similar to the garden in *El jardín de al lado*—is not subject to the synthesis of the literal and the figural senses (*Allegories*, p. 71):

> The shimmering of the fountain then becomes a much more disturbing movement, a vibration between truth and error that keeps the two readings from converging. The disjunction between the aesthetically responsive and the rhetorically aware reading, both equally compelling, undoes the pseudo-synthesis of inside and outside, time and space, container and content, part and whole, motion and stasis, self and understanding, writer and reader, metaphor and metonymy, that the text has constructed. It functions like an oxymoron, but since it signals a logical rather than a representational incompatibility, it is in fact an aporia. It designates the irrevocable occurrence of at least two mutually exclusive readings and asserts the impossibility of a true understanding, on the level of the figuration as well as of the themes.
>
> (72)

Beyond de Man's notion of unreadability, both the garden and the novel(s) studied characterize the proliferation of texts and intratexts in which to write, to read

and to narrate about writing, reading, and narrating become the story-telling and the story-told. To write and to read the palimpsest is to rewrite and to reread *El jardín de al lado*.

Notes

1. We can see how Henry James explores a poetics of rereading through the image of replotting the footprints that were "originally" traced. See *The Art of the Novel: Critical Prefaces by Henry James* (1934), foreword R. W. B. Lewis, intro. Richard P. Blackmur (Boston: Northeastern University Press, 1984).

2. Paul de Man, *Allegories of Reading: Figural Language in Rousseau, Nietzsche, Rilke, and Proust* (New Haven: Yale University Press, 1979, p. 4.

3. José Donoso, *El jardín de al lado* (Barcelona: Seix Barral, 1981), p. 29. All subsequent parenthetical page references are to this edition.

4. Paul de Man, "Autobiography as De-facement," *MLN* 94 (1979), p. 919.

5. Another scene where there is an evident exchange and superimposition of texts takes place at the house of a Peruvian movie producer. Julio and Katy are watching slides of the jungle, which are part of an unsuccessful project for a film based on Vargas Llosa's *La casa verde*. Katy diverts Julio's attention from the slides to her own story (confession) of the political assassination of her lover: "A medida que avanzaba el relato de Katy sobreimpuesto al relato del peruano, estas afectaciones se van perdiendo y Katy queda como desnuda, comovida, haciendo un alegato apasionado, certero, en contra del estado policial en que se ha convertido su país" (p. 183). What we see in the end, through the slides of *La casa verde*, are the footprints left by Katy's painful experience, rather than a fictional recreation of another pseudopolitical endeavor.

6. Lucille Kerr, "Authority in Play: José Donoso's *El jardín de al lado*," *Criticism* 25 (1983), pp. 41-65.

7. In his "*El jardín de al lado*: La escritura y el fracaso del éxito," *Revista Iberoamericana* 49 (1983), pp. 249-67, Oscar Montero presents, among other things, an examination of the correlations between Donoso's *Historia personal del "boom"* (1972) and *El jardín*: "Se trata, en cierto modo, de . . . una nueva versión de los hechos en la cual el fracaso del escritor Julio Méndez, cuyos valores literarios recuerdan los del Donoso de *Historia*, corresponde implícitamente al éxito de Donoso según otro modelo del quehacer literario" (pp. 451-52).

8. The reader is constantly reminded of the contrast between the beauty of the garden(s), Chile's political turbulence and Julio's internal storm as an

exile. The images of the garden, the jail and the novel are framed within one space that struggles to contain both the intra- and extra-textual manuscripts that are being written and read.

Alfred J. MacAdam (essay date 1987)

SOURCE: MacAdam, Alfred J. "Countries of the Mind: Literary Space in Joseph Conrad and José Donoso." In *Textual Confrontations: Comparative Readings in Latin American Literature,* pp. 61-87. Chicago: University of Chicago Press, 1987.

[*In the following chapter from his book on comparative literature, MacAdam compares and contrasts Joseph Conrad's* Nostromo *and Donoso's* A House in the Country, *finding in each work a break with literary tradition.*]

[Jorge Luis] Borges begins his 1938 review of *Absalom, Absalom!* by comparing Faulkner to Joseph Conrad:

> I know of two kinds of writer: one whose obsession is verbal procedure, and one whose obsession is the work and passions of men. The former tends to receive the derogatory label "Byzantine" and to be exalted as a "pure artist." The other, more fortunate, has known such laudatory epithets as "profound," "human," "profoundly human," and the flattering abuse of "primal." . . . Among the great novelists, Joseph Conrad was the last, perhaps, who was as interested in the procedures of the novel as in the destiny and personality of his characters. The last, until Faulkner's sensational appearance on the scene.[1]

Borges's association of Conrad with Faulkner reflects the powers of his imagination: In reviewing Faulkner, he looks beyond the southern, regional writer and discovers an artist concerned with both character and the problems of narrative structure. That is, he reminds us that Faulkner is as concerned with technique as he is with his obsessive themes. He then casts about for a parallel and finds Conrad: The mere act tells the critic a great deal about levels of reader response. On the one hand, Borges acknowledges that in the works of both there is the immediate appeal of theme and character, but he points out at the same time that there is another, perhaps more occult dimension to their writing, their modification of their immediate narrative tradition.

Borges has always had an antipathy toward the novel, preferring, when he condescends to speak favorably about extended fictions, what he calls, in his 1940 prologue to Adolfo Bioy Casares's novella *The Invention of Morel,* "the novel of adventures,"[2] fictions that have (according to him) a rigorously organized cause-and-effect plot. His sibylline remarks prod us into speculation: What are the "procedures of the novel" Borges

contrasts in that prologue with the "destiny and personality" of the characters? Except for his insistence in his 1932 essay "Narrative Art and Magic"[3] on the need for unity of plot, Borges goes no further with his "morphology of the novel":

> To my knowledge, no one has yet attempted a history of the forms of the novel, a morphology of the novel. Such a hypothetical and just history would emphasize the name of Wilkie Collins, who inaugurated the curious method of entrusting the narration of a work to the characters; of Robert Browning, whose vast narrative poem, *The Ring and the Book* (1868), details the same crime ten times, through ten months and ten souls; of Joseph Conrad, who at times showed two interlocutors guessing and reconstructing the story of a third. Also— with obvious justice—of William Faulkner.[4]

This is a curious list and a curious aesthetics of the novel, one vaguely based on the idea of the literary text's tendency, as the Russian Formalists would have it, to call attention to its mechanisms, in effect to make the display of its mechanisms a part of its very structure. Collins's *The Moonstone,* Browning's *The Ring and the Book,* and Conrad's *The Secret Agent*—if this is the novel by Conrad to which Borges alludes—are all eccentric works that constitute a parodic commentary on novelistic Realism.

What interests Borges is an author's subtle revolt against tradition and his almost imperceptible challenge to his readers to take note of his experiment. This is why Borges does not include Joyce or Virginia Woolf in the list: Their innovations are blatant attempts to modify both the narrative tradition and the reader's relationship to the text. Borges certainly admires these daring innovators, as his essays on Joyce and Woolf demonstrate, but his personal affinities lie with the kind of writer he includes in the list above, those whose experiments are veiled by an outward adherence to convention.

After 1932, the mature Borges is much more interested in the ironic parody of literary conventions rather than in an avant-garde assault on any literary establishment, as his own fictions prove. What makes Borges a fascinating if idiosyncratic critic is his ability to find aspects of the writers he likes that few critics ever see, for example, the idea that Joseph Conrad is as important a writer in his parodic manipulations of narrative structure as he is in the creation of intense psychological portraits. Borges's assertions about Conrad make us see Conrad in a different light and make us question our received notions about him. This is especially true of *Nostromo* (1904),[5] usually read as a political novel. Eloise Knapp Hay defines *Nostromo* in this way:

> *Nostromo* is primarily a novel of ideas, and its theme (seen especially in the contrast between the materialisms of the idealist Gould and the simple Nostromo)

evolves as a revelation of the logic of ideas in history. With the demise of Martin Decoud, and the ascent of Dr. Monygham in the last part of the novel, however, we mark a rejection—characteristic of Conrad—of ideas, of intellectuality, and an invocation of moral sensibility . . . as the proper guide for political action.[6]

Hay dissects *Nostromo* in order to find the organization of its intellectual structure, but she loses patience with the novel as an aesthetic structure:

> In short, I find that this disorderly presentation (in Part I) of material contributes greatly to the novel's "dramatic impenetrability" (as Morton Dauwen Zabel calls it) and its "hollow" reverberation (F. R. Leavis). It has not the chronological suggestiveness of *Lord Jim,* where the reader need not wonder distractedly for two hundred pages whether his human interest—the only worthy interest in a novel—is to be given anywhere a worthy object.
>
> (p.176)

Hay does not explain what she means by "human interest," but it no doubt has something to do with Borges's second type of writer, the one "whose obsession is the work and passions of men." Hay's dissatisfaction with the first part of *Nostromo* typifies the attitude of most Conrad critics since F. R. Leavis. Hay's reaction and her comparison of *Nostromo*'s "disorderly presentation of materials" with *Lord Jim*'s "chronological suggestiveness" reflect an all-too-common trend in Anglo-American literary criticism: What is unclear or ambiguous is not good. Even if, as Leavis says, *Nostromo* is "one of the great novels of the language,"[7] it is flawed.

There is something unsettling in this mixture of literary criticism and aesthetic evaluation: The critic wants to show the patterns of Conrad's political novels, but she also wants to tell us that *Nostromo* does not meet some unspecified standard. Conrad critics, from Leavis to Hay, have subordinated Conrad's "verbal procedures" to his themes. In doing so they have reawakened the ancient (and false) opposition of form to content; they have, in short, not read Conrad as a novelist but as an essayist. He is "good" when he presents his subjects in an orderly way and he is "bad" when he does not. A reading of *Nostromo* that would take Conrad's "verbal procedures" into account and think of them as consubstantial with his themes is possible.

We see this already in Leavis's essay on Conrad, where he states:

> What doesn't seem to be a commonplace is the way in which the whole book forms a rich and subtle but highly organized pattern. Every detail, character and incident has its significant bearing on the themes and motives of this. The magnificence referred to above addresses the senses, or the sensuous imagination; the pattern is one of moral significance.
>
> (p.232)

Leavis gestures toward the structure of *Nostromo,* but immediately returns to his primary concern, theme. *Nostromo*'s plot does, however, clarify the relationship between theme and structure and shows just how subtle an innovator Conrad is.

Eloise Knapp Hay's remark about *Lord Jim*'s "chronological suggestiveness"—which *Nostromo* certainly lacks—is an unwitting insight. It is precisely Conrad's eccentricity, his being an *outsider,* an interloper in the Western tradition and not a native-born English novelist that we see in the structure of *Nostromo.* He eschews chronology and the progressive view of history that informs the nineteenth-century European novel, and this links him to the parodic literature of twentieth-century Latin America. His attitudes are shared by authors like Alejo Carpentier, García Márquez, and José Donoso,[8] all of whom tamper with our received ideas of history and, like Conrad, invent imaginary lands where they present their theories of history. All of these writers have contributed ironic chapters to the history of literary utopias, especially insofar as utopias are set, as they have been since More, in the Americas.

If we read *Nostromo* as a parodic utopia, we see that "Conrad's supreme triumph in the evocation of exotic life and colour" (Leavis, pp.231-32) is a feat of illusory realism, that the setting holds up a moral mirror to Europe and is not necessarily a recreation of the exotic. We are back on Caliban's island, but it is no longer a theater of marvels; now it is merely the scene of sordid capitalist exploitation.

In *Nostromo,* it is not Prospero's magic but the American millionaire Holroyd (or "holy rood," the grotesque cross of evangelical capitalism) and his money that bring Conrad's imaginary Costaguana out of its pastoral torpor. The precapitalist territory has a history but it is cyclical rather than linear, a history of violence that begins with the Spanish *conquistadores* who discover silver and enslave Indians to mine it. The rule of the Spaniards is broken in the wars of independence, but the ideals of leaders like Simón Bolívar—whose lamentations about the "ungovernable" nature of Spanish America are quoted in *Nostromo* (pt. 2, chap. 5, p.161)—disintegrate during chaotic internecine struggles. Spanish American history after liberation is a series of civil wars in which opposing parties fight merely for power and from which the people receive no benefit. Order in that world is synonymous with control, and violence is the customary method either to maintain control or to overthrow it. The intention of the political idealists in that community is to end the history of cyclical repetition and to create a linear history like that of Europe, a history of evolving institutions.

This idealism in personified in *Nostromo* on the political and the economic levels by José Avellanos and Charles Gould. Both weave elaborate fictions in order to explain their motives: Avellanos, a victim—almost a martyr—of the tyranny of Guzman Bento, is an aristocratic "constitutionalist." Which means, simply, that he is committed to peace at home and to business done in a businesslike way abroad. His thoughts on Costaguanan history are in his book *Fifty Years of Misrule* (or *History of Misrule*—it seems to have both titles), which deals with the government of Guzman Bento.[9] The text tells what was wrong with Costaguana and proposes a plan of action that would at least guarantee domestic tranquility. Conrad never gives the details of don José's ideas on government because he wants them to remain vague. Don José is a pathetic fugure in the novel, a man who sacrifices himself to a shapeless ideal that corresponds in no way to the everyday reality of Costaguana. The reader learns nothing about his ideas except that the current regime gives him "a specific mandate to establish the prosperity of the people on the basis of firm peace at home, and to redeem the national credit by the satisfaction of all just claims abroad" (p. 126). A "firm peace" implies a free hand for repression, just as the order "to redeem the national credit" suggests paying the exorbitant interest rates demanded by international financiers. His only reality, ultimately, is his book, a martyrology written by a martyr; his government is no government, just a benign form of business-as-usual.

Charles Gould, holder of the Gould Concession, the right to work the silver mine that lies at the heart of *Nostromo,* is a more complex figure than don José Avellanos. He inherits the Concession, a kind of albatross, from his father, who urges him to abandon it. But Gould, despite his father's warning or because of it, decides to restart the mining operations halted during Guzman Bento's regime. Why he does this is mysterious, although it may be part of an Oedipal, fathers-against-sons pattern that reappears throughout the text: Gould senior fails at running the mine, so Gould the son may outdo his father and recover his lost dignity. This possibility is barely mentioned in the novel, although in part 1, chapter 6, upon learning of his father's death, Gould remarks that it was the mine that killed him, but that it might not have, "if he had only grappled with it in a proper way!" (p.63).

The posthumous victory of the son is veiled in the kind of pious public spirit that don José Avellanos expresses. Gould senior was a martyr to Latin America's history, which he called "the appalling darkness of intrigue, bloodshed, and crime that hung over the Queen of Continents" (p.81). Conrad readers will instantly react to the word "darkness" in this context, the chaos that lies just under the surface of civilization as we know it, a darkness a militant West seeks to eradicate, although "the benign project of civilizing the dark places of the world becomes the conscious desire to annihilate everything which opposes man's absolute will."[10] Charles

Gould, responding to his father's laments, presents this idealized vision of why he intends to reopen the mine:

> What is wanted here is law, good faith, order, security. Anyone can declaim about these things, but I pin my faith to material interests. Only let the material interests once get a firm footing, and they are bound to impose the conditions on which alone they can continue to exist. That's how your money—making is justified here in the face of lawlessness and disorder. It is justified because the security which it demands must be shared with an oppressed people. A better justice will come afterwards. That's your ray of hope.
>
> (p.81)

Gould clearly envisions himself as a stage in a process: He will bring Costaguana out of its cycles of rebellion and tyranny into the history of evolving institutions. The idea sounds fine, but it involves some questionable actions, especially the subordination of liberty to the security that "money-making" demands and the hint that the "better justice" to come may be indefinitely postponed.

Conrad wonders at what point the "material interests" become an end instead of a means, at what point Gould will become another Kurtz. This is the central issue of the novel, namely, that the subordination of all things to material interests is a form of economic barbarism and that the power that grows out of the accumulation of material wealth is an irresistible temptation. Thus the silver mine that lies at the heart of the text, the reason why international capitalism, personified by the American Holroyd, extends its tentacles to Costaguana, is merely a symbol. It represents material interests, which, when linked to an international market economy, turn even Western history into a struggle for power. The barbarism Gould and Avellanos want to extirpate returns in a different guise: Instead of the cycles of tyranny and revolt, the new history will be the enslavement of all to the ego of one—Holroyd.

Holroyd is the "hidden god" of *Nostromo,* the first cause for whom Charles Gould is the efficient cause. He represents for Conrad a force that transcends both the idea of history as it is in Costaguana's cyclical mode and in the evolutionary mode as it was envisioned by Hegel. He is Marx's notion of capitalism as the progressive concentration of power and wealth in fewer and fewer hands. Holroyd is the United States, carving out an empire in the twentieth century without having to resort to military force. Holroyd knows the history of European colonialism and views it as a lost cause. His assessment of Europe's folly and the ultimate triumph of the United States as a colonial force is one of the most-often quoted passages in *Nostromo:*

> The Costaguana Government shall play its hand for all it's worth—and don't you forget it, Mr. Gould. Now, what is Costaguana? It is the bottomless pit of ten-per-

cent loans and other fool investments. European capital had been flung into it with both hands for years. Not ours, though. We in this country know just about enough to keep indoors when it rains. We can sit and watch. Of course, some day we shall step in. We are bound to. But there's no hurry. Time itself has got to wait on the greatest country in the whole of God's Universe. We shall be giving the word for everything: industry, trade, law, journalism, art, politics, and religion, from Cape Horn clear over to Smith's Sound, and beyond, too, if anything worth taking hold of turns up at the North Pole. And then we shall have the leisure to take in hand the outlying islands and continents of the earth. We shall run the world's business whether the world like it or not. The world can't help it—and neither can we, I guess.

(p.75)

Beyond Holroyd's bravado, there is a notion here that influences the shaping of *Nostromo,* an idea of history that becomes the shape of this book.

Because it uses an imaginary setting and because it subordinates the development of character to the presentation of ideas, *Nostromo* ought to be read as a satiric utopia. Costaguana, even though it is a composite of many Spanish American nineteenth-century republics, is a "no-place," a mirror held up, not to an exotic "other world," but to the prevailing situation of the West. International capitalism, the "material interests" alluded to so often in the text, recognizes no national boundaries. Holroyd is an American who understands the role the United States is destined to play in the coming phase of international "development," but even he recognizes that he is part of a process that has its own ontogeny. Holroyd is a species of "world-historical-figure," the embodiment of the principles he enunciates in the passage quoted above.

At the same time he postulates this deterministic view of history, Conrad argues that individuals can retain some degree of independence. In fact, the human drama of the novel (as opposed to the inhuman or superhuman drama of international capitalism) deals precisely with the notion of fidelity to self. Throughout his writings, Conrad classifies his characters according to their ability to live out the destinies they create—as the writer himself fashions destinies—for themselves: There are the MacWhirrs (*Typhoon*) who are what they do, individuals Conrad admires even if he relegates them to a lower rank, and the Lord Jims, whose relation to their professions is less fixed and who, because of their crises and changes, are more interesting psychologically.

In *Nostromo,* Captain Mitchell is of the MacWhirr type, as is the "Garibaldino," Giorgio Viola, both men of principle who never doubt their principles. Their tenacity enables them to survive, just as their blindness to anything but duty creates an irony: Their angelic perfection makes them fools. The burden of the more psy-

chologically complex characters is being aware of that irony, of experiencing a destructive type of *desenqaño* or loss of illusion. This experience, a major theme of the Spanish-speaking world in the seventeenth century, was originally religious in nature: The "man of the world" would awaken one day to his folly; the scales would fall from his eyes, and he would see the illusions of this world for what they are. He would then fix his sight on salvation and the next world. Conrad's *desengaño* is secular, an existential collapse whose most radical form destroys the skeptic Decoud.

Conrad's characters all need fictions in which to believe because the fiction and the believing—acts both in the sense of actions and in the sense of part-playing—make human life possible. As Alan Sandison says, this fidelity to oneself may be selfish, "but in preserving oneself one is preserving others."[11] This would seem to make Conrad into a precursor of Camus and other Existentialists, and in his concern for the integrity of the self and its continued existence in the face of doubt he does resemble them. This maintenance of the self through an act of will is Romantic in origin, and is one of the most heavily used themes in twentieth-century Western literature, both in tragic and comic plots and in ironic and nonironic narratives.

In *Nostromo,* Conrad subordinates that important theme to a meditation on history, and this subordination explains some of the novel's irony as well as its structure—which so many critics have found faulty. Eloise Knapp Hay's complaints (quoted above) about the "disorderly presentation of material" in part 1 of the novel and the seeming lack of "human interest—the only worthy interest in a novel" represent the general critical verdict on *Nostromo:* It is a great but flawed novel. A demurring point of view might counter that Conrad in all likelihood knew what he was doing when he wrote *Nostromo* and that his methods in part 1 might be a signal to the reader about how he wanted his book to be read.

A much later text, Garcia Máquez's *One Hundred Years of Solitude* (1967), illuminates Conrad's strategy. The first sentence of García Márquez's satiric romance refers to no discerible present moment, and alludes to events already transpired but not yet narrated: "Many years later, before the firing squad, Colonel Aureliano Buendia was to remember the day his father took him to see ice." García Márquez in this way gives the reader "memories" of the future: When an event takes place, it fulfills a prophecy made earlier in the book. The effect is the reduction of the chronological and sequential aspects of the text to a single point, as if the reader could experience the whole text simultaneously in spatial terms instead of bit by bit, in chronological order. The reader thus gets the same perspective on the whole the writer has as he produces the work.

In part 1 of *Nostromo,* "The Silver of the Mine," Conrad deliberately confuses the chronology of his story so that the reader will not know what is happening "now" or has already taken place. In chapter 2, Conrad introduces Captain Mitchell, a man absolutely committed to his work, totally competent and devoid of imagination. As if to contrast the orderly nature of Captain Mitchell with the chaos of Costaguana politics, Conrad tells an anecdote using Mitchell as a point of view: "On a memorable occasion he [Mitchell] had been called upon to save the life of a dictator. . . . Poor Señor Ribiera (such was the dictator's name) had come pelting eighty miles over mountain tracks after the lost battle of Socorro . . ." (p.23). At this point in the novel, the reader can have no idea of the importance of this anecdote nor of its relative position with regard to the "now" in which the narrative is set. What seems a casual anecdote is the climax of the text, the revolution that threatens to bring down the government, take the silver mine away from Gould, and sweep the country back into chaos. As we read "away" from Mitchell's anecdote, we read "towards" it in terms of the work's chronology and in terms of the number of pages we have to read to reach it. The "line" of the narrative, of course, twists in the process into a circle.

Readers of *One Hundred Years of Solitude* will recognize this narrative prestidigitation. They will recall how García Márquez constantly plays with the linear experience of reading by implanting memories of events to come in their minds. The result, both in *Nostromo* and *One Hundred years of Solitude,* is the turning of time into space. Jocelyn Baines defines the effects of Conrad's manipulation of narrative time in this way:

> The effect of these time shifts is almost to abolish time in *Nostromo.* The elimination of progression from one event to another also has the effect of implying that nothing is ever achieved. By the end of the book we are virtually back where we started; it looks as if the future of Costaguana will be very similar to her past.[12]

Nostromo is a desperate text and its desperation reappears in authors like Alejo Carpentier (in his *The Kingdom of this World*) and in García Márquez (in his *One Hundred Years of Solitude*). These writers take Conrad's despair—each clash of wills brings violence and bloodshed—to the point of a deathwish. Both Carpentier and García Márquez conjure up hurricanes (García Márquez's clearly inspired by Carpentier's) to blow their created worlds into oblivion, to turn each of them into a *tabula rasa* where history can be inscribed anew. Conrad, Carpentier, and García Márquez all echo Stephen Dedalus's complaint ("History is a nightmare from which I am trying to awake"), but none succeeds in transforming the nightmare into the utopian dream because all remain faithful to the real evidence of history before them.

It has fallen to José Donoso to take a first step towards accomplishing that task, a step he takes without turning his fiction into a utopia totally disconnected from reality. His *A House in the Country* shows how the cycles of revolution and repression, of the triumph of material interests may be broken: The drama of his text is tragic because his utopia is crushed, but it does inscribe the possibility of a new day, a new history, at least for Spanish America.

Like *Nostromo* and *One Hundred Years of Solitude,* *A House in the Country* is set in an imaginary land, during a vague period when horses have not yet been replaced by automobiles. And like the two earlier texts, *A House in the Country* deals with the colonial situation from the point of view of the *criollos,* those born in the country of European descent, with no Indian or negro ancestors. The *criollo* aspect of *Nostromo* is often overlooked by English and American readers: Charles Gould, while of English "blood," thinks himself a native of Costaguana, with as much right to act in order to change its history as any of its mixed-blood dictators.

A House in the Country also deals with *criollos,* not, like Charles Gould, of English ancestry, but those Conrad describes in *Nostromo* in this way: "the great owners of estates on the plain, grave, courteous, simple men, *caballeros* of pure descent, with small hands and feet, conservative, hospitable, and kind" (p.41). The manners of the Venturas, the *criollo* family Donoso scrutinizes in his novel, do not coincide exactly with Conrad's description, but they nevertheless consider themselves an elite, superior in nature to those around them. Their mere existence is, for them, proof that God himself intended them for their position in the world.

There are myriad Venturas, and their wealth, like that of the Goulds, derives from a mine. But unlike Charles Gould, who imagines himself a transitional figure in Costaguanan history—"material interests" would provide stability, which in turn would cause the people to renounce disorder and misrule—the Venturas are resolute defenders of the status quo. They subscribe to a doctrine similar to the divine right of kings and countenance no questioning of their authority. Thus, while Charles Gould deludes himself into thinking he can use self-interest to better his country, the Venturas believe that material interests and the nation itself exist in order to provide them with an income and servants. In both novels, blind egoism leads to calamity.

Where Conrad and Donoso differ is their attitude towards the dynamics of history. Conrad sees a difference between the first two periods of Costaguanan history, Spanish rule and anarchic independence, as primitive variations of what was to come: The Spanish *conquistadores* work the silver mine with slave labor; during independence, with the mine under English control, it becomes a convenient symbol of foreign intervention and imperialism. In the third phase of Costaguanan history, the mine becomes Costaguana's link to international capitalism, a symbol of the subordination of all human life to material interests. Conrad denounces this situation because it breeds future violence, which will come when the socialists and communists of his final chapter triumph over the Goulds. He is not pleased with this prospect, and the despair in his text results from his not seeing any escape from material interests except violence.

Donoso agrees, but sees this violence as necessary because it would eliminate the very basis of the Venturas' wealth and the subordination of human life to things. The revolution he envisions would abolish private property. This utopian aspect of Donoso's novel is an echo of Don Quijote's discourse to the goatherds (*Don Quijote,* bk. 1, chap. 11), where Don Quijote praises the golden age in which the words "yours" and "mine" did not exist. Cervantes may have intended this speech as a mockery of utopian schemes, but it does evoke the radical critiques of private property made by Christian humanists, especially Thomas More. Donoso's utopian attack on private ownership requires the reader to recall similar attacks made during the eighteenth century by Rousseau, and in the nineteenth century by Pierre Joseph Proudhon, which were later systematized by Marx and Engels. The gold of the mine in *A House in the Country* conjures up golden ages, the idealized past, the utopian present, and the *real* future predicted by Marx and Engels, all golden ages in which, paradoxically, gold would have no value.

Donoso's text chronicles a critical moment in the Ventura family history, one in which their concept of history as repetition and perpetual present suffers a shock. This shock derives precisely from the criticism of private property that has been a constant though subterranean current in Western thought since antiquity, a criticism that seeks, especially in the analysis of Marx and Engels, to prove that private property is a fiction and not a reality. Marx and Engels say that society, ours or the Venturas', is as it is because we assume private property to be a "fact of life":

> Property owners and proletarians evince the same human self-alienation. But the landowners find in this self-alienation their confirmation and their good, their power: In it they have the appearance of human existence. The proletarians feel annihilated in their self-alienation; it they see their impotence and the reality of an inhuman existence.[13]

The Venturas justify their ownership of property by having recourse to tradition. Their ancestors took control of the mine and the natives (Donoso never refers to them as Indians, thus preserving the abstract nature of those oppressed) who work it. The natives turn the gold

they mine into gold leaf, which they give to the Venturas in exchange for goods worth very little relative to the market value of the gold leaf. The Venturas sell the gold leaf to foreigners, transforming it into money and the power it creates. Their defense of this primitive colonialism, aside from their idea that since things have "always" been this way they must be right, is based on a differentiation they make between themselves and the natives.

Tradition says the natives are cannibals—although the Venturas have supposedly purged the active exercise of this vice out of them. Cannibals, according to the "authorities" that lie at the basis of the Spaniards' justification for the conquest of the New World, are not human because human beings, by definition, do not eat their own kind. Since the natives are not human, it is both legal and laudable to enslave them. This postulate, mocked during the Renaissance by Montaigne in his essay on the cannibals, is nothing more than a fiction engendered by the idea of private property. Once private property is taken as a fact it creates its own defenses—the enslavement of supposed cannibals is one example—and these defenses become an ideology and a morality: Since history and tradition support these customs, they must, according to the Venturas, be sanctioned by God himself. Any alteration of them would not only be treason but heresy as well.

Private property thus produces an order, a social structure: The Venturas are the apex and the natives the base of the social triangle. The intermediate classes are composed of two groups, the family servants, who are superior to the natives but who lack individual identity for the Venturas, and the Ventura children, Venturas *in potentia* but not yet Venturas. The servants constitute a private army, whose mission, aside from attending to the needs of the Venturas themselves, is to keep the Ventura children under surveillance. As Lidia, the Ventura who administers the staff, puts it each year in her address to new servants:

> These [children], she assured them in her harangue, were their enemies, intent on their destruction because they wanted to destroy everything stable by their questioning of rules. Let the servants be aware of the brutishness of beings who, because they were still children, had not yet acceded to the illuminated class of their elders, and were capable of anything with their abuse, their disobedience, their filth, their demands, their destruction, attacks, undermining of peace and order by means of criticism and doubt. They were fully capable of annihilating them, the servants, for being the guardians, exactly so, of this civilized order, which was so venerable it defied all criticism. The danger of the children was only inferior to that of the cannibals, of whom it was not impossible that they, the children, ignorant as they were and perhaps in no ill-intentioned way, might even unwittingly be the agents.

(pp. 40-41)

Similar to the children are the in-laws, necessary for the perpetuation of the family but not really part of it; it is an alliance of one in-law, some children, and some natives that threatens the Venturas' "civilized order."

The servants are another kind of threat: As long as they remain servants or serve as a police force to spy upon and keep order among the children, they are mere projections of the Venturas' will. But armed and imbued with a sense of mission, what one of the Venturas calls "the mystical code that has guided our family since time immemorial" (p.269), they do indeed become a menace. When they identify themselves totally with the values of the Venturas, they find they have something they did not have before, an identity and a role in history. The instant they make that discovery the Venturas become expendable because the values they inculcate into their servants are greater than the Venturas themselves. And the moment the Venturas show the slightest weakness or indecision, the servants realize that only they are pure enough to be the keepers of that great tradition.

Donoso's drama, the abortive revolution against personal property, is more obviously allegorical than Conrad's meditation on material interests in *Nostromo*. Conrad deals with the inhuman history of things—the international economy—and how human beings are incorporated into it. Readers expecting to find a human drama (or melodrama) are frustrated because they find a disordered, oblique story whose protagonist dies in an absurd confusion of identity. Donoso alienates his reader in quite a different fashion: He puts his reader on guard from the outset by constantly intervening in the narrative in his own voice just to remind the reader that his book is indeed a fiction. This authorial interruption is related to the concept of personal property at an aesthetic level, but its main effect is to destroy sentimental lines between reader and character, or any notion that *A House in the Country* is a portrait of life.

The allegorical possibilities in *A House in the Country* are immense precisely because Donoso constantly reminds us that the text is a fiction. We can read it, for example, as an allegory on the history of Chile, Donoso's homeland, at the time of the coup against Salvador Allende in 1973. In the novel, the adult Venturas and their servants go off on an excursion and leave their children alone in the huge summer house. The trip is to last a day, but it is extended magically into an entire year. The Venturas' decision to absent themselves could correspond to the free elections that brought Allende to power, a moment in which neither the Venturas (the oligarchic upper classes) nor their servants (the armed forces) chose to intervene in national politics.

Suddenly a leader appears: In the novel this is the supposedly man brother-in-law Adriano Gomara, a physician known for his benevolence towards the natives (the lowest classes). Adriano Gomara emerges as a leader because he can mediate between the various factions that materialize among the Ventura children and the natives. His improvised government collapses because he cannot control the more radical elements within the ranks of the children and natives and because he cannot match the violent repression that takes place when the Venturas send their servants back to the country house to reassert their values and to repossess their property.

The Venturas' attempt to reverse history fails: One of the Ventura children, Malvina, forms an alliance with the foreigners who buy the gold leaf as a first step in taking possession of the mine. The Venturas are doomed, just as the utopian project of Adriano Gomara to forge a society without private property is doomed, but the history is redefined as a linear, irreversible process of change. No system is permanent, not even that of the Venturas. Donoso ultimately resolves nothing. Like Alejo Carpentier and García Márquez he ends his text with a natural disaster, one that wipes out the adult Venturas. The surviving children remain in the summer house while the servants, Malvina, and the foreigners escape to the city. The reader may wonder whether the surviving children will form the nucleus of a revolutionary avant-garde, but Donoso refuses to feed any speculation, rejecting the idea of projecting the novel beyond its limits. This is the chronicle of the fall of the Venturas, but their world, the world of private property, continues to exist without them.

Throughout the text, Donoso struggles against the idea of the representational in literature: His constant intervention in the book, his insistence on speaking as the author and not merely as a narrator, his commentary on the progression of the plot, are all devices he uses to keep the reader from confusing art and life. In the second chapter, Donoso explains to a reader he imagines growing impatient with his authorial interruptions that:

> I do it with the modest goal of suggesting that the reader accept what I write as artifice. When I intervene from time to time in the story, I only do so in order to remind the reader of his distance from the material of this novel, a thing I want to keep as my own object, one I show, display, but never relinquish completely so the reader may confuse his own experience with it. If I succeed in getting the public to accept these authorial manipulations, they will recognize not only that distance but also the fact that the old narrative devices, so discredited these days, may produce results as substantial as those created by conventions dissimulated by "good taste" and its hidden arsenal of tricks.
>
> (p. 53)

Here we see Donoso wrestling with a phantom that has haunted him since his earliest publications, the legacy of Realism. Donoso found his place in the literary tradition by means of parody, especialy the parody of the Chilean novel of *costumbrista* tendency, with its minute depiction of Chilean life. Here he integrates his parodic literary personality with the central theme of his novel, private property. In the passage above he states that he does not, want the reader to identify himself with the characters, but he does not thwart this identification by means of some Brechtian "alienation effect." For Donoso, the traditional novel was aesthetically valid and, moreover, better as fiction than the contemporary novel, the French New Novel for example. That is, the obvious display of devices in a novel by Balzac or Trollope reminds today's readers they are reading a work of art and that they must not allow themselves to rework the text into their own image as they might be tempted to do with the kind of text that invites the reader to be a co-creator or literary accomplice. Donoso is also doing it because he wants to remind the reader that this book belongs to José Donoso.

He expresses the same possessive spirit at the end of the novel, when the narrator explains why it is so difficult for him to end the book:

> It's curious nevertheless—and this is the point I wanted to make—that even though I've made my characters non-psychological, unrealistic, and artificial, I have not been able to avoid connecting myself to them emotionally and to their world, from which it would be as impossible to separate them as it would be to separate, for example, one of Ucello's hunters from his meadow he crosses. In other words, despite my determination not to mix reality and art, it's terribly painful for me to say this farewell, a conflict that takes the literary form of my not wanting to leave them behind without finishing *their* stories—forgetting that they have no more or less of a story than the one I want to give them—instead of settling for finishing *this* story which, in some way I don't fully understand, is, no doubt of it, my own.

(p.492)

After reading these two passages it is impossible not to think of Jorge Luis Borges. The same desire to rebel against the idea that literature is a mirror held up to life, the same desire to make the literary text a work of art that should be enjoyed for itself and not for its fidelity to the real world—even Donoso's use of the word "artifice" reminds us that Borges called the second group of stories in *Ficciones* "Artifices"—all of this delineates the problems involved in being a writer in the twentieth century. Conrad ran great risks in *Nostromo* by constructing a text he knew would confound readers accustomed to nineteenth-century story-telling, readers used to psychologically complex main characters and stereotyped secondary characters. By diverting attention away from character toward structure, Conrad broke with his immediate tradition and revitalized the novel of ideas, whose origins lie in satire.

Donoso's dilemma as a late twentieth-century writer is that he wants to do something similar to what Conrad did—meditate on the relationship between things and people in an imaginary land—but he cannot separate that meditation from a self-conscious contemplation of himself as a writer producing such a text. The example of Milton trying to write an epic poem and feeling obliged to take into account not only the classical and Renaissance epic traditions but also any knowledge even vaguely related to his subject (sunspots for example) comes to mind: The more self-conscious the text becomes, the more complex the materials the artist feels obliged to manipulate grow, and the more the resultant text becomes the writer's projected self-image, his metaphoric autobiography. Like the man Borges describes at the end of *El Hacedor* (The Maker), who proposes to draw a map of the world only to discover after years of labor that he has succeeded in drawing a self-portrait, Donoso (and Borges) finds that he is his text.

The image of Mary Shelley's monster in *Frankenstein; or, the Modern Prometheus*[14] also comes to mind here: Frankenstein is a type for the artist who creates his work of art from the *disjecta membra* of tradition. The final product is not only monstrous, an involuntary caricature—what the Romantic artist always fears he will engender—but a monstrous double of the artist himself. Where the Romantic would attempt to save face by blaming his medium—language—for its incapacity to express his intuitions, the modern artist cannot shift responsibility for the monstrous nature of his text away from himself. The Romantic at least possesses an ego he wishes he could express and communicate to others; the modern writer ambiguously finds his self-justification in the act of writing. His published text is monstrous because it makes many demands on him—aesthetic, political, social—and is simultaneously a mirror in which he sees his own confused self-image.

To publish that self-image is precisely to disconnect it from the self, to send it into the world where, like Frankenstein's monster, it will take on other identities even as it usurps its creator's name. Loss of name is a loss of identity, and personal identity is one kind of personal property Donoso has great difficulty criticizing. This is in fact a theme that reappears throughout Donoso's writing, with great poignancy in ***The Obscene Bird of Night***, where the failed author Humberto Peñaloza vainly tries to recover all the copies of his only book because its mere existence in someone else's library constitutes a loss of identity. Publication as loss of identity is the twentieth century's peculiar and ironic contribution to the *topos* of writing as a means to achieve fame and immortality. For writers like Borges and Donoso, writing is a kind of affliction that ultimately renders the author anonymous.

Thus, the issue of private property has the same value in ***A House in the Country*** that the idea of material interests has in *Nostromo*. The difference lies in the degree of self-consciousness, the degree to which the author of each text wants to put himself as author on display before the reader. *Nostromo* stands at the beginning of the modern tradition because of its deliberate alienation of the reader who comes to the novel hoping to identify with its central character. ***A House in the Country*** continues that tradition of putting the mechanisms of the text on display the better to explore the possibilities of the subject. The example of Thackeray in *Vanity Fair,* with its famous concluding passage about the characters who seem so real being mere puppets the author-narrator now puts back into their box, provides some idea of how venerable this tradition of allegorical novel-writing is.

This is not simply to say that the novel incorporates an earlier satiric or allegorical tradition into itself—even if this is obviously true—but to demonstrate that the tradition of true-to-life characters, the creation of novels in which the reader is invited to identify himself with the characters, while dominant over a long period of the novel's history, is not the only novelistic tradition. At the same time, Donoso's remarks above (pp.82-83) point out that more than verisimilitude is involved in the creation of character: The author takes a proprietary interest in his characters because they are his creation, because in some way they reflect him. This is a different sort of sentimental relationship from that of the reader who identifies himself with a character, but the possessive aspects are the same.

This situation, in which the author asserts his rights over the text, dramatizes the problem of literary meaning. Not only will the author lose his identity through writing but he will also lose exclusive rights over the text, as it becomes a part of the literary tradition, something with its own meaning-producing devices. No matter how much the author-in-the-text may protest, the literary text after publication is no longer his: It becomes part of the tradition and part of every reader's experience. In every way, it resembles the summer house Donoso uses as the center of his novel: The Venturas erected the house as a monument to themselves, to their power. It is surrounded by a fence made of iron lances that separates it from the rest of the world and marks it as personal, private property. When the children, the natives, and Adriano Gomara take control of the house, they take away the fence, symbolically destroying the idea of the house as personal property.

The restoration effected by the servants produces a parody of the earlier situation: Once an object is inserted in time, it becomes part of time and changes. This principle may be applied to society itself as well as to the work of art once it leaves the artist's hands. The author-in-the-text is part of the text: His asides to the reader are part of the text and are therefore public

property. The author, like Frankenstein, possesses his text only as long as he refrains from redacting it; from then on it belongs to no one or anyone.

Like Conrad, Donoso reveals a horrifying reality to us without resolving it in any way. There is no escape from material interests, just as there is no escape from the delusion of personal property or individual identity. Both *Nostromo* and ***A House in the Country*** parody the Realist tradition, which they both admire, but which requires a worldview unacceptable to both. These are not revolutionary novels in the political sense, but they are apocalyptic texts that prefer to announce the death of an old tradition rather than the birth of a new one.

Notes

1. Jorge Luis Borges, *"Absalom, Absalom,"* *Borges: A Reader. A Selection from the Writings of Jorge Luis Borges,* ed. Emir Rodríguez Monegal and Alastair Reid (New York: E. P. Dutton, 1981), p. 93.

2. Jorge Luis Borges, "Prologue to *The Invention of Morel,*" (1940), in *Borges: A Reader,* pp. 122-24.

3. Jorge Luis Borges, "Narrative Art and Magic," in *Borges: A Reader,* pp. 34-38.

4. Jorge Luis Borges, *"The Wild Palms,"* (1939), in *Borges: A Reader,* pp. 93-94.

5. Joseph Conrad, *Nostromo: A Tale of the Seaboard* (Great Britain: Penguin Books, 1967). All quotations are from this edition.

6. Eloise Knapp Hay, *The Political Novels of Joseph Conrad: A Critical Study* (Chicago: University of Chicago Press, 1963), p. 214.

7. F. R. Leavis, *The Great Tradition* (New York: Doubleday, 1954), p. 231.

8. Carpentier in *El recurso del método,* García Márquez in *Cien años de soledad,* and José Donoso in *Casa de campo.* All quotations from *Casa de campo* (*A House in the Country*), are taken from the first edition (Barcelona: Seix Barral, 1978). All translations are mine.

9. José Avellanos's book certainly has a bizarre life (or halflife) within Conrad's novel, as Frederick R. Karl points out: "He [Conrad] actively deceived, saying that for the history of Costaguana he depended on the "History of Fifty Years of Misrule" by the late Don José Avellanos. Conrad's point is truly Borgean: inventing a book within his own book, he then uses his Author's Note to cite it as one of his principal sources. If he had to divulge anything, he would reveal only what he had borrowed from himself! He had, in fact, most definite sources for names, events, and places." This

revelation appears in Karl's biography of Conrad, *Joseph Conrad: The Three Lives* (New York: Farrar, Straus and Giroux, 1979), p. 542. Karl's chapter on *Nostromo* explains Conrad's ambiguous politics as well as his complex loyalties: the Pole, the European, the professional sailor, the artist.

10. J. Hillis Miller, *Poets of Reality: Six Twentieth-Century Writers* (Cambridge: The Belknap Press of Harvard University Press, 1966), p. 6. Hillis Miller is discussing "Heart of Darkness" in the passage quoted, but his ideas apply as well to *Nostromo.*

11. Alan Sandison, *The Wheel of Empire: A Study of the Imperial Idea in Some Late Nineteenth and Early Twentieth-Century Fiction* (London: Macmillan, 1967), p. 138.

12. Jocelyn Baines, *Joseph Conrad: A Critical Biography* (New York: McGraw-Hill, 1960), p. 301.

13. Karl Marx and Friedrich Engels, *Die heilige Familie, oder Kritik der Kritishen Kritik: gegen Bruno Bauer und Konsorten,* in *Werke,* vol. 2 (Berlin: Dietz Verlag, 1962), p. 37. (My trans.).

14. For a discussion of the relationship between Donoso's earlier work, *The Obscene Bird of Night,* and *Frankenstein,* see my *Modern Latin American Narratives: The Dreams of Reason* (Chicago: University of Chicago Press, 1977).

Bibliography of Works Cited

Adams, Robert Martin. *Nil: Episodes in the Literary Void During the Nineteenth Century.* New York: Oxford University Press, 1970.

Arenas, Reinaldo. *El mundo alucinante.* Mexico: Editorial Diógenes, 1969.

Aristotle. *Poetics,* trans. Gerald F. Else. Ann Arbor: University of Michigan Press, 1967.

Auden, W. H. *The Prolific and the Devourer,* ed. and pref. Edward Mendelson. *Antaeus* 42 (Summer, 1981).

———. *Spain.* Great Britain: Faber and Faber, 1937.

Bahlke, George W. *The Later Auden.* New Brunswick: Rutgers University Press, 1970.

Baines, Jocelyn. *Joseph Conrad: A Critical Biography.* New York: McGraw-Hill, 1960.

Bakhtin, Mikhail. *The Dialogic Imagination: Four Essays,* ed. Michael Holquist, trans. Caryl Emerson and Michael Holquist. Austin: University of Texas Press, 1981.

———. *Problems of Dostoevsky's Poetics.* ed. and trans. Caryl Emerson, intro. Wayne C. Booth. Theory and History of Literature, vol. 8. Minneapolis: University of Minnesota Press, 1984.

Benjamin, Walter. *Reflections: Essays, Aphorisms, Autobiographical Writings,* ed. and intro. Peter Demetz, trans. Edmund Jephcott. New York: Harcourt Brace Jovanovich, 1979.

Blake, William. *The Poetry and Prose of William Blake,* ed. David V. Erdman, commentary by Harold Bloom. Garden City: Doubleday, 1970.

Bloom, Harold. *The Anxiety of Influence: A Theory of Poetry.* New York: Oxford University Press, 1973.

———. *The Visionary Company.* Ithaca: Cornell University Press, 1971.

Borges, Jorge Luis. "La biblioteca total." *Sur* 59 (1939).

———. "El tintorero enmascarado Hákim de Merv," *Historia universal de la infamia.* Buenos Aires: Emecé Editores, 1967.

———. "Kafka y sus precursores," *Otras inquisiciones.* Buenos Aires: Emecé Editores, 1960.

———. "Magias parciales del *Quijote,*" *Otras inquisiciones.* Buenos Aires: Emecé Editores, 1960

———. "Profesión de fe literaria," *El tamaño de mi esperanza.* Buenos Aires: Editorial Proa, 1926.

———. Prologue to *La invención de Morel* by Adolfo Bioy Casares. Buenos Aires: Emecé Editores, 1968.

———. "Tlön, Uqbar, Orbis Tertius," *Ficciones (1935-1944).* Buenos Aires: Emecé Editores, 1967.

———. *Borges: A Reader,* ed. Emir Rodríguez Monegal and Alastair Reid. New York: E. P. Dutton, 1983.

Brombert, Victor. *La Prison Romantique.* Paris: Librairie José Corti, 1975.

Buell, Frederick. *W. H. Auden as Social Poet.* Ithaca: Cornell University Press, 1973.

Campbell, Roy. *Flowering Rifle.* London: Longmans, Green, 1939.

Carlyle, Thomas. *Critical and Miscellaneous Essays.* Boston: Phillips, Sampson and Co., 1858.

———. *The French Revolution.* New York: Modern Library, 1934.

———. *On Heroes, Hero-Worship and the Heroic in History.* London: Oxford University Press, 1928.

Carroll, Lewis. *The Annotated Alice: Alice's Adventures in Wonderland and Through the Looking-Glass,* ed. Martin Gardiner. New York: Bramhall House, 1960.

———. *The Annotated Snark,* ed. Martin Gardiner. New York: Simon and Schuster, 1962.

Cervantes, Miguel de. *The Life and Exploits of Don Quixote de la Mancha,* trans. Charles Jarvis. London: Jones and Co., 1831.

Chiampi, Irlemar. *O Realismo Maravilhoso: Forma e Ideologia no Romance Hispano-Americano.* São Paulo: Editora Perspectiva, 1980.

Conrad, Joseph. *Nostromo: A Tale of the Seaboard.* Great Britain: Penguin Books, 1967.

Cortázar, Julio. *Rayuela.* Buenos Aires: Editorial Sudamericana, 1963.

Culler, Jonathan. *The Pursuit of Signs: Semiotics, Literature, Deconstruction.* Ithaca: Cornell University Press, 1981.

da Cunha, Euclides. *Os Sertões,* ed. Afrânio Coutinho. In vol. 2 of *Obra Completa.* Rio de Janeiro: José Aguilar Editôra, 1966.

Cunninghame Graham, Robert B. *A Brazilian Mystic, Being the Life and Miracles of Antonio Conselheiro.* New York: Books for Libraries Press, 1971.

Curtius, Ernst Robert. "Spain's Cultural Belatedness." In *European Literature and the Latin Middle Ages,* trans. W. Trask, New York: Harper and Row, 1963.

di Battista, Maria. *Virginia Woolf's Major Novels: The Fables of Anon.* New Haven: Yale University Press, 1980.

Donoso, José. *Casa de Campo.* Barcelona: Seix Barral, 1978.

Elliott, Robert C. *The Power of Satire: Magic, Ritual, Art.* Princeton: Princeton University Press, 1970.

Fernández Retamar, Roberto. *Calibán.* Mexico: Editorial Diógenes, 1970.

Frank, Joseph. *The Widening Gyre.* New Brunswick: Rutgers University Press, 1963.

Frye, Northrop. *Anatomy of Criticism: Four Essays.* Princeton: Princeton University Press, 1957.

————. *The Great Code: The Bible and Literature.* New York: Harcourt Brace Jovanovich, 1982.

————. *The Secular Scripture: A Study of Romance.* Cambridge: Harvard University Press, 1976.

Fry, Paul H. *The Poet's Calling in the English Ode.* New Haven: Yale University Press, 1980.

Fuentes, Carlos. Interview: "The Art of Fiction, LXVIII." *The Paris Review* 82 (Winter 1981).

García Márquez, Gabriel. *Cien años de soledad.* Buenos Aires: Editorial Sudamericana, 1967.

Garnett, Richard. *Life of Thomas Carlyle.* London: Walter Scott, 1887.

Gattégno, Jean. *Lewis Carroll: Fragments of a Looking-glass,* trans. Rosemary Sheed. New York: Thomas Y. Crowell, 1976.

Giamatti, A. Bartlett, "Proteus Unbound: Some Versions of the Sea God in the Renaissance." In *The Disciplines of Criticism: Essays in Literary Theory, Interpretation, and History,* ed. P. Demetz, T. Greene, and L. Nelson, Jr. New Haven: Yale University Press, 1968.

Gledson, John. *The Deceptive Realism of Machado de Assis: A Dissenting Interpretation of 'Dom Casmorro.'* Liverpool Monographs in Hispanic Studies 3. Liverpool: Francis Cairns, 1984.

Godwin, William. *Caleb Williams,* ed. David McCracken. London: Oxford University Press, 1970.

Guiliano, Edward, ed. *Lewis Carroll Observed: A Collection of Unpublished Photographs, Drawings, Poetry, and New Essays.* New York: Clarkson N. Potter, 1976.

Gledson, John. *The Deceptive Realism of Machado de Assis: A Dissenting Interpretation of "Dom Casmurro."* Liverpool Monographs in Hispanic Studies, 3. Liverpool: Francis Cairns, 1984.

González Echevarría, Roberto. *The Pilgrim at Home.* Ithaca: Cornell University Press, 1977.

Guillén, Claudio, "Genre and Countergenre." *Literature as System: Essays Toward the Theory of Literary History.* Princeton: Princeton University Press, 1970.

Hardy, Florence Emily. *The Life of Thomas Hardy, 1840-1928.* New York: St. Martin's Press, 1962.

Hardy, Thomas. *The Dynasts: An Epic-Drama of the War with Napoleon in Three Parts, Nineteen Acts, and One Hundred and Thirty Scenes.* New York: St. Martin's Press, 1977.

Hartman, Geoffrey H. *Beyond Formalism: Literary Essays, 1958-1970.* New Haven: Yale University Press, 1971.

Hay, Eloise Knapp. *The Political Novels of Joseph Conrad: A Critical Study.* Chicago: University of Chicago Press, 1963.

Hegel. Georg Wilhelm Friedrich. *Estetica,* ed. and trans. Nicolao Merker and Niccola Vaccaro. Milan: Giulio Einaudi Editore, 1967.

Hemmings, F. W. J. *Balzac: An Interpretation of La Comédie Humaine.* New York: Random House, 1967.

Hesse, Everett W., and Williams, Harry F., eds. *La vida de Lazarillo de Tormes.* Madison: University of Wisconsin Press, 1969.

Hillis Miller, J. *Poets of Reality: Six Twentieth-Century Writers.* Cambridge: Belknap Press of Harvard University Press. 1966.

Hirsch, *Validity in Interpretation.* New Haven: Yale University Press, 1971.

Hynes, Samuel. *The Auden Generation: Literature and Politics in England in the 1930s.* Great Britain: Bodley Head, 1976.

Irby, James E. "Borges and the Idea of Utopia." *Books Abroad* (Summer 1971).

Iser, Wolfgang. *The Act of Reading: A Theory of Aesthetic Response.* Baltimore: Johns Hopkins University Press, 1978.

Jauss, Hans Robert, "Literary History as a Challenge to Literary Theory." *New Literary History* 3 (Autumn 1970).

———. *Aesthetic Experience and Literary Hermeneutics,* trans. Michael Shaw, intro. Wlad Godzich. Theory and History of Literature, vol 3. Minneapolis: University of Minnesota Press, 1982.

Karl, Frederick R. *Joseph Conrad: The Three Lives.* New York: Farrar, Straus and Giroux, 1979.

Leavis, F. R. *The Great Tradition.* New York: Doubleday, 1954.

Lukács, Georg. *The Theory of the Novel,* trans. Anna Bostock. London: Merlin Press, 1971.

Mac Adam, Alfred J. "Borges the *Criollo:* 1923-1932," *Review 28* (January-April, 1981).

———. *Modern Latin American Narratives: The Dreams of Reason.* Chicago: University of Chicago Press, 1977.

Marx, Karl, and Engels, Friedrich. *Die heilege Familie, odes Kritik der Kritishen Kritik: gegen Bruno Bauer und Konsorten.* In *Werke,* vol. 2. Berlin: Dietz Verlag, 1962.

Mendelson, Edward. *Early Auden.* New York: Viking Press, 1981.

Neruda, Pablo. *España en el corazón: himno a las glorias del pueblo en la querra (1936-1937).* Santiago de Chile: Ercilla, 1938.

Replogle, Justin. *Auden's Poetry.* Seattle: University of Washington Press, 1969.

Rimbaud, Arthur. Letter to Paul Demeny, May 15, 1871. *Oeuvres.* ed. Suzanne Bernard. Paris: Garnier, 1960.

Rimbaud. Great Britain: Penguin Books, 1966.

Rodríguez Monegal, Emir. *El Boom de la novela latinoamericana.* Caracas: Editorial Tiempo Nuevo, 1972.

———. "The Boom: a Retrospective." Interview with Rodríguez Monegal, *Review 33* (September-December, 1984).

———. "Carnaval/Antropofagia/Parodia." *Revista Iberoamericana,* nos. 108-9 (July-December, 1979).

———. *Jorge Luis Borges: A Literary Biography.* New York: E. P. Dutton, 1978.

———. "The Metamorphoses of Caliban." *Diacritics* (September 1977.

———. *El viajero inmóvil: introducción a Pablo Neruda.* Buenos Aires: Losada, 1966.

Rosenberg, Philip. *The Seventh Hero: Thomas Carlyle and the Theory of Radical Activism.* Cambridge: Harvard University Press, 1974.

Said, Edward W. *Beginnings: Intention and Method.* New York: Basic Books, 1975.

Sandison, Alan. *The Wheel of Empire: A Study of the Imperial Idea in Some Late Nineteenth and Early Twentieth-Century Fiction.* London: Macmillan, 1967.

Santí, Enrico Mario. *Pablo Neruda: The Poetics of Prophecy.* Ithaca: Cornell University Press, 1982.

Sarduy, Severo. *Escrito sobre un cuerpo.* Buenos Aires: Editorial Sudamericana, 1969.

Shelley, Mary. *Frankenstein or, The Modern Prometheus.* Afterword by Harold Bloom. New York: New American Library, 1965.

Sicard, Alain. *El pensamiento poético de Pablo Neruda.* Madrid: Editorial Gredos, 1981.

Spitzer, Leo, "Interpretation of an Ode by Paul Claudel." *Linguistics and Literary History.* Princeton: Princeton University Press, 1967.

Thomas, Hugh. *The Spanish Civil War.* New York: Harper and Row, 1963.

Thomson, Clive. "Bakhtin's "Theory" of Genre." In *Studies in 20th Century Literature* 9, no. 1. Special Issue on Mikhail Bakhtin, ed. Clive Thomson (Fall 1984).

Vargas Llosa, Mario. *La guerra del fin del mundo.* Barcelona: Plaza y Janés, 1981.

Vidal, Hernán. *Literatura hispanoamericana e ideología liberal: surgimiento y crisis (una problemática sobre la dependencia en torno a la narrativa del Boom).* Buenos Aires: Ediciones Hispamérica, 1976.

Weintraub, Stanley. *The Last Great Cause: The Intellectuals and the Spanish Civil War.* Boston: Weybright and Talley, 1968.

Wellek, René, and Warren, Austin. *Theory of Literature.* Third ed. New York: Harcourt, Brace and World, 1962.

White, Hayden. *Metahistory: The Historical Imagination in Nineteenth Century Europe.* Baltimore: Johns Hopkins University Press, 1973.

Wilkins, Simon, ed. *Sir Thomas Browne's Works.* London: William Pickering, 1835.

Woolf, Virginia. *Orlando.* New York: Harcourt, Brace, 1928.

Wright, George T. *W. H. Auden.* New York: Twayne, 1967.

Wright, Walter F. *The Shaping of the Dynasts: A Study in Thomas Hardy.* Lincoln: University of Nebraska Press, 1967.

Lucille Kerr (essay date summer 1988)

SOURCE: Kerr, Lucille. "Conventions of Authorial Design: José Donoso's *Casa de campo.*" *Symposium: A Quarterly Journal in Modern Literature* 42, no. 2 (summer 1988): 133-52.

[*In the following essay, Kerr analyzes the metafictional elements of* Casa de campo.]

In José Donoso's **Casa de Campo** the conventions of reading mimetic fiction confront the conventions of reading reflexive writing. The novel juxtaposes and turns between at least two apparently distinct modes of discourse, two seemingly disparate ways of reading and writing narrative fiction. The fictions proposed by **Casa de campo** take us from a reading of the novel as a reflexive commentary on the state of things in modern fiction to a reading of its fiction as both a nineteenth-century family story and a political allegory. Within its pages Donoso's novel also produces the image of an author who is master over the text in which he himself appears but who can also be viewed as mastered by the fictions from which his image emerges. This figure turns between disguising and disclosing, questioning and supporting, different, but complementary, conventions of reading and writing.

There is little, if any, doubt that **Casa de campo** makes it possible for us to turn from one reading of its fictional story to another. We may read it "directly" as the chronicle of events in the life of the Ventura y Ventura family at their summer estate. We may read it "indirectly" as the chronicle of events in Chile in the early 1970s or as a more general tale about Spanish American history. The first, a more or less "literal" reading, accepts the novel as a quasi-realistic, though also ironic, presentation of fictional events and characters located in or around the **Casa de campo.**[1] The second, an essentially figurative reading, understands the story as a political allegory of the history of Chile in particular and/or Spanish America in general.[2] However, Donoso's novel is also a novel about writing novels and about the conventions that bind together narratives that appear to be either realistic or reflexive, fictions whose emphasis is mimetic or allegorical.

Casa de campo is a curious mixture of pages that relate its primary fictional story and passages that present the self-conscious commentaries by the author-narrator pre-

sumed to be responsible for that other "primary" material. Donoso's novel undermines, however, the primariness of its fiction and the privilege of the discourse that presents it. The novel turns with equal force between a reading that focuses on the fictional story (a story that can also be interpreted allegorically) to one that explores the writing of such forms of fiction. It moves us from a reading based on assumptions of referentiality (the referents are at once fictive and real, they are the fictional characters or the historical figures seen "through" them) and one that privileges principles of textuality and reflexivity.[3] Indeed, **Casa de campo** can be read as a novel that deals with the writing of one or the other kind of story.

Let us turn to both the novel's fictional story and its reflexive commentaries to see how **Casa de campo** proposes such readings. The fiction revolves around the Ventura y Ventura family, at whose *casa de campo,* located on property called Marulanda, most of the action is set. At the time of the main episodes (a summer during which the family stays at the country house), Marulanda is inhabited by three groups of characters: the Ventura family, composed of a total of forty-six adults and children;[4] the family's "army" of servants, which, headed by a Mayordomo, maintains order at the house; and the area's native inhabitants, who mine the gold from which the Venturas' wealth and power are derived.

The event that serves as catalyst for the story's major developments is the adults' picnic excursion to an idyllic retreat in a distant part of Marulanda.[5] Accompanied by all the servants, the parents embark on their outing, apparently abandoning their children at the *casa de campo.* Strangely enough, the excursion is lived by the adults as a trip of one day while it is experienced by the children as an absence of a whole year. This undelimitable time becomes a time of discord, disorder, and destruction at the summer house. In the temporary absence of the adults and servants, the children and the natives split into opposing camps to battle for control of the house and its grounds. Some follow Adriano Gomara (a Ventura by marriage only who had been declared insane and imprisoned by the elder Venturas), who is released once the adults depart, while others ally themselves with opposing factions as each group vies for power over the others.

Though the return of the parents, preceded by their servants, restores some kind of order, it does not return everything to the way things are at the beginning of the novel. Authorized by the Ventura adults, for whom they act, the servants restore an approximation of order by violently suppressing the children's and natives' resistance to their control. However, that order is also left in question at the novel's end. For when the parents themselves return, they are accompanied by a group of foreigners, to whom they plan to sell the property. However, it is this group of potential partners that is joined by the once-loyal Ventura servants and together they abandon both the former masters of the property and the decaying, but not yet totally destroyed, *casa de campo*.[6]

As convention would have it, the more or less representational discourse that presents the story focuses on the "third-persons" (i.e., the characters) who figure as fictional entities of the story and subjects of the narrative.[7] The omniscient narrator with whom the power and plan of narration reside, and who apparently is responsible for the way things do (or do not) get told, is a narrating subject who remains more or less "out of sight." I say "more or less" for several reasons. First, the narrator's discourse or "voice" turns from a posture of identification with to a position that is ironically distanced from (and at times seems to make parodic or caricaturesque gestures toward[8]) the characters and events in the fiction. That is, the narrative discourse fluctuates between emphasizing that there is indeed a narrator "behind" the fictional story that is being told and covering up or disguising the presence of a subject from whose position and perspective everything is known and narrated.[9]

Another fiction proposed by the novel is that this knowledgeable narrator is also its author, who reveals himself throughout the novel. This subject's visibility becomes a significant feature of the text as the narrator intermittently speaks not only to tell the story that is the principal object of narration but also to talk about his work as the author who has fashioned it. In fact, his visibility is fleshed out—in a sense literalized—when he incorporates himself into the text as a participant in a conversation held with a "real" person, upon whom, supposedly, one of his fictional characters of the same name (one Silvestre Ventura) has been based (395-403). The conversation between the unnamed author-character and the named person-character deals with the novel itself, as the "real" author, en route to his publisher with a copy of *Casa de campo* under his arm, meets the "real" Silvestre and comes to discuss it with him. His interlocutor responds to a reading of some of the novel's pages and the fiction it proposes with statements that elicit from the fictive author comments about the intentions and assumptions he has held while writing the novel.

Their conversation revolves mainly around the question of verisimilitude which also becomes the focus of the author-narrator's "postscript" that follows (404-5). Their meeting is a meeting of disparate positions on the relation between the literary and the extra-literary, between fiction and reality: that of Silvestre, who can't understand why this author has changed reality, thereby misrepresenting him and his family, and that of the author, who has written with the intention of deforming, making unrecognizable, that very reality (398-401). The one

desires literature to be realistic in a photographic, literal way: to copy accurately, to reproduce faithfully the "real" referents named in its pages. The other aims to undermine such a form of realism, putting in its place another kind of reality by rewriting the appearance of its apparently realistic models. "Realism" as a set of conventions that present directly images of the real, the author-character asserts, is a theory and a practice of the past. One simply can't write a novel as if one were living in the nineteenth century or as if the twentieth century had never occurred.

Yet, this is in a way just what Donoso does. Or, rather, by writing precisely from the perspective of a twentieth-century author rooted in both the literary practices and the political history of his own time, Donoso has managed to produce a text that returns us with equal force to the powers, as well as problems, of nineteenth-century conventions. If the authorial commentaries turn us away from the fictional story to consider reflexively the conventions of narrative fiction, they also fix our attention on both nineteenth- and twentieth-century literary practices that are simultaneously employed in *Casa de campo*. And, if the fictional story, interspersed with the author-narrator's ironic remarks and reflexive comments, turns us toward a reading of its characters and events as signifiers that belie an allegorical meaning,[10] it also keeps our gaze fixed on the development of its narrative and the invented world to which we have to adhere if we are to understand what it "really" means, if we are to read through it to the political history it also figures.

In the encounter between the "real" author and "real" person and in the authorial commentary that follows it, we have a good example of how *Casa de campo* turns our gaze (as well as its own focus) to what we might call its literary concerns, its reflexive inquiry. Throughout its pages *Casa de campo* develops a self-conscious commentary on, a critical analysis and theoretical discussion of, the story being told, the techniques that are used to tell it, and the framework of literary history within which the whole enterprise might be situated. The discourse we might call reflexive thus takes as its object the referential discourse—the Ventura narrative itself—that unfolds alongside it.

For example, in the numerous comments to his reader (these are "direct addresses" if we privilege the idea of the text as a communication between author and reader; they are "asides" if we privilege the idea of the novel as telling a story from which the fictive author's commentaries digress), the author-narrator draws attention to his unconventional approach to the conventions of narrative fiction. He openly refers to the novel as a text he has authored (e.g., 13, 166, 237, 363, 391-92); draws attention to his role as a narrator (e.g., 42, 52, 73); highlights the relationship between his role as an author and that of his readers (e.g., 104, 229, 310, 477); draws attention to his characters as characters (e.g., 174, 303-4, 318, 371-72, 394, 457); interprets events, or explains the meaning of characters' actions, or makes connections between narrative episodes (e.g., 166, 229, 466, 477); asserts or puts into question the authority of his own authorial intentions (e.g., 302, 349, 391-92, 492); makes implicit or explicit comparisons between disparate narrative conventions (e.g., 53, 334, 492-93). It is only in his function as narrator that this privileged subject tells what happens in Marulanda. In his function as author, he comments on his own characters and discusses how he has decided to tell, or not to tell, the Ventura family story. Throughout, he acknowledges the virtual presence of his interlocutor—the reader to whom he repeatedly refers and for whom he develops his explanations of the positions that his novel is meant to take.

This authorial subject is, of course, the novel's fictive author and thus but another artificial figure proposed by the text.[11] The imaginary conversation between this author and Silvestre Ventura is also emblematic of how the text disguises, while also seeming to display, its artifice (i.e., its textuality). It is a scene that purports to distinguish clearly between what is artificial and what is real, what is inside and what is outside the novel's fiction. It is a scene that is presented as a hypothetical "real" event whose artifice the novel's readers are asked to suppress while it is put forward. (The author-narrator says: "Supongamos que la siguiente entrevista tuvo—o hubiera podido tener—lugar" [395].) This momentary, conscious suspension of disbelief, in which author and reader are to participate together, turns us away from the Ventura family fiction to a "reality" outside it. This realm would appear to be a fictionalized depiction of the "reality" in which the author-narrator actually resides. It is the "real" world from which he has gathered material on which to base the representation of the Ventura fiction. It is the "real" world in which the writing of this novel has taken place and in which he, for a moment, transforms himself into a fictional character in dialogue with one of the models for that fiction.

In calling attention to the artificial status of the fictional world "below," from a position "above" (where the author "really" resides), the author-narrator appears to establish his distance and difference from that artifice. As we are well aware, however, this gesture is one that gives but another artificial turn to the text—a turn that produces its own realistic effect. For the position that never seems to be put into question is that of the subject who oversees the novel as a whole. The fictive author speaks of the text we read in an authoritative and apparently accurate manner. His reflexive observations draw our attention away from the represented fiction as realistic to the novel's narrative as artificial. However, in order to succeed with this distraction the author-

narrator actually proposes another realistic frame within the novel: the frame within which the fictive author himself speaks, the "real" position from which the authorial subject is able to take his reader into his confidence and declare the artificiality of the fictional world that his own discourse appears to frame. That frame, as we know, is itself part of the artifice it would claim to locate at a distance from the subject who speaks within it. Oddly enough, the comments that lead us to read the novel reflexively are given authority by the realistic appearance of the subject whose discourse forms that reflexive register.[12] We see, then, that the authorial image and voice that would lead us away from and outside the Marulanda fiction are part of the most powerful fiction of all. For this authorial fiction is but another representational effect of a discourse that proposes to "represent" nothing at all.

This author, who is himself but a well-disguised and thus verisimilar subject of artifice, is to be taken, appropriately enough, as an authority on the artificial. Indeed, as he himself emphasizes, his "intention" is to prove—or, rather, to prevent his reader from forgetting—that his novel is only an elaborate appearance. He thus claims that his text is to be taken as nothing more, and nothing less, than an artificial object. To that end, he explains early on why he finds it necessary to interrupt the fiction's flow, to erupt into the narrative and shift registers—that is, to move from a discourse that focuses on other fictional entities to one that centers on the author-narrator himself and the text over which he presides. For instance, at the beginning of chapter 2 he openly declares: "A estas alturas de mi narración, mis lectores quizás estén pensando que no es de 'buen gusto' literario que el autor tironee a cada rato la manga del que lee para recordarle su presencia, sembrando el texto con comentarios que no pasan de ser informes sobre el transcurso del tiempo o el cambio de escenografía. Quiero explicar cuanto antes que lo hago con el modesto fin de proponer al público que acepte lo que escribo como un artificio" (53).

Along with the many other self-conscious comments in the novel, this declaration of a literary intention would appear to situate itself on a level above the narrative, being as it is "outside" and "beyond" the fictional world proposed here. From within the realm of this "higher," more privileged discourse, the conventions of mimetic fiction are exposed, revealed for what they are: devices for creating an illusion of the real, techniques for making us suspend disbelief. It is from this perspective, then, that the novel demands that we read its story as nothing more than a fiction, as an artifice of whose conventional designs we are supposed to remain aware. The fictive author also admits, however, that this is precisely the kind of reading the novel attempts to undermine. He reveals that from within his own position as a privileged reader, from his superior position as a "real" and totally informed observer, he himself is unable to respond with or produce this kind of reading. Contrary to its author's stated intentions and techniques, then, the fiction in the face of which we are to remain distanced and of whose mechanisms we are to be critically aware manages to persuade even its own author of its "reality." The subject presumed to be most conscious of its artificiality is precisely the one brought under the spell of its representational powers.

In the final chapter—just before we find out how everything ends in *Casa de campo*—the narrating author uncovers the limits of his own readerly, and yet authorial, abilities. He confesses that his plan to create "personajes como seres a-psicológicos, inverosímiles, artificiales" (492) has somehow been foiled by those same fictional entities. He discloses that the presentation of those characters in the novel seems to have overpowered the intentions of the author responsible for their creation: "no he podido evitar ligarme pasionalmente a ellos y con su mundo circundante, del que es tan imposible extraerlos. . . . En otras palabras: pese a mi determinación de no confundir lo real con el arte, me está constando terriblemente esta despedida, conflicto que toma la forma literaria de no querer desprenderme de ellos sin terminar *sus* historias—olvidando que no tienen más historia que la que yo quiera darles—en vez de conformarme con terminar *esta* historia que, de alguna manera que no acabaré nunca de entender, es, sin duda, la mía" (492). This statement is at once a declaration of proprietary privilege and an acknowledgement of this author's failure to establish such rights and powers—such final authority—within or over the novel (see also Mac Adam).

The confessed contradiction revolves around a question of interpretation, a problem of reading. It raises questions about how to read the novel in relation to the various traditions to which it is bound and in relation to the various models of reading it calls to mind. If we were to read the narrative as the fictive author asserts he himself has been led to read it, we would read it as a discourse that represents a world which, in one way or another, gets taken as "real." However, as the narrative takes us inside the Ventura family story (the fictive reality produced by such a reading), the allegorical potential of that narrative also takes us outside that fiction to the historical reality it appears to figure. And, as we read the fictive author's comments on that fiction, we are turned to a view of its referents as mere fabrications, while at the same time the author-narrator who reveals their artifice to us supplants their "real" world with his own.

If we read the novel allegorically, we read its discourse as both transparent (as referring to entities and events that acquire something of a life of their own beyond the text that simultaneously recedes into the background while that privileged meaning reveals itself to us) and as opaque (as referring to entities and events that point as much to their own textual reality and the "meaning" signaled by that surface of words as to the reality of the story through which they also appear). Such a reading would see the novel's political allegory as figured by the main events of the Marulanda tale during that one fateful summer/year. More specifically, that story appears to allegorize events surrounding Salvador Allende's rise to power and his fall; it also seems to figure events of Spanish American history from the time of discovery or the era of independence to the present. But, even though the novel proposes a political allegory that operates in different, but connected, registers at once (it can be read as moving between macrocosmic and microcosmic analogies between Spanish America and Chile), it seems to aim principally at the Chilean context.[13] The Venturas' abandonment of their house and children, the ensuing disorder and partial destruction of their property, the rise of a leader in the figure of Adriano Gomara, who accedes briefly to power only to be murdered during the period of violence imposed by the servant "army," and the subsequent restoration of order, with the return of the Ventura adults as figures of precarious authority—all these and other narrative elements can be read as allegorizing Chile's political history from around 1970, when Allende was elected, to 1973, when the military coup brought his government to an end.

Political history is thus figured by a fictional reality that, paradoxically, must be perceived as a surface, as an artificial textualized reality in order to point toward the other "truer" story it also tells, the other reality (or realities) it also represents. To recognize that other meaning is also to read *Casa de campo* as mere artifice—as an artifice that, by drawing attention to itself as unreal, also draws attention away from questions of textuality toward the historical events the novel's central fiction can be read to figure. Oddly enough, the reaffirmation of the text's artificial status is precisely what enables us to read it also as figuring the "real." To read *Casa de campo* as a political allegory is, by definition and convention, to read it as a textualized representation, a fundamentally "artificial" and reflexive structure, as well as a narrative that tells a potentially convincing story. Donoso's novel highlights this characteristic of political allegory and thereby reveals some connections between the different readings we may give to representational and reflexive writing. It also reminds us of the possible points of contact between allegory as an "old" (i.e., classical, medieval, or Renaissance) form of narrative and modern fiction.[14]

There is, in the end, a great deal of self-consciousness in the fictional narrative and not a small amount of representational force in the fictive author's self-conscious commentary. The one form of writing seems to uncover, even to figure, the workings of the other. For example, as stylized or parodic as its development may seem to be, and as ironic as its (author's) intentions may appear, the discourse that produces and presents the Venturas manages both to represent the fictional world to which the novel refers and to proclaim in so many ways that what is meant here is something other than what, on the surface, is seen or told (see note 10). And, what is meant by this fiction, the allegorical potential of the narrative would tell us, is something "real," something historically "true." However, the meanings toward which the narrative turns us pertain as much to the literary as to the historical, as much to the realm of the textual as to the political.

If we were to posit the tale of political history allegorized through the fiction (that is, the historical referents) as the only story being told here, we would be privileging a meaning, a reading, that Donoso's novel also undercuts. Such a reduction of meaning to a univocal, unambiguous, and fixed reading is countered by the novel's discursive opposition. The complex dialectical interaction of fictions moves us from one register to another, from one kind of meaning to another throughout the novel. The story of the Ventura family and all the events set in Marulanda is at least a two-pronged, double-directed tale (that is, both a quasi-realist and an allegorical story) that is developed in constant contact, even in direct competition, with another openly reflexive one (the "story" of the fictive author and the literary issues with which he attempts to deal). Each story, each reading has its own kind of authority; they are of course interconnected—indeed, inseparable.[15]

The fictive author's presence just behind, as well as above, the story being told, however, points not only to invisible meanings below the surface of events but also to visible concerns that are displayed upon it. The immediate issues of concern to this author—those about which he reveals his authorial positions—appear to be those which shape the literary theories and practices of readers and writers of texts such as Donoso's own *Casa de campo,* rather than (or not only) those which inform Chile's recent political history. Thus, there would certainly appear to be several directions in which to take our reading of *Casa de campo.* The choice of one reading or another would seem to be a choice in favor of one kind of discourse or another, one type of issue or another. The choice—indeed, the opposition itself—is perhaps misleading. It leads us astray of the issues that are held in common by these apparently opposing spheres and aims. For the discourse whose object is the at once representational and allegorical events in Marulanda also returns us to questions that connect up with those around which the novel's fictive author creates his self-conscious commentary. And the discourse

whose object appears to be principally literary theory and practice actually leads us back to some of the key issues addressed within the development of the Ventura narrative.

In both these registers—in the literarily reflexive and the representational/allegorical realms—we are never far from some consideration of the conventions of authority. Throughout its pages *Casa de campo* examines relations of authority that govern these seemingly distant spheres of action, relations that inform literary as well as political theory and practice. For example, such relations and conventions are presented through the clashes among the Ventura adults, their children, the servants, and the natives (and, thus, among the classes or institutions they might be seen to figure). Through that fiction, the novel explores how authority is legitimized or challenged, how power is exercised or eliminated in the real world as well as in narrative fiction. One of the conclusions, as it were, to such conflicts is that no single system or individual, group or leader, emerges as entirely legitimate or finally authoritative.[16]

Though the relatively stable and established hierarchical order of the Ventura family and its property is destroyed by the end of the text, the novel does not elevate another order to take its place nor any figure of authority to lead the way. The presentation of conflict between groups or classes of characters (i.e., adults vs. children) also presents divisions within them. For example, rather than constituting a single voice and vision, the children divide themselves into groups supporting one or another interest, opposing one or another agenda. Though figures of authority emerge to lead or govern (Adriano Gomara, Juvenal, the Mayordomo), none of these figures remains unchallenged or undefeated, no one character receives lasting or unified support (not even from the text's author). Each group's powers are sanctioned and struck down, each leader's authority is supported and then challenged. The question of who has the right to and who shall rule, control, or author(ize) the reality and relationships of Marulanda circulates not only in the characters' deeds but also in their words. Indeed, these issues are explicitly thematized in some of the fictional characters' own ruminations about the nature of power or the exercise of authority, and in the narrator's description of the significance of specific events or actions.

In effect, within Marulanda itself many characters are acutely aware of the structures of authority, the relations of power within which they are situated and in accordance with or against which they may act. We see this, for example, in Balbina's (Adriano Gomara's wife) analysis of her husband's relation to the natives on whose behalf he works: "Estoy segura que los nativos, que te creen una especie de dios y eso te encanta, te enredan con sus mentiras y tú simulas creérselas para dominarlos. Esas cosas me pertenecen: si tú eres dios, yo soy la esposa del dios y tengo derechos" (78); "No me engañes, Adriano mío: aunque supieras que te están dando de comer carne humana, lo que no es improbable, comerías para no arriesgar tu poder" (83). While her interpretation of Adriano's motives may or may not be entirely valid, the analytical force of her reading of the relations of power that bind her husband and the natives, as well as the privileges that such a relation may grant her as the wife of such a powerful person, unveils some of the realities governing relations that may appear on the surface as free of any kind of interest or constraint. Her reading of the situation also reveals the potential for reading (legitimately, it seems) any relationship as a relation with interests of power.[17]

The children who are, by definition, subject to parental authority, are acutely aware of how such relations are formed and how they shift. They too understand the contingent nature of those relationships and thus how each of their positions may be upheld or undermined. For instance, while plotting an apparently harmless challenge to their parents' order in their project to uproot the iron gate surrounding the estate, the brothers Clemente, Mauro, and Valerio acknowledge an understanding of the hierarchy of authority that informs their relations with one another as well as with the Ventura adults. After Clemente, the youngest, challenges the authority of his older brother Mauro ("Quiero cuestionar la autoridad que te has arrogado para desposeerme de mi juguete"), we are told that "Mauro abrazó al pequeñuelo, asegurándole que después, cuando tuvieran tiempo, y él comprendiera su propia autoridad en caso que la tuviera, la recobraría" (101). This incident is later analyzed by Valerio (a year younger than Mauro), who situates it within the context of their transgressive project: "El propósito de lo nuestro era sólo hacer algo prohibido, ajeno a la voluntad de nuestros padres, algo verdaderamente nuestro, no tribal, secreto pero sin consecuencias. Ahora . . . no hay leyes y por lo tanto no hay autoridad, por lo cual queda invalidada tanto la esencia misma de nuestro quehacer como tu autoridad para quitarle la pelota a Clemente" (103). The wielding of authority is authorized by the laws that govern and give shape to the familial order within which they find themselves. Without such a structure neither legitimate actions nor transgressive acts are possible—the (familial, social, or political) law authorizes as much as constrains all subjects of authority. This is the force of Valerio's declaration—a declaration that, of course, takes on its own authoritative tone.

The servants in Marulanda are perceived as the force that upholds the authority of the Ventura adults as well as the established order that empowers them. They nonetheless also represent a potential threat to the privilege of the masters whom they serve. Indeed, though the servants act as the agents for the Ventura adults and thereby exercise authority for them, they are, it is suggested, a possible threat to their masters' position and power. This reading of the servants' real or imagined role in Marulanda is offered, in fact, as a possible explanation for the novel's catalytic event. Juvenal, the eldest of the Ventura children, theorizes that a question of control, of power, may be at the heart of the adults' one-day/one-year excursion: "este paseo fue organizado para aplacar a los sirvientes, ya que en sus filas podía estar germinando el descontento: quizás nuestros padres les tengan miedo por haberles dado demasiado poder, y el propósito de complacerlos a ellos, a los sirvientes, estaría entonces detrás de todo el fasto familiar" (153).

Such a view of the servants' powers and of their actions as potentially subversive is strengthened by a scene such as the one in which Juan Pérez (the only servant with a given name in the novel) overhears the Mayordomo's plan to bring the Ventura children under control by regulating—indeed, authoring entirely—the reality in which they live. The narrator reveals his critically subversive analysis of his own superior's misdirected goal, describing his thoughts while working to restore a mural in the room where the Mayordomo discusses the plan:

> Con un toque lívido de su pincel aquí, un verdoso acá, él podía alterar a este lacayo enaltecido hasta dotarlo de la perspicacia suficiente para que comprendiera de una vez que la meta no era atrapar a los niños dentro de esa realidad que él estaba inventando, sino a los Ventura mismos cuando regresaran. Tarea por cierto más difícil. Pero como al fin y al cabo son las leyes las que crean la realidad, y no a la inversa, y quien tiene el poder crea las leyes, era sólo cuestión de conservarlo. ¡Que el Mayordomo no lo malgastara! ¡Que fuera con cuidado para que el poder, que siempre finalmente se agota, no se agotara antes de la llegada de la presa suprema!
>
> (330-31)

However, we see that this same character is also characterized as unable to master the mechanisms of power he appears to analyze so acutely:

> Juan Pérez no sabía vincularse con el poder más que por medio de maquinaciones clandestinas que lo tornaban vulnerable a cualquier emoción. Así, no calculó que las grandes alianzas suelen establecerse directa y fríamente, de fuerza a fuerza, prescindiendo de consideraciones ideológicas y personalistas de frágil constitución puesto que no encarnan más que la carencia de esa autoridad oficial, sorda, y ciega, que en definitiva es la única que cuenta.
>
> (434-35)

This analysis of how power works, how authority gets wielded is an analysis provided by the author-narrator, who, in providing such comments, reveals his own understanding of and interest in this topic. Thus it is not surprising that such an issue becomes both an implicit and explicit focus of attention not only in the parts of the novel that tell its story but also in the sections that present its author-narrator's comments. Indeed, such issues of authority are self-consciously emphasized in the fictive author's discussion of the conventions governing narrative fiction and in his description of the privileges accompanying his own authorial activity. More specifically, the author-narrator takes up the issues of his own authority—his own powers and privileges (or lack thereof) as an author and as a narrator—as he makes theoretical and practical comments about writing novels in general and *Casa de campo* in particular. He posits the relation between author and reader as a polite partnership in which the author-narrator performs with the permission of his textual partner (e.g., 37, 318). We know, of course, that requests such as "si mis lectores me permiten" can be read as formulaic conventional devices, as the rhetorical convention of false humility used by many a conventional author. Such a request may be read as either revealing or obscuring the fictive author's position—or, perhaps, as disclosing the position in which he turns from mastery over to submission beneath his own reader and text.

Indeed, in the author/reader relationship implicitly posited by the fictive author, his is the position from which details are organized, information is withheld, and mysteries are clarified (see for example, 104, cited in note 10). The fictive author's frequent explicit reminders of his own authority and privilege punctuate the novel's pages. For example, when describing the vastness of the country house's underground cellars, built atop ancient salt mines, he states:

> No es mi intención, aunque como narrador omnisciente tendría derecho a hacerlo, contar la historia de esos sótanos pretendiendo que es independiente de mi antojo, o que existe fuera de esta página. Ni topógrafo ni espeleólogo, ni minero ni ingeniero, no voy a levantar un plano de esta mina de sal tan vasta y tan vieja como la de Wieliczka. Aspiro sólo a establecer el proscenio para mi recitación, rico, eso sí de bastidores, bambalinas, telones y tramoyas, y complejo de utilería y vestaurio, pero matizado por la reserva, de modo que mi monólogo—no nos engañemos: no pretendo que esta narración sea otra cosa—cobre proyecciones que ni mi propia intención desconoce."
>
> (349; see also 371, where he refers to "la prerogativa del escritor")

This statement of narrative intention and textual control emphasizes the fictive author's confidence in his plan and the authority of his position as sole subject (and thus owner) of the narration. His passing declaration of a restricted knowledge (he is not an engineer, etc.) and, thus, a limited literary intention does not seem to undermine his position of authority. However, as we (and he) move closer to the novel's final pages, we see this

image of authority eroded. We hear the voice of the author-narrator declare his own subservience and attachment to the very text over which most of his earlier statements proclaim his control. It seems that, in becoming an authoritative author and teller of a powerful and meaningful tale, this author-narrator seems to produce a text that also masters him.

As noted above, this dilemma is addressed near the end of the text (490-93), when the question of the novel's ending (not only what happens at the end, but also how to make that end or any end happen) is raised. The author-narrator finds himself under the spell, as it were, of his own fiction. In confessing his loss of control, he would of course put his own authority into question. This confession, as we recall, turns us, along with the fictive author himself, from a position of omniscient mastery to one with a limited perspective and power over things, and back again. For the fictive author's final confession unveils from a different angle how we shift back and forth between reading this author as an omnipotent authority and reading him as no more powerful than any of his characters or readers. As we are turned (with the authorial figure) from one to another image of his powers and position, we are turned with the text from a reading that sees it all as verbal artifice to one that accepts the representation of a believable, though also ironically staged, fictional world.

The following passage, which immediately precedes the confession cited earlier, illustrates the fictive author's shifting reasonings about and readings of his own text:

> Aunque yo mismo siento una curiosidad omnívora por saber todo . . .—pero me doy cuenta que para saberlo tendría que escribir por lo menos otra novela; o, como en algunas novelas del siglo pasado, agregar un epílogo insatisfactoriamente esquemático para redondear cada destino—, me veo excluido en forma dolorosa de las infinitas posibilidades narrativas que tendrá que ocultar mi silencio, y para paliar la contradictoria angustia producida por la necesidad de abandonar el campo en el momento justo sin la cual no hay aite, me digo a mí mismo que la vida real, en efecto, está constituida por anécdotas a medio terminar, por personajes inexplicables, ambiguos, desdibujados, por historias sin transición ni explicación, sin comienzo ni fin y casi siempre tan sin significado como una frase mal construida. Pero sé que justificarme de este modo es apelar a un criterio mimético de la obra de arte, que en el caso de la presente novela es totalmente ajeno a mi empeño porque esta historia hubiera sido otra si la hubiera escrito en esa tesitura. Quitado el freno a pesar mío—el freno de no confundir lo literario con lo real—, se descencadena entonces el desmedido apetito de no ser sólo mi texto, sino más, mucho más que mi texto: ser todos los textos posibles.
>
> (491-92)

As the fictive author continues with his "Es curioso, sin embargo . . ." and goes on to reveal that he has been made to believe in his characters and artifice, his statement turns into a confession of "insecurity" as well: "siento una oleada de inseguridad: dudo de la validez de todo esto y de su belleza, lo que me hace intentar aferrarme a estos trozos de mi imaginación y prolongarles la vida para hacerlos eternos y frondosos. Pero no puede ser. Tienen que terminar aquí, porque debo recordar que si los artificios poseen vida, poseen también muerte para que no lleguen a devorar como monstruos al autor" (492-93; see also 396, where he refers to the "tyranny" of the fictional character over its creator).

It is no accident that these statements are made near the end of the novel. For, as the fictive author also emphasizes, the novel's impending ending is precisely what appears to cause this sense of "angustia." As he contemplates receding into silence—that is, disappearing altogether—he is literally faced with a loss of position. These confessions can also be read as the fictive author's attempt to retain control, his defense against a fiction to which he has in a way already surrendered himself. (We might also read the imaginary conversation between the authorial figure and Silvestre Ventura, noted above, not only as a device through which more reflexive commentary is included in the novel. It is also the scene in which the fictive author defends himself against one of his characters, a character who is permitted a very challenging appearance by his own author.) With the end of the novel comes the "death of the author" in the form of silence—an impending silence that is acknowledged as well as deferred (491, 493). However, to keep talking, as it were, is to give power once again to the fictive entities that have come to have power over him, to the fiction that is not supposed to convince us but which, nonetheless, leads its own author to succumb to its conventional designs. Indeed, this is how *Casa de campo* ends—we return to the fictional world of Marulanda, as the authorial voice recedes behind the narrative discourse that brings the story to a close.

The novel's ending does not close off, however, the question of the author-narrator's authority, nor does it establish any fictional/allegorical figure or any literary model or political institution as unquestionably authoritative and, thus, worthy of unconditional support or condemnation by *Casa de campo*. Donoso's novel develops, rather, an inquiry into the political and social, literary and textual relations that make the exercise of authority possible in different arenas (see note 17). The character's apparent awareness of such matters, the author-narrator's self-consciousness of his own privilege or powerlessness, and the Ventura story's development of individual, group, or institutional conflicts of power—these features of *Casa de campo* connect different registers of fiction that have been designed, it may appear, with some such aim in mind.

Indeed, in turning us to read its text one way, then another, *Casa de campo* seems to reveal as well as veil the authorial figure responsible for its design, an author who might appear to (want to) take positions on a number of different topics. However, we must also remember that the author still remains under cover, under the protection of the various fictions ("realistic" or "allegorical" or "reflexive") that serve as provocative disguises while seeming to uncover the subject responsible for the masquerade. The discourse we might call representational points at meanings also allegorical, thus appearing to disclose the "real" author along with the "real" meaning of the whole fiction. The discourse we might call reflexive points at the artifice of all that may appear real or even meaningful—the artifice that makes it possible for anything like the truth to be seen. Together these modes support one another, figuring the shifts between one or another kind of reading, one or another kind of narrative convention, that shapes *Casa de campo* and the issues under consideration within its pages.[18]

We thus see how *Casa de campo* questions, but nonetheless also affirms, the orders that inform the various fictions between which it dialectically shifts, the various "realities" to which it simultaneously, though alternately, refers. The dialectic of discourses and fictions, moreover, figures as much as represents the dialectic of authority to which the novel's "real" as well as fictive author is subject. For, if, from above the novel's reflexive and representational/allegorical fictions, there surfaces an image of an authorial subject who has plotted everything out from a superior position of authority, we should also remember that that image is itself but another conventional product of a text in which convention is dialectically certified and curtailed. *Casa de campo* thus takes an unconventional turn around issues both old and new as it explores in complementary registers the relations between the authority of convention and the conventions of authority.

Notes

1. I use "literal" in the sense of what is explicit, manifest, or visible, what refers, on the surface of things, mainly to what can at first glance be seen. To put it another way, our literal reading of the novel is a reading of its literal level—the story of the Ventura family to which the narrative openly refers. On the other hand, if we think of the term "literal" itself in the most literal way, such a reading would point up not the referential, but rather the linguistic and textual, properties of the novel's discourse. This kind of distinction is important for the differences I wish to mark between two apparently disparate models of reading or forms of narrative, and also the form of allegorical readings or writing. (This a form of writing with which Donoso appears to work.) In reading a text allegorically or as having been written with an alle-

gorical design, we deal with two "levels" (one literal or surface, the other allegorical or interpretative), two "meanings," within the same text. (These points draw on the comments of Bloomfield [esp. 312-15], Culler [esp. 267-68], and Quilligan [*Language of Allegory* 67]; see also Todorov [*The Fantastic* 61-62] on the literal versus the referential, representative, or descriptive and the literal versus the figurative.) I use the terms "realistic" or "realist" not, in the restricted sense, to designate nineteenth-century realist fiction, but in a more general sense to describe a writing that produces an appearance of reality in the form of a fictional world and whose language can thus be characterized generally as transparent. (See Jakobson for some fundamental distinctions on realism.) I am grateful to my colleague Barbara E. Kurtz for bringing to my attention some of the materials on allegory cited in this essay.

2. The most helpful treatments of the novel's political allegory are those of Bacarisse, Gutiérrez Mouat ("Discurso"), and Iñigo Madrigal. Though the history of Chile is privileged as the political allegory's referent by most critics, Iñigo Madrigal also acknowledges the broader historical contexts (i.e., Latin America as a whole from the time of discovery to the end of the 19th century, see esp. 9-11) and Bacarisse asserts that many of the novel's allegorical elements can be read as referring to other contexts as well—to "pre-revolutionary Cuba, or the *ochenio* of *odriísmo* in Peru" (323). Indeed, Bacarisse appears to privilege the broader context over the Chilean by stating that "the allegorical elements in this novel do *not* correspond exactly to conditions or events in Chile and . . . their associations are more general" (323). (See also note 6.) Gutiérrez Mouat points out some problems with Iñigo Madrigal's reading of the novel and, drawing on Quilligan's *Language of Allegory,* asserts that the novel "no es una alegoría sino meramente alegórica" ("Discurso" 205). These and other points he makes are generally very well taken. However, it is not inappropriate to describe Donoso's novel as a political allegory, since the adjective "political" identifies it not as a "narrative peopled by personified abstractions moving about a reechoing landscape of language" (Quilligan "Allegory, Allegoresis," 163), not as a text that exemplifies the established genre called "allegory" (see Quilligan *Language of Allegory*). It refers instead to a text that figures a specific politico-historical situation and whose fictional narrative can thus be read allegorically. (The most helpful discussions of allegory include the work of Honig, Fletcher, and Quilligan. On some features of political allegory, see for example Fletcher 324-28 and Bloom 170-71, 175-77. For Donoso's own characterization of his novel as an allegory and/or as a "symbolic" and "political" work, see Donoso/Martínez 72 and Donoso/Christ 42).

3. I emphasize the allegorical reading suggested by the novel as much as its allegorical elements or its overall identity as a political allegory. On the distinction between allegory and allegorical reading see Quilligan *Language of Allegory* and "Allegory, Allegoresis." The distinction between fictive and real referents is proposed by Linda Hutcheon 93-94; I was reminded of this terminological possibility by Suleiman 146. Cf. Gutiérrez Mouat ("Discurso" 222-25) on the opposition between allegorical and carnivalesque discourse in the novel. My comments on reflexivity draw on the work of Alter, Hutcheon, and Spires; another very helpful study, which came to my attention too late for inclusion in this article, is that of Siegle.

4. The novel provides a table of family relationships that identifies each member by name and age (9). On the "hyperbolic" character of the family genealogy, see Gutiérrez Mouat "Carnavalización" 60.

5. See Christ 306 and Iñigo Madrigal 12 for relevant points about the painterly origins of the outing.

6. Briefly, within the Chilean context, the possible allegorical correspondences (as pointed out by Iñigo Madrigal, Bacarisse, and Omaña) include the following: Marulanda = Chile, 1970-73; Ventura adults = the oligarchy; children = the middle class; servants = Armed Forces; Mayordomo = Pinochet; natives = lower classes or proletariat or Communists; foreigners = North Americans; Adriano Gomara = Salvador Allende; rise of Adriano Gomara as a leader of one faction of children and natives = Allende's election in 1970; return of servants and death of Adriano Gomara at the hands of the servants = military coup of 1973. As noted above, within the context of other countries' political history or that of Spanish America as a whole, other equivalents have also been suggested: Marulanda could be read as an exemplary Spanish American country during its neocolonial period or as pre-revolutionary Cuba or as the Peru in the 1950s; the different groups of characters could be read as generally figuring distinct social classes, the servants the military forces, and the natives the lower classes, just as they do in the Chilean model; and points of contact could be established between Adriano Gomara and Castro or Madero.

7. I mean to emphasize, of course, the difference between the characters as subjects of the narrative discourse (*récit* or *énoncé,* the narrative text itself, the narrative as produced by the narrator) in which they figure as entities named and described in the third person by the narrator and the narrator's po-

sition as subject of narration or the act of narrating (or *énonciation*) through which his identity as a first person is intermittently emphasized in Donoso's novel. On these and other related distinctions, see, for example, Bal *Narratology,* Chatman *Story and Discourse,* Genette *Narrative Discourse,* and Todorov *Littérature et signification.*

8. On the ironic, parodic, and carnavalesque features of the novel, see Gutiérrez Mouat and Solotorevsky.

9. See Baker for comments on the process of masking and unmasking that shapes the narrator's appearance. Gutiérrez Mouat and Solotorevsky also emphasize that metaphor in their discussions of *Casa de campo* as a carnavalesque text. Donoso himself is the first to identify the novel in terms of the logic and structures of carnival (Donoso/Martinez 64).

10. The author-narrator provides explicit signs that the novel, or parts of it, can be read as symbolic, if not altogether allegorical. He makes statements that openly propose the figurative value of events and characters directly to the reader or that suggest this kind of interpretation from within the fiction itself. For example: "la figura de Melania era de una vaga inmaterialidad. Su sonrisa fija, en cambio, su cabeza de trenzas negras enroscadas como las serpientes de una Medusa, adquirieron una intensidad *alegórica* que hizo temblar a Mauro" (98; emphasis added); "Mis lectores se estarán preguntando cuál era el secreto que produjo esta ruptura entre los hermanos [Mauro, Valerio, Alamiro and Clemente, who dig up the spears forming the estate's iron gate], y acusando al escritor de utilizar el desacreditado artilugio de retener información con el fin de azuzar la curiosidad del lector. La verdad es que me he propuesto arrastrarlo hasta este punto del relato para descubrir ahora, dando al hecho toda su magnitud, aquello que quiero colocar como *símbolo* al centro de mi historia" (104; emphasis added); "Es que Wenceslao, igual que mis demás niños, es un personaje *emblemático*" (372; emphasis added).

11. Mac Adam concludes his reading of the novel by acknowledging this point (263). The term "fictive author" is suggested by Spires 15-16.

12. This view of things would put into question Baker's identification of a "meta-text" within *Casa de campo;* see also Mac Adam.

13. As acknowledged in note 2, there is reason to question the exclusion of other referents in an allegorical reading of the novel; but it would be difficult to claim that the Chilean case is in fact not privileged by Donoso, and I therefore emphasize that context here. Among the readings of the novel that minimize or exclude entirely the matter of its political allegory are those of Martinez, Pérez Blanco, and Salgado.

14. Given the complexity of Donoso's novel as it shifts between discursive modes and also between registers of meaning within each of those modes, it should be read as more than an example of allegory as "the most self-reflexive and self-critical of narrative genres" (Quilligan, *Language of Allegory* 24). However, we might identify it as a contemporary example of how such reflexivity itself becomes an object of textual commentary in a novel that suggests a number of interpretations, among them a reading of its text as a political allegory. (See also Quilligan's suggestive points on "the resurgence of allegoresis in the various reader-oriented critical approaches to literature" and "the resurgence of allegorical narrative in contemporary fiction" [*Language of Allegory* 280]).

15. Allegory can be described as an "authoritarian" form of fiction, precisely because it preselects and privileges a certain meaning and thus limits the possibilities for interpretation (see Quilligan "Allegory, Allegoresis," 182-85; cf. Suleiman). Donoso's novel works with the ideas of the authoritarian or authoritative within its various registers, one of which appears to be allegorical. However, his text would appear to authorize readings that complement and compete with one another all at the same time. Thus one of the issues raised by the novel has to do with the degree to which interpretation is fixed or not in *Casa de campo.*

16. The subversion of the possibility of establishing any stable or final authority can be understood in terms of the novel's carnavalesque structure. For a consideration of the question of power from that perspective, which in many ways supports the present reading, see Gutiérrez Mouat, "Discurso" 234-41 and "Carnavalización" 62.

17. A reading of the novel as lending unconditional support to the figure of Adriano Gomara/Salvador Allende would have to come to terms with the novel's critique of the relations that appear to be inherent in any exercise of authority or power and the self-interests that obtain in such situations, regardless of the aims of the participating subjects. Balbina's self-interested critique is also a critique of the possible self-interests of an apparently selfless figure who is, in fact, enmeshed in relations of power. The novel's (some would say Donoso's) critique of the opposition (the other Venturas, the servants, the Mayordomo) can thus be read as an exploration of how authority comes to be exercised as well as an apparent "taking of position" for or against any individual or group. Indeed, the

author-narrator appears to undercut a reading that would stabilize his own opinions of such entities or even the institutions or events for which they might stand (for example, he stresses that he does not wish to "condenarlos a todos" [302], when describing actions of the servants/army). Thus, though the novel can be read as taking positions for or against specific characters or groups, it also undercuts readings that would fix its position in unconditional or univocal terms.

18. We might note that Donoso's novel can be read as putting into question and at the same time using effectively the conventions of realist fiction. *Casa de campo* appears to transform dated conventions into the most up-to-date strategies of modern fiction. For Donoso's comments about his interest in "recuperating" such a "dead language" as that of nineteenth-century prose fiction, see Donoso/ Christ 42-43.

Works Cited

Alter, Robert. *Partial Magic: The Novel as a Self-Conscious Genre.* Berkeley: U of California P, 1975.

Bacarisse, Pamela. "Donoso and Social Commitment: *Casa de campo.*" *Bulletin of Hispanic Studies* 60 (1983): 319-32.

Baker, Rilda L. "Perfil del narrador desenmascarado en *Casa de campo.*" *LA CHISPA '81: Selected Proceedings, February 26-28, 1981.* Ed. Gilbert Paolini. New Orleans: Tulane U, 1981. 35-41.

Bal, Mieke. *Narratology: Introduction to the Theory of Narrative.* Trans. Christine van Boheemen. Toronto: U of Toronto P, 1985. Trans. of *De theorie van vertellen en verhalen,* 2nd ed., 1980.

Bloom, Edward A. "The Allegorical Principle." *ELH* 18 (1951): 163-90.

Bloomfield, Morton W. "Allegory as Interpretation." *New Literary History* 3 (1972-73): 301-17.

Chatman, Seymour. *Story and Discourse: Narrative Structure in Fiction and Film.* Ithaca: Cornell UP, 1978.

Culler, Jonathan. "Literary History, Allegory, and Semiology." *New Literary History* 7 (1976-77): 259-70.

Donoso, José. *Casa de campo.* Barcelona: Seix Barral, 1978.

———. Interview. With Ronald Christ. *Partisan Review* 49 (1982): 23-44.

———. Interview. With Z. Nelly Martínez. *Hispamérica* 21 (1978): 53-74.

Fletcher, Angus. *Allegory: The Theory of a Symbolic Mode.* Ithaca: Cornell UP, 1964.

Genette, Gérard. *Narrative Discourse: An Essay on Method.* Trans. Jane E. Lewin. Ithaca: Cornell UP, 1980. Trans. of "Discours du récit." *Figures III.* 1972.

Gutiérrez Mouat, Ricardo. "Carnavalización de la literatura en 'Casa de campo' y 'Cien años de soledad.'" *Sin nombre* 13.1 (1983): 50-64.

———. "*Casa de campo:* La carnavalización del discurso alegórico." *José Donoso, impostura e impostación: la modelización lúdica y carnavalesca de una producción literaria* (Gaithersburg, Md.: Hispamérica, 1983). 197-248. (Also published in *Kañina* 7.2 [1983]: 59-76.)

Honig, Edwin. *Dark Conceit: The Making of Allegory.* 1959. New York: Oxford UP, 1966.

Hutcheon, Linda. *Narcissistic Narrative: The Metafictional Paradox.* Waterloo, Ontario: Wilfrid Laurier UP, 1980.

Iñigo Madrigal, Luis. "Alegoría, historia, novela (a propósito de *Casa de campo,* de José Donoso)." *Hispamérica* 21 (1978): 5-31.

Jakobson, Roman. "On Realism in Art." *Readings in Russian Poetics: Formalist and Structuralist Views.* Ed. Ladislav Matejka and Krystyna Pomorska. Cambridge: MIT P, 1971. 38-46.

Mac Adam, Alfred J. "José Donoso: *Casa de campo.*" *Revista iberoamericana* 47 (1981): 257-63.

Martínez, Z. Nelly. "*Casa de campo* de José Donoso: afán de descentralización y nostalgia de centro." *Hispanic Review* 50 (1982): 439-48.

Omaña, Balmiro. "De *El obsceno pájaro de la noche* a *Casa de campo.*" *Texto crítico* 22-23 (1981): 265-79.

Pérez Blanco, Lucrecio. "*Casa de campo,* de José Donoso, valoración de la fábula en la narrativa actual hispanoamericana." *Anales de la literatura hispanoamericana* 6.7 (1978): 259-89.

Quilligan, Maureen. *The Language of Allegory: Defining the Genre.* Ithaca: Cornell UP, 1979.

———. "Allegory, Allegoresis, and the Deallegorization of Language: The *Roman de la rose,* the *De planctu naturae,* and the *Parlement of Foules.*" *Allegory, Myth, and Symbol.* Ed. Morton W. Bloomfield. Cambridge: Harvard UP, 1981. 163-86.

Salgado, María A. "*Casa de campo* o la realidad de la apariencia." *Revista iberoamericana* 51 (1985): 283-91.

Siegle, Robert. *The Politics of Reflexivity: Narrative and the Constitutive Poetics of Culture.* Baltimore: Johns Hopkins UP, 1986.

Solotorevsky, Myrna. *José Donoso: incursiones en su producción novelística.* Valparaíso: Ediciones Universitarias de Valparaíso, 1983.

Spires, Robert C. *Beyond the Metafictional Mode: Directions in the Modern Spanish Novel.* Lexington: U of Kentucky P, 1984.

Suleiman, Susan Rubin. *Authoritarian Fictions: The Ideological Novel As a Literary Genre.* New York: Columbia UP, 1983.

Todorov, Tzvetan. *Littérature et signification.* Paris: Larousse, 1967.

————. *The Fantastic: A Structural Approach to a Literary Genre.* Trans. Richard Howard. Cleveland: P of Case Western U, 1973. Trans. of *Introduction à la littérature fantastique.* 1970.

Marie Murphy (essay date January-June 1989)

SOURCE: Murphy, Marie. "Language Put-On: José Donoso's *A House in the Country.*" *Latin American Literary Review* 17, no. 33 (January-June 1989): 50-59.

[*In the following essay, Murphy discusses the metafictional purposes of Donoso's use of the* mise en abyme *structure in* A House in the Country.]

While the Latin American new narrative interrogates many aspects of self-consciousness, within this tradition, José Donoso's *A House in the Country* provides one of the most exhaustive examinations of the art of the novel, overtly juxtaposing realistic and post-modern techniques. In this study, I examine the most evident display in *A House in the Country* of what is perhaps the central problematic in metafiction: the discrepancy between art and reality. I consider two instances of the *mise en abyme* structure, pointing to the role of artifice (and the artifice of language) in foregrounding a paradoxical search for history and reality in the novel. A narrative mapping of rhetorical strategies, in which the narrator addresses readers, is supplemented by a network of interior duplication with the device of the *mise en abyme.* Two of these, the excursion to a mythical lagoon and the children's play within the novel, mirror the larger frame of the novel, while simultaneously pointing to the characters' construction of reality and the structuring process of fiction. Lucien Dällenbach specifies three principal categories of this reflective device: the first has a relationship of similitude with the whole which contains it; the second is a reduplication in infinite regress; and the third includes the work it is contained in.

The play and excursion are both fictions of uncertain origins within the novel and their function is identical within the anecdote—mystifying an opposing group. That is, the excursion to the mythical lagoon is invented to distract the adults from recognizing and preempting the impending revolution while the play is designed to sidetrack the children from joining the revolt. In the first part of the novel, the powerful Ventura adults prepare for an excursion to a fabled lagoon, while many of the children engage in their favorite game, acting out the unscripted play *La Marquise Est Sortie à Cinq Heures.* Once the adults have departed, some children and the enslaved Indians revolt against the parents' authoritarian rule. The mythical lagoon and the play signal the Ventura's predilection for living in a fantasy world, refusing to face reality. Simultaneously, these two *mises en abyme* recall and exalt the *power of invention,* problematizing both terms: the nature of power and the creative explosiveness of language despite/ behind official versions of truth.

The novel is at once all places and no place, a site where reality and fantasy intersect in a textual construction whereby the parts reflect each other and the whole, while the boundaries between constituent elements are subverted. The novel begins with an excursion to a lagoon which does not exist; the central events overlap with those of the embedded play; and the fresco depicted comes alive while the characters recede into its two-dimensionality. Beyond the play of authority between implied author, narrator, characters and readers, the text challenges the perception of reality, its representability and ultimately its existence.

The disposition of the discourse and eternally evolving myth foreground the novel's tentative nature: second versions rewrite earlier versions; filters obscure initial situations; Celeste "sees" within blindness, Arabela sees through foggy glasses, Wenceslao sees in the dark— perception in space is as confused as the ambiguous time. Reading is countered by being read to, telling by listening, and roles are unstable in a symmetrical reversibility. The lack of center in terms of originating facts generates a continual superimposition of narrative aspects—a productivity whose finality is seemingly belied.

The text advertises itself as a fictional analogue of both sociological theories as seen in Berger's and Luckmann's work, in which "reality is socially constructed" (primarily through language)[1] and a concept expressed in S. J. Schmidt's article, "The Fiction is that Reality Exists." Schmidt relies upon constructivist epistemology which asserts that "the constructed world is a world of experiencing which consists of experience and does not assert 'truth' in terms of a correspondence to an ontological reality" (258). He concludes that reality is always a construct and its objective existence is a fiction, insofar as we cannot ascertain more than postulations of reality. Specifically with regard to the relationship between reality and fiction, he remarks:

> By emphasizing the role of conventions in directing the system's constructional work, we can illustrate how the status of reality, truth, meaning, and identity depends

on conventions that determine what kind of rules are individually or socially accepted for the consensual *confirmation* of reality, truth, meaning, and identity.

(263)

A House in the Country and its characters never stop affirming and confirming, even while paradoxically undermining and doubting, presence and reality. While the discourse's fictiveness and intratextual "origins" delineate a hazy world apart from reality, the uncanny resemblance to real events and social reality play against the solipsism of the text.

The excursion to the fabled lagoon introduces and is emblematic of the novel itself. The fitful beginning(s) of the narrative is echoed in the fruitless attempt to establish an original cause for the parents' trip. Likewise, the narrator continually journeys back in time to explain the hypothetical lagoon, made even more implausible by the rumors, guesses and ever-widening circle of participants in the making of this myth. Apparently Arabela, Wenceslao and Adriano invented the lagoon in collusion, hoping to tempt the adults away from the seat of power/gold. The lagoon begins as a fiction within the novel but the Venturas eventually accept its existence as self-evident, thus it becomes "real." As the children inquire about it, the parents fabricate answers in order in order to mask their bewilderment. Arabela's trumped-up maps and documents, one level beyond the oral quality of rumors, further imprison the adults in the seemingly incontrovertible verification of the written word. Yet the word only "verifies" textual uncertainty.

The narrator's explanation of the myth's origin clearly refers to the poetics of fiction as well as to the similar process of constructing reality. Fiction is created with voices and fragments which gradually build a substitute for reality, potentially mistaken by a naive reader for reality itself. Donoso's narrator ensures that we do not confuse his words with actual persons and events via his metanarrative. Realistic tokens of scenery and events are simultaneously proffered and denied the reader. The serpentine cavalcade moving toward the lagoon is a metaphor of the novel's succession of words which precariously stand in place of the absent world—figures traced and erased in one process. Insofar as the excursion refers to a pleasurable escape from ordinary constrictions, the conventions of fiction are displayed. The novel too makes a journey, with no destination other than itself, infinitely expandable with temporal and spatial digressions. The concept of narrative as physical displacement is suggested by the hierarchical arrangement of carriages in the cavalcade, recurring linear images (the cavalcade, train, sinuous carriage line and Marulanda's fence) and the replication of the excursion in a variety of minor trips—all metaphorically linked to the present of the narrative journey.

The excursion's counterpart, the play, is likewise an affirmation of the novel's irreality. A stylized version of the encompassing novel, it foregrounds the jockeying for power, as well as the continual production of myths and masquerades. It also reminds readers of the absence of love in a world where affection is a farce, hyperbolically reduced to a trivial love intrigue in *La Marquise*. The monolithic Marulanda society becomes even more unreal in the distorted mirror of the play. The already emblematic characters are here complete caricatures; artificial, self-dramatizing behaviour is explicit acting; the fantastical landscape and mansion literally become a stage and rumors a script. For example, The Perfidious Marquise accompanies her words "with an end-of-the-second-act cackle" (240); the narrator aspires "to construct a stage" for his recital and "Outside a bright sun, burnished as if by order of the Venturas, highlighted the flat azure sky" (228).

Although *La Marquise Est Sortie à Cinq Heures* is designed to uphold the adults' authority, it is undermined by deviations from the play's ostensible plot. The verbal duplicity by which every revolutionary event is redefined as a mere game with no transcendence succeeds for a time in upholding the status quo. The drama can only be defeated by the refusal to play by the rules. After the revolution and once Casilda steals the Ventura gold, the game no longer serves the parents' purposes, thus their most savage measures are invoked: the servants crush the insurrection with a violence heretofore unseen. . . .

The play's climax inaugurates a heightening of theatricality (connoting artifice and flight from reality) as well as its contradiction. While the instances of confused levels, linguistic games and play-acting increase in the second half of the novel, their thematic and structural opposite occurs. The anecdote itself inserts the reality of history and change, provoking the parents' brutality to become increasingly obvious. The narrator contradicts the adults' denial of time, insisting that to say that life will continue as before the attack is patently absurd. Furthermore, he counterpoints his own touted "exaggerated artificiality" with more traditionally "realistic" and detailed scenes of the hunger, torture and death experienced in the country house: "I must ask my reader to imagine . . . a scene steeped in desolation and death: screaming, running, and shooting in the charred and muddy park, and corpses of nameless natives floating on the laghetto" (218). The theatrical flavor is frequently laced with a more straightforward description and syntax than in earlier scenes.

Several passages are in this realistic vein: the deaths of Adriano and Arabela, Wenceslao's monologue and other scenes which painfully remind us of political repression in the world we know. Furthermore, some characters are portrayed in more depth and allowed a greater freedom of voice than at the beginning. While the use of artifice never abates, the prettified characterizations occasionally verge on the monstrification of *The Obscene Bird of Night.* The undercurrent of the grotesque, related to the relative "realism" of the earlier novel, is intratextually related to the discussion about the novel between the "author" and character/reader Silvestre. In a purportedly realistic scene, Silvestre is transformed from a relatively elegant caricature to his realistic analogue (fat, smelling of alcohol, etc.) and back again to his original characterization. Once more placed under narrative scrutiny toward the end of the novel, Silvestre and the other adults are re-transformed into their grotesque, more "realistic" versions: "How monstrous all the grown-ups had become during their absence! . . . And was Silvestre just one more lackey, wheezing, bound by the coils of his obesity?" (309). The switching of registers foregrounds the very literariness of literature while reflecting upon Donoso's own body of fiction. Nevertheless, it also connotes, albeit ironically, a realistic and critical view of the parents who can no longer appear merely prettified and artificial.

One of the novel's central concerns is the linkage between artifice and language; indeed, the language is as much put-on as the characters' costumes. The Ventura adults expect that language should provide a window onto the world. Furthermore, language should be univocal, such that totalized meaning is determined by those in power. The narrator demonstrates this world view by metaphors: the insistence upon the apparent Order of the Marulanda society, the lances in the fence forever fixed, the Majordomo's authority as conferred and symbolized by his gigantic uniform, and characters trapped in eternal immobility.

This monolithic attitude toward reality and language is assailed from within the very world of the adults. Language continually dysfunctions in a variety of ways. Names, for instance, are generalized, such that Juan Pérez is the same name given to a different employee every year. Thus the specificity of a name is belied by its more general function of designating a position. Even more dysfunctional, words are used to convey opposite meanings from the norm within the textual world: love is hate, one year is one day, etc. Language inadequately hides a lack of knowledge, as with the library's empty books, or myths about unexplainable origins.

Within the play, *La Marquise,* language takes on special significance because its artificiality parallels the grown-ups' intent to shut out reality yet the nature of language undermines their concurrent intent to *represent* the world to their liking. The "unlimited semiosis"[2] of language is foregrounded by a particularly chaotic display of signifiers in transformation. For instance, Juvenal describes the play as a fable, legend, fairy tale; the narrator calls it a masquerade; and Melania, a farce. The cousins are called children, spectators, crowd, actors, extras, while Mauro refers to Melania's perspiration as

"that very drop, not some other . . . sweat, tear, lymph, dew . . . anything, everything" (156). The children are indiscriminately referred to by their names from the novel or the play, and furthermore they exchange roles and names throughout the rest of the novel with greater frequency. Once Adriano enters the spectacle, Melania calls him "God the Father Almighty" and the designation is taken up as an ironic epithet by the narrator in later moments.

The impossibility of a univocal interpretation of events is understood by Wenceslao, as he observes Juvenal straining "for sights and sounds no doubt identical but opposite in meaning to those he himself had noticed" (165). Ultimately, the linguistic correlation between signifier and signified is as tenuous and unreal as the skewed masks, crude make-up and hallucinatory scenery, where the illusion of correspondence is destroyed by inadequate theatrical tricks. Nothing quite matches nor masks properly, a metaphor for the slippage of signs whose meaning can neither be totally limited nor transparent.

Insofar as the handling of language and voice within the play hyperbolically mirrors that of the novel as a whole, the drama is a *mise en abyme* which Dällenbach would categorize as a reflection of both the text's narrative and linguistic code. By exaggeration, the opacity of all language, as well as the deliberate miscommunication of the adults, children and narrator is underlined. The novel's stilted language becomes the "Marquisese," a garbled, invented speech of the children, ironically, not at all childlike: "The rosebud withers in the inky night, while the teeming jungle takes up its adamant cat-o'-nines to destroy the imperial orography of my blood" (309). The stereotypical banalities of the adults are parodied by the "Marquisese's" exalted tone. Learned, archaic words and complicated syntax mock the adults' (and the narrator's) rhythmic and anaphoric pontifications. The "Marquises," an embedded language within the novel, is furthermore framed by the metalanguage enveloping the characters' and the narrators' utterances. Words become "divinas palabras" which cast a spell over children and readers. The narrator and children are ambiguously caught and revelling in the play's frenetic discourse.

A final breakdown of linguistic description is demonstrated when foreign guests (and potential buyers of the estate) disbelieve the Ventura description of reality. Celeste Ventura extols Marulanda: "Don't you find the ochers of twilight . . . deliquescent as a golden shower cascading over Diana . . . ?" (299). One of the guests, thinking Celeste is an actress, wonders: "How I'm suppose to believe . . . that the whole thing isn't some pure invention . . . The subjectivity that colors your judgement of everything pertaining to the family is at total odds with reality seen from outside" (317).

The narrator, proclaiming the fact that language only alludes indirectly to reality, deliberately foregrounds the characters and story as linguistic constructs in his metanarrative. He indicates to readers that they should avoid the pitfalls of seeing through words directly to the world. Allen Thiher, writing about Nabokov, makes some observations which can be applied to *A House in the Country:*

> A hatred of mirrors, to paraphrase Borges, is a beginning of an understanding of postmodern fiction, for as producers of doubles mirrors augment the illusion of being and foster metaphysical illusions. One might suspect that Hermann shares some of Nabokov's aversions, for, as representations, mirror-images work best to trap the unsuspecting, like mirrors set for dull-witted birds.
>
> (99)

Language, inevitably limiting and structuring reality by virtue of grammatical rules and the constraints of the mind's and society's veils, is further problematized through the narrator's equivocation. Obtrusive metaphors and similes, as well as highly visible stylized construction, make words not mirrors but obstacles and challenges in constructing a parallel but different reality.

The parents' attempt to suppress reality and words not emanating from their authority is unmasked by the narrator's parody of the mystification functioning at all levels of the society. Some of the more lucid characters undermine or qualify events through the play with or questioning of words. The children's rebellion is as much for lances which are weapons as for lances as words. Mauro opts for a free-floating approach to language: each lance or word should be "regrouped in a thousand different ways and with a thousand fine distinctions, no longer slaves to the allegorial function that now held them prisoners in the form of a railing" (78-79). Arabela, in stark contrast to the servants' euphemistic speech, (for instance, "disappear" meaning "vanish in a puff of smoke"), clearly defines: "I mean, specifically, that you and your men have arrested him and taken him away" (242). Wenceslao and Agapito invent a language in order to communicate among themselves, circumventing the official discourse: the Mayordomo's men "were too dense to understand any language but their own, not even pig latin" (261). Both Wenceslao's secret language and the "Marquisese" recall the invented language (gíglico) of Cortázar's *Hopscotch,* which also plays against prosaic, "serious" and traditional discourse.[3]

The Marulanda oligarchy in some sense also invents a language but their power in conferring names is ultimately denied. We discover that, unbeknownst to the adults, the name Juan Pérez which generically referred to a series of gardeners, is the real name of one person who returned to Marulanda yearly. Ironically his role is quite different from that which they had envisaged, since he is a secret usurper among the faceless servants. The dysfunctional quality of language is not only obviated at microtextual levels, it is conveyed at the level of larger narrative units as well. Not only do words and things mismatch, the novel's static beginnings and floating references to time and space refuse the Balzacian fixing of story in history. The central catalysts of the story, the lagoon and play, never believable, lose their potency altogether. The play's allure is transcended by Arabela's death, and the lagoon is scoffed at by the foreigners who take over the property. Power and the power of monolithic discourse, inseparable in this novel, are diffused.[4]

The adults' mask of truth and the narrator's parody of their methods convey the multivalent meaning of the phrase "only appearances count" in the discourse. The exaggerated richness of painterly details betrays the novel's intent to reduce the symbolic depth of characters and plot to schematic designs as seen metaphorically in the real-seeming fresco—the novel's most vertiginous *mise en abyme*. Reality is transcribed onto the surface of a page, or for the characters, the flatness of the fresco into which they can be duped into entering. Readers too, like dull-witted birds, can be induced into walking into the allegorical fresco and seeing a categorical description of Chile, or other univocal reflections of reality.

While the novel refuses to, and cannot, make its narrative a mirror of history, it refracts in distorted fashion aspects of Latin American and Chilean society and history. The author and narrator indicate that *A House in the Country* is all novels in some fashion, "an adventure novel," "a political novel," "pure language."[5] It moves in and out of allegory and history but is always inscribed within the frame of fictionality in which a separate universe is created.

Not a historical novel, it shows ways of reading a created world in which some characters search not only for language/lances, but also for history. Wenceslao attempts to understand the contradictions in Adriano's revolution, recognizing the problems in his "ideal" society. He insists upon analyzing the movement from within itself, refusing both absolute pessimism and nonaction. Not only is the adult denial of history exposed, the failure of the divided children to carry out a program, to make history, is chronicled. History is not resolved since the end implies the continuation of the dilemmas present from the beginning, but the progress of the novel shows the emergence of a faint light of consciousness. Characters' integrity as individual subjects is questioned, origins are absent and the last third of the novel departs from its historical analogue. There is no final knot which ties up interpretation and illuminates the reader as to who will inevitably rule

Marulanda. Since history cannot be represented as something outside language, the narrator shows the process of constructing worlds with figures drawn and suspended within language:

> The dust cloud raised by the cavalcade was never to settle: the stubborn fog that shrouded not objects but depths left no impression on the eye, suggesting instead that everything in sight-house, railing, in short, the entire universe-might reasonably be taken as figures embroidered in white thread on a fabric of similar whiteness, from which it would be impossible to extract them.
>
> (340)

The displays of worlds in the process of reconstruction is neither a reduction of literature to mere play, refusing to speak, nor is it analogous to the opposite extreme practiced by the Ventura authorities where reality is denied, not merely put into question. Rather than narrating with what Henry James called the "tone of the historian," offering reality "without rearrangement," the narrator's feigned authoritarianism and the play between allegory and illusion dissolves the author's, narrator's, characters', reader's and reality's power into the plurality of language. Donoso invokes a "morality of form" in the sense Barthes spoke of, in that literature is the site of subversion, not dogma; problems, not answers.[6] No comforting verisimilitude, identification nor resolutions are allowed the reader. The *mise en abyme* device and frame-breaks in **A House in the Country** point simultaneously to the self-enclosed world of fiction and its opposite—the impossibility of clear borders between reader/author and reality/fiction.[7] The narrator as guide dismantles his own rhetoric and reality, yet paradoxically calls for a realistic view. While Donoso's text does not permit the sign to be "grimly weighted by its signified," nor the novel to be "grimly weighed" by History, as with Barthes' discussion of the sign, "there is meaning but this meaning does not permit itself to be 'caught': it remains fluid, shuddering with a faint ebullition" (Barthes, 1978, 97-98).

A House in the Country's discontinuities and vertiginous interior duplication foreground similarities, and above all, differences between myth, fiction and history. Whereas myth presupposes a fixed, natural order of things which supports the status quo, fiction is an agreement—the site of questioning, change and of mutual participation in creating discourses that do not pretend to be absolute. While fiction is written in history, fiction permits us to write an alternative to history. Whereas in the world of myth, ethical meaning is attributed to mere conventions, fiction admits that it is only a world of appearances, where conventions accepted as conventions are used to create new forms and meanings. The *mise en abyme* structure creates a texture, an aesthetic pleasure, in which the real is investigated and figured on the margins of language and literature.

Notes

1. Gutiérrez Mouat has referred to Berger and Luckmann's work in relation to Donoso's fiction in the notes to his Introduction.

2. Eco describes Charles Pierce's theories on unlimited semiosis: "The process of unlimited semiosis shows us how signification, by means of continual shiftings which refer a sign back to another sign or string of signs, circumscribes *cultural units* in an asymptotic fashion, without even allowing one to touch them directly, though making them accessible through other units . . . Semiosis explains itself by itself: this continual circularity is the normal condition of signification and even allows communicational processes to use signs in order to mention things and states of the world" (198).

3. The use of subversive and nonsensical languages in Donoso, in its interplay with theatricality and power, also recalls Severo Sarduy's *Cobra,* a novel which continually produces and finally almost eclipses meaning. Playfully akin to Donoso's "Marquisese" and Cortazar's "gíglico," Sarduy's Cobra signs mambos in Esperanto at one point.

4. Vincent Leitch discusses Foucault's ideas on the subject of the relationship of power to language: "he demonstrates that archival discourse expands, divides, and deploys knowledge and power in the interest of social control. The rules of discourse, particularly the exclusionary ones, direct powerful, though often unnoticed, socio-political practices" (154). The will-to-knowledge, as an implacable and anonymous force always susceptible to transformation, "summons 'truth' as a mask for its operation" (154-155).

5. Iñigo Madrigal quotes from an interview of Donoso where the latter describes his novel as an adventure novel and a political novel (6). Donoso's narrator describes the novel as "pure language."

6. Susan Sontag writes in her Introduction to *A Barthes Reader:* "Although Barthes agrees with Sartre that the writer's vocation has an ethical imperative, he insists on its complexity and ambiguity. Sartre appeals to the morality of ends. Barthes invokes 'the morality of form'—what makes literature a problem rather than a solution; what makes literature" (xix).

7. I agree with David Carroll's rejection of the idea of literature as being completely self-enclosed. He writes about the dogmatic formalism of some post-structural and structural critics, such as Jean Ricardou, who reduce the text to a "pure, linguistic system" whereby pre-texts are ignored: "The gradual elimination of all problems of the signified (of

representation, history, sense, etc.) alone can guarantee that fiction is really what this theory and practice project it as being, but the consequences of such a 'sacrifice'are evident" (177-180).

Works Cited

Barthes, Roland. *A Barthes Reader.* Ed. Susan Sontag. New York: Hill and Wang, 1983

————*Roland Barthes.* Trans. Richard Howard. New York: Hill and Wang, 1978.

Berger, Peter L. and Luckmann, Thomas. *The Social Construction of Reality: A Treatis in the Sociology of Knowledge.* Garden City, New York: Doubleday, 1966.

Carroll, David. *The Subject in Question: The Languages of Theory and the Strategies of Fiction.* Chicago: University of Chicago Press, 1982.

Cortazar, Julio. *Hopscotch.* Trans. Gregory Rabassa. New York: Pantheon, 1966.

Dällenbach, Lucien. "Intertexte et autotexte," *Poétique* 27 (1976): 282-96.

Donoso, José. *A House in the Country.* Trans. David Pritchard with Suzanne Jill Levine New York: Knopf, 1984.

————*The Obscene Bird of Night.* Trans. Hardie St. Martin and Leonard Mades Boston: Nonpareil, 1979.

Eco, Umberto. *The Role of the Reader.* Bloomington: Indiana University Press, 1979.

Gutiérrez Mouat, Ricardo. *José Donoso: Impostura e impostación: La modelización lúdica y carnavalesca de una producción literaria.* Gaithersburg, MD: Hispamérica 1983.

Iñigo Madrigal, Luis. "Alegoría, historia, novela, (a propósito de *Casa de campo.*" *Hispamérica* IX (1980): 5-31.

James, Henry. *The House of Fiction.* Ed. Leon Edel. London: Rupert Hart-David, 1957.

Leitch, Vincent B. *Deconstructive Criticism.* New York: Columbia University Press 1983.

Sarduy, Severo. *Cobra.* Trans. Suzanne Jill Levine. New York: E.P. Dutton, 1975.

Schmidt, S. J. "The Fiction is that Reality Exists: A Constructivist Model of Reality, Fiction, and Literature." *Poetics Today* 5.2 (1984): 253-274.

Thiher, Allen. *Words in Reflection: Modern Language Theory and Postmodern Fiction.* Chicago: University of Chicago Press, 1984.

Juan Carlos Lértora (essay date spring-summer 1989)

SOURCE: Lértora, Juan Carlos. "José Donoso's Narrative: The Other Side of Language." *Salmagundi* 82-83 (spring-summer 1989): 258-68.

[*In the following essay, Lértora addresses Donoso's questioning of the traditional functions of narrative fiction in light of Mikhail Bakhtin's theory of the carnival.*]

A characteristic trait of the narrative produced by Spanish American writers like Gabriel Garcia Márquez, Julio Cortázar, G. Cabrera Infante, M. Vargas Llosa, and José Donoso, is its attempt to explore human experience by way of the secret codes associated with the instincts, the unconscious and magic. The discourse that founds these narratives is situated in the labyrinthic space of the characters' consciousness. Characters are no longer conceived as representatives of social class or as psychological types, but as subjects of inner conflicts for which they cannot always find lucid or logical understanding or expression. Consciousness is assumed as chaos; it has its corollary in the language that expresses it, whose categories contradict the rational, "objective" thinking of a positivistic discourse in order to explore a new "logic" that, as paradoxical as it may seem, has its constantly changing center in human ambiguity. There is where this new coherence dwells, in the inner space created by new, sometimes dizzying associations that generate new meanings.

The narrative discourse is not monologic and assertive about the world it deploys, but polyphonic (in Bakhtin's sense of a "plurality of voices and consciences independent and distinct, expressing different worldviews"). The space of the discourse is shared by multiple narrators (or different and contradictory manifestations of one consciousness) that sustain different view points without a prevalent enunciating instance (or authoritarian narrative voice) that would sanction one particular discourse as carrier of the truth about the represented world. This multiplicity of discourses is yet another expression of the fundamental ambiguity that Donosian narrative develops and that has as a corollary the manifold or labyrinthine confusion of personal identity.

To this consideration of human being, unreachable in its complexity, corresponds a treatment of a narrative time that, heavily influenced by Henri Bergson's theory, flows and stands still at the same time. A broken chronology, inconstant flow, that disperses itself repeatedly, is consonant with the nature of the human situations it narrates: time and space are conceived as inseparable entities, constituting, as Bakhtin defines it, the *chronotope.* It is in this coordinate that José Donoso's narrative should be placed.

From the outset Donoso's narrative fiction has challenged the institutions and conventions that regulate language and determine our response to it. Even in such early works as **"The Blue Woman"** and **"The Poisoned Pastries"** (both written in English), as also in his collection of short stories—***Summertime***—, and his first novel, ***Coronation,*** a number of characteristic concerns begin to appear.

These early works deploy a constellation of recurrent meanings, which are also present in the later works, according to which the world is perceived as ominous, deteriorating, mad, grotesque. These categories signal the fundamental precariousness of the world and of human existence. They form the basis of a nihilism that finds expression in the merciless destruction of myths and beliefs which are customarily introduced in order to hide from us the tragic ambiguity of the human condition.

In Donoso's narrative, human relations and social institutions are considered by means of a discourse which finds, in the rupture of conventions, its best definition. In Donosian fiction characters who defend (and believe in) an apparent order of the world are relentlessly destroyed. Tragedy is brought on by the search for rational meaning in a world dominated by instinct and irrationality. The world is inevitably destined to end in the decadent, the absurd and the abominable, the zones whence characters derive their definition and destiny. The tragedy of human being is basically provoked by an obstinate search for a rational explanation in a world in which the instinctual and irrational prevail.

Already in ***Coronation,*** with its grotesque and carnivalesque ending (the crowning of a dying crazy old woman by her servants who dress her as a Queen), Donoso's narrative sets itself apart from the characteristic traditional realism of the previous generation of Latin American novelists. It explores yet other existential dimensions which place the fiction in a marked frame of irrealism, penetrating reality from a new, obverse perspective. Another work entitled ***This Sunday*** subverts the interior consciousness of its characters while revealing their degraded existence and their anguish before the terror which alienates them from the world they inhabit. Later works would refine tendencies that are unmistakably a part of Donoso's distinctive voice and vision.

Given the nature of the world he depicts, the exasperating quality of his narrative situations, and the ambiguous condition of his characters, the Donosian narrative is connected in a decisive way to the carnivalesque tradition, with all it contains of spectacle, transgression, fragmentation, transvestism, defiance of all rules and hierarchies, inversion of whatever is established; in sum, *le monde á l'envers.* That is why, in Donoso's fiction, antithesis and parody are central figures. Certain categories of the carnivalesque, again as formulated by Bakhtin,[1] are central to the understanding of this aspect of Donoso's narrative: "eccentricity, like intimate relations, is a special category for perceiving the carnivalesque nature of the world; it allows itself to open up (and to express itself in concrete form) to all that is normally repressed [. . .] It is necessary to add another category, that of profanity, sacrilege, and the whole system of debasement, carnival mockery, and the inconveniences having to do with generational forces of the land and of the body, the parodies of texts and sacred words."

El lugar sin limites[2] represents a considerable breakthrough for Donoso into the realm of the carnivalesque as described by Bakhtin. Its pessimistic portrayal of the condition of personal existence through the presence of the absurd and the total disintegration of the self goes further than his earlier works in its depiction of a world corroded in all its components. This novel is itself an anguished metaphor of an inverted utopia, an impossible paradise without God, love or solidarity; it is a version of a lost Paradise, or the antibiblical prediction.

Desecration in the novel works at all levels: that of the body, of identity, and of the official discourse that attempts to impose a false sense of order and generosity. The novel depicts the inversion (which along with transvestism and antithesis are, at the figurative level, its basis) of all social roles, and bitterly shows the absurdity of absolutes.

By showing the impossibility of categorically limiting dichotomies such as man/woman, good/evil (which in Donoso's earlier works functioned as structuring principles based on a clear appearance/reality opposition), ***El lugar sin limites*** presses towards a radical perception of the ambiguity which, for Donoso, is essential to the human condition. There is no one identity; there is no authenticity; we are all fragments, pieces, a human kaleidoscope.

This conception generates narrative structures without center, works in continuous self-transformation and mutation, and a discourse in constant displacement that shows the emptiness of everything, the nothingness which finds its greatest expression in ***The Obscence Bird of Night.*** In this work, the reader cannot differentiate between what is dream or hallucination, "reality" or fantasy; between what supposedly has taken place, and what can only be conjectured. This is a novel in which Donoso's grotesque realism achieves the standard defined by Bakhtin: "The images of the Romantic grotesque," Bakhtin writes, "usually express fear of the world and seek to inspire their reader with this fear"; "madness acquires a somber, tragic aspect of individual isolation" and "discloses the potentiality of an entirely different world, of another order, another way of life. It leads men out of the confines of the apparent (false) unity of the indisputable and stable."[3] Donoso's obsession with the diffuseness of individual identity gives shape to an alienating view in which the monstrous and the obscene, ritual and magic, regularly interact with objective reality.[4]

The novel depicts a world of hallucinatory indeterminacy, of constant interruption of narrative sequences, the elimination of absolute dichotomies, so that the "same" and the "other" complement each other, "are" each other. The rupture of chronology, and the total elimination of the narrator-protagonist-witness are but components of a relentless procedure in terms of which reality and fantasy freely intermingle. This is, of course, also the case for much contemporary Latin American fiction, a tendency described by the labels of "Magical Realism" or the "Fantastic."

In this novel reality is perceived from its underside, as it were, at a level prior to, even resistant to, that of coherent formulation. It depicts profanation of the body, or identity, but also profanation of any official language that attempts to impose the appearance of order, of harmony, of human generosity. Chaos rules, relentlessly producing substitutions, transformations, and distortions of personality. "El Mudito" is the unreliable narrator, character and witness of different stories that have, as a common element, ambivalence and sequential instability. Inversion, transvestism and transgression are structuring categories of the novel; accordingly, the configurating narrative discourse is also ambiguous, the "other side" of what traditionally constitutes narrative discourse. In *The Obscene Bird of Night* the reader has no way to formulate valid reading hypotheses, or to come up with definitive answers to the questions raised. Everywhere the reader is confronted by narrative procedures that interrogate themselves and continue to open up disturbing questions.

The Obscene Bird of Night expresses a deeply pessimistic conception of the world and of human being as essentially anchored in the absurd. The ceaseless, maze-like changes in spatial structure are just one more manifestation of the novel's lack of center; the subject of discourse is plural; in the discourse there is always a displacement of center. If there is any order in the novel, it is of a precarious sort whose fragile membrane is constantly threatened. At best, we are given an illusory, transitory order which in the end cannot sustain itself. Most of the story corresponds to the delirious inner discourse of the narrator-protagonist-witness, a discourse delivered without sequential organization and originated from different levels of a fragmented inner consciousness, the reflection of a disintegrated identity. Donoso creates a series of substitutions at both the level of *énonciation* and the level of *énoncé* (—Humberto

Peñaloza/writer/secretary/the seventh hag/giant head of papier maché/son of Iris Mateluna/dog of Iris Mateluna/ "imbunche"/light ashes dispersed by the wind—) so that the subject of the narrative enunciation is never fixed, and the narrative discourse does not have a stable generating center. Julia Kristeva explains this narrative feature when she says that "The mechanism of this mutation is insured by a *shifter* or specific connector: the MASK, which is the mark of alterity, the rejection of identity".[5] Bakhtin claims that the mask is related to "the merry negation of uniformity and similarity; it rejects conformity to oneself. The mask is related to transition, metamorphoses, the violation of natural boundaries."[6]

In *The Obscene Bird of Night,* the mask does not have a single specific symbolic value; it does not constitute a concrete entity. It gives way to other masks but there is no concrete personality at the end of this permutation process, no unique or authentic identity. As Donoso puts it: "It is my obsession with the no unity of human personality. Why am I so interested in disguises? Because they are ways of dissolving the unity of human being, of undoing the psychological unity, that horrible myth we have invented".[7]

This view of human life as fragmented is sharply shown in *Sacred Families.* In **"Chatanooga Choo Choo"** the characters are like manikins whose faces can be erased and later be painted in different ways *ad infinitum,* and whose limbs can be assembled and disassembled whichever way one wants. In **"Gaspard de la nuit,"** the main character exchanges his identity with a *clochard* of identical appearance, thus losing his own identity while "the other" is now "himself". With this, Donoso expresses his rejection of the myth that assures the unity of the self and emphasizes, instead, dispersion and ambiguity as main features of our condition.

By refusing to acquiesce in a stable image of apprehensible reality, Donoso's narrative questions the mimetic nature of fiction in general, and poses new ways to explore its possibilities. One interesting aspect of the larger theoretical problem is nicely signalled in *The Obscene Bird,* where the character "El Mudito" ("The Mute") is the narrator; but as his words can't be spoken, there can be no communication. And if that is so, can there be narration? At this level the *Obscene Bird* stands as a metaphor of the impossibility of conveying deep inner experience, the experience of an identity in crisis, for example. What seems real is narrated from the other side of language, not from the side that "tells" but from the side that cannot "tell," that can give at most only an incomplete view of what we might call "Reality."

By denying the traditional mimetic condition of narrative, Donoso seeks to convey what is essentially a project of liberation or, in bakhtinian terms, the "carnivalesque spirit": "The carnival-grotesque form exercises the same function: to consecrate inventive freedom, to permit the combination of a variety of different elements and their rapprochement, to liberate from the prevailing point of view of the world, from conventions and established truths, from clichés, from all that is humdrum and universally accepted. This carnival spirit offers the chance to have a new outlook on the world, to realize the relative nature of all that exists, and to enter a completely new order of things." It is this freeing of the individual from the stifling weight of conventions, from the rigidity and falseness of institutionalized rituals, a salient aspect of Donoso's fiction, which finds its best expression through a discourse that seeks to break away from that other discourse, generated from power, that presumes to hold the truth.

The image of power and its carnivalesque transgression is the organizing principle of *A House In The Country.* The novel is organized by means of a narrative-authorial discourse that attempts to control all components of the represented world, but which the fiction itself contradicts. Complementary to this discourse there is another, multilevel discourse, which gives the novel a polyphonic structure, generated by different groups of characters. Characters are organized in a series of circles, or rings, which in turn correspond to the structures of power in the society; accordingly, their discourses represent the variety of social discourses, the social heteroglossia. The novel becomes, then, the space in which different discursive practices meet. The old members of the Ventura family, representative of the old aristocracy, owners of the gold that they exchange for money to foreign investors, are at the outer circle. Inside this hierarchical ring we find the younger thirty-three Ventura cousins, who already are, in essence, a micro version of what they will be when they grow up: just like the old Venturas. At the time the story takes place, they plan an endless game whose title corresponds to Valéry's well known line: "La marquise est sortie á cinq heures." Among them, there are transvestites and homosexuals, some sadistic, some greedy, in anticipation of what their life will be.

The next circle consists of the servants who, by not owning anything (not even their lives), have no identity; they are anonymous to the Venturas, and they are "recognized" only by the function they have in their domestic tasks. However they do have some power: to watch the children after a certain hour at night and punish those who are caught breaking the house rules.

House In The Country is the space whose limits separate two worlds, two intertwined social orders, generating a chaotic rebellion which is quickly quelled, and whose end is also the dissolution of an aristocratic dynasty which gives birth to another that, in turn, destroys the former. This example of social cannibalism belies

the standard understanding of cannibalism used by the aristocracy as a way of reinforcing its power. Ironically enough, the so-called "cannibals" of the novel, who constitute the last of the three "circles" of characters, are revealed to us late in the novel as "vegetarians."

House In The Country is a novel open to different readings; it transcends a simplistic interpretation which would bind it, in a mechanical way, to a historical pretext that might function as its referent; that is to say, to Chilean history after the military coup. Even so there are plenty of "winks to the reader's complicity," as Cortázar would put it, and a number of "coincidences": The initials of *Adriano Gómara,* the doctor being held in a tower for the "insane" and "dangerous," correspond to the initials of the assassinated President, *Allende Gossens;* the servants would be the military; the Venturas, the richest of Chilean society; the darkening of the home, an allegory of Chile's isolation, an image of death, etc. More important, the novel symbolizes the structuring of human relations based mainly on the exercise of power at all interpersonal levels. But the different discourses that organize the novel are structured in such a way that ultimately *it is the nature of fiction* that emerges as the text's final objective. The narrative discourse explores its own structuring possibilities as textual productivity regulated by the needs of writing.

It is this same principle that supports the represented world of *La misteriosa desaparición de la marquesita de Loria,* and certain *novellas* included in *Sacred Families* and *Cuatro para Delfina.* These are not political texts in any traditional sense. However, they do express both an "historical and ethical responsibility," quite as Roland Barthes saw it as the task of writing to do. The more overt manifestation of this responsibility is to be found in *Curfew,* Donoso's latest novel. The action takes place in twenty four hours, and is centered on the wake and burial of Matilde Urrutia, Pablo Neruda's widow. As an allegorical novel, *Curfew* depicts life in Chile after more than a decade of dictatorship, showing social contradictions, misery, and most importantly, hopelessness. The main character, Mañungo Vera, is a returned exile who embodies many characteristics of the well know composer and singer Victor Jara, brutally assassinated by the Military Junta in the first days of their murderous coup. Here, as elsewhere in Donoso, political concerns are enmeshed in a matrix which contains a range of other issues, equally compelling and disturbing.

Donoso constantly questions the ontological status of fiction and challenges its traditional mimetic function. This questioning informs his conception of reality as incapable of allowing for true insight and of power as the main obstacle to genuine human interaction. The obsession with power, inauthenticity, masquerade, irrationality, and the fragmentary makes for a persistent and painful exploration of the dark side of human existence. The language, which is equal to the large purpose assigned to it, is the final mark of Donoso's mastery and of his commitment to the excesses and obliquities of the carnivalesque.

Notes

1. M. Bakhtin, *Rabelais And His World.*

2. Since there is no English translation for this novel, or for *La misteriosa desaparición de la marquesita de Loria,* or *Cuatro para Delfina,* I refer to their Spanish titles.

3. Bakhtin, *Ibid.*

4. As Donoso has stated, Ernesto Sábato's work in part influenced him as he was writing *The Obscene Bird of Night.* Donoso shares with Sábato the notion that the irrational is also a valid aesthetic category. Donoso states that Sábato's *On Heroes And Tombs* "made me realize that, to attempt to give rational form to something that I was living as an obsession, was a mistake not only of behaviour, but of literature; that the irrational could have the same, or greater, intellectual value than the rational, and sometimes can masquerade as the unclear rational; intelligence and irrationality are not contradictory terms. The irrational, the obsessive may have the significant literary status, that Sábato conferred upon it in *On Heroes And Tombs.*" José Donoso, *Historia personal del Boom.*

5. J. Kristeva, The Text of the Novel.

6. Bakhtin, *Ibid.*

7. "Novel as Happening", an interview with E. Rodriguez Monegal.

Fernando Alegría (eassay date summer 1992)

SOURCE: Alegriá, Fernando. "Good-bye to Metaphor: *Curfew.*" *The Review of Contemporary Fiction* 12, no. 2 (summer 1992): 77-79.

[*In the following essay, Alegría says that, in his later novel* Curfew, *Donoso abandons his usual metaphorical technique and offers an obvious condemnation of the Pinochet regime.*]

For years José Donoso has beaten the path of metaphor to express his way of feeling and understanding Chile, a path both difficult and dangerous. In a bold effort he produced a beautiful and well-structured synthesis of nostalgia, emotions, and sorrows. It was called *A House in the Country.* It deeply impressed readers in Spain and Latin America, but Chileans did not seem moved.

They were dazzled and amused by the novel; yet they couldn't get over a feeling of playfulness, of clues to be deciphered, and failed to grasp the profound tension that surely seized the author when he opened and closed the doors to his risky maze.

Today Donoso lays cards on the table that the reader will have to stack up again but that in the process will open wounds and leave scars, for *Curfew* is a detailed account of a love affair with Chile that Donoso held in reserve up to now. But the matter is no longer the loose threads that lead to the ruin of aristocratic families confronted by the onrush of lower-class daring. The uneasiness is of a different kind. The sadness that reverberates like an echo in Donoso's stories here begins to be recognized not in the issue of origins and traditions but in wrongs committed, lack of will, and recent failures in today's Chile.

For those who wonder if Donoso finally makes a pronouncement in this novel on the bleak record of Pinochet's military dictatorship, the answer is loud and clear: not only does he take a stand but states it in the harshest terms. Such a change, which might surprise some of his readers, was to be expected. The general's image—coarse, stubborn, cranky—is crumbling today, at century's end, eaten away from within. The country of *Curfew* is the survivor of a bloody and brutal nightmare in which everything is possible—torture, disappearance, treason, murder—under the drab cloak of a clever and monstrous lie. Perhaps the important thing is not so much to remember the facts (the media repeats them constantly) but to examine objectively what those crimes have done to the character of the Chilean people as they deal with the crisis. It is in this connection that Donoso abandons his typical metaphoric strategy and confronts the collapse of Chilean society in images and portraits bound to cause a stir—and resentment?—among his compatriots. Let me make clear that I'm not referring to literary clues of the kind proffered by the book's jacket to serve as bait for the reader's curiosity. Donoso is too experienced and skillful to fall into that trap. His portraits are like Picasso's: multiple planes and angles, a nose where one expects an eye, a grill in place of a head of hair, a profile that is not a profile but the smudge of a face, and a resemblance dissolved along collective lines.

Who are the characters, the singer Mañungo Vera, the collector Freddy Fox, the minor poet Don Celedonio, the tragic Judit, the legendary Fausta? Those familiar with Santiago's social and literary menagerie will have a field day identifying them—a somewhat useless pastime. To my mind, it is not the *who* that matters but the *what* they represent. Mañungo, for instance, is the artist who lost the motivation and inspiration for rebellion in his years of exile. So much time passed! So many guitars wielded like machine-guns! People got tired, but the charismatic performer grew even wearier, and now he suddenly returns to Chile without knowing the why or the wherefore. He will find the reason—will he ever! He will inadvertently become part of the drama, he will plunge into it, thinking to save himself thanks to his art and his boldness—he, the superstar of guerrilla rock—without realizing that he has fallen headlong into a fight to the death against the dictatorship. And Mañungo dives into it with Judit and Fausta, the ugly duckling Lopita and Don César, and the cherub Jean Pablo. In Chile no one seems to be able to help coming face to face with abuse, derision, the thrust of the knife, or escape hearing the death knell of curfew.

The narrator seems not to take sides. But in his own way he does. He skillfully keeps his distance in "Evening"—one of the three parts of the novel—and a little less in "Night." In "Morning," after a scene of torture, imprisonment, and death, the narrator goes along with Judit and joins the resistance. He covers a lot of ground. And he rubricates his commitment with a master stroke: the metaphoric tableau entitled "Chile in Miniature."

History is smoothly framed by the description of Matilde Neruda's funeral [January 1985-Ed.]. Neruda and Matilde always received José Donoso with a cordial embrace and offered him an unwavering friendship. Donoso witnessed the outrages committed against Matilde and watched her struggle till the end. Matilde and Pablo unwittingly gave the Chilean people the occasion to protest with all their strength and soul and without risking a major confrontation: their funeral in Santiago's General Cemetery. As is well known, Neruda and Matilde are buried in a wall just a short distance from Victor Jara [the popular folksinger tortured and killed by military henchmen in the National Stadium in the hours following the coup—Ed.], in the grounds that elsewhere I've called "the slum of death." It is the field of the poor, of wooden crosses, red geraniums, and little paper flags.

Donoso gathers his characters in La Chascona, the Nerudas' house at the foot of the San Cristóbal [a hill just blocks from downtown Santiago—Ed.]. There he lays out their lines of communication and alienation; that is the stage for their loving and forgetting, for their disdain and their rebelliousness; there one can measure what's left of the old social classes, and more than one life falls apart as others come together. From there the characters go out wandering through the leafy streets of the Barrio Alto [Santiago's wealthy district—Ed.] surrounded by the fragrance of flowers and watered lawns. They stop off at garbage dumps that once were palaces, share in the tasks of beggars and trash can inspectors, conspire, make love, flee, and disappear. La Chascona is an island: breached, devastated, besieged, defending with invisible weapons the integrity of an already de-

funct Chile. Its owners don't rest and neither do their living kin. The city is the site of a free-for-all between the living and the dead.

To orchestrate this vast and agitated *danse macabre* Donoso displays arresting allegories: a hellish interlude in which an aroused pack of street dogs rape an aristocratic but seedy little bitch. Judit saves her by shooting her dead, Judit, who lives in order to avenge her own interrupted violation. A ghost ship, the *Caleuche,* signals its witchery from the waterways of Chiloé, and a small scale model of Chile, inspired by Walt Disney, shows off next to a Burger King.

The final dialogue between Mañungo and the journalists defines the novel:

> "Why did you come back to Chile at this particular time?" the reporters asked.
>
> "To stay here."
>
> "For how long?"
>
> "Forever."
>
> "Didn't you say last night in Neruda's house that your visit would be short because you didn't understand the situation your country was in?"
>
> "Now I understand it." He thought for an instant and then went on. "I've changed my plans. In any case, after twenty hours in my country, I can assure you that I have never been clearer on any subject than I am on this matter of staying."
>
> "In order to define your political action?"
>
> "Could be."
>
> "Armed struggle?"
>
> "No, except in self-defense or to defend someone else."
>
> "Songs?"
>
> "I'd like that. But who knows if bombs won't turn out to be the only alternative? It's their fault. Because what can we do when they force us into violence by taking away all our hope? I am not justifying bombs, but I do understand them."
>
> (trans. Alfred MacAdam)

This dialogue defines *one* novel among others, because there are several novels in **Curfew.** The main one is explanatory, mournful, and one might say, tough, if it didn't leave such a lump in one's throat.

Antonio Benítez Rojo (essay date summer 1992)

SOURCE: "*The Obscene Bird of Night* as a Spiritual Exercise." *The Review of Contemporary Fiction* 12, no. 2 (summer 1992): 50-55.

[*In the following essay, Rojo discusses the survival of the individual in the seemingly hopeless world of* The Obscene Bird of Night.]

From time to time, in accordance with the prescription of the majority of the world's religions, all believers must perform a ritual of self-annihilation. This has to do, of course, with the enactment of death. Accordingly, practices such as fasting, sexual abstinence, physical penitence, silence, worldly withdrawal, and meditation often play a role. In general, these practices not only limit to a greater or lesser degree the natural appetites of the body, but also affect the social activities of the individual in everything from work to recreation. For a period of time the believer is supposed to remain in a state of limbo in which he negotiates with death, and one can call this Lent, Sabbath, or Ramadan.

After this metaphysical plunge the pious individual emerges convinced of the futility of worldly values and fortified in his faith. Though results are not usually enduring, the various religions provide innumerable opportunities to strengthen the soul in the daily renouncement of small pleasures and worldly honors. Any hour of any day can be used for prayer, penance, sacrifice, mystic trances, or meditation. In the Catholic faith one may recall the spiritual exercises instituted by Saint Ignatius of Loyola.

Of course not all of humankind believes in an afterlife; there are those who are atheists or agnostics, and those who subscribe in only a nominal fashion to some religion or belief. By this I mean to say that millions and millions of human beings do not feel obligated by any religious code to simulate death, in even the most trivial way. And yet all simulations of death, including deep reflections on the subject (which implies dying a little), are productive experiences. In effect, one must agree with the ancients that to submerge oneself under the crust of the earth, if possible while fasting, skeptically leaving behind the bulky garments of vanity, pride, and self-importance—even if only for a short time—will be more enlightening than any moral harangue arising from the fear of divine punishment. To approach death without the hope of eternal life, and brush against the ashen folds of its cloak as a ritual initiation to a higher plane of earthly existence, is the best moral exercise that anyone could undertake if one is sincere.

If one accepts this proposition, what incentive do the incredulous have to experiment with this useful and economic initiation? Here literary creation doubtless performs an important role, because it provides a half-dozen models that can successfully substitute for the most demanding spiritual exercises. Notice, from the Bronze Age to the present, the enormous number of heroes and heroines who descend to gloomy depths and later resurface in the warm light of victory. Or the affectionate feelings that characters like Don Quixote, Hamlet, and Colonel Aureliano Buendia arouse by the mere fact of having lived exemplarily in their madness, which is to say, in death. Or, beginning with the mino-

taur and ending with the lugubrious entities of Stephen King, the fascination that otherworldly creatures have for us, as if those who traffic in them are part of an unmentionable pact. Or the disturbing compassion we bestow on human freaks, no matter how low their condition. Isn't having been born Quasimodo a case of starting life half dead from the beginning? Or the suspicious tenacity with which we read expiatory books like *Crime and Punishment* and *Under the Volcano,* whose realism is perhaps more awful than any fantastic monstrosity ever imagined. Anyway, to continue, it's obvious that without being aware of it, the most skeptical reader has died and revived to his heart's content through the medium of literary catharsis. And of course for those who only read the newspaper, there are always the radio, movie, and TV versions.

In any case, world literature produces every now and then truly exceptional works within this popular and varied genre. In my experience as a reader, for example, I treasure the readings of the first editions of *Nausea,* Curzio Malaparte's *Skin, The Tin Drum, The Subterraneans, The Plague,* and **The Obscene Bird of Night.** If including this last work leaves me open to a charge of regionalistic or linguistic chauvinism, I can only respond sincerely that I have never read any book by a contemporary author more devastating than that novel by José Donoso.

On what do I base my judgment? Well, I think it's a matter of density, of saturation. This in the sense that Donoso's book superimposes several of the aforementioned models to induce in the reader the imaginary experience of self-annihilation. To begin with, there is the epigraph chosen by Donoso to inform the reader from where he took the title of his novel and, in passing, to prepare him for one of the most anguished journeys to nowhere ever seen in the history of literature. The quote isn't brief (it comes from a letter by Henry James, Sr., to his sons Henry and William) but it is necessary to recall it in its entirety to allow us to approach the novel productively:

> Every man who has reached even his intellectual teens begins to suspect that life is no farce; that it is not genteel comedy even; that it flowers and fructifies on the contrary out of the profoundest tragic depths of the essential dearth in which its subject's roots are plunged. The natural inheritance of everyone who is capable of spiritual life is an unsubdued forest where the wolf howls and the obscene bird of night chatters.

The remaining 500-plus pages of text should be read as a pragmatic reflection on James Senior. If a reader, through excessive haste or carelessness, misses that passage, he could end up thinking that Donoso's novel is unnecessarily long, that it is repetitive, that its settings hardly differ among themselves, that the subject matter lacks suspense and excitement, that its characters are intolerably paradoxical, that its narrative structure is chaotic, and that its discourse is abstruse. However, it would never enter the reader's mind that he had just finished reading a minor work: frivolous, badly written, unoriginal, in short, forgettable. It is indeed possible that the reader will arrive at an unjust conclusion: too bad about that book; it could have been a masterpiece but the editor wasn't very good. Of course, if the reader considers the James quote as the first paragraph of Donoso's text, he will know very well what to expect. He will know that he has just entered Diogenes' tub, where he will have to accommodate himself for several days in order to meditate upon the irreparable indecency of the world and of that which we call reality—that abject convention we use to deny ourselves the most elementary answers: where did we come from? why are we here? where are we going? This takes for granted that the reader "has reached his intellectual teens" and "is capable of spiritual life."

In any case, Donoso connects the epigraph with a shadowy antechamber to facilitate the reader's entrance to the rigorous labyrinth that is the novel. In effect, upon turning the page, one suddenly encounters the death of the aged Brígida, and one has no option but to attend her wake in the chapel or the House of Spiritual Exercises. Forty decrepit old women, three nuns, and five orphan girls live there. But, most importantly, the principal character, Humberto Peñaloza, lives there as well. His tortured body will serve as a sarcophagus for the readers both male and female through the grace of catharsis. It is obvious in the previous sentence that I have emphasized the idea that the reader's gender is not important. Either sex will be able to identify with the protagonist. The same thing happens with particulars such as age and profession because Humberto Peñaloza, like the narrator in Borges's "Lottery in Babylon," has performed the most diverse moral roles (victim, executioner, sinner, penitent) and has worn the masks of man, baby, crone, giant, deaf-mute, and writer. In short, Humberto Peñaloza is everything and nothing, and his physical disappearance in the last night of the novel—a necessarily eschatological night—symbolizes the ethical initiation of which I have spoken, beyond which the individual has to go on living with the gnawing certainty that nobody knows anything and that life is nothing more than this: the existential frustration of knowing that nobody knows anything, beginning with oneself. Once the anguish has reached this extreme point, one should reach a kind of hopeless serenity that has favorable repercussions on the individual and, by extension, on society.

In reality, Donoso's novel is an inverted epic where the laurels do not belong to the victor but to the vanquished, to him who knowing from the start that all is lost tries, as Ernest Hemingway would say, to give it his best shot. And not to win accolades but for the sake of self-fulfillment. History, of course, counts for naught here since every event, once extracted from its manipulating discourse, lacks all organic meaning. For Donoso, in accordance with his fortunate metaphor, history is no longer anything more than a miserable sack stuffed with old newspapers whose photos and headlines tell us nothing.

To comment at length upon what happens in the novel goes beyond the intent of this quick rereading. Nevertheless, I would have to point out that the paradoxical behavior of the characters is due to the fact that in the text several worlds—or, if one prefers, spaces of seclusion—coexist: for example, the space of the Rinconada and that of the House of Spiritual Exercises, each with its own language and narrative model. The first is a kind of bestiary full of deformed and lewd people (dwarfs, giants, the grotesquely obese, hunchbacks), nightmarish creatures who drag their monstrosity through the luxurious pavillions and gardens of the place. But the lives of these defective beings are not far removed from our own. In reality, these beings are the moral monsters we carry within, that dark Other that wavers between elemental passions and the grossest sentiments, this perverse and crippled Mr. Hyde whom we do not always succeed in keeping at bay; this obscene bird of night of which James spoke to his sons.

Superimposed on the Rinconada is the House of Spiritual Exercises, a labyrinth of humid cells, tumbledown rooms, and patios full of rubble. At one time it was a structure of piety dedicated to perfecting souls. Now it barely functions as a shelter for a group of invalid and sterile women. In my reading—and possibly in Donoso's as well—these useless cellars that are about to be abandoned symbolize religion. I'm not referring only to Christianity but to any religion or belief, to any hope for a hereafter, or to any faith in a transcendental locus of eternal redemption. One could say that God once lived in these ancient cellars or, rather, someone passing himself off as God, taking advantage of kind souls. But that God, false or inefficient, has died and all that is left are his remains: tattered angels, onearmed virgins, patched sheets, rags, bits of string, burlap bags, old newspapers, broken objects, and leftovers.

Humberto Peñaloza resides simultaneously in both spaces. He suspects he is a sinner but doesn't know what his sin is. His life, minuscule and mediocre, never quite comes together in the eyes of reason; it is a coming and going full of sound and fury signifying nothing. From this precarious observatory Humberto Peñaloza mythicizes reality, that is to say, whatever he doesn't understand inside or outside himself. So his desire to become someone worthy (like Don Jerónimo de Azcoitía) and to be desired by someone estimable (like Doña Inés) not only compels him to live in La Rinconada and in the House of Spiritual Exercises, but also in a third space which, like the others, has its own language and narrative codes: the space of myth. In effect, lost in the night and the turns of an indecipherable labyrinth, Humberto Peñaloza lives the life of the minotaur. As in myth, the notions of time and space are blurred. Furthermore, the characters with whom he interacts allude more to transpersonal symbols than to real people. There inside, in the shadowy passages of the labyrinth, one never quite knows who is who and who is the Other. Consequently, all life is multiple, a sequence of masks that one must put on so that one can try to know oneself better. In the end, with the years and the vicissitudes of life, things seem to become simpler. The masks begin to disappear by dint of resembling themselves. It is precisely at this critical juncture that Donoso's narrative discourse apprehends Humberto Peñaloza. For a moment, the reader who accompanies him in his anguished adventure has the illusion that he is going to emerge from the text with an answer. A futile hope. Suddenly an old woman comes, grabs Humberto Peñaloza by the scruff of the neck, and stuffs him in a burlap sack. She immediately sews the mouth of the sack closed and puts the package in another bag, and so on. Then the old woman throws the bundle on her shoulder and begins to wander about aimlessly. Outside the bundle (which suffocates us and denies us access to any revelation) it is dark and cold. The old woman huddles over a bonfire, falls asleep, and soon everything turns into ashes which the wind disperses. In the end Humberto Peñaloza and the reader are reduced to a black smear on the stones, and the spiritual exercises that Donoso proposes for unbelieving humanity end right here.

Is *The Obscene Bird of Night* a pessimistic novel? I think not, but one must conclude that it lacks the sugary flavor of metaphysical explanation. Perhaps it could be taken for a pessimistic work if nothing remained of the human being. But something does remain: a black smear that the trip to nowhere does not succeed in blotting out. Well—the reader with certain expectations will say—a black mark and nothing are the same. And I nevertheless would say no, they aren't the same, and I would refer the reader to a curious belief of the Navajo Indians.

This belief or tradition is related to the beautiful blankets that the Navajo weave and that can be purchased in any store specializing in handmade textiles. These Indians believe that the weaver's dedication in carrying out her task is so intense that, thread by thread, her spirit passes into the cloth. So that she won't lose her spirit in the symmetrical labyrinths of the design (which to the Navajo implies losing one's reason) the weaver leaves a loose thread that interrupts the pattern of the cloth in some place. The Navajo believe that this loose thread provides the spirit with an escape route, and thanks to it the spirit can return to the artisan's body.

Perhaps the most interesting aspect of this belief is that the "lifeline" is, at the same time, the weaver's signature. Naturally one will say that such a practice is useless, given that ultimately the loose thread becomes part of the geometric pattern of the design. But it is also true that the thread, even though it can be read as a necessarily unsuccessful path of escape, also speaks of the individual's desire to leave an identifying mark, a signature, as an irrevocable record of his plan of escape. It is in this sense that I read in the black spot the name of Humberto Peñaloza and also that of the reader.

Djelal Kadir (essay date summer 1992)

SOURCE: Kadir, Djelal. "Next Door: Writing Elsewhere." *The Review of Contemporary Fiction* 12, no. 2 (summer 1992): 60-69.

[*In the following essay, Kadir deconstructs the theme of the "other place" in* The Garden Next Door, *drawing parallels to the work of Dante, T. S. Eliot, Henry James, and George Eliot.*]

Next door is always in another space, another yearned-for place of the other yearning in perpetual unsituatedness. Writing's difficulty must inevitably be brooked in the writing. The predicament finds no necessary and sufficient conditions of absolution or amelioration in its predication. The assuasive slave does not reside in what is written but in what writing does not give up, in what and where writing does not yield, in the indomitable and untenable otherness that writing insinuates only as trace and never as presence or outright representation. The only hope is a partial and borderline suggestion, a promise that reverberates at the far and always further end(-lessness) of writing's unpredictable alterities. Thus, the passage from the "unsubdued forest where the wolf howls and the obscene bird of night chatters" (Henry James, Sr.) next door to "the laughter in the garden [of] echoed ecstasy / Not lost, but requiring" (T. S. Eliot) is no less an attempt to indemnify the scriptor's damned project, to recoup the light in the darkness, the dancing in the stillness, the hope in the enervation of hope, the scrawl in the blankness of the page. Donoso's peregrination from the *locus damnificus* of *The Obscene Bird of Night,* epigraphized by Henry James, Sr., to *The Garden Next Door,* punctuated at its pivotal turning point by Eliot, does not figure a felicitous pilgrimage to a *locus aomenus* that lies beyond the howl of requirements or the unrequited need for ragged salvaging. Writing's personification, as authorial persona or as hapless scribe, is always already circumscribed by a yearning world of writing that will never yet relinquish its differential otherness to the writer's solicitation. Thus, whether walled in, wrapped up, and packaged tightly—as is the case of Mudito the scrivener—or shut out, exiled, kept at voyeuristic distance—as is the writer and would-be novelist Julio Méndez in **The Garden Next Door**—there is a breach to be brooked, an impossibility to be countenanced, a divide to be negotiated. Traversing from here to there always figures a stray travesty that suspends the goal, extenuates distance, and attenuates direct bearing. The trajectory, then, becomes inexorably elliptical, the path unpredictably misleading.

This is Donoso's itinerary through **The Garden Next Door.** And his pilgrimage echoes in the citations of its epigraphs the circuitous journey of two wayfarers, Cavafis and James Joyce, two whose Virgilian services Donoso engages with allusive pathos throughout his peregrination. For launching as he does from the nightmarish port of his wakeful history, his exilic wanderings will have taken him by the end of the novel to the *mare nostrum*'s enchanted other shore, "next door" to the indigent home of the Alexandrian poet and its haunted geography. And Donoso's scriptor will have been baptismally immersed and metamorphosed in Ovidian fashion in the mysteries of the Kasbah of Tangier, leaving behind the trace of his impossible novel, the chronicle of its impossibility that elicits the sanction of an ambiguous and androgynous writing as coincidental script, the published novel of the "Glorious" other we retrace in readerly consumption. But if the antipodic mirror of Joyce and Cavafis opens as double door to the antechamber of Donoso's dark wood-become-a-garden-next-door, it is Eliot's Dante that serves as mirrored lamp and supple guidepost in steadying the wayward voyage through a shadowed forest and a sinuous path. And as the enervation courses through *néant,* through writing degree zero and blankness of the page, the recourse for the energy to salvage the journey citationally harkens to the third part of the second quadrivium from Eliot's *Four Quartets.* It is here, where the infernal whiteness ogling the scribe darkens to infernal shadow with triple intensity in its incipit and enjambs its first verse with a Stygian verve: "O dark, dark, dark. They all go into the dark"; there, where the opened abyss of the ensuing verse proffers its ineluctable promise to be won and its unhurried challenge to be vanquished: "The vacant interstellar spaces, the vacant into the vacant."

Donoso's self-conscious evocation of Dante's Eliot in this "middle way"—at the midpoint of his novel (page 111 of the Spanish edition) and in midcareer—enjoins his exilic itinerary to one of exile's most emphatic poets who, banished from his native Florence, would begin "Nel mezzo del camin" (*Inferno* 1:1) to explore the byways of the wayward path ("la via smarrita" [*Inferno* 1:3]) in the human comedy's divine way stations, or in "the divine comedy's human leaps and lapses" (the phrasing here belongs to Dante's inimitable translator Allen Mandelbaum), as he went on enduring the salt

taste of exile's bread and the vicissitudes of the path that descends and ascends the stairs of others (*Paradiso* 17:57-60). Eliot's *Four Quartets,* certainly its "East Coker" evoked by Donoso, is a polyphonous lament in which authorial predicament, historical circumstance, and epigonic anxiety converge into a scribal threnody with incorrigible hope:

> So here I am, in the middle way, having had twenty years—
>
> Twenty years largely wasted, the years of *l'entre deux guerres*—
>
> Trying to learn to use words, and every attempt
>
> Is a wholly new start, and a different kind of failure
>
> Because one has only learnt to get the better of words
>
> For the thing one no longer has to say, or the way in which
>
> One is no longer disposed to say it. And so each venture
>
> Is a new beginning, a raid on the inarticulate
>
> With shabby equipment always deteriorating
>
> In the general mess of imprecision and feeling,
>
> Undisciplined squads of emotion. And what there is to conquer
>
> By strength and submission, has already been discovered . . .
>
> ("East Coker," V)

Eliot goes on to end "East Coker" in an encyclical tone whose anaphoric tempo and driving cadenza leave Dante behind to echo in Ecclesiastes, but with a decidedly historical twist which resounds with the baneful circumstances of exilic experience and political trials that perennially haunt the dispossessed other among others' prepossessions. I refer to Eliot's coda here that gives voice to the motto of Mary Queen of Scots in the Tower of London: "In my end is my beginning."

Donoso's circuitous harkening to the beleaguered Dante and the woeful Mary Stuart through this Eliotic incorporation into the midsection of his novel underscores the emphatically political character of his writing. And by political here we are to understand a highly textured site whose map includes, at once, the politics of writing, the politics of gender, the politics of historical torsions, and the ideological distortions of political power whose self-serving claims displace and ostracize even would-be alterities as insufferable threat. Donoso's *Obscene Bird of Night* has already dramatized this allegory of power in the juxtapositions of oligarchical privilege to the desultory discards of social dispossession. In **The Garden Next Door,** he rends the allegorical mask, baring the *clef* of his *roman-fleuve* to the point that more than likely proves unbearable for some, not only for politicians and petty dictators, but for stalwart wardens of the literary institutions, as well as for homophobic *machos*. A writerly text that confronts its world and wordly circumstance, **The Garden Next Door** indeed unfolds within the reckoning of history's nightmare from which Stephen Dedalus, transposed to the epigrammatic head of Donoso's novel, is still trying to awake. And it unfolds, too, with the almost fateful inexorableness of ancient tragedy which that other Greek, Cavafis, at the epigraphic gateway of this Donoso script stoically embodies as Necessity. Donoso is not oblivious to this political constancy, to the allusive byways plotted by his novels that on the abacus of some might come up redundant. His response lies at the threshold of his Eliotic citation; just where Donoso stops citing, Eliot continues with studied and insistent reiteration:

> You say I am repeating
>> Something I have said before. I shall say it again.
> Shall I say it again? In order to arrive there,
> To arrive where you are, to get from where you are not,
>> You must go by a way wherein there is no ecstasy.
> In order to arrive at what you do not know
>> You must go by a way which is the way of ignorance.
> In order to possess what you do not possess
>> You must go by the way of dispossession.
> In order to arrive at what you are not
>> You must go the way in which you are not.
> And what you do not know is the only thing you know
> And what you own is what you do not own
> And where you are is where you are not.

> ("East Coker," III)

Eliot's antithetical enigmas undergo a transformation in Donoso. **The Garden Next Door** elevates this counterpoint to a high order of desperate intensity, to an instrument of cultural and historical diagnosis, to an austere device of authorial confession, to severe measure for probing the somber intensities of writing's vocation. The soundings of this scrutiny figure an echoic discourse, a heterocosm of crossed antitheses that resound in a mirror: splenetic yet compassionate, melancholy yet desiring, despairing yet auspicious, desolate yet expectant. As more extended antithesis, disconsolate pathos finds its antidote in the manifold otherness of juxtaposition. Disbelieving in the possibility of an apocalyptic absolution, shunning the univocal word of the self-convinced, suspicious of the ideological talisman, the orthodox emblem, the canonical cameo and the unproblematic deliverance they would proffer, Donoso's scripture is hellbent *not* on resolution but on rummaging, *not* on sacred salvation but on heterodox salvaging. As such, the site of this writing is a shifting ground, a mobile locus for the *convivio* of alterities. And the problematic mutability of this restive seeking that always devolves upon exilic shiftlessness finds its animation on the edgy and exercised marginalities of

the dispossessed, the contiguities of otherness that, instead of converging, engage in a compensatory exchange of their histories, in a conversative trade in sundry versions of their otherness and its unremitting difference. Thus, the garden next door in the Old World city in the heart of Spain is also the garden at home in the exilic memory of the New World city in Spanish America's Santiago, Chile. "Home is where one starts from," Eliot avers. But in the beginning is also the end, and in the end is the beginning. Eliot knew the atopicality of the predicament quite well, born as he was in Saint Louis, Missouri, a New World home, traveling as he was to "East Coker," Somerset Village, England, an Old World home of the Eliots' birth. The alterities are confounded and confounding. Antipodic (mirrored) symmetry implodes, problematically, into the disjunctions of a superimposed filiation that refuses to cohere; the antistrophe denies to be rendered into harmonized epode; the antithesis that stubbornly tries to cling to its adjacency comes up against its indomitableness. The garden next door scurries unremittingly next door; the home garden is no more at home and the next-door garden never has been home. Both are elsewhere, in antithetical filiation through mind's eye and memory's recollection. And the amenity of the genial garden now turns to "unsubdued forest" and "dark wood" where the wolf still howls and the obscene bird chatters once again. Thus, the neat antitheses derail from the straight path, Euclidian parallels flee into random ellipses, ordered dichotomies crisscross helter-skelter opening up to exponential increments of contingency. Within this complex, this novel's Stephen Dedalus—Julio Méndez's uncomprehended and unassimilable son—wanders off into his own creative exile only to haunt his parents' homeless homefront as deracinated and dispossessed supplement, as androgenous ephebe, as ambivalent hermaphrodite and scatalogical jewel out of Cavafis. For Bijou, Méndez's substitute son of ambivalent gender and unpredictable acts, of fathomless yet unassailable vulnerability and invisible resources, floats in randomness and contingency. He bursts on the scene as wayward waif and exile's scapegoat and ends as Virgilian father to his would-be paternal substitute. It is (s)he whom Julio Méndez invokes as psychopomp to guide him in his transformational passage through the infernal other world of the multifarious Kasbah of Tangier, just as he had done previously through the kasbah of Madrid, the multitudinous Rastro. Intrusively mercurial, like his kleptomaniac prototype Hermes, Bijou serves as catalyst in Julio Méndez's transvaluation of his bourgeois values, to the unveiling of the *fauxsemblants* that dissimulate the sanctioned little criminalities of bourgeois decency. It is through this hermaphroditic adolescent, this generational other to the middle-aged Julio Méndez that the latter begins the arduous and often painfully hysterical process of demythologizing the foundational myths in which his middle-class ethos and neuroses find their legitimation. And in a more profound and cataclysmic sense, it is this would-be Rimbaud of the Verlaine-Mathilde triangle, this *angelo musicante,* as Julio dubs him, who sends a seismic shudder to the complacently self-centered sexuality of Julio and Gloria Méndez's droll marriage (78). Though peremptorily repressed and dismissed, this awakening may well have been, nonetheless, the spark that would lead to Julio's acceptance of his own ambivalent and ambiguous sexuality and to his recognition of the rightful claims of the generic other, of Gloria as legitimate alterity, as real other and superior scriptorial talent. Any recognition of one's creative limitations as a writer figures an agonistic trial, especially exacerbated when coupled with the concession of primacy to the creative powers of the "weaker gender" on the part of a phallocentric agonist at midlife plagued by the insecurities and ambiguities of his own sexuality, as is the case here with Julio Méndez. On this reckoning, the antithetical stress within sexuality and scripture, gender and engendering, writing and authorial potency, serves as the animating force that propels the itinerary of Donoso's novel through the embattled way stations of its cathartic and purgatorial plot.

The Garden Next Door is a chastening scene of writing become a scene of recognition that, in turn, transmutes, again, by brawn of re-incorporation into a scene of writing. It figures a writer's self-recognition in a trial by fire which is the threat of failing potency. At the far end of this alchemical trial, however, Donoso's plot offers no orthodox purities in the "depuration." One finds, instead, a heterology, a heterodox intermingling of differential multiplicity, of "unnatural" ruptures that transgress received hierarchies of domesticity. And the exercise of writing falls to the subservient other; it devolves upon the dispossessed alterity, as it did once before in the case of Mudito the secretary, amanuensis and general domestic in the institutional hierarchies of oligarchic order. And, as was the case in ***The Obscene Bird of Night,*** institutional order(ing) in ***The Garden Next Door*** becomes subjected to a politics of substitution through the mediate pressures of writing's agency—the agency of scriptor and of scripture as sundry *pharmakos:* expiatory sacrifice and witness, martyr and attestor, dependent and scribal deponent. In the earlier work, the institution of power traces a clearer dialectic of antitheticality, rooted, as it is, in the destitution of those who would confer its privilege. Potency, whether sexual, generative, or scriptive, is not a possession but the consequent by-product of dispossession and, as such, its authority lies in the "powerless" other. In ***The Obscene Bird,*** the politics of this order finds its dramatic foregrounding, now as discursive predication, now as apostrophe: "[W]itnesses are the ones who have power" (205); "don't leave the room, Humberto, watch me . . . lend me your envy to make me potent . . . you're the owner of my potency, Humberto, you took it just as I took the wound on your arm, you can never leave me, I need your envious eyes beside me if I am to go on being a man" (185). And while the privileged apprehend the indispensable nature of the "dispensable" other, the latter is no less cognizant of the authorizing necessity of his otherness: "[S]tripped of everything of the Humberto I used to be, except the still active principle of my eyes. I am just another old woman, Don Jerónimo, I'm Iris's dog, let me rest . . . I've already served you, being a witness is the same as being a servant" (62); "sew me all up, not only my parched mouth, but also my eyes, *especially* my eyes, so their power will be buried deep under my eyelids . . . sew them up, old women, in that way I'll make Don Jerónimo impotent forever" (65).

Now, in ***The Garden Next Door,*** the antithesis moves beyond a linear dialectic or, one could say, it becomes truly dialectical in changing to a reversible scripture whose politics of substitution entail a mutual implication, a capability of the *pharmakos* (writing and scriptor) to author(ize) *and* usurp the other as the other at once, to privilege the other through a self-effacement which is simultaneously self-privileging of one's own position. In short, a typical strategy of the ironic turn. Within the reversibility of this scriptive *convivio,* otherness attains to a domesticity of unpredictable exchange that proscribes the possibility of domestication. The scribing "domestic" could well be, through the ruse of indeterminacy, the purveyor of the script for a master(ing) narrative. And what ultimately salvages Donoso's novel from the dirge of splenetic monody is precisely this indeterminate surprise, the irony of a Jamesian turn (Henry, Jr., this time) that catapults the narrative and its history into the "echoed ecstasy" of this oscillation within as well as between otherness. In this emphatically conversative economy of writerly compensation, a process of exchange constantly (re)capitulates writing to its otherness, the novel of the writing and the writing of the novel apprehending each other without monitory apprehensions. I do not mean to imply by this "capitulation" that writing crystallizes into immobile self-seizure whereby the novel in the writing and the writing in the novel mutually grip each other with inextricable and solipsistic stricture. Much to the contrary, the process I describe is indeterminately gripping, one in which every instance of attained security or privilege engenders a dispossession not only of the other but within the "secured" position, within the authorized and authored privilege itself. For, if this scriptive self-seizure figures a self-writing of writing, an "autograph," autography, as with autobiography, ultimately figures a critique, a critical enterprise and, as such, it is always bent on critical apprehension, always on a course of decision, adjudication, evaluation that does not run, cannot run out its course. The diagnostic project is always that, a dia-gnostic that proscribes a definitive gnosis. By virtue of its analytic task, diagnosis works as "anacalypsis" rather than as "apocalypsis," as cover-up, that is, rather than as disclosure. As diagnosis, in other words, the critical examination is always augmentative rather than subtractive. It figures a parting discernment that necessarily compounds rather than one that renders a reduction. And as writing, it is by its very nature redactive rather than reductive. In this sense, writing as autograph engenders not only the transgressive frames of the provisional diagnoses it inevitably must transgress, but it becomes generative, too, of a problematic and nonreductionist synonymity between critique and eros—because writing is a desperate demand for love. Certainly so in Donoso and unmistakably in *The Garden Next Door,* where exilic writing clamors for acceptance by and of the other. ("No necesito su amor para terminar mi novela," Julio Méndez cloyingly protests at one point [215].) Writing is always exilic by virtue of necessity. Necessarily exilic because it is engendered by an irredressable plaint, an insecure insufficiency with an unrequited necessity to become necessary. Destined to founder in this seeking, writing invariably encounters the greatest necessity of all, impossibility—the impossibility born of betrayal and self-betrayal, the impossibility of decisively and decidably breaching otherness, of comprehending and being comprehended by "next door" into home. If indemnifying acceptance can be an impossibility, there is, of course, the venue of surreptitious usurpation. And this is the recourse adopted by Donoso in *The Garden Next Door.* But, in the end, this Hermetic strategy proves no less treacherous. (Gloria must write a second novel that "confirms" the present, surreptitious first one. Does a writer ever know which is the "second" novel of confirmation? Is not each one a furtive first novel?) Thus, writing must go on seeking conciliation and indemnity in desultory versions of its own production, a production in which betrayal itself becomes scripted, embedded as a curse on the wandering exile in exile's multifarious contingencies. *The Garden Next Door* dwells precisely in/on this adversative site of writing's adversity, rehearsing the writer's betrayal by writing's insurmountable demands in the rendering of experience to scripture. Scribing itself entails more than sufficient indomitable adversity to allow for its domestication into instrumentality, into tractable medium for chronicling experience. In the end, as novel, *The Garden Next Door* does not comprise or circumscribe the novel being rewritten in the novel by the beset Julio Méndez. It is comprised, instead, by the (other) scripture of the other, the writing "next door" inside one's own borrowed home, if you will, that chronicles the vicissitudes of the novel's impossible writing, its precluded completion. We are left, in fact, with the incompletion and the impossibility of the novel being written, with the unbreachableness of Julio Méndez's revisioning and revisions as he goes on to essay endlessly revisionary

versions of writing as a professor of literature, as professor of writing's insatiable desire that knows no closures and admits of no indemnity. In this sense, Julio Méndez, the former political prisoner and exiled writer, recapitulates to writing's sententious sentence; he becomes "reconciled" to writing's irreconcilable corpus as yet another reading and writing scrawl. The story he leaves behind is a surreptitious production that displaces him as authorial persona, as will the many turns of textuality that inevitably will have undermined the proprietory authority of his professional/professorial illusions of mastery, turning him out, yet again, into exile's nowhereland. If writing be a demand for love, reading is no less a desperate clamoring to brook exclusion, to breach unbreachable otherness in unrequited yearning. As a professor of literature, Julio Méndez cannot escape this insight. It becomes doubly poignant, then, that he should be reading out loud to Gloria (214-15) the revised versions of his impossible, would-be novel while she, in fact, as it turns out, is the one authoring the novel of his writing's impossibility.

Within the economy of this reversible scripture, the novel we read is the ensuing difference, as in the above-cited enigmas of Eliot's antithetical way stations, that issues from the other's ineluctable intrusion to salvage writing's enterprise. Like Julio Méndez, like his most significant other, like Donoso, we oscillate between the writing's novel and the would-be novel in the writing. Rather than a ruse on the part of a self-privileging authority—authorial or feigned—this differential situation of unsituatedness translates into the fact that we all inhabit (and are inhabited by) a predicament of being caught between alterities, between here and there that leaves us in neither place. It is a volatile habitation, its predicament subject to the contingencies of unpredictable commutation. What Donoso's *Garden Next Door* does is to allegorically dramatize the allegory of this predicament. And, of course, I consciously emphasize "allegory" in the reiteration, lest we forget the shifting otherness this word's root etymons connote. Need I repeat Donoso's Eliot? I shall repeat Donoso's Eliot:

> In order to arrive at what you are not
>   You must go through the way in which you are not.
> And what you do not know is the only thing you know
> And what you own is what you do not own
> And where you are is where you are not

Within Donoso's text, this Eliotic allegory of scurrying finds its echoic parenthesis in another Eliot, George, on the one hand, the other parenthesis being Henry James. For Donoso situates the internal displacements of his novel between *Middlemarch* and *The Spoils of Poynton.* And what sustains, literally, materially, his *tandem* scriptors—the would-be novelist, Julio, and the novelist, Gloria—of his novel is a "tedious translation of George Eliot's *Middlemarch,* done in tandem with Gloria, a task that seemed eternal, but one which provided a modest but sure income" (13). When, finally, at long length, the reversible significance of this scriptive tandem is revealed by dint of a Jamesian twist, and Gloria's writing that gives voice to Julio's narration displaces the latter altogether from the ruse of narrative performance, then we read: "And while I [Gloria] read and write, he puts the final touches to his translation of *The Spoils of Poynton*." And then, in tandem, a self-referential reflection, an autographic-interpretive moment of reflexivity: "Some relationship to the sold Roma home [the family home in Santiago, Chile], whose sale allows us to live a bit better, with the auctioning and dispersal of its furnishings that might be Poynton's? I have read Julio's translation: it is daring, creative, a masterpiece. [¶] While I write this, I see him totally absorbed in its revision" (215).

Sustained by a version of *Middlemarch* in the beginning, "totally absorbed" into a revision of *The Spoils of Poynton* in the end, Donoso's ostensible scriptor and his ostensible script straddle in oscillation the vicissitudes of a family romance of Torys and Reformers in political strife, on the one hand, and of the dispersal and dispossession of a homefront and its heirlooms on the other. The first, authored by a woman writer, Marian Evans, with a male persona, George Eliot, becomes incorporated into *The Garden Next Door,* a novel with a male author and an ostensibly male narrator but with a female scriptor. The second, an equally androgynous script scripted by a Henry James whose authorial gender has its animus in the ambiguities of his own sexual otherness. This, too, subsumed by Donoso into the equivocal ruse of his graphic figures and into the ambiguity of Donoso's/Gloria's revising and "revised" scriptor. *The Garden Next Door,* the garden next door itself, comprises a daring embrace equally of the other and of its parentheses, allowing a suggestion of the multifarious other to which it situates itself in parenthetic relation. In that topical relationship, its problematic, internal otherness inverts its parentheses, turning its parenthetical bookends outward, opening up and up to a writing that endlessly seeks to unveil what may lie next door, and beyond the next.

Alicia Borinsky (essay date 1993)

SOURCE: Borinsky, Alicia. "Closing the Book—Dogspeech: José Donoso." In *Theoretical Fables: The Pedagogical Dream in Contemporary Latin American Fiction,* pp. 118-31. Philadelphia: University of Pennsylvania Press, 1993.

[*In this chapter from her full-length study of several contemporary Latin American writers, Borinsky takes a deconstructive approach to several works by Donoso, with particular reference to images of dogs as representations of omniscient hopelessness.*]

FEAR AND STORY-TELLING

García Márquez's *Love in the Time of Cholera* offers its French-speaking parrot as a way of parodying the continuation of francophilia with the pleasures of literature. In José Donoso's *A House in the Country*[1] we also encounter the use of French to allude to the puzzles of literary convention, this time in the form of a game called "La marquesa salió a las cinco" played by some characters in the novel; the game's title is a translation of Paul Valéry's much-quoted attack on the novelistic genre.[2] Since *A House in the Country* is not sparing in its use of direct French titles, phrases, and even whole songs, the choice of Spanish for Valéry's phrase rather than its quotation in the original produces an effect of parodical displacement.

A House in the Country focuses on some cousins left by their parents with a group of servants in their wealthy mansion which is surrounded by lands occupied by impoverished natives. In the course of the novel the reader is apprised of the children's anxiety that their parents will not come back from their trip and of the parents' ensuing revulsion toward the situation they face on their return. During the uncertain time between departure and return, the children play "La marquesa salió a las cinco," face diverse dangers, and engage in transgressive sexual practices. The servants rebel only to be kept in place. The carefully fenced mansion is violated as suspicions of cannibalism among natives and other characters contribute to the delineation of a society shaped by greed and brutality. *A House in the Country* is a polytonal work, featuring a straightforward realistic style, a highly allusive and florid mode reminiscent of the turn-of-the century Spanish American "modernistas,"[3] and a playful—at times erudite—use of quotations and foreign terms. The preliminary farewell to the parents initiates the reader into the intricate architecture of the mansion, whose layers hiding gold and family secrets yield, as well, a patchwork of Spanish discursive styles that implicitly constitute another journey, this time into literary tradition.

What are the secrets unveiled during these simultaneous journeys? One concerns the contents of the house library, a room filled with richly bound volumes, which is off limits to the children and in which Adriano Gomara, the unfortunate father of one of the cousins, is being held prisoner by the rest of the family. Arabela, the keeper of the room, is a cousin thought by all to possess an unusual degree of information. When cousin Wenceslao, a boy whose mother enjoys dressing him up as a girl, is told by Arabela that the library contains nothing but empty bindings made to order by their grandfather for the sake of appearances, he ponders in shock the source of Arabela's knowledge because he realizes that it could not be traced to her studying in the library, as he had originally thought.

How does she know so much? The answer in his head took the form of a stampede of other immediate questions: but is it true that she knows so much? Or do I only think so because I know so little myself, and do the grown-ups only think so when they go to consult her because it suits their purposes that she should?

(p. 17)

The narrator reassures us that the grown-ups had known all along that only bindings filled the four-story salon called "the library" and that the interdiction denying the children access to that room (issued on the pretext of protecting their eyesight from stress and their minds from being misguided) was, in fact, another exercise of the parents' persistent wish to domesticate their offspring by having them follow orders.

Arabela's knowledge becomes linked to books, only to underscore the point that the alleged source of her information is sheer make-believe. Once the hypothesis of her familiarity with the library's authors and languages is dismissed, she becomes all the more puzzling to Wenceslao and the reader because Arabela is made to embody a knowledge *around* reading, but without any source *in* reading. Her wisdom stems in large measure from her recognition that nothing can be found in that library. Arabela is superior to her cousins because she is unaffected by the authority of the contents of library shelves. She is also familiar with the pain of Adriano Gomara, whose screams are heard when he is not drugged or asleep. Made indifferent to Adriano's pain because of the frequency of his protests and cynical about what might be learned from reading books, Arabela laughs at Wenceslao's bewilderment. In this early scene of the novel, Wenceslao's emotion in finding his father and his realization that the library is fake are presented in counterpoint to Arabela's allowing the question about how she attains knowledge to be addressed. Is her knowledge a hypothesis—as Wenceslao thinks—needed by both children and grown-ups? Or is it something firmer, grounded untransferably in Arabela?

If in *Love in the Time of Cholera* Fermina's superior intuition generated the energy needed to put the book aside and engage in "life," Arabela's strength in *A House in the Country* lies in a different domain.[4] She laughs. Her laughter *against* the sentimentality attendant in Wenceslao's reunion with his father and the shock of her revelation about the library destroys the possibility of investing them with anything but detachment. Arabela's laughter empties this part of the novel of the feelings she derides. Thus although she implies (like Fermina) that the realm of books is to be left for something else, her pursuit of that other realm has the vertiginous nature of destructive humor rather than the safer, canonized trappings of love associated with Fermina.

Cruel laughter superimposed onto a basic and unredeemable fear, not love, is the grounding reality presented by *A House in the Country* as the "other" of literature capable of telling us about the emptiness of the bindings in the library. Is Arabela's message right? Are there not books in the library? Or, in other words, how *different* are the occurrences that make up the novel from those encountered in reading literature?

The game "La marquesa salió a las cinco," played without explicit reference to the original French, is a key to some of the answers provided by the novel. Organized by a cousin named Juvenal, whose imprecations to the rest of the children are reminiscent of the Roman satirist,[5] the children change roles and engage in a form of play-acting that soon causes them to blur the distinction between the game's make-believe and that other layer perceived in the novel as their reality: a reality forceful enough to generate a baby born of one of the couplings between cousins even though, according to the temporal frame of the novel, such an event would have been impossible. In opposition to Valéry's disparaging dictum about the genre of the novel, fiction unravels without recourse to pedestrian commonsensical statements. The upsetting of time generated by "La marquesa salió a las cinco" within the novel is a forceful denial of the implications of "La marquise est sortie à cinq heures."

Love in the Time of Cholera's Dr. Urbino died trying to catch a parrot that he had tried to teach French; his last words, "ca y est," are to be completed—the reader intuits—by his playful executioner in a combination of verbal obedience and creole triumph at having gotten rid of the cumbersome teacher, ca y est. In shifting "La marquise est sortie à cinq heures" to the active game of "La marquesa salió a las cinco," *A House in the Country* grounds literature in the humor of displacement. There may not be books in that library and, indeed, there is contempt for those who would flow toward them in search of a wisdom better found elsewhere. The entanglements and occurrences among characters are suggested as the best realization of what is merely hinted at in books.

The relationship between literature and life is doubly registered in *A House in the Country*. On the one hand, the children's game creates a level of fiction within fiction with limits blurred by the hypothesis of the birth of a "real" baby, echoing the expected birth in Donoso's novel *The Obscene Bird of Night*.[6] On the other hand, a narrator with a will to control and intervene in the creation of the plot frames this layer with his comments and even a casual encounter in the street with one of the family members portrayed in the book who refuses his account as fanciful and boring. The story we read has not been well told, he says. The effect, as in García Márquez's *One Hundred Years of Solitude*, is to make us think that we should reread the whole novel with a critical eye. Yet whereas in García Márquez we would effectively void the history of the family through the hypothetical reinterpretation triggered by the rereading, in *A House in the Country* the perspective of the Ventura family member encountered in the street produces a different effect. His view dims both the horror and the wealth housed in the mansion. Without its sharp edges, the story turns, as if in a moment of "La marquesa salió a las cinco," into an insipid narrative—Valéry's and, of course, Donoso's refused alternative. Fear becomes paradoxically recognized as essential to the interest in the characters and the pleasure of the reception of their story.

As Seen by a Hungry Dog

Is *A House in the Country* to be understood, then, as the rather bland but effective reinstatement of a narrator capable of undermining Valéry's condescension to novelistic efforts? Donoso's book offers a larger enclosure in this regard, one that renders the frictions between art and life in a different and more eloquent register.

Tapestries and paintings abound in the tale. Unlike books they hold clues to the interpretation of events to come and are regarded as important elements in the visual and interpretative matrix of the reading. Such is the case, for example, of the wall-hanging "L'embarquement pour Cythère"[7] that is described as the parents are planning their departure. If a painting or tapestry anticipates and in so doing *participates* in shaping an event, can it not be said that this visual object exercises control over the events outside its representation? One of the servants, Juan Pérez, undertakes the task of restoring a tapestry hanging in the mansion. As he is portrayed performing the work, it becomes immediately apparent that the fresco trompe l'oeil has the capacity to perceive. It is no mere adornment:

> This eye, muttered Juan Pérez—dipping his brush in sea-green glitter and dotting the pupil of the greyhound, which stood peering into the ballroom through a door he had pawed open—will be my eye. It will take in everything: when I am not around, it will be here to spy on them.
>
> (p. 227)

In restoring the trompe l'oeil, Juan Pérez renders a version of it that upsets the social order that distributes roles in the represented scene. The greyhound is neither a domestic pet nor a well-trained hunting dog; furthermore, Juan Pérez himself refuses to be the courtier in the picture and, instead, makes himself one with the dog's eye:

> But he wished to make it quite clear that he wasn't that courtier, he was this famished greyhound whose black ribs he was now accentuating with shadows. Everything he restored with his brush seemed to turn into a hallucinated freak. His henchmen, dangling on scaffolds and pulleys at various heights over the face of the fresco, were busy imperceptibly transforming the frol-

icsome goddesses into harpies, the rosy clouds into thunderheads. This dog would see with a detail as sharp as its hunger everything Juan Pérez couldn't see for himself, what with his nose stuck inches from the wall, surrounded by paint pots, his back to the room.

> (pp. 227-28)

Juan Pérez is the dog's eye; the dog's eye is Juan Pérez, but the dog sees more than Juan Pérez does in spite of being a product of his restoration. The dog stands guard in the fresco and redeems Juan Pérez of his subservient role in the family. Its frightening and famished stare forever keeps score.

The dog's hungry stare seems to move the brush restoring the fresco, turning the participants in the scene into hallucinated freaks. What have they seen to look that way? It is not what they see but the manner in which they are stared at. With no more room for frolicking framed by harmonious relationships of power and subservience, the dog has uncovered the capacity underlying the scene. The dog watches hungrily, framing what it perceives with the tendentiousness of its hatred; its gaze transforms. At war with its object of attention, it imposes a paralyzing watch. It is not attacking anybody, though; it is, most important, setting a tone for the scene and uncovering the nature of its elements.

Arabela spoke to the emptiness of the library and laughed off Adriano Gomara's pain. The dog—beyond words—is to complete the lessons of her humor, taking them one step further toward the representation of the social order of the house in the key of a famished stare. Not books but a fresco trompe l'oeil tells us, again, that what matters is something other, more weighty, than whatever is found in bound volumes. Do we dare call it "life"? The half-alive characters who mingle with the inhabitants of the fresco do not assert a stark opposition between art and life. On the contrary, they posit a deeper understanding of art that would permeate our interpretation of life.

We encounter a dog that has become silent narrator and reweaver of the tale in Donoso's *La misteriosa desaparición de la marquesita de Loria*.[8] This short novel starts out as a playful, early twentieth-century erotic tale. A young woman brought up in strict convent fashion is married and loses her husband soon afterward. Her widowhood is an initiation into intense and transgressive sexual pleasures. The atmosphere in which Blanca, the young woman who becomes the Marquise of Loria, lives is one of detailed luxury. The decor of her house is described at length, recalling the fascination of turn-of-the-century modernistas for the literary rendition of ornamental objects.

The harmony of the marquise's world is upset by an amorous relationship with a man who has a dog named Luna—"moon" in Spanish. Blanca's link to the dog is strong and unquestionable; a physical bond is forged from the beginning, so that when we read of Blanca's reaction upon encountering the dog in her house, we are not surprised:

> As she opened the door of her darkened bedroom she felt that her heart leaped in shock, leaving her breathless: there were those two eyes like two moons swimming in that infinite warm, dark, and aromatic space. She perceived a new horizon of potent primitive and essential smells. She did not turn on the lights. The eyes approached her slowly in the dark until she saw the bottom of the hollow pupils, the other side of those eyes whose iridescence came out in drops of saliva from the growling dog. With a growl suddenly become louder Luna launched itself over her, throwing her onto the floor on top of the shards of crystal, slapping her with its rough legs, taking her clothes off again with its hot body, biting her as though it were about to swallow up her satined body, her perfect breasts. . . .
>
> There they were, those two limpid eyes, like two blank continents, like two sheets of paper without any writing.
>
> (pp. 162-63)

Blanca is released by the dog, we are told, when "it realizes that she was dissolving herself in the first spasm of the night." The implication is that Blanca felt a voluptuous pleasure in having been ravished. The next morning Blanca looks at her battered body and, after hearing the sounds of the dog next door and seeing it later outside her window, decides not to tell anyone what happened. She breaks up with one of her suitors because "she suffered such boredom when she saw his black imploring eyes which lacked the essential" (p. 168) and devotes herself to a secret life of acknowledging her relationship with Luna.

Blanca (white) is the epither for Luna (moon). The bond between Luna and Blanca acquires the necessity of a noun and its epithet. Luna's destruction of Blanca's *modernista* context and its slide into shards and ruins is hyperbolized in Blanca's end. She disappears mysteriously after taking a ride with a man with whom she has sex. Accused of killing her, he defends himself from the charges by saying that she had been taken away by a huge animal, in the middle of the night. Although the man is incarcerated, accused of a crime of passion, the reader—sharing the secret about the bond joining Blanca and Luna—knows that his being put away does not solve the puzzle of the violence that swallowed up Blanca.

After seeing and being stared at by the emptiness at the bottom of Luna's eyes, Blanca cannot but have her ornamental context dismantled. She gives herself away to be ravished by the dog's hungry, revealing eyes. *La misteriosa desaparición de la marquesita de Loria* goes one step beyond in the articulation of the consequences of the dog's watch. Whereas the greyhound re-

stored by Juan Pérez is merely keeping guard, Luna becomes the privileged dismantler of useless ornament, the supreme ravisher, capable of revealing to Blanca the pain at the core of the pleasure precipitating her into their bond. Blanca and Luna, adjective and noun, also suggest a threat to the reader being watched every night by the white moon, "la blanca luna."

A BEAUTIFUL FACE, GREAT CLOTHES

Blanca's ornamental world, her furniture, clothes, and accessories, are destroyed by the emptiness of the dog's fury. The uncertainty about the "true" existence of the dog renders the impact of its destructive energy in a most disturbing form. The hypothesis of its existence being lodged within Blanca, rather than in an external form, incorporates the threat as an inescapable realization of the emptiness of the self. Blanca, white, is just an adjective for Luna, moon—the uncontrollable dark hole driving her into pleasure and final obliteration. As an epithet inextricably attached to her noun, the truth for Blanca is the realization of her annihilation.

The traces left by Blanca are "a silver brooch of her *cloche*, one French shoe, and her golden *Patek Philippe*" (p. 194). The fragments of objects she has bought are retrieved as the only signs of her hypothetical uniqueness. Blanca's manufacturing of her persona through the acquisition of things is part of a sustained figuration of the self in contemporary society elucidated in Donoso's works. One of the novellas in the volume *Tres novelitas burguesas*[9] (three novellas of the middle class)—translated into English as *Sacred Families* in a rendition that conveys the sarcasm of the original title but forgoes its emphasis on compulsive consumption— offers one of the most intense figurations of the disturbing nature of fashion in our society.

"Chatanooga Choochoo" introduces us to the lives of a group of well-to-do characters, frequent consumers of culture and objects. Among them is Sylvia, a model with a "perfect face" whose features have to be literally drawn for every photo opportunity. What was an intimation of emptiness for Blanca is a celebration of possibilities and profit for Sylvia:

> The feeling that Sylvia—that woman-adjective, woman decoration, that collapsible, foldable woman who represented all comforts of modern life and lacked everything, even individuality and togetherness—had magical powers and was therefore powerful, must have dominated my sleep. I could only remember fragments of my dreams, not capture them whole, and I woke up fearing Sylvia. The first thing I felt on opening my eyes was an uncontrollable urge to see her again. What face was she wearing today? What dress did she have on, she who depended so much on clothes? A scarf knotted a certain way could change her whole appearance, not just physically, but inside, as a person. . . . I desired her . . . I definitely wanted to continue my "af-

fair" with her; but more urgent than that, or perhaps what gave strength and shape to that urgency, was the need to erase her face with vanishing cream and throw myself into the delight of painting her and making her up again.

(pp. 46-47)

Dancing with her friend Magdalena to the tune of "Chattanooga Choochoo" at a party, Sylvia suggests a disconcerting twinhood. She who can be made up to look like anybody could also *be* at the bottom of everybody. Huidobro's eloquent celebration of the permanent nostalgia inflicted by the intense love for a woman, "Todas las mujeres se te parecen / ahora que no te pareces a ninguna"[10] (All women resemble you / now that you don't resemble anyone), is repeated in a darkly humorous mode. The narrator's attraction to Sylvia draws him to the void, suggests to him the possibility of an ultimate empowerment: being able to efface and make up a new face for her.

Vanishing cream and makeup are to be understood both in their literal meanings and as objects of consumption. Sylvia is the supreme cosmetic product in the novel, ideally faceless and manageable and, because of it, a promise of perfect beauty with each new product. Magdalena, the narrator's wife, has a face of her own but needs to fight its wish to come out from under the makeup, so that she can be the face on the magazine covers like Sylvia. In a scene referred to by the narrator as a "surrogate of lovemaking" (p. 50), he makes up Magdalena.

Making up Magdalena is rendered as a kind of initiation of the narrator into something that is simultaneously new and necessary; he does it naturally as if he were meant for the role. The exercise also brings back to him scenes from his childhood, important recollections that shaped his sense of who he was. The narrator is not involved in a mindless game; he has invested himself totally in an experience with the revelatory powers of love:

> It was a game, masquerade and mask . . . and I thought about my childhood, when in summer homes in the hills we would invent costumes, stick our heads inside transparent silk stockings that preserved our individual features while disguising them; on them we would paint other faces, the bad man's grim scowl, the princess's white, chaste face, the witch's mean beak, the old hag's wrinkles, the patriarch's moustache and beard—but always with our features preserved under the false, transparent skin of the silk stockings. Thus with Magdalena now, who wasn't Magdalena but a mutation of the Sylvia mask, and these in turn were every possible variation of the mythological faces that appeared in fashion magazines which in turn were infinite variations of a mask created by some makeup artist in collaboration with a manufacturer.

(p. 51)

Magdalena is able to approach Sylvia's look as though she were covering her face with a silk stocking. One snag and her own features might upset the perfection of the makeup. Attaining Sylvia's look is the opposite of copying from an original deemed to be more authentic, grounded more deeply into existence than its imitation. Magdalena does not have the blank-page face of Sylvia. Had she been faceless like her she would have been able to possess any face she wanted.

Magdalena being made up by her husband is a parody of the transforming powers of love. His pleasure in achieving the appearance he wants her to have suggests that the identification with fragments of representation provided by advertising and art is all we have for articulating the terms of our desire. But **"Chatanooga Choochoo"** does not present us an ideal couple with the compliant wife ready to follow, in a world of high consumption, the whims of her husband. The voluptuousness of the narrator's sexual encounter with Sylvia conveys the desperation of his will to dominate women. Sylvia, her head shaped like an egg, does not have a face when she is not wearing makeup; she cannot speak because she is mouthless. This state generates great tenderness in the narrator, who sees her as an ideal woman. When he feels like it, he follows her to the bathroom and cuts out a mouth for her in lipstick with the same ease with which he had made up Magdalena. It is as though he were perfecting a kind of lovemaking, delving further into implications of a privileged coupling. The first thing Sylvia does after the narrator creates a mouth on her face is sing "Chattanooga Choochoo." Then she kisses him:

> Abruptly she fell silent and, coming closer, she put her newly cut out mouth on mine and kissed me. Unable to resist the impulse, I took her in my arms and that kiss—which undoubtedly she had given me to test the effectiveness of her mouth in all its functions—made me experience the ultimate satisfaction of kissing and perhaps even of loving a woman who is not complete: the power of civilized man, who does not cut out tongues or put out chastity belts—primitive procedures—but who knows how to compel a woman's submission by removing or putting on her mouth, taking her apart by removing her arms, her hair in the form of a wig, her eyes in the form of false eyelashes, eyebrows, blue shadow on the lids, removing, by means of some curious mechanism, her sex itself, so she can only use it when he needs her, so that her entire being depends on a man's will—singing or not singing "Chattanooga Choochoo."

(p. 27)

Bioy Casares's *Asleep in the Sun*[11] renders a phantasy in its nightmarish resolution by having the man who institutionalizes his wife so that her soul may be transplanted for a dog's become the victim of exchanges he naively thought were under his control. His notion of ideal love is not to be realized in spite of the "scientific" means attempted to bring it into existence. Similarly, the will for total control in **"Chatanooga Choochoo"** makes a victim of the one who wants to exercise it. Sylvia and Magdalena watch the narrator and Ramon, Sylvia's husband, dressed in identical suits sing and move to the beat of "Chattanooga Choochoo" for them. The transformations affecting Sylvia and Magdalena are infectious; the men are also subjected to the submissive powers represented by the song. It is a minor song and the elements causing the submission are not part of a sinister culture of sexual dominance. They are, instead, the everyday gestures, perceptions, objects, and sounds that mold men and women.

Swept away by the monster Luna, Blanca in *La misteriosa desaparición de la marquesita de Loria* embodies desire as a self-destructive conundrum; her watch as *blanca luna*—white moon—over the characters in **"Chatanooga Choochoo"** uncovers the possibility of a more sinister and unavoidable emptiness with the same power as Luna's, this time embodied in the faceless stare of the lover in our dreams.

A Greyhound, a Yellow Dog, and Despair

Donoso's *La desesperanza*[12] (Hopelessness), translated into English as *Curfew,* was published in 1986 and, unlike his other works, deals explicitly with a political situation. Two characters, Mañungo and Judit, are stranded in the streets of Santiago de Chile after the curfew established by the military regime. If found out, their lives would be in jeopardy. The novel describes the events of that night in a straightforward manner, emphasizing the cruelty of the political conditions endured by the country at large.

Dogs are again a key to the understanding of what is at stake in the narrative. As Mañungo and Judit look for shelter in the deserted streets, Judit sees a group of rough male dogs in pursuit of a delicate looking small female dog. They run after her, succeeding at points in cornering her with the visible desire to violate her. The peril faced by the female dog is told from a perspective that, in humanizing her, makes her situation applicable to the one experienced by Judit. As in Cortázar's "Press Clippings" the scene of nocturnal violence acquires a claustrophobic generality.

> At a corner, they saw the pack of dogs on the opposite side of the street. The enormous, maddened dog, and underneath him, between his paws, with her fur sticking to her nakedness, the little white bitch waited, licking her chops, while the beast satisfied his trivial impulse. The other dogs formed a querulous and expectant circle around the male, who could not seem to mount the bitch to his satisfaction. As soon as she saw the little white dog, Judit pulled away from Mañungo, crossed the street oblivious of who might see or hear her, and shouted scat, leave her alone, pardon her. But the dogs were unwilling to leave the bitch, whose eyes

seemed even more deeply shadowed and decadent, her face more concentrated and pale, accepting that all dogs wanted to possess her. [. . .] Mañungo, just outside the circle, shouted to Judit to get away, to let the disgusting dogs do what they wanted. The dogs jumped around Judit, tearing her sleeves, her skirt, her blouse, staining her with their saliva, with their semen, with their blood, ready to rape her.

(p. 181)

Mañungo is outside the circle made by the dogs, echoing the position he has in Chilean political life because he has just arrived from Paris. Judit, inside the circle, suffers the dog's threat from within, as though her own destiny were intertwined with the fate of the pursuit.

The small female dog, having decided to submit to the pack's attack, is playing a survival game. She is the acquiescent victim in a dark apprenticeship imposed by the rule of force. But Judit interferes with her decision, she stands in the circle in an attempt to defend her. Suddenly Judit, who is holding a pistol, decides to use it.

> She aimed at the dogs. There were so many. All the same. All of them deserved to die, undifferentiated males sticking to her and sullying her. In the middle of the pack was the little white bitch, poised as if all this were taking place in a salon, revealing the effect of this fury unleashed by her situation only in her melancholy smile, as if she knew that while she couldn't escape her destiny, she could at least play. Judit did not reach the bitch because the dogs were biting her streaming legs. She was a yard away from her. Between them the seething mob heaved. It seemed that the little white dog was not upset, because from between the paws of the tan dog in the center of the infernal circle, tender, clean, tired, she smiled at Judit, her accomplice, her savior, her sister, who aimed the pistol and shot her in the head. The body twitched and the bitch fell dead.

(pp. 181-82)

The result of Judit's intervention in the conflict is the destruction of the small female dog's strategy for survival. Judit's solidarity with her has effectively denied her life and shown to Judit the uncertainty governing any effort to overcome violence. This scene stands as the best rendition of what the original Spanish title of the novel conveys, a hopelessness so pervasive that every effort to stop aggression turns into its opposite. The compliant victim, having understood the message delivered by the drooling pack, had opted for expanding the powers of the pack even further; Judit by executing her turned her into an unwilling martyr to an unstated cause.

Did the dog die in dignity? Or was her acquiescence enough to make her a member of the attacking pack? Cortázar's Noemí ("Press Clippings") and Puig's Molina (*The Kiss of the Spider Woman*) attempt to enter the realm in which all this may be explained; for

Donoso certain games hold a key to the answer. They are not, as in Cortázar's *Hopscotch,* preexisting games reinscribed through writing but, as in "La marquesa salió a las cinco," invented ones that serve to uncover as conventional what we think of as belonging to the nature of society.

The Obscene Bird of Night, a somber novel narrated by a character alternatively called Humberto Peñaloza or "El Mudito" (the mute), is the starting point for many of the figurations found in Donoso's later works. As in *A House in the Country,* a large architectural enclosure, this time a convent, serves as the theater for the occurrences in the novel. Masks and lovemaking are brought together, questioning the stability of the self, and a meditation about clothing and rags anticipates the poetics of self-destruction that shapes *La misteriosa desaparición de la marquesita de Loria,* "Atomo verde número cinco," as well as the novellas gathered in *Cuatro para Delfina.*[13]

A yellow female dog is mentioned in *The Obscene Bird of Night* as the witness of an unspeakable secret that joins a little girl, her father, and an old woman who is presented simultaneously as a nanny and a witch. The dog appears at key moments in the narrative as two characters make sexual contact but interrupt it, fearing the dog's gaze. The yellow dog, silent but capable of running away with a secret held by its stare, closes the novel when a group of toothless old women play a game called "la perra amarilla" (yellow bitch). Betting everything they have, these old women, portrayed as indistinguishable and hence anonymous, lose their dentures, the contents of their newspaper-wrapped packages, and, by implication, whatever may be understood as making up their lives.

The newspapers, which reproduce the events of the day, are also disseminated in the game thanks to the randomness of who wins and who loses. Every loss or win is illusory, though, because we are told that in the end the only winner is the yellow bitch, "la perra amarilla." The dog says nothing as it runs away, obliterating history as represented by the old newspapers and erasing the individuality of the old women by taking everything from them. It is a total sweep; the dog is the supreme and uninvited player.

Should we make the dog say its message? Is there a moral that could make its way through the dog and represent us, our point of view? "La perra amarilla," like the other dogs in Donoso's stories, is not there so that we may speak through her in a triumph of domestication. These dogs already exist beyond the ambiguity of Kafka's animal as quoted by Borges;[14] they have won the staring battle and will not be vehicles for a message. On the contrary, as they stand in paralyzing guard they dare us to articulate their silence and learn the lesson they already hungrily know about us.

Notes

1. José Donoso, *Casa de campo* (Madrid: Seix Barral, 1978); trans. David Pritchard with Suzanne Jill Levine, *A House in the Country* (New York: Vintage Books, 1984). Page numbers correspond to the English translation; in some cases I have modified the translation for accuracy.

2. I am indebted to Michel Rybalka, from Washington University in St. Louis, for the information on the probable source for this Valéry quotation: it appears cited by Breton in the second Surrealist manifesto. See André Breton. "Second manifeste du surréalisme" (Paris: Sagittaire, 1929).

3. I refer to the school led by Ruben Darío. Donoso's novel takes up some of this modernista's favorite motifs and reinscribes them in a sinister key. See, for example, the treatment of gold in the chapter bearing that title ("El Oro") (pp. 166-200). The continued references to power and the materiality of its objects in Donoso's fiction have led to more than one interpretation favoring analysis of ideologies. See, for example, Hugo Achúgar, *Ideología y estructuras narrativas en José Donoso* (Caracas: Centro de Estudios Rómulo Gallegos, 1979), and Ricardo Gutiérrez Mouat, "El desclasamiento como ideología y forma en la narrativa de José Donoso," in his *El espacio de la crítica* (Madrid: Orígenes, 1989).

4. Arabela's knowledge gives her a peculiar kind of power, attained in some of Donoso's other works by old women, as in *The Obscene Bird of Night,* or derelicts, as in "Gaspar de la Nuit."

5. The vaguely archaic names of the cousins, clashing with the more "modern" references in the text, reinforce the sense that part of the narrative is to be construed as transhistorical. The role Juvenal plays in building this effect is important, having developed a narrative strategy seen by some as characteristic of postmodernism. John Barth has noted Donoso's relationship to postmodernism in "Post-Modernism Revisited," *Review of Contemporary Fiction* 8 (Fall 1988): 16-24.

6. José Donoso, *El obsceno pájaro de la noche* (Madrid: Seix Barral, 1970).

7. The wall-hanging is also an allusion to Charles Baudelaire's "Un voyage à Cythère." The joint consideration of the wall-hanging and the poem delineates the deterioration and sorrow to take place in the novel. The final lines of the poem, "Ah! Seigneur! donnez moi la force et le courage / De contempler mon coeur et mon corps sans dégoût!" uncannily encapsulate the characters' fi-

nal despair. See Charles Baudelaire, "Un voyage à Cythère," *Les fleurs du mal,* in *Oeuvres complètes* (Paris: Bibliothèque de la Pléiade, 1961), pp. 111-13.

8. José Donoso, *La misteriosa desaparición de la marquesita de Loria* (Barcelona: Seix Barral, 1981). Page numbers are in accordance with this edition; my translation. See also Philip Swanson, "Structure and Meaning in *La misteriosa desaparición de la marquesita de Loria,*" *Bulletin of Hispanic Studies* 3 (July 1986): 247-56.

9. José Donoso, *Tres novelitas burguesas* (Barcelona: Seix Barral, 1973), trans. Andree Conrad, *Sacred Families* (New York: Knopf, 1977). Page numbers refer to the English edition.

10. See Vicente Huidobro, "Altazor," in his *Obras completas* (Santiago: Editorial Zig Zag, 1976).

11. See Chapter 5 herein, devoted to Adolfo Bioy Casares.

12. José Donoso, *La desesperanza* (Barcelona: Seix Barral, 1986), trans. Alfred MacAdam, *Curfew* (New York: Weidenfeld and Nicolson, 1988); quotations and page numbers are in accordance with the English translation.

13. José Donoso, *Cuatro para Delfina* (Barcelona: Seix Barral, 1982).

14. See the epigraph for Chapter 2.

Bibliography

Achúgar, Hugo. *Ideología y estructuras narrativas en José Donoso.* Caracas: Centro de Estudios Rómulo Gallegos, 1979.

Alazraki, Jaime, ed. *Jorge Luis Borges.* Madrid: Taurus, 1976.

Alexandrian, Sarane. *Hans Bellmer.* New York: Rizzoli, 1972.

Andreu, Jean. "Personnage, lecteur, auteur." *L'Arc* 80 (1981): 24-34.

Bacarisse, Pamela. *The Necessary Dream: A Study of the Novels of Manuel Puig.* Totowa, NJ: Barnes and Noble, 1988.

Barrenechea, Ana María. *La expresión de la irrealidad en la obra de Jorge Luis Borges.* México: Colegio de México, 1957.

————. "Horacio en el proceso de escritura de *Rayuela:* Pretexto y texto." *Sur* 350-51 (1982): 45-63. (Buenos Aires)

Barth, John. "Post-Modernism Revisited." *Review of Contemporary Fiction* 8 (Fall 1988): 16-24.

Bastos, María Luisa. *Relecturas: Estudios de textos hispanoamericanos.* Buenos Aires: Hachette, 1989.

Baudelaire, Charles. *Les fleurs du mal.* In *Oeuvres complètes.* Paris: Bibliothèque de la Pléiade, 1961.

Bioy Casares, Adolfo. *La aventura de un fotógrafo en La Plata.* Buenos Aires: Emecé, 1985.

————. *Dormir al sol.* Buenos Aires: Emecé, 1973. Translation by Suzanne Jill Levine, *Asleep in the Sun.* New York: Persea Books, 1978.

————. *El héroe de las mujeres.* Madrid: Alfaguara, 1979.

————. *La invención de Morel.* Buenos Aires: Losada, 1940. Translation by Ruth L. Simms, *The Invention of Morel and Other Stories.* Austin: University of Texas Press, 1985.

————. *Una muñeca rusa.* Barcelona: Tusquets, 1991.

————. *Plan de evasión.* Buenos Aires: Galerna, 1969; Barcelona: EDHASA, 1990. Translation by S. J. Levine, *A Plan for Escape,* New York: Gray Wolf, 1988.

Blanqui, Louis Auguste. *Instructions pour une prise d'armes: L'éternité par les astres et autres textes.* Paris: Société Encyclopédique Française et Éditions de la Tête de Feuilles, 1972.

Bloom, Harold, ed. *Jorge Luis Borges.* New York: Chelsea House, 1986.

Bombal, María Luisa. *La amortajada.* Santiago: Nascimento, 1941; Buenos Aires: Editorial Andina, 1968.

————. *La historia de Maria Griselda.* Valparaiso: Ediciones Universitarias de Valparaiso, 1977.

————. *New Islands and Other Stories.* Translation by Richard and Lucia Cunningham. Prologue by Jorge Luis Borges. New York: Farrar, Straus, Giroux, 1982.

————. *La última niebla.* Buenos Aires: Editorial Andina, 1973.

Bonk, Ecke. *Marcel Duchamp: The Box in a Valise.* Translation by David Britt. New York: Rizzoli, 1989.

Borges, Jorge Luis. *El aleph.* Buenos Aires: Translation by Norman Thomas di Giovanni, in collaboration with the author, *The Aleph and Other Stories.* New York: E. P. Dutton, 1970.

————. *Ficciones.* New York: Grove Press, 1962.

————. *El informe de Brodie.* Translation by Anthony Kerrigan et al., *Dr. Brodie's Report.* New York: Bantam, 1973. Buenos Aires: Emece, 1970.

————. *Libro de sueños.* Buenos Aires: Torres Agüero Editor, 1976.

————. *Obras completas.* Buenos Aires: Emecé, 1974, 1989.

————. *Obras completas en colaboración.* Buenos Aires: Emecé, 1979; Madrid: Siruela, 1989.

————. *A Personal Anthology.* New York: Grove Press, 1967.

Borges, Jorge Luis and Adolfo Bioy Casares. *Libro del cielo y del infierno.* Barcelona: EDHASA, 1971.

Borges, Jorge Luis con Margarita Guerrero. *El libro de los seres.* Buenos Aires: Editorial Kier, 1967. Translated by Norman Thomas di Giovanni, *The Book of Imaginary Beings.* New York: E. P. Dutton, 1970.

Borinsky, Alicia. *Figuras furiosas.* Paris: Revista Rio de la Plata, 1985.

————. *Macedonio Fernández y la teoría crítica: Una evaluación.* Buenos Aires: Editorial Corregidor, 1987.

————. "*Plan de evasión* de Adolfo Bioy Casares: La representación de la representación." In Donald Yates, ed., *Otros mundos, otros fuegos: Fantasía y realismo mágico en Iberoamérica.* East Lansing: Michigan State University, Latin American Studies Center, 1975.

Breton, André. *Second manifesté du surréalisme.* Paris: Sagittaire, 1929.

Cabrera Infante, Guillermo. "Manuel Puig." *El País,* July 24, 1990.

Canetti, Elias. *Ear Witness: Fifty Characters.* Translation by Joachim Neugroschel. New York: Farrar, Straus, Giroux, 1986.

Canto, Estela. *Borges a contraluz.* Espasa Calpe, 1989.

Carpentier, Alejo. *El recurso del metodo.* Buenos Aires: Siglo XXI, 1974.

Cortázar, Julio. *Deshoras.* México: Editorial Nueva Imagen, 1983.

————. *Final de juego.* Buenos Aires: Sudamericana, 1974; Madrid: Ediciones Alfaguara, 1982. Translation by Paul Blackburn, *End of the Game and Other Stories.* New York: Harper and Row, 1978.

————. *Historias de cronopios y de famas.* Buenos Aires: Ediciones Minotauro, 1962.

————. *Rayuela.* Buenos Aires: Editorial Sudamericana, 1963. Translation by Gregory Rabassa, *Hopscotch.* New York: Avon, 1975; Pantheon, 1987. Critical edition edited by Julio Ortega and Saúl Yurkievich. Madrid: CSIC, 1991.

————. *62, Modelo para armar.* Buenos Aires: Editorial Sudamericana, 1968. Translation by Gregory Rabassa, *62: A Model Kit.* New York: Random House, 1972.

————. *Ultimo round.* Madrid: Siglo XXI, 1967.

————. *La vuelta al día en ochenta mundos.* México: Siglo XXI, 1967.

————. *Queremos tanto a Glenda.* México: Nueva Imagen, 1980. Translation by Gregory Rabassa. *We Love Glenda So Much and Other Tales.* New York: Knopf, 1983.

Cortazar, Julio and Carol Dunlop. *Los autonautas de la cosmopista: Un viaje atemporal Paris-Marsella.* Barcelona: Muchnik Editores, 1986.

Cúneo, Dardo. *El romanticismo politico: Leopoldo Lugones, Roberto J. Payro, José Ingenieros, Macedonio Fernández, Manuel Ugarte, Alberto Gerchunoff.* Buenos Aires: Editorial Transición, 1955.

Derrida, Jacques. *La vérité en peinture.* Paris: Flammarion, 1978.

Donoso, José. *Casa de campo.* Madrid: Seix Barral, 1978. Translation by David Pritchard with Suzanne Jill Levine, *A House in the Country.* New York: Vintage, 1984.

————. *Cuatro para Delfina.* Barcelona: Seix Barral, 1982.

————. *La desesperanza.* Barcelona: Seix Barral, 1986. Translation by Alfred J. MacAdam, *Curfew.* New York: Weidenfeld and Nicolson, 1988.

————. *El obsceno párajo de la noche.* Madrid: Seix Barral, 1970. Translation by Hardie St. Martin and Leonard Mades, *The Obscene Bird of Night.* New York: Knopf, 1973.

————. *La misteriosa desaparición de la marquesita de Loria.* Barcelona: Seix Barral, 1981.

————. *Tres novelitas burguesas.* Barcelona: Seix Barral, 1973. Translation by Andrée Conrad, *Sacred Families.* New York: Knopf, 1977.

Duras, Marguerite. *Le ravissement de Lol V. Stein.* Paris: Gallimard, 1964.

Fernández, Macedonio. *Adriana Buenos Aires: Última novela mala.* Buenos Aires: Editorial Corregidor, 1974.

————. *Epistolario.* Edited with notes by Alicia Borinsky. Buenos Aires: Editorial Corregidor, 1991.

————. *Macedonio: Selected Writings in Translation.* Edited by Jo Anne Engelbert. Fort Worth, TX: Latitudes Press, 1984.

————. *Museo de la novela de la Eterna: Primera novela buena.* Buenos Aires: Centro Editor de América Latina, 1967; Editorial Corregidor, 1975.

————. *No toda es vigilia la de los ojos abiertos y otros escritos metafísicos.* Buenos Aires: Editorial Corregidor, 1967, 1990.

————. *Papeles de recienvenido y continuación de la nada.* Prologue by Ramón Gómez de la Serna. Buenos Aires: Losada, 1944; Centro Editor de América Latina, 1966; Editorial Corregidor, 1989.

————. "Para una teoría de la Humorística." In Macedonio Fernández, *Papeles de recienvenido.*

————. *Poemas.* México: Editorial Guarania, 1953.

Ferrari, Osvaldo and Jorge Luis Borges. *Diálogos últimos.* Barcelona: Seix Barral, 1992.

Foster, Hannah W. *The Coquette, or, The History of Eliza Wharton: A Novel, Founded on Fact, by a Lady of Massachusetts.* 1811. New York: Oxford University Press, 1986.

Foucault, Michel. *Les mots et les choses: Une archéologie des sciences humaines.* Paris: Gallimard, 1966.

Fuentes, Carlos. *Aura.* México: Era, 1962; Durham, Engl.: University of Durham, 1986.

García, Germán Leopoldo, ed. *Jorge Luis Borge, Arturo Jauretche y otros hablan de Macedonio Fernández.* Buenos Aires: Carlos Pérez Editor, 1969.

García Márquez, Gabriel. *El amor en los tiempos del cólera.* Barcelona: Bruguera, 1985. Translation by Edith Grossman, *Love in the Time of Cholera.* London: Penguin, 1988.

————. *La aventura de Miguel Littín clandestino en Chile.* Buenos Aires: Editorial Sudamericana, 1986.

————. *Cien años de soledad.* Buenos Aires: Editorial Sudamericana, 1967. Translation by Gregory Rabassa, *One Hundred Years of Solitude.* New York: Harper and Row, 1970; reprint Avon, 1974.

————. *Crónica de una muerte anunciada.* Bogotá: Editorial La Oveja Negra, 1981. Translation by Gregory Rabassa, *Chronicle of a Death Foretold.* New York: Knopf, 1983.

————. *El general en su laberinto.* Madrid: Mondadori, 1989. Translation by Edith Grossman, *The General in His Labyrinth.* New York: Knopf, 1990.

————. *La incréible y triste historia de la cándida Eréndira y de su abuela desalmada: Siete cuentos.* Madrid: Mondadori, 1972, 1987. Translation by Gregory Rabassa, *Innocent Erendira and Other Stories.* New York: Harper and Row, 1978.

————. *El otoño del patriarca.* Buenos Aires: Editorial Sudamericana, 1975. Translation by Gregory Rabassa, *The Autumn of the Patriarch.* New York: Avon, 1977.

Genette, Gerard. "L'utopie littéraire." In Genette, *Figures, essaies.* Paris: Éditions du Seuil, 1966.

Giacoman, Helmy F., ed. *Homenaje a Gabriel García Márquez.* Long Island City, NY: Las Américas, 1972.

Goloboff, Gerardo Mario. *Leer Borges.* Buenos Aires: Huemul, 1978.

González Bermejo, Ernesto. "Ahora doscientos años de soledad." *Triunfo* 441 (1970): 12-18.

Gooding, Mel. *Surrealist Games.* Boston: Shambhala Redstone Editions, 1993.

Green, James R. "*El beso de la mujer araña:* Sexual Repression and Textual Repression." In *La Chispa 81: Selected Proceedings of the Louisiana Conference on Hispanic Languages and Literatures,* pp. 131-39. New Orleans: Tulane University, 1981.

Gutiérrez Mouat, Ricardo. *El espacio de la crítica: Estudios de literatura chilena moderna.* Madrid: Orígenes, 1989.

Hancock, Joel. "Gabriel García Márquez's Erendira and the Brothers Grimm." *Studies in Twentieth Century Literature* 3, 1 (1978): 45-52.

Hidalgo, Alberto, Macedonio Fernández, Vicente Huidobro, Jorge Luis Borges, and others. *Indice de la nueva poesía americana.* México and Buenos Aires: Sociedad de Publicaciones El Inca, 1926.

Higonnet, Margaret. "Speaking Silences: Women's Suicide." In Susan Suleiman, ed., *The Female Body in Western Culture.* Cambridge, MA: Harvard University Press, 1986.

Hoffmann, E. T. A. *Tales.* Translation by L. J. Kent and E. C. Knight. Edited by Victor Lange. New York: Continuum, 1982.

Huidobro, Vicente. "Manifestos." In *Obras completas.* Volume 1. Santiago: Editorial Zig Zag, 1976.

Irby, James. "Borges, Carriego y el arrabal." In Jaime Alazraki, ed., *Jorge Luis Borges.* Madrid: Taurus, 1976.

Irwin, John. "The Journey to the South: Poe, Borges and Faulkner." *Virginia Quarterly Review* 67, 3 (Summer 1991): 417-31.

Jitrik, Noé. *Escritores argentinos: Dependencia o libertad.* Buenos Aires: Ediciones del Candil, 1967.

————. "Estructura y significado en *Ficciones* de Jorge Luis Borges." In Juan Fló, ed., *Contra Borges.* Buenos Aires: Galerna, 1978.

Kadir, Djelal. "The Architectonic Principle of *Cien años de soledad* and the Vichian Theory of History." *Kentucky Romance Quarterly* 24, 3 (1977): 251-61.

Kafka, Franz. "Dearest Father" (1919), as quoted by Borges, in Jorge Luis Borges, *The Book of Imaginary Beings,* p. 26. New York: E. P. Dutton, 1970.

Kerr, Lucille. *Suspended Fictions: Reading Novels by Manuel Puig.* Urbana: University of Illinois Press, 1987.

Lagos-Pope, María Inés. "Silencio y rebeldía: Hacia una valoración de María Luisa Bombal dentro la tradición de la escritura femenina." In M. Agosín, E. Gascón-Vera, and Joy Renjilian Burgy, eds., *Maria Luisa Bombal: Apreciaciones críticas.* Tempe, AZ: Bilingual Press, 1987.

Leduc, Violette. *L'affamée*. Paris: Gallimard, 1948, 1972.

Levine, Suzanne Jill. "Adolfo Bioy Casares y Jorge Luis Borges: La utopía como texto." *Revista Iberoamericana* 43 (July-December 1977): 415-32.

————. *Guía de Adolfo Bioy Casares*. Madrid: Fundamentos, 1982.

Lezama Lima, José. "Acerca de *Rayuela*." *Revista de Casa de las Américas* 7, 49 (July-August 1968): 68. (Havana)

Lindstrom, Naomi. "El discurso de *La amortajada*: Convención burguesa vs. conciencia cuestionadora." In M. Agosín, E. Gascón-Vera, and Joy Renjilian Burgy, eds., *María Luisa Bombal: Apreciaciones críticas,* pp. 147-61. Tempe, AZ: Bilingual Press, 1987.

————. *Macedonio Fernández*. Lincoln, NB: Society of Spanish and Spanish-American Studies, 1981.

Lispector, Clarice. *Laços de Familia*. Río: Editôra do Autor, 1960. Translation by Giovanni Pontiero, *Family Ties*. Austin: University of Texas Press, 1972.

Luchting, Wolfgang A. "Gabriel García Márquez: The Boom and the Wimper." *Books Abroad* 44 (Winter 1970): 26-30.

MacAdam, Alfred J. *El individuo y el otro: Crítica a los cuentos de Julio Cortázar*. Buenos Aires: Librería, 1971.

Marechal, Leopoldo. *Adán Buenosayres*. Buenos Aires: Editorial Sudamericana, 1966.

Martino, Daniel, ed. *ABC de Adolfo Bioy Casares: Reflexiones y observaciones tomadas de su obra*. Alcalá de Henares: Ediciones de la Universidad, 1991.

Masiello, Francine. "Jailhouse Flicks: Projections by Manuel Puig." *Symposium* 32 (Spring 1978): 15-25.

Masson, André. Illustration for *Justine. Obliques,* no. 12-13, p. 14. Éditions Borderie, 1977.

Mastretta, Angeles. *Mujeres de ojos grandes*. Buenos Aires: Planeta Sur, 1992.

McGuirk, Bernard, and Richard Cardwell. *Gabriel García Márquez: New Readings*. Cambridge: Cambridge University Press, 1987.

Mehlman, Jeffrey. "Pierre Menard, Author of *Don Quixote* Again." *L'esprit créateur* 22, 4 (Winter 1983): 22-37.

Mendoza, Plinio Apuleyo. *El olor de la guayaba*. Barcelona: Bruguera, 1982.

Merrim, Stephanie. "For a New (Psychological) Novel in the Works of Manuel Puig." *Novel* 17 (Winter 1984): 141-57.

Mignolo, Walter. "Emergencia, espacio 'mundos posibles': La propuestas epistemológicas de Jorge Luis Borges." *Revista Iberoamericana* 100-101 (1967): 337-56.

Molloy, Sylvia. *Las letras de Borges*. Buenos Aires: Editorial Sudamericana, 1979.

Nabokov, Vladimir. *Lectures on Don Quixote*. New York: Harcourt Brace Jovanovich, 1983.

————. *Strong Opinions*. New York: McGraw-Hill, 1973.

Naville, Pierre. *Le temps du surréel*. Paris: Galilée, 1977.

Nogue, Paul. "La vision dejouée." *Le Surréalisme au service de la Révolution,* p. 26. Paris: Éditions des Cahiers Libres, May 1933. Reprinted in *Le Surréalisme au service de la Révolution*. Paris: Jean-Michel Place, 1975.

Onetti, Juan Carlos. *Cuentos secretos: Periquitá el Aguador y otras máscaras*. Montevideo: Marcha, 1986.

————. *Dejemos hablar al viento*. 3rd ed. Barcelona: Bruguera, 1979.

————. *La muerte y la niña*. Buenos Aires: Editorial Corregidor, 1973.

————. *Obras completas*. Madrid: Aguilar, 1970.

————. *Tan triste como ella y otros cuentos*. Barcelona: Lumen, 1976.

Ortega, Julio. "Borges y la cultura hispanoamericana." *Revista Iberoamericana* 100-101 (1967): 257-68.

————. "Gabriel García Márquez: *Cien años de soledad*." In *La contemplación y la fiesta: Ensayos sobre la nueva novela latinoamericana*. Lima: Editorial Universitaria, 1968.

Oviedo, José Miguel. "Angeles abominables: Las mujeres en las historias fantásticas de Bioy Casares." In Oviedo, *Escrito al margen*. Bogotá: Procultura, 1982.

————. "*La aventura de un fotógrafo en La Plata*." *Vuelta* 120 (November 1986): 58-60.

Pacheco, José Emilio. *El principio del placer*. México: Joaquín Mortiz, 1972.

Palau de Nemes, Graciela. "Gabriel García Márquez: *El otoño del patriarca*." *Hispamérica* 4, 11-12 (1975): 172-83.

Palencia Roth, Michael. *Gabriel García Márquez: La línea, el círculo y las metamorfosis del mito*. Madrid: Gredos, 1983.

Peignot, Jerome and the group Change, eds. *Écrits de Laure*. Paris: Pauvert, 1977.

Pellón, Gustavo. "Manuel Puig's Contradictory Strategy: Kitsch Paradigms Versus Paradigmatic Strategies in *El beso de la mujer araña* and *Pubis angelical.*" *Symposium* 36 (1983): 186-201.

Penuel, A. M. "The Sleep of Vital Reason in García Márquez's *Crónica de una muerte anunciada.*" *Hispania* 68 (December 1985): 753-66.

Peret, Benjamin. "Ces animaux de la famille." *Le Surréalisme au service de la Révolution.* Paris: Gallimard, March 1, 1926. Reprinted in *Le Surréalisme au service de la Révolution.* Paris: Jean-Michel Place, 1976.

Pezzoni, Enrique. "Bioy Casares: Adversos milagros." In Pezzoni, *El escritor y su voces,* pp. 237-45. Buenos Aires: Editorial Sudamericana, 1986.

Picón Garfield, Evelyn. *Cortázar por Cortázar.* Veracruz, Mexico: Universidad Veracruzana, 1978.

Pizarnik, Alejandra. *Obras completas.* Buenos Aires: Editorial Corregidor, 1992.

Puig, Manuel. *El beso de la mujer araña.* Barcelona: Seix Barral, 1979. Translation by Thomas Colchie, *The Kiss of the Spider Woman.* New York: Knopf, 1979.

————. *Boquitas pintadas.* Barcelona: Seix Barral, 1972. Translation by Suzanne Jill Levine, *Heartbreak Tango: A Serial.* New York: E. P. Dutton, 1975.

————. *Cae la noche tropical.* Barcelona: Seix Barral, 1988. Translation by Suzanne Jill Levine, *Tropical Night Falling.* New York: Simon and Schuster, 1991.

————. *Maldición eterna a quien lea estas páginas.* Barcelona: Seix Barral, 1980.

————. *Pubis angelical.* Barcelona: Seix Barral, 1979. Translation by Elena Brunet, *Pubis Angelical: A Novel.* New York: Random House, 1986.

————. *Sangre de amor correspondido.* Barcelona: Seix Barral, 1982. Translation by Jan L. Grayson, *Blood of Requited Love.* New York: Vintage, 1984.

————. *La traición de Rita Hayworth.* Buenos Aires: Editorial Jorge Alvarez, 1968. Translation by Suzanne Jill Levine, *Betrayed by Rita Hayworth.* New York: E. P. Dutton, 1971.

Rama, Angel. "Un patriarca en la remozada galería de dictadores." *Eco* 29, 178 (1975): 408-43.

Rentería Mantilla, Alfonso, ed. *García Márquez habla de García Márquez: 33 reportajes.* Bogotá: Rentería, 1979.

Roa Bastos, Augusto. *Yo, el supremo.* Buenos Aires: Siglo XXI, 1975. Translation by Helen Lane, *I, the Supreme.* New York: Knopf, 1986.

Robbe-Grillet, Alain. "Adolfo Bioy Casares: *L'invention de Morel.*" *Critique* 69 (February 1963).

Rodríguez Luis, Julio. "*Boquitas pintadas:* Folletín unanimista?" *Sin nombre* 5, 1 (1974): 50-56.

Rodríguez Monegal, Emir. "Borges y la 'Nouvelle Critique.'" In Jaime Alazraki, ed., *Jorge Luis Borges,* pp. 267-87. Madrid: Taurus, 1976.

————. *Jorge Luis Borges: A Literary Biography.* New York: E. P. Dutton, 1978.

————. "*One Hundred Years of Solitude,* the Last Three Pages." *Books Abroad* 47 (1973): 485-89.

Schmucler, Héctor. "*Rayuela:* Judicio a la literatura." *Pasado y presente* (April-September 1965): 29-45. (Córdoba, Argentina)

Senda Nueva Ediciones. *Las desterradas del paraíso: Protagonistas en María Luisa Bombal.* New York: Senda Nueva Ediciones, 1983.

Singer, Isaac Bashevis. *Shosha.* New York: Avon, 1982.

Sosnowski, Saúl. *Borges y la Cábala: La búsqueda del verbo.* Buenos Aires: Hispamérica, 1976.

Sturrock, John. "Odium Theologicum." In Harold Bloom, ed., *Jorge Luis Borges.* New York: Chelsea House, 1986.

Sucre, Guillermo. *Borges, el poeta.* México: UNAM, 1967.

Suleiman, Susan. *Subversive Intent: Gender, Politics and the Avant-Garde.* Cambridge, MA: Harvard University Press, 1990.

Swanson, Philip. "Structure and Meaning in *La misteriosa desaparición de la marquesita de Loria.*" *Bulletin of Hispanic Studies* 3 (July 1986): 247-56.

Tamargo, Maribel. *La narrativa de Bioy Casares: El texto como escritura-lectura.* Madrid: Playor, 1983.

Valdivieso, Mercedes. "Social Denunciation in the Language of 'El Arbol' by María Luisa Bombal." *Latin American Literary Review* 4, 9 (1976): 70-77.

Vargas Llosa, Mario. *Gabriel García Márquez: Historia de un deicidio.* Barcelona: Seix Barral, 1971.

————. "García Márquez: From Aracataca to Macondo." *Review* 70 (1971): 129-42.

von Hagen, Victor W. *The Four Seasons of Manuela.* London: J. M. Dent and Sons, 1952.

Williams, Raymond L. "The Dynamic Structure of García Márquez's *El otoño del patriarca.*" *Symposium* 32 (Spring 1978): 56-75.

Yurkievich, Saúl. *Fundadores de la nueva poesía latinoamericana.* Barcelona: Seix Barral, 1971.

————. *Julio Cortázar: Al calor de tu sombra.* Buenos Aires: Legasa, 1987.

————. "La pujanza insumisa." In Julio Cortázar, *Rayuela,* critical edition by Julio Ortega and Saúl Yurkievich, pp. 661-74. Madrid: CSIS, 1991.

Sharon Magnarelli (essay date 1993)

SOURCE: Magnarelli, Sharon. "How to Read José Donoso." In *Understanding José Donoso,* pp. 3-13. Columbia: University of South Carolina Press, 1993.

[*In the following introductory chapter to her full-length study of Donoso, Magnarelli discusses several common themes in Donoso's work.*]

Critics disagree, often vehemently, about how to read the works of José Donoso. Many, particularly his early critics, have insisted on perceiving his works in a traditional, realistic, or naturalistic mode, specifically as social realism whose goal is to critique the Chilean bourgeois society. Donoso maintains, and it would be hard for the careful reader to disagree, that on some level his work always encompasses a fissure with realism or social reality and that the social message is only one aspect of his work. For Donoso, reality is little more than a word, and not a very reliable one at that. Unlike the static, tangible, objective entity implied by the term as it is generally used, reality is for Donoso always fluid, always provisional, always subjective—that is, subject to the individual's perception, which is frequently metamorphosed, if not created, by language. Thus when his character Santelices looks out of his office window, he perceives not a dark, mundane, empty, quiet patio in its nighttime tranquillity (as another might view it) but a jungle teeming with ferocious beasts and fraught with danger. Although the two perceptions are contradictory, one interpretation of the physical surroundings is no more valid than the other. As presented by the author, neither vision is completely accurate nor completely erroneous. Both evoke, if indeed on different planes or within different focal points, our complex world, which includes the psychological as well as the physical and, as Donoso recognizes, is a world that can never be grasped in its totality at any given moment or by any given perceiver. It is for this reason that Donoso's fiction invites, indeed exacts, such disparate and multivocal readings.

Thus Donoso's prose can never be read simplistically on one level alone. On the contrary, it demands multiple readings and interpretations (as does any good piece of literature). Although his fiction creates a cosmos that may parallel the realities of quotidian experience, those literary worlds are unequivocally different and subject to their own rules. Donoso's narrative universe is not simply a reflection of some external referent (generally labeled reality) but rather an artistic invention in which he employs metaphors and other literary tropes and figures in order to embody multifarious meanings and thereby highlight the plurality of that world.

For that reason, Donoso specifically deplores readers' attempts to reduce and simplify his prose by "boiling down the complexities of a metaphor to the false lucidity of one word."[1] As a result, he refuses to deal with symbols that have an exact correlative in reality. Furthermore, he wants his readers to see not just the "what" and the "why" but also the "how" of his prose. For him style and technique are as important as his thematic concerns. *How* we perceive is as much an issue in his prose as *what* we perceive. That is why the questions of art (literature), artistic (literary) techniques, and artistic materials (language, discourse) are so frequently the subject as well as the material of his work.

MASKS AND CHANGING FACES

The "how" in Donoso, his technique, is often an endless superimposition of layers or levels—hence the mask or the disguise that figures in so much of his work and that ultimately is less a mask than simply another version or perception. The result of this technique is often a multilayered product in which the layers have become either inseparable or indiscernible, and thus the hierarchy implicit in the layering or masking (first layer, second layer, one *above* the other) is rendered null and void. At the same time, the mask consistently functions in a paradoxical fashion. It not only distorts the purportedly hidden, covered "face" but also inevitably allows that veiled layer to peek through. In this respect, both his thematic and his stylistic masks emphasize the gesture of disguising while they blur the ostensibly distinct and separate layers, as they produce new perceptions that combine the previous ones. This technique is perhaps best metaphorized in the image of the package in *The Obscene Bird of Night.* In that novel numerous packages are wrapped again and again, becoming ever more bulky and unwieldy, not with the goal of hiding or protecting anything but rather just for the sake of wrapping, as one stratum is superimposed on another. Similarly, for the Chilean author, human personality or selfhood (ontological being in the world) is a series of masks or disguises, ever changing and ever (inter)changeable, with no ultimate coherence or integrity.

Thematically the question of mask is treated in two principal ways in the works of Donoso. At times the characters are shown to be so rigidly restricted by social structures that their "authentic" selves cannot show through; nor, perhaps, are they even conscious of having an "authentic" self apart from the social role. Again one of Donoso's points is that the mask is or becomes the self. Humberto of *The Obscene Bird of Night* wants nothing more than to don the mask of Don Jerónimo and to be him. The brothers of **"Paseo"** (**"The Walk"**), like those of *This Sunday,* never disclose their emotions but feign a self-sufficiency they surely do not feel. In other words the motif of the mask reveals itself in a form of transvestism. Sometimes it is a transvestism in the traditional sense of wearing the clothing of the opposite sex, as in *Hell Has No Limits,* but at other times it is an interchangeability of characters when one character places himself in the clothes and thus the social position of another, such as Mauricio and his double in **"Gaspard de la Nuit."** A similar commutation of characters is apparent in the relationship between Peta Ponce and Inés as well as that of Humberto and Don Jerónimo in *The Obscene Bird of Night,* while the device reaches its apogee in **"Chatanooga Choo-choo,"** in which not only are the characters replaceable one with another, but even their individual body parts are detachable and reusable on other characters.

On the level of technique this layering or mask manifests itself in a number of ways. One is the framing technique by means of which Donoso embeds one narrative within another. An example of this can be found in *This Sunday,* in which the grandparents' stories are embedded within the grandson's. Similarly, in *The Obscene Bird of Night* the story of the landowner's daughter and the nanny/witch is inscribed within the larger narrative of Inés's attempts to have her ancestor canonized, a narrative which in turn is embedded within the still larger frame narrative that tells the tale of the Casa de los Ejercicios Espirituales, the asylum for old servants and other discarded possessions. Within this frame narrative the story of the Rinconada is embedded, much as its narrator, Humberto/Mudito, is enclosed within the Casa and its tale. By enclosing this series of tales one within the other, Donoso produces a Chinese box effect while at the same time he highlights both the metaphoric and the metonymic relations among the stories. The stories relate to each other metaphorically in that they exhibit significant similarities and metonymically because they exist in physical proximity. Yet the metaphoric similarities tend to blur the differences among the stories and lead us to an erroneous assumption of identity between the frame story and the embedded one. In turn, it is the metonymic relation, the embedding or layering, that underlines the error of this assumption and reminds us that the individual situations are only similar in appearance (surface, mask) and not in essence.

Another stylistic layering technique is found in Donoso's frequent utilization of the simile X is like Y. More than the metaphor (X is Y), the simile evokes similarity while underlining difference. By saying "X is like Y," one concurrently implies that X is not Y. Thus, to say X is like Y is to allow us to perceive both X and Y, their points of contact *and* their divergence, as so

many Donoso masks do. Although the two entities blend, to some degree, neither totally loses its unique qualities while we are led to a new perception.

Although the mask is one of the most important techniques and motifs in Donoso's works, my reading of his fiction will necessarily center on seven additional topics. Like the question of mask, each of these seven topics must be analyzed as both content and technique, for the issues he raises are always treated in both dimensions.

THE BOURGEOISIE IN CHILE

It would be impossible to comprehend Donoso's works without some understanding of the Chilean bourgeoisie to which his family belonged and from which the majority of his characters proceed. Like many Latin American countries, Chile is defined by a rigid class structure and the institution of the extended family with its numerous servants. In this extended family system, unmarried female relatives and less affluent relatives reside with the more prosperous members of the family in a home governed, nominally at least, by a male patriarchal figure. Like most upper-middle-class children in Santiago, Donoso spent much of his childhood in a large home surrounded not only by his immediate family (parents and brothers) but also by relatives, predominantly female (two of them elderly), as well as numerous servants, also predominantly female. Because the female servants are frequently charged with the care and early education of the children, they inevitably exert considerable influence over those children, as his prose demonstrates. Yet this system of household servants should not to be confused with the slavery system of the Southern United States during the eighteenth and nineteenth centuries. Servants in Chilean society, in spite of their lack of education and the fact that they belong to a different socioeconomic class, consider themselves members of the family they serve and on some level are considered by the family as members, though honorary ones. The esteem granted those servants is surely evidenced by the fact that Donoso dedicated his first book to Teresa Vergara, the servant who effectively raised him. It is noteworthy too that traditionally, even in their old age, after they have outlived their function and usefulness within the household, the servants are provided for by the family. This structure is reflected in his works: in *The Obscene Bird of Night* one finds an asylum for aged servants, while in *This Sunday* the elderly Violeta is comfortably established in a house provided by the family she had long served.

Such a family structure, marked as it is by the presence of numerous female relatives and servants, combines with the frequent absence of the father figure (because of responsibilities away from the home or simply his greater freedom and mobility) to imbue the Chilean bourgeois society with a distinctly matriarchal flavor. Children grow up surrounded by figures of immediate if not ultimate authority who are female. It is for this reason that the old servants in *The Obscene Bird of Night* are characterized as witchlike with a combination of natural powers (probably those actually wielded by the female servants over the children) and supernatural powers (perhaps those the child feared the female servant might exert).

Throughout Donoso's work the complex status of the servants is underscored. Subordinate to their "masters," they nonetheless enjoy a position of tacit, though not always recognized, power to the extent that the life of the household and the family could not continue as it is without them. At the same time, they assume much of the responsibility of caring for the young children and enjoy a dimension of influence in this respect. In fact, in *A House in the Country,* they tyrannize the children, especially after curfew, when their jurisdiction is total. More important, as Donoso himself has noted on several occasions, the subculture of the servant class not only provides an inverted mirror of the dominant culture but also exposes the children of that dominant culture to set a of "unorthodox," alternative cultural myths, value systems, and hierarchies. By means of their interrelationships as well as the stories they tell the children, the servants provide and represent the "other," alternative society that exists contingent to but separate from the dominant one, both metaphorically and metonymically. The servants bridge the two worlds, belonging to both, yet are never completely subject to the rules, rituals, and social decorum of the dominant class. It is presumed the servants can do things and feel emotions denied to their more rigidly masked masters. This is perhaps the germinal experience from which Donoso has developed his perception of the world as a series of tangential layers.

For those members of Chilean society not privy to an extended upper-middle-class family with servants, a different, if indeed parallel, social structure is available: the pension, which simulates the extended family in many ways. It is generally governed by a matriarchal figure who either presides over the servants or performs the labors of cooking and cleaning herself. This same woman frequently controls, to a greater or lesser degree, the activities as well as the moral conduct of her lodgers. Because of their close living conditions, the boarders at the pension mirror the family in that each is likely to know the intimate details of the others' lives while, like siblings, they alternately support and rival one another.

Nevertheless, in Donoso's prose fiction, the pension often marks the inveterate isolation and impotence felt by protagonists such as Santelices. Although there is probably no moment in Donoso's work when the social, fa-

milial structure is presented in a positive light—it is always either a sham (as in *A House in the Country*) or on the brink of destruction (as in "The Walk" and *This Sunday*)—the institution of the pension is perceived as little more than an unfortunate imitation of the family structure.

NANNIES AND WITCHES: FEMALE POWER AND THE SUPERNATURAL

The matriarchal bent that characterizes the social institutions of the home and the pension results in a society of females who maintain, or at least are perceived to maintain, quite a different position from that of women in the United States. Although it is doubtful that women wield or have wielded control in any significant measure on the national level in Chile (at least not overtly), they apparently wield significant control on the familial level, and that produces an awe, if not fear, of those women, particularly in the male child. Thus in Donoso one finds the repeated themes of the nanny and the witch. Throughout Donoso's works it is women who are the powerful ones, often in an evil fashion, while men are frequently portrayed as weak, ineffectual, and pathetic. When, on rare occasion, the text depicts an ostensibly strong, powerful man, that power is undercut by females. For example, Don Jerónimo's power in *The Obscene Bird of Night* is effectively nullified by the nanny/witch Peta Ponce, and masculine "strength" proves to be a sham that masks latent homosexuality in *Hell Has No Limits.* At other moments those males are openly controlled or emasculated by powerful mother figures, like Santelices or Andrés (*Coronation*).

CHILDREN, GAMES, AND RITUALS

Children frequently assume leading roles in Donoso's fiction. *A House in the Country* and a number of his short stories provide examples of this thematic concern. At times the events of the plot are even told from a child's point of view, as in *This Sunday* and "The Walk." There are several reasons for this procedure. First, the child's perspective provides a means of manipulating point of view; the child can share the adult reader's values, tell events as she or he sees them, and yet be incapable of comprehending their significance. Obviously, the narrator who cannot grasp the meaning of an experience is incapable of selecting those events and details that merit narration. As a result, readers are left, as they often are in life, with a mixture of relevant and irrelevant information from which to draw conclusions. Through the child's eyes, then, not only can readers understand their own limited comprehension of what surrounds them but at the same time, paradoxically, they can come to a new understanding. Clearly, such is both the theme and technique of *This Sunday,* in which the story of the last years of the narrator's grandparents—their personal demise and the end of a social era—is embedded within his adult speculations about those moments of his childhood. The result is a multilayered and multivocal tale that dramatizes not a moment or even a process of comprehension but an ongoing state of ignorance. As in **"The Walk,"** the narrator understands little more at the end of the process (the narration from his adult perspective, the contemplation of things past) than he did at the beginning or as a child.

Another professed motivation of Donoso's for focusing on children and their antithesis, the elderly, is that both groups live in a form of anarchy. Like the servants, children and the elderly exist on the fringes of society and are not subject to all the rules, role playing, and hierarchies to which adults are subject. Their actions and language tend to be freer, less self-conscious, less manipulated and manipulative. At the same time, however, the children imitate the adult world and reproduce it on a microcosmic level. As a result, the reader is proffered a new perspective that underlines the absurdities of adult (the reader's) society.

His concern with children also leads Donoso to employ the motif of the child's game. Again, however, he proffers a thinly veiled allegory of adult life, for he posits that children's games reflect, in structure and content, the more formalized ritualistic behavior (social decorum) that shapes adult lives. Thus the games are simultaneously similar to and different from adult rituals, but it would be difficult to decide which exerts more influence over the other. Think, for example, of *La Marquise Est Sortie á Cinq Heures* (The Marquise Left at Five o' Clock), the theatrical game of *A House in the Country,* or the games in *This Sunday.* Donoso's suggestion is that each makes the other problematic: adult rituals are absurd because of the traces they retain from childhood games; the latter are perverse because they resemble, perhaps even consciously imitate, adult rituals.

The Inexplicable: The Call of the Wild

Throughout Donoso's works, one encounters an element of the inexplicable, often depicted (or at least interpreted) as an element of supernatural power. None of our empirical experience seems to provide explanations for the strange allure of Maya in *This Sunday,* the interchangeability of physical parts in **"Chatanooga Choo-choo,"** Mauricio's strange whistling in **"Gaspard de la Nuit,"** Matilde's fascination for the dog in **"The Walk,"** or the protagonist's obsession with pictures of wild animals in **"Santelices."** What leads Andrés to opt consciously for insanity in *Coronation*? What does the father hide behind his poncho in *The Obscene Bird*?

Questions such as these necessarily punctuate any reading of Donoso's fiction. One of his points is surely that one can never "know" anything unequivocally. In many cases this inexplicable something, this call to another level of nature or reality, is resolved both stylistically and thematically by eradication or disappearance. The texts often end without resolution, or the characters simply disappear while their world disintegrates. *This Sunday* and *Coronation* both conclude with the death of the characters and the disintegration of the world as they knew it. *The Obscene Bird of Night* concludes with the burning of all the packages and papers that presumably were the text the reader has just finished; Marta and Roberto disappear into the night in **"Atomo verde número cinco"** ("Green Atom Number Five"), as does Matilde in **"The Walk."**

The unusual conclusions, or even nonconclusions, of so many of Donoso's works pose a curious contradiction. On one level his works seem to open up, letting in the unexpected and the unnatural or supernatural. Yet all his works close up around that possibility and somehow cover or negate it. Indeed, in many of the works in which the main character disappears, a new closure is effectuated in two ways. First, on the level of plot, the society or family depicted turns its back on the disappearance or erasure and carries on with life as if nothing had happened. Thus the brothers return to their ritualistic existence in **"The Walk"** after Matilde disappears and never make any direct reference to her disappearance. After the highly unusual happenings in *A House in the Country,* the parents return and life ostensibly goes on as usual—for a while, at least, until nature (the thistledown) "swallows" one group and perhaps the other. This erasure functions on the stylistic level too, for the reference to the disappearance or inexplicable event is frequently followed by a number of paragraphs about mundane events and written in the most apparently naturalistic, prosaic, and transparent of languages. In this way, the discourse of the text also denies that anything unusual has happened and lures the reader back into a false sense of complacency even after having shattered that complacency.

Space

The ostensibly circular structure that dominates much of Donoso's work is reflected in his use of space. The majority of his works take place either within the city or inside a carefully delimited and defined space—most often the home or a building that evokes a homelike structure. Generally the outside, be it a natural setting, the city, or the rest of society, is viewed as threatening and dangerous. Still, on the few occasions when the action takes place out of doors, even that exterior space tends to be markedly limited and confined. For example, the vineyards of *Hell Has No Limits* are bounded even as they surround the town. The Venturas' fence defines the "safe" spaces and separates them from the threatening outside, nature. Significantly, once outside the physical confines, characters tend to disappear, to be swallowed by the external world.

Surely the enclosed physical spaces evoke closed psychological spaces. Characters in the Donoso texts can function only within a rigidly ordered society and universe. The outside or exterior always threatens to destroy that social, psychological order and control. Nonetheless, Donoso's works are also characterized by the number of windows and doors (or even fences) that allow the characters to glimpse the "external" world and feel its allure from a safe distance. At the same time, physical space tends to close in upon itself, as in *The Obscene Bird of Night,* in which Mudito's physical enclosure becomes ever smaller as the book draws to a conclusion. Obviously the delimitation of physical space mirrors the space limitations of the literary work, also closed, structured, and excluding the threatening outside while it paradoxically proffers a relatively unthreatening glimpse of that threatening other, the world outside the confines and rigid structure of the book or society. Space in Donoso's works is necessarily a projection of the mind, as is dramatically demonstrated in Santelices's projection of the jungle onto the patio of his office building (an enclosure within an already severely delimited world).

ART AND LANGUAGE: THE BLENDING OF CONTENT AND FORM

This depiction of space and the projection of mental rigidity reflect Donoso's preoccupation with art and literature or language. In much of Donoso's work the world is depicted as already a reproduction of some earlier works of art or literature. Western aesthetics, particularly since the nineteenth century, has generally viewed art as a reproduction or mimesis of reality, but Donoso continually demonstrates the degree to which the opposite is also true: reality (or what we perceive as and then insist is reality) is frequently a reproduction or mimesis of artistic works. For this reason, in many of his works the principal action is presented as fiction, as fantasy even within the work. For example, the principal action of *This Sunday,* the relationship of the grandparents to each other and that of the grandmother to Maya, is presented as the recollections, not necessarily reliable, of an adult who reviews his childhood. Within that principal action the narrator includes the grandfather's memories of his youth. The continual embedding of one story within the other, combined with a repeated undermining of the reliability of the narrators, marks the fictitiousness of those tales and their distance from what might be labeled reality. It marks them as already reproduction. In this way Donoso suggests that art is not merely a mirror of some external reality; art and reality mutually influence, shape, and mold each other.

At the same time, language and the embedding technique, like the fences, doors, and windows, frequently provide limiting structures, for, consciously and intentionally or not, Donoso continually proposes that we perceive what we have words for and tend not to perceive what we cannot name. Like art and literature, language shapes and limits perception. When confronted with a situation for which we have no word, we perceive nothing. Thus an inability to name leads logically to the erasure or disappearance that so often marks the conclusion of his works.

As we examine the trajectory of Donoso's prose over the course of forty years, we shall find that some combination of these eight characteristics is present in every work.

Note

1. Ronald Christ, "An Interview with José Donoso," *Partisan Review* 49, 1 (1982): 30.

Sharon Magnarelli (essay date 1993)

SOURCE: Magnarelli, Sharon. "*Sacred Families*: Reading and Writing Power." In *Understanding José Donoso,* pp. 119-32. Columbia: University of South Carolina Press, 1993.

[*In the following essay, Magnarelli explores the ways in which Donoso's ostensibly realistic portrayal of bourgeois life in* Sacred Families *actually conceals a more complex examination of the power of representational aesthetic works.*]

Although *Tres novelitas burguesas* (*Sacred Families,* literally "Three Bourgeois Novellas"), published in 1973 by Seix Barral, returns to the shorter genres of Donoso's earlier career, it nonetheless proffers a prolongation and amplification of the themes and preoccupations of *The Obscene Bird of Night.* As was the case in his masterpiece, the major concerns of the trilogy are art and discourse, their power, and the effect they exercise on bourgeois society. In these works Donoso probes the instruments of representational art and shows them to be the same instruments by which our social structures are created.[1] Paradoxically, however, *Sacred Families* has elicited and surely will continue to inspire readings that perceive the text only in terms of social realism, for in it Donoso has abandoned, at least superficially, much of the overt fantasy and linguistic play of *The Obscene Bird.*[2] To the extent that *Sacred Families* has met readers' demands for an ostensibly realistic, representational portrayal of society, it should delight the casual reader and the student of history or sociology. Nonetheless, I suggest that the work's ostensible realism and mimesis are masks that undermine the representational mode they seem to support. In fact, Donoso spotlights the art and language that bring the text (and most of our social and psychological structures) into existence, challenges them, and undermines our belief in their ability to represent. And more important, he subtly examines how those media lead us to perceive power where little exists, where, underlying the mask of power, there lies only an intrinsic impotence from which our attention has been diverted. Thus, like the works discussed in previous chapters (particularly *The Obscene Bird of Night*), *Sacred Families* must be read for its aesthetic as well as its psychological and sociological messages, for the trilogy of novellas again underscores the interrelations among art and society (social structures) while it highlights the inevitable, if at times disguised, artificiality of them all.

Donoso's preoccupation with language and art is already underscored in the titles of the individual stories; each refers to another work of art—linguistic, musical, or pictorial. **"Chatanooga Choo-choo,"** the title of the first story, refers to a North American song of the big band era and thus to both a musical and a linguistic work of art. As Charles M. Tatum has noted, the song evokes the postwar evasionist period; that evasionism is reflected in both the words of the song and in the society portrayed.[3] **"Green Atom Number Five"** is the name of a painting by the protagonist of that story, and **"Gaspard de la Nuit"** refers to the musical composition by Ravel and indirectly to the prose poem of the same name by Aloysius Bertrand.[4] In each novella Donoso examines the status and nature of another work of art while he indirectly considers his own creation and being. At the same time each artistic creation to which he alludes is characterized by the fact that it is distanced in both time and mode from any "origin"; it is overtly artistic re-creation. Mauricio whistles "Gaspard de la Nuit," which repeats the musical composition for orchestra, which imitates the prose poem by Bertrand based on the work by Hoffmann. Anselmo and Ramón repeat the "Chatanooga Choo-choo" number performed earlier by Sylvia and Magdalena, which copies the 1940s creation, already conspicuously artificial and unconnected to a social reality. Similarly, the title of Roberto's painting highlights the fact that it is the fifth variation on the same theme. The additional fact that he had considered naming it according to its weight underscores the nonreferentiality, its distance from what we might label sociopolitical reality.

Plot and Technique/Being and Power

The setting of the stories of *Sacred Families* has moved from Chile to Barcelona and given the work a more cosmopolitan, international flavor. Although each narrative is autonomous (at least in terms of plot), each relies on the same cast of characters in that Barcelona setting. With the exception of Sylvia, a major character in both the first and the last narrative, the protagonists of each story are the secondary characters in the other stories, as each is placed in a slightly different context and viewed from a different perspective. Nonetheless,

all the stories address the theme of possession and how individuals define themselves by means of possession or appropriation, socially, sexually, or linguistically.

"Chatanooga Choo-choo" recounts events of a week in the life of two Barcelona couples: Ramón and Sylvia, Magdalena and Anselmo. The action of the story (although not the narrative itself) begins at a social gathering, where Sylvia and Magdalena, identically dressed, perform a song-and-dance number to the North American tune "Chatanooga Choo-choo." The story concludes a week later at a similar gathering when Anselmo and Ramón, also identically attired, perform the same song-and-dance number, demonstrating that the former controllers are now the controlled. In the interim we learn that Sylvia's face may be erased at any moment (reducing it to a blank, white ovoid) and repainted according to the desire of the man at hand. A night at the weekend home of Sylvia and Ramón leads Anselmo to have a brief affair with Sylvia, during which he paints and then erases her face and she steals his penis or makes it disappear. During the week that separates the two performances of "Chatanooga Choo-choo," Sylvia teaches Magdalena the technique of dismantling her husband when he becomes vexatious or superfluous. Thus in this narrative the identities of the characters—their existence, form, and personality—are directly and immediately dependent on the whim and will of another, while inversely and paradoxically each is responsible for shaping another, for providing the other with the "possessions" or features that mark being and personality. In this respect, power shifts according to context.

The males, who seem all-powerful early in the text as they erase and re-create Sylvia's features, prove less powerful than the reader may have imagined. In fact, our initial perception of their power is based to a large degree on our (mis)perception and unquestioning acceptance of the first, unilateral rendition of a situation that proves bilateral or even multilateral. Although the narrative technique proffers at least two narrative voices (Anselmo's and that of a more omniscient narrator who tells what Anselmo cannot), the beginning of the story is narrated by Anselmo. Because of the naturalness with which he paints the scene and presents his "point of view," it does not occur to the reader to distrust his rendition, his "superior" vision. Furthermore, since at the start we have no access to information other than Anselmo's narration, we accept his version and view him (and by implication Ramón) as powerful because he says he is. The suggestion is that as "readers" in the world, we tend to react the same way; we are deluded by the discursive spectacle of power and presume that power to be unilateral and unidirectional: we accept someone's rendition of events as fact because it has been presented as natural and indubitable, because someone has *said* that is how it is. Thus, paradoxically, while Donoso's characters and plot may not be totally representational, his technique is; that is, it accurately reflects how discourse functions in the world as it leads us to erroneous conclusions and perceptions of power. As we are afforded more information, however, we learn that the power is far less unilateral than Anselmo (and by implication we, as readers) had imagined. On the contrary, we soon discover that the women have the power to deprive the men of their penises (the emblem of manliness and being), to dismantle those men, and to pack them away until they have further need of them. What at the beginning of the story seemed "natural," an unalienable truth proffered by a reliable narrator, not only proves questionable but finally undermines the realistic deceit. In this manner Donoso leads us to question all our knowledge and sociopolitical "givens." Nonetheless, the overt "unnaturalness" of the final version (the dismantling of the men) precludes our facilely falling into another perceptual trap. It is not merely a matter of power's being inverted or changing hands (from male to female) in this story. Instead, our basic assumptions about power and being are challenged. Power is not either/or but and/also.

In terms of technique, it should be noted that while Anselmo narrates (that is, controls the discourse), he governs our perception, leading us to view him as all-powerful as he creates Sylvia by projecting his desires onto her, as Ramón did earlier, thus making her a mirror of their desires—paradoxically a reflection of the self. But even then their control is not absolute, for although she is their creation, Sylvia still exhibits some degree of autonomy and challenges their control. As a result she must be continually eliminated, erased (or at least her appendages, mouth, and facial features must be), so they can try again to (re)create the ideal embodiment of their desires, an embodiment with no desire apart from theirs. This task proves impossible. At the same time, although Anselmo thoroughly enjoys what he perceives as his absolute power, Sylvia's quasi powerlessness and helplessness necessarily convert him into her slave, for he must perform for her the tasks she cannot. Still, once her mouth and, by implication, her power of speech are returned to her, she begins to take control of the discourse and command him to perform menial tasks (close the curtains, repaint her face as she wants it), ever more demanding and less subtle. Eventually she fully "repossesses" the discourse when she "steals" his penis, and he is forced into relative silence (he cannot tell Magdalena about it and thus isolates himself from her), while she and Magdalena converse at will.[5] It is also at this point in the narrative that the other, ostensibly more omniscient narrator enters to supply a perception of power that differs significantly from Anselmo's.

In the next narrative, **"Green Atom Number Five,"** Marta and Roberto, a childless upper-middle-class couple, have installed themselves in their "definitive apartment." They have gone to every expense and effort to surround themselves with perfect and carefully selected objects, which, they believe, reflect their unique personalities (like Sylvia's face). The irony, of course, is that these personalities are not "individual"; they are merely vacuous reflections of others' masks, for the rooms have been created and the objects combined with considerable influence from others, much as Sylvia's features were created by others and reflected their desires. As soon as everything in this apartment is finally and definitively positioned, various items begin to disappear or are stolen (like Anslemo's penis), beginning with Roberto's painting, "Green Atom Number Five." As the objects continue to vanish, Roberto and Marta discover that, after fifteen years of marriage, neither of them possesses anything that belongs to him or her alone; everything is shared (not unlike the male organs in **"Chatanooga Choo-choo"**). What they never realize is that not only is everything communal property, shared between the two of them, but that, in turn, all (like their language and aesthetic taste) is shared with the rest of their society: neither of them has anything that is unique, proper (belonging to the self), not shared with the rest of their group. Again possession and uniqueness are shams; a comforting mirage of proprietorship is provided by art and discourse. Furthermore, although Donoso focuses here on the theme of possession already predominant in some of his earlier works, in this novella he highlights the vacuity of possession for the sake of possession. Roberto's painting is of no value, but both characters want to be able to declare it theirs. Similarly, Roberto insists that the extra room *belongs* to him. Empty and thus devoid of any intrinsic or extrinsic value, it is nonetheless his mirror, for it metaphorically reflects his own emptiness and the fact that he has (possesses) nothing, not even a unique personality.

On the thematic level, the story concludes as the two have gotten lost in the streets and alleyways (a labyrinthian setting reminiscent of the conclusion of *This Sunday*) they entered in search of the painting. Having assaulted and robbed the taxi driver, they attack each other and are left naked, glaring at each other, "lacking memory of past or thought of future, possessing only this narrow present of violence in the midst of empty space" (137/187). Deprived of their possessions (masks), they are reduced to emptiness and gratuitous violence.

Technically, however, the conclusion of the novella is significantly more complex and more open-ended than is immediately apparent, for discursively it reflects a desire for definitiveness, closure, and possession (like the apartment and life style of the bourgeois couple), while it underscores the lack thereof as it proffers multiple and perhaps self-contradictory alternatives (again in a reflection of **"Chatanooga Choo-choo"**): "like two animals that separate in the moment before pouncing on each other to destroy or to possess, or turn their backs and flee . . . into the vast, empty space" (137/187-88). What stands out in this plot resolution is that it resolves little, for the ostensibly omniscient narrator fails to authorize a single, unequivocal explanation of events. Instead he offers a series of alternative, antithetical possibilities (signaled by "or") that would appear to be mutually exclusive. First, he states that the couple is *like* animals—a simile that calls attention to itself as it reminds us that the couple simultaneously are and are not animals. Surely, one characteristic that separates people from animals is that the latter cannot possess. Marta and Roberto are acting like animals—without possessions—but all along they have presented themselves with the mask or veneer of polite civilization—with possessions, which, like art and discourse, disguised their animal nature. But specifically, they are like animals that either separate only briefly before coming together or flee in separate directions, not coming together. If we opt for the first conjecture, that they will eventually come together, we are faced with yet two more alternatives: they come together to destroy or to possess. Ultimately, however, the ostensible antitheses here are conflated and dissolve, for their results are identical. Whether they hate and destroy or love and possess, they each metaphorically devour (dispossess) the other. And whether they devour the other or turn and flee they still find themselves alone, vulnerable, always surrounded and threatened by that vast, menacing other(ness), all that is outside the self and threatens to dispossess one of the possessions that mark and define self.

Mauricio, the protagonist of the final novella, **"Gaspard de la Nuit,"** handles the problem by actively seeking dispossession before he is passively dispossessed. He has recently come to live with his mother, Sylvia (of the first narrative). Unconcerned about the things that interest other boys of his age, he passes his days whistling the Ravel composition "Gaspard de la Nuit" and wandering through the streets trying to entangle others in his tune: "it was audible music . . . halting the woman and proving to her that she wasn't free, that she was dependent on other powers; and from the frontier of her consciousness, Mauricio at last plunged into her . . . calling to her, commanding her" (159-60/215). The story concludes when Mauricio exchanges clothes and identities with the nameless street urchin (who looks like him) after their respective symbolic baptisms in the swamp and waterfalls. The unknown boy returns to Sylvia's apartment and proves to be the ideal son Sylvia needed to complete the cast of her bourgeois mother-son comedy (147/198). Thus Mauricio is freed of all identity and ties, free to pursue whatever it is he seeks, significantly freed of all artistic impulses as epitomized by his whistling. (After he exchanges identities he can

no longer whistle "Gaspard de la Nuit.") One of the problems that Sylvia had sensed all along with Mauricio was his lack of desire to possess. He does not want anything (155/209). The "new" Mauricio (the street urchin), however, desires possessions and thus can be defined by Sylvia.

Although the reader might be inclined to view this conclusion as the most positive of the three, careful consideration of its language challenges such a perception. At the final encounter of the old Mauricio (now the nameless street urchin) and the new Mauricio (formerly the nameless street urchin), the latter recalls Sylvia's words "I don't know how you could stand life before, living there . . ." (205/273; Donoso's ellipsis). As he whistles his (in)famous music, that same "there" is recalled in the thoughts of the old Mauricio, who recognizes that he no longer needs to whistle and that he cannot limit himself, but should leave. Specifically, he is going to leave by *going down* to the *other side* and continuing to walk (beyond *there*) toward other things. But is it not precisely from there and those things (social possessions) that he was trying to escape? Has anything been achieved here other than the bidirectional illusion of possession/dispossession?

Like that of **"Chatanooga Choo-choo,"** the narrative technique of **"Gaspard de la Nuit"** is predicated on a displacement of power as it subtly proffers more than one narrator or narrative position. At the same time, the text proffers numerous (often overlooked) narrative corrections which suggest that the situation might vary from what the discourse has initially posited. Although the opening words of the text take us back to the first novella as they recall Sylvia's artificiality (mirror, tweezers, *Vogue*), we soon learn that the ever changeable and malleable Sylvia is about to assume yet another "mask"—that of mother, a role still imposed by a male, this time her son Mauricio. Ironically, although the narrator notes that the latter's arrival threatens to fix Sylvia and Ramón's life into an artificial routine, his ensuing description of their present life specifically highlights its routine and artificiality; contrary to what the reader has been told, Mauricio would have no real effect on it. Later the narrative correction is more overt when the reference to "Ramón's ex-partner's wedding" is rectified to "Jaime Romeu's *daughter's* wedding" (141/192; Donoso's emphasis), a modification that subtly emphasizes the role of perspective in relation to possession: whose wedding is it, anyway? Similarly, because the tale opens with Sylvia and initially focuses on her (although she is not the narrator), we are likely to view her as the powerful, "castrating" mother who metaphorically devour Mauricio, the innocent, dull, powerless son. But the narrative technique undermines this perception too; soon after we discover that although such is precisely his fear, in fact, his music is described as an aggression against her (and others) and threatens to devour her: "the circle Mauricio's music was tracing would conquer and devour her" (151/204). Power is indeed in the eyes of the beholder.

The narrative power play continues as the reader accompanies Mauricio on his walk and sees from his perspective. Now he is the powerful one who attempts to violate others with his music until, in an unexpected inversion of power, the man in the brown suit, whom he had believed he was stalking, stalks him. Mauricio becomes a "frightened boy running home to Mama" (165/222) when that man proves to be only a "counterfeiter who had made him believe he [Mauricio] was powerful" (165/221), that is, until the man he was about to execute in his music and imagination stares at him with sad eyes and indicates the rest room sign. Note that it only takes a look (and a reasonably impotent one at that) to "reawaken Mauricio's childlike vulnerability" (165/221). Again power shifts quickly and easily.

Perhaps even more significant in regard to the question of power in this narrative is the presence of Sylvia. Throughout the three narratives, the characters who believe they have power generally do not. Sylvia is the character in the first narrative who initially allows Anselmo and Ramón to believe they are powerful, when in fact she controls them as much as they control her. Might not the same be the case here? Has Mauricio accomplished anything at the end of **"Gaspard de la Nuit,"** or have the covert powers of Sylvia merely led him to believe he is choosing a new life? After all, as the story concludes, she finally has the son she wanted (one in her own image). Again Donoso dramatizes the difficulty of identifying the source of power and the impossibility of finding it fixed and stable.

As in *The Obscene Bird,* then, two of the thematic concerns of *Sacred Families* are being and power. As has been demonstrated, being proves to be ever precarious, inherently superficial, and structured by the other person (who does or does not allow the self to continue to possess), while power inevitably proves to be other and differently located than what appearances had suggested. Thus the perfect object woman, the mannequin-like Sylvia of **"Chatanooga Choo-choo,"** who can be dismantled and recreated at the whim and to the specifications of any male, proves to be far less helpless and controllable than was first suggested by the males' dreams of domination. In **"Chatanooga Choo-choo"** not only does she metamorphose from a silent, helpless blob of raw material to a potent being who gives orders and controls Anselmo's acts and "creativity" (as he paints her face), but she even manages to deprive him of his manliness and by implication his personhood by taking "away the thing that endowed [him] with gravity and unity as a person" (35/54)—his penis. In fact, in the first story she is literally the castrating mother/female that she is only metaphorically or covertly in the

last. In either case, the reader is left to wonder how much of her castrating power is genuine (even within the fiction) and how much of it is imagined, a fear projected by the male characters (Mauricio and Anselmo). Donoso proposes that it may all be a question of point of view, of discursive structures and strategies imposed on society and supposed reality.

Indeed, all three narratives might be read as the literalization of the sociopsychological desires and fears already outlined in Donoso's previous works. **"Chatanooga Choo-choo"** dramatizes, first, the male desire for and fantasy of the object, adjective woman, pure decoration and dependency, created in his own image, fashioned for the whim of the moment. That dream of power, however, is followed by the dramatization of a fear of castration. Since the male organ is envisioned (imagined and imaged) as the center and essence of being or personhood, castration leads to that loss of personhood and individuality so feared in *The Obscene Bird of Night.*[6] What is particularly interesting about the novellas, however, is the fact that the males' fears, literally and figuratively realized in the first narrative but only potentially plotted in the last, are but inversions of their desires. **"Green Atom Number Five"** similarly literalizes the desire for something definitive and unchanging in a world of constant mutation but terminates in a frightening drama of loss, dispossession, and the metaphoric defrocking of the trappings of culture and civilization. Finally, **"Gaspard de la Nuit"** simultaneously dramatizes the desire to invade and violate the other (Mauricio's music) coupled with the fear of invasion and violations (Mauricio's perception of Sylvia's relationship to him). In this sense, the final novella circles back to the preoccupations of the first and demonstrates that desire and fear are predicated on perspective (thus the importance of narrative technique): one's desire to control another is the inverse (and by implication a mirror reflection) of the other's fear of that control. Similarly, one's "power" depends on another's "impotence," and vice versa. At the same time, **"Gaspard de la Nuit"** juxtaposes the dream (desire) to be someone and the dream (desire) to shed one's social role/mask and disappear into the freedom of nonidentity. Again it is all a question of perspective, point of view, where one is located or locates oneself in relation to power. And power is frequently imaged here in terms of the erotic, particularly in **"Gaspard de la Nuit,"** in which Mauricio repeatedly seeks to "penetrate" or "plunge into" others but sees their relation to him as penetration of the reverse type: as violation or rape.

READING THE WRITING

While students of naturalism or sociology may be offended by the "unrealistic" dismantling of the literary characters in **"Chatanooga Choo-choo,"** they will no doubt attribute it to a *representation* of a Freudian dream of power. On the other hand, we must not neglect the importance of Donoso's analysis of language and representation themselves. In this text the literary character, a linguistic entity recognized as such, is overtly portrayed as a more or less arbitrary conglomeration of signs—signs, words, elements of meaning, which can be joined, separated, or erased at will. In many respects this novella underscores Sylvia as the literary character par excellence, an artificial repetition of an artificial repetition. Just as any literary character can never be more than an arbitrary grouping of nouns, adjectives, and verbs, Sylvia is overtly just that. Her creators, like the author, work with her blank white face as they would use a blank sheet of paper (or in the pictorial arts, a blank canvas). The creators write or paint, with other materials, on that blank space and create the character and personality they desire (or so they believe). As her creator puts on her cosmetics, he formulates her and assigns her qualifying signifiers. Inasmuch as she is even called "the woman-adjective" (46/ 70), there obviously is little difference between the symbolic act of painting her face, making her up—and in this sense, providing her with specific modifiers—and that of fashioning her in language, again supplying her with adjectives that restrict and specify.

The individual facial features selected from *Vogue* magazine have no relation to Sylvia until they are grouped and labeled "Sylvia." Donoso here emphasizes that the literary character is a mere assembly of words and that, contrary to our traditional manner of viewing the literary character, the group of signs from which each character's signifiers are chosen is finite and shared. His metaphor here is not different from the one in *The Obscene Bird of Night* when the old women are left alone among the ruins of the desecrated chapel. In the rubble they find pieces of statues of saints, pieces that postdate earlier artistic creations that no longer exist in the same manner. Much like Anselmo and Ramón, the old women join these preterit particles and components to fashion new saints, new characters. In both cases what varies and what gives significance to the conglomeration is the context, the juxtaposition (the interrelation of the signifiers), as much as the signifiers themselves. Although the characters of the Donoso text naively seem to believe that these groups of signifiers are unique, the text emphasizes the nonunique nature of them and the entities that result. Because adjectives are finite in number and must be shared and repeated, the result is an entity that is neither distinctive nor unique.

Furthermore, the novellas in many ways might be seen as self-reading; that is, Donoso seems to be perusing and interpreting his own work as it progresses. Closely related to the detective novel (which he will pursue more overtly in *La misteriosa desaparición de la Marquesita de Loria*), in which the protagonist's primary function is to find the clues and "read" or interpret them, "**Chatanooga Choo-choo**" at first focuses on Anselmo, who, like the detective, repeatedly tries to discover the significance of various events and of the words of others. He finds as he "reads," however, that the words are not directly related to a single, specific referent and signification; instead, each group of words allows for multiple interpretations (again it all depends on context and perspective). For example, the story's beginning pages examine Anselmo's attempts to interpret the words of Sylvia:

> As she passed [the chops], Sylvia persisted. "And Magdalena's taste is so marvelous . . . [literally, "Magdalena has such good taste"]"
>
> Had she tasted it, [in Spanish, "her"]? Maybe because she was passing the meat as she said this, it flashed through my mind that she meant a "taste" of Magdalena's that only I knew; the idea made me retreat before the anthropophagous Sylvia. But of course she meant a different kind of "taste": the "taste" that governed our visit to the houses that afternoon, providing us with a common language; a "taste" related to aesthetic judgment, ordained by the social milieu in which we lived.
>
> (4/13)

As the detective-like story concludes, Donoso demonstrates that Anselmo has become both the narrator and the detective (reader of clues) as well as the murderer (to the extent that he "erases" Sylvia) and the murdered victim (to the extent that Magdalena disassembles him).

With a similar emphasis on the act of reading and interpreting clues (detective story motifs), "**Green Atom Number Five**" culminates in the events that result from the reading of a small piece of paper on which the title of the painting and its weight (Pound-Ounces 204) are written. The words are (mis)read as the address at which the painting will be found, and it is this (mis)interpretation that leads to the destructive chaos of the conclusion. What becomes clear, then, is that Marta and Roberto's problem is not just social (as critics have suggested) but also linguistic or semiotic. The couple has failed to see the arbitrary and ephemeral relation between the signifier (both in the sense of words and in the sense of objects, possessions that they want to "reflect" their personalities) and the signified. They have simplistically found a one-to-one relation between the signifier and signified and have overlooked the fact that the attempt to capture a definitive signifier is but the first step in the erasure of the signified. They have buried themselves in signifiers as the significance has disappeared, and they have failed to understand that their signs must be the essence of plurality insofar as each is shared not only by more than one referent but also by more than one speaker, writer, or reader. In this respect, it cannot be irrelevant that the title of the story, "**Green Atom Number Five**," signals the nonreferentiality (vacuity) of art. Roberto's painting of the same name (art within a work of art) is abstract, art for the sake of art. It does not pretend to "reflect" reality, to represent or "say" anything. It cannot be "read" because it has no message. Ostensibly its only functions are related to its context(s)—temporary at that. It functions as a possession and thus a mark of power and individuality, or it functions as the final touch that marks the completion of the apartment (again possession and individuality). But Donoso's message is clear: as a potential symbol, the painting is inevitably "misread" like all else in this world of surfaces and masks.

"Gaspard de la Nuit" evinces interesting similarities in regard to the question of reading. When Mauricio first arrives in Barcelona, Sylvia struggles to establish a relationship with him, only to discover that there is something about him that makes her uncomfortable. That "something," in fact, is that she cannot find the words with which to label him and describe him, words that would limit and define him. She cannot "read him." Similarly, Mauricio views her efforts to find signifiers that are applicable to him and will define him as violation, which he hates but which he simultaneously tries to inflict on others through his music. To this extent and in connection with the other two stories, Donoso presents Sylvia, in this novella, as the realistic, naturalistic writer or reader. She seeks the right words to name and describe events, people, objects, emotions, and sensations; but Mauricio, like Donoso himself, objects to this limitation.

Thus, while **Sacred Families** unquestionably portrays bourgeois society and its fantasies, it is simultaneously and equally concerned with its own existence and status as well as those of any linguistic or artistic creation. If Donoso were attempting only to portray society, there would have been no need to make the stories so closely interrelated. Surely the correspondence of characters in the narratives underscores a linguistic concern. The characters, groups of signifiers united by a proper noun or name, are repeated in the three novellas just as all signifiers, all adjectives, are inevitably repeated, shared, and exchangeable.

Concurrently, the format of separating the text into three stories rather than joining it into one more or less unified novel emphasizes the isolation of the literary sign. While superficially shared and repeated, like all signs, each character is nevertheless isolated and distinct due to the context in which he or she is presented. Ultimately the Sylvia of **"Chatanooga Choo-choo"** bears no more resemblance to the Sylvia of **"Gaspard de la Nuit"** than if they were two distinctly named characters placed in similar social milieus. The mask worn (or face presented) by Sylvia in the first narrative must differ from that of the last narrative in spite of the repetition of the name and other signifiers because the context is different—in one she plays the femme fatale and in the other, the mother.

Surely Donoso's texts should not be understood simply as descriptions of external events. Instead, the trilogy is a self-portrait and a self-analysis—a text that reads itself as it is written. The author shows not only that language masks and violates but that it is ever interchangeable and supplemental because it can never be unique or proper (in the sense of possessed). Donoso is not just seeking the right words to describe what he has experienced; he is also trying to analyze an experience that is neither separate nor external but ultimately a part of and dependent on the process and the medium (language and discourse) itself. It is not a question of a transposition into words but an analysis of those words. In **Sacred Families** Donoso has shown creation and commentary to be synchronic and indivisible.

Notes

1. As Griselda Pollock has noted, "[Art] is one of the social practices through which particular views of the world, definitions and identities for us to live are constructed, reproduced, and even redefined." Pollock, *Vision and Difference: Femininity, Feminism, and the Histories of Art* (New York: Routledge, 1988), 30.

2. Hortensia R. Morell's *José Donoso y el surrealismo: Tres novelitas burguesas* (Madrid: Pliegos, 1990), which came into my hands after the writing of this chapter, is an intelligent exception to the general rule. In it she focuses on how the text is in continual dialogue with the precepts of surrealism, thus suggesting, both implicitly and explicitly, that the goal of the text is not realism but rather an ironic questioning of bourgeois values.

3. Charles M. Tatum, "Enajenación, desintegración, y rebelión en *Tres novelitas burguesas,*" *The American Hispanist* 2, 16 (1977): 13.

4. Aloysius Bertrand is the pseudonym of Jacques-Luis-Napoléon Bertrand, a French author born around 1807, from whom the French composer Maurice Ravel "borrowed" his title and the three sections of his composition for "Gaspard de la Nuit": Ondine (Water Nymph), Le Gibet (Gallows), and Scarbo (Beetle). Apparently, however, the Bertrand work had already been "borrowed" from German writer E. T. A. Hoffmann. For a detailed analysis of the relation among the works, see Hortensia R. Morrell, "El doble en 'Gaspard de la Nuit': José Donoso à la manière de Ravel, en imitación de Bertrand," *Revista de Estudios Hispánicos* 15 (1981): 211-220.

5. There is the suggestion that one of the reasons for the initial dismantling and erasing of her face by Ramón is that she talked too much in the presence of the two men. At the same time, Donoso seems to be mocking here some of the contemporary

psychoanalytical theorists who view discourse as a phallic activity.

6. Donoso takes an almost feminist, perhaps tongue-in-check attitude here in regard to the sociopsychological value placed on the male organ by psychoanalysts such as Jung, Freud, and Lacan.

José Donoso and Nivea Montenegro and Enrico Mario Santi (interview date April 1994)

SOURCE: Donoso, José, Nivea Montenegro, and Enrico Mario Santi. "A Conversation with José Donoso." *New Novel Review/Nouveau roman* 1, no. 2 (April 1994): 7-15.

[*In the following interview, Donoso speaks about his life, the history of the "Boom" period, and aspects of postmodernism.*]

[*Nivia Montenegro*]: *José Donoso's distinguished writing career began in the 1950's when he published his first short stories in his native Chile, and since then he has piled success upon success, both in Latin America and in the rest of the world with his many novels, most of which have been translated into several languages. No serious reader or scholar of modern Latin American literature can afford not to know such Donoso classics as* **Coronation, Hell Has No Limits, The Obscene Bird of Night, Charleston and other Stories, State of Siege, The Garden Next Door, Taratuta,** *among others. A frequent visitor to the United States, Mr. Donoso is a graduate of Princeton University, has been a Writer-in-Residence at the Iowa Writers' Workshop, and currently is a fellow at the prestigious Woodrow Wilson Center in Washington, D.C., where he is at work on another novel about which we hope he will talk to us today. What we have planned for this afternoon is simply a conversation with José Donoso on the general subject of the new Latin American novel, a subject he is most qualified to speak on. Not only is Mr. Donoso one of the outstanding protagonists of this important development in modern Latin American literature, but also is the author of* **The Boom in Spanish American literature, A Personal History.** *Joining us in our discussion will be CMC and Scripps College Visiting Professor Enrico Mario Santí.*

[*José Donoso*]: Thank you very much. I feel very privileged to be here with you. Let me tell you that I have suggested this format, above all, because I am such a bad public speaker. I write a lot, but I talk less, in general, except in private. I do like to answer questions, and I can deal with that much better, than I can with a prolonged presentation. I would be very glad to answer your questions toward the end of this period. Meanwhile, we'll see how we can develop this with my two distinguished friends.

We just finished reading in class your novel **The Garden Next Door.** *There are several questions that you explore there which I'd like to ask you about. One of them, I think, is that the novel concerns, in part, an ongoing struggle, between a husband and a wife, who also happen to be either writing or trying to write a book. As we gather towards the end of the novel, one character, Gloria, is, or seems to be, successful in publishing, while the other, Julio, the husband, gets his manuscript rejected. Would you care to elaborate about, perhaps, the relationship of the two characters, whom you mention in* **A Personal History of the Boom:** *the figure of the writer versus the figure of the author?*

What can I say? The first thing I must say, of course, is that of all my novels it's the most autobiographical. I remember once when Russian television came to my house in Santiago and my wife came down to say hello, everybody said, "Ah, Gloria!" I don't really know how happy she was. But still, it is the story of a couple very much in a position such as the one my wife and I had together both in Spain, in several cities in Spain, and mainly in Sitges and in Madrid. The author and the novelist in this case are like two sides, two extremes, of a playing card. They complement and they value each other, they are one and the other, the same person. My wife was, before I met her, a painter who had had several reasonably successful shows in Buenos Aires and in other Latin American cities as well as in Egypt, in Cairo, where she lived as a young girl. When I met her, I told her, first of all, that I thought her painting stank, it was very bad, and that everybody was really making a fool of her by telling her she had a talent for painting, whereas I thought she had none. I also said that I thought that perhaps she could write, as she had been involved in writing articles for several magazines, and she clearly enjoyed literature, her intelligent enjoyment of literature in general. Then we got married. I told her that if she wanted to marry me she had to do two things: one was to learn how to drive a car because I never would, and the other one was to read Proust because if she hadn't read Proust we wouldn't have anything to talk about. She accomplished both things very well.

I met my wife in Buenos Aires, actually, as I was on the first leg of my trip on a voyage to all the countries of Latin America with my pockets full of letters of recommendation to the writers of all the whole continent signed by, especially, Pablo Neruda. Pablo and his wife went to my house the last night I was in Santiago to help me pack with my friends, I myself am very incapable in that sense, and they filled my pockets with letters. Eventually we lived in Mallorca, and in Barcelona where we met Carmen Balcells, who in the novel is the formidable Noria Monclús, and my wife started to want to write her own version of things. She has always been a woman of the world, a very worldly person, she has always gone to parties and met people in all sorts of places. Best of all, she's a great raconteur who tells a story much better than what I could ever hope to. Generally in conversation, in a group, when I want to tell an anecdote, I turn to her and say: "Please tell that story," because I know that she knows how incapable I feel of facing a social audience.

And so, she arrived at the conclusion that she wanted, somehow, to sum up her life. She struck on this idea of dividing her life into a series of parties: three parties in Cairo, one party in Madrid, another party in Iowa City and another party in Paris, and so forth, lots of parties, giving an account of what the atmosphere at these different places was all about. I think she has great narrative talent and I've always told her that. She has always wanted to write a novel, to write a narrative piece, and there were times when I think that our vision of the world overlapped: I didn't know whether I was telling my story or I was telling hers. There was a confusion of identity at that point and I think it is this confusion, this interchangeability of identities, which I have lived through so many times with her, that makes *The Garden Next Door* work.

But funny enough, it wasn't the book that I had started out to write with that idea. What I did start to write about was our experience of being expatriates, of living in Madrid, of living in Sitges, of being poor, of undergoing several depressions, of being unsuccessful. This is something which is sort of inside the novel, it's the "innards" of the novel. And I think that, biographically at least, it is this interchangeability, this communal experience, this *one* experience shared, that happens to be the backbone of the novel, in reality. I started out by writing about this experience, but I didn't know how to end the novel. And I gave the novel to my editors without the ending, until I went through reading the galleys, which I returned, then they were sent back to me in the form of page proofs. It was only in the page proofs that I deleted all the end that I had in the other novel, and in about two or three days I wrote, in quite a frenzy, the end as you know it. So that is my experience of writing and of my interchangeability of being an author with the identity of my wife.

[Enrico Mario Santí]: I have another question concerning **The Garden Next Door.** *It refers to that aspect of the novel that pokes fun at your other novelist friends and your novelist peers. People like Cortázar, García Márquez, and even a certain "Marcelo Chiriboga," whose identity I hope you will reveal to us today. The question has to do with whether you think that the new Latin American novel, which of course, these novelists represent, along with you, has come to the point now where we can actually make fun of it? Do you happen to think that we should?*

Oh, I think that it's important that we do make fun of them, more than anything else. I think that if one is not able to make fun of oneself, one is of little account. Some people have asked me whether I know if **The Garden Next Door** is in any way autobiographical, and how can it be autobiographical since the author in **The Garden Next Door** is an unsucessful writer while I have been a moderately successful one. My answer is always the same: that I think I nurse the incompetent and the failure in myself. I do not want to be too far from being a failure because I fear that if one loses sight of the possibility of failure in oneself, one tends to be a swollen-head lacking in irony. I think that this being able to face oneself as a failure is a help. I think that I poke fun at my writer friends, people who are writing in the same generation, because I fear that this experience of being a writer in that period was such a heady experience, such a glamorous experience it was. In a way, too, it was an experience of commonality. And I think it was dangerous, that this would go to our heads.

Well, does this mean that you are "Marcelo Chiriboga"?

No, but I'm going to be. Let me explain this to you. Right now I am in residence at the Wilson Center in Washington, D.C., and I'm writing two books. One book is on the travels of Sir Richard Burton when Sir Richard went to Chile in the 1870's or so I think it was. He left us no account of that two-month trip, so I make up the elements of that voyage which is uncharted and undocumented. That is one project. Another project is a novel about an Iowa girl, plump and delightful and happy-go-lucky, who falls in love with a professor, who teaches the Boom in the Midwest. This professor happens to be a Chiribogista—a specialist in the literature of Chiriboga, which is something I make up in the novel. I also make up a body of criticism surrounding Chiriboga, so that he's an invention, he's a literary character which I will continue with in this novel that I'm writing.

You mentioned something about the experience of commonality in your living abroad and meeting other Latin American writers of your generation. In rereading your **Personal History of the Boom,** *I remember how you explain a little bit what it meant for you to leave Chile at that time and to go to Mexico and to meet other writers who were doing exciting things at that moment. I thought that it must have been a good experience. It made me think of when I talked, for example, to contemporary Cuban writers, usually they have positive things to say about writers from other countries. But it's very hard to get them to comment positively on writers from within their own country. So perhaps going abroad, then, releases you from the provinciality* *and the pressures of competition, whatever that is. I wonder, too, what it meant, not only in personal terms but for your writing, to be away from Chile for a number of years.*

One of the curious things is that I've always been extremely interested in painting. As an undergraduate at Princeton I took a course on the Northern Renaissance and the later painting in the north of Europe with a professor Dewald. At that time the Kunsthistorische Museum of Vienna sent a huge exhibition of its recently recovered treasures to the Metropolitan Museum of Art, in New York. It included any number of precious materials, including a collection of painting, which I thought was very important. A few weeks after I arrived in the United States, I suddenly walked out into the hall of my dorm, and there, in the middle of the hall there was an easel, Vermeer's famous painting "The Artist in His Studio," which I had collected reproductions of as a young man. But suddenly it was right on my doorstep, the absolute thing, the genuine thing. There's a feeling: leaving Chile, which is a very remote country, meant being in touch, or coming in touch with the originals of many things which I had not known until then, except by reproduction, in literature, and other areas. And so, when we finally came to Europe, or came to the United States and Europe, or went to Mexico and then the United States and then Europe, I met all these great figures I had only read about. I sat at a table with Alejo Carpentier, for instance, whose work I admired a great deal. Suddenly, the whole of this movement of literature became alive, as a possibility. There was a remoteness of anything except local reknown as a young man. Suddenly, it opened up, it was possible to write things that counted in the great world beyond. I think, probably, one of the experiences of being Chilean is the fact of its remoteness. The way that it is separated from everything else by the cordillera and the Pacific Ocean. It's a very very narrow strip, as you know, and thus narrowness is also part of our experience. An isolation, a being in one way unique, in another way very limited. And it's good to have the limits well defined, but it is also very constraining. And the fact of being Chilean, going abroad meant also the possibility of jumping over these great hurdles, something that I couldn't do but with the imagination.

I remember when I married—I married very late in life, when I was 36, my wife was a year younger—and we settled down in our first home together. I remembered that somebody gave me as a wedding present, a typewriter, and I set it down in the corridor, the verandah of our house. We had a dog, and María del Pilar sat for several drawings I made, and then one day, I said, "I'm going to start writing a novel." And I said, I want to write a novel which is not like the novels of the other Latin American writers. I wanted to write a very Chilean novel, I wanted to write a novel which was very

much our own, which defines us very much. I wanted to write a very simple, straightforward, parable of a novel. And that year I started writing **The Obscene Bird of Night,** which I finished eight years afterwards. It was neither thin nor simple, but rather complex and different. But in any case, it did mean this jumping of frontiers, done first of all through my desire of emulation of certain writers—Alejo Carpentier, Carlos Fuentes, the first Vargas Llosa. These were, somehow, the models I wanted to reach, these were achievements that I envied and wanted very much, and this helped me in a way, to become a writer with a wider scope than merely the Chilean one.

Pepe, my class, too, has just finished reading **The Garden Next Door,** *and I wonder if we could broach the subject of your technique in that particular novel and also in the other novel, or short novel, that has just recently been translated into English,* **Taratuta.** *Some critics and some reviewers have said that in both of these works, and in fact, what could be called the latest trend of your narrative, there is a turn toward what, for lack of a better term, we could call a "postmodern" turn. That is, if I may be so bold as to attempt to define it, there is a deliberate confusing of the telling and the told, bringing the reader into the writer's workshop. I wonder if you could tell us a little bit about what made you go in this direction, or if this is something deliberate in you. Is there some sort of a common spirit or common turn in a number of other novelists, let's say, and do you feel yourself as part of this trend in general?*

Well, I think that it is true that in some ways the novel could be termed postmodern, or could be called what I assume is postmodern, which I'm not too clear about, as nobody very much is. But on another level, you must acknowledge that my novels, especially the last ones, on one level are postmodern and are involved with the confusion of the telling and the told, but on another level, they preserve a sort of sociological and, somehow, political meaning. This is, I think, why I never could hope to be termed "magical realist" at all. I could perhaps be a "critical realist," or what have you. I mean, you choose the words. They all define and I try to escape these definitions. But surely there's a valuation of the social experience, I have tended lately to hack it up into pieces, and to give it in fragments, which is, again, a very postmodern thing. I did it, of course, before I ever knew anything about the postmodern. Not to say that I feel like a precursor or anything like that. But it's there, it was a necessity. Somehow, the body of a novel, let's say, of the novel of experimentation, such as my generation of writers wrote it, the novel of, let's say, Vargas Llosa, *Conversation in the Cathedral,* the novels by Onetti, or those by Fuentes, they allude, I think, to an already-made vocabulary of images. They were explorations into the European and American novel of experimentation. I mean, it was all of Faulkner again, in many ways in a different guise, a different Faulkner, but nevertheless many things had been taken from Faulkner, as they had been taken from Virginia Woolf or from, as Gabriel García Márquez recognizes in his own case, as a direct influence on him, of *Orlando*, of James, Joyce, and so forth. I mean, they had a vocabulary, a way of looking at things. But I think things broke up later on. In Carlos Fuentes, say, it was *Terra nostra*, for instance, where things don't cohere, and there is this strange feeling of bringing into his texts other texts. As there is, I think, in these two novels of mine the life of other texts also in it. This is something that I was fairly cautious of doing in these novels. The other day I saw a movie called "Rosenkrantz and Gilderstern Are Dead." I don't know if you saw that movie: it's great. Somehow it reminded me of what I had been doing in *Taratuta,* in this seeing only fragments, of marking the impossibility of being a witness to the whole truth. The whole truth is not given to us, we see fragments of it, loose fragments of it. This is, I think, what *Taratuta* is. And we think we see one thing and we're seeing something else. We don't know who is seeing what, and where, and when. This is the play that goes on in *Taratuta,* and this, I think, is very definitely postmodern.

It's interesting that you are relating the whole question of a postmodern narrative, at one level, to a postmodern politics, on the other. Is what you're saying that in juxtaposing these two levels, just as we cannot have a complete story in the narrative, we cannot have a complete story in politics?

Oh, by all means. I mean, I mean, we have the story as fragments given to us by the media, as the discourse of politicians, as the poetry of Pablo Neruda. All different levels and different fragments of politics. But the overall theoretical and all-embracing truth is to be doubted, and our possibility of achieving that is to be very much in doubt at this point. I mean, something, this is, I think, in a way, an influence not only of politics itself but an influence of the media. I think the media is so important to our lives that it has transformed it. I mean, it has transformed our taste, our possibility of drawing things, of understanding, and everything else.

In, in reading your **Personal History of the Boom,** *which came out I think '70, '71?*

Yes.

—where you give a very personal and very detailed and informative view of what the Boom meant to somebody who was in it, as it was happening. I wonder how now, 20, 22 years later, it looks to you if you look back on it? For example, what has it meant, what do you think is perhaps, if any, its most important impact, contribution? Is it in literary terms or in commercial terms?

I think it's made a difference in one way. I think that for the generation of writers which, for lack of a better term, we call the Boom, and whose frontiers are very ill-defined, something happened. There was an army of classical writers to whom younger people could look up. I mean, it's extraordinary in Latin America at this point, very few people read anything beyond the Boom, except in very specialized classes. Seeing it in perspective, I think it's a partial perspective because I think another perspective will come which will put that perspective into perspective, speaking in postmodern terms. And I think that is important. But there is one, there's one stage, which is somehow being accomplished and to which the younger people in Latin America apply to. And I think the younger writers in our countries, not essentially the following generation, but the generation after, the one that follows, are either rebelling against or learning from—both being ways of learning—from this group of writers who have now become classics . . . or classics quote-unquote, of course.

Well, I was going to ask you to shift perspectives, and look at it from the perspective of the younger generation, because you talk in the book—but, I guess you already, in a way, did that—you talk about your "literary grandfathers" and about what that sort of ominous presence meant for you as a writer, and for the generation of weak literary fathers that followed. You as a young writer trying to, precisely, escape from those limits and constraints. I wonder, from the point of view of the younger writers, both in Chile and in other countries, what it has meant for them, this being a very positive experience, in the sense that Latin America has been put on the literary map, international map. I wonder also if you now are the ominous grandfather that they want to break away from.

I think probably in a way, yes. They want to break away from what we have done, if I may be so bold as to use "we" in a very broad sense. I think the younger generation, the young men and women writing now, though I must say that this generation in Latin America has not given very interesting women writers. For instance, comparing the literature of Buenos Aires, twenty, thirty years ago, the feminine literature of Buenos Aires compared to the feminine literature today was much greater and much stronger than now; incredibly so. But, how did I get involved in this?

I don't know, but you get out by yourself!

You sound very worried about this.

Well, it's all a question of the ending of, of *The Garden Next Door.*

Scott Pollard (essay date January-June 1995)

SOURCE: Pollard, Scott. "Gender, Aesthetics and the Struggle for Power in José Donoso's *El obsceno pájaro de la noche.*" *Latin American Literary Review* 23, no. 45 (January-June 1995): 18-42.

[*In the following essay, Pollard demonstrates how Donoso posits and then subverts the notion of patriarchy as the basis for Chilean society.*]

> Majority implies a state of domination, not the reverse. It is not a question of knowing whether there are more mosquitos or flies than men, but of knowing how "man" constituted a standard in the universe in relation to which men necessarily (analytically) form a majority. The majority in a government presupposes the right to vote, and not only is established among those who possess that right but is exercised over those who do not, however great their number; similarly, the majority in the universe assumes as pregiven the right and power of man . . . man is the molar entity par excellence.
>
> (Deleuze and Guattari, *A Thousand Plateaus,* 291-2)

Hand in hand with the rise of the fortunes of the left in Chile in the late 1930s, *la generación del 38* was a group of strongly committed writers who linked their aesthetic production with a revolutionary political end, "la salvación de la clase desposeída" (Guerra Cunningham 169), but by the late 1940s their vision of a socialist transformation of Chilean society had failed. Centrist Christian Democrats had come to power again, and the bourgeois status quo reasserted itself. As a member of the following *generación de 50,* José Donoso came to maturity as a writer in the face of his predecessors' failure. He rejected not only their political ends, but their historicizing aesthetics. And though his early novels, culminating in *El obsceno pájaro de la noche,* stand as an extended critique of the Chilean upper class, through them Donoso develops another critical standard, supplanting a conventional, class-bound perspective with gender: that is, just as Deleuze and Guattari conclude that man is the "molar entity par excellence"— *the* universal standard, *the* basis for all social and political organizations—so does Donoso make clear in *El obsceno pájaro* that patriarchy is the ground on which the class structure of Chilean society is built.

Though this "male" may seem universal, it is neither absolute nor eternal. For Deleuze and Guattari, any movement away from the masculine—toward a marginal form—is a "becoming," and they posit women as a necessary component of any such movement: "It is perhaps the special situation of women in relation to the man-standard that accounts for the fact that becomings, being minoritarian, always pass through a becoming-woman." If a society is going to change radically and fundamentally, if the masculine given is to be revised beyond recognition—beyond its essence as gender—

then feminine alterity is responsible for the first move. The narrative of *El obsceno pájaro* is a product of that move.

In the novel, a patriarchal identity constitutes the organizational center and surface of bourgeois society, the superstructure that is to be serviced by all other sectors of society. Moreover, that "I"—as embodied by Jerónimo de Azcoitía—is an idealized *objet d' art* that stands as the patriarchy's greatest and most visible product, its "standard," and as such all social material is enclosed within it. Jerónimo de Azcoitía is the ideal male: as presented, nothing less than sheer physical perfection. And around him, the world organizes itself, unable to resist the attractions of such beauty and wanting only to share in its transcendence. To invoke Keats, "Beauty is truth, truth beauty." Yet in *El obsceno pájaro,* truth and beauty do not exist in a realm of pure, aesthetic abstraction, as they do on the urn. Instead, they are instrumental for a patriarchal social organization. Truth and beauty are fashioned into an I-ideal, and around it society is made over into a redundant signifier. Anything which does not fit onto the signifying surface—all otherness— disappears underneath that surface as an absent support mechanism. This phallocentric art would construct a society that privileges "the conscious, undistorted, invariant, and nameable vision of male firstness" (Calderón 32). But beneath the inexorable preeminence of the masculine veneer, Donoso installs an invisible, feminized social material, which constitutes a fluid, boundless and selfless force—an explicitly anti-aesthetic discourse—that struggles to penetrate and lodge itself onto the patriarchal surface in order to radically revise the face of society and the very nature of subjectivity.

The novel is told, to be a little tongue and cheek, from the perspective of a confused escapee from a bourgeois concentration camp. Humberto Peñaloza has been taken in by the sheer physical and ideological beauty which is Jerónimo de Azcoitía. Later, he becomes conscious of how he has been exploited and would escape before that exploitation has exhausted his very being. Yet, in spite of the dangers he recognizes, Humberto remains attracted to the ideal self that Don Jerónimo represents to him, and the novels yaws between the poles of attraction and repulsion.

Broadly conceived, the novel is a (re)telling of Humberto Peñaloza's sad and downtrodden life, a first-person account of his exploitation at the hands of Jerónimo. More importantly, throughout the novel Mudito/Humberto pursues a transformation and reconceptualization of the world, which is meant to provide him an escape from exploitation. He uses his narrative to expose and destroy Jerónimo's artifice, undermine the attraction, and facilitate his escape from the exploitative social strictures which created Jerónimo and privileged an idealized, masculine "I" as its highest aesthetic production. Mudito's paradigm for this elimination is the old women of *La Casa de la Chimba de los Ejercicios Espirituales,* a soon-to-be decommissioned convent and a long-neglected piece of the Azcoitía family empire. *La Casa* is the site which initiates and give form to Humberto's narrative, revision, revelation, manifestation and escape (all these things). Within its milieu, there is no unified "I" or transcendent identity, no single voice or organizational center, no Great Story that must be told or plot that must be followed. Instead, there is a constant flux of human material, discourses and voices which subvert all attempts at exploitation and repression: the freakish heart of Bakhtin's carnival. Mudito adopts this powerfully decrepit selflessness to create a decentering, multivoiced narrative technique that will shatter the patriarchal "I" and expose the repressed material trapped behind its aesthetic veneer. Ideally, as the minoritarian grows exponentially—like a cancer—the presence of the majoritarian-masculine should shrink and disappear: if only Mudito could give over his attraction to Jerónimo, which he cannot.

In the novel, women are *the* source of transgression. The multiplicity of interconnected feminine voices and narratives that Humberto uses—that is, Peta Ponce, the *chonchón* myth, the yellow bitch, Inés *beata/bruja,* the female milieu of *La Casa,* the seven witches, the *imbunche*—constitute a constant and continuous threat to patriarchy's great Chilean representative, the Azcoitía family empire. Sharon Magnarelli categorizes the women who populate the novel as witches, the powerless yet mysteriously powerful who remain outside the control of patriarchy. In her chapter on *El obsceno pájaro* in *The Lost Rib,* she reaches the following conclusion:

> Thus, the witch is no doubt the true heretic who challenges or perhaps just ignores the patriarchal authority of our society and religion, thus undermining the very foundation of society as we know it, for she understands, as did Henry James and as does Donoso, that "the natural inheritance of everyone . . . is an unsubdued forest."
>
> (168)

Magnarelli attributes two very different actions to the witch. Either she self-consciously challenges patriarchy, or she ignores it, a non-action that lacks all self-consciousness. Of the two, it is the latter that best describes the women of *La Casa,* who seem utterly unaware of anything outside their small, selfless milieu. Thus, they are something of a "natural" contradiction to patriarchy, but, given their reclusive existence, they demonstrate no desire to act upon the disruptive quality of their otherness. Moreover, because of this natural state, the women have no discourse. Patriarchy comes to the text already constituted as such, bringing with it a well-established history and tradition, whereas the

feminine is new, essentially without history or tradition, and is only constituted as a discourse by Mudito as a weapon he can use to undermine Azcoitía hegemony.

But the history that Mudito writes is not a simple, straightforward revision, an unproblematic presentation of a pristine otherness. Rather, it is an ambivalent and contentious history of an aesthetic struggle, a history caught between the age-old effort to maintain the integrity of the patriarchal veneer and the newly-manifested desire to wholly liquidate it. Humberto presents Jerónimo de Azcoitía as a consummate artist, executor of his own image, classical in proportion and effortlessly realized. For Hector Calderón, he is Humberto's ego-ideal (35), the Father who Humberto did not even know that he was looking for until the epiphanic moment when a well-formed, dormant desire/discourse awakens to manifest itself incontrovertibly. Watching Jerónimo walking toward him on a downtown Santiago street, Humberto is acutely aware of the subtle nuances of the other's dress, and when Jerónimo inadvertently touches Humberto's arm with his glove surrender is absolute and unconditional, for Humberto sees Jerónimo as nothing less than a perfect aesthetic object, flesh as art, and would be a part of it:

> Por la vereda avanzaba entre el gentío alegre de esa mañana un hombre alto, fornido pero gracioso, de cabello muy rubio, de mirada airosa encubierta por algo que yo interpreté como un elegante desdén, vestido como jamás soñé que ningún osara vestir: todo era gris, muy claro, perla, paloma, humo . . . unos guantes ni grises ni cáscara ni amarillo pasar junto a mí en el gentío mañanero ese guante que usted llevaba empuñado me rozó aqui, en el brazo, justo en este sitio: lo estoy sintiendo ahora, quemándome todavía después de tantos años. Entonces, al mirarlo a usted, don Jerónimo, un boquete de hambre se abrió en mí y por él quise huir de mi propio cuerpo enclenque para incorporarme al cuerpo de esa hombre que iba pasando.
>
> (Donoso 90)

Neither Jeronimo's appearance nor Humberto's desire in any way disrupt the social order but, rather, reinforce it, because both are wholly mastered by the same set of, what Magnarelli calls, "discursive edifices" (*Understanding José Donso* 98). In other words, Humberto's reaction to Jerónimo is a formal one, a predictable and proper expression of desire, one which is necessary, given the social hierarchy to which he is subjected. At this moment, sense is sensibility. As the concrete realization of a set of ideals, or as their finest aesthetic expression, Jerónimo is the image of the absolute mastery of desire, and that image has the capacity to master not only Humberto's but all desires that come within its scope (that is, enforce its standard).

Deleuze and Guattari believe that art (visual, written, musical) marks the limits of a social domain. For them, ornamentation functions ideologically. As we saw with

Jerónimo, the Azcoitía patriarchy uses art to produce an ideal image of itself—the veneer it presents to the world and, through metonymic association, by which it would be judged. "Jerónimo de Azcoitía" is not merely a name associated with a simple symbol for an autonomous, self-sufficient and self-generating individual free of all social ties and dependencies—a "natural" man. Instead, that name is a function of an entire social domain, its particular "signature":

> expressive qualities, or matters of expression, are necessarily appropriative and constitute a having more profound than being. Not in the sense that these qualities belong to a subject, but in the sense that it carries or produces them. These qualities are signatures, but signature, the proper name, is not the constituted mark of a subject, but the constituting mark of a domain or abode.
>
> (316)

To complement the image of Jerónimo in the recognition scene, Donoso also offers an Azcoitía family history. Again, we are faced with the ideological function of art, though this time the social territory is producing a narrative of itself, a beautiful story which justifies its existence as center of power and by which it would be judged. The basic form of this history is an aristocratic hermeneutic to which all familial material must conform.

Once Humberto is captured by Jerónimo, his life should be an easy one to chart. To escape from his family's anonymous existence, he becomes involved in a café society of would-be intellectuals and decides to pursue a career as a writer. As a writer, he would have an identity, or, to invoke Calderón's insight, his life would finally have a "plot" (33). Humberto would have the power to create something as aesthetically appealing as Jerónimo de Azcoitía himself, and through association with the beautiful words that he composed Humberto would take on a significance not unlike that of his idol. When Humberto and Jerónimo meet at the *museo antropológico* and the latter agrees to finance Humberto's book, it would seem that life and art are converging and that dreams do come true. Even when Jerónimo locks the copies of the book up in his library, though, subverting Humberto's effort to achieve social visibility, he offers Humberto an enticing compensation, hiring him as his personal secretary. Humberto would not only be closer to his ego-ideal, but as his agent Humberto can *be* Jerónimo thus needing no longer to struggle to merely be *like* him. Captured, sucked in and suckered, Humberto should be grateful when Jerónimo then gives him the chance to write the next chapter in the great Azcoitía family romance. No longer struggling, Humberto is now an artist with a commission. Moreover, he has been given the kind of plot that, if handled well, just might make him a reputation.

As secretary, scriptor, and historian for Jerónimo and the Azcoitía family, Humberto's job is to extend the family history by fitting the material he is given into the Azcoitía narrative formula. In the recognition scene, Jerónimo is little more than a body, a raw material which his family and class have shaped into an ideal image of itself. Humberto is hired to continue to give shape to that image, utilizing the strict guidelines of the aforementioned hermeneutic. Yet Humberto really does not write this narrative—the effortless veneer, the beautiful story—but only tells of how such a story is written. We see through the penetrating gaze of a metanarratological consideration:

> Las reglas y las fórmulas, el ritual tan fijo y tan estilizado como los símbolos de la heráldica, que iban regulando el proceso del noviazgo, inscribían su propia figura y la de Inés, entrelazadas, como iban debajo de los árboles cargados de fruta, como en un medallón de piedra: este medallón no era más que una etapa del friso eterno compuestos por muchos medallones, y ellos, los novios, encarnaciones momentáneas de designios mucho más vastos que los detalles de sus sicologías individuales.
>
> (256)

This set of medallions, which we could entitle "The Life of Jerónimo de Azcoitía," is only part of a much larger set. As its current subject, Jerónimo serves as both central signifier and sign of the Azcoitía bourgeois domain. To use an ugly Barthian neologism, he signifies "Azcoitíaicity," in which a present group of social signs (language-objects)—courtship, love, marriage, family—is taken up into a mythic system that asserts the family's eternal and divinely sanctioned right to power. As such, Jerónimo does not merely function as static artifice but as the most active disseminatory agent within the circulatory system of the Azcoitía signifying regime. Jerónimo may be an *objet d' art,* but he is also an "author" (editor?) to whose formal structures Humberto is supposed to adhere. Yet Jerónimo himself cannot maintain the form.

Immediately after Jerónimo's marriage, his wife, Inés, introduces him to her nursemaid, Peta Ponce. Peta was created by the Azcoitía domain (in one genealogy, she is an actual offspring) to nurture its art, in this case the life (or perhaps it would be better to say image) of Inés. Recognizing the threat, Jerónimo would leave her behind and block her presence from the family history:

> El montón de andrajos se organizó para dar respuesta humana a la exclamación de Inés. Entre la vieja y la niña se entabló un diálogo que Jerónimo no estaba dispuesto a tolerar. Este escena no calzaba dentro de ningún medallón de piedra eterna. Y sicalzaba en alguno era en la otra serie, en la leyenda enemiga que contradecía a la suya, la de los condenados y los sucios que se retuercen a la siniestra de Dios Padre Todo poderoso.
>
> (159)

Jerónimo's enduring reaction to all challenges to the family history is aesthetic. Donoso presents the Azcoitía family history as "un friso eterno compuestos por muchos medallones," and to neutralize Peta's threat and salvage the purity of that history Jerónimo places her into another set of medallions, one which has nothing to do with his own. She is a "mountain of rags" who is rightfully part of "la leyenda enemiga." Life can be saved through an artful contrivance, but when she gives him a set of beautifully monogrammed handkerchiefs he finds history to have been inexorably violated in spite of his efforts:

> Dentro del paquete encontró tres pañuelos blancos de la batista más fina, con ribetes e iniciales tan ricamente bordados que lo hicieron estremecerse. ¿Cómo era posible que hubieran salido de debajo de ese catre, de los manos verrugosas de esa vieja? Eran los tres pañuelos más bellos y perfectos que había visto en su vida . . . si alguna vez soñó con pañuelos, eran éstos, su fragilidad, su equilibrio, este finura, sí, había soñado con estos pañuelos, exactos, estos pañuelos que tenía en sus manos . . . , esa vieja se introdujo en su suenño y se los robó.
>
> (159)

The transcendent can only come to mortals in the form of a dream, and only then to Kings and Heroes, but to Jerónimo it comes from under the cot of an old woman. Peta's handkerchiefs corrupt the family's divine history. Jerónimo can no longer see the world as a mirror—redundant signifier of his family's grand, master narrative—and he must concede to the presence of something Other. Now out of the land of redundant signification, Jerónimo, too, is forced to create a new kind of narrative, one that is still "closed, structured, and excluding the threatening outside while it paradoxically proffers a relatively unthreatening glimpse of that threatening other" (*Understanding José Donoso* 12). Patriarchal repression still functions, and, though no longer totalizing, it still has the capacity to create another kind of safe narrative.

But now Jerónimo finds himself on a slippery slope. It took all of his genius to neutralize Peta Ponce, and he makes a monumental effort to do the same with Boy and the *La Rinconada*, where he would create a monstrously inverse form of his own ideal existence. Moreover, he lays upon Humberto the responsibility of transforming this inverted material into the Azcoitía family romance, where Jerónimo is the hero who not only saves the family from imminent destruction but expands it—its organizing principle—into new realms. Humberto may be Jerónimo's designated ghost-writer—the *real* writer of Jerónimo's story—but he doesn't have the genius, either, to make the material that his benefactor palms off on him fit the form that Jerónimo cannot make work. The Azcoitía signifying regime is blocked, and as one of its functionaries, with his imagination

wholly inscribed within it, Humberto, too, can be nothing but blocked. Interestingly enough, at this point of personal as well as patriarchal crisis, Humberto develops a critical consciousness and becomes aware of the discourse that has motivated him and the exploitation he has suffered at the hands of Jerónimo: all of which forms the seed-bed for the narrative Humberto (now Mudito) produces in *La Casa*. Among the old women, Mudito writes of the beautiful veneer as well as the difficulties, adjustments, and failures that Jerónimo suffers in his attempts to shape the anonymous material to (re)produce his infallible image: thus, the revealing story about Jerónimo's meeting with Peta Ponce.

Yet, as Alicia Borinsky has pointed out, Humberto's newly acquired critical consciousness does not give him any distance from the material he narrates, for just as he deconstructs Jerónimo's story so does he deconstruct his own: "La autocrítica incorporada como tema en la novela y la autocrítica asumida como condición inherente a la narración, sin establecer distancias que permitan la distinción de momentos en los cuales un narrador privilegiado se desdobla en contemplar la obra" (281). Thus, the narrative of *El obsceno pájaro* itself is neither family romance nor some other kind of safe, distanced form of narrative; rather, it is open, intimate and subversive, where patriarchal discourse is refigured into its others *and vice-versa*. Moreover, only in a milieu like that of *La Casa* can this kind of infinitely transgressive narrative take root and grow.

The myth of the *niña-beata/niña-bruja* stands easily as the novel's most disseminated trope of subversion, where patriarchy produces the justification for its existence, its own annulment, and acts as the origin of the novel's feminine discourse as well. The myth is a patriarchal fantasy—source of the Azcoitía family's transcendent origin and the interpretive key to its history—but it is narrated by the women of *La Casa*. Identifying with the *bruja/beata,* they take their own peculiar pleasure in the retelling (a pleasure not sanctioned by the patriarchal arbiters who "originated" the myth). In it, both conflict and morality are gender based: the good, dominant, male order and its vast land holdings are threatened by an evil, subterranean, feminine force outside of its knowledge and control. The flashpoint of the conflict is the only woman in a family of nine men. Within the patriarchal order of things, she exists solely to please the men. She is the delicate filigree to their world, softening its edges with her feminine arts, which are taught her by a peasant nurse (a Peta Ponce figure) who is the only remotely maternal figure in the myth. Though they make up an *islafemenina* which the men consider "inaccessible para ellos, pero no peligrosa," the knowledge that the two women share ultimately constitutes an independent community which threatens patriarchal authority.

The conflict of the myth manifests itself in a competition for control of the girl. According to patriarchy's neurotic discourse, the nurse becomes a witch who steals the girl's body, gains sadomasochistic dominance over it, then uses the poor creature for her own perverse and evil ends. Through her power, the nurse creates two inexorably bound monstrosities, transforming the girl into a *Chonchón* (flying head) and herself into a *perra amarilla* (yellow bitch). At night, the latter leads the former over the family's land, and together they bring drought and pestilence: "malos tiempos, años de cosechas miserables, de calor y sequía, de animales envenenados y de niños que nacían muertos o con seis dedos en una mano"(33). Within the patriarchal myth, otherness can only make itself felt as threat and violation.

The father destroys this clandestine power when he enters his daughter's room and raises his poncho to hide her from sight. In doing so, he splits the bond between the two women, breaking the power of the nurse, taking his daughter back under his control while diverting attention to the nurse, turning her into a scapegoat. René Girard's concept of the monstrous double best describes the relationship between the women:

> In the collective experience of the *monstrous double* the differences are not eliminated, but muddied and confused. All the doubles are interchangeable, although their basic similarity is never formally acknowledged. They thus occupy the equivocal middle ground between difference and unity that is indispensable to the process of sacrificial substitution—to the polarization of violence onto a single victim who substitutes for all the others. The monstrous double gives the antagonists, incapable of perceiving that nothing actually stands between them (or their reconciliation), precisely what they need to arrive at the compromise that involves unanimity *minus* the victim of the generative expulsion.
>
> (*Violence and The Sacred* 161)

Initially, both women are monstrous and equally susceptible to being sacrificed. But as the community initiates the ritual of sacrifice, they are separated. One is loaded with the community's collective guilt, victimized and expunged, while the other is purified and sacrilized. The girl, as member of the family, is most internal to the community and fills the role of "the victim of the generative expulsion" as the father's poncho "polarizes the violence onto a single victim." It keeps the girl inside, denying any similarity to the nursemaid, while simultaneously differentiating the latter by loading her with all of the community's evil. When the father raises his poncho, he purifies the girl while simultaneously directing all communal violence against the old woman. She is the only monstrous thing in sight and, thus, becomes the sacrifice. In a final move to purify the patriarchal landscape of all traces of evil, the father puts his daughter in a convent, where any last

vestiges of a feminine Other can be contained. The last act of the myth is a purely ideological one. The girl is transformed from *niña-bruja* to *niña-beata* and becomes the family's link to the divine, the center and source of family history and the transcendent justification for its perpetuation. The male masters the female, figures her as both monstrous and divine, and only then places her at the very center of his life. The patriarchy is really doing little more here than performing its conventional disseminatory function, yet, though the feminine evil may be transformed into patriarchal good, Mudito's narrative (or, rather, Mudito's penchant for the metanarratological) insures that, for the reader, the ideological facade is not enough to hide the fact that this mythifying sign system has retained a feminine monstrosity at the very core of its self-image and has, thus, co-opted the seed of its own destruction.

Sharon Magnarelli points to the figure of the *bruja* as a particularly patriarchal creation, commenting that "it may seem absurd to attribute such fortuitous happenings to the workings of a witch, but for many centuries witches have been presumed, even by the supposedly intelligent, to be able to wreak just such havoc" (*The Lost Rib* 156). The witch is a way to explain the inexplicable, to divert attention from the absence of explanation. She is created in a void; thus, in the myth, the nurse/witch substitutes for the cacique's inability to explain the hardships his land has suffered. In the discourse of patriarchal myth-making, Magnarelli notes that, grammatically, the witch functions as an ellipsis, a diversionary tactic meant to draw attention away from the masculine *aporia*. Another blank space is created by the father when he raises his poncho to shield his daughter from view. Once again, the nurse acts as substitute. In the myth, what the father supposedly sees is a *chonchón*, but Donoso adds the possibility that he finds his daughter either in bed with her lover or giving birth: as Magnarelli adds, "whatever the father saw in the daughter's room was in some way threatening to the house full of males" (*The Lost Rib* 163). The ellipsis diverts attention from everyday explanations, because, to maintain its exalted, majoritarian self-image—just as Jerónimo does with *la leyenda enemiga*—the patriarchy would see itself as part of a grand, supernatural cosmogony, where conflicts are of epic proportion and resolutions extreme. The daughter becomes a monster and the nurse a witch who has brought a blight upon the land. Only the sacrificial killing of one and the banishment of the other behind the sacred walls of a convent can save the purity of this masculine world (that is, its self-image). The simple truths of adultery or childbirth out of wedlock could act as concrete proof of the imperfect and partial control the men have over their world. They create an ellipsis out of their "perfection" and turn an old woman into a witch.

This supplement, though, lasts just long enough to substantiate masculine perfection, then it, too, like everything else in the myth that falls outside the ideal limits of patriarchy, is put under erasure. In the myth's final ellipsis, the *niña-bruja* disappears under the sign of the *niña-beata.* A minor disfiguring of the patriarchal narrative is transformed into a disfigurement of epic proportions, which is then excised heroically, and the scars that remain are miraculously re-figured through a kind of narrative plastic surgery. Yet, behind the new beauty of the saintly child sits witchcraft, monstrosity, femininity, adultery and illicit childbirth, all hidden at the core of patriarchal self-justification. And it takes Mudito's narrative to penetrate the patriarchal ellipsis, reveal the fear of disfigurement that motivates it, and release all the disfiguring material to consciousness. We end up with a narrative that explicitly contravenes the family romance.

The Azcoitía family's founding myth of *Inés-beata* is a derivative of the *niña-beata. Inés-beata* lived in the family-owned convent. Though in the present moment of the novel, it is a place that is utterly marginalized, *La Casa* was once a sign of the Azcoitía family's power. Through her divinity, *Inés-beata* saved the convent from an earthquake which decimated the rest of Santiago, and the family traces its divine origin back to her and the place that she saved. As centerpiece of the family's power, *La Casa* took on a State function as a locus where the Chilean elite gathered. It is the site of the mastered female, upon which patriarchy has built its empires. But *La Casa* is also the place where the female reasserts herself against the male to create her own, independent existence. The place where the otherness of the feminine is most repressed—where the sign of repression is most stuffed with otherness—is also the place where it reasserts itself most strongly, where the previously closed narrative opens. When the old women tell the tale of the *niña-beata/niña-bruja,* they privilege the myth's threatening presence—as embodied by the witch, the *chonchón* and *perra amarilla*—and found their own differential identity in it. Traditionally, the convent in Latin America has been used as a depository for the human refuse of mainstream society (that is, old maids, children conceived out of wedlock to upper class women, the unemployable). Yet, as much as the convent originates as a means of patriarchal waste disposal and containment, the waste is neither contained nor disposed of, and it becomes the breeding grounds for the recalcitrant presence of the feminine Other.

The old women of *La Casa* remain ineffably beyond patriarchy's grasp, never in danger of becoming one more redundant signifier: exactly the kind of milieu Mudito needs to attack Jerónimo and his own past self (Humberto) as well as to save his skin as a writer. In *La Casa,* Mudito finds the necessity and inspiration to write. Moreover, its decrepit but liberating discourse

gives him the tools to create a new kind of narrative and possibly succeed where Jerónimo was unable to with *La Rinconada,* if Mudito can only handle the material. Oddly enough, at the primary site of the novel's feminine discourse, a well-formed patriarchal desire reawakens itself.

To double back to the beginning, it is in *La Casa* and with the old women that the narrative of *El obsceno pájaro* initiates itself. (In a sense, patriarchy is already in danger, almost an anachronism.) Now, under the women's control, Humberto's autobiography becomes an inverted image of the *Ur*-myth of the Chilean patriarchy, a narrative of the mastered phallus. Seven of the old women form a secret coven, called *las siete brujas,* around the orphan Iris Mateluna to protect her "virgin birth." They transform the teenager's false pregnancy into a personalized version of the myth of the second coming: since they "birthed" and cared for the divine child, he would intercede for them and provide a direct ascent to heaven. The novel begins when Mudito interjects himself into the coven to become the seventh witch after its founding member, la Brígida, dies. Though the child is their savior and functions as the centerpiece of their lives, he has no power to refigure the old women as redundant signifiers of a traditional, masculine, Christian mythos. Rather, as center he is a deprivileged figure, controlled and manipulated by a decentralized complex of feminine forces. In such circumstances, as Calderón has pointed out, Mudito the narrator cannot maintain himself as an ideal Jamesian center-of-consciousness in control of all that he perceives (42). Moreover, though powerful already, the women gain strength through a progressive emasculation of the "child." As much as Humberto is author of this fiction because he gives it language, he is also its object, the material out of which the fiction is fashioned. As his identities slip, Mudito becomes the seventh witch as well as the miraculous child, reduced to a specter of the patriarchy he once represented: with a shrinking body, his penis strapped to his leg, and finally castrated by Iris Mateluna, he is no longer narrator but image of the impossibility of patriarchal signification (that is, traditional narrative) in *La Casa.*

Yet, it is important to note that what Donoso does not offer us in this narrative is a feminine inversion of masculine transcendence: the mastered phallus does not become iconic. Instead, Donoso demythologizes the original transcendent figuration of the child. At the end of the novel, after the convent has been decommissioned and the money has dried up, Humberto quickly becomes a means to an economic end when the old women go out begging on the streets and use him as an easy source of pathos. As the novel progresses, Donoso removes more and more of the ideological support structures that lend stability to a milieu, thus forcing the signifier to do nothing more than slip, *in every direction.* The divine chariots do not arrive to provide the women a direct ascent to heaven. White microbuses take them to a convalescent home in a better neighborhood. Yet, given the senescent chaos of the old women, the microbuses resemble the wished-for chariots that the seven witches originally intended to conjure up. The child performed his expected duties, and the narrative closes. Yet, even though the old women believe that the child saved them, what we see is not a central signifier coming from on high to take up the poor, the weak, and the oppressed and finally give them their due: the bogus promise of transcendence. Instead it is one of their own, la Brígida, who "saves" them through her transgression, mastery and exploitation of patriarchal territory and its economic laws. She pays for the old women's respectable escape.

La Brígida, the absent woman whose death begins the novel, offers one of the novel's most peculiar reversals: the rich servant. She worked her entire life for Raquel Ruiz and her husband. He was an investor, and La Brígida entrusted some of her money with him, but soon she was the one making the decisions about what to buy, when to buy and when to sell. She mastered the mainstream economy to become a financial wizard, not through the rational study of its rules but through the whispered, incantatory *Dicen* of the old women/witches of *La Casa*. As a result, she inverts class relations, and transforms her employers into her "servants," though she never stops being their servant: as she cleans their house, they look after her burgeoning financial empire. Though she may have a knack for capital accumulation, she will not take an identifiable position within the social mainstream. She would assert her power over capital and remain invisible, beyond reification and beyond comprehension. Through the mystical *Dicen* she creates an *isla femenina* that is nearly impervious to patriarchal co-optation. She feminizes capital. The only mistake that Brígida makes is to spend money on her death. In the typical Catholic elision of materialism and divinity, she buys herself an elaborate funeral procession to make herself visible to God—an act meant to guarantee her a place in the firmament as compensation for the suffering and anonymity of her life. Yet, her visibility is only temporary, because the family crypt she inhabits is on loan to her from Raquel Ruiz, who will reclaim it at her own death, thereby erasing Brígida's violation of the social surface. As readers, we do not see just a prettified, airbrushed "After" image of a restored aristocratic order; rather, we know what had disfigured it, how and why the disfigurement was removed, and that the restoration work carried out by Raquel Ruiz is no more than skin deep.

La Brígida's money becomes worthwhile and takes on a feminized quality when it is finally used to take the women out of *La Casa*, yet they hardly experience her at all. It is no more than a subtle, barely detectable force which takes them up and impels them away from *La Casa*. As such, La Brígida no longer functions as a monstrous, transcendent woman of epic proportions transgressing the patriarchal frame. Her actions are both subtler and more humble. Given the tenuous, anarchic organization of the women, their narrative has no violatable frame because it has no teleological center, and, consequently, La Brígida and her money are really no more than another twist in their episodic plot. Moreover, Donoso explicitly demythologizes her absence to demonstrate the concrete, economic actions which brought about the removal. She is not a mysterious, subterranean being. At the end of the novel, La Brígida has been reconfigured as a concrete, feminine, non-patriarchized force, and she has lost the transcendent, monstrous attributes by which patriarchal history has insistently mythologized and oppressed women.

Yet, as much as Mudito's narrative founds itself as an open, critical, and feminized discourse, it is also Mudito's last desperate attempt to save what remains of his identity (literally, his penis) from Jerónimo and his unstoppable signifying/image-making regime. After losing eighty percent of his body to the residents of *La Rinconada* in the fever-dream—where he becomes their personal factory outlet for normal body parts—Humberto is reduced to little more than his potency. It is all that remains of his tenuous identity, and he flees the hospital when Jerónimo comes to assert his ultimate right, claiming that potency as his own. Ironically, it is the lack of an individuated subjectivity in *La Casa* that most attracts Mudito, because its worthlessness functions as an effective hiding place, an ellipsis behind which the "I" can disappear. Within the context of this "mundo al revés," Mudito conceives of the anarchical milieu of the old women as a protective enclosure and, potentially, another kind of closed narrative. Mudito presents the history of a failed man and thereby disassociates himself from the patriarchal ideal to more freely identify with the feminine milieu within which he has sequestered himself. Magnarelli sees Mudito as "a transvestite . . . lurking behind the verbal mask of the other characters" ("Amidst the Illusory Depths" 269). His purpose may be to use the women of *La Casa* in his story to undo the signifying chains that have bound him to Jerónimo and guarantee his escape, but as a transvestite Mudito only hides behind the roles he takes on in *La Casa*. He does not integrate into the decrepit life of the convent but merely uses it as a cover for his still well-formed desire for identity.

Perversely, he would shroud that desire in roles that are antithetical to it. Thus, emasculation—what William Rowe calls "self-elimination" (10)—becomes a way by which Mudito can adopt a series of identities to protect the phallus (the last piece of his old self). He becomes the seventh witch, the miraculous child, and finally the *imbunche* in order to embed himself further in the nonreifiable milieu of the women. Ironically, though, he is as much a reified material for the women as he had been for Jerónimo: by substituting for these different roles/bodies, Mudito as readily fulfills the requirements of the women's narrative as he had those of Jerónimo's. By acting out those substitutions, and in spite of his anonymity, Mudito maintains a clear, self-conscious distance in *La Casa.* Thus, his identity remains intact, and phallocentrism lives on at the very site of its subversion. Or, to approach Mudito's narrative from another angle, if in the transformation from man to woman to sexless child to package, we see a clear escape trajectory not only away from a patriarchal center *but from gender definition as well,* this kind of transformation (an ever-increasing lack) is also nothing more than another mask to hide the phallus. By trying to preserve something (himself) in a material (*La Casa*) that is endemic to it, Mudito embarks on a task as Sisyphian as Jerónimo's with *La Rinconada.* He is only capable of producing a cycle of discourses that transgress their own limits to reveal (revel in) otherness. In other words, as much as Mudito would like to protect himself through an act of self-abnegation and the reconstitution of *La Casa* as an anti-patriarchal fortress—as much as he would like to believe that *La Casa,* in its own perverse way, could provide him the truth he needs to finally dominate the world—his deconstructive narrative simultaneously revives the desire for a patriarchal identity while pulling down the fortress from within, leaving Mudito at square one. He had hoped for some kind of mastery but ultimately can only chase his own "tale," and the cycle spins on *ad infinitum* until the women of *La Casa* finally intervene to end it.

For Ricardo Guttiérez Mouat, in *El obsceno pájaro* Donoso has translated "un proyecto de liberación en términos de un encierro" (146). Given the spatial logic of the novel, a liberated space can only be approached through a series of ever-shrinking enclosures. Spaces become less and less formal, less able to be represented, until there is no form (no representation) at all. All the large spaces of the novel have been explicitly socialized, and thus they embody the danger of co-optation, reification and refiguration for those who inhabit them. A large space is a trap, and an individual becomes a part of somebody else's (his) public art. Thus, paradoxically, only at the moment of infinite smallness is there the possibility of a free, liberated expanse. Correlatively, the reduction of body and space are contiguous and parallel processes in the novel. While caught in the mainstream, Humberto remains whole, a faithful reproduction of Jerónimo. Even in his dream of the organ factory, hyper-reification not only insures the integrity of Humberto's body but its capacity to infinitely reproduce its own totality as well. Upon escaping the hospital—the last, purely hegemonic space Humberto inhabits—he nevertheless loses that ideological and reproductive integrity, having left eighty percent of his body behind. Only in such a reduced state can he fit the requisites of the marginal space of *La Casa* and the liberated anonymity of the old women. Though within the realm of a patriarchal sign system the breakdown of the body indicates reification, in *La Casa* the sloughing off of body parts is an end in itself and thus a means by which capture can be avoided. With nothing of value, refiguration into redundant signification seems impossible.

Yet, because he holds onto a desire for identity, he cannot fully integrate himself into the feminine milieu of *La Casa,* and what he manages is a mimetic act—a conventional narrative trope—adapting the feminine Other as a mask. As retired servants, they have been exhausted by the society which they served—that is, they suffer from the exhaustion of being that Humberto most feared. Yet, paradoxically, Mudito would use their exhaustion as a sign behind which to protect his essential, inexhaustible self. While in the sphere of Azcoitía hegemony, the mask is the aesthetic veneer hiding the family's monstrous mechanisms of power. In *La Casa,* the mask takes on a set of obverse functions. There, the act of masking is a movement, where every attempt Mudito makes to maintain his desire for identity merely results in the dissolution of that desire. Z. Nelly Martínez best describes the dissolution of the "I" when she speaks of the mask as a displacement and differal of the center in a signifier which is always other:

> La imagen que en el espejo le devuelve—una incontrolable sucesión de máscaras falaces en las que, sin embargo, se reconoce esporádicamente—despedaza definitivamente su identidad y lo arroja en la penumbra de un mundo interno, caótico y fluido . . . , en el que por ser todos los otros, termina siendo nadie . . . la abigarrada polifonía de la descentralización . . . derrota al personaje.
>
> (60)

Outside *La Casa,* the mask is nothing more than a patriarchal figure, a key means of preserving the "I," a redundant signifier, a static and highly formalized allegory of a patriarchal ideal. Inside, Mudito would exploit this now anachronistic form. But by trying to adapt it to the unstable flux of the feminine milieu he loses the authorial distance that mimesis would have given him outside *La Casa.* As a result, every construction of a mask-I relation fails. Mudito wanted to hide behind the sign of exhaustion, but ironically the sign exhausts him, dissolving rather than preserving his sense of self. Yet Mudito's only response to this, his third failure as a writer, is to reposit the patriarchal figure again and again. His imagination has reached its limit, and, like Sisyphus, he can do no more.

Because mask and identity can no longer maintain a conventional phallocentric structure, the constant slippage and incommensurability between the two results in a desperate, ever-quickening, hyperactive movement aimed at a perennially distant and unattainable ideal. Mudito loses control of the speed and trajectory of his escape, but he still does not become one with the indistinguishable flux of old women, because, though that phallocentric structure may have dissolved, its spectral presence and teleological motivation do not. Martínez claims that the act of masking ultimately destroys the integrity of the mask as well as the "I" behind it; as such, Mudito is not destroyed solely by the world of *La Casa* but by the desire for identity introduced into a milieu which could not support the formal necessities of that desire. Yet, that desire, even in the smallest space it occupies—the *imbunche* sack—does not extinguish itself but, rather, perpetuates itself until the women of *La Casa* (in particular, Peta Ponce) arrange for its final conflagration. Mudito may be exhausted when he comes to *La Casa,* and he may exhaust himself further through the very act of narration itself (through narratives that never resolve), but not until the women finally extinguish Mudito's desire can the ego-ideal that has long driven it be expunged: never deinscribed but only destroyed.

The women finally resolve the neverending story of *El obsceno pájaro* through the figure of the *imbunche*. In Chilean folklore, witches steal "poor innocents" (like the *niña-beata*) and sew up the nine orifices. It is the figure—crafted by artisans—of absolute feminine mastery and, thus, stands as the most dangerous threat to patriarchal domination. In *La Casa,* the *imbunche* is developed in two ways. It takes on mythic status through the narrative of the *niña-bruja/beata,* where the *chonchón* is equated with the *imbunche* as a means of totalized mastery. It is also developed in a much more concrete way through the proliferation of the packages in which the old women wrap the detritus of their lives. As *imbunche*, Mudito does not become the mythic creature; rather, mastered by the old women in the way they master everything, he becomes its poorer reincarnation, the package. These packages contain nothing, neither origin nor presence. Thus, once Mudito is wrapped, the phallus, theoretically, should be eradicated, and with it the desire for identity. Yet the *imbunche* simultaneously revives the threatening presence of Peta Ponce and the desire for identity. Mudito hears "alguien que se agita en un rincón afuera, hay alguien, hay afuera," and, desiring this self-validating Other, bites and claws his way out of the layers of sacks to reach the Being on the other side. In the process, he recovers his organs—his mouth, his eyes, his ears. As he takes on human form, the ideal of the name, the validation of being, revives itself: "tengo que seguir royendo porque hay alguien afuera esperándome para decirme mi nombre y quiero oírlo y masco y muerdo y rajo" (472).

To prevent this transgressive cycle from producing one more deconstructive turn, Peta Ponce sews up all the tears in the sack, denying Mudito's desire and closing the open narrative. This closure does not signify the return of the repressive form of the family romance. Rather, it creates an irrevocable sense of intimacy that negates Mudito's last safety net, critical distance, dissolving the line between storyteller and story. In the scene when she gives Jerónimo the gift of the embroidered handkerchiefs, Peta Ponce is a presence which has begun to disrupt the masculine domain. Now, sewing again, she dominates it, preventing its return. Only with history disrupted can Peta work to shut up man, shut up being, and bury the narrator's nostalgia for subjectivity: "Y durante siglos espero que se forme otra capa geológica con el detritus de los millones de vidas que dicen que existen, para que sepulte de nuevo mi nostalgia." Caught within the sack, Mudito loses the critical distance he had maintained throughout his navigation of *La Casa* and the writing of the metanarrative of the life of Jerónimo de Azcoitía. Now, he has nothing on which to exercise his desire, nothing from which to construct a narrative but himself. Reduced to an infinitesimal size, one among the garbage of millions, still driven, Mudito narrates one more time—one more angst-ridden piece of paranoia—and finally exhausts himself: the only available fuel for his unquenchable desire.

Other than Mudito's smoldering pile of ashes, at the end of the novel there are the old women transported in white microbuses, with a load of pumpkins, to a new convalescent home. In this rather comic scene, the women are no longer dangerous and have retreated to their pleasant, self-less existence. They are blithely unaware that La Brígida and her absent mastery of finance as well as the powerful, subterranean *Dicen* are now providing for them. Unlike Humberto, Jerónimo, and the rest of Chilean society, their lives do not need a "recognizable plot" (Calderón, 34), because they have no desire to be part of some grand sociohistorical narrative. Their desires are not well-formed, and therein lies the danger of making them the subject of a narration. Humberto was easily co-opted into Jerónimo's story, because he had been prepared his entire life for such a co-optation. The discursive forces at work in Chilean society had shaped Humberto and his desires to fit snugly into an aristocratic social order. Jerónimo does not even have to try to make Humberto fit—he just does—and, at least initially, there is no danger of rebellion, subversion, or transgression.

But the retired servants who populate *La Casa* are another matter. They have been used up and have lost the integrity of their once, well-formed desires. And because they are an unstable material, Mudito can neither make them fit into a narrative nor use them to give shape to one; he cannot make them act as protectors, no matter how much he struggles with them. In fact, because Mudito struggles, because the discursive forces that shaped him seem to have been suspended in *La Casa,* he himself is in danger. As the lone arranger of *La Casa,* without the weight of social discourse behind him, Mudito has a nearly impossible task. Jerónimo was not a genius but merely the conduit through which a powerful signifying regime expressed itself. Mudito is no genius either, and all he has to back him up is the specter of that once powerful signifying regime. As such, the narrative structure he creates is weak. Mudito needs material he can read, make sense of, and out of which he can construct a narrative, but the old women are unreadable, and—because Mudito has no other recourse, no other material he can turn to—they cause Mudito's fragile signifying regime to crash. In *La Casa,* the impulse to narrate has met its match. We could say that Mudito's story is the story of narrative desire finding itself out of its element and failing to digest an innenarrable material. If in the novel there is something we can identify as a "new" writing, perhaps it is the product of this incommensurable tension: narrative beyond its limits, without the safety net of critical distance.

It is important to note, however, that *El obsceno pájaro* is not all "about" a long and pathetic process of self-destruction. The twentieth century canon may have bestowed on Donoso the ability to imagine the apocalyptic end of a social order and even of civilization itself, both of which we glimpse in the novel. He sees clearly enough to recognize the patriarchal roots of a class-bound society and women's capacity to subvert such a society, and Donoso endows his female characters with substantial power. In such a decadent milieu, they rupture an entrenched, deep-seated complex of class, family and identity. In Donoso's universe, "Man" can no longer function as the standard. "He" is neither majoritarian nor molar but an entity cobbled together by a vast complex of minorities. Yet, in spite of this powerful reconceptualization of the Chilean bourgeoisie, Donoso does not attempt to build another historical master-narrative. Instead, he adopts a far more local strategy: of all the narrative threads that wend their way through the novel, only that of the convent's *isla femenina* survives. Donoso does not redeem, recuperate or retool history, but simply saves a small community of dispossessed old women from a disgraceful end. Thus, the end of *El obsceno pájaro* is not hopeless but pragmatic, empowered by a simple vision: a single, practical step toward the creation of a different kind of world.

Works Cited

Barthes, Roland. *Mythologies.* Annette Lavers, trans. New York: Hill and Wang, 1972.

Borinsky, Alicia. "Repeticiones y máscaras: *El obsceno pájaro de la noche*" in *Modern Language Notes,* 1973 March, 281-294.

Calderón, Héctor. "Ideology and Sexuality, Male and Female in *El obsceno pájaro de la noche*" in *Ideologies and Literature,* 1:3, 1985, 31-50.

Cunningham, Lucía Gúerra. *Texto e ideología en la narrativa chilena.* Minneapolis: The Prisma Institute, 1987.

Deleuze, Gilles and Guattari, Felix. *A Thousand Plateaus.* Minneapolis: University of Minnesota Press, 1987.

Donoso, José. *El obsceno pájaro de la noche.* Barcelona: Editorial Argos Vergara, 1970.

Girard, René. *Violence and The Sacred.* Baltimore: The Johns Hopkins University Press, 1979.

Gutiérrez Mouat, Ricardo. *José Donoso: Impostura e impostación.* Gaithersberg: Ediciones Hispamérica, 1984.

Magnarelli, Sharon. "Amidst the Illusory Depths: The First Person Pronoun and *El obsceno pájaro de la noche*" in *Modern Language Notes,* 93, 1978, 267-284.

———. *The Lost Rib: Female Characters in the Spanish American Novel.* Lewisberg: Bucknell University Press, 1985.

———. *Understanding José Donoso.* Columbia: University of South Carolina Press, 1993.

Martínez, Z. Nelly. "*El obsceno pájaro de la noche:* la productividad del texto" in *Revista Iberoamericana,* 110-111, enero-junio, 1980, 51-65.

Rowe, William. "José Donoso: *El obsceno pájaro de la noche* as Test Case for Psychoanalytic Interpretation" in *Modern Language Review,* 1983 July, 78 (3), 588-596.

Philip Swanson (essay date 1995)

SOURCE: Swanson, Philip. "José Donoso and *La misteriosa desaparición de la marquesita de Loria.*" In *The New Novel in Latin America: Politics and Popular Culture after the Boom,* pp. 92-113. Manchester: Manchester University Press, 1995.

[*In the following chapter from his book on Latin American literature after the "Boom," Swanson presents a semiotic reading of* La misteriosa desaparición de la marquesita de Loria, *including commentary on the ideas of previous critics of the work.*]

In a newspaper article in 1982, José Donoso lamented the almost exclusive association of Latin American fiction with long, complex, experimental, 'totalising' works and asked: '¿No ha llegado un momento de ruptura para la novela latinoamericana, de cambio . . . ?'.[1] A couple of years previously, in 1980, he had published

La misteriosa desaparición de la marquesita de Loria, probably the most surprising departure from his very own long, complex, experimental, 'totalising' novel from the height of the Boom, *El obsceno pájaro de la noche.* Though much Donoso criticism, partly due to a compliance with the ahistorical agenda of certain schools of literary theory, stresses the continuity of his work, it is pretty plain that there is a quite dramatic change of some kind in his writing after 1970.[2] In particular, there is an apparent reduction in complexity in the shape of the utilisation of popular or conventional genres and the abandonment of tortuous narrative structures. In *Casa de campo,* for instance, which replaces the technique or gimmick of authorial efface-ment, typical (in part) of the Boom, with the fore-grounding of a conventional narratorial or authorial figure, the narrator comments: 'en la hipócrita no-ficción de las ficciones en que el autor pretende eliminarse siguiendo reglas preestablecidas por otras novelas, o buscando fórmulas narrativas novedosas . . . , veo un odioso puritanismo que estoy seguro que mis lectores no encontrarán en mi escritura'.[3] Yet, as has already been proposed in the opening chapter, the narratorial/ authorial stance of *Casa de campo* is, despite the rela-tive accessibility of the text, highly problematic. This is dramatised most obviously in the encounter between the narrator-cum-author as character 'José Donoso' and Silvestre, one of his own literary creations: the author is (impossibly) on his way to his publisher's with the final manuscript of the novel under his arm, but his plans are derailed by the insistences of Silvestre, who, inciden-tally, bears little relation to the Silvestre of the rest of 'Donoso's' narrative. What this suggests is that there is, after all, continuity with the ideas of the earlier work, most notably the question of the relationship between art and society or reality, but that they are being treated or explored in a new or, indeed, novel way. The post-Boom Donoso can be seen, in other words, as, rather than fragmenting the notion of authority through a con-spicuously labyrinthine narrative structure, destabilising it instead via the subversion of narratorial power from within. *La misteriosa desaparición de la marquesita de Loria* can thus be seen, as with the novels by Vargas Llosa and Fuentes and other novels considered in this book, to similar and differing degrees, as a power struggle between 'author' or, as it really is in this case, narrator and the rival claims of character(s) within the text. Donoso's novel pits an implied male narrator us-ing both the sense of closure implicit in the popular and the authority implicit in High culture to keep in check or even destroy a potentially threatening female pres-ence who is herself associated with the popular and has her own pretensions to authority. The seemingly light-est, most titillating and least openly political Donosian post-Boom text, then, problematises the popular and be-comes political through the very processes of its own deceptive articulation.

As in other works by the Chilean author, *La marquesita de Loria,* as we shall from now on call it for short, is based around a false binarism which one might dub order-versus-chaos. One pole (identity, power, conven-tion, rationality, order—often linked with masculinity and adulthood) is opposed to and threatened by the other (fragmentation, rebellion, instinct, irrationality, chaos—often linked with 'femininity' or 'femaleness' and youth or old age). The distinction is, of course, a myth and therefore the former, dreading rupture and contamination, seeks to impose itself on and therefore create the illusion of separation from the latter. The fa-miliar and/or popular tone of the present text may be taken as an attempt to naturalise and thus disguise and neutralise this process. For example, the documentary style gives a comforting impression of truth and knowledge. The novel opens with this tone ('La joven marquesa viuda de Loria, nacida Blanca Arias en Man-agua, Nicaragua, era . . .'[4] and repeats it in the account of the marquis' death: 'Ese invierno andaba mucha dif-teria por Madrid: falleció dos días después del miér-coles de carnaval, Francisco Javier Anacleto Quiñones, marqués de Loria, antes de cumplir los veintiún años, dejando a toda su parentela desconsolada, muy espe-cialmente a su joven viuda - nacida Blanca Arias, hija del recordado diplomático nicaragüense . . .' (40-1). The narrator seems to come across as a compiler who is effortlessly familiar with his material: 'si queremos ser rigurosos hay que precisar que . . .' or 'sería dema-siado tedioso describir las ocasiones en que . . .' (13, 35). Yet the same casual strain with which the final chapter opens ('Todavía corre por Madrid la leyenda . . .' [173]) gives the game away. The legend referred to is that of the strange grey dog with golden-grey eyes who disturbs courting couples in the Madrid park, the Retiro. The redundant adverb 'todavía' indicates a cer-tain over-anxiety behind the narrator's jocular tone. Moreover, in designating the legend, highly ambigu-ously, as 'una alucinación histérica que, hay que confe-sar, puede no ser fruto sólo de fantasías coincidentes' (174), he appears to deny its veracity while trying to look as if he is not. Why does he introduce the story if it is only immediately to problematise it? Could it be to slur the integrity of his own protagonist, Blanca, who the reader knows thinks she has a relationship with a grey dog with golden-grey eyes which no one else seems to have seen? But why should the narrator want to discredit Blanca? Possibly because she represents a threat to the sense of order inscribed in the documen-tary style. Partly, this is the threat to the male of female power and sexuality, but it is also that Blanca under-mines order by dissolving the binary division: synthe-sising Europe and Latin America, power and submis-sion, even human and animal and male and female, she is drawn to a male dog with a female name, Luna (see 77), she is reflected in him and possibly is him (insofar as it is hinted that he may be her unconscious) or maybe becomes him at the end (when she is alleged to be devoured by a dog-like creature), and, in any case, seems to find union with the dark, unexplained 'other side' he represents (e.g. 163). In a sense, then, she brings the narrative face to face with what it would prefer to ignore or not to see. Why else is her shocking and unexplained disappearance simply passed over and displaced by the cheery epilogue of the conventional documentary narrator wrapping up the life-stories of the 'normal' characters who remain behind? The disappearance, indeed, is the crucial fulcrum of this contest. Given the documentary style, the title of the book suggests a case history, yet the words 'misteriosa' and 'desaparición' imply a problem and no solution—order threatened by chaos again. Furthermore, the two main sources of popular culture utilised here are those of erotica and detective fiction.[5] Both involve (in different ways) concealment and uncovering, their culmination being closure through disclosure (climactic fulfilment in the former, solving of the mystery in the latter). In *La marquesita de Loria* there is only closure: erotic fulfilment does not take place and the mystery of the disappearance remains unexplained. The 'official' narrative tidies things up neatly by ignoring what it would rather not see, but an implied reader might feel that what the novel is really about is what it keeps secret, what it hides, what it suppresses.

The broad outline given above can now be developed in more detail. The key issue is the significance (or lack of it) of Blanca's disappearance. The question is whether it is in some way wilful (on Blanca's part) or contrived (on the part of the narrator—or perhaps other characters acting as his surrogates). Sharon Magnarelli—in what must, nonetheless, be credited as a superbly constructed essay—denies Blanca much agency of substance. She does not really separate her from the literary forms the novel parodies or pastiches. Adding Spanish American *modernismo* to erotic and detective fiction (Rubén Darío is referred to on a number of occasions and his 'Era un aire suave . . .' is quoted playfully in the penultimate chapter and parallels aspects of the story of the novel), she claims that all three forms are predicated upon the urge to disguise an inherent absence and, by extension, the vacuity of the society they echo (102). Blanca, who is virtually synonymous with the text in Magnarelli's reading, is much the same. In a Barthesean nod to the idea of eroticism as a form of discourse, the critic gives Blanca's autoeroticism a linguistic meaning, saying that, in the novel, 'many of the linguistic constructs are devoted to the protagonist's self-admiration, as she "sees" herself, either mentally or in mirrors and pools of water, and as she "writes" herself in her internal monologues, carefully edits the script, sets the scene and then watches herself perform, both sexually and otherwise' (105). With Magnarelli's trademark linguistic parallel established, it is not long before there is talk of language ceasing to signify and becoming mere covering (117), Blanca herself, as her name suggests, representing this very state of affairs (though somewhat peculiarly, one might be forgiven for thinking, if language does not 'signify' anything). Blanca, as a kind of pseudo-narrator, narcissistically projects her own erotic desire on to others, needing to be and assuming she is being seen and lusted after by them. The closeness of her relationship with Luna epitomises this condition, for his eyes—with which she becomes utterly fascinated—are blank, like mirrors, empty reflections of her. With no identity other than the stereotypical practices and consumer items she sports, 'Blanca herself is an absence, enshrouded in signifiers which evoke not her but rather the elite society in which she moves' (107). And, moreover, that society is itself given over to burying its emptiness or 'nothingness' with layers of meaningless covering or adornment. So, for Magnarelli, Blanca's disappearance is the conclusion of the theme of absence made present. Blanca did not really disappear. Because she was never really there.

Notwithstanding the central contradiction concerning the representative or otherwise powers of language, Magnarelli marshalls considerable textual evidence which could be seen to support her argument (especially with regard to the projection of the wish to be seen and desired). Her point is reinforced by the link forged between Blanca and *modernismo* as well as with erotica and mysteries. A number of swan images crop up in relation to Blanca's life and, at one stage, echoing her earlier erotic adventure at the opera *Lohengrin* she sees herself, now widowed, in the waters of the Retiro as 'un maravilloso cisne negro entre tantos blancos' (46). The swan, of course, is the classic *modernista* image, so Blanca is again living in reflections, in literature rather than life, in a literature, moreover, that is most commonly associated with 'l'art pour l'art', style, surface, decoration—not with depth or substance. The language of the novel might even be said to mimic that of *modernismo*. There is the quotation in the penultimate chapter and Blanca's 'cuerpo fantaseoso' is at one stage said to be in an 'estado de sinestesia' (47), while Magnarelli identifies a proliferation of adjectivisation. A feature of the text is indeed the qualification of nouns by unnecessary adjectives or adjectivisation, as in, for example: 'sacó de su bolsillo un peine de carey y brillantes' (65). The qualification is, like Blanca in Magnarelli's reading, non-functional, sheer excess, mere supplement—if anything, it points to the absence or emptiness that characterises the high society in which the marchioness moves. Erotic and detective stories, the conventions of which the novel also mimics, are similarly surplus to meaningful requirements. 'All three forms of discourse are privileges of a leisured class—a class which consumes them and is portrayed within them, a class which has time, money and energy in excess of those used in "productive" or reproductive activities' (Magnarelli, 113).

Reducing *La marquesita de Loria* to 'empty signifiers' (122), Magnarelli's conclusion would seem to be that there is no significance to Blanca's disappearance, that it merely follows the internal logic of a narrative that the protagonist herself appears to dominate or even manipulate. Yet even Magnarelli acknowledges that 'Blanca is portrayed as conditioned by and a product of the social, artistic mythology which envelopes (*sic*) and surrounds her' (107). This may not seem to grant her much agency, but it opens the way for a reading that might begin to. An aspect of Blanca's 'conditioning', should one choose to read it this way, is that her 'natural' or 'authentic' Latin American self is swamped and distorted by European values (symbolised most obviously by the clothes, accessories and perfumes with European names with which she 'covers' herself). On the very first page it is said that, after her parents leave her in Madrid to return to their native Nicaragua, the marchioness

> se había convertido ya en una europea cabal, sustituyendo esos ingenuos afectos por otros y olvidando tanto las sabrosas entonaciones de su vernáculo como las licencias femeninas corrientes en el continente joven, para envolverse en el suntuoso manto de los prejuicios, rituales y dicción de su flamante rango . . . - en el fondo todo había sido tan fácil como descartar un huipil en favor de una túnica de Paul Poiret.
>
> (11-2)

Lucrecio Pérez Blanco sees the novel as being about loss of an American identity: 'si Blanca, símbolo de Hispanoamérica, desaparece y no se encuentra rastro alguno suyo, es porque la descomposición no deja rastro del propio ser. El mestizaje de sangre, que pide un comportamiento coherente y distinto de quien mezcló la sangre, puesto que el nuevo ser es distinto, se destruye, se descompone por falta de coherencia'.[6] The difficulty here is that the novel can also be seen as problematising the very idea of an 'authentic' 'Latin American' identity that Pérez Blanco appears to believe in. Surely if European identity (which seems here to amount to little more than a stream of conventions, fashions and designer goods) is a construct, then so is a Latin American identity which takes for granted 'las licencias femeninas corrientes en el continente joven' or, in a later example, 'esa pasmosa vocación para las perversiones que suele darse aparejada con la ternura en las hembras del trópico' (34). Examining Blanca's enraptured look at the opera, Casilda 'no pudo sino meditar cómo algunos seres muy primitivos, por ejemplo esta linda muchacha, tienen una pureza tal que les facilita la comprensión de lo más inaccesiblemente selecto del arte' (23). Of course, the reason for Blanca's rapture is not any primitive tropical purity but the fact that she is being surreptitiously masturbated by Paquito. Given that it is later revealed that Casilda has the hots for Blanca and given the Frenchwoman's fetishistic use of the term 'primitivo' to describe the young widow's image (115),

it can be seen that Blanca's native primitiveness is itself a cultural invention: it is little more than the erotic cliché (especially in the arts) of the member of a dominant group's fetishistic desire for 'difference' in the form of a 'young girl', a 'bit of rough', a 'black man' or whatever (it is worth noting, especially for Casilda, that Blanca and her family are also bound up with notions of cultural and racial inferiority). In fact, Blanca's sexual adventures, following the series format typical of erotic literature, rehearse many of the usual clichés. By the time she is faced, in the second-to-last chapter, with a ménage-à-trois involving a lesbian romp and male cross-dressing, she is 'mortalmente aburrida' (162). In the final chapter, it is after the clichéd violent encounter on the back seat of her Isotta-Fraschini with her own 'bit of rough', the chauffeur Mario, that she walks away and disappears forever. Does this not intimate some degree of consciousness and action on the marquesita's part? And does not the relieved tone of the tacked-on epilogue of the final four pages, which restores order and surveys the smug and materially satisfactory lives of the characters who survive the marchioness, also imply Blanca's challenge to and rejection of the lifestyle of the others? As Ricardo Gutiérrez-Mouat comments, referring to erotic play, though he could equally be referring to material indulgence, 'ante este aburguesamiento del carnaval erótico, a la marquesita no le queda otra solución que protagonizar el misterio de su propia desaparición'.[7] And in this respect *modernismo,* for Gutiérrez-Mouat, has a wider sociopolitical significance beyond that suggested by adjectivisation. What Darío represents is the propagation through literature of a falsely naturalised myth of Latin American identity, 'la impostación de un yo ficticio y artificial, y la apropiación de esta impostura a través de la lengua poética' (267). Blanca, it might be argued—in her rejection of social and sexual clichés, her relationship with Luna and her disappearance—breaks with both normalising social constructs and with the artistic constructs that underpin them. In one sense she is clearly the marquesa Eulalia from 'Era un aire suave . . .', 'maligna y bella', who toys with her lovers and 'ríe, ríe, ríe'. Yet Darío's poem ends with the lines: 'Yo el tiempo y el día y el país ignoro; I pero sé que Eulalia ríe todavía, I ¡y es crüel y eterna su risa de oro!'.[8] As Magnarelli has already pointed out (115), these lines indicate that the poet sees Eulalia as nothing but his own personal literary creation. If Donoso's novel uses the language of Darío's *modernismo,* one might therefore be inclined to infer that Blanca's actions in the text represent a rebellion against her linguistic construction and fixing. Her struggle is to transcend the restrictions that the narrative seeks to impose on her.

The relationship between protagonist and narrator raises important questions about representation. In particular, it raises questions about High and Low and about male representations of the female or, indeed, the 'feminine'.

The implied narratorial perspective of *La marquesita de Loria* can be taken as masculine. This is, by and large (and with some notable exceptions), the usual viewpoint of erotic or detective fiction; the tone here is purportedly authoritative and clearly masculine in, say, its comments on women; and the real author is, of course, a man. Also the theme of Blanca 'being seen', as well as the motifs of painting, the female model and the male artist, all suggest the male gaze. As has already been mentioned, the marquesita tends to perceive herself in terms of other people's looks of desire and, on top of this, she pictures herself as a Paul Chabas *baigneuse* and poses nude for the painter Archibaldo Arenas. Feminist art historian Linda Nochlin comments that 'the acceptance of woman as object of the desiring male gaze in the visual arts is so universal that for a woman to question, or to draw attention to this fact, is to invite derision, to reveal herself as one who does not understand the sophisticated strategies of high culture and takes art too "literally", and is therefore unable to respond to aesthetic discourses'.[9] For a woman to challenge the validity of the female nude or the sexualisation of the representation of the female, this would be 'undermined by authorized doubts, by the need to please, to be learned, sophisticated, aesthetically astute—in male-defined terms, of course' (Nochlin, 32). Applying the painter-(female) nude relationship to the narrator-(female) character relationship in Donoso's novel, we can deduce that Blanca's sexual exhibitionism and narcissism is simply her internalisation of the implied male narrator's urge to see and portray her as sex object. What appears to be narration from Blanca's viewpoint in her sexual fantasies may actually often be the subtle and naturalising imposition of the dominant masculine narratorial viewpoint, which is not as neutral, distant, detached or playfully light-hearted as it seems. This is the Foucaultian notion that 'symbolic power is invisible and can be exercised only with the complicity of those who fail to recognise either that they submit to it or that they exercise it' (Nochlin, 2). Yet this is equally a pattern of power and potential resistance. To quote Foucault:

> In effect, what defines a relationship of power is that it is a mode of action which does not act directly and immediately upon others. Instead it acts upon their actions: an action upon an action, on existing actions or on those which may arise in the present or the future. . . . A power relationship can only be articulated on the basis of two elements which are indispensable if it is really to be a power relationship: that 'the other' (the one over whom power is exercised) be thoroughly recognised and maintained to the very end as a person who acts; and that, faced with a relationship of power, a whole field of responses, reactions, results, and possible inventions may open up.[10]

Blanca, then, can acquire consciousness and contest her representation. She sees through the painter Archibaldo and leaves him; and she abandons too the narrator's attempted imposition of an erotic narrative by forsaking sexual high jinks, turning to Luna and disappearing.

What is beginning to emerge from behind the mask of a seemingly straightforward and amusing sophisticated pastiche of a popular genre is a more complex picture in which the mask itself is the very ploy activated to disguise the underlying reality of a power battle. Essentially a battle between a male narrator and his female protagonist, it is revealed by the (absent) presence of a further implied narrator (or, rather, implied author) who appeals to the insight and understanding of an implied reader. The reader is encouraged to see between the lines, in other words, and spot the limitations or inconsistencies of the projected narrator. The reader is the real detective in this mystery story and the villain he or she catches in the act is none other than the male narrator himself. An obvious example is the epilogue. The official narrator tries to 'close' the narrative by adopting a chirpy tone and describing a society enjoying harmony and satisfaction. Yet the alert reader cannot fail to notice his complete avoidance of or inability to explain or discuss the nature or implications of the marchioness's disappearance. The casual final line of the text, referring to the walks taken by Archibaldo and his new wife (incidentally, Blanca's sister—perhaps a more ruly and socially appropriate version of the marquesita?) 'seguidos por Luna, su gran y fiel perro gris' (198) is another pointer for the reader to pick up. The sheer unproblematic timbre of this statement must prompt the reader to feel that the official narrator is concealing something or refusing to face something, for he is simply glossing over the fact that Luna had previously appeared (at least) to have gone off to Blanca's, been involved in her disappearance, and is possibly still—in some phantasmal manifestation—haunting the shady corners of the Retiro to this day. A clue to assist the reader in deciphering this tendency is already given earlier in the presentation of Archibaldo Arenas. As a painter of portraits, he is like the narrator as compiler or chronicler, that is one who copies or reproduces reality in his art. Yet a detail reveals that he actually falsifies reality: he paints Tere Castillo as a 'pescadora gallega' when she is in fact a high society 'andaluza' (57). The implication is that the narrator does the same sort of thing. An example is the story of the death of the marquis, Paquito. Paquito's death is caused by complications arising from a bad cold which was aggravated when, insufficiently dressed, he left a fancy-dress ball early with Blanca in poor weather conditions. But two differing explanations as to why he left are given.[11] The first, fleetingly given shortly before the documentary-style death announcement quoted earlier as if by the official narrator, is that he 'fled', 'pegado a las faldas de Blanca porque tanta algarabía le causaba desazón', too scared to tell his mother he is going (40). This is a clear image of male weakness. The second (and more memorably expressed) version, presented more from Blanca's point of view, is that his determination to confront his mother and her alleged lover fills him with strength and energy, producing a huge erection and the determination to take his wife straight home and 'violarla' (51). What this indicates at the very least is that the narrator is at some level untrustworthy. Or, worse, that he is uneasy and manipulative. If the second version is from Blanca's viewpoint, then the narrator has manufactured her internalisation of the supposedly typical female (but actually male) fantasy of powerful male sexual potency. Blanca's 'point of view' here is really a narrative manipulation so that she is made to validate what is actually a projection of the male narrator's desire for sexual security. But surely, in the narrator's own terms, the first 'official' version, rather than Blanca's, should be the truth. This version though would confirm male weakness—which seems to be the truth anyway—for Paquito is, in fact, impotent. Thus the driving force behind the narrative power struggle is actually male sexual anxiety.

Fundamentally, it is the sense of order guaranteed by faith in binary logic that is felt to be in jeopardy. Political historian Carole Pateman says women have traditionally been perceived as 'potential disrupters of masculine boundary systems of all sorts', while Elaine Showalter, quoting Toril Moi, states that 'women's social or cultural marginality seems to place them on the borderlines of the symbolic order, both the "frontier between men and chaos", and dangerously part of chaos itself, inhabitants of a mysterious and frightening wild zone outside of patriarchal culture'.[12] It follows that the more the 'presence' of woman, the greater the sense of peril in man. Hence the narrator's need in *La marquesita de Loria* to impose himself on Blanca and assert his own presence in the epilogue. His anxiety suggests two possible things: that he is threatened by Blanca's leaving him, her independence, her departure from his familiar erotic narrative into an altogether less sure world; or that he gets rid of her himself, that he makes her disappear rather than confront what she is exposing herself and therefore exposing him to. The threat of greater female presence can be related to Showalter's comments on the emergence of the so-called New Woman at the *fin-de-siècle* (a world not dissimilar from the 1920s Madrid setting of Donoso's novel and with explicit parallels in Showalter's book to the current *fin-de-siècle*). Echoing the earlier remarks here, she discusses misogyny in *fin-de-siècle* painting: 'there images of female narcissism, of the *femme fatale* and the sphinx, of women kissing their mirror images, gazing at themselves in circular baths, or engaging in autoerotic play mutate by the end of the century into savagely "gynecidal" visions of female sexuality' (10). This is all remarkably like what happens to Blanca. Her self-consciousness and solitary sexual experiments do evolve in a deadly direction: two men die after sex with her and she, on a number of occasions, mentally verba-

lises the fatal power of her flesh. Moreover, Showalter's New Woman was particularly worrisome because her anarchic sense of sexual independence was thought to threaten the institution of matrimony (38) and presumably the male privileges that traditionally went with it. It is interesting in this respect that Blanca's thirst for carnal knowledge, 'este enloquecedor anhelo de lo desconocido' (46), takes off after the death of her husband. The widow is a traditionally troublesome image for the male: the idea of the Merry Widow, like Blanca, financially and therefore sexually independent, sexually experienced but unconstrained. Or there is the Black Widow, bringing death and associated with dark forces, again like Blanca with her mysterious canine companion, her links with the moon and the black women of the Caribbean with their tarot cards. The widow, of course, traditionally wears a veil, as does Blanca in her mourning outfit. Veils are strongly identified with female sexuality and the male gaze. According to Showalter, the veil traditionally represented the hymen (hence the conventional link with chastity) and 'Nature' in scientific or medical discourse was often likened to a woman whose secrets would be yielded when unveiled by man. But the veiled woman also connoted mystery and her 'secrets' were linked to the riddles of birth and death. Indeed Freud's reading of the image of the veiled woman in terms of the myth of the Medusa is the background to his theory of the male castration complex. To unveil woman is to confront the genitalised head of the Medusa, the upward displacement of the *vagina dentata*. The discovery of the female sexual organs incurs simultaneously the fear of decapitation or castration. This may well explain all the talk of penises in *La marquesita de Loria*—a projection of the narrator's male anxiety on to Blanca. Hard, 'iron' rods are frequently evoked yet the truth is that don Mamerto's penis is tiny, Almanza needs a corset to keep his up and Paquito's goes flaccid at the crucial moments. As Mary Ann Doane says, in her study of *femmes fatales* and veiling in cinema, 'the phallus actually becomes important only insofar as it might be absent, it might disappear. It assumes meaning only in relation to castration'.[13]

Veils, sexuality, decapitation and castration, decadence and the idea of the *femme fatale* are elements which all combine in the story and myth of Salome (a focus of Showalter's analysis), which finds interesting echoes of itself in *La marquesita de Loria*. As Showalter reminds us, she was painted by Gustave Klimt as an elegant lady of the *Belle Epoque* who holds the severed head casually by her side—another parallel with the narratorial fear that underlies the glamorous portrait of Donoso's 1920s high-society marchioness. More intriguing still is Oscar Wilde's play *Salome*, particularly his 1893 edition accompanied by the drawings of Aubrey Beardsley. *La marquesita de Loria* is also accompanied by illustrations from old editions of *La Es-*

fera, which—though much less sinister and suggestive—display certain period similarities with Beardsley's. The first drawing from *Salome* depicts the moon in a somewhat sexual context and its title was changed from *The Man in the Moon* to *The Woman in the Moon,* again echoing aspects of *La marquesita de Loria:* fear and mystery represented by the moon and Luna, sexual ambiguity and the dissolution of binary divisions. A further vague connection is the linking of the moon to death and disappearance. The Page of Herodias urges Narraboth to look at the moon rather than at Salome and later laments: '. . . now he has killed himself. . . . Well, I knew that the moon was seeking a dead thing, but I knew not that it was he whom she sought. Ah! Why did I not hide him from the moon?' This makes us think both of Blanca's withdrawal from sexuality in favour of a disappearance involving Luna and the male narrator's dual fear of female sexuality and chaos. But what Salome represents above all is the enthralling and terrifying unveiling of the female self. The widow's veil of the marquesita de Loria expresses not only her disquieting blurring of boundaries (the veil is neither complete exposure nor complete concealment) but is also relieved of its connotations of chastity, modesty and unavailability: 'la joven marquesa viuda de Loria paseaba por los senderos del Retiro luciendo para ojos desconocidos . . . el misterio de su luto. Pero de sus orejas se cimbraban dos lágrimas de oro facetado cuyo brillo trascendía los velos del duelo con perversos guiños impuestos por la ligereza del paso de la joven' (55). Within a few pages, the wind has lifted her veils and she is receiving copious *piropos* (59). Then she initiates her post-marital sex life and causes the death of the diminutively-endowed don Mamerto. All of this is a symbolic returning of the male gaze and part of a process of breaking with the self-image of woman as male sex object. What is more, it exposes the constructed nature of the masculine othering of women. The face behind the veil is probably normal after all. As Cixous says, 'You only have to look at the Medusa straight on to see her. And she's not deadly. She's beautiful and she's laughing'.[14] It is the fear of looking straight on that makes the marquesita disappear or at least makes the disappearance be ignored.

Effectively, what happens in *La marquesita de Loria* is that Blanca is both object and agent. She connotes what Laura Mulvey terms '*to-be-looked-at-ness*' in her seminal essay on female representation in film, 'Visual Pleasure and Narrative Cinema',[15] while at the same time marks the transition from heroine as reflection of the hero's dynamics to heroine with agency. Yet even without or before agency, so the theory goes, the male unconscious has to deal with castration anxiety (based on 'the visually ascertainable absence of the penis'), since even 'the woman as icon, displayed for the gaze and enjoyment of men, the active controllers of the look, always threatens to evoke the anxiety it originally

signified' (Mulvey, 13). Mulvey sees two avenues of escape for the male unconscious, both of which would seem to correspond to strategies employed (or attempted) by the implied male narrator of *La marquesita de Loria.* One is fetishistic scopophilia, 'a complete disavowal of castration by the substitution of a fetish object or turning the represented figure itself into a fetish so that it becomes reassuring rather than dangerous' (Mulvey, 13-4). This is clearly essayed in *La marquesita de Loria* but does not seem to work. The other is voyeurism, involving 'preoccupation with the re-enactment of the original trauma (investigating the woman, demystifying her mystery), counterbalanced by the devaluation, punishment or saving of the guilty object' (Mulvey, 13). Certainly, the narrator subjects the case of the marchioness to investigation and tries to devalue her by presenting her as sex-crazed and shallow. It is important to remember that the narrator adopts a playful, ironic tone more often than a documentary approach: this, coupled with the mocking adjectivisation mentioned earlier, allows him to appear superior and deflate Blanca. Yet he fails to demystify her mystery and fails, it can be argued, to devalue her. Perhaps then he manages to punish her. *Salome* ends with Herod calling for the woman's death. In Bram Stoker's *Dracula,* another *fin-de-siècle* work with evident links to *La marquesita de Loria,* Lucy's sexualised vampiric impurity (echoes of Blanca and Luna) is corrected by men decapitating her (Freud's Medusa-related castration anxiety again) and driving a stake through her heart (the relieved flaunting of the phallus). Blanca, meantime, is destroyed by a horrific monster (so Mario claims) and the world is put right again by the epilogue.[16] Returning now to the sketches from *La Esfera,* their arrangement suggests a similar urge to punish and regain control. The drawings, which precede each chapter, all of women, all suit the period tone of the text and may be taken to parallel it closely. The first three (of eight) all correspond to the action in the chapter concerned— widowhood, a masked ball, a woman alone in her bedroom. This all suggests strong narratorial control and organisation. Yet in the third chapter, the woman portrayed appears to be looking out straight ahead. This is the only picture in which the woman's eyes are not covered or turned away. Is this a breakdown in the power of the male gaze (control) and a pointer to Blanca's self-discovery or self-assertion? It could well be, because the illustration preceding the next chapter (the fourth)—a woman in a tennis dress—indicates a crumbling of the rigidly ordered parallels since it refers to an episode which does not take place until the sixth chapter. Indeed the next three illustrations bear no clear-cut relation to the chapters at all. Narratorial command of the entirety of the text is being undermined, it seems. But the placing of the final illustration reestablishes control. It is of a woman and a sporty motor car, alluding to Blanca's final and probably fatal journey in the last chapter. And here the woman is looking away and, for the first time in the drawings, is veiled. The inference may well be that the male narrator is back in charge, female modesty is restored, the female threat will be destroyed. Not so fast, though. The veil is an ambiguous image, problematising boundaries as much as fixing them. And, in the most important illustration of them all, the one in colour, on the cover, the female figure is looking right out at the other looker, eyes wide open and clear, returning the gaze, even, given the intensity of the eyes, acting as the gazing subject rather than the gazed-at object. Maybe the protagonist does get one over on her narrator after all.

The point is that there is something of a truth to both views of the outcome of the battle, for Blanca does not score a 'triumph' in any conventional sense and the narrator does manage to restore a semblance of order. The outcome is similar to that of Donoso's early story **'Paseo'** (and maybe, too, a variation on it, *Este domingo*) where an orderly but strangely uncomfortable narrator recalls the unexplained disappearance during his childhood of his aunt with a mysterious dog. The narrator's life is controlled but wanting, while the aunt's disappearance is seen as both a collapse into chaos and a glimpse of fulfilment or meaning. So what Blanca achieves is to transcend false, sterile and limiting notions of order, but that achievement—though potentially meaningful for her—is presented as dark and perturbing because it erodes the order-predicated binary logic upon which conventional narrative, society and even 'civilisation' depend. Turning now to examine this process more closely, the first thing to notice—before even considering Blanca's 'alternative'—is the unsettled nature of the narrative itself. The narrative depends in part on the illusion of documentary realism. Also, in mimicking a popular genre, it depends on the illusion of a comfortingly familiar format. Yet many narratorial interventions have a tongue-in-cheek quality about them (simple random examples would be the references to 'el banquete—si de banquete puede calificarse tan rústico ágape' or Almanza's 'retazos de fandangos absolutamente irrepetibles' [31, 155]). The language too is often exaggeratedly stylised (a good example here is the account of Blanca's erotic-cum-romantic visit to Archibaldo's studio where a short time lapse is described four times in eight pages as 'un siglo', there are three 'maravillosos' in a single paragraph and the first kiss ('dulce beso') of the encounter 'los haría—como lo aseguraban todos los novelistas—vibrar al unísono' and 'parecía haber encendido otra luz en el estudio' [122-30]). Moreover, there is a dramatic intervention towards the end in the report of the chauffeur's reaction to the disappearance: '. . . montó en el Isotta-Fraschini para ir a toda velocidad al puesto de policía más cercano, donde contó lo que el autor de esta historia acaba de contar en este capítulo y que está a punto de terminar' (193-4). In one sense, such interventions reinforce nar-

rative authority, by signposting a relaxed and superior organiser or creator. At the same time though, they disrupt the mode of documentary realism, question the popular genre feel of the text, conflict often—in terms of tone—with the events narrated, and betray an anxiety over narratorial presence (the last quotation immediately preceding the narratorial imposition of the order-restoring epilogue in the face of Blanca's chaotic disappearance). The text then seems to lack the '*colle logique*' which Barthes sees as fundamental to the 'readerly' text.[17] It is this rupturing of narratorial security which allows us to read Blanca's story as that which generates the textual discomfort.[18]

The essential feature of Blanca's story is the displacement of her sexual or material quest (voiced as a quest for knowledge and fulfilment [e.g. 12, 46-7]) and linked to a desire for gratification through power (e.g. 14, 58ff) by its opposite.[19] Sexual situations from the start are juxtaposed with instances of death or the appearance of morally sterile characters like Almanza. The lengthy and delayed build-up to the highly-charged description of the eventual sexual *rencontre* with Archibaldo Arenas (which promises to be the pinnacle of satisfaction) is almost immediately undone by Blanca's sense of disappointment and virtually instant abandonment of him. This is a pivotal encounter, for Archibaldo not only represents the meaninglessness of the sexual-material quest, he also provides Luna, the key figure in the displacement of the quest. Luna, of course, may not exist as such in a conventional sense (none of her staff notices him, Archibaldo does not miss him and he is still with her at the end).[20] He is, thus, part of Blanca, the unconscious side she has learned to suppress but is now beginning to see. Either way, it is what he represents that matters. And it is the opposite to Archibaldo. The painter's lemon-grey eyes turn out to be merely black and empty (120, 166, 168); instead Blanca immerses herself in the lemon-grey eyes of 'ese perro terrible y maravilloso' in a way she never could in anyone else's (166). The eyes (which are like two moons) are linked to the black or half-caste women who read tarot cards and talked of witchcraft to Blanca as a child:[21]

> . . . las mestizas de su niñez en las noches de miedo le señalaban las dos lunas idénticas en el horizonte (i.e. the moon and its reflection) para calmarla. ¿Pero por qué había producido esta hecatombe doméstica, Luna, su Luna, su perro querido a quien, ahora se daba cuenta, había echado de menos durante todo el día, sobre todo a sus ojos suspendidos en el horizonte mismo de su imaginación.
>
> (141-2)

Luna is part of a dark other side and is wreaking havoc in her world yet is what she really wants. He is an alternative to the material (he literally destroys the sumptuous but redundant elegance of her 'alcoba de raso color *fraise ecrasé*' [12] converting it into 'esa fétida ruina que la satisfacía' [170]) and the sexual (increasingly tiresome erotic incidents are juxtaposed sharply with the thrill of her return to Luna [140, 162-3, 184] and the erotic—or pornographic—cliché of the sexual encounter of woman and animal pointedly does not materialise [143]), offering her a unity or possibility of completion—'dos lunas que eran una sola' (106)—which she has been lacking in her life so far. The climax comes when she abandons the known world altogether by disappearing with the animal into 'la oscuridad total donde sólo podían existir los remansos lunares de los ojos de Luna' (189), seemingly devoured by a dog-like creature (193). All that remains of her are an ornate handgun, a silver clasp, a French shoe and a classy gold watch—all fetishistic images of the material and sensuous world she has left behind. There is no body. The narrator may have got rid of her.[22] But her 'absence' might also be his castration fear and her assertion of freedom from the male gaze. Blanca rejects the role that is written for her and undermines the very epistemological and ontological categories that give shape to society's script.

A final point concerning the narrator-marquesita dialectic is its relationship to that of Europe and Latin America. As has already been suggested, the post-Boom and even the postmodern in Latin America are concepts very much wrapped up with questions of intertextuality and cultural transnationalism, with two broad tendencies (sometimes different, sometimes convergent) emerging, one involving play and interaction with popular or mass culture, the other supposedly more popular-rooted and involving greater local cultural and political specificity. *La marquesita de Loria* is certainly not the latter (in the sense that, say, *testimonio* is) but it does come between two books dealing very obviously with Latin American politics (*Casa de campo* in 1978 and *El jardín de al lado* in 1981), the latter precisely dealing with the link with European perspectives. And interestingly enough, Donoso has defined the modern Latin American novel as 'being about identification, a search for national identity and for personal identity'.[23] Blanca's personal identity does have a strong continental and intercontinental dimension. Denoting and connoting her tropical provenance, her beauty is routinely described with terms like 'sus lindos brazos de criolla' (14) and her genital region is referred to with terms like 'vegetación' and 'selva' (at one stage 'su vellón casi no animal' [101]). The dangerous beauty and sexuality of the *femme fatale,* which needs to be contained, is thus identified with 'Latin Americanness'. The containment is effected by European discourse. Blanca is like a 'continente vacío' (167), to be filled with European signifiers. Displaying the complicity characteristic of the Foucaultian notion of power, she allows her identity to be remodelled via European fashions and practices and rewritten via the European-style narrator's pastiche of Spanish erotic fiction. However, while Blanca is

moulded by Europe as she is by the narrative, her Latin Americanness is resistant. Even the fragrance of L'Heure Bleue cannot conceal her 'ardiente aroma de criolla' (57). And she vows to hit back at accusations of *cursilería* (96): 'ella, al fin y al cabo, era una bravía hembra del continente nuevo, del que no se avergonzaba pese a que eligiera cubrirlo con un barniz de civilización, barniz que estaba dispuesta a romper en cuanto le conviniera' (74). Part of the marquesita's challenge to narratorial authority, then, is also implicitly a challenging of eurocentrism. Again, if the narrator is implied as European or Europeanist as well as male, then the implied reader will recognise the (implied) author as Latin American. The truth is, though, that Blanca, educated as she is 'tanto por las negras del trópico como por las monjas de España' (13), is both. As is the author, who is as much part of a European and North American cultural tradition as he is of a Latin American one.[24] Indeed the entire Blanca-narrator dialectic and the issues it has raised here draw attention to the deeply intratextual and intertextual construction of the novel. 'You must acknowledge', Donoso has remarked, 'that my novels, especially the last ones, on one level are postmodern and are involved with the confusion of the telling and the told, but on another level, they preserve a sort of sociological and, somehow, political meaning' (Montenegro and Santí, 12-3). Perhaps Donoso manages to achieve this balance—in this work at least, if not necessarily in the more overtly political *Casa de campo*—because the novel neither seeks the inscription of a strong authorial voice as in *La tía Julia y el escribidor* nor particularly seeks to reconcile a clear political agenda with the problematisation of the relationship between literature and reality as in *La cabeza de la hidra.* Oddly enough, *La misteriosa desaparición de la marquesita de Loria* has received very scant critical attention. This is probably because it has been considered frivolous and superficial. Yet it is the very subtlety of the interaction between the surface and what lies behind it that makes this novel one which does manage, without undoing itself, to be European and Latin American, popular and serious, at the same time.

Notes

1. José Donoso, 'Dos mundos americanos', *El Mercurio (Artes y Letras),* 14 Nov. 1982, p. 1.

2. Sharon Magnarelli's impressive work is an obvious example of the application of a theoretical model which brings out similar 'themes' across a variety of differing works. See her *Understanding José Donoso,* University of South Carolina Press, Columbia, 1993. All references to Magnarelli in this chapter will be to her 'Disappearance Under the Cover of Language: The Case of the Marquesita de Loria' in *Studies on the Works of José Donoso,* ed. Miriam Adelstein, Edwin Mellen Press, Lewiston/Queenston/Lampeter, 1990, pp.

101-29. For a discussion of the evolution in Donoso's work from Boom to post-Boom, see, for example, my *José Donoso: The Boom and Beyond*, Francis Cairns, Liverpool and Wolfeboro, 1988.

3. José Donoso, *Casa de campo*, 3rd ed., Seix Barral, Barcelona, 1980, p. 54.

4. José Donoso, *La misteriosa desaparición de la marquesita de Loria*, Seix Barral, Barcelona, 1980, p. 11.

5. Donoso himself describes the novel both as a take-off of Spanish erotic fiction of the 1920s and as a whodunnit in 'A Conversation between José Donoso and Marie-Lise Gazarian Gautier', in *The Creative Process in the Works of José Donoso*, ed. Guillermo I. Castillo-Feliú, Winthrop Studies on Major Modern Writers, Rock Hill, 1982, p. 15.

6. Lucrecio Pérez Blanco, 'Acercamiento a una novela de denuncia social: *La misteriosa desaparición de la marquesita de Loria* de José Donoso', *Revista de Estudios Hispánicos*, XVI, 1982, p. 400.

7. Ricardo Gutiérrez-Mouat, *José Donoso: impostura e impostación*, Hispamérica, Gaithersburg, 1983, p. 252.

8. Rubén Darío, *Poesías completas*, Aguilar, Madrid, 1961, pp. 615-17.

9. Linda Nochlin, *Women, Art, and Power and Other Essays*, Harper and Row, New York, 1988, pp. 29-30.

10. Michel Foucault, 'The Subject and Power', in *Michel Foucault, Beyond Structuralism and Hermeneutics*, eds. Hubert L. Dreyfus and Paul Rabinow, 2nd ed., University of Chicago Press, Chicago, 1983, p. 220.

11. Magnarelli offers a more or less opposite interpretation to the one given here, though her comments on the point of view in each version concur roughly with mine. See pp. 103-4 and pp. 124-5 n. 11.

12. Elaine Showalter, *Sexual Anarchy: Gender and Culture at the Fin-de-Siècle*, Penguin, New York, 1990, pp. 7-8. Showalter quotes Carol Pateman from Susan Aiken *et al.*, 'Trying Transformations: Curriculum Legislation and the Problem of Resistance', *Signs*, XII, 1987, p. 261 and Toril Moi, *Sexual/Textual Politics*, Routledge, London and New York, 1985, p. 167. My comments on the New Woman, the Veiled Woman, Salome and *Dracula* draw on Showalter. The quotation from Oscar Wilde is from Showalter, *Sexual Anarchy*, p. 155.

13. Mary Ann Doane, *Femmes Fatales: Feminism, Film Theory, Psychoanalysis*, Routledge, New York and London, p. 45. The central fear of the disappearance of the phallus becomes a literal reality in Donoso's 'Chatanooga Choochoo' from *Tres novelitas burguesas*, another story inverting traditional notions of sexual power.

14. Hélène Cixous, 'The Laugh of the Medusa', in *New French Feminisms*, ed. Elaine Marks and Isabelle de Courtivron, University of Massachusetts Press, Amherst, 1980, p. 255. Quoted in Showalter, *Sexual Anarchy*, p. 156.

15. Laura Mulvey, 'Visual Pleasure and Narrative Cinema', *Screen*, XVI, 1975, p. 11.

16. The pattern of this epilogue is inverted in an interesting way in Donoso's *El jardín de al lado*, where the narrative of an insecure male author turns out, in the final chapter, to be actually that of his wife. In a remark which may intimate male sexual insecurity, Donoso has commented that: 'Julio (the author character) se transforma en mujer. . . . Él busca una transformación todo el tiempo, quiere ser otro: no se da cuenta de que quiere ser *otra* en el fondo'. See my 'Una entrevista con José Donoso', *Revista Iberoamericana*, LIII, 1987, p. 997.

17. Roland Barthes, *S/Z*, Seuil, Paris, 1970, p. 162.

18. This sort of pattern is discussed in more detail in my 'Structure and Meaning in *La misteriosa desaparición de la marquesita de Loria*', *Bulletin of Hispanic Studies*, LXIII, 1986, pp. 247-56.

19. The quest is both material and sexual in that both are perceived as sources of possible satisfaction and forms of power, but—more fundamentally—the latter depends on the former, since it is wealth and status which allow for unquestioned sexual freedom and adventure.

20. Intriguingly, though, Luna does not appear to be present when Blanca visits Archibaldo's studio.

21. It is a motif of much Donoso fiction that women, servants, the elderly, the poor, blacks or other races are associated with witchcraft or the dark side: in other words, they represent an alternative or threat to the dominant order whose sense of survival depends on the repression of that which it would prefer not to have to deal with.

22. Given that the novel can be seen as a whodunnit, Blanca's 'killer' might well be the narrator. The fact that a shot is heard and a gun is found might, on the other hand, indicate a suicide, reinforcing perhaps the idea of Blanca's agency and choice and her rejection of society. Magnarelli suggests a possible scenario wherein Casilda would be the

killer (p. 126 n. 22), presumably framing Mario—whose prosecution she vigorously pursues (*Marquesita*, p. 194)—for the crime.

23. Amalia Pereira, 'Interview with José Donoso', *Latin American Literary Review,* XV, 1987, p. 58.

24. In a recent interview, Donoso admits also that his generation of writers from Latin America were exploring the 'already-made vocabulary of images' of the European and North American novel of experimentation. See Nivia Montenegro and Enrico Mario Santí, 'A Conversation with José Donoso', *New Novel Review* I, no. 2, 1994, p. 13.

Bibliography of Works Cited

Adelstein, Miriam. ed., *Studies on the Works of José Donoso,* Edwin Mellen Press, Lewiston/Queenston/Lampeter, 1990.

Agosín, Marjorie. 'Isabel Allende: *La casa de los espíritus*', *Revista Interamericana de Bibliografía*', XXXV, 1985, pp. 448-58.

Aiken, Susan Hardy. *et al.,* 'Trying Transformations: Curriculum Legislation and the Problem of Resistance', *Signs,* XII, 1987, pp. 255-75.

Allende, Isabel. *La casa de los espíritus,* 18th ed., Plaza y Janés, Barcelona, 1985.

———. 'La magia de las palabras', *Revista Iberoamericana,* LI, 1985, pp. 447-52.

Alonso, Carlos J. '*La tía Julia y el escribidor:* The Writing Subject's Fantasy of Empowerment', *PMLA,* CVI, 1991, pp. 46-59.

———. *The Spanish American Regional Novel,* Cambridge University Press, Cambridge, 1990.

Alvarez-Borland, Isabel. 'Identidad cíclica de *Tres tristes tigres*', *Revista Iberoamericana,* LVII, 1991, pp. 215-33.

Aneja, Anu. 'The Mystic Aspect of *L' Ecriture Féminine:* Hélène Cixous' *Vivre l'Orange*', *Qui Parle,* III, 1989, pp. 189-209.

Bacarisse, Pamela. *The Necessary Dream: A Study of the Novels of Manuel Puig,* University of Wales Press, Cardiff, 1988.

———. *Impossible Choices: The Implications of the Cultural References in the Novels of Manuel Puig,* University of Wales Press, Cardiff, 1993.

Bakhtin, Mikhail. *Problems of Dostoevsky's Poetics,* Ardis, Ann Arbor, 1973.

———. *Rabelais and His World,* MIT Press, Cambridge, 1968.

Barbosa, Maria José Somerlate. '*A hora da estrela* and the Tangible Reality of Fiction', *Romance Languages Annual,* I, 1989, pp. 379-83.

Barthes, Roland. *Essais critiques,* Seuil, Paris, 1964.

———. *S/Z,* Seuil, Paris, 1970.

Beardsell, Peter R. '*Don Segundo Sombra* and *Machismo*', *Forum for Modern Language Studies,* XVII, 1981, pp. 302-11.

Bell-Villada, Gene H. *García Márquez: The Man and His Work,* University of North Carolina Press, Chapel Hill, 1990.

Berger, John. *Ways of Seeing,* Penguin, London, 1972.

Bernard, Maité. 'Verdad y mentira del escribidor en *La tía Julia y el escribidor* de Mario Vargas Llosa', *Tropos,* XVII, 1991, pp. 33-46.

Bevan, David. ed., *Literature and Revolution,* Rodopi, Amsterdam and Atlanta, 1989.

Beverley, John. *Against Literature,* University of Minnesota Press, Minneapolis and London, 1993.

Boldy, Steven. 'Julio Cortázar: *Rayuela*', in Philip Swanson, ed., *Landmarks in Modern Latin American Fiction,* Routledge, London and New York, 1990, pp. 118-40.

Bordwell, David and Kristin Thompson. *Film Art,* Addison-Wesley Publishing Co., Reading/Menlo Park/London/Amsterdam/Don Mills/Sydney, 1980.

Boschetto, Sandra M. 'Dialéctica metatextual y sexual en *La casa de los espíritus* de Isabel Allende', *Hispania,* LXXII, 1989, pp. 526-32.

Brushwood, John S. 'Sobre el referente y la transformación narrativa en las novelas de Carlos Fuentes y Gustavo Sainz', *Revista Iberoamericana,* XLVII, 1981, pp. 49-54.

Cabrera Infante, Guillermo. *La Habana para un infante difunto,* Seix Barral, Barcelona, 1979.

———. 'The Invisible Exile', in John Glad, ed., *Literature in Exile,* Duke University Press, Durham and London, 1990, pp. 34-40.

———. *Tres tristes tigres,* Seix Barral, Barcelona, 1965.

Cano Gaviria, Ricardo. *El buitre y el ave fénix: conversaciones con Mario Vargas Llosa,* Anagrama, Barcelona, 1972.

Cánovas, Rodrigo. 'Los espíritus literarios y políticos de Isabel Allende', *Revista Chilena de Literatura,* XXXII, 1988, pp. 119-29.

Castillo, Debra. *Talking Back: Toward a Latin American Feminist Criticism,* Cornell University Press, Ithaca and London, 1992.

Castillo-Feliú, Guillermo I. *The Creative Process in the Works of José Donoso,* Winthrop Studies on Major Modern Writers, Rock Hill, 1982.

Castro-Klarén, Sara. *Understanding Mario Vargas Llosa,* University of South Carolina Press, Columbia, 1990.

Cervantes, Miguel de. *Don Quijote de la Mancha,* Juventud, Barcelona, 1971.

Cixous, Hélène. *Reading with Clarice Lispector,* edited, translated and introduced by Verena Andermatt Conley, University of Minnesota Press, Minneapolis and London, 1990.

————. 'The Laugh of the Medusa', in Elaine Marks and Isabelle de Courtivron, eds., *New French Feminisms,* University of Massachusetts Press, Amherst, 1980, pp. 245-64.

Close, A.J. *Miguel de Cervantes: Don Quijote,* Cambridge University Press, Cambridge, 1990.

Cornejo Polar, Antonio. ed., *José Donoso: la destrucción de un mundo,* Fernando García Cambeiro, Buenos Aires, 1975.

Cortínez, Verónica. 'Polifonía: entrevista a Isabel Allende y Antonio Skármeta', *Revista Chilena de Literatura,* XXXII, 1988, pp. 78-89.

Dapaz Strout, Lilia. 'Más allá del principio del placer del texto: Pascal, Puig y la pasión de la escritura: "El misterio de la celda siete"', *Hispanic Journal,* LI, 1983, pp. 87-99.

Darío, Rubén. *Poesías completas,* Aguilar, Madrid, 1961.

Di Antonio, Robert E. *Brazilian Fiction: Aspects and Evolution of the Contemporary Narrative,* University of Arkansas Press, Fayetville and London, 1989.

Doane, Mary Ann. *Femmes Fatales: Feminism, Film Theory, Psychoanalysis,* Routledge, London and New York, 1991.

Donoso, José. *Casa de campo,* 3rd ed., Seix Barral, Barcelona, 1980.

————. 'Dos mundos americanos', *El mercurio (Artes y letras),* 14 Nov. 1982, p. 1.

————. *El jardín de al lado,* Seix Barral, Barcelona, 1981.

————. *El obsceno pájaro de la noche,* 6th ed., Seix Barral, Barcelona, 1979.

————. *Historia personal del 'boom',* Anagrama, Barcelona, 1972.

————. *La misteriosa desaparición de la marquesita de Loria,* Seix Barral, Barcelona, 1980.

Dreyfus, Hubert L. and Paul Rabinow, *Michel Foucault: Beyond Structuralism and Hermeneutics,* 2nd ed., University of Chicago Press, Chicago, 1983.

Duncan, J. Ann. *Voices, Visions and a New Reality: Mexican Fiction Since 1970,* Pittsburgh University Press, Pittsburgh, 1986.

Durán, Gloria. 'The Fuentes Interviews in Fact and in Fiction', *Mester,* XI, 1982, pp. 16-24.

Earle, Peter G. 'Literature as Survival: Allende's *The House of the Spirits*', XXVIII, 1987, pp. 543-54.

Ezquerro, Milagros. *Essai d'analyse de 'El beso de la mujer araña' de Manuel Puig,* Institut d'études hispaniques et hispano-americaines, Université de Toulouse-Le Mirail, Toulouse, 1981.

Faris, Wendy B. *Carlos Fuentes,* Frederick Ungar, New York, 1983.

Fernández Moreno, César. ed., *América latina en su literatura,* Siglo XXI, Mexico, 1972.

Fiddian, Robin. 'A Prospective Post-script: Apropos of *Love in the Times of Cholera*', in Bernard McGuirk and Richard Cardwell, eds., *Gabriel García Márquez: New Readings,* Cambridge University Press, Cambridge, 1987, pp. 191-205.

————. 'Carlos Fuentes: *La muerte de Artemio Cruz*', in Philip Swanson, ed., *Landmarks in Modern Latin American Fiction,* Routledge, London and New York, 1990, pp. 96-117.

Filer, Malva E. 'La ciudad y el tiempo mexicano en la obra de Gustavo Sainz', *Hispamérica,* XIII, 1984, pp. 95-102.

Fitz, Earl E. *Clarice Lispector,* Twayne, Boston, 1985.

Foster, Douglas. 'Isabel Allende Unveiled', *Mother Jones,* XIII, 1988, pp. 42-46.

Foucault, Michel. *Les Mots et les choses,* Gallimard, Paris, 1966.

————. 'The Subject and Power', in Hubert L. Dreyfus and Paul Rabinow, *Michel Foucault: Beyond Structuralism and Hermeneutics,* 2nd ed., University of Chicago Press, Chicago, 1983, pp. 208-26.

Franco, Jean. 'Going Public: Reinhabiting the Private', in George Yúdice, Jean Franco, and Juan Flores, *On Edge: The Crisis of Contemporary Latin American Culture,* University of Minnesota Press, Minneapolis and London, 1992, pp. 65-83.

————. *Spanish American Literature Since Independence,* Ernest Benn, London, 1973.

————. 'The Critique of the Pyramid and Mexican Narrative After 1968', in Rose S. Minc, ed., *Latin American Fiction Today,* Montclair State College and Hispamérica, Takoma Park, n.d., pp. 49-60.

Frye, Northrop. *Anatomy of Criticism,* Penguin, Harmondsworth, 1991.

Fuentes, Carlos. *La cabeza de la hidra,* Argos Vergara, Barcelona, 1979.

———. *La nueva novela hispanoamericana,* Joaquín Mortiz, Mexico, 1969.

———. *Myself with Others,* Picador, London, 1988.

García Márquez, Gabriel. *Cien años de soledad,* 50th ed., Sudamericana, Buenos Aires, 1978.

García Ramos, Juan Manuel. *La narrativa de Manuel Puig (Por una crítica en libertad),* Secretariado de publicaciones de la Universidad de La Laguna, La Laguna, 1982.

García Serrano, M. Victoria. 'Un pre-texto problemático: la advertencia de *Tres tristes tigres*', *Hispanófila,* XXXIV, 1991, pp. 89-92.

Gass, W. H. 'The First Seven Pages of the Boom', *Latin American Literary Review,* XXIX, 1987, pp. 33-56.

Gazarian Gautier, Marie-Lise. 'A Conversation between José Donoso and Marie-Lise Gazarian Gautier', in Guillermo I. Castillo-Feliú, *The Creative Process in the Works of José Donoso,* Winthrop Studies on Major Modern Writers, Rock Hill, 1982, pp. 1-13.

Geisdorfer Feal, Rosemary. *Novel Lives: The Fictional Autobiographies of Guillermo Cabrera Infante and Mario Vargas Llosa,* University of North Carolina Press, Chapel Hill, 1986.

Gerdes, Dick. *Mario Vargas Llosa,* Twayne, Boston, 1985.

Gilkison, Jean. 'The Appropriation of the Conventions of Romance in Isabel Allende's *De amor y de sombra*', paper given at the Association of Hispanists of Great Britain and Ireland, Belfast, 1991.

Glad, John. ed., *Literature in Exile,* Duke University Press, Durham and London, 1990.

Gnutzmann, Rita. *Cómo leer a Mario Vargas Llosa,* Júcar, Madrid, 1992.

González Echevarría, Roberto. *Alejo Carpentier: The Pilgrim at Home,* Cornell University Press, Ithaca and London, 1977.

———. *La ruta de Severo Sarduy,* Ediciones del Norte, Hanover, 1987.

Guibert, Rita. 'Guillermo Cabrera Infante: conversación sobre *Tres tristes tigres*', in Julio Ortega, *et al., Guillermo Cabrera Infante,* Fundamentos, Madrid, 1974, pp. 19-46.

Gutiérrez-Mouat, Ricardo. *José Donoso: impostura e impostación,* Hispamérica, Gaithersburg, 1983.

Gyurko, Lanin A. 'Individual and National Identity in Fuentes' *La cabeza de la hidra*', in Rose S. Minc, ed., *Latin American Fiction Today,* Montclair State College and Hispamérica, Takoma Park, n.d., pp. 33-48.

Hall, Kenneth E. *Guillermo Cabrera Infante and the Cinema,* Juan de la Cuesta, Newark, 1989.

Harper, Ralph. *The World of the Thriller,* The Press of Case Western Reserve University, Cleveland, 1969.

Herrero, Javier. 'Carlos Fuentes y las lecturas modernas del *Quijote*', *Revista Iberoamericana,* XLV, 1979, pp. 555-62.

Janes, Regina. 'No More Interviews', *Salmagundi,* XLIII, 1979, pp. 87-95.

Jones, Ann Rosalind. 'Writing the Body: Toward an Understanding of *L'Ecriture Féminine*', in Elaine Showalter, ed., *The New Feminist Criticism: Essays on Women, Literature and Theory,* Pantheon-Random House, New York, 1985, pp. 361-77.

Jones, Julie. 'The Dynamics of the City: Gustavo Sainz's *La princesa del Palacio de Hierro*', *Chasqui,* XII, 1982, pp. 14-23.

Kafalenos, Emma. 'The Grace and Disgrace of Literature: Carlos Fuentes' *The Hydra Head*', *Latin American Literary Review,* XV, 1987, pp. 141-58.

Kerr, Lucille. *Reclaiming the Author: Figures and Fictions from Spanish America,* Duke University Press, Durham and London, 1992.

———. *Suspended Fictions: Reading Novels by Manuel Puig,* University of Illinois Press, Urbana, 1987.

King, John. ed., *Modern Latin American Fiction,* Faber and Faber, London, 1987.

Koldewyn, Phillip. '*La cabeza de la hidra:* residuous del colonialismo', *Mester,* XI, 1982, pp. 47-56.

Kristeva, Julia. 'La femme, ce n'est jamais ça', *Tel Quel,* LIX, 1974, pp. 19-24.

———. *La Révolution du langage poétique,* Seuil, Paris, 1974.

———. 'Le mot, le dialogue et le roman', in *Semiotiké,* Seuil, Paris, 1969.

Lacan, Jacques. *Ecrits: A Selection,* translated by A. Sheridan and edited by J.-A. Miller, Tavistock, London, 1977.

Leclerc, Annie. *Parole de femme,* Grasset, Paris, 1974.

Levine, Linda, and Jo Anne Engelbert. 'The World Is Full of Stories', *Review,* XXXIV 1980, pp. 18-20.

Lévy, Isaac Jack, and Juan Loveluck. eds., *Simposio Carlos Fuentes: Actas,* University of South Carolina Press, Columbia, n.d.

Lewis, Marvin A. *From Lima to Leticia: The Peruvian Novels of Mario Vargas Llosa,* University Press of America, Lanham and London, 1983.

Lipski, John M. 'Paradigmatic Overlapping in *Tres tristes tigres*', *Dispositio,* I, 1976, pp. 33-43.

Lispector, Clarice. *A hora da estrela,* Francisco Alves, Rio de Janeiro, 1992.

Ludmer, Josefina. '*Tres tristes tigres:* órdenes literarios y jerarquías sociales', *Revista Iberoamericana,* XLV, 1979, pp. 493-512.

Magnarelli, Sharon. 'Disappearance Under the Cover of Language: The Case of the Marquesita de Loria', in Miriam Adelstein, ed., *Studies on the Works of José Donoso,* Edwin Mellen Press, Lewiston/Queenston/Lampeter, 1990, pp. 102-29.

———. 'The Diseases of Love and Discourse: *La tía Julia y el escribidor* and *María*', *Hispanic Review,* LIV, 1986, pp. 195-205.

———. *The Lost Rib: Female Characters in the Spanish-American Novel,* Associated University Presses, London and Toronto, 1985.

———. *Understanding José Donoso,* University of South Carolina Press, Columbia, 1993.

Malcuzynski, M.-Pierrette. '*Tres tristes tigres,* or the Treacherous Play on Carnival', *Ideologies and Literature,* III, 1981, pp. 33-56.

Marks, Elaine and Isabelle de Courtivron. eds., *New French Feminisms,* University of Massachusetts Press, Amherst, 1980.

Martin, Gerald. *Journeys Through the Labyrinth: Latin American Fiction in the Twentieth Century,* Verso, London and New York, 1989.

———. 'Mario Vargas Llosa: Errant Knight of the Liberal Imagination', in John King, ed., *Modern Latin American Fiction,* Faber and Faber, London, 1987, pp. 205-33.

———. 'On "Magical" and Social Realism in García Márquez', in Bernard McGuirk and Richard Cardwell, eds., *Gabriel García Márquez: New Readings,* Cambridge University Press, Cambridge, 1987, pp. 95-116.

———. Review of Philip Swanson, *José Donoso: The 'Boom' and Beyond, Bulletin of Latin American Research,* VIII, 1989, pp. 130-1.

Martín, José Luis. *La narrativa de Vargas Llosa,* Gredos, Madrid, 1974.

Martínez, Z. Nelly. 'José Donoso', *Hispamérica,* XXI, 1978, pp. 53-74.

McCracken, Ellen. 'Vargas Llosa's *La tía Julia y el escribidor:* The New Novel and the Mass Media', *Ideologies and Literature,* III, 1980, pp. 54-69.

McGuirk, Bernard and Richard Cardwell. eds., *Gabriel García Márquez: New Readings,* Cambridge University Press, Cambridge, 1987.

Merrim, Stephanie. 'A Secret Idiom: The Grammar and Role of Language in *Tres tristes tigres*', *Latin American Literary Review,* VIII, 1980, pp. 96-117.

———. 'Through the Film Darkly: Grade "B" Movies and Dreamwork in *Tres tristes tigres* and *El beso de la mujer araña*', *Modern Language Studies,* XV, 1985, pp. 300-12.

———. '*Tres tristes tigres:* antimundo, antilenguaje, antinovela', *Texto crítico,* XI, 1985, pp. 133-52.

Millington, Mark I. 'Voces múltiples en Cabrera Infante', paper given at the Primer Congreso Anglo-Hispano, Huelva, 1992. Subsequently published in Alan Deyermond and Ralph Penny, eds., *Actas del Primer Congreso Anglo-Hispano.* Tomo II: *Literatura.* Castalia, Madrid, 1993, pp. 353-62.

Mimoso-Ruiz, Duarte. 'Aspects des "media" dans *El beso de la mujer araña* de Manuel Puig (1976) et *La tía Julia y el escribidor* de Mario Vargas Llosa (1977)', *Les Langues Néo-latines,* LXXVI, 1982, pp. 29-47.

Minc, Rose S. ed., *Latin American Fiction Today,* Montclair State College and Hispamérica, Takoma Park, n.d.

Minta, Stephen. *Gabriel García Márquez: Writer of Colombia,* Jonathan Cape, London, 1987.

Moi, Toril. ed., *French Feminist Thought: A Reader,* Basil Blackwell, Oxford, 1987.

———. *Sexual/Textual Politics,* Routledge, London and New York, 1990.

Monaco, James. *How to Read a Film,* Oxford University Press, Oxford and New York, 1977.

Montenegro, Nivia and Enrico Mario Santí. 'A Conversation with José Donoso', *New Novel Review,* I, no. 2, 1994, pp. 7-15.

Mora, Gabriela. 'Las novelas de Isabel Allende y el papel de la mujer como ciudadana', *Ideologies and Literature,* II, 1987, pp. 53-61.

Mulvey, Laura. 'Visual Pleasure and Narrative Cinema', *Screen,* XVI, 1975, pp. 6-18.

Muñoz, Elías Miguel. 'La utopía sexual en *El beso de la mujer araña* de Manuel Puig', *Alba de América,* July-December 1984, pp. 49-60.

Nelson, Ardis L. *Cabrera Infante in the Menippean Tradition,* Juan de la Cuesta, Newark, 1983.

———. '*Tres tristes tigres* y el cine', *Kentucky Romance Quarterly,* XXIX, 1982, pp. 391-404.

Nochlin, Linda. *Women, Art, and Power and Other Essays,* Harper and Row, New York, 1988.

Nunes, Benedito. 'Clarice Lispector ou o naufrágio da introspecçao', *Remate de Males,* IX, 1989, pp. 63-70.

Oliveira Filho. Odil José de, 'A voz do narrador em *O beijo da mulher aranha*', *Revista de Letras,* XXIV, 1984, pp. 53-60.

Ortega, Julio. *Poetics of Change: The New Spanish American Narrative,* University of Texas Press, Austin, 1984.

———. *et al., Guillermo Cabrera Infante,* Fundamentos, Madrid, 1974.

Osorio, M. 'Entrevista con Manuel Puig', *Cuadernos para el diálogo,* CCXXXI, 1977, pp. 51-3.

Oviedo, José Miguel. '*La tía Julia y el escribidor,* or the Coded Self-portrait', in Charles Rossman and Alan Warren Friedman, eds., *Mario Vargas Llosa: A Collection of Critical Essays,* University of Texas Press, Austin and London, 1978, pp. 166-81.

Pellón, Gustavo. 'Manuel Puig's Contradictory Strategy: Kitsch Paradigms *versus* Paradigmatic Structure in *El beso de la mujer araña* and *Pubis angelical*', *Symposium,* XXXVII, 1983, pp. 186-201.

Pereira, Amalia. 'Interview with José Donoso', *Latin American Literary Review,* XV, 1987, pp. 57-67.

Pérez Blanco, Lucrecio. 'Acercamiento a una novela de denuncia social: *La misteriosa desaparición de la marquesita de Loria* de José Donoso', *Revista de Estudios Hispánicos,* XVI, 1982, pp. 399-410.

Pérez Galdós, Benito. *Obras completas,* Aguilar, Madrid, 1961.

Pérez Luna, Elizabeth. 'Con Manuel Puig en Nueva York', *Hombre de Mundo,* III, no. 8, 1978, pp. 69-78 and 104-7.

Polo García, Victorino. 'De *Tres tristes tigres* a *La Habana para un infante difunto,* un espejo para el camino', *Revista Iberoamericana,* LVIII, 1992, pp. 557-66.

Promis Ojeda, José. 'La desintegración del orden en la novela de José Donoso', in Antonio Cornejo Polar, ed., *José Donoso: la destrucción de un mundo,* Fernando García Cambeiro, Buenos Aires, 1975, pp. 13-42.

Puig, Manuel. *Bajo un manto de estrellas,* Seix Barral, Barcelona, 1983.

———. *El beso de la mujer araña,* 2nd ed., Seix Barral, Barcelona, 1981.

Purdie, Susan. *Comedy: The Mastery of Discourse,* Harvester Wheatsheaf, Hemel Hempstead, 1993.

Quinlan, Susan Canty. *The Female Voice in Contemporary Brazilian Narrative,* Peter Lang, New York, 1991.

Rama, Angel. *La novela latinoamericana 1920-1980,* Instituto Colombiano de Cultura, Bogotá, 1982.

Reedy, Daniel R. 'Del beso de la mujer araña al de la tía Julia: estructura y dinámica interior', *Revista Iberoamericana,* XLVII, 1981, pp. 109-16.

Ricardou, Jean. *Nouveau problèmes du roman,* Seuil, Paris, 1978.

———. *Pour une théorie du nouveau roman,* Seuil, Paris, 1971.

Riley, E. C. *Don Quixote,* Allen and Unwin, London, 1986.

Rodríguez Monegal, Emir. *El arte de narrar,* Monte Avila, Caracas, n.d.

Rojas, Mario A. '*La casa de los espíritus* de Isabel Allende: un caleidoscopio de espejos desordenados', *Revista Iberoamericana,* LI, 1985, pp. 917-25.

Rossman, Charles and Alan Warren Friedman, eds., *Mario Vargas Llosa: A Collection of Critical Essays,* University of Texas Press, Austin and London, 1978.

Rowe, William. 'Liberalism and Authority: The Case of Mario Vargas Llosa', in George Yúdice, Jean Franco, and Juan Flores, *On Edge: The Crisis of Contemporary Latin American Culture,* University of Minnesota Press, Minneapolis and London, 1992, pp. 45-64.

———, and Vivian Schelling. *Memory and Modernity: Popular Culture in Latin America,* Verso, London and New York, 1991.

Sagarzazu, María Elvira. 'New Concerns for the Novel: A Latin American Viewpoint', in David Bevan, ed., *Literature and Revolution,* Rodopi, Amsterdam and Atlanta, 1989, pp. 163-9.

Sainz, Gustavo. *La princesa del Palacio de Hierro,* Océano, Mexico, 1982.

Sarduy, Severo. 'El barroco y el neobarroco', in César Fernández Moreno, ed., *América latina en su literatura,* Siglo XXI, Mexico, 1972, pp. 167-84.

———. 'Notas a las notas a las notas . . . a propósito de Manuel Puig', *Revista Iberoamericana,* XXXVII, 1971, pp. 555-67.

Shaw, D. L. 'Concerning the Interpretation of *Cien años de soledad*', *Ibero-Amerikanisches Archiv,* III, 1977, pp. 318-29.

———. *Nueva narrativa hispanoamericana,* Cátedra, Madrid, 1981.

———. Review of John King, ed., *Modern Latin American Fiction, Modern Language Review,* LXXXIV, 1989, p. 510.

———. 'Towards a Description of the Post-Boom', *Bulletin of Hispanic Studies,* LXVII, 1989, pp. 87-94.

Showalter, Elaine. *Sexual Anarchy: Gender and Culture at the Fin-de-siècle,* Penguin, New York, 1990.

————. ed., *The New Feminist Criticism: Essays on Women, Literature and Theory,* Pantheon-Random House, New York, 1985.

Siemens, William L. 'Guillermo Cabrera Infante and the Divergence of Revolutions: Political versus Textual', in David Bevan, ed., *Literature and Revolution,* Rodopi, Amsterdam and Atlanta, 1989, pp. 107-19.

————. *Worlds Reborn: The Hero in the Modern Spanish American Novel,* West Virginia University Press, Morgantown, 1984.

Smith, Paul Julian. *The Body Hispanic,* Oxford University Press, Oxford, 1989.

Smyth, Edmund J. ed., *Postmodernism and Contemporary Fiction,* Batsford, London, 1991.

Souza, Raymond D. *Major Cuban Novelists: Innovation and Tradition,* University of Missouri Press, Columbia and London, 1976.

Strassfield, Michael. *The Jewish Holidays,* Harper and Row, New York, 1985.

Swanson, Philip. *Cómo leer a Gabriel García Márquez,* Júcar, Madrid, 1991.

————. *Jose Donoso: The 'Boom' and Beyond,* Francis Cairns, Liverpool and Wolfeboro, 1988.

————. ed., *Landmarks in Modern Latin American Fiction,* Routledge, London and New York, 1990.

————. 'Structure and Meaning in *La misteriosa desaparición de la marquesita de Loria*', *Bulletin of Hispanic Studies,* LXIII, 1986, pp. 247-56.

————. 'Una entrevista con José Donoso', *Revista Iberoamericana,* 53, 1987, pp. 995-8.

Tittler, Jonathan. 'Carlos Fuentes', *Diacritics,* September 1980, pp. 46-56.

Vargas Llosa, Mario. *La tía Julia y el escribidor,* Seix Barral, Barcelona, 1977.

Vieira, Nelson H. 'A expressão judaica na obra de Clarice Lispector', *Remate de Males,* IX, 1989, pp. 207-9.

Waugh, Patricia. *Metafiction,* Routledge, London and New York, 1984.

Williams, Raymond L. 'The Reader and the Recent Novels of Gustavo Sainz', *Hispania,* LXV, 1982, pp. 383-7.

Williamson, Edwin. 'Magical Realism and the Theme of Incest in *One Hundred Years of Solitude*', in Bernard McGuirk and Richard Cardwell, eds., *Gabriel García Márquez: New Readings,* Cambridge University Press, Cambridge, 1987, pp. 45-63.

Wilson, Jason. 'Guillermo Cabrera Infante: An Interview in a Summer Manner with Jason Wilson', in John King, ed., *Modern Latin American Fiction,* Faber and Faber, London, 1987, pp. 305-25.

Yúdice, George. '¿Puede hablarse de postmodernidad en América Latina?', *Revista de Crítica Literaria Latinoamericana,* XXIX, 1989, pp. 105-28.

————. Jean Franco, and Juan Flores, eds., *On Edge: The Crisis of Contemporary Latin American Culture,* University of Minnesota Press, Minneapolis and London, 1992.

Janet Pérez (essay date January 1997)

SOURCE: Pérez, Janet. "Masks, Gender Expectations, Machismo and (Criss) Cross-Gender Writing in the Fiction of José Donoso." *Hispanófila* 119 (January 1997): 47-58.

[*In the following essay, Pérez analyzes the way Donoso critiques gender stereotyping and the cult of machismo by using cross-gender themes and symbols in his writing.*]

Criticism of Donoso to date has tended to categorize his works as social realism or even neo-naturalism during an early period up to the late 1960s and publication of *El obsceno pájaro de la noche,* [hereafter abbreviated *EOPN*] and as experimental thereafter. Those novels published after *EOPN*—a work so fragmented, contradictory, multivocal and multivalent as to defy most efforts at interpretation—have been comparably traditional in format and structure, so that views of Donoso as a social realist have not entirely disappeared, even though freudian, jungian and neo-freudian interpretations are also common and some structuralist and deconstructionist readings have appeared. Donoso in fact is neither as simplistic as early readings of his works of the 1950s and 1960s suggest, nor as impossibly obscure and unintelligible as some reactions to *EOPN* indicate. As Sharon Magnarelli points out, his "fiction invites, indeed exacts . . . disparate and multivocal readings. [It] can never be read simplistically" (3).

Among the oft-mentioned aspects of Donoso's writing are his treatment of the decadence of the Chilean bourgeoisie,[1] the crumbling of feudal structures and the "decay of an oligarchy."[2] The presence of numerous contradictions, use of multiple layers of reality and meaning, unstable identities and gender roles, consistent use of masks, role-playing and role reversal, and depiction of identity crises render his characters complex, even in the early works. Many commentators focus upon sexual problems,[3] highly visible in Donoso's fiction. But his work has not been read specifically from the perspective of the interface between social and sexual expectations, gender roles and models, employing the filter of *machismo* as a cultural gender imposition. Such an approach would be compatible with extant critical commentary on Donoso, and has the potential of identifying common ground between earlier approaches, a point of contact or intersection between social, historical, sociological, cultural, sociopolitical, economic, psychological, freudian and jungian readings and interpretations based on recent critical theory (structural, semiotic, deconstructionist, etc.).

Numerous Donoso characters lend themselves to readings as subversions of the *macho* stereotype, and consideration of gender roles is a basic prerequisite to understanding his depiction of Chilean society. While extended families in Chile are ostensibly ruled by patriarchs, reality within the home frequently approaches the matriarchal model, with the mother or nanny governing the child's existence and often holding the home together. Such, indeed, was the experience of Donoso's formative years, with a distant and unreliable father replaced by various elderly maternal relatives, possibly inspiring the powerful, witchlike females in his fiction. Small wonder, then, that ideal, intact families are seldom found in Donoso's work, and men "are frequently portrayed as weak, ineffectual and pathetic. When, on rare occasions, the text depicts an ostensibly strong, powerful man, that power is undercut by females" (Magnarelli 8). A repeated type is the male who has been emasculated or rendered impotent by a powerful mother figure (e.g., Andrés in *Coronación,* Álvaro in *Este domingo*). Elsewhere, exaggeratedly "masculine" behavior conceals self-doubt or masks latent homosexuality (Pancho in *El lugar sin límites,* Mario in *Coronación*).

This study examines passages relevant to Donoso's subversion of *machismo* and similar normative gender types, analyzing his peculiar use of cross-gender writing which incorporates the layering technique characteristic of other aspects of his fiction. Donoso does not simply, as a male writer, adopt the feminine gender perspective, role and attributes to write from the viewpoint of a female character, but sometimes adds other layers of reality or masquerade, for example, adopting the perspective of an ostensible female who ultimately proves to be a male homosexual and transvestite (in *El lugar sin límites*) or employing the putative masculine perspective of a character, supposedly the husband and narrator-protagonist, who is subsequently revealed not as "himself" but as the wife, who has adopted or usurped the husband's identity and point of view, making him a character—the narrator-protagonist—in *her* novel (*El jardín de al lado*). Given such added complexities, Donoso's technique might be termed "criss-cross gender writing" to distinguish it from more straightforward approaches.

Examining gender roles and expectations in relation to certain major motifs of Donoso's fiction, such as the mask, can illuminate prior interpretation and open additional avenues of meaning. The mask or disguise sometimes appears when characters are too repressed or insecure to reveal their true selves. The novelist himself calls attention to his use of disguise and the significance in his work of impersonation:

> ¿Por qué me interesan tanto los disfraces? ¿Por qué me interesan los travesti (sic)? ¿Por qué me interesa en *Coronación* la locura de la señora? ¿Por qué en *Este domingo* los disfraces tienen un lugar tan importante? Es porque éstas son maneras de deshacer la unidad del ser humano. Deshacer la unidad psicológica, ese mito horrible que nos hemos inventado.
>
> (Quoted by Rodríguez Monegal 525)

Such devices function equally well to subvert stereotypes, which obviously form part of what Donoso terms the horrible myth of psychological unity; indeed, a premise of unity and similarity underlies stereotyping per se. And sexual or gender stereotypes are among the most basic and widespread. Masks, costumes, cross-dressing, disguises and games, instances of identity and/or gender exchange, role reversals, and varying degress of failure to conform to or live up to stereotypical expectations are among techniques employed by Donoso which function to subvert antiquated, outmoded or unrealistic class and gender paradigms. Cross-gender writing, while not necessarily subversive, may be used effectively to parody or undermine.

Magnarelli points out that the motif of the mask sometimes "reveals itself in a form of transvestism . . . wearing the clothing of the opposite sex [as in *El lugar sin límites*] . . . but at other times, it is an interchangeability of characters when one places himself in the clothes and thus the social position of the other" (5). Identity transfer is carried to extremes of the absurd when characters exchange not only clothing and names but body parts, as in *El obsceno pájaro* and **"Chatanooga Choo-choo,"** both featuring detachable, reusable sexual organs and other parts of the body. Donoso's writings of the 1970s and 1980s, his exile fiction, abound in "homosexuality, schizophrenia, sterility, absence, estrangement, the double and role reversal" (Pérez 36) which may indeed be metaphors of exilic experience,[4] but also represent alternatives to assuming stereotyped gender roles, alternatives implying rejection, which provide other perspectives from which to view traditional, patriarchally-sanctioned gender models. Much like the fluid, Protean, changing identities in *EOPN,* the fragmented or multivocal "yo" undermines narrative reliability through its very multiplicity which Cirlot states is reductive and degrading.

Oscar Montero sees Donoso as deliberately trying to undermine the authority of the text, a patriarchal authority based upon traditional hierarchies of discourse. Clearly, efforts at such subversion would be in harmony with subversion of gender stereotypes, social class limitations, and patriarchally prescribed roles, and would probably have similar origins. Gutiérrez Mouat examines the ludic and carnivalesque aspects of Donoso's fiction, noting that play (juego) is typically juvenile and solitary, carnival adult and collective (25). Carnival, obviously, reinforces mask motifs and vice versa. Citing Bakhtin to the effect that the carnival is "funcional, no sustantivo" (27), Gutiérrez Mouat argues that it is an adjectival phenomenon whose function is to modify what convention has defined as stable or fixed (a category implicitly subsuming stereotypes). Bakhtin holds that "carnival celebrates change itself"—pure metamorphosis—but most readers of Donoso will agree that his ends are less celebratory and more serious, involving existential, ontological and social aims. The carnival function in Donoso, given its linkages to masks and to the the key theme of (multiplicity of) identity, underscored by the writer himself, probably transcends the "adjectival."

Aspects of Donoso's fiction lend themselves to a feminist reading, especially in the subversion of patriarchal norms and restrictions, undermining or reversing expectations of *machista* behavior, and the enclosure and perjorative treatment of women. Inversion, parody and deformation are seen by Bakhtin as carnivalesque techniques, and all are frequently used by Donoso to subversive ends. Gutiérrez Mouat maintains that "la temática de Donoso parte de una concepción del yo . . . como máscara, como protagonista de un rol, como personaje de un guión" (31), a concept rendering it logical to use techniques such as cross-gender writing (or criss-crossing), and motifs of replaceable identities and interchangeable body parts, much like changing the mask. This critic asserts that Donoso's view of society and social interaction is "como juego de actores cuyos roles están inscritos en un 'guión' social generalizado, cognoscible y transmitible" (33). The notion of the generalized, transmitted script recalls the *commedia dell'arte* with its stereotypical figures and unwritten but mutually understood scripts. Just as the *commedia dell'arte* masks or figures acquired easily recognizable characteristics (making their identities transferrable, interchangeable among members of a troupe), so also do such gender types as the *macho:* the word evokes mental images almost as concrete as do the names of Harlequin or Polichinella.

Interestingly, many of Donoso's works take place in houses—domestic, feminized spaces as opposed to the "man's world" (business, politics, professions and public spaces).[5] Indeed, the huge, rambling, labyrinthine, crumbling house is paradigmatic in his fiction, with its physical decay and decadence constituting a visible, Expressionistic symbol of the moral decay of those within, as seen in **Coronación, Este domingo,** and **Casa de campo,** as well as with the collapse of the convent "Casa de la Encarnación de la Chimba" in **EOPN.** Such humanized, decaying or declining houses are Donoso's hallmarks, as distinctive and recognizable as his neurotic, disguised, aberrant characters.

Among the most ludic and carnivalesque of all of Donoso's fiction is **Casa de campo.** The elaborate episodes of the cousins' stylized performances of "La Marquesa Salió a Las Cinco" constitute both an escape from adult control and a preparation for adult roles (cf. 95), allowing the novelist to satirize gender expectations, e.g., "la obligación número uno—si no la única—de las mujeres era justamente ser bonita" (96). A feminist could hardly have said it better! One grotesquely Expressionistic episode which clearly subverts gender expectations involves the "make-believe" housewifery in imitation of an earlier feast of roast pig shared by men of the family, whereby Mignon prepares a meal for her father, roasting her little sister Aída as a *cochinito* with an apple stuffed in her mouth. Upon viewing the ghastly repast, the father beats Mignon to a bloody, lifeless pulp with a log of firewood (85-87).

Another feminine role expectation or patriarchal norm subverted is the view of women as destined irrevocably to an unending child-bearing function: "Mauro solía tenderse sobre el cuerpo de Melania en un ruboroso simulacro del amor, un episodio más de La Marquesa Salió a Las Cinco, y debajo de la cama salía chillando una bandada de pequeñuelos desnudos participando en la parodia de un multitudinario alumbramiento" (150). By contrast, an episode between three male cousins involves a moralizing lecture by the homosexual Juvenal when he visits the bedroom and finds two younger boys masturbating: "cuidado: de esto que han estado haciendo a ser maricones que se disfrazan de marquesas y entornan los ojos al tocar el piano, como yo, hay un solo paso" (155). Neither these edifying thoughts nor Juvenal's pride in his "difference" as the only *maricón* among the thirty-three cousins prevent his climbing into bed with the younger boys and furthering their delinquency.

Not only sexual stereotypes and gender expectations but social distances are satirized, as the cousins play at lackeys and *mayordomos,* lords and ladies. The ritualistic, artificial nature of social intercourse is summarized in the codified hypocrisy of family laws: "el primer mandamiento era que jamás nadie debía enfrentarse con nada, que la vida era pura alusión y ritual y símbolo" (182); logically, reality is avoided and disguised: "se podía hacer todo, sentirlo todo, desearlo todo, aceptarlo todo, siempre que no se nombrara" (182). This clear allusion to the power of appearances and *el qué dirán,* the notion that what matters socially is not reality but what people think, occurs repeatedly throughout Donoso's work, explaining why masks and disguises acquire such visibility and significance. *Machismo* and gender stereotypes, as masks, when subverted or removed from the scene, permit manifestation of underlying authenticity or reality.

One may subvert stereotypes directly, portraying them in circumstances which make visible their limitations or shortcomings, via ridicule, parody or travesty. But one may also subvert indirectly, substituting other models, an approach which has the effect of suggesting alternatives or insinuating that the stereotype is not fully pervasive. Attaching positive attributes to alternative types functions to strengthen this latter approach. Both models appear in Donoso's fiction. Andrés, the wealthy bachelor in **Coronación** (a logical candidate for a *macho* or Don Juan) instead is depicted as bored, compulsive, repressed, a fearful introvert. Mario, his young lower-class rival for the favors of Estela, encarnates the archetypal *macho,* but his bullying behavior also underscores the shortcomings of the paradigm: ready to exploit Estela and her love by making her his accomplice in theft, he beats and insults her after her eleventh-hour decision not to be his partner in crime. In **Este domingo,** retired barrister and law professor Álvaro Vives is remembered by his grandson not as the womanizer he believes himself to be, but as an absurd, obsessive, self-centered, spoiled, immature hypochondriac. Álvaro, an archetypal male chauvinist, voices the most negative *machista* attitudes; for example, he scornfully refers to his wife's charitable, nurturing, caregiving personality by comparing her to a bitch nursing pups (22, 25, 28, 68), perhaps out of resentment at not being the focus of her attention. Taking social inequities for granted, Álvaro abuses master-servant relationships, impregnating the family maid and rationalizing that servants' role in life is to accept the master's sexual advances. Too irresponsible to acknowledge his paternity of Violeta's child, he is unable to function sexually with his social equals, i.e., without feeling superior: he manages to make love to his wife only by imagining her to be a servant. Obsessed with eroticism, he has repeated affairs, one resulting in the woman's suicide, but proves essentially impotent with women who are sexually demanding rather than maternal, subservient and submissive. Donoso's exploration of Álvaro's neuroses and fetishism, his egocentrism and inability to accept responsibility underscores the abyss between appearance and reality, between the mask of *machismo* and the insecure, spoiled, aging adolescent concealed beneath.

One of Donoso's most interesting characters and his most extensive early use of cross-gender writing appear in **El lugar sin límites** (1966). Manuel/a, a fiftyish transvestite, a male homosexual with a feminine psyche, refers to him/herself via feminine adjectives in interior monologues which for some fifty pages appear to convey a woman's thoughts. Only later does it become evident that beneath the red flamenco dancer's dress, Manuel/a possesses male genitalia, and is in fact Japo-

nesita's biological father. Pancho Vega, the local bully super-*macho* and would-be don Juan, abuses and beats Manuel/a, leaving "her" for dead, but his sadistic attack is clearly sexual, a cruel, violent possessing which reveals Pancho's repressed homosexuality, cowardice and insecurity. Pancho's visible emblem, the phallic red truck, fails to assure his masculinity despite his noisy horn-blowing and careening about the village, and his partial demonstration of self-sufficiency and power, achieved by repaying his loan to the patriarch don Alejo, does not restore his full *machista* prestige, already violated and diminished by don Alejo's public scoldings and Octavio's taunts. Beneath his mask, this blustering bully remains insecure, doubt-filled, his gender identity the victim of arrested development (as Donoso suggests by Pancho's lacking a father and the years the boy was forced to spend as the playmate of Alejo's daughter. In this, he incorporates the freudian psychoanalytic model of male homosexuality whose central thesis is that the condition is "caused by a disturbed upbringing and developmental arrest").[6] Magnarelli concludes that "Pancho's gratuitous and exaggeratedly 'macho' violence toward Manuela is fraught with eroticism" (69) and "his treatment of Manuela is certainly a form of rape" (70). By contrast, Manuel/a thinks as a woman, realizing or acknowledging maleness, only when pain from the beating forces the admission. While biologically male, Manuel/a has assumed the feminine gender identity to the point of feeling superior to biological females (Japonesita and the prostitutes), fantasizing that "she" can show them what a *real* woman is (LSL 111). Cross-gender writing in this case surrenders its mask once Manuel/a's gender is revealed, although the character persistently clings to the feminine identity long after the reader knows that this psychic entity is biologically male. Only briefly and nearly at the end does s/he revert to masculine adjectives, upon realization in final moments of lucidity that not being biologically female could prove fatal. In subsequent novels, Donoso uses his growing expertise in more recent liberal psychology to foreground the extent to which gender identity and roles may be masks.

In **El obsceno pájaro de la noche,** infertility becomes a metaphor subverting *machismo*. Don Jerónimo incorporates both class and gender stereotypes: patriarch par excellence, noble landowner and handsome, desirable male, representing power, aristocratic privilege, and the abuses thereof. Jerónimo and his wife Inés fail for years to conceive a son, finally engendered during a magical copulation involving identity substitutions. In the several variations of this hallucinatory event, the primal pair Jerónimo-Inés is repeatedly replaced and successively re-composed of Humberto and Inés; Humberto and the old servant Peta Ponce; Jerónimo and Peta Ponce (thereby subverting myths of race as well as class and identity). Each time, there are suggestions that the old servant possesses witchlike powers, that hers may be the real and ultimate authority. Regardless of progenitors, the monstrous offspring "Boy" (who has neither boyhood nor boyish appearance) encarnates negative visions of hereditary aristocracy, of which he is the anachronistic continuation.

Protagonist-narrator, Humberto, a "counterhero" in Barthes' terminology, lives in a fantasy world populated by obsessive fears, the phantoms of his frustrated desires, a universe of ongoing psychic deterioration only exacerbated by his occasional contacts with those in the external world, especially Jerónimo, who has repeatedly affirmed his own *machismo* or phallic power via symbolic castration of Humberto, his erstwhile secretary. Humberto's attempts to climb the social ladder (fulfilling his father's wishes and affirming his own identity), force him to seek Jerónimo's aid to publish his book—the tangible manifestation of his identity, subsequently appropriated by his employer and locked away. Humberto is similarly "robbed" of his heroism and near-martyrdom when wounded in a political skirmish as Jerónimo attributes Humberto's blood to himself. Finally, he suffers various operations, organ transplants, implants, and castration by Jerónimo's evil surgeon in La Rinconada. In sequences reminiscent of Nazi experiments, 80% of his body parts are replaced with monster parts. While no commentators of this novel have managed to discern where reality ends and Humberto's imagination or hallucinations begin, Donoso implies that some part of the atmosphere of floating paranoia comes as a reaction to Jerónimo's own insecurity and irrational fear of being cuckolded. For Enrique Luengo, *EOPN* "es una búsqueda por resolver el enigma de la identidad personal . . . penetra en la complejidad síquica de una mente extraviada que vive un proceso imaginativo exacerbado." In various ways, Humberto's plight results from paternal desire and gender expectations—i.e., that he succeed economically and socially—which exceed his capabilities. Not only are such expectations unrealistic given the rigid social structure of Chile, but they do not allow for variations in individual potential. For Humberto, schizophrenia is the result. Donoso explores other negative results of demands imposed by gender stereotypes and models in *El jardín de al lado*.

"Chatanooga Choo-choo" (*Tres novelitas burguesas*), set among the haute bourgeoisie of contemporary Barcelona, features two couples, Ramón and Sylvia, Magdalena and Anselmo. Initially, the identically-dressed women perform a song-and-dance routine; at story's end a week later, this skit is repeated by the identically-attired men, obviously suggesting some kind of gender-role reversal. A critique of easy sexuality, drugs and materialism, the story presents Sylvia as a mannequin, a mirror of masculine desire, a decorative object whose features can be erased at will and re-painted to please the man of the moment. Not only does this story employ exaggeration and fantasy to subvert the *machista* concept of woman as sex object, but it ultimately turns the tables. Anselmo, during a brief affair with Sylvia, paints and erases her face; she then appropriates his penis, but not until after having first shown his wife Magdalena how to disassemble him. In both cases, character identity—including gender role identity—depends upon the Other. Anselmo, the initial narrator and self-proclaimed voice of power and authority, leads readers to several erroneous perceptions, which are blamed upon the visibly castrating female. Later, a more nearly omniscient narrator replaces Anselmo and gives a different version. Not only does Donoso subvert *machismo* via real or imagined castration, but he also questions the phallocentric authority of the text by offering competing versions.

El jardín de al lado (1981), one of Donoso's most sustained exercises in [criss]cross-gender writing, centers upon Julio Méndez and his wife Gloria, impoverished Chilean exiles living in Spain, who accept the chance to spend the summer (circa 1980) in a luxurious Madrid flat in exchange for caring for a Chilean painter's dog and Siamese cat. Méndez, a former English professor jailed for a week during the recent revolutionary coup, was so terrified by his imprisonment that he fled to Spain upon release. Factors undermining his already shaky *machismo* include realization of his cowardice, inability to find work, and rejection of his novel of imprisonment, all of which contribute to a subsequent identity crisis. The stagnating marriage, obsession with his dead father and moribund mother, and unsuccessful struggles to overcome his fear enough to visit his dying mother's bedside occupy Julio more than the work of revising his novel. He and Gloria use alcohol to get through the days and drugs to make it through the nights. Depressed at Julio's criticisms (due to her not bringing in money), Gloria hysterically rejects Méndez: "grita y me quiere arañar, chillando que soy el culpable de su vida destrozada, de su incapacidad para enfrentar cualquier lucha, incluso cualquier acción o proyecto porque yo la he devorado" (201). Carlos, her psychotherapist, speaks for Donoso when he places the blame in the broad context of gender and culture: "como el fracaso de algo mayor, de una educación, de una clase, de un mundo, de un momento en la historia" (202). Significantly, however, he does not exculpate the husband: "—Tal vez algo de culpa tendrás—sugiere Carlos.—No sé, no creo . . ." (ibid). Informing Julio's inability to accept, even theoretically, some portion of responsibility, some chance that Gloria may be right, is the traditional patriarchal concept of women as hysterical and intellectually inferior.

Gloria's apparent failed suicide attempt, coinciding with Julio's mother's death and severance of his last roots in Chile, provides the stimulus for completing the revisions and resubmitting his novel. Unable to confess his failure upon receiving a second rejection, Julio informs Gloria the novel has been accepted and proposes a visit to their son in Marrakesh. Purloining one of their host's paintings, he sells it to a dealer. Returning to Gloria with money and plane tickets, he is momentarily transformed: "Me acerco: el falso triunfador, el macho falsificado" (231); for the first time in many months, he makes love to his wife, whereby Donoso subtly underscores the interdependency between *machismo* and the appearance of success or power. Julio's crime, their trip which resembles flight more than a vacation, and filial guilt at having refused his mother's dying wish, combine to produce an acute identity crisis in Tangiers. Flight and denial or avoidance having been his solutions before, Julio opts for switching identities with a beggar, a barely-conscious addict. The night he decides upon this symbolically suicidal identity switch, he leaves the hotel on the pretext of a brief errand.

Up to this point, Julio has ostensibly narrated events, but an unexpected change of narrator/narrative perspective in the final part reveals that the entire narrative is a novel written by Gloria who has done her own cross-gender writing by adopting Julio's identity, gender, perspective and profession or avocation. Gloria's novel is accepted by the same publisher who twice rejected Julio's. At the same time that Gloria emerges as a woman unknown to her husband despite a quarter-century of matrimony, Donoso shows the exiled writer reverting to a non-entity, his *machismo* eroded, his hopes as a writer dashed, his role as speaking voice supplanted by that of his wife. Actually, Julio proves unable to stand the rigors accompanying his new [non-]identity and returns to his wife the next day. Months later, Gloria recalls that when she overheard the phone call rejecting Julio's novel,

> mezclado con mi compasión y mi dolor, sentí . . . un componente de vengativa alegría ante su fracaso, el fracaso del macho de la familia, cuyo deber es el triunfo que saca a los suyos de la pobreza . . . misión ante la sociedad que ambos despreciamos en su contenido actual, pero de cuya forma todavía dependemos. Fue esta derrota final de Julio lo que más me ayudó a salir de mi depresión; necesitaba verlo menos fuerte.
>
> (255-56)

Gloria's resentment of Julio as the *macho* who has failed in his duty is exacerbated by her long-time resentment against her father who forced her into the Procrustean bed of an unwanted gender role, and this latent anger is momentarily transferred to Julio as well: "¿No estaba expiando Julio con su fracaso la culpa de mi padre, que me sacó de cuarto año de las monjas a los catorce años, yo, la primera de la clase, que soñaba con ser médico?" (256). Gloria envied Julio's educational opportunity, which both she and Donoso suggest that she might have used better. Ignoring their intelligence, her father condemns Gloria and her equally bright sisters to boring conventional marriages and "vidas con-

sumistas" instead of giving their intellects a chance to develop and allowing them to become productive members of society. His patriarchal tyranny not only deprived the girls of any right of career choice, but was short-sighted in a rapidly-changing world where it suddenly became necessary for Gloria to contribute to the family income. Gloria's literary success, enabling the couple to establish a home in exile, provides the respite necessary for Julio to find a teaching job. These details form the essential ingredients of Donoso's critique of the failures and wasted potential that result from gender stereotyping. As have various recent feminist writers as well, he shows that not only do such reactionary gender-role impositions deny education and equal opportunity to talented women, but also impose expectations of success or triumph upon men, which many cannot meet. Rather than blame individuals, Donoso targets the norms, the cultural expectations and gender stereotypes which deny women their self-realization, and still judge men—including those that heredity and socialization have predisposed to be Milquetoasts—by the Procrustean standard of *machismo*.

Notes

1. For example, Antonio Cornejo Polar, "*El obsceno pájaro de la noche:* la reversibilidad de la metáfora," in *José Donoso: La destrucción de un mundo* (Buenos Aires: Editorial Fernando García Cambeiro, 1975). See especially page 110.

2. Charles M. Tatum, "*El obsceno pájaro de la noche:* The Demise of a Feudal Society," *Latin American Literary Review* 1, 2 (Spring 1973) 99-105.

3. Silvia Martínez D'Acosta, *Dos ensayos literarios: Barrios y Donoso* (Miami: Ediciones Universal, 1976) suggests that Humberto [in *El obsceno pájaro*] experiences homosexual attraction toward don Jerónimo, the suppression/repression of which leads to paranoia. Hernán Vidal, *José Donoso: Surrealismo y rebelión de los instintos* (Gerona: Ediciones Aubi, 1972) uses Jungian theory to analyze Humberto's schizophrenic behavior as a result of alienation from society and inability to gain access to the upper class, wealth and power desired. George McMurray, *José Donoso* (Boston: Twayne Publishers, 1979) also bases his analysis on the mental state of the protagonist.

4. Janet Pérez, "Paradigms of Exile in Donoso's Spanish Fiction," *The Literature of Emigration and Exile,* eds. James Whitlark and Wendell Aycock (Lubbock: Texas Tech University Press, 1992) 33-42. I have argued in this essay that such identity problems are emblematic of exilic alienation, but are simultaneously intertwined with gender role and gender identity issues, often subverting the stereotype.

5. While the present study was in press, I examined Flora González Mandri, *José Donoso's House of Fiction* (Detroit: Wayne State University Press, 1995), subtitled "A Dramatic Construction of Time and Place." This critic examines Donoso's work in the context of "melodrama" and the house as "the scene for its theatrical deployment," according to Carlos J. Alonso (cited on cover). I would concur that space, for Donoso, is much more important than my essay has been able to recognize, given the specificity of its focus. González Mandri's Chapter 5, "The Androgynous Narrator in *El jardín de al lado*," treats some relevant issues such as transformations and "writing disguises," but does not directly address cross-gender writing strategies.

6. For explanation of this concept see Robert M. Friedman, "The Psychoanalytic Model of Male Homosexuality: A Historical and Theoretical Critique" in *Toward a New Psychology of Men. Psychoanalytic and Social Perspectives*. Edited by Robert M. Friedman and Leila Lerner. New York: The Guilford Press, 1986. 79-116.

Works Cited

Bakhtine, Mikhail. *Problems of Dostoyevsky's Poetics*. Trans. R. W. Rotsel. Michigan: Ardis, 1973.

Barthes, Roland. *The Pleasure of the Text*. Trans. Richard Miller. New York: Hill and Wang, 1984.

Cirlot, Juan Eduardo. *A Dictionary of Symbols*. Trans. Jack Sage. New York: The Philosophical Library, 1962.

Donoso, José. *Casa de campo*. Barcelona: Seix Barral, 1978.

———. *El jardín de al lado*. Barcelona: Seix Barral, 1981.

———. *Tres novelitas burguesas*. Barcelona: Seix Barral, 1973.

González Mandri, Flora. *José Donoso's House of Fiction*. Detroit: Wayne State University Press, 1995.

Gutiérrez Mouat, Ricardo. *José Donoso: Impostura e impostación*. Gaithersburg, MD: Hispamerica, 1983.

Luengo, Enrique. *José Donoso: Desde el texto al metatexto*. Concepción: Editora Aníbal Pinto, 1992.

Magnarelli, Sharon. *Understanding José Donoso*. Columbia: U of South Carolina P, 1993.

Montero, Oscar. "Donoso by Donoso: An Introduction to the Writer's Notebooks." Unpublished paper cited by Gutiérrez Mouat, 12.

Rodríguez Monegal, Emir. "José Donoso: La novela como Happening." *Revista Iberoamericana* 76-77 (July-December 1971). 525.

Mary Lusky Friedman (essay date summer 1999)

SOURCE: Friedman, Mary Lusky. "The Genesis of *La desesperanza* by José Donoso." *Studies in Twentieth Century Literature* 23, no. 2 (summer 1999): 255-74.

[*In the following essay, Friedman examines the working notes for* La desesperanza *and concludes that the novel evolved from Donoso's preoccupation with the ambivalence between parents and children and the possibility of identity transformed.*]

These days a special apology must be made for studying the process by which a writer makes a literary text. So politically incorrect has it become to consider a writer's intentions that some critics nowadays not only look askance at a writer's diaries and notes but even sidestep the term "work," which alludes to the creation of literature by a particular human being. What amounts to postmodern prudishness about the conception and gestation of a work of art needs resisting. Often a look at the process by which a work is made sheds light on the reasons why it works upon us. This is certainly the case with the novel *La desesperanza* (published in English under the title *Curfew*) by the Chilean writer José Donoso. The seven hundred pages of notes Donoso made as he shaped his 1986 narrative about an exile's return to Chile offer an illuminating counterpoint to the finished book. They reveal an artist feeling his way, with few preconceptions about how the novel should be, toward a successful expression of a unifying theme that he seldom articulated even for himself.

This theme, which Donoso identifies in his earliest notes only to lose sight of it again, is "the ambivalent relationship of a human being to his roots" (53: 16).[1] It is natural that Donoso should have wished to express his protagonist's ambivalence for Chile; Mañungo Vera, the fictional folksinger who is at the center of the tale, reenters Santiago (as Donoso himself had done) while Augusto Pinochet is still in power, and simultaneously feels deep affection for his homeland and disillusionment with it. However, another sort of ambivalence—the ambivalence that colors the relationship between parent and child—figures importantly in the novel as well. So thoroughly does it affect Donoso's way of conceiving the book that it surely springs from a deeper source than a facile association of "patria" (or, in English, "motherland") with literal parents. Although, as we shall see, one can find evidence of parent-child ambivalence in the finished novel, Donoso's working papers dramatically reveal how crucial this second kind of ambivalence was to his conception of *La desesperanza.* Time and again, as he imagined characters and elaborated the plot, Donoso mobilized and reintroduced the motif of conflicting emotions felt by children for parents and parents for children. In sowing his narrative with multiple expressions of ambivalence, Donoso deploys a powerful device: he recalls the reader to the archaic emotional world of the small child, whose opposing passions for its parents are the heritage of us all. By relating these passions and the guilt that they inspire to the experience of his repatriot hero and of other figures in the novel, Donoso deepens his treatment of his characters, forges a link between their experience and that of the reader, and redeems from topicality a novel that initially was read as a comment on a social moment that by now has passed.

This essay examines Donoso's creative turnings and changes of heart as, over a period of some five years, he shaped *La desesperanza*. I argue that at many points Donoso, consciously or not, devised textual strategies to express ambivalence between children and parents, and that this recurring motif shapes the narrative in important ways. Understanding the degree to which this is so helps a reader to identify significant currents in the finished book. Beyond that, it enables an interpreter of Donoso's narratives to perceive a relationship between parent-child ambivalence and the theme of the mutability of self, a dominant issue in all of Donoso's work.

Much of the commentary on Donoso's writing focuses on the idea that, as Sharon Magnarelli puts it, "human personality or selfhood (ontological being in the world) is a series of masks or disguises, ever changing and ever (inter)changing, with no ultimate coherence or integrity" (4). Donoso himself is on record as having expressed "una duda muy fuerte, una no-creencia en la unidad de la personalidad humana" 'a very strong doubt, a non-belief in the unity of the human personality' (Rodríguez Monegal 521). Yet critics find different meanings in the theme of identity as Donoso uses it. Some, like George McMurray, view the Chilean's treatment of this motif primarily as social criticism, condemnation of the distorting effects imposed by social determinants of identity—family relationships and economic class. Postmodernist critics, on the other hand, cite the mercurial identities of Donoso's heroes as proof that, for the Chilean, not only meaning but being itself must be ever-deferred.[2] Still other critics, perhaps influenced by Donoso's evident familiarity with psychoanalysis, see the unsteady selves he depicts as feeble egos, susceptible of being understood in psychological terms. These critics have invoked a variety of psychological theories to account for the experience of Donoso's figures. Pamela Bacarisse, for example, applies R.D. Laing's definition of schizophrenia to Humberto Peñaloza, the protagonist of *El obsceno pájaro de la noche* (1970), while Silvia Martínez Dacosta, using insights from ego psychology, argues that the same figure offers a case study of paranoia. Taking a different tack, Amadeo López explores Lacan's formulation of the Oedipus complex to find the cause of Humberto's "naufragio de la identidad" 'shipwreck of identity' (121) in failed relationships to weak father figures. C.G. Jung,

too, has inspired several readings of Donosan texts, most notably Hernán Vidal's *José Donoso: Surrealismo y la rebelión de los instintos* and Richard Callan's interpretation of **"Gaspard de la nuit."**

Following the lead of this third group of critics, I propose to interpret, in the light of still another psychoanalytic idea, Donoso's theme of identity transformed. The notes he made as he developed *La desesperanza* show that again and again, in developing his novel, he resorted to literary techniques that reflect the psychic process of "splitting," a defense mechanism identified by Freud but much studied by Melanie Klein and her followers. Children, Klein argues, shield themselves from their own anger at parental figures, an anger that invites parental retaliation, by splitting the image of a symbolic parent (or of the self) into entirely good and entirely bad aspects (Klein 99-110; Kernberg 29). Literature sometimes bears witness to this psychic process; Bruno Bettelheim, noting that "all young children sometimes need to split the image of their parent into its benevolent and threatening aspects to feel fully sheltered by the first" (68), shows that fairy tales regularly contain split images of symbolic parents. Fairy godmothers coexist with witches and evil stepmothers, and helpful genies with giants. Donoso's narratives, like fairy tales, are filled with paired characters who function as split images of a single being. Often—one might think of Alvaro and Maya in *Este domingo* (1966) or Inés de Azcoitía and Peta Ponce in *El obsceno pájaro de la noche*—one member of the pair is aristocratic (idealized) and the other destitute (devalued).[3] In itself, Donoso's penchant for creating paired characters suggests that he employs as literary technique what psychoanalysts call "splitting." His working papers for *La desesperanza* strongly confirm this idea. They show that his way of developing both characters and plot often entails either splitting into idealized figures and sinister alter egos characters who function symbolically as parents or children, or creating a forking plot that actualizes both poles of parent-child ambivalence. I do not wish to suggest that Donoso employed these techniques deliberately, or even that he intended to insert the motif of ambivalence in his text; his notes contain no explicit reference either to the techniques or, apart from the phrase I have quoted, to the theme itself. However, we shall see that consistently Donoso relied on splitting of characters and plot as favored means of developing his text.

Before *interpreting* Donoso's practices, though, one must have a clear idea of how he proceeded as he created *La desesperanza*. What is most striking about his notes, particularly those he made in 1985, is the degree to which Donoso resists analyzing what he creates. He begins by imagining characters who interest him, and whom he at first conceives not as participants in a story but as entities in themselves. Placing them in a situation whose outcome he has not prescribed—for example, Mañungo Vera's homecoming or Matilde Neruda's wake—he makes exhaustive and quite repetitive character sketches that are ever more detailed, tirelessly reworking the personal history and motivation of each character as he orders and reorders the plot. The story grows as, little by little, Donoso imagines how his fictional creatures might interact, or how their pasts might plausibly intersect. Donoso does not "know" as he writes how Mañungo's relationship with the female protagonist Judit will turn out, or whether or why Mañungo will decide in the end to remain in Chile. He seldom asks himself what the novel's main themes ought to be, never discusses imagery and hardly ever considers technical questions such as point of view. Attentive to the characters, he develops the plot sequentially, in an exploratory way, essaying ways to take each next step and usually settling definitively on one before advancing in his creation of the argument.

Donoso created **La desesperanza** in two sustained working sessions, one between December 1980 and December 1981 and the other between January and August 1985. In the first of these he planned a work that portrays Mañungo Vera's return with his son to his native town in a remote area of Southern Chile. This initial version of the story casts Mañungo's ambivalence to his homeland primarily by portraying him torn between two women, one idealized and the other sinister. On the one hand, Mañungo renews his love for his former primary school teacher and musical mentor Ulda Ramírez, a strong, passionate woman politically committed to the Left. On the other, he is attracted to his 18-year-old cousin Lidia Veloso, the self-centered daughter of a local right-wing strongman. Drawn to both lovers, who represent opposing ideological views, Mañungo impregnates both women. Finally, reluctantly giving Ulda up, he marries Lidia, embracing a stifling life devoid of music (Lidia, according to one version, buries Mañungo's guitar). Then, when Lidia falls into the sea and drowns on their wedding night, Mañungo flees across the mountains, renouncing his birthplace in favor of a larger world where he can resume his musical career.

In this original plot one can clearly see the splitting of the female "protagonist" into good and bad components. Donoso consciously contrasts the two women, at one point even reverting to a commonplace of Latin American fiction and proposing that Ulda stand for civilization and Lidia for barbarism (53: 1). It is harder to see that this doubling reflects ambivalence between parent and child; although Ulda's age and her nurturing of Mañungo early in his life suggest the maternal, Lidia Veloso is very young to be a symbolic mother. Yet she ingratiates herself with Mañungo by cultivating a rapport with his four-year-old son, using maternal ministrations to further her love interest. The importance of Mañungo's symbolic mothers in the finished novel—

throughout the book he yearns for reunion with lost mother figures, particularly Matilde Neruda and Ulda—permits one to speculate that Donoso's original doubling of female characters may also express a son's ambivalence for symbolic mothers. Moreover, Donoso invents in the 1981 notes two mysterious and powerful witches, evidence that from the outset he meant to portray highly charged maternal characters. One, an Indian woman named Clemencia, cohabits with Mañungo's widower father. By turns protecting and malevolent, she sometimes plays the role of a dangerous mother figure in the original plot, in one version of which she makes the pregnant Lidia miscarry. Still another ominous old woman, the seaweed seller Doña Petronila, figures in the early notes, as well. One of the only scenes in the finished novel that Donoso drafted in 1981 portrays the encounter in a small ferry boat of Doña Petronila and a youth who resembles Mañungo. Unfortunately, Donoso's copybooks do not contain the early manuscript of this scene, so it is impossible to know what characteristics Donoso first assigned to her.

The way Donoso develops Mañungo himself in his 1981 notes also shows his bent for creating "split" characters. In two ways he creates doubles for his protagonist. Planning a metanovelistic part of the plot, Donoso casts himself as a presence in the text, a narrator/character relating parts of the story in the first person. Like Mañungo, the Donoso character is an artist just returned from years abroad, and his experience parallels the singer's own. This doubling of Mañungo does not presuppose a symbolic division of the main character into "good" and "bad" aspects. However, the other alter ego Donoso creates for his protagonist, a hippie named Arturo Vergara, is more clearly a foil for the charismatic Mañungo. The complex way this character relates to parental figures reveals how compelling Donoso found the motif of ambivalence and shows one of his preferred techniques for portraying it. Arturo, fleeing to Chiloé to escape wealthy bourgeois parents who are pressing him to repay a loan, takes refuge under false colors with a credulous couple named Don Darío and Doña Nina.[4] Arturo's hosts shelter the young man because he intimates that he is a political refugee sought by the government. They sympathize with him because their own son has disappeared, a possible victim of right-wing repression. This remarkably complex subplot shows Donoso "splitting" both the figure of the parents and that of the child. In Arturo, Donoso creates a ne'er-do-well son who contrasts both with Mañungo, the idealized prodigal returned home, and with the couple's own "good" son. Moreover, Arturo is endowed with two sets of "parents," the real ones, who persecute him, and Darío and Nina, who protect him from harm.

After a year of intense work on his Chilote novel Donoso turned aside from it, perhaps displeased with its melodramatic and unworkable plot. When he returned to Mañungo's story in 1985, it was with a changed idea of what the novel should be. Whereas before he had provisionally called the novel "El Regreso" 'The Return,' a title that focuses on Mañungo Vera, he now settles on "La desesperanza" 'Hopelessness,' which alludes not to an individual protagonist but to Chile as a whole. An epigraph from *Bleak House* describing a nightmarish London confirms Donoso's intention of portraying a whole society: "Come night, come darkness, for you cannot come too soon or stay too long by such a place as this." Rereading, as he plans the first scenes of his text, both *Bleak House* and *Les misérables,* he admires Dickens's "grand intelligent construction of the real world" (1: 72) and Hugo's "vision of a nocturnal Paris that is ragged and solitary and terrible" (1: 14). With these masters in mind, he girds himself to convey the "desesperanza" of Santiago in early 1985, just after the death of Matilde Neruda while the city languished in a state of siege. The death of Neruda's widow struck Donoso as symbolic of the end of an era. "Matilde's Death Signifies Hopelessness," Donoso reflects, "the end of something, of a world, the end of the UP [Unidad Popular] and what it stood for"(1: 4).

Donoso now plans a novel divided into two parts. The first, subtitled "Funeral," will set Mañungo Vera's return to Santiago against the backdrop of Matilde Neruda's wake and burial. The second, "Fiesta," will depict the singer's welcome in Chiloé. These contrasting subtitles suggest that Donoso conceives a plot that will split Mañungo's experience of Chile into two parts, the first an experience of bereavement and despair in Santiago and the second of reunion with the community where he was raised. Thus, although Donoso will ultimately give up this bipartite schema, he starts work in 1985 with a plot that expresses ambivalence for Chile.

The "desesperanza" Donoso first conceives is the despairing tone of the country as a whole. He first thinks of it not in particular connection to Mañungo—only slowly will Donoso come to portray Matilde Neruda's death as the loss of a mother figure for the singer—but as the mood prevailing at Matilde's wake. He begins work on the plot of Part I by sketching ten characters attending the wake, among whom are a woman friend of the Nerudas, a humane minor writer, the head of Communist Youth, a rapacious oligarch, and a young Communist woman—characters who become, respectively, Fausta, Celedonio, Lisboa, Freddy Fox, and Judit in the final text. He then maps a plot in which Mañungo returns to Santiago and experiences firsthand the state of collapse into which Unidad Popular has sunk. Repelled by the dehumanizing opportunism of the Communists, who exploit Matilde Neruda's death for political effect, the singer decamps with his son for Chiloé.

Having sketched the outlines of Part I, Donoso enthusiastically turns to his female lead, at first setting her apart from other figures in the Santiago section of the book and casting her heroically as "*the only one not affected by hopelessness*" (1: 26, Donoso's emphasis). Modeling her largely on a woman he knew, a Communist from a wealthy Chilean family who had been jailed and tortured under Pinochet, Donoso from the outset conceives his female protagonist as unsusceptible to love, hardened by having been raped in prison both by men and by a dog trained by the police to sexually terrorize women. Significantly, he does not at first show her as prey to guilt. Wholly devoted to left-wing activism and in particular to a defense of the women who suffered with her in prison, she will, Donoso plans, seek her jailer during the curfew hours and have an intense but short-lived encounter with Mañungo. The singer will ultimately shy away from her, rejecting Judit's unskeptical commitment to a political cause and horrified by her bloodthirstiness.

Donoso almost immediately discards his idea that Judit is immune from despair; "it's hopelessness that makes criminals of us all" (1: 42), he has her say. He now plans to convey the "monstrification" (1: 42) of Santiago's citizens in his portrayal of Judit. Later, Donoso will complicate his understanding of his female lead. He will ascribe her emotional barrenness to guilt, and account for that guilt by providing Judit with ambivalent relationships with parental figures.

Donoso plans for Mañungo to separate from Judit at the end of Part I and journey to Chiloé in search of a wholesome, simple life. However, the "Fiesta" promised by the title of his projected Part II never materializes. Indeed, as Donoso, vacationing in Chiloé in January and February of 1985, reimmerses himself in Chilote life, he notes how completely his reaction to the place has changed. Whereas on his 1981 trip to the island Donoso had been much impressed with the beauty of Chiloé's glaciers, volcanoes, and lakes, he now sees in Chiloé "total hopelessness on an ecological-metaphysical-symbolic level"(1: 66). Attending the Festival of the Virgin of Caguash, he is struck by its drabness, the primitivism of the religious icons, and the deformity of many of the congregants. "They're all like *degenerates* [degenerados]," he writes, "undernourished, poor, lots of dwarfs, lots of people with defective hips, lame, others with clouded vision or completely blind, or with only one eye . . . the man without an arm . . . the man cut off at the waist" (1: 69, Donoso's emphasis). These sufferers, one of whom he will later recreate as the beggar king Don César, come to the Festival to offer their pain to Christ, but unlike their Spanish counterparts, fail to redeem their distress in colorful dress, drunkenness, and dance. Noting "the absence of any orgiastic feeling," Donoso is depressed by proceedings whose "pain is never transubstantiated into something else" (1: 69).

Donoso has, in effect, exchanged an idealized vision of Chiloé for a depreciated one, subjecting even the setting of his book to the process of "splitting." He now perceives Chiloé not as more wholesome than Santiago but as analogous to it, and visualizes Part II of his text as a section that, structurally and thematically, will parallel Part I. Mañungo, having seen and walked away from the values of the Chilean Left after an intense twenty-four hours in Santiago, will encounter in the space of a second day spent in Chiloé the sinister attitudes of the political Right.

Thus far Donoso has not probed much the psychology of Mañungo or Judit. In particular, he has not begun to link Mañungo's personal history and motivation with the topic of "la desesperanza." Now, planning the end of the novel, he imagines that Mañungo should die in a freak accident on the train as he leaves Chiloé after an unhappy visit there. Alternatively, Mañungo should take some "action . . . that demonstrates and dramatizes his hopelessness, which is not only political but also creative and personal, a dramatic action that will also reveal the generalized hopelessness . . . of people in general" (1: 89). It is now that Donoso begins to explore Mañungo's inner being. The singer should, he thinks, impregnate Lidia Veloso out of perverse self-destructiveness. Or he should commit a crime. It is important to note that Donoso hits upon the idea of Mañungo's guilt—evidenced in his self-destructiveness and in the commission of an actual crime—before he explores very much his protagonist's psychology. The many elaborations of the novel's ending that Donoso essays as he spins out the rest of the plot rationalize Mañungo's guilt in various ways. Significantly, these multiple versions of the ending also insistently deploy fathers and children in an array of ambivalent relationships.

Exactly whose death should bring the novel to a close remains an open question. If Mañungo's *father* were to die, the writer speculates, the death would symbolize the loss of "the land, tradition, origins" (1: 66). Quickly, though, Donoso abandons this idea and considers the death of Mañungo's *son* as a possible way to end the book. Analyzing the singer's relationship to Jean-Paul, Donoso posits that Mañungo feels guilt because he often wishes for his son's death, "as if death for a beloved person is the only hope of salvation" for Mañungo himself (1: 91). Donoso returns repeatedly in his notes to an anecdote he has heard about a Chilote man who, by sacrificing his daughter to the ghost ship, or Caleuche, saved his warehouse from a disastrous fire in Castro during the 1930s. Following this line of thought, Donoso imagines that Jean-Paul and not Mañungo might die leaning out the train window on the journey back to Santiago, at a moment when Mañungo is angry with his son and wishes him dead. Implicitly, Donoso is casting around for the right sort of "crime" for Mañungo to commit. One possible alternative is filicide.

As he elaborates reasons for Mañungo's guilt, Donoso in effect splits his protagonist by inventing Lopito, an alcoholic failed artist who inopportunely intrudes in Mañungo's doings during the night and day the novel depicts. Donoso does not, it must be said, consciously conceive of Lopito as an alter ego for Mañungo but as a foil for him.[5] Lopito's Dostoyevskian abjection, Donoso thinks, will evoke a second kind of guilt in Mañungo, who has escaped in exile the hard lot of Chileans like Lopito who remained at home.

Lopito is destined to have a complex role in *La desesperanza.* Eventually he will double both Mañungo and Mañungo's son. Mañungo sees in the grotesque drunkard what he himself might have become had he not left Chile. Like Lopito, he has had a brief affair with Judit. And both men harbor ambivalent feelings for their children. However, Donoso also develops Lopito as an emotionally needy substitute for Mañungo's son. The failed poet demands that Mañungo stay with him instead of returning to Jean-Paul in the hotel, and Lopito's body is described in the finished text as "casi infantil" 'almost infantile' (305).

Moreover, no sooner has Donoso invented Lopito than he wonders whether he should kill him off toward the end of Part II. (Lopito, he thinks, might try to vindicate himself by participating in a small political rally and be killed by a stray bullet.) Shortly before, Donoso had planned that the novel should end with Jean-Paul's death. Although he does not at first think of Lopito's death as a substitute for Jean-Paul's, or as the central event in the denouement of the novel, he will eventually develop the plot in just this way; after Matilde's funeral Lopito is arrested and dies in police custody and Mañungo, outraged at the mistreatment of his friend, vows to remain in Chile and take responsibility for Lopito's orphaned child. The ending Donoso finally elects economically plays out both aggression against one symbolic child (Lopito) and righteous defense of another (Lopito's daughter).

At this point in his development of the novel Donoso had an experience that changed his ideas about Mañungo's fate. On January 30, 1985, during his stay in Chiloé, Donoso and his wife María Pilar attended a meeting of the Comité de Defensa de Derechos del Pueblo and Mujeres de Chile. Seated rows behind his wife, Donoso was alarmed to see that, when the police broke up the meeting, María Pilar was among those detained. He volunteered for arrest himself in order to protect her. The couple received privileged treatment because of Donoso's fame and were released before their fellow prisoners, but not before Donoso had failed to secure from the officials at the jail a necessary medication. Donoso immediately resolves to use this dramatic experience in his novel; indeed, even before he records his own experience in his notes Donoso sketches a fictionalized version of it that substitutes Mañungo for his wife and himself. Mañungo, he imagines, will hope to expiate guilt at his non-participation in Chile's ills by being arrested. Ultimately, though, Donoso will modify this idea and subject Lopito, not the singer, to arrest, making the pathetic poet a scapegoat while assigning Mañungo the role he himself had played of trying to protect a hapless detainee.

Returning to his chronological development of Part I, Donoso spends six weeks elaborating the wake scene and Judit's adventures with Mañungo during the curfew hours. In working and reworking the wake scene, which he models on the concert in Tantamount House in Aldous Huxley's novel *Point Counter Point,* Donoso gradually creates a polyphonic texture by imagining the many tensions among the mourners. It may be useful to follow his method of conceiving character by following his invention of a single exemplary figure.

Ada Luz, Matilde Neruda's self-effacing friend, recommends herself for this kind of analysis. Donoso's technique of relating her little by little to other characters exemplifies his procedure with every other figure in the scene. Moreover, a false start he makes in conceiving Ada Luz reveals Donoso's continuing interest in the parent-child motif. Donoso first imagines Ada Luz as a mousy little woman reminiscent of Esther Summerson in *Bleak House.* He imagines that Ada Luz has heard Matilde wish that a left-wing priest say a mass over her remains. Donoso begins his development of Ada Luz by endowing her with an exiled stepson. "The son of her dead husband is the center of her world," Donoso writes, and then, feeling his way: "They won't let him return from exile. He could return, but it's not worth it for him to come for a month to visit his 'mother,' she thinks that if she were his real mother he would come back" (2: 93). Donoso, in other words, makes Ada Luz a doting would-be mother to an almost-son. This curiously equivocal mother-son relationship stands at first at the center of Ada Luz's emotional life. Little by little, however, Donoso relates Ada Luz to others in the wake scene, and as he does so he invents other human ties that ultimately supplant her motherly concerns. Her acquaintance with Lisboa, which begins when she asks the Communist Party to intercede to bring her stepson home, evolves into an amorous involvement. Then Donoso connects her to Judit by making Ada Luz one of the victims of rape imprisoned with her. Finally, he imagines that Lopito pesters Ada Luz so that she will rent him a room. By the end of the wake scene he has enmeshed Ada Luz in a web of relationships that make superfluous her devotion to a distant stepson. Nonetheless, Donoso's original portrayal of Ada Luz shows him still intrigued with parent-child relations.

As he elaborates the wake scene and the events of the night Judit and Mañungo share, Donoso also builds ambivalence into his conception of Judit. He aims to con-

vey "Judit's madness, her mental imbalance, how she suddenly goes off into a completely blighted, irrational world" (2: 142). Originally, he had envisioned Judit not as painfully neurotic but as emotionally blocked, and had not tried to account for this facet of her character. Now he explores Judit's psychology, making of his female lead a volatile person prey to intense ambivalence. Beginning with the idea that Judit, for reasons unspecified, pursues Mañungo throughout Part I of the book, Donoso soon makes her interest in Mañungo coexist with, and be subordinate to, her pursuit of a another man, the officer in the CNI (National Information Agency, Chile's secret police) who was in charge of her detention. By developing the plot in this way Donoso provides a plausible mission for his female lead, as well as a reason for her to conscript Mañungo during the curfew hours and a way to make him witness a political act. Curiously, though, by constructing a sort of double pursuit of two men whose voices she associates, one beneficent and the other an enemy, Donoso starts to portray Judit's ambivalence toward male figures, which he develops in several other ways as the novel evolves. Very soon, for example, he imagines that Judit should both hate her victimizer and be attracted to him. Then, ascribing Judit's emotional sterility to guilt, Donoso seeks reasons for the guilt and hits on the idea that the CNI man *saved* her from rape that her fellow prisoners were not spared—that is, that her jailer was in some sense her benefactor, too. And, in a bizarre turn of the plot that Donoso considers for a time and ultimately rejects, Judit is at one time convinced that the CNI man and the bureaucrat who issued her a false passport, a secret ally, are the same man. In developing Judit, then, Donoso relates her to men who, alternately or simultaneously, injure and protect her. The plot he devises to reveal his female protagonist expresses both poles of her ambivalence for figures who, like symbolic parents, exert power over her.

In writing the first draft of the wake and night walk scenes Donoso has for a time deflected his attention from Mañungo Vera. Now, reminding himself that Mañungo is the protagonist, Donoso sets about restoring to him pride of place. His reflections on Mañungo now revert to Chiloé. Donoso evokes Castro in the 1930s, when it was a city of *palafitos,* or primitive houses on stilts, and invents Mañungo's mother, killed there in the 1960 earthquake. In thinking of Mañungo as bereft of a mother, Donoso takes an important step toward expressing his hero's nostalgia for Chile as a yearning for absent mother figures.

He also returns to the Chilote myth of the Caleuche, one of several Chilote legends to which he alludes in his 1981 notes. Mañungo, he decides, should ride on the Caleuche, according to Chilote lore a ship manned by one-legged *brujos* (male witches) who spirit away shipwrecked sailors to a city under the sea. However,

Donoso begins with no clear idea what his hero's ride on the Caleuche should mean. Mañungo, he first thinks, will board the mysterious ghost ship in a dream-like scene, then jump overboard and escape, as though the vessel symbolized a diabolical Chile, or perhaps the Chilean Left Wing. Then he wonders whether Mañungo and Lidia should make love in a small boat, "bewitched by love" (2: 180), making the mythical ship with its *brujos* represent passion. Ultimately, however, Donoso returns to the idea of Mañungo's guilt; because he escapes the Caleuche, the singer is "maldito"—cursed or unholy. Alluding again to the proprietor who saved his warehouse by allowing the Caleuche to carry off his daughter, Donoso now takes an important next step. "SHIP OF ART," he muses. "The witch is the ARTIST: he causes death" (2: 206). Not only will Mañungo occasion someone's death, but he will do so *because he is an artist*. Listing Chilote elements he wishes to include, Donoso begins:

> artist—artist—brujo
> ship of art (Caleuche)
> artist-brujo-killing
> As the "artist," Mañungo becomes a murderer.
> He kills Lidia Veloso out of love and
> he kills someone for political reasons.
>   . . . . .
> Jail for Mañungo.
>
>   (2: 227)

Enthused though he is by this Chilote material, Donoso is brought up short when, after sketching an ending to Part I, he turns to the Chilote half of the novel. Almost immediately, faced with the awkwardness of transporting his Santiago characters to Chiloé, he abandons the idea of writing Part II, deciding instead to incorporate Chilote material in Part I as flashbacks. Enumerating aspects of Part II he intends to insert in the Santiago chapters, Donoso begins: "1. The artist as criminal, the artist-witch of the Chilote tradition, absolutely central to this novel. 2. The Caleuche, as the Ship of art . . ." (2: 233).

Now Donoso faces the task of relating Mañungo's criminality—which before he had ascribed to filicide—to his status as an artist. He has written a story in which left-wing friends press Mañungo to declare his opposition to the regime, whether by wearing a red armband, singing the protest song "Santiago ensangrentado" at Matilde's wake or accepting the mantle as Neruda's successor. Determined to champion "the essential immorality of the artist," Donoso will make Mañungo's aloofness from Chilean politics his (admirable) transgression:

> the artist-witch, the artist-criminal. He simply does not choose, he sits on the sidelines waiting and waiting for himself, watching and watching himself, and if he consumes himself in that watching of himself, well, so be

it. . . . Mañungo knows that he's immoral . . . but on another level the acceptance of his personal despair, as part of the despair of the country and the world, is clearheadedness, which is perhaps another form of hope . . . what he believes has to be free, not stifled, not programmatic. He rejects the tyranny of the historical moment.

>   (2: 234)

Having modified his view of "desesperanza" and made it a positive stance, Donoso changes the fate of Lopito. Initially he had considered having Lopito die at a political rally, trying to redeem himself by vocal adherence to the anti-Pinochet cause. Donoso now rejects this facile martyrdom, wondering whether he should end the novel with Lopito's death "en un acto de bella locura" 'in a beautiful act of madness' (2: 237), that is to say, an affirmation of "desesperanza." Perhaps, he thinks, Lopito should die reciting Rimbaud or Baudelaire at Matilde's funeral, a noble gesture that would cast Lopito, like Mañungo, as an advocate of politically disinterested art.

One might think that Donoso had turned aside from the motif of ambivalence of child for parent and parent for child. However, inventing the "bella locura" that should result in Lopito's death, he devises scenes that repeatedly cast Lopito in conflicted parent-child relationships. The scene evolves through the following versions:

1. Lopito distinguishes himself at Matilde's funeral in some unspecified way. Jean-Paul accuses him of being drunk and they fight. Mañungo intervenes to defend his son and feels guilty when Lopito is arrested.

2. Lopito is arrested for defending an old man roughly treated by police.

3. Lopito is arrested when he defends Don César, a leader among Santiago's mendicants, whose tricycle has been destroyed.

4. A beggar boy named Arturo cries when he finds his tricycle wrecked outside the cemetery. Lopito defends Arturo when an angry policeman threatens to take the lad to jail. Lopito is furious at the unfairness of the police but abuses the child.

5. Leaving the cemetery, Lopito meets Arturo and asks him about his father and Don César. Arturo entertains the children of Lopito, Mañungo and Judit, named Lopita, Jean-Paul and Marilú respectively, until they find Arturo's wrecked tricycle. When the police accuse Arturo of stealing wire from old funeral wreaths, Lopito defends him. Both Lopito and Arturo are taken away by the police, who release Arturo. Arturo witnesses Lopito's death and brings word to the other characters in Chile in Miniature.

6. Jean-Paul and Marilú laugh at Lopita at the cemetery and Lopito intervenes to save her. A policeman then laughs at Lopita and tells Lopito not to bother the other two children.

7. Lopito, drunk, strikes Lopita when she begs him to stop the other children from teasing her.

8. Jean-Paul and Marilú leave Lopita out of their game. Lopito takes Lopita by the hand but is violent with her and makes her cry. Outside the cemetery the other two children again mistreat Lopita. When Lopito comes to her defense a policeman accuses him of mistreating Jean-Paul and Marilú.

It would be hard to imagine a set of variants that more insistently express ambivalence between symbolic fathers and children. In every version, someone attacks an old man or child and usually someone comes to the victim's defense. Split portrayals of parents and children proliferate. Each rendering contains "good" and "bad" parents—Mañungo and Lopito in version 1, Lopito and the police in version 4 and 5, Lopito and Lopito himself in versions 6 and 8—and in many of the variants "good" child-victims coexist with children who torment. By splitting the images of parent and child, Donoso expresses on the level of the plot raw ambivalence in the parent-child relationship the story paints. The finished novel elides Lopito's aggressiveness to children, showing only his furious defense of Lopita when a policeman laughs at her. However, prior versions of the scene show how persistently Donoso at first portrays both poles of parental ambivalence.

These variants also give evidence that, as Donoso plans the end of his book, he suddenly alters his principals' role in the symbolic family relations that underlie the plot. Both of his main characters, until late in the book, function primarily as symbolic children vis-à-vis their own parents; Mañungo mourns the death of a symbolic mother in Matilde and achieves a mysterious *rapprochement* with Ulda in his dreams, while Judit inhabits a world where symbolic fathers alternately betray and protect her. At the end of the novel, though, Donoso shows both Mañungo and Lopito embracing a paternal role, Lopito as "bad" or ineffectual father and Mañungo as his "good" counterpart. The variants summarized above show Donoso in the process of shifting his view of Lopito from symbolic son, protecting an older man in variants 2 and 3, to symbolic father in the last five versions of the scene. Ultimately, Donoso will dramatize Mañungo's spiritual renewal by showing him transformed from prodigal son into the protecting surrogate father of Lopita.

Donoso moves toward this resolution intuitively at first, not following conscious intent. A Freudian slip he makes in his notes for variant 4—he calls Arturo "Arturo's son," quickly correcting himself, "no, 'Arturo,' his name is Arturo" (2: 327)—shows him ascribing the name of a son to his father. In another way, too, the novel encodes a reversal of father-son roles, although in a way no reader of the novel could detect. Between the time he finished a first draft and the publication of the finished work Donoso changed the name of the beggar boy from Arturo to Darío. In his 1981 notes he had created a young hippie named Arturo sheltered by a be-

nevolent older man named Darío. Whether Donoso consciously recalled these two discarded characters when he put the finishing touches on his text is impossible to say. Yet by assigning what originally was a father figure's name to a symbolic son, Donoso confirms privately the direction the end of the novel takes.

It remains to show how Donoso develops Judit. Unlike Mañungo, she never assumes the role of parent, turning aside at the end of the book from the painful task of consoling Lopita after her father's death. As Donoso develops Judit's story, he continues to portray her as a child relating to "good" and "bad" symbolic parents. We have already seen that her pursuit of the equivocally evil CNI man, whom she strangely identifies both with Mañungo and with a bureaucrat who saves her life, expresses her ambivalence for parent figures. In creating the rest of her story Donoso provides her with two other sets of symbolic parents. It is as he begins to detail Judit's early history, to be narrated to Mañungo during the night walk scene, that Donoso first alludes in his notes to Don César. The beggar king is both friend to Judit—he hides her while she is living underground—and potential betrayer; Arturo warns Judit that Don César has turned informant for the secret police. Himself a "split" father figure, Don César coexists in the text with Arturo's own less treacherous father, who proffers competing advice about the CNI man's whereabouts.

Fausta and Celedonio, too, serve as parent figures for Judit in the thrilling account of her escape from Chile. Originally Donoso invented these two without envisioning them as a couple. In complicating the relationships among the characters during the wake scene he makes them long-time lovers. However, in narrating Judit's deliverance, Donoso replaces the real parents of the woman on whose life he models Judit with Fausta and Celedonio. "I love the idea of Fausta and Celedonio as parents" (2: 263), he delightedly reflects. In this case, of course, Judit's "good" symbolic parents are not paired with "bad" counterparts, except insofar as the CNI itself embodies malevolent authority.

We have seen that Donoso, by invoking the conflicted and intense relations between parents and children as he creates the plot and characters of *La desesperanza,* grounds his story of an exile's return in a powerful experience of ambivalence that all his readers share. Evidence of this ambivalence survives in the finished text in Mañungo's relationship to maternal female characters and in Judit's tortured relationships with men. Yet the finished novel foregrounds another theme as well, that of transformation of self, which is central to many of Donoso's works. *La desesperanza* portrays Mañungo as a man who strives not only to restore his connection to his homeland, but to alter his being in the process of doing it. By reboarding the Caleuche, which Donoso finally depicts as the Chilote ship of art, Mañungo will be transformed. It is worth knowing that nowhere in his copious notes for the first draft of *La desesperanza* does Donoso mention the idea of transformation of self. This crucial motif, which Donoso incorporates late in his development of the text, grows out of his treatment of ambivalence between parents and children, for in the end it is Mañungo's assumption of a father's role that enacts the transformation of his being and confirms his reconciliation to an imperfect homeland. The novel ends as Mañungo, determined to defend the grotesque Lopita after her father's death, raises her on his shoulders and strides toward the matronly Fausta. This final reunion with his symbolic mother, and with Chile itself, is part and parcel of his transformation from needy child to responsible parent. It is also a transformation that resolves, in a moving moment of fictive grace, Mañungo's ambivalence toward maternal figures and toward the children for whom he must care.

By studying the complex process by which Donoso arrived at the final text of *La desesperanza* one can see that, in the case of this novel at least, the writer progressed in a particular way. For Donoso, character was destiny; both plot and theme evolved as he probed to discover who his fictional figures were. Consistently, in deepening his characters and relating them to one another, Donoso resorted to favored techniques, chief among them the Kleinian splitting of character and of plot. In doing so, he embedded in the novel time and again the compelling issue of ambivalence between parent and child. The fact that the overt central theme of the finished work—Mañungo's ability to transform himself—grows belatedly out of a welter of renderings of this primal ambivalence is suggestive indeed. Many of Donoso's narratives return to the idea that human identity may alter. They explore, now with hope, now with dread, the prospect that the self may be radically transformed. A look at Donoso's creation of *La desesperanza* leads one to wonder whether in other of his texts as well the theme of parent-child ambivalence coexists with and underlies the central Donosan theme of identity transformed.

Notes

1. I am grateful to Mr. Donoso for permitting me to study his working notes for *La desesperanza,* which are housed at the Princeton University Library. They consist of some 200 pages dated December 1, 1980 to December 10, 1981, handwritten in copybooks 52 and 53, and 500 typewritten sheets dated January 16 to August 23, 1985 and paginated in two series, the first of 93 pages and the second of 407. References to these notes are made in parentheses in the text, and refer either to copybook and page or to series and page. I have translated quotations from the notes into English.

2. Z. Nelly Martínez, for example, in a Derridian reading of *El obsceno pájaro de la noche,* writes that Humberto Peñaloza, the narrator, "se exhibe como un juego infinito de diferencias y de diferimientos" 'exhibits himself as an infinite game of differences and deferrals' (59).

3. Donoso's critics regularly point out his use of paired opposites. George McMurray notes the consistency with which Donoso, as early as *Coronación* (1957), pairs upper- and lower-class characters (68-70, 79, 84-85), and by 1985 Philip Swanson, who examines not just paired characters but binary opposition generally, has a considerable critical literature to review in his own study "Binary Elements in *El obsceno pájaro de la noche.*" Until now, critics have seen Donoso's use of opposites as a structuring device, but have not related it to Kleinian splitting and the idea of ambivalence.

4. Don Darío and Doña Nina are the names of a real couple Donoso met in 1981 on the island of Chiloé.

5. In an interview with Ricardo Gutiérrez Mouat, Donoso expresses surprise at the idea that Mañungo and Lopito might be considered as doubles (Gutiérrez Mouat 13).

Works Cited

Bacarisse, Pamela. "*El obsceno pájaro de la noche:* A Willed Process of Evasion." *Forum for Modern Language Studies* 15 (1975): 114-29.

Bettelheim, Bruno. *The Uses of Enchantment: The Meaning and Importance of Fairy Tales.* New York: Vintage Books, 1977.

Callan, Richard J. "'Gaspard de la Nuit': Crucial Breakthrough in the Growth of Personality." *The Creative Process in the Works of José Donoso.* Ed. Guillermo I. Castillo-Feliú. Winthrop Studies on Major Modern Writers. Rock Hill, SC: Winthrop College, 1982. 129-39.

Donoso, José. *Curfew.* Trans. Alfred MacAdam. New York: Weidenfeld & Nicolson, 1988.

———. *La desesperanza.* Barcelona: Seix Barral, 1986.

———. Unpublished working notes for *La desesperanza.* Notebooks 52 and 53, ms., and unbound ts. (series 1 and 2). Donoso papers. Princeton University Library.

Gutiérrez Mouat, Ricardo. "Beginnings and Returns: An Interview with José Donoso." *The Review of Contemporary Fiction* 12.2 (1992): 11-17.

Kernberg, Otto. *Borderline Conditions and Pathological Narcissism.* New York: Jason Aronson, 1975.

Klein, Melanie. "Notes on Some Schizoid Mechanisms." *International Journal of Psychoanalysis* 27 (1946): 99-110.

López, Amadeo. "Búsqueda del padre, lugar del reconocimiento en *El obsceno pájaro de la noche,* de José Donoso." *Revista chilena de literatura* 46 (1994): 121-32.

Magnarelli, Sharon. *Understanding José Donoso.* Columbia, S.C.: U of South Carolina P, 1993.

Martínez, Z. Nelly. "*El obsceno pájaro de la noche:* la productividad del texto." *Revista Iberoamericana* 46 (1980): 51-66.

Martínez Dacosta, Silvia. *Dos ensayos literarios sobre Eduardo Barrios y José Donoso.* Miami: Universal, 1976.

McMurray, George R. *José Donoso.* Boston: Twayne, 1979.

Rodríguez Monegal, Emir. "José Donoso: La novela como Happening." *Revista Iberoamericana* 76-77 (1971): 517-36.

Swanson, Philip. "Binary Elements in *El obsceno pájaro de la noche.*" *Revista de Estudios Hispánicos* 19.1 (1985): 101-16.

Vidal, Hernán. *José Donoso: Surrealismo y rebelión de los instintos.* Barcelona: Aubi, 1972.

Alejandro Herrero-Olaizola (essay date March 2000)

SOURCE: Herrero-Olaizola, Alejandro. "Consuming Aesthetics: José Donoso in the Field of Latin American Literary Production." *Modern Language Notes* 115, no. 2 (March 2000): 323-39.

[*In the following essay, Herrero-Olaizola uses Donoso's novel* El jardín de al lado *as a commentary on the cultural production of the "Boom" period, with special attention to the influence of the Seix Barral publishing company.*]

In spite of the disagreements on how to interpret and contextualize the publishing accomplishments of the "Boom" writers, almost everyone would acknowledge the need to ask how the institutions of literature—editors, literary agents, scholars, readers, publishing houses, authors, etc.—interacted in the production of contemporary Latin American narrative.[1] This essay evaluates the field of cultural production of the "Boom" through the interaction of Latin American writers (Mario Vargas Llosa, Gabriel García Márquez, José Donoso, Mauricio Wácquez, Jorge Edwards, Alfredo Bryce Echenique, among others) with the Barcelona intelligentsia

of the 1960s and 1970s (writers like Juan and Luis Goytisolo, Juan Marsé, Esther Tusquets, Juan Benet; and editors such as Carlos Barral and José María Castellet), and looks at how this interaction benefited the prominent Catalan publishing industry as well as the diffusion of Latin American narrative internationally. In particular, this essay focuses on Seix Barral's editorial policies favoring the distribution of the literary works of many Latin American writers in the 1960s and 1970s. In this sense, the case of José Donoso (1924-1996) is particularly relevant to evaluate the interaction among "Boom" writers and the Barcelona intelligentsia since he was a member of this group whose production was mainly published by Seix Barral.[2] Despite his role as agent/reporter/writer of the "Boom" Donoso has disregarded the Latin American publishing success as "anecdotal," and has insisted that "the Spanish American novel began to speak an international language" in a clear departure from "the regional taste and aesthetic values" (9-10) that dominated the novel before 1960.

In a recent essay on Seix Barral's publishing partner in Mexico, Editorial Joaquín Mortiz, Danny Anderson proposes to study the role of publishing houses as "cultural institutions" than "can provide a broader basis for understanding why and how texts become important works of literature" (34). "Rather than following changes in narrative trends," he adds, "one can establish histories of publishing houses that promoted certain kinds of literature, and at various moments achieved qualified and temporary degrees of cultural hegemony" (35). What Anderson's analysis suggests is that by tracing the marketing strategies generated by the publishing houses that distributed the "Boom" one may well be in a position to decipher the aesthetic program behind it. In order to explain how such aesthetic program was marketed, one has to examine the strategies of publishing houses and how they may relate to the literary creation, success and distribution of Latin American literature.

In an attempt to contextualize the strategies used by Seix Barral, and how they may be understood within the aesthetic program of the *nueva novela,* I propose in this essay a two-fold analysis based upon Pierre Bourdieu's model of literary production as laid out in *The Field of Cultural Production.* First, I map out the aesthetic and marketing program behind Seix Barral in order to examine its role as an agent of cultural production for Latin America; and, secondly, I explore its literary ramifications through a close reading of José Donoso's 1981 novel **El jardín de al lado** as a case study of the cultural production of the "Boom" period and its publishing industry in the Spanish literary market of the 1970s and beyond. I situate the "Boom" and *nueva novela* as part of the larger framework of the field of cultural production by looking into the institutions of literature and the social structures in which they appear. Furthermore, I am interested in exploring how such a theoretical framework becomes not simply thematized but also problematized from the writer's point of view in the process of literary production in Donoso's novel.

In order to examine the "Boom's" literary success within the context of Barcelona's cultural milieu, it may be useful to refer to some of Bourdieu's notions pertaining to what he calls "the field of cultural production." For Bourdieu the literary field, as any other social formation, is part of a hierarchical structure which consists of a series of fields (the economic field, the educational field, the political field, and the cultural field, etc.), "each of them with its own functioning and its own relations" (6). Whereas in the economic field agents battle for the acquisition of economic capital, in the cultural (or literary) field competition often concerns the acquisition of symbolic capital which is found in the accumulation of recognition, consecration and prestige (7). Bourdieu proposes that the field of cultural production is "an economic world reversed" where economic success (i.e., writing a best-seller) may impede consecration and symbolic power in the literary field. This distinction between economic and symbolic capital is paramount for the understanding of how the publishing industry operates within the literary field. Books have economic and symbolic value since they are priced according to their printing costs as well as other elements that cannot be measured in economic terms, such as the author's reputation, the critical reception, or the publisher's fame. For Bourdieu, "symbolic goods are a two-faced reality, a commodity and a symbolic object" whose cultural and commercial value "remain relatively independent" (113).

Whereas for Bourdieu the interaction of the symbolic and the economic becomes a key element to establish two sub-fields of production, restricted—that is, production for other producers such as museums, galleries, libraries, the educational system, etc.—and large-scale for the public at large, most publishing houses that distributed the works of the "Boom" appeared to have aimed at the field of restricted production and yet reached over the public at large. In a sense, the oscillatory movement between "Boom" and *nueva novela* present in these publishing houses would make this so-called "economic world reversed" take—yet another—turn or reversal, since their investment in symbolic capital (ie, creating a name, being identified as an avant-garde publisher, etc) ultimately provided economic returns produced from the consolidation of symbolic capital. Seix Barral's symbolic capital was based in part on the construction of Barcelona as a production site of the avant-garde, and its marketing depended on its annual literary prize *Premio Biblioteca Breve*. Editor Carlos Barral became an agent whose "symbolic investment" was to attract the Latin American writers to channel a more international distribution of their works.

In this case, the "Boom" writers and Seix Barral become what Bourdieu would call "agents occupying the diverse available positions" in the field so that they can "engage in competition for control of their interests" (6-7): while the Latin American writers compete for the production and distribution of their works and of their names, Seix Barral aims at gaining financial benefits and literary acclaim in marketing them.

There seem to be two strategies that most clearly contributed to resituating the position of Seix Barral within the literary field: a new market identity and an international visibility. In the 1960s Carlos Barral, a co-owner of the publishing house with Víctor Seix and also a leader of the editorial review board, was interested in expanding toward the Latin America market, which had been a major source of income for the publishing house in the 1930s. In his memoirs *Los años sin excusa* (1977), Barral talks about his interest in changing the market identity of the publishing house: "it was a matter of building up a backlist with the most important and exotic new authors. Later, it would not take long to impose the contents of this literary period on the Spanish-speaking markets with an intelligent presentation" (139) [my translation].

To create a new market identity of his publishing house Barral followed the scope of French literary journals and publishers—such as *NRF, Les Temps Modernes* and *Minuit*—to make a list of international authors. As explained by Danny Anderson, this process "consists of the systematic use of a network of social relationships," which, in Seix Barral's case, included members of the Barcelona intelligentsia as well as "published writers and prominent intellectuals who had already achieved prestige of their own" (10). Indeed, Barral looked for the validation of international editors and writers to establish Seix Barral's space for a select group of readers in order to make his publishing enterprise a sort of hybrid between what Bourdieu calls restricted and large-scale production. The new market identity would give the publishing house the cachet it needed to accumulate symbolic capital—mainly in the form of literary success and prestige—as well as economic capital which would then come from the large-scale production of some of the items in Seix Barral's backlist.

As Bourdieu reminds us the literary field is contained within the field of power, and Barral's new market identity had to "agree" with the political structure of the time. Despite the censorship of all printed materials under the Franco regime (1939-1975), Barral's project for an avant-garde readership went forward. Oddly enough, the process of changing Seix Barral's market identity coincided with the opening up that characterized the last phase of the regime (1959-75). From 1959 on, the new government of "technocrats" proposed economic reforms geared toward the creation of a consumer society in Spain (Dravasa 208-09). This expansion, based on the *Planes de Desarrollo* [Economic Development Plans], was designed to improve the infrastructures of the country by creating a "booming" tourist industry from which Spain could obtain an important source of revenue. As part of the new economic plan, they tried to break down Spain's international isolation by launching a massive campaign to export Spanish products world-wide. Indeed, the Latin American market was one of Franco's targets ever since Spain had lost its control of the publishing industry in Latin America after the fall of the Republic in 1939.[3]

Indeed, these changes in the configuration of "the field of cultural production" were not at odds with Barral's attempt to create a new and more international reputation of his publishing house. Even though it would seem a contradiction for Franco's government to allow and sponsor the distribution of Latin American writers who had sided with the Cuban Revolution, the field of power had been altered by the government's new international liberalism. As Bourdieu reminds us the relation between the field of power and the literary field is one of containment as well as autonomy since their relation operates in terms of "economic and political principles of hierarchization" (37). While Barral's change to a new market identity was geared toward gaining more symbolic capital for Seix Barral, the new printing law and the Economic Development Plans favored the consolidation of such autonomy.

It is from this point on that Seix Barral's image as an avant-garde publisher (or in Spanish as *editorial cultural*) begins to overlap with a strategy of international visibility due, on the one hand, to the economic reforms, and, on the other, to Barral's own network of international editors. While the strategy of a new market identity relies heavily on what Anderson calls "markers of prestige"—quality, openness to innovation, interest in international high culture, cosmopolitanism, etc. (13)—, Barral's project for international visibility was based on a greater distribution of Seix Barral's backlist thanks to the publicity generated by literary prizes. Through the combination of these two strategies, Seix Barral became what Bourdieu would call an "agent of consecration" competing in the field of restricted production for "the power to grant cultural consecration" (121). More specifically, an agent of consecration for the "Boom" writers as well as for Barcelona's avant-garde status within the field of cultural production.

In this sense, I would argue that the creation of three literary prizes by Carlos Barral—the *Premio Biblioteca Breve,* the *Prix Formentor,* and the *Prix International de Litterature*—may be seen as part of the agency of consecration.[4] The idea behind these prizes had to do not only with consecration, but also with the internationalization of the publishing house and the reinforce-

ment of its avant-garde readership. It is from this experience with the Formentor group of editors that Carlos Barral began his efforts to resituate Seix Barral's role within the field of literary production, and launched a strategy of international visibility for the Barcelona publishing house. As part of Barral's strategy to increase the visibility of his pro-Latin America enterprise, he convinced the Formentor group to award the 1961 *Prix International* to Jorge Luis Borges, undoubtedly the precursor of the "Boom" writers. The success of Borges's work in the international market was a key factor in the new direction of Seix Barral.

Once he had managed to convince his partners of this new direction, Barral orchestrated the creation of an annual literary prize which would be a springboard for the distribution of the Latin American Boom writers, the *Premio Biblioteca Breve.* Barral himself describes in his memoirs the prize as "an instrument of editorial strategy or maneuvering [which] ended up being a wonderful cultural toy . . . it began to gain prestige, especially all over the Americas . . . and became the cornerstone of a possible literary policy for the discovery of Spanish American literature" (1988:79-84). Indeed, the prestige or symbolic capital acquired by Seix Barral in the early 1960s was transformed into an economic success with the 1962 *Premio Biblieteca Breve.* That year the winner was La *ciudad y los perros,* written by an unknown young Peruvian writer, Mario Vargas Llosa. His book rapidly sold out, and by 1971 there had been 16 editions of the text and more than 135, 000 copies sold world-wide. This was quite an accomplishment for an avant-garde publishing house, since at the time most new titles in Spain sold an average of 3,000 copies. According to José Donoso this award launched Vargas Llosa internationally as well as Seix Barral; their names were linked from that moment on to the success of the Latin American novel of the 1960s (1977:72). Furthermore, Seix Barral's visibility derived also from the fact that while most books from Spanish publishers had something (as Donoso puts it) "suspiciously old" about them, this publishing house—in its quest for a new market identity and international visibility—made these novels appealing to the general public with "audacious, brilliant, and up-to-date" covers. For Donoso, Seix Barral's books became "the envy of all" Latin American writers who "had to put up with the total lack of style and the defective presentation of" their novels elsewhere (1977:73).[5]

The establishment of Seix Barral in the literary field of the "Boom"—through the strategies of a new market identity and international visibility—meant that contemporary Latin American novels were now largely distributed in Europe. Although Seix Barral at first aimed toward a restricted and more elitist production in line with the aesthetic renovation of the *nueva novela,* it was able soon to combine its symbolic investments with a rather large-scale distribution of Latin American fiction geared toward the general public. As Bourdieu points out, "these two fields of production [restricted and largescale], opposed as they are, coexist" (128). The terms "Boom" and *nueva novela* may be conceptualized revising this notion of coexistence: the marketing of an elitist aesthetics—such as the *nueva novela*—for popular consumption appears to go beyond the coexistence of restricted and large-scale production, and more in line with terms such as superimposition—or even—takeover. Therefore, one may argue that both terms, "Boom" and *nueva novela,* can be reconciled without discarding their complementary nature.

This dual concept of contemporary Latin American narrative as a commercial enterprise as well as an aesthetic renovation becomes part of José Donoso's fictions and essays. While he maintains that the crisis at Seix Barral "broke up the most influential agent for the internationalization of the Spanish American novel" (1977:108) during the 1960s, he acknowledges that the circle around the Barcelona intelligentsia continued to be associated with prestige and literary success. The literary success of Latin Americans in Barcelona did not end with the crisis at Seix Barral since Barral Editores—the new publishing house founded by Carlos Barral—maintained a similar market identity and international visibility of an avant-garde publisher from Barcelona.[6]

Indeed, by looking at my assessment of the "Boom" and *nueva novela,* it seems clear that markers of symbolic capital—like association with the avant-garde, being published by Seix Barral, belonging to the Barcelona intelligentsia—are key elements of economic as well as of literary success. It is precisely from this point of view, how aesthetics are "consumed" in the "Boom" that I wish to frame my reading of José Donoso's novel *El jardín de al lado* (1981). What I propose is to read Donoso's novel as a case study for the marketing of the aesthetic renovation of the *nueva novela* in the context of the Spanish publishing industry, that is, an analysis of the "consuming of aesthetics" to which the title of this essay refers.[7]

The novel tells a first-person account of an exiled Chilean author, Julio Méndez, in his quest for literary success among the "Boom" writers. After moving to Sitges—an enclave for Latin Americans as well as international expatriates (40km south of Barcelona)—with his wife Gloria, a translator and an article reviewer, Julio tries to publish his book manuscript, a fiction based on his 6-day imprisonment in Chile immediately after the 1973 coup d'etat against Salvador Allende. At the beginning of *El jardín de al lado,* we learn that Julio's novel—written between 1973 and 1980—has been rejected by his literary agent, Núria Monclús, whose powerful editorial network includes all major publishing houses and editors in Spain, as well as many

writers associated with the "Boom." Julio's fixation with the literary success mediated by Barcelona's publishing industry fuels his desire to rewrite the manuscript into what he calls "una obra maestra superior a esas literatura de consumo, hoy tan de moda, que ha encumbrado a falsos dioses como García Márquez, Marcelo Chiriboga, and Carlos Fuentes" (13). To help in the process of rewriting, a friend of the Mendez's, Chilean artist Pancho Salvatierra (literally, "Savior of the Land"), invites them to house-sit in Madrid for the summer so that Julio can peacefully work on his novel while Gloria devotes her time to translations and articles. While in Madrid, Julio will complete the revisions of the manuscript, partly inspired by his constant peeping into the neighbor's garden which resembles his mother's garden in Chile. In spite of the inspiration coming from "the garden next door," Julio's revised manuscript is rejected again by Núria Monclús. Julio, confused and frustrated by his lack of literary success, sells one of Pancho's paintings and goes off to Morocco with his wife Gloria. Their experience in Tangier becomes a turning point for the couple's story as well as for the novel: while Julio decides to relocate in Morocco to look for new sources for his literary success, Gloria prefers to go back to their Barcelona environment. Julio's first person narration stops at this point, the end of the penultimate chapter, and gives way to Gloria's final account of the story in the sixth and last chapter of the novel. Gloria's takeover as a first person narrator relocates the novel back in Barcelona, and more specifically at a luncheon with Núria Monclús, where both women discuss the publication of Gloria's—and not Julio's—first novel. *El jardín de al lado* concludes with Núria's intriguing question to Gloria: "—¿Bueno no es éste el capítulo que falta, el que no has escrito . . . ? (264). Ultimately, there is no real ending to the story since the reader faces a sort of cliffhanger: Who is writing this "missing chapter"? From what exact manuscript does it come from, Julio's or Gloria's, or from a composite text? Has Gloria been the narrator all along? Is there also a missing chapter in Donoso's text?

El jardín de al lado can be read as Donoso's tongue-in-cheek recreation of his *Historia personal del boom* as well as a *roman à clef* of the Barcelona publishing industry (Julio and Gloria as José and María Pilar Donoso, Núria Monclús as Carmen Balcells, the real agent of the Boom writers in Barcelona, etc.). Indeed, Donoso fictionalizes the mechanisms of marketing literary success by an inversion of his own success into the failure of Julio, perhaps proposing that a new generation of Latin Americans writers, women in particular, are "taking over" the field of literary production. This is the new marketing model that Núria Monclús is looking for as she admits it to Gloria in the final chapter: "Se necesitan más novelistas como tú" (248). One may read the implications of the narratorial switch as constructing a particular gender-based theory of authority in the text—as suggested by Lucille Kerr and Priscilla Meléndez—, which would open up a possible discussion of the "Boom" in terms of male vs. female notoriety. What strikes me about the narratorial switch in regard to my earlier definition of "Boom" / *nueva novela* is that Donoso's novel is placed in a time frame which favors the marketing of Latin American women writers, the late 1970s and early 1980s. In this sense, Gloria's take-over might also be read as underscoring the literary success of writers like Isabel Allende, Luisa Valenzuela, Rosario Ferré, Elena Poniatowska or Cristina Peri Rossi whose notoriety as members of the "Boom" phenomenon came after that of male authors in the 1960s and early 1970s. As Montero points out, Donoso appears to fictionalize "a different model of the literary task" (451: [my translation]), one in which his position as a male author has been altered by changes in the literary field. Such changes are anticipated by Núria's remarks about the future of Gloria's career: "Esta novela es extraordinaria, pero la prueba de fuego es la segunda" (248).

Interestingly, the Méndez came to Barcelona in 1973, but the production of "their" literary work takes place around 1980, the time of the literary success of women in the "Boom" (and for some "post-Boom") phenomenon. Within this literary field Julio constantly belittles—and yet envies—the literary success of exclusively male authors of the "Boom" like García Márquez, Fuentes, Vargas Llosa, Cortázar and the fictional Marcelo Chiriboga since they are part of "el insorpotable oropel de falsedades comerciales" (118) that have been become an integral part of the Barcelona publishing industry. For Julio, the "Boom" moved away from—what Bourdieu calls—the restricted into the large-scale production. The authors themselves have acquired star-like status and have started production for the public at large, rather than for other cultural producers. Julio's remarks seem to point toward Bourdieu's assessment that in the literary field, "the writer . . . writes not only for a public, but for a public of equals who are also competitors" in that field because "few people depend as much as artists do for their self-image upon the image of others, and particularly other writers and artists" (116). In this sense Julio is constantly measuring his image against that of the Boom writers. He is obsessively aware of this type of competition in the literary field: "¿Vería yo mi nombre allá arriba—pese a la contraria superagente mafiosa—entre los de Vargas Llosa, Roa Bastos, Marcelo Chiriboga, Carlos Fuentes y Ernesto Sábato?" (35). Indeed, Julio's rhetorical question ponders his ability to enter the literary field of the "Boom," a field "ruled" in the fiction by the all-mighty Núria Monclús. Julio knows that in order to achieve literary success in the Barcelona milieu he needs to occupy—what Bourdieu calls—an "available position to engage in competition for control of the interests or resources which are specific" to the literary field (6). For Julio, the exclusion from that particular field translates into failure, and impedes his return to Chile: "No puedo volver. ¿Cómo? ¿Sin un libro publicado en España, con la cola entre las piernas . . . ?" (165).[8]

Furthermore, Núria's reputation in the text as the "legendaria *capomafia* del grupo de célebres novelistas lationoamericanos" (44) underscores that much of the literary success of the "Boom" revolves around her power figure. In Bourdieu's terms, Núria would be an agent of consecration who has already acquired the power to grant cultural consecration within the literary field of the "Boom." Moreover, she is often identified as generator of economic capital, as a "catalana mercenaria que no era más que un mercader de literatura" (29). It is precisely Núria's capabilities as producer of symbolic as well as economic capital that Julio—and perhaps Gloria—pursue since they would also be competing in the literary field for symbolic capital, namely the literary success coming from the Barcelona publishing industry.

It is crucial to understand that in the literary field fictionalized in Donoso's novel, Núria dictates literary trends in the editorial industry in Barcelona but has also managed to control the economic capital upon which such industry is based: "se murmuraba que esta diosa tiránica era capaz de hacer y deshacer reputaciones, de fundir y fundar editoriales y colecciones, de levantar fortunas y hacer quebrar empresas" (44). Julio's exaggeration of Núria's powers does not correspond with the parameters of diffusion of Latin American literature of Seix Barral, Joaquín Mortiz or Sudamericana; rather, it presents a critique of the commercialization and business-like structures by which most publishers seem to function in the novel. In equivalent terms, Donoso describes in *Historia personal* the "real" literary agent of the Boom writers in Barcelona, Carmen Balcells, as a power figure who "seemed to have in her hands the strings that made us all dance like marionettes" (106).

Thanks to Núria's role the literary field of the Boom appears to have moved from the field of restricted into the field of large-scale production. For Gutiérrez Mouat, "the emergence of a culture industry in Latin America coincided with the modernization of the Latin American Novel, a revival that culminated in the boom of the 1960s" (67). This expansionary movement in Latin American narrative—against which Julio is determined to fight—has been framed by Jean Franco with the term *"autores superestrella"* [author-superstars], typical of the age of mass culture. Indeed, one of Núria's interest in the literary field is to promote the star status of Latin American writers. Julio's novel lacks the star qualities of other greats of the "Boom" since his revised manuscript—in Núria's words—is just "pura retórica, imitación de lo que está de moda entre los escritores latinoamericanos de hoy" (224).

By contrast, Núria seems to grant cultural consecration to the literary works of a fictional Ecuadorian writer who has become an *autor superestrella* of the Barcelona milieu, Marcelo Chiriboga. This super-star of the Latin American Boom assumes the role of the competitor of Julio within the literary field: Julio's self-image relies on the literary success of Chiriboga's masterpiece and best-seller *La caja sin secreto* [The Box Without Secret]. At first, Julio appears to despise Marcelo for being "el más insolentemente célebre de todos los integrantes del dudoso boom" (132). However, he later on succumbs to Chiriboga's literary success when, in the closing section of chapter 5, Julio admits:

> Mi novela es una mierda. La prosa de Chiriboga, en cambio, tiene una simplicidad deceptiva que se disuelve bajo la lengua, embargando los pulmones y el ser entero con un aroma que la corteza de su lenguaje no hacía esperar . . . Quisiera escribir como Chiriboga. Pero no puedo.
>
> (242)

Indeed, Julio—as a competitor of the literary field—is constantly measuring the quality of his own prose against Chiriboga's, and in so doing, he is proposing two models of writing which coincide with the trends of the commercial or editorial "boom" and aesthetic renovation *(nueva novela)*. While Julio insists on the documentary nature of his novel, he appears to criticize the excessive formalism and linguistic experimentation in the works of Cortázar, Fuentes, or Vargas Llosa. Julio considers their works as excessively cosmopolitan, lacking the kind of political commitment he brings into his novel with his ordeal in a Chilean prison (46). Interestingly, Chiriboga's master-piece is literally an empty box, "a box without any secrets," without any—let's say—political, testimonial or historical content, and yet shows great mastery of the language. The excessive formalism of Chiriboga's work, according to Julio, has become the key to marketing its literary success: "La obra de Chiriboga es una obra inerte, en el fondo una invención de esa bruja de las finanzas que es Núria Monclús" (139). Curiously, Chiriboga is the only fictional author of the Boom in *El jardín de al lado,* even though his literary persona has reappeared as a "real novelist" in Fuentes's *El naranjo* (1993), and as the subject of university research in Donoso's 1993 novel *Donde van a morir los elefantes.* One may read Chiriboga's presence, then, as the epitome of the marketing of Latin American fiction since his literary success in fiction appears to have surpassed the realm of the literary. The playfulness of his literary persona is also highlighted by the fact that his name is phonetically close to *chirigota* (Spanish for joke, laughing stock). Chiriboga's persona, therefore, appears to be in contrast with the literary persona of—what González calls—the "strong, male, politically committed figure," and more in line with the "new public role of the Latin American writer" (109), which Jean Franco would call *autor-superestrella.*

In the end, all the writers in Donoso's novel appear to lack the literary qualities Julio claims to have: Chiriboga is more of a "laughing stock" and a puppet in Núria's marketing plots than an accomplished writer, Gloria—despite her success, or her "glory"—is not an accomplished writer since she does not have a second novel and her first one appears to be incomplete, and the many real Boom writers mentioned in the text—Fuentes, Vargas Llosa, Roa Bastos, Sábato, Cortázar, etc—are also discarded because "desconocían la experiencia de primera mano como participantes en una tragedia colectiva" (46).

Moreover, it seems that one cannot study the "Boom" without addressing its own "awareness" of the field of cultural production in which its literary works appear. Many Boom writers, in this respect, enjoy autonomy with respect to the field by being critical of it. As Bourdieu points out, "the field of restricted production tends to develop its own criteria for the evaluation of its products, thus achieving the truly cultural recognition accorded by the peer group whose members are both privileged clients and competitors" (115). This is particularly true of the restricted production initially launched by Seix Barral, incidentally the kind of production Julio Méndez is looking for. While in Donoso's novel cultural legitimacy comes from the peer group of fictional and real characters—Fuentes, Cortázar, Chiriboga, García Márquez, Núria Monclús, etc—, Seix Barral's legitimacy for the distribution of Latin American culture is also based on the participation of the real peer group members—like García Márquez and Vargas Llosa—who became, for instance, participants in the evaluation process of the *Premio Biblioteca Breve.*

In closing, my reading of José Donoso's works underscores that the marketing of literary success of Latin American narrative after 1960s cannot be simply contextualized in economic terms since the marketing of an elitist aesthetics for popular consumption raises the question of how symbolic capital can become a commodity on the real economic market. In this sense, my reading of the "Boom" as a distinct—and yet concurrent—manifestation of the *nueva novela* helps to understand how this literary period oscillates from elitist to popular, from restricted to large-scale production, from the politically-committed author to the *autor-superestrella,* ultimately presenting a case of consuming aesthetics.

Notes

1. Ángel Rama sees the "Boom" as a movement toward the globalization of Latin America based on advertising strategies, and David Viñas as lacking

any aesthetic common denominator among its writers. For Emir Rodríguez Monegal the initial link between the "Boom" writers' support for the Cuban revolution and their "revolutionary" use of language was transformed into "an editorial phenomenon": "the result of a decision in the industry to launch a product they thought they could sell, the new Latin American prose fiction" (Mac Adam 30). Rodríguez Monegal refers to three factors that generated this oscillatory movement between a cultural revolution and an industrial boom: the role of Seix Barral, the creation of literary journals such as *Marcha, Primera Plana, Mundo Nuevo* and *Libre,* and the increasing number of translations and film adaptations of Latin American novels. Carlos Fuentes avoids the term "Boom" and focuses on *nueva novela as* defined by the modernization of Latin American fiction and its renovation of language, themes, and narrative structures.

2. Seix Barral has published eleven literary works by Donoso—*Coronación* (1958), *Este domingo* (1966), *Cuentos* (1971), *El obsceno pájaro de la noche* (1970), *Tres novelitas burguesas* (1973), *El lugar sin límites* (1976), *Casa de campo* (1978), *La misteriosa desaparición de la marquesita de Loria* (1980), *El jardín de al lado* (1981), *Cuatro para Delfina,* and *La desesperanza* (1986)—and two editions of his memoirs *Historia personal del boom* (1972, 1983). However, Donoso minimizes the importance of the marketing strategies by Seix Barral—and other publishing houses of the time, Joaquín Mortiz in Mexico, or Losada, Emecé, Jorge Álvarez and Sudamericana in Argentina—by pointing out that "the popularity of the contemporary Spanish American novel" goes beyond "the publicity mechanism." He cites Sudamericana's modest launching of *One Hundred Years of Solitude* as an example of a novel that becomes a world-wide best-seller without such editorial support (69-70; [all English quotations are from *The Spanish American Boom: A Personal History*]).

3. To illustrate the successful expansion into the Latin American market supported by the government's policies, one can look at data from the *Instituto Nacional del Libro Español* (National Book Institute) in 1957 only 3,000 new titles were published in Spain, by 1969 the numbers went up to 13,000. Also in 1969, 900 publishers were registered, and more than 82% of the books printed in Spain were headed for the Latin American market, mainly Argentina (18%), Mexico (13%), Venezuela (10%), and Chile (10%) (Dravasa 212-16). During the last decade of the Franco regime, new regulations concerning printed materials took effect based on the *Ley de Prensa e Imprenta* [The Printing and Publishing Law] authored by Manuel

Fraga Iribarne in 1966. With this new law the government claimed to put an end to the censorship of printed materials with its banner "la censura ya no existe" [censorship no longer exists]. Despite the government's claim, all printed material still had to receive the seal of approval of the *Ministerio de Información y Turismo,* and therefore censorship continued. Nonetheless, the new law did change the way in which manuscripts were evaluated by the censors. Manuel Abellán in "La censura franquista y los escritores latinoamericanos" argues that the law allowed for a larger distribution of Latin American texts, since many of their works were authorized for printing as long as they were not distributed in Spain. The government's expansion policies toward the Latin American market were also supported by the many restrictions on importing books from abroad, particularly from Cuba and Argentina, two of the most notable competitors for the literary distribution of the Latin American Boom. (see Abellán 1980, Cisquella, Santana 1992 and 1994, Sivona).

4. The Formentor and International Prizes were created by a consortium of six publishers from France (Gallimard), Spain (Seix Barral), Italy (Einaudi), England (Weidenfeld & Nicholson), Germany (Rowohlt Verlag), and the U.S. (Grove Press)—who were later joined by seven more editors from Portugal, Canada, the Netherlands, and the Scandinavian countries. They met once a year at the Formentor Hotel in Majorca to award the Formentor Prize to the best unpublished manuscript, and the International Prize to recognize an established author of world stature. Each prize carried a $10,000 award and the publication of the author's work by the 13 publishers. The *Premio Biblioteca Breve*—which carried an award of less than $2,000 and the publication of the winning manuscript—was officially open to literary works from Spain and Latin America, but in reality the selection of manuscripts by members of the jury (Joan Petit, Jose María Castellet, Luis Goytisolo) was subject to internal recommendations as well as the editorial policies of Carlos Barral (see p. 80-on, *Cuando las horas veloces).* It is no surprise that Barral's supervision of the prize between 1959 and 1969 resulted in five Latin American winners and two finalists (see Appendix).

5. Seix Barral marketed Latin American texts in three different collections: *Biblioteca Breve*—with its foldable jacket that will turn into a paperback version called *Biblioteca de Bolsillo*—, *Biblioteca Nueva Narrativa Hispánica*—distributed through the publishing house outlets in Barcelona, Caracas, Mexico—and the lesser known *Biblioteca Universal Formentor.*

6. This, indeed, relates to my earlier assessment of Barral's investments in symbolic capital within the literary field of the "Boom." In this sense, an ad for Barral Editores in the second issue of *Libre,* clearly showed the continuation of Carlos Barral's line of symbolic investment in literary success: "Manténganse en Vanguardia, siga a Barral [Keep up with the Avant-Garde, Follow Barral] (*Libre* 2, 1971-72).

7. I wish to thank Catherine Nickel for suggesting the phrase "consuming aesthetics" and for her kindness in reading an earlier version of this manuscript. My gratitude also goes to Ross Chambers for reading the first draft of this essay.

8. According to Flora Gónzalez, Julio's failure also suggests that the "androgynous" nature of Donoso's double narrator unveils "the image of the literary agent, Núria Monclús, as a castrating female" (105), without a single book published, Julio, *literally,* must hide his tail.

Bibliography

Abellán, Manuel. *Censura y creación literaria en España (1939-1976).* Barcelona: Ediciones Península, 1980.

————. "La censura franquista y los escritores latinoamericanos." *Letras Peninsulares* (Spring 1992): 11-21

Anderson, Danny J. "Creating Cultural Prestige: *Editorial Joaquín Mortiz." Latin American Research Review* 31.2 (1996): 3-41.

Barral, Carlos. *Los años sin excusa.* Barcelona: Seix-Barral, 1978.

————. *Los años de penitencia.* Madrid: Alianza Editorial, 1975.

————. *Cuando las horas veloces.* Barcelona: Tusquets, 1988.

Bourdieu, Pierre. *The Field of Cultural Production.* Ed. Randal Johnson. New York: Columbia, 1993.

Bufkin, E. C., ed. *Foreign Literary Prizes.* New York: Bowker Co., 1980.

Cisquella, Georgina et al. *Diez años de represión cultural: la censura de libros durante la Ley de Prensa (1966-76).* Barcelona: Anagrama, 1977.

Cortínez, Verónica. "La parroquia y el universo: *Historia personal del 'Boom'* de José Donoso." *Revista chilena de literatura* 48 (1996): 13-22.

Dravasa, Maider. "El 'Boom' y Barcelona: Literatura y poder." Diss. Yale Univ., 1991.

Donoso, José. *The Spanish American Boom: A Personal History.* New York: Columbia UP, 1977.

————. *Historia personal del 'boom' (new edition).* Barcelona: Seix-Barral, 1983.

————. *El jardín de al lado.* Barcelona: Seix-Barral, 1981.

————. *The Garden Next Door.* Trans. Hardie St. Martin. New York: Grove Press, 1992.

Feal, Rosemary. "Veiled Portraits: Donoso's Interartistic Dialogue in *El jardín de al lado." MLN* 103 (1988): 46-55.

Franco, Jean. "Narrador, Autor, Superestrella: la narrativa latinoamericana en la época de cultura de masas." *Revista iberoamericana* 114-115 (1981): 129-148.

Fuentes, Carlos. *La nueva novela hispanoamericana.* Mexico: Joaquín Mortiz, 1969.

González, Flora. *José Donoso's House of Fiction.* Detroit: Wayne State UP, 1995.

Gutiérrez Mouat, Ricardo. "Aesthetics, Ethics, and Politics in Donoso's *El jardín de al lado." PMLA* 106 (1991): 60-70.

Joset, Jacques. "El imposible *Boom* de José Donoso." *Revista iberoamericana* 48 (118-119) (1982): 91-101.

Kerr, Lucille. *Reclaiming the Author: Figures and Fictions from Latin America.* Durham: Duke UP, 1992.

Libre. 1971-72.

Mac Adam, Alfred J. "The Boom: A Retrospective." *Review: Latin American Literature and Arts* 33 (1984): 30-36.

Meléndez, Priscilla. "Writing and Reading the Palimpsest: Donoso's *El jardín de al lado." Symposium* 41 (Fall 1987): 200-213.

Montero, Oscar. *"El jardín de al lado:* La escritura y el fracaso del éxito" 49 (123-124) (1983): 449-67.

Rama, Ángel, ed. *Más allá del boom: literatura y mercado.* Mexico: Marcha, 1981.

Santana, Mario. "El 'boom' en Espana: una historia necesaria. *"Letras peninsulares* 5.1 (1992): 75-94.

————. "La mies y la cizaña: narrativa hispanoamericana y sistema literario en la España de los años 60." *Actas del XXIX Congreso del Instituto Internacional de Literatura Iberoamericana.* Barcelona: PPU, 1994. 599-607.

Sinova, Justino. *La censura de Prensa durante el franquismo (1936-1951).* Madrid: Espasa-Calpe, 1989.

Shaw, Donald L. "The Post-Boom in Spanish American Fiction. *"Studies in 20th-Century Literature* 19.1 (special issue, 1995): 11-27.

Tola de Habich, Fernando and Patricia Grieve. *Los españoles y el boom.* Caracas: Editorial Tiempo Nuevo, 1971.

Viñas, David. "Pareceres y disgresiones en torno a la nueva narrativa latinoamericana." *Más allá del boom: literatura y mercado.* Ed. Ángel Rama. Mexico: Marcha, 1981. 13-50.

FURTHER READING

Criticism

Baker, Robert. "José Donoso's *El obsceno pájaro de la noche*: Thoughts on 'Schizophrenic' Form." *Revista de Estudios Hispanicos* 26, no. 1 (January 1992): 37-60.
Examines what *El obsceno pájaro de la noche* suggest about "the postmodern historical moment."

Feal, Rosemary Geisdorfer. "Veiled Portraits: Donoso's Interartistic Dialogue in *El jardín de al lado. MLN* 103, no. 2 (March 1988): 398-418.
Discusses the connection between the masked narrator in *El jardín de al lado* and the novel's "dialogue" between the art forms of literature and painting.

Friedman, Mary Lusky. "The Chilean Exile's Return: Donoso versus García Márquez." *The Americas Review: A Review of Hispanic Literature and Art of the USA* 18, nos. 3-4 (Fall-Winter 1990): 211-17.
Explores the differences in Donoso's and Márquez's respective 1986 publications documenting the return of exiles to Chile after the end of the Pinochet government.

———. "The Artistry of *La desesperanza* by José Donoso." *Hispania* 78, no. 1 (March 1995): 13-24.
Examines the narrative strategies which underlie *La desesperanza,* a novel in which Donoso portrays the bleakness of the Pinochet era.

Kogan, Marcela. "Stormy Adventures of the Spirit." *Americas* 39, no. 6 (November-December 1987): 8-13.
Interview in which Donoso reflects on his life, career, and experiences as a member of the Latin American Boom generation.

Mandri, Flora González. "The Androgynous Narrator in *El jardín de al lado.*" In *José Donoso's House of Fiction: A Dramatic Construction of Time and Place,* pp. 109-22. Detroit: Wayne State University Press, 1995.
Analyzes Donoso's technique of using apparently distinct male and female voices in *El jardín de al lado* that, in the end, are actually the voice of a single female narrator.

Pollard, Scott. "Artists, Aesthetics, and Family Politics in Donoso's *El obsceno pájaro de la noche* and James's *The Golden Bowl.*" *Comparatist: Journal of the Southern Comparative Literature Association* 23, (May 1999): 40-62.
Discusses Donoso's *El obsceno pájaro de la noche* in terms of the premodern literary mode of Henry James's *The Golden Bowl.*

Additional coverage of Donoso's life and career is contained in the following sources published by the Gale Group: *Concise Dictionary of World Literary Biography,* **Vol. 3;** *Contemporary Authors,* **Vols. 81-84, 155;** *Contemporary Authors New Revision Series,* **Vols. 32, 73;** *Contemporary Literary Criticism,* **Vols. 4, 8, 11, 32, 99;** *Dictionary of Literary Biography,* **Vol. 113;** *DISCovering Authors Modules: Multicultural Authors; Hispanic Literature Criticism,* **Ed. 1;** *Hispanic Writers,* **Eds. 1, 2;** *Latin American Writers; Latin American Writers Supplement,* **Ed. 1;** *Literature Resource Center; Major 20th-Century Writers,* **Eds. 1, 2;** *Reference Guide to Short Fiction,* **Ed. 2;** *Short Story Criticism,* **Vol. 34; and** *World Literature and Its Times,* **Vol. 1.**

Helen Hooven Santmyer
1895-1986

American novelist, short story writer, poet, and essayist.

The following entry provides criticism on Santmyer's works from 1984 through 1998. For criticism prior to 1984, see *CLC,* Volume 33.

INTRODUCTION

Santmyer had a modest literary output beginning in the 1920s, but fame did not reach her until the publication of her 1982 novel *". . . And Ladies of the Club."* Thanks to some effective promotion and a selection by the Book-of-the-Month Club, this story of Midwestern small-town life became a bestseller when Santmyer was in her eighties. Thereafter critics and the public took a new interest in Santmyer's other works as well.

BIOGRAPHICAL INFORMATION

Helen Hooven Santmyer was born on November 25, 1895, in Cincinnati, Ohio, but spent much of her life in Xenia, a small city in the southwestern part of the state, where both sides of her family had deep roots. Santmyer never stopped calling Xenia home, in spite of occasional forays elsewhere in the United States and abroad. She led a happy and rather conventional childhood, with plenty of time to develop her love of reading. In 1914 she entered Wellesley College in Massachusetts, where she was encouraged to pursue a writing career. After a brief stint working for a suffragette organization in New York City, she became secretary to an editor of *Scribner's* magazine, where she was exposed to a number of famous writers such as Sinclair Lewis and F. Scott Fitzgerald. In 1921 she returned home to Xenia to care for her ailing mother. Her father's largesse allowed her to spend three years at Oxford University in England, where she received a degree in literature in 1927. During this period she also produced her first novel, continuing her literary efforts when she returned to Ohio. After a brief time in California with her family, she began to teach at Cedarville College near Xenia, becoming dean of women and chair of the English department. In the mid-1950s she left teaching to become a reference librarian at the Dayton and Montgomery County Library until her retirement in 1959, living and travelling with her longtime friend Mildred Sandoe. In the mid-1960s, using notes she had accumu-

lated over the years, she began work on what was to become *". . . And Ladies of the Club,"* not completing the manuscript until 1975. Santmyer professed to be as shocked as anyone else when the 1984 reissue of the book provoked such a worldwide literary reaction. At the time in poor health and in a nursing home, she was able to enjoy her newfound success only until 1986, when she died on February 21, from complications of emphysema.

MAJOR WORKS

Santmyer's first novel, the semi-autobiographical *Herbs and Apples* (1925), tells the story of a girl from Ohio who longs to go to New York to pursue a writing career but is thwarted by the onset of World War I. Her 1929 novel, *The Fierce Dispute,* focuses on a child whose mother and grandmother are engaged in a struggle for control of her future. *Ohio Town* (1962) is a collection of essays recalling the sights and sounds of Xenia in

Santmyer's youth. Santmyer's *". . . And Ladies of the Club"* attracted scant attention when it was first published by Ohio State University Press in 1982. When this saga of the lives of members of a small city women's club from 1868 to 1932 was reprinted by G. P. Putnam's Sons in 1984, however, it became the selection of the Book-of-the-Month Club, was widely reviewed, and brought a great deal of press attention to the elderly Santmyer. A posthumous novel, *Farewell, Summer,* appeared in 1988.

CRITICAL RECEPTION

Santmyer's early books were little noticed and little reviewed. The same could be said of *". . . And Ladies of the Club"* in its initial incarnation in 1982. Through a series of fortunate coincidences, the Putnam edition of 1984 became the publishing sensation of that year, remaining on the bestseller list for thirty-seven weeks. The story of a nearly ninety-year-old lady who had supposedly worked on a book for fifty years was irresistible to the national news media. Many critics were kind to Santmyer, noting her faithfulness to detail and her accurate evocation of life at the turn of the century and beyond. Others found the book unnecessarily long, compared it unfavorably with books like *Main Street* and *My Ántonia,* or accused the publisher of unduly promoting a mediocre book for its publicity value. Because of the success of *". . . And Ladies of the Club,"* Santmyer's other works, particularly *Ohio Town,* were reissued and also gained a modest amount of critical attention.

***

PRINCIPAL WORKS

Herbs and Apples (novel) 1925
The Fierce Dispute (novel) 1929
Ohio Town 1962 (essays)
". . . And Ladies of the Club" (novel) 1982; reprinted in 1984
Farewell, Summer (novel) 1988

***

CRITICISM

Trudy Krishner (review date 27 January 1984)

SOURCE: Krishner, Trudy. "The Goal of a Lifetime Won at Last." *Christian Science Monitor* (27 January 1984): 19.

[*In the following review, Krishner gives a preview of* ". . . And Ladies of the Club," *noting its fortunate selection by the Book-of-the-Month Club and G. P. Putnam's Sons.*]

For Helen Santmyer, success has come somewhat later than it does in most careers. Miss Santmyer, an 88-year-old retired librarian, is being hailed as the literary equivalent of Grandma Moses.

Her novel about small-town life, which she began in the 1920s and finally finished as a nursing home resident in the 1980s, has been published by a university press and is about to be republished in large, lucrative editions by the Book-of-the-Month Club and G. P. Putnam's Sons.

Suddenly Helen Hooven Santmyer is a literary celebrity. Reporters and photographers invade her nursing home accommodations in this quiet southwestern Ohio town. And, as the headlines indicate, the story is of triumph—the goal of a lifetime finally achieved.

Miss Santmyer's 1,344-page novel, *". . . And Ladies of the Club,"* spans the years 1868-1932 in the small fictional Ohio town of Waynesboro. It follows a group of women across the generations.

Work on it absorbed Miss Santmyer's attention year after year, decade after decade. In the '20s she conceived of the book as a kind of answer to Sinclair Lewis, the tart-tongued novelist who, she felt, had gotten life in small-town America all wrong. She became intent on responding to his *Main Street,* which made her so angry that, even decades after its publication in 1920, she seethed when she thought about it. Her friends and acquaintances weren't small, petty people. "They were strong, independent people," she says. "I wanted to paint a picture of what those men and women did."

Her own book would tell the true story of small-town life, the life she knew best, the life circumscribed by the courthouse, the church, the school, the railway station, and the cemetery. She spent her childhood years here before going east to Wellesley College, where she graduated in 1918. She published a book and then went abroad in 1924 to Oxford University to study the beginnings of the novel. "They gave me a bachelor of letters degree," she remembers, laughing. "It was a degree they invented for American students who already had their bachelor's, and they couldn't think of what else to give them."

She returned to Xenia in the late '20s to care for her mother and father, then served for many years as dean of women and head of the English Department at Cedarville College in southwestern Ohio. Later she worked as a reference librarian in Dayton.

She depicted small-town life in a collection of essays called *Ohio Town,* published in 1962. After completing *Ohio Town,* she turned back more earnestly to her novel.

"Helen worked on the revision of the book from 1976 on," says her friend Mildred Sandoe. And she didn't let ill health and hospitalization stop her. "She would ask me to bring [the manuscript] out to her, and I would read it to her, and she would make sugestions from the bed," Miss Sandoe recalls. In 1982 Ohio State University Press published *". . . And Ladies of the Club."*

Now it's making even bigger waves. Selection by the Book-of-the-Month Club assures an author of a wide reading audience, and, in this case, a six-figure advance against royalties. "The standard advance is $85,000," says club president Al Silverman, "but in this case we're paying $110,000."

And, since G. P. Putnam's Sons has contracted for rights to republish the novel in hard cover in August, sales are likely to be even higher.

Negotiations for adaptation of the book as a TV miniseries or feature film are under way. About the prospect of seeing her book on screen, Miss Santmyer is less than sanguine. "Movies ruin books," she says. "They take the love affairs and blow everything all out of proportion."

Carolyn See (review date 10 June 1984)

SOURCE: See, Carolyn. "The Time When Women Belonged." *Los Angeles Times Book Review* (10 June 1984): 1.

[*In the following review, See paints* ". . . And Ladies of the Club" *as a ponderous yet valuable look at the realities of small-town life.*]

What we will be looking at here in a shamefully short review is a true literary curiosity, an artifact much more than a novel, a monument of words, a tool for the student of American history, a private compilation, a channeling of tremendous, idiosyncratic effort.

Most people interested in publishing must know by now that *". . . And Ladies of the Club"* is the life's work of an obscure woman already living out her days in a nursing home. They know this book was printed in a small edition by the Ohio State University Press. All this is unusual enough, but the truly miraculous aspects of this curious story are that this book was then picked up by a successful commercial publisher and has been made a main selection of the Book-of-the-Month Club. It must be a throwback to a certain kind of philanthropy, a respect for culture as such, the culture described within the pages of this vast volume.

There are problems with this unending narrative, physical and cultural problems aplenty. To read *". . . And Ladies of the Club,"* you're going to have to pick it up.

It's chunky and thick, about the size, shape and weight of a five-pound sack of sugar. Its almost 1,200 pages are a mild deception. The print in this book is excruciatingly small: if the type size were in any way normal, the pages might run close to 2,000.

The cultural obstacles are almost certainly more enervating. We live in the 20th Century, but in style, subject matter, treatment, and above all, pace, this is precisely a 19th-Century novel, not merely in length, but in gentility. There are no murders, sex scenes, jokes or adventures here. And—to get the last caveat out of the way— Helen Hooven Santmyer is no Tolstoy, or even a George Eliot. There is no structure here, no particular novelistic cunning or guile. Readers cannot fairly expect to put down this volume with characters like Natasha or Mr. Casuabon imprinted forever in their brains: This is a novel of ordinary life, in an ordinary Midwestern town, whose inhabitants are born, marry, reproduce, grow old and die. That is all.

Yet *". . . And the Ladies of the Club"* is a valuable book, a meticulous, painstaking journey through our American past. It begins in the year 1868, at a commencement on the shaded lawns of the Waynesboro Female College. We see for the first time Anne Alexander and Sally Cochran, young ladies dressed in the height of fashion, graduates on the brink of life, who will both within a year and a half be wives and mothers. Anne will marry John Gordon, a morose young doctor still reeling from his experiences in the Civil War, and Sally's life will be spent with John's friend, Ludwig Rausch, an enterprising young businessman who buys up a decaying rope business and becomes actively involved in local politics.

But just as important as these two marriages, Santmyer suggests, is the founding of the Waynesboro Women's Club. The club, at its beginning, consists of a dozen ladies who agree to meet on Wednesday afternoons, "fortnightly," to read and criticize papers on literature and history. The charter membership includes Anne and Sally, those two fresh young graduates; Mrs. Ballard, wife of the judge, and her two old-maid daughters; several more old-maid schoolteachers, and one calculating teacher who has just snagged a rather dim Civil War general. . . .

And life "begins," at least in the eyes of Anne and Sally. We see postwar politics from their point of view; the serious rifts in the Republican party, the different economic policies that determine depression and recovery. We see the rope business and exactly how it grows—and how you make rope. Again, from the woman's point of view, we watch the dissensions between the Protestant sects: the unfashionable, shabby Baptists; the comparatively liberal Presbyterians, and the rock-ribbed, bigoted and oppressive Reformed Presbyterians, who won't drink, dance, sing hymns or observe Christmas. We see—at a distance—the untouchable, socially impossible, Roman Catholics, made up entirely of the Irish working class.

We see, then, people trying to make a life, make *their* lives, within a set of rules, mostly self-inflicted, that would seem impossibly stultifying. We read, at the end of the book, that its writer considered this account to be an answer to Sinclair Lewis, "whose *Main Street* had made her so angry that after a decade, she seethed when she thought of it." But *". . . And Ladies of the Club"* is more damning by far than that cranky little volume, simply by its exhaustive description of small-town American life.

This is a society where, even to visit your best girlfriend, you don't venture out without gloves, hat, parasol, card case. A society where marriages may be placed in jeopardy if one person wants to see an amateur theatrical and the other considers it certain damnation. Where families are broken because of one *mouthful* of beer. Where even the "good guys," Sally Cochran Rausch, for instance, can rant that a wife with a Catholic *mother* "will never be received in society."

This is a picture of a society so stultifying that by Page 700 or so the reader is beaten, knowing that there is no point, outside of grim determination, in going on reading, because there will simply be more lemonade: "When Rose had filled the glasses and withdrawn, the two women exchanged the usual amenities before settling down to business. A polite inquiry as to Mr. Cochran's health was answered as politely." And so on. Forever. For lifetimes.

It must be Santmyer's submerged contention that within these strictures, of course, life *did* go on, and women contributed much to it. There are those "Glorious Fourths," with fried chicken, fireworks, grand marches. The women's club, besides writing papers and keeping up with contemporary literature, is responsible, first, for a subscription library, and then a public one—although most of the population is scandalized by the thought of Negroes and Irish touching the books and making them "filthy."

The women sponsor lectures, lead a temperance crusade. And the stultifying closeness and emphasis on "correct" behavior has peculiar positive effects: When Anne's womanizing husband allows a cousin of his—on whom he has fathered a child—to come to Waynesboro, Anne can welcome her with almost open arms, secure in the conviction that a woman who, again, wants to be "received" into society, must behave with perfect prudence and circumspection.

This book is too long, too thick, too dense, too detailed to be summed up in one review. A reader may object that the pages and pages and *pages* of time spent in discussion of local Ohio politics are interesting in terms of history, but exhausting in a novel, and wonder that although we see Anne and Sally year by year, from the time they're 18 until they're 80, we don't know a great deal more about them at the end than at the beginning.

What this book is—no more, no less—is a mirror on daily life in a small American town. Infidelity, sickness, death are all submerged in who is going to give whom a ride home from the club, who's going to take cakes to the bereaved, who's going to answer the door, who's going to warm the sheets, who's going to call the undertaker. The theme, if there is one, is—given this life, what do you do with it? Anne, whose husband is unfaithful and gloomy, whose children both die, who never gets to go anywhere, who evolves from being a devout Presbyterian to a mild skeptic, is sure of one thing only. In spite of *everything,* the trivial and the everyday, we are put in this life to enjoy it, and she sets about this task with the same sad persistence she would employ to write one of her club papers.

Michael Malone (essay date 21-28 July 1984)

SOURCE: Malone, Michael. ". . . And Ladies of the G.O.P." *Nation* 129 (21-28 July 1984): 52-4.

[*In the following essay, Malone takes a jaundiced view of* ". . . And Ladies of the Club," *asserting that it is graceless and of dubious literary quality.*]

Properly publicized, nothing succeeds like failure, particularly when its hucksters belong to the industry that inflicted the initial wound. Hollywood, for example, adores films excoriating its powerful heartlessness and takes sentimental satisfaction in rewarding its own victims: Ingrid Bergman wins an Oscar for having been ostracized by those who give Oscars. Publishing is no different: it fervently gloats over how many times it turned down William Kennedy's *Ironweed* before wreathing the book in loot and laurel. An even noisier lemming rush chased John Kennedy O'Toole's *A Confederacy of Dunces.* Eleven years after its young author, depressed by innumerable rejections of his novel, committed suicide, his mother persuaded Walker Percy to persuade Louisiana State University Press to publish the book. It became a best seller and won the Pulitzer Prize in 1981.

As Reagan would say, here we go again. In 1982, Ohio State University Press printed a few hundred copies of a 1,176-page novel called *". . . And Ladies of the Club,"* by Helen Hooven Santmyer, an octogenarian resident of a nursing home in a small southwestern Ohio town. The book received a few regional reviews and sold modestly. Now, in *The New York Times Book*

Review of June 24, a full-page ad announces that G. P. Putnam's Sons has 200,000 copies of this same novel in print; the book is praised in a long review by Vance Bourjaily and listed (before publication) as number two on the *Times* best-seller list. Book-of-the-Month Club has paid $110,000 to make *". . . And Ladies of the Club"* its main selection; Berkeley Books has paid $400,000 for the paperback rights; and *Family Circle* is serializing Miss Santmyer's encyclopedic tome of middle-American social, theological and political mores from 1868 to 1932 as "an unforgettable love story." A mini-series is apparently in the works. This book, in industry lingo, has legs.

It has legs without the sex or shootouts or glitz that usually accompany such limbs. It has legs without the grace of style or joy of creativity that occasionally accompany such limbs. Its legs have nothing to do with its enormous body (it's longer than *War and Peace*), nor its circumscribed soul. *Ladies* [*". . . And Ladies of the Club,"*] is an earnest, intelligent, stolidly written, leaden-crafted, Sears, Roebuck catalogue of the lives of a great many earnest, stolid, well-off, white Protestant Republican citizens who reside in a small southwestern Ohio town and think its values the center and circumference of the moral universe. The book is village Victorian; the legs are modern Manhattan. Having legs means a novel will walk briskly off the shelf to the cash register, like any other successfully promoted product. Just as literature need not be bad (or good) to fail—Thackeray's *Vanity Fair* was rejected eighteen times—so it need not be bad (or good) to succeed with a helping leg up. Byron's *Childe Harold* sold like *The Michael Jackson Story* because society was agog with scandalous rumors about its author. Many writers who have made their way into the canon were boosted there, in fact, by one leg or another. If not "mad, bad and dangerous to know," they were flamboyantly self-destructive, or hermits, or died young, or fought bulls, or were censored. We're only human; we like a star.

Helen Hooven Santmyer is now a star, a celebrity product, famous for writing a very long book over a very long time at a very advanced age, and for having her book left forlorn by the hearth at first and then whisked off to the ball to marry the Prince of Fortune. As a journalist from *The Washington Post* put it, apparently in all seriousness,

> The bare account of how she produced the work over the years, in her spare time, in sickness and in health, in itself provides an astonishing testament. She wrote it all out in longhand, on a ledger. . . . Let us pause to praise . . . a really good example of the lone and worthy human triumphing in the end. Amid the hog wallow of phonies, hucksters, hustlers, and other assorted Great I Ams . . . rises the name of Helen Hooven Santmyer. She stands apart for fulfilling the American—the universal—dream of achieving a life's ambition. Her hard work has paid off at age 88.

The fact that all this sounds like the sort of speech that would start Reagan weeping into the flag has a lot to do with *why* *". . . And Ladies of the Club"* is the right best seller for our neo-Gilded Age. But first, *how?*

THE MAKING OF A BEST SELLER

Again, we have a mother to thank. One Grace Sindell, overhearing a woman tell her Shaker Heights librarian that *Ladies* was the best book she'd ever read, passed the novel along to her son Gerald (a Hollywood "writer/producer/director") who passed it along to one Stanley Corwin (a producer, once highly placed in New York publishing) who passed it along to an old college pal, one Owen Laster (of the William Morris Agency). He was "overwhelmed by its quality" and passed it along to Phyllis Grann, president and publisher of G. P. Putnam's. She was "mesmerized" by its quality and, having purchased the novel "solely on the basis of its literary merit," planned a 50,000-copy first printing. Perhaps Laster mentioned that Sindell and Corwin (who had, of course, already flown to Ohio and bought up the trade rights from a startled O.S.U. Press) were planning a miniseries. Touting *Ladies* as a new *Forsyte Saga*, Putnam's sold the work to Book-of-the-Month Club, where president Al Silverman, "captured" by its quality, crowned it "The Great Middle American Novel," and chairman Edward Fitzgerald added, "There is no way we won't sell more than 100,000 copies of that book."

We are now up to January, 1984. Who knows how many (or how few) people have, at this point, actually read, word by word, this discursive, repetitious and often exhaustingly dull four and a half pounds of paper. *". . . And Ladies of the Club"* is not the longest novel in the world (that honor goes, I believe, to Jules Romains's *Men of Good Will*), but as Putnam's publicist points out, it's twice as long as *Gone With the Wind*. I am not a particularly slow reader, and it took me months to trudge my way dutifully through its wrist-wrenching bulk. Moreover, I love long novels with lots of characters, like *War and Peace,* I love Victorian town novels, like *Middlemarch,* I love Great Middle American Novels, like *My Antonia,* I love fat pedestrian family sagas, like *The Forsyte Saga.* I love *Gone With the Wind.* Had *Ladies* been anywhere near as good as the least of these, I would have loved it. But it wasn't and I didn't.

Why I was assigned to read it, why CBS and NBC and ABC and *Time* and *Newsweek* and *Life* rushed to Xenia to tree Santmyer in her nursing home, has little to do with the "Dickensian richness" that Mr. Kefauver of O.S.U. Press saw in those eleven boxes of manuscript she sent him and a great deal to do with the leader-of-the-pack status of *The New York Times*.

On January 12, an article titled "Happy End for Novelist's 50-Year Effort," accompanied by a photo of Santmyer, appeared on the front page of *The Times*. By next day the blitz was on, and out in Xenia, Ohio, at Hospitality Home East, stunned administrators were fielding phone calls as if they were Swifty Lazar. Those dusty copies Mr. Kefauver hadn't been able to sell vanished, except for one he hid in a vault. "Just extraordinary," said he, and sold Santmyer's nonfiction *Ohio Town* (1963) to Harper & Row for $25,000. Harper also optioned her first two novels, *Herbs and Apples* (1925) and *The Fierce Dispute* (1929), though both were already in the public domain. They also bought, sight unseen, her unpublished *Farewell to Summer.* If she has any short stories up in the attic, she should pack them off to Manhattan at once.

The early media flurry sketched a Grandma Moses portrait of Santmyer warbling her woodnotes wild for a half-century to defend small-town virtues against the (surely by now somewhat faded) sneers of Sinclair Lewis. The author, who appears to be a sharp-minded and impressively unflappable woman, made it clear that she is no literary naif. She studied at Oxford, she published books, she worked for Scribner's, she taught English, she was a reference librarian and a college dean. While she took notes for *Ladies* for decades (I suspect *Ohio Town* is one such notebook), major work did not begin until she was seventy, and while she intensely disliked *Main Street,* she has not devoted her life to wreaking revenge on Lewis. Abandoning the Grandma Moses approach, *Family Circle* described Santmyer as "a forerunner of the modern single career-woman." (Unlike most of the women in her book, she has never married.)

THE MESSAGE OF A BEST SELLER

Whether as ur-feminist or "champion of the small town and of late bloomers everywhere," as *Life* has it, Santmyer is first and foremost *old.* And old is in, from Madison Avenue ("Where's the beef?") to Publishers' Row (note the fuss over 77-year-old Harriet Doerr's first novel, *Stones for Ibarra*). More than old, Santmyer is a defender, like the President, of "Old America"—that mythical Eden where happy, decent, solvent, paternalistic, family-faithful, Good Christian People of the Middle Class live protected by white picket fences from the soot of the fallen world. "Such is our comfortable tradition and sure faith," as Lewis says in the preface to *Main Street.* It is interesting to see journalists contrasting Santmyer's Waynesboro with Lewis's "embittered" Gopher Prairie, Anderson's "twisted" Winesburg and Masters's "morbid" Spoon River—as if we'd slid back a half century and "revolt from the village" literature was freshly shocking. Of course, we *have* slid back, and the conservative character of Santmyer's book is a key to its success. Raised a Calvinist Republican, the author gives every indication of sharing the political views of her protagonists. Asked why she ended the novel in 1932, she snapped, "What I thought of the

New Deal wasn't fit to print." Her heroine, Ann (symbol of devoted loving-kindness), regrets dying and leaving the country in the hands of "that bland patronizing demagogue," F.D.R. "Where did all those votes come from? Poor white trash must have crawled out like worms from under stones."

The novel is loosely centered around sweet brunet Ann and saucy blond Sally, and their Civil War veteran husbands, John (a good but gloomy doctor) and Ludwig (a benevolent industrialist). The politics of all four, from age 17 to 70, are as right as Reagan. John: "I didn't fight to set the nigger free." Ludwig: "Our labor force probably doesn't know the meaning of the word [union], and we could replace them easily enough anyway." Sally (after her son gets "an Irish washerwoman's child" pregnant): "What is the use of money if we can't use it to get out of mistakes like this?" Woodrow Wilson is a "pusillanimous pedagogue"; Eugene Debs, a "jailbird"; Populism, "incredible folly"; and, according to these victors of the Civil War, "Negroes would rather fish than work anyday."

The women pass their days paying calls, retiring to have babies, planning theatrical Christmas parties and subscription libraries, writing literary papers for their Women's Club and talking politics, on which subject they are quite *au courant*. There is far more discussion of the need for protective tariffs and the resumption of the gold standard than of their "unforgettable love story." In comparison, Carol Kennicott, with her yearning for romance and her interior-decorating notions of revolution against Main Street, seems astonishingly innocent. An inordinate amount of *Ladies* is given over to secondhand nitty-gritty convention politicking, for Ludwig, Mark Hanna's pal, is a bigwig among delegates. We need to remember that, during the postwar years, various gangs of Ohio Republicans were running the country: Grant, the eighteenth President; Hayes, the nineteenth; Garfield, the twentieth; Harrison, the twenty-third; McKinley, the twenty-fifth; Taft, the twenty-seventh; and Harding, the twenty-ninth. The election of each is a major subject of gossip in this novel. That the Ohioans (from the Whiskey Ring to the Teapot Dome) were as inept and/or corrupt a bunch of mediocrities as ever sat in the Oval Office now occupied by Harding's true heir is a view vigorously poohpoohed by Santmyer's Waynesboroeans. What's good for the G.O.P. is "for the good of the country." Bad times (the Panic of 1873, the Depression) are ultimately troublesome only because they temporarily threaten Ludwig's cordage factory. Of Ohioan Coxey's March to Washington with thousands of unemployed, we hear nothing. Presumably, those sorts would rather fish than work. For the rest, prosperity always triumphs in the end.

But it is as a writer and not as an apologist for reactionary nostalgia that Santmyer must be judged. Indeed, she has wisely judged herself in the person of a novel-writing young woman who appears toward the book's end, her heart set "on being famous," ready to "do a long book about the 60s, 70s, and 80s, covering several generations of life in a small midwestern town." "She laughed at herself ruefully. She was no Galsworthy, much less . . . a Proust."

Exactly so. And while this novel is a prodigious feat of endurance and, in a way, an act of bravery, the result is work and not art. Much has been made of its "thick-textured tapestry of life," but I found the attention to setting curiously sporadic and diffuse—like blurred and spotted rotogravures. Naturally in so long and minutely paced a domestic saga, historical particulars do add up. Slowly, sewing machines, public schools and horseless carriages appear. If not an artist's selective eye for the revelatory detail, Santmyer has a research librarian's eye for the accurate detail, the "iron-gray faille, whose skirt had a deep box-plaited flounce, an overskirt of lilacs foulard." This parenthetical facsimile of life (how a class of people dressed, wed, celebrated, died, worshipped) has in itself the interest (if not the liveliness) of the Lisle Letters or Mary Chestnut's diary. But as Santmyer devotes far more descriptive space to Ludwig's rope factory (her father ran one) than to anything else, we learn rather more about hemp delivery and cable-lay than most readers will find riveting.

More troublesome, she lacks a writer's ear and consequently, her characters lack voices. The middle class speak the writerly prose of the narrator, rather formal even among intimates: "You agree with me that Julia is a completely frigid woman." "It is in your power to make him as happy as it is possible for a man like John to be, who is by temperament moody and unstable, and who is still suffering the nervous traumatism consequent to the war." The faithful blacks speak Uncle Remus: "Res' yo'se'f on yonde' chair." Conversations are repeated again and again as if the author as well as the characters had forgotten they'd already said all this. Talk swings from the mundane—John: "Has the paper come?" Ann: "How could the paper get through this snow?" John: "That was stupid of me. We'll probably not get a paper"—to the philosophical—John to Ann: "It is in the small ways in which love expresses itself that make in the end for happiness, not the overwhelming passion"—to the sociological—Ann to her grandchildren: "Once people get the notion the government has an obligation to support its citizens, there'll be no end to what they'll demand. America will be on a long toboggan slide downhill to Socialism." Dialogue is used in awkward ways to refresh the reader's memory. Why should Sally need to tell Ann, whom she has seen almost daily for fifty years, that her son "seems to be doing very well as a customer's man in the brokerage firm where his father-in-law's a partner"?

Santmyer has listed among her own favorite writers Dickens, Twain, Balzac and "the Russians." Those are good choices. I wish she could have learned from them extravagance and passion and proportion. In her *Comédie Humaine,* life is kept in ledgers, summer to fall, winter to spring, year by changeless year. It's not that nothing happens; there are immense events—fires, floods, polio epidemics—and domestic calamities—infidelity, divorce, drug addiction, runaways, a probable lesbian's suicide—social scandals and endless deaths, both sudden and lingering. But there are so many of them and most are so patly foreshadowed and so matter-of-factly fulfilled that our response is blunted. Santmyer's detached, summarizing approach works most effectively, and movingly, on her portraits of the cramped, dwindled valiant lives and solitary deaths of three spinsters. There are secondary characters (an elderly suffragette and temperance activist, a bright socialist lawyer, a wry newspaper owner) who struck me as far more interesting than the central figures but who get short shrift. Santmyer also has a talent for the caustic riposte which I wish she had allowed herself to indulge, especially as so much of the book is gossip of a not especially good-hearted kind, among folk with the "universal desire to be the first with the news, particularly bad news."

Fellow members of the real Xenia Women's Club have described Helen Hooven Santmyer as "reticent and austere." Something of that quality stiffens her pen in *". . . And Ladies of the Club."* She said she worried people wouldn't think the book dramatic because there wasn't enough violence in it, "nothing hysterical." In fact, it isn't dramatic because there isn't enough drama in it; the author seems to shy away from scenes, not squeamish about their subject matter so much as their fictive nature, as if fiction-making itself were a bit silly. "These things don't happen except in cliché-filled banal novels." "A novelist couldn't have worked things out better," is the embarrassed response to a coincidence. But the great novelists were no more afraid of life's continual clichés and coincidences than they were tempted to use fact to justify fiction.

Asked what she thought of *Ladies,* Santmyer replied, "I think there's something there, but I don't think I can put it into words." She said of her earlier novels, "They never sold enough to make me rich." Well, *Ladies* has made her both rich and famous. The Xenia Chamber of Commerce is preparing a brochure to lead tourists through the fictional sites in the town. Similar steps were taken by the good folk of Sauk Centre, Minnesota ("The Original Main Street"), and of Clyde, Ohio (Winesburg), and of Red Cloud, Nebraska ("Willa Cather Country"). I suggest that anyone who wants to read a "Great Middle American Novel" should go find a copy of *My Antonia,* or *Winesburg, Ohio,* or *Main Street* and *Babbitt,* or *Main-Travelled Roads,* or *Tom Sawyer.* All of those put together are still not as long as *". . . And Ladies of the Club."*

Anne Barry (essay date autumn 1984)

SOURCE: Barry, Anne. "Helen Hooven Santmyer: 'I Awoke One Morning and Found Myself Famous' (Lord Byron)." *Ohioana Quarterly* 27 (autumn 1984): 88-9.

[*In the following essay, Barry describes the successful saga of* ". . . And Ladies of the Club," *emphasizing the Ohioana Award given to Santmyer in 1983.*]

The first item on the *New York Times* News Quiz for Saturday 14 January was: "Posing for this photograph, the first anyone has been permitted to take of her, was a new experience for 88-year-old Helen Hooven Santmyer, but her other novel experience was even more noteworthy. What was it?"

Readers of *Ohioana Quarterly* know it concerned her second Ohioana-Award book, *". . . And Ladies of the Club."* Readers have also seen her photograph, taken with her permission, in several issues of the *Quarterly.* But Miss Santmyer was "discovered" by the national press when it was announced that her 1,334-page novel about life in small-town Ohio was a main selection of the Book-of-the-Month Club.

G. P. Putnam's Sons first printing is 150,000 copies and paperback rights have been auctioned for $396,000. *Life* magazine (June 1984) has featured Miss Santmyer and the bestseller she published at age 88. The book is also being serialized in *Family Circle* magazine and adapted for a television miniseries. Several Ohio communities are striving to attract the eye of the TV producers, as a 1974 tornado in Greene County destroyed most of the novel's locale: Xenia, transformed into the fictional town of Waynesboro, from 1868 to 1932.

When the Ohio State University Press in 1982 first published 1,500 copies of *". . . And Ladies of the Club"* at $35.00 each, *Ohioana Quarterly* was one of the few publications to review the book. Don E. Weaver in the spring 1983 issue, under the headline "A Great Ohio Novel," wrote, "Miss Santmyer is a very facile writer with a simple easy style. She can handle tragedy and scandal, happiness and success without resort to hyperbole or turgid rhetoric. Reading her prose is sheer pleasure." For this book Miss Santmyer received the 1983 Ohioana Book Award in fiction. (She had previously won a nonfiction award for *Ohio Town* in 1963.) The novel was nearly fifty years in the writing, interrupted by her writing her reminiscences of Xenia in *Ohio Town.* (Harper & Row will reprint *Ohio Town* in paperback and has options on her other previous books.)

A resident for two years of Hospitality Home East in Xenia, Miss Santmyer weighs only 80 lbs. and is confined to a wheelchair. She is nearly blind from cataracts and tires very quickly because of her emphysema. The national publicity, interviews for the "MacNeil-Lehrer Report," CBS, ABC, NBC, and a crew of German filmmakers have exhausted her.

"I have no plans for the money, but it'll be awfully nice to have it," she says. After she graduated from Wellesley, where she was encouraged to become a writer, she worked as a secretary to the editor of *Scribner's* magazine. She earned a second degree from Oxford University but was never able to afford a return trip to Europe. She published two novels (**Herbs and Apples, The Fierce Dispute**) in the 1920s and returned to Xenia in 1929. "I never got rich from those books," she says. "An occasional royalty, but they never sold enough to make me rich."

From 1935 to 1953 she was dean of women and head of the English department at Cedarville College in Ohio. Later she was a reference librarian in Dayton. One of the reasons it took so long to write *". . . And Ladies of the Club"* was that she could only write part time. "That was the trouble, I always had to earn a living while I wrote."

After a lifetime of obscurity, with great perseverence and undaunted by illness, Helen Hooven Santmyer has gained national fame and much-deserved recognition as a distinguished Ohio author. Her novel, written in longhand in a bookkeeper's ledgers—eleven boxes full—is longer than *Gone with the Wind* and may well become an equal classic of regional history.

The Ohio State University Press, which still holds the copyright, will use the income it shares with Miss Santmyer to publish books that don't make large profits—scholarly works that require considerable editing and appeal only to a limited market. Or to have the courage to publish a novel weighing 4.2 lbs. that is the same size as *Who's Who!*

Robert F. Fleissner (review date June 1986)

SOURCE: Fleissner, Robert. Review of *". . . And Ladies of the Club,"* by Helen Hooven Santmyer. *CLA Journal* 29 (June 1986): 486-89.

[*In the following review, Fleissner defends* ". . . And Ladies of the Club" *against charges of racism.*]

Because Central State University hosted a most successful conference on Helen Hooven Santmyer's bestselling novel, *". . . And Ladies of the Club,"* in January, 1985, it is particularly important to come to terms with the issue of race. A number of prominent reviewers (for example, in *Newsweek* and in the *New York Times*) have pinpointed racism as a defect in this work.

But is it? Owing to the fact that our campus is only four miles from where she resides, I have had the opportunity to interview her and her friends, who have staunchly defended her on this point. At one point, I seriously considered jettisoning the conference because of its apparently controversial nature, but close study of the text made me desist. In this essay, I should like to consider some ten key points seriatim on the novel's attitude toward blacks.

1. The Zack episode. When I first picked up the novel, I automatically turned to the page describing how a black worker in a rope factory gets into an accident and is tended by Dr. Gordon. His name may sound a bit odd and as though it is making fun of him, at first, but upon careful reading we recognize that it is meant respectfully as an abbreviation of Zachariah (of Biblical vintage). Zack argues that if his leg has to be amputated, he will not be good for anything (p. 318). At first, this description struck me as possibly racist; however, when I brought it up in class, a freshman thought that the worker's feeling was entirely understandable and even acceptable in terms of the historical setting of the novel (at this time, 1878). It is important, therefore, to retain the awareness that Miss Santmyer is, before anything else, historical in her approach.

2. One reviewer of the book referred to the ignominious fact that a black is cited as having a "prehensile foot" (p. 348). Although, granted, the allusion may appear unduly grotesque, even simian if taken literally, the heroine's own daughter, Binny, is described at another point as a "monkey" (p. 545). The evolutionary argument will not hold water.

3. On the very next page, John Jordan is described as sensitive to prejudice against blacks or (at least) to the notion of keeping blacks from advancing: his son refers to "the Enemy," whereupon Mr. Jordan responds, "'Enemy! Who's the enemy?'" He then "frowned, fork suspended, thinking of the colored children who lived in the East End." (The reference is obliquely to that section of Xenia, Ohio, which is a few miles from our campus and which is almost entirely black.) Surely the father's remonstrance is meant to be antiracist.

4. Captain Bodien dresses down a black servant with strong language later in the book (p. 733); his voice is gruff and military, corresponding with his title, but he is not necessarily thereby guilty of bias. For he also uses strong language toward a priest who had been looking after his wife, going so far as to ask for his rifle. This personage is not one to be envied; he himself certainly *can* be thought of as biased. But that does not mean that he mirrors the novelist herself.

5. The description of the cook Martha's death seems very sincerely expressed (pp. 846-47), given an acceptance of Fundamentalism, but it is possible to read into

it other meanings. For instance, a certain tacky quality emerges: Martha never married, but apparently did not want to be thought of as a virgin, saying "I wouldn' want yo' to think Ah neve' had me a man"; then on the very same page, a bit later, she expresses strong Christian spiritual beliefs. (A colleague of mine felt that her dialect was unauthentic, but that is beside the point.) Evidently the author wanted us to feel that Martha was humanized, not hypocritical, however. Her mistress' reaction after her death certainly may give the impression of condescension: "'Such faith should be rewarded; maybe we all get the Heaven we believe in.'" But on the other hand, it does not hurt to take it literally, too.

6. On the matter of educating blacks, Miss Santmyer has this to say:

> The Southern [blacks], according to Rachel, have been effectively disenfranchised over the last ten years, and if they can't vote, what hope is there of getting decent schools for them? Or of getting away from what amounts to bondage to the land: they're all sharecroppers and never get out of debt to the landowners. I could see she was right: What was the point of all that fighting, if the [black] isn't any better off than he was before?

Such writing is hardly eloquent, but it is honest and realistic, pointing to an attempt on the part of Northerners after the Civil War to come to terms with their inheritance.

7. Along the same lines, the Woman's Club (which the novel mainly concerns) decided to have a paper read on the writer Tourgée because "he has done such fine work against the Klan and for the cause of the [blacks.]" (p. 555). Thus, if individual women in the club may not have been always unbiased, the Club as a whole, at least, was striving toward a sense of equality.

8. The strong emphasis upon the Republican Party and its politics in the novel hardly can be said to be *opposed* to what blacks were after then, because, since they followed Lincoln's party, they naturally were then on the Republican side, too. This point is often made in the novel, for what it is worth.

9. Regardless of how authentic or unauthentic the dialect here used by blacks is, and how irrelevant it may seem to modern readers, it does relate to that used also by such a noted poet of the area as Paul Lawrence Dunbar; it need not be thought of merely as "gibberish," as one reviewer put it.

10. True, blacks are cited in this novel as servants and having low-class, low-paying jobs. This situation strikes some modern readers as uncomfortable, yet it merely reflects the author's attempt to be objective.

To sum up, if we say that Santmyer's portrayal of blacks is racist, we would have to say that she is also anti-Catholic because of her portrayal of poor-white Irish

Americans, anti-Presbyterian because of her portrait of the Reverend McCune, anti-German because of the Club's final reaction to the Rausches, and where do we stop with such special pleading? It might be mentioned, in passing, that one reviewer (in the *New York Times*) criticized her for being anti-Jewish because of her description of the Klein family as mercenary; however, in point of fact the Kleins are Lutheran, and the passing references to Jews at times, though apprehensive perhaps, are complimentary.

Is it not then demeaning—not only to Santmyer, but to black people—for an ambitious work like this, one which has such strong moral messages (Aurelius' *Meditations,* for example, being cited in exemplary fashion throughout), to be labeled prejudiced simply owing to its attempt to be objectively fair about nineteenth-century social realities, without excessive sentimentality? The novel may not be The Great American one in all respects—for example, its style is not distinguished enough for that—but it is a remarkably accurate picture of life in this area from the time of the end of the Civil War to Franklin Delano Roosevelt. Not all the characters are likable, but that is true of many important novels; and besides, there is no reason to think that Santmyer intended it otherwise.

Sybil Steinberg (review date 9 October 1987)

SOURCE: Steinberg, Sybil. Review of *The Fierce Dispute,* by Helen Hooven Santmyer. *Publishers Weekly* 232 (9 October 1987): 79.

[*In the following brief review, Steinberg gives an unfavorable assessment of Santmyer's second novel* The Fierce Dispute.]

The success of "*. . . And Ladies of the Club*" has prompted reissue of the author's earlier works. [*The Fierce Dispute*], her second, was originally published in 1929—and the years have not been kind. Dated in form and content, it is what was once called a "woman's book," but a contemporary audience will find its simple sentimentality tame. In the Ohio town familiar to readers of Santmyer's other works, a genteel matriarchy lives in a once magnificent, now dilapidated family manse behind a locked iron gate. The trio, consisting of the disapproving grandmother, Mrs. Baird, her shamed daughter Hilary and granddaughter Lucy Anne, live cut off from the rest of the community. The tension between mother and daughter for the child's spirit and affection propels the plot, which hinges on the mystery surrounding the child's father, a musician, and the rosewood piano in the attic. For all its gothic posing, dark glances and histrionic dialogue, this is a colorless novel in which the few psychological insights are not sufficient to invest the narrative with vitality or credibility.

Rose Russell Stewart (review date 19 May 1988)

SOURCE: Stewart, Rose Russell. "A Midsummer Romance in 1905." *Blade* (19 May 1988): F7.

[*In the following review, Stewart notes a pleasant sense of nostalgia in Santmyer's posthumous novel* Farewell, Summer.]

After a long, difficult day of meeting the demands of family, work, and community, how nice it is to settle down to a book that doesn't force my emotions to stretch from one end to another.

Farewell, Summer is a novella that relieves its reader of emotional upheavals by discussing current or historical turmoils. Rather, it amuses with fond childhood memories.

The author so expertly describes the scenery of country life that in some instances it appears the characters are dropped in merely to bring human vibrancy to a relaxed, beautiful, rural setting.

Imagine this: "The water made a rainbow in the sun over the row of cabbages, and you could smell the fresh dampness as far as the summer kitchen." Or, "In Grandmother's yard were petunias and verbenas and marigolds—all the strong-colored flowers of midsummer."

And: "We were in the heat of summer then. Days were long heavy, somnolent; locusts sang in all the trees, a stupefying chorus. It was too hot to do anything but read, or swing lazily in the hammock without reading. I looked for locust shells on the tree trunks and collected them. The heat made one childish; I lay on the grass . . ."

Farewell, Summer takes me back to my own childhood summers, in hilly country with weeping willows to swing on. On these long, languid summers where I was surrounded with relatives, we cousins conjured up foolishness and listened in on grown folks' conversations.

These thoughts kept popping into my mind while reading Helen Hooven Santmyer's book, as they are the very things Santmyer's Elizabeth Lane does—engage in child-like fun while surrounded by very adult goings on.

After years away as a writer and scholar, Elizabeth returns to the small Ohio town of Sunbury with the intentions of working on one book, but being there revives memories buried the years she was away. They must be written about now.

Although heat and passion are hardly the gist of *Farewell Summer,* the story takes some twists and turns that one might be more apt to find in a novel about an adult love triangle.

The year is 1905, and Elizabeth at 11 is in love with a Texas cousin who'd come to Ohio for the summer. Hers is not a love of wanton passion; rather she is very fond of Steve, and cares a great deal for him.

Steve, although a sensitive boy with great depth, is described as the "Wild West cousin." His affection, however, focuses on another cousin, Damaris. And he has things in mind other than being simply "kissing cousins."

Damaris denies her emotions and turns Steve away. She determined as a child to not marry, a decision reinforced by her desire to become a nun. Heartbroken and lovesick, Steve leaves Ohio and heads for Texas—only to find tragedy waiting for him.

It turns out that one of the relatives brought Steve to Ohio in hopes that he and Damaris would fall in love and marry. It is not clear how far or how close Steve and Damaris are as cousins because there are so many relatives to try to keep up with. The obvious intention of an incestuous relationship that could have developed is not acceptable, even though it is presented tastefully, innocently.

Farewell, Summer is full of kinship expressions that modern America may no longer be familiar with—almost everyone is addressed as "cousin," and that makes one want to go home, be enveloped in family, and rethink wonderful memories of growing up.

This last novel by the late Helen Hooven Santmyer—also the author of *". . . And Ladies of the Club," Ohio Town, Herbs and Apples,* and *The Fierce Dispute*—should surely be put on your list of those to read, particularly if you need a hiatus from urban life.

Sally A. Myers (review date summer/autumn 1998)

SOURCE: Myers, Sally A. Review of Loris Troyer's *Portage Pathways* and Santmyer's *Ohio Town. Northwest Ohio Quarterly* (summer/autumn 1998): 167-70.

[*In the following review of a reissue of* Ohio Town, *Myers says that this book of essays is superior to Santmyer's more famous* ". . . And Ladies of the Club."]

Loris C. Troyer's *Portage Pathways* and Helen Hooven Santmyer's *Ohio Town* reflect two very different approaches to local history, from counties at opposite ends of the state. Troyer, an editor emeritus of the Ravenna-Kent *Record-Courier,* chronicles important people and events in a portion of the old Western Reserve. Troyer's book is a compilation of columns on Portage County history written after his retirement in 1982. Santmyer, a former professor of English, librarian, and dean of women who published several books in her lifetime,

writes a more impressionistic work, portraying the life of the Greene County town of Xenia by focusing on the places which figured strongly in people's lives. A reissue of a work first published in 1962, Santmyer's book is a valuable resource for local historians in the wake of the 1974 tornado which devastated Xenia. . . .

Santmyer is better known for her ponderous 1982 work of fiction, *". . . And Ladies of the Club,"* than for the non-fictional *Ohio Town.* The novel gained her some notoriety at the time of its re-publication in 1984 thanks to some effective promotion by the Book-of-the-Month Club. *Ohio Town,* originally published in 1962 and now reissued in paperback with added photoplates, is really a better book. Its prose is pleasing, even graceful, and its vignettes of life in Xenia before the First World War give the reader a sense of verisimilitude and provide a paradigm for the history of small American towns everywhere.

This is no *Winesburg, Ohio,* however. Unlike many well-known writers of her generation, Santmyer does not cast a cynical eye on her hometown, but rather looks upon it with bemused nostalgia. She views places and people of Xenia from the point of view of the young person she once was and tries to reconstruct the ambiance of town life for the reader. In the chapter entitled "The Courthouse," for instance, she points to the pre-eminence of the courthouse clock tower, "which can be read from as far away as you can see" (11) and literally marks out the times of people's lives with its chime. She resurrects the sights, sounds, and smells of an old-fashioned downtown and the history of many of the venerable homes in Xenia which "have their names and pedigrees" (79).

Santmyer does not neglect the "other side" of town, however. In "The East End," she tells the story of the section reserved for African-Americans, who comprised more of the town's population than in many comparably sized Ohio towns. Santmyer portrays a relationship between blacks and whites which was "easy and comfortable" (94) even if the races did not live together. One wonders whether black residents perceived their lives in terms quite so beneficent.

She also paints vivid pictures of schoolroom life in the early 1900's: "a noisy roomful of children in motion, where chalk, erasers, spitballs, and wet sponges filled the air" (170), a place where every commencement ceremony "included a valedictory, and a Latin as well as an English salutatory" and children respectfully watched "slim, wide-hatted girls with roses coming down tree-shaded streets" (176).

Santmyer laments the passages of certain institutions like the old opera house, whose lectures and musical and theatrical productions chronicled the cultural history of the town. She also remembers how "[n]o one of my generation grew up in any county seat in America without consciousness of a certain relationship between himself and the railroad" and regrets that the younger generation will likely not know "how exciting it is to step on a Pullman" or "to have seen the end of your own train whipping around a curve behind you" (250).

In short, if Troyer's historical notes are those of a journalist dedicated to "the facts," Santmyer's are those of a poet. While Troyer, for example, chronicles many of the important people and events associated with the Kent Town Hall, Santmyer remembers general impressions, like the "consciousness of the [courthouse] tower with its four-faced clock, the goose-girl drinking fountain on the Main Street curb, the spread of lawn, and the trees in the square" (3). Troyer's book is mostly an interesting source of information and local color for those interested in the old Western Reserve. Santmyer's transcends specific facts but lets the reader step into history.

FURTHER READING

Biography

Quay, Joyce Crosby. *Early Promise, Late Reward: A Biography of Helen Hooven Santmyer.* Manchester, Conn.: Knowledge, Ideas, and Trends, Inc., 1995, 134 p.

> Self-published, chronological biography of Santmyer written by an Ohio native who interviewed Santmyer and did extensive research among her papers.

Criticism

Bourjaily, Vance. "The Other Side of 'Main Street.'" *The New York Times Book Review* (24 June 1984): 7.

> Bourjaily favorably reviews ". . . And Ladies of the Club" as a fascinating re-creation of the life of a small town.

Brownmiller, Susan. "'. . . And Ladies of the Club' Life, Death, Boredom on Main Street." *The Chicago Tribune,* (10 June 1984): 13.

Explains that Santmyer's writing in ". . . And Ladies of the Club" is occasionally inspired but mostly limited in perspective.

Filler, Louis. "An Ohio Masterpiece: Prospects for Renewal." In *The Unbought Grace of Life: Essays in Honor of Russell Kirk,* edited by James E. Person, Jr., pp. 106-14. Peru, Ill.: Sherwood Sugden & Company, 1994.

> A reevaluation of ". . . And Ladies of the Club."

Hill, Eldon. Review of *Ohio Town,* by Helen Hooven Santmyer. *Indiana Magazine of History* 59, no. 1 (March 1963): 294-95.

> Favorable review of *Ohio Town.*

Kaufman, Joanne. Review of *Ohio Town,* by Helen Hooven Santmyer. *The New York Times Book Review* (16 September 1984): 31.

> Presents a generally favorable assessment of Santmyer's book of essays.

Lyons, Gene. "Sunny Side of the Street." *Newsweek* (18 June 1984): 93.

> Lyons says that ". . . And Ladies of the Club" is more of a publishing event than a good work of literature.

Marnell, Francis X. "Main Street Revisited." *National Review* 36, no. 19 (5 October 1984): 54-5.

> A favorable review which touts ". . . And Ladies of the Club" as a counterpart to *Main Street.*

McDowell, Edwin. "Happy End for Novelist's 50-Year Effort." *The New York Times* (12 January 1984): A1.

> McDowell describes publication plans for ". . . And Ladies of the Club" and chronicles Santmyer's long route to literary fame.

Review of *Herbs and Apples,* by Helen Hooven Santmyer. *The Saturday Review of Literature* 2, no. 16 (14 November 1925): 301.

> An early, mostly unfavorable, review of Santmyer's first novel.

Review of ". . . And Ladies of the Club" by Helen Hooven Santmyer. *Time* 124 (9 July 1984): 84.

> Brief review of ". . . And Ladies of the Club," stating that Santmyer's novel has been oversold by its publisher and is also rather dull.

Additional coverage of Santmyer's life and career is contained in the following sources published by the Gale Group: *Contemporary Authors,* **Vols. 1-4R, 118;** *Contemporary Authors New Revision Series,* **Vols. 15, 33;** *Contemporary Literary Criticism,* **Vol. 33;** *Dictionary of Literary Biography Yearbook,* **1984;** *Literature Resource Center; Major 20th-Century Writers,* **Ed. 1; and** *Twentieth-Century Romance and Historical Writers.*

The Time Machine

H. G. Wells

(Born Herbert George Wells) English autobiographer, novelist, essayist, journalist, and short story writer.

The following entry presents criticism on Wells's novella *The Time Machine* (1895). For additional coverage of his life and works, see *TCLC,* Volumes 6, 12, and 19.

INTRODUCTION

Published in book form in 1895, *The Time Machine* is regarded as the best-known of Wells's "scientific romances" and one of the most influential stories about time travel ever written. Although the story was not the first to explore the concept of time travel, it is significant for its pseudoscientific explanation of how time travel could possibly occur. The novella initially appeared in serialized form as "The Chronic Argonauts" in *Science School Journal* in April 1888; it was then revised and published as *The Time Machine* in *National Observer* in 1894 and the *New Review* in January 1895. Wells revised the story again for the Atlantic Edition, which was published in 1924. Since its initial appearance in book form, *The Time Machine* has never gone out of print.

PLOT AND MAJOR CHARACTERS

Written in a conversational tone, *The Time Machine* opens with an unnamed narrator professing his admiration for his mentor, the older scientist known only as the Time Traveller. The narrator reflects on the disappearance of the Time Traveller three years before and contends that he is telling the story to attest to the powers of the human imagination and as a warning of what the future can bring. He describes the Thursday night dinners the Time Traveller used to give at his home for a group of his friends. It was at one of these occasions that the Time Traveller first asserted that the Fourth Dimension not only existed, but that time travel was possible. In fact, he showed his friends a small model of his new invention, a time machine. The assembled group is shocked when he makes the machine disappear before their eyes. On the next Thursday, the Time Traveler further astounds his waiting guests when he ap-

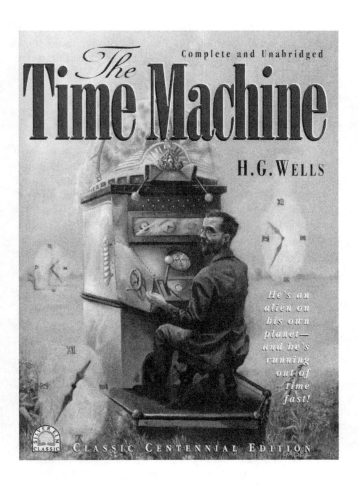

Book cover illustration by Matt Gabel of the 1995 Worthington Press edition of The Time Machine.

pears suddenly in the dining room, disheveled, dirty, and limping. He explains that since their last meeting he has traveled to the year 802,701, where he expected to find amazing technological and cultural progress. Instead, he finds a race of beings he calls the Eloi, a diminutive, weak people who live together in harmony. Yet he is surprised to find the Eloi bereft of intellectual curiosity and fearful of the dark. The reason for this becomes clear to him when darkness falls and he discovers a second species, the Morlocks, described as primordial, predatory creatures who live below the surface and feed on the Eloi after dark. The Time Traveller chronicles his many adventures in the future, including rescuing Weena, an Eloi and love interest, from drowning; unearthing the truth of what happened to the human race; and escaping a group of marauding Morlocks. The Time Traveller then journeys even further into the future, where he discovers the extinction of all human life on Earth. When he travels thirty million years into the future, he finds no signs of life at all. He begs his skeptical guests to heed his warning: the human race cannot be allowed to devolve into the primitive Eloi and Morlocks. He then announces that he will return to the future in an attempt to further understand what awaits the human race. The Time Traveller never returns from his last journey.

MAJOR THEMES

Critics have found parallels between the narrator's and Time Traveller's relationship in *The Time Machine* and that of the dual protagonists in Joseph Conrad's tale "Heart of Darkness." Most commentators have focused on major thematic concerns embodied by the conflict between the Eloi and Morlock races. The story is often perceived from a Darwinian perspective; it has been noted that Wells often employed the theory of evolution as a motif in his scientific romances. Some critics have focused on Wells's concept of the duality of the individual: in the story, the Time Traveller asserts that the contradictory characteristics of the Eloi and Morlock exist within the individual and are held together by love and intellectual interest. Other commentators have interpreted the novella from a Marxist perspective: in this vein, the Morlocks represent the proletariat and the Eloi are viewed as the bourgeois class. With this interpretation, *The Time Machine* is considered a sociopolitical commentary on turn-of-the-century England. Autobiographical aspects of the story have been investigated, as issues of class were another recurring theme in Wells's life and work. Moreover, some scholars have argued that *The Time Machine* can also be perceived as an exploration of the dualities between aestheticism and utilitarianism as well as pastoralism and technology. The utopian and mythological qualities of *The Time Machine* have been a rich area for critical discussion.

CRITICAL RECEPTION

Upon its publication in book form in 1895, *The Time Machine* was hailed as a masterpiece. Yet the novella was classified as a scientific romance, a genre considered by many—including Wells himself—as inconsequential. It wasn't until Bernard Bergonzi's study, *The Early H. G. Wells: A Study of the Scientific Romances* (1960), that critics began to take Wells's work seriously and catapulted *The Time Machine* into the ranks of classic English literature. It was Bergonzi who first dis-

cussed the mythological aspects of the novella. Reviewers have investigated its profound influence on the genre of science fiction and later generations of authors, such as Jorge Louis Borges, George Orwell, and Aldous Huxley. Some critics have proclaimed Wells as "the father of modern science fiction." *The Time Machine* is still one of Wells's best-known works. The book has been translated into many languages, and has inspired cinematic adaptations and literary sequels.

PRINCIPAL WORKS

"The Chronic Argonauts" (short story) 1888

Select Conversations with an Uncle (Now Extinct), and Two Other Reminiscences (short stories) 1895

The Stolen Bacillus and Other Incidents (short stories) 1895

The Time Machine (novella) 1895

The Wonderful Visit (novel) 1895

The Island of Dr. Moreau (novel) 1896

The Wheels of Chance (novel) 1896

The Invisible Man: A Grotesque Romance (novel) 1897

The Plattner Story and Others (short stories) 1897

Thirty Strange Stories (short stories) 1897

Certain Personal Matters: A Collection of Material, Mainly Autobiographical (autobiography) 1898

The War of the Worlds (novel) 1898

Tales of Space and Time (short stories) 1899

When the Sleeper Wakes (novel) 1899

The First Men in the Moon (novel) 1901

Anticipations of the Reaction of Mechanical and Scientific Progress upon Human Life and Thought (nonfiction) 1902

The Sea Lady: A Tissue of Moonshine (novel) 1902

Mankind in the Making (nonfiction) 1903

Twelve Stories and a Dream (short stories) 1903

The Food of the Gods, and How It Came to Earth (novel) 1904

Kipps: A Monograph (novel) 1905

A Modern Utopia (novel) 1905

The Future in America: A Search after Realities (nonfiction) 1906

First and Last Things: A Confession of Faith and a Rule of Life (nonfiction) 1908

New Worlds for Old (nonfiction) 1908

Tono-Bungay (novel) 1908

The History of Mr. Polly (novel) 1910

The Country of the Blind and Other Stories (short stories) 1911

The Door in the Wall and Other Stories (short stories) 1911

Floor Games (juvenilia) 1911

The New Machiavelli (novel) 1911

Marriage (novel) 1912

The Passionate Friends: A Novel (novel) 1913

War and Common Sense (nonfiction) 1913

Social Forces in England and America (essays) 1914

The War That Will End War (essays) 1914

The World Set Free: A Story of Mankind (novel) 1914

The Research Magnificent (novel) 1915

The War and Socialism (nonfiction) 1915

God, the Invisible King (nonfiction) 1917

Joan and Peter (novel) 1918

The Salvaging of Civilization: The Probable Future of Mankind (nonfiction) 1921

A Short History of the World (nonfiction) 1922

Men Like Gods (novel) 1923

The Dream (novel) 1924

A Year of Prophesying (essays) 1924

The Short Stories of H. G. Wells (short stories) 1927

The Open Conspiracy: Blue Prints for a World Revolution (nonfiction) 1928

The King Who Was a King: An Unconventional Novel (novel) 1929

Selections from the Early Prose Works of H. G. Wells (nonfiction) 1931

The Work, Wealth and Happiness of Mankind (nonfiction) 1931

The Shape of Things to Come: The Ultimate Revolution (novel) 1933

Experiment in Autobiography: Discoveries and Conclusions of a Very Ordinary Brain (Since 1866) (autobiography) 1934

The New America: the New World (nonfiction) 1935

Brynhild (novel) 1937

World Brain (essays and speeches) 1938

The Fate of Man (nonfiction) 1939

All Aboard for Ararat (novel) 1940

The Rights of Man; or, What Are We Fighting For? (nonfiction) 1940

Guide to the New World: A Handbook of Constructive World Revolution (nonfiction) 1941

The Pocket History of the World (nonfiction) 1941

Phoenix: A Summary of the Inescapable Conditions of World Reorganisation (nonfiction) 1942

Crux Ansata: An Indictment of the Roman Catholic Church (nonfiction) 1943

'42 to '44: A Contemporary Memoir upon Human Behavior during the Crisis of the World Revolution (nonfiction) 1944

The Happy Turning: A Dream of Life (nonfiction) 1945

Henry James and H. G. Wells: A Record of Their Friendship, Their Debate on the Art of Fiction, and Their Quarrel (letters) 1958

Selected Short Stories (short stories) 1958

Arnold Bennett and H. G. Wells: A Record of a Personal and a Literary Friendship (letters) 1960

Journalism and Prophecy, 1893-1946: An Anthology (essays and lectures) 1964

H. G. Wells's Literary Criticism (essays) 1980

The Man with the Nose and Other Uncollected Short Stories (short stories) 1984

The Complete Short Stories (short stories) 1987

Bernard Shaw and H. G. Wells (letters) 1995

The Correspondence of H. G. Wells (letters) 1996

CRITICISM

Bernard Bergonzi (essay date 1960)

SOURCE: Bergonzi, Bernard. "*The Time Machine*: An Ironic Myth." In *H. G. Wells: A Collection of Critical Essays,* edited by Bernard Bergonzi, pp. 39-55. Englewood Cliffs, N.J.: Prentice-Hall, 1976.

[*In the following essay, originally published in 1960, Bergonzi underscores the mythical qualities of* The Time Machine *and outlines the major thematic concerns of the novella.*]

H. G. Wells seems so essentially a writer of the first half of the twentieth century that we tend to forget that if he had died in 1900 at the age of thirty-four he would already have had a dozen books to his credit. He first established his reputation by the scientific romances written during these early years of his literary career, and they have remained popular. Historically considered, they are of interest as the forerunners of much latter-day science fiction. Yet, in my opinion, more substantial claims can be made for them. They are often compared with the work of Jules Verne, but this is a misleading comparison even if a plausible one. Wells himself wrote in 1933, "there is no resemblance whatever between the anticipatory inventions of the great Frenchman and these fantasies." His early romances, in fact, despite their air of scientific plausibility, are much more works of pure imagination. They are, in short, *fantasies,* and the emphasis should be on "romance" rather than "scientific." And like other kinds of literary romance they are distinguished by a quality which may reasonably be called symbolic, even if not specifically allegorical. Indeed, I would claim that Wells's early fiction is closer to the symbolic romances of Hawthorne or Melville, or to a complex fantasy like *Dr. Jekyll and Mr. Hyde,* or even to the fables of Kafka, than it is to the more strictly scientific speculations of Verne. This at least, is the assumption on which I base the following examination of *The Time Machine,* Wells's first novel, which appeared in 1895. This approach has already been hinted at by one of the best of Wells's modern critics, V. S. Pritchett, who has written:

> Without question *The Time Machine* is the best piece of writing. It will take its place among the great stories of our language. Like all excellent works it has meanings within its meaning . . .[1]

An earlier writer on Wells, Edward Shanks, remarked:

> If I were to say that many of Mr. Wells's early books have a poetic quality I should run the risk of conveying a false impression. Luckily they have a peculiar quality which enables them to bear a special description. They are, in their degree, myths; and Mr. Wells is a myth-maker.[2]

Shanks expanded his remarks with particular reference to *The Island of Dr. Moreau,* though they apply equally to *The Time Machine*:

> These passages suggest one interpretation of the book. But it is a myth, not an allegory; and whereas an allegory bears a single and definite interpretation, a myth does not, but can be interpreted in many ways, none of them quite consistent, all of them more alive and fruitful than the rigid allegorical correspondence.

Pritchett has referred to *The Time Machine* as a "poetic social allegory." But this narrows the effective range of the work too much; though on one level the "allegory," or in Shanks's more appropriate term, the "myth," does operate in social terms, its further significance is biological and even cosmological. Structurally, *The Time Machine* belongs to the class of story which includes James's *Turn of the Screw,* and which Northrop Frye has called "the tale told in quotation marks, where we have an opening setting with a small group of congenial people, and then the real story told by one of the members." As Frye observes:

> The effect of such devices is to present the story through a relaxed and contemplative haze as something that entertains us without, so to speak, confronting us, as direct tragedy confronts us.[3]

The aesthetic distancing of the central narrative of *The Time Machine,* "the time traveller's story," is carefully carried out. At the end of the book, the traveller says:

> No, I cannot expect you to believe it. Take it as a lie—or a prophecy. Say I dreamed it in the workshop. Consider I have been speculating upon the destinies of our race, until I have hatched this fiction. Treat my assertion of its truth as a mere stroke of art to enhance its interest. And taking it as a story, what do you think of it?

The manifest disbelief of all his friends other than the storyteller—one of them "thought the tale a 'gaudy lie'"—is balanced by the apparent evidence of his sojourn in the future, the "two strange white flowers" of an unknown species. In fact, Wells demands assent by apparently discouraging it.

The opening chapters of the novel show us the inventor entertaining his friends, a group of professional men, in the solid comfort of his home at Richmond. They recall the "club-man" atmosphere with which several of Kipling's short stories open, and their function in the narrative is to give it a basis in contemporary life at its most ordinary and pedestrian: this atmosphere makes the completest possible contrast with what is to come: an account of a wholly imaginative world of dominantly paradisal and demonic imagery, lying far outside the possible experience of the late Victorian bourgeoisie. These chapters are essential to Wells's purpose, since they prevent the central narrative from seeming a piece of pure fantasy, or a fairy story, and no more. The character of the time traveller himself—cheerful, erratic, and somewhat absurd, faintly suggestive of a hero of Jerome K. Jerome's—has a similar function. In the work of other popular writers of fantastic romance in the nineties, such as Arthur Machen and M. P. Shiel (both clearly deriving from Stevenson), a "weird" atmosphere is striven after from the very beginning and the dramatic power is correspondingly less.

Once the reader has been initiated into the group of friends, he is prepared for whatever is to come next. First the model time machine is produced—"a glittering metallic framework, scarcely larger than a small clock, and very delicately made. . . . There was ivory in it, and some crystalline substance"—and sent off into time, never to be seen again. Then we are shown the full scale machine, and the account of it is a brilliant example of Wells's impressionistic method:

> I remember vividly the flickering light, his queer, broad head in silhouette, the dance of the shadows, how we all followed him, puzzled but incredulous, and how there in the laboratory we beheld a larger edition of the little mechanism which we had seen vanish from before our eyes. Parts were of nickel, parts of ivory, parts had certainly been filed or sawn out of rock crystal. The thing was generally complete, but the twisted crystalline bars lay unfinished upon the bench besides some sheets of drawings, and I took one up for a better look at it. Quartz it seemed to be.

The assemblage of details is strictly speaking meaningless but nevertheless conveys very effectively a sense of the machine without putting the author to the taxing necessity of giving a direct description.

The central narrative of *The Time Machine* is of a kind common to several of Wells's early romances: a central character is transferred to or marooned in a wholly alien environment, and the story arises from his efforts to deal with the situation. This is the case with the time traveller, with the angel in *The Wonderful Visit* and with Prendick in *The Island of Dr. Moreau,* while Griffin in *The Invisible Man* becomes the victim of his environment in attempting to control it. Though Wells is a writer of symbolic fiction—or a myth-maker—the symbolism is not of the specifically heraldic kind that we associate, for instance, with Hawthorne's scarlet letter, Melville's white whale, or James's golden bowl. In Wells the symbolic element is inherent in the total fictional situation, rather more in the manner of Kafka.

When, for instance, we are shown in *The Time Machine* a paradisal world on the surface of the earth inhabited by beautiful carefree beings leading a wholly aesthetic existence, and a diabolic or demonic world beneath the surface inhabited by brutish creatures who spend most of their time in darkness in underground machine shops, and only appear on the surface at night, and when we are told that these two races are the descendents respectively of the present-day bourgeoisie and proletariat, and that the latter live by cannibalistically preying on the former—then clearly we are faced with a symbolic situation of considerable complexity, where several different "mythical" interpretations are possible.

The time traveller—unlike his predecessor, Nebogipfel (hero of **"The Chronic Argonauts,"** Wells's first version of *The Time Machine,* published in a student magazine in 1888), and his successors, Moreau and Griffin—is not a solitary eccentric on the Frankenstein model, but an amiable and gregarious bourgeois. Like Wells himself, he appears to be informed and interested in the dominant intellectual movements of his age, Marxism and Darwinism. Wells had come across Marx at South Kensington, and though in later years he was to become extremely anti-Marxist, in his immediate post-student days he was prepared to uphold Marxian socialism as "a new thing based on Darwinism." However doubtfully historical this may be, the juxtaposition of the two names is very important for Wells's early imaginative and speculative writing. The time traveller, immediately after he has arrived in the world of 802701, is full of forebodings about the kind of humanity he may discover:

> What might not have happened to men? What if cruelty had grown into a common passion? What if in this interval the race had lost its manliness, and had developed into something inhuman, unsympathetic, and overwhelmingly powerful? I might seem some old-world savage animal, only the more dreadful and disgusting for our common likeness—a foul creature to be incontinently slain.

At first, however, his more fearful speculations are not fulfilled. Instead of what he had feared, he discovers the Eloi, who are small, frail and beautiful. He is rather shocked and then amused by their child-like ways and manifest lack of intellectual powers—"the memory of my confident anticipations of a profoundly grave and intellectual posterity came, with irresistible merriment, to my mind." Such a "grave and intellectual posterity" had in fact been postulated by Bulwer Lytton in *The Coming Race,* 1871, a work, which it has been suggested had some influence on *The Time Machine,* though the resemblances are very slight. But it is quite possible that Wells was here alluding to Bulwer Lytton's romance, as well as to the wider implications of optimistic evolutionary theory.

Subsequently the traveller becomes charmed with the Eloi and the relaxed communism of their way of life. They live, not in separate houses, but in large semi-ruinous buildings of considerable architectural splendour, sleeping and eating there communally. Their only food is fruit, which abounds in great richness and variety, and they are described in a way which suggests the figures of traditional pastoral poetry: "They spent all their time in playing gently, in bathing in the river, in making love in a half-playful fashion, in eating fruit and sleeping." Later the traveller takes stock of their world:

> I have already spoken of the great palaces dotted about among the variegated greenery, some in ruins and some still occupied. Here and there rose a white silvery figure in the waste garden of the earth, here and there came the sharp vertical line of some cupola or obelisk. There were no hedges, no signs of proprietary rights, no evidences of agriculture; the whole earth had become a garden.

There appear to be no animals, wild or domestic, left in the world, and such forms of life as remain have clearly been subject to a radical process of selection:

> The air was free from gnats, the earth from weeds or fungi; everywhere were fruits and sweet and delightful flowers; brilliant butterflies flew hither and thither. The ideal of preventive medicine was attained. Disease had been stamped out. I saw no evidence of any contagious diseases during all my stay. And I shall have to tell you later that even the processes of putrefaction and decay had been profoundly affected by these changes.

Man has, in short, at some period long past obtained complete control of his environment, and has been able to manipulate the conditions of life to his absolute satisfaction. The "struggle for existence" has been eliminated, and as a result of this manipulation the nature of the species has undergone profound modification. Not only have the apparent physical differences between male and female disappeared, but their mental powers have declined as well as their physical. The human race, as it presents itself to the traveller, is plainly in its final decadence. The Eloi, with their childlike and sexually ambiguous appearance, and their consumptive type of beauty, are clearly reflections of *fin de siècle* visual taste. *The Time Machine* is in several respects a book of its time, for speculations about decadence and degeneration were much in the air in the eighties and early nineties, reaching their peak in Max Nordau's massive work of destructive criticism, *Degeneration.* Wells certainly knew the English edition of this book, which appeared in March 1895, when *The Time Machine* was already completed, for he makes a satirical reference to it in his second novel, *The Wonderful Visit,* published the following October.

In the world that the traveller surveys, aesthetic motives have evidently long been dominant as humanity has settled down to its decline. "This has ever been the fate of energy in security; it takes to art and to eroticism, and then comes languour and decay." But in the age of the Eloi even artistic motives seem almost extinct. "To adorn themselves with flowers, to dance, to sing in the sunlight; so much was left to the artistic spirit, and no more." The implied comment on *fin de siècle* aestheticism is, again, unmistakable. The first chapter of the time traveller's narrative is called "In the Golden Age," and the following chapter, "The Sunset of Mankind": there is an ironic effect, not only in the juxtaposition, but in the very reference to a "golden age." Such an age, the *Saturnia regna,* when men were imagined as living a simple, uncomplicated and happy existence, before in some way falling from grace, was always an object of literary nostalgia, and traditionally thought of as being at the very beginning of man's history. Wells, however, places it in the remotest future, and associates it not with dawn but with sunset. The time traveller sees the Eloi as leading a paradisal existence, and his sense of this is imparted to the reader by the imagery of the first part of his narrative. They are thoroughly assimilated to their environment, where "the whole earth had become a garden," and "everywhere were fruits and sweet and delicious flowers; brilliant butterflies flew hither and thither." Their appearance and mode of life makes a pointed contrast to the drab and earnest figure of the traveller:

> Several more brightly-clad people met me in the doorway, and so we entered, I, dressed in dingy nineteenth-century garments, looking grotesque enough, garlanded with flowers, and surrounded by an eddying mass of bright, soft-coloured robes and shining white limbs, in a melodious whirl of laughter and laughing speech.

The writing here suggests that Wells was getting a little out of his depth, but the intention is clearly to present the Eloi as in some sense heirs to Pre-Raphaelite convention. This implicit contrast between the aesthetic and the utilitarian, the beautiful and idle set against the ugly and active, shows how *The Time Machine* embodies another profound late-Victorian preoccupation, recalling, for instance, the aesthetic anti-industrialism of Ruskin and Morris. The world of the Eloi is presented as not only a golden age, but as something of a lotos land, and it begins to exercise its spell on the traveller. After his immediate panic on discovering the loss of his machine, he settles down to a philosophic resignation:

> Suppose the worst? I said. Suppose the machine altogether lost—perhaps destroyed? It behoves me to be calm and patient, to learn the way of the people, to get a clear idea of the method of my loss, and the means of getting materials and tools; so that in the end, perhaps, I may make another. That would be my only hope, a poor hope, perhaps, but better than despair. And, after all, it was a beautiful and curious world.

The traveller's potential attachment to the Eloi and their world is strengthened when he rescues the little female, Weena, from drowning, and begins a prolonged flirta-tion with her. This relationship is the biggest flaw in the narrative, for it is totally unconvincing, and tends to embarrass the reader (Pritchett has referred to the "faint squirms of idyllic petting.") But though the traveller feels the attraction of the kind of life she represents, he is still too much a man of his own age, resourceful, curious and active, to succumb to it. As he says of himself, "I am too Occidental for a long vigil. I could work at a problem for years, but to wait inactive for twenty-four hours—that is another matter."

But it is not long before he becomes aware that the Eloi are not the only forms of animal life left in the world, and his curiosity is once more aroused. He realises that Weena and the Eloi generally have a great fear of darkness: "But she dreaded the dark, dreaded shadows, dreaded black things." Here we have the first hint of the dominant imagery of the second half of the narrative, the darkness characteristic of the Morlocks, and the ugly, shapeless forms associated with it, contrasting with the light and the brilliant colours of the Eloi and their world. Looking into the darkness one night just before dawn the traveller imagines that he can see vague figures running across the landscape, but cannot be certain whether or not his eyes have deceived him. And a little later, when he is exploring one of the ruined palaces, he comes across a strange creature—"a queer little ape-like figure" that runs away from him and disappears down one of the well-like shafts that are scattered across the country, and whose purpose and nature had puzzled the traveller on his arrival: "My impression of it is, of course, imperfect; but I know it was a dull white, and had strange large greyish-red eyes; also that there was flaxen hair on its head and down its back." The traveller now has to reformulate his ideas about the way the evolutionary development of man has proceeded: "Man had not remained one species, but had differentiated into two distinct animals." He has to modify his previous "Darwinian" explanation by a "Marxist" one: "it seemed clear as daylight to me that the gradual widening of the merely temporary and social difference between the Capitalist and the Labourer was the key to the whole position." Even in his own day, he reflects, men tend to spend more and more time underground: "There is a tendency to utilise underground space for the less ornamental purposes of civilisation." Even now, does not an East-end worker live in such artificial conditions as practically to be cut off from the natural surface of the earth?" Similarly the rich have tended to preserve themselves more and more as an exclusive and self-contained group, with fewer and fewer social contacts with the workers, until society has stratified rigidly into a two-class system. "So, in the end, above ground, you must have the Haves, pursuing pleasure and comfort and beauty, and below ground the Have-nots; the workers getting continually adapted to the conditions of their labour." The analysis represents, it will be seen, a romantic and pessimistic variant of orthodox Marxist thought: the implications of the class-war are accepted, but the possibility of the successful proletarian revolution establishing a classless society is rigidly excluded. Thus, the traveller concludes, the social tendencies of nineteenth century industrialism have become rigidified and then built in, as it were, to the evolutionary development of the race. Nevertheless, he is still orthodox enough in his analysis to assume that the Eloi, despite their physical and mental decline, are still the masters and the Morlocks—as he finds the underground creatures are called—are their slaves. It is not long before he discovers that this, too, is a false conclusion.

Soon enough, despite his dalliance with Weena, and her obvious reluctance to let him go, the traveller decides that he must find out more about the Morlocks, and resolves to descend into their underworld. It is at this point that, in Pritchett's phrase, "the story alters its key, and the Time Traveller reveals the foundation of slime and horror on which the pretty life of his Arcadians is precariously and fearfully resting."[4] The descent of the traveller into the underworld has, in fact, an almost undisplaced mythical significance: it suggests a parody of the Harrowing of Hell, where it is not the souls of the just that are released but the demonic Morlocks, for it is they who dominate the subsequent narrative. During his "descent into hell" the traveller is seized by the Morlocks, but he keeps them at bay by striking matches, for they recoil from light in any form, which is why they do not normally appear on the surface of the earth by day. During his brief and confused visit to their world he sees and hears great machines at work, and notices a table spread for a meal. He observes that the Morlocks are carnivorous, but does not, for a time, draw the obvious conclusion about the nature of the meat they are eating. However, it is readily apparent to the reader. The Morlocks have a complex symbolic function, for they not only represent an exaggerated fear of the nineteenth century proletariat, but also embody many of the traditional mythical images of a demonic world. This will soon be apparent if one compares Wells's account of them and their environment with the chapter on "Demonic Imagery" in Northrop Frye's *Anatomy of Criticism*. As Frye writes:

> Images of perverted work belong here too: engines of torture, weapons of war, armour, and images of a dead mechanism which, because it does not humanise nature, is unnatural as well as inhuman. Corresponding to the temple or One Building of the Apocalypse, we have the prison or dungeon, the sealed furnace of heat without light, like the city of Dis in Dante.[5]

Indeed nothing is more remarkable about *The Time Machine* than the way in which its central narrative is polarised between opposed groups of imagery, the paradisal (or, in Frye's phrase, the apocalyptic) and the demonic, representing extreme forms of human desire and repulsion.

A further significance of the Morlocks can be seen in the fact that they are frequently referred to in terms of unpleasant animal life: thus they are described as, or compared with, "apes," "lemurs," "worms," "spiders," and "rats." One must compare these images with the traveller's original discovery that all forms of non-human animal life—with the apparent exception of butterflies—had been banished from the upper world, whether noxious or not. There is a powerful irony in his subsequent discovery that the one remaining form of animal life, and the most noxious of all, is a branch of humanity. Furthermore this confusion of human and animal—with its origin in some kind of imaginative perturbation over the deeper implications of Darwinism—was to provide the central theme of *The Island of Dr. Moreau.*

The traveller narrowly escapes with his life from the Morlocks and returns to the surface to make another reappraisal of the world of 802701. The image of the "golden age" as it has presented itself to him on his arrival has been destroyed: "there was an altogether new element in the sickening quality of the Morlocks—a something inhuman and malign." He has to reject his subsequent hypothesis that the Eloi were the masters, and the Morlocks their slaves. A new relationship has clearly evolved between the two races; the Eloi, who are in terror of dark and moonless nights, are in some way victims of the Morlocks, though he is still not certain precisely how. His experience underground has shattered his previous euphoria (symbolically perhaps an end of the paradisal innocence in which he has been participating), and his natural inventiveness and curiosity reassert themselves. He makes his way with Weena to a large green building that he has seen in the distance many miles off, which he later calls "the Palace of Green Porcelain." On their way they spend a night in the open: the traveller looks at the stars in their now unfamiliar arrangements and reflects on his present isolation.

> Looking at these stars suddenly dwarfed my own troubles and all the gravities of terrestrial life. I thought of their unfathomable distance and the slow inevitable drift of their movements out of the unknown past into the unknown future. I thought of the great precessional cycle that the pole of the earth describes. Only forty times had that silent revolution occurred during all the years that I had traversed. And during these few revolutions all the activity, all the traditions, the complex organisations, the nations, languages, literatures, aspirations, even the mere memory of Man as I knew him, had been swept out of existence. Instead were these frail creatures who had forgotten their high ancestry, and the white Things of which I went in terror. Then I thought of the Great Fear that was between the two species, and for the first time, with a sudden shiver, came the clear knowledge of what the meat I had seen might be. Yet it was too horrible! I looked at little Weena sleeping beside me, her face white and star-like under the stars, and forthwith dismissed the thought.

The traveller's knowledge of the world of the Eloi and the Morlocks, and the relation between them, is almost complete. When they reach the Palace of Green Porcelain, he finds, as if to belie his reflections on the disappearance of all traces of the past, that it is a vast museum: "Clearly we stood among the ruins of some latter-day South Kensington!" The museum, with its semi-ruinous remains of earlier phases of human achievement, puts the traveller once more in a direct emotional relation with the past, and, by implication, with his own age. Here, the Arcadian spell is finally cast off. He remembers that he is, after all, a late-Victorian scientist with a keen interest in technology. He is intrigued by various great machines, some half destroyed, and others in quite good condition:

> You know I have a certain weakness for mechanism, and I was inclined to linger among these: the more so as for the most part they had the interest of puzzles, and I could make only the vaguest guesses at what they were for. I fancied that if I could solve their puzzles I should find myself in possession of powers that might be of use against the Morlocks.

The Morlocks, after all, are a technological race, and if he is to defend himself against them—as he has decided he must—he must match himself against their mechanical prowess. The images of machinery in this part of the narrative are sufficient to suggest to the reader the presence of the Morlocks, and before long the traveller sees footprints in the dust around him, and hears noises coming from one end of a long gallery, which mean that the Morlocks are not far away. He breaks an iron lever off one of the machines to use as a mace. By now, his feelings for the Morlocks are those of passionate loathing: "I longed very much to kill a Morlock or so. Very inhuman, you may think, to want to go killing one's own descendants! But it was impossible, somehow, to feel any humanity in the things." Since the Morlocks on one level stand for the late nineteenth century proletariat, the traveller's attitude towards them clearly symbolises a contemporary bourgeois fear of the working class, and it is not fanciful to impute something of this attitude to Wells himself. From his schooldays in Bromley he had disliked and feared the working class in a way wholly appropriate to the son of a small tradesman—as various Marxist critics have not been slow to remark. The traveller's gradual identification with the beautiful and aristocratic—if decadent—Eloi against the brutish Morlocks is indicative of Wells's own attitudes, or one aspect of them, and links up with a common theme in his realistic fiction: the hypergamous aspirations of a low-born hero towards genteel heroines: Jessica Milton in *The Wheels of Chance,* Helen Walsingham in *Kipps,* Beatrice Normandy in *Tono-Bungay,* and Christabel in *Mr. Polly.*

Wells's imagination was easily given to producing images of mutilation and violence, and the traveller's hatred of the Morlocks gives them free rein. The reader is further prepared for the scenes of violence and destruction which end the traveller's expedition to the museum by his discovery of "a long gallery of rusting stands of arms," where he "hesitated between my crowbar and a hatchet or a sword." But he could not carry both and kept the crowbar. He contented himself with a jar of camphor from another part of the museum, since this was inflammable and would make a useful weapon against the Morlocks. By now we have wholly moved from the dominantly paradisal imagery of the first half of the narrative to the demonic imagery of the second. Instead of a golden age, or lotos land, we are back in the familiar world of inventiveness and struggle.

When Weena and the traveller are once more outside the museum and are making their way homeward through the woods, he decides to keep the lurking Morlocks at bay during the coming night by lighting a fire. He succeeds only too well, and before long discovers that he has set the whole forest ablaze. Several Morlocks try to attack him, but he fights them off with his iron bar. He then discovers the creatures all fleeing in panic before the advancing fire: in the confusion Weena is lost. There are some powerful descriptions of the Morlocks' plight:

> And now I was to see the most weird and horrible thing, I think, of all that I beheld in that future age. This whole space was as bright as day with the reflection of the fire. In the centre was a hillock or tumulus, surmounted by a scorched hawthorn. Beyond this was another arm of the burning forest, with yellow tongues already writhing from it, completely encircling the space with a fence of fire. Upon the hillside were some thirty or forty Morlocks, dazzled by the light and heat and blundering hither and thither against each other in their bewilderment. At first I did not realise their blindness, and struck furiously at them with my bar, in a frenzy of fear, as they approached me, killing one and crippling several more. But when I watched the gestures of one of them groping under the hawthorn against the red sky, and heard their moans, I was assured of their absolute helplessness and misery in the glare, and I struck no more of them.

Eventually, on the following morning, the traveller gets back to the neighbourhood of the White Sphinx, whence he had started. Everything is as it was when he left. The beautiful Eloi are still moving across the landscape in their gay robes, or bathing in the river. But now his disillusion with their Arcadian world and his realisation of the true nature of their lives is complete.

> I understood now what all the beauty of the over-world people covered. Very pleasant was their day, as pleasant as the day of the cattle in the field. Like the cattle they knew of no enemies, and provided against no needs. And their end was the same.

Here we have the solution to a riddle that was implicitly posed at the beginning of the traveller's narrative. Soon after his arrival among the Eloi he had found that there were no domestic animals in their world: "horses, cattle, sheep, dogs, had followed the Ichthyosaurus into extinction." Yet the life led by the Eloi is clearly that contained in conventional literary pastoral, and the first part of the traveller's narrative partakes of the nature of pastoral—but it is a pastoral world without sheep or cattle. And a little later, during his speculations on the possibilities of eugenic development, he had reflected:

> We improve our favourite plants and animals—and how few they are—gradually by selective breeding; now a new and better peach, now a seedless grape, now a sweeter and larger flower, now a more convenient breed of cattle.

Something of the sort, he concludes, has brought about the world of 802701. But the paradox latent in the observation is only made manifest in his return from the museum, now possessing a complete knowledge of this world. There are no sheep or cattle in the pastoral world of the Eloi because they are themselves the cattle, fattened and fed by their underground masters. They are *both* a "sweeter and larger flower" and "a more convenient breed of cattle." Thus the complex symbolism of the central narrative of *The Time Machine* is ingeniously completed on this note of diabolical irony. Such knowledge has made the Arcadian world intolerable to the traveller. He is now able to escape from it: the Morlocks have produced his machine and placed it as a trap for him, but he is able to elude them, and travels off into the still more remote future.

The final part of the time traveller's narrative, the chapter called "The Further Vision," is an extended epilogue to the story of the Eloi and the Morlocks. The traveller moves further and further into the future, until he reaches an age when all traces of humanity have vanished and the world is given over to giant crabs. The earth has ceased to rotate, and has come to rest with one face always turned to the sun:

> I stopped very gently and sat upon the Time Machine, looking round. The sky was no longer blue. North-eastward it was inky black, and out of the darkness shone brightly and steadily the pale white stars. Overhead it was a deep Indian red and starless, and south-eastward it grew brighter to a growing scarlet where, cut by the horizon, lay the huge hull of the sun, red and motionless. The rocks about me were of a harsh, reddish colour, and all the trace of life that I could see at first was the intensely green vegetation that covered every projecting point on their south-eastern face. It was the same rich green that one sees on forest moss or on lichen in caves: plants which like these grow in a perpetual twilight.

The whole of this vision of a dying world is conveyed with a poetic intensity which Wells was never to recapture. The transition from the social and biological interest of the "802701" episode to the cosmological note of these final pages is extremely well done: the previous account of the decline of humanity is echoed and amplified by the description of the gradual death of the whole physical world. The traveller moves on and on, seeking to discover the ultimate mystery of the world's fate.

> At last, more than thirty million years hence, the huge red-hot dome of the sun had come to obscure nearly a tenth part of the darkling heavens. Then I stopped once more, for the crawling multitude of crabs had disappeared, and the red beach, save for its livid green liverworts and lichens, seemed lifeless. And now it was flecked with white. A bitter cold assailed me. Rare white flakes ever and again came eddying down. To the north-eastward, the glare of snow lay under the starlight of the sable sky, and I could see an undulating crest of hillocks pinkish-white. There were fringes of ice along the sea margin, with drifting masses further out; but the main expanse of that salt ocean, all bloody under the eternal sunset, was still unfrozen.

Finally, after an eclipse of the sun has reduced this desolate world to total darkness, the traveller returns to his own time, and the waiting circle of friends in his house at Richmond.

A contemporary reviewer paid special tribute to these final pages, and referred to "that last *fin de siècle,* when earth is moribund and man has ceased to be."[6] This reference to the *fin de siècle* is appropriate both in its immediate context and in a larger sense, for, as I have already suggested, *The Time Machine* is pre-eminently a book of its time, giving imaginative form to many of the fears and preoccupations of the final years of the nineteenth century. Max Nordau, in fact, had attacked these preoccupations and attitudes in a passage which curiously anticipates the themes and dominant images of *The Time Machine*:

> *Fin de siècle* is at once a confession and a complaint. The old Northern faith contained the fearsome doctrine of the Dusk of the Gods. In our days there have arisen in more highly developed minds vague qualms of a Dusk of the Nations, in which all suns and all stars are gradually waning, and mankind with all its institutions and creations is perishing in the midst of a dying world.[7]

Since *The Time Machine* is a romance and not a piece of realistic fiction, it conveys its meaning in poetic fashion through images, rather than by the revelation of character in action. It is, in short, a myth, and in Shanks's words, "can be interpreted in many ways, none of them quite consistent, all of them more alive and fruitful than the rigid allegorical correspondence." I have tried to indicate some of the thematic strands to be found in the work. Some of them are peculiarly of their period, others have a more general and a more fundamental human relevance. The opposition of Eloi and Morlocks can be interpreted in terms of the late nineteenth-century class struggle, but it also reflects an opposition between aestheticism and utilitarianism, pastoralism and technology, contemplation and action, and ultimately, and least specifically, between beauty and ugliness, and light and darkness. The book not only embodies the tensions and dilemmas of its time, but others peculiar to Wells himself, which a few years later were to make him cease to be an artist, and become a propagandist. Since the tensions are imaginatively and not intellectually resolved we find that a note of irony becomes increasingly more pronounced as the traveller persists in his disconcerting exploration of the world where he has found himself. *The Time Machine* is not only a myth, but an ironic myth, like many other considerable works of modern literature. And despite the complexity of its thematic elements, Wells's art is such that the story is a skilfully wrought imaginative whole, a single image.

Notes

1. *The Living Novel* (London, 1946), pp. 119-20.

2. *First Essays on Literature* (London, 1923), p. 158.

3. *Anatomy of Criticism* (Princeton, 1957), p. 202.

4. ["The Scientific Romances" in *The Living Novel*. It is the essay preceding this in the present volume.—Ed.]

5. *Anatomy of Criticism*, p. 150.

6. *Daily Chronicle*, 27 July, 1895.

7. *Degeneration* (London, 1895), p. 2.

Robert M. Philmus (essay date May 1969)

SOURCE: Philmus, Robert M. "*The Time Machine*; Or, The Fourth Dimension as Prophecy." *PMLA* 84, no. 3 (May 1969): 530-35.

[*In the following essay, Philmus analyzes Wells's own observations on* The Time Machine *and provides a stylistic examination of the novella.*]

The statements that H. G. Wells gave out in the twenties and thirties about his early "scientific romances" or "scientific fantasies," as he alternately called them, are not sympathetic to the spirit of these works written before the turn of the century. In general, he makes them out to be slighter in substance or more tendentious in tone than the serious reader coming upon them now would find them. Nevertheless, Wells does not attempt wilfully to mislead or mystify his readers in later assessments of his early romances; and in fact his own criticism is sometimes actively helpful in understanding his fiction.

Of particular importance are his various observations about *The Time Machine* (1895); and his Preface to the *Scientific Romances* especially—an indispensable account of the theory and practice of his science fiction—draws attention to two aspects of this early fantasy essential to interpreting it. The first of these concerns the Time Traveller's vision of the future, a vision which Wells characterizes as running "counter to the placid assumption" of the nineties "that Evolution was a pro-human force making things better and better for mankind." The second point, already implicit in this last remark from the Preface, is that *The Time Machine* is an "assault on human self-satisfaction."[1]

These observations can in effect be taken to summarize the findings of Bernard Bergonzi's study of *The Time Machine* as an "ironic myth" of degeneration and Mark R. Hillegas' analysis of it as "a serious attack on human complacency."[2] Neither of these studies explains, however, the Traveller's compulsion to resume his time-travelling, to return, presumably, to the world of the Eloi and the Morlocks; and it is towards an explanation of this response to the vision or prophecy of *The Time Machine* that my own interpretation is directed. It seems to me that Wells has structured his romance so as to educe the ultimate consequences of both the myth he develops and the several internal points of view towards it. Since the fantasy thus approaches the very postulates of his science fiction, I propose to examine its structure in detail, considering summarily but analytically the components of that structure: the Time Traveller's vision of the future, his interpretation of it, and the reaction of his audience to the prophetic report.[3]

I

To begin then with the Time Traveller's vision, "degeneration" is not, I think, a precise enough description of the backsliding of the human species into the less and less recognizably anthropomorphic descendants that the Traveller comes upon in the world of 802,701 and beyond. It is true that Wells himself used that term as early as 1891 in an essay outlining the abstract idea behind his vision of the future;[4] but in that same essay, entitled **"Zoological Retrogression,"** Wells also calls this process of reversion "degradation,"[5] which suggests the step-by-step decline from man to beast that he was to take up in *The Island of Doctor Moreau* (1896) as well. More accurately still, one can define the vision in *The Time Machine* of Homo sapiens gradually reduced to species lower and lower on the evolutionary scale as a vision of devolution.

The human ancestry of the degenerate species that the Traveller discovers in the "Golden Age" of 802,701 is scarcely discernible. The feeble and "childlike" Eloi (p. 38)[6] are more human than the "ape-like" and predatory Morlocks (p. 77) that emerge nightly from dark catacombs to prey upon the creatures of the "upper-world"; but while "modification of the human type" among the Morlocks has been "far more profound than among the

'Eloi'" (p. 84), the process of devolution has by no means reached an equilibrium. The oppressive, almost Manichean, threat to the sunlit paradise of the Eloi which the dark and demonic "underworld" of the Morlocks imposes becomes finally the impending destruction of the solar system itself,[7] foreshadowed in the total blackness of the solar eclipse which concludes the chapter called "The Further Vision."

The paradise-hell of the Eloi and the Morlocks in fact leads causally as well as temporally to what the Traveller sees as the further vision of devolution tending towards the extinction of all life. In an episode appearing in the *New Review* but deleted subsequently, he comes next upon a species more degraded than the Morlocks. Of this creature, which he likens to "rabbits or some breed of kangaroo," the Traveller reports: "I was surprised to see that the thing had five feeble digits to both its fore and hind feet—the fore feet, indeed, were almost as human as the fore feet of a frog. It had, moreover, a roundish head, with a projecting forehead and forward-looking eyes." As a result of his examination, he admits that "A disagreeable apprehension crossed my mind"; but he has no opportunity to observe "my grey animal, or grey man, whichever it was" at greater length because he perceives that he is being stalked by a monster similar to a gigantic centipede.[8] It is left for the reader to infer that at this point in the future the Eloi have devolved into creatures with "five feeble digits," in this case the victims of giant centipedes.

At the next stop in the distant future (in both the Heinemann and the *New Review* versions) all anthropomorphic life seems to have disappeared, and the Traveller sees instead "a thing like a huge white butterfly" and "a monstrous crab-like creature" (p. 137). He goes on until, thirty million years hence, it appears as if animal life has devolved out of existence. Plant life has degenerated to "livid green liverworts and lichens" (p. 139). Here he witnesses a solar eclipse which prefigures the end of the world.

> The darkness grew apace; a cold wind began to blow in freshening gusts from the east, and the showering white flakes in the air increased in number. From the edge of the sea came a ripple and whisper. Beyond these lifeless sounds the world was silent. Silent? It would be hard to convey the stillness of it . . . As the darkness thickened, the eddying flakes grew more abundant . . . and the cold of the air more intense. At last, one by one, swiftly, one after the other, the white peaks of the distant hills vanished into blackness. The breeze rose to a moaning wind. I saw the black central shadow of the eclipse sweeping towards me. In another moment the pale stars alone were visible. All else was rayless obscurity. The sky was absolutely black.
>
> (pp. 140-141)

In retrospect, it seems that the unbalanced struggle between the Eloi and the Morlocks prepares for this final vision, that a terrible logic compels the conclusion:

"The sky was absolutely black." "People unfamiliar with such speculations as those of the younger Darwin," the Time Traveller had remarked earlier, "forget that the planets must ultimately fall back one by one into the parent body" (p. 76). This is a vision hardly in accord with "Excelsior" optimism; on the contrary, it is precisely calculated to "run counter to the placid assumption . . . that Evolution was a pro-human force making things better and better for mankind."[9]

Indeed, the ideas Wells is dealing with are, as he stated in the early essay on **"Zoological Retrogression,"** an "evolutionary antithesis":

> . . . there is almost always associated with the suggestion of advance in biological phenomena an opposite idea, which is its essential complement. The technicality expressing this would, if it obtained sufficient currency in the world of culture, do much to reconcile the naturalist and his traducers. The toneless glare of optimistic evolution would then be softened by a shadow; the monotonous reiteration of 'Excelsior' by people who did not climb would cease; the too sweet harmony of the spheres would be enhanced by a discord, this evolutionary antithesis—degradation.
>
> (**"Retrogression,"** p. 246)

Wells goes on to illustrate "the enormous importance of degeneration as a plastic process in nature" and its "parity with evolution" by giving examples of species which have retrogressed and of vestigial features now observable which perhaps presage future degeneration. His concluding remarks are especially relevant to the vision presented in *The Time Machine*:

> There is, therefore, no guarantee in scientific knowledge of man's permanence or permanent ascendancy . . . The presumption is that before him lies a long future of profound modification, but whether this will be, according to his present ideals, upward or downward, no one can forecast. Still, so far as any scientist can tell us, it may be that, instead of this, Nature is, in unsuspected obscurity, equipping some now humble creature with wider possibilities of appetite, endurance, or destruction, to rise in the fulness of time and sweep *homo* away into the darkness from which his universe arose. The Coming Beast must certainly be reckoned in any anticipatory calculations regarding the Coming Man.
>
> (**"Retrogression,"** p. 253)

Clearly this speculation goes beyond the mere softening of the "glare of optimistic evolution" with a "shadow." The "opposite idea" dominates Wells's imagination—the vision of man's being swept away "into the darkness from which his universe arose"—of "life that . . . is slowly and remorselessly annihilated," as he says in "On Extinction"[10]—the vision, in other words, of *The Time Machine*. And his prophecy of the "Coming Beast"—in stories like **"The Sea Raiders"** (1896), *The War of the Worlds* (1898), and **"The Empire of the**

Ants" (1904), as well as in *The Time Machine*—though more literal than Yeats's vision of the Second Coming—is no less forceful in its dramatic impact.

II

The vision of the future as a devolutionary process, in reversing the expectations of "optimistic evolution," is not isolated in *The Time Machine* as an imaginative possibility for its own sake. The structure of the world of 802,701, for instance, suggests a critique of the pastoral utopia of Morris' *News from Nowhere* (1891) and other pre-Wellsian utopian romances, since the idyllic world of the Eloi is quite literally undermined by the machine-dominated world of the Morlocks. Thus the vision of the future in *The Time Machine* both reflects and evaluates man's "present ideals," a point that the Time Traveller emphasizes by insisting that the theories he has developed to explain the world of the future derive from what he sees in the present state of human affairs.

Although the Traveller revises his theories as he learns about the nature of the Morlocks, he temporarily settles on an etiological interpretation of the relationship between the effete (and virtually androgynous) Eloi and their more energetic predators. "The great triumph of Humanity I had dreamed of took a different shape in my mind. It had been no such triumph of moral education and general co-operation as I had imagined. Instead, I saw a real aristocracy, armed with perfected science and working to a logical conclusion the industrial system of today. Its triumph had not been simply a triumph over nature, but a triumph over nature and the fellow-man" (p. 84). To be sure, he himself reserves a doubt concerning this account of how the future world had come to be: "My explanation may be absolutely wrong. I still think it is the most plausible one." His ambivalence here reminds one, not accidentally, of his subsequent remark as to how the reader may accept this vision of the future. "Take it as a lie—or a prophecy . . . Consider I have been speculating on the destinies of our race, until I have hatched this fiction" (p. 145). Together, these statements suggest that any explanation of the imaginary world of the Eloi and the Morlocks is important only insofar as it makes it clear that the world projected in the fiction is prophecy; that is, the "working to a logical conclusion" of what can be observed in the world of the present.

The Time Traveller himself says that he has arrived at his explanation by extrapolating (to appropriate a useful word from the jargon of science fiction) from tendencies existing in the present:

> At first, *proceeding from the problems of our own age,* it seemed clear as daylight to me that the gradual widening of the present merely temporary and social difference between the Capitalist and the Labourer, was

the key to the whole position. No doubt it will seem grotesque enough to you—and wildly incredible!—and yet *even now there are existing circumstances* to point that way.

(pp. 81-82; my emphasis)

What this passage implies is that the procedure for interpreting the vision of *The Time Machine* recapitulates the process by which the fiction was "hatched"; so that the science-fictional method of prophecy is itself "the key to the whole position." Moreover, on the evidence of the Traveller's own theories, the future that Wells has projected does not, precisely speaking, embody only the consequences of "the industrial system of to-day," but also the consequences of the ideal which directs the course and uses of technological advance.

While they summarily describe a world resulting from man's present ideals, the Time Traveller's theories are also evaluative. In saying, for example, that "the great triumph of Humanity . . . had not been simply a triumph over nature" (as T. H. Huxley had urged[11]) "but a triumph over nature and the fellow-man," the Time Traveller makes a negative moral judgment: "moral education and general co-operation" had not been achieved. And condemnation is again entailed in his observation that the human intellect "had set itself steadfastly towards comfort and ease, a balanced society with security as its watchword"; for "Only those animals partake of intelligence that have to meet a huge variety of needs and dangers" (p. 130). The ideal (perfect security) therefore undermines the means of maintaining it (intelligence); and the result, the Traveller continues, is that "the upper-world man had drifted towards his feeble prettiness, and the underworld to mere mechanical industry. But that perfect state had lacked one thing even for mechanical perfection—absolute permanency" (pp. 130-131). This final interpretation, which elaborates on and at the same time supersedes his previous explanations, accounts more fully for the world of the Eloi and the Morlocks as it obviously impugns man's "present ideals." The ideal of subjugating man and nature to realize a state of "comfort and ease" is satirically judged by projecting its consequences as a vision of the future.

Both the Traveller's principle for interpreting the vision and the process by which that vision has been arrived at assume, therefore, that man's ideals to affect the course of evolution, that the world of 802,701 and beyond is the "working to a logical conclusion" of man's striving for comfort and ease. This point is made explicitly in the version of *The Time Machine* published in the *National Observer,* a version inferior in conception and structure to that put out by Heinemann, and one containing more cross-discussion between the Traveller (referred to as the Philosopher) and his fictive audience than Wells finally (and rightly) decided was necessary.

In the serialized episode called "The Refinement of Humanity: A.D. 12,203," the Philosopher remarks to a doctor in his audience:

> You believe that the average height, average weight, average longevity will all be increased, that in the future humanity will breed and sanitate itself into human Megatheria . . . But . . . what I saw is just what one might have expected. Man, like other animals, has been moulded, and will be, by the necessities of his environment. What keeps men so large and so strong as they are? The fact that if any drop below a certain level of power and capacity for competition, they die. Remove dangers, render physical exertion no longer a necessity but an excrescence upon life, abolish competition by limiting population . . . [and you get degeneration].
>
> Somewhere between now and then [i.e., 12,203] your sanitary science must have won the battle it is beginning now.[12]

Here and elsewhere in this early draft Wells does not really achieve any degree of detachment from the Philosopher; but at least passages such as this help to clarify how a vision antithetical to "the placid assumption of that time that Evolution was a pro-human force" can also illustrate the consequences of an ideal seemingly inseparable from that assumption—namely, the ideal of evolving towards greater and greater "comfort and ease."

As far as the Time Traveller's theories are necessary for understanding the prophecy, then, it is somewhat misleading to say that "This horrible degeneration [of the Eloi and the Morlocks] has occurred because mankind, as Huxley feared, was ultimately unable to control the cosmic or evolutionary process."[13] Rather, the Traveller implies, mankind apparently controlled the cosmic process too well, according to an ideal the consequences of which no one could foresee. One of those consequences is that by 802,701 no species has the intelligence any more to set limits on the struggle for existence, in which the defenseless Eloi fall victim to the carnivorous Morlocks. Among these descendants of homo sapiens, the struggle for survival—which, engendered by "Necessity," makes the "absolute permanency" of "mechanical perfection" impossible—now resumes the character that struggle takes among other animals. "Man," the Traveller reflects, "had been content to live in ease and delight upon the labours of his fellow-man, had taken Necessity as his watchword and excuse, and in the fulness of time Necessity had come home to him" (pp. 105-106). And once this "Necessity" reasserts itself, once, that is to say, man's descendants begin reverting to beasts, anthropomorphic life, according to the vision of *The Time Machine,* is irrevocably on the downward path of devolution.

III

This vision of social disintegration and devolution as a critique of the ideal of striving towards "ease and delight" can exist only in the dimension of prophecy, that dimension into which the critique can be projected and imaginatively given life—the world, in other words, of science fantasy.[14] The fourth dimension as a dimension in time is thus a metaphor: it is the dimension open to the imagination. "Our mental existences, which are immaterial and have no dimensions, are passing along the Time-Dimension" (p. 6), the Traveller had said in introducing his audience to the concept of this new dimension. As a world wherein the consequences of the accepted ideal can be envisioned, the fourth dimension provides a critical and comprehensive point of view from which to evaluate the present.

That at the beginning of *The Time Machine* no one except the Time Traveller has conceived of—or even can conceive of—this dimension already indicates a lack of imaginative (and critical) awareness on the part of his audience. His argument for a fourth dimension, prefaced by the caveat that "I shall have to controvert one or two ideas that are almost universally accepted" (pp. 1-2), meets with incomprehension and complacent skepticism. Quite predictably, his audience fails to take seriously—if the point is grasped at all—the relevance of the Time Traveller's vision. No one else seems to connect the vision of "The two species that had resulted from the evolution of man . . . sliding down towards, or . . . already arrived at, an altogether new relationship" (p. 97) with his preconception of an "inevitable tendency to higher and better things" (**"Retrogression,"** p. 247). Perhaps no one in the audience takes this vision seriously because, as Wells speculated elsewhere, "It is part of the excessive egotism of the human animal that the bare idea of its extinction seems incredible to it."[15] Certainly there is no sign that anyone among the listeners sees how, or that, this vision implicates his present ideals, which are responsible for the shape of the future. On the contrary, the reactions typifying the attitude of the audience are the skepticism of the Medical Man, who wants to analyze the flowers that the Traveller has brought back with him, and the arrant disbelief of the Editor, who considers the Traveller's account a "gaudy lie" (p. 148). Only the unidentified narrator of the entire *Time Machine* lies "awake most of the night thinking about it."

In fact, the Time Traveller himself does not seem to be wholly cognizant of the implications of his theories. If his etiology is correct, the cause of the degeneration he discovers exists in the present. Therefore, the burden of what he calls "moral education" remains here and now; and his return to the world of 802,701 would appear to be either a romantic evasion and of a piece with the sentimental "squirms of idyllic petting" that V. S. Pritchett finds embarrassing,[16] or a pessimistic retreat from a world "that must inevitably fall back upon and destroy its makers" (p. 152). In any case, the Traveller's point of view, though more comprehensive than that of the other characters, is still limited; and this limitation has its structural correlative in the fact that his narrative is related secondhand, as it were, three years after his disappearance, and comprises only a part—albeit a large part—of the fiction.

That the structure of **The Time Machine** encompasses, and thereby defines the limits of, the Traveller's point of view indicates that the romance follows an inner logic of its own, a logic, like that governing the Time Traveller's vision, which compels ultimate consequences from a given premise. Accordingly, the logic which necessitates the Traveller's vanishing into the world of his vision depends upon how he accepts that vision. His insistence that "The story I told you was true" (p. 148) implies that he takes his prophecy literally, that he allows it the same ontological status that he himself has. Thus to dramatize the assertion that his tale is literally true, he must go back into the world of the future: since he cannot accept it as fiction, as an invented metaphor, he must disappear into the dimension where his vision "exists." The demand that his vision be literally true, in other words, requires that the Traveller be no more real than it is; and his return to that world fulfills this demand.

In being subsumed in his vision, however, he also renders it no less real than any member of the fictive audience; so that one is forced to give the same degree of credibility to the futuristic fantasy as to the contemporary scene in which the Traveller relates his story. What the reader is left with, that is, is the prophecy, the metaphorical truth which mediates between the blind and complacent optimism evidenced by the fictive audience and the resultant devolution envisioned by the Time Traveller.

The Traveller's return to the world of 802,701, far from vitiating the impact of **The Time Machine,** reinforces its claim to integrity: by having the Time Traveller act out the ultimate consequence of his taking a prophetic myth literally, Wells illustrates the rigor that he has submitted himself to in satirizing certain "present ideals." The romance, as I see it, is thus rigorously self-contained in "working to a logical conclusion" both the myth of devolution that exposes tendencies "of our own age" and the various points of view regarding the truth of that prophetic myth.

According to this interpretation, Wells's experiment in fiction is comparable in the artistry of its narrative to the contemporaneous experiments of, say Joseph Conrad, who also wrote tales "told in quotation marks"[17] and who found in Wells an early admirer; and for the complexity of its structure and point of view, **The Time Machine** deserves the praise that Henry James in fact bestowed on it.[18]

Notes

1. *The Scientific Romances of H. G. Wells* (London, 1933), p. ix.

2. Bergonzi, "*The Time Machine*: An Ironic Myth," *Critical Quarterly,* II (1960), 293-305, and *The Early H. G. Wells: A Study of the Scientific Romances* (Toronto, 1961), pp. 42-61; Hillegas, "Cosmic Pessimism in H. G. Wells' Scientific Romances," *Papers of the Mich. Acad. of Sci., Arts, and Letters,* XLVI (1961), 657-658, and *The Future as Nightmare: H. G. Wells and the Anti-Utopians* (New York, 1967), pp. 24-34.

3. All published drafts of *The Time Machine* share these components, though the serialized versions appearing in the *National Observer* (1894) and the *New Review* (1895) differ from the first English edition, published by Heinemann, in many respects—not all of them minor. Sometimes these differences give insight into the meaning of Wells's fantasy, though the serialized versions of course count only as outside evidence for any interpretation. Otherwise they are of interest solely to a study of Wells's progress as a literary artist, a subject it is not my intention to discuss explicitly here.

Some evaluation of the merits of the Heinemann version of *The Time Machine* relative to the various previously published drafts, including the first American edition, can be found in Bergonzi's "The Publication of *The Time Machine* 1894-5," *RES,* N.S., IX (1960), 42-51.

4. The fact that Wells was familiar with the notion of degeneration at this early date would seem to reduce the possible extent of any influence on him of Max Nordau's *Degeneration* (1894), which Bergonzi adduces as a source for the vision of the future in *The Time Machine.*

5. "Zoological Retrogression," *The Gentleman's Magazine,* 7 Sept. 1891, p. 246.

6. All quotations from *The Time Machine* refer to the first English edition (London, 1895).

7. As Bergonzi observes of *The Time Machine,* "its central narrative is polarised between opposed groups of imagery, the paradisal . . . and the demonic" ("An Ironic Myth," p. 300).

8. *The Time Machine* in the *New Review,* XII (1895), 578-579.

9. *The Time Machine* is part of a reaction on the part of many writers of the late eighties and nineties to the strident optimism that permeated the official rhetoric of the Victorian age. See Bergonzi's discussion of the *fin du globe* in his *Early H. G. Wells,* pp. 3-14, et passim. Some material may also be found in Hillegas' *Future as Nightmare* (see n. 2 above), relevant to attitudes towards evolution during the period in which Wells was writing *The Time Machine.*

10. "On Extinction," *Chamber's Journal*, X (30 Sept. 1893), 623.

11. In "Evolution and Ethics" and other essays, Huxley declares that ethical man can exist only if he modifies the "cosmic process."

12. "The Refinement of Humanity," *National Observer*, N.S., XI (21 Apr. 1894), 581-582.

13. Hillegas, "Cosmic Pessimism," p. 658.

14. As late as *Men Like Gods* (1923), the utopian fantasy that takes place in the "F dimension," Wells has one of his characters say of another (neither has yet been initiated into Utopia): "He has always had too much imagination. He thinks that things that don't exist *can* exist. And now he imagines himself in some sort of scientific romance and out of our world altogether" (*Men Like Gods*, New York, 1923, pp. 21-22).

15. "The Extinction of Man," *Certain Personal Matters* (London, 1898 [1897]), p. 172. This essay first appeared in the *Pall Mall Gazette* for 23 Sept. 1894.

16. *The Living Novel* (London, 1946), p. 119.

17. Northrop Frye, *Anatomy of Criticism* (Princeton, N. J., 1957), pp. 202-203.

18. On 21 Jan. 1900, James wrote to Wells: "It was very graceful of you to send me your book—I mean the particular masterpiece entitled *The Time Machine,* after I had so *un*-gracefully sought it at your hands" (*Henry James and H. G. Wells,* ed. Leon Edel and Gordon N. Ray, Urbana, Ill., 1958, p. 63).

Jean-Pierre Vernier (essay date 1971)

SOURCE: Vernier, Jean-Pierre. "*The Time Machine* and Its Content." In *H. G. Wells, "The Time Machine," "The War of the Worlds": A Critical Edition,* edited by Frank D. McConnell, pp. 315-20. New York: Oxford University Press, 1977.

[*In the following essay, originally published in French in 1971, Vernier describes the variations of* The Time Machine *and discusses its universal appeal at the time of its publication.*]

The Time Machine has remained one of Wells's most popular books, and one of the most often reprinted. The circumstances of its publication are, in general, well enough known that here we need only recall them briefly. The Time Traveller appeared for the first time in the *Science Schools Journal,* in a story entitled "**The Chronic Argonauts**"; following are the principal transformations undergone by that original tale:[1]

A. "**The Chronic Argonauts,**" published in the *Science Schools Journal,* 1881.

B. Two different versions of the same story, written in 1889 and 1892. The texts were never published, and Geoffrey West is the only authority attesting to their existence.

C. In 1893, another version was written by Wells and published in series form in *The National Observer* during the spring of 1894. This is actually the earliest form of *The Time Machine.*

D. In 1894 Wells took up the story again, producing a new version serialized in *The New Review* beginning in January 1895. Except for a few details, this is the version Heinemann published in book form in June 1895. Preparing it for book form, Wells contented himself with rewriting the opening, making it more dramatic and less didactic, and excising a few episodes that unnecessarily slowed the plot development. But one highly interesting variation appears between the 1893 text and the 1894. In *The National Observer,* the last vision of a world where life has gradually disappeared due to the cooling of the sun is introduced only as a brief speculation within the final episode, while in *The New Review* this vision has been enlarged to the dimensions of the definitive version. We are dealing, then, with a slowly elaborated work, and one upon which Wells placed high hopes. In December 1894 he wrote to Miss Healey:

> You may be interested to know that our ancient "**Chronic Argonauts**" of the *Science Schools Journal* has at last become a complete story and will appear as a serial in the *New Review* for January. It's my trump card and if it does not come off very much I shall know my place for the rest of my career.[2]

To be sure, there is some exaggeration in this. We can hardly imagine Wells abandoning his writing career because of the failure of one book. On those rare occasions when an editor did reject his work, he simply revised, often restating the same ideas in altered form. But no such problem arose with *The Time Machine,* which was accorded a reception that must have surpassed even Wells's own hopes. In the *Review of Reviews,* W. T. Stead called him "a man of genius."[3] The sentiment was echoed by a number of reviewers, and indicates quite well the quality of praise lavished on Wells at the time. Unknown till then, he rapidly became one of the foremost literary figures of his age—an age when young talent was relatively rare. We may ask what allowed him to achieve such success. Should we assume that Wells, in 1894, expressed the preoccupations of his age so clearly that his readers saw in his work an illustration of their own confusing problems? Or should we, on the other hand, assume that *The Time Machine* offered them an escape from those problems?

Many critics have claimed to find in the adventures of the Time Traveller a satire against the age, a warning from Wells to his contemporaries. . . . Indeed, it is possible—though not certain—that Wells meant to apprise his contemporaries of the dangers of science and show them the faults inherent in their social organization. But this does not appear to have been the essential motive of the work. Wells himself, of course, came to subscribe to this reading and, in hindsight, located *The Time Machine* in the line of his propagandistic works which provided the ideological basis of the *Open Conspiracy*.[4] In *All Aboard for Ararat* (1940) Noah Lammock—one of Wells's numerous incarnations—is arguing with the Lord:

> "I never wrote *The Time Machine*," said Noah.
>
> "Why pretend?" said the Lord. "The same idea is the framework of your *Work, Wealth and Happiness of Mankind*. It is *World Brain*. It crops up more and more frequently in your books as you get older and repeat yourself more and more—"[5]

But this is merely one of Wells's constant attempts to impose upon his lifework a unity which is not, in fact, there. In 1894 the realm of pure ideas scarcely attracted him. And like most of his stories from the same period, *The Time Machine* rests upon a fundamental ambiguity—an ambiguity, moreover, as fecund as the ambiguity of poetry, revealing meaning upon meaning at levels at once parallel to each other and superimposed upon one another. As Bernard Bergonzi brilliantly indicates, the book's central episode is a metaphor for an extremely complex reality:

> The opposition of Eloi and Morlocks can be interpreted in terms of the late nineteenth-century class-struggle, but it also reflects an opposition between aestheticism and utilitarianism, pastoralism and technology, contemplation and action, and ultimately, and least specifically, between beauty and ugliness, and light and darkness. The book not only embodies the tensions and dilemmas of its time, but others peculiar to Wells himself, which a few years later were to make him cease to be an artist and become a propagandist.[6]

Certainly, despite Wells's own simplistic explanation of them, the Eloi and the Morlocks awaken archetypal responses in the reader. But that is not their only function.

The theme itself of time travel is called into play in a manner very characteristic of the period. Long before the book appeared, people had been discussing the plausibility of the hypothesis; and serious physicists had demonstrated that time travel is physically impossible. But that is a different problem from Wells's. Insofar as the reader is induced, by the narrative technique, to believe in the reality of the voyage, we have to admit that the writer has achieved his goal. What is significant—and what Paul Valéry saw splendidly—is that the "time" through which Wells's hero travels is wholly different from "time" as conceived by contemporary physics:

> Even Wells, in his famous story *The Time Machine,* employs and explores time *as it was,* old time, the time which was believed in *before* him. . . .[7]

It is no surprise, then, that the reader finds in the book characters who, fantastic as they may be, nevertheless betray familiar traits.

> The Eloi, with their childlike and sexually ambiguous appearance, and their consumptive type of beauty, are clear reflections of *fin de siècle* visual taste.[8]

Apparently, for the contemporary reader, the identification of these frail creatures with the aesthetes of the Decadent Movement was inevitable. And over against the Eloi, the Morlocks may illustrate the same process of identification even more clearly. They evoke the demons of popular tradition, descended from the Middle Ages through the period of the Gothic Novel. And their origin, as explained by Wells, makes them descendents of the working class of the end of the nineteenth century. And it matters little what kind of workers. Their appearance and habitat inevitably suggest the miners. And the miners, we know, represented for both the upper and the middle classes of the time a barely human species—a species requiring constant surveillance if one did not wish to fall prey to their natural savagery. We may assert that, for the middle class of the late nineteenth century, the existence of the miner represented a constant and ominous annoyance, an image of potential revolution very like the "terrorist with a knife" of the period between the two World Wars.

So that Wells presents to his predominantly middle class audience a society composed of two other classes, with neither of whom they can identify: on the one hand the descendents of the capitalists, a collection of dilettantes at the margin of society; and on the other the Morlocks descended from the proletarians, traditional enemies of the middle class. Furthermore, Wells shows no sympathy for either class: and the reader thus finds himself a pure spectator. This is so much the case, indeed, that the reader feels no indignation when the hero fights the Morlocks with fire: he can regard it only as man's affirmation of his superiority over creatures with whom he has nothing in common. The world from which these creatures come is not the reader's. And, doubtless, this is one reason why *The Time Machine* has no value as propaganda. The original Chapter Seven was titled, simply, *Explanation*. We are in the realm of fantasy, and there is no conscious urge to instruct or warn us. As Kingsley Amis correctly observes:

> When the Time Traveller finds that mankind will have become separated into two races, the gentle ineffectual Eloi and the savage Morlocks, the idea that these are descended respectively from our own leisured classes and manual workers comes as a mere explanation, a solution to the puzzle; it is not transformed, as it inevitably would be in a modern writer, into a warning about some current trend in society.[9]

The book, rather, is a series of hypotheses based upon the theory of evolution—not as Darwin and Huxley expounded it, but as it was popularized among the reading public. The divorce between the real world and the imaginative universe is total: *The Time Machine* is above all a work of art, and is typical of its age only to the extent that all art is a re-creation of the world of the moment within the artist's own vision. It appears, besides, that Wells himself is more concerned to make his reader admit the plausibility of his hypothesis—more concerned, that is, with problems of literary technique—than with the actual validity of such hypotheses. As he himself later said:

> It was still possible in *The Time Machine* to imagine humanity on the verge of extinction and differentiated into two decadent species, the Eloi and the Morlocks, without the slightest reflection upon everyday life. Quite a lot of people thought that idea was very clever in its sphere, very clever indeed, and no one minded in the least. It seemed to have no sort of relation whatever to normal existence.[10]

Perhaps it is just because *The Time Machine* seemed to be a game that readers and critics gave it such an enthusiastic welcome. They found there a new, original world, which was, nevertheless, not disturbing since it could not conceivably come into existence. But the game is far from being simply frivolous; and behind the descriptions of fantastic beings and worlds, there is manifested a peculiar disquiet. To be sure, we do not find a concerted attack on this or that aspect of the modern world: but the violence itself, which is such an essential element in all the stories of this period, clearly illustrates Wells's unrest. But *The Time Machine,* finally, is not one of those numerous works in which he acerbically criticized his society and eventually elaborated a complex social philosophy. It is a youthful work that owes its triumph above all to its literary genius and its exuberance. . . .

Doubtless, there is a typical *fin de siècle* attitude in Wells's obvious pleasure in imagining the end of our world, and in the evocative power of his description of the planet dying under a sun that grows more and more cold. But these achievements do not in any way surpass the limitations of an aesthetic game founded upon an intellectual hypothesis. We can scarcely argue that this hypothesis was ahead of its time. For it is only a point of departure, a pretext for a dream which, disturbing as it may be, remains nevertheless a dream.

Notes

1. This information is provided in Geoffrey West, *H. G. Wells: A Sketch for a Portrait* (London, 1930), pp. 287-296. A more detailed examination of the problem is found in the article of Bernard Bergonzi, "The Publication of *The Time Machine,* 1894-1895," *Review of English Studies* XI, 41 (February 1960): 42-51.

2. West, p. 102. Elizabeth Healey, a friend of Wells's at the Normal School of Science, remained his correspondent for nearly fifty years.

3. *Review of Reviews* XI (1895): 263. Stead, third editor of the sensationalist and widely-read *Pall Mall Gazette,* was one of the most important literary sponsors of his time.

4. The phrase for Wells's theory, maintained during his later years, that the intellectuals and scientists of the world should assume a benevolent dictatorship in order to introduce some measure of sanity into the counsels of international politics.

5. *All Aboard for Ararat* (London, 1940), p. 54.

6. Bernard Bergonzi, *The Early H. G. Wells* (Manchester, 1961), p. 61.

7. Paul Valéry, "Literature and Our Destiny," in *Remarks on the Modern World* (Paris, 1962), p. 252.

8. Bergonzi, pp. 48-49.

9. Kingsley Amis, *New Maps of Hell* (London, 1961), p. 33.

10. *The Fate of Man* (New York, 1939), p. 67.

Alex Eisenstein (essay date 1972)

SOURCE: Eisenstein, Alex. "Very Early Wells: Origins of Some Major Physical Motifs in *The Time Machine* and *The War of the Worlds.*" *Extrapolation* 13 (1972): 119-26.

[*In the following essay, Eisenstein traces Wells's formulation of the Morlocks and their underground environs in* The Time Machine *to his childhood home, Atlas House.*]

In *The Early H. G. Wells,*[1] Bernard Bergonzi treats the dualistic future world of *The Time Machine* mainly as an expression of the traditional mythic schism between Paradise and Perdition. To support his interpretation, he cites the contrasting imagery associated with the two distinct human habitats—and species—delineated in the story: descriptions of the upper realm and its people are predominately sunny and idyllic; those of the lower, somber and infernal.

Yet, beyond the demonic role he thus ascribes to the Morlocks, Professor Bergonzi further claims that these creatures "represent an exaggerated fear of the nineteenth century proletariat."[2] Of course, in terms of the tale's quasi-Darwinian rationale, they are literally the biological and social descendants of the working class, but Mr. Bergonzi attributes to them a much closer identity with the toiling masses: "Since the Morlocks on one level stand for the late nineteenth century proletariat, the Traveller's attitude towards them symbolizes a contemporary bourgeois fear of the working class, and it is not fanciful to impute something of this attitude to Wells himself. From his school days in Bromley he had disliked and feared the working class in a way wholly appropriate to the son of a small tradesman—as various Marxist critics have not been slow to remark."[3] A brief quotation from the last third of the narrative, establishing the protagonist's overwhelming desire (by then) to slaughter all Morlocks, immediately precedes the above discussion in its original context. With such a preface, Mr. Bergonzi's commentary strongly implies that a real-life corollary of this homicidal urge became a deepseated affliction of the Wellsian psyche.

This malign conjecture further suggests that the Morlocks must ultimately derive from that hypothetical antipathy for Victorian Labor. However, despite the ready assertion of "various Marxist critics," the formulation of these bestial hominids and their plutonian abode stems from other and more primary childhood referents.

First among the latter is Atlas House, the birthplace of Wells and home of his infancy and early childhood. Its particular situation and character reflect, to a large degree, the peculiar dichotomy of the world of A.D. 802,701. His father's crockery shop opened onto High Street, and directly behind the shop lay the small parlor of the Wells home. From this parlor, "a murderously narrow staircase with a twist in it led downstairs to a completely subterranean kitchen, lit by a window which derived its light from a grating on the street level, and a bricked scullery, which, since the house was poised on a bank, opened into the yard at the ground level below."[4] These lines from Wells's autobiography firmly establish his own feeling about the cellar rooms; although the lowest floor allowed direct access to level ground and open air, he thought of these rooms as "*completely subterranean.*" (The dim illumination from the grate doubtless served as a constant reminder of this subsurface condition.)

A fanciful extension of the underground status to the backyard should have been fairly automatic for any normally imaginative pre-school youngster, and especially for one who played there so long and so often that he "learnt its every detail."[5] Several of these physical details enhanced the subterranean aura. Beginning at the rear wall of the house, a brickwork pavement spread across half the yard,[6] thus linking it, by similarity of texture, to the indoor domain of the scullery. Large "erections in the neighbors' yards on either side" and "a boundary wall"[7] at the far end hemmed in the backyard, isolating it from the outer world—and, perhaps, vaulting upward like the steep sides of a pit. One adjunct of the yard actually simulated some gloomy catacomb: "Between the scullery and the neighbour's wall was a narrow passage covered over,"[8] where his father stored many piles of red earthenware for the shop. The cellar and the yard, in many of their dominant features, recall

the industrial character of the Morlock caverns. Together, they functioned as the apparent site of all the necessary work accomplished in the limited universe accessible to Wells as a toddler—the place where everything was produced, cleaned, or otherwise prepared for use above or below. All the fixtures on that level bespoke some form of utilitarian labor: "In the scullery was a small fireplace, a copper boiler for washing, a provision cupboard, a bread pan, a beer cask, a pump delivering water from a well into a stone sink, and space for coal . . . beneath the wooden stairs."[9] In the yard stood "a brick erection, the 'closet,' an earth jakes over a cesspool, . . . and above this closet was a rainwater tank. Behind it was the brick dustbin . . ."[10] and from the house, "an open cement gutter brought the waste waters of the sink to a soak away"[11] in the center of the half-paved yard. (Note the prevalence of metal, stone, and stone-like materials, and the numerous vessels for storage or processing, along with mechanisms and conduits for the conveyance of working fluids and the disposal of wastes.)

Even the plots adjacent to the yard can be identified with basic functions performed by the Morlocks in their underworld, or with the underworld itself. "On one hand was the yard of Mr. Munday, the haberdasher, . . . who had put up a greenhouse and cultivated mushrooms . . . ; and on the other, Mr. Cooper, the tailor, had built out a workroom in which two or three tailors sat and sewed."[12] On one hand, the "greenhouse" nurtured plants that commonly grow in dark, dank caverns; on the other, one of the notable vestigial "duties" remaining to the Morlocks lay in their capacity as clothiers for the Eloi.

But most important, the major occupation of the subsurface dwellers also loomed in the background of Atlas House. Beyond the boundary wall at the end of the yard spread "the much larger yard and sheds of Mr. Covell the butcher, in which pigs, sheep and horned cattle were harboured violently, and protested plaintively through the night before they were slaughtered."[13] This presence surely made an indelible impression on Wells, for it crops up again as the metaphoric essence of a subsequent major work, *The Island of Dr. Moreau.*

The concept of a hidden lower world exercised an even greater fascination for Wells, one that continued throughout his life. *First Men in the Moon,* though possibly somewhat derivative of Kepler's *Somnium,* clearly contains another surface elysium shielding a vast industrial substratum. The idea emerges, for perhaps its last public appearance, in a metaphor from the *Autobiography* that summarizes his early psychosexuality: "So at the age of seven . . . , I had already between me and my bleak protestant God, a wide wide world of snowy mountains, Arctic regions, tropical forests, prairies and deserts and high seas, . . . about which I was prepared to talk freely, and cool and strange below it all a cavernous world of nameless goddess mistresses of which I never breathed a word to any human being."[14]

A unique bibliographic discovery made by Wells in his early life probably accentuated his receptivity to the concept of a hidden world below; it also lends some credibility to the notion that the infernal aspects of the Morlock habitat indicate the real creative roots of this environmental motif. (Bergonzi does not make this claim outright, but he might easily believe as much, if one may judge from his emphasis of these aspects.) In the words of Wells:

> There was a picture in an old illustrated book of devotions, Sturm's *Reflections,* obliterated with stamp paper, and so provoking investigation. What had mother been hiding from me? By holding up the page to the light I discovered the censored illustration represented hell-fire; devil, pitchfork and damned, all complete and drawn with great gusto. But she had anticipated the general trend of Protestant theology at the present time and hidden hell away.[15]

Hell, of course, embodies the idea of an underworld without recourse to stamp-covered illustrations; nevertheless, the obscured drawing in Sturm was a physical metaphor of all such underworlds, and young Wells may have perceived it as such, if only unconsciously. Yet, among Wells's earliest experiences, all reading and even religious training must rank second to his awareness of Atlas House, for it preceded them all.

The quasi-subterranean kitchen of his birthplace pervaded his psyche to such a degree that he recreated it, under fictional circumstances fraught with gross improbability, in one of the most perilous scenes in *The War of the Worlds.* In the second chapter of Book Two, "The Earth Under the Martians," the narrator is trapped in an abandoned house that barely escapes total destruction when a Martian cylinder lands nearby:

> The fifth cylinder must have fallen right into the midst of the house we had first visited. The building had vanished, completely smashed, pulverised, and dispersed by the blow. . . . The earth all round it had splashed under that tremendous impact . . . and lay in heaped piles that hid the masses of the adjacent houses. . . . Our house had collapsed backward; the front portion, even on the ground floor, had been destroyed completely; by a chance the kitchen and scullery had escaped, and stood buried now under soil and ruins, closed in by tons of earth on every side save towards the cylinder. Over that aspect we hung now on the very edge of the great circular pit . . .[16]

The house is largely decimated, while the *kitchen and scullery* survive, though engulfed by earth on *three sides.* This result occurs despite the fact that the house collapses *backward.* Presumably, the kitchen is to the rear; how does the rear survive when the front is utterly demolished? It does so, of course, because the author contrived it so, by *fiat.* The event is not impossible, perhaps, but to me it seems most unlikely—compounding the coincidence of the landing itself. The *precise* physical situation must have held a fair amount of intrinsic significance for Wells; surely he could have trapped the narrator beside the impact crater in a manner less idiosyncratic or incredible?

If anyone might doubt that an edifice like Atlas House could adequately serve as model for an extensive subterranean world, he should consider the psychological effect of entering such a building on the first floor and then discovering *another* ground level below. Even from an adult observer, the first encounter with this situation may elicit a sense of suddenly penetrating a dimension of existence normally veiled beneath the mundane, surface world.

From infancy, of course, Wells became increasingly familiar with this bi-level arrangement; it could hardly have seemed very strange to him for all his youth, much less the rest of his life. Nevertheless, this condition does not preclude the possibility that the structure of Atlas House retained a powerful grip on his imagination; it merely indicates that such an influence probably developed in a fairly gradual manner. Still, at some early point in his life, there had to be a *first time* for Wells to experience and perceive the "odd" nature of Atlas House. Whether the metaphoric significance occurred to him immediately, or rather seeped slowly into his mental storehouse without conscious realization, cannot be determined by the literary tools and data currently available; indeed, that question may remain forever moot. Even so, the circumstantial evidence for a connection between early environs and fictional setting cannot be summarily dismissed—especially in view of the complementary origin of the Morlock race.

What of these Morlocks, then? What are their prototypes, if not—at least, not entirely—the imps of Satan that once infested Anglican dogma? What is the principal inspiration for this savage race, if not a similarly savage revulsion for the brutish workers of the world? The actual source again involves childhood fantasizing about Atlas House, this time spurred by a natural-science book Wells read at age seven: "There was Wood's *Natural History,* also copiously illustrated and full of exciting and terrifying facts. I conceived a profound fear of the gorilla, of which there was a fearsome picture, which came out of the book at times after dark [the gorilla, of course; not the picture] and followed me noiselessly about the house. The half landing was a favourite lurking place for this terror. I passed it whistling, but wary and then ran for my life up the next flight."[17] The Morlocks share all the insidious, nocturnal habits of the imaginary ape: like him, they emerge at night to ambush the dawdler from shadowed hideaways;

they clamber up from lower levels to chase and terrorize small and youthful innocents.

That the Morlock race is a literary amalgam of apes and several other creatures has never been a great secret; the story itself indicates as much, and Bergonzi duly notes this. Nevertheless, his own investigation of the early H. G. Wells never leads him to suspect (or betray that he does) the true bedrock origins of Wells's creations. The *real* psychological significance of the Morlocks lies not in any apprehensive loathing for the proletariat, but rather in a profound early fear of wild animals in general and specifically of the gorilla, conceived as a personal household nemesis. In conjunction with the metaphoric aura of the house, this fear-fantasy provided the essential basis for the vision of the future contained in *The Time Machine*. All else, even the ostensible, socio-scientific explanation in the story, are mere after-the-fact rationales overlaid on the germinal idea.

As mentioned above, Wells's first knowledge of wild animals soon crystallized into a fear of monumental proportions: ". . . I was glad to think that between the continental land masses of the world, which would have afforded an unbroken land passage for wolves from Russia and tigers from India, and this safe island . . . stretched the impassable moat of the English Channel."[18] Even much later, at age thirteen, he was still prone to bestial nemeses of the night, as in the following description of the terrors attending the weekend journey to his Uncle Tom's riverside inn, Surly Hall: "My imagination peopled the dark fields on either hand with crouching and pursuing foes. Chunks of badly trimmed hedge took on formidable shapes. Sometimes I took to my heels and ran. For a week or so that road was haunted by a rumour of an escaped panther . . . That phantom panther waited for me patiently; it followed me like a noiseless dog, biding its time. And one night on the other side of the hedge a sleeping horse sighed deeply, a gigantic sigh, and almost frightened me out of my wits."[19] The hobgoblin activities recorded here bear an acute resemblance to those executed by the malevolent ape of Atlas House; Wells evidently retained the primary image long after its inception.

A relevant sidelight on Morlock origins—the Wood volume also triggered in Wells inklings of the rigorous Darwinian principles he later acquired in formal sessions with T. H. Huxley: "Turning over the pages of the *Natural History,* I perceived a curious relationship between cats and tigers and lions and so forth, and to a lesser degree between them and hyenas and dogs and bears, and between them again and other quadrupeds, and curious premonitions of evolution crept into my thoughts."[20] This revelation reinforces the impression that this book was an important wellspring for the speculative constructs employed in *The Time Machine*.

In like manner the dominant apparition of *The War of the Worlds* can be traced to Wells's first direct encounter with the wider Universe. In his fourteenth year, while delving into an attic storeroom in Up Park (his second home), he uncovered the following treasure:

> . . . There was a box, at first quite mysterious, full of brass objects that clearly might be screwed together. I screwed them together, by the method of trial and error, and presently found a Gregorian telescope on a trip in my hands. I carried off the wonder to my bedroom. . . . I was discovered by my mother in the small hours, my bedroom window wide open, inspecting the craters of the moon. She had heard me open the window. She said I should catch my death of cold. But at the time that seemed a minor consideration.[21]

Here is the inanimate progenitor of the Martian war machine—both are tripodal devices assembled from cylinders. The parts of the telescope screw together, whereas the cylinders from Mars *un*screw to open. Both the telescope and the war machine involve optical systems—the first for concentrating distant radiation, the other for projecting concentrated radiation over considerable distance (the narrator repeatedly calls the heat-ray mechanism a "camera" or "projector").

The war machines are variously described, but most often as metallic and "glittering."[22] Nothing glitters like gold, of course—except, perhaps, the highly polished tube of a brass telescope; the cowled head of one of these monster machines is termed a "brazen hood"[23] soon after their initial appearance in the story.

The notion of three-legged fighting machines could have sprung from contemplation of any tripod-mounted apparatus—for instance a portrait camera, which possesses the same general attributes that qualify the telescope as a prototype. Even a ringstand or a milking stool could be prime suspects; one of the marching engines of holocaust is actually likened to a milking stool, in a passage describing its exotic mode of locomotion.[24] A telescope, of course, figures prominently in the first chapter; yet, somewhat later, British defenders introduce a much more suggestive instrument—the heliograph. But Wells never *built* a heliograph, nor did he handle a camera in his early years; tripod ringstands remained outside his direct experience until he entered the Normal School of Science in 1884, and his childhood acquaintance with milking stools was surely no better than second hand. Furthermore, the telescope—and only the telescope—engaged his mind and spirit with the remarkable vistas and wonders of Space. No other similar artifact affected his outlook to the extent, and in the direction, that this one did. Such examples as these illustrate how Wells's imagination transformed the objects of commonplace experience into the fundamental imagery of his fictions.

Notes

1. Bernard Bergonzi, *The Early H. G. Wells* (Manchester: Manchester University Press, 1961).

2. Bergonzi, p. 53.

3. Bergonzi, p. 56.

4. H. G. Wells, *Experiment in Autobiography* (New York: Macmillan, 1934), p. 22.

5. *Ibid.*, p. 23.

6. *Ibid.*, p. 23.

7. *Ibid.*, pp. 23 and 22, respectively.

8. *Ibid.*, p. 23.

9. *Ibid.*, p. 22. Elsewhere in the *Autobiography* (p. 48), Wells recaptures a vivid impression of the working ambience of "washing day, when the copper in the scullery was lit and all the nether regions were filled with white steam and the smell of soapsuds."

10. Wells, p. 22.

11. *Ibid.*, p. 23.

12. *Ibid.*, p. 23.

13. *Ibid.*, p. 22.

14. *Ibid.*, p. 58.

15. *Ibid.*, p. 29.

16. *Seven Science Fiction Novels of H. G. Wells* (New York: Dover), p. 406; *Seven Famous Novels by H. G. Wells* (Garden City: Garden City Publishing Co., 1934), p. 347; *TWOTW* (New York: Popular Library, 1962), p. 128.

17. Wells, *Autobiography,* p. 54. From the context, the half-landing in question is not clear (there were several, as the house possessed three stories above ground); however, inasmuch as meals were always eaten in the cellar kitchen, this anecdote probably refers to the landing between cellar and parlor, which would be passed on the way to bed after evening meal.

18. *Ibid.*, p. 95.

19. *Ibid.*, pp. 54-55.

20. *Ibid.*, p. 106.

21. Wells, *The War of the Worlds,* Ch. 10.

22. *Ibid.*, Ch. 10.

23. *Ibid.*, Ch. 10, para. 12.

24. *Ibid.*, Ch. 12, para. 8; Ch. 13, para. 2; Ch. 13, para. 44; *passim.*

William G. Niederland (essay date spring-summer 1976)

SOURCE: Niederland, William G. "The Birth of H. G. Wells's *Time Machine." American Imago* 35, nos. 1-2 (spring-summer 1978): 106-12.

[*In the following essay, originally delivered as a speech in 1976, Niederland considers the influence of Wells's childhood and personal experiences on* The Time Machine.]

One of the most influential writers in English of the early twentieth century, H. G. Wells's prodigious output—more than 150 books, as well as countless articles, reviews, and short stories—has remained psychologically unexplored. Many of Wells's works repeat certain themes of his own life and development and often project his personal experiences and tribulations onto mankind and its prognosticated future. The study of these themes in one of his most famous novels has led me to certain inferential conclusions.

Born in 1866, the year following the end of the American Civil War, he grew up at the height of the Victorian era, and lived through two world wars and the beginning of the atomic age. He died in 1946, one year after the bombing of Hiroshima.

His artistic career, which started in late adolescence, began with the writing of **The Time Machine,** a literary masterpiece that propelled him—a one-time apprentice in a cramped drapery store, and the son of poor parents, members of the British servant class—to world fame. **The Time Machine** was a most unusual tale, a pioneering venture into the realm of what is now termed science fiction.

In this brief communication, I shall attempt to present an outline of the main themes, influences, and fantasies which went into the creation of **The Time Machine.**

The machine is an ingenious device which enables its inventor, "the Time Traveler," to leave the present and travel in a few moments into the future. During the course of the trip, he witnesses the rise and fall of civilizations through various ages of human development. The Time Traveler and his machine finally come to rest in the year 802,701 A.D., when he encounters the humans of that period and finds them divided into two groups, the "Elois" and the "Morlocks."

Before going into this neatly split stage of humanity in the year 802,701, I wish to acquaint you with the Time Traveler's discussion, prior to his departure, with a number of invited guests, among them a medical man and a psychologist. This discussion forms the introduction to the story: "Clearly," the Time Traveler explains, "*any real body* must have extension in four directions; it must have length, breadth, thickness, and *duration*. But through *a natural infirmity of the flesh* . . . we are inclined to overlook this. . . . There are really four dimensions, three which we call planes of space, and *the fourth, time*" (italics added). Shortly thereafter, the Time Traveler takes off on his journey into the future.

A closer look at Wells's physical and mental condition at the time he began work on *The Time Machine* is required in order to understand his emphasis on "body" and "infirmity of the flesh," and the dimension of time. The first draft of *The Time Machine* goes back to 1886-87. Then titled **"The Chronic Argonauts,"** it gives the Time Traveler's name as "Nebo-gipfel," i. e., the man on the top of Mount Nebo. After numerous revisions prior to its publication in 1895, the final version omits the name and the Time Traveler becomes nameless. Yet his original, first-draft name is not without significance. Mount Nebo is part of the mountain range overlooking the land of Moab, northeast of the Dead Sea. It was from this summit that Moses, unable to enter the Promised Land, was allowed to see it before his death. The pertinent text in the Bible, a book which Wells's mother, a strictly religious and puritanical woman, was fond of quoting regularly, reads in part: "And Moses went up to Mount Nebo . . . and the Lord showed him all the land . . . there, in the land of Moab, Moses, the servant of the Lord, died . . .", in full view of the Promised Land.

The Bible was the most important treasure in the early Wells's household. In 1939, Wells wrote a personal letter of congratulation to Freud on the appearance of *Moses and Monotheism,* which he described as "so fascinating that I did not get to bed until one" in the morning. In his note to Freud, he added pertinent comments on Moses which reveal his thorough knowledge of the biblical text (Jones, *Life of Freud,* Vol. III).

A few months before he began work on *The Time Machine,* Wells fell ill with pulmonary tuberculosis—frequently a fatal disease in those days—from which he suffered for approximately ten years. In his autobiography (1934), he writes about the early stages of the illness, during which he composed (or should I say, invented?) the essential parts of *The Time Machine*:

> Apart from general fear of disease, disappointment and frustration which weighed *so heavily upon my imagination* during my consumptive phase, there were unpleasant minor fears and anxieties which I still recall acutely. Every time I coughed and particularly if I had a bout of coughing, there was the dread of tasting the peculiar tang of blood. And I remember as though it happened only last night, *the little tickle and trickle of blood in the lungs that precede a real hemorrhage.* Don't cough too soon? Don't cough too much? There was always the question how big the flow was to be, how long would it go on, and *what was to be the end of it this time* . . . dreading even to breathe. . . .
>
> (Italics added)

I leave open the question whether a patient suffering from tuberculosis can actually perceive the "tickle and trickle of blood" in a pulmonary cavity, as Wells records. Perhaps we have here the familiar oversensitivity to internal stimuli which Greenacre (1957)[1] mentions as an important component of a creative individual's heightened perceptivity.

Wells's medical history preceding the outbreak of tuberculosis includes a ruptured kidney, likewise accompanied by massive hemorrhage, and a fractured leg at age seven, i. e., bodily injuries which had immobilized him for varying periods of time. Throughout childhood, puberty, and postpuberty, he had suffered from serious undernourishment, frequent periods of starvation, and lack of maternal care. He remained an underfed, undersized, sickly looking individual until his thirties, later becoming a somewhat plump, short man of "commonplace appearance." He was a "replacement child," to use Pollock's apt wording. Two years before his birth, a sister, Fanny, had died of acute appendicitis. This sister had been mother's favorite, "a very bright, precocious, and fragile little girl . . . that had delighted mother's heart," according to Wells's description.

After the death of her only daughter Fanny, the mother had been in a state of serious depression not alleviated by the birth of H. G., the youngest, now, of three brothers. She remained pious, somber, and depressed throughout the rest of her life. Hence, apparently, the inadequate mothering that Wells experienced as a child (his early years were almost completely solitary [Dickson, 1969][2]); and this may have led to his later difficulties with women (broken marriages, unsatisfactory sexual experiences, etc.).

As for leg fracture at age seven, he consciously, if somewhat facetiously, later attributed his literary career to "two broken legs" which, in his words, altered the course of his life: the first, his own, introduced him to the delights of reading and studying, and the second, his father's, who became permanently lame after a leg fracture, when H. G. was eleven, caused the bankruptcy of the unsuccessful paternal crockery business. The father's partial crippling and debasement, his role as a mutilated (castrated) father figure, can be followed through many pages of Wells's autobiography and other works, including the final paragraph of *The Time Machine,* where the medical man is declared dead, the psychologist is paralyzed, and the remaining *dramatis personae,* originally present in the Time Traveler's home, "have as completely dropped out of existence as if they, too, had travelled off. . . ."

To return to the Time Traveler's experiences during his journey into the future, he encounters a strange type of mankind: the Elois and the Morlocks. The former are gentle, infantile, indescribably happy yet frail people who know nothing about art, literature, or work; they are four feet high, graceful and apparently sexless, that is, infants who live a playful existence during the day, though preyed upon by the beastly Morlocks as soon as daylight vanishes. The latter emerge from subterranean wells at night, chase after the sleeping Elois, and feed on them. The world is peopled by cannibalistic devourers, the Morlocks, and those who are devoured, the Elois. In other words, the Time Traveler finds in the year 802,701 A.D. a world of pregenital regression to oral and oral-sadistic levels. Apart from fossils of bygone civilizations, nothing else exists. "In thousands of generations," Wells writes, man has undergone a process of "human decay" and has regressed to "the childish simplicity of the little people" who are "mere fatted cattle" for cannibalistic, inhuman brutes.

There is a touching interlude in the story when the Time Traveler rescues a helpless young Eloi woman from drowning, and the rescued girl, Weena, clings to him in gratitude, as if she wished to offer herself to him in womanly love and affection. But this also ends soon, when they are surrounded by murderous Morlocks in a dark forest. She succumbs helplessly to the onslaught of the brutal creatures during a night filled with tenderness on the one hand, and relentless attack by the voracious Morlocks on the other. It is a nocturnal scene of utter distress, desolation, and fear. The girl Weena and the Elois in general appear to be modeled on the description of Wells's mother forever lamenting the loss of his fragile little sister Fanny.

As I have shown in previous papers concerning the effect of physical conditions (and their mental representations) on the creative process (1965, 1967, 1973)[3], the regression in the service of the ego (Kris, 1952)[4] should be extended—in my opinion—to the problem of *ego survival*. Under the spur of dreaded dissolution, the ego's ability to achieve what had previously been impossible appears to acquire a creative momentum of great intensity in gifted individuals. After a massive pulmonary hemorrhage, Wells wrote: "I must say this for chest diseases . . . they clear the mind like strong tea"; and again: "I have been dying for nearly two-thirds of a year . . . and I have died enough. *I stopped dying then and there . . . my real writing began*" (italics mine). In a letter of a much later date, Wells spoke of his creativeness as "a race against death," alluding to the antinomy between creativity and death, viewing the former as an effort to "stave off" the latter.

More specifically, for Wells, tuberculosis—a matter of life and death in his day—involved the issue of *time,* as the Time Traveler so clearly expounded at the beginning of the tale. What had seemed an imminent threat of death became for Wells the start of a new life

(rebirth). Thus, with respect to the creation of *The Time Machine,* the following restitutional steps can be discerned:

1. A forward leap in time, which denies the present and carries the author into a fantasied futuristic world, away from illness and the threat of death.

2. What purports to be a flight into future is, in reality, an unconscious regression to the *fantasied perfect state prior to* the multiple disabilities of the past and present (tuberculosis, ruptured kidney, early leg fracture, etc.).

3. The regression leads to narcissistic and oral levels as personified on the one hand by the narcissistically tinged lives of the Elois and the oral-sadistic, overtly cannibalistic Morlocks; it is they who raise the Elois like sheep, feed them, clothe them, and each night take some away and devour them. The dangers of the *night* had for the tubercular Wells a special meaning, as can be found in other writings by him, for instance: "Night, the mother of fear and mystery, was coming upon me . . . suddenly the night became terrible. I found myself sitting up in bed, staring at the dark. . . ."

4. As a consequence, the defensive-regressive mechanisms—once set in motion by the time voyager—take their full course to reach the protective and life-giving, i. e., birth-giving, mother. Fusing and identifying with her, the author is himself able to give birth to a new creation. At the same time the infantile omnipotence, best illustrated by the Time Traveler's capacity to travel forward and backward as and when he wishes, is regained in full in an attempt to master the misery and dread of the present through the control of time and duration.

An analytic inquiry into the symbolic meaning of the Time Traveler's landing time supports the foregoing interpretations. The then desperately ill Wells chose as his landing time the year:

802701 A.D.

Thus he expanded the time and created a feeling of infinite time in the following way—unconsciously, I tentatively suggest:

> The first part of the year chosen by the author symbolizes the feeding mother *in actu,* as it were: the double 0 in the number 8, the central 0 and the 2—all breasts, i. e., mother; and the second part of the figure is likewise characterized, in addition to the phallic numbers 7 and 1 (father), by the maternal 0 in the center. In a letter written much later to a woman then very close to him, Rebecca West, Wells said that much of his life and work was "*a race against death,*" a statement which in my opinion confirms the foregoing points. But the Time Traveler, in his ingenious vehicle (mother), had all the time in the world, of course, like an infant at mother's breast—in timeless fusion with the early mother.

Thus, Wells wove the story of his disease and early struggle with death into the haunting chapters of the

H. G. Wells

novel which, incidentally, contains several direct references to tuberculosis and illness. The first parts of the book were composed by him at the onset, the later parts and revisions at the end of his disease. Thus the birth of H. G. Wells's first—and, many believe, his most enduring—masterpiece, *The Time Machine.*

Notes

1. Greenacre, P. (1957): The Childhood of the Artist. *Psa. Study of the Child,* XII, 9-36.

2. Dickson, L. (1969): *H. G. Wells—His Turbulent Life and Times.* New York, Atheneum, 1969.

3. Niederland, W. G. (1965): Narcissistic Ego Impairment in Patients with Early Physical Malformations. *Psa. Study of the Child,* XX, 518-533.

   ———. (1967): Clinical Aspects of Creativity. *American Imago,* XXIV, 6-34.

   ———. (1973): Psychoanalytic Concepts of Creativity and Aging. *J. Geriatric Psychiatry,* VI, 160-168.

4. Kris, E. (1952): *Psychoanalytic Explorations in Art.* New York, Internat. Univ. Press, 1952.

Alex Eisenstein (essay date July 1976)

SOURCE: Eisenstein, Alex. "*The Time Machine* and the End of Man." *Science Fiction Studies* 3, no. 2 (July 1976): 161-65.

[*In the following essay, Eisenstein investigates the cycle of evolution as illustrated in* The Time Machine.]

As many critics have observed, H. G. Wells was preoccupied very early with speculations on evolution, in particular the evolution of Man and the prospects of intelligent life, whatever its origins. *The Time Machine* (1895), *The War of the Worlds* (1898), and *The First Men in the Moon* (1901) are the best known examples of his interest in such matters, but certain of his shorter works also reflect this concern. Frequently, Wells would recapitulate and refine his major ideas, mining old essays for new story material or refashioning the elements of one tale in the context of another; various scholars have explored the interpenetration of these works in some detail.

In **"The Man of the Year Million"** (essay, 1893)[1] and *The War of the Worlds,* Wells outlined one model for the ultimate evolution of humankind. In both works, the culmination of higher intelligence is a globular entity, brought about by the influence of steadily advancing technology. In each case, it mainly consists of a great, bald head, supported on large hands or equivalent appendages, with thorax vestigial or entirely absent. The Martian is a direct analogue of the Man of the Year Million, as Wells himself indicated by citing his own essay in the body of the novel (§2:2).[2] The Selenite master-race of *First Men* is a kindred expression of this vision of enlarged intellect—especially the Grand Lunar, with its enormous cranium, diminutive face, and shriveled body. Of more special relevance to the Martians are the malignant cephalopods of **"The Sea Raiders"** (1896) and **"The Extinction of Man"** (essay, 1894), and as well the predatory specimen in **"The Flowering of the Strange Orchid"** (1894).

At least one scholar has referred to **"The Man of the Year Million"** as "another version" of *The Time Machine,* apparently because the domeheads take refuge underground from the increasing rigors of a cooling surface.[3] This connection is rather tenuous, at best; by such criteria, *First Men* also might be deemed a variant of *The Time Machine.* In fact, the Further Vision of the latter constitutes a curious inversion of the above essay, but scholars and critics have failed to perceive this relation. Their failure depends on a more primary error, which is this—the notion that Man is extinct at the climax of the novel.

That the progeny of Man is *not* absent from the final moments of the Further Vision should be evident from a passage that appeared (until recently) only in the serial version. This deleted episode is a philosophic bridge, a key to what happens at world's end. It introduces the successors of Eloi and Morlock: a hopping, kangaroo-like semblance of humanity and a monstrous, shambling centipede. According to Robert Philmus, "these two species must have descended in the course of time from the Eloi and the Morlocks; and again the 'grey animal, or grey man, whichever it was' is the victim of the carnivorous giant insects."[4]

Philmus accentuates the elements of degeneration and regression in Wells's Darwinian conjectures; thus he asserts that *The Time Machine* embodies a vision of the hominid line "irrevocably on the downward path of devolution."[5] The general validity of this viewpoint cannot be disputed; nevertheless, the extreme construction he places upon it leads him considerably astray. Though Wells used terms like "retrogression," "degradation," and "degeneration" in his essays, they were for him *relative* terms only. He would hardly have portrayed Man as reverting *literally* into so primitive a creature; such "devolution," I submit, is not in the Wellsian mode.

Philmus may have been encouraged in this faulty genealogy by the Traveller's observations of the Elysian world of the Eloi, which seems devoid of animal life, excepting a few sparrows and butterflies (§4b/288; §5a/292).[6] Of course, this stricture need not apply to the murky lower world, which could easily harbor all sorts of vermin. If butterflies prosper above, in a world of flowers, then centipedes should thrive below, in a realm of meaty table scraps and other waste. And at journey's end, "a thing like a huge white butterfly" makes a brief display, as a demonstration of what has survived the English sparrow (§11/328).

The Morlocks of Millennium #803, moreover, are not a race destined for perpetual dominance. This much is made clear by numerous facets of their existence—their lack of light, the disrepair of much of their machinery, their crude and inefficient method of harvesting Eloi. Although the Time Traveller refers to the Eloi as "cattle" and supposes that they may even be bred by the Morlocks (§7/311), the rest of the book does not show the latter practicing much in the way of husbandry. Indeed the absence of other land animals in the lush upper world may well be the result of earlier predations by the Morlocks. So the best assumption is that the relationship between the two races is unstable—that the Morlocks are depleting their latest dietary resource, which must eventually go the way of its predecessors.

The kangaroo-beast, therefore, can only be a tribe descended from the Morlocks, now scavenging the surface in the long twilight. The irony of the new situation is evident, and quite typical of the many ironic aspects of the novel: the hound is now the hare, the erstwhile predator has become the current prey.

The ancestry of this pathetic creature is confirmed by its morphology. Consider the appearance of the Morlock: "a queer little ape-like figure," "dull white," with "flaxen hair on its head and down its back" (§5b/299), and a "chinless" face, with "great, lidless, pinkish-grey eyes" (§6/306). Compare that with the Traveller's description of the later species: "It was . . . covered with a straight greyish hair that thickened about the head into a Skye terrier's mane. . . . It had, moreover, a rounded head, with a projecting forehead and forward-looking eyes, obscured by its lank hair" (325). The ape-like brow-ridge is a tell-tale vestige of the Morlocks, as well as the lank hair that now shields the creature's eyes. The shaggy visage identifies the kangaroo-man as a once-nocturnal animal only recently emerged from darkness. Another indicative trait is its rabbit-like feet, which are compatible with the "queer narrow footprints" of the Morlocks (§5a/292).

From a close inspection the Traveller surmises the nature of the beast: "A disagreeable apprehension flashed across my mind. . . . I knelt down and seized my capture, intending to examine its teeth and other anatomical points which might show human characteristics . . ." (326). He might also be looking for the signs of yesterday's carnivore.

This Morlock offspring is no longer extant in the climactic scene of the Further Vision, but it is not the Last Man observed by the Traveller. He arrives in the era of the giant land-crabs, then passes on to the time of the great eclipse, where nothing seems to stir—at first:

> I looked about me to see if any traces of animal life remained. . . . But I saw nothing moving, in earth or sky or sea. The green slime alone testified that life was not extinct. . . . I fancied I saw some black object flopping about . . . but it became motionless as I looked at it, and I judged that my eye had been deceived, and that the black object was merely a rock.

A neaby planet encroaches on the bloated sun; the eclipse progresses, becomes total, and then the shadow of heaven recedes:

> I shivered, and a deadly nausea seized me. . . . I felt giddy and incapable of facing the return journey. As I stood sick and confused I saw again the moving thing upon the shoal. . . . It was a round thing, the size of a football perhaps . . . and tentacles trailed down from it; it seemed black against the weltering blood-red water, and it was hopping fitfully about. Then I felt I was fainting. But a terrible dread of lying helpless in that remote and awful twilight sustained me while I clambered into the saddle.
>
> (§11/329-30)

The kangaroo-men hop about on elongated feet; the men of the year million hop about on great soft hands; the thing on the shoal hops about on a trailing mass of tentacles. This similarity in modes of locomotion is hardly a literary accident. In contrast, the Sea-Raiders never hop, but creep along at a steady pace when traversing solid ground.

In general form the Last Creature resembles a large cephalopod. Is it a primitive survivor from the ocean deeps, like *Haploteuthis* in **"The Sea-Raiders,"** or is it a being like the Martians, the hypertrophic end-product of intelligent life? Most of the evidence points to the latter—a highly specialized and atrophied edition of genus *Homo*. Note particularly the size of the creature; it is about "the size of a football"—which is to say, about the size of a human head.

The Time Traveller contracts a "terrible dread of lying helpless" in the dying world soon after he becomes fully aware of the thing on the shoal. There seems to be a special revulsion attached to this monster, even though it can hardly pose a real threat to the Traveller. Before it commands his attention, he feels "incapable of facing the return journey"; afterward, the "dread of lying helpless" in its presence impels him to turn back forthwith. Consciously, the Traveller does not perceive the human ancestry of this apocalyptic organism, but apparently the unconscious realization of its true nature makes him flee the final wasteland. Not the oppressive conditions, nor the extinction of Man, nor even the approaching oblivion triggers his retreat; rather, he recoils from the knowledge, however submerged, of what Man has become.

And what has Man become? Certainly not the inflated intellect of a Martian, nor that of a Sea-Raider, despite the somatic affinities. In one important respect, the Last Man differs greatly from these other fantastic creations: it is a being without a face. Even *Haploteuthis* has a definite, mock-human visage—"a grotesque suggestion of a face." To be sure, the super-minds in the Wellsian canon—the million-year domeheads, the Martians, the Grand Lunar—all suffer from facial attrition, yet certain features, especially the eyes, always remain. Not so with the fitful creature on the beach; the swollen surface of its body seems utterly blank, devoid of perceptual apparatus, and its aimless, reflexive actions indicate that it is virtually mindless. In the end, then, Man has become little more than a giant polyp.

All these transmuted beings emphasize two primary functions of life: ingestion and cerebration. The intelligent Sea-Raiders, for example, come to earth in seach of a better feed. Both the Martians and the domeheads have actually surrendered their alimentary canals to cortical advances, and the Martians, like the man-eating squids, also come to Earth for new sustenance. The mindless tropism of the Strange Orchid impels it to siphon off human blood, whereas the Martians strive for the same end with a ruthless deliberation.

The ultimate survivor of *The Time Machine* is not a great brain; as with a polyp, therefore, all that is left is a great ravening stomach. (For this, too, its size is appropriate.) Here, in counterpoint to the Martian terror, is the Wellsian image of ultimate horror.

And so we confront a symbolic paradox: the same emblem represents both the zenith and the nadir of mentality; the opposition of head and stomach, of mind and body, is fused in this one corporeal form. In Wells's iconography, it stands for the ultimate degeneration, whether of body or mind. He disapproved less, we may suppose, of the absolute intellect, reserving his greatest dread for the other, the mindless all-devouring. Yet there can be little doubt that, despite sardonic ambiguities, as in **"The Man of the Year Million"** and *The First Men in the Moon,* he truly preferred neither; his best wish was that Man should master himself without ever losing the essence of humanity. To this end Wells devoted most of his long and active life, even unto *Mind at the End of Its Tether* (1945), where a faint hope still lingers that some ultra-human entity will arise to survive the impending decline of *Homo sapiens*. This was Wells's last desperate hope, and a very feeble one it was; nevertheless, near the end of his life, amid sickness and depression, that glimmer remained. As the nameless narrator of *The Time Machine* insists, when faced with the inevitable disintegration of Man: "If that is so, it remains for us to live as though it were not so" (Epilogue/335).

Notes

1. First published in *The Pall Mall Gazette,* Nov 9, 1893, this essay, with title changed to "Of a Book Unwritten," appears in *Certain Personal Matters* (UK 1897), as does the other essay mentioned in this paragraph, "The Extinction of Man."

2. Another avatar appears in "The Plattner Story," against a setting remarkably suggestive of the Further Vision. Plattner, who is blown through a fourth *spatial* dimension, finds himself on a barren landscape of dark *red* shadows, backed by a *green* sky-glow. He watches the *rise* of a giant green sun, which reveals a deep cleft nearby. A multitude of bulbous creatures float upward, like so many bubbles, from this chasm. These are the "Watchers of the Living," literally the souls of the dead: "they were indeed limbless; and they had the appearance of human heads beneath which a tadpole-like body swung" (para. 26). Significantly, Wells had referred to his Men of the Year Million as "human tadpoles."

In many respects, this realm of the afterlife is a striking reversal of *The Time Machine*'s terminal wasteland, yet quite recognizably akin to it.

3. Gordon S. Haight, "H. G. Wells's 'The Man of the Year Million'," *Nineteenth-Century Fiction* 12 (1958): 323-26.

4. Robert M. Philmus, *Into the Unknown* (US 1970), pp 70-71.

5. *Ibid.,* p. 75.

6. §7/311 = Chapter 7 in the standard form of the text (i.e., as published in the Atlantic Edition, the *Complete Short Stories,* and almost all editions since 1924), or Page 311 of *Three Prophetic Novels of H. G. Wells* (Dover Publications, 1960). The chapterings of the standard and Dover forms (with "a" and "b" added for convenience) collate as follows: 1a = 1; 1b = 2; 2 = 3; 3 = 4; 4a = 5; 4b = 6; 5a = 7; 5b = 8; 6 = 9; 7 = 10; 8 = 11; 9 = 12; 10 = 13; 11 = 14; 12a = 15; 12b = 16; Epilogue = Epilogue. The deleted passage, pages 325-27 of the Dover text, would appear between the first and second paragraphs of Chapter 11 in the standard text.

Patrick Parrinder (essay date November 1976)

SOURCE: Parrinder, Patrick. "*News from Nowhere, The Time Machine* and the Break-Up of Classical Realism." *Science Fiction Studies* 3, no. 3 (November 1976): 265-74.

[*In the following essay, Parrinder views William Morris's* News from Nowhere *and Wells's* The Time Machine *as "symptoms of cultural upheaval," particularly the end of classical realism at the end of the nineteenth century.*]

Critics of SF are understandably concerned with the integrity of the genre they study. Yet it is a commonplace that major works are often the fruit of an interaction of literary genres, brought about by particular historical pressures. Novels such as *Don Quixote, Madame Bovary* and *Ulysses* may be read as symptoms of cultural upheaval, parodying and rejecting whole classes of earlier fiction. My purpose is to suggest how this principle might be applied in the field of utopia and SF. While Morris's *News from Nowhere* and Wells's *The Time Machine* have many generic antecedents, their historical specificity will be revealed as that of conflicting and yet related responses to the break-up of classical realism at the end of the nineteenth century.[1]

Patrick Brantlinger describes *News from Nowhere* in a recent essay[2] as "a conscious anti-novel, hostile to virtually every aspect of the great tradition of Victorian fiction." In a muted sense, such a comment might seem self-evident; Morris's book is an acknowledged master-piece of the "romance" genre which came to the fore as a conscious reaction against realistic fiction after about 1880. Yet *News from Nowhere* is radically unlike the work of Rider Haggard, R. L. Stevenson or their fellow-romancers in being a near-didactic expression of left-wing political beliefs. William Morris was a Communist, so that it is interesting to consider what might have been his reaction to Engels' letter to Margaret Harkness (1888), with its unfavorable contrast of the "point blank socialist novel" or "Tendenzroman" to the "realism" of Balzac:

> That Balzac thus was compelled to go against his own class sympathies and political prejudices, that he *saw* the necessity of the downfall of his favourite nobles, and described them as people deserving no better fate; and that he *saw* the real men of the future where, for the time being, they alone were to be found—that I consider one of the greatest triumphs of Realism, and one of the grandest features in old Balzac.[3]

It is not clear from the wording (the letter was written in English) whether Engels saw Balzac's far-sightedness as a logical or an accidental product of the Realist movement which in his day extended to Flaubert, Zola, Turgenev, Tolstoy and George Eliot. Engels' disparagement of Zola in this letter has led many Marxists to endorse Balzac's technical achievement as a realist at the expense of his successors. Yet the passage might also be read as a tribute to Balzac's social understanding and political integrity, without reference to any of the formal doctrines of realism. What is certain is that the "triumph" Balzac secured for the Realist school was in part a personal, moral triumph, based on his ability to discard his prejudices and see the true facts. Engels's statement seems to draw on two senses of the term "realism," both of which originated in the nineteenth century. Nor, I think, is this coincidence of literary and political valuations accidental. The fiction of Stendhal, Balzac and Flaubert in particular is characterized by the systematic unmasking of bourgeois and romantic attitudes. In their political dimension, these novelists inherit a tradition of analysis going back to Machiavelli, and which is most evident in Stendhal, who was not a professional writer but an ex-administrator and diplomat. Harry Levin defines the realism of these novelists as a critical, negational mode in which "the truth is approximated by means of a satirical technique, by unmasking cant or debunking certain misconceptions."[4] There are two processes suggested here: the writer's own rejection of cant and ideology, and his "satirical technique." Both are common to many SF novels, including *The Time Machine,* although in terms of representational idiom these are the opposite of "realistic" works. *News from Nowhere,* on the other hand, is the utopian masterpiece of a writer who in his life went against his class sympathies and joined the "real men of the future," as Balzac did by implication in his books. Morris has this in common with Engels (who distrusted him personally). Hostile critics have seen his socialist works as merely a transposition of the longings for beauty, chivalry and vanquished greatness which inform his early poetry. As literary criticism this seems to me shallow. Nor do Morris's political activities provide evidence of poetic escapism or refusal to face the facts. It was not by courtesy that he was eventually mourned as one of the stalwarts of the socialist movement.[5]

On the surface, *News from Nowhere* (1890) was a response to a utopia by a fellow-socialist—Edward Bellamy's *Looking Backward,* published two years earlier. Morris reviewed it in *The Commonweal,* the weekly paper of the Socialist League, on 22 June 1889. He was appalled by the servility of Bellamy's vision of the corporate state, and felt that the book was politically dangerous. He also noticed the subjectivity of the utopian form, its element of self-revelation. Whatever Bellamy's intentions, his book was the expression of a typically Philistine, middle-class outlook. *News from Nowhere* was intended to provide a dynamic alternative to Bellamy's model of socialist aspiration; a dream or vision which was ideologically superior as well as creative, organic and emotionally fulfilling where Bellamy's was industrialized, mechanistic and stereotyped. Morris was strikingly successful in these aims. The conviction and resonance of his "utopian romance" speak, however, of deeper causes than the stimulus provided by Bellamy.

News from Nowhere is constructed around two basic images or *topoi*: the miraculous translation of the narrator into a better future (contrasted with the long historical struggle to build that future, as described in the chapter "How the Change Came"), and the journey up the Thames, which becomes a richly nostalgic passage towards an uncomplicated happiness—a happiness which proves to be a mirage, and which author and reader can only aspire to in the measure in which they take up the burden of the present. Only the first of these *topoi* is paralleled in Bellamy. The second points in a quite different direction. *News from Nowhere* is a dream taking place within a frame of mundane political life—the meeting at which "there were six persons present, and consequently six sections of the party were represented, four of which had strong but divergent Anarchist opinions" (§1). The dream is only potentially a symbol of reality, since there is no pseudo-scientific "necessity" that things will evolve in this way. The frame occasions a gentle didacticism (in dreams begin responsibilities), but also a degree of self-consciousness about the narrative art. "Guest," the narrator, is both a third person ("our friend") and Morris himself; the change from third- to first-person narration is made at the end of the opening chapter. Morris's subtitle, furthermore, refers to the story as a "Utopian Romance." Many objections which have been made to the book reflect the reader's discomfiture when asked to seriously imagine a world in which enjoyment and leisure are not

paid for in the coin of other people's oppression and suffering. It could be argued that Morris should not have attempted it—any more than Milton in *Paradise Lost* should have attempted the task of justifying the ways of God to men. Morris, however, held a view of the relation of art to politics which emphatically endorsed the project of imagining Nowhere.

One of his guises is that of a self-proclaimed escapist: "Dreamer of dreams, born out of my due time, / Why should I strive to set the crooked straight?" *News from Nowhere* stands apart from these lines from *The Earthly Paradise* (1868-70), as well as from the majority of Morris's prose romances. Together with *A Dream of John Ball* (1888) it was addressed to a socialist audience and serialized in *The Commonweal. News from Nowhere* retains some of the coloration of *John Ball*'s medieval setting, but, for a Victorian, radical medievalism could serve as an "estranging," subversive technique. Two of the major diagnoses of industrial civilization, Carlyle's *Past and Present* and Ruskin's essay "The Nature of Gothic," bear witness to the power of such medievalist imagination. Morris's own influential lectures on art derive from "The Nature of Gothic," and are strenuous attempts to "set the crooked straight" even at the cost of violent revolution and the destruction of the hierarchical and predominantly "literary" art of the bourgeoisie.[6] It is easy to find gaps between his theory of culture and his practice in literature and the decorative arts.[7] Nonetheless, his attack on middle-class art finds important expression in *News from Nowhere,* which is an attempt to reawaken those aspirations in the working class which have been deadened and stultified under capitalism. Genuine art for Morris does more than merely reflect an impoverished life back to the reader: "It is the province of art to set the true ideal of a full and reasonable life before [the worker], a life to which the perception and creation of beauty, the enjoyment of real pleasure that is, shall be felt to be as necessary to man as his daily bread."[8] *News from Nowhere,* however deficient in political science, is a moving and convincing picture of a community of individuals living full and reasonable lives. The "enjoyment of real pleasure"[9] begins when the narrator wakes on a sunny summer morning, steps out of his Thames-side house and meets the boatman who, refusing payment, takes him for a leisurely trip on the river.

Morris's attack on the shoddiness of Victorian design and the separation of high art from popular art was pressed home in his lectures. In *News from Nowhere* he turns his attention to another product of the same ethos—the Victorian novel. Guest's girl-friend, Ellen, tells him that there is "something loathsome" about nineteenth-century novelists.

> Some of them, indeed, do here and there show some feeling for those whom the history-books call "poor," and of the misery of whose lives we have some in-

kling; but presently they give it up, and towards the end of the story we must be contented to see the hero and heroine living happily in an island of bliss on other people's troubles; and that after a long series of sham troubles (or mostly sham) of their own making, illustrated by dreary introspective nonsense about their feelings and aspirations, and all the rest of it; while the world must even then have gone on its way, and dug and sewed and baked and carpentered round about these useless—animals.

[§22]

Morris introduced his poem *The Earthly Paradise* as the tale of an "isle of bliss" amid the "beating of the steely sea"; but the "hero and heroine" evoked by Ellen are also clearly from Dickens. (The "dreary introspective nonsense" might be George Eliot's.) Guest is seen by the Nowherians as an emissary from the land of Dickens (§19). Both Morris and Bellamy shared the general belief that future generations would understand the Victorian period through Dickens's works. In *Looking Backward,* Dr Leete is the spokesman for a more bourgeois posterity:

> Judged by our standard, he [Dickens] overtops all the writers of his age, not because his literary genius was highest, but because his great heart beat for the poor, because he made the cause of the victims of society his own, and devoted his pen to exposing its cruelties and shams. No man of his time did so much as he to turn men's minds to the wrong and wretchedness of the old order of things, and open their eyes to the necessity of the great change that was coming, although he himself did not clearly foresee it.

[§13]

Not only Morris would have found this "Philistine." But Morris's Ellen and Bellamy's Dr Leete are on opposite sides in the ideological debate about Dickens's value, which continues to this day. One of the earliest critics to register Dickens's ambiguity was Ruskin, who denounced *Bleak House* as an expression of the corruption of industrial society, while praising *Hard Times* for its harshly truthful picture of the same society.[10] Morris, too, was divided in his response. When asked to list the world's hundred best books, he came up with 54 names which included Dickens as the foremost contemporary novelist. The list was dominated by the "folk-bibles"—traditional epics, folktales and fairy tales—which he drew upon in his romances.[11] Dickens's humour and fantasy appealed to the hearty, extrovert side of Morris stressed by his non-socialist friends and biographers.[12] Yet he also reprinted the "Podsnap" chapter of *Our Mutual Friend* in *The Commonweal*,[13] and inveighed against Podsnappery and the "counting-house on the top of a cinder-heap" in his essay "How I Became a Socialist." It is the world of the counting-house on the cinder-heap—the world of *Our Mutual Friend*—whose negation Morris set out to present in *News from Nowhere.*

Not only do the words "our friend" identify Guest on the opening page, but one of the earliest characters Morris introduces is Henry Johnson, nicknamed Boffin or the "Golden Dustman" in honour of a Dickensian forebear. Mr. Boffin in *Our Mutual Friend* is a legacy-holder earnestly acquiring some culture at the hands of the unscrupulous Silas Wegg; Morris's Golden Dustman really is both a cultured man and a dustman, and is leading a "full and reasonable life." He has a Dickensian eccentricity, quite frequent among the Nowherians and a token of the individuality their society fosters. This character, I would suggest, is strategically placed to insinuate the wider relation of Morris's "Utopian Romance" to nineteenth-century fiction.

The tone of *News from Nowhere* is set by Guest's initial outing on the Thames. Going to bed in mid-winter, he wakes to his boat-trip on an early morning in high summer. The water is clear, not muddy, and the bridge beneath which he rows is not of iron construction but a medieval creation resembling the Ponte Vechhio or the twelfth-century London Bridge. The boatman lacks the stigmata of the "working man" and looks amazed when Guest offers him money. This boat-trip is a negative counterpart to the opening chapter of *Our Mutual Friend,* in which Gaffer Hexam, a predatory Thames waterman, and his daughter Lizzie are disclosed rowing on the river at dusk on an autumn evening. Southwark and London Bridges, made of iron and stone respectively, tower above them. The water is slimy and oozy, the boat is caked with mud and the two people are looking for the floating corpses of suicides which provide a regular, indeed a nightly, source of livelihood. Dickens created no more horrifying image of city life. His scavengers inaugurate a tale of murderousness, conspiracy and bitter class-jealousy. Morris's utopian waterman, by contrast, guides his Guest through a classless world in which creativity and a calm Epicureanism flourish.

Two further Dickensian parallels centre upon the setting of the river. The Houses of Parliament in *News from Nowhere* have been turned into the Dung Market, a storage place for manure. Dickens scrupulously avoids the explicitly excremental, but in *Hard Times* he calls Parliament the "national cinder-heap," and a reference to the sinister dust-heaps of *Our Mutual Friend* may also be detected both here and in "How I Became a Socialist." It seems the Nowhereians have put the home of windbags and scavengers to its proper purpose. In the second half of *News from Nowhere,* Guest journeys up-river with a party of friends; this again, perhaps recalls the furtive and murderous journey of Bradley Headstone along the same route. Headstone tracks down Eugene Wrayburn, his rival for the love of Lizzie Hexam. Guest's love for Ellen, by contrast, flourishes among friends who are free from sexual jealousy. Yet jealousy has not disappeared altogether, for at Mapledurham the travellers hear of a quarrel in which a jilted lover attacked his rival with an axe (§24). Shortly afterwards, we meet the Obstinate Refusers, whose abstention from the haymaking is likened to that of Dickensian characters refusing to celebrate Christmas. Even in the high summer of Nowhere, the dark shadow of Dickens is occasionally present, preparing for the black cloud at the end of the book under which Guest returns to the nineteenth century.

News from Nowhere has a series of deliberate echoes of Dickens's work, and especially of *Our Mutual Friend.* Such echoes sharpen the reader's sense of a miraculous translation into the future. In chapters 17 and 18 the miracle is "explained" by Hammond's narrative of the political genesis of Nowhere—a narrative which recalls the historiographical aims of novelists such as Scott, Disraeli and George Eliot. These elements of future history and Dickensian pastiche show Morris subsuming and rejecting the tradition of Victorian fiction and historiography. The same process guides his depiction of the kinds of individual and social relationships which constitute the ideal of a "full and reasonable life." Raymond Williams has defined the achievement of classical realism in terms of the balance it maintains between social and personal existence: "It offers a valuing of a whole way of life, a society that is larger than any of the individuals composing it, and at the same time valuing creations of human beings who, while belonging to and affected by and helping to define this way of life, are also, in their own terms, absolute ends in themselves. Neither element, neither the society nor the individual, is there as a priority."[14] SF and utopian fiction are notorious for their failure to maintain such a balance. But the achievement that Williams celebrates should be regarded, in my view, not as an artistic unity so much as a *coalition* of divergent interests. Coalitions are produced by the pressures of history; by the same pressures they fall apart. In mid-Victorian fiction, the individual life is repeatedly defined and valued in terms of its antithesis to the *crowd,* or *mass society.* The happiness of Dickens's Little Dorrit and Clennam is finally engulfed by the noise of the streets; characters like George Eliot's Lydgate and Gwendolen Harleth are proud individuals struggling to keep apart from the mass, while their creator sets out to record the "whisper in the roar of hurrying existence."[15] The looming threat of society in these novels is weighed against the possibility of spiritual growth. George Eliot portrays the mental struggles of characters who are, in the worldly sense, failures. She cannot portray them achieving social success commensurate with their gifts, so that even at her greatest her social range remains determinedly "provincial" and she can define her characters' limitations with the finality of an obituarist. She cannot show the source of change, only its effects and the way it is resisted. Dickens's despair at the irreducible face of society led him in his later works to fantasize it, portraying it as throttled by monstrous institutions and pre-

sided over by spirits and demons. His heroes and heroines are safe from the monstrous tentacles only in their "island of bliss." One reason why Dickens's domestic scenes are so overloaded with sentimental significance is that here his thwarted utopian instincts were forced to seek outlet. The house as a miniature paradise offsets the hell of a society.

It should not be surprising that a novelist such as Dickens possessed elements of a fantastic and utopian vision.[16] They are distorted and disjointed elements, whereas Morris in *News from Nowhere* takes similar elements and reunites them in a pure and uncomplex whole. Several of his individual characters display a Dickensian eccentricity, and they all have the instant capacity for mutual recognition and trust which Dickens's good characters show. Yet this mutual trust is all-embracing; it no longer defines who you are, since it extends to everybody, even the most casual acquaintances (Hammond, the social philosopher of Nowhere, explains that there are no longer any criminal classes, since crimes are not the work of fugitive outcasts but the "errors of friends" [§12]). Guest's sense of estrangement in Nowhere is most vivid in the early scenes where he is shown round London. Not only has the city become a garden suburb and the crowds thinned out, but the people he meets are instinctively friendly, responding immediately to a stranger's glance. They are the antithesis of Dickens's crowds of the "noisy and the eager and the arrogant and the forward and the vain," which "fretted, and chafed, and made their usual uproar."[17] The friendly crowd is such a paradox that Morris's imagination ultimately fails him slightly, so that he relapses into Wardour Street fustian:

> Therewith he drew rein and jumped down, and I followed. A very handsome woman, splendidly clad in figured silk, was slowly passing by, looking into the windows as she went. To her quoth Dick: "Maiden, would you kindly hold our horse while we go in for a little?" She nodded to us with a kind smile, and fell to patting the horse with her pretty hand.
>
> "What a beautiful creature!" said I to Dick as we entered.
>
> "What, old Greylocks?" said he, with a sly grin.
>
> "No, no," said I; "Goldylocks,—the lady."
>
> [§6]

Morris here is feeling his way toward the authentically childlike view of sexual relationships which emerges during the journey up-river. Guest begins to enjoy a gathering fulfillment, movingly portrayed but also clearly regressive. Annie at Hammersmith is a mother-figure, Ellen a mixture of sister and childhood sweetheart. Guest, though past his prime of life, feels a recovery of vigour which is, in the event, illusory; his fate is not to be rejuvenated in Nowhere but to return to the nineteenth century, strengthened only in his longing for change. Though he shares his companions' journey to the haymaking, his exclusion from the feast to celebrate their arrival is another inverted Dickensian symbol.[18] The return to the present is doubly upsetting to the "happy ending" convention (seen for example in Bellamy); for it is not a nightmare but a stoical affirmation of political responsibility. Guest's last moments in Nowhere show him rediscovering the forgotten experience of alienation and anonymity.

Dickens and George Eliot were moralists in their fiction and supporters of social and educational reform outside it. Morris worked to improve Victorian taste while coming to believe that there were no "moral" or "reformist" solutions to the social crisis. It was the perspective of the labour movement and the revolutionary "river of fire"[19] which enabled him to reassemble the distorted affirmation of a Dickens novel into a clear, utopian vision. His vision draws strength from its fidelity to socialist ideals and to Morris's own emotional needs. But Morris, for all his narrative self-consciousness, can only register and not transcend what is ultimately an aesthetic impasse. His book is *News from Nowhere, or An Epoch of Rest*; it shows not only the redemption of man's suffering past but his enjoyment of Arcadian quietism. In Nowhere pleasure may be had "without an afterthought of the injustice and miserable toil which made my leisure" (§20). Morris omits to describe how in economic terms leisure is produced, and how in political terms a society built by the mass labour movement has dispersed into peaceful anarchism. He stakes everything on the mood of "second childhood":

> "Second childhood," said I in a low voice, and then blushed at my double rudeness, and hoped that he hadn't heard. But he had, and turned to me smiling, and said: "Yes, why not? And for my part, I hope it may last long; and that the world's next period of wise and unhappy manhood, if that should happen, will speedily lead us to a third childhood: if indeed this age be not our third. Meantime, my friend, you must know that we are too happy, both individually and collectively to trouble ourselves about what is to come hereafter."
>
> [§16]

It is true that the passage hints at further labours of social construction lying in store for man. Morris, however, prefers not to contemplate them. One is forced to conclude that in *News from Nowhere* the ideal of the perfection of labour is developed as an alternative to the dynamism of Western society. We are left with the irresolvable ambiguity of the Morrisian utopia, which peoples an exemplary socialist society with characters who are, in the strict sense in which Walter Pater had used the term, decadents.[20]

H. G. Wells first listened to Morris at socialist meetings at Hammersmith in the 1880s. Even for a penniless South Kensington science student, attending such meetings was an act of social defiance. But, as he later recalled, he soon forgot his "idea of a council of war, and . . . was being vastly entertained by a comedy of picturesque personalities."[21] He saw Morris as trapped in the role of poet and aesthete, yet in *A Modern Utopia* (1905) he readily acknowledged the attractiveness of a Morrisian earthly paradise:

> Were we free to have our untrammelled desire, I suppose we should follow Morris to his Nowhere, we should change the nature of man and the nature of things together; we should make the whole race wise, tolerant, noble, perfect—wave our hands to a splendid anarchy, every man doing as it pleases him, and none pleased to do evil, in a world as good in its essential nature, as ripe and sunny, as the world before the Fall.[22]

Wells, in effect, accuses Morris of lacking intellectual "realism." His response to this appears to far less advantage in *A Modern Utopia,* however, than it does in his dystopian works beginning with *The Time Machine* (1895). *A Modern Utopia* is an over-ambitious piece of system-building, reflecting its author's eclectic search for a "new aristocracy" or administrative elite; *The Time Machine* is a mordantly critical examination of concepts of evolution and progress and the future state, with particular reference to *News from Nowhere.*

While Guest wakes up in Hammersmith, the Time Traveller climbs down from his machine in the year 802,701 A.D. at a spot about three miles away, in what was formerly Richmond. The gay, brightly-dressed people, the verdant park landscape and the bathing in the river are strongly reminiscent of Morris. The Eloi live in palace-like communal buildings, and are lacking in personal or sexual differentiation. On the evening of his arrival, the Time Traveller walks up to a hilltop and surveys the green landscape, murmuring "Communism" to himself (§6). The reference is to Morris rather than to Marx (whose work and ideas Wells never knew well). Wells has already begun his merciless examination of the "second childhood" which Morris blithely accepted in Nowhere.

From the moment of landing we are aware of tension in the Time Traveller's responses. He arrives in a thunderstorm near a sinister colossus, the White Sphinx, and soon he is in a frenzy of fear. The hospitality of the Eloi, who shower him with garlands and fruit, does not cure his anxiety. Unlike most previous travellers in utopia, he is possessed of a human pride, suspicion and highly-strung sensitivity which he cannot get rid of. He reacts with irritability when asked if he has come from the sun in a thunderstorm: "It let loose the judgment I had suspended upon their clothes, their frail light limbs and fragile features. A flow of disappointment rushed across my mind. For a moment I felt that I had built the Time Machine in vain" (§5). When they teach him their language, it is he who feels like a "schoolmaster amidst children," and soon he has the Eloi permanently labelled as a class of five-year-olds.

The apparent premise of *The Time Machine* is one of scientific anticipation, the imaginative working-out of the laws of evolution and thermodynamics, with a dash of Marxism added. Critics sometimes stress the primacy of the didactic surface in such writing.[23] But *The Time Machine* is not exhausted once we have paraphrased its explicit message. Like *News from Nowhere,* it is a notably self-conscious work. Wells's story-telling frame is more elaborate than Morris's, and Robert M. Philmus has drawn attention to the studied ambiguity Wells puts in the Time Traveller's mouth: "Take it as a lie—or a prophecy. Say I dreamed it in the workshop" (§16).[24] One of his hero's ways of authenticating his story is to expose the fabrications of utopian writers. A "real traveller," he protests, has no access to the "vast amount of detail about building, and social arrangements, and so forth" found in utopian versions (§8). He has "no convenient cicerone in the pattern of the Utopian books" (§8). He has to work everything out for himself by a process of conjecture and refutation—a crucial feature of *The Time Machine* which does much to convey the sense of intellectual realism and authenticity. The visit to the Palace of Green Porcelain parallels Guest's visit to the British Museum, but instead of a Hammond authoritatively placed to expound "How the Change Came," the Time Traveller must rely on habits of observation and reasoning which his creator acquired at the Normal School of Science.

In *The Time Machine* Wells uses a hallowed device of realistic fiction—the demonstration of superior authenticity over some other class of fictions—in a "romance" context. His aim is, in Levin's words, to "unmask cant" and debunk misconceptions. The truths he affirms are both of a scientific (or Huxleyan) and a more traditional sort. The world of Eloi and Morlocks is revealed first as devolutionary and then as one of predator and prey, of *homo homini lupus.* This must have a political, not merely a biological significance. No society, Wells is saying, can escape the brutish aspects of human nature defined by classical bourgeois rationalists such as Machiavelli and Hobbes. A society that claims to have abolished these aspects may turn out to be harbouring predatoriness in a peculiarly horrible form. This must become apparent once we can see the *whole* society. In Morris's Nowhere, part of the economic structure is suppressed; there is no way of knowing what it would have been like. In *The Time Machine* it is only necessary to put the Eloi and Morlocks in the picture together—whether they are linked by a class relationship, or a species relationship, or some evolutionary combination of the two—to destroy the mirage of utopian communism. The Dickensian society of scavengers cannot be so lightly dismissed.

In contrast to Morris's mellow Arcadianism, *The Time Machine* is an aggressive book, moving through fear and melodrama to the heights of poetic vision. The story began as a philosophical dialogue and emerged from successive revisions as a gripping adventure-tale which is also a mine of poetic symbolism. To read through the various versions is to trace Wells's personal discovery of the "scientific romance."[25] *The Time Machine* in its final form avoids certain limitations of both the Victorian realist novel and the political utopia. An offshoot of Wells's use of fantasy to explore man's temporal horizons is that he portrays human nature as at once more exalted and more degraded than the conventional realist estimate.

Imagining the future liberates Wells's hero from individual moral constraints; the story reveals a devolved, simian species which engages the Time Traveller in a ruthless, no-holds-barred struggle. The scenario of the future is a repository for symbolism of various kinds. The towers and shafts of the story are recognizably Freudian, while the names of the Eloi and Morlocks allude to Miltonic angels and devils. The Time Traveller himself is a variant of the nineteenth-century romantic hero. Like Frankenstein, he is a modern Prometheus. The identification is sealed in the Palace of Green Porcelain episode, where he steals a matchbox from the museum of earlier humanity, whose massive architectural remains might be those of Titans. But there is no longer a fit recipient for the gift of fire, and the Time Traveller's matches are only lit in self-defence. We see him travel to the end of the world, alone, clasped to his machine on the sea-shore. When he fails to return from his second journey we might imagine him as condemned to perpetual time-travelling, as Prometheus was condemned to perpetual torture.

There are few unqualified heroes in Victorian realistic fiction (this is a question of generic conventions, not of power of characterization). The zenith of the realist's art appears in characters such as Lydgate, Dorothea, Pip and Clennam, all of whom are shown as failures, and not often very dignified failures. They are people circumscribed and hemmed in by bourgeois existence. Intensity of consciousness alone distinguishes theirs from the average life of the ordinary member of their social class. As against this, Wells offers an epic adventurer who (like Morris's knights and saga-heroes) is close to the supermen of popular romance. His hero is guilty of sexual mawkishness and indulges in Byronic outbursts of temperament. But what distinguishes him from the run-of-the-mill fantasy hero is the epic and public nature of his mission. As Time Traveller he takes up the major cognitive challenge of the Darwinist age. He boasts of coming "out of this age of ours, this ripe prime of the human race, when Fear does not paralyse and mystery has lost its terrors" (§10). The retreat of superstition before the sceptical, scientific attitude dictated that the exploit of a modern Prometheus or Faust should be told in a scaled-down, "romance" form. Nonetheless, the Time Traveller shares the pride of the scientists, inventors and explorers of the nineteenth century, and not the weakness or archaism of its literary heroes.

There is a dark side to his pride. The scene where he surveys the burning Morlocks shows Wells failing to distance his hero sufficiently. The Time Traveller is not ashamed of his cruel detachment from the species he studies, nor does he regret having unleashed his superior "firepower." His only remorse is for Weena, the one creature he responded to as "human," and Wells hints that her death provides justification for the slaughter of the Morlocks. This rationalization is a clear example of imperialist psychology; but Wells was both critic and product of the imperialist ethos. Morris, who was so sharp about Bellamy, would surely have spotted his vulnerability here. It is not merely the emotions of scientific curiosity which are satisfied by the portrayal of a Hobbesian, dehumanized world.

News from Nowhere and **The Time Machine** are based on a fusion of propaganda and dream. Their complexity is due in part to the generic interactions which I have traced. Morris turns from the degraded world of Dickens to create its negative image in a Nowhere of mutual trust and mutual fulfilment. Wells writes a visionary satire on the utopian idea which reintroduces the romantic hero as explorer and prophet of a menacing future. Both writers were responding to the break-up of the coalition of interests in mid-Victorian fiction, and their use of fantasy conventions asserted the place of visions and expectations in the understanding of contemporary reality. Schematically, we may see Wells's SF novel as a product of the warring poles of realism and utopianism, as represented by Dickens and Morris. More generally, I would suggest that to study the aetiology of works such as *News from Nowhere* and **The Time Machine** is to ask oneself fundamental questions about the nature and functions of literary "realism."

Notes

1. I use "realism" in a broadly Lukacsian sense, to denote the major representational idiom of 19th-century fiction. See e.g. Georg Lukacs, *Studies in European Realism* (US 1964). I also argue that "realism" in literature cannot ultimately be separated from the modern non-literary senses of the term. No sooner is a convention of literary realism established than the inherently dynamic "realistic outlook" starts to turn against that convention.

2. Patrick Brantlinger, *"News from Nowhere*: Morris's Socialist Anti-Novel," *Victorian Studies* 19(1975):35ff. This article examines Morris's aesthetic in greater depth than was possible here, with conclusions that are close to my own.

3. Karl Marx and Frederick Engels, *On Literature and Art,* ed. Lee Baxandall and Stefan Morawski (US 1974), p 117.

4. Harry Levin, *The Gates of Horn* (US 1966), p 55.

5. The best political biography is E. P. Thompson, *William Morris: Romantic to Revolutionary* (UK 1955).

6. Morris's published lectures are reprinted in his *Collected Works,* ed. May Morris, vols. 22-23 (UK 1914), and some unpublished ones in *The Unpublished Lectures of William Morris,* ed. Eugene D. LeMire (US 1969). Three recent (but no more than introductory) selections are: *William Morris: Selected Writings and Designs,* ed. Asa Briggs (US-UK 1962); *Political Writings of William Morris,* ed. A. L. Morton (US—UK 1962); and *William Morris, Selected Writings,* ed. G. H. Cole (US 1961).

7. Morris took up the practice of handicrafts in 1860 and became, in effect, an extremely successful middle-class designer. His theories of the unity of design and execution were often in advance of his workshop practice. See e.g. Peter Floud, "The Inconsistencies of William Morris," *The Listener* 52(1954):615ff.

8. Morris, "How I Became a Socialist" (1894).

9. See note 6.

10. Ruskin commented on *Bleak House* in "Fiction— Fair and Foul," published in the *Nineteenth Century* (1880-1), and on *Hard Times* in *Unto This Last* (1860).

11. *Collected Works* 22:xiii ff.

12. J. W. Mackail records somewhat fatuously that "In the moods when he was not dreaming of himself as Tristram or Sigurd, he identified himself very closely with . . . Joe Gargery and Mr Boffin."—*The Life of William Morris* (UK 1901), 1:220-21. Cf. Paul Thompson, *The Work of William Morris* (UK 1967), p 149.

13. See E. P. Thompson (Note 5) pp 165-67. I have not managed to locate this in the files of *The Commonweal.*

14. Raymond Williams, *The Long Revolution* (UK 1961), p 268.

15. George Eliot, Introduction to *Felix Holt* (1866).

16. The fantastic and utopian elements in Dickens are associated with his genius for satire and melodrama: with his vision of the interlocking, institutional character of social evil, and his delight in sharp and magical polarizations between the

strongholds of evil and those of beauty and innocence. The elements of traditional romance in Dickens's vision make him an exaggerated, but by no means unique case; a utopian element could, I think, be traced in every great novelist.

17. Dickens, *Little Dorrit,* §34.

18. Tom Middlebro' argues that both river and feast are "religious symbols"—"Brief Thoughts on *News from Nowhere,*" *Journal of the William Morris Society* 2(1970):8. If so, this was true for Dickens as well, and I would see him as Morris's immediate source. The symbolism of the feast is present in all Dickens's works and has been discussed by Angus Wilson, "Charles Dickens: A Haunting," *Critical Quarterly* 2(1960):107-08.

19. Morris, "The Prospects of Architecture in Civilization" in *Hopes and Fears for Art* (1882).

20. Pater describes the poetry of the Pleiade as "an aftermath, a wonderful later growth, the products of which have to the full the subtle and delicate sweetness which belong to a refined and comely decadence." Preface to *The Renaissance* (1873). The compatibility of one aspect of Pater's and Morris's sensibility is suggested by the former's review of "Poems by William Morris," *Westminster Review* 34(1868):300ff.

21. *Saturday Review* 82(1896):413.

22. Wells, *A Modern Utopia* §1:1.

23. See e.g. Joanna Russ's remarks on *The Time Machine,* SFS 2(1975):114-15.

24. Robert M. Philmus, *Into the Unknown* (US 1970), p 73.

25. The most telling contrast is with the *National Observer* version (1894). For a reprint of this and an account of Wells's revisions of *The Time Machine* see his *Early Writings in Science and Science Fiction,* ed. Robert M. Philmus and David Y. Hughes (US 1975), pp 47ff.

David J. Lake (essay date March 1979)

SOURCE: Lake, David J. "The White Sphinx and the Whitened Lemur: Images of Death in *The Time Machine.*" *Science Fiction Studies* 6, no. 1 (March 1979): 77-84.

[In the following essay, Lake considers Wells's use of imagery in The Time Machine.*]*

There is widespread agreement that *The Time Machine* is H. G. Wells' finest scientific romance; many critics would go further and call it the best of all his fictions.

A sample remark is that of V. S. Pritchett in *The Living Novel*: "Without question *The Time Machine* is the best piece of writing. It will take its place among the great stories of our language. Like all excellent works it has meanings within its meaning. . . ."[1] Pritchett here indicates a main reason for *The Time Machine*'s greatness: its richness of suggestion. Bernard Bergonzi, in one of the most detailed studies so far of the novel, has emphasized its mythic quality.[2] Certainly the vision of a future decadent world polarized between the paradisal Eloi and the demonic Morlocks has the quality of great myth, and like myth is multivalent: the sociological interpretation is obvious (and indicated by Wells in the text), and beyond that there is an easy underground shaft to Freud as it were. But the notion of "myth" is not enough to explain the excellence of *The Time Machine.* Myths can always be handled badly or superficially; but in fact Wells has given his myth a nearly perfect embodiment. It is the details of his writing that count. In particular, I submit that a large part of the excellence of *The Time Machine* derives from its systematic imagery. And the images are largely organized in a system of colors.[3]

Bergonzi (p. 217, note 43) has drawn attention to the White Sphinx which dominates the Time Traveller's first impression of the future world—and not incidentally adorned the cover of the first British edition in 1895. But Bergonzi's interpretation of this as a typical fin-de-siecle motif is insufficient. I would like now to examine two questions: first, why a sphinx; and second, why a white one?

The answer to the first question must be fairly obvious in outline; but even here we have richness of suggestion. In Wells' earlier *National Observer* version of the story,[4] the main features of the scene are already there: the white marble sphinx beside a silver birch tree in a hailstorm, the sphinx's sightless but watching eyes, its faint smile, its spread wings. In the final version (chap. 3:27),[5] Wells has added the detail: "It was greatly weather-worn, and that imparted an unpleasant suggestion of disease". Later (chap. 5:44) Wells combines the whiteness with the dilapidation in the adjective "leprous".

This Sphinx really does dominate the story; and not just the Time Traveller's first impression either. It strikes the first really sinister note, suggesting the decay of the future world, and also a mysterious threat to the hero. Its wings are spread, not folded, to suggest a flying bird of prey; as we see from the development of that idea soon after the initial description: "I felt naked in a strange world. I felt as perhaps a bird may feel in the clear air, knowing the hawk wings above and will swoop" (chap. 3:28). And the swoop duly takes place, when the Morlocks drag the time machine into the pedestal of the sphinx. Thus the symbol is also an efficient cause in the story; which is an excellent way to use symbols, and not only in SF.[6]

We can focus the sphinx symbol a little more clearly if we recall the most famous sphinx of mythology, the one which confronted Oedipus. The answer to that sphinx's riddle was simply Man—the creature who goes on four legs in infancy, stands firm on two legs in manhood, and totters three-legged on a staff in old age. And precisely the rise and fall of Man is the subject, or a main subject, of **The Time Machine.** I submit therefore that this leprous, crumbling sphinx represents the "three-legged" stage, the decay of Man in the future world. Its whiteness is the whiteness not only of leprosy but also of bone, its sightless eyes are those of a human skull. It stands for immediate decay and the menace of imminent death.

It is really astonishing to notice how often the color *white* appears in the text. The sphinx is hardly ever mentioned without being called "white," even though there are no other sphinxes about. And there are many other white things. Already in that first future scene we have the white sphinx, the *silver* birch tree, the *white* hailstones. The birch might suggest a rather colder climate than is presented for the year 802,701; and the hailstones are in a sense the first hostile move against the hero, and foreshadow the "white flakes" of snow in the end-of-the-world Further Vision (chap. 11:108).[7] Then again there is the whiteness of the Eloi: "white limbs" (chap. 4:33), suggesting once more decadence. There are several instances of over-lush white flowers. But above all, there is the whiteness of the Morlocks.

Of course the Morlocks' pallor is explained scientifically as due to their underground habitat (chap 5:62). But as in the case of the sphinx, their color is insisted upon again and again. For instance, here is the first view of them:

> The moon was setting, and the dying moonlight and the first pallor of dawn were mingled in a ghastly half-light. The bushes were inky black, the ground a sombre grey, the sky colorless and cheerless. And up the hill I thought I could see ghosts. Three several times, as I scanned the slope, I saw white figures. Twice I fancied I saw a solitary white, ape-like creature. . . .
>
> (chap. 5:57)

This passage is a rich example of Wells' excellent handling of colour symbolism. *White* and its shades are here associated with *setting, dying,* ghastliness and cheerlessness. The setting moon—later in the story, the waning moon—perfectly combines the ideas of whiteness and of death, since the moon looks whitish and is a dead planet. *Grey* is a variant of *white* which is also from time to time applied to the Morlocks: it is "colourless and cheerless", suggesting an absence of the colors of life. And here the greyish-whiteness of the

Morlocks is attached to the idea of *ghosts.* The following paragraph expands on the "ghost" idea. So at their first appearance, the Morlocks are associated with death, and the uncanny whiteness of things which were once alive but are so no longer. Then again we have, near the beginning of the next chapter:

> I felt a peculiar shrinking from these pallid bodies. They were just the half-bleached colour of the worms and things one sees preserved in spirit in a zoological museum. And they were filthily cold to the touch. Probably my shrinking was largely due to the sympathetic influence of the Eloi, whose disgust of the Morlocks I now began to appreciate.
>
> (chap. 6:66)

Of course, the disgust felt by the Eloi turns out to be the horror of death. We notice also in this passage that the Morlocks are "filthily cold" and compared to dead biological specimens. One important meaning of the Morlocks, I submit, is simply Death itself. Their name alone suggests that: the first syllable is surely from *mors,* the Latin for "death". And Wells was a fairly good Latin scholar, quoting (for instance) from Horace's Odes, Book I, repeatedly in the first two chapters of *Love and Mr. Lewisham.*[8] It is the corpse that is *filthily* cold and pallid (*pallida Mors* in Horace's famous Ode I.4) and that, like the Morlocks, stinks. The danger of the Morlocks is that they may *lock* one into *rigor mortis,* or into the underworld-grave.

I do not mean at all to deny that the Morlocks also carry other suggestions: the working classes, dangerous animals,[9] and so forth. The suggestion of *ape,* or degenerate ape-man, is particularly strong. But why should apes be cold to the touch? There is no scientific justification for that, so the force behind it must be symbolic; and not of apehood. (Of course it might suggest a sub-mammalian class of animals; but this suggestion, being essentially privative, does not exclude the worse negation.) And in the paragraph next after the one just quoted, there is a striking phrase which combines the "ape" and the "death" suggestions. Here the Traveller anticipates in the waning moon "the appearances of these unpleasant creatures from below, these whitened Lemurs. . . ." (chap. 6:66).

"Lemur" here is a beautiful pun. Biologically, it signifies a pro-simian, a lower primate which goes on all fours. But it also and originally in Latin signified a *ghost.* Here, then, the word suggests sub-apes and ghosts at once. And why the curious adjective *whitened*? Could this not be an echo of Matthew 23:27— "whited sepulchers" in the King James Version? It is probably not the only echo of that gospel in the story, for there is also "abominable desolation" in "The Further Vision" (chap. 11:107), which recalls the words "abomination of desolation" in Matthew 24:15. If I am right about the biblical associations, then both words of the phrase "whitened Lemurs" carry overtones of death and the grave. This is in addition to the "ape" motif, and blends perfectly with it. For the post-human ape and the post-human ghost are equally ex-men; the "simian" stoop of the Morlocks is also the stoop of Oedipus' "three-legged" old man dropping into the grave. The death-motif of the Morlocks also blends well with the demonic motif noted by Bergonzi (p. 53). The phrase "damned souls" (chap. 9:99) combines both suggestions.

The deathly associations of the Morlocks explain most of their horror. What is being repressed, what erupts from the well-shafts under the waning moon, is the fear of personal and racial death. The Time Traveller reacts by these things with an emotion which is quite excessive if it merely embodies the fear of dangerous animals or the descendants of the proletariat. Time and again it is made clear that his emotion is not merely fear but also horror and hatred. This rises to a climax towards the end of his stay in that world, when he feels a positive longing to kill Morlocks. He comments: "Very inhuman, you may think, to want to go killing one's own descendants! But it was impossible, somehow, to feel any humanity in the things" (chap. 8:86-87). No indeed: the Time Traveller does not regard the Morlocks as human, because he has subconsciously equated them with the great and last Enemy; they are symbolically that white cold death which will eventually overwhelm the Earth and every descendant of mankind.

This, indeed, is the most fundamental theme of the whole story: death, and the vain attempt to transcend death. The Time Traveller must remain nameless, because he is not a particular individual, he is all of us. We are all time travellers, but as things are, our voyages can seldom stretch further than seventy or eighty years. The most glorious thing, the exhilaration about a Time Machine is that it enables the Traveller (who is Man) to transcend his own lifetime. Yet in Wells' romance the whole endeavor is shown to be ultimately vain. At the end of things waits the inevitable cold death. And meanwhile, the Morlocks are the hated harbingers.

The Time Traveller's horror and hatred of them erupts most obviously during the fight and fire in the woods (chap. 9). When the Morlocks are blinded and dying in the fire, he makes the strange comment: "And now I was to see the most weird and horrible thing, I think, of all that I beheld in that future age" (chap. 9:97). This is surprising. Why is this scene more horrible than that in the Underworld, for instance? But it is so to the Traveller: later on he is persuaded that he is dreaming a nightmare, and screams and prays and even bites himself in a passionate desire to awake (chap. 9:98). Moreover, by

this time it is fairly clear that Weena has died of sheer terror. It would seem, therefore, that this scene of the "thirty or forty Morlocks" blundering about the fires incarnates their essential horror until the horror is unbearable. It is, we may say, Hell and Death brought to the surface; and it is here that the Morlocks are called "damned souls".

It is now necessary to explore the story's color symbolism a little further. Darko Suvin has persuasively outlined the essential polarity of red, black, and green.[10] In this fight-and-fire scene the predominant colour is *red*: naturally enough, the fire produces a "red sky", and makes the foliage a "red canopy". It is, I believe, reasonable to regard red in *The Time Machine* as another color connected with death, subsidiary to white but important enough at times. We have the red of the first sunset in the future, where the association with racial death is explicit: "The ruddy sunset set me thinking of the sunset of mankind" (chap. 4:39). Red is the color of dying heat, as incandescence drops towards invisibility. This, probably, is why the brightest star in the future sky is a red one (chap. 7:79)—all the stars are on the wane. Above all we see this in the last sunset of the Further Vision, where the earth has ceased rotating, and the sun, fixed symbolically (without astronomical necessity) in the west, is a "huge red-hot dome", and makes the ocean "all bloody under the eternal sunset" (chap. 11:107-108). In this end-of-the-world scene the main colors are red (sun, rocks, ocean), white (snow, ice), and black (a monster, and the final eclipse). These are all colors of death. And all these colors are present in the fire scene in the wood: "But at last, above the subsiding red of the fire, above the streaming masses of black smoke and the whitening and blackening tree stumps, and the diminishing numbers of these dim creatures, came the white light of the day" (chap. 9:98).

Red is the color not only of ending (sunset), and hell (fire), but also of blood. The Traveller sees red meat in the Underworld (chap. 6:70)—a dismembered Eloi corpse. And inevitably the Morlocks have greyish-*red* eyes (chap. 5/60). Where white and grey are deadly by negation, red functions as a positive menace.

Green, as noted by Suvin, is usually a life color; but in the "Further Vision" I think it sometimes carries a different suggestion. Thus we have the "poisonous-looking green" of the lichens (chap. 11:107), also "livid green" (108), where the association with paleness suggests that green also is here becoming a "deadly" color—as it is almost throughout **"The Plattner Story"**.

Purple is also used occasionally; I think with a suggestion of over-ripe decadence. The first sunset is "purple and crimson" (chap. 4:39). Some of the Eloi wear purple (chap. 3:29) or purple and white (chap. 4:31) tunics. And the first flowers the Traveller sees in the future are rhododendrons, and "I noticed that their mauve and purple blossoms were dropping in a shower under the beating of the hailstones" (chap. 3:26). If the purple flowers can symbolize the decadent Eloi, then here we have a first hint of them "dropping" under the violent onslaught of the Morlocks. That initial downpour may be associated with the Morlocks by a simile describing its end: "The grey downpour was swept aside and vanished like the trailing garments of a ghost" (chap. 3:28). Both *grey* and *ghost,* as we have seen, have associations with the Morlocks. Thus the various colors of the first scene hint at the coming drama before the actors appear, like the overture to an opera.

But from the beginning to the end of the story, it is above all the color *white* which recurs, and I think always carrying suggestions of decadence or death. Immediately after the Traveller's arrival, in the area near the sphinx he sees "strange white flowers, measuring a foot perhaps across the spread of the waxen petals" (chap. 4:32). And the very last image in the Epilogue is that of Weena's *white* flowers ("*not unlike very large white mallows*", chap. 7:76), her last gift to the Traveller. They are "shrivelled now," but they provide a touching funeral wreath for the human race.

It is a superficial defect of *The Time Machine* that there is a logical hiatus between the Eloi-Morlock world and the "Further Vision" of the ultimate cold-death. The decadence of the Eloi is due to human choice in our own civilization, and perhaps it need not be so; whereas the ultimate doom is the effect of thermo-dynamics, and inevitable no matter how wisely we manage our affairs. There is also a hiatus in the story line between the two parts of the Traveller's adventure: in the first and main part he is menaced by the Morlocks, in the second by various monsters[11] and the final cold. I would claim that the logical and structural gap is bridged by symbolic identification: the Morlocks are the ghostly harbingers of the End. And because the End is brought on by blind, sub-human forces, the Morlocks have to be blind (in daylight) and sub-human too—in defiance of extrapolative logic. For if the Eloi are made decadent by a too easy life, why should the subterranean workers be made decadent by a hard one? Would not their grim conditions in fact lead to selection for intelligence, for survival of the cunningest? And their blindness in daylight could only have arisen after a breakdown of their former electric lighting—but no such breakdown could have occurred if they had remained intelligent. But none of this matters much, because Wells is motivated not by scientific but poetic logic. And in the greater kinds of science fiction, poetry counts for much more than science.

As a matter of fact, apart from the lack of light in the Underworld there is very little evidence for a breakdown in Morlock society in the final text of *The Time Machine.* In the *National Observer* version of 1894 several of the underworld machines were described as "disused and broken down";[12] but in the final text the whole scene is much vaguer, more poetic, and full of the usual color imagery (chap. 6:70). It is notable that all the ghostly and deathly hints about the Morlocks in this scene and elsewhere, apart from their name, seem to have been developed by Wells *after* the *National Observer* version.[13] This must be a case of inspired revision. In the final version, too, there is much less argument as to how the Morlocks might have lost their intelligence, and much more poetic suggestion. And this, I believe, is why *The Time Machine* is great: because it uses the techniques of poetry. In this novel, imagery is used as Shakespeare uses it. The "running images" in *The Time Machine* are as consistent and persistent as those in *Hamlet* or *Macbeth.*

Moreover, whiteness and silvery moonlight symbolize death not only in *The Time Machine* but also in a great many other of Wells' works of the 1890s and 1900s. They are prominent images in the deadly ending of the fantasy novel *The Sea Lady* (1902) and in the fable-story **"The Beautiful Suit"** (1909). They likewise figure notably in passages in *The Island of Dr. Moreau* (1896) and *Tono-Bungay* (1909). Moreau himself is frequently described as "white-haired": we first meet him as an unnamed "massive white-haired man" (chap. 5) a couple of pages after Prendick has had bad dreams and seen the "ghostly faint white beam" of a waning moon in his cabin (chap. 4). Other significances may attach to Moreau: he may be looked upon, for example, as the God of Evolution; but since Death is the great instrument of Evolution, it may be that the first syllable of his name, like the first syllable of "Morlock," derives from *mors* (or the French *mort*). And so at last we have the description of Moreau lying dead under the moon: ". . . his massive face, calm even after his terrible death, and with the hard eyes open, staring at the dead white moon above" (chap. 19). In the next sentence, the narrator watches "that ghastly pile of silvery light and ominous shadows." The effects of deadly radio-active "quap" in *Tono-Bungay* constantly include *whitening.* Thus we hear of "white dead mangroves," "bone-white dead trees," "dirty shingle and mud, bleached and scarred." Every man at the nearby station dies of the white disease "like a leper" (III.i.4). And the gleam of this quap is like "diluted moonshine" (III.iv.4).

There is not much moonlight in *The First Men in the Moon* (1901), principally because for much of the novel we are on the moon itself. The whiteness of snow, however, is associated with death in one extremely powerful scene. Cavor and Bedford arrive on the moon in what looks like a drift of snow; but they soon realize that most of this is frozen air. They witness the morning "resurrection of the frozen air" (chap. 7). Much later, when Bedford is trying to escape through the lunar evening, we have some of the best writing in the book:

> And as I stood there, stupid and perplexed . . . something very, very soft and light and chill touched my hand for a moment and ceased to be, and then a thing, a little white speck drifted athwart a shadow. It was a tiny snowflake, the first snowflake, the herald of the night.
>
> . . . . .
>
> Over me, about me, closing in on me, embracing me ever nearer, was the Eternal, that which was before the beginning and that which triumphs over the end; that enormous void in which all light and life is but the thin and vanishing splendour of a falling star, the cold, the stillness, the silence—the infinite and final Night of space.

(chap. 18)

Before he escapes, the whiteness is upon Bedford himself. "The frost gathered on my lips, icicles hung from my moustache and beard, I was white with the freezing atmosphere" (chap. 18).

Most notably of all, both ***The Invisible Man*** (1897) and **"The Cone"** (1895) are thoroughly permeated with "whiteness=death" symbolism.[14] The death-symbolism of the colors black, red, and white pervades Wells' short story, reaching a climax on pp. 302-03 in the Atlantic Edition text. Here the wisps of steam in the moonlight are called "an instant succession of ghosts coming up from the black and red eddies, a white uprising. . . ." Horrocks, a grim engineer (and, as his name suggests, a proto-Morlock) murders the poet Raut (a proto-Eloi); in his last moments Raut sees his murderer as a "gesticulating figure . . . bright and white in the moonlight" (I, 305). Above all, Horrocks himself says that the vapor of the furnace is "white as death"—a striking phrase which Raut repeats to himself (I, 303).

If my analysis above is a true one, then the success of ***The Time Machine*** has implications for all science fiction that aspires to greatness. Outstanding achievement would seem to depend not only of peculiar generic virtues, but also and even more on the virtues of good mythical and symbolic fiction outside the SF genre: in particular on the handling of imagery.

Notes

1. *The Living Novel* (UK 1946), pp. 119-20.

2. *The Early H. G. Wells: A Study of the Scientific Romances* (UK 1961), pp. 42, 45.

3. This has already been noted briefly by various critics, e.g. Darko Suvin, "A Grammar of Form and a Criticism of Fact: *The Time Machine* as a Structural Model for Science Fiction," in D. Suvin and R. M. Philmus, eds., *H. G. Wells and Modern Science Fiction* (US 1977), pp. 91, 101. See also the long discussion of Wells' color symbolism in Wolfgang Schepelmann, *Die englische Utopie in Uebergang: von Bulwer-Lytton bis H. G. Wells* (Wien, 1975), pp. 218-73, passim, and the briefer references on red and white in the cosmological imagination (including *The Time Machine*) in Hélène Tuzet, *Le Cosmos et l'imagination* (Paris, 1965), p. 449ff. et passim.

4. Reprinted in Robert M. Philmus and David Y. Hughes, eds., *H. G. Wells: Early Writings in Science and Science Fiction* (US 1975), pp. 57-90. Hereafter cited as *Early Writings*.

5. *The Time Machine* appeared in its substantially final form in the Heinemann edition of 1895; the present standard text (with minor verbal revisions, deleted headings, and altered chaptering) is that of the Atlantic Edition, 1924. I give references to chapter and page of this edition. Thus, chap. 3:27 means Chapter 3, page 27 of the Atlantic Edition, Vol. I.

6. For instance, the poisoned skull in *The Revenger's Tragedy* (1607) is both a symbol of death and a murder weapon.

7. This was noted by Jack Williamson, *H. G. Wells: Critic of Progress* (US 1973), p. 50

8. Lewisham translates Odes I.19 and I.14 in these two chapters. See also Wells' *Experiment in Autobiography* (1934; UK 1966), I, 139-41 for his early acquaintance with Latin. "Morlock" may, however, partly derive from English words such as "mortal".

9. Alex Eisenstein, in "Origins of Some Major Physical Motifs in *The Time Machine* and *The War of the Worlds*," *Extrapolation* 13, no. 2 (May 1972), 119-26, has argued (p. 123) that the Morlocks derive from Wells' "profound early fear of wild animals in general and specifically of the gorilla," and that "this fear-fantasy provided the essential basis for the vision of the future contained in the *The Time Machine*. All else, even the ostensible, socio-scientific explanation in the story, are mere after-the-fact rationales overlaid on the germinal idea. [This fear may have contributed to Wells' creation of] the Morlocks, but "essential basis" seems much too strong. Moreover, the Morlocks never suggest large apes like gorillas, but always small primates, such as lemurs. The meaning of *The Time Machine* must be sought in the text itself, not in the early biography of the author.

10. "A Grammar of Form . . ." *loc. cit.* p. 101.

11. Eisenstein, in "*The Time Machine* and the End of Man," *SFS* 9 (July 1976), 163, makes a good case for regarding the black monster on the shoal as

the last descendant of the Morlocks. If we can accept this, then there is another symbolic linkage between the parts of the story. The Morlock line is still the enemy, but with a color change from white to the more final death color, black.

12. *Early Writings,* p. 83.

13. At least, so it seems from the texts which have survived. But there may be a minor bibliographic mystery here. In the *National Observer* articles, there seems to be a hiatus between the instalments of April 28 and May 19, 1894, entitled "The Sunset of Mankind" and "In the Underworld" respectively; see *Early Writings,* pp. 78-82. After the briefest reference to Morlocks on p. 78, "In the Underworld" begins: "'I have already told you,'" said the Time Traveller, "that it was customary on the part of the delightful people of the upper world to ignore the existence of these pallid creatures of the caverns, and consequently when I descended among them I descended alone.'" But in fact there is no previous reference to any attitude of the upperworlders to the Morlocks; we are not even told that the Morlocks dwelt in "caverns", much less that the hero was about to descend among them. So it is possible that somehow Wells' first full-scale description of the Morlocks may be lost.

14. "The Cone" was first published September 18, 1895, a few months after the final version of *The Time Machine.* Space will not permit the necessarily lengthy discussion of *The Invisible Man*'s complex imagery.

Mark M. Hennelly, Jr. (essay date summer 1979)

SOURCE: Hennelly, Mark M., Jr. "*The Time Machine*: A Romance of 'The Human Heart'." *Extrapolation* 20, no. 2 (summer 1979): 154-67.

[*In the following essay, Hennelly relates Wells's scientific writings to his* The Time Machine *and explores different aspects of the novella, particularly the roles of the Narrator and Time Traveller.*]

> I felt I lacked a clue. I felt—how shall I put it? Suppose you found an inscription, with sentences here and there in excellent plain English, and interpolated therewith, others made up of words, of letters even, absolutely unknown to you? Well, on the third day of my visit, that was how the world of Eight Hundred and Two Thousand Seven Hundred and One presented itself to me!
>
> (pp. 57-58)[1]

The reader of H. G. Wells's *The Time Machine* (1895) shares these insecurities with the Time Traveller since the full meaning of his "strange adventures" (p. 95),

and especially the enigmatic conclusion, remain "absolutely unknown" after the book is closed, that is, not wholly intelligible as allegories of either Huxlian devolution or Marxian dialectical materialism. Although both science and sociology inform the tale, Wells's own oxymoronic label for his favorite early genre explicitly identifies *The Time Machine* as a "scientific *romance,*" not scientific naturalism or realism. Consequently, the missing "clue" to the meaning of this "unknown" Romance world is not blatantly supplied by either the "excellent plain English" of the nameless Narrator or that of the Time Traveller himself.

In the preface to the Random House edition (1931) of *The Time Machine,* Wells describes his style in the "Chronic Argonauts," the first version of his Romance, as "the pseudo-Teutonic, Nathaniel Hawthorne style."[2] Later in *Experiment In Autobiography* (1934), he details more fully the genesis of the tale and Hawthorne's influence: "I began a romance, very much under the influence of Hawthorne, which was printed in the *Science Schools Journal,* the "Chronic Argonauts." . . . It was the original draft of what later became *The Time Machine,* which won me recognition as an imaginative writer."[3] But as Hawthorne's famous distinction between the Novel and the Romance in his "Preface" to *The House of the Seven Gables* implies, both of Wells's narrative interlocutors, especially the first Narrator, are concerned with "a very minute fidelity" to the "probable" and not the "possible." Both supply answers from the external, scientific, and "ordinary course of man's experience" although, admittedly, the nature of the experience they are attempting to explain is of the "Marvellous." Both fail to understand that often in the scientific Romance, the scientific is simply an externalization of, an extrapolation of, the psychological. In fact, in an 1897 interview, Wells refuses to accept that realism and the psychological Romance could ever be totally separate since "the scientific episode which I am treating insists upon interesting me, and so I have to write about the effect of it upon *the mind of some particular person.*"[4] Both speakers neglect, then, what Hawthorne calls "the truth of the human heart," that is, the balanced and unified psychological experience which must be interpolated from ambiguous, external clues. And as Wells himself admits in "Bye-Products in Evolution" (1895), "the logical student of evolution" is "invariably puzzle[d]" by aesthetics, but "with regard to the subtle mechanism of mind, we are even more in the dark than when we deal with chemical equilibrium."[5] Consequently, Hawthorne's later advice for understanding the dream-world of his story, "the topsy-turvey commonwealth of sleep," suggests the value of the same kind of reading for Wells's Romance, which is repeatedly called a dreamlike adventure: "Modern psychology, it may be, will endeavor to reduce these alleged necromanies [the nightmares of the Maules and Pyncheons] within a system instead of rejecting them as altogether fabulous"

(Chapt. 1). In "The Custom House" opening of *The Scarlet Letter*, Hawthorne defines the world of his Romances even more relevantly: "a neutral territory, somewhere between the real world and fairy-land, where the Actual and the Imaginary may meet, and each imbue itself with the nature of the other." The Time Traveller's perplexed imaginings upon return to the actual present suggest the same neutral territory:

> Did I ever make a Time Machine, or a model of a Time Machine? Or is it all only a dream? They say life is a dream, a precious poor dream at times—but I can't stand another that won't fit. It's madness. And where did the dream come from? . . . [*sic*] I must look at that machine. If there is one!
>
> (p. 96)

The consequences of exploring this neutral territory to search for the "truth of the human heart" in **The Time Machine** illuminate some of those "unknown" words and letters, which puzzle both the Time Traveller and the reader, and consequently demonstrate that attention to morality is as essential as attention to biology for the understanding of the Romance. Thus, this journey forward in time is actually a journey inward and downward in psychological space; the future macrocosm is the present introcosm. Although this thesis precludes a detailed examination of Wells's early essays on science, Robert Philmus and David Hughes's collection of these writings supports this critical *volte-face* by indicating that 1895 is the watershed year when "The view of nature's laws disposing of what man proposes gives way to the idea of 'artificial' evolution, man's consciously taking charge of his future by shaping his sociocultural environment, over which he can exert control" (**Early Writings**, p. x). At any rate, after taking a brief survey of previous readings, we will discuss Wells's psychologizing with respect to the Narrator, the frame story of the Dinner Guests, the three worlds of the future, and finally the Time Traveller himself.

The Time Machine has not received the critical coverage it deserves; but scholarly response has clearly isolated three major lines of inquiry—scientific, autobiographical, and mythic. Robert Philmus, for example, most cogently explains the anti-Darwinian and Marxian (or anti-Marxian?) issues by discussing the themes of survival of the unfittest or least human in the Eloi and Morlocks and by implying Wells's ambivalent attitude toward the leisure and proletariat classes. For Philmus, consequently, the novel (not Romance) becomes an oracle of devolution:

> This vision of social disintegration and devolution as a critique of the ideal of striving towards "ease and delight" can exist only in the dimension of prophecy, that dimension into which the critique can be projected and imaginatively given life—the world, in other words, of science fantasy.[6]

From a different critical vantage point, Alex Eisenstein traces the genesis of Wells's future shock to his past personal history while growing up at Atlas House where the topography approximated the split-levels of 802,701 and where his reading of Strum's *Reflections* and his viewing of the illustration of an ape from Wood's *Natural History* jointly spawned a fear of simian creatures like the Morlocks.[7] Finally, although Bernard Bergonzi also discovers scientific and socialistic allegories in the tale, he alone stresses its *Romance* genre while locating archetypal patterns:

> Since **The Time Machine** is a romance and not a piece of realistic fiction, it conveys its meaning in poetic fashion through images, rather than by the revelation of character in action. It is, in short, a myth. . . . The opposition of Eloi and Morlocks can be interpreted in terms of the late nineteenth-century class struggle, but it also reflects an opposition between aestheticism and utilitarianism, pastoralism and technology, contemplation and action, and ultimately, and least specifically, between beauty and ugliness, and light and darkness.[8]

Agreeing with Bergonzi's premise concerning genre, but strongly disagreeing with his dismissal of "character," we can now abandon sociology and biology for psychology and morality.

The primary Narrator in **The Time Machine** plays a far more significant role than that Eugene D. LeMire credits him with—namely, taking advantage of "the supreme moment of the raconteur . . . the moment of the long cigar and tall tale."[9] That is, he does not simply narrate the tale; but he is also a character in it, one whose point of view naturally colors his narration, whose sensibilities consequently transcend those of the caricatured and wooden Dinner Guests, and who finally serves as a go-between, or mediator between the personalities of the Guests and the Time Traveller and between the Time Traveller and the reader. In an important sense, then, the Narrator is a surrogate for the reader in the Romance; and though less well-drawn, he functions much like Marlowe in *Lord Jim*, or better still, lawyer Utterson in *Dr. Jekyll and Mr. Hyde*, a tale whose use of *Doppelgängers* is very similar to **The Time Machine**'s.

Thus, the Narrator's "inadequacy" parallels the Time Traveller's own avowed problems (pp. 94-95) in accurately and credibly describing "strange adventures":

> In writing it down I feel with only too much keenness the inadequacy of pen and ink—and, above all, my own inadequacy—to express its quality. You read, I will suppose, attentively enough; but you cannot see the speaker's white, sincere face in the bright circle of the little lamp, nor hear the intonation of his voice.
>
> (pp. 36-37)

At issue here, however, is not only the partial identification between Narrator and Time Traveller, but also the thematic emphasis upon empirical verification, or direct involvement with experience (rather than scienfitic or aesthetic detachment), and upon the reader's own active role in interpretively filling in many thematic spaces which the narrative leaves blank. While the Narrator, like Coleridge's Wedding-Guest, seems "better than" the other, more sceptical, shallow Dinner Guests because he "lay awake most of the night thinking about" the tale (p. 96), he does more than provide an example for sensitive reader response. Unlike Utterson, who vanishes from the last pages of Stevenson's Romance and thereby fails to register either a normative or ironic moral reaction to Jekyll-Hyde's disintegration, he finally editorializes significantly on the Time Traveller's concluding and pivotal disappearance. His commentary, though, *apparently* fails to accept the moral inferences of the Traveller's quest. Thus, the reader is tempted either to believe the Narrator's own ignorant yet guarded, optimistic prognosis for the future or to accept the Traveller's ambiguous account of the "unknown." In this latter case, suspecting the simplistic moral tag of the Narrator, as he likewise would in "The Rime of the Ancient Mariner," the reader himself must reinterpret the narrative "clues" for a specific psychological and moral message. The Narrator, at any rate, believes that

> the future is still black and blank—is a vast ignorance, lit at a few casual places by the memory of his story. And I have by me, for my comfort, two strange white flowers, gifts from Weena—shrivelled now, and brown and flat and brittle—to witness that even when mind and strength had gone, gratitude and mutual tenderness still lived on in the heart of man.
>
> (p. 98)

Recalling the Time Traveller's earlier caution to the "untravelled" or inexperienced listener of a tale and his anecdote regarding the futility of an African trying to understand an industrial city (pp. 56-57), the reader is certainly invited to side with the Traveller and to dismiss the Narrator as morally naive, a Pollyanna who is neither sadder nor wiser but rather blithefully ignorant of "the heart of man." However, the narrative problem is not so easily resolved and really cannot be simplified into the *either-or* logic argued above, just as the same narrative dislocation cannot be so easily solved in *The Island of Dr. Moreau* where, before his "cure," the Narrator finds "Beast People" alive and unwell in England, while afterward he perceives only "the shining souls of men." However, in *The Time Machine* both commentaries can be accommodated by correctly understanding the Romance-meaning of the Traveller's return journey. And after comparing present and future societies, we will attempt this understanding.

The narrative frame's dramatization of late Victorian society has escaped critical notice entirely, except for Philmus's brief allusion to Northrop Frye's discussion of "tales 'told in quotation marks,'"[10] LeMire's reference to the "peculiar abstract names of the characters" and the "ironic comment on the stupidities of class-conflict in Wells' own world,"[11] and finally Philmus and Hughes's recognition of "the unimaginative complacency . . . exemplified by his audience" and of the fact that somehow this audience's "narrow scope of consciousness is responsible for cosmic catastrophe" (*Early Writings,* p. 55). However, and again as in *Dr. Jekyll and Mr. Hyde,* this well-ordered wasteland of insecure, repressed, yet self-satisfied bachelors foreshadows the chaotic future with its schizophrenic upper and lower worlds. Thus, with the Narrator caught between, the microcosmic cross section of upper class gentility apparently contrasts with the hard-working discipline of the Time Traveller, much as the warm and leisurely setting of the smoking room contrasts with the cold (p. 96) and mechanical atmosphere of the scientific laboratory, and as finally the tropical, lotus world of the Eloi contrasts with the cooler, subterranean machine-shop of the Morlocks. In fact, as so often occurs in the allegorical Romance, the tale's very first paragraph provides a threshold symbol for this apparent Jekyll-Hyde polarity by pitting Eloi "laziness" against Morlock "earnestness":

> The fire burned brightly, and the soft radiance of the incandescent lights in the lilies of silver caught the bubbles that flashed and passed in our glasses. Our chairs, being his patents, embraced and caressed us rather than submitted to be sat upon, and there was that luxurious after-dinner atmosphere when thought runs gracefully free of the trammels of precision. And he put it [some recondite matter] to us in this way—marking the points with a lean forefinger—as we sat and lazily admired his earnestness over this new paradox (as we thought it) and his fecundity.
>
> (p. 25)

As in Stevenson's Romance, however, the real point here is not (or not *simply*) an acknowledgement of Victorian duality, both cultural and psychological, but rather as we shall see, a condemnation of such duality and a moral plea for recognizing the essential, paradoxical unity of a well-balanced and whole personality system. Time Traveller and Guests are One; the Hebraic Morlocks must lie down with the Hellenic Eloi to achieve psychological harmony. Put in another way, the Guests need first to realize they are Eloi (who are called a "wretched aristocracy in decay," p. 75) and then actualize the Morlock side of themselves; while the Time Traveller must realize that essentially he has been acting like a Morlock and then also accept his Eloi half. Specifically, what all the character groupings share is the common flaw of *misoneism*—an obsessive hatred and fear of novelty and temporal change. This taboo threat not only reappears throughout *The Time Machine,* but it is constantly enfleshed in the imagery and finally constitutes, of course, the tale's primary subject matter. As the Time Traveller learns, "There is no intelligence where there is no change and no need of change" (p. 87). Wells's scientific essays repeatedly emphasize this same point with regard to external adaptation or, to use Wells's term, "plasticity." In **"The Rate of Change in Species"** (1894), for instance, he predicts that in the event of "some far-reaching change effected in the conditions of life on this planet," large organisms like mankind "driving on the old course by virtue of the inertia of their too extensive lives, would have scarcely changed in the century, and, being no longer fitted to the conditions around them, would dwindle and—if no line of retreat offered itself—become extinct" (*Early Writings*, p. 130). The results of this "inertia" are personified in the hedonistic Eloi who exist in "indolent serenity" (p. 62) only for the present; they haven't learned from the mistakes of the past, nor do they, believing as they do in "absolute permanency" (p. 88), foresee a changeable future. The Morlocks, conversely, labor only for the future overthrow and domination of the Eloi. The indolent Guests serenely indulge in the immediate and present gratification of their pleasure principles—cigars and sherry forever. When the Time Traveller's narrative disturbs this reverie, they discount it, deem it a "gaudy lie" (p. 96), or compulsively check their watches (p. 95) in order to escape, ironically, from this tale of time and change back to the narcotics of their own smoking rooms or the peaceful sleep of their boudoirs.[12] To complete this pattern, though we anticipate ourselves, the Time Traveller, as his name suggests, has attempted to cheat "the inevitable process of decay" (p. 76) by his ivory-tower existence in the laboratory, and more specifically by his machine which is an unnatural attempt to control time, to escape the present. Thus, none of the characters realize, at least at the beginning of the Romance, that their misoneism has reduced them to "a very splendid array of fossils" (p. 76) like those decaying in the Palace of Green Porcelain.

This museum, or giant time-capsule, brings us to the first world of the future, the divided-self of the Eloi and Morlocks. Ostensibly, these "two species" appear to be separate and distinct, polarized races with antithetical, not complementary, cultures:

> The two species that had resulted from the evolution of man were sliding down towards, or had already arrived at an altogether new relationship from that of master-slave. The Eloi, like the Carlovingian kings, had decayed to a mere beautiful futility. They still possessed the earth on sufferance: since the Morlocks, subterranean for innumerable generations, had come at last to find the daylit surfaces intolerable. And the Morlocks made their garments, I inferred, and maintained them in their habitual needs, perhaps through the survival of an old habit of service (p. 70). . . . And so these inhuman sons of men—! I tried to look at the thing in a scientific spirit. After all, they were less human and more remote than our cannibal ancestors of three or four thousand years ago. And the intelligence that would

> have made this state of things a torment had gone. Why should I trouble myself? These Eloi were mere fatted cattle, which the ant-like Morlocks preserved and preyed upon—probably saw to the breeding of.

> (pp. 74-75)

I quote this description at length not only to indicate the seeming differences between the two races, but more importantly for the sake of comparing it with passages from Robert Lewis Stevenson and Carl Jung, which will be discussed shortly. The point is twofold. First of all, apparent differences cloak an essential unity—both peoples share the same pigmy size, the same whitish color, and the same curious laugh. Secondly, but most important, both share a symbiotic cosmology whose convex towers and concave wells form one balanced and total circle. In fact, while learning to identify with *both* Eloi *and* Morlocks, the Time Traveller discovers this architectural unity: "After a time, too, I came to connect these wells with tall towers standing here and there upon the slopes" (p. 56). Again, as a scientific footnote to the Romance theme, we should recall that in a 1904 essay, **"The Scepticism of the Instrument,"** Wells criticizes "formal logic" for being unable to cope with what he calls the concept of "complementarity," that is, for creating an apparent conflict where there exists essential unity (see *Early Writings*, pp. 6-7). And as Philmus and Hughes indicate, "As early as **'Zoological Retrogression'** (1891), he uses the term 'opposite idea' not as a synonym for 'antithesis' or 'negation,' but in the sense of 'essential complement'" (*Early Writings*, pp. 6-7). In addition, Wells's essays stressed more and more the importance of cooperation, rather than competition, among species. In **"Ancient Experiments in co-operation"** (1892), for example, he writes: "the cooperative union of individuals to form higher unities, underlies the whole living creation" (*Early Writings*, p. 191). In this same essay, cooperative unity seems to carry an internal as well as external significance.

> It is as startling and grotesque as it is scientifically true, that man is an aggregate of amoeboid individuals in a higher unity, and that such higher unities as may be reasonably likened to man . . . have united again into yet higher individual unities, and that, therefore, there is no impossibility in science that in the future men should not coalesce into similar unified aggregates.

> (*Early Writings*, p. 192)[13]

In **"Mr. Marshall's Doppelganger"** (1897) and again in the significantly titled *The Secret Places Of The Heart* (1922), Wells blatantly dramatizes this internal theme of the divided self. But, he also implies that the symbiotic macrocosm of the future is actually an image of the ruptured relationship between modes and levels of consciousness. The last chapter of Stevenson's Romance, "Henry Jekyll's Full Statement Of the Case," employs much the same rhetoric but makes the psychological nature of this relationship more clearly than Wells does:

> . . . man is not truly one, but truly two. . . . I learned to recognize the thorough and primitive duality of man; I saw that, of the two natures that contended in the field of my consciousness, even if I could rightly be said to be either, it was only because I was radically both. . . . It was the curse of mankind that these incongruous faggots were thus bound together—that in the agonized womb of consciousness, these polar twins should be continuously struggling. How, then, were they dissociated?[14]

The answer to this pivotal question, which is also central to the meaning of both the Beast People in *The Island of Dr. Moreau* and the Eloi-Morlock division in *The Time Machine,* is that society, epitomized here by high Victorian obsession with order, security, and intelligence and its repressive terror of chaos, impulse, and desire, has "dissociated" these "polar twins." In fact, in **"Morals and Civilization"** (1897), Wells links such repression to static inertia, or misoneism: "It is no inevitable force which changes militant into static civilizations. As much as anything it is the demoralisation due to security,—a disorganization of the forces of moral suggestion" (*Early Writings,* p. 226). And Jung's commentary on "visionary" literature in "Psychology And Literature" addresses this same compulsive "security" and the consequent "primitive duality of man" (which ought ideally to be a unity), thereby helping to explain why the Traveller "had a vague sense of something familiar" (p. 71) from what he "had seen in the Underworld" (p. 71):[15]

> But the primordial experiences rend from top to bottom the curtain upon which is painted the picture of an ordered world, and allow a glimpse into the unfathomable abyss of the unforn and of things yet to be. Is it a vision of other worlds, or of the darknesses of the spirit, or of the primal beginnings of the human psyche? . . . We are reminded of nothing in everyday life, but rather of dreams, night-time fears, and the dark uncanny recesses of the human mind. . . . However dark and unconscious this night-world may be, it is not wholly unfamiliar. Man has known it from time immemorial, and for primitives it is a self-evident part of their cosmos. It is only we who have repudiated it because of our fear of superstition and metaphysics, building up in its place an apparently safer and more manageable world of consciousness in which natural law operates like human law in a society. The poet now and then catches sight of the figures that people the night-world—spirits, demons, and gods; he feels the secret quickening of human fate by a suprahuman design, and has a presentiment of incomprehensible happenings in the pleroma. In short, he catches a glimpse of the psychic world that terrifies the primitive and is at the same time his greatest hope.[16]

Comparing this account with Wells's own tell-tale description of the origin of his Romances, we can certainly see its significance:

> I found that, taking almost anything as a starting point and letting my thoughts play about with it, there would presently come out of the darkness, in a manner quite inexplicable, some absurd or vivid little nucleus. Little men in canoes upon sunlit oceans would come floating out of nothingness, incubating the eggs of prehistoric monsters unawares; violent conflicts would break out amidst the flower beds of suburban gardens. I would discover I was peering into remote and mysterious worlds ruled by an order, logical indeed, but other than our common sanity.[17]

However, by revealing the general danger of *repudiating* darkness for light and the *greatest hope* in reconciling the two in Wells's "mysterious worlds," cited above, Jung's insights only diagnose a portion of the disease of the human heart. The Palace of Green Porcelain and the White Sphinx provide clues to the rest of the mystery. Both symbols deal with time, change, and misoneism. The Palace, "this ancient monument of an intellectual age" (p. 77), is complex. Its fossilized treasures not only warn against the vanity of human wishes and the "futility of all ambition" (p. 79), such as the Time Traveller's and the Morlocks' emphases on future glory, but it also admonishes hedonists like the Dinner Guests and Eloi who live only for the present and thus court no great expectations. Neither response can arrest "the inevitable process of decay" (p. 76); and both sins of wasting time render the sinners into "dessicated mummies in jars" (p. 77), like the "stuffed animals" who are wasted by time in the museum.

The White Sphinx, on the other hand, parallels the temporal dimensions of the Time Machine and the Palace by placing the blighted worlds of the future, and thus the world of the present, in their proper wasteland context as it overlooks "a tangled waste of beautiful bushes and flowers, a long-neglected and yet weedless garden" (p. 44). Although, in a sense, the Time Traveller finally fulfills the redemptive function of Oedipus, the riddle of this Sphinx has not yet been solved by a questing hero; and thus the sought-for answer, which admits change and time in the three ages of man, has not provided renewing, spring rains. The Sphinx's "white leprous face" (p. 51), "weather-worn" condition, and "unpleasant suggestion of disease" (p. 40), all indicate that wasteland sterility has infected even this major symbol of potential health. Finally, the Sphinx, like the "griffins' heads" (p. 47) and the "Faun" (p. 72), implies the unification of a dual nature; and consequently these three sole survivors of past art are all imaginative reminders of the Romance's psychological theme. As Wells indicates in **"Human Evolution, An Artificial Process,"** published the year following *The Time Machine* and vital to its understanding, civilized man is a compound of "an inherited factor, the natural man, . . . the culminating ape" and "an acquired factor, the artificial man, the highly plastic creature of tradition, suggestion, and reasoned thought" (**Early Writings**, p. 217). Such a compound certainly suggests the symbiotic Morlocks and Eloi, as do the following remarks whose moral psychologizing is as true of **The Time Machine** as of **The Island of Dr. Moreau**: "in this view, what we call Morality becomes the padding of suggested emotional habits necessary to keep the round Palaeolithic savage in the square hole of the civilised state. And Sin is the conflict of the two factors—as I have tried to convey in my **Island of Dr. Moreau**" (p. 217). Wells concludes the essay by hoping that men "have the greatness of heart" to create "a social organization . . . cunningly balanced" (p. 218) between savagery and civilization (p. 218).

However, the subsequent future worlds, of the giant butterflies and crabs and finally of the great "Silence," are dramatic condemnations of the wasteland's denial of the "truth of the human heart" and thus seem to refute Wells's dream of balance. The wish-fulfillment of misoneism has already cursed the earth in the next world since stellar motion is "growing slower and slower" (p. 90) and the sun has "halted motionless upon the horizon" (p. 90). Now the changeless wasteland no longer betrays even a semblance of the Eloi's Eden. The "eternal sea" (p. 91) and "perpetual twilight" (p. 90) reflect "the sense of abominable desolation that hung over the world" (p. 91). Finally, the "huge white butterfly" and "monster crab" (p. 91) are the only survivors of psychological devolution; they are the end-products of, and commentaries upon, the anemic Eloi and blood-thirsty Morlocks. Remembering Stein's classification of humanity into butterflies and beetles in *Lord Jim,* we might reinterpret his metaphor to suggest that caterpillars (crabs) and butterflies are, in essence, the same creature; and it is for this reason that the Greeks were so fond of viewing the butterfly as an emblem of the total psyche. Again, dualistic appearances cloak an inner, unified reality. A "thousand years or more" later (p. 92), the "eternal sunset" (p. 92) is replaced by the Silence, or "black central shadow of the eclipse" (p. 93); and this *Gotterdämmerung* leaves the world in "rayless obscurity" (p. 93), totally without solar change. In a startling and haunting last image, which recalls the false dichotomy between spectators and participants in the previous worlds and starkly joins the human and subhuman, the Traveller describes the final mutant form of life as the hybrid of a soccerball (British football) and octopus: "It was a round thing, the size of a football perhaps, or, it may be, bigger, and tentacles trailed down from it . . . it was hopping fitfully about" (p. 93). This, then, is the end-result of fear of change and fear of unifying the contraries of the human heart.

The previous discussions of the Narrator, the Dinner Guests, and the future worlds, however, make most sense when viewed in the light of the Time Traveller's "growing knowledge" (p. 81). This repeated *gnostic* theme, which is rooted in the Romance, branches out into several different but related genres—the *Bildungsroman,* the myth of the hero, and, as I have argued elsewhere,[18] the Victorian novel which focuses upon some major crisis in epistemology. Most generally, the Time Traveller's reiterated "pale" but also "animated" (see pp. 25 and 36) personality suggests that he, and by extension his wasted culture, is caught between two worlds: one, of pleasure, is externalized in feeble aristocracy like the Eloi and is all but dead; the other, of labor and thought (see p. 88 for Morlock thought), is personified by the Morlocks and is powerless to be born without the correct kind of ideological conception. Like the mythic questers of old and like each individual personality, the Time Traveller can insure this conception by "boldly penetrating . . . underground mysteries" (p. 65), that is, by harrowing hell, reconciling spirit and sense, discovering the hidden truth of the human heart, and living fully in the present.

Specifically, as indicated before, the Time Traveller must admit the Morlock side of himself and integrate this with his more deeply suppressed Eloi side. However, at the tale's outset in London, he is blithefully ignorant of both halves of his heart; and so once in the future, he immediately feels "naked in a strange world" (p. 41). This stripping away of his old personality masks prepares him for his inevitable identity crisis—"my mind was already in revolution" (p. 62) he admits in 802,701. The Time Traveller verbalizes it on the scientific level as "Man had not remained one species, but had differentiated into two distinct animals" (p. 61). After feeling initial disgust for the Morlocks (machinists and meat-eaters like himself) and condescension toward the Eloi (whose enervated spontaneity still highlights his own emotional sterility), the Traveller identifies with both in order to reintegrate these now "distinct animals." Having first struck "in a frenzy of fear" (p. 85) at the Morlocks during the forest fire, he significantly empathizes with their plight: "I was assured of their absolute helplessness and misery in the glare, and I struck no more of them" (p. 85). Previously, in the Palace of Green Porcelain, he had recognized his own "certain weakness for mechanism" (p. 77) and then therapeutically and thematically "felt that *I was wasting my time* in this academic examination of machinery" (p. 78, italics mine). This newly-discovered "knowledge" is put into practice when the Time Traveller, who in previous drafts is called The Philosopher, spontaneously "turned to Weena. 'Dance,' I cried to her in her own tongue" (p. 79). Thus Morlock and Eloi are joined; and, unlike Dr. Moreau's Beast People, their extremes are tempered. Earlier in his quest for the truth of the human heart, the Traveller feels that "my growing knowledge would lead me back" to solve "the mystery of the bronze doors under the sphinx" (p. 55), or, implicitly, the mysterious unity of the future world. And even here he anticipates the redeeming solution to the Sphinx's riddle, which would best prepare him and his culture to accept "the wear of time" (p. 79): "To sit among all those unknown things [the mysteries of the Sphinx] before a puzzle like that is hopeless. That way lies monomania. Face this world. Learn its ways, watch it, be careful of too many hasty guesses at its meaning. In the end you will find clues to it all" (p. 55). Thus like any good scientist, but also like any good Romancifier, the Traveller learns in the new world by employing the "experimental method," constantly testing hypotheses against experience, both external and internal.

In **"Human Evolution, An Artificial Process,"** Wells predicts that only in "Education lies the possible salvation of mankind from misery and sin" (***Early Writings,*** p. 219). And through his Romance, the Time Traveller certainly tries to dramatize to the Narrator, the Dinner Guests, and, by extension, the Victorian audience at large what Wells means by "Education," that is, that desired balance between savagery and civilization, between past and present. But what of the Victorian wasteland? Does the Time Traveller *educate* and thereby redeem it; or does he reject it? Put another way, is his final role that of a savior, as when he saves Weena from drowning; or is his final role that of a destroyer, as when the forest fires he lights burns her to death? These questions are as complex, but as thematically significant, as the riddle of the Sphinx since the meaning of his enigmatic return journey back to the future depends upon our answers. If the future is taken realistically, as it would be in a scientific *novel,* then the Traveller's withdrawal from the present merely confirms his sins against time and his escapist obsession with the future. This reading, then, effectively negates the success of his first wonderful visit into the future. If, on the other hand, the future is considered as an allegory of the present, as it should be in the psychological Romance, then the Time Traveller's return journey does not indicate the hero's escape from his destiny but rather suggests a simple redirection of his quest.[19] The Dinner Guests believe the Time Traveller to be either delirious or duplistic, and thus his new-found "knowledge" has not yet saved them. He consequently returns with trusty "kodak" (p. 97) in hand to gather empirical proof for these doubting Thomases. But as the Narrator reports, "he has never returned" (p. 98). Has he failed and been killed by the Morlocks, whom by now he should certainly *know* how to handle? Has he escaped to settle down with the pretty Eloi, perhaps even returning prior to the death of Weena to save her again, before the fact, by committing another sin against time? There is obviously no textual evidence for this reading. Is the future merely a *possible* future, a potential schizophrenia which will only be realized if the current wasteland

mentality is not cured; and thus the Time Traveller, attempting to verify this ominous portent to the Guests, is destroyed by his own dualism? Or, following the conditions of the Romance, which the Narrator fails to understand, has he simply returned to the allegorical present to save both the Eloi and the Morlocks and thereby redeem the realistic present of Victorian England?

The Traveller's symbolic identification with Prometheus throughout the tale supports this last hypothesis and thus sustains the Narrator's belief that "gratitude and a mutual tenderness still lived on in the heart of man." As the Traveller explains during the unrelieved darkness of the Eloi's night: "In this decadence, too, the art of fire-making had been forgotten on the earth" (p. 82); and then he begins to educate Weena about the magic of matches. Thus on the realistic level, he brings the gift of fire to the future as Prometheus had brought it from the gods to the human world; on the psychological, or Romance level, he brings back "foreknowledge" (the Greek meaning of *Prometheus*) from the Eloi (*Lord* or *God* in the Bible) and Morlocks to the Dinner Guests in the *educating* form of his Romance. Whether his return journey is intended to help the future or bring help from the future, the meaning is the same; and the Narrator's optimism is implicitly upheld. For the Time Traveller at least, time is no longer out of joint; and his Romance-quest has revealed the unified and balanced truth of the human heart.

In conclusion, as R. H. Hutton's review in the *Spectator* (July 13, 1895) implies, it is indeed a pity that Wells's own Victorian audience, like the Dinner Guests, did not as yet understand this truth and remained wasteland unbelievers:

> We have no doubt that, so far as Mr. Wells goes, his warning is wise. But we have little fear that the languid, ease-loving, and serene temperament will ever paralyse the human race after the manner he supposes, even though there may be at present some temporary signs of the growth of the appetite for mere amusement.[20]

Notes

1. *The Time Machine/The War of the Worlds,* with an introduction by Isaac Asimov (Greenwich, Connecticut: Fawcett Publications, Inc., 1968); all quotations will be taken from this edition, which is one of the more generally available, and noted within the text.

2. (New York: Random House, 1931), p. ix.

3. (London: Victor Gollancz and The Cresset Press, 1934), I, 309.

4. *To-day,* 2 (Sept., 1897), as quoted in Bernard Bergonzi's *The Early H. G. Wells: A Study Of The Scientific Romances* (Manchester: The University

Press, 1961), p. 44, italics mine. The interested reader should consult this book-length study of the genre of the scientific romance, especially Chapter 2 which deals with *The Time Machine*.

5. *Early Writings In Science And Science Fiction By H. G. Wells*, eds. Robert Philmus and David Y. Hughes (Berkeley and Los Angeles: Univ. of California Press, 1975), pp. 204-05. This collection will subsequently be noted within the text as *Early Writings*.

6. "'*The Time Machine*'; or, the Fourth Dimension as Prophecy," *PMLA*, 84 (1969), 534.

7. "Very Early Wells: Origins of Some Physical Motifs in *The Time Machine* and *The War Of The Worlds*," *Extrapolation*, 13 (1972), 119-126 *passim*.

8. "*The Time Machine*: An Ironic Myth," *Critical Quarterly* 2 (1960), 305; this essay later makes up part of Bergonzi's chapter on *The Time Machine* in his study of the scientific romances. See note 4.

9. "H. G. Wells And The World Of Science Fiction," *Univ. of Windsor Review*, 2 (1967), 60.

10. Philmus, 535; the reference is to *Anatomy of Criticism*, (Princeton: Princeton Univ. Press, 1957), pp. 202-203.

11. LeMire, 61-62.

12. Discussing the tale as a scientific treatise, Alfred Borrello confirms Wells's condemnation of misoneistic tendencies: "The species, he believed, is cursed with a fundamental yearning for the *status quo*, for a changeless existence in which life proceeds at the same pointless pace as it always proceeded—witness its desire for a never-ending Heaven," in *H. G. Wells: Author in Agony* (Carbondale and Edwardsville: Southern Illinois Univ. Press, 1972), p. 13.

13. See Borrello's discussion of the lack of cultural "individuality" in the Morlocks and Eloi, pp. 11-12.

14. It is interesting to note here that Wells's Victorian audience saw no relationship between his Romance and Stevenson's—even though it could not help linking the two tales. For example an unsigned review in the *Daily Chronicle* (July 27, 1895) reads: "No two books could well be more unlike than *The Time Machine* and *The Strange Case of Dr. Jekyll and Mr. Hyde*, but since the appearance of Stevenson's creepy romance we have had nothing in the domain of pure fantasy so bizarre as this 'invention' by Mr. H. G. Wells." This review is reprinted in *H. G. Wells: The Critical Heritage*, ed. Patrick Parrinder (London and Boston: Routledge and Kegan Paul, 1972), p. 38.

15. Here the specific reference is to the resemblance between the meat in the Underworld and the bodies of the Eloi.

16. Reprinted in *The Spirit in Man, Art, and Literature*, trans. R. F. C. Hull (Princeton: Princeton Univ. Press, 1971), pp. 90-91, 95-96. For the sake of unity, I have combined excerpts from a series of paragraphs dealing with "visionary" literature.

17. Quoted in Kenneth Young's *H. G. Wells* (Essex: Longman Group Ltd., 1974), pp. 13-14.

18. "*Dracula*: The Gnostic Quest and Victorian Wasteland," *English Literature in Transition*, 20 (1977), 13-26. This essay also clarifies the relationships between gnosticism, the wasteland theme, and Victorian literature.

19. See Philmus' relevant description of the future as a fourth dimension, fantasy world, 534-535.

20. Reprinted in *H. G. Wells: The Critical Heritage*, p. 36.

Frank Scafella (essay date November 1981)

SOURCE: Scafella, Frank. "The White Sphinx and *The Time Machine*." *Science Fiction Studies* 8, no. 3 (November 1981): 255-65.

[*In the following essay, Scafella detects certain parallels between* The Time Machine *and the fable of Oedipus and the Sphinx.*]

> The fable [of the Sphinx] is an elegant and a wise one, invented apparently in allusion to Science; especially in its application to practical life . . . Sphinx proposes to men a variety of hard questions and riddles which she received from the Muses . . . when they pass from the Muses to Sphinx, that is from contemplation to practice, . . . they begin to be painful and cruel; and unless they be solved and disposed of, they strangely torment and worry the mind, pulling it first this way and then that, and fairly tearing it to pieces.
>
> —Francis Bacon, "Sphinx; or, Science" from *The Wisdom of the Ancients*

1. Soon after crash landing his Time Machine in the land of the Morlocks and the Eloi, H. G. Wells's Time Traveller stands up to look around him. What should he see immediately before him but a gigantic Sphinx, "a colossal figure, carved apparently in some white stone [while] all else of the world was invisible."

> It was very large, for a silver birch-tree touched its shoulder. It was of white marble, in shape something like a winged sphinx, but the wings, instead of being carried vertically at the sides, were spread so that it seemed to hover. The pedestal, it appeared to me, was of bronze, and was thick with verdigris. It chanced that

the face was towards me; the sightless eyes seemed to watch me; there was the faint shadow of a smile on the lips. It was greatly weather-worn, and that imparted an unpleasant suggestion of disease.[1]

A diseased sphinx, as white as Melville's whale, blind, with wings outspread in mock flight and on its face the grin of the fabled Cheshire Cat stands in the Time Traveller's way and holds him in fascination. It is only by an act of sheer will that "at last I tore my eyes from it for a moment, and saw . . . that the sky was lightening with the promise of the sun" (3:18).

We do not know what prompted Wells to imagine his Time Traveller face to face with the Sphinx at the very opening of his narrative, but that he did so is significant. For one thing, it means that *The Time Machine* must be read as a variation of Oedipus's encounter with the Sphinx on the road to Thebes. For another, the Sphinx, according to Bacon, is a symbol of Science.[2] For still another, the White Sphinx is alluded to or figures directly in the action on 15 of the 70-odd pages of the narrative. Moreover, in the presence of the White Sphinx the Time Traveller experiences a variety of psychic states which range from the awe of his initial awareness through dread and despair to a resolve to hold himself in check by the exercise of reason. This sequence of emotions charts a transformation in the mind of the Time Traveller from an essentially contemplative to an intensely practical mode of response to the world. It would be too much to suggest, by way of Bacon, that *The Time Machine* is thus an allegorical rendering of the fable of Oedipus and the Sphinx. Nevertheless, certain parallels between that fable and the Time Traveller's adventures are direct and highly suggestive of the emergence, establishment, and predicament of the scientist in the modern world—especially when one examines the Time Traveller's experience in the world of 802,701 in light of Bacon's interpretation of the fable as an allegory of the nature of knowledge as it is employed in contemplation and in practice. By playing Bacon off against Wells and Wells against Bacon, we can augment our appreciation of *The Time Machine* as a scientific romance.

2. The Time Traveller's initial awareness of the White Sphinx coincides with the shattering of his presupposition of finding "incredible advancement in knowledge" and a "profoundly grave and intellectual posterity" in the future to which his Time Machine transports him. Far from grave and intellectual, however, the first beings to greet him, the Eloi, appear effeminate and childlike. "A flow of disappointment rushed across my mind," he says. And there, towering above him, is the "Sphinx of white marble, which had seemed to watch me all the while with a smile at my astonishment" (4:21). As in the ancient fable of Oedipus and the Sphinx, so here: the appearance of the Sphinx coincides

with the posing of a hard question or riddle. And from that moment onward, there is no help for the Traveller but to answer the riddle correctly or be devoured.

"Now of the Sphinx's riddles there are in all two kinds," says Bacon; "one concerning the nature of things, another concerning the nature of man" (p. 419). So far as the nature of things is concerned, the world of 802,701 poses no riddles for the Time Traveller. "The whole earth had become a garden" (4:25), he knows, through the organized effort of mankind to subjugate Nature, to "readjust the balance of animal and vegetable life to suit our human needs". He is witness to the completion of this readjustment "for all Time"—no insects, no weeds, no fungi, no disease, no toil, no commerce, luscious fruits and flowers, a "social paradise" (4:26). But so far as the nature of man is concerned, there is indeed a riddle to be solved. For in this "garden" world of the future the Time Traveller has "happened upon humanity upon the wane." How does he explain this paradox? Through what process of readjustment has man come to the state of the Eloi? Why is it that the subjugation of Nature to human needs has led to atrophy of knowledge and intellect? At first the answer to these questions seems simple enough to the Time Traveller. He is at leisure when he first answers the riddle of the nature of man, seated on top of a hill on a bench of griffins' heads (a mythical monster closely associated with the Sphinx), looking out upon "as sweet and fair a view as I have ever seen" (4:25). At this moment the riddle does not trouble the Time Traveller deeply for, as Bacon observes, "so long as the object of meditation and inquiry is merely to know, the understanding is not oppressed or straitened by it, but is free to wander and expatiate, and finds in the very uncertainty of conclusion and variety of choice a certain pleasure and delight" (p. 419). With the sweet and fair view of the world around and no restrictions on the time he might take to contemplate that world and the creatures who inhabit it, the Time Traveller moves with ease to the following conclusion about the nature of man as he has found him in the Eloi. "Humanity had been strong, energetic, and intelligent, and had used all its abundant vitality to alter the conditions under which it lived. And now came the reaction of the altered conditions." Whereas the pain and necessity of readjustment forced man to exercise intelligence, self-restraint, patience, and decision to channel his "restless energy" of mind in constructive enterprises, under the conditions of perfect comfort and security that energy "takes to art and eroticism," and then comes "langour and decay." Thus "the exquisite beauty of the buildings I saw was the outcome of the last surgings of the now purposeless energy of mankind before it settled down into perfect harmony with the conditions under which it lived" (4:27).

Everything is fine with the Time Traveller, then, so long as he is free merely to contemplate the nature of the

Eloi. Indeed, he takes pleasure in dallying since there is no pragmatic reason for pressing on to certainty about his hypothesis. In this mood of quiet contemplation, "musing over this too perfect triumph of man" (5:28), the sun sets and the Time Traveller's casual gaze begins to search out familiar objects as he determines to descend the hill to sleep. "I looked for the building I knew," he says. "Then my eye travelled along to the figure of the White Sphinx upon the pedestal of bronze, growing distinct as the light of the rising moon grew brighter. I could see the silver birch against it. There was the tangle of rhododendron bushes, black in the pale light, and there was the little lawn" on which the Time Machine had landed. Then "I looked at the lawn again," he says, and suddenly the mood of contemplation is shattered. "A queer doubt chilled my complacency," he confesses, for "the Time Machine was gone!" (5:28). In this instant the question or riddle of the Eloi, like the hard questions posed to ancient travellers by the Sphinx, suddenly passes "from contemplation to practice, whereby there is necessity for present action, choice and decision," and here the riddle begins to be "painful and cruel." For unless such questions are "solved and disposed of," says Bacon, "they strangely torment and worry the mind, pulling it first this way and then that, and fairly tearing it to pieces" ("Sphinx," p. 419).

The discovery of his loss of the Time Machine throws the Time Traveller into emotional turmoil. "At once, like a lash across the face, came the possibility of losing my own age, of being left helpless in this strange new world" (5:28). The time of contemplation is now past; the occasion for practical action, choice, and decision is at hand, and if he does not act quickly the Traveller is lost forever. For if the wretched captives of Sphinx could not at once solve and interpret the dark and perplexed riddles that she propounded to them, says Bacon, "as they stood hesitating and confused she cruelly tore them to pieces" (p. 418). The bare thought of the loss of his Time Machine grips the Time Traveller at the throat and stops his breathing. He plunges down the hill and into the rhododendron bushes in a passion of fear, in excessive dread, cursing aloud, feeling faint and cold, and running about furiously. He is possessed of blind anger, frenzy, anguish of mind, horrible fatigue, and despair. He beats the bushes with clenched fists, sobbing and bawling like an angry child, blundering about, screaming and crying upon God, maddened. And all the while "above me towered the Sphinx, upon the bronze pedestal, white, shining, leprous, in the light of the rising moon. It seemed to smile in mockery of my dismay." For what causes dismay is "the sense of some hitherto unsuspected power, through whose intervention my invention had vanished." At length he falls to the ground at the pedestal of the White Sphinx and lies "weeping with absolute wretchedness . . . I had exhausted my emotion" (5:30). Thus the Time Travel-

ler, taken unawares, finds himself in a paradigmatic human situation symbolized in the Oedipus myth: either exercise reason to gain control over paralyzing fear, or be devoured by the Sphinx.

3. If the Time Traveller is unaware of the paradigmatic nature of his predicament, Wells was not. As we have seen, the Time Traveller's initial encounter with the Sphinx results in his experience of a sequence of emotion and thought at once typical of the Oedipus narrative and representative of the transition that takes place in the human mind as it shifts from an artistic or purely philosophical to a scientific grasp of the world. Having been drained emotionally, and having been placed beyond confidence in his first hypothesis about the Eloi by his "sense of some hitherto unsuspected power," the Time Traveller finds himself on just such a verge of consciousness as Wells speaks of (autobiographically) in **"The Rediscovery of the Unique"** (1891). His set views of the world of 802,701 have been "decimated . . . as a pestilence thins a city"; his theory of life among the Eloi has received "such a twist as tall towers sometimes get from lively yet conservative earthquakes"; and his new relationship to the world is perhaps best characterized by the final paragraph of the essay.

> Science is a match that man has just got alight. He thought he was in a room—in moments of devotion, a temple—and that his light would be reflected from and display walls inscribed with wonderful secrets and pillars carved with philosophical systems wrought into harmony. It is a curious sensation, now that the preliminary splutter is over and the flame burns up clear, to see his hands lit and just a glimpse of himself and the patch he stands on visible, and around him, in place of all that human comfort and beauty he anticipated—darkness still.[3]

Not only does the Time Traveller thus come to see his immediate situation clearly but he begins to reason with himself "to be calm and patient, to learn the way of the people, to get a clear idea of the method of my loss, and the means of getting materials and tools" to make another machine if he cannot recover the original one. He begins to probe the world around for answers, as the true scientist must.

It does not take him long to determine that the method of his loss is a secret of the bronze doors in the pedestal under the White Sphinx. Nor does it take him long to see that no amount of force will cause these doors to open. The Sphinx divulges its secrets to no man by force or cunning. "Patience," says the Time Traveller to himself.

> If you want your machine again you must leave that Sphinx alone . . . You will get it back as soon as you can ask for it . . . Face this world. Learn its ways, watch it, be careful of too hasty guesses at its meaning. In the end you will find clues to it all.

(5:32)

Implicit in the Time Traveller's resolve to "leave that Sphinx alone" is his recognition that the Sphinx will not, in and of itself, afford him access to what is unique about the nature of man in 802,701. Access to that uniqueness will come, he concludes, only as a result of mastering the problems of the world. So "I determined to put the thought of my Time Machine and the mystery of the bronze doors under the sphinx as much as possible in a corner of memory, until my growing knowledge would lead me back to them in a natural way" (5:32). His discovery of the Morlocks, "the bleached, obscene, nocturnal Thing" that lives in the deep darkness of wells, is his first major clue to an understanding of his loss and the method of recovering his machine. For even though his discovery of the Morlocks raises as many questions as it answers ("What, I wondered, was this Lemur doing in my scheme of a perfectly balanced organization? How was it related to the indolent serenity of the beautiful Upper-worlders? And what was hidden down there, at the foot of that shaft?"), "my mind was already in revolution; my guesses and impressions were slipping and sliding to a new adjustment. I had now a clue to the import of these wells . . . [and] to the mystery of the ghosts; to say nothing of a hint at the meaning of the bronze gates and the fate of the Time Machine" (5:39). Unlike the scientist who might seek to keep his original suspicion of a perfectly balanced organization intact by experimental verification, the Time Traveller lets his original theory go as he begins to make his investigation into the nature of the Morlocks more searching and minute. His acquisition of knowledge about the Morlocks and the Eloi thus presents us with a paradigm of the true scientist's approach to the world.

From the point of view of the reader, at least two additional observations should be made about the Time Traveller's decision to leave the Sphinx alone in his attempt to recover his Time Machine. First, the White Sphinx is not a monster with volition of its own (as is the Sphinx that blocks Oedipus's way); it is a statue, a symbol, a work of art. Neither the Time Traveller nor the narrator follows out the implications of this fact, but the Traveller is obviously aware that the White Sphinx manifests certain sharp variations from the classical Sphinx with which he is familiar: "the wings, instead of being carried vertically at the sides, were spread so that it seemed to hover," and so on. Moreover, the Traveller fails to make explicit a connection between the White Sphinx and the Morlocks that the sightless eyes and diseased aspect invite. Mention of the Morlock as a "bleached, obscene, nocturnal Thing" should leave little doubt in the reader's mind that the White Sphinx is an outward and visible sign of the inward and spiritual condition to which man as Morlock has fallen.[4] Furthermore, it would seem that the reader is justified in pointing out that the White Sphinx thus brings with it into Wells's romance the most ancient of its associations,

those with the conditions of disorder or chaos. In the *Enuma elish,* a creation myth dating from the beginning of the second millennium before our era, the Sphinx is a monster born of Tiamat, the primordial mother and embodiment of the disorder that preceded the creation of the world. For "when Marduk had been created ('A God was engendered, most able and wisest of gods'), Tiamat, inflamed with rage, gave birth to monsters— viper, dragon, sphinx, great lion, mad dog, scorpion-man."[5] Living under the oppression of the great order that exists among the Eloi, the Morlocks give birth to the White Sphinx, symbol of the great disorder that reigns among men in the Under-world. Thus the problem that the Traveller faces in the White Sphinx is to determine just what the nature of the disorder is that the statue projects, and the Sphinx itself will not give him the solution to that problem.

Second, the Sphinx is a symbol of science.

> Science, being the wonder of the ignorant and unskillful, may not be absurdly called a monster [says Bacon]. In figure and aspect it is represented as many-shaped, in allusion to the immense variety of matter with which it deals. It is said to have the face and voice of a woman, in respect to its beauty and facility of utterance. Wings are added because the sciences and the discoveries of science spread and fly abroad in an instant; the communication of knowledge being like that of one candle with another, which lights up at once. Claws, sharp and hooked, are ascribed to it with great elegance, because the axioms and arguments of science penetrate and hold fast the mind, so that it has no means of evasion or escape.
>
> (p. 419)

If so (and I wager that Wells intended it this way), *The Time Machine* presents us with a paradox so far as science itself is concerned. Here we find science diseased primarily because of the uses to which Man has put it. Symbolized in the White Sphinx, science (in the long view) is to become a mockery of its true nature: in place of a sober countenance, the Traveller finds a sly and condescending grin; the swift communication of knowledge from man to man, and from generation to generation, ceases even as Sphinx spreads her wings to show all the world that she can fly; and "that ghastly whiteness it is which imparts such an abhorrent mildness, even more loathsome than terrific, to the dumb gloating of [its] aspect." These words from *Moby-Dick* are appropriate since what the Time Traveller beholds in the White Sphinx Ishmael beholds in the white whale:

> the one visible quality in the aspect of the dead which most appals the gazer, . . . the marble pallor lingering there; as if indeed that pallor were as much the badge of consternation in the other world, as of mortal trepidation here. . . . Nor even in our superstitions do we fail to throw the same snowy mantle round our phantoms; all ghosts rising in the milk-white fog—Yea,

while these terrors seize us, let us add, that even the king of terrors, when personified by the evangelist, rides on his pallid horse.[6]

One side of the paradox, then, has science as a shroud, dormant, corpse-like, a phantom of her true self. On the other side, however, it is only by way of science, the patient acquisition of knowledge through study of the natural world, that the Time Traveller can regain his own age and circumvent the fate prophesied for him and for all mankind in this phantom of his vision. It is by the very gifts of science—the match and the Time Machine in particular—that the Traveller not only regains his own time, but lives to tell his tale so that those with eyes to see and ears to hear may avoid the fate that was almost his.

4. If the Time Traveller's response to his predicament is representative of the scientific method of achieving discernment and knowledge, we have in *The Time Machine* a model of Wells's own deepest hopes for and misgivings about the nature and role of science in the modern world. If so, we cannot regard Wells's attitude in 1895 as unequivocally pessimistic. It may be that the evidence before us leaves us no alternative but to conclude that Wells was less pessimistic about science itself than he was about the use to which scientists were putting it. Certainly the Time Traveller's actions manifest what Alfred North Whitehead calls the genius of science, namely "the instinctive faith that there is an Order of Nature which can be traced in every detained occurrence."[7] The true scientist, that is, approaches the world in confidence that, in the words of Robert Andrew Millikan,

> the universe is rationally intelligible, no matter how far from a complete comprehension of it we may now be, or indeed may ever come to be. [Science] believes in the absolute uniformity of nature. It views the world as a mechanism, every part and every movement of which fits in some definite, invariable way into the other parts and the other movements; and it sets itself the inspiring task of studying every phenomenon in the confident hope that the connections between it and the other phenomena can ultimately be found.[8]

The emphasis on instinctive faith, Order, Nature, rational intelligibility, and what Whitehead calls "a vehement and passionate interest in the relation of general principles to irreducible and stubborn facts" Wells's Time Traveller manifests in his actions. His attitude (to borrow an apt figure from Steven Marcus), expresses

> the faith which our culture has inherited that there is nothing that cannot be rationally understood and thus taught and learned . . . Our culture is probably incorrigible in this virtually dogmatic innocence, and indeed it is difficult to imagine our own existence if we try to subtract from it the conviction that it is really highly preferable to live in the light we continue to generate rather than in the darkness we have cast out and replaced.[9]

From the perspective of Wells's Time Traveller, the vantage point of one who holds the match of science in his hand and is permitted to see, not the ultimate order and original form of the universe itself but merely "his hands lit and just a glimpse of himself and the patch he stands on visible," certainty about the ultimate order of things may never be his to hold. But his patient and steady investigations into the natural order of things move him inevitably in that direction. What he must avoid is the rational manipulation of nature through experimental verification to prove the theories he holds about the ultimate order of the world of 802,701; and he must also forego the temptation to employ his knowledge of that world to mold nature to fit his own human needs. Perhaps it was because he saw science moving in the direction of serving human needs primarily that Wells became pessimistic, not about science itself but about the uses to which scientists put it.

In Wells's thinking about science (so far, at least, as *The Time Machine* and **"The Rediscovery of the Unique"** are concerned), emphasis falls not on mind, reason, order, principle, or rational intelligibility but on method, technique, technology. It is with micrometer, microscope, polarizer, and microchemical tests that the natural scientist perceives the uniqueness of otherwise apparently identical crystals of a precipitate. The Time Machine and matches serve something of the same function for the Time Traveller. "When I started with the Time Machine," says the Traveller,

> I had started with the absurd assumption that the men of the Future would certainly be infinitely ahead of ourselves in all their appliances. I had come without arms, without medicine, without anything to smoke . . . even without enough matches. If only I had a Kodak! I could have flashed that glimpse of the Under-world in a second, and examined it at leisure.

> (6:45)

Appliances—arms, medicine, matches, Kodak, and the Time Machine itself—embody more significance in the Wellsian view of the nature and function of science than any idea, virtue, or particular quality of sense or sensibility supposed to be inherent in the human psyche or the universe at large. It is machinery, appliances, that provide the occasion for the sustenance, if not the creation, of that peculiar quality which makes the Morlock, however loathsome, a creature more creative and self-sustaining than the Eloi. For "the Under-world being in contact with machinery, which, however perfect, still needs some little thought outside habit, had probably retained perforce rather more initiative, if less of every other human character, than the Upper." Surely it is this insight, arrived at by way of "learn[ing] this world," that the Time Traveller has in mind when, after the night in the forest and the loss of Weena to the Morlocks and sitting once more on the bench of griffins' heads, he observes that "for once, at least, I grasped the mental operations of the Morlocks" (10:64). Their initiative with machinery is the clue that explains both the loss of the Time Machine and the method of its recovery. By way of the Machine the Morlocks seek to trap the Time Traveller for meat, and seeing this he walks willingly through the bronze doors which slide open at his approach, knowing that all he need do is to replace the levers that set it in motion and be returned to the 19th century, his own age.

5. The dominating presence of the White Sphinx, then, causes *The Time Machine* to bulge toward myth and allegory. What might otherwise have been a novel thus becomes SF or "scientific romance." For *The Time Machine* begins and ends as a novel might; reality is rendered realistically as the Time Traveller's friends gather in his home and (when all is said and done) depart from it. Yet even the names of the Time Traveller's friends, which appear only at the beginning and the ending, suggest that this is more than a novel. The Time Traveller, the Medical Man, the Psychologist, the Editor, Blank, Dash, and Chose are all one-dimensional characters. Even the narrator remains nameless and impersonal since the focus of *The Time Machine* is not on character but on plot. For if in the novel "character is more important than action and plot," the romance clearly "prefers action [and plot] to character."[10]

Nevertheless Frank McConnell and Samuel Hynes regard *The Time Machine* as a novel and interpret the role of its narrator as if they were dealing with a narrative rendered realistically rather than with a romance. The narrator reacts "to the Traveller's theories and tales with ordinary doubt," they write, because

> he is simply the ordinary man refusing to acknowledge what his imagination cannot endure. So at the end he offers his own hearty but ill-founded hopes: 'I, for my own part, cannot think that these latter days of weak experiment, fragmentary theory, and mutual discord are indeed man's culminating time!' And he offers, as reasons for comfort, the flowers that the Traveller brought back from the Golden Age, 'to witness that even when mind and strength had gone, gratitude and a mutual tenderness still lived on in the heart of man.' But the reader who had read the story must feel the bitter irony of that foolish comfort; for mind and strength had indeed gone, but fear had not, and the preying of man upon man had not, and where is the comfort in *that*?[11]

In the first place, the narrator is not simply the ordinary man who doubts what his imagination cannot encompass; he is a man for whom the Time Traveller's story has had the salutary effect of putting a whole new aspect on the face of things. Far from being the one who doubts, he is the only one of the Traveller's immediate audience not to dismiss the tale of the Morlocks and the Eloi as either incredible or a lie. When the Traveller finishes his story, his audience sits around him "in the dark," says the narrator,

and little spots of colour swam before them. The Medical Man seemed absorbed in the contemplation of our host. The Editor was looking hard at the end of his cigar—the sixth. The Journalist fumbled for his watch. The others, as far as I remember, were motionless.

(12:71)

Each has his attention focused on something other than the story that he has just heard. The Journalist is concerned about the lateness of the hour and of getting home. The Editor, on his way home, dismisses the story as a "gaudy lie." Only the narrator continues to be held by the story of the Morlocks and the Eloi. "The story was so fantastic and incredible," he says, "the telling so credible and sober. I lay awake most of the night thinking about it" (12:72). The narrator recognizes in the sober and credible manner of its telling, in its very atmosphere and tone, that the Traveller's story is not a fabrication but a faithful description of an actual experience in a real place. It is this that elicits the narrator's belief and elevates his thought to a new and unexpected level of reality. For the Time Traveller's story awakens in the narrator the twin desires "to survey the depths of space and time" and "to hold communion with other living things."[12] If when all is said and done the narrator takes comfort in anything, it is the manifold possibilities of Time Travel.

Second, this awakening of belief and desire within the narrator not only opens him to other worlds but to discipleship. He returns to the Time Traveller's house next day; he would hear and see more of this man who tells such credible and sober tales of his travels in the fantastic and incredible realm. In the Traveller the narrator recognizes a kindred spirit if not a mentor. As if in direct verification that he might be chosen for a disciple, chance affords the narrator the rare privilege, at the Time Traveller's house next day, of touching the Time Machine itself. "I stared for a minute at the Time Machine and put out my hand and touched the lever," he says. And what happens in the moment of this touch marks the narrator as a Time Traveller too, if only in imagination. For at his touch "the squat substantial-looking mass swayed like a bough shaken by the wind." The narrator's touch and the instantaneous movement of the machine attest to his having been awakened to the Time Traveller within himself. It is, therefore, no surprise to the reader when (subsequently) the Time Traveller says to the narrator, "I know why you came," and then affords him the high and rare privilege of actually seeing the Traveller depart into the incredible realm once more. The narrator opens the laboratory door just as the Time Traveller departs on his second trip into the future, and here is what he sees.

> I seemed to see a ghostly, indistinct figure sitting in a whirling mass of black and brass for a moment—a figure so transparent that the bench behind with its sheets of drawings was absolutely distinct; but this phantasm

vanished as I rubbed my eyes. The Time Machine had gone. . . . I felt an unreasonable amazement. I knew that something strange had happened, and for the moment could not distinguish what the strange thing might be . . . Then I understood . . . I stayed on, waiting for the Time Traveller; waiting for the second, perhaps still stranger story, and the specimens and photographs he would bring with him.[13]

Third, and finally, it is not the narrator's experience here that is important in and of itself (as it would be in the novel), but the function that he serves in the narrative. He is the master link between the reader and the fantastic realm into which the Time Traveller ventures. In the manner of the Time Traveller himself, but as one who believes from hearing rather than from actual experience (as the reader must also), the narrator represents the fantastic and the incredible in a sober and credible way. It is the story that counts, not the teller of the tale, because

where the novelist would arouse our interest in character by exploring his origin, the romancer will probably do so by enveloping it in mystery. Character itself becomes, then, somewhat abstract and ideal, so much so in some romances that it seems to be merely a function of plot. The plot we may expect to be highly colored. Astonishing events may occur, and these are likely to have a symbolic or ideological, rather than a realistic, plausibility. . . . [Thus] the romance will more freely veer toward mythic, allegorical, and symbolic forms.[14]

It matters very little, then, whether the narrator is an ordinary man; what matters fundamentally is that he be a true believer. Then the reader will be confident that the story he is told, however fantastic and incredible, is rendered accurately and in minute detail, with that kind of faithfulness to mood and tone, atmosphere and incident that is commonly found in the recounting of experiences that have changed one's life. In such narrations it matters very little who the narrator is *as a person,* for it is the action and the story that he tells that are important. **The Time Machine** is just such a narration and there at its very beginning is the Sphinx, the most ancient of mythical creatures and as enigmatic to the narrator as it is to the Time Traveller himself. This mystery is passed on directly to the reader. And the reader is left not with the burden of having to believe or not believe, but with the very same obligation that has fallen to the Time Traveller and to the narrator in his turn: each must make some sense of the riddle thus posed. The Time Traveller makes sense of it all by way of leaving the Sphinx alone. The narrator's mode of making sense is, in the best mythological sense, wonderful participation in the Time Traveller's experience through a faithful rendering of it. But the reader must face the Sphinx directly if he is to make sense, as I have tried to do here, of its peculiar kind of sense-making.

Notes

1. H. G. Wells, *Three Novels: The Time Machine, The War of the Worlds, The Island of Doctor Moreau* (London: Heinemann, 1963), 3:18.

2. In *Francis Bacon: Selected Writings,* with an Introduction and Notes by Hugh G. Dick (NY: The Modern Library, 1955), pp. 417-20.

3. In H. G. Wells, *The Time Machine and The War of the Worlds: A Critical Edition,* ed. Frank D. McConnell (NY: Oxford, 1977), p. 344.

4. See Robert M. Philmus, *Into the Unknown: The Evolution of Science Fiction from Francis Godwin to H. G. Wells* (Berkeley & Los Angeles, 1970), in which it is argued that what I have called "fallen" should be understood as "devolution," as the "gradual reduction of Homo sapiens to species lower and lower on the evolutionary scale" (pp. 70ff.). Philmus points out that the Time Traveller views man's decline as "degeneration"; Wells's own term for this process was "degradation"—all of which goes to show that the White Sphinx forces author, protagonist, reader *and* critic to formulate his own answer to the riddle of man's future.

5. Paul Ricoeur, *The Symbolism of Evil,* trans. Emerson Buchanan (NY, 1967), p. 178.

6. Herman Melville, *Moby-Dick,* Chapter 42, "The Whiteness of the Whale."

7. Alfred North Whitehead, *Science and the Modern World* (NY, 1958), p. 4.

8. Robert Andrew Millikan, "The Spirit of Modern Science," in *Science and Literature,* ed. Frederick H. Law (NY, 1929), p. 311.

9. In a review of *Havelock Ellis: A Biography, New York Times Book Review,* June 22, 1980, p. 29.

10. Richard Chase, *The American Novel and its Tradition* (NY, 1957), p. 13. Even though Chase is concerned primarily with American romance, his guiding assumption is "that the American novel is obviously a development from the English tradition" (p. 3), a tradition of which Wells is no small part.

11. In McConnell, *The Time Machine,* pp. 352-53.

12. J. R. R. Tolkien argues that these desires are basic both to the creation and the appreciation of Fantasy or Fairy-Stories. "Eloi and Morlocks live far away in an abyss of time so deep as to work an enchantment upon them. . . . This enchantment of distance, especially of distant time, is weakened only by the preposterous and incredible Time Machine itself. But we see in this example one of

the main reasons why the borders of fairy-story are inevitably dubious. The magic of Faerie is not an end in itself, its virtue is in its operations: among these are the satisfaction of certain primordial human desires," in particular the desires mentioned above. "On Fairy-Stories," in *The Tolkien Reader* (NY: Ballantine, 1966), p. 13.

13. There is a strong suggestion here that the Time Traveller thus becomes to the narrator as the Hebrew prophet, Elijah, is to his disciple, Elisha. "Elijah said to Elisha, 'Tell me what I can do for you before I am taken from you.' Elisha said, 'Let me inherit a double share of your spirit.' 'You have asked a hard thing,' said Elijah. 'If you see me taken from you, may your wish be granted; if you do not, it shall not be granted.' They went on, talking as they went, and suddenly there appeared chariots of fire and horses of fire, which separated them one from the other, and Elijah was carried up in the whirlwind to heaven" (II Kings 2:9-12).

14. Chase, *loc. cit.* (see note 10).

John Huntington (essay date 1982)

SOURCE: Huntington, John. Chapter on *The Time Machine*, by H. G. Wells. In *The Logic of Fantasy: H. G. Wells and Science Fiction*, pp. 41-55. New York: Columbia University Press, 1982.

[*In the following essay, Huntington perceives Wells's view of life in the future found in* The Time Machine *as a simplification of issues relevant at the time of the novella's publication.*]

Wells's use of balanced opposition and symbolic mediation as a way of thinking finds its most perfect form in *The Time Machine.* If the novella imagines a future, it does so not as a forecast but as a way of contemplating the structures of our present civilization.[1] At one level *The Time Machine* presents a direct warning about the disastrous potential of class division. But at a deeper level it investigates large questions of difference and domination, and rather than settling the issues, it constructs unresolvable conflicts that return us to the central dilemmas that have characterized the evolutionary debate. . . .

The Time Traveller's insights into the benefits of civilization are paradoxical. In his first interpretation of the meaning and structure of the world of 802,701 he finds a complex pleasure in the union of idyllic ease and evolutionary decline:

> To adorn themselves with flowers, to dance, to sing in the sunlight; so much was left of the artistic spirit, and no more. Even that would fade in the end into a con-

tented inactivity. We are kept keen on the grindstone of pain and necessity, and, it seemed to me, that here was that hateful grindstone broken at last!

> (p. 43)

If there is regret at lost keenness here, there is also joy at escaped hardship. By the end of the novella, when he realizes that the decline has not conferred quite the benefits he anticipated and that the structure of civilization has degenerated into a primitive horror in which the Morlocks, the slothlike descendents of the laboring class, slaughter and eat the Eloi, the species descended from the upper classes, he entertains a different set of conflicting emotions. Now he balances a sense of the ironic justice of this situation with an irrational sympathy for the humanoid Eloi:

> Then I tried to preserve myself from the horror that was coming upon me, by regarding it as a rigorous punishment of human selfishness. Man had been content to live in ease and delight upon the labours of his fellow-man, had taken Necessity as his watchword and excuse, and in the fulness of time Necessity had come home to him. I even tried a Carlyle-like scorn of this wretched aristocracy-in-decay. But this attitude of mind was impossible. However great their intellectual degradation, the Eloi had kept too much of the human form not to claim my sympathy, and to make me perforce a sharer in their degradation and their Fear.

> (p. 81)

If the moral view, which would find satisfaction in the Eloi enslavement, is not adequate to the situation, it nevertheless works against the sense of pity, which is also, in itself, inadequate. Such nodes of conflicting insights and feelings are the expressions of tensions developed by the brutal oppositions on which the whole novella is built.

We can isolate two large, separate realms of opposition which operate in *The Time Machine.* One, essentially spatial, consists of the conflict between the Eloi and the Morlocks. Though the Time Traveller first views the 802,701 world as free from opposition, the novella traces his discovery of the radical oppositions that actually define that world; what begins as a vision of benign decay and carefree pastoral ends up as a vision of entrapment wherein the economic divisions of the present have become biological and territorial. The other opposition is temporal; it entails the opposition between the civilization of 1895 and a set of increasingly less civilized, more purely natural worlds of the future. Of these, the world of the Eloi-Morlock conflict is of course the most important. Towards the end of the novella the Time Traveller moves further into the future; he sees darkness and cold advance on the earth until life is diminished to huge, sluggish crabs and then finally to a football-sized organism that hops fitfully on the tideless shore.[2]

Because the Time Traveller arrives in 802,701, not by a process of incremental progressions, but by a single leap, the structure of the novella poses a puzzle: what is the relation of the future to the present? The Time Traveller and the reader are engaged in the same activity: they try to understand the nature of the temporal contrast presented and then to discover connections. Like evolutionary biologists, they must first understand what distinguishes two species and then they must reconstruct the evolutionary sequence that links them; the difference between Eohippus and the modern horse is like that between the modern human and the Eloi or the Morlocks. Unlike the biologist, however, the Time Traveller and the reader are engaged in negotiating a pattern more complex than a simple genealogical sequence. We must figure out what bonds exist amidst the differences between the Time Traveller and his and our distant grandchildren. The mental act of reconstructing the evolutionary connection involves more than just taxonomic description; it is not simply a perceiving of a pure two-world system; it entails examining a whole series of ambiguous moral conflicts.

During the course of the novella, as the truth reveals itself and the meanings of the discovered oppositions change, one relation between the present and the future persists: the future is a *reduction* of the present.[3] The future offers a simplification of issues that is much like that which occurs in conventional pastoral: economic and social complexities have disappeared, and the issues of the world are those determined by elementary human nature. But to compare *The Time Machine* to a pastoral is somewhat misleading; though both diminish the importance of civilized forms and conventions, in *The Time Machine* the main agent of change is a biological regression not found in the conventional pastoral. The inhabitants of the future have lost much of the erotic, intellectual, and moral energy that we generally associate with human beings and which it is the purpose of the usual pastoral to liberate. The society of the future is reduced to what in 1895 might be considered childish needs and pleasures, and it is under the terms of this radical diminution that the systems of spatial opposition work.

Such a reduction certainly simplifies social issues, but the first question it raises is how human or how bestial are these distant cousins of present-day humanity. The split between the Eloi and the Morlocks raises this question from opposite directions: the Eloi seem subhumans, the Morlocks superanimals. The Time Traveller certainly considers Weena the most human creature he finds in the future, but as he acknowledges, he tends to think of her as more human than she is.[4] Her humanoid appearance tends to obscure how much she is a pet rather than a human companion. At the other extreme, the Morlocks, though they too are supposedly descended from present-day humanity, because they look like sloths, always seem bestial to the Time Traveller. For much of his time in 802,701 he does not realize their importance; he treats them first as "ghosts," then as lower animals, then as servants to the Eloi. Even at the end when he comprehends their domination of the Eloi he never really conceives of them as human. Thus the novella sets up a symmetrical illusion: the Eloi, because of their appearance, seem more human than they are; the Morlocks, again because of appearance, seem less.

The Time Traveller's relation to the Eloi engages special problems because it involves, not simply identification, but affection across the abyss of species difference. Critics have found the Time Traveller's attention to his "little woman" disturbing and have treated the hints of repressed sexuality, of pedophilia, as a novelistic blunder.[5] I would suggest, however, that the unease generated by this relationship is apt, for at issue is the whole puzzle of human relations to nonhumans. The Time Traveller himself is confused by Weena. He can treat her as an equal and contemplate massacring Morlocks when he loses her, but he also forgets her easily. The tension and the ambiguities of their relationship derive from the impossibility of defining either an identity or a clear difference. To render such a state Wells plays on the inherently ambiguous relationship between adults and children.

The puzzle of Weena's sexuality is reflected and reversed by the Time Traveller's relation to the Morlocks. When he first meets the Eloi he allows them to touch him: "I felt other soft little tentacles upon my back and shoulders. They wanted to make sure I was real. There was nothing in this at all alarming" (p. 30). Similar behavior by the Morlocks, however, leads the Time Traveller to an hysterical smashing of skulls. At first, the touch of the Morlocks is hardly distinguishable from that of the Eloi: it is as if "sea anemones were feeling over my face with their soft palps" (p. 57). But this same intimate approach becomes sinister as the Time Traveller becomes aware of the Morlocks' real intent, and he feels horror later, at night in the forest, when he becomes aware that "Soft little hands, too, were creeping over my coat and back, touching even my neck" (p. 93). The reasons for the different reactions to this intimate approach are obvious; what we need to observe, however, is the area of identity here. If the repressed sexuality of the relation with Weena leads to a passive and childish activity (weaving flowers, dancing to burning matches), the Morlocks' almost seductive aggression leads to an antipathy which generates violence and ingenious invention.[6]

The central mystery of Eloi and Morlock humanity and of the Time Traveller's relation to it is emblematized by the statue of the sphinx that the Time Traveller sees when he first arrives in 802,701. The symbol works at a number of levels. It stands for the paradox of a progress that is a regression: the future is represented by a monument that we associate with early civilization. Thus, the future is a return to the past, to the childhood, so to speak, of human society. The sphinx herself is also a poser of riddles: when Oedipus met her she asked him the riddle of man who appears in different forms. This connection is clearly in Wells's mind, for no sooner has the Time Traveller seen the statue than he begins speculating about the possibilities of the human form in this distant future. But it is in her own appearance that the sphinx raises the most perplexing puzzle, for she represents a literal combination of human and animal: woman and lion. We ask whether Weena is a woman or not, whether a Morlock is a beast or not; here in the sphinx we have a creature which is both. The sphinx marks the cut; it is a union of a crucial opposition and, like the flying man, points to the possibility of transcending the contradiction. This important mediating symbolism is repeated in a striking but diminished form by the statue of a Faun which the Time Traveller later discovers (p. 77), another literal mixture of human and animal.[7]

Just as the sphinx and the faun render visually the puzzle of the relation of human and beast and offer a union of the supposed dichotomy, they also denote the areas of human and animal activity that have been diminished by the decline into the future. The sphinx, the poser of riddles, is a figure of the very intellectual prowess that the childish creatures of the future lack. Similarly, the faun embodies the sexual energy that is noticeably absent. Thus, while the statues link the human and the animal, they do so ironically; they suggest a potential for accomplishment and for civilization of which the Eloi and the Morlocks are biologically incapable.

While such issues of the relation of present-day humanity to these future creatures pervade the novella, the opposition between the Eloi and the Morlocks themselves, of which the Time Traveller becomes increasingly aware as he learns more about the future's underworld, has an important social meaning. In the split between the two species we see a split intrinsic to technological civilization itself. This is no dark secret of the tale, of course:[8] the Time Traveller's final interpretation of how the split developed refers directly back to the division of labor in contemporary England. But the values that initially caused the split persist in the far future, and, in ways that are not generally recognized, the two species represent and at the same time parody values that belong, not merely to British capitalist civilization, but to all technological cultures. Though the Morlocks are hairy, have an apelike posture, cannot bear light, and live in burrows of a sort, any simple equation of them with the lower animals won't do. They live amidst thudding machines, and their habitat is artificially ventilated. The passage down which the Time Traveller climbs to visit them has a ladder with iron rungs. Unlike the Eloi, the Morlocks function as a group; they are individually weak, but they cooperate. Thus, though their specific intellectual and emotional capacities remain largely unknown, symbolically they subsume one aspect of what we admire in civilization: organized technological mastery. And the Eloi with their trivial, careless aestheticism embody the alternative leisure aspect of civilization, the pure delight in beauty, gaity, play. They live for these and as much as possible avoid even thinking about necessity and pain. The Morlock-Eloi split may be the result of today's class divisions, but in its final form it expresses two high and apparently contradictory values of human civilization: mastery and aesthetic leisure.[9]

The landscape of the future becomes an extension of the contradictions represented in Eloi and Morlock. The surface of the countryside, while much hedged and walled, is devoid of meaningful divisions; the ruined castles of the Eloi hardly differentiate inside and outside; at one time the Time Traveller even gets lost because the field in which he has landed is indistinguishable from any other; only the presence of the statue of the sphinx defines it. But a radically different world exists beneath the Eloi pastoral, and so it is *down* that the Time Traveller must go to find an alternative. Up and down, therefore, become an important expression of the basic Eloi-Morlock opposition. The same opposition is expressed in the opposition between light and dark. The imbalance of the opposition is symbolized by the fact that the Morlocks can intrude on the Eloi above-ground preserve at night.

The cut between the two opposed realms is marked most concretely by the strange palace of green porcelain that the Time Traveller visits when seeking to recover his lost time machine. The building is made of material that reminds the Time Traveller of Chinese porcelain and has an oriental look to it; it seems a special version of the palaces the Eloi inhabit. But within this aestheticized exterior is a museum of technology, a "latter-day South Kensington." It thus partakes of both the worlds of Eloi aesthetics and Morlock technology. But most importantly it blurs the line between up and down. As he walks along one of the galleries, the Time Traveller finds himself unexpectedly underground. He confesses he wasn't even aware of the slope. And then, as if to underline the importance of this transition, but also to offer a new way of treating it, the editor, a person who appears nowhere else in the novella, supplies a curious footnote: "It may be, of course, that the floor did not slope—but that the museum was built into the side of a hill" (p. 85). By translating the up-down division into a lateral one, the museum ingeniously mediates the division's absolute separation. That is not to say that it resolves the split: Weena is still afraid of the dark, and the Time Traveller retreats back to the light. But it is an important symbolic possibility in an otherwise destructive and rigid opposition.

Though a treasury of the present in the future, the museum of green porcelain also stands for the important mediating possibilities of modern technology in the face of the future's natural antithesis. The diminished intelligence of the creatures of the future prevents them from understanding or using the museum; only the Time Traveller is capable of realizing the museum's potential. The Time Traveller thus becomes the main mediator in the future system of static oppositions because by means of his human intelligence, passion, and morality he is able to bridge its dichotomies. He reconciles in himself the masterful and aesthetic aspects of culture that are at war in the future: at the end of the story he displays to his audience a flower, the token of Eloi aestheticism and affection, but he also vigorously demands a piece of meat, a token of Morlock carnivorousness. The future is a horror in part because the divisions that are for us in the present still capable of modification and correction have become a purely natural competition, a predatory antithesis that does not allow for exchange or change. The Time Traveller offers some hope because by using tools and by acting ethically he is able to break down the bounds of the otherwise rigid, hostile evolutionary categories.

It is his mastery of fire that gives the Time Traveller his most distinctive mediating power. That power is complex, however, and as in the cases of the other mediating images, involves contradiction and operates on a number of planes of meaning simultaneously. In *The Time Machine* fire defines civilized humanity. It is an image of both domestic security and war. It has an aesthetic function and a technological one. Finally, it is an emblem of the paradox of degenerative progress that dominates the whole novella.

The Time Traveller himself makes the link between fire and present-day humanity when he observes how rare fire is in nature:

> I don't know if you have ever thought what a rare thing flame must be in the absence of man and in a temperate climate. The sun's heat is rarely strong enough to burn, even when it is focussed by dewdrops, as is sometimes the case in more tropical districts. Lightning may blast and blacken, but it rarely gives rise to wide-spread fire. Decaying vegetation may occasionally smoulder with the heat of its fermentation, but this rarely results in flame. In this decadence, too, the art of fire-making had been forgotten on the earth. The red tongues that went licking up my heap of wood were an altogether new and strange thing to Weena.
>
> (p. 92)

Implicit in the absence of fire is the question we have looked at earlier of the actual "humanity" of either the Eloi or the Morlocks. In this formulation of the issue, fire is a symbol of human control over nature, a control that the future has lost. Such innocence has ambiguous

value; earlier in the story, before the Time Traveller has realized that the Eloi are victims, he approves of such ignorance. It is night; he has lost his time machine; searching for it he blunders into the dilapidated hall of the Eloi and, after striking a match, demands his machine from them. Their confusion conveys two things to him: that "they had forgotten about matches" and that they had forgotten about fear (p. 46). The link between the two forgettings is casual but significant. To forget about matches is to lose as aspect of today's technology, to revert to a primitive state in which tools are unknown. But to forget fear, one would expect, is to live in a world of complete security, to have escaped the primitive natural situation in which fear is necessary for survival. Thus, while the forgetting of matches suggests regression, the forgetting of fear suggests progress. At this early stage in his acquaintance with the future the Time Traveller interprets both forgettings as the privileges of progress, as the evidence of a carefree pastoral idyll. Under these circumstances the paradox that progress has led to regression is not dismaying.

So long as he does not understand the real situation of the future the Time Traveller has no conception of the importance his mastery of fire has, and he uses his matches merely to entertain the Eloi, to make them dance and laugh. The irony of such trivialization is that it actually prevents knowledge, as is clear in the following passage:

> I proceeded, as I have said, to question Weena about this Underworld, but here again I was disappointed. At first she would not understand my questions, and presently she refused to answer them. She shivered as though the topic was unendurable. And when I pressed her, perhaps a little harshly, she burst into tears. They were the only tears, except my own, I ever saw in that Golden Age. When I saw them I ceased abruptly to trouble about the Morlocks, and was only concerned in banishing these signs of her human inheritance from Weena's eyes. And very soon she was smiling and clapping her hands, while I solemnly burned a match.
>
> (p. 66)

By using fire as a toy the Time Traveller diverts Weena from exhibiting "signs of her human inheritance." His instinct to avert tears is understandable, but the completeness with which the concern for Weena's innocence overrides the concern with the facts about the Morlocks has signs of panic. The other time that the Time Traveller uses matches to entertain the Eloi is also after they have been "distressed" by his inquiries about the Morlocks (p. 61). In both cases the match is used for entertainment at the expense of further knowledge, to sustain a complacent happiness which is, in fact, an illusion.

Though he is capable of using matches to preserve an innocent decorum, the Time Traveller is not simply a Victorian gentleman intent on preventing children from learning or expressing the grim truth. The match may be a toy, but it is also an instrument for seeing. When he first looks for the time machine the Time Traveller uses a match. When he looks down one of the Morlock wells he uses a match. And when he enters the underworld he uses a match: "The view I had [of the Morlocks' cavern] was as much as one could see in the burning of a match" (p. 70). When two paragraphs later he chides himself for coming to the future ill-equipped, the Time Traveller emphasizes the importance of matches for his investigation: though he might prefer a "kodak," the match, feeble as it is, is the single "tool" that he has brought. For the Time Traveller to be master of fire is for him to have an intellectual dominance, and the safety match becomes a symbol of that aspect of present-day technology.

Intellectual dominance leads to other kinds of dominance. The ambiguous potential of fire is most forcefully realized when the Time Traveller uses it, not for entertaining or seeing, but as a weapon. The match becomes an important defensive tool which allows the Time Traveller to move across the boundaries of this world. And after he visits the green porcelain palace and comes away with matches and camphor, the Time Traveller begins to use fire as a tool of aggression. With the intention of "amaz[ing] our friends," he sets a pile of wood on fire. Now when Weena wants to dance and play with the light, the Time Traveller prevents her. A little later he is forced to start a second fire.

What is important for our understanding of the symbol is that the fires fail him in diametrically opposite ways. The second, beside which he goes to sleep, goes out and the Morlocks, unhindered by the fire, almost overcome him. But the first, forgotten and left behind, starts a forest fire which threatens to destroy even the Time Traveller himself. We have here an expression of the danger of dependence on the very technology that allows for mastery: it can either fail to perform even its elementary expectations, or it can go wild and overperform. In both cases the human is betrayed by his own technological sophistication. Fire, which up to this point has been a symbol of technology's ability to mediate, here develops its own destructive opposition between too much and too little. The puzzle that a dependence on technology presents is again rendered a little later in the novella when the Time Traveller, mounted on the time machine's saddle, confidently tries to light a match to drive off the assaulting Morlocks and discovers that he has safety matches that won't strike without the box.

Yet it is just at the moments when fire gets out of control that the Time Traveller performs his most radical mediations. When the fire goes out he is forced to lay about with his other tool, a makeshift club, and when he is overtaken by the forest fire he comes to feel pity for the Morlocks. In both cases, though in different ways, he bridges the distance between himself and these alien beings.

In the first instance what starts as an act of self-defence becomes more aggressive until the Time Traveller is enjoying destroying others:

> It was indescribably horrible in the darkness to feel all these soft creatures heaped upon me. I felt as if I was in a monstrous spider's web. I was overpowered, and went down. I felt little teeth nipping at my neck. I rolled over, and as I did so my hand came against my iron lever. It gave me strength. I struggled up, shaking the human rats from me, and holding the bar short, I thrust where I judged their faces might be. I could feel the succulent giving of flesh and bone under my blows, and for a moment I was free.
>
> (p. 95)

The striking word, "succulent," in the last sentence conveys both the pleasure the Time Traveller gets from such battery and the strange similarity between such violent activity and Morlock cannibalism. The Time Traveller here reveals himself as like the Morlocks and quite unlike the passionless and passive Eloi.

A more direct acknowledgment of his union with the Morlocks occurs after the first fire overtakes them all and the Time Traveller stops clubbing the "human rats" and becomes a victim with them. "I followed in the Morlocks' path" (p. 96). In the face of the larger catastrophe of the forest fire, the discriminations and hostilities that have kept the Time Traveller and the Morlocks apart are abandoned, and the Time Traveller, "assured of their absolute helplessness and misery in the glare," refrains from his aggressions. Even when the thought of the "awful fate" of Weena whom he has lost in the confusion moves him "to begin a massacre of the helpless abominations" about him, the Time Traveller "contains" himself.

The logical distinctions to be made at this point are complex. The Time Traveller is both identical with the Morlocks and separate from them. In the morning, exhausted, shoeless, with grass tied to his feet to protect them from the hot soil, he is only remotely the master scientist. He has been reduced to a bare forked thing and forced to acknowledge his bond in suffering with the other creatures of this world. But with the difference between himself and the Morlocks overwhelmed by their common fate as victims of the fire, the Time Traveller reasserts a distinction, not by exhibiting mastery of some sort over the others, but by restraining himself, by mastering his own brutal nature.

The Time Traveller's self-control has a complex symbolic function. It marks his difference from both Morlock and Eloi, since neither species seems capable of such conscious mastery of the self. It is his ability—a distinctly human ability—to bridge distinctions, to recognize an area of identity within a difference, that sets him apart from the other forms of life which will presumably remain locked in opposition. The Time Traveller is able to assert an ethical view in the face of the evolutionary competition that rules the future. He offers the promise of, if not resolving, at least comprehending the problems inherent in the conflict between evolution and ethics. In place of absolute antagonism between classes and between species, he acknowledges momentarily the bonds that extend across those divisions. Such an act of sympathizing with a different creature is an important gesture in Wells; we will explore it more fully in the next chapter. What interests us right now, however, is not the particular thematic issue, but its structural fitness: the act both acknowledges difference and momentarily bridges that difference. In this way it reflects the central pattern of *The Time Machine* itself: its art is to create emblems of difference and separation and then to meditate on the balances, the antitheses and the identities that are possible.

In saying that reconciling both sides of a conflict is the central act of *The Time Machine,* I do not mean to suggest that the novella is without explicit moral point. The Time Traveller's latest interpretation of the division between Eloi and Morlock foresees and fears the transformation of an economic social division into a biological one, of an ethical issue into an evolutionary one. Clearly, Wells's moral point here is to impress on an audience which tends to accept the economic divisions of civilization as "natural" the horror of what it would mean if that division were truly natural. More narrowly, one may perhaps legitimately examine the novella as a treatise on possible evolutionary directions and study it as a prediction of sorts. But in isolating such moral ideas in the novella, one needs to be aware of the danger of distorting the deepest mechanisms of Wells's imagination: he is not the sort of writer who hides an esoteric meaning which is available only to the painstaking exegete. The difficulty one has deriving a clear reading of the future from *The Time Machine* comes from the large, unresolved oppositions of the tale. Instead of trying to "settle" ambiguities, to find out the one true reading, we should focus on the specific and powerful contradictions the story sets up. To see contradiction clearly in all its appalling and irresolvable conflict, and then to try by whatever imaginative means possible to mediate that disjunction: that is the true and deep moral of *The Time Machine.*

In the last paragraphs of the novella Wells offers us an explicit instance of how to read this way, to accept both sides of a contradiction. The Time Traveller has disappeared on his second journey three years ago, and the narrator speculates about his fate.[10] Wells here enforces ambiguity. And one understands why: any plot resolu-

tion would resolve the earlier tensions in such a way as to diminish the complexity of the whole vision. In this final stasis of opposition, not only does the frame distance us, as Robert Philmus has argued,[11] but the narrator proposes an attitude diametrically contrary to that of the Time Traveller. "I, for my own part," the narrator confesses,

> cannot think that these latter days of weak experiment, fragmentary theory, and mutual discord are indeed man's culminating time! I say, for my own part. He, I know—for the question had been discussed among us long before the Time Machine was made—thought but cheerlessly of the Advancement of Mankind, and saw in the growing pile of civilization only a foolish heaping that must inevitably fall back upon and destroy its makers in the end.
>
> (p. 117)

Here again we see the two attitudes of promise and hubris implicit in the symbolism of the matches. And then the narrator tries to combine the two in a single stance: if the Time Traveller's vision of bleak decline is the true one, the narrator argues, "it remains for us to live as though it were not so." He finally settles on an image that echoes the more hellish imagery of the novella itself and also alludes to the image of the feeble light shed by the match of science at the end of **"The Rediscovery of the Unique"**: "But to me the future is still black and blank—is a vast ignorance, lit at a few casual places by the memory of his story."[12]

We see Wells here balancing pessimism and optimism. But the novella achieves an even more essential balance between a vision of change and a vision of no change. If we recall the two realms of opposition with which we began this essay, we can see that they themselves create an opposition. The horror of the split between the Eloi and the Morlocks lies in the fact that the divisions of modern civilization have not changed but have, by a process of speciation, become intrinsic in nature. But the other opposition, that between the present and the future, is a vision of change, of entropic decline. The first opposition implies that the essential injustice, the conflict of classes, will not change. On the other hand, the second opposition argues that in spite of all humans might do, things will change. The processes of entropy and evolution will continue, and any vision of humanity's place in the universe must take into account these large movements that are outside our control. This conflict between a vision of change and a vision of stasis undermines any simple thematic reading at the deepest level. Viewed as a prediction, the novella contradicts itself: the economic pessimism foresees a grim permanence; the cosmic pessimism sees an equally grim movement. And if the cosmic has the last word, that does not disqualify the economic: in terms of mere hundreds of thousands of years the cosmic process, by dividing the classes into species, merely confirms the continuity of the economic. Only on the scale of millions of years does the division of classes cease to be a controlling factor. So we face a problem as we try to derive a message from *The Time Machine.* But the problem is not a flaw: such unresolved, antithetical conflict is central to the way Wells's imagination works and gives his fiction a profundity, based on the ambiguities of human desire and experience, that is rare in thought about the future.

It may help us see exactly what Wells has achieved in *The Time Machine* if we briefly observe how George Pal in his film of *The Time Machine* (1960) avoids facing the very conflicts that define Wells's work. First of all, Pal erases the issue of evolution and ethics by making the Morlocks monsters and the Eloi simply badly educated humans. Though for a while the film allows us to think there may be a genetic problem, by the end the Eloi, who have spoken English from the beginning, show that they are human in every way: they become social; Weena, a starlet, falls in love; a male Eloi learns to fight; they use records (the talking rings); and in the end the Time Traveller (here H. George Wells) returns with books to repair the educational gap that has prevented the Eloi from succeeding. These people are not involved in any evolutionary or cosmic process; they are simply humans living in a "dark age." And while the Eloi are beautiful humans who can be reindoctrinated, the Morlocks represent nothing but horror. More than simply a softening of Wells's pessimism has taken place here: the intellectual tensions of the conflicts, both between the present and the future and between the values represented by the Eloi and the Morlocks, have disappeared.

If Pal ignores the biological issue so central to Wells, he evades the economic issue as well. In place of Wells's vision of class difference developing into species difference, Pal gives us a vague history of the first part of our century as it is defined by its wars. We know that the wars went on and that the bombs got more destructive until finally the human race "split." The conflict is not in capitalism itself, but in the opposition of capitalism and communism. The clear hint is that the Morlocks are, loosely, the Russians; the story of the Time Traveller's final return to revive Eloi culture is, thus, an allegory of the liberation of peoples oppressed by totalitarian communism. The sense of catastrophe, individual, social, racial, cosmic, that so darkens Wells's end, is entirely missing from Pal's. Like Nunez in Wells's **"The Country of the Blind,"** the film George seeks a society he can dominate, and this time there seems no chance of the kind of ironic development that keeps Nunez from ruling the country of the blind.

It is important that we understand how Pal has changed the very nature of the story's thought. Wells's myth develops systematically a set of logical oppositions as a way of making us confront contradictions latent in our society and begin to think anew about our civilization, but Pal's myth lacks a logical base; our values and our civilization, except that they have wars, are not questioned. The future need only be returned to the present for all to be well; it can be "cured" by discipline and books. Wells has created a static nightmare which has the virtue of forcing us to reconsider our own world; Pal, by envisioning a change, a restoration, has freed himself from that stasis but has also avoided thought about the need for change in the present or the future. He has robbed Wells's story of the essence of its conflict and replaced intellectual tension with melodramatic conventions that inspire unreflective affirmation.

Notes

1. The novella has often been casually lumped with other of Wells's more obviously prophetic novels. The Dover text is entitled, *Three Prophetic Novels of H. G. Wells* and includes along with *The Time Machine,* "A Story of the Days to Come" and *When the Sleeper Wakes.* The urge to see the novella as a serious exercise in extrapolation of the potentials of the human future persists. On the other hand, Robert Philmus, "The Logic of 'Prophecy' in *The Time Machine,*" in Bernard Bergonzi, ed., *H. G. Wells: A Collection of Critical Essays* (Englewood Cliffs, N.J.: Prentice-Hall, 1976), pp. 56-68, despite his title, is not concerned with prediction. What he calls the "dimension of 'prophecy'" (p. 65) is a narrative device common to much fiction.

2. The structure of this decline has been analysed by Darko Suvin in "*The Time Machine* versus *Utopia* as Structural Models for SF," in *Metamorphoses of Science Fiction,* pp. 223-33.

3. The argument of this paragraph owes much to Fredric Jameson's seminal essay, "World Reduction in Le Guin: The Emergence of Utopian Narrative," *Science-Fiction Studies* (1975), 2:221-30.

4. "She always seemed to me, I fancy, more human than she was, perhaps because her affection was so human." *The Time Machine,* p. 82.

5. V. S. Pritchett's distaste for the "Faint squirms of idyllic petting" has found numerous sympathetic readers. See Pritchett's "The Scientific Romances," *The Living Novel,* p. 125.

6. Even when he meets the Eloi, the Time Traveller's first thoughts are violent: "They looked so frail that I could fancy flinging the whole dozen of them about like nine-pins" (p. 30). The obvious but important difference between this "fancy" and his treatment of the Morlocks is that here he is able to resist acting on such fantasies.

7. Mark M. Hennelly, Jr., "*The Time Machine*: A Romance of 'the Human Heart,'" *Extrapolation*

(1979), 20:154-67, has observed the Sphinx and the faun as "unification of dual nature" (p. 163).

The Sphinx may have been suggested to Wells by a passage in Huxley: "However shocking to the moral sense this eternal competition of man against man and of nation against nation may be; however revolting may be the accumulation of misery at the negative pole of society, in contrast with that of monstrous wealth at the positive pole; this state of things must abide, and grow continually worse, so long as Istar holds her way unchecked. It is the true riddle of the Sphinx; and every nation which does not solve it will sooner or later be devoured by the monster itself has generated." "The Struggle for Existence in Human Society" (1888), in *Evolution and Ethics and Other Essays,* p. 212.

8. Bergonzi has sketched some basic oppositions: "The opposition of Eloi and Morlocks can be interpreted in terms of the late nineteenth-century class struggle, but it also reflects an opposition between aestheticism and utilitarianism, pastoralism and technology, contemplation and action, and ultimately, and least specifically, between beauty and ugliness, and light and darkness." *The Early H. G. Wells,* p. 61. Contemplation hardly seems appropriate to describe the Eloi.

9. This is a recurrent opposition and puzzle in science fiction of this century. See my "From Man to Overmind: Arthur C. Clarke's Myth of Progress," in Joseph D. Olander and Martin Greenberg, eds., *Arthur C. Clarke* (New York: Taplinger, 1977), pp. 211-22.

10. No hint is given by the Time Traveller of the destination of his second voyage into time. Philmus, perhaps influenced by George Pal's film of 1960 (discussed below), twice suggests he returns to 802,701 ("The Logic of 'Prophecy' in *The Time Machine,*" pp. 57, 67), but that seems doubtful. Such a return is certainly not one of the possibilities the narrator imagines in the "Epilogue."

11. "The Logic of 'Prophecy' in *The Time Machine,*" p. 67.

12. See the last paragraph of "The Rediscovery of the Unique," *Early Writings in Science and Science Fiction,* pp. 30-31, discussed in chapter 1 above.

Robert J. Begiebing (essay date fall 1984)

SOURCE: Begiebing, Robert J. "The Mythic Hero in H. G. Wells's *The Time Machine.*" *Essays in Literature* 11, no. 2 (fall 1984): 201-10.

[*In the following essay, Begiebing discusses the Time Traveller as the archetype of the mythic hero.*]

In 1915 Van Wyck Brooks hinted at an important quality of H. G. Wells's vision when he said that the author's intelligence is "exuberant" with a "very genuine religious instinct" that Wells "lavished" upon "the social process itself." And in 1922 and 1946 two foreign writers, Evgeny Zamyatin and Jorge Luis Borges, commented on Wells's timeless symbolic processes and mythmaking. But it was in the 1960's that critics began to focus on the archetypal dimensions of Wells's "scientific romances." Bernard Bergonzi argued in 1960 and 1961 that Wells's early fantasies were closer to the fables of Hawthorne, Melville, and Kafka than to science. In support of his argument, Bergonzi quoted both V. S. Pritchett, who saw *The Time Machine* as a "great story . . . that has meanings within meanings," and Edward Shanks, who saw Wells as a "mythmaker." Bergonzi's mythic analysis focused on the "paradisal and demonic" imagery in Wells's first novel and the ironic use of the pastoral myth of the Golden Age. Bergonzi also reminded us that Wells contrasted himself to Jules Verne (whom Wells saw as dealing with "possible things" based on present science) by placing his own work in the class of the *Golden Ass of Apuleius, True Histories of Lucian,* and *Frankenstein.* Since Bergonzi, critics such as Patrick Parrinder and Robert Philmus have written of Wells's "barrier-breaking heroes," "ideological fables," "primordialism," and "mythic mode." And in the later 70's Jean-Pierre Vernier, agreeing with Bergonzi's view of the ironic pastoral myth, argued that *The Time Machine* awakens "archetypal responses in the reader."[1]

Wells's biographers Norman and Jeanne MacKenzie also have argued that Wells is distinguished by the "symbolic power" of his stories. The MacKenzies remind us that Wells compared his early creative process to a dreaming in which, the MacKenzies say, "powerful and primitive emotions were translated" into visual images and "patterns of archetypal thought," a pattern of thought Wells himself intimated in his Preface to *The Country of the Blind and Other Stories* in 1911:

> I found that, taking almost anything as a starting point and letting my thoughts play about it, there would presently come out of the darkness, in a manner quite inexplicable, some absurd or vivid little nucleus. Little men in canoes upon sunlit oceans . . . , violent conflicts would break out amidst the flowerbeds of suburban gardens; I would discover I was peering into remote and mysterious worlds ruled by an order logical indeed but other than our common sanity.[2]

I am suggesting that if there can be little doubt now about the archetypal dimension of Wells's scientific romances, then clarifying one so far unexamined but central mythic pattern in *The Time Machine* may increase our understanding of that novel's unity and power, and, subordinately, may make one connection, perhaps not adequately recognized, between Wells's first novel and much of his later work. The mythic pattern I refer to is that which Joseph Campbell calls the great "monomyth" of the hero. Wells's otherwise nameless Time Traveller is, to use Wells's own phrase, one of "the active, strong, and subtle." By his violent journey into a mysterious and misunderstood dimension, the hero gains a wisdom that could, but probably will not, be the salvation of his species. And it was just this salvation of his species to which H. G. Wells later devoted his lifework, a devotion for which he was, finally, censured and ridiculed.

Although he wears the face and dress of a late nineteenth-century scientist, the Time Traveller exhibits at least three characteristics of the primordial heroic figure. These characteristics, as they appear in the art and religion of diverse cultures, have been delineated by such students of the mythic hero as Carl Jung, Erich Neumann, Mircea, Eliade, and Joseph Campbell. If the faces, forms, and quests of the hero are as vast and changeable as the hundreds of cultures that have recreated him, the three characteristics I find in Wells's novel are central to the heroic figure generally, as Campbell's work especially makes clear. Indeed, it is Campbell who best summarizes for us the social, psychological, and spiritual qualities of the hero and his quest.

> Beyond the threshold . . . the hero journeys through a world of unfamiliar yet strangely intimate forces, some of which severely threaten him (tests), some of which give magical aid (helpers). When he arrives at the nadir of the mythological round, he undergoes a supreme ordeal and gains his reward . . . represented as . . . sacred marriage . . . father atonement . . . apotheosis, or again—if the powers have remained unfriendly to him—his theft of the boon he came to gain . . . ; intrinsically it is an expansion of consciousness and therewith of being (illumination, transfiguration, freedom). The final work is that of the return. . . . At the return threshold the transcendental powers must remain behind; the hero reemerges from the kingdom of dread (return, resurrection). The boon that he brings restores the world (elixir).[3]

"The changes," Campbell continues, "rung on the simple scale of the monomyth defy description."

The first characteristic of the mythic hero is that he is an extraordinary individual among his fellows—in his powers of perception, his courage and ability to take risks and endure suffering, and his capacity to assert himself and his vision effectively, he is set apart from the mass of humanity. Wells's Time Traveller is certainly an extraordinary man, and the device of the frame story emphasizes this point. By his curiosity, perceptiveness, intelligence, and courage, the first in Wells's series of millenarian heroes stands in sharp contrast to the mundane abilities of his guests—a group of professional and scientific men who serve as foils to the hero. In their dialogue with the Time Traveller, they express only common sense, complacency, positivism, and un-

derstood consciousness. If the Traveller's theories are admittedly based on the most advanced thought of "scientific people," he is the kind of scientist who sees the possibilities within the theories as even the scientific people do not. To the physician, the experiment with the model machine has to be "some sleight-of-hand trick or other" that the "common sense of the morning" will settle. To the psychologist it is "an ingenious paradox and trick." And even the "joyous" and "irreverent" editor and journalist, who represent a *fin de siècle* flaccid anarchism, raise objections, resort to caricature, and heap ridicule on the whole "gaudy lie." By their lack of comprehension they reveal the uncommon imagination and power of the hero. He is an eccentric to them, a man whose "earnestness" and "fecundity" they admire if not understand. He is a source of amusement, is "one of those fellows who are too clever to be believed; you never felt that you saw all around him," and is so whimsical that they "distrusted him." Wells's hero is, then, also described as a kind of Trickster figure, a seeming "quack" and magician whose playfulness runs even to Christmas apparitions. "Things that would have made the fame of a less clever man seemed tricks in his hands. It is a mistake to do things too easily."[4]

Not only does the hero see and understand things the guests do not, he has the unusual courage to follow his vision, to chase a theory down dark, rustling corridors at the risk of sanity and life. Indeed, the "full temerity" of his voyage comes to the hero as he slows down his machine and contemplates the most horrible possibilities of the future. But the risk, he assures himself, is unavoidable, "one of the risks a man has got to take." And upon his return, at the threshold of his laboratory, the danger, the suffering, the harrowing test of the voyage is clear:

> He was in an amazing plight. His coat was dusty and dirty, and smeared with green down the sleeves; his hair disordered, and it seemed to me greyer—either with dust or dirt or because its colour had actually faded. His face was ghastly pale; his chin had a brown cut on it—a cut half healed; his expression was haggard and drawn, as by intense suffering. For a moment he hesitated in the doorway, as if he had been dazzled by the light.[5]

The second mythic characteristic of Wells's hero lies in the nature of his quest. The heroic journey—however actual it may in one sense seem or be—is a voyage into self as much as, or more than, a physical journey. Here, deep in the self, he meets the helpful and threatening forces with which he must deal, and through or against whom he must earn his own transformation: the wisdom of expanded consciousness and the means of salvation he imparts to others upon his return.

Wells certainly suggests that the voyage may be read as a journey into deepest self. The Traveller's time theory is above all a theory of a fourth dimension that is attached, in his words, "to our mental existences." The only factor that distinguishes time from the three spatial dimensions is that our bodies move in space, but "our consciousness moves along" time. At many points the voyage is dreamlike: "For the most part of that night," he says of the Dark Nights in the woods battling Morlocks, "I was persuaded it was a nightmare." And of Weena's death, he says: "Now, in this old familiar room, it is more like the sorrow of a dream than an actual loss." And he will invite skeptical listeners to interpret his tale as the dream of a man sleeping in his laboratory and, therefore, either a "lie—or a prophecy" (pp. 88-89, 99). The passage to that laboratory is like the passage to the realm of dreams too. It is a "long, draughty corridor" of "flickering light," along which one sees "the dance of shadows" and the "queer, broad head in silhouette" of the Traveller. The imagery of the voyage itself has the hallucinatory quality of a dream. Night follows day "like the flapping of a black wing." The whole "surface of the earth" is "melting and flowing under my eyes" (pp. 22, 30-31).

One's immersion in this realm is a dreadful adventure, a kind of death from one world to be born into another: "I suppose a suicide who holds a pistol to his skull feels much the same wonder at what will come next as I felt then," the Traveller says of the beginning of his voyage. His sensations vary from excessive unpleasantness to "hysterical exhilaration" and a "certain curiosity and therewith a certain dread." And upon his arrival, the conflicting images of the demonic and the paradisal act as threshold symbols of the strangely primordial realm he has entered. Hail stones assault flower blossoms. Colossal stone figures and buildings loom beyond the rhododendrons; a white sphinx suggests mystery and disease. Soon he is "groping among moon-lit ruins and touching strange creatures in the black shadows" (pp. 29-33).

Like Odysseus and a host of heroes before him, the Traveller's survival during the quest and his return depend on, as the Traveller puts it, "force and cunning." Like his predecessors, too, the Traveller meets helpers and threats among the unfamiliar but strangely intimate forces he encounters. Weena, of course, despite her slight consciousness and her diminutive stature, is friend, guide, and object of "a miniature flirtation." She provides "signs of the human inheritance," such as fear, that warn him; she offers flowers that, in the end, become symbols of "gratitude and mutual tenderness," of that human sympathy which, with "mind and strength," threatens to die out in the world. "Nor until it was too late did I clearly understand what she was to me. For by . . . showing in her weak, futile way that she cared for me, the little doll of a creature presently gave my return to the neighbourhood . . . almost a feeling of coming home" (pp. 55, 63, 104). She is the "child," as even the Traveller repeatedly calls her, the princess, one

face of the Nourishing Mother, who deep in the heroic journey, reveals the lost potential, the unconscious source of life in the hero and humanity. Dreading darkness, playfully clapping and dancing before the fire lost to the Upper-worlders, Weena is indeed a child of light, the one whom the hero had hoped to bring back to his own time, yet can do so only metaphorically through his tale.[6]

And like his mythic progenitors, the Traveller is the fire-starter, he who battles the dark, destructive side of world and mind with the creative power in himself. The task of the hero, as Campbell and Jung have argued, is to carry life energy—symbolized by fire—across the "difficult thresholds of transformation" and change the "patterns of consciousness and unconscious life."[7] When he descends to the "Under-world" (to use Wells's own term), the hero battles the destructive human potential, or the bestial insanity, faced at this deepest point of the journey, symbolized by the devouring Terrible Mother in myth and, in Wells's novel, by that "subterranean species of humanity" the cannibal Morlocks—those "bleached, obscene, nocturnal things"—and by the "leprous," mocking, white sphinx, one gateway to this Under-world.[8] Here, in the blackness beneath, the only security against the Morlock is fire: "they did not seem to have any fear of me apart from the light" (p. 66). And when these "damned souls" bring the Under-world to the Upper-world during the "Dark Nights," it is with fire again that the hero—feeling a "strange exultation"—defeats them. Here, in what Campbell calls the nadir of the heroic journey, the Time Traveller knows primitive dread: "I had slept, and my fire had gone out, and the bitterness of death came over my soul. . . . I felt as if I was in a monstrous spider's web" (p. 86).

More important than the particular qualities and unities of the timeless heroic quest itself, however, are the wisdom gained and the message or boon with which the hero returns. Wells's hero returns with a prophecy that he conveys as compulsively as Coleridge's sea voyager. "I want to tell it" he says. "Badly. . . . I've lived eight days as no human being ever lived before!" (p. 28). The message is that which, in a variety of ways and degrees of effectiveness, Wells would speak throughout his life: though humanity as a species has been granted the rare opportunity to do otherwise, it stands to lose all that which its positive potential suggests it can develop—courage, humane assertiveness, perceptiveness, intellect, consciousness, endurance, and wholeness of vision.

> I grieved to think how brief the dream of human intellect had been. It had committed suicide. It had set itself steadfastly towards comfort and ease, a balanced society with security and permanency as its watchword, it had attained its hopes—to come to this at last. . . . No doubt in that perfect world there had been no unemployed problem, no social question left unsolved. And a great quiet had followed. . . .

Nature never appeals to intelligence until habit and instinct are useless. There is no intelligence where there is no change and no need of change. Only those animals partake of intelligence that have to meet a huge variety of needs and dangers.

(p. 90)

Stasis and temporary social or technological success lead to psychic, and even physical, decadence, to Eloi and Morlock, to exquisite and fragile children or to soulless beast-men whose only organizing principles are obeisance to machinery and a devouring of humankind.

Wells arrived early at a conception of the degeneration of self and civilization, and he connected the root of all the possibilities and symptoms of degeneracy to that "human selfishness" whose "rigorous punishment" reaches far into the future of the race (p. 75). Such degeneracy is what Erich Neumann called "sclerosis of consciousness" in his own study of the mythic hero's task:

Typical . . . is the state of affairs in America, though the same holds true for practically the whole Western hemisphere. Every conceivable sort of dominant rules the personality. . . . The grotesque fact that murders, brigands, gangsters, thieves, forgers, tyrants and swindlers, in a guise that deceives nobody, have seized control of collective life is characteristic of our time. . . . Worship of the "beast" is by no means confined to Germany; it prevails wherever . . . the aggravating complexities of civilized behavior are swept away in favor of bestial rapacity. . . . [The] integration of the personality, its wholeness, becomes the supreme ethical goal upon which the fate of humanity depends.[9]

The mindless sensuality of Eloi is no less destructive of self and civilization than the bestial rapacity of the Morlock—both adequately symbolized by Wells's headless faun in the garden. "All traditions, the complex organizations, the nations, languages, aspirations . . . had been swept out of existence," the Time Traveller tells us, and "from the bottom of my heart I pitied this last rill from the great flood of humanity" (pp. 73-74). Neither the "too perfect triumph" of technology, nor the rapacity of vain and selfish power strugglings or wars between classes and nations, nor the comfort and ease that tempt at every turn can be the salvation of the species. Survival must be based not on these attributes of modern civilization but on some other integrating wholeness of vision—which vision Wells would spend the rest of his life struggling to articulate. If at times Wells slipped and turned toward that "too perfect triumph of man" that led toward Eloi and Morlock, as his son Anthony West has suggested, he was nevertheless fighting the old prophetic battle to change patterns of consciousness.[10]

Wells's first fictional hero, then, endures a quest, as we have seen, that traces the traditional patterns of the hero myth central to diverse cultures. Even the return of the hero to the fourth dimension at the end of the novel is not anomalous to the heroic pattern. Frequently, as Campbell points out, the hero may "refuse the responsibility" to return "into the kingdom of humanity" where the boon "redounds to the renewing of humanity," or having returned to mankind, may pass again back into the realm discovered in the quest. Indeed, it is by the freedom to pass back and forth between the world of time and the timeless world of the quest—"permitting the mind to know the one by virtue of the other," that one recognizes the hero as "Master of Two Worlds." For it is in combining the eternal symbols and experience with the historical moment that the myth conveys its truth, not in the lasting physical presence of the hero in his time.[11]

Yet even if we limit our consideration of the heroic journey to Wells's hero specifically, that hero's ultimate return to the dimension of the vision can be seen as an affirmation rather than a denial of his prophetic value for Wells's theme. As Robert Philmus has argued, for example, the Traveller by vanishing into the other world accepts his vision literally and demands that it be not only metaphorically true:

The Traveller's return . . . far from vitiating the impact of *The Time Machine,* reinforces its claim to integrity: by having the Time Traveller act out the ultimate consequence of his taking the myth literally, Wells illustrates the rigor that he has submitted himself to in satirizing certain "present ideals." The romance, as I see it, is thus rigorously self-contained in "working to a logical conclusion" both the myth of devolution that exposes tendencies "of our own age" and the various points of view regarding the truth of that prophetic myth.[12]

The prophecy, the wisdom gained, is, for the traditional hero as for Wells's first hero, a new pattern of consciousness, a revolutionary vision against entropy and degeneration that may destroy the old canon and build a new.[13] If the wisdom learned from the heroic journey in *The Time Machine* is the awareness of the avenues to human degeneracy, a degeneracy connected in Chapter 11 to the cosmos, it remains for each generation to avoid the fate of "energy in security," to renew for itself—so long as it is a cosmic possibility—its physical power and its positive psychic evolution. If the Traveller "saw in the growing pile of civilization only a foolish heaping that must inevitably fall back upon and destroy its makers in the end," as the narrator tells us, it also "remains for us to live as though it were not so" (p. 104).

As late as 1942 in his D.Sc. thesis at London University, Wells argued that our collective survival lay "in some sort of super-individual, a brave new *persona*" that would integrate the whole human social organism, "the ecology of Homo sapiens." Human ecology Wells defined as the science of working out "biological, intellectual, and economic consequences" to enable us to see the possibilities of the future.[14] What the hero brings to his culture is what Campbell calls the "primitive health" or new consciousness of interrelationships—the ecology if you will—of humanity, nature, and social order.

There is a continuity in much of Wells's work, I am suggesting, that builds upon his first novel's hero and upon that hero's earned wisdom. And perhaps our understanding of Wells will benefit from other critics' still closer examination of that continuity. Let me suggest a few sources of this continuity in closing.

The Invisible Man (1897) presents another visionary scientist among "floundering yokels." Yet he is motivated, even to the point of murder, by pride, vanity, and paranoiac dreams of power. This time it is through a flawed or false hero and his "evil experiment" that Wells defines human degeneracy-through-selfishness by depicting again the death of human sympathy and by warning of the dangers of uncontrolled rational intellect. And this novel and its theme were directly preceded and initially developed by *The Island of Dr. Moreau* (1896) in which an earlier Rappaccini-like scientist dreams of Godlike power and argues for the uselessness of concepts such as pleasure and pain while extolling the delights of "intellectual desires." The theme of responsibility for one's actions and for others (even other creatures) is suggested through the vivisectionist, who is unaware of his victims' agonies and of his responsibilities for his grotesque creations. Yet when the narrator Pendrick returns to London, he sees the beast in all humanity and wonders if God, too, had blundered, if progress or evolution is even possible.

The War of the Worlds (1898) then carries forward Wells's program for the total reform of humanity and social order by warning, as his first hero did, of the dangers of becoming over-specialized prisoners of technology, like the Martians, or of becoming prisoners of the decadence born of the naive yet supreme confidence in the future as progress. And from this point onward to the end of his life, in fiction and nonfiction, Wells will frequently focus on the possible avenues of salvation for the species. *Anticipations* (1901), which Wells accurately called the "keystone to the main arch of my work," more emphatically focuses his concern for secular salvation through revolutionary change: "I'm going to write, talk, preach revolution for the next five years," he promised. It is at this point that Wells approaches a "new synthesis" through his search for a group of heroic individuals, a search that moves from the "New Republicans" to the "Open Conspiracy," to the "Samuari" of *A Modern Utopia* (1905), and beyond, Wells searches for offshoots, if at times terminal branches, of the heroic personality of the Time Traveller.

In 1933-34 Wells looked back on *Utopia* in his autobiography and continued to argue that through the creation of a heroic class we may attain the knowledge to outrun catastrophe. And widest knowledge he continues to attach, as in *Utopia,* to the best in humanity: to individual uniqueness and liberty, to dynamic society and state, to pluralism of morality, to originality of mind, to courage, self-sufficiency, renunciation, and to endurance. Even economics, Wells argues, like all social theories or institutions, must be attached to human psychology or forever flounder dangerously.

To the end of his life, Wells maintained the thread of continuity that reached back to the Time Traveller's prophecy. In *Mind at the End of Its Tether* (1945), it is ordinary man who is at the end, and only an extraordinary minority of the highly adaptable (or "Over-Man") may survive. We have come so far, Wells said, outside the order of Nature, have become so much the evolutionary objects of some new, implacable, universal hostility, that we perch on the brink of extinction, perch quite beyond "quantitative adjustments," so that we will have to move so steeply up or steeply down the evolutionary chain that few indeed, if any, may now adapt. Wells concludes his final prophetic warning with two points that return us to the message of his earliest hero. First, the only fight worth the effort is the heroic battle for human advancement, however great the odds now, as if even Hiroshima "were not so." Better, Wells reminds us, to end as a species in "dignity, kindliness and generosity, and not like drunken cowards in a daze or poisoned rats in a sack." And second, the chief form of human adaptability for survival will be a revolutionary change of consciousness, that "mental adaptability" which the mythic hero has always earned and prophesied to humankind.[15]

As Wells's first hero said, and as so many of Wells's later works echoed, "What, unless biological science is a mass of errors, is the cause of human intelligence and vigour? Hardship and freedom: conditions under which the active, strong, and subtle survive and the weaker go to the wall; conditions that put a premium upon the loyal alliance of capable men, upon self-restraint, patience, and decision" (p. 44). If the first part of these words sounds like mere Social Darwinism, and in one sense it does, the second part has new significance for the post-Hiroshima generation.

Notes

1. Van Wyck Brooks, *The World of H. G. Wells* (New York: Kennerley, 1915), pp. 168-71; Evgeny Zamyatin, "Herbert Wells," *A Soviet Heretic: Essays of Yevgeny Zamyatin,* trans. Mirra Ginsburg (Chicago: Univ. of Chicago Press, 1970), pp. 259-90; Jorge Luis Borges, "The First Wells," *Other Inquisitions: 1937-1952,* trans. Ruth L. C. Simms

(Austin: Univ. of Texas Press, 1964), pp. 81-88. Bernard Bergonzi, *"The Time Machine*: An Ironic Myth,*"* in *H. G. Wells: A Collection of Critical Essays,* ed. Bernard Bergonzi (Englewood Cliffs, NJ: Prentice-Hall, 1976), pp. 39-53, hereafter cited as *Critical Essays,* and Bernard Bergonzi, *The Early H. G. Wells* (Manchester: Manchester Univ. Press, 1961), pp. 16-20, 42-43, 49-61. See also Patrick Parrinder, *H. G. Wells* (Edinburgh: Oliver & Boyd, 1970), and Robert M. Philmus, *Into the Unknown: The Evolution of Science Fiction from Francis Godwin to H. G. Wells* (Berkeley: Univ. of California Press, 1970). Jean-Pierre Vernier, *"The Time Machine* and Its Context,*"* in *The Time Machine, The War of the Worlds: A Critical Edition,* trans. and ed. Frank D. McConnell (New York: Oxford Univ. Press, 1977), pp. 314-320, hereafter cited as *Critical Edition.*

2. *Norman and Jeanne MacKenzie, H. G. Wells* (New York: Simon and Schuster, 1973), pp. 118-19.

3. *The Hero with a Thousand Faces* (New Jersey: Princeton Univ. Press, 1968), pp. 245-46. Hereafter cited as *Hero.*

4. The Trickster is one face of the mythic hero, see esp. *Critical Edition,* pp. 18-20, 22-24. And cf. *Hero,* pp. 44-45, 90, 184.

   On the subject of the guests' response to Wells's hero's tale, Campbell again is helpful. Upon returning from his journey the hero always meets the "return blow of reasonable queries, hard resentment, and good people at a loss to comprehend." How to "communicate to people who insist on the exclusive evidence of their senses the message of the all-generating void"—that is the problem the hero faces "throughout the millenniums of mankind's prudent folly," *Hero,* pp. 216, 218. Erich Neumann, in *The Origins and History of Consciousness* (New Jersey: Princeton Univ. Press, 1973), adds that the hero is ever the "outsider" who brings into conflict his "new images" and values (from an inner compelling voice) with the collective, the old order, thereby sacrificing friendship and normal living. See esp. pp. 375, 378.

5. *Critical Edition,* p. 25. Future references are cited in parentheses.

6. Carl Jung, *Symbols of Transformation,* trans. R. F. C. Hull. Vol. 5 (New Jersey: Princeton Univ. Press, 1956), pp. 242, 272, 292-93, 300-01. Hereafter cited as *Symbols.* Cf. Neumann's discussion of the "mythological goal of the dragon fight" for the captive woman in *Consciousness,* pp. 105, 201; and the *Critical Edition,* pp. 54-56, 63, 71.

7. *Symbols,* pp. 121, 149, 170, 212, and *Hero,* pp. 8, 10. When Wells and Jung met in 1923, Wells found Jung's collective unconscious similar to his own concept of the "Mind of the Race"; see MacKenzie, pp. 338, 346.

8. To the Traveller the Sphinx represents disease and the mysteries "which I could not face" of the Under-world (p. 64). She seems to hover, to watch him, to smile in mockery, and the Traveller finally realizes that he cannot defeat her or open her mysteries by force so much as, like Oedipus, by craft and cunning (pp. 36, 50). And somehow this "crouching white shape" seems to him connected to the riddles of how mankind has evolved (pp. 33, 36, 50). The Sphinx is the traditional symbol of the dragon devourer, the Terrible Mother, the guardian of the mysteries of destruction and regeneration or creative evolution. It is her defeat that allows for the enthronement or prophecy of the Good Mother. See *Consciousness,* pp. 161-62, 324.

9. Neumann, *Consciousness,* pp. 391-92.

10. Anthony West, "H. G. Wells," in *Critical Essays,* pp. 10, 12-13, 20. West suggests that Wells strayed from his "deeper intuitions" during his "middle period" of scientific utopianism beginning around 1901 with *Anticipations.* But, West argues, Wells returned in later years to his belief that virtue does not reside in intellect alone. The idea of revolutionary change, West reminds us, was the *sine qua non* of Wells's utopias. West is on this point in considerable contrast to Frederick Karl in "Conrad, Wells and the Two Voices," *PMLA,* 88 (1973), 1049-65. Karl argues that after the scientific romances especially, Wells, unlike Conrad, was an "ahistorical" ameliorist in the liberal, utilitarian, scientific tradition.

11. See *Hero,* esp. pp. 193, 229, 356, 358. Campbell's examples range from Buddha, the Hindu Muchukunda, saints dying in supernal ecstasy, and to numerous heroes "fabled to have taken up residence forever" in the realm discovered in the journey. "The last act in the biography of the hero is that of the death or departure"; yet he remains a "synthesizing image" of the historical and the timeless worlds.

12. Robert Philmus, *"The Time Machine*; or, the Fourth Dimension as Prophecy," *PMLA,* 84 (1969), 530-35.

13. Campbell argues that the mythic hero is always connected to larger cosmic forces and that he is therefore an "evolutionary" hero leading humanity to further stages of development in social, artistic, and spiritual realms. He is the "creative power" of things becoming; see *Hero,* esp. 315, 336-37. Compare Neumann, *Consciousness,* p. 131. Both

Neumann and Mircea Eliade have argued equally emphatically for the hero as "revolutionary" figure who "brings to birth those forms the age is most lacking," who restores a balance to his age, and who "regenerates time" as a representative of eternal powers and truths. See *Consciousness,* pp. 376-77, 381, and Eliade, *The Myth of the Eternal Return* (New York: Pantheon Books, 1954), esp. pp. 35-47, 55-57, 69, 87-88.

14. See MacKenzie, pp. 163, 437.

15. See Wells, *Mind at the End of Its Tether* (London: William Heinemann, 1945), esp. pp. 4, 18, 30, 34. Campbell's and Neumann's argument for the significance of the timeless heroic quest in the mid- and late-twentieth century world is remarkably similar to Wells's, but especially as the argument culminates in *Tether.* Campbell, to take one instance, also emphasizes the delicate ecology of planetary community now as a new, dangerous stage in human evolution as much in need as preceding stages of some new heroic consciousness. The whole thing is being worked out, Campbell argues, on a level deeper than the boundaries of nationalism or ego-consciousness; it is being worked out, toward success or failure, in the collective unconscious and on the "titanic battle-fields" of the planet, and it is bound to be a "long and very frightening process." It is man who has become the "alien presence" and "mystery" whose "image of society is to be reformed" toward non-nationalistic and non-egocentric systems. The "whole destiny" of a species is to be, or not, atoned. See *Hero,* esp. pp. 388-90. Neumann similarly argues, in his appendices most clearly, that the global revolution of modern times is an evolutionary storm-center. The regeneration of the species toward some new stage of advancement must go beyond mere re-collectivization as well as beyond mere nationalism and egocentricity or selfishness. See *Consciousness,* pp. 422, 436, 441.

Veronica Hollinger (essay date July 1987)

SOURCE: Hollinger, Veronica. "Deconstructing *The Time Machine.*¹" *Science Fiction Studies* 14, no. 42 (July 1987): 201-21.

[*In the following essay, Hollinger explores aspects of time travel in literature, contending that* The Time Machine *achieves an ironic deconstruction of Victorian scientific positivism.*]

Time is, of all modes of existence, most obsequious to the imagination. . . .

—Samuel Johnson

The idea of time travel has for many years exercised the ingenuity not only of SF writers, but of scientists and philosophers as well; neither the equations of quantum physics nor the rules of logic have managed definitively to prove or to disprove the possibility that this most paradoxical of SF concepts may some day be realized.[2] The purpose of this present essay is to examine some aspects of time travel within the framework of Derridean deconstruction, since, as I hope to demonstrate, the time-travel story always achieves a deconstruction of certain received ideas about the nature and structure of time. It may be that deconstructive activity of some kind is characteristic of all SF, in which case this present application of post-structuralist critical theory may serve to suggest new approaches to other SF motifs. The final two sections of this essay focus in detail upon H. G. Wells's *The Time Machine* (1895), the novella which first applied technology to time travel and which remains the most influential time-travel story ever written. Anticipating post-structuralist strategies by a good many years, *The Time Machine* accomplishes its own ironic deconstruction of Victorian scientific positivism, couched in the very language of the system which it sets out to undermine. And this, as I will discuss below, is the very essence of the deconstructive enterprise.

1. Time travel is a sign without a referent, a linguistic construction originating in the metaphorical spatialization of temporality. As Mark Rose observes, "the visualization of time as a line generated the idea of time travel" (p. 108). To write about time travel, therefore, is necessarily to have performed a kind of reading, to have interpreted time in order to structure it as the "space" through which a traveller can undertake a journey. As linguistic construction, time travel is never "true," but its very status as pure sign gives rise to one of its most valuable functions within the SF genre: the time-travel story provides literary metaphors of our ideas about the nature of time; it is a means of working out the logical (and the not-so-logical) implications of our interpretations of this most nebulous aspect of human experience.

As in all SF, the relationship in time-travel stories between narrative event and empirical reality can be characterized as either analogical or extrapolative. The analogical tendency is exhibited, for example, in James Tiptree, Jr's "Houston, Houston, Do You Read?" (1976), in which time travel is used both to literalize Tiptree's critique of contemporary sexual chauvinism and to demystify the signifying coerciveness of concepts such as "feminine" and "masculine." Her fictional future is relatively discontinuous with contemporary reality. At the other end of the spectrum, a novel like Gregory Benford's *Timescape* (1980) emphasizes the interrelationships among present, past, and future in very direct ways, concerned as it is with the short-term effects of recent ecological carelessness. No matter what the reigning tendency of a particular story, however, time travel is itself always metaphorical, the result of a "false" condensation of time with space.[3] *The Time Machine,* for example, offers itself as a prophetic warning of the decline of the human race and this "devolution" is the apparently direct result of the class divisiveness of Wells's contemporary social situation. Nevertheless, the "scientific" rationale for the temporal journey which makes possible this warning is developed solely through spatial metaphors. The Time Traveller's central contention is that "there is no difference between Time and any of the three dimensions of Space except that our consciousness moves along it" (*TTM* [*The Time Machine*] 1:5).

It is indicative of the changes that have occurred in scientific and philosophical "discursive formations" (to borrow a term from Michel Foucault) that SF no longer defines itself solely as an extrapolative genre. This is due in large part to the comprehensive realization that reality is constituted by language; that the language from within which we speak constantly mediates between the self and experience of reality. Ferdinand de Saussure's insight into the arbitrary nature of the bond between sign and referent, his conclusion that "every means of expression used in society is based, in principle, on collective behaviour or—what amounts to the same thing—on convention" (p. 68), indicates both the contingency and indeterminacy of these linguistic mediations. We are led to the unavoidable conclusion that experience of reality is always already interpretation, since "without language, thought is a vague, uncharted nebula [a happily fortuitous SF metaphor]. There are no pre-existing ideas, and nothing is distinct before the appearance of language" (Saussure: 112). Like other literary metaphors, a time-travel story is a metaphor once removed, a metaphor of a metaphor which may or may not have any direct relationship with objective reality, since that reality is screened from direct apprehension by the very language through which we speak of it. Language speaks of time in spatial metaphors and produces the concept of travel in time.[4]

Rose suggests that the metaphorical tendency in contemporary SF far outweighs its predictive intent. In his initial distinction between fantasy and SF, he discusses analogy and extrapolation in the following terms:

> it may be useful . . . to conceive the opposition between fantasy and science fiction in terms of Roman Jakobson's distinction between metaphor and metonymy as poles of literary behavior. The changed worlds of fantasy are presented as literary substitutions for reality; they are related to the empirical world paradigmatically or metaphorically. . . . The changed worlds of science fiction, however, are presented as logical extensions of reality; they are related to the empirical world syntagmatically or metonymically. This is

what is meant when science fiction is called an extrapolative form.

> (Rose: 21-22)[5]

Recognizing that "both principles are at work in science fiction as in all discourse" (p. 22), Rose nevertheless notes a shift in emphasis from metonymy to metaphor in more recent SF, which has resulted in "a radical reinterpretation of the genre" (p. 16). We may conclude from this that time travel is not the anomaly it might at first appear to be, since its overtly metaphorical function is now the rule of the genre, rather than the exception.[6] Darko Suvin (pp. 222-42) has suggested *The Time Machine* as a "structural model" for SF; in the present context, it offers itself as a linguistic paradigm as well.[7]

Suvin has defined SF as a genre "whose main formal device is an imaginative framework alternative to the author's empirical environment" (p. 8). From this perspective, time travel is "a means of reality displacement" (p. 71) similar to space travel, in that it functions to introduce the reader into the alternative framework of the SF text as an "extension and exaggeration of some facet of our experience into [*sic*] another setting" (Lindsay: 126). Extending beyond such generic displacement, however, time travel also achieves a displacement specific to itself, and this is its subversion of certain traditional approaches to the question of time. This holds true whether the stories in which it appears offer themselves to the reader as metaphorical commentaries, as exercises in extrapolation, or as blends of both.

It will be useful at this point (for critical theory can be as much a force for defamiliarization as SF itself)[8] to continue this discussion of the particular nature and function of time travel from within the context of Derridean deconstruction. Jacques Derrida's (anti)philosophical strategies are so named because they recognize the impossibility of effecting any complete or permanent breakdown of the conventionalized modes of thought from within which we interpret human reality. Derrida cautions that

> it is not a question of 'rejecting' these notions; they are necessary, and, at least at present, nothing is conceivable for us without them. It is a question at first of demonstrating the systematic and historical solidarity of the concepts and gestures of thought that one often believes to be innocently separated.

> (*OG*, pp. 13-14)

Both SF and post-structuralist theory in general are involved in the processes of defamiliarization: SF achieves a "cognitive estrangement"[9] through its displacement of the social/political/cultural present, while deconstruction seeks to expose the conventional nature of the "gestures of thought" of the Western metaphysical tradition. Thus both call attention to the historical contingency of their subject matter.[10] On the other hand, both SF and deconstruction must speak from within the contexts which they seek to defamiliarize: there is no getting outside of the discourses of consensus reality. Derrida is at his most succinct here: "il n'y a pas de hors-texte" (*OG*, p. 158). There is no vantage point outside the boundaries of the observable, no privileged observer, no completely innocent reading of "reality."

2. Time travel is always potentially deconstructive, effecting as it does a displacement of the human "here and now" upon which we tend to base our interpretations of reality. Its immediate fascination for writers, as for scientists and logicians, is the fact that time-travel stories are always constructed around and within paradox, "the contradiction that at each different moment we occupy a different moment from the one which we are then occupying—that five minutes from now, for example, [we] may be a hundred years from now" (Williams: 105). The time traveller experiences diachrony (succession) as synchrony (simultaneity), but the effect is not simply a reversal of these two perspectives, because the time-travel story does not abandon the notion of historical change, which tends to result when synchrony is privileged over diachrony. The result is rather a paradoxical movement in which the narrative synchronicity of temporal events highlights rather than hides differences in times. The instantaneous displacement of the time traveller from one moment to another creates an *immediate* juxtaposition of differences which our habitual sense of the successivity of events renders less discontinuous and jarring than it in fact is.

At the heart of the time-travel motif is the "scandal" of temporal paradox. The Grandfather Paradox is the best-known version of this peril of backward time travel. Larry Niven develops it as follows:

> At the age of eighty your grandfather invents a time machine. You hate the old man, so you steal the machine and take it sixty years back into the past and kill him. How can they suspect you?
>
> But you've killed him before he can meet your grandmother. Thus you were never born. He didn't get a chance to build the time machine either.
>
> But then you can't have killed him. Thus he may still sire your father, who may sire you. Later there will be a time machine . . .
>
> You and the machine both do and do not exist.
>
> (Niven: 111)[11]

As Niven concludes, "with the Grandfather Paradox operating, the effect, coming before the cause, may cause the cause never to come into effect, with results that are not even self-consistent" (p. 113). This variation of the time-travel story leads the reader to "the point at which thought encounters an *aporia*—or self-engendered paradox beyond which it cannot press" (Norris: 49).

The structure of the time-loop story creates another version of temporal paradox. Readers who try to unravel the threads of Robert A. Heinlein's "All You Zombies—" (1959) will find themselves ensnared in the same time-loop which traps its protagonist: through time travel and sex change, he is his own mother and father; trapped in a process of endless supplementation, he must repeatedly travel into the past to (re)create himself.[12]

Heinlein's brilliant exercise in solipsism is a virtual dramatization of Derrida's (non)concept of the *supplement,* which he develops in his deconstruction of the nature/culture opposition. As Derrida demonstrates, the concept of the supplement contains two differing significations. At its most obvious, it is a surplus, an addition to full presence: "it cumulates and accumulates presence" (*OG*, p. 144). Thus, for example, culture supplements nature, and writing supplements speech. Traditionally, nature and speech are privileged over culture and writing, which are considered to be supplementary constructs. In addition, however (as its own "supplementary" implication), the supplement compensates for a *lack* of full presence and comes to replace that which it supplements: "it intervenes or insinuates itself *in-the-place-of*" (*OG*, p. 145: emphasis in original).[13]

In demonstrating the impossibility of arriving at the origin of the "entity" (his protagonist Jane), Heinlein dramatizes the *always already* supplemented nature of that entity. At which point did Jane enjoy a pure un(re)created state if s/he is caught in the deterministic strands of an endless time-loop? "All You Zombies—" is the fictional analogue of the Derridean contention that "the apparent addition/substitution of the supplement actually *constitutes* the seemingly unsupplemented entity" (Leitch: 172; emphasis in original). Heinlein's Jane is always already supplemented by his/her trips into the past to repeat the act of (re)creation: "the indifferent process of supplementarity has always already *infiltrated* presence" (*OG*, p. 163; emphasis in original).[14] Heinlein's story is arguably the masterpiece of its type, but the disturbing play of supplementarity is inherent in any time-loop situation, from Robert Silverberg's hard-bitten "Absolutely Inflexible" (1956) to the parodic "Seventh Voyage" of Stanislaw Lem's *Star Diaries* (1964).

3. As I suggested earlier, to write about time travel is always already to have performed a reading; that is, it requires that the writer has first interpreted time in order to structure it as space. Since scientific discourse is one of the frameworks within which all SF is written, the revolution which overturned the Newtonian scientific paradigm has necessarily had an effect upon how time-travel stories read time. This scientific revolution accounts for a major shift in the development of the

motif, since interpretation of time is a crucial differentium between the Newtonian and Einsteinian worldviews.[15] As James Ziegler explains:

> To Newton time was a constant, to be measured in the same way that mass, density, and volume are measured. To Einstein time is relative in the same way that mass, density, and volume are relative. Since mass, density, and volume change as their velocities change, time also changes—hence the popular term *fourth dimension.*
>
> (p. 74)

If the reading of time takes place within the paradigm of Classical Physics, temporal structure will tend to be linear, homogeneous, and consecutive; on the other hand, relative time is nothing if not a "post-structure," tending towards heterogeneity and indeterminacy. Or, to invoke an analogous set of metaphors developed by Roland Barthes, Newtonian time is read as Work (*œuvre*), Einsteinian time as Text (*texte*).[16]

Before exploring this analogy, however, it is necessary to review the implications of the several sets of binary oppositions that have appeared in my own text. I have already made use of Rose's Jakobsonian distinction between metonymy and metaphor, and two more polarities have just been introduced: the opposition between the Newtonian and Einsteinian scientific paradigms and Barthes' opposition of the Work to the Text. While each of these is a functional opposition in this present analysis, it should not be supposed that they are in any *fundamental* sense truly antithetical. Indeed, the configuration of binary oppositions, as the principal structural convention of our mental operations, is the prime target of Derridean deconstruction.[17] Derrida's deconstruction of the "proper" discourse of philosophy (in his essay "White Mythology: Metaphor in the Text of Philosophy"), as it demonstrates the metaphorical nature of all language, leads inevitably to the conclusion that, so far from standing in opposition to metaphor, metonymy may in fact be defined as a special case of metaphor. Nor does Relativity Theory consider Newtonian science in opposition to itself: "Relativity does not . . . contradict classical physics. It simply regards the old concepts as limiting cases that apply solely to the familiar experiences of [human beings]" (Barnett: 58).

Hence, if my contention that time may be read as either Work or Text is to hold up, it is necessary to "supplement" Barthes' argument, to recognize that all literary productions are texts (or intertexts, for that matter—a more radically heterogeneous view of literary discourse). The Work, best exemplified in the world-view of the 19th-century realist novel, is a limiting case of Text, one more consonant with "the familiar experiences" of human reality, which we tend to interpret in linear, causal patterns, as logical structures. It is *différance*

which defines and which "invites us to undo the need for balanced equations, to see if each term in an opposition is not after all an accomplice of the other" (Spivak: lix). In place of presence, of center, of secure ground upon which to base our knowledge of reality, Derrida offers the "play" of *différance* as the (non)principle of reality. *Différance,* a Derridean neologism which conflates the effects of both deferral and difference, is the gap between signifier and signified, between sign and referent, between our interpretations of the world and the world "in itself."[18]

Barthes makes the distinction between Work and Text in "From Work to Text," a product of his later, post-structuralist, career. Recognizing that the idea of the Work arises from within the same epistemological matrix (or *epistemè*) as does Classical Physics, he writes of it as "a traditional notion that has long been and still is thought of in what might be called Newtonian fashion" (p. 74). The implication here, of course, is that the Text is to be aligned with Einsteinian "fashion." Derrida has also recognized the post-structuralist affinities of relativistic science. In his seminal essay "Play, Structure and Sign in the Discourse of the Human Sciences," he observes that "the Einsteinian constant is not a constant, is not a center. It is the very concept of variability—it is, finally, the concept of the game" (p. 267). Relativity becomes identified with free play and *différance,* the (non)principles of the "post-structure."

Time-travel stories influenced by Newtonian fashions rely heavily upon an interpretation of time-as-Work, which limits the free play of both narrative event and structure: the Newtonian universe is "a closed system operating by fixed rules that [can] be discovered by reason based on observation" (Ziegler: 70). Newton's idealist physics defined time as absolute: in Book One of his *Principia Mathematica* (1687), he writes that "absolute, true and mathematical time, of itself and from its own nature, flows equably without relation to anything external" (quoted in Thayer, p. 17). Absolute Time (functioning like a kind of metaphysical Greenwich Mean Time) joins the company of transcendental signifieds, the centers which determine the fixed nature of metaphysical structures. By the 19th century, the concept of Absolute Time had given way to a belief in Natural Law as the organizing principle which secured and determined the nature and structure of time.

In many ways, ***The Time Machine*** appears to be an exemplary demonstration of time as Newtonian Work. Wells's Traveller journeys through one dimension of a rational universe which is itself a fixed structure, a totality whose "truth" is, at least potentially, accessible to scientific discovery. The Victorian scientist is presented as an intelligent and competent reader of time future, the quintessential privileged observer, the subject who enjoys a vantage point hundreds of thousands of years removed from the object of his study.[19]

Because time is a linear and homogeneous Work, the Time Traveller moves along a fixed time-line into a future which is the direct and apparently inevitable result of his present (time read as classic realist novel). His ability to return to this present (as opposed to any other "present") is never in question. As he gazed at the stars of the far future (he tells his listeners), he "thought of their unfathomable distance, and the slow inevitable drift of their movements from the unknown past into the unknown future" (1:79). This "inevitable drift" of the stars is both a fact of Wells's narrative universe and a resolutely spatial metaphor for the fixed structure of time.

Inevitability is a keynote of time-as-Work. The "devolution" which Wells saw threatening the society of his own day is figured first in bio-sociological decline and then repeated in the entropic decay of the Solar System (scientifically determined according to the Second Law of Thermodynamics).[20] At the level of narrative event, the logic of Wells's reading seems to require the final disappearance of the Traveller himself from the text.[21] The most powerful event in **The Time Machine** is a dramatically visual depiction of this vast determination: the Traveller at the terminal beach, a helpless and horrified spectator at the end of the world. Wells's epilogue seems to suggest that time future is as fixed as time past: "If that is so, it remains for us to live as though it were not so" (12:117). Nothing to be done. Interpreted within the framework of the Newtonian world-view, the Narrator's rather enigmatic conclusion invites this fatalistic reading.

When time is read as Work, SF tends to function metonymically—that is, as extrapolation—since temporal structure is comprised of a rational and successive series of cause-and-effect events. Temporal free play is usually limited to forward movement in time; the "scandal" of temporal paradox is quite firmly excluded from the game. This may be the reason that most early time-travel stories limit themselves to trips into the future. Examples would include the optimistic anticipation of Edward Bellamy's best-selling utopia, *Looking Backward, 2000-1887* (1888), and the "death-watch" anxieties of John W. Campbell's twin stories "Twilight" (1934) and "Night" (1935), which together offer Campbell's own version of the triumph of entropy. These future journeys provide some protection against the dangers (to narrative event and/or to the discourse of the text) of temporal paradox. One of the earliest stories to admit the potential for temporal paradox, Mark Twain's *A Connecticut Yankee in King Arthur's Court* (1889), dissolves finally into a metaphysical negation of reality, conveniently erasing temporal structure altogether. In place of the majestic drift of the stars in **The Time Machine,** Hank Morgan in *A Connecticut Yankee* refers to his life as "this pathetic drift between the eternities" (18:161).

4. When the Einsteinian scientific paradigm displaces the Newtonian, SF is invited to explore what we might call the infinite free play of temporal structure, the play of time-as-Text, heterogeneous, indeterminate, and uncentered, completely at odds with the notion of fixed structure. Considered in this context, Derrida's explication of the concept of centered structure implicates Classical Physics in the game of Western metaphysics:

> The concept of centered structure is in fact the concept of a freeplay based on a fundamental ground, a freeplay which is constituted upon a fundamental immobility and a reassuring certitude, which is itself beyond the reach of the freeplay. With this certitude anxiety can be mastered, for anxiety is invariably the result of a certain mode of being implicated in the game, of being caught by the game, of being as it were from the very beginning at stake in the game.
>
> ("Play, Sign and Structure," p. 248)

Derrida's (anti)philosophy is clearly a product of the same *episteme* which produced the Principle of Indeterminacy. This holds, in part, that "the very act of observing alters the object being observed" (Heisenberg: 24). The scientist as well as the philosopher is implicated in the game. We may also see in the Principle of Complementarity, by which contemporary physics recognizes both the wave and particle properties of light, a recognition of the fundamental *différance* in the nature of reality.

Relativity offers a new (non)definition of both space and time:

> space and time are forms of intuition, which can be no more divorced from consciousness than can our concepts of color, shape, or size. Space has no objective reality except as an order or arrangement of the objects we perceive in it, and time has no independence apart from the order of events by which we perceive it.
>
> (Barnett: 19)

Scientific discourse admits its own status as metaphor. Time has no reality outside of our interpretations and it invites a potentially vast variety of possible "readings." Time is read as Work in a reality defined by discourse that upholds the traditional hierarchical opposition between science and fiction, in which science is the privileged term. In post-structuralist epistemology, of which Relativity Theory is one expression, this opposition has been subverted. Science, no longer privileged, has become subsumed under fiction as a particular system of discourse, and this has greatly expanded the possibilities for SF's explorations of the nature and structure of time.[22]

Jorge Luis Borges has left us one of the most memorable figurations of this new awareness of time in his story "The Garden of Forking Paths" (1944), which concerns a book which is also a labyrinth, a remarkable image of time-as-Text. Borges writes that the author of this book did not think of time as absolute and uniform. He believed in an infinite series of times, in a dizzily growing, ever spreading network of diverging, converging parallel times. This web of time—the strands of which approach one another, bifurcate, intersect or ignore each other through the centuries—embraces *every* possibility.

(p. 156)[23]

Borges's radical postmodern philosophy is echoed in less extreme form in many SF stories which function within the Einsteinian paradigm. The fixed time-line of *The Time Machine* loses its privileged status in the face of the heterogeneity of times of the relative universe. Such offshoots of the time-travel story as alternate and parallel world stories, which frequently include the ideas of multiple time-tracks and branching time-lines, are extensions of this reading of time-as-Text. James Blish's *Jack of Eagles* (1952), for example, is an early novel which suggests the possibility of a split in the time-line. Larry Niven explores some of the darker implications of a universe of universes created by endlessly branching time-lines in his story "All the Myriad Ways" (1968). Alternate times and multiple time-tracks shape stories such as Philip K. Dick's *The Man in the High Castle* (1962), in which Germany and Japan have won World War II. Norman Spinrad's *The Iron Dream* (1972), which is "really" Adolph Hitler's 1953 award-winning novel, *The Lord of the Swastika,* also fits into this category. In many of these stories, scientific relativity finds its analogue in a serious exploration of cultural relativity.

Time-as-Text invites us not only to read it, but to participate in writing it as well, to admit our active role in the creation of the structure, our complicity in the game: "the Text requires an attempt to abolish (or at least to lessen) the distance between writing and reading, not by intensifying the reader's projection into the Work, but by linking the two together in a single unifying process" (Barthes: 79). Because Wells's Time Traveller reads the future as logical and determined extrapolation of his present, he confirms the inevitability of devolution and apocalypse, a confirmation which severely limits the freedom of the human subject to shape events in time. Relativity has contributed to the restoration of this freedom in many SF stories. Marge Piercy's *Woman on the Edge of Time* (1976), for example, posits at least two opposing futures which are potential in the present, and one of these, a feminist utopia, uses time travel in an effort (whose outcome is left open) to ensure its actualization. Benford's *Timescape* (1980) assumes an even greater freedom to write time: the doomed world of 1998 successfully uses time travel to warn the world of 1962 of its impending ruin; the result is a split in the time-line, as the world of 1962 veers towards its new future, while the "old" future continues to decline. Writing time in this instance includes (re)writing the past.

Even when a time-travel story inscribes itself within the Newtonian paradigm (as many still continue to do), it is (at least, from a "postmodern" perspective) always already deconstructive of any mechanical reading of the universe. *The Time Machine* can once again provide the model for this particular textual activity. We have already seen, for example, some of the effects of Wells's reading of time-as-Work: the determinate nature of time, the linearity of temporal structure, and the apparently extrapolative tendency which develops from this view of time. But by the very fact that this is a time-travel story, narrative activity disruptive of specific aspects of the 19th-century positivist world-view is already at play within the text.

In the first place, in order to postulate time travel as one of the givens of his narrative universe, Wells had to separate the subjective time of his Traveller from the objective time by which his temporal perceptions are supposedly determined. Private time breaks free of public time. This situation is analogous to Derrida's subversion of the *langue/parole* (language as system/language as individual speech-act) hierarchy erected by Saussurean structural linguistics. This deconstruction of the opposition between public and private time also anticipates Relativity Theory, which, in Stephen Kern's delightful image, has "filled the universe with clocks each telling a different correct time" (p. 19). Kern identifies the collusion between the normative and the coercive, between "the authority of uniform public time" and "centralized public authority" (p. 16) which is implicit in the idea of a public time. Now there is no more privileged Time, only an infinite number of individual times which together constitute the illusion of an absolute and universal Time.

As a consequence of this subversion of public time, the concept of "now" becomes displaced from its privileged point on the time-line: this is the characteristic gesture of displacement particular to the language of time travel. "Now" is no longer "here" but "there." There is no longer a privileged "now" of any empirical force. Within the discourse of the time-travel story, "now" becomes shifting and unstable, indicative of any point in the past, present, or future inhabited by the subjective present of the time traveller.[24] Language recognizes temporal subjectivity; it is always limited to private time. No words exist to fix the absolute present, the Now, while narrating the time traveller's experiences in the past or future relative to that absolute present. Wells's Narrator demonstrates this linguistic peculiarity as he speculates on the Time Traveller's "present" whereabouts: "He may even now—if I may use the phrase—be wandering on some plesiosaurus-haunted Oolitic coral reef, or beside the lonely saline lakes of the Triassic Age" (12:117).

As as point of reference, the time traveller acts as both the functional (not absolute) center of the temporal structure and as a floating signifier released from any fixed relationship to that structure. Time-travel stories, then, are never "really" versions but are always subversions of traditional temporal structure; their absolute rejection of an absolute Present works to negate the very concept of temporal Presence, "temporal presence as point . . . of the now or of the moment" (*OG,* p. 12).

5. In an important early essay, **"The Rediscovery of the Unique"** (1891). Wells demonstrates his anticipation of several key Derridean concepts. The focus of the essay is the "rediscovery" of difference: "*All being is unique,* or, nothing is strictly like anything else. It implies . . . that we only arrive at the idea of similar beings by an unconscious or deliberate disregard of an infinity of small differences" (Philmus & Hughes: 23; Wells's emphasis). Even more significant is Wells's conclusion:

> [The "human delusion" of sameness] has grown with the growth of the mind, and is, we are quite prepared to concede, a necessary feature of thought. We may here remark, parenthetically, that we make no proposal to supersede ordinary thinking by a new method . . . This . . . is outside the scope of the present paper, and altogether premature.
>
> (*ibid.,* pp. 25-26)

According to Derrida, the present moment is no more conducive to new methods of thinking than was the late 19th century:

> the movements of deconstruction do not destroy structures from the outside. They are not possible and effective, nor can they take accurate aim, except by inhabiting those structures. Inhabiting them *in a certain way.*
>
> (*OG,* p. 24; emphasis in original)

Wells's answer to this dilemma, that there is no ground upon which to base any attack upon conventionalized systems of thought outside of those systems themselves, proves to be the same as Derrida's. Just as Derridean deconstruction is a profoundly ironic enterprise, one which, in the words of Paul de Man, "splits the subject into an empirical self that exists in a state of inauthenticity and a self that exists only in the form of a language that asserts the knowledge of its inauthenticity" (p. 197), so *The Time Machine* is a profoundly ironic text. It simultaneously inhabits the world of Classical Physics and ironizes that world-view. We have already seen how the classical definition of time is crucial to the logic of the narrative events and to the Time Traveller's interpretations of these events. It will therefore be worthwhile to examine in more detail the cumulative effects of Wells's ironization of the Newtonian paradigm on the "meaning" of his novella.

An implicit confession of disloyalty to the classical world-view is embedded in the very title of this "exemplary" Newtonian production. While "the time machine"

refers to the invention by which the Victorian scientist moves into the far future, Wells's title invites at least two more readings. Mark Rose points out that the machine of the title is also "the relentless turning of history . . . a diabolic mechanism whose workings lead to death" (p. 101). Time is the machine which will eventually crush the life out of the very universe. A third reading reminds us, self-reflexively, that the time machine is the story itself, which creates the time of its particular narrative universe. Although Wellsian time travel is a direct literalization of linguistic metaphor—diachrony treated as synchrony—his story-as-time-machine works its own considerable deconstruction upon the time machine of Classical Physics.[25]

Robert M. Philmus and David Y. Hughes have discussed in some detail the subversion of the Newtonian worldview which takes place on the level of narrative event in *The Time Machine.* They link this to the rising influence of evolutionary theory in the latter half of the 19th century:

> The newly posited entanglement of species in the destiny of one another reopened the question of 'humanity's' relation to (the rest of) nature and to the universe at large in part because it rendered the concept of isolation (itself a spatial concept) anachronistic, if not obsolete.
>
> (p. 3)

Wells's repudiation of "the anthropocentric fallacy" (Philmus & Hughes: 8) is demonstrated both in the disappearance of the human race from the universe of the far future and in the disappearance of the Time Traveller himself from the universe of the story.[26] What is of interest within the terms of this present discussion is that there is a parallel attack against such a centrist perspective in the text's ironically compromised sense of commitment to the ideal of logocentrism as well, an ideal framed by the same *epistemè* from within which the intellectual conventions of scientific positivism were developed. The very discourse of Wells's text subverts the notion of full presence through its ironic treatment of this traditional metaphysical concept. This can most clearly be seen in the development of the "frame story" within which the events of *The Time Machine* occur. There is a constant tension between the logocentric idealism of Wells's Narrator and the events which he reports at second hand.

Vincent Leitch explains that

> the logocentric system always assigns the origin of truth to the *logos*—to the spoken word, or to the Word of God. Moreover, the being of the entity is always determined as *presence*: the 'object' of science and metaphysics is characteristically the 'present entity.' In these circumstances, the full presence of the voice is valued over the mute signs of writing. . . . Writing represents a fall from full speech.
>
> (p. 25)

It is this hegemony of Speech over Writing that Derrida criticizes in Saussure; Wells's Narrator is a supporter of the same metaphysics of presence and would undoubtedly agree with Saussure (p. 30) that "writing obscures language; it is not a guise for language but a disguise." The "truth" of the Traveller's story is apodictically proven through his own account of it. a convention used in the 19th century to support the fictional truths of texts as disparate as *Jane Eyre* (1848), *David Copperfield* (1850), and *Dracula* (1897) (although, as a compendium of written reports, *Dracula* is already contaminated by a fall from immediate presence).

Wells's Narrator is so extremely conscious of the truth-value of the present voice that he enters the following disclaimer for his own second-hand account:

> In writing it down I feel with only too much keenness the *inadequacy of pen and ink*—and, above all, my own inadequacy—to express [the] quality [of the original narration]. You read, I will suppose, attentively enough; but you cannot know the speaker's white, sincere face . . . nor hear *the intonation of his voice.*
>
> (2:21-22; my emphasis)

Derrida reminds us that writing in the logocentric system is always the sign of a double absence: "the absence of the signatory, to say nothing of the absence of the referent" (*OG*, p. 40). *The Time Machine* calls particular attention to these absences, since the only I/eye-witness disappears from the text. Committed as Wells's novella apparently is to the tradition in which Presence supports the truth of narrative event, it nevertheless informs us at the end that "the Time Traveller vanished three years ago. And, as everybody knows now, he has never returned" (12:117). This last-minute supplementary information changes the very essence of the narrative: the presence of the Time Traveller has, in fact, *always already* been an absence. This is further underlined by a strange and seemingly irrelevant occurrence which takes place during the Time Traveller's exploration of the Palace of Green Porcelain. He recounts that, "yielding to an irresistible impulse, I wrote my name upon the nose of a steatite monster from South America that particularly took my fancy" (8:89). The unnamed Traveller has at last named himself, but that name exists on a monument from the past buried in a museum in the future—never in the present. Presence is always already past or to come: it is never immediate. If, as Derrida defines it, "a written signature implies the actual or empirical non-presence of the signer" ("Signature Event Context," p. 194), then Wells's text here reinforces the absence at its core, since not only the "signer" but his very signature is lost in time.

6. Paralleling this subversion of logocentrism in Wells's text is the displacement of the human subject from the center to the periphery of natural structure, and, finally, to a point outside the picture altogether. This movement is analogous to the reversal of the evolutionary process which the Traveller discovers to be the fate of humanity. If we view the time from which the Traveller embarks as one in which humanity is the center and meaning of the natural world, then the world of 802,701 is one in which the Eloi and the Morlocks are less central and more marginal—that is, less "human" and more "natural"—than before; in the distant future at the end of the world, humanity is no longer even a peripheral presence but a complete absence. In this extreme displacement of the subject, only the object, the world of nature, remains. The "object" has overwhelmed the "subject" in a deconstructive reversal of the traditional scientific conviction of the power of the Cartesian *res cognans* over the *res extensa*. *The Time Machine,* to borrow the words of Paul de Man, is an ironic treatment of "the purely instrumental, reified character of [our] relationship to nature." It demonstrates that "Nature can at all times treat [us] as if [we] were a thing and remind [us] of [our] factitiousness, whereas [we are] quite powerless to convert even the smallest particle of nature into something human" (p. 196). Under these circumstances, the gestures of "observation" and "reason" become sadly diminished and ineffectual. Humanity as transcendental signified, the ground of the Time Traveller's explorations into the future, has been removed as part of the narrative equation; and any "meaning" based on such a ground has vanished with it.

This is supported by the ironic role played by the figure of the White Sphinx in the text. The various references to the Oedipus myth in *The Time Machine* (noted in Ketterer: 340-41, and Huntington: 44-45) are focussed upon this inscrutably "colossal figure" with its "unpleasant suggestion of disease" (*TTM* 3:27); the answer to its ancient riddle is also the answer which correctly interprets the world of 802,701. Only now the riddle of the Sphinx might more suitably be: "What is missing from this picture?" In each case, the answer is the same: "Man"; but while the original question bespeaks presence, the revision in *The Time Machine* points to absence. The discourse of Wells's text is also constituted by absence, so that the Time Traveller is a correlative on the textual level of the absence repeated on the level of narrative event.[27] The end result of the Time Traveller's readings of the future is absence, just as his absence is the final note in our reading of *The Time Machine.*

In his early writings, Wells explored both absolutist and psychologistic approaches in his discussions of the nature of time, oscillating between concepts of cosmic determinism and human free will in his earlier versions of *The Time Machine.* Philmus and Hughes (pp. 47-56) demonstrate the balance achieved in the final version between Wells's idea of "the universe rigid"[28] and the theory that time is a subjective phenomenon, stressing Wells's ultimate adherence to a principle of complementarity in what has become the definitive edition of the text. In like manner, John Huntington emphasizes that "the coexistence of opposites is a fundamental element in all of Wells's early fiction," and cites the juxtaposition of the world of 802,701 against the present world of *The Time Machine* as one example of what he terms "this two world structure" (p. 21). He goes on to argue that "by a series of fairly simple transformations a number of other oppositions in Wells's early fiction derive from this . . . structure" (p. 22), such as "the moral opposition" (p. 33) represented by the scientist and the anarchist of **"The Stolen Bacillus"** (1895). What is of interest here is Huntington's contention that the typical Wellsian opposition, that between nature and culture, is an ironic one, maintaining as it does "a constant and balanced reciprocity[;] . . . the one cannot exist without the other" (p. 22). The two world(view)s which are woven together throughout both narrative events and textual discourse in *The Time Machine* function in a manner similar to Huntington's "two world structure." As he concludes, "in such a structure neither world in itself holds our interest; what is important is the two of them together and the linked oppositions they establish" (*ibid.*). (We might observe here once again that oppositions as *oppositions* tend to exist "in the eye of the beholder"; as a rule, they are *effects* produced by difference rather than fundamental antitheses.)

The end result of the presence of these complementary world-views is a play between narrative metonymy (*The Time Machine* as extrapolative work) and textual metaphor (*The Time Machine* as figurative text), which is as integral to its structure as is the play between present and future. There is an implicit insistence upon this in the Time Traveller's invitation to his listeners (which is also a self-reflexive moment of textual duplicity):

> Take it as a lie—or a prophecy. Say I dreamed it in the workshop. Consider I have been speculating upon the destinies of our race until I have hatched this fiction. Treat my assertion of its truth as a mere stroke of art to enhance its interest. And taking it as a story, what do you think of it?

                                                                      (12:112)

The Time Machine is essentially an exercise in *aporia*, an oscillation between the desire for presence and the awareness of absence, between the objectivity of extrapolation and the subjectivity of metaphor, between—one is tempted to add, given its historical moment—the 19th century and the 20th century.

The Narrator's acknowledgment of human ineffectuality in the face of a determined future—his "If that is so, it remains for us to live as though it were not so" (12:117)—begins to take on additional resonance at this point, in view of the complementary existence of both world-views in the text. Balanced against the deterministic universe of the Newtonian paradigm is the refutation of that very paradigm. If the future is not, after all, a fixed and determined one, then perhaps the refusal on the part of humanity to read time as though it were inevitable might avert the devolution to which the Traveller bears witness.[29]

Certainly *The Time Machine* is about "making a difference"; its narrative defamiliarizes apparently natural class-structures by taking them to their biosociological extremes; its discourse achieves at least a partial displacement of the logocentric system through a comparable act of deconstruction. Like the (anti)philosophy of deconstruction, it both admits the ineluctability of our metaphysical structures and effects a defamiliarization of those structures. It acknowledges its inevitable inscription within the logocentric system of Classical Physics at the same time as it inhabits that system "in a certain way," with an ironic skepticism which questions some of its own fundamental narrative commitments.

In 1933, in his **"Preface to the Scientific Romances,"** Wells referred to *The Time Machine* as an "assault on human self-satisfaction" (p. v). The strategic position occupied by *The Time Machine* accomplishes much more than simply an overt attack upon 19th-century moral complacency, however; in its deconstruction of some fundamental aspects of traditional logocentric discourse, it looks forward to the projects of much contemporary critical theory. It attempts at once to displace a smug humanity from its privileged position at the center of creation and to remind us of our ineluctable ties to the natural world. And what, after all, is the aim of post-structuralist theory if not a continuation, in another form, of that same "assault on human self-satisfaction"?

Notes

1. This essay was in part made possible through a grant from the Social Sciences and Humanities Research Council of Canada.

2. See, for example, Larry Dwyer's essay, "Time Travel and Changing the Past," for a discussion of the implications of the Einstein-Maxwell equations and Kurt Gödel's solutions to the field equations of general relativity "which permit closed timelike lines to exist in spacetime" (p. 344). Dwyer's is only one of many philosophical attempts to justify at least the logical possibility of time travel. Other challenging discussions include David Lewis's "The Paradoxes of Time Travel" and Paul Horwich's "On Some Alleged Paradoxes of Time Travel."

3. Donald Davidson points out that "most metaphors are false" (p. 39). For his discussion of this aspect of metaphor, see "What Metaphors Mean," pp. 39-41.

4. Time travel is the result of a kind of linguistic extrapolation, then, even as it functions as literary metaphor. I am indebted to David Ketterer for this observation.

5. Rose is applying the distinctions between metaphor and metonymy drawn by Jakobson in his "Two Aspects of Language and Two Types of Aphasic Disturbance." See especially, Jakobson, pp. 76-82.

6. The most overtly "metonymical" trend in SF today is probably cyberpunk, which may be one of the reasons that it stands out as a "movement." The sensibility of a novel like William Gibson's *Neuromancer* (1984), for instance, is firmly rooted in technological extrapolation, although it is by no means devoid of metaphorical content. Cyberpunk seems to be an SF current flowing against the contemporary tide.

7. In his recent essay, "*Futurological Congress* as Metageneric Text," Robert M. Philmus has discussed several aspects of generic self-reflexivity in *The Time Machine,* demonstrating its value as a model in this context as well. The heterogeneity of meaning of Wells's title, to which I refer below, is also a key factor in Philmus's analysis. See especially pp. 313-15.

8. Terry Eagleton writes, for example, that "the genuinely theoretical question is always violently estranging, a perhaps impossible attempt to raise to self-reflexivity the very enabling conditions of a range of routinized practices . . ." (p. 89).

9. Suvin's definition of the genre, which is the most useful yet devised, reads in full: "SF is . . . a literary genre whose necessary and sufficient conditions are the presence and interaction of estrangement and cognition, and whose main formal device is an imaginative framework alternative to the author's empirical environment" (pp. 7-8).

10. Carl Freedman has made a similar point about the conjunction of SF and critical theory, which I will quote at length, because of its importance:

> It is . . . a matter of the shared perspectives between SF and critical theory, of the dialectical standpoint of the SF tendency, with its insistence upon historical mutability, material reducibility, and, at least implicitly, Utopian possibility. In a sense, SF is of all genres the one most devoted to historical specificity: for the SF world is not only one different in time or place from our own, but one whose chief interest is precisely the dif-

ference that such difference makes, and, in addition, one whose difference is nonetheless contained within a cognitive continuum with the actual. . . .

(p. 186-87)

11. This is never posed as a "Father Paradox." It is as if the SF community is evading the Oedipal aspects implicit in its favorite model of temporal paradox.

12. Even a narrative line as uncomplicated as that of *The Terminator* (1984) creates the potential for endless repetition which the viewer must tacitly ignore in order to collaborate in the closure of the film.

13. The sign, for example, "is always the supplement of the thing itself" (*OG,* p. 145), at the same time as it stands in for the full presence which it both defers and differs from. The aim of Derrida's argument is to deny the notion of origin, of the unsupplemented entity. Nature is a construct of culture; speech of a larger writing (hence Derrida's *grammatological* undertaking); "the thing in itself" of the sign used to "replace" it. For a useful summary of Derrida's theories of the *supplement,* see Leitch, pp. 169-78.

14. As Leitch explains, the *always already* "works to insert the *supplement* into any seemingly simple or pure metaphysical conceptualization" (p. 171).

15. My initial thinking about the effects of Relativity on the development of the time-travel motif was generated by Andrew Gordon's excellent essay, "Silverberg's Time Machine." Gordon discusses, for example, the disparity of subject and form in many time-travel stories: "the problem is that time-travel stories have been trying to deal with twentieth-century conceptions of time in narrative forms borrowed from the 19th-century" (p. 348). These narrative forms, of course, were developed to explain the reality created by nineteenth-century scientific metaphors.

16. Since availing myself of Barthes' distinction between *oeuvre* and *texte,* I have come across another instance of the same application to quite different circumstances. This suggests to me that the Barthian treatment of *oeuvre* and *texte* is a flexible notion with potential for a wide range of applications. See Patrice Pavis's discussion of *oeuvre* and *texte* (pp. 2-12).

17. In "Signature Event Context," Derrida draws attention to the political character of such oppositions:

> an opposition of metaphysical concepts . . . is never a confrontation of two terms, but a hierarchy and the order of a subordination. Decon-

struction cannot be restricted or immediately pass to a neutralization: it must . . . put into practice a *reversal* of the classical opposition *and* a general *displacement* of the system. It is on that condition alone that deconstruction will provide the means of *intervening* in the field of oppositions it criticizes and that is also a field of non-discursive forces.

(p. 195; emphasis in original)

18. In her Preface to *Of Grammatology,* Gyatri Spivak neatly exemplifies the dual effects of *différance* in her discussion of the nature of the sign: "Such is the strange 'being' of the sign: half of it is always 'not there' [the signified, which is constantly deferred] and the other half always 'not that' [the signifier, which is always different from that which it signifies]" (p. xvii).

19. As Spivak points out, however, "the description of the object is as contaminated by the patterns of the subject's desire as is the subject constituted by that never-fulfilled desire" (p. lix).

20. In his "Preface" to the 1931 Random House edition, Wells draws attention to his application of the Second Law of Thermodynamics in *The Time Machine* (pp. ix-x).

21. See Philmus's discussion of this point in his "*The Time Machine*: or, the Fourth Dimension as Prophecy" (pp. 534-35).

22. British physicist Michael Shallis writes: "the world exists for us only in the form we clothe it. Our descriptions or explanations define our world. Our technology manifests our explanations" (p. 197).

23. Borges demonstrates a more pragmatic approach to the subject, however, in his ironic "A New Refutation of Time." After developing arguments which seem to deny the objective reality of time, he nevertheless concludes that "denying temporal succession, denying the self, denying the astronomical universe, are apparent desperations and secret consolations. . . . Time is the substance I am made of. . . . The world, unfortunately, is real; I, unfortunately, am Borges" (p. 222). Borges thus neatly sums up the apparent impossibility of reconciling contemporary scientific descriptions of "reality" with our human experience of it.

24. The separation of private from public time, or as Hilary Putnam phrases it, "the relativistic notion of *proper* time" (p. 669), has been recognized as the only route logic can take to defend the philosophical possibilities of time travel. See, for example, Putnam's essay, "It Ain't Necessarily So" and David Lewis's "The Paradoxes of Time Travel."

25. Even this "obvious" reading suggests the play of *différance*: Philmus and Hughes (p. 48) draw attention to the fact that Wells's "invention" includes not only the machine itself, but "the notion of travelling through time" and, even more importantly, "its rationale."

26. The formal irony of *The Time Machine* has elsewhere been identified by Bernard Bergonzi, for example, in his "*The Time Machine*: An Ironic Myth," and by Hughes in his "H. G. Wells: Ironic Romancer."

27. I am here distinguishing between two aspects of *The Time Machine* as narrative fiction, based upon Shlomith Rimmon-Kenan's structuralist distinctions (pp. 3-4). The first is that aspect of "written discourse," or "text," through which "all the items of the narrative content are filtered"; in the case of *The Time Machine,* the text is permeated by the absence of the Time Traveller, necessitating a secondary Narrator and a second-hand "translation." The second aspect is that of the "story," "the narrated events" of the fiction, which in the present instance include the final disappearance of humanity from the world as well as the "actual" disappearance of the Traveller himself.

28. Although the original version of Wells's essay entitled "The Universe Rigid" has been lost, he includes what might be considered an "abstract" of this lost essay in the first book version of *The Time Machine,* published in the United States by Henry Holt. This "abstract" probably gives a much truer idea of the original argument than does the reconstruction undertaken by Wells nearly 40 years after the fact in his 1934 *Experiment in Autobiography* (see Philmus & Hughes, pp. 4-5, 51-53).

29. I am indebted to David Y. Hughes for this reminder of possible alternative readings of the Narrator's conclusion.

Works Cited

Barnett, John. *The Universe and Dr Einstein.* 2nd ed. rev. [1957]; rpt. NY: Bantam, 1968.

Barthes, Roland. "From Work to Text" [1971]; rpt. in *Textual Strategies: Perspectives in Post-Structuralist Criticism,* ed. Josué V. Harari (Ithaca, NY: Cornell UP, 1979), pp. 73-81.

Bergonzi, Bernard. "*The Time Machine*: An Ironic Myth," *Critical Quarterly,* 2 (Winter 1960): 293-305.

Borges, Jorge Luis. "The Garden of Forking Paths" [1944], in *The Traps of Time,* ed. Michael Moorcock, trans. Helen Temple & Ruthven Todd (Harmondsworth, UK: Penguin, 1968), pp. 145-57.

———. "A New Refutation of Time," trans. James E. Irby, in *The Discontinuous Universe: Selected Writings in Contemporary Consciousness,* ed. Sallie Sears & Georgianna W. Lord (NY: Basic Books, 1972), pp. 208-23.

Davidson, Donald. "What Metaphors Mean," in *On Metaphor,* ed. Sheldon Sacks (Chicago: Chicago UP, 1979), pp. 29-45.

De Man, Paul. "The Rhetoric of Temporality," in *Interpretation: Theory and Practice,* ed. Charles S. Singleton (Baltimore: Johns Hopkins UP, 1969), pp. 173-209.

Derrida, Jacques. "Différance," in *Speech and Phenomena and Other Essays on Husserl's Theory of Signs,* trans. David B. Allison & Newton Garver (Evanston, IL: Northwestern UP, 1973), pp. 129-60.

————. *Of Grammatology* [1967], trans. Gyatri Chakravorty Spivak. Baltimore: Johns Hopkins UP, 1976.

————. "Signature Event Context," trans. Samuel Weber & Jeffrey Mehlman, *Glyph,* 1 (1977): 172-97.

————. "Structure, Sign and Play in the Discourse of the Human Sciences" [1967], in *The Structuralist Controversy: The Languages of Criticism and the Sciences of Man,* ed. Richard Macksey & Eugene Donato (Baltimore: Johns Hopkins UP, 1972), pp. 247-72.

————. "White Mythology: Metaphor in the Text of Philosophy," *New Literary History,* 6 (Autumn 1974): 5-74.

Dwyer, Larry. "Time Travel and Changing the Past," *Philosophical Studies,* 27 (1975): 341-50.

Eagleton, Terry. *The Function of Criticism: From "The Spectator" to Post-Structuralism.* London: Verso Editions, 1984.

Freedman, Carl. "Science Fiction and Literary Theory," SFS, 14 (1987): 180-200.

Gordon, Andrew. "Silverberg's Time Machine," *Extrapolation,* 23 (1982): 345-61.

Heisenberg, Werner. *Physics and Philosophy: The Revolution in Modern Science* [1958]; rpt. NY: Harper & Row, 1962.

Horwich, Paul. "On Some Alleged Paradoxes of Time Travel," *Journal of Philosophy,* 72 (Aug. 1975): 432-44.

Huntington, John. *The Logic of Fantasy: H. G. Wells and Science Fiction.* NY: Columbia UP, 1982.

Hughes, David Y. "H. G. Wells: Ironic Romancer," *Extrapolation,* 6 (1965): 32-38.

Jakobson, Roman. "Two Aspects of Language and Two Types of Aphasic Disturbances," in *Fundamentals of Language* (The Hague: Mouton, 1956), pp. 53-82.

Kern, Stephen. *The Culture of Time and Space, 1880-1918.* Cambridge, MA: Harvard UP, 1983.

Ketterer, David. "Oedipus as Time Traveller," SFS, 9 (1982): 340-41.

Leitch, Vincent. *Deconstructive Criticism: An Advanced Introduction.* NY: Columbia UP, 1983.

Lewis, David. "The Paradoxes of Time Travel," *American Philosophical Quarterly,* 13 (Apr. 1976): 145-52.

Lindsay, Clarence. "H. G. Wells, Viktor Shlovsky, and Paul de Man," in *The Scope of the Fantastic: Theory, Technique, Major Authors,* ed. Robert A. Collins & Howard D. Pearce (Westport, CT: Greenwood Press, 1985), pp. 125-33.

Niven, Larry. "The Theory and Practice of Time Travel," in his *All the Myriad Ways* (1971; rpt. NY: Ballantine, 1981), pp. 125-33.

Norris, Christopher. *Deconstruction: Theory and Practice.* NY: Methuen, 1982.

Pavis, Patrice. "The Classical Heritage of Modern Drama: The Case of Postmodern Theatre," *Modern Drama,* 29 (Mar. 1986): 1-22.

Philmus, Robert M. "*Futurological Congress* as Metageneric Text," SFS, 13 (1986): 313-28.

————. "*The Time Machine*: or, The Fourth Dimension as Prophecy," *PMLA,* 84 (1969): 530-35.

————. & David Y. Hughes (eds.) *H. G. Wells: Early Writings in Science and Science Fiction.* Berkeley: California UP, 1975.

Putnam, Hilary. "It Ain't Necessarily So," *Journal of Philosophy,* 59 (1962): 658-71.

Rimmon-Kenan, Shlomith. *Narrative Fiction: Contemporary Poetics.* NY: Methuen, 1983.

Rose, Mark. *Alien Encounters: Anatomy of Science Fiction.* Cambridge, MA: Harvard UP, 1981.

Saussure, Ferdinand de. *Course in General Linguistics,* trans. Wade Baskin, ed. Charles Bally & Albert Sechehaye. NY: McGraw-Hill, 1966.

Shallis, Michael. *On Time: An Investigation into Scientific Knowledge and Human Experience.* Markham, Ont.: Penguin, 1983.

Spivak, Gyatri Chakravorty. "Preface" to *Of Grammatology,* pp. ix-lxxxvii (see Derrida).

Suvin, Darko. *Metamorphoses of Science Fiction: On the Poetics and History of a Literary Genre.* New Haven: Yale UP, 1979.

Thayer, H. S. (ed.). *Newton's Philosophy of Nature: Selections from his Writings.* NY: Hafner, 1953.

Twain, Mark. *A Connecticut Yankee at King Arthur's Court* [1889]; rpt. Harmondsworth, UK: Penguin, 1971.

Wells, H. G. "Preface" to *The Time Machine* (NY: Random House, 1931), pp. vii-x.

————. "Preface" to *The Scientific Romances of H. G. Wells* (London: Victor Gollancz, 1933), pp. iii-vi.

————. *The Time Machine* [1895], in *The Works of H. G. Wells,* The Atlantic Edition, (London: T. Fisher Unwin, 1924), I:3-118.

Williams, Donald C. "The Myth of Passage," *Journal of Philosophy,* 48 (1951); rpt. in *The Philosophy of Time,* ed. Richard M. Gale (Garden City, NY: Doubleday-Anchor, 1967), pp. 98-116.

Ziegler, James D. "Primitive, Newtonian, and Einsteinian Fantasies: Three Worldviews," in *The Scope of the Fantastic* (*see* Lindsay), pp. 125-33.

Kathryn Hume (essay date spring 1990)

SOURCE: Hume, Kathryn. "Eat or Be Eaten: H. G. Wells's *The Time Machine.*" *Philological Quarterly* 69, no. 2 (spring 1990): 233-51.

[*In the following essay, Hume investigates the function of oral fantasies and imagery in* The Time Machine.]

"It is very remarkable that this is so extensively overlooked," says the Time Traveller, speaking of time as the fourth dimension.[1] Similarly remarkable is the way we have overlooked the comprehensive functions of oral fantasies in *The Time Machine.* They play a fourth dimension to the other three of entropy, devolution, and utopian satire. They ramify, by regular transformations, into those other three; into the social and economic worlds of consumption and exploitation; and into the realm of gender anxieties. They transform the ideological commonplaces from which the text constructs its reality. They create a network of emotional tensions that subliminally unites the three time frames: Victorian England, the Realm of the Sphinx, and the Terminal Beach. At the same time, this nexus of related images undercuts and fragments the logical, scientific arguments being carried out on the surface of the tale.

The Time Machine is the first of Wells's scientific romances to achieve canonical status.[2] In their eagerness to elevate and assimilate this text, however, critics have lost awareness that some of its parts are not explained by their normal critical strategies. One such feature to disappear from critical discourse is the failure of any coherent social message to emerge from the world of the Eloi and Morlocks. Another partly repressed feature is the disparity between the Time Traveller's violent emotions and the experiences that evoke them.[3] A third feature lost to view is the dubious logic that binds the two futuristic scenarios.

I would like to approach the text with both the oral image complex and these elided mysteries in mind. What emerges will not fill the gaps in the narrative logic; the text resists such treatment, for reasons that will be shown. Rather, I wish to explore the hidden dynamics of emotion and logic. Since the semes attached to eating, consumption, and engulfment point in so many directions, I shall start instead with the public ideologies of power, size and gender. Then we can explore their symbolic manifestations as fantasies of being eaten or engulfed; as equations involving body size, intelligence, and physical energy; and as gender attributes projected on the world. Once sensitized to these concerns, we can examine the two future scenarios and their relationship to the Victorian frame. By exploring the interplay of ideology with its symbolic distortions, we will better sense what the text represses, and why despite (or even because of) this hidden material, the book has such disturbing power.

IDEOLOGICAL ASSUMPTIONS

Ideology, used here in Roland Barthes' sense, means the unexamined assumptions as to what is natural and inevitable and hence unchangeable. One realizes these "inevitabilities" to be historical and contingent most readily by comparing cultures, for within a culture, the ideological is taken to be "real."

The part of the general ideology relevant here consists of a nexus of values that include power, body size, and gender. Separating the values even to this extent is artificial; they intertwine tightly, and in turn link to other values such as dominance, exploitation, race, physical height, and bodily strength. They also merge with political and social and military power. The form taken by this family of assumptions in England made the British Empire possible.

Let us assume you are a nineteenth-century Briton—white, male, and a member of the politically powerful classes. You are also nominally Christian and equipped with the latest weaponry. You could expect to march into any country not blessed with most of these characteristics and expropriate what you wanted, be it raw material, cheap labor, land, or valuables. Such power gives the ability to exploit and consume. The so-called inferior races had no choice, since their technology was insufficient to resist British force. The Traveller's outlook is very much that of the nineteenth-century Briton among the aliens. His strength, technological know-how, and culture elevate him in his own mind. He scribbles his name on a statue, much as other nineteenth-century Britons carved theirs on Roman and Greek temples. To the empire builders, killing Africans or Indians was not "really" murder; they were Other and hence less than truly human. While the Traveller controls his impulse to massacre Morlocks (and is even praised for his restraint by one critic),[4] he smashes at their skulls in a way he would never dream of doing in Oxford Street. He is outraged (as well as frightened) when his trespassing machine is impounded. In the "kangaroo" and "centipede" episode found in the *New Review* serialization of the novel, his immediate impulse is to hit one of the kangaroo-like creatures on the skull with a rock. When examination of the body suggests that it is of human descent, he feels only a flash of "disagreeable apprehension," evidently directed toward this proof of Man's degeneration, not at his own murderous action. His regret at leaving the body (possibly just unconscious) to the monstrous "centipede" appears to be regret at the loss of a scientific specimen, not guilt at leaving this "grey animal . . . or grey man" to be devoured.[5] He protects himself from any acknowledgment of this self-centeredness by viewing his urges as scientific, but ultimately he sees himself as having the right to whatever he wants, and cherishes himself for being the only "real" human and therefore the only creature with rights.

Part of this superiority stems from physical size, the second element in the ideology and one closely linked to power. Size generally permits a man to feel superior to women, and a British man to feel superior to members of shorter races. In English, size is a metaphor used to indicate that which is valuable, good, desirable. "Great," "high," and "large" are normally positive markers.[6]

In the two paragraphs that encompass the narrator's first language lesson and his response to it, we find the word "little" used eight times. Attached in his mind to the littleness of the Eloi is their "chatter," their tiring easily, their being "indolent" and "easily fatigued," and their "lack of interest" (p. 35). Littleness and its associated debilities are so grotesquely prominent that one cannot help note this obsession with the inferiority attaching to bodies of small size. What the narrator thinks will shape and limit what he hears and sees. When he first hears the Eloi (p. 29), they look and sound like "men" running. Later, his senses register "children": "I heard cries of terror and their little feet running" (p. 46).

The ideological inferiority of littleness is reinforced for readers by the Traveller's reactions to artifacts of the prior civilization. He admires and wonders at the "ruinous splendor" consisting of "a great heap of granite, bound together by masses of aluminium, a vast labyrinth of precipitous walls" (p. 36). He cannot describe such a building without expressing this admiration for sheer size: the buildings are "splendid," "colossal," "tall," "big," "magnificent," "vast," "great," and "huge." He never wonders whether the size was functional and if so, how. Nor does he speculate on whether it was achieved through slave labor, as were the colossal monuments of antiquity which it resembles, with its "suggestions of old Phoenician decorations" (p. 33). He simply extends automatic admiration to such remains because of their impressive size.

The third element in the common ideology, besides power and size, is gender. Power and size support the superior status of maleness. Wells extends this prejudice to the point of defining humanity as male. Early in his narrative, the Time Traveller recounts his fear that "the race had lost its manliness" (p. 28). No sooner does he identify the Eloi as shorter than himself than they become "creatures" and are quickly feminized with such terms as "graceful," "frail," "hectic beauty," "Dresden china type of prettiness." All later descriptions use codes normally applied to women or children: mouths small and bright red, eyes large and mild, a language that sounds sweet and liquid and cooing and melodious. Ultimately, he equates loss of manliness with loss of humanity.

To sum up the ideological assumptions: the text shows as natural and inevitable the interconnection of power, size and male gender. Wells was to prove capable of challenging the politics of power in later scientific romances. He questions the might-makes-right outlook of Empire in his reference to the Tasmanians in *The War of the Worlds* (1898), and in Dr. Moreau's parodic imposition of The Law on inferior beings (1896). Callousness towards non-British sentients is rebuked by Cavor, who is shocked by Bedford's slaughter of Selenites in *The First Men in the Moon* (1901). However, though power may be somewhat negotiable to Wells, size and maleness remain positively marked throughout the scientific romances. In *The Food of the Gods* (1904), size automatically conveys nobility of purpose, and this idealized race of giants consists so exclusively of men that it will have trouble propagating.

If this text merely echoed the ideology of its times, *The Time Machine* (1895) would be drab and predictable. The symbolic enlargements and distortions of these values are what create the images and tensions that make it interesting, so let us turn to them.

SYMBOLIC TRANSFORMATIONS OF IDEOLOGY

Power belongs to the same family of values as "exploitation" and "consumption." These terms from the political and economic spheres take on added resonances when they emerge as oral fantasies about eating and being eaten. As Patrick A. McCarthy points out, cannibalism lies at the heart of this darkness, or so at least the Traveller asseverates.[7] Actually, the evidence for cannibalism is far from complete, as David Lake observes, and the narrator may be jumping to totally unwarranted conclusions. However the notion of humans as fatted kine for a technologically superior group will reappear in *The War of the Worlds,* so it evidently held some fascination for Wells. The latter book certainly makes the connection between eating people and economic exploitation,[8] a parallel made famous by Swift's "Modest Proposal."

The putative cuisine of the Morlocks is only the most obvious of the oral fantasies. "Eat or be eaten" is a way of characterizing some social systems, but in Wells's futures, the words are literally applicable, and the text regales us with variations upon the theme of eating. The Time Traveller fears that the Morlocks will feed upon him as well as on Eloi. In the extra time-frame of the *New Review* version, the centipede appears to be hungry. The crabs make clear their intentions to consume the Traveller. The Sphinx traditionally devoured those who could not guess her riddle; the Traveller's entering her pedestal constitutes but a slight displacement of entering her maw. The Victorian frame features a prominent display of after-dinner satisfactions (including drinks, cigars, and feminized chairs that embrace and support the men) and a meal at which the Traveller urgently gobbles his food. Oral fantasies also take the forms of engulfment: one can be overwhelmed, drowned, swallowed by darkness, or rendered unconscious. Both in the narrator's dreams and in his physical adventures, we find several such threats of dissolution.

Norman Holland observes that "the single most common fantasy-structure in literature is phallic assertiveness balanced against oral engulfment,"[9] exactly the pattern of **The Time Machine.** Typical of the phallic stage anxieties is the exploration of dark, dangerous, and congested places. Time travel and other magic forms of travel are common omnipotence fantasies at this stage of development. So is the pre-oedipal polarization of agents into threatening and non-threatening, and the focus on a single figure. Opposing this phallic quest are oral anxieties. One such wave of anxiety oozes forth as the engulfing embraces of night (e.g., "dreaming . . . that I was drowned, and that sea-anemones were feeling over my face with their soft palps"—p. 57). Another such anxiety grips the narrator when he faces the yawning underworld; indeed, upon escaping from below, he collapses in a dead faint. The threat of being eaten, and the enfolding gloom of the Terminal Beach are two others.

The protagonist faces engulfment of body and mind. When he returns to his own time, he responds with typical defenses against oral anxieties; he eats something ("Save me some of that mutton. I'm starving for a bit of meat"—p. 18), and he tells his tale. Holland observes that "a common defense against oral fusion and merger is putting something out of the mouth . . . usually speech" (p. 37).

This fantasy content forecloses many options for plot development. Within the economy of oral anxieties, the subject eats or is eaten; there is no third way. When the Time Traveller finds himself on the Terminal Beach, where nothing appears edible or consumable or exploitable, he cannot assert his status as eater. Evidently, he

subliminally accepts power relationships in terms of this binary fantasy, and thus dooms himself to being devoured through sheer default of cultural imagination. His technological magic may permit him to withdraw physically, but psychically, he is more defeated than triumphant at the end. Like his strategic withdrawal from the underworld, his departure is a rout. We note that although he returns home, he does not long remain. He is swallowed up by past or future.[10]

The commonplace assumptions in this text about bodily size undergo equivalent amplifications and distortions that affect the plot. We find elaborate equations between bodily size, intelligence, and bodily energy. Some of these simply reflect the science of the day. Researchers were establishing averages for sizes and weights of male and female brains, and followed many dead-end theories as they tried to prove what they were looking for: superiority of men over women and of whites over darker races. Furthermore, many scientists were convinced that the First Law of Thermodynamics, conservation of energy, applied to mental "energy" as well as physical.

> Food was taken in, energy (including thought) emerged, and the energy was "an exact equivalent of the amount of food assumed and assimilated." In Hardaker's crudely quantitative universe bigger was definitely better, and men were bigger.[11]

If the human race dwindles in size, so will its brain size, so will intelligence, and so will physical energy. Thus much is good science of the day. The text moves from science to symbolism, however, in linking the First and Second Laws of Thermodynamics and implying that energy loss in the universe will directly diminish the mental and physical energy of humanity. Although Wells does not state this explicitly, he apparently accepted it. The loss of culture and security would otherwise have reversed the devolutionary decline as the descendants of humans had once more to struggle for existence. This reason for species degeneration remains implicit, but it clearly follows the fantastic elaboration of ideology and science.

The explicit reason given for degeneration is Darwinian. The Traveller decides that strength and size must have declined because they were no longer needed for survival: "Under the new conditions of perfect comfort and security, that restless energy, that with us is strength, would become weakness. . . . And in a state of physical balance and security, power, intellectual as well as physical, would be out of place" (p. 42). Such a safe society dismays him. He relishes swashbuckling physical action, and is loath to consider a world that would exclude it. Indeed the Morlocks provide him with a welcome excuse to exercise powers not wanted in London. "I struggled up, shaking the human rats from me, and, holding the bar short, I thrust where I judged their faces might be. I could feel the succulent giving of flesh and bone under my blows, and for a moment I was free" (p. 95). "Succulent" is highly suggestive, relating as it does to the realm of the edible.

The equivalence of body, mind, and energy determines major features of the futuristic scenarios. We find something like medieval planes of correspondence. As the cosmos runs down, men will lose energy individually—a linkage no more logical than the Fisher-King's thigh wound causing sterility to fall upon the crops of his realm. Given this as a textual assumption about reality, however, we can see that clever, efficient and adaptive beings are impossible, although a setting like the Terminal Beach would call forth precisely such a humanity in the hands of other writers.

Gender, the third ideological element, undergoes a different kind of symbolic transformation. The traditional semes of "masculine" and "feminine"—whether culturally derived or natural—are widely familiar and even transcend cultural boundaries. Semes of the masculine include such constelled values as culture, light, the Sun, law, reason, consciousness, the right hand, land, and rulership. The feminine merges with chaos, darkness, the Moon, intuition, feeling, the left hand, water, and the unconscious.[12] The dialogue between them in some cultures involves balance; in the West, however, we find masculine consciousness fighting off or being overwhelmed by the feminine powers associated with unconsciousness. Thus the eat-consume-overwhelm nexus also enters the story as an attribute of gender.

Much of what troubles us in the realm of the Sphinx derives its power from the text's manipulation of these values. The grotesque is frequently formed from the mingling of characteristics from two "naturally" separate sets, man and beast, for instance. Despite cultural changes since the turn of the century, the traditional assumptions about gender are well enough ingrained in us by reading, if nothing else, to give the story's grotesques most of their original power. Wells attaches but also denies "feminine" and "masculine" attributes to both Eloi and Morlocks. The resulting contradictions prevent us from resolving the tensions roused by these grotesques into the kinds of reality that we are culturally conditioned to find comfortable.

The Eloi at first appear to be the only race, and then the superior of the two. Their life consists of a pastoral idyll, sunlight, and apparent rulership. Thanks to happiness, beauty, absence of poverty, and uninterrupted leisure, their life better fits our notion of Haves than Havenots. However, closer inspection shows them to be small, lacking in reason, deficient in strength, passively fearful, ineffectual, and ultimately just not "masculine" enough to be plausible patriarchal rulers, the standard against which they are implicitly held. In the *National Observer* version the Eloi have personal flying machines, but Wells ultimately deprived them of anything so technical. For all that they are feminized, however, they lack positive identity with the feminine, so we cannot reconcile them to our sense of the real by means of that pattern.

The Morlocks, by virtue of living in the dark and underground, seem first of all sinister, but secondarily are marked with symbolism of the unconscious and hence the feminine. Their access to the innards of the Sphinx reinforces the latter. Confusing our judgment, however, is their possible control of the machines, a power linked in Western eyes with the masculine rather than the feminine. Likewise, their apparently predatory aggression, their hunting parties (if such they be) fit "masculine" patterns. However, they seem deficient in strength and size to the Traveller, and their inability to tolerate light makes them obviously vulnerable in ways not befitting a "master" race. When comparing the two races, we find that both have traits associated with ruling and exploiting. The Eloi apparently live off the labor of the Morlocks while the latter apparently live off the flesh of the former. However, both are "feminized" in ways that render them less than masterful. These ambiguities in the cultural symbol system cannot be resolved. The traits associated with each race remain in uneasy tension, and contribute to the difficulty that critics have had in putting labels to the two races.

Power, size, and gender; oral fantasies, the laws of thermodynamics as applied to bodies and thought, and the grotesque: this peculiar mixture propels the story and gives it much of its intensity, its disturbing power. However, these concepts are not entirely consistent and harmonious. The conflicts they generate undermine the narrative logic and thereby dissolve the coherence of the ideas Wells was exploring. As we move to the future scenarios, we will note the gaps in the logic.

IN THE RIDDLING REALM OF THE SPHINX

Almost any way we approach this addled utopia, we find irreducible ambiguity. Does *The Time Machine* seriously concern a possible—albeit distant—future, or is futurity only a metaphoric disguise for the present? Darko Suvin focuses on the biological elements of the story, so he views the futurity as substantial and important. Others who focus on entropy or time travel likewise assume the significance of the futurity.[13] After all, without a real time lapse, anatomical evolution would be impossible. Alternately, the "future" settings may be read as versions of Wells's present. "If the novella imagines a future, it does so not as a forecast but as a way of contemplating the structures of our present civilization."[14] Social warnings of danger 800,000 years away will inevitably fail to grip. Hence, the reality of time in this text—Wells's cherished fourth dimensional time—depends upon whether readers are focusing on biological or social systems.

Even if the critic ruthlessly simplifies to one or the other, interpretations go fuzzy at the edges or lead to contradiction. The biological reading appears at first to be straightforward. Wells asks, "what if progress is not inevitable and devolution can happen as well as evolution?" The Traveller decides that the Eloi degenerate because they no longer need to fight for survival—an interesting argument to present to the increasingly nonphysical Victorian society. The need for serious, bodily rivalry makes utopia a dangerous goal, and social restraint unhealthy. Wells thus raises a genuine problem, but does not develop it.

The social reading is yet more disturbing in its inability to satisfy the expectation of coherence. Oppressing the working class is dangerous as well as inhumane, and if we continue along such lines, the Haves will fall prey to the Havenots. At first glance, this seems like an unexceptionable social warning about mistreating the Workers. Somewhat unexpectedly, Wells treats the situation not as a revolution devoutly to be desired, but as a nightmarish terror. He evidently could not work up much sense of identification with the exploited. Hence the dilemma: not improving conditions leads to nightmare, but improving them in the direction of equality gets us back to utopia and its degeneration. If one accepts the biological message—physical competition—one must ignore the social message; if one accepts the social—improved conditions—one must ignore the biological. Wells offers us no way to accept both.

Since these two approaches lead to contradiction, one might try to escape the ambiguity by generalizing the referents of Eloi and Morlocks. Then one can read this as a parable about human nature,[15] or opt for Bergonzi's approach, and see the struggle between Eloi and Morlocks as polysemous. They are Pre-Raphaelite aesthetes and proletarians, and their struggle variously resonates with "aestheticism and utilitarianism, pastoralism and technology, contemplation and action, and ultimately . . . beauty and ugliness, and light and darkness" (Bergonzi, p. 305). If you are content, with Bergonzi, to call the tale "myth" and agree that meaning in myth is always multiple, you have one solution to the problem of interpretation. Otherwise, you must accept that the Eloi and Morlocks do not form coherent portraits. Their unstable identities—e.g., Morlocks as underclass or rulers—seem better likened to the duck/rabbit optical illusion, which has two embedded forms but which we are compelled to see as only one at a given time. The Eloi are an upper class in terms of pleasant material living conditions and freedom from toil, but they are an exploited class if they are being kept as cattle. The same double-identity obscures any explanation of the Mor-

locks. I have argued elsewhere that another possibility is that the two represent a dual assessment of the middle class alone: on the surface, we find an idealized and ineffectual claim to sweetness and light and vague aestheticism, but the vicious, exploitive side of bourgeois power, which preys upon the helpless, is hidden (Hume, pp. 286-87). We can (and will) make many other such equations because each reader's assumptions will activate different voices within the text. Resolution, though, is unlikely. The two races have been rendered permanently ambiguous through their clashing qualities.

They also resist interpretation because of the disparity between the Traveller's emotions and what he actually experiences. The Morlocks are only guilty of touching him and of trying to keep him from leaving them. They use no weapons, and they attempt to capture rather than kill him. They may be interested in studying him or in trying to establish communication. After all, as Lake points out, the Morlocks apparently visit the museum out of curiosity. The Traveller is as ready to jump to dire conclusions as Bedford is in *The First Men in the Moon.* What pushes him to such extremes of fear and loathing may be his deep uneasiness over code violations. The grotesque mixing of masculine and feminine and of human and animal seem to produce in him much the sort of panic and hostility as that felt by some people towards transvestites and physical freaks.

Even the Sphinx plays her part in such confusions. "The State" and its powers are conventionally symbolized by the masculine, the father, the lawgiver. Wells's symbols for government are patriarchal in other romances, and his heroes either rebel against this oedipal oppressor or make their way into patriarchal power and identify with it. Dr. Moreau is such a threatening father, indeed a not-very-displaced castrating father. Almost all the clashes over authority in *The Food of the Gods* are put in terms of fathers and sons. The Invisible Man's hatred for established authority causes him to act in a way that literally kills his father. The Martians allow the protagonist to project his dissatisfactions with the social system onto an enemy, and with the defeat of the enemy, take up a patriarchal role and uphold the status quo.

The Sphinx, though, is female, the spawn of chaos.[16] She looms over the landscape, evidently the symbol of a ruling power, present or past, but also a grotesque yoking of beast and woman. (The other ornaments in her realm—a griffin and a faun—are also hybrids.) Bram Dijkstra has explored the Sphinx in late nineteenth-century art. He sees her renditions there as embodying tensions between the sexes that reflect male fears of

> a struggle between woman's atavistic hunger for blood—which she regarded as the vital fluid of man's seminal energies and hence the source of that material strength she craved—and man's need to conserve the

nourishment that would allow his brain to evolve. Woman was a perverse instrument of the vampire of reversion, and by giving in to her draining embrace, men thought, they must needs bleed to death.

(Dijkstra, p. 332)

In the art of this era, then, we find the same configuration of man being consumed, that consumption being carried out in such a way as to diminish not only his manly strength but also his intelligence. Oral fantasies here merge with the peculiarly end-of-the-century way of construing conservation of energy in physical and mental terms. Wells's world ruled by the Sphinx is indeed one bled of its masculinity and mental power, a world of reversion.

Wells's susceptibility to such oral anxieties is underlined by another gap in the logic. The oral fears emerge in a curiously skewed form. Haves normally exploit, "eat," or consume Havenots in a capitalist system; that is how the image usually enters socio-economic discourse. In *The Time Machine,* however, the cannibalistic urges are instead projected onto the Havenots. One finds a similar reversed logic in the martial fiction of America and England in the period of 1870 to the 1920s. Those white, Anglo-American populations who were spreading empire and invading the Philippines or carrying out wars in India and Africa entertained themselves with invasion tales in which they themselves were the victims. *The War of the Worlds* is just such an invasion tale, probably the greatest to emerge out of this literary type in England. Wells likens Martian treatment of Britons to British treatment of Tasmanians. America battened on fictions about the Black Menace, the Yellow Menace, the Red Menace, not to mention fears that England, Canada, or Mexico would invade America. Throughout the same period, America was stripping Native Americans of land and lynching Blacks, and sending armies to the Philippines and Haiti.[17] Whether Wells is using this trick of mind to characterize his protagonist, or whether Wells himself is denying political guilt and replacing it with self-justifying political fears simply is not clear. The application of the cannibalistic fantasy to the exploited group remains a notable gap in the logical fabric of the whole.

What are we to make of this adventure in the realm of the Sphinx, then? A rather mixed message, at best. Utopias by most definitions eliminate competition. This proves a dangerous ideal, because so safe an environment would encourage bodily weakness, and then degeneration of mind and feminization. In other words, beware Socialism! However, the paradise of capitalists is a world in which the Great Unwashed lives underground, its misery unseen and ignored. This too leads to degeneration, as we see, because it also abolishes real struggle. Without the chance or need to compete—literally to destroy or exploit or "consume"—man devolves,

according to Wells's ideology. The importance of competition comes out when we realize its relevance to power, size, and masculine behavior patterns, and its status as guarantor of intelligence. This competitive violence appears to be the most consistently upheld value in the first adventure, but even such struggle is undermined by the arguments in the second adventure, the excursion to the Terminal Beach. There entropy, by means of the planes of correspondences, cancels the energizing effect of struggling for existence.

THE TERMINAL BEACH: A JOURNEY TO THE INTERIOR

"Journey to the interior" nicely condenses what happens here. *The Time Machine* as a totality consists of a trip to the interior of some unknown land, as found in *She, Henderson the Rain King, Heart of Darkness,* and *The Lost Steps.* The foray from 800,000 to thirty million years into the future is an embedded journey to the interior, a *mise en abîme* repetition. Call the Terminal Beach a mindscape reached by being eaten. The Traveller enters the Sphinx much as Jonah or Lucian enter their respective whales.[18] Entropy may supply the logic that links the two scenarios, but the emotional unity derives from oral fantasies.

The Terminal Beach actually consists of two scenes and several fractional visions. The crab-infested litoral comes first, then the world in which life lingers in the form of a black, flapping, tentacled "football." The eclipse and snowflakes both belong to the second scene, increasing its inhospitability. However, both form a continuum of desolation and an invitation to despair.

That the Traveller's responses need not be quite so bleak becomes clear if we contrast Wells's handling this situation with what might be called the Germinal Beach in Arthur C. Clarke's *2010.* There, new life is discovered, but the physical conditions are much the same as in Wells, and Clarke clearly had both of Wells's beaches in mind. Clarke's setting consists of ice and water, where Wells has water, pebbles, and ice. Clarke's tragic snowflakes result from the ruptured space ship. Clarke offers a huge, slow-moving, semi-vegetative creature. Both authors suggest the frailty of life through flickering, flapping, flopping, intermittent movement. In *The Time Machine,* day and night "flap" as the Traveller zooms into the future; the black creature on the strand flops, a screaming butterfly flutters, crab mouths flicker, the sea surface ripples. The larval stages of Clarke's life-form remind the speaker of flowers and then butterflies, and then flop about like stranded fish. Wells eclipses the sun to squeeze the last drop of symbolic value out of the light and darkness; Clarke has his observer break their artificial light so that the phototropic life-form will return to the sea. The Time Traveller sees "a curved pale line like a vast new moon" (p. 107) and as the eclipse passes off, notes "a red-hot bow in the sky" (p. 109); Clarke's Dr. Chang notes that "Jupiter was a huge, thin crescent" (p. 81),[19] and a few pages after this scene, another character stares at a picture of Earth as a thin crescent looming above the Lunar horizon.

Even in the most distant future, the Time Traveller can breathe the atmosphere and can escape any immediate danger by pulling a lever, yet he despairs. Clarke's Chinese astronaut will die as soon as his oxygen runs out, yet he remains scientifically alert and basically excited and pleased, although the level of life visible in each scene is roughly the same: non-human, non-intelligent, and probably scarce. Clearly the two authors perceive the landscapes from different vantages. To Clarke, Europa is the key to hegemony of the outer planets, the source of "the most valuable substance in the Universe" (p. 66). With Europa's water and cold fusion, settlers would enjoy virtually unlimited power for themselves plus fuel for their spaceships. By contrast, the Time Traveller sees nothing worth colonizing in either scene, nothing to exploit or utilize, nothing to consume. Wells and Clarke are at one in valuing worlds for what we can exploit.

Again, Wells disturbs his Traveller by violating his codes for normal reality. Instead of finding light and dark, he finds all liminal and borderline colors and values: palpitating greyness, steady twilight (p. 104), a sun that glows dully, and a beach on which there are no waves, only an oily swell. An eclipse is suitably liminal as well, a state that produces neither true day nor true night. In addition to being in a permanently transitional phase, his world is also liminal with regards to land and water. The ocean has approached over the millennia; what was high land in Victorian London and 800,000 years later is about to be overwhelmed by the advancing ocean. Light and land, often mindscape equivalents to mind and body, are threatened by the encroaching, engulfing forces of darkness and water. Insofar as sea and darkness have symbolic associations with the unconscious and the feminine, this threat repeats both the gender and oral anxieties seen in the earlier adventure.

One's first instinct upon reading the Terminal Beach chapter is to interpret it solely as a funereal rhapsody on entropy, as a look at the inevitable death of the sun and the ramifications of this eventuality for mankind. George H. Darwin provided Wells with ideas about tidal friction and slowed rotation. The Book of Revelation contributes water-turned-blood. These simple transformations, plus the narrator's depression at what he finds, make the bleakness and hopelessness seem natural and inevitable. I would argue that to some degree they are actually cultural and ideological.

One has only to look at *The War of the Worlds* or even *The First Men in the Moon* to see very different fic-

tional responses to apparently dead-end situations. The protagonists in those stories, or various lesser characters, face new situations with the same sort of scientific curiosity and engagement shown by Clarke's Dr. Chang. They are not foolish optimists, but a bleak and threatening situation is cause for intellectual stimulation, for forming and confirming theories, for taking pride in observing new phenomena, for striving against the environment. The Time Traveller, though, seemingly suffers an entropic loss of his own energy as he observes that life in general has lost the struggle. The point of failure, however, actually came where Wells's thermodynamic fantasy overcame his Darwinian science. When the social system eventually disintegrated, the descendents of Eloi and Morlocks should have improved through survival of the fittest. His assumptions about mind, energy, and body, though, render his fictional creations helpless long before the final scenes. That helplessness was dictated by a fantastic distortion of the laws of thermodynamics, not by the laws themselves, so here again, we find the amplifications and elaborations of basic ideologies affecting plot. Mankind disappears because of one such fantasy; the Traveller's panic takes its form from another.

In superficial regards, *The Time Machine* is obviously enough a social satire to justify our expecting a reasonably coherent warning. The doubled identities of both Eloi and Morlocks turns them into the literary equivalent of an optical illusion. Coherence can no more emerge from them than from Escher's drawing of water flowing downhill in a circle. Scientifically, *The Time Machine* explores entropic decline, but refuses to give us ingenious humanity striving ever more ferociously to put off the inevitable. Humanity has already degenerated irreversibly through the exercise of what is generally considered its higher impulses. Even that would be a warning, but Wells undercuts it with his thermodynamic fantasies, which would bring about similar degeneration in any case through the links he posits among body and mind and energy. Thus do some of the rather fierce undercurrents in this romance break up its arguments, leaving them as stimulating fragments rather than logical structures. The powerful emotions both expressed by the Traveller and generated in readers are tribute to the sub-surface currents, especially the oral-stage anxieties. The torment they represent is most clearly seen in the blind, defensive, totally illogical projection of savagery and cannibalism upon the group most apparently exploited. Like the imperialistic nations fantasizing their own humiliation at the hands of invaders, Wells's Traveller, and possibly Wells himself, are projecting behavior upon others in ways that suggest considerable repressed social guilt.

The return of the repressed is important to the dynamics of this tale. I will finish my arguments with one further variant on that theme. When the Time Traveller seeks the ruler of the pastoral realm, he seeks an Absent Father, and finds instead the Sphinx, avatar of threatening femininity. Within the classical Greek world view, "man" is the proud answer to the Sphinx's riddle, and man as Oedipus vanquishes the feminine and chaotic forces from Western civilization. In **The Time Machine,** "man" is no longer as proud an answer, and man has no power to prevent the lapse from order towards entropy. One might even argue that this time-travelling Oedipus is to some degree the criminal responsible for the status quo, for the ideologies he embodies have limited his culture's vision and rendered alternatives invisible. The Greeks and their civilization based on patriarchal structures banished the Sphinx. Here, she returns, and she succeeds in swallowing humanity after all.

Notes

1. The Atlantic edition of *The Works of H. G. Wells,* 1 (New York: Charles Scribner's Sons, 1924): 4-5.

2. Bernard Bergonzi rendered *The Time Machine* orthodox by bestowing upon it two charismatic labels: "ironic" and "myth." See "*The Time Machine*: An Ironic Myth," *Critical Quarterly* 2 (1960): 293-305.

3. See David J. Lake, "Wells's Time Traveller: An Unreliable Narrator?" *Extrapolation* 22, no. 2 (1981): 117-26.

4. John Huntington sees this mastery of his actions as index to the protagonist's superiority over both Eloi and Morlocks, since they lack such self-control. See *The Logic of Fantasy: H. G. Wells and Science Fiction* (Columbia U. Press, 1982), p. 51.

5. For details of this and many other variants, including a previously unpublished draft of an excursion into the past, see *The Definitive Time Machine: A Critical Edition of H. G. Wells's Scientific Romance,* with introduction and notes by Harry M. Geduld (Indiana U. Press, 1987), quotations from p. 179.

6. In her utopian novel, *The Dispossessed,* Ursula Le Guin calls our attention to this unthinking esteem for height by replacing commendatory terms based on size with those based on centrality.

7. See McCarthy's "*Heart of Darkness* and the Early Novels of H. G. Wells: Evolution, Anarchy, Entropy," *Journal of Modern Literature* 13, no. 1 (1986): 37-60.

8. See Kathryn Hume, "The Hidden Dynamics of *The War of the Worlds,*" *PQ* 62 (1983): 279-92; Wells developed the connection more forcefully in the serialized version.

9. Norman N. Holland, *The Dynamics of Literary Response* (New York: W. W. Norton, 1975), p. 43.

10. For an argument in favor of the Traveller's being a traditional monomyth hero, and hence triumphant, see Robert J. Begiebing, "The Mythic Hero in H. G. Wells's *The Time Machine,*" *Essays in Literature,* 11 (1984): 201-10. Wells's many escape endings are analyzed by Robert P. Weeks in "Disentanglement as a Theme in H. G. Wells's Fiction," originally published in *Papers of the Michigan Academy of Science, Arts, and Letters* 39 (1954), reprinted in *H. G. Wells: A Collection of Critical Essays,* edited by Bernard Bergonzi (Englewood Cliffs, New Jersey: Prentice-Hall, 1976), pp. 25-31. Interestingly, Wells considered another kind of ending, at least in response to editorial pressures. In the version of this story serialized in *The National Observer,* the story ends with the Traveller referring to hearing his child crying upstairs because frightened by the dark. This *ad hoc* family man, however, may result from hasty termination of the serial. Henley, as editor, liked Wells's work while his replacement, Vincent, did not. See Geduld for such variants.

11. For the nineteenth-century science behind all the assumptions about body size and energy, see Cynthia Eagle Russett, *Sexual Science: The Victorian Construction of Womanhood* (Harvard U. Press, 1989), p. 105.

12. In other words, Yin, Yang, and Jung. These symbolic clusters of values are discussed and illustrated throughout both the following Jungian studies by Erich Neumann: *The Origins and History of Consciousness,* Bollingen Series 42 (Princeton U. Press, 1970) and *The Great Mother: An Analysis of the Archetype,* Bollingen Series 47 (Princeton U. Press, 1972).

13. Darko Suvin, *Metamorphoses of Science Fiction: On the Poetics and History of a Literary Genre* (Yale U. Press, 1979), chapter 10. For an analysis of time travel, see Veronica Hollinger, "Deconstructing the Time Machine," *Science-Fiction Studies* 14 (1987): 201-21.

14. Huntington, p. 41. Others focusing on social issues include Patrick Parrinder, "*News from Nowhere, The Time Machine* and the Break-Up of Classical Realism," *Science-Fiction Studies* 3, no. 3 (1976): 265-74, and Wayne C. Connely, "H. G. Well's [sic] *The Time Machine*: It's [sic] Neglected Mythos," *Riverside Quarterly* 5, no. 3 (1972): 178-91.

15. Stephen Gill sees the Morlocks as "the bestial nature of human beings." Hennelly sees it about the failure to reconcile the contraries in the human heart, and Lake explores it as a protest against death. See Gill, *Scientific Romances of H. G. Wells: A Critical Study* (Cornwall, Ontario: Vesta

Publications, 1975), p. 38, and Mark M. Hennelly, Jr., "*The Time Machine*: A Romance of 'The Human Heart,'" *Extrapolation* 20, no. 2 (1979): 154-67; and David J. Lake, "The White Sphinx and the Whitened Lemur: Images of Death in *The Time Machine*," *Science-Fiction Studies* 6, no. 1 (1979): 77-84.

16. See Frank Scafella, "The White Sphinx and *The Time Machine*," *Science-Fiction Studies* 8, no. 3 (1981): 255-65, p. 259. Bram Dijkstra explores the *fin de siècle* fascination with sphinxes in art in *Idols of Perversity: Fantasies of Feminine Evil in Fin-de-Siècle Culture* (Oxford U. Press, 1986), pp. 325-32.

17. For an analysis of the British version of such invasion jitters, see Cecil Degrotte Eby, *The Road to Armageddon: The Martial Spirit in English Popular Literature, 1870-1914* (Duke U. Press, 1987). For the American version, see H. Bruce Franklin, *War Stars: The Superweapon and the American Imagination* (Oxford U. Press, 1988).

18. Two mindscapes similarly reached in a physical interior are Harlan Ellison's "Adrift Just Off the Islets of Langerhans: Latitude 38° 54' N, Longitude 77° 00' 13" W," and Norman Spinrad's "Carcinoma Angels." In the latter, the protagonist psychically descends into his own body to kill cancer cells. He "finally found himself knee-deep in the sea of his digestive juices lapping against the walls of the dank, moist cave that was his stomach. And scuttling towards him on chitinous legs, a monstrous black crab with blood-red eyes, gross, squat, primeval." The Wellsian intertext enriches the cancer/crab wordplay. "Carcinoma Angels" is found in *Dangerous Visions,* ed. Harlan Ellison (London: Victor Gollancz, 1987), 513-21, quotation, p. 521.

19. The "Germinal Beach" occurs on pp. 77-82 of Arthur C. Clarke, *2010* (London: Granada, 1983).

David C. Cody (essay date fall 1993)

SOURCE: Cody, David C. "Faulkner, Wells, and the 'End of Man'." *Journal of Modern Literature* 18, no. 4 (fall 1993): 465-74.

[*In the following essay, Cody judges the influence of* The Time Machine *on William Faulkner's 1950 Nobel Prize speech.*]

> We finish thus; and all our wretched race
> Shall finish with its cycle, and give place
> To other beings, with their own time-doom;
> Infinite eons ere our kind began;

> Infinite eons after the last man
> Has joined the mammoth in earth's tomb and womb.

—James Thomson, "The City of Dreadful Night" (1874)

> Why should we bear with an hour of torture, a moment of pain,
> If every man die for ever, if all his griefs are in vain,
> And the homeless planet at length will be wheel'd thro' the silence of space,
> Motherless evermore of an ever-vanishing race,
> When the worm shall have writhed its last, and its last brother-worm will have fled
> From the dead fossil skull that is left in the rocks of an earth that is dead?. . . .
> Have I crazed myself over their horrible infidel writings? O yes,
> For these are the new dark ages, you see, of the popular press,
> When the bat comes out of his cave, and the owls are whooping at noon,
> And Doubt is lord of this dunghill and crows to the sun and the moon,
> Till the Sun and the Moon of our science are both of them turn'd into blood
> And Hope will have broken her heart, running after a shadow of good. . . .

—Alfred, Lord Tennyson, "Despair: A Dramatic Monologue" (1881)

One must err to grow and the writer feels no remorse for this youthful effort. Indeed he hugs his vanity very pleasantly at times when his dear old Time Machine crops up once more in essays and speeches, still a practical and convenient way to retrospect or prophecy.

—H. G. Wells, Preface (1931) to *The Time Machine* (1895)

In his 1950 Nobel Prize speech, William Faulkner contemplates the ultimate fate of mankind in a nuclear age and considers the role that the writer might play in helping to determine that fate. In one of the most famous passages he would ever write, he suggests that the young writer of his day, although living in the debilitating shadow of "a general and universal fear so long sustained by now that we can even bear it," must "teach himself that the basest of all things is to be afraid; and, teaching himself that, forget it forever, leaving no room in his workshop for anything but the old verities and truths of the heart, the old universal truths lacking which any story is ephemeral and doomed—love and honor and pity and pride and compassion and sacrifice."[1] "Until he relearns these things," Faulkner insists, "he will write as though he stood among and watched the end of man. I decline to accept the end of man. It is easy enough to say that man is immortal simply because he will endure: that when the last ding-dong of doom has clanged and faded from the last worthless rock hanging tideless in the last red and dying evening, that even then there will still be one more sound: that of his puny inexhaustible voice, still talking. I refuse to accept this. I believe that man will not merely endure: he will prevail" (p. 4).[2] Although the Nobel Speech is addressed to "the young man or woman writing today" and although it concerns itself with "our tragedy today" ("There are no longer questions of the spirit," Faulkner writes, ". . . There is only the question: when will I be blown up?"), it has as one of its central themes the crucial importance of remembering or re-learning the "old universal truths" which mankind is in danger of forgetting. Faulkner insists that man is immortal not merely because he will "endure," but because he is possessed of a soul, "a spirit capable of compassion and sacrifice and endurance" which will permit him, in the end, to "prevail," and he makes the point too that "the poet's voice" is one of the "props" or "pillars" that will help man to do so: "The poet's, the writer's duty," he informs us, "is to write about these things. It is his privilege to help man endure by lifting his heart, by reminding him of the courage and honor and hope and pride and compassion and pity and sacrifice which have been the glory of his past" (p. 4).[3]

The Speech, then, is emphatic in its defence of the "old verities and truths of the heart." Whether Faulkner's life's work is in fact "uplifting" in this sense—whether he really did believe, that is, that his own work signified an affirmative belief—is a complex question that is not easily resolved. In the Speech, however, Faulkner contrasts his own efforts on behalf of mankind with the work of other writers who have failed in their duty because they have written as though they "stood among and watched the end of man." He does not identify such writers by name, but that oddly detailed reference to a "last worthless rock hanging tideless in the last red and dying evening" gives us some sense of what he had in mind—for although it has been plausibly suggested that in the Speech as a whole he disparages the pessimistic view of man's future that had been expressed by Joseph Conrad in his essay "Henry James: An Appreciation," the very specificity of that apocalyptic reference makes it clear that Faulkner is in fact recalling the climacteric scene in H. G. Wells's *The Time Machine: An Invention* (1895).[4]

We do not know when Faulkner first encountered Wells's "scientific romance"—which purports, of course, to be the narrative of a traveller who has quite literally "stood among and watched the end of man"—but we do know that his personal library at Rowan Oak contained a copy of a special limited edition published in 1931, with a preface by the elderly Wells and remarkable "designs" in color by W. A. Dwiggins.[5] In the penultimate chapter of *The Time Machine,* the Time Traveller moves forward into the distant future, watching as the earth's rotation upon its axis gradually slows, the planet eventually coming to rest "with one face to the sun, even as in our own time the moon faces the earth" (77). As he begins to slow his motion through time, "the dim outlines of a desolate beach" gradually

become visible, and when he comes to rest he finds himself in a world very different from the one he has left behind:

> The sky was no longer blue. North-eastward it was inky black, and out of the blackness shone brightly and steadily the pale white stars. Overhead it was a deep Indian red and starless, and south-eastward it grew brighter to a glowing scarlet where, cut by the horizon, lay the huge hull of the sun, red and motionless. The rocks about me were of a harsh reddish colour. . . . [T]he machine was standing on a sloping beach. The sea stretched away to the south-west, to rise into a sharp bright horizon against the wan sky. There were no breakers and no waves, for not a breath of wind was stirring.

> (p. 77)

It was on this desolate beach, clearly, with its tideless sea brooding beneath a red and dying sun, that Faulkner first stumbled over his "last worthless rock." It is not a pleasant place, and the Time Traveller—appalled by the "abominable desolation," but "drawn on by the mystery of the earth's fate"—decides to venture still further into the future. When he halts once more, "more than thirty million years hence," he finds himself upon the same stretch of beach, now lying cold and apparently lifeless in a dying world in which "the huge red-hot dome of the sun had come to obscure nearly a tenth part of the darkling heavens." Here, troubled by "a certain indefinable apprehension," he watches as "an inner planet passing very near to the earth" gradually eclipses the sun. [. . .] As the eclipse becomes total, the silence, cold, and darkness grow overwhelming, but one final epiphany awaits him:

> A horror of this great darkness came on me. The cold, that smote to my marrow, and the pain I felt in breathing, overcame me. I shivered, and a deadly nausea seized me. Then like a red-hot bow in the sky appeared the edge of the sun. . . . As I stood sick and confused I saw again the moving thing upon the shoal—there was no mistake now that it was a moving thing—against the red water of the sea. It was a round thing, the size of a football perhaps, or, it may be, bigger, and tentacles trailed down from it; it seemed black against the weltering blood-red water, and it was hopping fitfully about. Then I felt that I was fainting. But a terrible dread of lying helpless in that remote and awful twilight sustained me while I clambered upon the saddle.

> (p. 80)

In much of the horror literature produced in the late Victorian and Edwardian periods, characters experience symptoms such as nausea, sickness, and confusion after an encounter with the "uncanny"—Freud's *unheimlich*—or with what we have more recently come to refer to as the "abject." In her *Powers of Horror* (1982), Julia Kristeva defines "abjection" as that which "disturbs identity, system, order. What does not respect borders, positions, rules. The in-between, the ambiguous, the composite."[6] Such encounters appear so frequently in the horror literature of the *fin de siècle* that they might almost be called a defining characteristic of the genre, just as the literature itself was a symptom of the intense anxiety which existed in the culture that engendered it. In Kipling's "The Strange Ride of Morrowbie Jukes" (1885), for example, the protagonist, caught up in his Imperialist nightmare, compares his "inexplicable terror" to "the overpowering nausea of the Channel passage—only my agony was of the spirit and infinitely more terrible."[7] We might also recall the "horror and revolting nausea" experienced by the doctor who witnesses the ghastly demise of Helen Vaughn in Arthur Machen's "The Great God Pan" (1890); the "horror" and "loathing" with which Basil Hallward views the infamous portrait in Wilde's *The Picture of Dorian Gray* (1891); and the "horrible feeling of nausea" that overcomes Jonathan Harker when he meets the Count in Bram Stoker's *Dracula* (1897): in all such descriptions, the response is triggered by the realization that an ontological border (between the normal and the abnormal, the safe and the unsafe) has been violated.[8] In this sense, the Time Traveller's nausea is due not merely to the cold and the thin atmosphere which he encounters in the future, but also to his realization—not as mere theory or hypothesis, but as fact—that mankind has no place there. Faulkner's young writers, attempting to create in a time when not the century, but the world itself seemed about to come to an end, were similarly distressed—and so, if the speech is any indication, was Faulkner himself.

To appreciate the relevance of Faulkner's reference to *The Time Machine,* then, we must be cognizant, as Faulkner himself obviously was, of the various implications of that final moment of horror, which is given particular emphasis in Wells's narrative not merely because the encounter itself marks the culmination of the Time Traveller's adventuring (the round object the size of a football is the last sight he sees before he flees back to the relative safety of the late-nineteenth century) and not merely because it provides us with a glimpse of the end of life on earth. In his preface to the 1931 edition of *The Time Machine,* the elderly Wells noted that although his romance "seems a very undergraduate performance to its now mature writer, as he looks it over once more," it nevertheless "goes as far as his philosophy about human evolution went in those days" (p. ix). During the Victorian period as a whole, of course, and during the *fin de siècle* in particular, the prevailing "philosophy about human evolution" underwent a remarkable transformation. For many years, many more or less eminent Victorians, equating technological advances with moral ones, had attempted to reconcile the moral values of Christianity with what was (ostensibly, at least) morally neutral Darwinian thought: their tendency, inevitably, was to distort the latter so that in

various ways it could be made to reinforce belief in human "Progress," both spiritual and material. By 1895, however, the great age of Victorian optimism was already over, and in this sense *The Time Machine* reflects an ongoing ideological crisis within late-Victorian culture itself, as the heirs of Darwin asserted the primacy (and the purity) of their own vision, which was much less overtly anthropocentric. It is only a slight exaggeration to suggest, as two recent critics have done, that by 1895 "the conventional pieties of romantic Christianity seemed on the verge of being finally destroyed by the overwhelming evidence for Darwinian materialism."[9]

The groundwork for such destruction, however, had been laid much earlier. In 1834, for example, William Whewell had noted in his Bridgewater Treatise on *Astronomy and General Physics Considered with Reference to Natural Theology* that all planets orbiting the sun were gradually losing velocity because of the resistance offered by an "ethereal medium":

> It may be millions of millions of years before the earth's retardation may perceptibly affect the apparent motion of the sun; but still the day will come (if the same Providence which formed the system, should permit it to continue so long) when this cause will entirely change the length of our year and the course of our seasons, and finally stop the earth's motion round the sun altogether. The smallness of the resistance, however small we choose to suppose it, does not allow us to escape this certainty.[10]

By 1852, seven years before the first publication of Darwin's *The Origin of Species,* Lord Kelvin and others had already formulated the Second Law of Thermodynamics, and Kelvin himself had stated that "Within a finite period of time past, the earth must have been, and within a finite period to come, the earth must again be, unfit for the habitation of man as at present constituted."[11] In his *The Conservation of Energy* (1873), Balfour Stewart would note that "We are led to look to an end in which the whole universe will be one equally heated inert mass, and from which everything like life or motion or beauty will have utterly gone away."[12] In his *Degeneration* (1893), the eccentric Max Nordau would suggest that even the "degenerate" art and music and literature of the day betokened doom: "The old Northern faith contained the fearsome doctrine of the Dusk of the Gods. In our days there have arisen in more highly-developed minds vague qualms of a Dusk of the Nations in which all suns and all stars are gradually waning and mankind with all its institutions and creations is perishing in the midst of a dying world."[13] Many of the most prominent scientists of the period agreed that in the long term at least, the prospects for continued human existence were grim; this view is also reflected in such dark and anxiety-ridden poems as James Thomson's "The City of Dreadful Night" (1874) and the elderly Tennyson's "Despair: A Dramatic Monologue" (1881).

The same premise, of course, shaped *The Time Machine.* Looking back in 1931 on the *weltanschauung* that had prevailed during his youth, Wells would note that "the geologists and astronomers of that time told us dreadful lies about the 'inevitable' freezing up of the world—and of life and mankind with it. There was no escape, it seemed. The whole game of life would be over in a million years or less. They impressed this upon us with the full weight of their authority . . ." (ix-x). That Darwin himself eventually accepted this pessimistic vision of the future of mankind, and that he too found the idea profoundly disturbing, is made clear in one of his letters to J. D. Hooker, dating from Feb. 9, 1865:

> I quite agree how humiliating the slow progress of man is, but everyone has his own pet horror, and this slow progress or even personal annihilation sinks in my mind into insignificance compared with the idea or rather I presume certainty of the sun some day cooling and we all freezing. To think of the progress of millions of years, with every continent swarming with good and enlightened men, all ending in this, and with probably no fresh start until this our planetary system has been again converted into red-hot gas. Sic transit gloria mundi, with a vengeance. . . .[14]

The same point would later recur in William James's *The Varieties of Religious Experience* (1902), although James inverted the central metaphor:

> The lustre of the present hour is always borrowed from the background of possibilities it goes with. Let our common experiences be enveloped in an eternal moral order; let our suffering have an immortal significance; let Heaven smile upon the earth, and deities pay their visits; let faith and hope be the atmosphere which man breathes in;—and his days pass by with zest; they stir with prospects, they thrill with remoter values. Place round them on the contrary the curdling cold and gloom and absence of all permanent meaning which for pure naturalism and the popular scientific evolutionism of our time are all that is visible ultimately, and the thrill stops short, or turns rather to an anxious trembling.

> For naturalism, fed on recent cosmological speculations, mankind is in a position similar to that of a set of people living on a frozen lake, surrounded by cliffs over which there is no escape, yet knowing that little by little the ice is melting, and the inevitable day drawing near when the last film of it will disappear, and to be drowned ignominiously will be the human creature's portion. The merrier the skating, the warmer and more sparkling the sun by day, and the ruddier the bonfires at night, the more poignant the sadness with which one must take in the meaning of the total situation.[15]

Wells's "imaginative romance," then, is a dramatization of the views of those "geologists and astronomers" who were proponents of "popular scientific evolutionism"

and of their counterparts in physics, biology, and even philosophy. As a literary fantasy, *The Time Machine* owes a great deal to works by Swift, Poe, Stevenson, Twain, and Kipling; as a modern myth, it echoes ancient legends concerning the Twilight of the Gods; but as a presumably scientific Jeremiad, it is most obviously and specifically indebted to the thought of Thomas Henry Huxley, the great rationalist and defender of Darwin whose lectures on Biology and Zoology had greatly impressed Wells during his first year (1884) as a student at the Normal School of Science.[16] In his influential essay "Evolution and Ethics" (first presented as a Romanes lecture, in 1893), Huxley acknowledged that to the popular mind, "evolution" meant "progressive development," but he emphasized that "every theory of evolution must be consistent not merely with progressive development, but with indefinite persistence in the same condition and with retrogressive modification."[17] It was Huxley's definition of the latter term as "progress from a condition of relative complexity to one of relative uniformity" that provided Wells with the "central idea" for the work that would eventually become *The Time Machine.* "The theory of evolution," Huxley wrote, "encourages no millennial anticipations. If, for millions of years, our globe has taken the upward road, yet, some time, the summit will be reached and the downward route will be commenced. The most daring imagination will hardly venture upon the suggestion that the power and intelligence of man can ever arrest the procession of the great year" (p. 85). Fascinated by the concept of "degeneration following security," Wells would vividly describe its ultimate consequences in the penultimate chapter of *The Time Machine,* in which the "round thing" encountered on the dying beach is, in fact, the last representative of degenerate "man"—man as he would appear after thirty million years of inexorable "progress" on a "downward route" dictated by laws of physics and thermodynamics.

It is this denial of the possibility that man might somehow "prevail," then, that Faulkner condemns in a Speech which implicitly contrasts the uplifting "old verities and truths of the heart" with the deeply pessimistic premise underlying Wells's late-Victorian nightmare. In this sense, Faulkner's Speech, always viewed as a classic affirmation of the values of humanism, is also a profoundly conservative work in which he adopts the traditional stance of the Biblical prophet—or of the Victorian sage. Ignoring his own prolonged flirtation with literary Decadence and with the implicitly nihilistic attitudes of the Lost Generation, Faulkner condemns Wells because in writing *The Time Machine* he had contributed to rather than helped to alleviate the potentially overwhelming anxieties that would eventually begin to cripple modern literature. Hence Faulkner's invocation of implicitly Victorian virtues in the Speech itself, and hence the relevance of the fact that in the midst of an attempt to "uplift the hearts" of the young writers who lived in the shadow of a possible nuclear holocaust, he would invoke—as epitomizing a decadent and enervating sense of imminent and inevitable doom—a work written fifty-five years earlier (and two years before Faulkner himself had been born) in the midst of another period of cultural malaise.[18] Even in this sense, however, his choice of *The Time Machine* as a text to react against was singularly apt, for as Wells informs us, the Time Traveller "thought but cheerlessly of the Advancement of Mankind, and saw in the growing pile of civilization only a foolish heaping that must inevitably fall back upon and destroy its makers in the end" (p. 86). In declining to accept "the end of man," then, Faulkner is rejecting the very premise that haunts the conclusion of *The Time Machine*—the assumption that life itself has no ultimate or transcendent meaning.

The connection between Faulkner's Nobel Prize Speech and Wells's work does not end there, however, for in declining to accept the end of man, Faulkner was also echoing or recapitulating a memorable conversation that Wells had had in 1906 with Theodore Roosevelt, then President of the United States. Roosevelt, of course, was a staunch advocate of American expansionism—his best-known literary work, *The Winning of the West,* being in effect, as David Wrobel has noted, "a study of American imperialism and its march across the continental mainland."[19] Many years afterwards, in his *Experiment in Autobiography* (1934), Wells recalled the conversation and brooded over its implications:

> It is a curious thing that as I talked with President Roosevelt in the garden of the White House there came back to me quite forcibly that undertone of doubt that has haunted me throughout this journey. After all, does this magnificent appearance of beginnings, which is America, convey any clear and certain promise of permanence and fulfilment whatever? . . . Is America a giant childhood or a gigantic futility, a mere latest phase of that long succession of experiments which has been and may be for interminable years—may be, indeed, altogether until the end—man's social history?

> I can't now recall how our discursive talk settled towards this, but it is clear to me that I struck upon a familiar vein of thought in the President's mind. He hadn't, he said, an effectual disproof of a pessimistic interpretation of the future. If one chose to say America must presently lose the impetus of her ascent, that she and all mankind must culminate and pass, he could not conclusively deny that possibility. Only he chose to live as if this were not so.

> That remained in his mind. Presently he reverted to it. He made a sort of apology for his life, against the doubts and scepticisms that, I fear, must be in the background of the thoughts of every modern man who is intellectually alive. He mentioned my *Time Machine.* . . . He became gesticulatory, and his straining voice a note higher in denying the pessimism of that book as a credible interpretation of destiny. With one of those sudden movements of his he knelt forward in a garden-

chair—we were standing, before our parting, beneath the colonnade—and addressed me very earnestly over the back, clutching it and then thrusting out his familiar gesture, a hand first partly open and then closed.

> "Suppose, after all," he said slowly, "that should prove to be right, and it all ends in your butterflies and morlocks. That doesn't matter now. The effort's real. It's worth going on with. It's worth it. It's worth it—even so." . . .

> I can see him now and hear his unmusical voice saying, "The effort—the effort's worth it," and see the gesture of his clenched hand and the—how can I describe it?—the friendly peering snarl of his face, like a man with the sun in his eyes. He sticks in my mind at that, as a very symbol of the creative will in man, in its limitations, its doubtful adequacy, its valiant persistence, amidst perplexities and confusions. He kneels out, assertive, against his setting—and his setting is the White House, with a background of all America.[20]

In his Speech, then, Faulkner—himself speaking, as it were, "with a background of all America"—is also rehearsing the role played by Roosevelt when, acknowledging the possibility that it might all end in "butterflies and morlocks," proclaims that he nevertheless "chose to live as if this were not so." Both Roosevelt and Faulkner reject Wells's premise that America itself is a "gigantic futility," just as both refuse to accept the inevitability of "the end of man." Perhaps they do so because to do otherwise would be to admit that their own struggles and sacrifices, their own "anguish and travail"—Faulkner's as an artist, Roosevelt's as a "reformer"—had been in vain. Speaking as a writer, speaking to writers, and for writers, Faulkner also speaks—as sage and prophet—to all mankind, refusing to accept the Time Traveller's testimony that the writer's struggle to uplift the human heart is a pointless one. By implication, he offers himself as a writer who has both uplifted hearts and insisted that human existence is meaningful; in this crucial sense, the Nobel Speech is also an attempt on his part both to find meaning in his own existence and to define a philosophical perspective from which that existence can be judged. His ringing affirmation of humanist values upon the occasion of his receipt of the most prestigious of literary awards, then, may have been at least in part an attempt to respond to or forestall criticism of his own work; criticism grounded on the premise that his own work was not "uplifting." In the Speech, he undertakes both to enhance his status and reputation as an American man of letters and to influence or even to re-define the context within which his audience would receive and react to his own "life's work in the agony and sweat of the human spirit," and in a dramatic sense he uses the Speech to position himself as the very incarnation of what Wells, speaking of Roosevelt, had called the "very symbol of the creative will in man, in its limitations, its doubtful adequacy, its valiant persistence, amidst perplexities and confusions." The general outlines of this effort are readily visible in the portions of the Speech in which he proclaims the continuing importance of certain traditional values in a world which has come to neglect them. Faulkner does so, perhaps, because he feared that without that faith in the meaningfulness of his own life's work he would himself be consumed by the same "general and universal" fear of which he speaks so eloquently in the Nobel Speech and elsewhere—the fear that had preoccupied H. G. Wells as it had preoccupied Shakespeare: the old fear that all our yesterdays have but lighted fools the way to dusty death.

Notes

1. William Faulkner, "Speech of Acceptance upon the award of the Nobel Prize for Literature, delivered in Stockholm on the tenth of December, nineteen hundred fifty," in *The Faulkner Reader* (Random House, 1954), pp. 3-4. All citations from the Nobel Speech refer to this edition.

2. The reference to "the last worthless rock" is, of course, accompanied by a reference to "the last ding-dong of doom," otherwise the world's death-knell—a Faulknerian variation on the traditional Crack of Doom that is to herald the Day of Judgment. It is tempting to read this phrase as a deliberate echo or redaction of Shakespeare's reference to "the last syllable of recorded time" in the great nihilistic speech from *Macbeth* that had already provided Faulkner with the title for *The Sound and the Fury*. In this sense, the thrust of the Nobel Speech would also refute Macbeth's conclusion that life—the "walking shadow," the "poor player"—will "strut and fret his hour upon the stage" and then "be heard no more." What Faulkner meant by the word "prevail" is an interesting question in itself. One wonders whether he meant more than is implicit in the ambiguous vision, set forth four years afterwards in *A Fable,* of man's progress through the Universe as a sort of interplanetary Mad Hatter's Tea Party: "Oh, yes, he will survive it because he has that in him which will endure even beyond the last ultimate worthless tideless rock freezing slowly in the last red and heatless sunset, because already the next star in the blue immensity of space will be already clamorous with the uproar of his debarkation, his puny and inexhaustible voice still talking, still planning; and there too after the last ding dong of doom has rung and died there will be one sound more: his voice, planning still to build something higher and faster than ever before, yet it too inherent with the same old primordial fault since it too in the end will fail to eradicate him from the earth." [William Faulkner, *A Fable* (New York, 1954), p. 354.]

3. Joseph Blotner and several other critics have remarked the fact that three years later, in the preface to *The Faulkner Reader*, Faulkner would repeat that the writer's purpose was "to uplift man's heart," even though the source of this "hope and desire" may be "completely selfish, completely personal." [William Faulkner, *The Faulkner Reader* (Random House, 1954), p. x.] On this occasion he suggested that he remembered encountering the phrase as a boy in the preface to an unidentified book by the Polish novel Laureate Henryk Sienkiewicz. (Several commentators have noted that the book was *Pan Michael*, the third volume of a lengthy historical romance typical in its way of the nineteenth-century revival of interest in the medieval cult of chivalry). In fact, the passage appears at the end of the book, not in the preface, but this reference too suggests a connection between Faulkner's speech and his sense of the importance of the values of the past. His hortatory invocation of the "old verities and truths of the heart, the old universal truths lacking which any story is ephemeral and doomed—love and honor and pity and pride and compassion and sacrifice" as the proper study of "the young man or woman writing today" has a characteristically Victorian ring: we might, for example, compare it with the sentiment expressed by the young John Buchan, when in 1896 he reminded his reader that "The old noble commonplaces of love and faith and duty are always with us, since they are needful for the making of any true man or woman." [John Buchan, "Prefatory," in *Scholar-Gypsies* (Bodley Head, 1896).]

4. In 1967 Eric Solomon suggested that Faulkner owed "much of the rhetoric and many of the key ideas" in the speech to Conrad's essay on James, first published in the *North American Review* in 1905 and later reprinted in Conrad's *Notes on Life and Letters*. Conrad refers to the last day as a moment when some last artist "will formulate, strange as it may appear, some hope now to us utterly inconceivable." Solomon notes that Conrad and Faulkner employ "remarkable similar phrases and attitudes that reflect their essentially hopeful views of man's chances in a doom-ridden world." Christof Wegelin, writing in 1974, agreed that "the final paragraph of Faulkner's speech owed its rhetoric and its key ideas to Conrad," but concluded that "there is nothing in Conrad to match Faulkner's optimism" and went on to suggest that "while Faulkner expressed an essentially hopeful view, Conrad was at best dubious about man's end." Conrad suggests that "When the last aqueduct shall have crumbled to pieces, the last airship fallen to the ground, the last blade of grass have died upon a dying earth," a man "gifted with a power of expression and courageous enough to interpret the ultimate experience of mankind in

terms of his temperament, in terms of art" will be "moved to speak on the eve of that day without tomorrow—whether in austere exhortation or in a phrase of sardonic comment, who can guess?" Hence, presumably, Faulkner's sardonic glimpse of post-Doomsday man and his "puny inexhaustible voice, still talking." This stands in stark contrasts, obviously, to the Time Traveller's vision of the overwhelming silence that reigns at the end of things. See Eric Solomon, "Joseph Conrad, William Faulkner, and the Nobel Prize Speech," *Notes and Queries* (New Series XIV, 1967), pp. 247-48, and Christof Wegelin, "'Endure' and 'Prevail': Faulkner's Modification of Conrad," *Notes and Queries* (New Series XXI, 1974), pp. 375-76. For the relevant passage in Conrad's essay, see his *Notes on Life and Literature* (Doubleday, Page & Company, 1924), pp. 13-14. It may be worth noting that Conrad (a longtime friend who would in 1907 dedicate *The Secret Agent* to Wells, was himself indebted to *The Time Machine* both in the essay on Henry James and in such crucial works as *Heart of Darkness*. In any case the pages of Faulkner's copy of *Notes on Life and Literature* remained uncut, and we might also note that in describing his "last evening" Conrad refers only to the "feeble glow of the sun," and to the "last flicker of light on a black sky": his evening is neither "tideless" nor "red," and there is no reference to any rock, "worthless" or otherwise.

5. H. G. Wells, *The Time Machine* (Random House, 1931). All citations from *The Time Machine* refer to this edition. See Joseph Blotner's *William Faulkner's Library—A Catalogue* (University Press of Virginia, 1964), p. 75.

6. Julia Kristeva, *Powers of Horror: An Essay on Abjection* (Columbia University Press, 1982), p. 4.

7. Rudyard Kipling, *The Portable Kipling,* ed. Irving Howe (Viking, 1982), p. 14.

8. For relevant citations and insightful commentary see Susan J. Navarette's "The Physiology of Fear: Decadent Style and the Fin de Siècle Literature of Horror" (Doctoral Dissertation, Department of English, The University of Michigan, 1989), pp. 53-54. I am also indebted to Professor Navarette for bringing the relevant passage in Max Nordau's *Degeneration* to my attention.

9. See Samuel L. Hynes and Frank D. McConnell, "*The Time Machine* and *The War of the Worlds*: Parable and Possibility in H. G. Wells," in H. G. Wells, *The Time Machine; The War of the Worlds: A Critical Edition,* edited by Frank D. McConnell (Oxford University Press, 1977), p. 345.

10. William Whewell, *Astronomy and General Physics Considered with Reference to Natural Theology* (William Pickering, 1834), pp. 199-200.

11. Lord Kelvin, quoted in Sir William Thomson's *Mathematical and Physical Papers,* 5 Volumes (Cambridge University Press, 1882-1911), I: p. 514.

12. Balfour Stewart, *The Conservation of Energy* (H. S. King, 1873), p. 153.

13. Max Nordau, *Degeneration* (1893), (D. Appleton and Company, 1895), p. 2.

14. Charles Darwin, *More Letters of Charles Darwin,* 2 Vols. ed. Francis Darwin (D. Appleton and Company, 1903), vol. I, pp. 260-261.

15. William James, *The Varieties of Religious Experience* (1902), (Penguin Books, 1982), p. 141.

16. For information on this relationship, and for an interesting commentary on the genesis of the various versions of *The Time Machine,* see Harry M. Geduld's introduction to *The Definitive Time Machine: A Critical Edition of H. G. Wells's Scientific Romance* (Indiana University Press, 1987).

17. Thomas H. Huxley, "Evolution and Ethics," in *Evolution and Ethics and Other Essays* (AMS Press, 1970), p. 85. We might note in passing that Huxley begins his lecture with a summary of the plot of "Jack and the Bean-Stalk" and that it would appear that Wells also appropriated the basic structure of this fairy tale for *The Time Machine.*

18. Wells in middle age was guardedly optimistic about man's future, but by the time of his death in 1946 he had—as such works as *The Fate of Man* (1939) and *Mind at the End of its Tether* (1946) reveal—become increasingly bleak and pessimistic. As he wrote in *The Fate of Man* (Longmans, Green, & Co., 1939):

> There is no reason whatever to believe that the order of nature has any greater bias in favor of man than it had in favor of the icthyosaur or the pterodactyl. In spite of all my disposition to a brave looking optimism, I perceive that now the universe is bored with him, in [sic] turning a hard face to him, and I see him being carried less less and less intelligently and more and more rapidly, suffering as every ill-adapted creature must suffer in gross and detail, along the stream of fate to degradation, suffering, and death. . . . Adapt or perish, that is and always has been the implacable law of life for all its children. Either the human imagination and the human will to live, rises to the plain necessity of our case and a renascent Homo Sapiens stuggles on to a new, a harder, and a happier world dominion, or he blunders down the slopes of failure through a series of unhappy phases, in the wake of all the monster reptiles and beasts that have flourished and lorded it on the earth before him, to his ultimate extinction.

(pp. 247-48)

It is difficult to determine how familiar Faulkner was with Wells's later works, although Blotner also notes that Faulkner kept a copy of *The Outline of History* (1923) in the bookcase in his bedroom at Rowan Oak.

19. David M. Wrobel, *The End of American Exceptionalism* (University Press of Kansas, 1993), p. 66.

20. H. G. Wells, *Experiment in Autobiography* (The Macmillan Company, 1934), pp. 648-649.

Bruce David Sommerville (essay date winter 1994)

SOURCE: Sommerville, Bruce David. "*The Time Machine*: A Chronological and Scientific Revision." *Wellsian* 17 (winter 1994): 11-29.

[*In the following essay, Sommerville traces the complex chronological structure of* The Time Machine, *asserting that the accepted chronology of the novella "is erroneous and that the true chronology reveals a hidden series of events."*]

INTRODUCTION

For work having time as a major theme, it is rather odd that the chronology of H. G. Wells's *The Time Machine* has not been fully analysed. Its chronological structure is complex, comprising an outer framework of events set in the late Victorian atmosphere of the Time Traveller's Richmond home, and a more extensive inner core of events ostensibly set in the distant future.

The chronology of the outer framework will be explored in detail here. It will be shown that the accepted chronology of *The Time Machine* is erroneous and that the true chronology reveals a hidden series of events. The discussion below will establish the following points:

1 The chronology of the outer framework forms a puzzle, the solution of which reveals the Time Traveller to have hoaxed his guests, especially the narrator, Hillyer. The Time Traveller has not travelled in time but has dreamed his vision of the future after returning to his workshop from a cycling excursion.

2 The disappearance of the model time machine and the Time Traveller's final departure are optical illusions which, along with his theory of time and his dream, accord with contemporary theories of psychology and visual perception.

3 The relationship between the Time Traveller's hoax and the book's theme of evolutionary retrogression is best understood by viewing *The Time Machine* as an indictment of late nineteenth century complacency. The Time Traveller's deception of Hillyer is Wells's way of ridiculing the naïve optimism and complacency Hillyer displays in the Epilogue.

One result of this analysis of *The Time Machine* is a greater appreciation of its scientific basis, especially in the area of psychology. Autobiography is also important and indicates the whereabouts of the Time Traveller following his final "disappearance" on the "Time Machine".

The outer framework is here considered to include the passages describing the Time Traveller's departure and return. Unless stated otherwise, all references to *The Time Machine* are to the Heinemann edition of 1895.

1 THE CHRONOLOGICAL PUZZLE OF *THE TIME MACHINE*

There are eleven references to puzzles in *The Time Machine,* three on one page (111). If one takes this as a hint and reads carefully, contradictions can be found in the chronology of the Time Traveller's account which yield the solution to a puzzle and a new reading.

THE CHRONOLOGY OF THE OUTER FRAMEWORK

Literary critics and the Time Traveller's guests alike assume that the Time Traveller returns to his laboratory from the future at eight o'clock in the evening on the day of his departure. Geoffrey H. Wells (226) and Harry M. Geduld (11) both affirm this chronology which, to the best of my knowledge, has not been disputed. However, a close reading of the second paragraphs of Chapters 4 and 15 show this assumption to be wrong. Here is the Time Traveller's account of his departure on his machine on the second Thursday afternoon:

> Then I noted the clock. A moment before, as it seemed, it had stood at a minute or so past ten; now it was nearly half-past three!
>
> . . . The laboratory got hazy and went dark. Mrs Watchett came in, and walked, apparently without seeing me, towards the garden door. I suppose it took her a minute or so to traverse the place, but to me she seemed to shoot across the room like a rocket. I pressed the lever over to its extreme position. The night came like the turning out of a lamp, and in another moment came tomorrow.
>
> (28)

Note that Mrs Watchett traversed the laboratory after half-past three but before the night came.

In Chapter 15, where the Time Traveller describes his return from the future, he again encounters Mrs Watchett: "As I returned, I passed again across that minute when she traversed the laboratory. But now her every motion appeared to be the exact inversion of her previous ones" (142-43). According to his own account, the Time Traveller returns almost to his starting time, in the late afternoon, before nightfall. Yet at eight o'clock he belatedly greets his guests creating the impression that he had only just returned. He later upholds this false impression when telling how he stopped the machine and sat down on the bench:

> For a time my brain went stagnant. Presently I got up and came through the passage here, limping, because my heel was still painful, and feeling sorely begrimed. I saw the Pall Mall Gazette on the table by the door. I found the date was indeed today, and looking at the timepiece, saw the hour was almost eight o'clock.
>
> (144)

The words "For a time" and "Presently" imply a short duration between his return and his entry into the dining room. But the Time Traveller has spent several hours in his laboratory with a "stagnant" brain while his guests, unaware of this, have begun dinner in his absence. The Time Traveller's mind has been elsewhere for this period: "Around me was my old workshop again, exactly as it had been. I might have slept there, and the whole thing have been a dream" (143). The Time Traveller has dreamed the entire future adventure with the Eloi and Morlocks while sitting on the bench in his laboratory. Wherever he has travelled, he has not travelled in time. His claim to have done so is part of an elaborate hoax.[1] This interpretation is confirmed by another missing piece of time. In the second to last paragraph of Chapter 3 the Time Traveller prefaces his story by remarking: "I was in my laboratory at four o'clock, and since then . . . I've lived eight days . . . such days as no human being ever lived before!" (25). This statement does not square with the implication that he began his journey at half-past three and returned at eight o'clock.

The contradiction can be resolved by accepting the Time Traveller's claim to have been in his laboratory at four o'clock and by taking the statement "such days as no human being ever lived before" literally. His remarks are then clearly a hint that his vision of the future occurred in the laboratory after four o'clock as "no human being"—which includes the Time Traveller himself—has lived those eight days before four o'clock. It can thus be concluded that the Time Traveller's vision of the future was in the form of a dream which occurred between four o'clock and eight o'clock on the second Thursday evening after he returned to his laboratory and before he greeted his dinner guests. The chronological inconsistencies are a clue to understanding this.

The chronology of the rest of the evening supports this view. Allowing about three-quarters of an hour for the Time Traveller to wash, dress and dine, we can assume he begins his narrative at about a quarter to nine. He concludes four hours later, given by the Journalist's remark, "I'm hanged if it isn't a quarter to one" (146). The duration of the story concurs with that of the dream.

The Time Traveller openly admits his story is a dream when he says:

> No. I cannot expect you to believe it. Take it as a lie—or a prophecy. Say I have dreamed it in the workshop. Consider that I have been speculating upon the destinies of our race, until I have hatched this fiction.
>
> (145)

The ingenuity of his hoax is shown by his claim to have seen not only Mrs Watchett as he returned from the future, but also Hillyer, who "passed like a flash" (143). He also implies that he saw the whole party of guests as he returned, for to them he remarks, of the Time Machine, "It had come to rest again in the north-west, against the wall where you saw it" (143). At this stage, only three of his guests have seen the machine, and then only after dinner on the previous Thursday when it was in the south-east corner of the laboratory.

The Time Traveller's claims are prophecies: first, that Hillyer will return, which he does the next day; and second that the whole party will go to view the machine against the north-west wall, which they do after the Time Traveller concludes his story. Although seeming to confirm his story, both prophecies are realised by the Time Traveller. He perceives that Hillyer credits his story more than the other guests and shrewdly guesses that he will return to discuss time-travelling—indeed, prompts him to do so by naming him. The Time Traveller also arranges for the whole group to view the machine by rushing to the laboratory with the lamp to reassure himself of the machine's reality.

> Did I ever make a Time Machine, or a model of a Time Machine? Or is it only a dream? . . . I must look at that machine. . . .
>
> The Time Traveller put the lamp down on the bench and ran his head along the damaged rail. "It's all right now," he said. "The story I told you was true. *I'm sorry to have brought you out here in the cold.*" [my italics]
>
> (147-48)

The Time Traveller is a clever man indeed.

There is strong evidence that the chronological "faults" of the outer framework are deliberate and not the result of errors in writing or in publication. This evidence will now be reviewed.

THE PUZZLE: ACCIDENT OR DESIGN?

In June 1894, Wells reviewed Dr O.W. Owen's Sir Francis Bacon's Cipher Story. In "More Bacon", Wells describes Owen's efforts to uncover a cipher story hidden in some literary works attributed to Bacon, and notes the literary euphemisms that typified the age.

> Then language and thought alike were permeated by the spirit of Euphues, so that whereas we aim nowadays at subtlety of meaning and simplicity of expression, the ambition of the educated man of the early

seventeenth century was invariably to conceal a simply idiotic meaning beneath an imposing, brilliant, and even enigmatical form.

(4)

Two other unsigned essays published in April and May 1894 which discuss cryptograms and hidden symbols could also belong to Wells.[2]

The text of **The Time Machine** was revised by Wells before, during and after its serial publication in the *New Review* (Bergonzi "Publication of **The Time Machine**" 43-45). Apart from the two well-known major revisions to Chapters 1 and 14 of the Heinemann edition, I count forty-five minor revisions of the *New Review* version prior to its publication by Heinemann. None of these revisions changes the chronology of the outer framework. In 1924, Wells revised the text again for inclusion in **The Works of H. G. Wells,** Atlantic Edition (Preface vol 1 Atlantic Edition xxii). Despite re-reading and revising, Wells still made no changes to the chronology of the story. Given his writing on literary puzzles and his detailed revisions of **The Time Machine** (all of which left the chronology intact) it is clear that the chronological irregularities of the book are part of Wells's design. The work has been carefully and cleverly written.

The circumstances of the Time Traveller's return to his laboratory, however, indicate that he has *somehow* travelled *somewhere*. We will now examine the "how" and the "where" of the Time Traveller's journey.

THE MACHINE

The Time Traveller's dishevelled state when he enters the dining room at eight o'clock is described by Hillyer.

> His coat was dusty and dirty, and smeared with green down the sleeves; his hair disordered, and as it seemed to me greyer—either with dust or dirt or because its colour had actually faded. His face was ghastly pale; his chin had a brown cut on it—a cut half-healed; his expression was haggard and drawn, as by intense suffering.
>
> (20)

He is also lame, having on his feet only a pair of tattered, bloodstained socks (21) as well as having scarred knuckles (146). His condition resembles that of another of Wells's characters, Mr Hoopdriver of **The Wheels of Chance,** whose bruised ankles and legs were merely the visible sign of more extensive injuries.

> Fired by these discoveries, an investigatory might perhaps have pursued his inquiries further—to bruises on the shoulders, elbows, and even the finger joints, of the central figure of our story. He had indeed been bumped and battered at an extraordinary number of points.
>
> (8-9)

Hoopdriver's injuries were based on injuries Wells himself sustained while learning to ride the bicycle, as he makes clear in his autobiography: "The diamond frame had appeared but there was no free-wheel. You could only stop and jump off when the treadle was at its lowest point, and the brake was an uncertain plunger upon the front wheel" (543). The importance of cycling in Wells's life in the 1890s is described by David C. Smith, who states that Wells used his safety bicycle to explore the Thames valley (Smith "Little Wars for Little People" 127-28). In the text and notes of his biography of Wells, Smith also discusses cycling and its relationship to Wells's early journalism (**H. G. Wells** 136, 523).

In an early essay, **"Specimen Day",** Wells recounts a journey to Crawley on a tricycle. This essay has many points in common with the Time Traveller's account, some of which are best illustrated by a direct comparison:

"Specimen Day"

The road to Midhurst . . . goes up and down like a switch back.

(17)

We have a pleasant but all too short run together, and upset in a heap on as soft a parch of turf as I have ever fallen on.

(19)

. . . certain little misadventures on the road had made me, to say the least, dusty.

(18)

The Time Machine

There is a feeling exactly like that one has upon a switchback—of helpless headlong motion!

(29)

. . . I was sitting on soft turf in front of the overset machine.

(32)

His coat was dusty and dirty, and smeared with green down the sleeves. . . .

(20)

These autobiographical parallels indicate that in the interval between his two dinner engagements, the Time Traveller has been learning to ride a bicycle. He may have embarked on one or more cycling excursions, or a holiday. The Time Traveller's dream of the future occurs on his return, just as Hoopdriver was wont to "ride through Dreamland on wonderful dream bicycles that change and grow after a day's cycling" (**Wheels of Chance** 81). The Time Traveller's machine is no ordinary bicycle, being one of his own design made of nickel, ivory and quartz (15-16). Nevertheless, the most audacious part of his hoax is his act of passing off this bicycle to his guests as a machine capable of travelling in time.

Many references in the text of **The Time Machine** support the bicycle hypothesis. On stopping his machine suddenly, the Time Traveller falls off it: "Like an impatient fool, I lugged over the lever, and incontinently the thing went reeling over, and I was flung headlong through the air" (32). What is more, a brazen hint equating the Time Machine with a bicycle is given by Wells in his Preface to a later edition of **The Time Machine**: "So The Time Machine has lasted as long as the diamond-framed safety bicycle, which came in at about the date of its first publication".[3] The similarities between the Time Machine have been noted by other commentators but none identify the Time Traveller's absence, activities or physical condition with cycling.[4]

It is true that the claim that the Time Machine is a bicycle and the Time Traveller's vision is a dream demands a revision of the cardinal incidents in the book.

A REVISION OF THE TIME TRAVELLER'S ACTIVITIES

The Time Traveller invites his guests to dinner one Thursday evening, planning a hoax based on the construction of his own bicycle. After discussing space and time (1-7) and causing a model to disappear by means of an optical illusion (to be discussed below), he shows his guests the full-size machine in the laboratory, declaring his intention to explore time (16).

He completes his machine and takes a cycling holiday around the Thames valley, during which he has an accident, injures himself and damages the machine (148). The Time Traveller finds two flowers which are "sports" (146), that is, variations of a species type.[5] Given his lameness, it is probable that he loses his machine and has to walk a long way to recover it. He sends a note to his home stating that his return may be delayed (19).[6]

Reaching his laboratory at four o'clock in the afternoon on the second Thursday, he dismounts shakily and sits down on his bench. Exhausted, he falls asleep and has a dream in which his cycling experiences and his thoughts about the future of the human race are mixed together. Awakening just before eight o'clock, the Time Traveller approaches the dining room and, upon hearing this guests discussing the "ingenious paradox and trick" (19) of the previous week, decides to continue the hoax. He then washes, dresses, dines and imparts his vision (27-144). Most guests are sceptical, but the gullible Hillyer returns the following afternoon (148). Expecting his visit, the Time Traveller has set up a second optical illusion (see below). After asking Hillyer to wait for half an hour, the Time Traveller goes out of his labora-

tory, primes his illusion and departs on his machine in advance of Hillyer's (and the manservant's) entry (150-51). The hoax is completed by the Time Traveller's failure to return.

This solution to Wells's puzzle may, however, be only partial. Readers of his time could not have used the biographical details used here. We must, therefore, assume that the true series of events in The Time Machine can be discovered purely on internal evidence. The following passage, spoken by the Time Traveller, points to a cryptogram hidden in the work.

> I felt I lacked a clue. I felt—how shall I put it? Suppose you found an inscription, with sentences here and there in excellent plain English, and, interpolated therewith, others made up of words, of letters even, absolutely unknown to you? Well, on the third day of my visit, that was how the world of Eight Hundred and Two Thousand Seven Hundred and One presented itself to me!
>
> (71)

Note that the initial capitals of the date, when rearranged, spell "THE HOST". This probably refers to the Time Traveller and could form part of a longer message. As the cryptogram belongs to the inner core of the narrative, it is not my intention to deal with it here, but in a subsequent paper.

If, as I have argued, the Time Traveller has not physically travelled in time, how are we to understand his theory of time, his vision of the future, his demonstration of the model and his disappearance? These questions will now be addressed.

2 PRINCIPLES OF PSYCHOLOGY: THEORY, MODEL AND DREAM

Book reviews and articles by Wells published between 1893 and 1895 indicate that he was abreast of developments in psychology and visual perception. These theories underpin the outer framework of **The Time Machine**.

THE TIME TRAVELLER'S THEORY

By the early 1890s, physiologically-based theories of the perception of time were well-established in psychology. Herbert Spencer, who was a seminal influence on Wells, broaches the subject of temporal perception thus: "The doctrine that Time is knowable only by the succession of our mental states calls for little exposition: it is so well established a doctrine" (2: 209). In **"The Position of Psychology"**, a review of George Trumbull Ladd's *Psychology, Descriptive and Explanatory,* and C. Lloyd Morgan's *Psychology for Teachers,* Wells boldly criticises psychological research, showing a familiarity with the main trends in this science and the work of researchers such as William James and James Sully (715).

In *The Time Machine,* the Time Traveller provides a "proto-(William) Jamesian demonstration that time is a dimension of consciousness."[7] The nature of his discourse can best be understood by examining the emphasis placed on nervous physiology in contemporary theories of perception in such works as James's *Principles of Psychology* (1890) and Spencer's *Principles of Psychology* (1881).

When time is discussed in absolute or objective terms spatial analogies are used, with the similarities and differences between our perception of time and our perception of space being stressed (James 1: 610-11). For example, events are located in time in a certain succession or order, separated by intervals, just as objects are in space (1: 631 text and note; Spencer 21: 210-11, 217). However, James notes, a major difference is that our perception of time is limited to a few seconds (the present) while our perception of space is more extensive (1: 611). Spencer also articulates this by applying the term "co-existence" to our feelings of space, and "sequence" to our feelings of time (1: 210-11 et seq., 2: 208-9).

Subjectively, our perception of time is said to depend on principles of nervous action. The slow decline of nervous activity after a presentation (such as the after-images we see after looking at a bright light) gives rise to our sensation of the present which then fades into a sensation of immediate past as the nervous action passes into memory and is succeeded by a new presentation. Our perception of time is thus produced by a continual succession of nervous sensations, or feelings (James 1: 632-45; Spencer 1: 268; Sully Human Mind 1; 269-72).[8]

In Chapter 1 of *The Time Machine,* the Time Traveller relates space, time and consciousness by stressing extrinsic similarities between space and time, but noting the difference in our perception of them:

> . . . any real body must have extension in four directions: it must have Length, Breadth, Thickness and—Duration. But through a natural infirmity of the flesh which I will explain to you in a moment, we incline to overlook this fact. There are really four dimensions, three which we call the three planes of Space, and a fourth, Time. There is, however, a tendency to draw an unreal distinction between the former three dimensions and the latter because it happens that our consciousness moves intermittently in one direction along the latter from the beginning to the end of our lives.
>
> (2-3)

The Time Traveller proposes that time and space have common objective properties, such as extension, but a difference arises in our (subjective) perception of them. He calls the difference an "unreal distinction" due to a "natural infirmity of the flesh" because the distinction is a mental one produced by our nervous sensations. Successive nervous sensations cause us to perceive time as a sequence, or as the Time Traveller puts it, as an intermittent movement of consciousness. This discussion of space, time and consciousness is quite in accordance with psychological theory espoused by James and Spencer. Wells, however, uses a language suited to a popular readership.

The joining of the absolute standpoint—seen most clearly in the version which depicts a rigid physical universe extended in four dimensions—with the standpoint of human consciousness is not contradictory but complementary (Philmus & Hughes 51). However, it appears that Wells has leaned closer to the latter standpoint than commonly realised, for the Time Traveller's journey through time is in the form of a series of mental states, a dream. Contemporary scientific literature shows much common ground between psychology and visual perception.[9] James emphasises the role of visual sensations in temporal perception by describing how the world would appear to a being whose nervous system operates 1000 times more slowly than ours, creating the impression of a rapid movement through time.

> Winters and summers will be to him like quarters of an hour. Mushrooms and the swifter growing plants will shoot into being so rapidly as to appear instantaneous creations; annual shrubs will rise and fall from the earth like restlessly boiling-water springs; the motions of animals will be as invisible as are to us the movements of bullets and cannon-balls; the sun will scour through the sky like a meteor, leaving a fiery trail behind him. . . .
>
> (James 1: 639)

Similarly, the Time Traveller's successive sensations of the external world cover increasingly larger intervals as he moves forward in time.

> The slowest snail that ever crawled dashed by too fast for me. . . . the jerking sun became a streak of fire, a brilliant arch, in space; . . . I saw trees growing and changing like puffs of vapour, now brown, now green: they grew, spread, shivered, and passed away. I saw huge buildings rise up faint and fair, and pass like dreams. The whole surface of the earth seemed changed—melting and flowing under my eyes.
>
> (29-30)

The similarity of these two passages, together with the Time Traveller's Jamesian discussion of time, indicate the strong influence of theories of psychology and visual perception in the outer framework of *The Time Machine.* This intermediate field where psychology and physiology meet has also influenced Wells in his design of the Time Traveller's experiment with the model.

EXPERIMENTAL VERIFICATION

The two phenomena most relevant to the model's disappearance are: (i) the concept of presentation below the threshold; and (ii) the illusory nature of visual perception.

(i) The use by Wells of the phenomenon of "presentation below the threshold" (14-15) again indicates an acquaintance with psychology. Wells's knowledge of this could have come from a number of sources. Sully, for example, writes: "Every stimulus must reach a certain intensity before any appreciable sensation results. This point is known as the threshold or liminal intensity of sensation" (*The Human Mind* 1: 87). James Ward states that if the intensity of a presentation is less than a certain assignable value it is said to lie "below the threshold of consciousness" (19: 49).

(ii) Wells would have undoubtedly been struck by the importance of optical illusions for research in psychology. Optical illusions are discussed in detail by James (2: 86-103, 243-68), while Sully devotes an entire work to the psychology of illusions. Ladd deals with illusions in the context of suggestion, feeling and association:

> Our ideas, feelings, and volitions take part in determining how we shall see the spatial qualities and relations of any object. . . . Or—to say the same truth in more popular phrase—within given limits, we see what we think or imagine ought to be seen; what we are expecting to see; and what we by an act of will determine to see.
>
> (362-63)

The Time Traveller is portrayed as an expert in physical optics (114). Relevant to this field, as to psychology, were theories of colour vision. Researchers in both psychology and optics often employed "colour tops" because visual illusions resulted when the tops, with patterns on their flat upper surface, were spun.[10] In **"The Visibility of Colour"** (1895), Wells indicates a knowledge of colour vision and refers to the new Spectrum Top, a device mentioned some months earlier in *Nature*.[11] These concepts all bear on the demonstration of the model.

The Time Traveller places his model on a table before his guests. It is a "glittering metallic framework" about the size of a small clock, containing ivory, "some transparent crystalline substance," and brass (10). The Time Traveller then gets the Psychologist to push a little white lever to start the model. As Hillyer observes:

> One of the candles on the mantel was blown out, and the little machine suddenly swung round, became indistinct, was seen as a ghost for a second perhaps, as an eddy of faintly glittering brass and ivory; and it was gone—vanished! Save for the lamp the table was bare.
>
> (12-13)

The Time Traveller has made the model less visible by causing it to spin rapidly, like a top, so that the presentation of the framework approaches the threshold of perception. The framework-like construction of the model would allow things behind it to be visible through it, so enhancing the illusion. Moreover, the model is made of materials that are white, highly reflective or transparent, rather than opaque. The model is then no more appreciable than "the spoke of a wheel spinning" (15). The psychological phenomenon of suggestion also plays a part in this demonstration. Ladd emphasises the importance of suggestion in optical illusions:

> In the wider meaning of that much-abused word, all visual perception, true or false, our daily sights of the most practical and ordinary kind as well as the wildest hallucinations of the hypnotic dreamer or of the inmate of the madhouse—involve "suggestion."
>
> (364)

Before causing the model to disappear, the Time Traveller provides his guests with the appropriate suggestion. "'Presently'", he tells them, "'I am going to press the lever, and off the machine will go. It will vanish, pass into future time, and disappear'" (12). After his guests see what they expect to see, the Time Traveller stands and turns to the mantel to fill his pipe, removing the model as he does so. His guests are not observing his actions here, for, as Hillyer faithfully records, "We stared at each other" (13). The illusion of the model's disappearance may thus be explained in terms of psychology and colour vision. The disappearance of the full-sized Time Machine can be similarly explained.

THE TIME TRAVELLER'S DISAPPEARANCE

Hillyer's account of the Time Traveller's disappearance is vague, being qualified by the words "seemed", "indistinct" and "apparently". Here is his testimony:

> As I took hold of the handle of the door I heard an exclamation, oddly truncated at the end, and a click and a thud. A gust of air whirled round me as I opened the door, and from within came the sound of broken glass falling on the floor. The Time Traveller was not there. I seemed to see a ghostly, indistinct figure sitting in a whirling mass of black and brass for a moment—a figure so transparent that the bench behind with its sheets of drawings was absolutely distinct; but this phantasm vanished as I rubbed my eyes. The Time Machine had gone. Save for a subsiding stir of dust, the further end of the laboratory was empty. A pane of the skylight had, apparently, just been blown in.
>
> (150)

The Time Traveller has a reputation as a practical joker, having once shown his guests a ghost (16). The creation of such illusions was a common Victorian parlour trick involving a "magic lantern": a three-dimensional image was created seemingly in mid-air by reflecting a brightly-lit object onto a sheet of glass, and this probably explains the Time Traveller's ghost and his "disappearance".[12]

Expecting Hillyer to turn up, the Time Traveller has earlier removed a sheet of glass from the skylight to provide a reflective surface for his illusion, which is triggered by Hillyer touching the door handle. The sounds Hillyer hears are easily explained by a phonographic recording, and the gust of air arises as the door is opened between the "long, draughty corridor" (15) and the laboratory which has a hole in the skylight. Hillyer's perception of events accords with the suggestions arising from the Time Traveller's story.

If it is accepted that the Time Traveller has not travelled in time, we might expect that his dream vision of the future may be understood in terms of psychology. Again, we find evidence of this in Wells's early journalism.

ALTERNATIVE REALITY: THE TIME TRAVELLER'S DREAM

In his 1893 essay, **"The Dream Bureau",** Wells recounts a psychological explanation for dreams in which they are simply "the imperfect and exaggerated interpretation by the somnolent mind of the sensations that affect it, together with the flow of suggestions that naturally follow such impressions" (3). Wells discusses the work of the French scientist, Alfred Maury, on the origin of dream images, as does Sully who gives a very thorough account of Maury's researches into how the external and internal sensations that affect us while sleeping influence dream imagery (*Illusions* 10).

James considered dreams to be a perfectly valid alternative world where our perceptions arise from *re*-presentations from our memory rather than presentations from the external world.

> The world of dreams is our real world whilst we are sleeping, because our attention then lapses from the sensible world. Conversely, when we wake the attention usually lapses from the dream-world and that becomes unreal. . . . The dream holds true, namely, in one half of that universe; the waking perceptions in the other half.
>
> (2: 294n)

These presentations to the mind from the memory were considered to constitute a form of perception, Sully acknowledging that "recent psychology draws no sharp distinction between perception and recollection" (*Illusions* 10). Thus even the Time Traveller's dream can be brought within the science of psycho-physiology, presenting to the Time Traveller's mind a vivid alternative reality derived from his cycling memories, his thoughts on the human future and the associations arising therefrom.

The important role of psychology in the outer framework greatly strengthens the scientific foundation of **The Time Machine.** Commentators have erred in de-scribing the Time Traveller's theory and demonstration as "pseudo-scientific", "bogus" or "verbal flimflam".[13] On the contrary, the related areas of nervous action, visual perception, memory, suggestion and illusion, which underpin almost the entire outer framework, are informed by some of the major scientific works of Wells's day.

The question arises as to how the outer framework relates to the inner core, with its theme of human evolutionary degeneration. A comparison of the views of the Time Traveller and Hillyer will help clarify this.

3 EVOLUTION AND ETHICS: HILLYER VS THE TIME TRAVELLER

As Mark R. Hillegas argues, the theme of evolutionary retrogression in **The Time Machine** attempts to jolt the reading public out of its complacency by an imaginative presentation of the "cosmic pessimism" of the naturalist T. H. Huxley.[14] In his essays of the late 1880s and early 1890s, Huxley attacks the "optimistic dogma" that the evolutionary state of nature is "the best of all possible worlds". Hillegas's view accords with a comment made by Wells that **The Time Machine** depicted a future "that ran counter to the placid assumption of that time that Evolution was a pro-human force making things better and better for mankind" (Wells, Preface to **Scientific Romances** ix).

It is not my purpose here to discuss the inner core of **The Time Machine** further. Bearing in mind that the book can be viewed as an attack on the complacency inherent in optimistic evolutionism, the Time Traveller's motive for what I have argued is his deception of Hillyer can be more easily understood.

THE FOOLING OF HILLYER

The Epilogue of **The Time Machine** contrasts with the apparent pessimism of the Time Traveller with the dogged hopefulness of Hillyer, who writes:

> I, for my part, cannot think that these latter days of the weak experiment, fragmentary theory, and mutual discord are indeed man's culminating time! I say, for my own part. He, I know—for the question had been discussed among us long before the Time Machine was made—thought but cheerlessly of the Advancement of Mankind, and saw in the growing pile of civilization only a foolish heaping that must inevitably fall back upon and destroy its makers in the end. If this is so, it remains for us to live as though it were not so. But to me the future is still black and blank—is a vast ignorance, lit at a few casual places by the memory of his story.
>
> (152)

Some commentators cite this apparent ambiguity as revealing a deep conflict in Wells's own outlook, the Time Traveller's pessimistic view representing that of "a scientist who had gone to the end of science" and Hillyer's hopeful view constituting an "almost existential courage against the void" (Hynes & McConnell 353, 355). Or Wells could be *enforcing* ambiguity, showing us how to accept both sides of a contradiction by balancing the unresolved pessimism and optimism of the Epilogue (Huntington 52-53). The dichotomy is also said to reflect the problem of determinism and free will—the determinate evolutionary laws of the inner core being balanced by an affirmation of the importance of human responsibility where, at the level of individual action man must behave *as though* he were free" (Haynes 129).

However, the ambiguity of the Epilogue vanishes once we accept that the events of the outer framework constitute a hoax. Let us re-examine the views of the Time Traveller and Hillyer, and their relationship, in this light. Hillyer is an optimist. Despite the "fragmentary theory and mutual discord" of his time, he anticipates continued progress. Despite the Time Traveller's vision of evolutionary degeneration, Hillyer cannot think that it may occur, or that it may have already begun. The phrase "these latter days of weak experiment" implies an existing ebbing of intelligence about which Hillyer is unconcerned. With the words "for my own part" Hillyer opposes his view to that of the Time Traveller.

In fact, Hillyer is in reaction to the Time Traveller's vision. If that bleak future is true, "it remains for us to live as though it were not so" says Hillyer. This is not an existential courage against the void, but a romantic evasion by Hillyer of the Time Traveller's future. Hillyer is contented that the future remain "a vast ignorance."

The final sentence of *The Time Machine* reveals Hillyer's romantic view of the human story: "And I have by me, for my comfort, two strange white flowers—shrivelled now, and brown and flat and brittle—to witness that even when mind and strength had gone, gratitude and a mutual tenderness still lived on in the heart of man" (152). Hillyer sees the Time Traveller's flowers only as a source of comfort in the face of the harsh future he depicts. Hillyer's concern, like that of the ancestors of the Eloi and the Morlocks, is for comfort and security.

The Time Traveller's poor regard for Hillyer is shown by his "disappearance" when the latter arrives on the Friday afternoon, and the blatant lie the Time Traveller tells just before departing. Hillyer naïvely recalls his challenge to his friend:

> "But is it not some hoax?" I said. "Do you really travel through time?" "Really and truly I do." And he looked frankly into my eyes.
>
> (149)

The character of Hillyer, along with the complacent and optimistic views he represents, is the subject of devastating ridicule by Wells. The hoax of the outer framework supports the evolutionary arguments of the inner core by implying that those of Hillyer's views, therefore, are not Wells's views.

CONCLUSION

The outer framework of *The Time Machine* has been examined in detail. It has been shown that the book is constructed as a puzzle which, when solved, shows the Time Traveller's story to be a hoax. His vision of the future is a dream experienced after returning from a cycling excursion. However, the Time Traveller's activities could also be the subject of a cryptogram.

The Time Traveller's theory of time, his optical illusion and his dream are informed by an intermediate area of scientific research involving psychology and the physiology of visual perception. The hoax of the outer framework supports the theme of the work as a whole by ridiculing the optimistic and complacent outlook of the narrator, Hillyer. The Epilogue is not ambiguous, as the fooling of Hillyer shows that Wells favours the Time Traveller's view.

It is not my aim here to pursue the implications (if any) of this reading, except to propose that the dominant role of psychology and consciousness, culminating in the Time Traveller's dream, destroys the sense of the cosmic determinism superficially present in the work. At the deeper level the human mind predominates. If it could once be said that the role of consciousness "reaffirms the possibilities for human will in a Rigid Universe" (Philmus & Hughes 55) we must further ask whether Wells placed any credence in a rigid determinism at all.

An important feature to emerge here is the strong scientific foundation of *The Time Machine,* built from Wells's education in biology, his reading in psychology and colour vision, and his own science writing. The design of the book as an intellectual puzzle and the extensive revisions made to the text, indicate a brilliant conception and meticulous execution, where Wells has displayed a creativity almost rivalling that of his scientific coevals on whose work *The Time Machine* is based.

It remains only to suggest that the Time Traveller's final departure is simply the start of a second, more extensive, cycling holiday. His three-year absence (151) may be explained in terms of Robert P. Weeks's analysis of many of Wells's characters as being driven by a profound desire to escape social, evolutionary or scientific restrictions (Weeks 26-30). The escape of the Time Traveller may even reflect a desire by Wells to escape from some of all of the restrictions described by Weeks; a desire which surfaced in 1901 when Wells vanished for two months on his bicycle without informing his wife of his whereabouts (West 258-59).

In any case, soon after the publication of *The Time Machine,* Wells had a tandem bicycle made to his own plans by Humber, after which he and his wife began exploring the south of England on this machine (*Autobiography* 543). Perhaps the Time Traveller was not far behind.

Notes

1. A hint as to the role of the later chapter in uncovering this puzzle is given in the second to last paragraph of Chapter 7 where the Time Traveller, puzzling over the loss of his machines, says 'In the end you will find clues to it all' (65).

2. Philmus and Hughes attribute 'More Bacon' to Wells, and suggest that 'Mysteries of the Modern Press: Secret Marks in Printing', *Pall Mall Gazette* 58 (April 23 1894):3; and 'A Remarkable Literary Discovery: Francis Bacon the Author of "Box and Cox"'! *Pall Mall Gazette* 58 (May 3 1894):3, could also be by Wells.

3. H. G. Wells, Preface to a revised edition of *The Time Machine,* 1931 x.

4. See Williamson 52, Batchelor 10, Geduld 96, 192.

5. In 'Discoveries in Variation', Wells notes that lilies may sometimes have their floral organs in fives instead of threes, just as the Time Traveller's flowers have an unusual gynaeceum (312).

6. The presence of the note is another inconsistency discrediting the Time Traveller's tale. He would have no excuse for being late if he could really travel in time. Also, how could the note have been sent?

7. Philmus and Hughes, *Early Writings* 48. This comment refers to the first instalment of the 1894 *National Observer* series of articles by Wells on time travelling, but it is equally applicable to the Heinemann edition.

8. James, *Principles,* 1:632-45; Spencer, *Principles,* 1:268. For discussion of time perception see also James Sully, *The Human Mind: a Textbook of Psychology,* 2 vols. London: Longman, Green, 1892 1:269-72, 318-29; 2;343-45.

9. The German physiologist, Hermann von Helmholtz, discusses psychology extensively (see H Helmholtz, *Helmholtz's Treatise on Physiological Optics* vol. 3. Ed. James P.C. Southall. Menasha Wisconsin: Optical Society of America, 1925, 1-35; H. Helmholtz, Popular Lectures on Scientific Subjects. Trans. E. Atkinson. London: Longmans, Green, 1873, 197-99, 306-16. Conversely, Helmholtz's work is freely cited by psychological researchers).

10. See James, 2:23-24; Ladd, 106, 109; Sully, *Illusions* 56; Helmholtz, *Treatise* 215-24; Capt. W. de Abney, *Colour Vision, Being the Tyndall Lectures* delivered in 1894 at the Royal Institution. London: Sampson Low, Marston, 1895 (32-34).

11. H. G. Wells. 'The Visibility of Colour' *Pall Mall Gazette* 60 (March 7 1895):4. This is a review of Abney's Tyndall lecture (see above). Abney does not mention the Spectrum Top, but Wells was also reviewing books for *Nature* in late 1894 and may have read of the Spectrum Top there.

12. Frank D. McConnell, ed. H. G. Wells: *The Time Machine, The War of the Worlds: A Critical Introduction.* New York: Oxford UP, 1977 (22n). See also Geduld, who, in The Definitive Time Machine (98, 119) links the ghost trick to the Time Traveller's disappearance.

13. These comments are made by, respectively: Bernard Bergonzi, *The Early H. G. Wells: A Study of the Scientific Romance,* Manchester: Manchester UP, 1961 (33); Darko Suvin, *Metamorphoses of Science Fiction,* New Haven: Yale UP, 1979 (212); Robert Crossley, *H. G. Wells,* Mercer Island, Washington: Stamont House, 1986 (21).

14. Mark R Hillegas, 'Cosmic Pessimism in H. G. Wells's Scientific Romances' *Papers of the Michigan Academy of Science, Arts and Letters* 46 (1961): 656-57.

Works Cited

Bergonzi, Bernard. *The Early H. G. Wells: A Study of the Scientific Romances.* Manchester: Manchester UP, 1961.

Crossley, Robert. *H. G. Wells.* Mercer Island, Washington: Starmont House, 1986.

———. "The Publication of *The Time Machine* 1894-5." *Review of English Studies.* 11 (1960): 43-45.

Geduld, Harry M., ed. *The Definitive Time Machine: A Critical Edition of H. G. Wells's Scientific Romance.* Bloomington: Indiana UP, 1987.

Haynes, Roslynn D. *H. G. Wells: Discoverer of the Future.* London: Macmillan, 1980.

Helmholtz, H. *Popular Lectures on Scientific Subjects.* Trans E. Atkinson. London: Longmans, Green: 1873.

———. *Treatise on Physiological Optics.* 3 vols. Ed. James P. C. Southall. Menasha, Wisconsin: Optical Society of America, 1925.

Hillegas, Mark R. "Cosmic Pessimism in H. G. Wells's Scientific Romances." *Papers of the Michigan Academy of Science, Arts and Letters.* 46 (1961): 656-57.

Huxley, T. H. "The Struggle for Existence: A Programme." *Nineteenth Century* 23 (1888).

Huntington, John. *The Logic of Fantasy: H. G. Wells and Science Fiction.* New York: Columbia UP, 1982.

Hynes, Samuel L. & Frank D. McConnell. "*The Time Machine* and *The War of the Worlds*: Parable and Possibility in H. G. Wells." McConnell, *H. G. Wells: The Time Machine, The War of the Worlds: A Critical Edition.* New York: Oxford UP, 1977.

James, William. *The Principles of Psychology.* 2 vols. London: Macmillan, 1890.

Ladd, George Trumbull. *Psychology, Descriptive and Explanatory: A Treatise of the Phenomena, Laws, and Development of Human Mental Life.* London: Longmans, Green, 1894.

McConnell, Frank D., ed. *H. G. Wells: The Time Machine, The War of the Worlds: A Critical Edition.* New York: Oxford UP, 1977.

Philmus, Robert M. & David Y. Hughes, eds. *H. G. Wells: Early Writings in Science and Science and Science Fiction.* Berkeley: California UP, 1975.

Smith, David C. *H. G. Wells: Desperately Mortal.* New Haven: Yale UP, 1986.

———. "Little Wars for Little People: Sport, Games, and Leisure Time in the Work and Life of H. G. Wells." *Arete* 2 (1985): 127-28.

Spencer, Herbert. *The Principles of Psychology.* 3rd ed. 2 vols. London: Williams & Norgate, 1881.

Sully, James. *Illusions: A Psychological Study.* London: C. Kegan Paul, 1881.

———. *The Human Mind: A Textbook of Psychology.* 2 vols. London: Longmans, Green, 1892.

Suvin, Darko. *Metamorphoses of Science Fiction.* New Haven: Yale UP, 1979.

Ward, James. "Psychology." *Encyclopædia Britannica: A Dictionary of Arts, Sciences and General Literature.* 9th ed. 20 vols. Edinburgh: Adam & Charles Black, 1883.

Weeks, Robert P. "Disentanglement as a Theme in H. G. Wells's Fiction." *H. G. Wells: A Collection of Critical Essays.* Ed. Bernard Bergonzi. Englewood Cliffs NJ: Prentice Hall, 1976.

Wells, H. G. "Discoveries in Variation." *Saturday Review* 79 (1895): 312.

———. *Experiment in Autobiography: Discoveries and Conclusions of a Very Ordinary Brain.* 2 vols. London: Gollancz, 1934.

———. Prefaces. *The Atlantic Edition of the Works of H. G. Wells.* 28 vols. London: Unwin, 1924.

———. [unsigned] "The Dream Bureau: A New Entertainment." *Pall Mall Gazette* 57 (October 25 1893).

———. "The Position of Psychology." *Saturday Review* 78 (1894): 715.

———. *The Scientific Romances of H. G. Wells.* London: Victor Gollancz, 1933.

———. [H. G. Wells]. "'Specimen Day' (From a Holiday Itinerary)." *Science Schools Journal* 33 (October 1891): 17-19.

———. *The Time Machine: An Invention.* London: Heinemann, 1895.

———. *The Wheels of Chance: A Holiday Adventure.* Macmillan Colonial Library Series. London: Macmillan, 1986.

———. "The Visibility of Colour." *Pall Mall Gazette* 60 (March 7 1895): 4

Wells, Geoffrey H. *The Works of H. G. Wells 1887-1925: A Bibliography, Dictionary and Subject Index.* London: Routledge & Sons, 1926.

Patrick Parrinder (essay date 1995)

SOURCE: Parrinder, Patrick. "Possibilities of Space and Time (*The Time Machine*)." In *Shadows of the Future: H. G. Wells, Science Fiction and Prophecy*, pp. 34-48. Liverpool, United Kingdom: Liverpool University Press, 1995.

[*In the following essay, Parrinder explores the significance of time travel in Wells's fiction, particularly* The Time Machine.]

I

Towards the end of ***The Time Machine,*** the Traveller finishes the story of his adventures, pauses, and looks around at his listeners. He is like a lecturer waiting for the first question after his talk, and like many nervous lecturers he tries to start the ball rolling by interrogating the audience himself. "'No. I cannot expect you to believe it'", he begins. "'Take it as a lie—or a prophecy. Say I dreamed it in the workshop. . . . Treat my assertion of its truth as a mere stroke of art to enhance its interest. And taking it as a story, what do you think of it?'" (§12). There is another awkward silence, while the Time Traveller fiddles with his pipe, and the audience shift uneasily in their chairs. Then the newspaper editor says that their host ought to be a writer of stories. The narrator, who is not sure what to think, returns to the Traveller's house in Richmond the next day, just in time to speak with him before he departs on the second voyage, from which he never returns. As Robert Philmus has observed, within the narrative framework it is the Traveller's second disappearance and failure to return that proves the reality of time travel, establishing him as a prophet rather than a liar.[1]

For the narrator in the 'Epilogue', the Time Traveller's tale appears as a brief moment of enlightenment, like the flaring of the match in 'The Rediscovery of the Unique', amid the vast ignorance and darkness of the future. The light of prophecy is also the light of science—but it is the extent of the blackness that terrifies. Wells says something very similar in *The Future in America,* when he speaks of the loss of his belief in the imminence of the Christian apocalypse during his adolescence. The study of biology revealed to him an 'endless vista of years ahead' (p. 10). Space, too, appeared as an endless vista, and it is notable that in his early works Wells often uses the word figuratively to indicate a measure of time, as in the phrase 'a space of time'.[2] The complementarity of space and time in the Wellsian universe is summed up in the title of his 1899 volume of stories, *Tales of Space and Time.*

But travel in time with its prophetic associations engages Wells's imagination more intensely than journeys into space. Despite his reputation as the founder of modern science fiction, he took little or no interest in the fiction of spaceships and stellar travel. His rhetorical vision in *The Discovery of the Future* of beings who 'shall laugh and reach out their hands amid the stars' (p. 36) was to inspire other writers, though it corresponds to very little in Wells's own output. Apart from the mystical dream-narrative of his short story **'Under the Knife'**, *The First Men in the Moon* is his only narrative of a journey beyond the earth's atmosphere; and it is notable that Bedford, the narrator, experiences the dissolution of identity in 'infinite space' during the comparatively short return journey from the moon. He recounts this phase of his adventures in a detached, almost serene way, very different from the Time Traveller's 'hysterical exhilaration' (§3) as he rushes into the future. There is fear and trembling in Wells's imagination of time travel; in *The First Men in the Moon,* however, the experience of thrilling revelation is reserved not for the journey but for the discoveries that the two explorers make on the moon.

What, then, was the source of the exhilaration of time travel? It reflects the bias of Wells's scientific interests, in evolutionary biology and palaeontology rather than astronomy and physics, but it also has a more personal appeal, reflecting his imaginative 'impatience'. We can hardly avoid relating it both to the religious millennialism of his upbringing,[3] and to his intimations of an early death. The fundamental commonsense objection to time travel is the one put forward by Wells's fellow-

novelist Israel Zangwill, writing about *The Time Machine* in his *Pall Mall Magazine* column in September 1895. To travel forward more than a few years in time, Zangwill argued, is to travel through one's own death.[4] (It is also, one might add, to travel through the death of the machine: metal fatigue and corrosion are often swifter processes than the decay of the human body.) Admittedly, the idea of 'travelling through' death is misleading, since what the time machine achieves for its rider is the circumvention and bypassing of the ravages of time. Since he is still alive and has only aged by a few hours when he reaches 802,701, his journey takes place in a different time-frame from the one that he leaves behind and later re-enters.[5] Wells is aware of some at least of the paradoxes that beset all time-travel narratives. These are most obtrusive at the end of the story, when the narrator returns to Richmond the day after the Traveller's return and sees the Time Machine in the empty laboratory before meeting its inventor in the smoking-room. The Traveller has already passed through this moment in the empty laboratory twice, once on his journey forwards and once on his return journey; on the latter occasion he '"seemed to see Hillyer . . . but he passed like a flash"' (§12). If Hillyer is the narrator (as Geduld suggests),[6] the Traveller is seeing him either at this moment or on the occasion, somewhat later, when the narrator re-enters the laboratory. On that second occasion, the narrator catches sight of the ghostly figure of the Traveller on the machine, in the act of departure—or arrival—or both. There are further complications that could be teased out from the story's opening-up of such paradoxes.[7]

Before receiving his 'death warrant' after his footballing accident in 1887, Wells had written **'A Vision of the Past'**. Immediately after it, he wrote **'The Chronic Argonauts,'** the first version of *The Time Machine,* which is set in present time. At the end of **'The Chronic Argonauts'** the Reverend Elijah Cook returns from an involuntary voyage into the future, but we never hear his tale of what happened there. Wells's friends complained about the abrupt ending, but it was many years before he was able to write the promised sequel to his own satisfaction. When it eventually appeared in book form, it had been revised at least half a dozen times.[8] For six years (1888-94), we may say, Wells had hesitated on the brink of a genuinely prophetic narrative. His exultation once he had succeeded in giving the future a body and shape is perhaps mirrored in the pun (supposing it is a pun) in Section 4 of *The Time Machine,* when the Traveller reflects on the 'oddness of wells still existing'.

In **'The Chronic Argonauts'** there are two narratives, which Wells calls 'exoteric' and 'esoteric'. The exoteric or external story is told by 'the author' (that is, Wells himself), while the esoteric or internal one is told, in an incomplete and fragmentary form, by the Reverend Elijah Cook. The figure who never tells his story is Nebogipfel, the inventor of the time machine or 'Chronic Argo' himself. He only expounds the principles of time-travelling, in conversation with Elijah Cook. In the *National Observer* version of Wells's tale, published between March and June 1894, Nebogipfel, now rechristened or relabelled the Time Traveller, is constantly interrupted by his hearers. His mixture of philosophical argument and adventure narrative is punctuated by commentaries and outbursts of scepticism. The sheer imaginative power of his tale is never given full rein, as if some inhibition still curbed its author. As storytelling, this version is bungled just as **'The Chronic Argonauts'** is bungled.[9] But in the final version Wells's inhibitions are overcome, and, once we are with the Traveller on his voyage, the smoking-room setting of the tale is forgotten for very long stretches. The Delphic voice pours forth at last. The Traveller is now more than a mere narrative device. He is a heroic figure within the confines of the story, as well as an avatar of the visionary personality that Wells was discovering, with growing confidence, within himself.

II

When Dr Nebogipfel's unwilling passenger, the Rev. Elijah Cook, arrives back from his journey in **'The Chronic Argonauts'** he announces that he has several depositions to make. These concern a murder in the year 1862 (indicating that, unlike the Time Traveller, the Argonauts have gone both ways in time), an abduction in 4003 and a series of '"assaults on public officials in the years 17,901 and 2"'.[10] In the *National Observer* 'Time Machine', the world of the Eloi and Morlocks is set in AD 12,203. In the final version, the date, conveniently registered on the Time Machine's instrument panel, is 802,701. There follows the 'Further Vision', in which the Traveller journeys forward another twenty-nine million years. The reader of the different versions of **The Time Machine** succumbs to the spell of these mysterious numbers themselves—above all, the puzzling figure 802,701—but, beyond that, the meaning of such vast expanses of imaginary time calls out for explanation.

When the Time Traveller's guests encounter the idea of visiting the future, it is plain how limited their (and, by extension, our) horizons are. The Journalist dubs their host 'Our Special Correspondent in the Day after Tomorrow' (§2). The Editor wants a tip for next week's horse-racing. The Very Young Man suggests investing some money and travelling forward to collect the profits. Yet even the relatively modest *National Observer* voyage crossed a timespan of more than twice as long as recorded history. Wells's familiarity with the prehistoric vistas opened up by nineteenth-century geology and archaeology had shaped his vision of time travel. As a South Kensington student, he belonged to the first generation of young people to learn as a matter of

course about the Stone Age, the era of the dinosaurs, and the formation of the earth. This marvellous new field of knowledge, which rapidly became a staple of popular culture, is evoked in the Epilogue to **The Time Machine** where the narrator imagines the Traveller voyaging into Palaeolithic, Jurassic and Triassic times.

Humanity emerged at a relatively late point in the evolutionary chain, yet our race is still almost unimaginably old. In Wells's next scientific romance, Dr Moreau reminds the narrator that '"Man has been a hundred thousand [years] in the making"' (Ch. 14). Actually, Moreau's figure is a gross underestimate, as the chronological horizon of **The Time Machine** hints. In *The Outline of History,* Wells was to put the emergence of the subhuman *pithecanthropus erectus* at six hundred thousand years ago, though since the advent of radiocarbon dating this has been increased to 1.8 million years.[11] In September 1994 reports appeared of the discovery of a fruit-eating humanoid creature (possibly analogous to the Eloi on the evolutionary scale) said to be 4.4 million years old.

Before **The Time Machine** Wells had implied a possible chronology for future evolution in **'The Man of the Year Million'.** Then, in a discussion of **'The Rate of Change in Species'** (December 1894), he outlined the considerations that may have led him to lengthen the Time Traveller's journey from the ten thousand years of the *National Observer* version to eighty times as long. Wells claimed it was a little-noticed biological fact that the rate of possible change was governed by the gap between generations, and hence by the average age of maturity in a species. Evolution by natural selection—the strictly Darwinian model to which Wells and Huxley adhered—could not have brought about significant changes within the human species within recorded history, so that any such changes must be cultural, not natural in origin. Wells was determined to show the results of hypothetical natural evolution, not of artificial or eugenic processes in **The Time Machine.** The Traveller's voyage through the best part of a million years thus reflects both the probable age of the human species, in the understanding of Wells's contemporaries, and the minimum time needed for natural selection to produce new degenerate beings descended from present-day humanity.

The time-horizon of Wells's story is also affected by contemporary physical predictions of the future of the solar system. The Traveller reaches a point where not only humanity, but the sun's heat itself is manifestly on the wane. If the story of evolution pointed to the plasticity of biological species, Lord Kelvin's Laws of Thermodynamics portrayed the universe as a finite enclosure in which energy was limited. As a student, Wells had once engaged in a spoof demonstration of a perpetual motion machine (powered by a concealed electromagnet)[12]—a thermodynamic impossibility not unlike a time machine, since both depend on the ability to bypass the normal framework of what, in a lost article, he had called the 'Universe Rigid'.[13] The Second Law of Thermodynamics with its statement that energy always tends to disperse made it clear that the sun and other stars must eventually cool and burn out. *The Time Machine* reflects this entropic process, as well as Sir George Darwin's calculations of the effects of tidal drag on the earth's motion. Later in his life, however, Wells readily admitted that his astronomical predictions had been too gloomy.[14] The study of radioactivity had revealed that the source of the sun's heat was thermonuclear fusion rather than combustion; the sun was not a coal fire, so to speak, but a nuclear reactor. The predicted life of the solar system increased from the implied timescale of the 'Further Vision' to ten thousand million years, or perhaps a million million years.[15]

These are unimaginable and almost meaningless expanses of time, yet paradoxically *The Time Machine* renders a thirty million-year future thinkable. That is the 'virtual reality' effect of the story's mythical, apocalyptic hold over the reader. To ask how Wells manages it is to come up against the truism that our only models for imagining the future derive from our knowledge and understanding of the past. He could write of travelling one million or thirty million years ahead only in the light of the geologists' consensus that the earth was already much older than that, though precisely how much older was a matter of conjecture. Kelvin had estimated that the age of the oldest rocks was as little as twenty-five million years, while T. H. Huxley guessed at four hundred million. Summing up the controversy in *The Outline of History,* Wells is unable to arbitrate between these two. Reusing one of his favourite metaphors, he adds that 'Not only is Space from the point of view of life and humanity empty, but Time is empty also. Life is like a little glow, scarcely kindled yet, in these void immensities' (p. 8). In *The Time Machine* he had slightly prolonged that little glow.

III

Wells's use of geological chronology does not explain how he was able to depict the sub-civilisation of the Eloi and Morlocks at a precise date in the future, given in the final version as 802,701. Readers have often wondered why he settled on this curious figure. We may approach an answer by looking more closely at the sensations of time-travelling described in the story. Riding into the future, the Traveller observes the speeding-up of natural phenomena: the alternation of night and day until the two are indistinguishable, the flickering change of the seasons, the swift growth and disappearance of trees. This part of his narrative, which has the vertiginous effect of a constantly accelerating film, may make us wonder how fast he is travelling and how 'long' his

journey takes. At one point he mentions a speed of more than a year a minute, but if this were his average velocity it would take nearly eighteen months to reach 802,701. Travelling more rapidly later in the story, he approaches the 'Further Vision' at a speed of something like fifty years per second; but, in fact, five hundred years per second would be a more plausible average speed.[16] At that rate he could have reached the age of the Eloi and Morlocks in less than half an hour.

During his voyage he sees signs of changing civilisations as well as changing natural phenomena. "'I saw huge buildings rise up faint and fair, and pass like dreams'", he reports (§3). How often did this happen? "'I saw great and splendid architecture rising about me, more massive than any buildings of our own time, and yet, as it seemed, built of glimmer and mist'". There would have been no need to go forward three-quarters of a million years in order to see the architecture of successive human civilisations. Our knowledge of past history suggests that 800 years might have been enough. Even given vastly more durable building materials, 8000 years would have been amply sufficient. Assuming some degree of continuity in human civilisation, changes in architecture would normally take place far more frequently than the natural climatic changes that the Traveller also observes—"'I saw a richer green flow up the hillside, and remain there without any wintry intermission'" (§3)—let alone the species modifications that have produced the Eloi and Morlocks.

The order of the figures in 802,701 suggests a suitably entropic and cyclical 'running-down' number.[17] We can explain how Wells may have arrived at it, however, by the supposition that *The Time Machine* embodies not one future timescale but two. The two scales, those of historical time measured by the rise and fall of cultures and civilisations, and of biological time measured by the evolution and devolution of the species, are superimposed upon one another. To begin with, I suggest that Wells must have projected the invention of the Time Machine forward to the beginning of the twentieth century, so that the dinner party at Richmond may be imagined as taking place in 1901. (Analogously, the events of *The War of the Worlds*—which Wells began writing immediately after *The Time Machine* was published—also take place 'early in the twentieth century' (I,1).) He had already used the early twentieth century as baseline in **'The Chronic Argonauts,'** where the furthest point that we know to have been reached is the years 17,901-02: that is, a voyage of 16,000 years. In *The Time Machine* the world of the Eloi and Morlocks is located not 16,000 but 800,800 years after 1901—a significantly bifurcated number. The 800 years, enough to allow for the rise and fall of a civilisation or two in historical time, take us to 2701. To this figure Wells added a further 800,000 (that is, the best part of a million years) of evolutionary time. Supposing the number 802,701 to have been determined by a process such as this, its poetic appeal as a symbol of entropy would have ensured its adoption. Its significance—to be further explored in Chapter Five below—is that *The Time Machine* is plotted with both timescales, the evolutionary and the historiographic, in mind, though these are incompatible in certain respects. Without the 800-year timescale we cannot easily explain such crucial details as the survival of unmistakably classical forms of architecture into the far future, creating an essentially familiar landscape dominated by the Sphinx and surrounded by ruined palaces and gardens.

IV

The Sphinx and the decaying palaces are central to the symbolism of the story. The Sphinx is the symbol of foreboding and prophecy. The palaces and gardens suggest the landscape of neoclassical paintings and country houses, while alluding to a line of English utopian romances which would have been fresh in the minds of Wells's first readers: Richard Jefferies' *After London* (1885), W. H. Hudson's *A Crystal Age* (1887), and, above all, William Morris's *News from Nowhere* (1890). Morris's death in 1896 drew an affectionate if patronising acknowledgment from Wells in the *Saturday Review*—'His dreamland was no futurity, but an illuminated past', Wells wrote[18]—but a more wholehearted tribute, and one which hints at the strong connections between *News from Nowhere* and *The Time Machine*, appears at the beginning of *A Modern Utopia*:

> Were we free to have our untrammelled desire, I suppose we should follow Morris to his Nowhere, we should change the nature of man and the nature of things together; we should make the whole race wise, tolerant, noble, perfect . . . in a world as good in its essential nature, as ripe and sunny, as the world before the Fall. But that golden age, that perfect world, comes out into the possibilities of space and time. In space and time the pervading Will to Live sustains for evermore a perpetuity of aggressions.[19]

Chapter Five of *The Time Machine* in the first edition is titled 'In the Golden Age'. In Wells's vision, the 'possibilities of space and time' are not unlimited. In space and time what appears to be a Morrisian utopia can only be fatally flawed; no earthly paradise of this sort is possible. The words Eloi and Morlocks signify angels and devils, and the two races, the products of natural selection, are held together in a predatory and symbiotic relationship—a 'perpetuity of aggressions' without which neither could flourish.

The Time Machine is both an explicitly anti-utopian text, and one which deliberately recalls *News from Nowhere* at a number of points. Morris's pastoral, idyllic society is centred on Hammersmith in West London,

while the society of the Eloi is centred two or three miles upstream at Richmond. Both are placed in a lush parkland replacing the nineteenth-century industrial and suburban sprawl beside the River Thames. The Eloi, like the inhabitants of Nowhere and of most other contemporary socialist utopias, eat together in communal dining halls. William Guest, Morris's 'time traveller', learns about the history of twentieth- and twenty-first century England from an old man at the British Museum, while Wells's Traveller journeys to the Palace of Green Porcelain, an abandoned museum of the arts and sciences modelled on the Crystal Palace and the South Kensington Museum.[20] On the evening of his first day with the Eloi, the Traveller climbs to a hilltop, surveys the countryside and exclaims '"Communism"' (§4) to himself. The Communism he has in mind must be the pastoral utopia of Morris and Thomas More, rather than the revolutionary industrial society of Marx and Saint-Simon.

On two occasions the Time Traveller mocks at the artificiality of utopian narratives, as if to establish the superior authenticity of his own story. A '"real traveller"', he protests, has no access to the vast amount of detail about buildings and social arrangements to be found in these books (§5). He has '"no convenient cicerone in the pattern of the Utopian books"' (§5); instead, he has to work everything out for himself by trial and error. The emphasis is not on the exposition of a superior utopian philosophy but on the Traveller's own powers of observation and his habits of deductive and inductive reasoning. In terms of narrative structure as well as of evolutionary possibility, Wells claims to present a less self-indulgent, more realistic vision than Morris and his tradition could offer—as if the world of 802,701 were somehow less of a wish-fulfilment fantasy than Morris's Nowhere. The Time Traveller shows himself in the opening chapters to be a master of several sciences. He is a brilliant inventor and engineer, who is able by his own efforts to test the practical consequences of his theoretical discoveries in four-dimensional geometry.[21] He understands the principles of biology and psychology, and in studying the Eloi and Morlocks without the benefit of a guide he finds himself in the position of an anthropologist and ethnographer. Like an ethnographer in the field, he learns the language of his hosts and attempts to question them about 'taboo' topics such as the mysterious wells dotted across the countryside. At each stage, but always aware that he may lack some crucial information, he attempts to theorise his findings.[22] In a characteristic Wellsian touch, he reverses the usual relations between a nineteenth-century anthropologist and his subject-matter, comparing his account of the Eloi to the '"tale of London which a negro, fresh from Central Africa, would take back to his tribe"'—though he adds that the negro would find plenty of willing informants, and in any case, '"think how narrow the gap between a negro and a white man of our own times, and how wide the interval between myself and these of the Golden Age!"' (§5).

Admittedly, the Traveller often fails to live up to his ideal of scientific detachment. Unlike the utopias against which he is reacting, Wells's tale is a violent adventure story as well as something resembling a fieldwork report. The Traveller's behaviour in moments of crisis is typically hysterical, panic-stricken, negligent and, when he confronts the Morlocks, ruthless and desperate. In all this he embodies what Wells in *A Modern Utopia* was to call the Will to Live. Equally, the bloodthirstiness of Wells's anti-utopian realism invites the rejoinder that William Morris made in his review of Edward Bellamy's urban, collectivist utopia *Looking Backward*: 'The only safe way of reading a utopia is to consider it as the expression of the temperament of its author'.[23] *The Time Machine* debunks the utopian dream (a dream that would be reinstated in many of Wells's later works) en route to the discovery that the human species is engaged in a brutal struggle for survival which, in the long run, it cannot win—since all terrestrial life is doomed to extinction. Wells enables his Time Traveller to circumvent his own natural death—to cheat death, so to speak—only to inflict violent death on some of humanity's remote descendants, before going on to witness the collective death of the species and the environment that has sustained it.

In speaking of authorial temperament, Morris was invoking one of the principal categories of late nineteenth-century literary theory. He would have been aware of the widespread reaction against the claims to scientific objectivity made by the realist and naturalist movements; every work of art, it was argued, betrayed the imprint of its maker's personality.[24] To modern readers, once we have acknowledged the complexity and uniqueness of a text like *The Time Machine,* such appeals to personality and temperament have come to seem tautologous rather than illuminating. Nevertheless, we may say that when Wells's artistic imagination was at its most vivid, in the early scientific romances, it was also at its most violent. Ten years after the searing anti-utopianism of these books, he was ready to present his own, comparatively pacific vision of *A Modern Utopia.* As it happens, this apparent change of heart runs parallel with a dramatic improvement in his medical condition.

The cannibalistic Morlocks, the bloodsucking Martians and the bath of pain in which the vivisectionist Dr Moreau transforms wild animals into sham human beings were all conceived during the years in which Wells himself was often bedridden and spitting blood. Since tuberculosis had been (wrongly) diagnosed, it is significant that the first of the Eloi whom the Time Traveller meets face to face has the '"hectic beauty"' of a '"consumptive"' (§3). The Traveller feels intensely for this society of doomed consumptives, and, once he is armed with a rusty iron bar, he does his best to wreak havoc among the species that lives off them. Wells suffered a final serious relapse in 1898, after the completion of his early romances. He moved to the south coast and commissioned the architect Charles Voysey to build him a house on the cliffs at Sandgate, designed to accommodate the wheelchair to which he soon expected to be confined. But this soon became irrelevant to the needs of its resilient and indeed hyperactive owner.

As his self-identification with the consumptive Eloi came to seem groundless, so did the calculations of planetary cooling reflected in both *The Time Machine* and *The War of the Worlds* lose their sway over contemporary scientific opinion. In *The Interpretation of Radium* (1908)—the book which led Wells to envisage the possibility of atomic warfare—Frederick Soddy wrote that 'Our outlook on the physical universe has been permanently altered. We are no longer the inhabitants of a universe slowly dying from the physical exhaustion of its energy, but of a universe which has in the internal energy of its material components the means to rejuvenate itself perennially over immense periods of time'.[25] Wells's switch shortly before the First World War from entropic pessimism to a position much closer to Soddy's thermonuclear optimism followed his discovery of the internal energy and potential for self-renewal of his own body, so that he was doubly removed from the outlook of the author of *The Time Machine.*

V

However anti-utopian its outcome, the Time Traveller's voyage confirms that a kind of utopia had been achieved in the 'nearer ages', when, for example, disease had been stamped out, the processes of natural decay slowed if not halted, and population growth brought under control. Nature had been subjugated—for a time (§4). There emerged the monumental civilisation whose buildings and landscapes still dominated the age of the Eloi and Morlocks. It is the Traveller's fate to chart the seemingly inevitable decline that followed once the human species had reached its zenith, or what the narrator terms the 'manhood of the race' (Epilogue). Pursuing Wells's deterministic hypothesis of a necessary downward curve in human fortunes, he is a symbolic figure embarking on the central quest of the scientific romance, the journey towards, and beyond, the 'last man'.[26]

The Time Traveller is a variant on the heroes of nineteenth-century Gothic and romantic melodrama. He arrives in the future in the midst of a thunderstorm, but when he discovers that the Morlocks have removed his machine his elation gives way to a frenzy of despair.

His violent emotionalism is reminiscent of *Franken-stein*—a literary model which Wells acknowledged[27]—and, since Mary Shelley's romance is subtitled *The Modern Prometheus* in allusion to Prometheus's legendary role as the creator of humanity, it is interesting that the Time Traveller has a still better claim to Promethean ancestry. The name Prometheus means 'forethought'.[28] Just as Prometheus was one of the Titans, the Traveller is identified with the race of 'giants' who preceded the Eloi and Morlocks and built the great palaces. The Eloi recognise his semi-divine status when they ask, at the moment of his arrival, if he has come from the sun (p. 39). He brings a box of matches with him, and when they run out he steals another box from the Palace of Green Porcelain. Prometheus stole fire from Zeus and brought it down to earth as a gift concealed in a stalk of fennel, to show his friendship for suffering humanity. But neither the frugivorous Eloi nor the half-blind Morlocks are fit recipients for the gift of fire. Future humanity has degenerated so much that the Traveller's matches are used only as purposeless toys, or in self-defence against the Morlocks. In the end his playing with fire causes reckless destruction including, it would seem, the death of Weena who is the one friend he has made in the new world.

Pursuing the imaginative logic of the Time Traveller's identification with Prometheus, we can come to a possible solution to the mystery of his disappearance on his second voyage. Can it be that—punished for his daring in setting out to discover the future in defiance of the gods—his fate is to remain bound to his machine, condemned to perpetual time-travelling just as Prometheus was bound to a rock and condemned to perpetual torture? All that we know is that the narrator's question, 'Will he ever return?', must be answered in the negative. A life of torture, too, was the fate of another famous figure of Greek legend, with whom the Traveller must also be identified: Oedipus, who answered the riddle of the Sphinx, which was the riddle of human life. What the Traveller instinctively fears as he looks into the Sphinx's sightless eyes is the death of humanity and his own inability to survive in a post-human world: "'I might seem some old-world savage animal . . . a foul creature to be incontinently slain'" (§3). But he does not flinch from his self-appointed mission of traversing the valley of the shadow of death and reporting the Shape of Things to Come to the people of his own time: "'It is how the thing shaped itself to me, and as that I give it to you'" (§10).

Notes

1. Robert M. Philmus, 'The Logic of "Prophecy" in *The Time Machine*' in Bernard Bergonzi, ed., *H. G. Wells: A Collection of Critical Essays* (Englewood Cliffs, N.J.: Prentice-Hall, 1976), pp. 67-68.

2. See, for example, *The Time Machine*, §§ 3 and 4; 'How I Died', p. 182.

3. See Norman and Jeanne Mackenzie, *The Time Traveller: The Life of H. G. Wells* (London: Weidenfeld & Nicolson, 1973), especially pp. 24, 121-24.

4. Israel Zangwill, 'Without Prejudice', reprinted in Patrick Parrinder, ed., *H. G. Wells: The Critical Heritage*, pp. 40-42.

5. Recent discussions of this question include those by Roslynn D. Haynes in *H. G. Wells: Discoverer of the Future* (London and Basingstoke: Macmillan, 1980), p. 58, and by Harry M. Geduld in *The Definitive 'Time Machine': A Critical Edition of H. G. Wells's Scientific Romance*, ed. Geduld (Bloomington and Indianapolis: Indiana University Press, 1987), pp. 96-97.

6. *The Definitive 'Time Machine'*, p. 118.

7. See ibid., p. 120, n. 6.

8. Geoffrey West, *H. G. Wells: A Sketch for a Portrait*, pp. 288-94.

9. 'The Chronic Argonauts' and the '*National Observer* Time Machine' are reprinted in *The Definitive 'Time Machine'*, pp. 135-52 and 154-74 respectively.

10. *The Definitive 'Time Machine'*, p. 145.

11. Henry Gee, 'What's our line?', *London Review of Books*, 16:2 (27 January 1994), p. 19.

12. Geoffrey West, *H. G. Wells: A Sketch for a Portrait*, p. 61.

13. See H. G. Wells, 'Preface', *The Time Machine* (New York: Random House, 1931), p. ix.

14. Ibid., pp. ix-x.

15. See H. G. Wells, *The Discovery of the Future*, p. 17, n. 6.

16. 'Fifty years per second', because the dials of the Time Machine are calibrated in days, thousands of days, millions of days, and thousands of millions, and the Traveler reports that the 'thousands hand was sweeping round as fast as the seconds hands of a watch' (§11). If one complete revolution of the 'thousands' dial represents a million days, he is covering a million days a minute, or 46 years per second—but it would still take more than a week to traverse 30 million years. We may, of course, find the references to the dials highly implausible, especially as the time to be measured is not linear. If the dials measure terrestrial days, one must wonder how they cope with or allow for the slowing down of the terrestrial day to the point where a single solar revolution 'seemed to stretch through centuries' (§11)!

17. Cf. William Bellamy, *The Novels of Wells, Bennett and Galsworthy 1890-1910* (London: Routledge & Kegan Paul, 1971), p. 221.

18. H. G. Wells, 'The Well at the World's End', in *H. G. Wells's Literary Criticism,* p. 112.

19. H. G. Wells, *A Modern Utopia* (London: Chapman & Hall, 1905), p. 7. Subsequent page references in text.

20. This was the nineteenth-century name for what are now four separate museums clustered together in South Kensington: the Geological Museum, the Natural History Museum, the Science Museum and the Victoria and Albert Museum. It is to this Museum (not the district of London in which it is located) to which the Time Traveller refers when he describes the Palace of Green Porcelain as a '"latter-day South Kensington"' (§8).

21. The Time Traveller's discovery is that the fourth dimension is *Time*. In this he anticipates Einstein. The widespread popular view of the fourth dimension in the late nineteenth century was of an extra dimension of space, corresponding to the 'spirit world' and frequented by ghosts. See Michio Kaku, *Hyperspace: A Scientific Odyssey Through Parallel Universes, Time Warps, and The Tenth Dimension* (New York and Oxford: Oxford University Press, 1994), especially p. 84.

22. On two occasions his explanations make use of the contemporary anthropological concept of '"savage survivals"' (§4).

23. William Morris, 'Looking Backward', *Commonweal* (22 June 1889), p. 194.

24. One influential expression of this view was Henry James's essay 'The Art of Fiction' (1884). See *Henry James, Selected Literary Criticism,* ed. Morris Shapira (London: Heinemann, 1963), p. 66.

25. Frederick Soddy, *The Interpretation of Radium: Being the Substance of Six Free Popular Experimental Lectures Delivered at the University of Glasgow,* 3rd edn. (London: Murray, 1912), p. 248.

26. On 'last man' fictions see Patrick Parrinder, 'From Mary Shelley to *The War of the Worlds*; The Thames Valley Catastrophe', in David Seed, ed., *Anticipations: Essays on Early Science Fiction and Its Precursors* (Liverpool: Liverpool University Press, 1995), pp. 58-74.

27. See H. G. Wells, preface to *The Scientific Romances of H. G. Wells* (1933), reprinted in *H. G. Wells's Literary Criticism,* pp. 240, 241. Subsequent page references in text.

28. Robert Graves, *The Greek Myths* (Harmondsworth: Penguin, 1955), I, p. 148.

John S. Parrington (essay date October 1997)

SOURCE: Parrington, John S. "*The Time Machine*: A Polemic on the Inevitability of Working-Class Liberation, and a Plea for a Socialist Solution to Late-Victorian Capitalist Exploitation." *Cahiers Victoriens et Edouardiens* 46 (October 1997): 167-79.

[*In the following essay, Parrington provides a sociopolitical interpretation of* The Time Machine.]

H. G. Wells intended **The Time Machine** to be a polemic on the inevitability of a working-class rise to power and, an attempt to reveal why the achievement of revolutionary Socialism was necessary, as against Fabian parliamentary Socialism, the latter of which strives for Socialism without eliminating class struggle from society.

The Time Traveller's position in the book is interesting. He was a scientist of the Wellsian type in the sense that he was not a conventional late-Victorian inventor.

Throughout the story the reader is led to believe that the meetings held at the Time Traveller's home occurred not just in the two weeks described, but in several preceding weeks also. They were casual meetings in that different guests waded in and out of them without any apparent invitation or excuse. They were open, albeit to a select section of the community (i.e., the bourgeoisie, including a doctor, psychologist, provincial mayor, editor, etc.). The discussions were led by the Time Traveller himself and appeared to progress meeting by meeting, preparing the guests for what the Time Traveller revealed as his invention in the penultimate session.

It was in that session that the Time Traveller demonstrated his model Time Machine. Although the assembly generally considered the experiment hocus-pocus, the very act was a huge gamble. Why? Well, he did not only reveal the nature of his work, but he gave a demonstration of it to a group of potential Capitalists. To do so without having the Time Machine patented or without having previous guarantees of investment in his project seems extremely ingenuous. It was a security risk which put his experiment at the mercy of any spying scientific plagiarist who might have attended the meetings. In late-Victorian times this was unheard of and a more typical posture can be found in the actions of Griffin in **The Invisible Man,** who experiments on invisibility in secret for fear of losing his discovery to the senior professors around him.[1] Wells's major criticism of the scientific world of his day was of their secrecy and scheming which led to militarism and war. The Time Traveller obviously did not subscribe to the scientific secrecy of his contemporaries. From this starting point, the Time Traveller's personality becomes apparent.

For a scientific mechanic, the Narrator reveals early in the book a strange invention made by the Time Traveller saying:

> our chairs, being his patent, embraced and caressed us rather than submitted to be sat upon.[2]

A very strange invention by a man who strives to realise time travel! It seems that the Time Machine is not an end in itself. This is evidenced by the chairs. The Time Traveller makes things to improve human comfort. He reveals his secrets to the public rather than tender them out for maximum profit. His home is fitted with chairs to "embrace and caress" their users. This sounds like a man intent on advancing human comfort to the best of his ability, from chairs sat upon to societies to be lived in. Thus, his masterpiece is a Time Machine. What better way of maximising human comfort than by learning from future generations? Thus, when the Time Machine is built the Time Traveller chooses a revolutionary advance into the future rather than a reactionary descent into the past or, as Arnold Bennett puts it:

> the Time Traveller goes forward, not into the dark backward and abysm.[3]

Such is the Time Traveller's motive for time travel.

What does this motive tell us? It can mean but one thing: the Time Traveller is a Socialist. However, he desires Socialism without believing in its advent. This is revealed at the end when the narrator states:

> he, I know—for the question had been discussed among us long before the Time Machine was made—thought but cheerlessly of the advancement of mankind, and saw in the growing pile of civilization only a foolish heaping that must inevitably fall back upon and destroy its makers in the end
>
> (*TM* [*The Time Machine*], 303)

The Time Traveller's attitude is such that any political commitment would be pointless. To create a world where all people would be equal would only be possible by going forward and learning from our descendants. In this way, the Time Traveller could return to his own time and use his acquired knowledge for progress. This attitude may seem naive but it is the one he holds before journeying into the future.

So we understand the position at the beginning of the book. A disillusioned Socialist has built a Time Machine with the ambition of making fundamental discoveries from the future in order to return to his own time and prevent human degeneration. This plot goes hand in hand with Wells's later warning:

> human history becomes more and more a race between education and catastrophe.[4]

The Time Traveller is determined to obtain education in order to prevent human catastrophe.

Having determined the aims of the Time Traveller, we can now turn to his evolved perceptions of the social situation in the world of 802,701. On his arrival in the future, he quickly develops a Fabian Socialist critique of societal evolution. He anticipates, on his arrival in the year 802,701, that the people,

> would be incredibly in front of us in knowledge, art, everything.
>
> (*TM*, 226)

However, he learns otherwise when an Eloi asks him by sign whether he has come from the sun in the thunderstorm! This primitive intelligence, combined with the simplicity of their clothes, "their frail white limbs and fragile features" (*TM*, 226), make the Time Traveller revise his prejudgment. But despite the seeming lack of mental development made by the Eloi, the Time Traveller does not despair of humanity. His initial Fabian interpretation of the future remains and later, when he discovers the lack of private property and the abundance of collective living, he infers, "communism" (*TM*, 231). With this thought in his mind, he rapidly reassesses the world around him along that line of thinking:

> Seeing the ease and security in which these people were living, I felt that this close resemblance of the sexes was after all what one would expect; for the strength of a man and the softness of a woman, the institution of the family, and the differentiation of the occupations are mere militant necessities of an age of physical force. Where population is balanced and abundant, much child-bearing becomes an evil rather than a blessing to the state; where violence comes but rarely and offspring are secure, there is . . . no necessity . . . for an efficient family, and the specialisation of the sexes with reference to their children's needs disappear.
>
> (*TM*, 231)

It is clear from this passage that not only does the Time Traveller believe he is in a Socialist Utopia, but he also believes human evolution has proceeded beneficially for humanity. He is, in effect, drawing the equation that human evolution leads to Socialism. This again is a Fabian critique of the future: late-Victorian Capitalism need not be overthrown by revolution, as evolution will equalise society and create Socialism by design.

At this stage of the novel, therefore, Wells appears to be legitimising Fabian Socialist gradualism within a Capitalist society. The Time Traveller breaks off from his narrative in order to say more or less as much:

The science of our time has attacked but a little department of human disease, but, even so, it spreads its operations very steadily and persistently. Our agriculture and horticulture destroy a weed just here and there and cultivate perhaps a score or so of wholesome plants, leaving the greater number to fight out a balance as they can. We improve our favourite plants and animals . . . gradually by selective breeding . . . We improve them gradually, because our ideals are vague and tentative, and our knowledge is very limited; because nature, too, is shy and slow in our clumsy hands. Some day all this will be better organised, and still better . . . The whole world will be intelligent, educated, and co-operating; things will move faster and faster towards the subjugation of nature. In the end, wisely and carefully we shall readjust the balance of animal and vegetable life to suit our human needs.

(*TM*, 233)

This legitimisation of Fabianism, by extension, declares redundant the need for revolution as a means of replacing individualist society with collectivist society.

This is the situation by chapter four of the book. The reader is lured into a false security with futurity. One is made to believe that all is rosy in the garden of 802,701. The Time Traveller throws our vision of the future into chaos however on the last page of chapter four when he declares, concerning his theory of Eloi life:

very simple was my explanation, and plausible enough—as most wrong theories are!

(*TM*, 236)

Having revealed the Time Traveller's first impressions of the future, we must now analyse his revised vision as dictated by the new circumstances which challenge his applied Fabianism. In chapter five, the Time Traveller makes the fundamental discovery of the book. After encountering a Morlock and pondering over its significance, he declares:

gradually, the truth dawned on me: that man had not remained one species, but had differentiated into two distinct animals: that my graceful children of the Upperworld were not the sole descendants of our generation, but that this bleached, obscene, nocturnal Thing, which had flashed before me, was also heir to all ages.

(*TM*, 251)

With this discovery, the Time Traveller's Utopian image of the future crashes down before him. He ponders thus:

What, I wondered, was this Lemur doing in my scheme of a perfectly balanced organization? How was it related to the indolent serenity of the beautiful Upperworlders?

(*TM*, 252)

Having questioned the future in this way, a void exists in the Time Traveller's reasoning. But once he has discovered the Morlocks' subterranean habitation, which drives him to his logical conclusion:

What so natural, then, as to assume that it was in this artificial Underworld that such work as was necessary to the comfort of the daylight race was done?

(*TM*, 253)

With this discovery, the realisation of a class-divided inheritor-society occurs to the Time Traveller. By considering late-Victorian Britain, he deduces continued Capitalist divergence between the classes. The working class situation grew thus:

Proceeding from the problems of our own age, it seemed clear as daylight to me that the gradual widening of the present merely temporary and social difference between the Capitalist and the Labourer, was the key to the whole position . . . Even now there are existing circumstances to point that way. There is a tendency to utilize underground space for the less ornamental purposes of civilization; . . . there are underground workrooms and restaurants, and they increase and multiply. Evidently, I thought, this tendency had increased till industry had gradually lost its birthright in the sky. I mean that it had gone deeper and deeper into larger and even larger underground factories, spending a still increasing amount of its time therein . . . Even now, does not an East-end worker live in such artificial conditions as practically to be cut off from the natural surface of the earth?

(*TM*, 253)

The Time Traveller describes the ruling class evolution thus:

The exclusive tendency of richer people—due, no doubt, to the increasing refinement of their education, and the widening gulf between them and the rude violence of the poor—is already leading to the closing, in their interest, of considerable portions of the surface of the land . . . And this same widening gulf—which is due to the length and expense of the higher educational process and the increased facilities for and temptations towards refined habits on the part of the rich—will make that exchange between class and class, that promotion by intermarriage which at present retards the splitting of our species along lines of social stratification, less and less frequent.

(*TM*, 254)

Having determined the Victorian seeds of futurity's evils, he defines the end product of Victorian exploitative Capitalism in the following terms:

So in the end you must have the Haves, pursuing pleasure and comfort and beauty, and below-ground the Have-nots, the workers getting continually adapted to the conditions of their labour. Once they were there, they would no doubt have to pay rent, and not a little of it, for the ventilation of their caverns; and if they refused, they would starve or be suffocated for their arrears. Such of them as were so constituted as to be miserable and rebellious would die, and, in the end, the balance being permanent, the survivors would become as well adapted to the conditions of underground life, and as happy in their way, as the Upper-world people were to theirs.

(*TM,* 254)

The quotation of these lengthy passages has been necessary to make clear Wells's main argument of the book. The underground drudgery of the Morlocks and the relative luxury of the upper-world Eloi is a result of the continuation of late-Victorian Capitalism. The Capitalists' ownership of the land has driven the workers below ground and exploited their labour through the threat of suffocation and starvation. Throughout the rest of the book there is no evidence to suggest that this Capitalist evolution, as assumed by the Time Traveller, was wrong. The means by which class-division has continued is undeniably through the exploitation as described by the Time Traveller. However, Capitalist greed and individualism do not carry the day and the world of 802,701 has a curious twist in its tail, as the Time Traveller explains in the next section of the book.

The Time Traveller finally discovers the truth about the social order of 802,701 in chapter seven. He realises that:

the Upper-world people might once have been the favoured aristocracy, and the Morlocks their mechanical servants; but that had long since passed away.

(*TM,* 263)

The Time Traveller theorises that, although the Eloi may once have dominated the Morlocks, the old adage that 'necessity is the mother of invention' still applies and, as the Time Traveller explains:

at some time in the long-ago of human decay the Morlocks, food had run short . . . Even now man is far less discriminating and exclusive in his food than he was . . . His prejudice against human flesh is no deep-seated instinct . . . These Eloi were mere fatted cattle which the ant-like Morlocks preserved and preyed upon—probably saw to the breeding of.

(*TM,* 269)

Thus, from a position of advantage and privilege, the Capitalist descendants, the Eloi, have degenerated, through their mood of complacency, and the struggling masses, the Morlocks, asserted their power and reversed the status quo of late-Victorian society. Or, as the Time Traveller puts it, society has "committed suicide" (*TM,* 286). The way in which the Morlocks asserted their power was explained thus by the Time Traveller:

As I see it, the Upper-world man had drifted towards this feeble prettiness, and the Under-world to mere mechanical industry . . . The Underworld being in contact with machinery, which, however perfect, still needs some little thought outside habit, had probably retained perforce rather more initiative, and when other meat failed them, they turned to what old habit had hitherto forbidden.

(*TM,* 287)

So, from late-Victorian Capitalism the world has continued, making no efforts to level out the disproportionate spread of wealth. Capitalism was perpetuated by the ruling class and the exploited masses were left to live in conditions of poverty. This exploitative progression continued, it seems, for many thousands of years. Eventually however, the ruling class, or Eloi, lost all ability to manage the world due to the perfect nature of their exploitation. The Morlocks became unable to throw off their yoke and eventually came to accept the divisions of society. As the year 802,701 shows, that division developed to such an extent that humanity came to resemble two different species. However, Wells reveals that the exploitation of the Morlocks by the Eloi was doomed to fail. The repressive nature of the Eloi developed to such an extent that the Morlocks could not even maintain the basic lifestyle they came to know. Starvation occurred hand in hand with the Morlocks' development of oxygenation of their subterranean habitats. Once the Morlocks released themselves from dependence on the Eloi for oxygen they became, in effect, the ruling class. For the clothing and food which the Eloi drove the Morlocks to produce thus ceased to be obtainable under exploitative conditions. Although the Morlocks could not return to living on the earth's surface, they could turn the tables on the Eloi and in turn become exploiters. Michael Coren supports this point when he writes:

the [Morlock], forced to toil beneath the surface like its proletarian ancestors, has reversed the class equation and feeds on the flesh of the effete surface-dwellers.[5]

Hence the Morlocks became farmers of the Eloi and used their upperworld cousins as a readily-available food supply. It is this situation that the Time Traveller discovers. The point thus to be deduced from the story is that the working class is the inevitable inheritor of worldly power. Under Capitalism, the gruesome expropriation of the ruling class will occur as the Time Traveller describes. The working class's inevitable rise under a Capitalist system, however, does not herald the end of the need for a Socialist struggle. This is made evident by the last section of the book, where the Time Traveller travels on to the dusk of life on earth. By depicting the end of the world as being empty of human life, Wells is demonstrating the ultimate failings of a Capitalist society. Within a Capitalist society there is, by definition, a struggle between the Haves and the Have-nots. In a situation where that struggle is perpetuated by the maintenance of an exploitative society, only immediate class interests are protected and not long-term human stability. Hence, in *The Time Machine,* class struggle, through the continuation of a Capitalist system, has provoked the short-term exploitation of one class by another and not the long-term guarantee of human and earthly protection. In the book, human extinction is inevitable because an exploitative society is maintained. Michael Sherborne is therefore wrong when he writes that:

> the new world . . . is a savage mockery of the ill-conceived promises of Marxism.[6]

Rather, the vision of the year 802,701 highlights the need for Marx's proletarian revolution and reveals the inherent flaw in Fabian Socialism. This is where the attractions of revolutionary Socialism covertly enter the story. Although not verbalised by the Time Traveller, the inference from the book is that while Capitalism can only lead to human disintegration, true Socialism (i.e., a world devoid of class, racial or gender inequality and conflict) will lead to long-term comfort instead of short-term antagonism. With long-term planning, the end of the world can be anticipated and action to prevent human extinction can be taken. Although the Time Traveller reveals to his guests that the world is doomed if it follows its present course, there is nothing in the book to suggest that the future is fixed and unalterable. Indeed, Wells was later to write that:

> if the world does not please you, you can change it . . . You may change it into something sinister and angry, to something appalling, but it may be that you will change it to something brighter, something more agreeable.[7]

The belief in a Socialist solution to societal degeneration is inferred and therefore given hope by one character at one time in the book. That character is the Narrator and the time when he offers humanity hope is in the epilogue. The passage reads thus:

> [The Time Traveller] thought but cheerlessly of the advancement of mankind, and saw in the growing pile of civilization only a foolish heaping that must inevitably fall back upon and destroy its makers in the end. If that is so, it remains for us to live as if it were not so.
>
> (*TM*, 303)

"It remains for us to live as if it were not so." It is with these words that Wells transforms the novel from one of uncompromising pessimism to a symbol of hope for the future. The book represents a warning to humanity, not a definite vision of things to come. This, we believe, is where Patrick Parrinder errs when he writes:

> The Time Machine is an attack on Utopia.[8]

The book is actually, in the words of Brian Murray:

> the first in a long line of Wellsian attacks on the kind of crude industrial capitalism he watched operate in the closing decades of the nineteenth century,[9]

and shows a vision of how things could go. This interpretation was supported by Wells himself when he declared that the book was about:

the responsibility of men to mankind. Unless humanity hangs together, unless all strive for the species as a whole, we shall end in disaster.[10]

Finally, we could draw an interesting parallel with a novel reflecting a similar hope. In the latter stages of Charles Dickens's "A Christmas Carol", Ebenezer Scrooge is taken to a graveyard by the Ghost of Christmas yet to Come and is directed towards an untended grave. The passage reads as follows: 'Before I draw nearer to that stone to which you point,' said Scrooge, 'answer me one question. Are these the shadows of things that Will be, or are they shadows of things that May be, only?'

> Still the Ghost pointed downward to the grave by which it stood.
>
> 'Men's courses will foreshadow certain ends, to which, if persevered in, they must lead,' said Scrooge. 'But if the courses be departed from, the ends will change. Say it is thus with what you show me!'
>
> The Spirit was immovable as ever.
>
> Scrooge crept towards it, trembling as he went; and following the finger, read upon the stone of the neglected grave his own name, EBENEZER SCROOGE . . .
>
> 'No, Spirit! Oh, no, no.'
>
> The finger still was there.
>
> 'Spirit!' he cried, tight clutching at its robe, 'hear me! I am not the man I was. I will not be the man I must have been but for this intercourse. Why show me this, if I am past all hope!'
>
> For the first time the hand appeared to shake.
>
> 'Good Spirit,' he pursued, as down upon the ground he fell before it: 'Your nature intercedes for me, and pities me. Assure me that I yet may change these shadows you have shown me, by an altered life!'
>
> The kind hand trembled.
>
> '. . . I will not shut out the lessons that they teach. Oh, tell me I may sponge away the writing on this stone!'[11]

The message in this passage can easily translate into that conveyed in *The Time Machine*. The figure of Scrooge can symbolise late-Victorian Capitalism; the grave, future society; the Ghost of Christmas yet to Come, the Time Machine. Scrooge asks:

> Why show me this, if I am past all hope!
>
> (*CT,* 67)

The same question could be put to Wells regarding the future. Why did Wells show us his bleak picture of the future if it cannot be altered? Wells did believe that the shadows of the future revealed in *The Time Machine* may be altered by a change in social relationships. That change is offered by Socialism and it is Socialism that

Wells intended to propagate—by highlighting the degenerative effect of late-Victorian Capitalism. What Dickens expressed regarding the individual, Wells expressed about society: with the necessary willpower, change can occur. This is what the Narrator, at the end of *The Time Machine,* means when he says, regarding the Time Traveller's pessimistic prophecy:

> it remains for us to live as if it were not so.

The attitude of the Narrator is the attitude of Wells and the idea that society can be changed is the cornerstone message of the book.

Although things have changed between 1895 and today, the basic ruling principles of society are the same. Injustice and inequality remain. Racism and international exploitation as well as class division exist today as strongly, if not more so, than 100 years ago. Since *The Time Machine* was published, humanity has lost 100 years and the Socialist societal reconstruction of the world still remains as a job undone. The warnings of *The Time Machine* can aid us in the battle to fight injustice and we believe it was this message that H. G. Wells had in mind when he wrote this novel.

Notes

1. H. G. Wells, *The Invisible Man, The Secret Places of the Heart and God the Invisible King* (London: Odhams Press, Undated), 79.

2. H. G. Wells, *The Wheels of Chance & The Time Machine* (London: Dent 1935), 201.

3. A. Bennett quoted in Harris Wilson (ed.), *Arnold Bennett & H. G. Wells: A Record of a Personal and a Literary Friendship* (London: Rupert Hart-Davis, 1960), 274.

4. H. G. Wells, *The Outline of History, Volume II* (London: Cassell, 1925), 725.

5. Michael Coren, *The Invisible Man: The Life and Liberties of H. G. Wells* (London: Bloomsbury, 1993), 50.

6. Michael Draper, H. G. Wells (London: MacMillan, 1987), 38.

7. H. G. Wells, *The History of Mr. Polly* (London: Longmans, 1965), 184.

8. Patrick Parrinder (ed.,) *The Wellsian,* (N° 4). P. Parrinder "H. G. Wells's Journey Through Death", 1981, 19.

9. Brian Murray, *H. G. Wells* (London: Continuum, 1990), 90.

10. H. G. Wells quoted in David Smith: *H. G. Wells: Desperately Mortal* (Yale, 1986), 49.

11. Charles Dickens, *Christmas Tales* (London: Michael O'Mara Books, 1990), 67.

Jan Hollin (essay date 1999)

SOURCE: Hollin, Jan. "*The Time Machine* and the Ecotopian Tradition." *Wellsian* 22 (1999): 47-54.

[*In the following essay, Hollin discusses* The Time Machine *as an ecotopian novel.*]

In the following I should like to investigate the relationship between H. G. Wells's *The Time Machine* and utopian romances and utopian novels that envision an ecologically sound society and could thus be called ecotopian. I hope to demonstrate that *The Time Machine* is inter-linked with this literary genre because Wells addresses problems that lie at the very centre of the ecotopian discourse.

I would like to start by explaining what I mean by ecotopian writing because "ecotopian" is certainly not a widely used and well-established term. According to Krishan Kumar, William Morris's *News from Nowhere* (1890) can be considered as the "prototype" of ecotopian literature.[1] Contrary to technocratic anthropocentric attempts at subduing nature, Morris and his successors expressed reverence for the beauty of nature and showed the dependence of the individual on it as a source of physical regeneration and mental inspiration.

The term "ecotopian" is derived from the novels *Ecotopia* (1975) and *Ecotopia Emerging* (1981) by the American writer Ernest Callenbach. The societies described in ecotopian writing oscillate between two poles. On the one side, unrealistically harmonious human communities have transformed the earth into a paradisaic garden. On the other side, subsistent agrarian societies, which are more or less post-industrial, attempt to use only renewable resources. As far as the form is concerned, the ecotopian genre can be seen as an amalgamation of different genre influences that all meet in the author's attempt to create the vision of an ecologically sound society. Such a mixture can already be seen in *News from Nowhere* as is indicated in the subtitle in which William Morris calls his book a utopian romance.

In 1907, Robert Blatchford published *The Sorcery Shop,* which can be seen as a follow-up ecotopian romance to *News from Nowhere.* Robert Graves' *Seven Days in New Crete* (1949) and Aldous Huxley's last novel, *Island* (1962), could be seen as further English examples of the ecotopian genre. Furthermore, Charlotte Perkins Gilman's *Herland* (1915), Austin Wright's *Islandia* (1942 posthumously), Marge Piercy's *Woman on the Edge of Time* (1976) and Kim Stanley Robinson's *Pacific Edge* (1988) could be understood as American representatives of the ecotopian tradition.

These works of fiction share three characteristics which represent the central classifying elements of the ecotopian literary genre. First of all, ecotopias can be understood as counter-utopias to technocratic utopias that try to solve the problems of human society through technological progress and administrative improvement. Morris's *News from Nowhere,* for example, was written as a personal response after reading Bellamy's *Looking Backward.* Linked to this concept of an intertextual motivation is the second element that all ecotopian writing shares. It can be seen as an attempt to overcome the modern but also the postmodern feeling of having reached a *cul-de-sac* in human society. William Morris explained his reason for struggling to turn Nowhere into reality with a statement which may stand as the ecotopian motto: "So there I was in for a fine pessimistic end of life, if it had not somehow dawned on me that amidst all this filth of civilization the seeds of a great change, what we others call Social-Revolution, were beginning to germinate."[2]

Thirdly, I would see ecotopian romances and novels as a romanticizing of the utopian novel because nature and love build the very core of the ecotopian vision. In addition to this, counter-cultural notions of the Romantic Movement bear particular importance in the ecotopian vision of a better world. Shelley's propagation of vegetarianism and De Quincey's description of mind-expanding drugs, for instance, find their counterpart in ecotopian writing. Whereas traditionally utopian novels concentrate on the best way of adapting nature to human demands, ecotopian endeavours try to overcome such an anthropocentric approach and try to find a non-domineering position for humanity in the great chain-of-being. Since Thomas More's *Utopia* love has played a relatively unimportant role in the utopian discourse. Contrary to this, love stands at the centre of ecotopia. Love is seen as the very life force that makes life worth living and humanity's journey through the ages worth undertaking.

Contrary to pastoral and Arcadian literary forms, ecotopian writing does not delete industrialization and its effects from its fictitious macrocosm in an escapist way but aims at representing—more or less—realistic ways of transforming the world. Literary vraisemblance is the foundation of the ecotopian vision. This explains why the ecotopian aeon is designed as a catalogue of proposals open for discussion by the readers rather than as an eschatological prophecy of a Golden Age.[3] Ecotopian novels could thus be seen as a constructive answer to Karl Popper's criticism of utopian blueprints.

Following a central insight of ecology, ecotopian writing assumes growth and decay as the central processes of life on earth and thus overcomes the conceptual limitations of the western progressive paradigm in which the traditional utopian novel is rooted. Particularly after the Second World War, ecotopian writing seems to have followed the guideline which H. G. Wells set up for utopias after Charles Darwin: "the Modern Utopia must not be static but kinetic."[4] This might explain why, with the exception of feminist utopias, ecological utopias are the only literary utopias that have survived the rise of dystopian and the decline of eutopian literature after the Second World War.

To what extent is this ecotopian genre relevant for reading H. G. Wells's *The Time Machine*? First of all the prototype of the ecotopian genre, *News from Nowhere,* seems to be of particular importance because it represents a major influence on *The Time Machine.* Wells himself tells us in his *Experiment in Autobiography* that for him as a student Morris was one of the most impressive intellectual figures of the day:

> Socialism was then a splendid new-born hope . . . Wearing our red ties to give zest to our frayed and shabby costumes we went great distances through the gas-lit winter streets of London and by the sulphureous Underground Railway, to hear and criticize and cheer and believe in William Morris, Bernard Shaw, Hubert Bland, Graham Wallas and all the rest of them, who were to lead us to that millennial world.[5]

Even in his preface to *A Modern Utopia* in 1905, Wells points out that it would be wonderful if we could follow Morris to his Nowhere. But at the same time Wells emphasizes that he finds Morris's utopian design utterly unrealistic.[6]

Morris's vision of a better world, *News from Nowhere,* was first published in *The Commonweal,* the weekly paper of the Socialist League, in 39 instalments from January to October 1890 and came out in book form a year later. *News from Nowhere* was a major literary success and influenced *The Time Machine* in manifold ways. For Patrick Parrinder, Morrisian influence can be detected mainly in the setting of *The Time Machine*:

> Morris's pastoral, idyllic society is centred on Hammersmith, while the society of the Eloi is centred on Richmond; both are placed in a verdant parkland by the River Thames. Morris's narrator learns the history of his society by visiting the British Museum, while the Time Traveller journeys to the Palace of Green Porcelain, an abandoned science museum near Banstead. [. . .] On the evening of his first day with the Eloi the Time Traveller climbs to a hilltop, surveys the view and exclaims "Communism!" to himself: the Communism referred to must be the pastoral utopia of Morris and More, rather than the revolutionary industrial society of Marx and Engels.[7]

The thoughts of the Time Traveller when arriving in the future and his interpretation of the situation of the English future make one think that the Time Traveller had finished reading *News from Nowhere* just shortly before embarking on his journey through the ages. In a sense, the Time Traveller seems to have arrived in a post-Nowherian England. Right after stopping in the year 802,701 the Time Traveller is overwhelmed by the impression that England has been transformed into a garden with beautiful, delicate inhabitants. The warm climate that the traveller experiences recalls the romance-like Mediterranean weather of Nowhere. The disappearance of houses and cottages and the demeanour of the inhabitants give the Time Traveller the opinion that he has entered a communist age.

Almost immediately after arriving, this positive impression is mixed with negative sensation. The people of the future seem to have lost the interest characteristic of *Homo sapiens.* Whereas William Guest arrived in an England where the filthy capitalist past is still a living memory among older Nowherians, Wells's Time Traveller arrives, it seems, at a post-Nowherian England where innumerable generations of living the good life in an English paradise have transformed the English into an infantile lot with almost animal-like stupidity. Experiencing this change turns the Victorian visitor into a cultural pessimist who laments the decline of civilization: "This has ever been the fate of energy in security; it takes to art and to eroticism, and then come languor and decay."[8]

While the Time Traveller is still debating in interior monologues whether living in paradise is such a desirable lot for the human race, traces of the Morlocks and their actions are starting to deconstruct his first reading of the culture that he has entered through time travel. In this sense, it can be said that Wells's description of the Eloi mirrors Morris's merry Nowherians of the future, but by adding the cannibalistic Morlocks to the picture Wells satirizes Morris's idyllic vision of a peaceful post-industrial England of the future in a sarcastic way.—Actually, I think that 'sarcastic' is a very appropriate adjective in this context if you think about the etymology of the word.

The Time Machine can thus be read as H. G. Wells's attempt at pointing out the unrealistic parts in William Morris's utopian design: a Nowherian paradise on earth is not possible. For the Time Traveller it seems debatable whether such a society without toil and pain but also without challenges is at all desirable. In a sense the Time Traveller can be seen as a person taking up the line of argument that the old grumbler in *News from Nowhere* follows. The major part of *News from Nowhere* is a panegyric on the new utopian world; the old way of life is harshly criticized. It is only in the last third of the romance that we are confronted with a figure who is discontented with life in Nowhere: Ellen's grandfather, who belongs to the group of those grumbling about the new society. He is bored by the epoch of rest that he has to live in. He finds this earthly paradise without competition dull: "I think one may do

more with one's life than sitting on a damp cloud and singing hymns."[9] The praiser of past times believes that Guest's age, full of struggle, was much more exciting and tells the visitor, "you are brisker and more alive, because you have not wholly got rid of competition."[10]

In *The Sorcery Shop* Robert Blatchford follows Morris's utopian vision uncritically and restricts himself to adding decorous details like avid propagation for vegetarianism to the ecotopian picture. This might explain why Laurence Thompson comments about *The Sorcery Shop* in his biography of Robert Blatchford: "It is the dying voice of William Morris in a world thrilling to the new voice of H. G. Wells."[11] It seems though as if Robert Blatchford had sensed the epigonal anachronism that underlies his utopian romance and tried to update his vision of a better society by evoking the name of his famous contemporary: Nathaniel Fry, the wizard who in *The Sorcery Shop* acts as a cicerone to the ecotopian Manchester of the future, introduces himself as an artist who works for the company Wells and Wells.[12]

In contrast to Blatchford, later ecotopian writing takes up Wells's criticism of Morris. In *Seven Days in New Crete* Robert Graves demonstrates, just like H. G. Wells in ***The Time Machine,*** the possible danger of stagnation that an ecotopian society has to face. Furthermore, Graves illustrates why a fully harmonious society, a paradise, is not possible on earth. To quote the argument of the Old Raja in Aldous Huxley's ecotopian novel *Island*:

> One third, more or less, of all the sorrow [. . .] is unavoidable. It is the sorrow inherent in the human condition, the price we must pay for being sentient and self-conscious organisms, aspirants to liberation, but subject to the laws of nature and under orders to keep on marching, through irreversible time, through a world wholly indifferent to our well-being, towards decrepitude and the certainty of death.[13]

The same kind of anti-Morrisian realism is characteristic of the experience of the Time Traveller. The insight he gains through time travel goes beyond the knowledge that death is certain for everybody. He has experienced the end not only of mankind but also of life on earth. The Time Traveller is too puzzled and too overwhelmed by his experience to ponder how one should deal with the insight that all human endeavours seem so futile and vain in the end. He is so fascinated by his experience, in a sense, so addicted to time travel that he leaves the Victorian age after collecting a few items that he hopes to find helpful on his journey. This explains why writing down the story remains as a task for the narrator and not for the Time Traveller. It is also the narrator who tries to assess what has happened by adding an epilogue to the account of the Time Traveller. The tale of the future has somewhat sobered the narrator from utopian optimism but the flowers that Weena gave to the Time Traveller remain as symbols of the ec-otopian credo of love. These flowers, to quote from the interpretation by the narrator, "witness that even when mind and strength had gone, gratitude and a mutual tenderness still lived on in the heart of man."[14]

Notes

1. Cf. Krishan Kumar, *Utopianism* (Milton Keynes: Open University Press, 1991), p. 103: "Ernest Callenbach's *Ecotopia* (1975) appears to have named the form; but, as with the feminist utopia, the essence of the ecological utopia was presented much earlier, in William Morris's *News from Nowhere* (1890)."

2. William Morris, "How I became a Socialist", *Political Writings of William Morris,* ed. A. L. Morton (London: Lawrence and Wishart, 1973), p. 245.

3. Cf. For instance Ernest Callenbach, *Ecotopia: The Notebooks and Reports of William Weston* (Berkeley: Banyan Tree Books, 1975), p. 135: ". . . but evidently the Ecotopian revolution, whatever else it may have accomplished, has not touched the basic miseries of the human condition." And p. 144: "Still, it is doubtful if Ecotopians are happier than Americans. It seems likely that difference ways of life involve losses that balance the gains, and gains that balance the losses. Perhaps it is only that Ecotopians are happy, and miserable, in different ways from ourselves."

4. H. G. Wells, *A Modern Utopia* (Lincoln: University of Nebraska Press, 1967), p. 5. Cf. Also Bülent Somay, "Towards an Open-Ended Utopia", *Science-Fiction Studies* 11 (March 1984), pp. 25-38.

5. E. P. Thompson, *William Morris: Romantic to Revolutionary* (New York: Pantheon, 1976), pp. 552-3.

6. Wells, *A Modern Utopia,* p. 7: "Were we free to have our untrammel[l]ed desire, I suppose we should follow Morris to his Nowhere, we should change the nature of man and the nature of things together; we should make the whole race wise, tolerant, noble, perfect—wave our hands to a splendid anarchy, every man doing as it pleases him, and none pleased to do evil, in a world as good as its essential nature, as ripe and sunny, as the world before the Fall. But that golden age, that perfect world, comes out into the possibilities of space and time. In space and time the pervading Will to Live sustains for evermore a perpetuity of aggressions."

7. Patrick Parrinder, "*The Time Machine*: H. G. Wells's Journey through Death", *The Wellsian,* 4 (1981), p. 20. See also "*News from Nowhere, The Time Machine* and the Break-Up of Classical Realism", *Science-Fiction Studies,* 3.3 (1976), pp. 265-74, and Robert M. Philmus, "'A Story of Days to Come' and *News from Nowhere*: H. G. Wells as a Writer of Anti-Utopian Fiction", *English Literature in Transition,* 30.4 (1987), pp. 450-5.

8. H. G. Wells, *The Time Machine* (London: Dent, 1978), p. 38.

9. William Morris, *News from Nowhere,* ed. James Redmond (London: Routledge & Kegan Paul, 1970), p. 130.

10. Morris, *News from Nowhere,* p. 128. Cf. my article, "The Old Grumbler at Runnymede", *Journal of the William Morris Society,* 10.2 (Spring 1993), pp. 17-21.

11. Laurence Thompson, *Robert Blatchford: Portraits of an Englishman* (London: Victor Gollancz, 1951), p. 184.

12. Robert Blatchford, *The Sorcery Shop: An Impossible Romance* (London: The Clarion Press, 1907), pp. 5-6.

13. Aldous Huxley, *Island* (London: Grafton, 1976), p. 99.

14. Wells, *The Time Machine,* p. 105.

Martin T. Willis (essay date July 1999)

SOURCE: Willis, Martin T. "Edison as Time Traveler: H. G. Wells's Inspiration for his First Scientific Character." *Science Fiction Studies* 26, no. 2 (July 1999): 284-94.

[*In the following essay, Willis contends that Thomas Edison could be the inspiration for the character of the Time Traveler in* The Time Machine.]

Critics of H. G. Wells's **The Time Machine** have reached no conclusions about the character of, or inspiration for, the Time Traveler. Opinions differ greatly as to the personality of this central figure, with critics forming three distinct groups: those who see the Time Traveler as a poor example of the late Victorian scientist, those who view him as a scientific Everyman, and those who find him a reflection either of Wells himself or of some mythic precedent. Israel Zangwill, in a critique that appeared soon after the publication of the novel (1895), reflects the opinions of the first of these groups, arguing that the Time Traveler "behaves exactly like the hero of a commonplace sensational novel, with his frenzies of despair and his appeals to fate" (qtd. in Parrinder 40). A sizeable proportion of contemporary criticism agrees with this view. Robert J. Begiebing notes that Wells's hero is "a kind of Trickster figure, a seeming "'quack' and magician" (203) rather than a scientist; and John Batchelor defines the Time Traveler as "an ordinary, anonymous middle-class person" (9).

Obversely, Bernard Bergonzi—deservedly a well-regarded critic of Wells's work—suggests that the Time Traveler may at first appear as a sober bourgeois but remembers that "he is, after all, a late-Victorian scientist with a keen interest in technology" (55). John Huntington also places greater emphasis on the actions of the Time Traveler than on initial impressions, highlighting the club-making episode as indicative of an "ability to do more than serve machines the way the Morlocks do, but to improvise and invent" (40). Merritt Abrash obliquely lends his support to this critical position when he notes that "science is [the Time Traveler's] only topic of conversation" (5), while Brian Murray is outspoken in arguing that "*The Time Machine* features a central character, the 'Time Traveler,' who is not a ghoul; he is congenial, refined—precisely the sort of figure that Sir Richard Gregory had in mind when he praised Wells's ability to present "scientific workers" as "human beings" and not as the travesties in which they figure in novels and romances written without his intimate knowledge of them and their impulses" (Murray 88).

There remains a third view of the Time Traveler, however, one that seeks mythic or other models for this complex character. David Ketterer was the first critic to recognize the hero's mythological dimensions in *The Time Machine*: "It is tempting to identify him, by analogy at least, with H. G. Wells. However that may be, the analogue that Wells himself supplies is Oedipus" (340). Ketterer defends his interpretation by citing the similarities of the riddle, the image of the sphinx, the Time Traveler's limp, and the mythological allusions of the novel's conclusion. Begiebing likewise notes a mythical aspect to the central figure of Wells's novel, although he does not link the Time Traveler to a specific mythic or literary prototype. More generically, Begiebing believes that the Time Traveler "exhibits at least three characteristics of the primordial heroic figure" (202). Harry M. Geduld pursues Ketterer's suggestion that Wells himself can be found in the Time Traveler's character, suggesting that "a degree of self-idealization also seems evident in his depiction of the spare and solitary scientist of *The Time Machine*, but we must be extremely wary of any elaborate identification of the Time Traveler and H. G. Wells" (4). Brian Murray's criticism is more encompassing, agreeing with each of these critics in turn: "The Time Traveler stands for much that Wells would consistently praise: he is resourceful, intrepid, and intensely curious about the world he occupies; he is then linked to a long line of literary heroes, to Ulysses and Aeneas, bravely facing a series of hard tests and gaining wisdom as he goes" (89).

Disagreement among critics, then, is rife; and different interpretations of the Time Traveler may mark the work even of single commentators. There is consensus, however, on the protagonist of the short story that gave Wells the impetus for *The Time Machine*. Dr Nebogipfel, hero of **"The Chronic Argonauts,"** is commonly branded a poorly executed, quasi-magical figure whose necromantic leanings override and negate his scientific sensibilities and reduce the effectiveness of the story as a whole. As Bernard Bergonzi writes:

> Dr. Nebogipfel, though supposedly a scientist and F.R.S., is a strange character to have been produced by the keen young student who had studied under Huxley. In fact, he has very little to do with the atmosphere of progressive thinking and intellectual inquiry that had characterized the Royal College of Science in the eighties . . . and a great deal to do with a literary tradition exemplified by Mary Shelley's Frankenstein and Stevenson's Dr Jekyll. Stevenson's story had appeared in 1886, two years before Wells' romance. Nebogipfel is the scientist as magician or alchemist, rather than the sober investigator of the physical world, and substantially the same type is to recur in Wells' fiction as Dr Moreau, and Griffin, the Invisible Man. Nebogipfel, like Frankenstein, is of a solitary and secretive disposition. To this extent, too, he corresponds to the contemporary aesthetic ideal of the artist who must necessarily be isolated and suffering before he can create.
>
> (34-35)

Roslynn D. Haynes likewise views Dr Nebogipfel as a derivative of Mary Shelley's Frankenstein, physically as well as symbolically: "Dr Nebogipfel of **"The Chronic Argonauts"** seems at first to be merely an exaggerated alchemist figure, his face that of the sunken-eyed fanatic, his demeanour reminiscent of Frankenstein" (197). John Batchelor, too, emphasizes literary precedent when, in terminology similar to Haynes, he points out that "Dr. Nebogipfel seems part demon, part alchemist, an uneasily jocular descendant of Mary Shelley's Frankenstein and of Dr. Faustus" (9).

For the majority of critics, then, Nebogipfel and the Time Traveler have little in common as characters, despite the connection between **"The Chronic Argonauts"** and *The Time Machine*. Even critics who do not believe the Time Traveler is representative of the Victorian scientist still see a significant difference between the magician and trickster of the novel and the necromantic alchemist of the earlier story. The presumed disparity between the two protagonists is, however, illusory. Dr Nebogipfel and the Time Traveler—as well as the versions of these figures that appear in the interim Time Machine narratives—are far more closely connected than previous commentary has allowed. The continuity among the different protagonists is provided, I shall argue, by one historical figure: Thomas Edison. It was Edison who inspired H. G. Wells in creating the Time Traveler and all his prototypes.

While such a claim has not been made before with regard to Wells's writings, Edison did inspire other works of science fiction towards the end of the nineteenth century. The most important of these are Garrett Serviss's *Edison's Conquest of Mars* (1898), which can be categorized as a utopian version of Wells's own (largely dystopian) *The War of the Worlds* (1898), and Villiers de L'Isle-Adam's *L'Eve Future* (1886). The latter is the more interesting of the two for my purposes, for it characterizes Edison not only as a scientist and inventor but also as a figure of contemporary mythology, tied as closely to a necromantic as to a scientific tradition. The importance of this double image of Edison will be made clear as the present argument progresses. It is sufficient to highlight that writers of fiction were interested in Thomas Edison during the late 1800s, although Wells's own interest in Edison has not yet been remarked.

Towards the end of his career, Wells's knowledge of Edison is not in doubt. In *The Work, Wealth and Happiness of Mankind* (1932), Wells wrote enthusiastically of Edison's contribution to science and human endeavor generally, suggesting that "his was certainly the most ingenious mind that has ever devoted itself to the commercial application of science" (454). Furthermore, in a phrase that could as easily be applied to the Time Traveler as to the American inventor, Wells argues that Edison was "driven by an indefatigable curiosity" (455). While this late work is useful in highlighting Wells's appreciation of Edison's character and inventions, it does not, of course, go any way towards proving that the younger Wells—the Wells who wrote **"The Chronic Argonauts"** and *The Time Machine*—had any detailed knowledge of Edison's work or any intention of drawing on Edison in creating his fictional characters. For evidence of this, it is necessary to turn to Edison's career in the 1880s and 1890s and to what Wells may have known of it at that time.

During the years from 1888 to 1895—from Wells's first conception of *The Time Machine* and, logically, of the Time Traveler, to the published version of the novel[1]—Thomas Edison was at the peak of his career. In this seven-year span he recorded hundreds of patents, improved his revolutionary phonograph, and extended the use of electric lighting into the public sphere.[2] As Ronald W. Clark states in his biography of Edison, "between 1880 and 1890 Edison crossed that real but unidentifiable frontier which divides the famous from the celebrities" (149). The U.S. popular press had dubbed him the greatest living American and he was undoubtedly the world's best known living inventor. Edison recorded his first patent at twenty-one, earned and lost several fortunes during a long career, invented the first instruments to record and reproduce the human voice, brought electric light into homes world-wide, made the first piece of cinema complete with sound and movement, and continued to work at least a sixteen-hour day

almost to the point of his death in 1931 at the age of 84. During the late nineteenth century, he was viewed as the ultimate Victorian hero, displaying all the qualities so exalted at that time, as encapsulated by Thomas Hughes: "[Edison] was known to Americans and to the world as a plain-speaking man of inventive genius who, through self-education and discipline, applied his talents to the solution of practical problems of substance and intrinsic interest" (3).

Despite this aggrandizement, public perceptions of Edison were not entirely homogenous. While the general layman would certainly have respected Edison's scientific pragmatism, a segment of the population regarded him with some superstition. The rural community of Menlo Park, where Edison founded a laboratory, feared the scientific experiments taking place almost on their own doorstep. They called him "The Wizard of Menlo Park," a title that, fueled by the popular media, became synonymous with the practical inventor. The irony of these opposing perceptions of Edison is very clear: while the world heard of yet another empirical invention revealing sound common sense, they were also hearing that a wizard had been behind its construction.

In Britain, too, the popular press saw Edison as a mixture of scientist and magician. H. G. Wells would have been aware of this mixed persona, perpetuated in numerous articles, as *The Times* of 31 December 1878 testifies: "Mr Thomas Alva Edison's present sayings and doings are watched and noted with feverish anxiety both in the United States and in this country" (4). The same article, indeed, exhibits both the magical and scientific view of Edison, claiming at one point that "he is in the position of a skilful conjurer" (4) and at another that "he has a large factory and laboratory at Menlo Park . . . where many highly skilled artificers are employed in constructing elaborate machinery" (4).

H. G. Wells works different sides of this dual image of Edison throughout the long genesis of *The Time Machine*. The early short story **"The Chronic Argonauts"** plays heavily on "The Wizard of Menlo Park" persona. Dr. Nebogipfel inspires great interest in the small Welsh village of Llyddwdd when he arrives unannounced and immediately occupies the Old Manse. Curiosity very quickly becomes distrust, however, as Nebogipfel proves himself to be somewhat odd: "In almost every circumstance of life the observant villagers soon found his ways were not only not *their* ways, but altogether inexplicable upon any theory of motives they could conceive" (137). Edison inspired similar feelings when he arrived in the quiet Menlo Park area of New Jersey, as Ronald Clark has reported: "By the simple inhabitants of the region . . . he was regarded with a kind of uncanny fascination, somewhat similar to that inspired by Dr. Faustus of old, and no feat, however startling, would have been considered too great for his occult attainments" (73).

In short, Nebogipfel's arrival in a rural community, his construction of a laboratory for his work, and the reaction to this intrusion from the resident population parallels exactly Edison's move from his New York workshop to his Menlo Park research facilities in 1876. And one further aspect of Nebogipfel's transformation of the Old Manse even more firmly allies him with Edison. The narrative reveals how, late one evening,

> a strange whizzing, buzzing whirr filled the night air, and a bright flicker glanced across the dim path of the wayfarers. All eyes were turned in astonishment to the Old Manse. The house no longer loomed a black featureless block but was filled to overflowing with light. From the gaping holes in the roof, from chinks and fissures amid tiles and brickwork, from every gap which Nature or man had pierced in the crumbling old shell, a blinding blue-white glare was streaming, beside which the rising moon seemed a disc of opaque sulphur.
>
> (139)

The coming of electric light is viewed as a transcendental experience by the local inhabitants of Llyddwdd; Wells emphasizes their ignorance of scientific advancement.

The light bulbs sending their beams streaming from the windows of the Old Manse also, of course, highlight Wells's engagement with perhaps the best known of Thomas Edison's inventions, one heavily covered by both the popular and scientific press. As early as New Year's Day 1880, an article in *Nature* discussed Edison's electric lighting at Menlo Park and found it "bright, clear, mellow, regular, free from flickering or pulsations, while the observer gets more satisfaction from it than from gas" (215). Wells apparently suggests a connection between Nebogipfel's electric lighting and Edison's spectacle of electricity at Menlo Park.

Now Wells discarded the electric light episode in later versions of *The Time Machine*: the final published novel explicitly refers to the gas lighting in the Time Traveler's home. Such regression from a scientific advancement of the late nineteenth century to mid-Victorian technology appears, at first, incongruous: science fiction most often extrapolates on contemporary ingenuity, rather than looking back to the past. This would also seem to obscure any connection of Edison with the Time Traveler.

But I believe that the final omission of this scene fits into a pattern common to all Wells's science fiction. In his well known introduction to *Scientific Romances,* Wells states that his narrative practice is to "domesticate the impossible hypothesis" (viii) in order to make plausible that which seems fantastic. The failure of **"The Chronic Argonauts"** rests upon just this problem: Dr Nebogipfel is too easily seen as a necromantic figure rather than a "plausible" scientist. Wells's irony—

directed at the Welsh villagers—is not effective: in relying on the "Wizard of Menlo Park" component of Edison's myth in constructing Nebogipfel, that narrative becomes too overtly magical. In the versions of *The Time Machine* that were to follow **"The Chronic Argonauts"** (they were published in the *National Observer* and the *New Review,* respectively), Wells attempted to correct this bias, turning Nebogipfel into the Philosophical Inventor and discarding the Welsh village, the dark esotericism, and the electric light episode.

While Edison defined himself in phrasing similar to Wells's, suggesting in an interview that "I might be called a scientific inventor, as distinguished from a mechanical inventor" (Clark 67), the characteristics of the Philosophical Inventor in the *National Observer* and the *New Review* versions are at odds with the popular conceptions of Thomas Edison in the early 1890s. Indeed, the *New Review* version states that the Philosophical Inventor "was a mathematician of peculiar subtlety, and one of our most conspicuous investigators in molecular physics. . . . In the after-dinner hours he was ever a wide and variegated talker. . . . At these times he was as unlike the popular conception of a scientific investigator as a man could be" (175).

The discarding of the electrical light episode is a further example of the disguising of character that Wells attempts in his re-workings of the original tale. Although electricity itself has little connection with the necromancy that Dr. Nebogipfel epitomizes, the myth of the "wizard" Edison focused on his electrical experiments at Menlo Park. In the popular imagination, then, magic and the electrical light were, if not synonymous, at least well-linked. For this reason Wells's return to gas lighting in the final versions of his tale is no more than a further layer of domestication, a structuring of the commonplace and the traditional upon which the plausible foundations of his narrative are built. To have continued to emphasize electrical lighting—especially in the sensationalist manner of **"The Chronic Argonauts"**—would have been to upstage the most fantastic episodes of the narrative, which of course center on the time machine itself.

There do remain, regardless of Wells's alteration of the character of the Philosophical Inventor, echoes of Edison's myth both in the *National Observer* and the *New Review* versions. The protagonist in the *National Observer* version combines his professional and domestic affairs, with visitors appearing in his laboratory during the narrative—a domestic accommodation that parallels Edison's Menlo Park facilities. Although these characters are never named in the *National Observer* version, by the time of the *New Review* these visitors to the Philosophical Inventor's laboratory are given names: Blank, Dash and Chose. A ready comparison may be drawn here with Edison, who, inspired by his continued interest in telegraphy, nicknamed his first two children Dot and Dash.[3]

Other names in the *National Observer* version suggest further tenuous, though provocative, echoes of Edison's domestic life. In this version the Eloi woman Weena first appears, and her name remains unchanged in the final version of *The Time Machine.* Even granting the alteration in spelling, a parallel with Edison's own partner can be drawn. By the time of the writing of the *National Observer* narrative in the early 1890s, Edison had been married for several years to Mina, whose name is close to that of Wells's Eloi character both in linguistic form and pronunciation.

The clues from language do not end there. While revealing the model time machine to his collected guests, the German Officer—a character who does not survive Wells's later revisions—expresses his astonishment with the phrase "Gott in Himmel" (159)[4], a perfectly apt reaction to the spectacle he has just witnessed. This character and his German exclamation, however, also recall Edison's demonstration of the prototype phonograph. In the company of his assistant John Kreusi, Edison recited a nursery rhyme and then played back the phonograph recording. He, like the German Officer of Wells's tale, was astonished: "Kreusi, after hearing the phonograph reproduce Edison reciting 'Mary had a little lamb,' could only respond, 'Mein gott im Himmel' [sic]" (Hughes 12). Although the phrase itself is common, its appearance, in both cases, in connection with the demonstration of a previously unseen invention under very similar circumstances suggests more than coincidence.[5]

From **"The Chronic Argonauts"** to the *National Observer* through the *New Review,* the characterization of Wells's first scientific protagonist altered dramatically. These changes, however, had more to do with Wells's conception of the narrative as a plausible piece of scientific extrapolation than with the discarding of Edison after the first short story. Indeed, Thomas Edison remains integral to the construction of each central character. It remains vital, however, to see how far elements of Edison's myth can be traced in the character of the Time Traveler himself. For this the 1895 version of *The Time Machine*—the finished work in a sense[6]—must provide the basis for reference. And the close connections between Edison and Wells's protagonist are still evident throughout that final version.

While many of the critics I have discussed earlier view the Time Traveler as a theorist, for instance, it is clear that practical invention is just as strong an impulse. A dinner guest reveals that "our chairs, being his patents, embraced and caressed us rather than submitted to be sat upon" (3). The Time Traveler's impulse to build a

time machine rather than merely theorize over the scientific possibility of time travel surely marks him as working in the realm of the practical. Thomas Edison, similarly, decried the exclusively intellectual branches of scientific research that produce hypotheses and speculations but cannot apply them. Ronald Clark puts this succinctly in revealing that "preoccupation with development of a specific invention to meet a specific need was a feature of Edison's entire working life, and with it there went a contempt, barely concealed at times, for the man who dealt in theories rather than their practical application" (65). Furthermore, both Edison and the Time Traveler make practical provision for their "hands-on" philosophy. While Edison had a large-scale operation at Menlo Park, he also had a private workshop which, when he moved to West Orange later in his career, was connected to his own living quarters. Likewise the Time Traveler's laboratory, in which he builds his time machine, is at the rear of his suburban London house.

As for their actual working practices, parallels can again be found. Edison's methodology was "a curious combination of the personally intuitive and the strictly scientific" (Clark 71), a process of trial and error, of minor changes and alterations. The Time Traveler reveals a like-minded attitude in his examination of problems. During his sojourn in the future world of the Eloi and the Morlock, he puzzles for some time over the construction of the society of the year 802,701. Despite his limited knowledge, he immediately appraises the cultural situation: "'Communism,' said I to myself" (33). But later, the Time Traveler admits that his first theory was wholly wrong: "very simple was my explanation, and plausible enough—as most wrong theories are!" (38). Setbacks drive him to the discovery of new information, the continual evaluation of which brings him to his goal: a practical knowledge of the world of the far future.

Successful as the Time Traveler and Edison are in their trial and error approach to solving problems, it is undoubtedly a time-consuming and lengthy approach requiring much energy and dedication. Edison was renowned as an obsessive worker, spending days and nights in his workshops and catching only a few hours' sleep on his desktop when fatigued. He seemed incapable of relaxation when faced with a problem, preferring the frustration of repeated failure to giving up or retreating. The popular media were well aware of this trait in his character and Edison was cruelly lampooned by many humorous publications on the day of his first marriage, when a variety of cartoons depicted him in his laboratory in a frock-coat, holding aloft a light bulb while the wedding reception carried on the celebrations in the adjacent room. The Time Traveler, although never reaching this level of preoccupation, displays a similar restlessness and hatred of inactivity when confronted with a difficult problem. The clearest example of this occurs when he returns from a day-long expedition through his immediate surroundings to discover that the time machine is no longer parked on the grass in front of the statue of the white Sphinx. After recovering from his panic, and deducing that the time machine is now inside the Sphinx, the Time Traveler attempts vainly to break down the heavy doors that block his access to the interior. His strenuous actions produce no effect and "at last, hot and tired, I sat down to watch the place. But I was too restless to watch for long: I am too Occidental for a long vigil. I could work at a problem for years, but to wait inactive for twenty-four hours—that is another matter" (44). One need look no further than the mainstream Contemporary press to discover similar sentiments expressed about Edison himself. *The Times* reported during the 1870s that "having once undertaken to furnish a printing machine . . . [Edison] shut himself up in a room declaring he would remain there till he succeeded in getting the machine to his mind. He accomplished the task after 60 hours of continuous labour" (4).

Practicality and professional pragmatism are not the only qualities shared by the Time Traveler and Edison. Their ability to solve problems—particularly those that occur in the process of their own investigations—is accompanied by a flamboyance evident in both their personalities. The Time Traveler demonstrates this very early in the narrative when he provides his guests with the most eclectic of after-dinner entertainments—his model time machine:

> He [the Time Traveler] took one of the small octagonal tables that were scattered about the room, and set it in front of the fire, with two legs on the hearthrug. On this table he placed the mechanism. Then he drew up a chair, and sat down. The only other object on the table was a small shaded lamp, the bright light of which fell upon the model. There were also perhaps a dozen candles about, two in brass candlesticks upon the mantel and several in sconces, so that the room was brilliantly illuminated[. . .]. There was a minute's pause perhaps. The Psychologist seemed about to speak to me, but changed his mind. Then the Time Traveler put forward his finger towards the lever. "No," he said suddenly. "Lend me your hand." And turning to the Psychologist, he took that individual's hand in his own and told him to put out his forefinger. So that it was the Psychologist himself who sent forth the model Time Machine on its interminable voyage.
>
> (9-10)

The deference paid to the small model, the atmospheric illumination of the room, and the use of the Psychologist's finger all add to the theatrical spectacle the Time Traveler cleverly engineers. No mere presentation of fact or simple relation of events is good enough for the ingenious inventor to first reveal his remarkable discovery. Instead, he constructs a dramatic exhibition that has great impact upon the gathered witnesses.

This sense of showmanship was shared by Thomas Edison, who shrewdly realized that making an impression was often as important as providing a worthwhile invention. His demonstration of the electric lightbulb, first to a select group of important public figures and then to the general public, was just such a feat. As Thomas Hughes relates, "special trains from New York and elsewhere brought the prominent and the plain to view four houses illuminated, streets lit, and the laboratory glowing" (30). Equally spectacular was Edison's revelatory exhibition of the phonograph to reporters for *Scientific American*: he so excited and enthralled onlookers that "the editor had to stop the demonstration because the size of the crowd that had assembled threatened to collapse the office floor" (Hughes 13).

It can readily be seen, then, why interpretations of Wells's Time Traveler differ so markedly. A major influence on the character, Thomas Edison, was himself a man of paradox—utilitarian yet theatrical, necromantic yet scientific. In various versions of *The Time Machine,* Wells experimented with the different public personae of Edison: however unlikely it seems that any one figure could have influenced Dr Nebogipfel, the Philosophical Inventor, and the Time Traveler, these protagonists all share some aspect of the many-faceted personality and myth of Thomas Edison. In addition, details in the texts also locate roots of Wells's character in Edison's private world. A common thread can be seen to run from the early short story, **"The Chronic Argonauts,"** to the completed novel published in 1895. Nebogipfel explores the "Wizard of Menlo Park" side of the Edison myth, the Philosophical Inventor—although less explicitly representative—reveals some interesting biographical parallels, and the final protagonist, the Time Traveler, displays many of the characteristics of Edison as an indefatigable practical scientist.

In their roles as scientist and inventor, both Thomas Edison and the fully-fledged Time Traveler of the 1895 romance reveal marked similarities in technique, working practice, and personality. No longer should Wells's Time Traveler be seen as the cool scientific thinker, or a mythical hero in the epic mold, or an ordinary Victorian who is out of his depth in the world of the Eloi and Morlock. Rather he should be viewed as a subtle and complimentary portrait of the foremost scientist of the late nineteenth and early twentieth centuries, a man whose work offered as powerful a vision of the future as Wells's evocation of the year 802,701.

Notes

1. H. G. Wells began *The Time Machine* in 1888, with the short story "The Chronic Argonauts," published in the *Science Schools Journal* between April and June of that year. Further versions ap-

peared in the *National Observer* between March and June of 1894 and the *New Review,* which serialized the story from January to May 1895. The completed novel was first published in the United States in May 1895; this was closely followed by a more definitive edition published in Britain later that month. I recommend Harry M. Geduld's *The Definitive Time Machine,* which republishes "The Chronic Argonauts" and excerpts from the two later versions. This book was invaluable during my initial researches into the genesis of Wells's first scientific romance.

2. On the life and work of Thomas Edison, see in Works Cited the studies of Ronald W. Clark, Thomas P. Hughes, Nina Morgan, and Keith Ellis.

3. Ronald Clark makes note of this in his biography of Edison: "A daughter, named Marion [sic], was born the following year [1872]; four years later, a son christened Thomas and in 1879 a second son, William Leslie. Edison, still concentrating on the telegraph, nicknamed the first two children Dot and Dash" (32). I am unable to locate any publications contemporaneous with Wells's *Time Machine* narratives that tell this story and thereby prove that the nicknames were known to the wider public in the 1880s and 1890s.

4. This page reference refers to the reprinted version of the *National Observer* articles that can be found in Harry M. Geduld (154-174).

5. Although I find this parallel striking and undoubtedly suggestive I am unable, once again, to provide any evidence that the story of John Kreusi was told in contemporary publications. At the same time, it remains a piece of circumstantial evidence that is difficult to ignore.

6. This was the last major revision of *The Time Machine* story. All future alterations were minor.

Works Cited

Abrash, Merritt. "The Hubris of Science: Wells' Time Traveler." In *Patterns of the Fantastic II,* ed. Donald M. Hassler. Mercer Island, WA: Starmont, 1985. 5-11.

Anon. *Nature* 21 (Jan. 1, 1880): 215.

Anon. "Sketch of Edison." *Times* (Dec. 31, 1878): 4.

Batchelor, John. *H. G. Wells.* Cambridge: Cambridge UP, 1985.

Begiebing, Robert J. "The Mythic Hero in H. G. Wells's *The Time Machine.*" In *Essays in Literature* 11.2 (1984): 201-210.

Bergonzi, Bernard. *The Early H. G. Wells: A Study of the Scientific Romances.* Manchester: Manchester UP, 1961.

Clark, Ronald W. *Edison: The Man Who Made The Future.* London: Macdonald, 1977.

Ellis, Keith, *Thomas Edison: Genius of Electricity.* London: Priory, 1974.

Geduld, Harry M. *The Definitive Time Machine: A Critical Edition of H. G. Wells' Scientific Romance.* Bloomington: Indiana UP, 1987.

Haynes, Roslynn D., *H. G. Wells: Discoverer of the Future—The Influence of Science on His Thought.* London: Macmillan, 1980.

Hughes, Thomas P. *Thomas Edison: Professional Inventor.* London: HMSO, 1976.

Huntington, John. "The Science Fiction of H. G. Wells." In *Science Fiction: A Critical Guide,* ed. Patrick Parrinder. London: Longmans, 1979. 34-50.

Ketterer, David. "Oedipus as Time Traveler." *SFS* 9.3 (Nov. 1982): 340-341.

Morgan, Nina. *Thomas Edison.* Hove: Wayland, 1991.

Murray, Brian. *H. G. Wells.* New York: Continuum, 1990.

Wells, H. G. *The Scientific Romances.* London: Gollancz, 1933.

———. *The Work, Wealth and Happiness of Mankind.* London: Heinemann, 1932.

Zangwill, Israel. "Israel Zangwill on Time Travelling." In *H. G. Wells: The Critical Heritage.* Ed. Patrick Parrinder. London: Routledge, 1972. 40-42.

FURTHER READING

Criticism

Beaulieu, François O. "The Copy Texts of American Revised Editions of *The Time Machine.*" *The Wellsian* 22 (1999): 54-67.

    Traces the variations of the copy texts of the American revised editions of *The Time Machine.*

Berger, Roger A. "'Ask What You Can Do for Your Country': The Film Version of H. G. Wells's *The Time Machine* and The Cold War." *Literature Film Quarterly* 17, no. 3 (1989): 177-87.

    Contrasts the political themes of the book and cinematic versions of *The Time Machine.*

Bignell, Jonathan. "Another Time, Another Space: Modernity, Subjectivity, and *The Time Machine.*" *The Wellsian* 22 (1999): 34-47.

Reviews the cinematic adaptation of *The Time Machine.*

Derry, Stephen. "The Time Traveller's Utopian Books and His Reading of the Future." *Foundation,* no. 65 (1995): 16-24.

 Considers the impact of utopian literature on *The Time Machine.*

Mackerness, E. D. "Zola, Wells, and 'The Coming Beast'." *Science Fiction Studies* 8, no. 2 (July 1981): 143-48.

 Finds parallels between *The Time Machine* and the work of Emile Zola.

Person, James E., Jr. "A Timeless Science Fantasy Turns 100." *The Detroit News* (4 October 1995): 19A.

Reflects on Wells's life and work on the 100th anniversary of the publication of *The Time Machine.*

Suvin, Darko. "*The Time Machine* versus *Utopia* as a Structural Model for Science Fiction." *Comparative Literature Studies* 10 (1973): 334-52.

 Contends that *The Time Machine* and Thomas More's *Utopia* are "among the basic historical models for the structuring of subsequent science fiction."

Wasson, Richard. "Myth and the Ex-Nomination of Class in *The Time Machine.*" *The Minnesota Review* 15 (1980): 112-22.

 Maintains that *The Time Machine* "is a transitional work illustrating the displacement of the rhetoric of class in fiction."

Additional coverage of Wells's life and career is contained in the following sources published by the Gale Group: *Authors and Artists for Young Adults,* **Vol. 18;** *Beacham's Encyclopedia of Popular Fiction: Biography & Resources,* **Vol. 3;** *British Writers,* **Vol. 6;** *Children's Literature Review,* **Vol. 64;** *Concise Dictionary of British Literary Biography, 1914-1945;* *Contemporary Authors,* **Vols. 110, 121;** *Dictionary of Literary Biography,* **Vols. 34, 70, 156, 178;** *DISCovering Authors; DISCovering Authors: British Edition; Canadian Edition; DISCovering Authors Modules: Most-studied Authors* **and** *Novelists; DISCovering Authors 3.0; Exploring Short Stories; Literature and Its Times,* **Vol 3;** *Literature Resource Center; Major 20th-Century Writers,* **Eds. 1, 2;** *Reference Guide to English Literature,* **Ed. 2;** *Reference Guide to Short Fiction,* **Ed. 2;** *St. James Guide to Horror, Ghost & Gothic Writers; St. James Guide to Science Fiction Writers,* **Ed. 4;** *St. James Guide to Young Adult Writers; Science Fiction Writers; Short Stories for Students,* **Vol. 3;** *Short Story Criticism,* **Vol. 6;** *Something about the Author,* **Vol. 20;** *Supernatural Fiction Writers; Twayne's English Authors; Twentieth-Century Literary Criticism,* **Vols. 6, 12, 19;** *World Literature and Its Times,* **Vol. 4;** *World Literature Criticism;* **and** *Writers for Children.*

How to Use This Index

The main references

Calvino, Italo
    1923-1985 .... **CLC 5, 8, 11, 22, 33, 39,**
                  73; SSC 3, 48

list all author entries in the following Gale Literary Criticism series:

AAL = *Asian American Literature*
BLC = *Black Literature Criticism*
BLCS = *Black Literature Criticism Supplement*
CLC = *Contemporary Literary Criticism*
CLR = *Children's Literature Review*
CMLC = *Classical and Medieval Literature Criticism*
DC = *Drama Criticism*
HLC = *Hispanic Literature Criticism*
HLCS = *Hispanic Literature Criticism Supplement*
LC = *Literature Criticism from 1400 to 1800*
NCLC = *Nineteenth-Century Literature Criticism*
NNAL = *Native North American Literature*
PC = *Poetry Criticism*
SSC = *Short Story Criticism*
TCLC = *Twentieth-Century Literary Criticism*
WLC = *World Literature Criticism, 1500 to the Present*
WLCS = *World Literature Criticism Supplement*

The cross-references

See also CA 85-88, 116; CANR 23, 61;
DAM NOV; DLB 196; EW 13; MTCW 1, 2;
RGSF 2; RGWL 2; SFW 4; SSFS 12

list all author entries in the following Gale biographical and literary sources:

AAYA = *Authors & Artists for Young Adults*
AFAW = *African American Writers*
AFW = *African Writers*
AITN = *Authors in the News*
AMW = *American Writers*
AMWR = *American Writers Retrospective Supplement*
AMWS = *American Writers Supplement*
ANW = *American Nature Writers*
AW = *Ancient Writers*
BEST = *Bestsellers*
BPFB = *Beacham's Encyclopedia of Popular Fiction: Biography and Resources*
BRW = *British Writers*
BRWS = *British Writers Supplement*
BW = *Black Writers*
BYA = *Beacham's Guide to Literature for Young Adults*
CA = *Contemporary Authors*
CAAS = *Contemporary Authors Autobiography Series*
CABS = *Contemporary Authors Bibliographical Series*
CAD = *Contemporary American Dramatists*
CANR = *Contemporary Authors New Revision Series*
CAP = *Contemporary Authors Permanent Series*
CBD = *Contemporary British Dramatists*
CCA = *Contemporary Canadian Authors*
CD = *Contemporary Dramatists*
CDALB = *Concise Dictionary of American Literary Biography*
CDALBS = *Concise Dictionary of American Literary Biography Supplement*
CDBLB = *Concise Dictionary of British Literary Biography*
CMW = *St. James Guide to Crime & Mystery Writers*
CN = *Contemporary Novelists*

CP = Contemporary Poets
CPW = Contemporary Popular Writers
CSW = Contemporary Southern Writers
CWD = Contemporary Women Dramatists
CWP = Contemporary Women Poets
CWRI = St. James Guide to Children's Writers
CWW = Contemporary World Writers
DA = DISCovering Authors
DA3 = DISCovering Authors 3.0
DAB = DISCovering Authors: British Edition
DAC = DISCovering Authors: Canadian Edition
DAM = DISCovering Authors: Modules
   DRAM: Dramatists Module; **MST:** Most-studied Authors Module;
   MULT: Multicultural Authors Module; **NOV:** Novelists Module;
   POET: Poets Module; **POP:** Popular Fiction and Genre Authors Module
DFS = Drama for Students
DLB = Dictionary of Literary Biography
DLBD = Dictionary of Literary Biography Documentary Series
DLBY = Dictionary of Literary Biography Yearbook
DNFS = Literature of Developing Nations for Students
EFS = Epics for Students
EXPN = Exploring Novels
EXPP = Exploring Poetry
EXPS = Exploring Short Stories
EW = European Writers
FANT = St. James Guide to Fantasy Writers
FW = Feminist Writers
GFL = Guide to French Literature, Beginnings to 1789, 1798 to the Present
GLL = Gay and Lesbian Literature
HGG = St. James Guide to Horror, Ghost & Gothic Writers
HW = Hispanic Writers
IDFW = International Dictionary of Films and Filmmakers: Writers and Production Artists
IDTP = International Dictionary of Theatre: Playwrights
LAIT = Literature and Its Times
LAW = Latin American Writers
JRDA = Junior DISCovering Authors
MAICYA = Major Authors and Illustrators for Children and Young Adults
MAICYAS = Major Authors and Illustrators for Children and Young Adults Supplement
MAWW = Modern American Women Writers
MJW = Modern Japanese Writers
MTCW = Major 20th-Century Writers
NCFS = Nonfiction Classics for Students
NFS = Novels for Students
PAB = Poets: American and British
PFS = Poetry for Students
RGAL = Reference Guide to American Literature
RGEL = Reference Guide to English Literature
RGSF = Reference Guide to Short Fiction
RGWL = Reference Guide to World Literature
RHW = Twentieth-Century Romance and Historical Writers
SAAS = Something about the Author Autobiography Series
SATA = Something about the Author
SFW = St. James Guide to Science Fiction Writers
SSFS = Short Stories for Students
TCWW = Twentieth-Century Western Writers
WLIT = World Literature and Its Times
WP = World Poets
YABC = Yesterday's Authors of Books for Children
YAW = St. James Guide to Young Adult Writers

Literary Criticism Series
Cumulative Author Index

Anouilh, Jean (Marie Lucien Pierre) 1910-1987 . **CLC 1, 3, 8, 13, 40, 50; DC 8**
See also CA 123; 17-20R; CANR 32; DAM DRAM; DFS 9, 10; EW 13; EWL 3; GFL 1789 to the Present; MTCW 1, 2; RGWL 2, 3; TWA

Anthony, Florence
See Ai

Anthony, John
See Ciardi, John (Anthony)

Anthony, Peter
See Shaffer, Anthony (Joshua); Shaffer, Peter (Levin)

Anthony, Piers 1934- .... **CLC 35**
See also AAYA 11; BYA 7; CA 21-24R; CAAE 200; CANR 28, 56, 73, 102; CPW; DAM POP; DLB 8; FANT; MAICYA 2; MAICYAS 1; MTCW 1, 2; SAAS 22; SATA 84; SATA-Essay 129; SFW 4; SUFW 1, 2; YAW

Anthony, Susan B(rownell) 1820-1906 .... **TCLC 84**
See also FW

Antiphon c. 480B.C.-c. 411B.C. .... **CMLC 55**

Antoine, Marc
See Proust, (Valentin-Louis-George-Eugene-)Marcel

Antoninus, Brother
See Everson, William (Oliver)

Antonioni, Michelangelo 1912- .... **CLC 20, 144**
See also CA 73-76; CANR 45, 77

Antschel, Paul 1920-1970
See Celan, Paul
See also CA 85-88; CANR 33, 61; MTCW 1

Anwar, Chairil 1922-1949 .... **TCLC 22**
See Chairil Anwar
See also CA 121; RGWL 3

Anzaldua, Gloria (Evanjelina) 1942- .... **HLCS 1**
See also CA 175; CSW; CWP; DLB 122; FW; RGAL 4

Apess, William 1798-1839(?) .... **NCLC 73; NNAL**
See also DAM MULT; DLB 175, 243

Apollinaire, Guillaume 1880-1918 .... **PC 7; TCLC 3, 8, 51**
See Kostrowitzki, Wilhelm Apollinaris de
See also CA 152; DAM POET; DLB 258; EW 9; EWL 3; GFL 1789 to the Present; MTCW 1; RGWL 2, 3; TWA; WP

Apollonius of Rhodes
See Apollonius Rhodius
See also AW 1; RGWL 2, 3

Apollonius Rhodius c. 300B.C.-c. 220B.C. .... **CMLC 28**
See Apollonius of Rhodes
See also DLB 176

Appelfeld, Aharon 1932- ... **CLC 23, 47; SSC 42**
See also CA 133; 112; CANR 86; CWW 2; EWL 3; RGSF 2

Apple, Max (Isaac) 1941- .... **CLC 9, 33; SSC 50**
See also CA 81-84; CANR 19, 54; DLB 130

Appleman, Philip (Dean) 1926- .... **CLC 51**
See also CA 13-16R; CAAS 18; CANR 6, 29, 56

Appleton, Lawrence
See Lovecraft, H(oward) P(hillips)

Apteryx
See Eliot, T(homas) S(tearns)

Apuleius, (Lucius Madaurensis) 125(?)-175(?) .... **CMLC 1**
See also AW 2; CDWLB 1; DLB 211; RGWL 2, 3; SUFW

Aquin, Hubert 1929-1977 .... **CLC 15**
See also CA 105; DLB 53; EWL 3

Aquinas, Thomas 1224(?)-1274 ..... **CMLC 33**
See also DLB 115; EW 1; TWA

Aragon, Louis 1897-1982 .... **CLC 3, 22; TCLC 123**
See also CA 108; 69-72; CANR 28, 71; DAM NOV, POET; DLB 72, 258; EW 11; EWL 3; GFL 1789 to the Present; GLL 2; MTCW 1, 2; RGWL 2, 3

Arany, Janos 1817-1882 .... **NCLC 34**

Aranyos, Kakay 1847-1910
See Mikszath, Kalman

Arbuthnot, John 1667-1735 .... **LC 1**
See also DLB 101

Archer, Herbert Winslow
See Mencken, H(enry) L(ouis)

Archer, Jeffrey (Howard) 1940- .... **CLC 28**
See also AAYA 16; BEST 89:3; BPFB 1; CA 77-80; CANR 22, 52, 95; CPW; DA3; DAM POP; INT CANR-22

Archer, Jules 1915- .... **CLC 12**
See also CA 9-12R; CANR 6, 69; SAAS 5; SATA 4, 85

Archer, Lee
See Ellison, Harlan (Jay)

Archilochus c. 7th cent. B.C.- .... **CMLC 44**
See also DLB 176

Arden, John 1930- .... **CLC 6, 13, 15**
See also BRWS 2; CA 13-16R; CAAS 4; CANR 31, 65, 67; CBD; CD 5; DAM DRAM; DFS 9; DLB 13, 245; EWL 3; MTCW 1

Arenas, Reinaldo 1943-1990 .. **CLC 41; HLC 1**
See also CA 133; 128; 124; CANR 73, 106; DAM MULT; DLB 145; EWL 3; GLL 2; HW 1; LAW; LAWS 1; MTCW 1; RGSF 2; RGWL 3; WLIT 1

Arendt, Hannah 1906-1975 .... **CLC 66, 98**
See also CA 61-64; 17-20R; CANR 26, 60; DLB 242; MTCW 1, 2

Aretino, Pietro 1492-1556 .... **LC 12**
See also RGWL 2, 3

Arghezi, Tudor .... **CLC 80**
See Theodorescu, Ion N.
See also CA 167; CDWLB 4; DLB 220; EWL 3

Arguedas, Jose Maria 1911-1969 .... **CLC 10, 18; HLCS 1**
See also CA 89-92; CANR 73; DLB 113; EWL 3; HW 1; LAW; RGWL 2, 3; WLIT 1

Argueta, Manlio 1936- .... **CLC 31**
See also CA 131; CANR 73; CWW 2; DLB 145; EWL 3; HW 1; RGWL 3

Arias, Ron(ald Francis) 1941- .... **HLC 1**
See also CA 131; CANR 81; DAM MULT; DLB 82; HW 1, 2; MTCW 2

Ariosto, Ludovico 1474-1533 ... **LC 6, 87; PC 42**
See also EW 2; RGWL 2, 3

Aristides
See Epstein, Joseph

Aristophanes 450B.C.-385B.C. .... **CMLC 4, 51; DC 2; WLCS**
See also AW 1; CDWLB 1; DA; DA3; DAB; DAC; DAM DRAM, MST; DFS 10; DLB 176; RGWL 2, 3; TWA

Aristotle 384B.C.-322B.C. .... **CMLC 31; WLCS**
See also AW 1; CDWLB 1; DA; DA3; DAB; DAC; DAM MST; DLB 176; RGWL 2, 3; TWA

Arlt, Roberto (Godofredo Christophersen) 1900-1942 .... **HLC 1; TCLC 29**
See also CA 131; 123; CANR 67; DAM MULT; EWL 3; HW 1, 2; LAW

Armah, Ayi Kwei 1939- . **BLC 1; CLC 5, 33, 136**
See also AFW; BW 1; CA 61-64; CANR 21, 64; CDWLB 3; CN 7; DAM MULT, POET; DLB 117; EWL 3; MTCW 1; WLIT 2

Armatrading, Joan 1950- .... **CLC 17**
See also CA 186; 114

Armitage, Frank
See Carpenter, John (Howard)

Armstrong, Jeannette (C.) 1948- .... **NNAL**
See also CA 149; CCA 1; CN 7; DAC; SATA 102

Arnette, Robert
See Silverberg, Robert

Arnim, Achim von (Ludwig Joachim von Arnim) 1781-1831 ..... **NCLC 5; SSC 29**
See also DLB 90

Arnim, Bettina von 1785-1859 .... **NCLC 38**
See also DLB 90; RGWL 2, 3

Arnold, Matthew 1822-1888 ..... **NCLC 6, 29, 89; PC 5; WLC**
See also BRW 5; CDBLB 1832-1890; DA; DAB; DAC; DAM MST, POET; DLB 32, 57; EXPP; PAB; PFS 2; TEA; WP

Arnold, Thomas 1795-1842 .... **NCLC 18**
See also DLB 55

Arnow, Harriette (Louisa) Simpson 1908-1986 .... **CLC 2, 7, 18**
See also BPFB 1; CA 118; 9-12R; CANR 14; DLB 6; FW; MTCW 1, 2; RHW; SATA 42; SATA-Obit 47

Arouet, Francois-Marie
See Voltaire

Arp, Hans
See Arp, Jean

Arp, Jean 1887-1966 .... **CLC 5; TCLC 115**
See also CA 25-28R; 81-84; CANR 42, 77; EW 10

Arrabal
See Arrabal, Fernando

Arrabal, Fernando 1932- ... **CLC 2, 9, 18, 58**
See also CA 9-12R; CANR 15; EWL 3

Arreola, Juan Jose 1918-2001 .... **CLC 147; HLC 1; SSC 38**
See also CA 200; 131; 113; CANR 81; DAM MULT; DLB 113; DNFS 2; EWL 3; HW 1, 2; LAW; RGSF 2

Arrian c. 89(?)-c. 155(?) .... **CMLC 43**
See also DLB 176

Arrick, Fran .... **CLC 30**
See Gaberman, Judie Angell
See also BYA 6

Arriey, Richmond
See Delany, Samuel R(ay), Jr.

Artaud, Antonin (Marie Joseph) 1896-1948 .... **DC 14; TCLC 3, 36**
See also CA 149; 104; DA3; DAM DRAM; DLB 258; EW 11; EWL 3; GFL 1789 to the Present; MTCW 1; RGWL 2, 3

Arthur, Ruth M(abel) 1905-1979 ..... **CLC 12**
See also CA 85-88; 9-12R; CANR 4; CWRI 5; SATA 7, 26

Artsybashev, Mikhail (Petrovich) 1878-1927 .... **TCLC 31**
See also CA 170

Arundel, Honor (Morfydd) 1919-1973 .... **CLC 17**
See also CA 41-44R; 21-22; CAP 2; CLR 35; CWRI 5; SATA 4; SATA-Obit 24

Arzner, Dorothy 1900-1979 .... **CLC 98**

Asch, Sholem 1880-1957 .... **TCLC 3**
See also CA 105; EWL 3; GLL 2

Ash, Shalom
See Asch, Sholem

Ashbery, John (Lawrence) 1927- .. **CLC 2, 3, 4, 6, 9, 13, 15, 25, 41, 77, 125; PC 26**
See Berry, Jonas
See also AMWS 3; CA 5-8R; CANR 9, 37, 66, 102; CP 7; DA3; DAM POET; DLB 5, 165; DLBY 1981; EWL 3; INT CANR-9; MTCW 1, 2; PAB; PFS 11; RGAL 4; WP

Ashdown, Clifford
See Freeman, R(ichard) Austin

Ashe, Gordon
See Creasey, John

Ashton-Warner, Sylvia (Constance)
1908-1984 .... **CLC 19**
See also CA 112; 69-72; CANR 29; MTCW 1, 2

Asimov, Isaac 1920-1992 ..... **CLC 1, 3, 9, 19, 26, 76, 92**
See also AAYA 13; BEST 90:2; BPFB 1; BYA 4, 6, 7, 9; CA 137; 1-4R; CANR 2, 19, 36, 60; CLR 12, 79; CMW 4; CPW; DA3; DAM POP; DLB 8; DLBY 1992; INT CANR-19; JRDA; LAIT 5; MAICYA 1, 2; MTCW 1, 2; RGAL 4; SATA 1, 26, 74; SCFW 2; SFW 4; TUS; YAW

Askew, Anne 1521(?)-1546 .... **LC 81**
See also DLB 136

Assis, Joaquim Maria Machado de
See Machado de Assis, Joaquim Maria

Astell, Mary 1666-1731 .... **LC 68**
See also DLB 252; FW

Astley, Thea (Beatrice May) 1925- .. **CLC 41**
See also CA 65-68; CANR 11, 43, 78; CN 7; EWL 3

Astley, William 1855-1911
See Warung, Price

Aston, James
See White, T(erence) H(anbury)

Asturias, Miguel Angel 1899-1974 .... **CLC 3, 8, 13; HLC 1**
See also CA 49-52; 25-28; CANR 32; CAP 2; CDWLB 3; DA3; DAM MULT, NOV; DLB 113; EWL 3; HW 1; LAW; MTCW 1, 2; RGWL 2, 3; WLIT 1

Atares, Carlos Saura
See Saura (Atares), Carlos

Athanasius c. 295-c. 373 .... **CMLC 48**

Atheling, William
See Pound, Ezra (Weston Loomis)

Atheling, William, Jr.
See Blish, James (Benjamin)

Atherton, Gertrude (Franklin Horn)
1857-1948 .... **TCLC 2**
See also CA 155; 104; DLB 9, 78, 186; HGG; RGAL 4; SUFW 1; TCWW 2

Atherton, Lucius
See Masters, Edgar Lee

Atkins, Jack
See Harris, Mark

Atkinson, Kate 1951- .... **CLC 99**
See also CA 166; CANR 101; DLB 267

Attaway, William (Alexander)
1911-1986 .... **BLC 1; CLC 92**
See also BW 2, 3; CA 143; CANR 82; DAM MULT; DLB 76

Atticus
See Fleming, Ian (Lancaster); Wilson, (Thomas) Woodrow

Atwood, Margaret (Eleanor) 1939- ... **CLC 2, 3, 4, 8, 13, 15, 25, 44, 84, 135; PC 8; SSC 2, 46; WLC**
See also AAYA 12, 47; BEST 89:2; BPFB 1; CA 49-52; CANR 3, 24, 33, 59, 95; CN 7; CP 7; CPW; CWP; DA; DA3; DAB; DAC; DAM MST, NOV, POET; DLB 53, 251; EWL 3; EXPN; FW; INT CANR-24; LAIT 5; MTCW 1, 2; NFS 4, 12, 13, 14; PFS 7; RGSF 2; SATA 50; SSFS 3, 13; TWA; YAW

Aubigny, Pierre d'
See Mencken, H(enry) L(ouis)

Aubin, Penelope 1685-1731(?) .... **LC 9**
See also DLB 39

Auchincloss, Louis (Stanton) 1917- .. **CLC 4, 6, 9, 18, 45; SSC 22**
See also AMWS 4; CA 1-4R; CANR 6, 29, 55, 87; CN 7; DAM NOV; DLB 2, 244; DLBY 1980; EWL 3; INT CANR-29; MTCW 1; RGAL 4

Auden, W(ystan) H(ugh) 1907-1973 . **CLC 1, 2, 3, 4, 6, 9, 11, 14, 43, 123; PC 1; WLC**
See also AAYA 18; AMWS 2; BRW 7; BRWR 1; CA 45-48; 9-12R; CANR 5, 61, 105; CDBLB 1914-1945; DA; DA3; DAB; DAC; DAM DRAM, MST, POET; DLB 10, 20; EWL 3; EXPP; MTCW 1, 2; PAB; PFS 1, 3, 4, 10; TUS; WP

Audiberti, Jacques 1900-1965 .... **CLC 38**
See also CA 25-28R; DAM DRAM; EWL 3

Audubon, John James 1785-1851 . **NCLC 47**
See also ANW; DLB 248

Auel, Jean M(arie) 1936- .... **CLC 31, 107**
See also AAYA 7; BEST 90:4; BPFB 1; CA 103; CANR 21, 64, 115; CPW; DA3; DAM POP; INT CANR-21; NFS 11; RHW; SATA 91

Auerbach, Erich 1892-1957 .... **TCLC 43**
See also CA 155; 118; EWL 3

Augier, Emile 1820-1889 .... **NCLC 31**
See also DLB 192; GFL 1789 to the Present

August, John
See De Voto, Bernard (Augustine)

Augustine, St. 354-430 .... **CMLC 6; WLCS**
See also DA; DA3; DAB; DAC; DAM MST; DLB 115; EW 1; RGWL 2, 3

Aunt Belinda
See Braddon, Mary Elizabeth

Aunt Weedy
See Alcott, Louisa May

Aurelius
See Bourne, Randolph S(illiman)

Aurelius, Marcus 121-180 .... **CMLC 45**
See Marcus Aurelius
See also RGWL 2, 3

Aurobindo, Sri
See Ghose, Aurabinda

Aurobindo Ghose
See Ghose, Aurabinda

Austen, Jane 1775-1817 ...... **NCLC 1, 13, 19, 33, 51, 81, 95, 119; WLC**
See also AAYA 19; BRW 4; BRWC 1; BRWR 2; BYA 3; CDBLB 1789-1832; DA; DA3; DAB; DAC; DAM MST, NOV; DLB 116; EXPN; LAIT 2; NFS 1, 14; TEA; WLIT 3; WYAS 1

Auster, Paul 1947- .... **CLC 47, 131**
See also AMWS 12; CA 69-72; CANR 23, 52, 75; CMW 4; CN 7; DA3; DLB 227; MTCW 1; SUFW 2

Austin, Frank
See Faust, Frederick (Schiller)
See also TCWW 2

Austin, Mary (Hunter) 1868-1934 . **TCLC 25**
See Stairs, Gordon
See also ANW; CA 178; 109; DLB 9, 78, 206, 221, 275; FW; TCWW 2

Averroes 1126-1198 .... **CMLC 7**
See also DLB 115

Avicenna 980-1037 .... **CMLC 16**
See also DLB 115

Avison, Margaret 1918- .... **CLC 2, 4, 97**
See also CA 17-20R; CP 7; DAC; DAM POET; DLB 53; MTCW 1

Axton, David
See Koontz, Dean R(ay)

Ayckbourn, Alan 1939- ...... **CLC 5, 8, 18, 33, 74; DC 13**
See also BRWS 5; CA 21-24R; CANR 31, 59; CBD; CD 5; DAB; DAM DRAM; DFS 7; DLB 13, 245; EWL 3; MTCW 1, 2

Aydy, Catherine
See Tennant, Emma (Christina)

Ayme, Marcel (Andre) 1902-1967 ... **CLC 11; SSC 41**
See also CA 89-92; CANR 67; CLR 25; DLB 72; EW 12; EWL 3; GFL 1789 to the Present; RGSF 2; RGWL 2, 3; SATA 91

Ayrton, Michael 1921-1975 .... **CLC 7**
See also CA 61-64; 5-8R; CANR 9, 21

Aytmatov, Chingiz
See Aitmatov, Chingiz (Torekulovich)
See also EWL 3

Azorin .... **CLC 11**
See Martinez Ruiz, Jose
See also EW 9; EWL 3

Azuela, Mariano 1873-1952 .. **HLC 1; TCLC 3**
See also CA 131; 104; CANR 81; DAM MULT; EWL 3; HW 1, 2; LAW; MTCW 1, 2

Ba, Mariama 1929-1981 .... **BLCS**
See also AFW; BW 2; CA 141; CANR 87; DNFS 2; WLIT 2

Baastad, Babbis Friis
See Friis-Baastad, Babbis Ellinor

Bab
See Gilbert, W(illiam) S(chwenck)

Babbis, Eleanor
See Friis-Baastad, Babbis Ellinor

Babel, Isaac
See Babel, Isaak (Emmanuilovich)
See also EW 11; SSFS 10

Babel, Isaak (Emmanuilovich)
1894-1941(?) .... **SSC 16; TCLC 2, 13**
See Babel, Isaac
See also CA 155; 104; CANR 113; DLB 272; EWL 3; MTCW 1; RGSF 2; RGWL 2, 3; TWA

Babits, Mihaly 1883-1941 .... **TCLC 14**
See also CA 114; CDWLB 4; DLB 215; EWL 3

Babur 1483-1530 .... **LC 18**

Babylas 1898-1962
See Ghelderode, Michel de

Baca, Jimmy Santiago 1952- . **HLC 1; PC 41**
See also CA 131; CANR 81, 90; CP 7; DAM MULT; DLB 122; HW 1, 2

Baca, Jose Santiago
See Baca, Jimmy Santiago

Bacchelli, Riccardo 1891-1985 .... **CLC 19**
See also CA 117; 29-32R; DLB 264; EWL 3

Bach, Richard (David) 1936- .... **CLC 14**
See also AITN 1; BEST 89:2; BPFB 1; BYA 5; CA 9-12R; CANR 18, 93; CPW; DAM NOV, POP; FANT; MTCW 1; SATA 13

Bache, Benjamin Franklin
1769-1798 .... **LC 74**
See also DLB 43

Bachelard, Gaston 1884-1962 ...... **TCLC 128**
See also CA 89-92; 97-100; GFL 1789 to the Present

Bachman, Richard
See King, Stephen (Edwin)

Bachmann, Ingeborg 1926-1973 .... **CLC 69**
See also CA 45-48; 93-96; CANR 69; DLB 85; EWL 3; RGWL 2, 3

Bacon, Francis 1561-1626 .... **LC 18, 32**
See also BRW 1; CDBLB Before 1660; DLB 151, 236, 252; RGEL 2; TEA

Bacon, Roger 1214(?)-1294 .... **CMLC 14**
See also DLB 115

Barondess, Sue K(aufman)
1926-1977 .... **CLC 8**
See Kaufman, Sue
See also CA 69-72; 1-4R; CANR 1

Baron de Teive
See Pessoa, Fernando (Antonio Nogueira)

Baroness Von S.
See Zangwill, Israel

Barres, (Auguste-)Maurice
1862-1923 .... **TCLC 47**
See also CA 164; DLB 123; GFL 1789 to
the Present

Barreto, Afonso Henrique de Lima
See Lima Barreto, Afonso Henrique de

Barrett, Andrea 1954- .... **CLC 150**
See also CA 156; CANR 92

Barrett, Michele .... **CLC 65**

Barrett, (Roger) Syd 1946- .... **CLC 35**

Barrett, William (Christopher)
1913-1992 .... **CLC 27**
See also CA 139; 13-16R; CANR 11, 67;
INT CANR-11

Barrie, J(ames) M(atthew)
1860-1937 .... **TCLC 2**
See also BRWS 3; BYA 4, 5; CA 136; 104;
CANR 77; CDBLB 1890-1914; CLR 16;
CWRI 5; DA3; DAB; DAM DRAM; DFS
7; DLB 10, 141, 156; EWL 3; FANT;
MAICYA 1, 2; MTCW 1; SATA 100;
SUFW; WCH; WLIT 4; YABC 1

Barrington, Michael
See Moorcock, Michael (John)

Barrol, Grady
See Bograd, Larry

Barry, Mike
See Malzberg, Barry N(athaniel)

Barry, Philip 1896-1949 .... **TCLC 11**
See also CA 199; 109; DFS 9; DLB 7, 228;
RGAL 4

Bart, Andre Schwarz
See Schwarz-Bart, Andre

Barth, John (Simmons) 1930- ... **CLC 1, 2, 3,
5, 7, 9, 10, 14, 27, 51, 89; SSC 10**
See also AITN 1, 2; AMW; BPFB 1; CA
1-4R; CABS 1; CANR 5, 23, 49, 64, 113;
CN 7; DAM NOV; DLB 2, 227; EWL 3;
FANT; MTCW 1; RGAL 4; RGSF 2;
RHW; SSFS 6; TUS

Barthelme, Donald 1931-1989 ... **CLC 1, 2, 3,
5, 6, 8, 13, 23, 46, 59, 115; SSC 2, 55**
See also AMWS 4; BPFB 1; CA 129; 21-
24R; CANR 20, 58; DA3; DAM NOV;
DLB 2, 234; DLBY 1980, 1989; EWL 3;
FANT; MTCW 1, 2; RGAL 4; RGSF 2;
SATA 7; SATA-Obit 62; SSFS 3

Barthelme, Frederick 1943- .... **CLC 36, 117**
See also AMWS 11; CA 122; 114; CANR
77; CN 7; CSW; DLB 244; DLBY 1985;
EWL 3; INT CA-122

Barthes, Roland (Gerard)
1915-1980 .... **CLC 24, 83**
See also CA 97-100; 130; CANR 66; EW
13; EWL 3; GFL 1789 to the Present;
MTCW 1, 2; TWA

Barzun, Jacques (Martin) 1907- ..... **CLC 51,
145**
See also CA 61-64; CANR 22, 95

Bashevis, Isaac
See Singer, Isaac Bashevis

Bashkirtseff, Marie 1859-1884 .... **NCLC 27**

Basho, Matsuo
See Matsuo Basho
See also RGWL 2, 3; WP

Basil of Caesaria c. 330-379 .... **CMLC 35**

Bass, Kingsley B., Jr.
See Bullins, Ed

Bass, Rick 1958- .... **CLC 79, 143**
See also ANW; CA 126; CANR 53, 93;
CSW; DLB 212, 275

Bassani, Giorgio 1916-2000 .... **CLC 9**
See also CA 190; 65-68; CANR 33; CWW
2; DLB 128, 177; EWL 3; MTCW 1;
RGWL 2, 3

Bastian, Ann .... **CLC 70**

Bastos, Augusto (Antonio) Roa
See Roa Bastos, Augusto (Antonio)

Bataille, Georges 1897-1962 .... **CLC 29**
See also CA 89-92; 101; EWL 3

Bates, H(erbert) E(rnest)
1905-1974 .... **CLC 46; SSC 10**
See also CA 45-48; 93-96; CANR 34; DA3;
DAB; DAM POP; DLB 162, 191; EWL
3; EXPS; MTCW 1, 2; RGSF 2; SSFS 7

Bauchart
See Camus, Albert

Baudelaire, Charles 1821-1867 . **NCLC 6, 29,
55; PC 1; SSC 18; WLC**
See also DA; DA3; DAB; DAC; DAM
MST, POET; DLB 217; EW 7; GFL 1789
to the Present; RGWL 2, 3; TWA

Baudouin, Marcel
See Peguy, Charles (Pierre)

Baudouin, Pierre
See Peguy, Charles (Pierre)

Baudrillard, Jean 1929- .... **CLC 60**

Baum, L(yman) Frank 1856-1919 .. **TCLC 7,
132**
See also AAYA 46; CA 133; 108; CLR 15;
CWRI 5; DLB 22; FANT; JRDA; MAI-
CYA 1, 2; MTCW 1, 2; NFS 13; RGAL
4; SATA 18, 100; WCH

Baum, Louis F.
See Baum, L(yman) Frank

Baumbach, Jonathan 1933- .... **CLC 6, 23**
See also CA 13-16R; CAAS 5; CANR 12,
66; CN 7; DLBY 1980; INT CANR-12;
MTCW 1

Bausch, Richard (Carl) 1945- .... **CLC 51**
See also AMWS 7; CA 101; CAAS 14;
CANR 43, 61, 87; CSW; DLB 130

Baxter, Charles (Morley) 1947- . **CLC 45, 78**
See also CA 57-60; CANR 40, 64, 104;
CPW; DAM POP; DLB 130; MTCW 2

Baxter, George Owen
See Faust, Frederick (Schiller)

Baxter, James K(eir) 1926-1972 .... **CLC 14**
See also CA 77-80; EWL 3

Baxter, John
See Hunt, E(verette) Howard, (Jr.)

Bayer, Sylvia
See Glassco, John

Baynton, Barbara 1857-1929 .... **TCLC 57**
See also DLB 230; RGSF 2

Beagle, Peter S(oyer) 1939- .... **CLC 7, 104**
See also AAYA 47; BPFB 1; BYA 9, 10;
CA 9-12R; CANR 4, 51, 73, 110; DA3;
DLBY 1980; FANT; INT CANR-4;
MTCW 1; SATA 60, 130; SUFW 1, 2;
YAW

Bean, Normal
See Burroughs, Edgar Rice

Beard, Charles A(ustin)
1874-1948 .... **TCLC 15**
See also CA 189; 115; DLB 17; SATA 18

Beardsley, Aubrey 1872-1898 .... **NCLC 6**

Beattie, Ann 1947- ..... **CLC 8, 13, 18, 40, 63,
146; SSC 11**
See also AMWS 5; BEST 90:2; BPFB 1;
CA 81-84; CANR 53, 73; CN 7; CPW;
DA3; DAM NOV, POP; DLB 218, 278;
DLBY 1982; EWL 3; MTCW 1, 2; RGAL
4; RGSF 2; SSFS 9; TUS

Beattie, James 1735-1803 .... **NCLC 25**
See also DLB 109

Beauchamp, Kathleen Mansfield 1888-1923
See Mansfield, Katherine
See also CA 134; 104; DA; DA3; DAC;
DAM MST; MTCW 2; TEA

Beaumarchais, Pierre-Augustin Caron de
1732-1799 .... **DC 4; LC 61**
See also DAM DRAM; DFS 14, 16; EW 4;
GFL Beginnings to 1789; RGWL 2, 3

Beaumont, Francis 1584(?)-1616 .. **DC 6; LC
33**
See also BRW 2; CDBLB Before 1660;
DLB 58; TEA

**Beauvoir, Simone (Lucie Ernestine Marie
Bertrand) de** 1908-1986 .... **CLC 1, 2, 4,
8, 14, 31, 44, 50, 71, 124; SSC 35;
WLC**
See also BPFB 1; CA 118; 9-12R; CANR
28, 61; DA; DA3; DAB; DAC; DAM
MST, NOV; DLB 72; DLBY 1986; EW
12; EWL 3; FW; GFL 1789 to the Present;
MTCW 1, 2; RGSF 2; RGWL 2, 3; TWA

Becker, Carl (Lotus) 1873-1945 ..... **TCLC 63**
See also CA 157; DLB 17

Becker, Jurek 1937-1997 .... **CLC 7, 19**
See also CA 157; 85-88; CANR 60; CWW
2; DLB 75; EWL 3

Becker, Walter 1950- .... **CLC 26**

Beckett, Samuel (Barclay)
1906-1989 .. **CLC 1, 2, 3, 4, 6, 9, 10, 11,
14, 18, 29, 57, 59, 83; SSC 16; WLC**
See also BRWR 1; BRWS 1; CA 130; 5-8R;
CANR 33, 61; CBD; CDBLB 1945-1960;
DA; DA3; DAB; DAC; DAM DRAM,
MST, NOV; DFS 2, 7; DLB 13, 15, 233;
DLBY 1990; EWL 3; GFL 1789 to the
Present; MTCW 1, 2; RGSF 2; RGWL 2,
3; SSFS 15; TEA; WLIT 4

Beckford, William 1760-1844 .... **NCLC 16**
See also BRW 3; DLB 39, 213; HGG;
SUFW

Beckham, Barry (Earl) 1944- .... **BLC 1**
See also BW 1; CA 29-32R; CANR 26, 62;
CN 7; DAM MULT; DLB 33

Beckman, Gunnel 1910- .... **CLC 26**
See also CA 33-36R; CANR 15, 114; CLR
25; MAICYA 1, 2; SAAS 9; SATA 6

Becque, Henri 1837-1899 .... **NCLC 3**
See also DLB 192; GFL 1789 to the Present

Becquer, Gustavo Adolfo
1836-1870 .... **HLCS 1; NCLC 106**
See also DAM MULT

Beddoes, Thomas Lovell 1803-1849 .. **DC 15;
NCLC 3**
See also DLB 96

Bede c. 673-735 .... **CMLC 20**
See also DLB 146; TEA

Bedford, Denton R. 1907-(?) .... **NNAL**

Bedford, Donald F.
See Fearing, Kenneth (Flexner)

Beecher, Catharine Esther
1800-1878 .... **NCLC 30**
See also DLB 1, 243

Beecher, John 1904-1980 .... **CLC 6**
See also AITN 1; CA 105; 5-8R; CANR 8

Beer, Johann 1655-1700 .... **LC 5**
See also DLB 168

Beer, Patricia 1924- .... **CLC 58**
See also CA 183; 61-64; CANR 13, 46; CP
7; CWP; DLB 40; FW

Beerbohm, Max
See Beerbohm, (Henry) Max(imilian)

Beerbohm, (Henry) Max(imilian)
1872-1956 .... **TCLC 1, 24**
See also BRWS 2; CA 154; 104; CANR 79;
DLB 34, 100; FANT

Beer-Hofmann, Richard
1866-1945 .... **TCLC 60**
See also CA 160; DLB 81

Beg, Shemus
See Stephens, James

Begiebing, Robert J(ohn) 1946- .... **CLC 70**
See also CA 122; CANR 40, 88

Behan, Brendan 1923-1964 ...... **CLC 1, 8, 11, 15, 79**
See also BRWS 2; CA 73-76; CANR 33; CBD; CDBLB 1945-1960; DAM DRAM; DFS 7; DLB 13, 233; EWL 3; MTCW 1, 2

Behn, Aphra 1640(?)-1689 .. **DC 4; LC 1, 30, 42; PC 13; WLC**
See also BRWS 3; DA; DA3; DAB; DAC; DAM DRAM, MST, NOV, POET; DFS 16; DLB 39, 80, 131; FW; TEA; WLIT 3

Behrman, S(amuel) N(athaniel) 1893-1973 .... **CLC 40**
See also CA 45-48; 13-16; CAD; CAP 1; DLB 7, 44; IDFW 3; RGAL 4

Belasco, David 1853-1931 .... **TCLC 3**
See also CA 168; 104; DLB 7; RGAL 4

Belcheva, Elisaveta Lyubomirova 1893-1991 .... **CLC 10**
See Bagryana, Elisaveta

Beldone, Phil "Cheech"
See Ellison, Harlan (Jay)

Beleno
See Azuela, Mariano

Belinski, Vissarion Grigoryevich 1811-1848 .... **NCLC 5**
See also DLB 198

Belitt, Ben 1911- .... **CLC 22**
See also CA 13-16R; CAAS 4; CANR 7, 77; CP 7; DLB 5

Bell, Gertrude (Margaret Lowthian) 1868-1926 .... **TCLC 67**
See also CA 167; CANR 110; DLB 174

Bell, J. Freeman
See Zangwill, Israel

Bell, James Madison 1826-1902 .... **BLC 1; TCLC 43**
See also BW 1; CA 124; 122; DAM MULT; DLB 50

Bell, Madison Smartt 1957- ...... **CLC 41, 102**
See also AMWS 10; BPFB 1; CA 111, 183; CAAE 183; CANR 28, 54, 73; CN 7; CSW; DLB 218, 278; MTCW 1

Bell, Marvin (Hartley) 1937- .... **CLC 8, 31**
See also CA 21-24R; CAAS 14; CANR 59, 102; CP 7; DAM POET; DLB 5; MTCW 1

Bell, W. L. D.
See Mencken, H(enry) L(ouis)

Bellamy, Atwood C.
See Mencken, H(enry) L(ouis)

Bellamy, Edward 1850-1898 ...... **NCLC 4, 86**
See also DLB 12; NFS 15; RGAL 4; SFW 4

Belli, Gioconda 1949- .... **HLCS 1**
See also CA 152; CWW 2; EWL 3; RGWL 3

Bellin, Edward J.
See Kuttner, Henry

Belloc, (Joseph) Hilaire (Pierre Sebastien Rene Swanton) 1870-1953 .... **PC 24; TCLC 7, 18**
See also CA 152; 106; CWRI 5; DAM POET; DLB 19, 100, 141, 174; EWL 3; MTCW 1; SATA 112; WCH; YABC 1

Belloc, Joseph Peter Rene Hilaire
See Belloc, (Joseph) Hilaire (Pierre Sebastien Rene Swanton)

Belloc, Joseph Pierre Hilaire
See Belloc, (Joseph) Hilaire (Pierre Sebastien Rene Swanton)

Belloc, M. A.
See Lowndes, Marie Adelaide (Belloc)

Belloc-Lowndes, Mrs.
See Lowndes, Marie Adelaide (Belloc)

Bellow, Saul 1915- . **CLC 1, 2, 3, 6, 8, 10, 13, 15, 25, 33, 34, 63, 79; SSC 14; WLC**
See also AITN 2; AMW; AMWR 2; BEST 89:3; BPFB 1; CA 5-8R; CABS 1; CANR 29, 53, 95; CDALB 1941-1968; CN 7; DA; DA3; DAB; DAC; DAM MST, NOV, POP; DLB 2, 28; DLBD 3; DLBY 1982; EWL 3; MTCW 1, 2; NFS 4, 14; RGAL 4; RGSF 2; SSFS 12; TUS

Belser, Reimond Karel Maria de 1929-
See Ruyslinck, Ward
See also CA 152

Bely, Andrey .... **PC 11; TCLC 7**
See Bugayev, Boris Nikolayevich
See also EW 9; EWL 3; MTCW 1

Belyi, Andrei
See Bugayev, Boris Nikolayevich
See also RGWL 2, 3

Bembo, Pietro 1470-1547 .... **LC 79**
See also RGWL 2, 3

Benary, Margot
See Benary-Isbert, Margot

Benary-Isbert, Margot 1889-1979 .... **CLC 12**
See also CA 89-92; 5-8R; CANR 4, 72; CLR 12; MAICYA 1, 2; SATA 2; SATA-Obit 21

Benavente (y Martinez), Jacinto 1866-1954 .... **HLCS 1; TCLC 3**
See also CA 131; 106; CANR 81; DAM DRAM, MULT; EWL 3; GLL 2; HW 1, 2; MTCW 1, 2

Benchley, Peter (Bradford) 1940- .. **CLC 4, 8**
See also AAYA 14; AITN 2; BPFB 1; CA 17-20R; CANR 12, 35, 66, 115; CPW; DAM NOV, POP; HGG; MTCW 1, 2; SATA 3, 89

Benchley, Robert (Charles) 1889-1945 .... **TCLC 1, 55**
See also CA 153; 105; DLB 11; RGAL 4

Benda, Julien 1867-1956 .... **TCLC 60**
See also CA 154; 120; GFL 1789 to the Present

Benedict, Ruth (Fulton) 1887-1948 .... **TCLC 60**
See also CA 158; DLB 246

Benedikt, Michael 1935- .... **CLC 4, 14**
See also CA 13-16R; CANR 7; CP 7; DLB 5

Benet, Juan 1927-1993 .... **CLC 28**
See also CA 143; EWL 3

Benet, Stephen Vincent 1898-1943 ... **SSC 10; TCLC 7**
See also AMWS 11; CA 152; 104; DA3; DAM POET; DLB 4, 48, 102, 249; DLBY 1997; EWL 3; HGG; MTCW 1; RGAL 4; RGSF 2; SUFW; WP; YABC 1

Benet, William Rose 1886-1950 ..... **TCLC 28**
See also CA 152; 118; DAM POET; DLB 45; RGAL 4

Benford, Gregory (Albert) 1941- ..... **CLC 52**
See also BPFB 1; CA 69-72, 175; CAAE 175; CAAS 27; CANR 12, 24, 49, 95; CSW; DLBY 1982; SCFW 2; SFW 4

Bengtsson, Frans (Gunnar) 1894-1954 .... **TCLC 48**
See also CA 170; EWL 3

Benjamin, David
See Slavitt, David R(ytman)

Benjamin, Lois
See Gould, Lois

Benjamin, Walter 1892-1940 .... **TCLC 39**
See also CA 164; DLB 242; EW 11; EWL 3

Benn, Gottfried 1886-1956 .. **PC 35; TCLC 3**
See also CA 153; 106; DLB 56; EWL 3; RGWL 2, 3

Bennett, Alan 1934- .... **CLC 45, 77**
See also BRWS 8; CA 103; CANR 35, 55, 106; CBD; CD 5; DAB; DAM MST; MTCW 1, 2

Bennett, (Enoch) Arnold 1867-1931 .... **TCLC 5, 20**
See also BRW 6; CA 155; 106; CDBLB 1890-1914; DLB 10, 34, 98, 135; EWL 3; MTCW 2

Bennett, Elizabeth
See Mitchell, Margaret (Munnerlyn)

Bennett, George Harold 1930-
See Bennett, Hal
See also BW 1; CA 97-100; CANR 87

Bennett, Gwendolyn B. 1902-1981 .... **HR 2**
See also BW 1; CA 125; DLB 51; WP

Bennett, Hal .... **CLC 5**
See Bennett, George Harold
See also DLB 33

Bennett, Jay 1912- .... **CLC 35**
See also AAYA 10; CA 69-72; CANR 11, 42, 79; JRDA; SAAS 4; SATA 41, 87; SATA-Brief 27; WYA; YAW

Bennett, Louise (Simone) 1919- .... **BLC 1; CLC 28**
See also BW 2, 3; CA 151; CDWLB 3; CP 7; DAM MULT; DLB 117; EWL 3

Benson, A. C. 1862-1925 .... **TCLC 123**
See also DLB 98

Benson, E(dward) F(rederic) 1867-1940 .... **TCLC 27**
See also CA 157; 114; DLB 135, 153; HGG; SUFW 1

Benson, Jackson J. 1930- .... **CLC 34**
See also CA 25-28R; DLB 111

Benson, Sally 1900-1972 .... **CLC 17**
See also CA 37-40R; 19-20; CAP 1; SATA 1, 35; SATA-Obit 27

Benson, Stella 1892-1933 .... **TCLC 17**
See also CA 154, 155; 117; DLB 36, 162; FANT; TEA

Bentham, Jeremy 1748-1832 .... **NCLC 38**
See also DLB 107, 158, 252

Bentley, E(dmund) C(lerihew) 1875-1956 .... **TCLC 12**
See also CA 108; DLB 70; MSW

Bentley, Eric (Russell) 1916- .... **CLC 24**
See also CA 5-8R; CAD; CANR 6, 67; CBD; CD 5; INT CANR-6

Beranger, Pierre Jean de 1780-1857 .... **NCLC 34**

Berdyaev, Nicolas
See Berdyaev, Nikolai (Aleksandrovich)

Berdyaev, Nikolai (Aleksandrovich) 1874-1948 .... **TCLC 67**
See also CA 157; 120

Berdyayev, Nikolai (Aleksandrovich)
See Berdyaev, Nikolai (Aleksandrovich)

Berendt, John (Lawrence) 1939- ...... **CLC 86**
See also CA 146; CANR 75, 93; DA3; MTCW 1

Beresford, J(ohn) D(avys) 1873-1947 .... **TCLC 81**
See also CA 155; 112; DLB 162, 178, 197; SFW 4; SUFW 1

Bergelson, David 1884-1952 .... **TCLC 81**
See Bergelson, Dovid

Bergelson, Dovid
See Bergelson, David
See also EWL 3

Berger, Colonel
See Malraux, (Georges-)Andre

Berger, John (Peter) 1926- .... **CLC 2, 19**
See also BRWS 4; CA 81-84; CANR 51, 78; CN 7; DLB 14, 207

Berger, Melvin H. 1927- .... **CLC 12**
See also CA 5-8R; CANR 4; CLR 32; SAAS 2; SATA 5, 88; SATA-Essay 124

Black Tarantula
See Acker, Kathy
Blackwood, Algernon (Henry)
1869-1951 .... **TCLC 5**
See also CA 150; 105; DLB 153, 156, 178;
HGG; SUFW 1
Blackwood, Caroline 1931-1996 .... **CLC 6, 9,
100**
See also CA 151; 85-88; CANR 32, 61, 65;
CN 7; DLB 14, 207; HGG; MTCW 1
Blade, Alexander
See Hamilton, Edmond; Silverberg, Robert
Blaga, Lucian 1895-1961 .... **CLC 75**
See also CA 157; DLB 220; EWL 3
Blair, Eric (Arthur) 1903-1950 .... **TCLC 123**
See Orwell, George
See also CA 132; 104; DA; DA3; DAB;
DAC; DAM MST, NOV; MTCW 1, 2;
SATA 29
Blair, Hugh 1718-1800 .... **NCLC 75**
Blais, Marie-Claire 1939- .... **CLC 2, 4, 6, 13,
22**
See also CA 21-24R; CAAS 4; CANR 38,
75, 93; DAC; DAM MST; DLB 53; EWL
3; FW; MTCW 1, 2; TWA
Blaise, Clark 1940- .... **CLC 29**
See also AITN 2; CA 53-56; CAAS 3;
CANR 5, 66, 106; CN 7; DLB 53; RGSF
2
Blake, Fairley
See De Voto, Bernard (Augustine)
Blake, Nicholas
See Day Lewis, C(ecil)
See also DLB 77; MSW
Blake, Sterling
See Benford, Gregory (Albert)
Blake, William 1757-1827 .... **NCLC 13, 37,
57; PC 12; WLC**
See also AAYA 47; BRW 3; BRWR 1; CD-
BLB 1789-1832; CLR 52; DA; DA3;
DAB; DAC; DAM MST, POET; DLB 93,
163; EXPP; MAICYA 1, 2; PAB; PFS 2,
12; SATA 30; TEA; WCH; WLIT 3; WP
Blanchot, Maurice 1907- .... **CLC 135**
See also CA 144; 117; DLB 72; EWL 3
Blasco Ibanez, Vicente 1867-1928 . **TCLC 12**
See also BPFB 1; CA 131; 110; CANR 81;
DA3; DAM NOV; EW 8; EWL 3; HW 1,
2; MTCW 1
Blatty, William Peter 1928- .... **CLC 2**
See also CA 5-8R; CANR 9; DAM POP;
HGG
Bleeck, Oliver
See Thomas, Ross (Elmore)
Blessing, Lee 1949- .... **CLC 54**
See also CAD; CD 5
Blight, Rose
See Greer, Germaine
Blish, James (Benjamin) 1921-1975 . **CLC 14**
See also BPFB 1; CA 57-60; 1-4R; CANR
3; DLB 8; MTCW 1; SATA 66; SCFW 2;
SFW 4
Bliss, Reginald
See Wells, H(erbert) G(eorge)
Blixen, Karen (Christentze Dinesen)
1885-1962
See Dinesen, Isak
See also CA 25-28; CANR 22, 50; CAP 2;
DA3; DLB 214; MTCW 1, 2; SATA 44
Bloch, Robert (Albert) 1917-1994 .... **CLC 33**
See also AAYA 29; CA 146; 5-8R, 179;
CAAE 179; CAAS 20; CANR 5, 78;
DA3; DLB 44; HGG; INT CANR-5;
MTCW 1; SATA 12; SATA-Obit 82; SFW
4; SUFW 1, 2
Blok, Alexander (Alexandrovich)
1880-1921 .... **PC 21; TCLC 5**
See also CA 183; 104; EW 9; EWL 3;
RGWL 2, 3

Blom, Jan
See Breytenbach, Breyten
Bloom, Harold 1930- .... **CLC 24, 103**
See also CA 13-16R; CANR 39, 75, 92;
DLB 67; EWL 3; MTCW 1; RGAL 4
Bloomfield, Aurelius
See Bourne, Randolph S(illiman)
Blount, Roy (Alton), Jr. 1941- .... **CLC 38**
See also CA 53-56; CANR 10, 28, 61;
CSW; INT CANR-28; MTCW 1, 2
Blowsnake, Sam 1875-(?) .... **NNAL**
Bloy, Leon 1846-1917 .... **TCLC 22**
See also CA 183; 121; DLB 123; GFL 1789
to the Present
Blue Cloud, Peter (Aroniawenrate)
1933- .... **NNAL**
See also CA 117; CANR 40; DAM MULT
Bluggage, Oranthy
See Alcott, Louisa May
Blume, Judy (Sussman) 1938- .... **CLC 12, 30**
See also AAYA 3, 26; BYA 1, 8, 12; CA 29-
32R; CANR 13, 37, 66; CLR 2, 15, 69;
CPW; DA3; DAM NOV, POP; DLB 52;
JRDA; MAICYA 1, 2; MAICYAS 1;
MTCW 1, 2; SATA 2, 31, 79; WYA; YAW
Blunden, Edmund (Charles)
1896-1974 .... **CLC 2, 56**
See also BRW 6; CA 45-48; 17-18; CANR
54; CAP 2; DLB 20, 100, 155; MTCW 1;
PAB
Bly, Robert (Elwood) 1926- .... **CLC 1, 2, 5,
10, 15, 38, 128; PC 39**
See also AMWS 4; CA 5-8R; CANR 41,
73; CP 7; DA3; DAM POET; DLB 5;
EWL 3; MTCW 1, 2; PFS 17; RGAL 4
Boas, Franz 1858-1942 .... **TCLC 56**
See also CA 181; 115
Bobette
See Simenon, Georges (Jacques Christian)
Boccaccio, Giovanni 1313-1375 ... **CMLC 13,
57; SSC 10**
See also EW 2; RGSF 2; RGWL 2, 3; TWA
Bochco, Steven 1943- .... **CLC 35**
See also AAYA 11; CA 138; 124
Bode, Sigmund
See O'Doherty, Brian
Bodel, Jean 1167(?)-1210 .... **CMLC 28**
Bodenheim, Maxwell 1892-1954 .... **TCLC 44**
See also CA 187; 110; DLB 9, 45; RGAL 4
Bodenheimer, Maxwell
See Bodenheim, Maxwell
Bodker, Cecil 1927- .... **CLC 21**
See also CA 73-76; CANR 13, 44, 111;
CLR 23; MAICYA 1, 2; SATA 14, 133
Bodker, Cecil 1927-
See Bodker, Cecil
Boell, Heinrich (Theodor)
1917-1985 ..... **CLC 2, 3, 6, 9, 11, 15, 27,
32, 72; SSC 23; WLC**
See Boll, Heinrich
See also CA 116; 21-24R; CANR 24; DA;
DA3; DAB; DAC; DAM MST, NOV;
DLB 69; DLBY 1985; MTCW 1, 2; TWA
Boerne, Alfred
See Doeblin, Alfred
Boethius c. 480-c. 524 .... **CMLC 15**
See also DLB 115; RGWL 2, 3
Boff, Leonardo (Genezio Darci)
1938- .... **CLC 70; HLC 1**
See also CA 150; DAM MULT; HW 2
Bogan, Louise 1897-1970 .... **CLC 4, 39, 46,
93; PC 12**
See also AMWS 3; CA 25-28R; 73-76;
CANR 33, 82; DAM POET; DLB 45, 169;
EWL 3; MAWW; MTCW 1, 2; RGAL 4
Bogarde, Dirk
See Van Den Bogarde, Derek Jules Gaspard
Ulric Niven
See also DLB 14

Bogosian, Eric 1953- .... **CLC 45, 141**
See also CA 138; CAD; CANR 102; CD 5
Bograd, Larry 1953- .... **CLC 35**
See also CA 93-96; CANR 57; SAAS 21;
SATA 33, 89; WYA
Boiardo, Matteo Maria 1441-1494 .... **LC 6**
Boileau-Despreaux, Nicolas 1636-1711 . **LC 3**
See also DLB 268; EW 3; GFL Beginnings
to 1789; RGWL 2, 3
Boissard, Maurice
See Leautaud, Paul
Bojer, Johan 1872-1959 .... **TCLC 64**
See also CA 189; EWL 3
Bok, Edward W. 1863-1930 .... **TCLC 101**
See also DLB 91; DLBD 16
Boland, Eavan (Aisling) 1944- .. **CLC 40, 67,
113**
See also BRWS 5; CA 143; CANR 61; CP
7; CWP; DAM POET; DLB 40; FW;
MTCW 2; PFS 12
Boll, Heinrich
See Boell, Heinrich (Theodor)
See also BPFB 1; CDWLB 2; EW 13; EWL
3; RGSF 2; RGWL 2, 3
Bolt, Lee
See Faust, Frederick (Schiller)
Bolt, Robert (Oxton) 1924-1995 .... **CLC 14**
See also CA 147; 17-20R; CANR 35, 67;
CBD; DAM DRAM; DFS 2; DLB 13,
233; EWL 3; LAIT 1; MTCW 1
Bombal, Maria Luisa 1910-1980 .... **HLCS 1;
SSC 37**
See also CA 127; CANR 72; EWL 3; HW
1; LAW; RGSF 2
Bombet, Louis-Alexandre-Cesar
See Stendhal
Bomkauf
See Kaufman, Bob (Garnell)
Bonaventura .... **NCLC 35**
See also DLB 90
Bond, Edward 1934- .... **CLC 4, 6, 13, 23**
See also BRWS 1; CA 25-28R; CANR 38,
67, 106; CBD; CD 5; DAM DRAM; DFS
3,8; DLB 13; EWL 3; MTCW 1
Bonham, Frank 1914-1989 .... **CLC 12**
See also AAYA 1; BYA 1, 3; CA 9-12R;
CANR 4, 36; JRDA; MAICYA 1, 2;
SAAS 3; SATA 1, 49; SATA-Obit 62;
TCWW 2; YAW
Bonnefoy, Yves 1923- .... **CLC 9, 15, 58**
See also CA 85-88; CANR 33, 75, 97;
CWW 2; DAM MST, POET; DLB 258;
EWL 3; GFL 1789 to the Present; MTCW
1, 2
Bonner, Marita .... **HR 2**
See Occomy, Marita (Odette) Bonner
Bonnin, Gertrude 1876-1938 .... **NNAL**
See Zitkala-Sa
See also CA 150; DAM MULT
Bontemps, Arna(ud Wendell)
1902-1973 ..... **BLC 1; CLC 1, 18; HR 2**
See also BW 1; CA 41-44R; 1-4R; CANR
4, 35; CLR 6; CWRI 5; DA3; DAM
MULT, NOV, POET; DLB 48, 51; JRDA;
MAICYA 1, 2; MTCW 1, 2; SATA 2, 44;
SATA-Obit 24; WCH; WP
Booth, Martin 1944- .... **CLC 13**
See also CA 93-96; CAAE 188; CAAS 2;
CANR 92
Booth, Philip 1925- .... **CLC 23**
See also CA 5-8R; CANR 5, 88; CP 7;
DLBY 1982
Booth, Wayne C(layson) 1921- .... **CLC 24**
See also CA 1-4R; CAAS 5; CANR 3, 43;
DLB 67
Borchert, Wolfgang 1921-1947 .... **TCLC 5**
See also CA 188; 104; DLB 69, 124; EWL
3

Borel, Petrus 1809-1859 .... **NCLC 41**
See also DLB 119; GFL 1789 to the Present
Borges, Jorge Luis 1899-1986 ... **CLC 1, 2, 3, 4, 6, 8, 9, 10, 13, 19, 44, 48, 83; HLC 1; PC 22, 32; SSC 4, 41; TCLC 109; WLC**
See also AAYA 26; BPFB 1; CA 21-24R; CANR 19, 33, 75, 105; CDWLB 3; DA; DA3; DAB; DAC; DAM MST, MULT; DLB 113; DLBY 1986; DNFS 1, 2; EWL 3; HW 1, 2; LAW; MSW; MTCW 1, 2; RGSF 2; RGWL 2, 3; SFW 4; SSFS 4, 9; TWA; WLIT 1
Borowski, Tadeusz 1922-1951 .... **SSC 48; TCLC 9**
See also CA 154; 106; CDWLB 4; DLB 215; EWL 3; RGSF 2; RGWL 3; SSFS 13
Borrow, George (Henry)
1803-1881 .... **NCLC 9**
See also DLB 21, 55, 166
Bosch (Gavino), Juan 1909-2001 ..... **HLCS 1**
See also CA 204; 151; DAM MST, MULT; DLB 145; HW 1, 2
Bosman, Herman Charles
1905-1951 .... **TCLC 49**
See Malan, Herman
See also CA 160; DLB 225; RGSF 2
Bosschere, Jean de 1878(?)-1953 ... **TCLC 19**
See also CA 186; 115
Boswell, James 1740-1795 ... **LC 4, 50; WLC**
See also BRW 3; CDBLB 1660-1789; DA; DAB; DAC; DAM MST; DLB 104, 142; TEA; WLIT 3
Bottomley, Gordon 1874-1948 ..... **TCLC 107**
See also CA 192; 120; DLB 10
Bottoms, David 1949- .... **CLC 53**
See also CA 105; CANR 22; CSW; DLB 120; DLBY 1983
Boucicault, Dion 1820-1890 .... **NCLC 41**
Boucolon, Maryse
See Conde, Maryse
Bourget, Paul (Charles Joseph)
1852-1935 .... **TCLC 12**
See also CA 196; 107; DLB 123; GFL 1789 to the Present
Bourjaily, Vance (Nye) 1922- .... **CLC 8, 62**
See also CA 1-4R; CAAS 1; CANR 2, 72; CN 7; DLB 2, 143
Bourne, Randolph S(illiman)
1886-1918 .... **TCLC 16**
See also AMW; CA 155; 117; DLB 63
Bova, Ben(jamin William) 1932- ...... **CLC 45**
See also AAYA 16; CA 5-8R; CAAS 18; CANR 11, 56, 94, 111; CLR 3; DLBY 1981; INT CANR-11; MAICYA 1, 2; MTCW 1; SATA 6, 68, 133; SFW 4
Bowen, Elizabeth (Dorothea Cole)
1899-1973 . **CLC 1, 3, 6, 11, 15, 22, 118; SSC 3, 28**
See also BRWS 2; CA 41-44R; 17-18; CANR 35, 105; CAP 2; CDBLB 1945-1960; DA3; DAM NOV; DLB 15, 162; EWL 3; EXPS; FW; HGG; MTCW 1, 2; NFS 13; RGSF 2; SSFS 5; SUFW 1; TEA; WLIT 4
Bowering, George 1935- .... **CLC 15, 47**
See also CA 21-24R; CAAS 16; CANR 10; CP 7; DLB 53
Bowering, Marilyn R(uthe) 1949- .... **CLC 32**
See also CA 101; CANR 49; CP 7; CWP
Bowers, Edgar 1924-2000 .... **CLC 9**
See also CA 188; 5-8R; CANR 24; CP 7; CSW; DLB 5
Bowers, Mrs. J. Milton 1842-1914
See Bierce, Ambrose (Gwinett)
Bowie, David .... **CLC 17**
See Jones, David Robert

Bowles, Jane (Sydney) 1917-1973 ..... **CLC 3, 68**
See Bowles, Jane Auer
See also CA 41-44R; 19-20; CAP 2
Bowles, Jane Auer
See Bowles, Jane (Sydney)
See also EWL 3
Bowles, Paul (Frederick) 1910-1999 . **CLC 1, 2, 19, 53; SSC 3**
See also AMWS 4; CA 186; 1-4R; CAAS 1; CANR 1, 19, 50, 75; CN 7; DA3; DLB 5, 6, 218; EWL 3; MTCW 1, 2; RGAL 4
Bowles, William Lisle 1762-1850 . **NCLC 103**
See also DLB 93
Box, Edgar
See Vidal, Gore
See also GLL 1
Boyd, James 1888-1944 .... **TCLC 115**
See also CA 186; DLB 9; DLBD 16; RGAL 4; RHW
Boyd, Nancy
See Millay, Edna St. Vincent
See also GLL 1
Boyd, Thomas (Alexander)
1898-1935 .... **TCLC 111**
See also CA 183; 111; DLB 9; DLBD 16
Boyd, William 1952- .... **CLC 28, 53, 70**
See also CA 120; 114; CANR 51, 71; CN 7; DLB 231
Boyle, Kay 1902-1992 .... **CLC 1, 5, 19, 58, 121; SSC 5**
See also CA 140; 13-16R; CAAS 1; CANR 29, 61, 110; DLB 4, 9, 48, 86; DLBY 1993; EWL 3; MTCW 1, 2; RGAL 4; RGSF 2; SSFS 10, 13, 14
Boyle, Mark
See Kienzle, William X(avier)
Boyle, Patrick 1905-1982 .... **CLC 19**
See also CA 127
Boyle, T. C.
See Boyle, T(homas) Coraghessan
See also AMWS 8
Boyle, T(homas) Coraghessan
1948- .... **CLC 36, 55, 90; SSC 16**
See Boyle, T. C.
See also AAYA 47; BEST 90:4; BPFB 1; CA 120; CANR 44, 76, 89; CN 7; CPW; DA3; DAM POP; DLB 218, 278; DLBY 1986; EWL 3; MTCW 2; SSFS 13
Boz
See Dickens, Charles (John Huffam)
Brackenridge, Hugh Henry
1748-1816 .... **NCLC 7**
See also DLB 11, 37; RGAL 4
Bradbury, Edward P.
See Moorcock, Michael (John)
See also MTCW 2
Bradbury, Malcolm (Stanley)
1932-2000 .... **CLC 32, 61**
See also CA 1-4R; CANR 1, 33, 91, 98; CN 7; DA3; DAM NOV; DLB 14, 207; EWL 3; MTCW 1, 2
Bradbury, Ray (Douglas) 1920- .... **CLC 1, 3, 10, 15, 42, 98; SSC 29, 53; WLC**
See also AAYA 15; AITN 1, 2; AMWS 4; BPFB 1; BYA 4, 5, 11; CA 1-4R; CANR 2, 30, 75; CDALB 1968-1988; CN 7; CPW; DA; DA3; DAB; DAC; DAM MST, NOV, POP; DLB 2, 8; EXPN; EXPS; HGG; LAIT 3, 5; MTCW 1, 2; NFS 1; RGAL 4; RGSF 2; SATA 11, 64, 123; SCFW 2; SFW 4; SSFS 1; SUFW 1, 2; TUS; YAW
Braddon, Mary Elizabeth
1837-1915 .... **TCLC 111**
See also BRWS 8; CA 179; 108; CMW 4; DLB 18, 70, 156; HGG
Bradford, Gamaliel 1863-1932 .... **TCLC 36**
See also CA 160; DLB 17

Bradford, William 1590-1657 .... **LC 64**
See also DLB 24, 30; RGAL 4
Bradley, David (Henry), Jr. 1950- .... **BLC 1; CLC 23, 118**
See also BW 1, 3; CA 104; CANR 26, 81; CN 7; DAM MULT; DLB 33
Bradley, John Ed(mund, Jr.) 1958- . **CLC 55**
See also CA 139; CANR 99; CN 7; CSW
Bradley, Marion Zimmer
1930-1999 .... **CLC 30**
See Chapman, Lee; Dexter, John; Gardner, Miriam; Ives, Morgan; Rivers, Elfrida
See also AAYA 40; BPFB 1; CA 185; 57-60; CAAS 10; CANR 7, 31, 51, 75, 107; CPW; DA3; DAM POP; DLB 8; FANT; FW; MTCW 1, 2; SATA 90; SATA-Obit 116; SFW 4; SUFW 2; YAW
Bradshaw, John 1933- .... **CLC 70**
See also CA 138; CANR 61
Bradstreet, Anne 1612(?)-1672 ...... **LC 4, 30; PC 10**
See also AMWS 1; CDALB 1640-1865; DA; DA3; DAC; DAM MST, POET; DLB 24; EXPP; FW; PFS 6; RGAL 4; TUS; WP
Brady, Joan 1939- .... **CLC 86**
See also CA 141
Bragg, Melvyn 1939- .... **CLC 10**
See also BEST 89:3; CA 57-60; CANR 10, 48, 89; CN 7; DLB 14, 271; RHW
Brahe, Tycho 1546-1601 .... **LC 45**
Braine, John (Gerard) 1922-1986 . **CLC 1, 3, 41**
See also CA 120; 1-4R; CANR 1, 33; CDBLB 1945-1960; DLB 15; DLBY 1986; EWL 3; MTCW 1
Braithwaite, William Stanley (Beaumont)
1878-1962 .... **BLC 1; HR 2**
See also BW 1; CA 125; DAM MULT; DLB 50, 54
Bramah, Ernest 1868-1942 .... **TCLC 72**
See also CA 156; CMW 4; DLB 70; FANT
Brammer, William 1930(?)-1978 ...... **CLC 31**
See also CA 77-80
Brancati, Vitaliano 1907-1954 .... **TCLC 12**
See also CA 109; DLB 264; EWL 3
Brancato, Robin F(idler) 1936- .... **CLC 35**
See also AAYA 9; BYA 6; CA 69-72; CANR 11, 45; CLR 32; JRDA; MAICYA 2; MAICYAS 1; SAAS 9; SATA 97; WYA; YAW
Brand, Max
See Faust, Frederick (Schiller)
See also BPFB 1; TCWW 2
Brand, Millen 1906-1980 .... **CLC 7**
See also CA 97-100; 21-24R; CANR 72
Branden, Barbara .... **CLC 44**
See also CA 148
Brandes, Georg (Morris Cohen)
1842-1927 .... **TCLC 10**
See also CA 189; 105
Brandys, Kazimierz 1916-2000 .... **CLC 62**
See also EWL 3
Branley, Franklyn M(ansfield)
1915-2002 .... **CLC 21**
See also CA 33-36R; CANR 14, 39; CLR 13; MAICYA 1, 2; SAAS 16; SATA 4, 68, 136
Brant, Beth (E.) 1941- .... **NNAL**
See also CA 144; FW
Brathwaite, Edward Kamau
1930- .... **BLCS; CLC 11**
See also BW 2, 3; CA 25-28R; CANR 11, 26, 47, 107; CDWLB 3; CP 7; DAM POET; DLB 125; EWL 3
Brathwaite, Kamau
See Brathwaite, Edward Kamau

Deighton, Len .... **CLC 4, 7, 22, 46**
See Deighton, Leonard Cyril
See also AAYA 6; BEST 89:2; BPFB 1; CD-
BLB 1960 to Present; CMW 4; CN 7;
CPW; DLB 87

Deighton, Leonard Cyril 1929-
See Deighton, Len
See also CA 9-12R; CANR 19, 33, 68;
DA3; DAM NOV, POP; MTCW 1, 2

Dekker, Thomas 1572(?)-1632 ..... **DC 12; LC 22**
See also CDBLB Before 1660; DAM
DRAM; DLB 62, 172; RGEL 2

de Laclos, Pierre Ambroise Franois
See Laclos, Pierre Ambroise Francois

Delafield, E. M. .... **TCLC 61**
See Dashwood, Edmee Elizabeth Monica
de la Pasture
See also DLB 34; RHW

de la Mare, Walter (John)
1873-1956 . **SSC 14; TCLC 4, 53; WLC**
See also CA 163; CDBLB 1914-1945; CLR
23; CWRI 5; DA3; DAB; DAC; DAM
MST, POET; DLB 19, 153, 162, 255;
EWL 3; EXPP; HGG; MAICYA 1, 2;
MTCW 1; RGEL 2; RGSF 2; SATA 16;
SUFW 1; TEA; WCH

de Lamartine, Alphonse (Marie Louis Prat)
See Lamartine, Alphonse (Marie Louis Prat)
de

Delaney, Franey
See O'Hara, John (Henry)

Delaney, Shelagh 1939- .... **CLC 29**
See also CA 17-20R; CANR 30, 67; CBD;
CD 5; CDBLB 1960 to Present; CWD;
DAM DRAM; DFS 7; DLB 13; MTCW 1

Delany, Martin Robison
1812-1885 .... **NCLC 93**
See also DLB 50; RGAL 4

Delany, Mary (Granville Pendarves)
1700-1788 .... **LC 12**

Delany, Samuel R(ay), Jr. 1942- .... **BLC 1; CLC 8, 14, 38, 141**
See also AAYA 24; AFAW 2; BPFB 1; BW
2, 3; CA 81-84; CANR 27, 43, 115; CN
7; DAM MULT; DLB 8, 33; FANT;
MTCW 1, 2; RGAL 4; SATA 92; SCFW;
SFW 4; SUFW 2

De la Ramee, Marie Louise (Ouida)
1839-1908
See Ouida
See also CA 204; SATA 20

de la Roche, Mazo 1879-1961 .... **CLC 14**
See also CA 85-88; CANR 30; DLB 68;
RGEL 2; RHW; SATA 64

De La Salle, Innocent
See Hartmann, Sadakichi

de Laureamont, Comte
See Lautreamont

Delbanco, Nicholas (Franklin)
1942- .... **CLC 6, 13, 167**
See also CA 17-20R; CAAE 189; CAAS 2;
CANR 29, 55; DLB 6, 234

del Castillo, Michel 1933- .... **CLC 38**
See also CA 109; CANR 77

Deledda, Grazia (Cosima)
1875(?)-1936 .... **TCLC 23**
See also CA 205; 123; DLB 264; EWL 3;
RGWL 2, 3

Deleuze, Gilles 1925-1995 .... **TCLC 116**

Delgado, Abelardo (Lalo) B(arrientos)
1930- .... **HLC 1**
See also CA 131; CAAS 15; CANR 90;
DAM MST, MULT; DLB 82; HW 1, 2

Delibes, Miguel .... **CLC 8, 18**
See Delibes Setien, Miguel
See also EWL 3

Delibes Setien, Miguel 1920-
See Delibes, Miguel
See also CA 45-48; CANR 1, 32; HW 1;
MTCW 1

DeLillo, Don 1936- ..... **CLC 8, 10, 13, 27, 39, 54, 76, 143**
See also AMWS 6; BEST 89:1; BPFB 1;
CA 81-84; CANR 21, 76, 92; CN 7; CPW;
DA3; DAM NOV, POP; DLB 6, 173;
EWL 3; MTCW 1, 2; RGAL 4; TUS

de Lisser, H. G.
See De Lisser, H(erbert) G(eorge)
See also DLB 117

De Lisser, H(erbert) G(eorge)
1878-1944 .... **TCLC 12**
See de Lisser, H. G.
See also BW 2; CA 152; 109

Deloire, Pierre
See Peguy, Charles (Pierre)

Deloney, Thomas 1543(?)-1600 .... **LC 41**
See also DLB 167; RGEL 2

Deloria, Ella (Cara) 1889-1971(?) ..... **NNAL**
See also CA 152; DAM MULT; DLB 175

Deloria, Vine (Victor), Jr. 1933- ...... **CLC 21, 122; NNAL**
See also CA 53-56; CANR 5, 20, 48, 98;
DAM MULT; DLB 175; MTCW 1; SATA 21

del Valle-Inclan, Ramon (Maria)
See Valle-Inclan, Ramon (Maria) del

Del Vecchio, John M(ichael) 1947- .. **CLC 29**
See also CA 110; DLBD 9

de Man, Paul (Adolph Michel)
1919-1983 .... **CLC 55**
See also CA 111; 128; CANR 61; DLB 67;
MTCW 1, 2

DeMarinis, Rick 1934- .... **CLC 54**
See also CA 57-60, 184; CAAE 184; CAAS
24; CANR 9, 25, 50; DLB 218

de Maupassant, (Henri Rene Albert) Guy
See Maupassant, (Henri Rene Albert) Guy
de

Dembry, R. Emmet
See Murfree, Mary Noailles

Demby, William 1922- .... **BLC 1; CLC 53**
See also BW 1, 3; CA 81-84; CANR 81;
DAM MULT; DLB 33

de Menton, Francisco
See Chin, Frank (Chew, Jr.)

Demetrius of Phalerum c.
307B.C.- .... **CMLC 34**

Demijohn, Thom
See Disch, Thomas M(ichael)

Deming, Richard 1915-1983
See Queen, Ellery
See also CA 9-12R; CANR 3, 94; SATA 24

Democritus c. 460B.C.-c. 370B.C. . **CMLC 47**

de Montaigne, Michel (Eyquem)
See Montaigne, Michel (Eyquem) de

de Montherlant, Henry (Milon)
See Montherlant, Henry (Milon) de

Demosthenes 384B.C.-322B.C. ...... **CMLC 13**
See also AW 1; DLB 176; RGWL 2, 3

de Musset, (Louis Charles) Alfred
See Musset, (Louis Charles) Alfred de

de Natale, Francine
See Malzberg, Barry N(athaniel)

de Navarre, Marguerite 1492-1549 ..... **LC 61**
See Marguerite d'Angouleme; Marguerite
de Navarre

Denby, Edwin (Orr) 1903-1983 .... **CLC 48**
See also CA 110; 138

de Nerval, Gerard
See Nerval, Gerard de

Denham, John 1615-1669 .... **LC 73**
See also DLB 58, 126; RGEL 2

Denis, Julio
See Cortazar, Julio

Denmark, Harrison
See Zelazny, Roger (Joseph)

Dennis, John 1658-1734 .... **LC 11**
See also DLB 101; RGEL 2

Dennis, Nigel (Forbes) 1912-1989 ...... **CLC 8**
See also CA 129; 25-28R; DLB 13, 15, 233;
EWL 3; MTCW 1

Dent, Lester 1904(?)-1959 .... **TCLC 72**
See also CA 161; 112; CMW 4; SFW 4

De Palma, Brian (Russell) 1940- ...... **CLC 20**
See also CA 109

De Quincey, Thomas 1785-1859 ..... **NCLC 4, 87**
See also BRW 4; CDBLB 1789-1832; DLB
110, 144; RGEL 2

Deren, Eleanora 1908(?)-1961
See Deren, Maya
See also CA 111; 192

Deren, Maya .... **CLC 16, 102**
See Deren, Eleanora

Derleth, August (William)
1909-1971 .... **CLC 31**
See also BPFB 1; BYA 9, 10; CA 29-32R;
1-4R; CANR 4; CMW 4; DLB 9; DLBD
17; HGG; SATA 5; SUFW 1

Der Nister 1884-1950 .... **TCLC 56**

de Routisie, Albert
See Aragon, Louis

Derrida, Jacques 1930- .... **CLC 24, 87**
See also CA 127; 124; CANR 76, 98; DLB
242; EWL 3; MTCW 1; TWA

Derry Down Derry
See Lear, Edward

Dersonnes, Jacques
See Simenon, Georges (Jacques Christian)

Desai, Anita 1937- .... **CLC 19, 37, 97**
See also BRWS 5; CA 81-84; CANR 33,
53, 95; CN 7; CWRI 5; DA3; DAB; DAM
NOV; DLB 271; DNFS 2; EWL 3; FW;
MTCW 1, 2; SATA 63, 126

Desai, Kiran 1971- .... **CLC 119**
See also CA 171

de Saint-Luc, Jean
See Glassco, John

de Saint Roman, Arnaud
See Aragon, Louis

Desbordes-Valmore, Marceline
1786-1859 .... **NCLC 97**
See also DLB 217

Descartes, Rene 1596-1650 .... **LC 20, 35**
See also DLB 268; EW 3; GFL Beginnings
to 1789

De Sica, Vittorio 1901(?)-1974 .... **CLC 20**
See also CA 117

Desnos, Robert 1900-1945 .... **TCLC 22**
See also CA 151; 121; CANR 107; DLB
258; EWL 3

Destouches, Louis-Ferdinand
1894-1961 .... **CLC 9, 15**
See Celine, Louis-Ferdinand
See also CA 85-88; CANR 28; MTCW 1

de Tolignac, Gaston
See Griffith, D(avid Lewelyn) W(ark)

Deutsch, Babette 1895-1982 .... **CLC 18**
See also BYA 3; CA 108; 1-4R; CANR 4,
79; DLB 45; SATA 1; SATA-Obit 33

Devenant, William 1606-1649 .... **LC 13**

Devkota, Laxmiprasad 1909-1959 . **TCLC 23**
See also CA 123

De Voto, Bernard (Augustine)
1897-1955 .... **TCLC 29**
See also CA 160; 113; DLB 9, 256

De Vries, Peter 1910-1993 ..... **CLC 1, 2, 3, 7, 10, 28, 46**
See also CA 142; 17-20R; CANR 41; DAM
NOV; DLB 6; DLBY 1982; MTCW 1, 2

Dewey, John 1859-1952 .... **TCLC 95**
See also CA 170; 114; DLB 246, 270;
RGAL 4

Dexter, John
See Bradley, Marion Zimmer
See also GLL 1

Dexter, Martin
See Faust, Frederick (Schiller)
See also TCWW 2

Dexter, Pete 1943- .... **CLC 34, 55**
See also BEST 89:2; CA 131; 127; CPW;
DAM POP; INT 131; MTCW 1

Diamano, Silmang
See Senghor, Leopold Sedar

Diamond, Neil 1941- .... **CLC 30**
See also CA 108

Diaz del Castillo, Bernal
1496-1584 .... **HLCS 1; LC 31**
See also LAW

di Bassetto, Corno
See Shaw, George Bernard

Dick, Philip K(indred) 1928-1982 ... **CLC 10,
30, 72; SSC 57**
See also AAYA 24; BPFB 1; BYA 11; CA
106; 49-52; CANR 2, 16; CPW; DA3;
DAM NOV, POP; DLB 8; MTCW 1, 2;
NFS 5; SCFW; SFW 4

Dickens, Charles (John Huffam)
1812-1870 .... **NCLC 3, 8, 18, 26, 37, 50,
86, 105, 113; SSC 17, 49; WLC**
See also AAYA 23; BRW 5; BRWC 1; BYA
1, 2, 3, 13, 14; CDBLB 1832-1890; CMW
4; DA; DA3; DAB; DAC; DAM MST,
NOV; DLB 21, 55, 70, 159, 166; EXPN;
HGG; JRDA; LAIT 1, 2; MAICYA 1, 2;
NFS 4, 5, 10, 14; RGEL 2; RGSF 2;
SATA 15; SUFW 1; TEA; WCH; WLIT
4; WYA

Dickey, James (Lafayette)
1923-1997 .... **CLC 1, 2, 4, 7, 10, 15, 47,
109; PC 40**
See also AITN 1, 2; AMWS 4; BPFB 1;
CA 156; 9-12R; CABS 2; CANR 10, 48,
61, 105; CDALB 1968-1988; CP 7; CPW;
CSW; DA3; DAM NOV, POET, POP;
DLB 5, 193; DLBD 7; DLBY 1982, 1993,
1996, 1997, 1998; EWL 3; INT CANR-
10; MTCW 1, 2; NFS 9; PFS 6, 11;
RGAL 4; TUS

Dickey, William 1928-1994 .... **CLC 3, 28**
See also CA 145; 9-12R; CANR 24, 79;
DLB 5

Dickinson, Charles 1951- .... **CLC 49**
See also CA 128

Dickinson, Emily (Elizabeth)
1830-1886 ... **NCLC 21, 77; PC 1; WLC**
See also AAYA 22; AMW; AMWR 1;
CDALB 1865-1917; DA; DA3; DAB;
DAC; DAM MST, POET; DLB 1, 243;
EXPP; MAWW; PAB; PFS 1, 2, 3, 4, 5,
6, 8, 10, 11, 13, 16; RGAL 4; SATA 29;
TUS; WP; WYA

Dickinson, Mrs. Herbert Ward
See Phelps, Elizabeth Stuart

Dickinson, Peter (Malcolm) 1927- .. **CLC 12,
35**
See also AAYA 9; BYA 5; CA 41-44R;
CANR 31, 58, 88; CLR 29; CMW 4; DLB
87, 161, 276; JRDA; MAICYA 1, 2;
SATA 5, 62, 95; SFW 4; WYA; YAW

Dickson, Carr
See Carr, John Dickson

Dickson, Carter
See Carr, John Dickson

Diderot, Denis 1713-1784 .... **LC 26**
See also EW 4; GFL Beginnings to 1789;
RGWL 2, 3

Didion, Joan 1934- . **CLC 1, 3, 8, 14, 32, 129**
See also AITN 1; AMWS 4; CA 5-8R;
CANR 14, 52, 76; CDALB 1968-1988;
CN 7; DA3; DAM NOV; DLB 2, 173,
185; DLBY 1981, 1986; EWL 3; MAWW;
MTCW 1, 2; NFS 3; RGAL 4; TCWW 2;
TUS

Dietrich, Robert
See Hunt, E(verette) Howard, (Jr.)

Difusa, Pati
See Almodovar, Pedro

Dillard, Annie 1945- .... **CLC 9, 60, 115**
See also AAYA 6, 43; AMWS 6; ANW; CA
49-52; CANR 3, 43, 62, 90; DA3; DAM
NOV; DLB 275, 278; LAIT 3; MTCW 1,
4, 5; MTCW 1, 2; NCFS 1; RGAL 4;
SATA 10; TUS

Dillard, R(ichard) H(enry) W(ilde)
1937- .... **CLC 5**
See also CA 21-24R; CAAS 7; CANR 10;
CP 7; CSW; DLB 5, 244

Dillon, Eilis 1920-1994 .... **CLC 17**
See also CA 147; 9-12R, 182; CAAE 182;
CAAS 3; CANR 4, 38, 78; CLR 26; MAI-
CYA 1, 2; MAICYAS 1; SATA 2, 74;
SATA-Essay 105; SATA-Obit 83; YAW

Dimont, Penelope
See Mortimer, Penelope (Ruth)

Dinesen, Isak .... **CLC 10, 29, 95; SSC 7**
See Blixen, Karen (Christentze Dinesen)
See also EW 10; EWL 3; EXPS; FW; HGG;
LAIT 3; MTCW 1; NCFS 2; NFS 9;
RGSF 2; RGWL 2, 3; SSFS 3, 6, 13;
WLIT 2

Ding Ling .... **CLC 68**
See Chiang, Pin-chin
See also RGWL 3

Diphusa, Patty
See Almodovar, Pedro

Disch, Thomas M(ichael) 1940- ... **CLC 7, 36**
See also AAYA 17; BPFB 1; CA 21-24R;
CAAS 4; CANR 17, 36, 54, 89; CLR 18;
CP 7; DA3; DLB 8; HGG; MAICYA 1, 2;
MTCW 1, 2; SAAS 15; SATA 92; SCFW;
SFW 4; SUFW 2

Disch, Tom
See Disch, Thomas M(ichael)

d'Isly, Georges
See Simenon, Georges (Jacques Christian)

Disraeli, Benjamin 1804-1881 ... **NCLC 2, 39,
79**
See also BRW 4; DLB 21, 55; RGEL 2

Ditcum, Steve
See Crumb, R(obert)

Dixon, Paige
See Corcoran, Barbara (Asenath)

Dixon, Stephen 1936- .... **CLC 52; SSC 16**
See also AMWS 12; CA 89-92; CANR 17,
40, 54, 91; CN 7; DLB 130

Doak, Annie
See Dillard, Annie

Dobell, Sydney Thompson
1824-1874 .... **NCLC 43**
See also DLB 32; RGEL 2

Doblin, Alfred .... **TCLC 13**
See Doeblin, Alfred
See also CDWLB 2; EWL 3; RGWL 2, 3

Dobroliubov, Nikolai Aleksandrovich
See Dobrolyubov, Nikolai Alexandrovich
See also DLB 277

Dobrolyubov, Nikolai Alexandrovich
1836-1861 .... **NCLC 5**
See Dobroliubov, Nikolai Aleksandrovich

Dobson, Austin 1840-1921 .... **TCLC 79**
See also DLB 35, 144

Dobyns, Stephen 1941- .... **CLC 37**
See also CA 45-48; CANR 2, 18, 99; CMW
4; CP 7

Doctorow, E(dgar) L(aurence)
1931- .... **CLC 6, 11, 15, 18, 37, 44, 65,
113**
See also AAYA 22; AITN 2; AMWS 4;
BEST 89:3; BPFB 1; CA 45-48; CANR
2, 33, 51, 76, 97; CDALB 1968-1988; CN
7; CPW; DA3; DAM NOV, POP; DLB 2,
28, 173; DLBY 1980; EWL 3; LAIT 3;
MTCW 1, 2; NFS 6; RGAL 4; RHW;
TUS

Dodgson, Charles L(utwidge) 1832-1898
See Carroll, Lewis
See also CLR 2; DA; DA3; DAB; DAC;
DAM MST, NOV, POET; MAICYA 1, 2;
SATA 100; YABC 2

Dodson, Owen (Vincent) 1914-1983 .. **BLC 1;
CLC 79**
See also BW 1; CA 110; 65-68; CANR 24;
DAM MULT; DLB 76

Doeblin, Alfred 1878-1957 .... **TCLC 13**
See Doblin, Alfred
See also CA 141; 110; DLB 66

Doerr, Harriet 1910- .... **CLC 34**
See also CA 122; 117; CANR 47; INT 122

Domecq, H(onorio Bustos)
See Bioy Casares, Adolfo

Domecq, H(onorio) Bustos
See Bioy Casares, Adolfo; Borges, Jorge
Luis

Domini, Rey
See Lorde, Audre (Geraldine)
See also GLL 1

Dominique
See Proust, (Valentin-Louis-George-Eugene-
)Marcel

Don, A
See Stephen, Sir Leslie

Donaldson, Stephen R(eeder)
1947- .... **CLC 46, 138**
See also AAYA 36; BPFB 1; CA 89-92;
CANR 13, 55, 99; CPW; DAM POP;
FANT; INT CANR-13; SATA 121; SFW
4; SUFW 1, 2

Donleavy, J(ames) P(atrick) 1926- .... **CLC 1,
4, 6, 10, 45**
See also AITN 2; BPFB 1; CA 9-12R;
CANR 24, 49, 62, 80; CBD; CD 5; CN 7;
DLB 6, 173; INT CANR-24; MTCW 1,
2; RGAL 4

Donnadieu, Marguerite
See Duras, Marguerite
See also CWW 2

Donne, John 1572-1631 ..... **LC 10, 24; PC 1,
43; WLC**
See also BRW 1; BRWC 1; BRWR 2; CD-
BLB Before 1660; DA; DAB; DAC;
DAM MST, POET; DLB 121, 151; EXPP;
PAB; PFS 2, 11; RGEL 2; TEA; WLIT 3;
WP

Donnell, David 1939(?)- .... **CLC 34**
See also CA 197

Donoghue, P. S.
See Hunt, E(verette) Howard, (Jr.)

Donoso (Yanez), Jose 1924-1996 ... **CLC 4, 8,
11, 32, 99; HLC 1; SSC 34; TCLC 133**
See also CA 155; 81-84; CANR 32, 73; CD-
WLB 3; DAM MULT; DLB 113; EWL 3;
HW 1, 2; LAW; LAWS 1; MTCW 1, 2;
RGSF 2; WLIT 1

Donovan, John 1928-1992 .... **CLC 35**
See also AAYA 20; CA 137; 97-100; CLR
3; MAICYA 1, 2; SATA 72; SATA-Brief
29; YAW

Don Roberto
See Cunninghame Graham, Robert
(Gallnigad) Bontine

Doolittle, Hilda 1886-1961 . **CLC 3, 8, 14, 31, 34, 73; PC 5; WLC**
See H. D.
See also AMWS 1; CA 97-100; CANR 35; DA; DAC; DAM MST, POET; DLB 4, 45; EWL 3; FW; GLL 1; MAWW; MTCW 1, 2; PFS 6; RGAL 4

Doppo, Kunikida .... **TCLC 99**
See Kunikida Doppo

Dorfman, Ariel 1942- .... **CLC 48, 77; HLC 1**
See also CA 130; 124; CANR 67, 70; CWW 2; DAM MULT; DFS 4; EWL 3; HW 1, 2; INT CA-130; WLIT 1

Dorn, Edward (Merton)
1929-1999 .... **CLC 10, 18**
See also CA 187; 93-96; CANR 42, 79; CP 7; DLB 5; INT 93-96; WP

Dor-Ner, Zvi .... **CLC 70**

Dorris, Michael (Anthony)
1945-1997 .... **CLC 109; NNAL**
See also AAYA 20; BEST 90:1; BYA 12; CA 157; 102; CANR 19, 46, 75; CLR 58; DA3; DAM MULT, NOV; DLB 175; LAIT 5; MTCW 2; NFS 3; RGAL 4; SATA 75; SATA-Obit 94; TCWW 2; YAW

Dorris, Michael A.
See Dorris, Michael (Anthony)

Dorsan, Luc
See Simenon, Georges (Jacques Christian)

Dorsange, Jean
See Simenon, Georges (Jacques Christian)

Dos Passos, John (Roderigo)
1896-1970 ... **CLC 1, 4, 8, 11, 15, 25, 34, 82; WLC**
See also AMW; BPFB 1; CA 29-32R; 1-4R; CANR 3; CDALB 1929-1941; DA; DA3; DAB; DAC; DAM MST, NOV; DLB 4, 9, 274; DLBD 1, 15; DLBY 1996; EWL 3; MTCW 1, 2; NFS 14; RGAL 4; TUS

Dossage, Jean
See Simenon, Georges (Jacques Christian)

Dostoevsky, Fedor Mikhailovich
1821-1881 .. **NCLC 2, 7, 21, 33, 43, 119; SSC 2, 33, 44; WLC**
See Dostoevsky, Fyodor
See also AAYA 40; DA; DA3; DAB; DAC; DAM MST, NOV; EW 7; EXPN; NFS 3, 8; RGSF 2; RGWL 2, 3; SSFS 8; TWA

Dostoevsky, Fyodor
See Dostoevsky, Fedor Mikhailovich
See also DLB 238

Doughty, Charles M(ontagu)
1843-1926 .... **TCLC 27**
See also CA 178; 115; DLB 19, 57, 174

Douglas, Ellen .... **CLC 73**
See Haxton, Josephine Ayres; Williamson, Ellen Douglas
See also CN 7; CSW

Douglas, Gavin 1475(?)-1522 .... **LC 20**
See also DLB 132; RGEL 2

Douglas, George
See Brown, George Douglas
See also RGEL 2

Douglas, Keith (Castellain)
1920-1944 .... **TCLC 40**
See also BRW 7; CA 160; DLB 27; EWL 3; PAB; RGEL 2

Douglas, Leonard
See Bradbury, Ray (Douglas)

Douglas, Michael
See Crichton, (John) Michael

Douglas, (George) Norman
1868-1952 .... **TCLC 68**
See also BRW 6; CA 157; 119; DLB 34, 195; RGEL 2

Douglas, William
See Brown, George Douglas

Douglass, Frederick 1817(?)-1895 ..... **BLC 1; NCLC 7, 55; WLC**
See also AFAW 1, 2; AMWC 1; AMWS 3; CDALB 1640-1865; DA; DA3; DAC; DAM MST, MULT; DLB 1, 43, 50, 79, 243; FW; LAIT 2; NCFS 2; RGAL 4; SATA 29

Dourado, (Waldomiro Freitas) Autran
1926- .... **CLC 23, 60**
See also CA 25-28R; 179; CANR 34, 81; DLB 145; HW 2

Dourado, Waldomiro Autran
See Dourado, (Waldomiro Freitas) Autran
See also CA 179

Dove, Rita (Frances) 1952- . **BLCS; CLC 50, 81; PC 6**
See also AAYA 46; AMWS 4; BW 2; CA 109; CAAS 19; CANR 27, 42, 68, 76, 97; CDALBS; CP 7; CSW; CWP; DA3; DAM MULT, POET; DLB 120; EWL 3; EXPP; MTCW 1; PFS 1, 15; RGAL 4

Doveglion
See Villa, Jose Garcia

Dowell, Coleman 1925-1985 .... **CLC 60**
See also CA 117; 25-28R; CANR 10; DLB 130; GLL 2

Dowson, Ernest (Christopher)
1867-1900 .... **TCLC 4**
See also CA 150; 105; DLB 19, 135; RGEL 2

Doyle, A. Conan
See Doyle, Sir Arthur Conan

Doyle, Sir Arthur Conan
1859-1930 .... **SSC 12; TCLC 7; WLC**
See Conan Doyle, Arthur
See also AAYA 14; BRWS 2; CA 122; 104; CDBLB 1890-1914; CMW 4; DA; DA3; DAB; DAC; DAM MST, NOV; DLB 18, 70, 156, 178; EXPS; HGG; LAIT 2; MSW; MTCW 1, 2; RGEL 2; RGSF 2; RHW; SATA 24; SCFW 2; SFW 4; SSFS 2; TEA; WCH; WLIT 4; WYA; YAW

Doyle, Conan
See Doyle, Sir Arthur Conan

Doyle, John
See Graves, Robert (von Ranke)

Doyle, Roddy 1958(?)- .... **CLC 81**
See also AAYA 14; BRWS 5; CA 143; CANR 73; CN 7; DA3; DLB 194

Doyle, Sir A. Conan
See Doyle, Sir Arthur Conan

Dr. A
See Asimov, Isaac; Silverstein, Alvin; Silverstein, Virginia B(arbara Opshelor)

Drabble, Margaret 1939- ...... **CLC 2, 3, 5, 8, 10, 22, 53, 129**
See also BRWS 4; CA 13-16R; CANR 18, 35, 63, 112; CDBLB 1960 to Present; CN 7; CPW; DA3; DAB; DAC; DAM MST, NOV; POP; DLB 14, 155, 231; EWL 3; FW; MTCW 1, 2; RGEL 2; SATA 48; TEA

Drapier, M. B.
See Swift, Jonathan

Drayham, James
See Mencken, H(enry) L(ouis)

Drayton, Michael 1563-1631 .... **LC 8**
See also DAM POET; DLB 121; RGEL 2

Dreadstone, Carl
See Campbell, (John) Ramsey

Dreiser, Theodore (Herman Albert)
1871-1945 .... **SSC 30; TCLC 10, 18, 35, 83; WLC**
See also AMW; AMWR 2; CA 132; 106; CDALB 1865-1917; DA; DA3; DAC; DAM MST, NOV; DLB 9, 12, 102, 137; DLBD 1; EWL 3; LAIT 2; MTCW 1, 2; NFS 8; RGAL 4; TUS

Drexler, Rosalyn 1926- .... **CLC 2, 6**
See also CA 81-84; CAD; CANR 68; CD 5; CWD

Dreyer, Carl Theodor 1889-1968 ...... **CLC 16**
See also CA 116

Drieu la Rochelle, Pierre(-Eugene)
1893-1945 .... **TCLC 21**
See also CA 117; DLB 72; EWL 3; GFL 1789 to the Present

Drinkwater, John 1882-1937 .... **TCLC 57**
See also CA 149; 109; DLB 10, 19, 149; RGEL 2

Drop Shot
See Cable, George Washington

Droste-Hulshoff, Annette Freiin von
1797-1848 .... **NCLC 3**
See also CDWLB 2; DLB 133; RGSF 2; RGWL 2, 3

Drummond, Walter
See Silverberg, Robert

Drummond, William Henry
1854-1907 .... **TCLC 25**
See also CA 160; DLB 92

Drummond de Andrade, Carlos
1902-1987 .... **CLC 18**
See Andrade, Carlos Drummond de
See also CA 123; 132; LAW

Drummond of Hawthornden, William
1585-1649 .... **LC 83**
See also DLB 121, 213; RGEL 2

Drury, Allen (Stuart) 1918-1998 .... **CLC 37**
See also CA 170; 57-60; CANR 18, 52; CN 7; INT CANR-18

Dryden, John 1631-1700 ..... **DC 3; LC 3, 21; PC 25; WLC**
See also BRW 2; CDBLB 1660-1789; DA; DAB; DAC; DAM DRAM, MST, POET; DLB 80, 101, 131; EXPP; IDTP; RGEL 2; TEA; WLIT 3

Duberman, Martin (Bauml) 1930- ..... **CLC 8**
See also CA 1-4R; CAD; CANR 2, 63; CD 5

Dubie, Norman (Evans) 1945- .... **CLC 36**
See also CA 69-72; CANR 12, 115; CP 7; DLB 120; PFS 12

Du Bois, W(illiam) E(dward) B(urghardt)
1868-1963 ..... **BLC 1; CLC 1, 2, 13, 64, 96; HR 2; WLC**
See also AAYA 40; AFAW 1, 2; AMWC 1; AMWS 2; BW 1, 3; CA 85-88; CANR 34, 82; CDALB 1865-1917; DA; DA3; DAC; DAM MST, MULT, NOV; DLB 47, 50, 91, 246; EWL 3; EXPP; LAIT 2; MTCW 1, 2; NCFS 1; PFS 13; RGAL 4; SATA 42

Dubus, Andre 1936-1999 ..... **CLC 13, 36, 97; SSC 15**
See also AMWS 7; CA 177; 21-24R; CANR 17; CN 7; CSW; DLB 130; INT CANR-17; RGAL 4; SSFS 10

Duca Minimo
See D'Annunzio, Gabriele

Ducharme, Rejean 1941- .... **CLC 74**
See also CA 165; DLB 60

Duchen, Claire .... **CLC 65**

Duclos, Charles Pinot- 1704-1772 .... **LC 1**
See also GFL Beginnings to 1789

Dudek, Louis 1918- .... **CLC 11, 19**
See also CA 45-48; CAAS 14; CANR 1; CP 7; DLB 88

Duerrenmatt, Friedrich 1921-1990 ... **CLC 1, 4, 8, 11, 15, 43, 102**
See Durrenmatt, Friedrich
See also CA 17-20R; CANR 33; CMW 4; DAM DRAM; DLB 69, 124; MTCW 1, 2

Duffy, Bruce 1953(?)- .... **CLC 50**
See also CA 172

Eden, Emily 1797-1869 .... **NCLC 10**
Edgar, David 1948- .... **CLC 42**
See also CA 57-60; CANR 12, 61, 112;
CBD; CD 5; DAM DRAM; DFS 15; DLB
13, 233; MTCW 1
Edgerton, Clyde (Carlyle) 1944- ...... **CLC 39**
See also AAYA 17; CA 134; 118; CANR
64; CSW; DLB 278; INT 134; YAW
Edgeworth, Maria 1768-1849 .... **NCLC 1, 51**
See also BRWS 3; DLB 116, 159, 163; FW;
RGEL 2; SATA 21; TEA; WLIT 3
Edmonds, Paul
See Kuttner, Henry
Edmonds, Walter D(umaux)
1903-1998 .... **CLC 35**
See also BYA 2; CA 5-8R; CANR 2; CWRI
5; DLB 9; LAIT 1; MAICYA 1, 2; RHW;
SAAS 4; SATA 1, 27; SATA-Obit 99
Edmondson, Wallace
See Ellison, Harlan (Jay)
Edson, Russell 1935- .... **CLC 13**
See also CA 33-36R; CANR 115; DLB 244;
WP
Edwards, Bronwen Elizabeth
See Rose, Wendy
Edwards, G(erald) B(asil)
1899-1976 .... **CLC 25**
See also CA 110; 201
Edwards, Gus 1939- .... **CLC 43**
See also CA 108; INT 108
Edwards, Jonathan 1703-1758 .... **LC 7, 54**
See also AMW; DA; DAC; DAM MST;
DLB 24, 270; RGAL 4; TUS
Edwards, Sarah Pierpont 1710-1758 .. **LC 87**
See also DLB 200
Efron, Marina Ivanovna Tsvetaeva
See Tsvetaeva (Efron), Marina (Ivanovna)
Egoyan, Atom 1960- .... **CLC 151**
See also CA 157
Ehle, John (Marsden, Jr.) 1925- ...... **CLC 27**
See also CA 9-12R; CSW
Ehrenbourg, Ilya (Grigoryevich)
See Ehrenburg, Ilya (Grigoryevich)
Ehrenburg, Ilya (Grigoryevich)
1891-1967 .... **CLC 18, 34, 62**
See Erenburg, Il'ia Grigor'evich
See also CA 25-28R; 102; EWL 3
Ehrenburg, Ilyo (Grigoryevich)
See Ehrenburg, Ilya (Grigoryevich)
Ehrenreich, Barbara 1941- .... **CLC 110**
See also BEST 90:4; CA 73-76; CANR 16,
37, 62; DLB 246; FW; MTCW 1, 2
Eich, Gunter
See Eich, Gunter
See also RGWL 2, 3
Eich, Gunter 1907-1972 .... **CLC 15**
See Eich, Gunter
See also CA 93-96; 111; DLB 69, 124;
EWL 3
Eichendorff, Joseph 1788-1857 .... **NCLC 8**
See also DLB 90; RGWL 2, 3
Eigner, Larry .... **CLC 9**
See Eigner, Laurence (Joel)
See also CAAS 23; DLB 5; WP
Eigner, Laurence (Joel) 1927-1996
See Eigner, Larry
See also CA 151; 9-12R; CANR 6, 84; CP
7; DLB 193
Einhard c. 770-840 .... **CMLC 50**
See also DLB 148
Einstein, Albert 1879-1955 .... **TCLC 65**
See also CA 133; 121; MTCW 1, 2
Eiseley, Loren
See Eiseley, Loren Corey
See also DLB 275
Eiseley, Loren Corey 1907-1977 .... **CLC 7**
See Eiseley, Loren
See also AAYA 5; ANW; CA 73-76; 1-4R;
CANR 6; DLBD 17

Eisenstadt, Jill 1963- .... **CLC 50**
See also CA 140
Eisenstein, Sergei (Mikhailovich)
1898-1948 .... **TCLC 57**
See also CA 149; 114
Eisner, Simon
See Kornbluth, C(yril) M.
Ekeloef, (Bengt) Gunnar
1907-1968 .... **CLC 27; PC 23**
See Ekelof, (Bengt) Gunnar
See also CA 25-28R; 123; DAM POET
Ekelof, (Bengt) Gunnar 1907-1968
See Ekeloef, (Bengt) Gunnar
See also DLB 259; EW 12; EWL 3
Ekelund, Vilhelm 1880-1949 .... **TCLC 75**
See also CA 189; EWL 3
Ekwensi, C. O. D.
See Ekwensi, Cyprian (Odiatu Duaka)
Ekwensi, Cyprian (Odiatu Duaka)
1921- .... **BLC 1; CLC 4**
See also AFW; BW 2, 3; CA 29-32R;
CANR 18, 42, 74; CDWLB 3; CN 7;
CWRI 5; DAM MULT; DLB 117; EWL
3; MTCW 1, 2; RGEL 2; SATA 66; WLIT
2
Elaine .... **TCLC 18**
See Leverson, Ada Esther
El Crummo
See Crumb, R(obert)
Elder, Lonne III 1931-1996 ..... **BLC 1; DC 8**
See also BW 1, 3; CA 152; 81-84; CAD;
CANR 25; DAM MULT; DLB 7, 38, 44
Eleanor of Aquitaine 1122-1204 ... **CMLC 39**
Elia
See Lamb, Charles
Eliade, Mircea 1907-1986 .... **CLC 19**
See also CA 119; 65-68; CANR 30, 62; CD-
WLB 4; DLB 220; EWL 3; MTCW 1;
RGWL 3; SFW 4
Eliot, A. D.
See Jewett, (Theodora) Sarah Orne
Eliot, Alice
See Jewett, (Theodora) Sarah Orne
Eliot, Dan
See Silverberg, Robert
Eliot, George 1819-1880 ...... **NCLC 4, 13, 23,**
41, 49, 89, 118; PC 20; WLC
See also BRW 5; BRWC 1; BRWR 2; CD-
BLB 1832-1890; CN 7; CPW; DA; DA3;
DAB; DAC; DAM MST, NOV; DLB 21,
35, 55; RGEL 2; RGSF 2; SSFS 8; TEA;
WLIT 3
Eliot, John 1604-1690 .... **LC 5**
See also DLB 24
Eliot, T(homas) S(tearns)
1888-1965 ...... **CLC 1, 2, 3, 6, 9, 10, 13,**
15, 24, 34, 41, 55, 57, 113; PC 5, 31;
WLC
See also AAYA 28; AMW; AMWC 1;
AMWR 1; BRW 7; BRWR 2; CA 25-28R;
5-8R; CANR 41; CDALB 1929-1941;
DA; DA3; DAB; DAC; DAM DRAM,
MST, POET; DFS 4, 13; DLB 7, 10, 45,
63, 245; DLBY 1988; EWL 3; EXPP;
LAIT 3; MTCW 1, 2; PAB; PFS 1, 7;
RGAL 4; RGEL 2; TUS; WLIT 4; WP
Elizabeth 1866-1941 .... **TCLC 41**
Elkin, Stanley L(awrence)
1930-1995 .. **CLC 4, 6, 9, 14, 27, 51, 91;**
SSC 12
See also AMWS 6; BPFB 1; CA 148;
9-12R; CANR 8, 46; CN 7; CPW; DAM
NOV, POP; DLB 2, 28, 218, 278; DLBY
1980; EWL 3; INT CANR-8; MTCW 1,
2; RGAL 4
Elledge, Scott .... **CLC 34**
Elliot, Don
See Silverberg, Robert

Elliott, Don
See Silverberg, Robert
Elliott, George P(aul) 1918-1980 .... **CLC 2**
See also CA 97-100; 1-4R; CANR 2; DLB
244
Elliott, Janice 1931-1995 .... **CLC 47**
See also CA 13-16R; CANR 8, 29, 84; CN
7; DLB 14; SATA 119
Elliott, Sumner Locke 1917-1991 ..... **CLC 38**
See also CA 134; 5-8R; CANR 2, 21
Elliott, William
See Bradbury, Ray (Douglas)
Ellis, A. E. .... **CLC 7**
Ellis, Alice Thomas .... **CLC 40**
See Haycraft, Anna (Margaret)
See also DLB 194; MTCW 1
Ellis, Bret Easton 1964- ...... **CLC 39, 71, 117**
See also AAYA 2, 43; CA 123; 118; CANR
51, 74; CN 7; CPW; DA3; DAM POP;
HGG; INT CA-123; MTCW 1; NFS 11
Ellis, (Henry) Havelock
1859-1939 .... **TCLC 14**
See also CA 169; 109; DLB 190
Ellis, Landon
See Ellison, Harlan (Jay)
Ellis, Trey 1962- .... **CLC 55**
See also CA 146; CANR 92
Ellison, Harlan (Jay) 1934- ... **CLC 1, 13, 42,**
139; SSC 14
See also AAYA 29; BPFB 1; BYA 14; CA
5-8R; CANR 5, 46, 115; CPW; DAM
POP; DLB 8; HGG; INT CANR-5;
MTCW 1, 2; SCFW 2; SFW 4; SSFS 13,
14, 15; SUFW 1, 2
Ellison, Ralph (Waldo) 1914-1994 .... **BLC 1;**
CLC 1, 3, 11, 54, 86, 114; SSC 26;
WLC
See also AAYA 19; AFAW 1, 2; AMWR 2;
AMWS 2; BPFB 1; BW 1, 3; BYA 2; CA
145; 9-12R; CANR 24, 53; CDALB 1941-
1968; CSW; DA; DA3; DAB; DAC;
DAM MST, MULT, NOV; DLB 2, 76,
227; DLBY 1994; EWL 3; EXPN; EXPS;
LAIT 4; MTCW 1, 2; NCFS 3; NFS 2;
RGAL 4; RGSF 2; SSFS 1, 11; YAW
Ellmann, Lucy (Elizabeth) 1956- ..... **CLC 61**
See also CA 128
Ellmann, Richard (David)
1918-1987 .... **CLC 50**
See also BEST 89:2; CA 122; 1-4R; CANR
2, 28, 61; DLB 103; DLBY 1987; MTCW
1, 2
Elman, Richard (Martin)
1934-1997 .... **CLC 19**
See also CA 163; 17-20R; CAAS 3; CANR
47
Elron
See Hubbard, L(afayette) Ron(ald)
Eluard, Paul .... **PC 38; TCLC 7, 41**
See Grindel, Eugene
See also EWL 3; GFL 1789 to the Present;
RGWL 2, 3
Elyot, Thomas 1490(?)-1546 .... **LC 11**
See also DLB 136; RGEL 2
Elytis, Odysseus 1911-1996 .... **CLC 15, 49,**
100; PC 21
See Alepoudelis, Odysseus
See also CA 151; 102; CANR 94; CWW 2;
DAM POET; EW 13; EWL 3; MTCW 1,
2; RGWL 2, 3
Emecheta, (Florence Onye) Buchi
1944- .... **BLC 2; CLC 14, 48, 128**
See also AFW; BW 2, 3; CA 81-84; CANR
27, 81; CDWLB 3; CN 7; CWRI 5; DA3;
DAM MULT; DLB 117; EWL 3; FW;
MTCW 1, 2; NFS 12, 14; SATA 66; WLIT
2

Emerson, Mary Moody
1774-1863 .... **NCLC 66**
Emerson, Ralph Waldo 1803-1882 . **NCLC 1,**
38, 98; PC 18; WLC
See also AMW; ANW; CDALB 1640-1865;
DA; DA3; DAB; DAC; DAM MST,
POET; DLB 1, 59, 73, 183, 223, 270;
EXPP; LAIT 2; NCFS 3; PFS 4, 17;
RGAL 4; TUS; WP
Eminescu, Mihail 1850-1889 .... **NCLC 33**
Empedocles 5th cent. B.C.- .... **CMLC 50**
See also DLB 176
Empson, William 1906-1984 ... **CLC 3, 8, 19,**
33, 34
See also BRWS 2; CA 112; 17-20R; CANR
31, 61; DLB 20; EWL 3; MTCW 1, 2;
RGEL 2
Enchi, Fumiko (Ueda) 1905-1986 ..... **CLC 31**
See Enchi Fumiko
See also CA 121; 129; FW; MJW
Enchi Fumiko
See Enchi, Fumiko (Ueda)
See also DLB 182; EWL 3
Ende, Michael (Andreas Helmuth)
1929-1995 .... **CLC 31**
See also BYA 5; CA 149; 124; 118; CANR
36, 110; CLR 14; DLB 75; MAICYA 1,
2; MAICYAS 1; SATA 61, 130; SATA-
Brief 42; SATA-Obit 86
Endo, Shusaku 1923-1996 ..... **CLC 7, 14, 19,**
54, 99; SSC 48
See Endo Shusaku
See also CA 153; 29-32R; CANR 21, 54;
DA3; DAM NOV; MTCW 1, 2; RGSF 2;
RGWL 2, 3
Endo Shusaku
See Endo, Shusaku
See also DLB 182; EWL 3
Engel, Marian 1933-1985 .... **CLC 36**
See also CA 25-28R; CANR 12; DLB 53;
FW; INT CANR-12
Engelhardt, Frederick
See Hubbard, L(afayette) Ron(ald)
Engels, Friedrich 1820-1895 .. **NCLC 85, 114**
See also DLB 129
Enright, D(ennis) J(oseph) 1920- .. **CLC 4, 8,**
31
See also CA 1-4R; CANR 1, 42, 83; CP 7;
DLB 27; EWL 3; SATA 25
Enzensberger, Hans Magnus
1929- .... **CLC 43; PC 28**
See also CA 119; 116; CANR 103; EWL 3
Ephron, Nora 1941- .... **CLC 17, 31**
See also AAYA 35; AITN 2; CA 65-68;
CANR 12, 39, 83
Epicurus 341B.C.-270B.C. .... **CMLC 21**
See also DLB 176
Epsilon
See Betjeman, John
Epstein, Daniel Mark 1948- .... **CLC 7**
See also CA 49-52; CANR 2, 53, 90
Epstein, Jacob 1956- .... **CLC 19**
See also CA 114
Epstein, Jean 1897-1953 .... **TCLC 92**
Epstein, Joseph 1937- .... **CLC 39**
See also CA 119; 112; CANR 50, 65
Epstein, Leslie 1938- .... **CLC 27**
See also AMWS 12; CA 73-76; CAAS 12;
CANR 23, 69
Equiano, Olaudah 1745(?)-1797 . **BLC 2; LC**
16
See also AFAW 1, 2; CDWLB 3; DAM
MULT; DLB 37, 50; WLIT 2
Erasmus, Desiderius 1469(?)-1536 ...... **LC 16**
See also DLB 136; EW 2; RGWL 2, 3;
TWA
Erdman, Paul E(mil) 1932- .... **CLC 25**
See also AITN 1; CA 61-64; CANR 13, 43,
84

Erdrich, Louise 1954- .... **CLC 39, 54, 120;**
NNAL
See also AAYA 10, 47; AMWS 4; BEST
89:1; BPFB 1; CA 114; CANR 41, 62;
CDALBS; CN 7; CP 7; CPW; CWP;
DA3; DAM MULT, NOV, POP; DLB 152,
175, 206; EWL 3; EXPP; LAIT 5; MTCW
1; NFS 5; PFS 14; RGAL 4; SATA 94;
SSFS 14; TCWW 2
Erenburg, Ilya (Grigoryevich)
See Ehrenburg, Ilya (Grigoryevich)
Erickson, Stephen Michael 1950-
See Erickson, Steve
See also CA 129; SFW 4
Erickson, Steve .... **CLC 64**
See Erickson, Stephen Michael
See also CANR 60, 68; SUFW 2
Ericson, Walter
See Fast, Howard (Melvin)
Eriksson, Buntel
See Bergman, (Ernst) Ingmar
Ernaux, Annie 1940- .... **CLC 88**
See also CA 147; CANR 93; NCFS 3
Erskine, John 1879-1951 .... **TCLC 84**
See also CA 159; 112; DLB 9, 102; FANT
Eschenbach, Wolfram von
See Wolfram von Eschenbach
See also RGWL 3
Eseki, Bruno
See Mphahlele, Ezekiel
Esenin, Sergei (Alexandrovich)
1895-1925 .... **TCLC 4**
See also CA 104; RGWL 2, 3
Eshleman, Clayton 1935- .... **CLC 7**
See also CA 33-36R; CAAS 6; CANR 93;
CP 7; DLB 5
Espriella, Don Manuel Alvarez
See Southey, Robert
Espriu, Salvador 1913-1985 .... **CLC 9**
See also CA 115; 154; DLB 134; EWL 3
Espronceda, Jose de 1808-1842 ..... **NCLC 39**
Esquivel, Laura 1951(?)- ... **CLC 141; HLCS**
1
See also AAYA 29; CA 143; CANR 68, 113;
DA3; DNFS 2; LAIT 3; MTCW 1; NFS
5; WLIT 1
Esse, James
See Stephens, James
Esterbrook, Tom
See Hubbard, L(afayette) Ron(ald)
Estleman, Loren D. 1952- .... **CLC 48**
See also AAYA 27; CA 85-88; CANR 27,
74; CMW 4; CPW; DA3; DAM NOV,
POP; DLB 226; INT CANR-27; MTCW
1, 2
Etherege, Sir George 1636-1692 .... **LC 78**
See also BRW 2; DAM DRAM; DLB 80;
PAB; RGEL 2
Euclid 306B.C.-283B.C. .... **CMLC 25**
Eugenides, Jeffrey 1960(?)- .... **CLC 81**
See also CA 144
Euripides c. 484B.C.-406B.C. .... **CMLC 23,**
51; DC 4; WLCS
See also AW 1; CDWLB 1; DA; DA3;
DAB; DAC; DAM DRAM, MST; DFS 1,
4, 6; DLB 176; LAIT 1; RGWL 2, 3
Evan, Evin
See Faust, Frederick (Schiller)
Evans, Caradoc 1878-1945 ... **SSC 43; TCLC**
85
See also DLB 162
Evans, Evan
See Faust, Frederick (Schiller)
See also TCWW 2
Evans, Marian
See Eliot, George
Evans, Mary Ann
See Eliot, George

Evarts, Esther
See Benson, Sally
Everett, Percival
See Everett, Percival L.
See also CSW
Everett, Percival L. 1956- .... **CLC 57**
See Everett, Percival
See also BW 2; CA 129; CANR 94
Everson, R(onald) G(ilmour)
1903-1992 .... **CLC 27**
See also CA 17-20R; DLB 88
Everson, William (Oliver)
1912-1994 .... **CLC 1, 5, 14**
See also BG 2; CA 145; 9-12R; CANR 20;
DLB 5, 16, 212; MTCW 1
Evtushenko, Evgenii Aleksandrovich
See Yevtushenko, Yevgeny (Alexandrovich)
See also RGWL 2, 3
Ewart, Gavin (Buchanan)
1916-1995 .... **CLC 13, 46**
See also BRWS 7; CA 150; 89-92; CANR
17, 46; CP 7; DLB 40; MTCW 1
Ewers, Hanns Heinz 1871-1943 ..... **TCLC 12**
See also CA 149; 109
Ewing, Frederick R.
See Sturgeon, Theodore (Hamilton)
Exley, Frederick (Earl) 1929-1992 .... **CLC 6,**
11
See also AITN 2; BPFB 1; CA 138; 81-84;
DLB 143; DLBY 1981
Eynhardt, Guillermo
See Quiroga, Horacio (Sylvestre)
Ezekiel, Nissim 1924- .... **CLC 61**
See also CA 61-64; CP 7; EWL 3
Ezekiel, Tish O'Dowd 1943- .... **CLC 34**
See also CA 129
Fadeev, Aleksandr Aleksandrovich
See Bulgya, Alexander Alexandrovich
See also DLB 272
Fadeev, Alexandr Alexandrovich
See Bulgya, Alexander Alexandrovich
See also EWL 3
Fadeyev, A.
See Bulgya, Alexander Alexandrovich
Fadeyev, Alexander .... **TCLC 53**
See Bulgya, Alexander Alexandrovich
Fagen, Donald 1948- .... **CLC 26**
Fainzilberg, Ilya Arnoldovich 1897-1937
See Ilf, Ilya
See also CA 165; 120
Fair, Ronald L. 1932- .... **CLC 18**
See also BW 1; CA 69-72; CANR 25; DLB
33
Fairbairn, Roger
See Carr, John Dickson
Fairbairns, Zoe (Ann) 1948- .... **CLC 32**
See also CA 103; CANR 21, 85; CN 7
Fairfield, Flora
See Alcott, Louisa May
Fairman, Paul W. 1916-1977
See Queen, Ellery
See also CA 114; SFW 4
Falco, Gian
See Papini, Giovanni
Falconer, James
See Kirkup, James
Falconer, Kenneth
See Kornbluth, C(yril) M.
Falkland, Samuel
See Heijermans, Herman
Fallaci, Oriana 1930- .... **CLC 11, 110**
See also CA 77-80; CANR 15, 58; FW;
MTCW 1
Faludi, Susan 1959- .... **CLC 140**
See also CA 138; FW; MTCW 1; NCFS 3
Faludy, George 1913- .... **CLC 42**
See also CA 21-24R

Faludy, Gyoergy
  See Faludy, George
Fanon, Frantz 1925-1961 .... **BLC 2; CLC 74**
  See also BW 1; CA 89-92; 116; DAM
  MULT; WLIT 2
Fanshawe, Ann 1625-1680 .... **LC 11**
Fante, John (Thomas) 1911-1983 ..... **CLC 60**
  See also AMWS 11; CA 109; 69-72; CANR
  23, 104; DLB 130; DLBY 1983
Farah, Nuruddin 1945- ...... **BLC 2; CLC 53,
  137**
  See also AFW; BW 2, 3; CA 106; CANR
  81; CDWLB 3; CN 7; DAM MULT; DLB
  125; EWL 3; WLIT 2
Fargue, Leon-Paul 1876(?)-1947 .... **TCLC 11**
  See also CA 109; CANR 107; DLB 258;
  EWL 3
Farigoule, Louis
  See Romains, Jules
Farina, Richard 1936(?)-1966 .... **CLC 9**
  See also CA 25-28R; 81-84
Farley, Walter (Lorimer)
  1915-1989 .... **CLC 17**
  See also BYA 14; CA 17-20R; CANR 8,
  29, 84; DLB 22; JRDA; MAICYA 1, 2;
  SATA 2, 43, 132; YAW
Farmer, Philip Jose 1918- .... **CLC 1, 19**
  See also AAYA 28; BPFB 1; CA 1-4R;
  CANR 4, 35, 111; DLB 8; MTCW 1;
  SATA 93; SCFW 2; SFW 4
Farquhar, George 1677-1707 .... **LC 21**
  See also BRW 2; DAM DRAM; DLB 84;
  RGEL 2
Farrell, J(ames) G(ordon)
  1935-1979 .... **CLC 6**
  See also CA 89-92; 73-76; CANR 36; DLB
  14, 271; MTCW 1; RGEL 2; RHW; WLIT
  4
Farrell, James T(homas) 1904-1979 . **CLC 1,
  4, 8, 11, 66; SSC 28**
  See also AMW; BPFB 1; CA 89-92; 5-8R;
  CANR 9, 61; DLB 4, 9, 86; DLBD 2;
  EWL 3; MTCW 1, 2; RGAL 4
Farrell, Warren (Thomas) 1943- ...... **CLC 70**
  See also CA 146
Farren, Richard J.
  See Betjeman, John
Farren, Richard M.
  See Betjeman, John
Fassbinder, Rainer Werner
  1946-1982 .... **CLC 20**
  See also CA 106; 93-96; CANR 31
Fast, Howard (Melvin) 1914-2003 .. **CLC 23,
  131**
  See also AAYA 16; BPFB 1; CA 1-4R, 181;
  CAAE 181; CAAS 18; CANR 1, 33, 54,
  75, 98; CMW 4; CN 7; CPW; DAM NOV;
  DLB 9; INT CANR-33; MTCW 1; RHW;
  SATA 7; SATA-Essay 107; TCWW 2;
  YAW
Faulcon, Robert
  See Holdstock, Robert P.
Faulkner, William (Cuthbert)
  1897-1962 .... **CLC 1, 3, 6, 8, 9, 11, 14,
  18, 28, 52, 68; SSC 1, 35, 42; WLC**
  See also AAYA 7; AMW; AMWR 1; BPFB
  1; BYA 5; CA 81-84; CANR 33; CDALB
  1929-1941; DA; DA3; DAB; DAC; DAM
  MST, NOV; DLB 9, 11, 44, 102; DLBD
  2; DLBY 1986, 1997; EWL 3; EXPN;
  EXPS; LAIT 2; MTCW 1, 2; NFS 4, 8,
  13; RGAL 4; RGSF 2; SSFS 2, 5, 6, 12;
  TUS
Fauset, Jessie Redmon
  1882(?)-1961 .. **BLC 2; CLC 19, 54; HR
  2**
  See also AFAW 2; BW 1; CA 109; CANR
  83; DAM MULT; DLB 51; FW; MAWW

Faust, Frederick (Schiller)
  1892-1944(?) .... **TCLC 49**
  See also Austin, Frank; Brand, Max; Challis,
  George; Dawson, Peter; Dexter, Martin;
  Evans, Evan; Frederick, John; Frost, Fred-
  erick; Manning, David; Silver, Nicholas
  See also CA 152; 108; DAM POP; DLB
  256; TUS
Faust, Irvin 1924- .... **CLC 8**
  See also CA 33-36R; CANR 28, 67; CN 7;
  DLB 2, 28, 218, 278; DLBY 1980
Fawkes, Guy
  See Benchley, Robert (Charles)
Fearing, Kenneth (Flexner)
  1902-1961 .... **CLC 51**
  See also CA 93-96; CANR 59; CMW 4;
  DLB 9; RGAL 4
Fecamps, Elise
  See Creasey, John
Federman, Raymond 1928- .... **CLC 6, 47**
  See also CA 17-20R; CAAS 8; CANR 10,
  43, 83, 108; CN 7; DLBY 1980
Federspiel, J(uerg) F. 1931- .... **CLC 42**
  See also CA 146
Feiffer, Jules (Ralph) 1929- ...... **CLC 2, 8, 64**
  See also AAYA 3; CA 17-20R; CAD; CANR
  30, 59; CD 5; DAM DRAM; DLB 7, 44;
  INT CANR-30; MTCW 1; SATA 8, 61,
  111
Feige, Hermann Albert Otto Maximilian
  See Traven, B.
Feinberg, David B. 1956-1994 .... **CLC 59**
  See also CA 147; 135
Feinstein, Elaine 1930- .... **CLC 36**
  See also CA 69-72; CAAS 1; CANR 31,
  68; CN 7; CP 7; CWP; DLB 14, 40;
  MTCW 1
Feke, Gilbert David .... **CLC 65**
Feldman, Irving (Mordecai) 1928- ..... **CLC 7**
  See also CA 1-4R; CANR 1; CP 7; DLB
  169
Felix-Tchicaya, Gerald
  See Tchicaya, Gerald Felix
Fellini, Federico 1920-1993 .... **CLC 16, 85**
  See also CA 143; 65-68; CANR 33
Felsen, Henry Gregor 1916-1995 ...... **CLC 17**
  See also CA 180; 1-4R; CANR 1; SAAS 2;
  SATA 1
Felski, Rita .... **CLC 65**
Fenno, Jack
  See Calisher, Hortense
Fenollosa, Ernest (Francisco)
  1853-1908 .... **TCLC 91**
Fenton, James Martin 1949- .... **CLC 32**
  See also CA 102; CANR 108; CP 7; DLB
  40; PFS 11
Ferber, Edna 1887-1968 .... **CLC 18, 93**
  See also AITN 1; CA 25-28R; 5-8R; CANR
  68, 105; DLB 9, 28, 86, 266; MTCW 1,
  2; RGAL 4; RHW; SATA 7; TCWW 2
Ferdowsi, Abu'l Qasem 940-1020 . **CMLC 43**
  See also RGWL 2, 3
Ferguson, Helen
  See Kavan, Anna
Ferguson, Niall 1964- .... **CLC 134**
  See also CA 190
Ferguson, Samuel 1810-1886 .... **NCLC 33**
  See also DLB 32; RGEL 2
Fergusson, Robert 1750-1774 .... **LC 29**
  See also DLB 109; RGEL 2
Ferling, Lawrence
  See Ferlinghetti, Lawrence (Monsanto)
Ferlinghetti, Lawrence (Monsanto)
  1919(?)- ..... **CLC 2, 6, 10, 27, 111; PC 1**
  See also CA 5-8R; CANR 3, 41, 73;
  CDALB 1941-1968; CP 7; DA3; DAM
  POET; DLB 5, 16; MTCW 1, 2; RGAL 4;
  WP

Fern, Fanny
  See Parton, Sara Payson Willis
Fernandez, Vicente Garcia Huidobro
  See Huidobro Fernandez, Vicente Garcia
Fernandez-Armesto, Felipe .... **CLC 70**
Fernandez de Lizardi, Jose Joaquin
  See Lizardi, Jose Joaquin Fernandez de
Ferre, Rosario 1942- ...... **CLC 139; HLCS 1;
  SSC 36**
  See also CA 131; CANR 55, 81; CWW 2;
  DLB 145; EWL 3; HW 1, 2; LAWS 1;
  MTCW 1; WLIT 1
Ferrer, Gabriel (Francisco Victor) Miro
  See Miro (Ferrer), Gabriel (Francisco
  Victor)
Ferrier, Susan (Edmonstone)
  1782-1854 .... **NCLC 8**
  See also DLB 116; RGEL 2
Ferrigno, Robert 1948(?)- .... **CLC 65**
  See also CA 140
Ferron, Jacques 1921-1985 .... **CLC 94**
  See also CA 129; 117; CCA 1; DAC; DLB
  60; EWL 3
Feuchtwanger, Lion 1884-1958 .... **TCLC 3**
  See also CA 187; 104; DLB 66; EWL 3
Feuillet, Octave 1821-1890 .... **NCLC 45**
  See also DLB 192
Feydeau, Georges (Leon Jules Marie)
  1862-1921 .... **TCLC 22**
  See also CA 152; 113; CANR 84; DAM
  DRAM; DLB 192; EWL 3; GFL 1789 to
  the Present; RGWL 2, 3
Fichte, Johann Gottlieb
  1762-1814 .... **NCLC 62**
  See also DLB 90
Ficino, Marsilio 1433-1499 .... **LC 12**
Fiedeler, Hans
  See Doeblin, Alfred
Fiedler, Leslie A(aron) 1917-2003 ..... **CLC 4,
  13, 24**
  See also CA 9-12R; CANR 7, 63; CN 7;
  DLB 28, 67; EWL 3; MTCW 1, 2; RGAL
  4; TUS
Field, Andrew 1938- .... **CLC 44**
  See also CA 97-100; CANR 25
Field, Eugene 1850-1895 .... **NCLC 3**
  See also DLB 23, 42, 140; DLBD 13; MAI-
  CYA 1, 2; RGAL 4; SATA 16
Field, Gans T.
  See Wellman, Manly Wade
Field, Michael 1915-1971 .... **TCLC 43**
  See also CA 29-32R
Field, Peter
  See Hobson, Laura Z(ametkin)
  See also TCWW 2
Fielding, Helen 1959(?)- .... **CLC 146**
  See also CA 172; DLB 231
Fielding, Henry 1707-1754 .... **LC 1, 46, 85;
  WLC**
  See also BRW 3; BRWR 1; CDBLB 1660-
  1789; DA; DA3; DAB; DAC; DAM
  DRAM, MST, NOV; DLB 39, 84, 101;
  RGEL 2; TEA; WLIT 3
Fielding, Sarah 1710-1768 .... **LC 1, 44**
  See also DLB 39; RGEL 2; TEA
Fields, W. C. 1880-1946 .... **TCLC 80**
  See also DLB 44
Fierstein, Harvey (Forbes) 1954- ..... **CLC 33**
  See also CA 129; 123; CAD; CD 5; CPW;
  DA3; DAM DRAM, POP; DFS 6; DLB
  266; GLL
Figes, Eva 1932- .... **CLC 31**
  See also CA 53-56; CANR 4, 44, 83; CN 7;
  DLB 14, 271; FW
Filippo, Eduardo de
  See de Filippo, Eduardo
Finch, Anne 1661-1720 .... **LC 3; PC 21**
  See also DLB 95

Garnett, David 1892-1981 .... **CLC 3**
See also CA 103; 5-8R; CANR 17, 79; DLB 34; FANT; MTCW 2; RGEL 2; SFW 4; SUFW 1

Garos, Stephanie
See Katz, Steve

Garrett, George (Palmer) 1929- .. **CLC 3, 11, 51; SSC 30**
See also AMWS 7; BPFB 2; CA 1-4R; CAAE 202; CAAS 5; CANR 1, 42, 67, 109; CN 7; CP 7; CSW; DLB 2, 5, 130, 152; DLBY 1983

Garrick, David 1717-1779 .... **LC 15**
See also DAM DRAM; DLB 84, 213; RGEL 2

Garrigue, Jean 1914-1972 .... **CLC 2, 8**
See also CA 37-40R; 5-8R; CANR 20

Garrison, Frederick
See Sinclair, Upton (Beall)

Garro, Elena 1920(?)-1998 .... **HLCS 1**
See also CA 169; 131; CWW 2; DLB 145; EWL 3; HW 1; LAWS 1; WLIT 1

Garth, Will
See Hamilton, Edmond; Kuttner, Henry

Garvey, Marcus (Moziah, Jr.)
1887-1940 .... **BLC 2; HR 2; TCLC 41**
See also BW 1; CA 124; 120; CANR 79; DAM MULT

Gary, Romain .... **CLC 25**
See Kacew, Romain
See also DLB 83

Gascar, Pierre .... **CLC 11**
See Fournier, Pierre
See also EWL 3

Gascoyne, David (Emery)
1916-2001 .... **CLC 45**
See also CA 200; 65-68; CANR 10, 28, 54; CP 7; DLB 20; MTCW 1; RGEL 2

Gaskell, Elizabeth Cleghorn
1810-1865 .... **NCLC 5, 70, 97; SSC 25**
See also BRW 5; CDBLB 1832-1890; DAB; DAM MST; DLB 21, 144, 159; RGEL 2; RGSF 2; TEA

Gass, William H(oward) 1924- . **CLC 1, 2, 8, 11, 15, 39, 132; SSC 12**
See also AMWS 6; CA 17-20R; CANR 30, 71, 100; CN 7; DLB 2, 227; EWL 3; MTCW 1, 2; RGAL 4

Gassendi, Pierre 1592-1655 .... **LC 54**
See also GFL Beginnings to 1789

Gasset, Jose Ortega y
See Ortega y Gasset, Jose

Gates, Henry Louis, Jr. 1950- ... **BLCS; CLC 65**
See also BW 2, 3; CA 109; CANR 25, 53, 75; CSW; DA3; DAM MULT; DLB 67; EWL 3; MTCW 1; RGAL 4

Gautier, Theophile 1811-1872 .. **NCLC 1, 59; PC 18; SSC 20**
See also DAM POET; DLB 119; EW 6; GFL 1789 to the Present; RGWL 2, 3; SUFW; TWA

Gawsworth, John
See Bates, H(erbert) E(rnest)

Gay, John 1685-1732 .... **LC 49**
See also BRW 3; DAM DRAM; DLB 84, 95; RGEL 2; WLIT 3

Gay, Oliver
See Gogarty, Oliver St. John

Gay, Peter (Jack) 1923- .... **CLC 158**
See also CA 13-16R; CANR 18, 41, 77; INT CANR-18

Gaye, Marvin (Pentz, Jr.)
1939-1984 .... **CLC 26**
See also CA 112; 195

Gebler, Carlo (Ernest) 1954- .... **CLC 39**
See also CA 133; 119; CANR 96; DLB 271

Gee, Maggie (Mary) 1948- .... **CLC 57**
See also CA 130; CN 7; DLB 207

Gee, Maurice (Gough) 1931- .... **CLC 29**
See also AAYA 42; CA 97-100; CANR 67; CLR 56; CN 7; CWRI 5; EWL 3; MAI-CYA 2; RGSF 2; SATA 46, 101

Geiogamah, Hanay 1945- .... **NNAL**
See also CA 153; DAM MULT; DLB 175

Gelbart, Larry (Simon) 1928- .... **CLC 21, 61**
See Gelbart, Larry
See also CA 73-76; CANR 45, 94

Gelbart, Larry 1928-
See Gelbart, Larry (Simon)
See also CAD; CD 5

Gelber, Jack 1932- .... **CLC 1, 6, 14, 79**
See also CA 1-4R; CAD; CANR 2; DLB 7, 228

Gellhorn, Martha (Ellis)
1908-1998 .... **CLC 14, 60**
See also CA 164; 77-80; CANR 44; CN 7; DLBY 1982, 1998

Genet, Jean 1910-1986 .. **CLC 1, 2, 5, 10, 14, 44, 46; TCLC 128**
See also CA 13-16R; CANR 18; DA3; DAM DRAM; DFS 10; DLB 72; DLBY 1986; EW 13; EWL 3; GFL 1789 to the Present; GLL 1; MTCW 1, 2; RGWL 2, 3; TWA

Gent, Peter 1942- .... **CLC 29**
See also AITN 1; CA 89-92; DLBY 1982

Gentile, Giovanni 1875-1944 .... **TCLC 96**
See also CA 119

Gentlewoman in New England, A
See Bradstreet, Anne

Gentlewoman in Those Parts, A
See Bradstreet, Anne

Geoffrey of Monmouth c.
1100-1155 .... **CMLC 44**
See also DLB 146; TEA

George, Jean
See George, Jean Craighead

George, Jean Craighead 1919- .... **CLC 35**
See also AAYA 8; BYA 2, 4; CA 5-8R; CANR 25; CLR 1; 80; DLB 52; JRDA; MAICYA 1, 2; SATA 2, 68, 124; WYA; YAW

George, Stefan (Anton) 1868-1933 . **TCLC 2, 14**
See also CA 193; 104; EW 8; EWL 3

Georges, Georges Martin
See Simenon, Georges (Jacques Christian)

Gerhardi, William Alexander
See Gerhardie, William Alexander

Gerhardie, William Alexander
1895-1977 .... **CLC 5**
See also CA 73-76; 25-28R; CANR 18; DLB 36; RGEL 2

Gerson, Jean 1363-1429 .... **LC 77**
See also DLB 208

Gersonides 1288-1344 .... **CMLC 49**
See also DLB 115

Gerstler, Amy 1956- .... **CLC 70**
See also CA 146; CANR 99

Gertler, T. .... **CLC 34**
See also CA 121; 116

Gertsen, Aleksandr Ivanovich
See Herzen, Aleksandr Ivanovich

Ghalib .... **NCLC 39, 78**
See Ghalib, Asadullah Khan

Ghalib, Asadullah Khan 1797-1869
See Ghalib
See also DAM POET; RGWL 2, 3

Ghelderode, Michel de 1898-1962 ..... **CLC 6, 11; DC 15**
See also CA 85-88; CANR 40, 77; DAM DRAM; EW 11; EWL 3; TWA

Ghiselin, Brewster 1903-2001 .... **CLC 23**
See also CA 13-16R; CAAS 10; CANR 13; CP 7

Ghose, Aurabinda 1872-1950 .... **TCLC 63**
See Ghose, Aurobindo
See also CA 163

Ghose, Aurobindo
See Ghose, Aurabinda
See also EWL 3

Ghose, Zulfikar 1935- .... **CLC 42**
See also CA 65-68; CANR 67; CN 7; CP 7; EWL 3

Ghosh, Amitav 1956- .... **CLC 44, 153**
See also CA 147; CANR 80; CN 7

Giacosa, Giuseppe 1847-1906 .... **TCLC 7**
See also CA 104

Gibb, Lee
See Waterhouse, Keith (Spencer)

Gibbon, Lewis Grassic .... **TCLC 4**
See Mitchell, James Leslie
See also RGEL 2

Gibbons, Kaye 1960- .... **CLC 50, 88, 145**
See also AAYA 34; AMWS 10; CA 151; CANR 75; CSW; DA3; DAM POP; MTCW 1; NFS 3; RGAL 4; SATA 117

Gibran, Kahlil 1883-1931 . **PC 9; TCLC 1, 9**
See also CA 150; 104; DA3; DAM POET, POP; EWL 3; MTCW 2

Gibran, Khalil
See Gibran, Kahlil

Gibson, William 1914- .... **CLC 23**
See also CA 9-12R; CAD 2; CANR 9, 42, 75; CD 5; DA; DAB; DAC; DAM DRAM, MST; DFS 2; DLB 7; LAIT 2; MTCW 2; SATA 66; YAW

Gibson, William (Ford) 1948- ... **CLC 39, 63; SSC 52**
See also AAYA 12; BPFB 2; CA 133; 126; CANR 52, 90, 106; CN 7; CPW; DA3; DAM POP; DLB 251; MTCW 2; SCFW 2; SFW 4

Gide, Andre (Paul Guillaume)
1869-1951 ..... **SSC 13; TCLC 5, 12, 36; WLC**
See also CA 124; 104; DA; DA3; DAB; DAC; DAM MST, NOV; DLB 65; EW 8; EWL 3; GFL 1789 to the Present; MTCW 1, 2; RGSF 2; RGWL 2, 3; TWA

Gifford, Barry (Colby) 1946- .... **CLC 34**
See also CA 65-68; CANR 9, 30, 40, 90

Gilbert, Frank
See De Voto, Bernard (Augustine)

Gilbert, W(illiam) S(chwenck)
1836-1911 .... **TCLC 3**
See also CA 173; 104; DAM DRAM, POET; RGEL 2; SATA 36

Gilbreth, Frank B(unker), Jr.
1911-2001 .... **CLC 17**
See also CA 9-12R; SATA 2

Gilchrist, Ellen (Louise) 1935- .. **CLC 34, 48, 143; SSC 14**
See also BPFB 2; CA 116; 113; CANR 41, 61, 104; CN 7; CPW; CSW; DAM POP; DLB 130; EWL 3; EXPS; MTCW 1, 2; RGAL 4; RGSF 2; SSFS 9

Giles, Molly 1942- .... **CLC 39**
See also CA 126; CANR 98

Gill, (Arthur) Eric (Rowton Peter Joseph)
1882-1940
See Gill, Eric
See also CA 120; DLB 98

Gill, Eric 1882-1940 .... **TCLC 85**
See Gill, (Arthur) Eric (Rowton Peter Joseph)

Gill, Patrick
See Creasey, John

Gillette, Douglas .... **CLC 70**

Gilliam, Terry (Vance) 1940- .... **CLC 21, 141**
See Monty Python
See also AAYA 19; CA 113; 108; CANR 35; INT 113

Gillian, Jerry
See Gilliam, Terry (Vance)
Gilliatt, Penelope (Ann Douglass)
1932-1993 .... **CLC 2, 10, 13, 53**
See also AITN 2; CA 141; 13-16R; CANR
49; DLB 14
Gilman, Charlotte (Anna) Perkins (Stetson)
1860-1935 ..... **SSC 13; TCLC 9, 37, 117**
See also AMWS 11; BYA 11; CA 150; 106;
DLB 221; EXPS; FW; HGG; LAIT 2;
MAWW; MTCW 1; RGAL 4; RGSF 2;
SFW 4; SSFS 1
Gilmour, David 1946- .... **CLC 35**
Gilpin, William 1724-1804 .... **NCLC 30**
Gilray, J. D.
See Mencken, H(enry) L(ouis)
Gilroy, Frank D(aniel) 1925- .... **CLC 2**
See also CA 81-84; CAD; CANR 32, 64,
86; CD 5; DLB 7
Gilstrap, John 1957(?)- .... **CLC 99**
See also CA 160; CANR 101
Ginsberg, Allen 1926-1997 .... **CLC 1, 2, 3, 4,**
6, 13, 36, 69, 109; PC 4; TCLC 120;
WLC
See also AAYA 33; AITN 1; AMWC 1;
AMWS 2; BG 2; CA 157; 1-4R; CANR
2, 41, 63, 95; CDALB 1941-1968; CP 7;
DA; DA3; DAB; DAC; DAM MST,
POET; DLB 5, 16, 169, 237; EWL 3; GLL
1; MTCW 1, 2; PAB; PFS 5; RGAL 4;
TUS; WP
Ginzburg, Eugenia .... **CLC 59**
Ginzburg, Natalia 1916-1991 .... **CLC 5, 11,**
54, 70
See also CA 135; 85-88; CANR 33; DFS
14; DLB 177; EW 13; EWL 3; MTCW 1,
2; RGWL 2, 3
Giono, Jean 1895-1970 .... **CLC 4, 11; TCLC**
124
See also CA 29-32R; 45-48; CANR 2, 35;
DLB 72; EWL 3; GFL 1789 to the
Present; MTCW 1; RGWL 2, 3
Giovanni, Nikki 1943- ...... **BLC 2; CLC 2, 4,**
19, 64, 117; PC 19; WLCS
See also AAYA 22; AITN 1; BW 2, 3; CA
29-32R; CAAS 6; CANR 18, 41, 60, 91;
CDALBS; CLR 6, 73; CP 7; CSW; CWP;
CWRI 5; DA; DA3; DAB; DAC; DAM
MST, MULT, POET; DLB 5, 41; EWL 3;
EXPP; INT CANR-18; MAICYA 1, 2;
MTCW 1, 2; PFS 17; RGAL 4; SATA 24,
107; TUS; YAW
Giovene, Andrea 1904-1998 .... **CLC 7**
See also CA 85-88
Gippius, Zinaida (Nikolayevna) 1869-1945
See Hippius, Zinaida
See also CA 106
Giraudoux, Jean(-Hippolyte)
1882-1944 .... **TCLC 2, 7**
See also CA 196; 104; DAM DRAM; DLB
65; EW 9; EWL 3; GFL 1789 to the
Present; RGWL 2, 3; TWA
Gironella, Jose Maria 1917-1991 ..... **CLC 11**
See also CA 101; EWL 3; RGWL 2, 3
Gissing, George (Robert)
1857-1903 .... **SSC 37; TCLC 3, 24, 47**
See also BRW 5; CA 167; 105; DLB 18,
135, 184; RGEL 2; TEA
Giurlani, Aldo
See Palazzeschi, Aldo
Gladkov, Fedor Vasil'evich
See Gladkov, Fyodor (Vasilyevich)
See also DLB 272
Gladkov, Fyodor (Vasilyevich)
1883-1958 .... **TCLC 27**
See Gladkov, Fedor Vasil'evich
See also CA 170; EWL 3

Glancy, Diane 1941- .... **NNAL**
See also CA 136; CAAS 24; CANR 87;
DLB 175
Glanville, Brian (Lester) 1931- .... **CLC 6**
See also CA 5-8R; CAAS 9; CANR 3, 70;
CN 7; DLB 15, 139; SATA 42
Glasgow, Ellen (Anderson Gholson)
1873-1945 .... **SSC 34; TCLC 2, 7**
See also AMW; CA 164; 104; DLB 9, 12;
MAWW; MTCW 2; RGAL 4; RHW;
SSFS 9; TUS
Glaspell, Susan 1882(?)-1948 ..... **DC 10; SSC**
41; TCLC 55
See also AMWS 3; CA 154; 110; DFS 8;
DLB 7, 9, 78, 228; MAWW; RGAL 4;
SSFS 3; TCWW 2; TUS; YABC 2
Glassco, John 1909-1981 .... **CLC 9**
See also CA 102; 13-16R; CANR 15; DLB
68
Glasscock, Amnesia
See Steinbeck, John (Ernst)
Glasser, Ronald J. 1940(?)- .... **CLC 37**
Glassman, Joyce
See Johnson, Joyce
Gleick, James (W.) 1954- .... **CLC 147**
See also CA 137; 131; CANR 97; INT CA-
137
Glendinning, Victoria 1937- .... **CLC 50**
See also CA 127; 120; CANR 59, 89; DLB
155
Glissant, Edouard (Mathieu)
1928- .... **CLC 10, 68**
See also CA 153; CANR 111; CWW 2;
DAM MULT; EWL 3; RGWL 3
Gloag, Julian 1930- .... **CLC 40**
See also AITN 1; CA 65-68; CANR 10, 70;
CN 7
Glowacki, Aleksander
See Prus, Boleslaw
Gluck, Louise (Elisabeth) 1943- .. **CLC 7, 22,**
44, 81, 160; PC 16
See also AMWS 5; CA 33-36R; CANR 40,
69, 108; CP 7; CWP; DA3; DAM POET;
DLB 5; MTCW 2; PFS 5, 15; RGAL 4
Glyn, Elinor 1864-1943 .... **TCLC 72**
See also DLB 153; RHW
Gobineau, Joseph-Arthur
1816-1882 .... **NCLC 17**
See also DLB 123; GFL 1789 to the Present
Godard, Jean-Luc 1930- .... **CLC 20**
See also CA 93-96
Godden, (Margaret) Rumer
1907-1998 .... **CLC 53**
See also AAYA 6; BPFB 2; BYA 2, 5; CA
172; 5-8R; CANR 4, 27, 36, 55, 80; CLR
20; CN 7; CWRI 5; DLB 161; MAICYA
1, 2; RHW; SAAS 12; SATA 3, 36; SATA-
Obit 109; TEA
Godoy Alcayaga, Lucila 1899-1957 .. **HLC 2;**
PC 32; TCLC 2
See Mistral, Gabriela
See also BW 2; CA 131; 104; CANR 81;
DAM MULT; DNFS; HW 1, 2; MTCW 1,
2
Godwin, Gail (Kathleen) 1937- ..... **CLC 5, 8,**
22, 31, 69, 125
See also BPFB 2; CA 29-32R; CANR 15,
43, 69; CN 7; CPW; CSW; DA3; DAM
POP; DLB 6, 234; INT CANR-15;
MTCW 1, 2
Godwin, William 1756-1836 .... **NCLC 14**
See also CDBLB 1789-1832; CMW 4; DLB
39, 104, 142, 158, 163, 262; HGG; RGEL
2
Goebbels, Josef
See Goebbels, (Paul) Joseph
Goebbels, (Paul) Joseph
1897-1945 .... **TCLC 68**
See also CA 148; 115

Goebbels, Joseph Paul
See Goebbels, (Paul) Joseph
Goethe, Johann Wolfgang von
1749-1832 ... **NCLC 4, 22, 34, 90; PC 5;**
SSC 38; WLC
See also CDWLB 2; DA; DA3; DAB;
DAC; DAM DRAM, MST, POET; DLB
94; EW 5; RGWL 2, 3; TWA
Gogarty, Oliver St. John
1878-1957 .... **TCLC 15**
See also CA 150; 109; DLB 15, 19; RGEL
2
Gogol, Nikolai (Vasilyevich)
1809-1852 .... **DC 1; NCLC 5, 15, 31;**
SSC 4, 29, 52; WLC
See also DA; DAB; DAC; DAM DRAM,
MST; DFS 12; DLB 198; EW 6; EXPS;
RGSF 2; RGWL 2, 3; SSFS 7; TWA
Goines, Donald 1937(?)-1974 ... **BLC 2; CLC**
80
See also AITN 1; BW 1, 3; CA 114; 124;
CANR 82; CMW 4; DA3; DAM MULT,
POP; DLB 33
Gold, Herbert 1924- ... **CLC 4, 7, 14, 42, 152**
See also CA 9-12R; CANR 17, 45; CN 7;
DLB 2; DLBY 1981
Goldbarth, Albert 1948- .... **CLC 5, 38**
See also AMWS 12; CA 53-56; CANR 6,
40; CP 7; DLB 120
Goldberg, Anatol 1910-1982 .... **CLC 34**
See also CA 117; 131
Goldemberg, Isaac 1945- .... **CLC 52**
See also CA 69-72; CAAS 12; CANR 11,
32; EWL 3; HW 1; WLIT 1
Golding, William (Gerald)
1911-1993 ..... **CLC 1, 2, 3, 8, 10, 17, 27,**
58, 81; WLC
See also AAYA 5, 44; BPFB 2; BRWR 1;
BRWS 1; BYA 2; CA 141; 5-8R; CANR
13, 33, 54; CDBLB 1945-1960; DA;
DA3; DAB; DAC; DAM MST, NOV;
DLB 15, 100, 255; EWL 3; EXPN; HGG;
LAIT 4; MTCW 1, 2; NFS 2; RGEL 2;
RHW; SFW 4; TEA; WLIT 4; YAW
Goldman, Emma 1869-1940 .... **TCLC 13**
See also CA 150; 110; DLB 221; FW;
RGAL 4; TUS
Goldman, Francisco 1954- .... **CLC 76**
See also CA 162
Goldman, William (W.) 1931- ...... **CLC 1, 48**
See also BPFB 2; CA 9-12R; CANR 29,
69, 106; CN 7; DLB 44; FANT; IDFW 3,
4
Goldmann, Lucien 1913-1970 .... **CLC 24**
See also CA 25-28; CAP 2
Goldoni, Carlo 1707-1793 .... **LC 4**
See also DAM DRAM; EW 4; RGWL 2, 3
Goldsberry, Steven 1949- .... **CLC 34**
See also CA 131
Goldsmith, Oliver 1730-1774 .... **DC 8; LC 2,**
48; WLC
See also BRW 3; CDBLB 1660-1789; DA;
DAB; DAC; DAM DRAM, MST, NOV,
POET; DFS 1; DLB 39, 89, 104, 109, 142;
IDTP; RGEL 2; SATA 26; TEA; WLIT 3
Goldsmith, Peter
See Priestley, J(ohn) B(oynton)
Gombrowicz, Witold 1904-1969 .... **CLC 4, 7,**
11, 49
See also CA 25-28R; 19-20; CANR 105;
CAP 2; CDWLB 4; DAM DRAM; DLB
215; EW 12; EWL 3; RGWL 2, 3; TWA
Gomez de Avellaneda, Gertrudis
1814-1873 .... **NCLC 111**
See also LAW
Gomez de la Serna, Ramon
1888-1963 .... **CLC 9**
See also CA 116; 153; CANR 79; EWL 3;
HW 1, 2

Goncharov, Ivan Alexandrovich
1812-1891 .... **NCLC 1, 63**
See also DLB 238; EW 6; RGWL 2, 3

Goncourt, Edmond (Louis Antoine Huot) de
1822-1896 .... **NCLC 7**
See also DLB 123; EW 7; GFL 1789 to the
Present; RGWL 2, 3

Goncourt, Jules (Alfred Huot) de
1830-1870 .... **NCLC 7**
See also DLB 123; EW 7; GFL 1789 to the
Present; RGWL 2, 3

Gongora (y Argote), Luis de
1561-1627 .... **LC 72**
See also RGWL 2, 3

Gontier, Fernande 19(?)- .... **CLC 50**

Gonzalez Martinez, Enrique
1871-1952 .... **TCLC 72**
See also CA 166; CANR 81; EWL 3; HW
1, 2

Goodison, Lorna 1947- .... **PC 36**
See also CA 142; CANR 88; CP 7; CWP;
DLB 157; EWL 3

Goodman, Paul 1911-1972 ..... **CLC 1, 2, 4, 7**
See also CA 37-40R; 19-20; CAD; CANR
34; CAP 2; DLB 130, 246; MTCW 1;
RGAL 4

Gordimer, Nadine 1923- ...... **CLC 3, 5, 7, 10,
18, 33, 51, 70, 123, 160, 161; SSC 17;
WLCS**
See also AAYA 39; AFW; BRWS 2; CA
5-8R; CANR 3, 28, 56, 88; CN 7; DA;
DA3; DAB; DAC; DAM MST, NOV;
DLB 225; EWL 3; EXPS; INT CANR-28;
MTCW 1, 2; NFS 4; RGEL 2; RGSF 2;
SSFS 2, 14; TWA; WLIT 2; YAW

Gordon, Adam Lindsay
1833-1870 .... **NCLC 21**
See also DLB 230

Gordon, Caroline 1895-1981 . **CLC 6, 13, 29,
83; SSC 15**
See also AMW; CA 103; 11-12; CANR 36;
CAP 1; DLB 4, 9, 102; DLBD 17; DLBY
1981; EWL 3; MTCW 1, 2; RGAL 4;
RGSF 2

Gordon, Charles William 1860-1937
See Connor, Ralph
See also CA 109

Gordon, Mary (Catherine) 1949- .... **CLC 13,
22, 128; SSC 59**
See also AMWS 4; BPFB 2; CA 102;
CANR 44, 92; CN 7; DLB 6; DLBY
1981; FW; INT CA-102; MTCW 1

Gordon, N. J.
See Bosman, Herman Charles

Gordon, Sol 1923- .... **CLC 26**
See also CA 53-56; CANR 4; SATA 11

Gordone, Charles 1925-1995 .. **CLC 1, 4; DC
8**
See also BW 1, 3; CA 150; 93-96, 180;
CAAE 180; CAD; CANR 55; DAM
DRAM; DLB 7; INT 93-96; MTCW 1

Gore, Catherine 1800-1861 .... **NCLC 65**
See also DLB 116; RGEL 2

Gorenko, Anna Andreevna
See Akhmatova, Anna

Gorky, Maxim .... **SSC 28; TCLC 8; WLC**
See Peshkov, Alexei Maximovich
See also DAB; DFS 9; EW 8; EWL 3;
MTCW 2; TWA

Goryan, Sirak
See Saroyan, William

Gosse, Edmund (William)
1849-1928 .... **TCLC 28**
See also CA 117; DLB 57, 144, 184; RGEL
2

Gotlieb, Phyllis Fay (Bloom) 1926- .. **CLC 18**
See also CA 13-16R; CANR 7; DLB 88,
251; SFW 4

Gottesman, S. D.
See Kornbluth, C(yril) M.; Pohl, Frederik

Gottfried von Strassburg fl. c.
1170-1215 .... **CMLC 10**
See also CDWLB 2; DLB 138; EW 1;
RGWL 2, 3

Gotthelf, Jeremias 1797-1854 .... **NCLC 117**
See also DLB 133; RGWL 2, 3

Gottschalk, Laura Riding
See Jackson, Laura (Riding)

Gould, Lois 1932(?)-2002 .... **CLC 4, 10**
See also CA 77-80; CANR 29; MTCW 1

Gould, Stephen Jay 1941-2002 .... **CLC 163**
See also AAYA 26; BEST 90:2; CA 205;
77-80; CANR 10, 27, 56, 75; CPW; INT
CANR-27; MTCW 1, 2

Gourmont, Remy(-Marie-Charles) de
1858-1915 .... **TCLC 17**
See also CA 150; 109; GFL 1789 to the
Present; MTCW 2

Govier, Katherine 1948- .... **CLC 51**
See also CA 101; CANR 18, 40; CCA 1

Gower, John c. 1330-1408 .... **LC 76**
See also BRW 1; DLB 146; RGEL 2

Goyen, (Charles) William
1915-1983 .... **CLC 5, 8, 14, 40**
See also AITN 2; CA 110; 5-8R; CANR 6,
71; DLB 2, 218; DLBY 1983; EWL 3;
INT CANR-6

Goytisolo, Juan 1931- .... **CLC 5, 10, 23, 133;
HLC 1**
See also CA 85-88; CANR 32, 61; CWW
2; DAM MULT; EWL 3; GLL 2; HW 1,
2; MTCW 1, 2

Gozzano, Guido 1883-1916 .... **PC 10**
See also CA 154; DLB 114; EWL 3

Gozzi, (Conte) Carlo 1720-1806 .... **NCLC 23**

Grabbe, Christian Dietrich
1801-1836 .... **NCLC 2**
See also DLB 133; RGWL 2, 3

Grace, Patricia Frances 1937- .... **CLC 56**
See also CA 176; CN 7; EWL 3; RGSF 2

Gracian y Morales, Baltasar
1601-1658 .... **LC 15**

Gracq, Julien .... **CLC 11, 48**
See Poirier, Louis
See also CWW 2; DLB 83; GFL 1789 to
the Present

Grade, Chaim 1910-1982 .... **CLC 10**
See also CA 107; 93-96; EWL 3

Graduate of Oxford, A
See Ruskin, John

Grafton, Garth
See Duncan, Sara Jeannette

Grafton, Sue 1940- .... **CLC 163**
See also AAYA 11; BEST 90:3; CA 108;
CANR 31, 55, 111; CMW 4; CPW; CSW;
DA3; DAM POP; DLB 226; FW; MSW

Graham, John
See Phillips, David Graham

Graham, Jorie 1951- .... **CLC 48, 118**
See also CA 111; CANR 63; CP 7; CWP;
DLB 120; EWL 3; PFS 10, 17

Graham, R(obert) B(ontine) Cunninghame
See Cunninghame Graham, Robert
(Gallnigad) Bontine
See also DLB 98, 135, 174; RGEL 2; RGSF
2

Graham, Robert
See Haldeman, Joe (William)

Graham, Tom
See Lewis, (Harry) Sinclair

Graham, W(illiam) S(idney)
1918-1986 .... **CLC 29**
See also BRWS 7; CA 118; 73-76; DLB 20;
RGEL 2

Graham, Winston (Mawdsley)
1910- .... **CLC 23**
See also CA 49-52; CANR 2, 22, 45, 66;
CMW 4; CN 7; DLB 77; RHW

Grahame, Kenneth 1859-1932 .... **TCLC 64**
See also BYA 5; CA 136; 108; CANR 80;
CLR 5; CWRI 5; DA3; DAB; DLB 34,
141, 178; FANT; MAICYA 1, 2; MTCW
2; RGEL 2; SATA 100; TEA; WCH;
YABC 1

Granger, Darius John
See Marlowe, Stephen

Granin, Daniil .... **CLC 59**

Granovsky, Timofei Nikolaevich
1813-1855 .... **NCLC 75**
See also DLB 198

Grant, Skeeter
See Spiegelman, Art

Granville-Barker, Harley
1877-1946 .... **TCLC 2**
See Barker, Harley Granville
See also CA 204; 104; DAM DRAM;
RGEL 2

Granzotto, Gianni
See Granzotto, Giovanni Battista

Granzotto, Giovanni Battista
1914-1985 .... **CLC 70**
See also CA 166

Grass, Guenter (Wilhelm) 1927- ... **CLC 1, 2,
4, 6, 11, 15, 22, 32, 49, 88; WLC**
See also BPFB 2; CA 13-16R; CANR 20,
75, 93; CDWLB 2; DA; DA3; DAB;
DAC; DAM MST, NOV; DLB 75, 124;
EW 13; EWL 3; MTCW 1, 2; RGWL 2,
3; TWA

Gratton, Thomas
See Hulme, T(homas) E(rnest)

Grau, Shirley Ann 1929- .... **CLC 4, 9, 146;
SSC 15**
See also CA 89-92; CANR 22, 69; CN 7;
CSW; DLB 2, 218; INT CA-89-92,
CANR-22; MTCW 1

Gravel, Fern
See Hall, James Norman

Graver, Elizabeth 1964- .... **CLC 70**
See also CA 135; CANR 71

Graves, Richard Perceval
1895-1985 .... **CLC 44**
See also CA 65-68; CANR 9, 26, 51

Graves, Robert (von Ranke)
1895-1985 .. **CLC 1, 2, 6, 11, 39, 44, 45;
PC 6**
See also BPFB 2; BRW 7; BYA 4; CA 117;
5-8R; CANR 5, 36; CDBLB 1914-1945;
DA3; DAB; DAC; DAM MST, POET;
DLB 20, 100, 191; DLBD 18; DLBY
1985; EWL 3; MTCW 1, 2; NCFS 2;
RGEL 2; RHW; SATA 45; TEA

Graves, Valerie
See Bradley, Marion Zimmer

Gray, Alasdair (James) 1934- .... **CLC 41**
See also CA 126; CANR 47, 69, 106; CN
7; DLB 194, 261; HGG; INT CA-126;
MTCW 1, 2; RGSF 2; SUFW 2

Gray, Amlin 1946- .... **CLC 29**
See also CA 138

Gray, Francine du Plessix 1930- ..... **CLC 22,
153**
See also BEST 90:3; CA 61-64; CAAS 2;
CANR 11, 33, 75, 81; DAM NOV; INT
CANR-11; MTCW 1, 2

Gray, John (Henry) 1866-1934 ...... **TCLC 19**
See also CA 162; 119; RGEL 2

Gray, Simon (James Holliday)
1936- .... **CLC 9, 14, 36**
See also AITN 1; CA 21-24R; CAAS 3;
CANR 32, 69; CD 5; DLB 13; EWL 3;
MTCW 1; RGEL 2

Guevara (Serna), Ernesto
1928-1967 .... **CLC 87; HLC 1**
See Guevara, Che
See also CA 111; 127; CANR 56; DAM
MULT; HW 1

Guicciardini, Francesco 1483-1540 ..... **LC 49**

Guild, Nicholas M. 1944- .... **CLC 33**
See also CA 93-96

Guillemin, Jacques
See Sartre, Jean-Paul

Guillen, Jorge 1893-1984 . **CLC 11; HLCS 1;**
PC 35
See also CA 112; 89-92; DAM MULT,
POET; DLB 108; EWL 3; HW 1; RGWL
2, 3

Guillen, Nicolas (Cristobal)
1902-1989 .... **BLC 2; CLC 48, 79; HLC**
1; PC 23
See also BW 2; CA 129; 125; 116; CANR
84; DAM MST, MULT, POET; EWL 3;
HW 1; LAW; RGWL 2, 3; WP

Guillen y Alvarez, Jorge
See Guillen, Jorge

Guillevic, (Eugene) 1907-1997 .... **CLC 33**
See also CA 93-96; CWW 2

Guillois
See Desnos, Robert

Guillois, Valentin
See Desnos, Robert

Guimaraes Rosa, Joao 1908-1967 .... **HLCS 2**
See also CA 175; LAW; RGSF 2; RGWL 2,
3

Guiney, Louise Imogen
1861-1920 .... **TCLC 41**
See also CA 160; DLB 54; RGAL 4

Guinizelli, Guido c. 1230-1276 ...... **CMLC 49**

Guiraldes, Ricardo (Guillermo)
1886-1927 .... **TCLC 39**
See also CA 131; EWL 3; HW 1; LAW;
MTCW 1

Gumilev, Nikolai (Stepanovich)
1886-1921 .... **TCLC 60**
See Gumilyov, Nikolay Stepanovich
See also CA 165

Gumilyov, Nikolay Stepanovich
See Gumilev, Nikolai (Stepanovich)
See also EWL 3

Gunesekera, Romesh 1954- .... **CLC 91**
See also CA 159; CN 7; DLB 267

Gunn, Bill .... **CLC 5**
See Gunn, William Harrison
See also DLB 38

Gunn, Thom(son William) 1929- .. **CLC 3, 6,**
18, 32, 81; PC 26
See also BRWS 4; CA 17-20R; CANR 9,
33; CDBLB 1960 to Present; CP 7; DAM
POET; DLB 27; INT CANR-33; MTCW
1; PFS 9; RGEL 2

Gunn, William Harrison 1934(?)-1989
See Gunn, Bill
See also AITN 1; BW 1, 3; CA 128; 13-
16R; CANR 12, 25, 76

Gunn Allen, Paula
See Allen, Paula Gunn

Gunnars, Kristjana 1948- .... **CLC 69**
See also CA 113; CCA 1; CP 7; CWP; DLB
60

Gunter, Erich
See Eich, Gunter

Gurdjieff, G(eorgei) I(vanovich)
1877(?)-1949 .... **TCLC 71**
See also CA 157

Gurganus, Allan 1947- .... **CLC 70**
See also BEST 90:1; CA 135; CANR 114;
CN 7; CPW; CSW; DAM POP; GLL 1

Gurney, A. R.
See Gurney, A(lbert) R(amsdell), Jr.
See also DLB 266

Gurney, A(lbert) R(amsdell), Jr.
1930- .... **CLC 32, 50, 54**
See Gurney, A. R.
See also AMWS 5; CA 77-80; CAD; CANR
32, 64; CD 5; DAM DRAM; EWL 3

Gurney, Ivor (Bertie) 1890-1937 ... **TCLC 33**
See also BRW 6; CA 167; PAB; RGEL 2

Gurney, Peter
See Gurney, A(lbert) R(amsdell), Jr.

Guro, Elena 1877-1913 .... **TCLC 56**

Gustafson, James M(oody) 1925- ... **CLC 100**
See also CA 25-28R; CANR 37

Gustafson, Ralph (Barker)
1909-1995 .... **CLC 36**
See also CA 21-24R; CANR 8, 45, 84; CP
7; DLB 88; RGEL 2

Gut, Gom
See Simenon, Georges (Jacques Christian)

Guterson, David 1956- .... **CLC 91**
See also CA 132; CANR 73; MTCW 2;
NFS 13

Guthrie, A(lfred) B(ertram), Jr.
1901-1991 .... **CLC 23**
See also CA 134; 57-60; CANR 24; DLB 6,
212; SATA 62; SATA-Obit 67

Guthrie, Isobel
See Grieve, C(hristopher) M(urray)

Guthrie, Woodrow Wilson 1912-1967
See Guthrie, Woody
See also CA 93-96; 113

Guthrie, Woody .... **CLC 35**
See Guthrie, Woodrow Wilson
See also LAIT 3

Gutierrez Najera, Manuel
1859-1895 .... **HLCS 2**
See also LAW

Guy, Rosa (Cuthbert) 1925- .... **CLC 26**
See also AAYA 4, 37; BW 2; CA 17-20R;
CANR 14, 34, 83; CLR 13; DLB 33;
DNFS 1; JRDA; MAICYA 1, 2; SATA 14,
62, 122; YAW

Gwendolyn
See Bennett, (Enoch) Arnold

H. D. .... **CLC 3, 8, 14, 31, 34, 73; PC 5**
See Doolittle, Hilda

H. de V.
See Buchan, John

Haavikko, Paavo Juhani 1931- .. **CLC 18, 34**
See also CA 106; EWL 3

Habbema, Koos
See Heijermans, Herman

Habermas, Juergen 1929- .... **CLC 104**
See also CA 109; CANR 85; DLB 242

Habermas, Jurgen
See Habermas, Juergen

Hacker, Marilyn 1942- . **CLC 5, 9, 23, 72, 91**
See also CA 77-80; CANR 68; CP 7; CWP;
DAM POET; DLB 120; FW; GLL 2

Hadrian 76-138 .... **CMLC 52**

Haeckel, Ernst Heinrich (Philipp August)
1834-1919 .... **TCLC 83**
See also CA 157

Hafiz c. 1326-1389(?) .... **CMLC 34**
See also RGWL 2, 3

Haggard, H(enry) Rider
1856-1925 .... **TCLC 11**
See also BRWS 3; BYA 4, 5; CA 148; 108;
CANR 112; DLB 70, 156, 174, 178;
FANT; MTCW 2; RGEL 2; RHW; SATA
16; SCFW 4; SFW 4; SUFW 1; WLIT 4

Hagiosy, L.
See Larbaud, Valery (Nicolas)

Hagiwara, Sakutaro 1886-1942 .... **PC 18;**
TCLC 60
See Hagiwara Sakutaro
See also CA 154; RGWL 3

Hagiwara Sakutaro
See Hagiwara, Sakutaro
See also EWL 3

Haig, Fenil
See Ford, Ford Madox

Haig-Brown, Roderick (Langmere)
1908-1976 .... **CLC 21**
See also CA 69-72; 5-8R; CANR 4, 38, 83;
CLR 31; CWRI 5; DLB 88; MAICYA 1,
2; SATA 12

Haight, Rip
See Carpenter, John (Howard)

Hailey, Arthur 1920- .... **CLC 5**
See also AITN 2; BEST 90:3; BPFB 2; CA
1-4R; CANR 2, 36, 75; CCA 1; CN 7;
CPW; DAM NOV, POP; DLB 88; DLBY
1982; MTCW 1, 2

Hailey, Elizabeth Forsythe 1938- ..... **CLC 40**
See also CA 93-96; CAAE 188; CAAS 1;
CANR 15, 48; INT CANR-15

Haines, John (Meade) 1924- .... **CLC 58**
See also AMWS 12; CA 17-20R; CANR
13, 34; CSW; DLB 5, 212

Hakluyt, Richard 1552-1616 .... **LC 31**
See also DLB 136; RGEL 2

Haldeman, Joe (William) 1943- .... **CLC 61**
See Graham, Robert
See also AAYA 38; CA 53-56, 179; CAAE
179; CAAS 25; CANR 6, 70, 72; DLB 8;
INT CANR-6; SCFW 2; SFW 4

Hale, Janet Campbell 1947- .... **NNAL**
See also CA 49-52; CANR 45, 75; DAM
MULT; DLB 175; MTCW 2

Hale, Sarah Josepha (Buell)
1788-1879 .... **NCLC 75**
See also DLB 1, 42, 73, 243

Halevy, Elie 1870-1937 .... **TCLC 104**

Haley, Alex(ander Murray Palmer)
1921-1992 .... **BLC 2; CLC 8, 12, 76**
See also AAYA 26; BPFB 2; BW 2, 3; CA
136; 77-80; CANR 61; CDALBS; CPW;
CSW; DA; DA3; DAB; DAC; DAM MST,
MULT, POP; DLB 38; LAIT 5; MTCW
1, 2; NFS 9

Haliburton, Thomas Chandler
1796-1865 .... **NCLC 15**
See also DLB 11, 99; RGEL 2; RGSF 2

Hall, Donald (Andrew, Jr.) 1928- ...... **CLC 1,**
13, 37, 59, 151
See also CA 5-8R; CAAS 7; CANR 2, 44,
64, 106; CP 7; DAM POET; DLB 5;
MTCW 1; RGAL 4; SATA 23, 97

Hall, Frederic Sauser
See Sauser-Hall, Frederic

Hall, James
See Kuttner, Henry

Hall, James Norman 1887-1951 ..... **TCLC 23**
See also CA 173; 123; LAIT 1; RHW 1;
SATA 21

Hall, (Marguerite) Radclyffe
1880-1943 .... **TCLC 12**
See also BRWS 6; CA 150; 110; CANR 83;
DLB 191; MTCW 2; RGEL 2; RHW

Hall, Rodney 1935- .... **CLC 51**
See also CA 109; CANR 69; CN 7; CP 7

Hallam, Arthur Henry
1811-1833 .... **NCLC 110**
See also DLB 32

Halleck, Fitz-Greene 1790-1867 .... **NCLC 47**
See also DLB 3, 250; RGAL 4

Halliday, Michael
See Creasey, John

Halpern, Daniel 1945- .... **CLC 14**
See also CA 33-36R; CANR 93; CP 7

Hamburger, Michael (Peter Leopold)
1924- .... **CLC 5, 14**
See also CA 5-8R; CAAE 196; CAAS 4;
CANR 2, 47; CP 7; DLB 27

Hamill, Pete 1935- .... **CLC 10**
See also CA 25-28R; CANR 18, 71

Hartmann von Aue c. 1170-c. 1210 .... **CMLC 15**
See also CDWLB 2; DLB 138; RGWL 2, 3

Hartog, Jan de
See de Hartog, Jan

Haruf, Kent 1943- .... **CLC 34**
See also AAYA 44; CA 149; CANR 91

Harwood, Ronald 1934- .... **CLC 32**
See also CA 1-4R; CANR 4, 55; CBD; CD 5; DAM DRAM, MST; DLB 13

Hasegawa Tatsunosuke
See Futabatei, Shimei

Hasek, Jaroslav (Matej Frantisek)
1883-1923 .... **TCLC 4**
See also CA 129; 104; CDWLB 4; DLB 215; EW 9; EWL 3; MTCW 1, 2; RGSF 2; RGWL 2, 3

Hass, Robert 1941- ... **CLC 18, 39, 99; PC 16**
See also AMWS 6; CA 111; CANR 30, 50, 71; CP 7; DLB 105, 206; EWL 3; RGAL 4; SATA 94

Hastings, Hudson
See Kuttner, Henry

Hastings, Selina .... **CLC 44**

Hathorne, John 1641-1717 .... **LC 38**

Hatteras, Amelia
See Mencken, H(enry) L(ouis)

Hatteras, Owen .... **TCLC 18**
See Mencken, H(enry) L(ouis); Nathan, George Jean

Hauptmann, Gerhart (Johann Robert)
1862-1946 .... **SSC 37; TCLC 4**
See also CA 153; 104; CDWLB 2; DAM DRAM; DLB 66, 118; EW 8; EWL 3; RGSF 2; RGWL 2, 3; TWA

Havel, Vaclav 1936- ..... **CLC 25, 58, 65, 123; DC 6**
See also CA 104; CANR 36, 63; CDWLB 4; CWW 2; DA3; DAM DRAM; DFS 10; DLB 232; EWL 3; MTCW 1, 2; RGWL 3

Haviaras, Stratis .... **CLC 33**
See Chaviaras, Strates

Hawes, Stephen 1475(?)-1529(?) .... **LC 17**
See also DLB 132; RGEL 2

Hawkes, John (Clendennin Burne, Jr.)
1925-1998 .. **CLC 1, 2, 3, 4, 7, 9, 14, 15, 27, 49**
See also BPFB 2; CA 167; 1-4R; CANR 2, 47, 64; CN 7; DLB 2, 7, 227; DLBY 1980, 1998; EWL 3; MTCW 1, 2; RGAL 4

Hawking, S. W.
See Hawking, Stephen W(illiam)

Hawking, Stephen W(illiam) 1942- . **CLC 63, 105**
See also AAYA 13; BEST 89:1; CA 129; 126; CANR 48, 115; CPW; DA3; MTCW 2

Hawkins, Anthony Hope
See Hope, Anthony

Hawthorne, Julian 1846-1934 .... **TCLC 25**
See also CA 165; HGG

Hawthorne, Nathaniel 1804-1864 ... **NCLC 2, 10, 17, 23, 39, 79, 95; SSC 3, 29, 39; WLC**
See also AAYA 18; AMW; AMWC 1; AMWR 1; BPFB 2; BYA 3; CDALB 1640-1865; DA; DA3; DAB; DAC; DAM MST, NOV; DLB 1, 74, 183, 223, 269; EXPN; EXPS; HGG; LAIT 1; NFS 1; RGAL 4; RGSF 2; SSFS 1, 7, 11, 15; SUFW 1; TUS; WCH; YABC 2

Haxton, Josephine Ayres 1921-
See Douglas, Ellen
See also CA 115; CANR 41, 83

Hayaseca y Eizaguirre, Jorge
See Echegaray (y Eizaguirre), Jose (Maria Waldo)

Hayashi, Fumiko 1904-1951 .... **TCLC 27**
See Hayashi Fumiko
See also CA 161

Hayashi Fumiko
See Hayashi, Fumiko
See also DLB 180; EWL 3

Haycraft, Anna (Margaret) 1932-
See Ellis, Alice Thomas
See also CA 122; CANR 85, 90; MTCW 2

Hayden, Robert E(arl) 1913-1980 ..... **BLC 2; CLC 5, 9, 14, 37; PC 6**
See also AFAW 1, 2; AMWS 2; BW 1, 3; CA 97-100; 69-72; CABS 2; CANR 24, 75, 82; CDALB 1941-1968; DA; DAC; DAM MST, MULT, POET; DLB 5, 76; EWL 3; EXPP; MTCW 1, 2; PFS 1; RGAL 4; SATA 19; SATA-Obit 26; WP

Hayek, F(riedrich) A(ugust von)
1899-1992 .... **TCLC 109**
See also CA 137; 93-96; CANR 20; MTCW 1, 2

Hayford, J(oseph) E(phraim) Casely
See Casely-Hayford, J(oseph) E(phraim)

Hayman, Ronald 1932- .... **CLC 44**
See also CA 25-28R; CANR 18, 50, 88; CD 5; DLB 155

Hayne, Paul Hamilton 1830-1886 . **NCLC 94**
See also DLB 3, 64, 79, 248; RGAL 4

Hays, Mary 1760-1843 .... **NCLC 114**
See also DLB 142, 158; RGEL 2

Haywood, Eliza (Fowler)
1693(?)-1756 .... **LC 1, 44**
See also DLB 39; RGEL 2

Hazlitt, William 1778-1830 ...... **NCLC 29, 82**
See also BRW 4; DLB 110, 158; RGEL 2; TEA

Hazzard, Shirley 1931- .... **CLC 18**
See also CA 9-12R; CANR 4, 70; CN 7; DLBY 1982; MTCW 1

Head, Bessie 1937-1986 ...... **BLC 2; CLC 25, 67; SSC 52**
See also AFW; BW 2, 3; CA 119; 29-32R; CANR 25, 82; CDWLB 3; DA3; DAM MULT; DLB 117, 225; EWL 3; EXPS; FW; MTCW 1, 2; RGSF 2; SSFS 5, 13; WLIT 2

Headon, (Nicky) Topper 1956(?)- ..... **CLC 30**

Heaney, Seamus (Justin) 1939- ..... **CLC 5, 7, 14, 25, 37, 74, 91; PC 18; WLCS**
See also BRWR 1; BRWS 2; CA 85-88; CANR 25, 48, 75, 91; CDBLB 1960 to Present; CP 7; DA3; DAB; DAM POET; DLB 40; DLBY 1995; EWL 3; EXPP; MTCW 1, 2; PAB; PFS 2, 5, 8, 17; RGEL 2; TEA; WLIT 4

Hearn, (Patricio) Lafcadio (Tessima Carlos)
1850-1904 .... **TCLC 9**
See also CA 166; 105; DLB 12, 78, 189; HGG; RGAL 4

Hearne, Vicki 1946-2001 .... **CLC 56**
See also CA 201; 139

Hearon, Shelby 1931- .... **CLC 63**
See also AITN 2; AMWS 8; CA 25-28R; CANR 18, 48, 103; CSW

Heat-Moon, William Least .... **CLC 29**
See Trogdon, William (Lewis)
See also AAYA 9

Hebbel, Friedrich 1813-1863 .... **NCLC 43**
See also CDWLB 2; DAM DRAM; DLB 129; EW 6; RGWL 2, 3

Hebert, Anne 1916-2000 .... **CLC 4, 13, 29**
See also CA 187; 85-88; CANR 69; CCA 1; CWP; CWW 2; DA3; DAC; DAM MST, POET; DLB 68; EWL 3; GFL 1789 to the Present; MTCW 1, 2

Hecht, Anthony (Evan) 1923- ...... **CLC 8, 13, 19**
See also AMWS 10; CA 9-12R; CANR 6, 108; CP 7; DAM POET; DLB 5, 169; EWL 3; PFS 6; WP

Hecht, Ben 1894-1964 ..... **CLC 8; TCLC 101**
See also CA 85-88; DFS 9; DLB 7, 9, 25, 26, 28, 86; FANT; IDFW 3, 4; RGAL 4

Hedayat, Sadeq 1903-1951 .... **TCLC 21**
See also CA 120; EWL 3; RGSF 2

Hegel, Georg Wilhelm Friedrich
1770-1831 .... **NCLC 46**
See also DLB 90; TWA

Heidegger, Martin 1889-1976 .... **CLC 24**
See also CA 65-68; 81-84; CANR 34; MTCW 1, 2

Heidenstam, (Carl Gustaf) Verner von
1859-1940 .... **TCLC 5**
See also CA 104

Heifner, Jack 1946- .... **CLC 11**
See also CA 105; CANR 47

Heijermans, Herman 1864-1924 .... **TCLC 24**
See also CA 123; EWL 3

Heilbrun, Carolyn G(old) 1926- .... **CLC 25**
See Cross, Amanda
See also CA 45-48; CANR 1, 28, 58, 94; FW

Hein, Christoph 1944- .... **CLC 154**
See also CA 158; CANR 108; CDWLB 2; CWW 2; DLB 124

Heine, Heinrich 1797-1856 .... **NCLC 4, 54; PC 25**
See also CDWLB 2; DLB 90; EW 5; RGWL 2, 3; TWA

Heinemann, Larry (Curtiss) 1944- .. **CLC 50**
See also CA 110; CAAS 21; CANR 31, 81; DLBD 9; INT CANR-31

Heiney, Donald (William) 1921-1993
See Harris, MacDonald
See also CA 142; 1-4R; CANR 3, 58; FANT

Heinlein, Robert A(nson) 1907-1988 . **CLC 1, 3, 8, 14, 26, 55; SSC 55**
See also AAYA 17; BPFB 2; BYA 4, 13; CA 125; 1-4R; CANR 1, 20, 53; CLR 75; CPW; DA3; DAM POP; DLB 8; EXPS; JRDA; LAIT 5; MAICYA 1, 2; MTCW 1, 2; RGAL 4; SATA 9, 69; SATA-Obit 56; SCFW 1; SFW 4; SSFS 7; YAW

Helforth, John
See Doolittle, Hilda

Heliodorus fl. 3rd cent. - .... **CMLC 52**

Hellenhofferu, Vojtech Kapristian z
See Hasek, Jaroslav (Matej Frantisek)

Heller, Joseph 1923-1999 . **CLC 1, 3, 5, 8, 11, 36, 63; TCLC 131; WLC**
See also AAYA 24; AITN 1; AMWS 4; BPFB 2; BYA 1; CA 187; 5-8R; CABS 1; CANR 8, 42, 66; CN 7; CPW; DA; DA3; DAB; DAC; DAM MST, NOV, POP; DLB 2, 28, 227; DLBY 1980; EWL 3; EXPN; INT CANR-8; LAIT 4; MTCW 1, 2; NFS 1; RGAL 4; TUS; YAW

Hellman, Lillian (Florence)
1906-1984 .. **CLC 2, 4, 8, 14, 18, 34, 44, 52; DC 1; TCLC 119**
See also AAYA 47; AITN 1, 2; AMWS 1; CA 112; 13-16R; CAD; CANR 33; CWD; DA3; DAM DRAM; DFS 1, 3, 14; DLB 7, 228; DLBY 1984; EWL 3; FW; LAIT 3; MAWW; MTCW 1, 2; RGAL 4; TUS

Helprin, Mark 1947- .... **CLC 7, 10, 22, 32**
See also CA 81-84; CANR 47, 64; CDALBS; CPW; DA3; DAM NOV, POP; DLBY 1985; FANT; MTCW 1, 2; SUFW 2

Helvetius, Claude-Adrien 1715-1771 .. **LC 26**

Helyar, Jane Penelope Josephine 1933-
See Poole, Josephine
See also CA 21-24R; CANR 10, 26; CWRI 5; SATA 82

Hugo, Victor (Marie) 1802-1885 .... **NCLC 3, 10, 21; PC 17; WLC**
See also AAYA 28; DA; DA3; DAB; DAC; DAM DRAM, MST, NOV, POET; DLB 119, 192, 217; EFS 2; EW 6; EXPN; GFL 1789 to the Present; LAIT 1, 2; NFS 5; RGWL 2, 3; SATA 47; TWA

Huidobro, Vicente
See Huidobro Fernandez, Vicente Garcia
See also EWL 3; LAW

Huidobro Fernandez, Vicente Garcia
1893-1948 .... **TCLC 31**
See Huidobro, Vicente
See also CA 131; HW 1

Hulme, Keri 1947- .... **CLC 39, 130**
See also CA 125; CANR 69; CN 7; CP 7; CWP; EWL 3; FW; INT 125

Hulme, T(homas) E(rnest)
1883-1917 .... **TCLC 21**
See also BRWS 6; CA 203; 117; DLB 19

Hume, David 1711-1776 .... **LC 7, 56**
See also BRWS 3; DLB 104, 252; TEA

Humphrey, William 1924-1997 .... **CLC 45**
See also AMWS 9; CA 160; 77-80; CANR 68; CN 7; CSW; DLB 6, 212, 234, 278; TCWW 2

Humphreys, Emyr Owen 1919- .... **CLC 47**
See also CA 5-8R; CANR 3, 24; CN 7; DLB 15

Humphreys, Josephine 1945- ..... **CLC 34, 57**
See also CA 127; 121; CANR 97; CSW; INT 127

Huneker, James Gibbons
1860-1921 .... **TCLC 65**
See also CA 193; DLB 71; RGAL 4

Hungerford, Hesba Fay
See Brinsmead, H(esba) F(ay)

Hungerford, Pixie
See Brinsmead, H(esba) F(ay)

Hunt, E(verette) Howard, (Jr.)
1918- .... **CLC 3**
See also AITN 1; CA 45-48; CANR 2, 47, 103; CMW 4

Hunt, Francesca
See Holland, Isabelle (Christian)

Hunt, Howard
See Hunt, E(verette) Howard, (Jr.)

Hunt, Kyle
See Creasey, John

Hunt, (James Henry) Leigh
1784-1859 .... **NCLC 1, 70**
See also DAM POET; DLB 96, 110, 144; RGEL 2; TEA

Hunt, Marsha 1946- .... **CLC 70**
See also BW 2, 3; CA 143; CANR 79

Hunt, Violet 1866(?)-1942 .... **TCLC 53**
See also CA 184; DLB 162, 197

Hunter, E. Waldo
See Sturgeon, Theodore (Hamilton)

Hunter, Evan 1926- .... **CLC 11, 31**
See McBain, Ed
See also AAYA 39; BPFB 2; CA 5-8R; CANR 5, 38, 62, 97; CMW 4; CN 7; CPW; DAM POP; DLBY 1982; INT CANR-5; MSW; MTCW 1; SATA 25; SFW 4

Hunter, Kristin 1931-
See Lattany, Kristin (Elaine Eggleston) Hunter

Hunter, Mary
See Austin, Mary (Hunter)

Hunter, Mollie 1922- .... **CLC 21**
See McIlwraith, Maureen Mollie Hunter
See also AAYA 13; BYA 6; CANR 37, 78; CLR 25; DLB 161; JRDA; MAICYA 1, 2; SAAS 7; SATA 54, 106; WYA; YAW

Hunter, Robert (?)-1734 .... **LC 7**

Hurston, Zora Neale 1891-1960 .... **BLC 2; CLC 7, 30, 61; DC 12; HR 2; SSC 4; TCLC 121, 131; WLCS**
See also AAYA 15; AFAW 1, 2; AMWS 6; BW 1, 3; BYA 12; CA 85-88; CANR 61; CDALBS; DA; DA3; DAC; DAM MST, MULT, NOV; DFS 6; DLB 51, 86; EWL 3; EXPN; EXPS; FW; LAIT 3; MAWW; MTCW 1, 2; NFS 3; RGAL 4; RGSF 2; SSFS 1, 6, 11; TUS; YAW

Husserl, E. G.
See Husserl, Edmund (Gustav Albrecht)

Husserl, Edmund (Gustav Albrecht)
1859-1938 .... **TCLC 100**
See also CA 133; 116

Huston, John (Marcellus)
1906-1987 .... **CLC 20**
See also CA 123; 73-76; CANR 34; DLB 26

Hustvedt, Siri 1955- .... **CLC 76**
See also CA 137

Hutten, Ulrich von 1488-1523 .... **LC 16**
See also DLB 179

Huxley, Aldous (Leonard)
1894-1963 ..... **CLC 1, 3, 4, 5, 8, 11, 18, 35, 79; SSC 39; WLC**
See also AAYA 11; BPFB 2; BRW 7; CA 85-88; CANR 44, 99; CDBLB 1914-1945; DA; DA3; DAB; DAC; DAM MST, NOV; DLB 36, 100, 162, 195, 255; EWL 3; EXPN; LAIT 5; MTCW 1, 2; NFS 6; RGEL 2; SATA 63; SCFW 2; SFW 4; TEA; YAW

Huxley, T(homas) H(enry)
1825-1895 .... **NCLC 67**
See also DLB 57; TEA

Huysmans, Joris-Karl 1848-1907 ... **TCLC 7, 69**
See also CA 165; 104; DLB 123; EW 7; GFL 1789 to the Present; RGWL 2, 3

Hwang, David Henry 1957- .. **CLC 55; DC 4**
See also CA 132; 127; CAD; CANR 76; CD 5; DA3; DAM DRAM; DFS 11; DLB 212, 228; INT CA-132; MTCW 2; RGAL 4

Hyde, Anthony 1946- .... **CLC 42**
See Chase, Nicholas
See also CA 136; CCA 1

Hyde, Margaret O(ldroyd) 1917- ..... **CLC 21**
See also CA 1-4R; CANR 1, 36; CLR 23; JRDA; MAICYA 1, 2; SAAS 8; SATA 1, 42, 76

Hynes, James 1956(?)- .... **CLC 65**
See also CA 164; CANR 105

Hypatia c. 370-415 .... **CMLC 35**

Ian, Janis 1951- .... **CLC 21**
See also CA 187; 105

Ibanez, Vicente Blasco
See Blasco Ibanez, Vicente

Ibarbourou, Juana de 1895-1979 ..... **HLCS 2**
See also HW 1; LAW

Ibarguengoitia, Jorge 1928-1983 ...... **CLC 37**
See also CA 113; 124; EWL 3; HW 1

Ibn Battuta, Abu Abdalla
1304-1368(?) .... **CMLC 57**
See also WLIT 2

Ibsen, Henrik (Johan) 1828-1906 .... **DC 2; TCLC 2, 8, 16, 37, 52; WLC**
See also AAYA 46; CA 141; 104; DA; DA3; DAB; DAC; DAM DRAM, MST; DFS 1, 6, 8, 10, 11, 15, 16; EW 7; LAIT 2; RGWL 2, 3

Ibuse, Masuji 1898-1993 .... **CLC 22**
See Ibuse Masuji
See also CA 141; 127; MJW; RGWL 3

Ibuse Masuji
See Ibuse, Masuji
See also DLB 180; EWL 3

Ichikawa, Kon 1915- .... **CLC 20**
See also CA 121

Ichiyo, Higuchi 1872-1896 .... **NCLC 49**
See also MJW

Idle, Eric 1943-2000 .... **CLC 21**
See Monty Python
See also CA 116; CANR 35, 91

Ignatow, David 1914-1997 .... **CLC 4, 7, 14, 40; PC 34**
See also CA 162; 9-12R; CAAS 3; CANR 31, 57, 96; CP 7; DLB 5; EWL 3

Ignotus
See Strachey, (Giles) Lytton

Ihimaera, Witi 1944- .... **CLC 46**
See also CA 77-80; CN 7; RGSF 2

Ilf, Ilya .... **TCLC 21**
See Fainzilberg, Ilya Arnoldovich
See also EWL 3

Illyes, Gyula 1902-1983 .... **PC 16**
See also CA 109; 114; CDWLB 4; DLB 215; EWL 3; RGWL 2, 3

Immermann, Karl (Lebrecht)
1796-1840 .... **NCLC 4, 49**
See also DLB 133

Ince, Thomas H. 1882-1924 .... **TCLC 89**
See also IDFW 3, 4

Inchbald, Elizabeth 1753-1821 ...... **NCLC 62**
See also DLB 39, 89; RGEL 2

Inclan, Ramon (Maria) del Valle
See Valle-Inclan, Ramon (Maria) del

Infante, G(uillermo) Cabrera
See Cabrera Infante, G(uillermo)

Ingalls, Rachel (Holmes) 1940- .... **CLC 42**
See also CA 127; 123

Ingamells, Reginald Charles
See Ingamells, Rex

Ingamells, Rex 1913-1955 .... **TCLC 35**
See also CA 167; DLB 260

Inge, William (Motter) 1913-1973 ..... **CLC 1, 8, 19**
See also CA 9-12R; CDALB 1941-1968; DA3; DAM DRAM; DFS 1, 5, 8; DLB 7, 249; EWL 3; MTCW 1, 2; RGAL 4; TUS

Ingelow, Jean 1820-1897 .... **NCLC 39, 107**
See also DLB 35, 163; FANT; SATA 33

Ingram, Willis J.
See Harris, Mark

Innaurato, Albert (F.) 1948(?)- .. **CLC 21, 60**
See also CA 122; 115; CAD; CANR 78; CD 5; INT CA-122

Innes, Michael
See Stewart, J(ohn) I(nnes) M(ackintosh)
See also DLB 276; MSW

Innis, Harold Adams 1894-1952 .... **TCLC 77**
See also CA 181; DLB 88

Insluis, Alanus de
See Alain de Lille

Iola
See Wells-Barnett, Ida B(ell)

Ionesco, Eugene 1912-1994 ... **CLC 1, 4, 6, 9, 11, 15, 41, 86; DC 12; WLC**
See also CA 144; 9-12R; CANR 55; CWW 2; DA; DA3; DAB; DAC; DAM DRAM, MST; DFS 4, 9; EW 13; EWL 3; GFL 1789 to the Present; MTCW 1, 2; RGWL 2, 3; SATA 7; SATA-Obit 79; TWA

Iqbal, Muhammad 1877-1938 .... **TCLC 28**
See also EWL 3

Ireland, Patrick
See O'Doherty, Brian

Irenaeus St. 130- .... **CMLC 42**

Irigaray, Luce 1930- .... **CLC 164**
See also CA 154; FW

Iron, Ralph
See Schreiner, Olive (Emilie Albertina)

Li Ho 791-817 .... **PC 13**

Liliencron, (Friedrich Adolf Axel) Detlev
    von 1844-1909 .... **TCLC 18**
    See also CA 117

Lille, Alain de
    See Alain de Lille

Lilly, William 1602-1681 .... **LC 27**

Lima, Jose Lezama
    See Lezama Lima, Jose

Lima Barreto, Afonso Henrique de
    1881-1922 .... **TCLC 23**
    See also CA 181; 117; LAW

Lima Barreto, Afonso Henriques de
    See Lima Barreto, Afonso Henrique de

Limonov, Edward 1944- .... **CLC 67**
    See also CA 137

Lin, Frank
    See Atherton, Gertrude (Franklin Horn)

Lincoln, Abraham 1809-1865 .... **NCLC 18**
    See also LAIT 2

Lind, Jakov .... **CLC 1, 2, 4, 27, 82**
    See Landwirth, Heinz
    See also CAAS 4

Lindbergh, Anne (Spencer) Morrow
    1906-2001 .... **CLC 82**
    See also BPFB 2; CA 193; 17-20R; CANR
    16, 73; DAM NOV; MTCW 1, 2; SATA
    33; SATA-Obit 125; TUS

Lindsay, David 1878(?)-1945 .... **TCLC 15**
    See also CA 187; 113; DLB 255; FANT;
    SFW 4; SUFW 1

Lindsay, (Nicholas) Vachel
    1879-1931 .... **PC 23; TCLC 17; WLC**
    See also AMWS 1; CA 135; 114; CANR
    79; CDALB 1865-1917; DA; DA3; DAC;
    DAM MST, POET; DLB 54; EXPP;
    RGAL 4; SATA 40; WP

Linke-Poot
    See Doeblin, Alfred

Linney, Romulus 1930- .... **CLC 51**
    See also CA 1-4R; CAD; CANR 40, 44,
    79; CD 5; CSW; RGAL 4

Linton, Eliza Lynn 1822-1898 .... **NCLC 41**
    See also DLB 18

Li Po 701-763 .... **CMLC 2; PC 29**
    See also WP

Lipsius, Justus 1547-1606 .... **LC 16**

Lipsyte, Robert (Michael) 1938- ...... **CLC 21**
    See also AAYA 7, 45; CA 17-20R; CANR
    8, 57; CLR 23, 76; DA; DAC; DAM
    MST, NOV; JRDA; LAIT 5; MAICYA 1,
    2; SATA 5, 68, 113; WYA; YAW

Lish, Gordon (Jay) 1934- ... **CLC 45; SSC 18**
    See also CA 117; 113; CANR 79; DLB 130;
    INT 117

Lispector, Clarice 1925(?)-1977 .... **CLC 43;
    HLCS 2; SSC 34**
    See also CA 116; 139; CANR 71; CDWLB
    3; DLB 113; DNFS 1; FW; HW 2; LAW;
    RGSF 2; RGWL 2, 3; WLIT 1

Littell, Robert 1935(?)- .... **CLC 42**
    See also CA 112; 109; CANR 64, 115;
    CMW 4

Little, Malcolm 1925-1965
    See Malcolm X
    See also BW 1, 3; CA 111; 125; CANR 82;
    DA; DA3; DAB; DAC; DAM MST,
    MULT; MTCW 1, 2; NCFS 3

Littlewit, Humphrey Gent.
    See Lovecraft, H(oward) P(hillips)

Litwos
    See Sienkiewicz, Henryk (Adam Alexander
    Pius)

Liu, E. 1857-1909 .... **TCLC 15**
    See also CA 190; 115

Lively, Penelope (Margaret) 1933- .. **CLC 32,
    50**
    See also BPFB 2; CA 41-44R; CANR 29,
    67, 79; CLR 7; CN 7; CWRI 5; DAM
    NOV; DLB 14, 161, 207; FANT; JRDA;
    MAICYA 1, 2; MTCW 1, 2; SATA 7, 60,
    101; TEA

Livesay, Dorothy (Kathleen)
    1909-1996 .... **CLC 4, 15, 79**
    See also AITN 2; CA 25-28R; CAAS 8;
    CANR 36, 67; DAC; DAM MST, POET;
    DLB 68; FW; MTCW 1; RGEL 2; TWA

Livy c. 59B.C.-c. 12 .... **CMLC 11**
    See also AW 2; CDWLB 1; DLB 211;
    RGWL 2, 3

Lizardi, Jose Joaquin Fernandez de
    1776-1827 .... **NCLC 30**
    See also LAW

Llewellyn, Richard
    See Llewellyn Lloyd, Richard Dafydd Vivian
    See also DLB 15

Llewellyn Lloyd, Richard Dafydd Vivian
    1906-1983 .... **CLC 7, 80**
    See Llewellyn, Richard
    See also CA 111; 53-56; CANR 7, 71;
    SATA 11; SATA-Obit 37

Llosa, (Jorge) Mario (Pedro) Vargas
    See Vargas Llosa, (Jorge) Mario (Pedro)
    See also RGWL 3

Lloyd, Manda
    See Mander, (Mary) Jane

Lloyd Webber, Andrew 1948-
    See Webber, Andrew Lloyd
    See also AAYA 1, 38; CA 149; 116; DAM
    DRAM; SATA 56

Llull, Ramon c. 1235-c. 1316 .... **CMLC 12**

Lobb, Ebenezer
    See Upward, Allen

Locke, Alain (Le Roy)
    1886-1954 .... **BLCS; HR 3; TCLC 43**
    See also BW 1, 3; CA 124; 106; CANR 79;
    DLB 51; RGAL 4

Locke, John 1632-1704 .... **LC 7, 35**
    See also DLB 31, 101, 213, 252; RGEL 2;
    WLIT 3

Locke-Elliott, Sumner
    See Elliott, Sumner Locke

Lockhart, John Gibson 1794-1854 .. **NCLC 6**
    See also DLB 110, 116, 144

Lockridge, Ross (Franklin), Jr.
    1914-1948 .... **TCLC 111**
    See also CA 145; 108; CANR 79; DLB 143;
    DLBY 1980; RGAL 4; RHW

Lockwood, Robert
    See Johnson, Robert

Lodge, David (John) 1935- .... **CLC 36, 141**
    See also BEST 90:1; BRWS 4; CA 17-20R;
    CANR 19, 53, 92; CN 7; CPW; DAM
    POP; DLB 14, 194; INT CANR-19;
    MTCW 1, 2

Lodge, Thomas 1558-1625 .... **LC 41**
    See also DLB 172; RGEL 2

Loewinsohn, Ron(ald William)
    1937- .... **CLC 52**
    See also CA 25-28R; CANR 71

Logan, Jake
    See Smith, Martin Cruz

Logan, John (Burton) 1923-1987 .... **CLC 5**
    See also CA 124; 77-80; CANR 45; DLB 5

Lo Kuan-chung 1330(?)-1400(?) .... **LC 12**

Lombard, Nap
    See Johnson, Pamela Hansford

Lomotey (editor), Kofi .... **CLC 70**

London, Jack 1876-1916 .. **SSC 4, 49; TCLC
    9, 15, 39; WLC**
    See London, John Griffith
    See also AAYA 13; AITN 2; AMW; BPFB
    2; BYA 4, 13; CDALB 1865-1917; DLB

8, 12, 78, 212; EXPS; LAIT 3; NFS 8;
    RGAL 4; RGSF 2; SATA 18; SFW 4;
    SSFS 7; TCWW 2; TUS; WYA; YAW

London, John Griffith 1876-1916
    See London, Jack
    See also CA 119; 110; CANR 73; DA; DA3;
    DAB; DAC; DAM MST, NOV; JRDA;
    MAICYA 1, 2; MTCW 1, 2

Long, Emmett
    See Leonard, Elmore (John, Jr.)

Longbaugh, Harry
    See Goldman, William (W.)

Longfellow, Henry Wadsworth
    1807-1882 .... **NCLC 2, 45, 101, 103; PC
    30; WLCS**
    See also AMW; AMWR 2; CDALB 1640-
    1865; DA; DA3; DAB; DAC; DAM MST,
    POET; DLB 1, 59, 235; EXPP; PAB; PFS
    2, 7, 17; RGAL 4; SATA 19; TUS; WP

Longinus c. 1st cent. - .... **CMLC 27**
    See also AW 2; DLB 176

Longley, Michael 1939- .... **CLC 29**
    See also BRWS 8; CA 102; CP 7; DLB 40

Longus fl. c. 2nd cent. - .... **CMLC 7**

Longway, A. Hugh
    See Lang, Andrew

Lonnbohm, Armas Eino Leopold 1878-1926
    See Leino, Eino
    See also CA 123

Lonnrot, Elias 1802-1884 .... **NCLC 53**
    See also EFS 1

Lonsdale, Roger ed. .... **CLC 65**

Lopate, Phillip 1943- .... **CLC 29**
    See also CA 97-100; CANR 88; DLBY
    1980; INT 97-100

Lopez, Barry (Holstun) 1945- .... **CLC 70**
    See also AAYA 9; ANW; CA 65-68; CANR
    7, 23, 47, 68, 92; DLB 256, 275; INT
    CANR-7, -23; MTCW 1; RGAL 4; SATA
    67

Lopez Portillo (y Pacheco), Jose
    1920- .... **CLC 46**
    See also CA 129; HW 1

Lopez y Fuentes, Gregorio
    1897(?)-1966 .... **CLC 32**
    See also CA 131; HW 1

Lorca, Federico Garcia
    See Garcia Lorca, Federico
    See also DFS 4; EW 11; RGWL 2, 3; WP

Lord, Bette Bao 1938- .... **AAL; CLC 23**
    See also BEST 90:3; BPFB 2; CA 107;
    CANR 41, 79; INT CA-107; SATA 58

Lord Auch
    See Bataille, Georges

Lord Brooke
    See Greville, Fulke

Lord Byron
    See Byron, George Gordon (Noel)

Lorde, Audre (Geraldine)
    1934-1992 .. **BLC 2; CLC 18, 71; PC 12**
    See Domini, Rey
    See also AFAW 1, 2; BW 1, 3; CA 142; 25-
    28R; CANR 16, 26, 46, 82; DA3; DAM
    MULT, POET; DLB 41; FW; MTCW 1,
    2; PFS 16; RGAL 4

Lord Houghton
    See Milnes, Richard Monckton

Lord Jeffrey
    See Jeffrey, Francis

Loreaux, Nichol .... **CLC 65**

Lorenzini, Carlo 1826-1890
    See Collodi, Carlo
    See also MAICYA 1, 2; SATA 29, 100

Lorenzo, Heberto Padilla
    See Padilla (Lorenzo), Heberto

Loris
    See Hofmannsthal, Hugo von

Medoff, Mark (Howard) 1940- .... **CLC 6, 23**
See also AITN 1; CA 53-56; CAD; CANR 5; CD 5; DAM DRAM; DFS 4; DLB 7; INT CANR-5

Medvedev, P. N.
See Bakhtin, Mikhail Mikhailovich

Meged, Aharon
See Megged, Aharon

Meged, Aron
See Megged, Aharon

Megged, Aharon 1920- .... **CLC 9**
See also CA 49-52; CAAS 13; CANR 1

Mehta, Ved (Parkash) 1934- .... **CLC 37**
See also CA 1-4R; CANR 2, 23, 69; MTCW 1

Melanter
See Blackmore, R(ichard) D(oddridge)

Meleager c. 140B.C.-c. 70B.C. ...... **CMLC 53**

Melies, Georges 1861-1938 .... **TCLC 81**

Melikow, Loris
See Hofmannsthal, Hugo von

Melmoth, Sebastian
See Wilde, Oscar (Fingal O'Flahertie Wills)

Meltzer, Milton 1915- .... **CLC 26**
See also AAYA 8, 45; BYA 2, 6; CA 13-16R; CANR 38, 92, 107; CLR 13; DLB 61; JRDA; MAICYA 1, 2; SAAS 1; SATA 1, 50, 80, 128; SATA-Essay 124; WYA; YAW

Melville, Herman 1819-1891 ..... **NCLC 3, 12, 29, 45, 49, 91, 93; SSC 1, 17, 46; WLC**
See also AAYA 25; AMW; AMWR 1; CDALB 1640-1865; DA; DA3; DAB; DAC; DAM MST, NOV; DLB 3, 74, 250, 254; EXPN; EXPS; LAIT 1, 2; NFS 7, 9; RGAL 4; RGSF 2; SATA 59; SSFS 3; TUS

Members, Mark
See Powell, Anthony (Dymoke)

Membreno, Alejandro .... **CLC 59**

Menander c. 342B.C.-c. 293B.C. .... **CMLC 9, 51; DC 3**
See also AW 1; CDWLB 1; DAM DRAM; DLB 176; RGWL 2, 3

Menchu, Rigoberta 1959- .. **CLC 160; HLCS 2**
See also CA 175; DNFS 1; WLIT 1

Mencken, H(enry) L(ouis)
1880-1956 .... **TCLC 13**
See also AMW; CA 125; 105; CDALB 1917-1929; DLB 11, 29, 63, 137, 222; MTCW 1, 2; NCFS 4; RGAL 4; TUS

Mendelsohn, Jane 1965- .... **CLC 99**
See also CA 154; CANR 94

Menton, Francisco de
See Chin, Frank (Chew, Jr.)

Mercer, David 1928-1980 .... **CLC 5**
See also CA 102; 9-12R; CANR 23; CBD; DAM DRAM; DLB 13; MTCW 1; RGEL 2

Merchant, Paul
See Ellison, Harlan (Jay)

Meredith, George 1828-1909 ... **TCLC 17, 43**
See also CA 153; 117; CANR 80; CDBLB 1832-1890; DAM POET; DLB 18, 35, 57, 159; RGEL 2; TEA

Meredith, William (Morris) 1919- .... **CLC 4, 13, 22, 55; PC 28**
See also CA 9-12R; CAAS 14; CANR 6, 40; CP 7; DAM POET; DLB 5

Merezhkovsky, Dmitry Sergeyevich
1865-1941 .... **TCLC 29**
See also CA 169

Merimee, Prosper 1803-1870 ... **NCLC 6, 65; SSC 7**
See also DLB 119, 192; EW 6; EXPS; GFL 1789 to the Present; RGSF 2; RGWL 2, 3; SSFS 8; SUFW

Merkin, Daphne 1954- .... **CLC 44**
See also CA 123

Merlin, Arthur
See Blish, James (Benjamin)

Merrill, James (Ingram) 1926-1995 .. **CLC 2, 3, 6, 8, 13, 18, 34, 91; PC 28**
See also AMWS 3; CA 147; 13-16R; CANR 10, 49, 63, 108; DA3; DAM POET; DLB 5, 165; DLBY 1985; INT CANR-10; MTCW 1, 2; PAB; RGAL 4

Merriman, Alex
See Silverberg, Robert

Merriman, Brian 1747-1805 .... **NCLC 70**

Merritt, E. B.
See Waddington, Miriam

Merton, Thomas (James)
1915-1968 . **CLC 1, 3, 11, 34, 83; PC 10**
See also AMWS 8; CA 25-28R; 5-8R; CANR 22, 53, 111; DA3; DLB 48; DLBY 1981; MTCW 1, 2

Merwin, W(illiam) S(tanley) 1927- ... **CLC 1, 2, 3, 5, 8, 13, 18, 45, 88; PC 45**
See also AMWS 3; CA 13-16R; CANR 15, 51, 112; CP 7; DA3; DAM POET; DLB 5, 169; INT CANR-15; MTCW 1, 2; PAB; PFS 5, 15; RGAL 4

Metcalf, John 1938- .... **CLC 37; SSC 43**
See also CA 113; CN 7; DLB 60; RGSF 2; TWA

Metcalf, Suzanne
See Baum, L(yman) Frank

Mew, Charlotte (Mary) 1870-1928 .. **TCLC 8**
See also CA 189; 105; DLB 19, 135; RGEL 2

Mewshaw, Michael 1943- .... **CLC 9**
See also CA 53-56; CANR 7, 47; DLBY 1980

Meyer, Conrad Ferdinand
1825-1905 .... **NCLC 81**
See also DLB 129; EW; RGWL 2, 3

Meyer, Gustav 1868-1932
See Meyrink, Gustav
See also CA 190; 117

Meyer, June
See Jordan, June (Meyer)

Meyer, Lynn
See Slavitt, David R(ytman)

Meyers, Jeffrey 1939- .... **CLC 39**
See also CA 73-76; CAAE 186; CANR 54, 102; DLB 111

Meynell, Alice (Christina Gertrude Thompson) 1847-1922 .... **TCLC 6**
See also CA 177; 104; DLB 19, 98; RGEL 2

Meyrink, Gustav .... **TCLC 21**
See Meyer, Gustav
See also DLB 81

Michaels, Leonard 1933- .... **CLC 6, 25; SSC 16**
See also CA 61-64; CANR 21, 62; CN 7; DLB 130; MTCW 1

Michaux, Henri 1899-1984 .... **CLC 8, 19**
See also CA 114; 85-88; DLB 258; GFL 1789 to the Present; RGWL 2, 3

Micheaux, Oscar (Devereaux)
1884-1951 .... **TCLC 76**
See also BW 3; CA 174; DLB 50; TCWW 2

Michelangelo 1475-1564 .... **LC 12**
See also AAYA 43

Michelet, Jules 1798-1874 .... **NCLC 31**
See also EW 5; GFL 1789 to the Present

Michels, Robert 1876-1936 .... **TCLC 88**

Michener, James A(lbert)
1907(?)-1997 .. **CLC 1, 5, 11, 29, 60, 109**
See also AAYA 27; AITN 1; BEST 90:1; BPFB 2; CA 161; 5-8R; CANR 21, 45, 68; CN 7; CPW; DA3; DAM NOV, POP; DLB 6; MTCW 1, 2; RHW

Mickiewicz, Adam 1798-1855 . **NCLC 3, 101; PC 38**
See also EW 5; RGWL 2, 3

Middleton, Christopher 1926- .... **CLC 13**
See also CA 13-16R; CANR 29, 54; CP 7; DLB 40

Middleton, Richard (Barham)
1882-1911 .... **TCLC 56**
See also CA 187; DLB 156; HGG

Middleton, Stanley 1919- .... **CLC 7, 38**
See also CA 25-28R; CAAS 23; CANR 21, 46, 81; CN 7; DLB 14

Middleton, Thomas 1580-1627 ...... **DC 5; LC 33**
See also BRW 2; DAM DRAM, MST; DLB 58; RGEL 2

Migueis, Jose Rodrigues 1901- .... **CLC 10**

Mikszath, Kalman 1847-1910 .... **TCLC 31**
See also CA 170

Miles, Jack .... **CLC 100**
See also CA 200

Miles, John Russiano
See Miles, Jack

Miles, Josephine (Louise)
1911-1985 .... **CLC 1, 2, 14, 34, 39**
See also CA 116; 1-4R; CANR 2, 55; DAM POET; DLB 48

Militant
See Sandburg, Carl (August)

Mill, Harriet (Hardy) Taylor
1807-1858 .... **NCLC 102**
See also FW

Mill, John Stuart 1806-1873 .... **NCLC 11, 58**
See also CDBLB 1832-1890; DLB 55, 190, 262; FW 1; RGEL 2; TEA

Millar, Kenneth 1915-1983 .... **CLC 14**
See Macdonald, Ross
See also CA 110; 9-12R; CANR 16, 63, 107; CMW 4; CPW; DA3; DAM POP; DLB 2, 226; DLBD 6; DLBY 1983; MTCW 1, 2

Millay, E. Vincent
See Millay, Edna St. Vincent

Millay, Edna St. Vincent 1892-1950 .... **PC 6; TCLC 4, 49; WLCS**
See Boyd, Nancy
See also AMW; CA 130; 104; CDALB 1917-1929; DA; DA3; DAB; DAC; DAM MST, POET; DLB 45, 249; EXPP; MAWW; MTCW 1, 2; PAB; PFS 3, 17; RGAL 4; TUS; WP

Miller, Arthur 1915- ...... **CLC 1, 2, 6, 10, 15, 26, 47, 78; DC 1; WLC**
See also AAYA 15; AITN 1; AMW; AMWC 1; CA 1-4R; CABS 3; CAD; CANR 2, 30, 54, 76; CD 5; CDALB 1941-1968; DA; DA3; DAB; DAC; DAM DRAM, MST; DFS 1, 3; DLB 7, 266; LAIT 1, 4; MTCW 1, 2; RGAL 4; TUS; WYAS 1

Miller, Henry (Valentine)
1891-1980 .... **CLC 1, 2, 4, 9, 14, 43, 84; WLC**
See also AMW; BPFB 2; CA 97-100; 9-12R; CANR 33, 64; CDALB 1929-1941; DA; DA3; DAB; DAC; DAM MST, NOV; DLB 4, 9; DLBY 1980; MTCW 1, 2; RGAL 4; TUS

Miller, Jason 1939(?)-2001 .... **CLC 2**
See also AITN 1; CA 197; 73-76; CAD; DFS 12; DLB 7

Miller, Sue 1943- .... **CLC 44**
See also AMWS 12; BEST 90:3; CA 139; CANR 59, 91; DA3; DAM POP; DLB 143

Miller, Walter M(ichael, Jr.)
1923-1996 .... **CLC 4, 30**
See also BPFB 2; CA 85-88; CANR 108; DLB 8; SCFW; SFW 4

Millett, Kate 1934- .... **CLC 67**
See also AITN 1; CA 73-76; CANR 32, 53, 76, 110; DA3; DLB 246; FW; GLL 1; MTCW 1, 2

Millhauser, Steven (Lewis) 1943- .... **CLC 21, 54, 109; SSC 57**
See also CA 111; 110; CANR 63, 114; CN 7; DA3; DLB 2; FANT; INT CA-111; MTCW 2

Millin, Sarah Gertrude 1889-1968 ... **CLC 49**
See also CA 93-96; 102; DLB 225

Milne, A(lan) A(lexander)
1882-1956 .... **TCLC 6, 88**
See also BRWS 5; CA 133; 104; CLR 1, 26; CMW 4; CWRI 5; DA3; DAB; DAC; DAM MST; DLB 10, 77, 100, 160; FANT; MAICYA 1, 2; MTCW 1, 2; RGEL 2; SATA 100; WCH; YABC 1

Milner, Ron(ald) 1938- .... **BLC 3; CLC 56**
See also AITN 1; BW 1; CA 73-76; CAD; CANR 24, 81; CD 5; DAM MULT; DLB 38; MTCW 1

Milnes, Richard Monckton
1809-1885 .... **NCLC 61**
See also DLB 32, 184

Milosz, Czeslaw 1911- ...... **CLC 5, 11, 22, 31, 56, 82; PC 8; WLCS**
See also CA 81-84; CANR 23, 51, 91; CD-WLB 4; CWW 2; DA3; DAM MST, POET; DLB 215; EW 13; MTCW 1, 2; PFS 16; RGWL 2, 3

Milton, John 1608-1674 ..... **LC 9, 43; PC 19, 29; WLC**
See also BRW 2; BRWR 2; CDBLB 1660-1789; DA; DA3; DAB; DAC; DAM MST, POET; DLB 131, 151; EFS 1; EXPP; LAIT 1; PAB; PFS 3, 17; RGEL 2; TEA; WLIT 3; WP

Min, Anchee 1957- .... **CLC 86**
See also CA 146; CANR 94

Minehaha, Cornelius
See Wedekind, (Benjamin) Frank(lin)

Miner, Valerie 1947- .... **CLC 40**
See also CA 97-100; CANR 59; FW; GLL 2

Minimo, Duca
See D'Annunzio, Gabriele

Minot, Susan 1956- .... **CLC 44, 159**
See also AMWS 6; CA 134; CN 7

Minus, Ed 1938- .... **CLC 39**
See also CA 185

Miranda, Javier
See Bioy Casares, Adolfo
See also CWW 2

Mirbeau, Octave 1848-1917 .... **TCLC 55**
See also DLB 123, 192; GFL 1789 to the Present

Mirikitani, Janice 1942- .... **AAL**
See also RGAL 4

Miro (Ferrer), Gabriel (Francisco Victor)
1879-1930 .... **TCLC 5**
See also CA 185; 104

Misharin, Alexandr .... **CLC 59**

Mishima, Yukio ... **CLC 2, 4, 6, 9, 27; DC 1; SSC 4**
See Hiraoka, Kimitake
See also BPFB 2; GLL 1; MJW; MTCW 2; RGSF 2; RGWL 2, 3; SSFS 5, 12

Mistral, Frederic 1830-1914 .... **TCLC 51**
See also CA 122; GFL 1789 to the Present

Mistral, Gabriela
See Godoy Alcayaga, Lucila
See also DNFS 1; LAW; RGWL 2, 3; WP

Mistry, Rohinton 1952- .... **CLC 71**
See also CA 141; CANR 86, 114; CCA 1; CN 7; DAC; SSFS 6

Mitchell, Clyde
See Ellison, Harlan (Jay)

Mitchell, Emerson Blackhorse Barney
1945- .... **NNAL**
See also CA 45-48

Mitchell, James Leslie 1901-1935
See Gibbon, Lewis Grassic
See also CA 188; 104; DLB 15

Mitchell, Joni 1943- .... **CLC 12**
See also CA 112; CCA 1

Mitchell, Joseph (Quincy)
1908-1996 .... **CLC 98**
See also CA 152; 77-80; CANR 69; CN 7; CSW; DLB 185; DLBY 1996

Mitchell, Margaret (Munnerlyn)
1900-1949 .... **TCLC 11**
See also AAYA 23; BPFB 2; BYA 1; CA 125; 109; CANR 55, 94; CDALBS; DA3; DAM NOV, POP; DLB 9; LAIT 2; MTCW 1, 2; NFS 9; RGAL 4; RHW; TUS; WYAS 1; YAW

Mitchell, Peggy
See Mitchell, Margaret (Munnerlyn)

Mitchell, S(ilas) Weir 1829-1914 .... **TCLC 36**
See also CA 165; DLB 202; RGAL 4

Mitchell, W(illiam) O(rmond)
1914-1998 .... **CLC 25**
See also CA 165; 77-80; CANR 15, 43; CN 7; DAC; DAM MST; DLB 88

Mitchell, William 1879-1936 .... **TCLC 81**

Mitford, Mary Russell 1787-1855 ... **NCLC 4**
See also DLB 110, 116; RGEL 2

Mitford, Nancy 1904-1973 .... **CLC 44**
See also CA 9-12R; DLB 191; RGEL 2

Miyamoto, (Chujo) Yuriko
1899-1951 .... **TCLC 37**
See Miyamoto Yuriko
See also CA 170, 174

Miyamoto Yuriko
See Miyamoto, (Chujo) Yuriko
See also DLB 180

Miyazawa, Kenji 1896-1933 .... **TCLC 76**
See also CA 157; RGWL 3

Mizoguchi, Kenji 1898-1956 .... **TCLC 72**
See also CA 167

Mo, Timothy (Peter) 1950(?)- ... **CLC 46, 134**
See also CA 117; CN 7; DLB 194; MTCW 1; WLIT 4

Modarressi, Taghi (M.) 1931-1997 ... **CLC 44**
See also CA 134; 121; INT 134

Modiano, Patrick (Jean) 1945- .... **CLC 18**
See also CA 85-88; CANR 17, 40, 115; CWW 2; DLB 83

Mofolo, Thomas (Mokopu)
1875(?)-1948 .... **BLC 3; TCLC 22**
See also AFW; CA 153; 121; CANR 83; DAM MULT; DLB 225; MTCW 2; WLIT 2

Mohr, Nicholasa 1938- .... **CLC 12; HLC 2**
See also AAYA 8, 46; CA 49-52; CANR 1, 32, 64; CLR 22; DAM MULT; DLB 145; HW 1, 2; JRDA; LAIT 5; MAICYA 2; MAICYAS 1; RGAL 4; SAAS 8; SATA 8, 97; SATA-Essay 113; WYA; YAW

Mojtabai, A(nn) G(race) 1938- ..... **CLC 5, 9, 15, 29**
See also CA 85-88; CANR 88

Moliere 1622-1673 ..... **DC 13; LC 10, 28, 64; WLC**
See also DA; DA3; DAB; DAC; DAM DRAM, MST; DFS 13; DLB 268; EW 3; GFL Beginnings to 1789; RGWL 2, 3; TWA

Molin, Charles
See Mayne, William (James Carter)

Molnar, Ferenc 1878-1952 .... **TCLC 20**
See also CA 153; 109; CANR 83; CDWLB 4; DAM DRAM; DLB 215; RGWL 2, 3

Momaday, N(avarre) Scott 1934- ...... **CLC 2, 19, 85, 95, 160; NNAL; PC 25; WLCS**
See also AAYA 11; AMWS 4; ANW; BPFB 2; CA 25-28R; CANR 14, 34, 68; CDALBS; CN 7; CPW; DA; DA3; DAB; DAC; DAM MST, MULT, NOV, POP; DLB 143, 175, 256; EXPP; INT CANR-14; LAIT 4; MTCW 1, 2; NFS 10; PFS 2, 11; RGAL 4; SATA 48; SATA-Brief 30; WP; YAW

Monette, Paul 1945-1995 .... **CLC 82**
See also AMWS 10; CA 147; 139; CN 7; GLL 1

Monroe, Harriet 1860-1936 .... **TCLC 12**
See also CA 204; 109; DLB 54, 91

Monroe, Lyle
See Heinlein, Robert A(nson)

Montagu, Elizabeth 1720-1800 .... **NCLC 7, 117**
See also FW

Montagu, Mary (Pierrepont) Wortley
1689-1762 .... **LC 9, 57; PC 16**
See also DLB 95, 101; RGEL 2

Montagu, W. H.
See Coleridge, Samuel Taylor

Montague, John (Patrick) 1929- ..... **CLC 13, 46**
See also CA 9-12R; CANR 9, 69; CP 7; DLB 40; MTCW 1; PFS 12; RGEL 2

Montaigne, Michel (Eyquem) de
1533-1592 .... **LC 8; WLC**
See also DA; DAB; DAC; DAM MST; EW 2; GFL Beginnings to 1789; RGWL 2, 3; TWA

Montale, Eugenio 1896-1981 ... **CLC 7, 9, 18; PC 13**
See also CA 104; 17-20R; CANR 30; DLB 114; EW 11; MTCW 1; RGWL 2, 3; TWA

Montesquieu, Charles-Louis de Secondat
1689-1755 .... **LC 7, 69**
See also EW 3; GFL Beginnings to 1789; TWA

Montessori, Maria 1870-1952 ...... **TCLC 103**
See also CA 147; 115

Montgomery, (Robert) Bruce 1921(?)-1978
See Crispin, Edmund
See also CA 104; 179; CMW 4

Montgomery, L(ucy) M(aud)
1874-1942 .... **TCLC 51**
See also AAYA 12; BYA 1; CA 137; 108; CLR 8; DA3; DAC; DAM MST; DLB 92; DLBD 14; JRDA; MAICYA 1, 2; MTCW 2; RGEL 2; SATA 100; TWA; WCH; WYA; YABC 1

Montgomery, Marion H., Jr. 1925- .... **CLC 7**
See also AITN 1; CA 1-4R; CANR 3, 48; CSW; DLB 6

Montgomery, Max
See Davenport, Guy (Mattison, Jr.)

Montherlant, Henry (Milon) de
1896-1972 .... **CLC 8, 19**
See also CA 37-40R; 85-88; DAM DRAM; DLB 72; EW 11; GFL 1789 to the Present; MTCW 1

Monty Python
See Chapman, Graham; Cleese, John (Marwood); Gilliam, Terry (Vance); Idle, Eric; Jones, Terence Graham Parry; Palin, Michael (Edward)
See also AAYA 7

Moodie, Susanna (Strickland)
1803-1885 .... **NCLC 14, 113**
See also DLB 99

Moody, Hiram (F. III) 1961-
See Moody, Rick
See also CA 138; CANR 64, 112

Moody, Minerva
See Alcott, Louisa May

Naylor, Gloria 1950- ..... **BLC 3; CLC 28, 52, 156; WLCS**
See also AAYA 6, 39; AFAW 1, 2; AMWS 8; BW 2, 3; CA 107; CANR 27, 51, 74; CN 7; CPW; DA; DA3; DAC; DAM MST, MULT, NOV, POP; DLB 173; FW; MTCW 1, 2; NFS 4, 7; RGAL 4; TUS

Neff, Debra .... **CLC 59**

Neihardt, John Gneisenau 1881-1973 .... **CLC 32**
See also CA 13-14; CANR 65; CAP 1; DLB 9, 54, 256; LAIT 2

Nekrasov, Nikolai Alekseevich 1821-1878 .... **NCLC 11**
See also DLB 277

Nelligan, Emile 1879-1941 .... **TCLC 14**
See also CA 204; 114; DLB 92

Nelson, Willie 1933- .... **CLC 17**
See also CA 107; CANR 114

Nemerov, Howard (Stanley) 1920-1991 .... **CLC 2, 6, 9, 36; PC 24; TCLC 124**
See also AMW; CA 134; 1-4R; CABS 2; CANR 1, 27, 53; DAM POET; DLB 5, 6; DLBY 1983; INT CANR-27; MTCW 1, 2; PFS 10, 14; RGAL 4

Neruda, Pablo 1904-1973 .. **CLC 1, 2, 5, 7, 9, 28, 62; HLC 2; PC 4; WLC**
See also CA 45-48; 19-20; CAP 2; DA; DA3; DAB; DAC; DAM MST, MULT, POET; DNFS 2; HW 1; LAW; MTCW 1, 2; PFS 11; RGWL 2, 3; TWA; WLIT 1; WP

Nerval, Gerard de 1808-1855 ... **NCLC 1, 67; PC 13; SSC 18**
See also DLB 217; EW 6; GFL 1789 to the Present; RGSF 2; RGWL 2, 3

Nervo, (Jose) Amado (Ruiz de) 1870-1919 .... **HLCS 2; TCLC 11**
See also CA 131; 109; HW 1; LAW

Nesbit, Malcolm
See Chester, Alfred

Nessi, Pio Baroja y
See Baroja (y Nessi), Pio

Nestroy, Johann 1801-1862 .... **NCLC 42**
See also DLB 133; RGWL 2, 3

Netterville, Luke
See O'Grady, Standish (James)

Neufeld, John (Arthur) 1938- .... **CLC 17**
See also AAYA 11; CA 25-28R; CANR 11, 37, 56; CLR 52; MAICYA 1, 2; SAAS 3; SATA 6, 81; SATA-Essay 131; YAW

Neumann, Alfred 1895-1952 .... **TCLC 100**
See also CA 183; DLB 56

Neumann, Ferenc
See Molnar, Ferenc

Neville, Emily Cheney 1919- .... **CLC 12**
See also BYA 2; CA 5-8R; CANR 3, 37, 85; JRDA; MAICYA 1, 2; SAAS 2; SATA 1; YAW

Newbound, Bernard Slade 1930-
See Slade, Bernard
See also CA 81-84; CANR 49; CD 5; DAM DRAM

Newby, P(ercy) H(oward) 1918-1997 .... **CLC 2, 13**
See also CA 161; 5-8R; CANR 32, 67; CN 7; DAM NOV; DLB 15; MTCW 1; RGEL 2

Newcastle
See Cavendish, Margaret Lucas

Newlove, Donald 1928- .... **CLC 6**
See also CA 29-32R; CANR 25

Newlove, John (Herbert) 1938- .... **CLC 14**
See also CA 21-24R; CANR 9, 25; CP 7

Newman, Charles 1938- .... **CLC 2, 8**
See also CA 21-24R; CANR 84; CN 7

Newman, Edwin (Harold) 1919- ...... **CLC 14**
See also AITN 1; CA 69-72; CANR 5

Newman, John Henry 1801-1890 . **NCLC 38, 99**
See also BRWS 7; DLB 18, 32, 55; RGEL 2

Newton, (Sir) Isaac 1642-1727 ...... **LC 35, 53**
See also DLB 252

Newton, Suzanne 1936- .... **CLC 35**
See also BYA 7; CA 41-44R; CANR 14; JRDA; SATA 5, 77

New York Dept. of Ed. .... **CLC 70**

Nexo, Martin Andersen 1869-1954 .... **TCLC 43**
See also CA 202; DLB 214

Nezval, Vitezslav 1900-1958 .... **TCLC 44**
See also CA 123; CDWLB 4; DLB 215

Ng, Fae Myenne 1957(?)- .... **CLC 81**
See also CA 146

Ngema, Mbongeni 1955- .... **CLC 57**
See also BW 2; CA 143; CANR 84; CD 5

Ngugi, James T(hiong'o) .... **CLC 3, 7, 13**
See Ngugi wa Thiong'o

Ngugi wa Thiong'o
See Ngugi wa Thiong'o
See also DLB 125

Ngugi wa Thiong'o 1938- .... **BLC 3; CLC 36**
See Ngugi, James T(hiong'o); Ngugi wa Thiong'o
See also AFW; BRWS 8; BW 2; CA 81-84; CANR 27, 58; CDWLB 3; DAM MULT, NOV; DNFS 2; MTCW 1, 2; RGEL 2

Niatum, Duane 1938- .... **NNAL**
See also CA 41-44R; CANR 21, 45, 83; DLB 175

Nichol, B(arrie) P(hillip) 1944-1988 . **CLC 18**
See also CA 53-56; DLB 53; SATA 66

Nicholas of Cusa 1401-1464 .... **LC 80**
See also DLB 115

Nichols, John (Treadwell) 1940- .... **CLC 38**
See also CA 9-12R; CAAE 190; CAAS 2; CANR 6, 70; DLBY 1982; TCWW 2

Nichols, Leigh
See Koontz, Dean R(ay)

Nichols, Peter (Richard) 1927- .... **CLC 5, 36, 65**
See also CA 104; CANR 33, 86; CBD; CD 5; DLB 13, 245; MTCW 1

Nicholson, Linda ed. .... **CLC 65**

Ni Chuilleanain, Eilean 1942- .... **PC 34**
See also CA 126; CANR 53, 83; CP 7; CWP; DLB 40

Nicolas, F. R. E.
See Freeling, Nicolas

Niedecker, Lorine 1903-1970 ..... **CLC 10, 42; PC 42**
See also CA 25-28; CAP 2; DAM POET; DLB 48

Nietzsche, Friedrich (Wilhelm) 1844-1900 .... **TCLC 10, 18, 55**
See also CA 121; 107; CDWLB 2; DLB 129; EW 7; RGWL 2, 3; TWA

Nievo, Ippolito 1831-1861 .... **NCLC 22**

Nightingale, Anne Redmon 1943-
See Redmon, Anne
See also CA 103

Nightingale, Florence 1820-1910 ... **TCLC 85**
See also CA 188; DLB 166

Nijo Yoshimoto 1320-1388 .... **CMLC 49**
See also DLB 203

Nik. T. O.
See Annensky, Innokenty (Fyodorovich)

Nin, Anais 1903-1977 ..... **CLC 1, 4, 8, 11, 14, 60, 127; SSC 10**
See also AITN 2; AMWS 10; BPFB 2; CA 69-72; 13-16R; CANR 22, 53; DAM NOV, POP; DLB 2, 4, 152; GLL 2; MAWW; MTCW 1, 2; RGAL 4; RGSF 2

Nisbet, Robert A(lexander) 1913-1996 .... **TCLC 117**
See also CA 153; 25-28R; CANR 17; INT CANR-17

Nishida, Kitaro 1870-1945 .... **TCLC 83**

Nishiwaki, Junzaburo
See Nishiwaki, Junzaburo
See also CA 194

Nishiwaki, Junzaburo 1894-1982 .... **PC 15**
See Nishiwaki, Junzaburo
See also CA 107; 194; MJW; RGWL 3

Nissenson, Hugh 1933- .... **CLC 4, 9**
See also CA 17-20R; CANR 27, 108; CN 7; DLB 28

Niven, Larry .... **CLC 8**
See Niven, Laurence Van Cott
See also AAYA 27; BPFB 2; BYA 10; DLB 8; SCFW 2

Niven, Laurence Van Cott 1938-
See Niven, Larry
See also CA 21-24R; CAAS 12; CANR 14, 44, 66, 113; CPW; DAM POP; MTCW 1, 2; SATA 95; SFW 4

Nixon, Agnes Eckhardt 1927- .... **CLC 21**
See also CA 110

Nizan, Paul 1905-1940 .... **TCLC 40**
See also CA 161; DLB 72; GFL 1789 to the Present

Nkosi, Lewis 1936- .... **BLC 3; CLC 45**
See also BW 1, 3; CA 65-68; CANR 27, 81; CBD; CD 5; DAM MULT; DLB 157, 225

Nodier, (Jean) Charles (Emmanuel) 1780-1844 .... **NCLC 19**
See also DLB 119; GFL 1789 to the Present

Noguchi, Yone 1875-1947 .... **TCLC 80**

Nolan, Christopher 1965- .... **CLC 58**
See also CA 111; CANR 88

Noon, Jeff 1957- .... **CLC 91**
See also CA 148; CANR 83; DLB 267; SFW 4

Norden, Charles
See Durrell, Lawrence (George)

Nordhoff, Charles (Bernard) 1887-1947 .... **TCLC 23**
See also CA 108; DLB 9; LAIT 1; RHW 1; SATA 23

Norfolk, Lawrence 1963- .... **CLC 76**
See also CA 144; CANR 85; CN 7; DLB 267

Norman, Marsha 1947- .... **CLC 28; DC 8**
See also CA 105; CABS 3; CAD; CANR 41; CD 5; CSW; CWD; DAM DRAM; DFS 2; DLB 266; DLBY 1984; FW

Normyx
See Douglas, (George) Norman

Norris, (Benjamin) Frank(lin, Jr.) 1870-1902 .... **SSC 28; TCLC 24**
See also AMW; BPFB 2; CA 160; 110; CDALB 1865-1917; DLB 12, 71, 186; NFS 12; RGAL 4; TCWW 2; TUS

Norris, Leslie 1921- .... **CLC 14**
See also CA 11-12; CANR 14; CAP 1; CP 7; DLB 27, 256

North, Andrew
See Norton, Andre

North, Anthony
See Koontz, Dean R(ay)

North, Captain George
See Stevenson, Robert Louis (Balfour)

North, Captain George
See Stevenson, Robert Louis (Balfour)

North, Milou
See Erdrich, Louise

Northrup, B. A.
See Hubbard, L(afayette) Ron(ald)

North Staffs
See Hulme, T(homas) E(rnest)

Oliver, Mary 1935- .... **CLC 19, 34, 98**
    See also AMWS 7; CA 21-24R; CANR 9, 43, 84, 92; CP 7; CWP; DLB 5, 193; PFS 15

Olivier, Laurence (Kerr) 1907-1989 . **CLC 20**
    See also CA 129; 150; 111

Olsen, Tillie 1912- ... **CLC 4, 13, 114; SSC 11**
    See also BYA 11; CA 1-4R; CANR 1, 43, 74; CDALBS; CN 7; DA; DA3; DAB; DAC; DAM MST; DLB 28, 206; DLBY 1980; EXPS; FW; MTCW 1, 2; RGAL 4; RGSF 2; SSFS 1; TUS

Olson, Charles (John) 1910-1970 .. **CLC 1, 2, 5, 6, 9, 11, 29; PC 19**
    See also AMWS 2; CA 25-28R; 13-16; CABS 2; CANR 35, 61; CAP 1; DAM POET; DLB 5, 16, 193; MTCW 1, 2; RGAL 4; WP

Olson, Toby 1937- .... **CLC 28**
    See also CA 65-68; CANR 9, 31, 84; CP 7

Olyesha, Yuri
    See Olesha, Yuri (Karlovich)

Omar Khayyam
    See Khayyam, Omar
    See also RGWL 2, 3

Ondaatje, (Philip) Michael 1943- .... **CLC 14, 29, 51, 76; PC 28**
    See also CA 77-80; CANR 42, 74, 109; CN 7; CP 7; DA3; DAB; DAC; DAM MST; DLB 60; MTCW 2; PFS 8; TWA

Oneal, Elizabeth 1934-
    See Oneal, Zibby
    See also CA 106; CANR 28, 84; MAICYA 1, 2; SATA 30, 82; YAW

Oneal, Zibby .... **CLC 30**
    See Oneal, Elizabeth
    See also AAYA 5, 41; BYA 13; CLR 13; JRDA; WYA

O'Neill, Eugene (Gladstone) 1888-1953 ...... **TCLC 1, 6, 27, 49; WLC**
    See also AITN 1; AMW; AMWC 1; CA 132; 110; CAD; CDALB 1929-1941; DA; DA3; DAB; DAC; DAM DRAM, MST; DFS 9, 11, 12, 16; DLB 7; LAIT 3; MTCW 1, 2; RGAL 4; TUS

Onetti, Juan Carlos 1909-1994 ... **CLC 7, 10; HLCS 2; SSC 23; TCLC 131**
    See also CA 145; 85-88; CANR 32, 63; CD-WLB 3; DAM MULT, NOV; DLB 113; HW 1, 2; LAW; MTCW 1, 2; RGSF 2

O Nuallain, Brian 1911-1966
    See O'Brien, Flann
    See also CA 25-28R; 21-22; CAP 2; DLB 231; FANT; TEA

Ophuls, Max 1902-1957 .... **TCLC 79**
    See also CA 113

Opie, Amelia 1769-1853 .... **NCLC 65**
    See also DLB 116, 159; RGEL 2

Oppen, George 1908-1984 ..... **CLC 7, 13, 34; PC 35; TCLC 107**
    See also CA 113; 13-16R; CANR 8, 82; DLB 5, 165

Oppenheim, E(dward) Phillips 1866-1946 .... **TCLC 45**
    See also CA 202; 111; CMW 4; DLB 70

Opuls, Max
    See Ophuls, Max

Origen c. 185-c. 254 .... **CMLC 19**

Orlovitz, Gil 1918-1973 .... **CLC 22**
    See also CA 45-48; 77-80; DLB 2, 5

Orris
    See Ingelow, Jean

Ortega y Gasset, Jose 1883-1955 ...... **HLC 2; TCLC 9**
    See also CA 130; 106; DAM MULT; EW 9; HW 1, 2; MTCW 1, 2

Ortese, Anna Maria 1914-1998 .... **CLC 89**
    See also DLB 177

Ortiz, Simon J(oseph) 1941- .... **CLC 45; NNAL; PC 17**
    See also AMWS 4; CA 134; CANR 69; CP 7; DAM MULT, POET; DLB 120, 175, 256; EXPP; PFS 4, 16; RGAL 4

Orton, Joe .... **CLC 4, 13, 43; DC 3**
    See Orton, John Kingsley
    See also BRWS 5; CBD; CDBLB 1960 to Present; DFS 3, 6; DLB 13; GLL 1; MTCW 2; RGEL 2; TEA; WLIT 4

Orton, John Kingsley 1933-1967
    See Orton, Joe
    See also CA 85-88; CANR 35, 66; DAM DRAM; MTCW 1, 2

Orwell, George . **TCLC 2, 6, 15, 31, 51, 128, 129; WLC**
    See Blair, Eric (Arthur)
    See also BPFB 3; BRW 7; BYA 5; CDBLB 1945-1960; CLR 68; DAB; DLB 15, 98, 195, 255; EXPN; LAIT 4, 5; NFS 3, 7; RGEL 2; SCFW 2; SFW 4; SSFS 4; TEA; WLIT 4; YAW

Osborne, David
    See Silverberg, Robert

Osborne, George
    See Silverberg, Robert

Osborne, John (James) 1929-1994 .... **CLC 1, 2, 5, 11, 45; WLC**
    See also BRWS 1; CA 147; 13-16R; CANR 21, 56; CDBLB 1945-1960; DA; DAB; DAC; DAM DRAM, MST; DFS 4; DLB 13; MTCW 1, 2; RGEL 2

Osborne, Lawrence 1958- .... **CLC 50**
    See also CA 189

Osbourne, Lloyd 1868-1947 .... **TCLC 93**

Oshima, Nagisa 1932- .... **CLC 20**
    See also CA 121; 116; CANR 78

Oskison, John Milton 1874-1947 .... **NNAL; TCLC 35**
    See also CA 144; CANR 84; DAM MULT; DLB 175

Ossian c. 3rd cent. - .... **CMLC 28**
    See Macpherson, James

Ossoli, Sarah Margaret (Fuller) 1810-1850 .... **NCLC 5, 50**
    See Fuller, Margaret; Fuller, Sarah Margaret
    See also CDALB 1640-1865; FW; SATA 25

Ostriker, Alicia (Suskin) 1937- .... **CLC 132**
    See also CA 25-28R; CAAS 24; CANR 10, 30, 62, 99; CWP; DLB 120; EXPP

Ostrovsky, Aleksandr Nikolaevich
    See Ostrovsky, Alexander
    See also DLB 277

Ostrovsky, Alexander 1823-1886 .. **NCLC 30, 57**
    See Ostrovsky, Aleksandr Nikolaevich

Otero, Blas de 1916-1979 .... **CLC 11**
    See also CA 89-92; DLB 134

Otto, Rudolf 1869-1937 .... **TCLC 85**

Otto, Whitney 1955- .... **CLC 70**
    See also CA 140

Ouida .... **TCLC 43**
    See De la Ramee, Marie Louise (Ouida)
    See also DLB 18, 156; RGEL 2

Ouologuem, Yambo 1940- .... **CLC 146**
    See also CA 176; 111

Ousmane, Sembene 1923- .. **BLC 3; CLC 66**
    See Sembene, Ousmane
    See also BW 1, 3; CA 125; 117; CANR 81; CWW 2; MTCW 1

Ovid 43B.C.-17 .... **CMLC 7; PC 2**
    See also AW 2; CDWLB 1; DA3; DAM POET; DLB 211; RGWL 2, 3; WP

Owen, Hugh
    See Faust, Frederick (Schiller)

Owen, Wilfred (Edward Salter) 1893-1918 ... **PC 19; TCLC 5, 27; WLC**
    See also BRW 6; CA 141; 104; CDBLB 1914-1945; DA; DAB; DAC; DAM MST, POET; DLB 20; EXPP; MTCW 2; PFS 10; RGEL 2; WLIT 4

Owens, Louis (Dean) 1948-2002 .... **NNAL**
    See also CA 137, 179; CAAE 179; CAAS 24; CANR 71

Owens, Rochelle 1936- .... **CLC 8**
    See also CA 17-20R; CAAS 2; CAD; CANR 39; CD 5; CP 7; CWD; CWP

Oz, Amos 1939- .... **CLC 5, 8, 11, 27, 33, 54**
    See also CA 53-56; CANR 27, 47, 65, 113; CWW 2; DAM NOV; MTCW 1, 2; RGSF 2; RGWL 3

Ozick, Cynthia 1928- .... **CLC 3, 7, 28, 62, 155; SSC 15**
    See also AMWS 5; BEST 90:1; CA 17-20R; CANR 23, 58; CN 7; CPW; DA3; DAM NOV, POP; DLB 28, 152; DLBY 1982; EXPS; INT CANR-23; MTCW 1, 2; RGAL 4; RGSF 2; SSFS 3, 12

Ozu, Yasujiro 1903-1963 .... **CLC 16**
    See also CA 112

Pabst, G. W. 1885-1967 .... **TCLC 127**

Pacheco, C.
    See Pessoa, Fernando (Antonio Nogueira)

Pacheco, Jose Emilio 1939- .... **HLC 2**
    See also CA 131; 111; CANR 65; DAM MULT; HW 1, 2; RGSF 2

Pa Chin .... **CLC 18**
    See Li Fei-kan

Pack, Robert 1929- .... **CLC 13**
    See also CA 1-4R; CANR 3, 44, 82; CP 7; DLB 5; SATA 118

Padgett, Lewis
    See Kuttner, Henry

Padilla (Lorenzo), Heberto 1932-2000 .... **CLC 38**
    See also AITN 1; CA 189; 131; 123; HW 1

Page, James Patrick 1944-
    See Page, Jimmy
    See also CA 204

Page, Jimmy 1944- .... **CLC 12**
    See Page, James Patrick

Page, Louise 1955- .... **CLC 40**
    See also CA 140; CANR 76; CBD; CD 5; CWD; DLB 233

Page, P(atricia) K(athleen) 1916- ...... **CLC 7, 18; PC 12**
    See Cape, Judith
    See also CA 53-56; CANR 4, 22, 65; CP 7; DAC; DAM MST; DLB 68; MTCW 1; RGEL 2

Page, Stanton
    See Fuller, Henry Blake

Page, Stanton
    See Fuller, Henry Blake

Page, Thomas Nelson 1853-1922 .... **SSC 23**
    See also CA 177; 118; DLB 12, 78; DLBD 13; RGAL 4

Pagels, Elaine Hiesey 1943- .... **CLC 104**
    See also CA 45-48; CANR 2, 24, 51; FW; NCFS 4

Paget, Violet 1856-1935
    See Lee, Vernon
    See also CA 166; 104; GLL 1; HGG

Paget-Lowe, Henry
    See Lovecraft, H(oward) P(hillips)

Paglia, Camille (Anna) 1947- .... **CLC 68**
    See also CA 140; CANR 72; CPW; FW; GLL 2; MTCW 2

Paige, Richard
    See Koontz, Dean R(ay)

Paine, Thomas 1737-1809 .... **NCLC 62**
    See also AMWS 1; CDALB 1640-1865; DLB 31, 43, 73, 158; LAIT 1; RGAL 4; RGEL 2; TUS

Peake, Mervyn 1911-1968 .... **CLC 7, 54**
　　See also CA 25-28R; 5-8R; CANR 3; DLB
　　15, 160, 255; FANT; MTCW 1; RGEL 2;
　　SATA 23; SFW 4
Pearce, Philippa
　　See Christie, Philippa
　　See also CA 5-8R; CANR 4, 109; CWRI 5;
　　FANT; MAICYA 2
Pearl, Eric
　　See Elman, Richard (Martin)
Pearson, T(homas) R(eid) 1956- .... **CLC 39**
　　See also CA 130; 120; CANR 97; CSW;
　　INT 130
Peck, Dale 1967- .... **CLC 81**
　　See also CA 146; CANR 72; GLL 2
Peck, John (Frederick) 1941- .... **CLC 3**
　　See also CA 49-52; CANR 3, 100; CP 7
Peck, Richard (Wayne) 1934- .... **CLC 21**
　　See also AAYA 1, 24; BYA 1, 6, 8, 11; CA
　　85-88; CANR 19, 38; CLR 15; INT
　　CANR-19; JRDA; MAICYA 1, 2; SAAS
　　2; SATA 18, 55, 97; SATA-Essay 110;
　　WYA; YAW
Peck, Robert Newton 1928- .... **CLC 17**
　　See also AAYA 3, 43; BYA 1, 6; CA 81-84,
　　182; CAAE 182; CANR 31, 63; CLR 45;
　　DA; DAC; DAM MST; JRDA; LAIT 3;
　　MAICYA 1, 2; SAAS 1; SATA 21, 62,
　　111; SATA-Essay 108; WYA; YAW
Peckinpah, (David) Sam(uel)
　　1925-1984 .... **CLC 20**
　　See also CA 114; 109; CANR 82
Pedersen, Knut 1859-1952
　　See Hamsun, Knut
　　See also CA 119; 104; CANR 63; MTCW
　　1, 2
Peeslake, Gaffer
　　See Durrell, Lawrence (George)
Peguy, Charles (Pierre)
　　1873-1914 .... **TCLC 10**
　　See also CA 193; 107; DLB 258; GFL 1789
　　to the Present
Peirce, Charles Sanders
　　1839-1914 .... **TCLC 81**
　　See also CA 194; DLB 270
Pellicer, Carlos 1900(?)-1977 .... **HLCS 2**
　　See also CA 69-72; 153; HW 1
Pena, Ramon del Valle y
　　See Valle-Inclan, Ramon (Maria) del
Pendennis, Arthur Esquir
　　See Thackeray, William Makepeace
Penn, William 1644-1718 .... **LC 25**
　　See also DLB 24
PEPECE
　　See Prado (Calvo), Pedro
Pepys, Samuel 1633-1703 ... **LC 11, 58; WLC**
　　See also BRW 2; CDBLB 1660-1789; DA;
　　DA3; DAB; DAC; DAM MST; DLB 101,
　　213; NCFS 4; RGEL 2; TEA; WLIT 3
Percy, Thomas 1729-1811 .... **NCLC 95**
　　See also DLB 104
Percy, Walker 1916-1990 .... **CLC 2, 3, 6, 8,**
　　14, 18, 47, 65
　　See also AMWS 3; BPFB 3; CA 131; 1-4R;
　　CANR 1, 23, 64; CPW; CSW; DA3;
　　DAM NOV, POP; DLB 2; DLBY 1980;
　　1990; MTCW 1, 2; RGAL 4; TUS
Percy, William Alexander
　　1885-1942 .... **TCLC 84**
　　See also CA 163; MTCW 2
Perec, Georges 1936-1982 .... **CLC 56, 116**
　　See also CA 141; DLB 83; GFL 1789 to the
　　Present; RGWL 3
**Pereda (y Sanchez de Porrua), Jose Maria
　　de** 1833-1906 .... **TCLC 16**
　　See also CA 117
Pereda y Porrua, Jose Maria de
　　See Pereda (y Sanchez de Porrua), Jose
　　Maria de

Peregoy, George Weems
　　See Mencken, H(enry) L(ouis)
Perelman, S(idney) J(oseph)
　　1904-1979 .. **CLC 3, 5, 9, 15, 23, 44, 49;**
　　SSC 32
　　See also AITN 1, 2; BPFB 3; CA 89-92;
　　73-76; CANR 18; DAM DRAM; DLB 11,
　　44; MTCW 1, 2; RGAL 4
Peret, Benjamin 1899-1959 .... **PC 33; TCLC
　　20**
　　See also CA 186; 117; GFL 1789 to the
　　Present
Peretz, Isaac Leib 1851(?)-1915
　　See Peretz, Isaac Loeb
　　See also CA 201
Peretz, Isaac Loeb 1851(?)-1915 ...... **SSC 26;
　　TCLC 16**
　　See Peretz, Isaac Leib
　　See also CA 109
Peretz, Yitzhkok Leibush
　　See Peretz, Isaac Loeb
Perez Galdos, Benito 1843-1920 ..... **HLCS 2;
　　TCLC 27**
　　See Galdos, Benito Perez
　　See also CA 153; 125; HW 1; RGWL 2, 3
Peri Rossi, Cristina 1941- .. **CLC 156; HLCS
　　2**
　　See also CA 131; CANR 59, 81; DLB 145;
　　HW 1, 2
Perlata
　　See Peret, Benjamin
Perloff, Marjorie G(abrielle)
　　1931- .... **CLC 137**
　　See also CA 57-60; CANR 7, 22, 49, 104
Perrault, Charles 1628-1703 ... **DC 12; LC 2,
　　56**
　　See also BYA 4; CLR 79; DLB 268; GFL
　　Beginnings to 1789; MAICYA 1, 2;
　　RGWL 2, 3; SATA 25; WCH
Perry, Anne 1938- .... **CLC 126**
　　See also CA 101; CANR 22, 50, 84; CMW
　　4; CN 7; CPW; DLB 276
Perry, Brighton
　　See Sherwood, Robert E(mmet)
Perse, St.-John
　　See Leger, (Marie-Rene Auguste) Alexis
　　Saint-Leger
Perse, Saint-John
　　See Leger, (Marie-Rene Auguste) Alexis
　　Saint-Leger
　　See also DLB 258; RGWL 3
Perutz, Leo(pold) 1882-1957 .... **TCLC 60**
　　See also CA 147; DLB 81
Peseenz, Tulio F.
　　See Lopez y Fuentes, Gregorio
Pesetsky, Bette 1932- .... **CLC 28**
　　See also CA 133; DLB 130
Peshkov, Alexei Maximovich 1868-1936
　　See Gorky, Maxim
　　See also CA 141; 105; CANR 83; DA;
　　DAC; DAM DRAM, MST, NOV; MTCW
　　2
Pessoa, Fernando (Antonio Nogueira)
　　1898-1935 ..... **HLC 2; PC 20; TCLC 27**
　　See also CA 183; 125; DAM MULT; EW
　　10; RGWL 2, 3; WP
Peterkin, Julia Mood 1880-1961 ...... **CLC 31**
　　See also CA 102; DLB 9
Peters, Joan K(aren) 1945- .... **CLC 39**
　　See also CA 158; CANR 109
Peters, Robert L(ouis) 1924- .... **CLC 7**
　　See also CA 13-16R; CAAS 8; CP 7; DLB
　　105
Petofi, Sandor 1823-1849 .... **NCLC 21**
　　See also RGWL 2, 3
Petrakis, Harry Mark 1923- .... **CLC 3**
　　See also CA 9-12R; CANR 4, 30, 85; CN 7

Petrarch 1304-1374 .... **CMLC 20; PC 8**
　　See also DA3; DAM POET; EW 2; RGWL
　　2. 3
Petronius c. 20-66 .... **CMLC 34**
　　See also AW 2; CDWLB 1; DLB 211;
　　RGWL 2, 3
Petrov, Evgeny .... **TCLC 21**
　　See Kataev, Evgeny Petrovich
Petry, Ann (Lane) 1908-1997 .. **CLC 1, 7, 18;
　　TCLC 112**
　　See also AFAW 1, 2; BPFB 3; BW 1, 3;
　　BYA 2; CA 157; 5-8R; CAAS 6; CANR
　　4, 46; CLR 12; CN 7; DLB 76; JRDA;
　　LAIT 1; MAICYA 1, 2; MAICYAS 1;
　　MTCW 1; RGAL 4; SATA 5; SATA-Obit
　　94; TUS
Petursson, Halligrimur 1614-1674 .... **LC 8**
Peychinovich
　　See Vazov, Ivan (Minchov)
Phaedrus c. 15B.C.-c. 50 .... **CMLC 25**
　　See also DLB 211
Phelps (Ward), Elizabeth Stuart
　　See Phelps, Elizabeth Stuart
　　See also FW
Phelps, Elizabeth Stuart
　　1844-1911 .... **TCLC 113**
　　See Phelps (Ward), Elizabeth Stuart
　　See also DLB 74
Philips, Katherine 1632-1664 . **LC 30; PC 40**
　　See also DLB 131; RGEL 2
Philipson, Morris H. 1926- .... **CLC 53**
　　See also CA 1-4R; CANR 4
Phillips, Caryl 1958- .... **BLCS; CLC 96**
　　See also BRWS 5; BW 2; CA 141; CANR
　　63, 104; CBD; CD 5; CN 7; DA3; DAM
　　MULT; DLB 157; MTCW 2; WLIT 4
Phillips, David Graham
　　1867-1911 .... **TCLC 44**
　　See also CA 176; 108; DLB 9, 12; RGAL 4
Phillips, Jack
　　See Sandburg, Carl (August)
Phillips, Jayne Anne 1952- .... **CLC 15, 33,
　　139; SSC 16**
　　See also BPFB 3; CA 101; CANR 24, 50,
　　96; CN 7; CSW; DLBY 1980; INT
　　CANR-24; MTCW 1, 2; RGAL 4; RGSF
　　2; SSFS 4
Phillips, Richard
　　See Dick, Philip K(indred)
Phillips, Robert (Schaeffer) 1938- .... **CLC 28**
　　See also CA 17-20R; CAAS 13; CANR 8;
　　DLB 105
Phillips, Ward
　　See Lovecraft, H(oward) P(hillips)
Piccolo, Lucio 1901-1969 .... **CLC 13**
　　See also CA 97-100; DLB 114
Pickthall, Marjorie L(owry) C(hristie)
　　1883-1922 .... **TCLC 21**
　　See also CA 107; DLB 92
Pico della Mirandola, Giovanni
　　1463-1494 .... **LC 15**
Piercy, Marge 1936- .... **CLC 3, 6, 14, 18, 27,
　　62, 128; PC 29**
　　See also BPFB 3; CA 21-24R; CAAE 187;
　　CAAS 1; CANR 13, 43, 66, 111; CN 7;
　　CP 7; CWP; DLB 120, 227; EXPP; FW;
　　MTCW 1, 2; PFS 9; SFW 4
Piers, Robert
　　See Anthony, Piers
Pieyre de Mandiargues, Andre 1909-1991
　　See Mandiargues, Andre Pieyre de
　　See also CA 136; 103; CANR 22, 82; GFL
　　1789 to the Present
Pilnyak, Boris 1894-1938 . **SSC 48; TCLC 23**
　　See Vogau, Boris Andreyevich
Pinchback, Eugene
　　See Toomer, Jean

Sandburg, Carl (August) 1878-1967 . **CLC 1, 4, 10, 15, 35; PC 2, 41; WLC**
See also AAYA 24; AMW; BYA 1, 3; CA 25-28R; 5-8R; CANR 35; CDALB 1865-1917; CLR 67; DA; DA3; DAB; DAC; DAM MST, POET; DLB 17, 54; EXPP; LAIT 2; MAICYA 1, 2; MTCW 1, 2; PAB; PFS 3, 6, 12; RGAL 4; SATA 8; TUS; WCH; WP; WYA

Sandburg, Charles
See Sandburg, Carl (August)

Sandburg, Charles A.
See Sandburg, Carl (August)

Sanders, (James) Ed(ward) 1939- .... **CLC 53**
See Sanders, Edward
See also BG 3; CA 13-16R; CAAS 21; CANR 13, 44, 78; CP 7; DAM POET; DLB 16, 244

Sanders, Edward
See Sanders, (James) Ed(ward)
See also DLB 244

Sanders, Lawrence 1920-1998 .... **CLC 41**
See also BEST 89:4; BPFB 3; CA 165; 81-84; CANR 33, 62; CMW 4; CPW; DA3; DAM POP; MTCW 1

Sanders, Noah
See Blount, Roy (Alton), Jr.

Sanders, Winston P.
See Anderson, Poul (William)

Sandoz, Mari(e Susette) 1900-1966 .. **CLC 28**
See also CA 25-28R; 1-4R; CANR 17, 64; DLB 9, 212; LAIT 2; MTCW 1, 2; SATA 5; TCWW 2

Sandys, George 1578-1644 .... **LC 80**
See also DLB 24, 121

Saner, Reg(inald Anthony) 1931- .... **CLC 9**
See also CA 65-68; CP 7

Sankara 788-820 .... **CMLC 32**

Sannazaro, Jacopo 1456(?)-1530 .... **LC 8**
See also RGWL 2, 3

Sansom, William 1912-1976 . **CLC 2, 6; SSC 21**
See also CA 65-68; 5-8R; CANR 42; DAM NOV; DLB 139; MTCW 1; RGEL 2; RGSF 2

Santayana, George 1863-1952 .... **TCLC 40**
See also AMW; CA 194; 115; DLB 54, 71, 246, 270; DLBD 13; RGAL 4; TUS

Santiago, Danny .... **CLC 33**
See James, Daniel (Lewis)
See also DLB 122

Santmyer, Helen Hooven
1895-1986 .... **CLC 33; TCLC 133**
See also CA 118; 1-4R; CANR 15, 33; DLBY 1984; MTCW 1; RHW

Santoka, Taneda 1882-1940 .... **TCLC 72**

Santos, Bienvenido N(uqui)
1911-1996 .... **CLC 22**
See also CA 151; 101; CANR 19, 46; DAM MULT; RGAL 4

Sapir, Edward 1884-1939 .... **TCLC 108**
See also DLB 92

Sapper .... **TCLC 44**
See McNeile, Herman Cyril

Sapphire
See Sapphire, Brenda

Sapphire, Brenda 1950- .... **CLC 99**

Sappho fl. 6th cent. B.C.- ...... **CMLC 3; PC 5**
See also CDWLB 1; DA3; DAM POET; DLB 176; RGWL 2, 3; WP

Saramago, Jose 1922- ..... **CLC 119; HLCS 1**
See also CA 153; CANR 96

Sarduy, Severo 1937-1993 .... **CLC 6, 97; HLCS 2**
See also CA 142; 89-92; CANR 58, 81; CWW 2; DLB 113; HW 1, 2; LAW

Sargeson, Frank 1903-1982 .... **CLC 31**
See also CA 106; 25-28R; CANR 38, 79; GLL 2; RGEL 2; RGSF 2

Sarmiento, Domingo Faustino
1811-1888 .... **HLCS 2**
See also LAW; WLIT 1

Sarmiento, Felix Ruben Garcia
See Dario, Ruben

Saro-Wiwa, Ken(ule Beeson)
1941-1995 .... **CLC 114**
See also BW 2; CA 150; 142; CANR 60; DLB 157

Saroyan, William 1908-1981 ... **CLC 1, 8, 10, 29, 34, 56; SSC 21; WLC**
See also CA 103; 5-8R; CAD; CANR 30; CDALBS; DA; DA3; DAB; DAC; DAM DRAM, MST, NOV; DLB 7, 9, 86; DLBY 1981; LAIT 4; MTCW 1, 2; RGAL 4; RGSF 2; SATA 23; SATA-Obit 24; SSFS 14; TUS

Sarraute, Nathalie 1900-1999 .... **CLC 1, 2, 4, 8, 10, 31, 80**
See also BPFB 3; CA 187; 9-12R; CANR 23, 66; CWW 2; DLB 83; EW 12; GFL 1789 to the Present; MTCW 1, 2; RGWL 2, 3

Sarton, (Eleanor) May 1912-1995 ..... **CLC 4, 14, 49, 91; PC 39; TCLC 120**
See also AMWS 8; CA 149; 1-4R; CANR 1, 34, 55; CN 7; CP 7; DAM POET; DLB 48; DLBY 1981; FW; INT CANR-34; MTCW 1, 2; RGAL 4; SATA 36; SATA-Obit 86; TUS

Sartre, Jean-Paul 1905-1980 . **CLC 1, 4, 7, 9, 13, 18, 24, 44, 50, 52; DC 3; SSC 32; WLC**
See also CA 97-100; 9-12R; CANR 21; DA; DA3; DAB; DAC; DAM DRAM, MST, NOV; DFS 5; DLB 72; EW 12; GFL 1789 to the Present; MTCW 1, 2; RGSF 2; RGWL 2, 3; SSFS 9; TWA

Sassoon, Siegfried (Lorraine)
1886-1967 .... **CLC 36, 130; PC 12**
See also BRW 6; CA 25-28R; 104; CANR 36; DAB; DAM MST, NOV, POET; DLB 20, 191; DLBD 18; MTCW 1, 2; PAB; RGEL 2; TEA

Satterfield, Charles
See Pohl, Frederik

Satyremont
See Peret, Benjamin

Saul, John (W. III) 1942- .... **CLC 46**
See also AAYA 10; BEST 90:4; CA 81-84; CANR 16, 40, 81; CPW; DAM NOV, POP; HGG; SATA 98

Saunders, Caleb
See Heinlein, Robert A(nson)

Saura (Atares), Carlos 1932-1998 .... **CLC 20**
See also CA 131; 114; CANR 79; HW 1

Sauser, Frederic Louis
See Sauser-Hall, Frederic

Sauser-Hall, Frederic 1887-1961 ...... **CLC 18**
See Cendrars, Blaise
See also CA 93-96; 102; CANR 36, 62; MTCW 1

Saussure, Ferdinand de
1857-1913 .... **TCLC 49**
See also DLB 242

Savage, Catharine
See Brosman, Catharine Savage

Savage, Thomas 1915- .... **CLC 40**
See also CA 132; 126; CAAS 15; CN 7; INT 132; TCWW 2

Savan, Glenn (?)- .... **CLC 50**

Sax, Robert
See Johnson, Robert

Saxton, Robert
See Johnson, Robert

Sayers, Dorothy L(eigh)
1893-1957 .... **TCLC 2, 15**
See also BPFB 3; BRWS 3; CA 119; 104; CANR 60; CDBLB 1914-1945; CMW 4; DAM POP; DLB 10, 36, 77, 100; MSW; MTCW 1, 2; RGEL 2; SSFS 12; TEA

Sayers, Valerie 1952- .... **CLC 50, 122**
See also CA 134; CANR 61; CSW

Sayles, John (Thomas) 1950- . **CLC 7, 10, 14**
See also CA 57-60; CANR 41, 84; DLB 44

Scammell, Michael 1935- .... **CLC 34**
See also CA 156

Scannell, Vernon 1922- .... **CLC 49**
See also CA 5-8R; CANR 8, 24, 57; CP 7; CWRI 5; DLB 27; SATA 59

Scarlett, Susan
See Streatfeild, (Mary) Noel

Scarron 1847-1910
See Mikszath, Kalman

Schaeffer, Susan Fromberg 1941- ..... **CLC 6, 11, 22**
See also CA 49-52; CANR 18, 65; CN 7; DLB 28; MTCW 1, 2; SATA 22

Schama, Simon (Michael) 1945- ..... **CLC 150**
See also BEST 89:4; CA 105; CANR 39, 91

Schary, Jill
See Robinson, Jill

Schell, Jonathan 1943- .... **CLC 35**
See also CA 73-76; CANR 12

Schelling, Friedrich Wilhelm Joseph von
1775-1854 .... **NCLC 30**
See also DLB 90

Scherer, Jean-Marie Maurice 1920-
See Rohmer, Eric
See also CA 110

Schevill, James (Erwin) 1920- .... **CLC 7**
See also CA 5-8R; CAAS 12; CAD; CD 5

Schiller, Friedrich von 1759-1805 ...... **DC 12; NCLC 39, 69**
See also CDWLB 2; DAM DRAM; DLB 94; EW 5; RGWL 2, 3; TWA

Schisgal, Murray (Joseph) 1926- .... **CLC 6**
See also CA 21-24R; CAD; CANR 48, 86; CD 5

Schlee, Ann 1934- .... **CLC 35**
See also CA 101; CANR 29, 88; SATA 44; SATA-Brief 36

Schlegel, August Wilhelm von
1767-1845 .... **NCLC 15**
See also DLB 94; RGWL 2, 3

Schlegel, Friedrich 1772-1829 .... **NCLC 45**
See also DLB 90; EW 5; RGWL 2, 3; TWA

Schlegel, Johann Elias (von)
1719(?)-1749 .... **LC 5**

Schleiermacher, Friedrich
1768-1834 .... **NCLC 107**
See also DLB 90

Schlesinger, Arthur M(eier), Jr.
1917- .... **CLC 84**
See also AITN 1; CA 1-4R; CANR 1, 28, 58, 105; DLB 17; INT CANR-28; MTCW 1, 2; SATA 61

Schmidt, Arno (Otto) 1914-1979 ...... **CLC 56**
See also CA 109; 128; DLB 69

Schmitz, Aron Hector 1861-1928
See Svevo, Italo
See also CA 122; 104; MTCW 1

Schnackenberg, Gjertrud (Cecelia)
1953- .... **CLC 40; PC 45**
See also CA 116; CANR 100; CP 7; CWP; DLB 120; PFS 13

Schneider, Leonard Alfred 1925-1966
See Bruce, Lenny
See also CA 89-92

Schnitzler, Arthur 1862-1931 ..... **DC 17; SSC 15; TCLC 4**
See also CA 104; CDWLB 2; DLB 81, 118; EW 8; RGSF 2; RGWL 2, 3

Somers, Jane
See Lessing, Doris (May)

Somerville, Edith Oenone
1858-1949 .... SSC 56; TCLC 51
See also CA 196; DLB 135; RGEL 2; RGSF 2

Somerville & Ross
See Martin, Violet Florence; Somerville, Edith Oenone

Sommer, Scott 1951- .... CLC 25
See also CA 106

Sondheim, Stephen (Joshua) 1930- . CLC 30, 39, 147
See also AAYA 11; CA 103; CANR 47, 67; DAM DRAM; LAIT 4

Sone, Monica 1919- .... AAL

Song, Cathy 1955- .... AAL; PC 21
See also CA 154; CWP; DLB 169; EXPP; FW; PFS 5

Sontag, Susan 1933- .... CLC 1, 2, 10, 13, 31, 105
See also AMWS 3; CA 17-20R; CANR 25, 51, 74, 97; CN 7; CPW; DA3; DAM POP; DLB 2, 67; MAWW; MTCW 1, 2; RGAL 4; RHW; SSFS 10

Sophocles 496(?)B.C.-406(?)B.C. .... CMLC 2, 47, 51; DC 1; WLCS
See also AW 1; CDWLB 1; DA; DA3; DAB; DAC; DAM DRAM, MST; DFS 1, 4, 8; DLB 176; LAIT 1; RGWL 2, 3; TWA

Sordello 1189-1269 .... CMLC 15

Sorel, Georges 1847-1922 .... TCLC 91
See also CA 188; 118

Sorel, Julia
See Drexler, Rosalyn

Sorokin, Vladimir .... CLC 59

Sorrentino, Gilbert 1929- .. CLC 3, 7, 14, 22, 40
See also CA 77-80; CANR 14, 33, 115; CN 7; CP 7; DLB 5, 173; DLBY 1980; INT CANR-14

Soseki
See Natsume, Soseki
See also MJW

Soto, Gary 1952- ... CLC 32, 80; HLC 2; PC 28
See also AAYA 10, 37; BYA 11; CA 125; 119; CANR 50, 74, 107; CLR 38; CP 7; DAM MULT; DLB 82; EXPP; HW 1, 2; INT CA-125; JRDA; MAICYA 2; MAIC-YAS 1; MTCW 2; PFS 7; RGAL 4; SATA 80, 120; WYA; YAW

Soupault, Philippe 1897-1990 .... CLC 68
See also CA 131; 147; 116; GFL 1789 to the Present

Souster, (Holmes) Raymond 1921- .... CLC 5, 14
See also CA 13-16R; CAAS 14; CANR 13, 29, 53; CP 7; DA3; DAC; DAM POET; DLB 88; RGEL 2; SATA 63

Southern, Terry 1924(?)-1995 .... CLC 7
See also AMWS 11; BPFB 3; CA 150; 1-4R; CANR 1, 55, 107; CN 7; DLB 2; IDFW 3, 4

Southey, Robert 1774-1843 .... NCLC 8, 97
See also BRW 4; DLB 93, 107, 142; RGEL 2; SATA 54

Southworth, Emma Dorothy Eliza Nevitte
1819-1899 .... NCLC 26
See also DLB 239

Souza, Ernest
See Scott, Evelyn

Soyinka, Wole 1934- .. BLC 3; CLC 3, 5, 14, 36, 44; DC 2; WLC
See also AFW; BW 2, 3; CA 13-16R; CANR 27, 39, 82; CD 5; CDWLB 3; CN 7; CP 7; DA; DA3; DAB; DAC; DAM DRAM, MST, MULT; DFS 10; DLB 125; MTCW 1, 2; RGEL 2; TWA; WLIT 2

Spackman, W(illiam) M(ode)
1905-1990 .... CLC 46
See also CA 132; 81-84

Spacks, Barry (Bernard) 1931- .... CLC 14
See also CA 154; CANR 33, 109; CP 7; DLB 105

Spanidou, Irini 1946- .... CLC 44
See also CA 185

Spark, Muriel (Sarah) 1918- ..... CLC 2, 3, 5, 8, 13, 18, 40, 94; SSC 10
See also BRWS 1; CA 5-8R; CANR 12, 36, 76, 89; CDBLB 1945-1960; CN 7; CP 7; DA3; DAB; DAC; DAM MST, NOV; DLB 15, 139; FW; INT CANR-12; LAIT 4; MTCW 1, 2; RGEL 2; TEA; WLIT 4; YAW

Spaulding, Douglas
See Bradbury, Ray (Douglas)

Spaulding, Leonard
See Bradbury, Ray (Douglas)

Spelman, Elizabeth .... CLC 65

Spence, J. A. D.
See Eliot, T(homas) S(tearns)

Spencer, Anne 1882-1975 .... HR 3
See also BW 2; CA 161; DLB 51, 54

Spencer, Elizabeth 1921- .... CLC 22; SSC 57
See also CA 13-16R; CANR 32, 65, 87; CN 7; CSW; DLB 6, 218; MTCW 1; RGAL 4; SATA 14

Spencer, Leonard G.
See Silverberg, Robert

Spencer, Scott 1945- .... CLC 30
See also CA 113; CANR 51; DLBY 1986

Spender, Stephen (Harold)
1909-1995 .... CLC 1, 2, 5, 10, 41, 91
See also BRWS 2; CA 149; 9-12R; CANR 31, 54; CDBLB 1945-1960; CP 7; DA3; DAM POET; DLB 20; MTCW 1, 2; PAB; RGEL 2; TEA

Spengler, Oswald (Arnold Gottfried)
1880-1936 .... TCLC 25
See also CA 189; 118

Spenser, Edmund 1552(?)-1599 ..... LC 5, 39; PC 8, 42; WLC
See also BRW 1; CDBLB Before 1660; DA; DA3; DAB; DAC; DAM MST, POET; DLB 167; EFS 2; EXPP; PAB; RGEL 2; TEA; WLIT 3; WP

Spicer, Jack 1925-1965 .... CLC 8, 18, 72
See also BG 3; CA 85-88; DAM POET; DLB 5, 16, 193; GLL 1; WP

Spiegelman, Art 1948- .... CLC 76
See also AAYA 10, 46; CA 125; CANR 41, 55, 74; MTCW 2; SATA 109; YAW

Spielberg, Peter 1929- .... CLC 6
See also CA 5-8R; CANR 4, 48; DLBY 1981

Spielberg, Steven 1947- .... CLC 20
See also AAYA 8, 24; CA 77-80; CANR 32; SATA 32

Spillane, Frank Morrison 1918-
See Spillane, Mickey
See also CA 25-28R; CANR 28, 63; DA3; MTCW 1, 2; SATA 66

Spillane, Mickey .... CLC 3, 13
See Spillane, Frank Morrison
See also BPFB 3; CMW 4; DLB 226; MSW; MTCW 2

Spinoza, Benedictus de 1632-1677 .. LC 9, 58

Spinrad, Norman (Richard) 1940- ... CLC 46
See also BPFB 3; CA 37-40R; CAAS 19; CANR 20, 91; DLB 8; INT CANR-20; SFW 4

Spitteler, Carl (Friedrich Georg)
1845-1924 .... TCLC 12
See also CA 109; DLB 129

Spivack, Kathleen (Romola Drucker)
1938- .... CLC 6
See also CA 49-52

Spoto, Donald 1941- .... CLC 39
See also CA 65-68; CANR 11, 57, 93

Springsteen, Bruce (F.) 1949- .... CLC 17
See also CA 111

Spurling, Hilary 1940- .... CLC 34
See also CA 104; CANR 25, 52, 94

Spyker, John Howland
See Elman, Richard (Martin)

Squires, (James) Radcliffe
1917-1993 .... CLC 51
See also CA 140; 1-4R; CANR 6, 21

Srivastava, Dhanpat Rai 1880(?)-1936
See Premchand
See also CA 197; 118

Stacy, Donald
See Pohl, Frederik

Stael
See Stael-Holstein, Anne Louise Germaine Necker
See also EW 5; RGWL 2, 3

Stael, Germaine de
See Stael-Holstein, Anne Louise Germaine Necker
See also DLB 119, 192; FW; GFL 1789 to the Present; TWA

Stael-Holstein, Anne Louise Germaine Necker 1766-1817 .... NCLC 3, 91
See Stael; Stael, Germaine de

Stafford, Jean 1915-1979 .. CLC 4, 7, 19, 68; SSC 26
See also CA 85-88; 1-4R; CANR 3, 65; DLB 2, 173; MTCW 1, 2; RGAL 4; RGSF 2; SATA-Obit 22; TCWW 2; TUS

Stafford, William (Edgar)
1914-1993 .... CLC 4, 7, 29
See also AMWS 11; CA 142; 5-8R; CAAS 3; CANR 5, 22; DAM POET; DLB 5, 206; EXPP; INT CANR-22; PFS 2, 8, 16; RGAL 4; WP

Stagnelius, Eric Johan 1793-1823 . NCLC 61

Staines, Trevor
See Brunner, John (Kilian Houston)

Stairs, Gordon
See Austin, Mary (Hunter)
See also TCWW 2

Stalin, Joseph 1879-1953 .... TCLC 92

Stampa, Gaspara c. 1524-1554 .... PC 43
See also RGWL 2, 3

Stampflinger, K. A.
See Benjamin, Walter

Stancykowna
See Szymborska, Wislawa

Standing Bear, Luther
1868(?)-1939(?) .... NNAL
See also CA 144; 113; DAM MULT

Stannard, Martin 1947- .... CLC 44
See also CA 142; DLB 155

Stanton, Elizabeth Cady
1815-1902 .... TCLC 73
See also CA 171; DLB 79; FW

Stanton, Maura 1946- .... CLC 9
See also CA 89-92; CANR 15; DLB 120

Stanton, Schuyler
See Baum, L(yman) Frank

Stapledon, (William) Olaf
1886-1950 .... TCLC 22
See also CA 162; 111; DLB 15, 255; SFW 4

Starbuck, George (Edwin)
1931-1996 .... CLC 53
See also CA 153; 21-24R; CANR 23; DAM POET

Stark, Richard
See Westlake, Donald E(dwin)

Staunton, Schuyler
See Baum, L(yman) Frank

Tomalin, Claire 1933- .... **CLC 166**
    See also CA 89-92; CANR 52, 88; DLB
    155

Tomasi di Lampedusa, Giuseppe 1896-1957
    See Lampedusa, Giuseppe (Tomasi) di
    See also CA 111; DLB 177

Tomlin, Lily .... **CLC 17**
    See Tomlin, Mary Jean

Tomlin, Mary Jean 1939(?)-
    See Tomlin, Lily
    See also CA 117

Tomline, F. Latour
    See Gilbert, W(illiam) S(chwenck)

Tomlinson, (Alfred) Charles 1927- .... **CLC 2,
    4, 6, 13, 45; PC 17**
    See also CA 5-8R; CANR 33; CP 7; DAM
    POET; DLB 40

Tomlinson, H(enry) M(ajor)
    1873-1958 .... **TCLC 71**
    See also CA 161; 118; DLB 36, 100, 195

Tonson, Jacob fl. 1655(?)-1736 .... **LC 86**
    See also DLB 170

Toole, John Kennedy 1937-1969 ..... **CLC 19,
    64**
    See also BPFB 3; CA 104; DLBY 1981;
    MTCW 2

Toomer, Eugene
    See Toomer, Jean

Toomer, Eugene Pinchback
    See Toomer, Jean

Toomer, Jean 1892-1967 .. **BLC 3; CLC 1, 4,
    13, 22; HR 3; PC 7; SSC 1, 45; WLCS**
    See also AFAW 1, 2; AMWS 3, 9; BW 1;
    CA 85-88; CDALB 1917-1929; DA3;
    DAM MULT; DLB 45, 51; EXPP; EXPS;
    MTCW 1, 2; NFS 11; RGAL 4; RGSF 2;
    SSFS 5

Toomer, Nathan Jean
    See Toomer, Jean

Toomer, Nathan Pinchback
    See Toomer, Jean

Torley, Luke
    See Blish, James (Benjamin)

Tornimparte, Alessandra
    See Ginzburg, Natalia

Torre, Raoul della
    See Mencken, H(enry) L(ouis)

Torrence, Ridgely 1874-1950 .... **TCLC 97**
    See also DLB 54, 249

Torrey, E(dwin) Fuller 1937- .... **CLC 34**
    See also CA 119; CANR 71

Torsvan, Ben Traven
    See Traven, B.

Torsvan, Benno Traven
    See Traven, B.

Torsvan, Berick Traven
    See Traven, B.

Torsvan, Berwick Traven
    See Traven, B.

Torsvan, Bruno Traven
    See Traven, B.

Torsvan, Traven
    See Traven, B.

Tourneur, Cyril 1575(?)-1626 .... **LC 66**
    See also BRW 2; DAM DRAM; DLB 58;
    RGEL 2

Tournier, Michel (Edouard) 1924- .... **CLC 6,
    23, 36, 95**
    See also CA 49-52; CANR 3, 36, 74; DLB
    83; GFL 1789 to the Present; MTCW 1,
    2; SATA 23

Tournimparte, Alessandra
    See Ginzburg, Natalia

Towers, Ivar
    See Kornbluth, C(yril) M.

Towne, Robert (Burton) 1936(?)- ..... **CLC 87**
    See also CA 108; DLB 44; IDFW 3, 4

Townsend, Sue .... **CLC 61**
    See Townsend, Susan Lilian
    See also AAYA 28; CA 127; 119; CANR
    65, 107; CBD; CD 5; CPW; CWD; DAB;
    DAC; DAM MST; DLB 271; INT 127;
    SATA 55, 93; SATA-Brief 48; YAW

Townsend, Susan Lilian 1946-
    See Townsend, Sue

Townshend, Pete
    See Townshend, Peter (Dennis Blandford)

Townshend, Peter (Dennis Blandford)
    1945- .... **CLC 17, 42**
    See also CA 107

Tozzi, Federigo 1883-1920 .... **TCLC 31**
    See also CA 160; CANR 110; DLB 264

Tracy, Don(ald Fiske) 1905-1970(?)
    See Queen, Ellery
    See also CA 176; 1-4R; CANR 2

Trafford, F. G.
    See Riddell, Charlotte

Traill, Catharine Parr 1802-1899 .. **NCLC 31**
    See also DLB 99

Trakl, Georg 1887-1914 .... **PC 20; TCLC 5**
    See also CA 165; 104; EW 10; MTCW 2;
    RGWL 2, 3

Tranquilli, Secondino
    See Silone, Ignazio

Transtroemer, Tomas (Goesta)
    1931- .... **CLC 52, 65**
    See also CA 129; 117; CAAS 17; CANR
    115; DAM POET; DLB 257

Transtroemer, Tomas Gosta
    See Transtroemer, Tomas (Goesta)

Transtromer, Tomas
    See Transtroemer, Tomas (Goesta)

Transtromer, Tomas (Goesta) 1931-
    See Transtroemer, Tomas (Goesta)

Transtromer, Tomas Gosta
    See Transtroemer, Tomas (Goesta)

Traven, B. 1882(?)-1969 .... **CLC 8, 11**
    See also CA 25-28R; 19-20; CAP 2; DLB
    9, 56; MTCW 1; RGAL 4

Trediakovsky, Vasilii Kirillovich
    1703-1769 .... **LC 68**
    See also DLB 150

Treitel, Jonathan 1959- .... **CLC 70**
    See also DLB 267

Trelawny, Edward John
    1792-1881 .... **NCLC 85**
    See also DLB 110, 116, 144

Tremain, Rose 1943- .... **CLC 42**
    See also CA 97-100; CANR 44, 95; CN 7;
    DLB 14; RGSF 2; RHW

Tremblay, Michel 1942- .... **CLC 29, 102**
    See also CA 128; 116; CCA 1; CWW 2;
    DAC; DAM MST; DLB 60; GLL 1;
    MTCW 1, 2

Trevanian .... **CLC 29**
    See Whitaker, Rod(ney)

Trevor, Glen
    See Hilton, James

Trevor, William .. **CLC 7, 9, 14, 25, 71, 116;
    SSC 21, 58**
    See Cox, William Trevor
    See also BRWS 4; CBD; CD 5; CN 7; DLB
    14, 139; MTCW 2; RGEL 2; RGSF 2;
    SSFS 10

Trifonov, Iurii (Valentinovich)
    See Trifonov, Yuri (Valentinovich)
    See also RGWL 2, 3

Trifonov, Yuri (Valentinovich)
    1925-1981 .... **CLC 45**
    See Trifonov, Iurii (Valentinovich)
    See also CA 103; 126; MTCW 1

Trilling, Diana (Rubin) 1905-1996 . **CLC 129**
    See also CA 154; 5-8R; CANR 10, 46; INT
    CANR-10; MTCW 1, 2

Trilling, Lionel 1905-1975 .... **CLC 9, 11, 24**
    See also AMWS 3; CA 61-64; 9-12R;
    CANR 10, 105; DLB 28, 63; INT CANR-
    10; MTCW 1, 2; RGAL 4; TUS

Trimball, W. H.
    See Mencken, H(enry) L(ouis)

Tristan
    See Gomez de la Serna, Ramon

Tristram
    See Housman, A(lfred) E(dward)

Trogdon, William (Lewis) 1939-
    See Heat-Moon, William Least
    See also CA 119; 115; CANR 47, 89; CPW;
    INT CA-119

Trollope, Anthony 1815-1882 .... **NCLC 6, 33,
    101; SSC 28; WLC**
    See also BRW 5; CDBLB 1832-1890; DA;
    DA3; DAB; DAC; DAM MST, NOV;
    DLB 21, 57, 159; RGEL 2; RGSF 2;
    SATA 22

Trollope, Frances 1779-1863 .... **NCLC 30**
    See also DLB 21, 166

Trotsky, Leon 1879-1940 .... **TCLC 22**
    See also CA 167; 118

Trotter (Cockburn), Catharine
    1679-1749 .... **LC 8**
    See also DLB 84, 252

Trotter, Wilfred 1872-1939 .... **TCLC 97**

Trout, Kilgore
    See Farmer, Philip Jose

Trow, George W. S. 1943- .... **CLC 52**
    See also CA 126; CANR 91

Troyat, Henri 1911- .... **CLC 23**
    See also CA 45-48; CANR 2, 33, 67; GFL
    1789 to the Present; MTCW 1

Trudeau, G(arretson) B(eekman) 1948-
    See Trudeau, Garry B.
    See also CA 81-84; CANR 31; SATA 35

Trudeau, Garry B. .... **CLC 12**
    See Trudeau, G(arretson) B(eekman)
    See also AAYA 10; AITN 2

Truffaut, Francois 1932-1984 ... **CLC 20, 101**
    See also CA 113; 81-84; CANR 34

Trumbo, Dalton 1905-1976 .... **CLC 19**
    See also CA 69-72; 21-24R; CANR 10;
    DLB 26; IDFW 3, 4; YAW

Trumbull, John 1750-1831 .... **NCLC 30**
    See also DLB 31; RGAL 4

Trundlett, Helen B.
    See Eliot, T(homas) S(tearns)

Truth, Sojourner 1797(?)-1883 ...... **NCLC 94**
    See also DLB 239; FW; LAIT 2

Tryon, Thomas 1926-1991 .... **CLC 3, 11**
    See also AITN 1; BPFB 3; CA 135; 29-32R;
    CANR 32, 77; CPW; DA3; DAM POP;
    HGG; MTCW 1

Tryon, Tom
    See Tryon, Thomas

Ts'ao Hsueh-ch'in 1715(?)-1763 .... **LC 1**

Tsushima, Shuji 1909-1948
    See Dazai Osamu
    See also CA 107

Tsvetaeva (Efron), Marina (Ivanovna)
    1892-1941 .... **PC 14; TCLC 7, 35**
    See also CA 128; 104; CANR 73; EW 11;
    MTCW 1, 2; RGWL 2, 3

Tuck, Lily 1938- .... **CLC 70**
    See also CA 139; CANR 90

Tu Fu 712-770 .... **PC 9**
    See Du Fu
    See also DAM MULT; TWA; WP

Tunis, John R(oberts) 1889-1975 ..... **CLC 12**
    See also BYA 1; CA 61-64; CANR 62; DLB
    22, 171; JRDA; MAICYA 1, 2; SATA 37;
    SATA-Brief 30; YAW

Tuohy, Frank .... **CLC 37**
    See Tuohy, John Francis
    See also DLB 14, 139

Author Index

Wycherley, William 1640-1716 .... **LC 8, 21**
See also BRW 2; CDBLB 1660-1789; DAM
DRAM; DLB 80; RGEL 2
Wylie, Elinor (Morton Hoyt)
1885-1928 .... **PC 23; TCLC 8**
See also AMWS 1; CA 162; 105; DLB 9,
45; EXPP; RGAL 4
Wylie, Philip (Gordon) 1902-1971 ... **CLC 43**
See also CA 33-36R; 21-22; CAP 2; DLB
9; SFW 4
Wyndham, John .... **CLC 19**
See Harris, John (Wyndham Parkes Lucas)
Beynon
See also DLB 255; SCFW 2
Wyss, Johann David Von
1743-1818 .... **NCLC 10**
See also JRDA; MAICYA 1, 2; SATA 29;
SATA-Brief 27
Xenophon c. 430B.C.-c. 354B.C. ... **CMLC 17**
See also AW 1; DLB 176; RGWL 2, 3
Xingjian, Gao 1940-
See Gao Xingjian
See also CA 193; RGWL 3
Yakumo Koizumi
See Hearn, (Patricio) Lafcadio (Tessima
Carlos)
Yamada, Mitsuye (May) 1923- .... **PC 44**
See also CA 77-80
Yamamoto, Hisaye 1921- .... **AAL; SSC 34**
See also DAM MULT; LAIT 4; SSFS 14
Yamauchi, Wakako 1924- .... **AAL**
Yanez, Jose Donoso
See Donoso (Yanez), Jose
Yanovsky, Basile S.
See Yanovsky, V(assily) S(emenovich)
Yanovsky, V(assily) S(emenovich)
1906-1989 .... **CLC 2, 18**
See also CA 129; 97-100
Yates, Richard 1926-1992 .... **CLC 7, 8, 23**
See also AMWS 11; CA 139; 5-8R; CANR
10, 43; DLB 2, 234; DLBY 1981, 1992;
INT CANR-10
Yeats, W. B.
See Yeats, William Butler
Yeats, William Butler 1865-1939 .... **PC 20;**
TCLC 1, 11, 18, 31, 93, 116; WLC
See also BRW 6; BRWR 1; CA 127; 104;
CANR 45; CDBLB 1890-1914; DA; DA3;
DAB; DAC; DAM DRAM, MST, POET;
DLB 10, 19, 98, 156; EXPP; MTCW 1,
2; NCFS 3; PAB; PFS 1, 2, 5, 7, 13, 15;
RGEL 2; TEA; WLIT 4; WP
Yehoshua, A(braham) B. 1936- .. **CLC 13, 31**
See also CA 33-36R; CANR 43, 90; RGSF
2; RGWL 3
Yellow Bird
See Ridge, John Rollin
Yep, Laurence Michael 1948- .... **CLC 35**
See also AAYA 5, 31; BYA 7; CA 49-52;
CANR 1, 46, 92; CLR 3, 17, 54; DLB 52;
FANT; JRDA; MAICYA 1, 2; MAICYAS
1; SATA 7, 69, 123; WYA; YAW
Yerby, Frank G(arvin) 1916-1991 ..... **BLC 3;**
CLC 1, 7, 22
See also BPFB 3; BW 1, 3; CA 136; 9-12R;
CANR 16, 52; DAM MULT; DLB 76;
INT CANR-16; MTCW 1; RGAL 4; RHW
Yesenin, Sergei Alexandrovich
See Esenin, Sergei (Alexandrovich)
Yevtushenko, Yevgeny (Alexandrovich)
1933- ...... **CLC 1, 3, 13, 26, 51, 126; PC**
40
See Evtushenko, Evgenii Aleksandrovich
See also CA 81-84; CANR 33, 54; CWW
2; DAM POET; MTCW 1

Yezierska, Anzia 1885(?)-1970 .... **CLC 46**
See also CA 89-92; 126; DLB 28, 221; FW;
MTCW 1; RGAL 4; SSFS 15
Yglesias, Helen 1915- .... **CLC 7, 22**
See also CA 37-40R; CAAS 20; CANR 15,
65, 95; CN 7; INT CANR-15; MTCW 1
Yokomitsu, Riichi 1898-1947 .... **TCLC 47**
See also CA 170
Yonge, Charlotte (Mary)
1823-1901 .... **TCLC 48**
See also CA 163; 109; DLB 18, 163; RGEL
2; SATA 17; WCH
York, Jeremy
See Creasey, John
York, Simon
See Heinlein, Robert A(nson)
Yorke, Henry Vincent 1905-1974 ..... **CLC 13**
See Green, Henry
See also CA 49-52; 85-88
Yosano Akiko 1878-1942 .... **PC 11; TCLC 59**
See also CA 161; RGWL 3
Yoshimoto, Banana .... **CLC 84**
See Yoshimoto, Mahoko
See also NFS 7
Yoshimoto, Mahoko 1964-
See Yoshimoto, Banana
See also CA 144; CANR 98; SSFS 16
Young, Al(bert James) 1939- ... **BLC 3; CLC**
19
See also BW 2, 3; CA 29-32R; CANR 26,
65, 109; CN 7; CP 7; DAM MULT; DLB
33
Young, Andrew (John) 1885-1971 ...... **CLC 5**
See also CA 5-8R; CANR 7, 29; RGEL 2
Young, Collier
See Bloch, Robert (Albert)
Young, Edward 1683-1765 .... **LC 3, 40**
See also DLB 95; RGEL 2
Young, Marguerite (Vivian)
1909-1995 .... **CLC 82**
See also CA 150; 13-16; CAP 1; CN 7
Young, Neil 1945- .... **CLC 17**
See also CA 110; CCA 1
Young Bear, Ray A. 1950- ... **CLC 94; NNAL**
See also CA 146; DAM MULT; DLB 175
Yourcenar, Marguerite 1903-1987 ... **CLC 19,**
38, 50, 87
See also BPFB 3; CA 69-72; CANR 23, 60,
93; DAM NOV; DLB 72; DLBY 1988;
EW 12; GFL 1789 to the Present; GLL 1;
MTCW 1, 2; RGWL 2, 3
Yuan, Chu 340(?)B.C.-278(?)B.C. . **CMLC 36**
Yurick, Sol 1925- .... **CLC 6**
See also CA 13-16R; CANR 25; CN 7
Zabolotsky, Nikolai Alekseevich
1903-1958 .... **TCLC 52**
See also CA 164; 116
Zagajewski, Adam 1945- .... **PC 27**
See also CA 186; DLB 232
Zalygin, Sergei -2000 .... **CLC 59**
Zamiatin, Evgenii
See Zamyatin, Evgeny Ivanovich
See also RGSF 2; RGWL 2, 3
Zamiatin, Evgenii Ivanovich
See Zamyatin, Evgeny Ivanovich
See also DLB 272
Zamiatin, Yevgenii
See Zamyatin, Evgeny Ivanovich
Zamora, Bernice (B. Ortiz) 1938- .. **CLC 89;**
HLC 2
See also CA 151; CANR 80; DAM MULT;
DLB 82; HW 1, 2
Zamyatin, Evgeny Ivanovich
1884-1937 .... **TCLC 8, 37**
See Zamiatin, Evgenii; Zamiatin, Evgenii
Ivanovich
See also CA 166; 105; EW 10; SFW 4

Zangwill, Israel 1864-1926 ... **SSC 44; TCLC**
16
See also CA 167; 109; CMW 4; DLB 10,
135, 197; RGEL 2
Zappa, Francis Vincent, Jr. 1940-1993
See Zappa, Frank
See also CA 143; 108; CANR 57
Zappa, Frank .... **CLC 17**
See Zappa, Francis Vincent, Jr.
Zaturenska, Marya 1902-1982 ..... **CLC 6, 11**
See also CA 105; 13-16R; CANR 22
Zeami 1363-1443 .... **DC 7; LC 86**
See also DLB 203; RGWL 2, 3
Zelazny, Roger (Joseph) 1937-1995 . **CLC 21**
See also AAYA 7; BPFB 3; CA 148; 21-
24R; CANR 26, 60; CN 7; DLB 8; FANT;
MTCW 1, 2; SATA 57; SATA-Brief 39;
SCFW; SFW 4; SUFW 1, 2
Zhdanov, Andrei Alexandrovich
1896-1948 .... **TCLC 18**
See also CA 167; 117
Zhukovsky, Vasilii Andreevich
See Zhukovsky, Vasily (Andreevich)
See also DLB 205
Zhukovsky, Vasily (Andreevich)
1783-1852 .... **NCLC 35**
See Zhukovsky, Vasilii Andreevich
Ziegenhagen, Eric .... **CLC 55**
Zimmer, Jill Schary
See Robinson, Jill
Zimmerman, Robert
See Dylan, Bob
Zindel, Paul 1936-2003 ...... **CLC 6, 26; DC 5**
See also AAYA 2, 37; BYA 2, 3, 8, 11, 14;
CA 73-76; CAD; CANR 31, 65, 108; CD
5; CDALBS; CLR 3, 45, 85; DA; DA3;
DAB; DAC; DAM DRAM, MST, NOV;
DFS 12; DLB 7, 52; JRDA; LAIT 5;
MAICYA 1, 2; MTCW 1, 2; NFS 14;
SATA 16, 58, 102; WYA; YAW
Zinov'Ev, A. A.
See Zinoviev, Alexander (Aleksandrovich)
Zinoviev, Alexander (Aleksandrovich)
1922- .... **CLC 19**
See also CA 133; 116; CAAS 10
Zoilus
See Lovecraft, H(oward) P(hillips)
Zola, Emile (Edouard Charles Antoine)
1840-1902 ...... **TCLC 1, 6, 21, 41; WLC**
See also CA 138; 104; DA; DA3; DAB;
DAC; DAM MST, NOV; DLB 123; EW
7; GFL 1789 to the Present; IDTP; RGWL
2; TWA
Zoline, Pamela 1941- .... **CLC 62**
See also CA 161; SFW 4
Zoroaster 628(?)B.C.-551(?)B.C. ... **CMLC 40**
Zorrilla y Moral, Jose 1817-1893 .... **NCLC 6**
Zoshchenko, Mikhail (Mikhailovich)
1895-1958 .... **SSC 15; TCLC 15**
See also CA 160; 115; RGSF 2; RGWL 3
Zuckmayer, Carl 1896-1977 .... **CLC 18**
See also CA 69-72; DLB 56, 124; RGWL
2, 3
Zuk, Georges
See Skelton, Robin
See also CCA 1
Zukofsky, Louis 1904-1978 ... **CLC 1, 2, 4, 7,**
11, 18; PC 11
See also AMWS 3; CA 77-80; 9-12R;
CANR 39; DAM POET; DLB 5, 165;
MTCW 1; RGAL 4
Zweig, Paul 1935-1984 .... **CLC 34, 42**
See also CA 113; 85-88
Zweig, Stefan 1881-1942 .... **TCLC 17**
See also CA 170; 112; DLB 81, 118
Zwingli, Huldreich 1484-1531 .... **LC 37**
See also DLB 179

Literary Criticism Series
Cumulative Topic Index

This index lists all topic entries in Gale's *Classical and Medieval Literature Criticism* (CMLC), *Contemporary Literary Criticism* (CLC), *Drama Criticism* (DC), *Literature Criticism from 1400 to 1800* (LC), *Nineteenth-Century Literature Criticism* (NCLC), *Short Story Criticism* (SSC), and *Twentieth-Century Literary Criticism* (TCLC). The index also lists topic entries in the Gale Critical Companion Collection, which includes the following publication: *Harlem Renaissance* (HR).

Topic Index

TCLC Cumulative Nationality Index

TCLC-133 Title Index

ISBN 0-7876-6337-9

90000